THE BUILDINGS OF ENGLAND

FOUNDING EDITOR: NIKOLAUS PEVSNER
JOINT EDITORS: BRIDGET CHERRY AND JUDY NAIRN
ADVISORY EDITOR: JOHN NEWMAN

DEVON

BRIDGET CHERRY AND NIKOLAUS PEVSNER

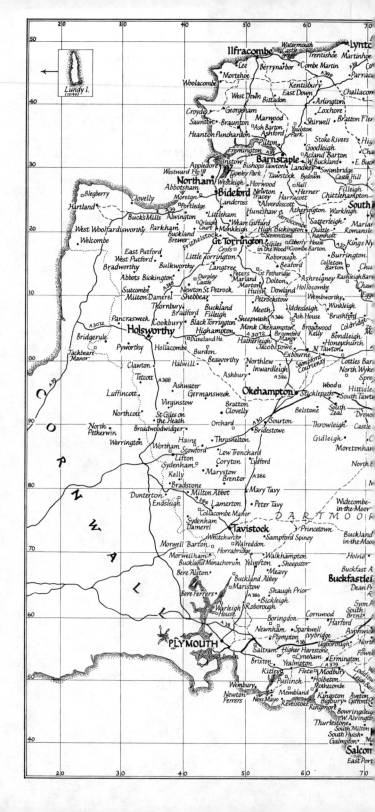

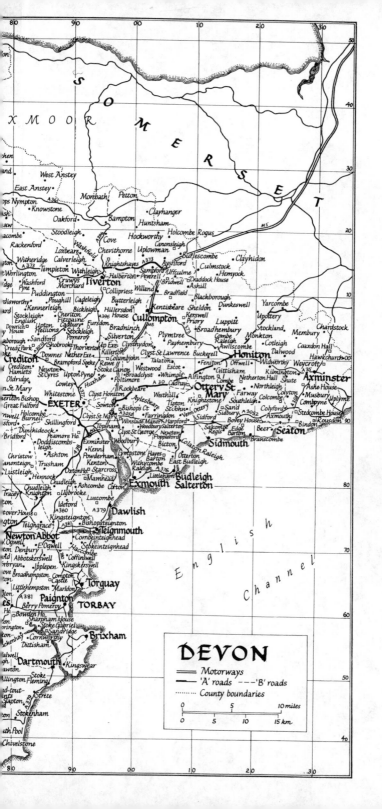

DEVON

Motorways
'A' roads --- 'B' roads
.... County boundaries

0   5   10 miles
0   5   10   15 km

Devon

BY

BRIDGET CHERRY

AND

NIKOLAUS PEVSNER

THE BUILDINGS OF ENGLAND

PENGUIN BOOKS

PENGUIN BOOKS
Published by the Penguin Group
27 Wrights Lane, London w8 5TZ, England

Viking Penguin Inc., 40 West 23rd Street, New York, New York 10010, USA
Penguin Books Australia Ltd, Ringwood, Victoria, Australia
Penguin Books Canada Ltd, 2801 John Street, Markham, Ontario, Canada L3R 1B4
Penguin Books (NZ) Ltd, 182–190 Wairau Road, Auckland 10, New Zealand

Penguin Books Ltd, Registered Offices: Harmondsworth, Middlesex, England

—

First published in two volumes 1952:
North Devon by Nikolaus Pevsner
South Devon by Nikolaus Pevsner

Second edition, extensively revised, 1989

—

ISBN 0 14 071050 7

—

Copyright © Bridget Cherry, 1989,
and copyright © Nikolaus Pevsner, 1952, 1989
All rights reserved

—

Printed in Great Britain
by Butler & Tanner Ltd, Frome and London
Set in Linotron Plantin
by Wyvern Typesetting Ltd, Bristol

TO W. G. HOSKINS

CONTENTS

MAP REFERENCES

The numbers printed in italic type in the margin against the place names in the gazetteer of the book indicate the position of the place in question on the index map (pages 2–3), which is divided into sections by the 10-kilometre reference lines of the National Grid. The reference given here omits the two initial letters (formerly numbers) which in a full grid reference refer to the 100-kilometre squares into which the country is divided. The first two numbers indicate the *western* boundary, and the last two the *southern* boundary, of the 10-kilometre square in which the place in question is situated. For example, South Molton (reference 7020) will be found in the 10-kilometre square bounded by grid lines 70 and 80 on the *west* and 20 and 30 on the *south*; Tavistock (reference 4070) in the square bounded by grid lines 40 and 50 on the *west* and 70 and 80 on the *south*.

The map contains all those places, whether towns, villages, or isolated buildings, which are the subject of separate entries in the text.

PREFACE

BY BRIDGET CHERRY

When Dr Nikolaus Pevsner and his wife undertook the tour of Devon in 1949 for the volumes that were published in 1952 as *North Devon* and *South Devon*, numbers 4 and 5 of the *Buildings of England* series, they charted a county whose rural landscape had barely been touched by the C20. Inland there had been little to disrupt the ancient pattern of agricultural settlement. The declining population of the earlier C20 had left the Regency and Victorian character of the seaside resorts undisturbed. Only the flattened centres of Exeter and Plymouth were abrupt exceptions, brutal reminders of the Second World War.

Today, Devon is still predominantly rural, and is still a delight to visit, but it is a county that is changing rapidly, and whose distinctive architectural heritage needs to be guarded sensitively if more is to survive than picture-postcard prettiness. The countryside may look unchanged, but the traditional way of life is in decline. Farmhouses and manor houses remain, but less often with the continuity of ownership which used to be such a marked feature of the county. Barns, shippons, and linhays frequently shelter humans rather than produce and animals, and larger houses have often been subdivided, so that instead of single families one may find communities of new residents from outside the county. As access to Devon has been eased by motorways and faster trains (and even airports), the population has increased at a rate that is one of the highest in the country (19 per cent over the last thirty years). It is not a balanced population; the increase is concentrated in the south and east, and so far the influx has been largely of retired people, who constitute over 40 per cent of the inhabitants of some of the south coast resorts. But even in many country parishes the numbers have grown, and in addition there are now over three million annual visitors. In the South Hams district in 1981 one in eleven homes was used for holiday accommodation, while in Torbay the 115,582 local residents were augmented by 76,400 visitors during the peak season.

The architectural repercussions of these changes are most readily visible in the larger towns. Torquay's skyline was callously disrupted by towers of flats and hotels already from the 1960s. At both Plymouth and Exeter the low-key post-war reconstruction has been upstaged by shopping and office developments of the last ten years. Barnstaple is likewise in the throes of transformation on the eve of the arrival of the North Devon motorway. At Exeter many good buildings have been lost unnecessarily since the war, but there has been a noticeable change of heart from the early 1970s onwards; the more recent arrivals are on the whole not too damaging to the townscape. Moreover, there can be positive sides to these changes: new money can mean the recondition-ing of old buildings, as at Southernhay, Exeter. However, too often coherent old centres have been fragmented by destructive inner ring

roads and ugly car parks, with little compensating restoration. Newton Abbot and Teignmouth are among the worst examples. Plymouth,
still Devon's only major city, has suffered similarly, and here there is
also a deplorable history of neglect of some of the city's best buildings.
In Plymouth, but also all over the county, until very recently conservation efforts have been directed almost exclusively towards buildings
not later than the C17; towns or areas whose main interest lies in their
legacy of Regency or Victorian buildings (much of Plymouth,
Teignmouth, or Ilfracombe, for example) have been correspondingly
neglected. There has been a dispiriting lethargy about worthwhile
individual buildings: *Foulston*'s Egyptian House, Devonport, the C19
Roman Catholic church at Barnstaple (possibly designed by *Pugin*),
and *Sedding*'s admirable All Saints clergy house at Plymouth have all
been in need of attention for many years. Victorian churches of all
denominations are among the urban buildings most at risk from both
demolition and major alterations (*see* Torquay). The smaller towns
have fared better (except for Tiverton, horribly maltreated in the
1960s). Several – Bideford, Tavistock, Totnes, for example – are some
of the most delightful in England. But they need to be guarded
carefully both from becoming tourist stage sets, and from being
swamped by out-of-scale housing, a special danger in popular coastal
towns such as Dartmouth and Sidmouth.

In the countryside there have been fewer major losses. Some minor
churches have been converted to other uses, although this has been
less common than in other rural counties. Among major country
houses, the most tragic loss was Dunsland House, destroyed by fire in
1967; demolitions include the early C19 Annery House, Monkleigh,
and *William White*'s Winscott, St Giles-in-the-Wood. Others stand
gutted or derelict (Blackborough and Haine). But there have been
some remarkable rescue operations and repairs by private owners
(Compton Castle, Canonteign, Stedcombe House, and, more contro-
versially but spectacularly, Boringdon). Among the houses owned by
the National Trust (which range from medieval Shute Barton to
Lutyens's Castle Drogo) the most spectacular transformation has been
the reinstatement of the High Victorian decoration of *William Burges*'s
Knightshayes. Conservation can provide a welcome opportunity to
arrive at a better understanding of a complicated building history. The
repair of English Heritage's medieval complexes of Bowhill, Exeter,
and Leigh Barton, and the excavations at Okehampton Castle, have all
been illuminating. So has the examination of the guest house at
Buckfast Abbey, the excavation of Protector Somerset's remarkable
work at Berry Pomeroy, and, not least, the conservation of the W front
of Exeter Cathedral.

Houses in private occupation can be investigated less easily, and
their intricate history often remains unrecorded. It is these buildings
that are most at risk, coming under increasing pressure as they are
adapted to meet the needs both of a rising, affluent population and of
the holidaymaker. Insensitive internal alterations and conversions
may not only be visually disruptive to the historic fabric, but can too
easily abruptly destroy the fragile evidence of centuries of gradual
evolution.

Our understanding of this evolution has developed rapidly over the
last thirty-five years. The value of Devon buildings as historical
evidence has been underlined by the work of W. G. Hoskins and his

many followers; and the burgeoning study of architectural history has made it possible to perceive their national significance more clearly. Both Pevsner's own work and the *Buildings of England* series in general played an important role in developing this broader architectural appreciation, but the Devon volumes came too early to be able to do more than briefly sketch the interest of some of the untrodden fields. Indeed, Pevsner felt the need to say in 1952 that 'the present state of research does not really justify a guide book such as this'. The first editions could draw on a century's accumulated antiquarian research on churches and, to a lesser extent, on medieval houses; other material available was much thinner. The books broke new ground by paying attention, albeit briefly, to little explored topics such as Regency seaside architecture, the Plymouth Docks, and c19 public buildings. However, Victorian church restorations and furnishings were still rarely a subject for appreciation, and the books barely touched on other matters that have since proved fruitful fields for investigation – above all, Devon's exceptionally well preserved early rural buildings. By drawing on new work on such topics, it is to be hoped that this volume presents a more rounded picture of the buildings of Devon than was possible in 1952. If this is so, it is due not only to recent published research (*see* Further Reading) but to the fact that this book is very much a cooperative effort, produced with the assistance of many willing helpers.

   Both introduction and gazetteer have as their base the entries in the first edition, but have been extensively rewritten and enlarged. The authors of those sections of the introduction for which I am not responsible are named in the text; I am much indebted to all of them, but would like to pay special tribute here to the late Alec Clifton-Taylor, whose essay on building stones is sadly the last of the many valuable contributions he made to this series. The gazetteer also includes many specialist contributions; to distinguish their authorship in the text would be excessively complicated and disruptive, so the various responsibilities must be explained here. The entries on pre-historic archaeological sites are the work of Frances Griffith, those on industrial archaeology of Professor Walter Minchinton; in both cases the emphasis has been on sites where there is something for the visitor to see. Medieval castles are largely by Dr Robert Higham; Deborah Griffiths helped on Berry Pomeroy, Stuart Blaylock on Exeter. The selection of chapels included was made by Roger Thorne, assisted by the research of Christopher Stell. The farmhouse entries, a major contribution to the book, are by Peter Beacham. For these (as for chapels) the wealth of material made it necessary to be selective; the farmhouses included were chosen because they were especially instructive examples of the different types whose general development is discussed in the introduction. The account of Exeter Cathedral uses as its base the revised version by Dr Priscilla Metcalf in Pevsner and Metcalf, *The Cathedrals of England* (1985). The source of nearly all the details of c19 work on churches (and of many contributions to the relevant parts of the introduction) was Dr Chris Brooks, originator (with Joanna Cox and Martin Cherry) of the c19 Devon Churches Project based at Exeter University. Much information was generously provided by other people, as the acknowledgements make clear. For the rest, and for the balance of what is included, I must bear the responsibility.

The decision to publish this much-expanded material as one large book instead of two smaller ones is based on the premise that this is a more satisfactory arrangement for most users than an arbitrary division into two substantial volumes which would in any event be neither pocket-sized nor pocket-money-priced. In order to save space, we have omitted the glossary. We have also eliminated the alphabetical cross-references in the text, providing instead a very full index of places and buildings. There is also – a new departure for *The Buildings of England* – an index of patrons and residents. Buildings outside towns are generally described under civil parishes; at the end of each parish entry there are cross references to those major houses and castles and other settlements which have their own entries. All places with a gazetteer entry are shown on the general map at the beginning of the book.

The general principles of inclusion in the gazetteer are those established in other volumes of *The Buildings of England*: all churches and major secular buildings of up to 1800 appear, but a more selective approach has been adopted for lesser buildings primarily of local interest, and for buildings of the C19 and C20. In this volume the special interest both of the lesser rural buildings and of C19 churches and furnishings has demanded that many be given more space than would have been allocated in early volumes in the series. Major church furnishings should be as complete as space and information permit, with the exception, in most cases, of bells, hatchments, plain fonts, and plate. Movable furnishings in houses are not described. Parentheses are used to indicate the occasional new entry or detail that has not been seen either by me or by any other contributor. I owe it to all house-owners to state that inclusion of a building in the book does not imply that it is open to the public, and it also needs to be said, particularly in the case of the lesser buildings where we have not tried to be all-inclusive, that omission or very cursory mention should not be taken to imply that a building is necessarily of no interest. It would be a dull county where there were no possibilities for new discoveries or re-evaluations. Comments on errors and omissions will, as always, be welcome.

ACKNOWLEDGEMENTS

The springboard for this book was the volumes on *North* and *South Devon*, of 1952, so it is appropriate to acknowledge first the people whose groundwork over thirty years ago provided the base. The primary debt is to Sir Nikolaus Pevsner, as will be obvious. The extensive preliminary extracting of information was done by R. Schilling, with assistance from Katherine Michaelson and Mary Mouat. Among those who helped in Devon were G.W. Copeland; E. Hart, Head Verger of Exeter Cathedral; E. J. Coombe, Devon County Librarian; N.S.E. Pugsley, Exeter City Librarian; W.G. Hoskins; H.P.R. Finberg; Amery Adams of the Devonshire Association; Bruce Oliver; and Alfred E. Blackwell of the North Devon Athenaeum, Barnstaple. The first editions were also indebted to the early statutory lists of historic buildings then being compiled by the Ministry of Housing and Local Government, to the indexes of Victorian churches and of Victorian stained glass, respectively compiled by H.S. Goodhart Rendel and T.D. Kendrick, and to the collections of the National Buildings Record, then under the care of Cecil Farthing.

The National Buildings Record has become the National Monuments Record, and Devon local history is now gathered together in the West Country Studies Library at Exeter: this new edition owes much to the invaluable collections of both institutions and to the help of their staffs. Both the Further Reading (*see* p. 116) and the long list of names that follows here demonstrate how interest in historic buildings has vastly expanded over the last few decades. Very many people made work on this book both enjoyable and rewarding. I am indebted to them all, and these brief acknowledgements do scant justice to the friendship and help which I received from so many who care about Devon buildings.

The chief collaborators have been mentioned in the Preface, but several of them did far more than write their pieces. Peter Beacham, as County Conservation Officer, was an unfailing source of advice and encouragement on every possible subject, and also read the whole of the gazetteer in typescript; Chris Brooks, as Secretary of the Devon Buildings Group, was a mine of useful information on far more than C19 churches. This revision of Devon proceeded at the same time as the Department of the Environment's major resurvey of buildings of architectural and historic interest, largely carried out by the firm of Architecton. I am grateful to all those involved in this work who shared their discoveries with me, and discussed numerous problems, especially Peter Chapman, Martin Cherry, Joanna Cox, Michael Laithwaite, John Schofield, and John Thorp. Michael Laithwaite in addition contributed much to the entries on Totnes houses from his own research, improved the accounts of Barnstaple and Ilfracombe, and provided useful advice on other topics; and John Thorp was an invaluable guide to the houses of Topsham and Bideford. At Exeter I had the knowledgeable guidance of the City Archaeological Unit under Dr Chris Henderson, and at the cathedral much assistance from Dr John Allan, and also from Audrey Erskine. On more recent Exeter matters I was helped by Michael Stocks and John Clark of the Planning Department, and by notes from members of the Civic Society, among whom Hazel Harvey was especially helpful. At Plymouth Jonathan Coad guided me round the Dockyard, Tim Brown introduced me to the suburbs, Joyce Knight of the Plymouth Athenaeum provided useful notes, and James Barber and Cynthia Gaskell-Brown of the Plymouth Museum and A. B. Fenton of the Planning Department patiently answered numerous questions. At Torbay I could not have managed without the constructive assistance of Alan Taylor of the Torbay Planning Department. Among others who acted as instructive guides as well as providing information, I must especially thank Paul Pearn, M. Allen of the Tiverton Civic Society, and Geoffrey Hoare at Budleigh Salterton.

Our files of over thirty years produced many comments and corrections in response to the first edition; among them I must acknowledge the especially helpful notes from A. W. Everett, A. F. Cornelius, G. W. Copeland, and Alec Clifton-Taylor, and also from Howard Colvin, Geoffrey Frankiss, Dr W. F. B. Lloyd, E. W. Masson Phillips, and Diana Woolner. Among the many people who provided information especially for the new edition, often making their own unpublished research available, I am particularly indebted to Michael Sayer, who most generously gave me access to the material he had prepared for an intended Burke–Savile guide to country houses, including much on family history, and who also read and commented on the gazetteer. I must also thank Peter Reid, who kept me up to date with recent information on country houses, Marjorie Rowe and the staff of the Devon Record Office, and Sheila Stirling of the Devon and Exeter Institute. On modern buildings I was helped by information from Basil Bird, former county architect, E. H. Surgey of Plymouth Architect's Department, and many planners and architects of the district councils.

I received much other specialized help, without which this book would be very much the poorer. I am especially grateful to Ian Allen (H. T. North); Dr J. Allibone (Devey and Salvin); W. P. Authers (Tiverton); Colin Baylis (Walter Cave, and a most helpful list of other Arts and Crafts work); Stuart Blaylock (Exeter); Ursula Brighouse (Woodbury); Alan Brooks (references to c 19 schools); Stewart Brown (Buckfast Abbey); A. W. Champniss (lists of organ cases); Peter Child (buildings in East and North Devon); Peter Christie (Bideford); R. Coates (the records of the Rolle estates); Peter Cormack (early c 20 stained glass); Professor J. M. Crook (references to c 19 architects from the *Builder*); Ivy Davidson (Modbury); Anthony Emery (medieval Dartington); Denis Evinson (lists of R.C. churches); L. Fairweather (Salcombe); Dr Richard Gem (churches); Hilary Grainger (Ernest George); S. Hardaway (Torquay); Hugh Harrison (the work of Herbert Read); W. A. Hatch (Ashburton); Rodney Hubbuck (c 19 stained glass); Anna Hulbert (painted work in churches); Charles Hulland (rural buildings in mid Devon); Sally Jeffrey (John James); Harriet Jordan (T. H. Mawson); R. J. Joy (Dartmoor Prison); Alison Kelly and J. H. Havill (Coade stone); Francis Kelly (churches); A. F. Langham (Lundy); Peter Laws (the Seddings); Audrey Lloyd (Alexander Lauder); Jonathan Lomas (buildings in North Devon); John Longhurst (Ilfracombe); Barbara Mann (Chulmleigh and district); Hugh Meller (National Trust properties); Father Charles Norris of Buckfast (stained glass); Caroline Oboussier (Topsham); W. Pearce (South Molton); Alan Powers (buildings of the 1930s); Margaret Richardson (Lutyens and Maufe); J. G. M. Scott (clocks and bells); Harry Gordon Slade (Berry Pomeroy and Bowhill); Professor M. J. Swanton (church furnishings); F. K. Theobald (Moretonhampstead); Adam White (c16 and c17 monuments).

The helpfulness of many house owners and incumbents of churches made visits a pleasure and correspondence less of a chore; while my excursions in Devon were made especially enjoyable through the hospitality of Peter and Chrissie Beacham, Chris Brooks and Joanna Cox, Paul and Eileen Pearn, and Michael and Averil Swanton. The book was speeded on its way through help in the office from Jeffrey West and Patience Trevor, and through the typing skills of Averil Swanton, Judith Heaver, and Helen Torok. As with other volumes in this series, Susan Rose-Smith organized the illustrations with her usual efficiency, and among those who took photographs specially for the book I owe particular thanks to George Hall and Colin Westwood. The maps and plans are the work of Reginald and Marjorie Piggott and Richard Andrews; the farmhouse introduction drawings are by Robert Weston. John Newman, our consultant editor, gave wise advice, and the final text has been improved immeasurably by the editing and indexing skills of my co-editor Judy Nairn.

INTRODUCTION

Devon is the largest of the old English counties after Yorkshire and Lincolnshire.* In population however it ranks only eighth in the modern non-metropolitan counties, and although the 1981 figure of 932,000 is a sizeable increase since 1951 (when it was 797,738), in many areas people and buildings are still thinly scattered. Consequently, it is the variety of landscape rather than the architectural wealth of the county that will first strike the visitor. It ranges from the subtropical fertility of Salcombe to the grim blizzards of Princetown on Dartmoor, from the flattish dull plains in the centre to the 'English Switzerland' of Lynton and the valleys behind which were so dear to the Mid-Victorians. All that can be said about the county throughout is that it is hilly and well wooded everywhere, and that its landscape features are on a large scale, as England goes, and never niggling. 1 Otherwise, Exmoor, the W fringes of which reach into Devon, is different from Dartmoor, a little more melodious, less forbidding in outline, and lacking the granite outcrops which are the unforgettable 3 feature of Dartmoor. The north coast is different from the south, though both have their lush combes. The south coast has many 2 estuaries, the north really only one, the estuary formed by the confluence of Torridge and Taw below Bideford and Barnstaple, The south against that has, from E to W, the Axe, the Otter, the Exe, the Teign, the Dart, the Yealm, and the combined Plym, Tavy, and Tamar. The extensive winding creeks of the south find no parallel in the north. The colour of the rocks in the north is grey, in the south red.

The geological complexity of Devon is reflected in the county's varied building materials, discussed in the account that follows. While Dartmoor offers the richest evidence for prehistoric activity, the most important modern settlements are on or near the coast. The largest, Plymouth (population 243,895) – of special interest for its domestic, military, and naval architecture, especially of the C18 and early C19 – is followed by Torbay (population 115,582), a modern administrative combination of the seaside towns of Torquay, Paignton, and Brixham. 5 Exeter, the only major Roman settlement, with a cathedral from the 12 C11 and a C20 university, comes only third, with 95,621.

The prosperity of Devon owed much to the exploitation of Dartmoor's mineral wealth, but still more to the growth of the wool and cloth trade, especially from the later Middle Ages to the C17. The county is rich in good buildings of this period, both in the small inland market towns (Ashburton, Chagford, Cullompton, Tiverton, and Totnes have some of the best) and in the ports on the estuaries: Dartmouth and Topsham in the south, Barnstaple and Bideford in the north. Those interested in the development of the seaside resort will

* 1,661,000 acres until 1974. The small areas then transferred to Cornwall (North Petherwin, Werrington) have been retained in this volume.

also find plenty to study, from the early *cottages ornés* of Sidmouth to the late Victorian terraces of Ilfracombe. But Devon is not essentially an urban county; picturesque villages abound, of cob-walled houses (especially in the east and south) or of granite (around Dartmoor), and so do medieval churches with their furnishings, while some of the most
4 rewarding buildings are the isolated manor houses and farmhouses, incorporating centuries of gradual development, which lie hidden away in the remote countryside.

BUILDING STONES

BY ALEC CLIFTON-TAYLOR

No English county contains so great a variety of building materials as Devon. No English cathedral incorporates so many different kinds of stone as Exeter. A survey of the building materials of this county is not therefore easy, more particularly as so much of the walling is hidden under plaster rendering, whitewash or colour-wash.

Our finest building stones, the Jurassic limestones with which the adjoining counties of Dorset and Somerset are so generously endowed, are not found in Devon, apart from a little Blue Lias, not very good, on the eastern fringe of the county, close to Lyme Regis. So Devon buildings are mostly deficient in refinements, especially carved detail. But sturdy they certainly are. 'Every Devon landowner, even the smallest,' said W. G. Hoskins in what, after over thirty years, is still one of the best books ever written about this county,* had building stone somewhere on his land: the surface of the county is pitted with these little overgrown quarries that have produced only one house and its outbuildings and boundary walls.' Stone of some kind was in fact available here almost everywhere. The only other widely distributed material was cob.

Devon's two kinds of limestone are sharply contrasted. Beer is a Cretaceous stone occurring on the south-east coast, west of Seaton. It was mostly worked by means of adits, galleries driven more or less horizontally into the hillside: one of them is now accessible to tourists. Being close to the sea, it could be loaded on to ships with no great difficulty. It has had a very long if somewhat chequered history. The stone was used extensively, especially in East Devon, by the church builders of the c 15 and early c 16. It came into its own again for a while in the Victorian period, and has been used intermittently, but not very much, in the present century. For a chalk-stone it is comparatively hard and shelly, and in this clean country air it will sometimes prove to be durable. It is of little use in a polluted atmosphere, and even in small towns, as at the churches of Tiverton, Cullompton, and Totnes (s porch), it has weathered very badly. It is seen to much better advantage internally, where its light tone can be aesthetically a great asset, as in Exeter Cathedral. At the quarry it is at first so soft that large blocks can be cut out like cheese, but as with many limestones it

* *Devon*, Collins, 1954. I should like to acknowledge my indebtedness to him.

hardens on exposure to the air. It is therefore the easiest to carve of all the Devon stones, and was much in demand in East and South Devon for ornamental work. In churches it was easily the best stone available for capitals, mouldings, and occasionally for much more elaborate undertakings like the screens at Totnes. In houses it provided the material for some imposing Elizabethan chimneypieces, even at farmhouse level, as at Poltimore, Farway, a few miles north of Beer.

Very different are the Devonian limestones: older by nearly three hundred million years, and much tougher. They are found in a number of limited areas between the estuaries of the Exe and the Tamar, and are seen to good effect in the predominantly grey towns of Torquay, Newton Abbot, and especially Plymouth, where even in the C19 this stone continued to be widely used in preference to brick. Some of these Devon limestones could be polished to look like marble. Ashburton marble, dark grey with thin pink and white veins, was used for C18 fireplaces, and a great variety of polished Devonian limestones were exploited by the Victorians to provide reredoses, pulpits, fonts, and pavements streaked and splashed with many different colours. The development of machine polishing gave High Victorian architects throughout the country the perfect material for polychromatic display. The most important centres for marble-working were the Turnchapel and Orestone quarries near Plymouth and the St Marychurch works of Blackler and Sons.

Devon has no fewer than five varieties of sandstone, all of which have been used for building in their own areas. As with the limestones, the youngest occur in the eastern part of the county. From the ridge of Upper Greensand east of Sidmouth came the material sometimes known as malmstone, quarried at Salcombe Regis. This is a pleasing greenish stone, but although in some demand in the late Middle Ages it was rarely worked in later times until in 1982 it was used for repairs to Exeter Cathedral.

Within the New Red sandstone series, both the Triassic and the Permian stones were at one time much sought after. The former can be seen at Sidmouth and at Ottery St Mary, where its colour is a neutral grey-brown; but the Permian stone was employed much more extensively. The earliest recorded use was in 1341–2 when, as Dr Hoskins has noted, fifty loads were brought from Whipton quarry, just outside Exeter, for the cathedral. Many small quarries, and in the neighbourhood of Exeter several larger ones, were worked for this stone for a century and a half from c. 1390. Churches from Cullompton to Paignton display it to excellent advantage, and further west too, for a long thin tongue stretches along the Vale of Crediton, almost to Hatherleigh. Permian sandstone in Devon is often bright red, as evinced by the coastal scenery between Dawlish Warren and Teignmouth familiar to countless travellers by rail. But the interior of the collegiate church at Crediton reveals an exquisite and most unusual blending of pink, purple-pink and blue-grey. Although tougher than the Greensand stone, it is only moderately durable, but it could be ashlared, and for the carver this was always one of the most congenial of the county's materials.

To the Carboniferous sandstones belong the Culm Measures, which yielded, from a profusion of small local quarries, the stone for more of the county's churches than any other. Most of those in central Devon are of Culm Measures sandstone; and a humble-looking material it is,

generally attractive neither in colour nor texture. Though there are
sometimes hints of red, the usual colour is a sombre brownish-grey;
and since it could usually be procured only in small hard pieces, the
coursing is rough and the texture very rubbly. Where, as for instance
at Coldridge, the window traceries, buttress facings, and other dressings are of grey granite, the effect is better; here too the abundance of
silver-green lichen, to which this stone is happily much prone, is very
welcome. At Bondleigh the church path is composed of little flaggy
pieces laid vertically: quite a pretty effect.

Of the same age as the Old Red sandstone of Herefordshire, but
differently constituted, are the Devonian sandstones. These are not
confined to Devon, but in this county they only occur towards the
northern and southern extremities, providing the material for nearly
all the churches north of South Molton and Barnstaple and for a good
many of those south of Totnes and Ivybridge. All the quarries were,
again, small and purely local. Devonian sandstones are also very hard
and not amenable to carving, but aesthetically they are preferable to
those from the Culm Measures. They could be obtained in somewhat
larger pieces, and their colours are rather more pleasing; at Combe
Martin church, for instance, there are pale shades of grey, pink, and
fawn: a gentle, sensitive combination. More often, however, the greys
predominate.

From the Upper Greensand, between the Blackdown Hills, and the
coast of East Devon, came another building stone which has not
always received the attention which it deserves: chert. It is sometimes
mistaken for flint, with which it has much in common, for chert is also
a form of silica, occurring as nodules and in thin beds. But the average
size of the boulders is considerably larger. Colyton church is largely
built of them, and some of these are 10–12 in. long and others 5–6 in.
high. The average size is not less than 4 in. by 2. As with flints,
technique improved steadily, until by the C 19 this intractable stone
could be squared. At Feniton the projection for the organ added in
1877 displays wonderfully masoned blocks of chert, squared and rock-
faced and measuring up to 6 by 13 in. The colours are quite different
from flint. The most usual colour is milky brown, but there are toffee
browns too, and suggestions of amethyst. Some of it is shiny and
glassy, with the consistency and semi-transparency of horn. It can be
most attractive. Other churches at which it can be seen to advantage
are Axminster, Awliscombe, and Kentisbeare, and a good secular
example is the gatehouse of Shute Barton.

Budleigh Salterton pebble bed deserves just a brief mention. It
occurs between the Triassic and the Permian beds of the New Red
sandstone, and was formed from the gravel of a large river which,
aeons ago, flowed northwards from France. The liver-coloured pebbles, all beautifully rounded and largely quartzite, can be seen in field
and garden walls and farm buildings, and occasionally in patterned
floors, on the hills west of the Otter, between Budleigh and Talaton.

Among the igneous rocks which yielded building stone in Devon,
granite undoubtedly holds pride of place. But because of the difficulty
of quarrying, almost all the granite used before the C 19 was moorstone: blocks of stone, some very large, lying about on the surface of
the land on the fringes of Dartmoor. This stone had been used for dry
walling since prehistoric times. Aplite, a type of granite from near
Meldon, was used as dressed stone at Okehampton and Gidleigh

castles in the C14. In the following century granite was in considerable demand for church arcades and window tracery, and it was later used also for bridges and such utility objects as cattle troughs, gatepiers, and stiles, as well as for field walls. It might, moreover, travel considerable distances. For example, at Sutcombe, north of Holsworthy, the church, as we should expect, is built of Culm Measures sandstone, but, inside, the Tudor N arcade is in Dartmoor granite, and a very pleasing example of it, sparkling cream-grey, with a specially grainy texture. For domestic building, dressed moorstone blocks, largely confined to the area around Dartmoor, were used already in the late medieval period for longhouses. The well-known Caroline Almshouses at Moretonhampstead are all moorstone, laid random on the side-walls, but carefully squared, no doubt with much labour, on the front, where, however, the open arcade also illustrates very clearly how difficult it was to attain any degree of refinement in granite at this time: undercut capitals, for example, were an impossibility. Granite continued to be worked during the C18, especially after the opening of the quarries at Haytor, and was occasionally used for large houses, as at Stover, near Teigngrace.

Further quarries were opened on Dartmoor for the building of Princetown gaol in 1806. In 1819 granite provided the material for the beautiful old lighthouse in the centre of Lundy Island; there was no transport problem here, for the whole of that island is granite. During the C19 methods of quarrying granite made great strides, and considerable quantities were exported: for example, to London in 1864, for the first part of the Thames Embankment. The most famous C20 granite building, not only in Devon but anywhere, is Lutyens's Castle Drogo.

Rather like granite, though without its sparkle, is white elvan, which is a quartz porphyry, and not really white but pale buff-grey. This is confined to the south-west corner of the county; the principal quarries were on Roborough Down, not far from Buckland Abbey. It can be seen at a number of churches on the south-western fringe of Dartmoor, among them Walkhampton, Sheepstor, Meavy, and Shaugh Prior; also at Plympton (both churches). This stone has a curious pitted appearance, but time has shown that here it is very durable. Elvans are more finely textured than granite, and very useful therefore for church arcades, window mullions, and dressings. The colour is usually light grey with a hint of buff.

As a glance at a geological map will reveal, the height of complexity is reached in the southern part of the county. Here, in addition to all the varieties of stone already described, Devon builders also made use of the basic igneous rocks, of which one of the commonest is basalt, a volcanic lava, more finely grained than granite, because, at the time of its formation, it cooled and crystallized more rapidly. Stone of this kind, also known as trap, was used first at Exeter, by the Romans for the town walls and by the Normans for Rougemont Castle; the source for both was the quarry of Northernhay, very close by. Various other quarries a few miles away to the west and north of the city were later to supply stone not only for churches but for domestic and other buildings, too, until well into the C19. Volcanic ash deposited in water would ultimately consolidate into a solid and hard rock known as basaltic tuff. At Totnes, this was readily available in the town and across the Dart and, although not suitable for architectural features, this reddish-brown stone was used extensively here for walling. Near Tavistock the monks owned Hurdwick quarry, the source of a metamorphosed tuff notable for its very distinctive greenish colour. Tavistock is largely built of this stone, which can also be seen in many churches round about. Close to, Hurdwick stone will be seen to have a pitted surface which seems to simulate decay.

There is also a green stone at Totnes; this is dolerite, a volcanic rock similar to basalt, which outcrops at Cornworthy, between Totnes and Dartmouth. At Dartmouth it was used in early Tudor times for part of the castle.

The tally of Devon building stones is still not complete. Slate, both for masonry and as a roofing material, made a significant contribution in every century from the twelfth to the nineteenth. Many small quarries and a few large ones, widely distributed and mostly over-grown today, serve to remind us of how important slate used to be. Specially notable was the area between Dartmouth and Kingsbridge, where slate used not only for houses, barns, and boundary walls, but for churches too, is much in evidence. The largest quarry was at Charleton, close to the Salcombe estuary near Kingsbridge, whence, as there was convenient water transport, a great deal was exported, especially in the c15 to Holland. Another big quarry was at Mill Hill, two miles west of Tavistock, where the unexpected range of colours is very pleasurable. In the north, between Barnstaple and Lynton, the Devonian slate is darker and less agreeable: this can be seen for example at Kentisbury.

In former times Devon produced a great deal of roofing slate, and very attractive it was, both for its texture and for its warm-hued colours. A great deal was exported too: the Pipe Rolls for 1180 record that 800,000 slates were sent from Totnes for the castle at Winchester, and another 100,000 for Porchester. The quarries were to the south of the town: one, Englebourne, was still working until within the present century. Unfortunately, however, Devon slate has not proved very durable; much of it had to be replaced by the tougher product from Delabole in Cornwall, or, much worse aesthetically, by Welsh slate.

Between the mid c17 and the mid c19 slate was also much in demand as a covering for house walls at some places, notably Plymouth, Totnes, Ashburton, and Topsham. Although attractive shapes can occasionally be seen (far less often though than in Germany and France), most hung slate in Devon is plain, and the object was strictly practical: to provide additional protection against bad weather. It is not always realized that many kinds of stone, including even granite, are by no means always impervious to damp, especially in the wetter parts of the country: slate-hanging helped to render them more waterproof. To apply the slates it was usually necessary to attach wooden battens to the face of the wall. Only of course with a fissile stone like slate, possessing the natural property of being easy to split apart, was this a practical proposition.

Apart from slate, the main roofing material was thatch, attractive because of its cheapness and its ready availability. The usual material until the introduction of the combine-harvester was wheat-straw, although at one time rye-straw was also used in certain areas, and, round the perimeter of Dartmoor, where no corn was grown, heather provided a rustic substitute. Today the material generally employed for thatching in Devon is wheat reed, or 'Devon reed', as it is known here. The term is strictly a misnomer, for it is not reed but long straw, specially grown for the thatcher to a length of about 3 ft, and preserved from bruising in the threshing drum by being passed through a special device known as a comber. What relates it to true reed is the manner in which it is laid, with the butts of the stalks forming the exposed surface of the roof, as distinct from the small flat bundles laid in overlapping courses, which is the method with straw. Good thatched roofs of combed wheat reed, of which Devon can still show a large number, may last fifty years, and vie with Norfolk reed itself in appearance.

The main alternative to stone was cob (*see* Farmhouse Introduction). Timber-framed exteriors are uncommon, except for town-house fronts of the C16–17. Wood was, however, an indispensable accompaniment to much of the stonework. Where the walls are of slate-stone, Culm Measures sandstone, or chert, the more refined features, such for example as the door frames and the mullions of the windows, may be of Beer stone or granite, but often they are oak. And even in churches, recourse was occasionally had to wood for the arcades: central Devon has two examples, Nymet Rowland and Dowland. At both churches it is apparent that the oak was regarded as a practicable or economical substitute for stone; stone forms have been imitated exactly, and it is apparent that good stone, had it been available, would have done the job better. Internally, of course, in churches and houses alike, the role of timber has always been of prime importance.

Brick did not become widespread as a building material until the late C17, although, because of its fire-resisting qualities, it was used already in the C16 for ovens and chimneys. Some of the earliest bricks were imported from Holland. They are of a distinctive type, small and buff-yellow, and can be seen in many C17 houses in Topsham and also in Dartmouth. Holland provided the principal foreign market for Devonshire serges, so it is likely that the bricks came back as ballast. Another port, Bideford, also has good brickwork of the 1690s.

During the C18 the adoption of brick became gradually more widespread, although largely confined to towns. In 1731 Tiverton suffered a devastating fire; nearly all the rebuilding was carried out in brick. By the end of the century it had become the usual material in the towns of East Devon, and most notably at Exeter. Much was destroyed by bombs in 1941, but parts of the Southernhay estate laid out between 1773 and 1810, all in mellow red brick, happily survive. A good many of these brick houses, especially in coastal resorts like Sidmouth, were covered with that favourite Regency material, stucco, and painted. In the later C19, the distinctive hard pale yellow brick from Marland, near Barnstaple, was much used in North Devon; it dominates late Victorian resorts such as Ilfracombe. At Plymouth, on the other hand, as already observed, brick did not come into general use even in the C19 and it may still sit uneasily in Devon's countryside.

PREHISTORIC AND ROMAN DEVON:

THE VISIBLE EVIDENCE

BY TOM GREEVES

Structures associated with permanent settlement have been features of the Devon landscape for at least five and a half thousand years, and many of them from the prehistoric period still survive in a sufficiently well-preserved state for us to be able to recover something of their original form and design. These structures include places of burial and worship, houses, field systems, and defensive sites, each broad type containing many variations within it. Of course, people were living within what is now the county of Devon for many thousands of years before the date of the earliest surviving structures. Evidence of human occupation at least 40,000 years ago has been found at Kent's Cavern, Torquay, which is one of the oldest and most important archaeological sites in the country.

The great upland area of Dartmoor, containing approximately 125,000 acres of moorland, has the greatest surviving concentration of visible field remains of the prehistoric period. This is due partly to the robust nature of the granite of which many of the structures were built, and partly to the relative lack of exploitation of the moorland environment in later periods. Important, though often more subtle, visible evidence of prehistoric occupation also exists on the Devon tracts of Exmoor. Despite some encroachment by medieval and later features, there are areas both of Dartmoor and Exmoor that can with some truth be spoken of as PREHISTORIC LANDSCAPES, so complete is the range of structures visible in a virtually unaltered environment. Elsewhere in the county upstanding prehistoric remains tend to be islands within a modern farmed landscape, though groupings of sites may well exist in any area of unimproved land such as coastline or upland heath.

Modern archaeological techniques – in particular field-walking and aerial reconnaissance – are beginning to uncover evidence of settlement, burial, and extensive human intervention in the landscape of lowland Devon, and the invisible archaeological potential of the country's cultivated fields demonstrates the widespread extent of prehistoric activity throughout the county.

The visible prehistoric structures date roughly from the last three thousand years B.C. They fall broadly into three categories: those concerned with burial and worship; settlements of villages, farms, and fields; and defensive sites.

STRUCTURES OF BURIAL AND WORSHIP include the most widespread surviving prehistoric feature of the Devon landscape: the BARROW. About 1300 have been positively identified already (see Further Reading). The majority were places of burial, either inhumation or cremation, but some probably had other functions: the largest, for example, may well have served as territorial markers, and others, intimately connected with stone rows and circles, etc., apparently formed part of a coherent ritual design. Few have been precisely dated, but a dozen radiocarbon determinations and analogies with sites elsewhere in the country suggest that the great majority of them fall between *c.* 3000 and 1000 B.C.

The earliest and some of the most impressive structures form a small group of chambered tombs, probably for collective burial. One of the most striking is Spinsters' Rock at Drewsteignton, a bare megalithic framework of three granite orthostats, each about 6 ft high, supporting a massive capstone. The stones collapsed in 1862 but were restored in the same year, apparently not quite accurately. However, the un-dressed slabs and the simple supporting technique for the capstone illustrate clearly the building method of the period. The similar slabs lying on the ground at the s end of a massive long barrow at Corringdon Ball Gate, South Brent, must represent a collapsed chamber. The barrow itself has maximum dimensions of about 130 by 65 by 6 ft high. Its approximate N–S orientation is paralleled by the remains of cham-bered long cairns at Cuckoo Ball (where the chamber is at the N end) and Butterdon Hill, both in Ugborough parish. A recently discovered long cairn N of Postbridge, Lydford, confirms the penetration of these early tomb types into the heart of Dartmoor. This one, too, has a possible collapsed chamber (though no large stones) at its higher, N end.

The most detailed structural evidence for a large chambered cairn has been provided by a unique example in lowland Devon, discovered incorporated into a later hedge-bank at Broadsands, Torbay. It is a polygonal chamber, about 11 by 7 by 5¼ ft high, constructed of local limestone slabs up to 5 ft high with drystone walling in between them. It had been roofed by at least two slabs. A short passage, 12½ ft long by nearly 4 ft wide and similarly constructed, led to the chamber. The original cairn mound was probably circular and about 40 ft in diameter. Evidence of inhumations was found. It is probable that earthen long barrows previously existed in lowland Devon. The only confirmed example has recently been destroyed near Tiverton.

The more usual ROUND BARROWS and CAIRNS display great architectural variety which is often apparent to the field observer. About half the known round barrows of the county survive on Dartmoor. They vary greatly in size, the largest being the central one at Three Barrows, South Brent. It is 130 ft in diameter and 8 ft high, but many are less than 30 ft in diameter. It is a common misconception that all barrows have substantial mounds of turf or stone; in fact many consist, as field evidence, only of a low ring bank, perhaps 3–6 ft wide, enclosing a level area or one with a small low mound in its centre. Good examples of such RING CAIRNS are to be seen at Cosdon, South Tawton; Gripper's Hill, Dean Prior; Saddlesborough, Shaugh Prior; and Headon Down, Cornwood. Many more 'conventional' barrow mounds appear to have a ring-cairn element, for example the apparently Wessex-type bell barrow on Piles Hill, Ugborough, and the northernmost of Two Barrows, Manaton.

Mounded barrows on Dartmoor often have a RETAINING CIRCLE of stone slabs, frequently leaning outwards and usually not con-tiguous. Setta Barrow, High Bray, is a good example on Exmoor, and on Dartmoor are Grim's Grave, Shaugh Prior, in the Plym valley, and Down Tor, Walkhampton. The relation of the circle to the mound can vary considerably. The type with a double or triple ring of stones is clearly related to the multiple concentric STONE RINGS found under certain cairns (e.g. near Grey Wethers, Lydford, and at Glasscombe,

Ugborough) or more or less free-standing (also at Glasscombe). They are usually constructed of small stones, often about 8 in. long by 4 in. wide by 4 in. high; larger stones are to be seen at Yellowmead, Sheepstor, and Shovel Down, Gidleigh.

Of the six small cairns excavated on Shaugh Moor, Shaugh Prior, in the late 1970s (only four of them visible as earthwork features), two proved to be ring cairns, three small ones had stone kerbs (i.e. similar to the retaining circle), and one was a stone cairn. Pits containing charcoal were found beneath most of them, but there was no evidence of human burial. Radiocarbon tests yielded a date in the first half of the second millennium B.C.

Many barrows contained CISTS, i.e. pits or chests lined with stone slabs or, occasionally, wood. Nearly two hundred stone cists have been recorded on Dartmoor alone, and many can still be seen, especially in the Plym valley on SW Dartmoor. Mostly they consist of two side slabs, two shorter end slabs, and a cover-stone.

Construction materials for barrow mounds include turf and clay (sometimes burnt), turf covering a central cairn, stones covering turf, and many others. Beyond Dartmoor it is more common to see barrows with surrounding ditches, e.g. at Five Barrows, North Molton; on Parracombe Common; and in the parish of Farway.

Equally important is the grouping of the barrows and their association with other ritual features. Ring cairns and mounded barrows are often found next to each other, and occasionally linear groups occur, as on Affaland Moor, Clawton; at Chapman Barrows, Challacombe and Parracombe; and on Crownhill Down, Sparkwell. CAIRNFIELDS – small stone heaps, sometimes twenty or thirty together, occasionally associated with short lengths of straggling wall – have also been identified on Dartmoor, for example at White Hill, Peter Tavy, and at Rowter Marsh, Lydford. They may have had a ritual function, have been stone clearance heaps for primitive agriculture, or – perhaps most likely – some combination of both.

Devon is especially rich in STONE ROWS, which clearly had a religious or ritual function, and perhaps also the secular one of defining territories. More than seventy are known on Dartmoor, single, double, or triple, and ranging in length from about 30 yards to just over 2 miles. Most of the stones are less than 3 ft in height, but on Staldon Moor, Cornwood, they are consistently large: up to nearly 8 ft tall. Generally, the stones are regularly spaced within the row, and have their long axes following the direction of the row. There is commonly a cairn at the higher end – more than sixty such cases are known on Dartmoor. The hypothesis that many of the rows were products of several phases of construction is supported by field evidence, as at Merrivale, Walkhampton, where the northernmost pair changes distinctly in character and slightly in alignment about halfway along its length, and near Glasscombe Corner, Ugborough, where a row is double for part of its length and single for the rest. A few rows occur in North Devon; one at Yelland, Fremington, is in what is now an inter-tidal zone of the Taw estuary.

A rarer type of structure is the impressive free-standing STONE CIRCLE, of which about a dozen are known on Dartmoor. Most are between 80 and 100 ft in diameter and consist of 30 to 36 evenly spaced stones enclosing a level area. The stones are mostly no more than 3 ft in height but can nevertheless be quite substantial slabs, as at Mardon,

Moretonhampstead. Although not apparently dressed, they seem to have been carefully chosen to create an impression of regularity, most marked at the restored circles at Grey Wethers, Lydford.

On the Devonshire parts of Exmoor there are no certain stone circles, but there are several enigmatic groups known as STONE SETTINGS, such as that on Longstone Allotment, Challacombe, where five stones are arranged in a quadrilateral.

These brief typological descriptions cannot of course do justice to the remarkable concentrations of prehistoric ritual structures in some parts of the county, especially on Dartmoor, where at least half a dozen major centres appear to have formed the focus of religious and other activity, just as medieval and present-day parish churches have done. Drizzlecombe, Sheepstor, in the Plym valley has one of the finest groupings, and here and at Merrivale, Walkhampton; Shovel Down, Gidleigh; and Fernworthy, Lydford, stone rows, stone circles, and barrows can be found clustered together, reflecting the complexity and sophistication of prehistoric society over probably at least 1,500 years. Comparable ritual complexes also existed in lowland Devon, but these are now known only from cropmark evidence.

Our second category of prehistoric sites comprises SETTLEMENTS OF VILLAGES, FARMS, AND FIELDS. One of the earliest known dwellings within the county was excavated on Haldon Hill near Exeter. It was a rectangular timber-framed structure with wattle-and-daub walls, on a foundation of small stones, measuring about 20 by 13 ft inside. It probably dates from the centuries around 3000 B.C.

On both Dartmoor and Exmoor one can still see the foundations of HOUSES and FIELD SYSTEMS dating from the second millennium B.C. onwards. On Dartmoor perhaps as many as 5,000 house sites are still visible, besides vast areas of field systems. The Dart Valley system, comprising some 7,500 acres, adjoins the Rippon Tor complex, which may once have covered 11,000 acres, making these the largest prehistoric field systems yet identified in Britain.

REAVES are linear boundaries which divide the moor into blocks of land similar to our modern parishes, with common land on the higher ground. Some also form the upper 'terminal' boundary of a network of fields. One of these physical boundaries has been traced for more than six miles. They now have the appearance of low stony banks, about 3–6 ft wide and up to about 3 ft high. The course of the major reaves is typically sinuous, and in some places 'gang-junctions' – a sudden change in direction or style of construction – suggest a meeting-point of two building teams. Excavated evidence from Holne Moor has shown that many of the reaves were neatly faced with stone, most commonly on the 'outside', i.e. towards the open grazing land rather than the lower-altitude fields. What seem to be gateways are visible in some of the reaves. Excavation on Shaugh Moor, Shaugh Prior, and on Holne Moor, Holne, has shown that the stone reaves were preceded by an earthen bank and ditch, and on Shaugh Moor there was evidence of timbers of a possible hurdlework fence along part of the original boundary. Most of the Dartmoor reaves were built in the mid second millennium B.C., and they can provide important clues to relative chronology, for some cut across stone rows, apparently slighting them (e.g. at Shovel Down, Gidleigh, and at Hurston Ridge, Chagford), while others seem to respect them (Holne Moor, Holne; Merrivale, Walkhampton).

The surviving buildings – known as HUT CIRCLES – of the prehistoric people of Dartmoor are as varied as the barrows. Evidence from Holne Moor, Holne, and Gould Park, North Bovey, has proved the existence of substantial free-standing timber structures both preceding and contemporary with the stone phase. A stone house on Holne Moor was found to have had an internal timber lining. Other evidence recoverable by excavation includes sophisticated use of drains and ditches for coping with surface water, and evidence of postholes for the timber uprights supporting roofs of organic material. The visible foundations range in diameter from around 9 to 36ft and must represent a wide range of functions, not necessarily connected with living quarters. An entrance is often visible. Some of the walls have an inner and outer facing of large stone slabs; others use small stones in a relatively unsophisticated drystone technique, as on Shaugh Moor (site excavated and now destroyed). These buildings were by no means all low and cramped; the area covered by many equals that of some of the medieval longhouses, and several still have wall slabs standing to a height of between 3 and 6ft, as at Metherel, Chagford; near Haytor, Ilsington; and on Vogwell Down, Manaton. Some, like those between Merrivale and Foggintor in Walkhampton parish, have internal subdivisions. Some are conjoined, as at Broadun, Lydford, others terraced into the hill-slope, as at Gould Park, North Bovey. On the edge of the moor, especially below about 800ft, less stone is used, presumably reflecting a greater availability of turf and wood, and structures seem to be more frequently terraced into the hillside, as on Hanger Down, Cornwood. Such sites are more closely comparable with the few known house sites on Exmoor (e.g. Parracombe Common).

Hut circles can occur singly; in clusters of 6–10 buildings, sometimes among fields, as on Holne Moor, Holne, and at Kestor, Chagford; in substantial, straggling, unenclosed groups of up to ninety, as at Watern Oke, Lydford; and in complex enclosed settlements defined by substantial walls, as at Riders Rings, South Brent. Some of these enclosures, or 'pounds' as they are commonly known on Dartmoor, are very large: the one at Broadun, Lydford, contains some forty buildings within an area of 14 acres, and that at Whittenknowles Rocks, Sheepstor, is of a similar size and capacity.

Although Grimspound, Manaton, has an imposing entrance, other enclosures do not; indeed on Shaugh Moor, Shaugh Prior, there was one enclosure, with five huts, which had no entrance at all, though an unusually thick stretch of enclosure wall led the excavator to speculate about the possibility of access by means of a stile. This enclosure (now engulfed by china-clay working) is particularly important as it produced evidence of a structural sequence of about a thousand years, at the start of which the settlement of five hut circles was unenclosed. Moreover, none of the huts produced evidence of a hearth, which raises the question of whether or not they were seasonally occupied.

Traces of late prehistoric field systems do exist on the limestone plateau of south Devon, between Newton Abbot and Torbay, especially in the parishes of Ipplepen, Kingskerswell, and Torbryan. Sub-rectangular enclosures and other features are defined by stony banks rarely more than 20in. high. At Dainton, Ipplepen, extensive evidence of human occupation and metallurgical activity was found by excavation in advance of quarrying.

DEFENSIVE SITES. Because of their greater resistance to cultivation, hilltop sites with substantial earthworks or stone 'fortifications' are still widely distributed throughout the county, redressing the bias towards Dartmoor which has been evident in discussing other structures. At Hembury, Payhembury, in East Devon a substantial hilltop was occupied by at least 3500 B.C. and probably rather earlier. The site, defined by a series of interrupted ditches dug across a natural spur, was occupied again in the later prehistoric period, when massive ramparts were constructed, and then, briefly, by the Roman army (see below).

Most of the visible remains of the many HILLFORTS scattered throughout Devon belong to the first millennium B.C. The large defensive sites with single or multiple ramparts closely set together, found principally in the east of the county, resemble others in southern Britain. Dumpdon, Luppitt, and Hembury, Payhembury, are examples in East Devon; Countisbury near Lynton another in the N of the county. Surface features on all these sites are largely restricted to the impressive ramparts and the complex entrances. At Hembury excavation has produced evidence for a box-rampart with massive timber posts. Elsewhere – particularly W of the Exe and on Exmoor – the ramparts are spaced more widely, perhaps to provide corrals for stock in a pastorally based economy. Good examples of the type are Clovelly Dykes, Clovelly, and Milber Down, Haccombe with Coombe.

Some of the hill-slope enclosures with a single rampart appear to be related to the Cornish 'rounds'. These smaller sites, perhaps representing an enclosed hamlet or single farm, are visible throughout the county, and recent aerial survey has identified many others (including enclosed settlements that could never qualify for the name 'hillfort') whose above-ground traces have been wholly destroyed.

In addition, Devon has its share of spectacular promontory forts and cliff castles occupying uncompromisingly defensive and frequently inhospitable sites. Good examples are at Bolt Tail, Malborough, and at Hillsborough, Ilfracombe. Inland, a fine defended promontory may be seen at Halstock, Okehampton Hamlets, where a substantial outer bank (of which one end has been obliterated) cuts off the only stretch which is not protected by steep drops to the river below.

With the notable exception of the city walls of Exeter, there are few visible structures within the county that can, with any confidence, be assigned to the period of ROMAN OCCUPATION in the first four centuries A.D. Substantial stone remains of the bath house of the legionary fortress of c. A.D. 50–70 survive beneath the Cathedral Green at Exeter, but are not at present displayed. The city walls of Exeter follow the line of defences for the enlarged civil Roman town of Isca Dumnoniorum, and date from the end of the second century A.D. They enclose 93 acres and have a circuit of 1.45 miles, from which nearly three-quarters survives. The base of the wall is over 10 ft wide. Although many of the Roman facing blocks were replaced with similar stone before the C14, enough still exists to give a good impression of the scale and quality of Roman building technique.

Outside Exeter, many new discoveries of sites have been made in recent years, largely through aerial photography. Most are of Roman military forts, often visible only as cropmarks; some have slight earthwork remains, as at Cullompton, or preserve part of their extent in the shape of modern field boundaries, as at Woodbury, just S of

Axminster. Villas have been excavated at Holcombe, Uplyme, and at Seaton, but no upstanding remains survive. At Sourton Down, Sourton, a conspicuous earthwork, consisting of a square platform defined by two ditches and with a causeway on its SW side, has been interpreted as a possible Roman signal station.

INDUSTRIAL DEVON

BY WALTER MINCHINTON

If industrial archaeology is concerned, as it properly should be, with the whole range of man's industrial activity and not just with the period of the Industrial Revolution, then our survey begins with the early evidence of such activity in Devon which largely depended upon the natural resources of the county. This is provided by TINNERS' MILLS (including blowing houses) used to process tin produced by streaming on Dartmoor. Fine examples dating from the late Middle Ages can be seen at Henglake, South Brent; Merrivale, Walkhampton; Glaze Meet, Ugborough; and Norsworthy, Walkhampton. Stone was early dressed for bridges, buildings, millstones, and other purposes. At Beer and elsewhere stone was quarried from the Middle Ages, but until the C19 most of the granite used was collected from clitters (surface boulders) on Dartmoor. Representative of the QUARRYING industry are the limestone quarries at Ashburton, Beer, Plymouth, Torquay, and Westleigh, the granite workings at Haytor, Ilsington, and at Merrivale, Walkhampton, and the lava and breccia quarries of the Exeter district (Pocombe and Heavitree respectively).

To facilitate travel in a county of high rainfall and many streams and rivers, our predecessors made tracks and roads and built bridges. Inevitably later development has overlaid or replaced much of their work, but two well-known tracks across Dartmoor survive, the Abbot's Way (or Jobbers' Road) from Buckfastleigh to Whitchurch, and the King Way from Tavistock to Okehampton. Of the number of clapper BRIDGES the most notable are in Lydford parish on Dartmoor, at Postbridge and Bellever. More elaborate are the remains of the Old Exe Bridge at Exeter, recently excavated. At Barnstaple, Bideford, Clyst St Mary, Horrabridge, Staverton, and elsewhere, medieval bridges, sometimes widened, are still used.

If tin was the first of the economic resources of Devon to be exploited, wool was the second. Taking advantage of the rich pastures of the county, farmers reared sheep to provide wool. WOOLLEN CLOTH manufacture was for long a domestic industry, but the introduction of the water-driven fulling mill in the C13 made the finishing processes more capital-intensive. While little survives in a physical sense directly of the medieval Devon cloth industry, as discussed elsewhere, the chantries of the parish churches of Cullompton and Tiverton bear witness to the wealth to which it gave rise, and Tuckers Hall, Fore Street, Exeter is the hall of the Guild of Weavers, Tuckers (or Fullers) and Shearmen. Though the importance of clothmaking declined from the early C19, wooden-shuttered wool lofts can still be seen in Ashburton and Buckfastleigh, and former factory buildings at Buckfastleigh, Culmstock, North Tawton, Ottery St Mary, and Uffculme. In Axminster is the building where CARPETS were made. Two industries, LACE and PAPER, developed on a factory basis when woollen cloth declined. Early C19 lace factories are to be found at Tiverton (where John Heathcoat set up manufacture) and Barnstaple, while paper mills were clustered mainly in Exeter and the Culm valley at Cullompton, Hele (Bradninch), and Silverton, but also at Ivybridge and at Tuckenhay.

Agriculture too was a major industry, based largely on sheep and cattle. FARMHOUSES are the subject of a separate introduction, but we shall discuss here the evidence of other buildings ancillary to farming activity. From the C16 until the late C19 lime was strewn by farmers on the soil to reduce its acidity. Over 370 LIMEKILNS are still to be found in many parts of the county, along the coasts, in the valleys of the Exe, the Dart, the Tamar, the Taw, and the Torridge, and in the Kingsbridge estuary, and on inland sites such as the banks of the Grand Western Canal as well. Their form varies, and no typology is as yet available. Horses were used to work machinery for threshing and cider-making, among other things, and the ROUNDHOUSES which housed the machinery are still to be seen attached to some barns. A few POUNDS, used to impound stray animals, survive, as at Bicton, Great Torrington, and Sidbury. There are good examples of ICEHOUSES at Bicton, Killerton, and Yealmpton. ASH HOUSES (for storing ashes to be used as fertilizer) can be seen on some farms, for example at North Bovey. At Braunton there is an OPEN FIELD, and other field systems are visible at Challacombe, Manaton, and at Halsanger Common, N of Ashburton. LAND RECLAMATION schemes were carried out by *James Green* at Budleigh Salterton, W of the Otter, and at Chelson along the east banks of the Plym near Plymouth. On Dartmoor (for example at Trowlesworthy, Shaugh Prior, and at Ditsworthy, Sheepstor) and elsewhere in the county (e.g. on the cliff south of Noss Mayo) WARRENS were constructed to encourage the breeding of rabbits both for fur and food.

To grind corn, wind power was employed, particularly from about 1780 to 1830, and remains of nine WINDMILL TOWERS survive, five of them in a ring around Torbay; but from before Domesday Devon was a county of water power rather than wind power. Many WEIRS impounded water, and a distinctive tumbling weir is to be found at Ottery St Mary. There are still many WATERMILLS, some converted to private dwellings, as at Deerbridge Mill, Slapton, others used as tourist attractions, as at Ilfracombe and Otterton; only a few are still operating commercially as corn mills, for example at Harbertonford, Monk Okehampton, and Thorverton (turbine). There are also farm mills, as at Ashton in the Teign valley and at Yeo, Chagford. Water power was also used for such other purposes as sawmilling and paper- and sailcloth-making, as well as to facilitate the drainage of mines on Dartmoor. The need of farmers for tools was met, as at Dunsford and Sticklepath, by edge-tool factories. In indented estuaries in the county, TIDEMILLS at Kingsbridge, Plymstock (Plymouth), Stoke Gabriel, Topsham, and Totnes supplemented other sources of power in the grinding of corn.

As is usual in agricultural counties, many of the towns had BREWERIES, most of which have disappeared. Good examples remain however at Dartmouth (now a pottery works) and Uffculme, while in Exeter several have found alternative uses. Disused malt-houses can be seen in Exeter and Newton Abbot (Tuckers' Maltings), and there is a fine thatched former malthouse at Crediton. At Plymouth, Coates Gin Distillery, founded in 1793, continues to operate in a late C18/early C19 building which incorporates a C15 hall.

MINING continued from the later Middle Ages into modern times. Its high noon in Devon was the first two-thirds of the C19, when a wide range of minerals was produced. Of these, copper and arsenic were the most important, but lead, iron, silver, and tin were also extracted. Apart from spoil heaps, little now remains of all this activity. There are ruined engine houses at Wheal Betsy, Mary Tavy; Wheal Exmouth, Canonteign; and the Druids Mine, Ashburton. In the Tamar Valley are the stacks and flues of Devon Great Consols and Gawton (both in Tavistock Hamlets). Morwellham is a restored copper port. The most important sites on Dartmoor are Birch Tor and Vitifer, North Bovey; Eylesbarrow, Sheepstor; and Ramsley, South Zeal. In North Devon, some evidence of early mining remains near Combe Martin and North Molton.

Using local clay, POTTERY, less widespread than formerly, is still manufactured at Barnstaple, Heathfield (Bovey Tracey), and Honiton. At Bovey Tracey some pottery kilns survive. BRICKS were also made in various parts of the county and are still produced in Exeter and at Steer Point, Brixton, near Plymouth.

In the C19 water power was replaced by STEAM in Devon's manufacturing industries. Steam flour-mills were built at Barnstaple, Exeter, North Tawton, Plymouth, Tiverton, and elsewhere, although many have now been demolished as flour-milling, like so many other industries, has become more centralized. Paper-mills acquired steam engines (as at Ivybridge and Trew's Weir, Exeter), as did cloth-making. The only steam engine still working – as a tourist attraction – is at Coldharbour Mill in Uffculme, which also has a large industrial waterwheel. At Dartmouth, the birthplace of the inventor, a *Newcomen* engine brought from outside the county is on display. Of recent years the number of CHIMNEYSTACKS too has been sharply reduced. Steam has given way to electricity.

Along with flour-milling and brewing, cloth manufacture and mining were Devon's major industries, but the wide range of other activities included ENGINEERING, as at Tavistock (Gill & Rundles early C19 foundry), Kingsbridge, Exeter, and Plymouth. Of the many village FORGES, examples can be seen at Branscombe and at Cockington, Torbay. There is still a LEATHER WORKS operating in Colyton. On Dartmoor, at Two Bridges, Lydford, there was a GUNPOWDER WORKS (1855).

With two coastlines and several navigable rivers, water provided the main means for the transport of goods before the improvement of the roads and the coming of the railways. QUAYS were constructed, for example at Appledore, Bideford, Lynmouth, and places along the Tamar. Harbour walls created sheltered ports at Clovelly (1587) and Ilfracombe (1760, 1824–9, 1873), and at Torquay and Brixham (the major fishing port, 1799–1804), Torbay. Morwellham was an up-river port. WAREHOUSES are to be found at Appledore, Dartmouth, Exeter (1835), Plymouth, Totnes, and elsewhere; CUSTOM HOUSES include those at Exeter (1680–1) and Topsham (at both of which the frame of the King's Beam for weighing dutiable goods remains), and at Dartmouth (1739) and Plymouth (1586, 1810). [148]

Safety at sea was improved by the construction of LIGHTHOUSES. On Lundy the Old Lighthouse of 1819, built on high ground and so of little use in fog, was replaced in 1897 by the North and South Lights. Of *Smeaton*'s tower, the third Eddystone lighthouse (1759), the top part has been rebuilt on Plymouth Hoe. LIFEBOAT STATIONS have altered their character, but early ones can be seen at Exmouth and Salcombe. At Plymouth the safety of the harbour was greatly increased by the construction between 1811 and 1844 of the BREAKWATER designed by *John Rennie*, and *Brunel*'s DOCKS at Millbay were built in 1859. Among the port industries were SHIPBUILDING (slipways survive at Salcombe and Topsham; at Appledore are the site of the Richmond dry dock and the recent covered shipbuilding yard), SAILMAKING (early C19 sail lofts at Appledore and Topsham), and ROPEMAKING (rope walks at Bideford and Dartmouth). The most impressive site is the Royal Naval Dockyard at Devonport, Plymouth, started in 1691 by *Edmund Dummer* and developed ever since. The best surviving groups are the gun wharf of 1718–25, the later C18 roperies, [154] *Rennie*'s victualling yard of 1825–33, the largely Edwardian steam [146] yard, and the new covered repair sheds.

Because water transport was widely available, road improvement came comparatively late to Devon, and the packhorse reigned generally until after 1750 and in some places as late as 1830. Between the 1750s and the 1840s, thirty-two turnpike trusts were founded in Devon to improve roads for wheeled traffic. The oldest of the eighty or so surviving TOLL HOUSES, a rare thatched one at Newton Poppleford, is of 1758, but most date from between 1815 and 1845. The so-called Copper Castle at Honiton is the only one to retain its gates. The toll house at Shaldon Bridge, Teignmouth, was the last to operate in Devon, c. 1827–1948. A few MILESTONES are still in place, and there are several ROADSIDE MONUMENTS of note such as the direction post at East Budleigh of c. 1580 and the Coalbrookdale dolphin lamp-posts at Barnstaple.

With road improvement in the C19 many more BRIDGES were built. Cowley Bridge over the Exe at Exeter by *James Green* is of 1813, the bridge at Totnes, designed by *Charles Fowler*, of 1826–8. At Exeter, the little iron bridge of 1814 in the Close was followed in 1834 by a more impressive structure spanning the Longbrook Valley: the North Road Iron Bridge. St Saviour's Bridge, Ottery St Mary, is of 1851. The oldest surviving concrete bridge in England, built in 1877, is at Seaton, and at Thorverton there is an early (1908) reinforced concrete bridge.

Navigation between Exeter and the sea, interrupted by the construction of weirs on the Exe, was restored by the earliest pound-lock CANAL in Devon – and in England too – built by *John Trew* between 1560 and 1566 and improved and extended on a number of later occasions. Other canals were built in the late C18 and early C19 to solve local transport problems and not to provide a network of communications: the Grand Western (1810–14, *John Rennie*), running E from Tiverton through Halberton and Sampford Peverell, the Stover (1790–2) from Teigngrace, joining the Teign at Newton Abbot, the Tavistock (1803–17, *John Taylor*), with its warehouses and tunnel, running W to Morwellham on the Tamar, the Cann Quarry (1829) at

Plympton St Mary, the Rolle, beginning in Great Torrington, with the Beam aqueduct built by *James Green* in 1825–7, which now carries the drive to Beam College, and the Bude Canal (1819–25), its inclines also designed by *James Green*.

RAILED TRANSPORT was provided first by tramways. The Haytor Granite Tramway, built by George Templer of Stover to enable granite to be brought from the quarries in the parish of Ilsington to the Stover Canal at Teigngrace in 1820, had granite rails, some of which are still in position. A number of mineral railways and tramways followed to exploit the resources of Dartmoor and the Tamar Valley. More important was the arrival at Exeter of the main line of the Bristol & Exeter Railway in 1844. To complete the link with Plymouth, *Isambard Kingdom Brunel*, the engineer for the South Devon Railway, chose a route which ran through St Thomas (Exeter) on a substantial sixty-two-arch viaduct, down the Exe, and then along the coast from Dawlish to Teignmouth. It required considerable engineering works, particularly tunnels and a protective sea wall. The railway was originally designed as a broad-gauge line operated on the atmospheric principle as far as Newton Abbot (1847–8), the power being provided by stationary engines rather than moving locomotives. Of the ENGINE HOUSES, the most obvious is that at Starcross and the most complete that at Torre, Torquay (Torbay). Between Newton Abbot and Plymouth, where the railway arrived in 1849, the route was designed for single-line atmospheric working, and the gradients over which steam and now diesel locomotives still labour are fiercer than if the line had been designed for their operation. Of the series of magnificent timber VIADUCTS (later replaced by stone) that were built by Brunel to bridge the valleys as the line skirted the southern edge of Dartmoor the original stone piers can still be seen at Glazebrook, South Brent; Bittaford, Ugborough; Slade, Cornwood; and Ivybridge. At Plympton the road crosses the railway by one of the most oblique BRIDGES Brunel ever built – 63 degrees off the square. His major achievement was the Royal Albert Bridge at Plymouth (1859), which carries the railway across the Tamar from Devon to Cornwall. On the old Southern Railway's lines there are several viaducts between Plymouth and Gunnislake in Cornwall, notably the one at Calstock, Bere Alston, built of concrete blocks by *Richard Church* in 1907; others are at Holsworthy on the old line to Bude, reinforced concrete of 1898, and the massed concrete Cannington viaduct of 1900–3 at Uplyme, on the Lyme Regis branch. The wrought-iron and steel girder viaduct at Meldon, Okehampton, was built in two sections by *W. R. Galbraith* and *R. F. Church* in 1874 and 1879. The brick Chelfham viaduct (1898 by *Frank W. Chanter*) carried the narrow-gauge Lynton & Barnstaple Railway over the river Yeo at Bratton Fleming. Notable stations are at Axminster (1859, *Sir William Tite*), Crediton (1854, *Brunel*), Dawlish (1848, *Brunel*; 1873, *J. P. Margery*), Exeter St Davids (1864, *Henry Lloyd* and *Francis Fox*, and 1910–12), and Torre, Torquay (1848, *Brunel*). TUNNELS are at Marley Head, Rattery (1848), White Ball, Holcombe Rogus, partly in Somerset (1843), and Devonport, Plymouth (1858 and 1883). CLIFF RAILWAYS exist at Lynton (1890) and at Babbacombe, Torquay (1926).

WATER is essential for human existence. Water from wells and streams met the needs of many, but with the growth of towns in the high Middle Ages steps had to be taken to augment supplies. The underground passages at Exeter were constructed from the late C12, and the Tiverton leat dates from the C13. Drake's leat to supply Plymouth was built in the late C16. Elsewhere in villages water was obtained from conduits or pump houses. Public conduits exist at Beer, Dartmouth, Denbury, Hemyock, Modbury, and elsewhere, and pumps at Ipplepen, Shaldon (Teignmouth), and Torbryan, for example. From the late C19 large quantities of water were obtained from reservoirs like Burrator, Sheepstor (1898), Avon, South Brent (1956), and Meldon, Okehampton (1972). They have impressive retaining dams. To assist distribution, several water towers of steel or reinforced concrete were erected, for example at Broadclyst, Clovelly, Dunkeswell, and East Prawle (Chivelstone). Late C19 cast-iron public urinals have been preserved at Plymouth and Colyford station.

Among English counties Devon was comparatively quick to install HYDRO-ELECTRICITY PLANTS at Okehampton from 1889 (where the dam on the Okement is visible), at Lynton (1890), and at Chagford (after 1891). The modern plants at Mary Tavy and Morwellham, together with Chagford, make Devon the largest producer of hydro-electricity in England. An unusually ornate early ELECTRICITY GENERATING STATION remains at Haven Banks, Exeter (1903–5 by *Donald Cameron*). GASHOLDERS with varying degrees of ornamentation are still prominent in many places; most are spiral holders, introduced in the 1930s, but at Newton Abbot there is also quite an elaborate example of the earlier column-guided type (others remain at Barnstaple and at Coxside, Plymouth).

Devon's mineral wealth was located far from settlements, so HOUSING was provided for mine-workers at Haytor (Ilsington), Tavistock, Morwellham, and elsewhere, and for workers in that Dartmoor successor to mining, the china clay industry, at Lee Moor, Shaugh Prior. Other industrial housing can be found at Tiverton, where John Heathcoat built houses for his lace-workers. In Exeter, the Improved Industrial Dwellings at Kendal Close, Blackboy Road, are the only survivors of a number of later C19 blocks.

In the TWENTIETH CENTURY mining has declined but quarrying continues; ball clay is extracted at Bovey Tracey and in North Devon, and china clay at Lee Moor, Shaugh Prior. The majority of the stone now quarried is only for road aggregate. Textiles have declined sharply. Gasholders have been demolished as natural gas has replaced coal gas, and railway lines have been closed, with stations and other buildings finding new uses. New industrial buildings, mainly on estates round Exeter, Plymouth, Barnstaple, Torbay, and other places, have contributed little of architectural distinction, but the covered shipyards at Appledore and at Devonport, Plymouth, are impressive structures, and the out-of-town supermarkets, though not elegant, have wide internal spans. For the most part, because of expense, stone has been replaced as a building material by brick – not all made within the county – steel, and concrete.

As rail has shrunk, so roads have grown. Three of the earliest prestressed concrete bridges in Britain were built in 1955 after the Lynton floods. The coming of the motorway involved cuttings, embankments, viaducts, and bridges. Construction commenced in Devon with the Cullompton bypass in 1969, and the M5 was completed beyond Exeter in 1977; the two prestressed concrete viaducts over the

Exe at Topsham and at Exminster are 757 and 330 yards long. The
improvement of the A38 to Plymouth in 1974 involved the construction of a variety of concrete and steel bridges – largely the work of
Devon County Council staff – including one with two arches at
Chudleigh spanning 150ft. A slender road suspension bridge, contrasting with the massiveness of the Brunel bridge, was built over the
Tamar from Plymouth to Saltash in Cornwall in 1961.

When Daniel Defoe wrote about Devon in the early C18, he
described it as a prosperous, populous, industrial county; in the late
C20 it is none of these. When they can serve as tourist attractions, the
remains of past economic activity are safeguarded. The work of
distinguished engineers such as *Isambard Kingdom Brunel*, *James
Green*, *Thomas Newcomen*, *John Rennie*, *John Smeaton*, and *John
Taylor*, and of architects like *Charles Fowler* and *Sir William Tite*, can
be seen. But elsewhere the buildings and structures where our
forefathers earned a living are under threat. The writings of industrial
archaeologists have shown, however, that Devon is not just a county of
cream teas and golden sands, red cliffs and thatched cottages but one
where over the centuries a whole range of industrial occupations have
been carried on in home, workshop, factory, and mine.

CHURCHES AND THEIR FURNISHINGS:

MEDIEVAL TO MID SEVENTEENTH CENTURY

The earliest group of Christian remains, mostly from the fringes of
Dartmoor (Lustleigh, Stowford, Yealmpton; others now at Tavistock),
belongs to the PRE-CONQUEST PERIOD. It consists of a number of
inscribed stones, probably of the C6–7. The names (some of them of
Irish settlers) are in Latin, and in a few cases in Ogham script as well.
Many churches are dedicated to Celtic missionaries of the C6 and C7
(Brannock, Nectan, Petrock, etc.), and even if some of these names
are later adoptions, their occurrence suggests that some ecclesiastical
centres existed at this time. What happened when the SAXONS began
to penetrate Devon in the C7 is obscure, although we know that the
Saxon St Boniface, who was born at Crediton in 680, was educated at a
monastery in Exeter. But architectural evidence of this early period is
almost non-existent. The small, completely plain crypt at Sidbury,
discovered in the C19, has no datable features, although it could have
originated as an early mausoleum which was later incorporated in the
church. There are a few decorated cross shafts. The best is at Colyton,
with lively inhabited scrolls, probably of the C9/10; other fragments
9 survive at Copplestone, Colebrooke; Dolton (converted to a font); and
St Nicholas Exeter. Sidbury has a slab with carved interlace. Nothing
is known of the pre-Conquest buildings of the monastic foundations of
Tavistock and Buckfast, nor of those of the most important early
foundations with secular canons, such as Hartland and Plympton.
Only at Exeter is there a little late Saxon evidence: excavations

revealed the apsed, aisleless C11 minster church which preceded the cathedral; long and short work (also probably late Saxon) survives at St Martin, and was found at St George (from which now only a reset doorway survives); while at St Olave, the odd small tower may be a survival from an C11 palace chapel.

Architectural remains become more copious after the NORMAN CONQUEST. The major monuments are in Exeter: the two elaborately decorated transeptal towers of the C12 cathedral (a type of tower unique in England) are incorporated in the later rebuilding; loose fragments suggest that the C12 church had a giant order of columns of West Country type. At St Nicholas Priory there is the late C11 groined undercroft of the W range and fragments of sophisticated late C12 carved work. There were many new foundations at this time,* but very little is left of contemporary monastic work. The plans of the churches at Buckfast and Plympton are known from excavations, but the most complete remains of this period are of the Premonstratensian abbey at Torre, Torquay (Torbay): here there are foundations of the church, early undercrofts to the W range, and an excellent late C12 transitional doorway to the chapter house. Otherwise all that need be noted from the C12 are the core of the gatehouse at Tavistock, remains of gateways at Buckfast and Plympton, and a modest doorway at Kerswell.

Stone parish churches were probably widespread in the C12, and very possibly earlier, but subsequent enlargement and rebuilding have obscured much of the evidence. The most usual reminders of the C12 and C13 are towers. Their solidity preserved them, for it needed considerable pride and money to pull down a tower and replace it by one bigger and better. Most of the early towers are unbuttressed. Some, especially N of Bolt Head, have corbel tables below the battlements. The majority are at the W end of the church, often so slim in girth as to make the nave appear wide behind them. Sidbury is an exception; elaborately treated, with flat buttresses, twin arched belfry windows, and, most remarkably, a ground-floor rib-vault – the earliest in Devon – with unmoulded rectangular ribs supported by caryatid capitals. Early transeptally placed towers are also found (as in Cornwall). There are at least eighteen, most of them in North Devon, this balance probably explained by the more energetic later medieval rebuilding which took place in the richer south. Those of Barnstaple, Braunton, and Ilfracombe are especially impressive. Was their inspiration the twin transeptal towers of Exeter, or should one look to an older tradition of free-standing bell-towers? Like those of the cathedral, the towers of the parish churches appear to have been built as virtually self-contained structures, unlike the storeyed side-chambers or *porticus* of Saxon churches. Crossing towers are less frequent, although a number exist which are of C12 or C13 origin (Aveton

*The main post-Conquest foundations are as follows. Benedictine: Otterton (an alien priory), before 1087; Totnes, *c.* 1090; Pilton, by the C12: Modbury (an alien priory), *c.* 1140; Cowick, Exeter, before 1144; Polsloe, Exeter (nuns), before 1160. Cluniac: Barnstaple, *c.* 1107; Kerswell, early C12; St James Exeter, before 1146. Cistercian: Buckfast (a refoundation, at first Savignac), 1146; Dunkeswell, 1201; Newenham, Axminster, 1247; Buckland, 1278. Augustinian canons: Plympton (a refoundation), 1121; Marsh Barton, Exeter (a cell of Plympton in 1142); Hartland (a refoundation, at first Arrouasian), after 1161; Frithelstock, *c.* 1220. Augustinian nuns: Canonsleigh, after 1161; Cornworthy, early C13. Premonstratensian canons: Torre, Torquay, 1196.

13 Gifford, Axminster, Branscombe, Colyton, Crediton, Kingsbridge, Shute, Tawstock).

Aisleless cruciform churches, once probably quite common, have generally been enveloped by later medieval additions – sometimes lopsidedly, so that an early transept remains on one side, a Perp aisle on the other. Occasionally the early cruciform plan survives complete, as at West Down or West Ogwell (the latter as late as *c.* 1300). A few unenlarged buildings are even simpler, for example the two-cell plan 31 of Honeychurch, or the single cell of St Michael Brentor. Aisled churches of this period are rare. St Mary Arches Exeter is the only one 7 remaining with two regular arcades, an elegant mid C12 work. The evidence suggests that Braunton may also have had two aisles, but only their outer walls remain. More frequently a single aisle was added to an earlier building. Surviving C12 examples are most often on the N side: Farway, Hawkchurch, North Petherwin, Salcombe Regis, Sidbury.

Later centuries showed the greatest respect for carved Norman doorways and for fonts. Of DOORWAYS, nearly all on the S side of the church, there are many examples, although none of as much exuberance as elsewhere in England. Among the most accomplished, with orders with chevron and other decoration, are the reset doorways at Axminster and Paignton (Torbay), the latter a polychrome effort in two types of stone. Bishopsteignton (like Paignton, a manor of the Bishop of Exeter) has an especially rich doorway with beakhead, and a tympanum as well, remarkable chiefly for its ruthless barbarity. Tympana generally do not compete favourably with those of other counties. Other places where Norman CARVING can be studied are 8 Bondleigh, Chulmleigh, Down St Mary (another tympanum), Hawk-church (especially good), High Bickington, and Membury. In North Devon there are three doorways of almost identical design, at Buck-land Brewer, Shebbear, and West Woolfardisworthy (Woolsery). Sidbury is again exceptional in having a little sculpture not attached to a doorway.

Norman FONTS in Devon number more than a hundred. They fall into several groups. The most elementary resembles an eggcup without any pronounced structural articulation (Bridgerule). Elemen-tary also is the font in the form of a square early Norman block capital: plain, as at Clovelly and Instow; or with the four semicircular surfaces decorated, as at High Bickington. Alternatively, the font is treated like a scalloped capital: three scallops at Weare Giffard; five scallops at Nether Exe; decorated bowl and scallops at Hartland. The most usual structurally articulated form is the goblet, a roughly circular bowl on a columnar or conically tapering shaft. One group of these in red sandstone is frequent S of a line from Plymouth via Ivybridge to Newton Abbot. The decoration is a palmette frieze with cable-moulding along the upper rim and sometimes chevron towards the bottom of the bowl. The cable may be replaced by a row of small saltire crosses (Cornworthy, cf. Fowey in Cornwall), and the palmettes supplemented or replaced by rosettes in circles (Combeinteignhead, 10 Buckland in the Moor), running scrolls (Farringdon), or even such motifs as incised dragons (Dean Prior). There are some rare, more ambitious square bowls with big coarse human faces at the corners and usually rosettes in circles, 'trees of life', or other motifs at the sides (a common Cornish type), for example Bratton Clovelly and Ashwater. A curious variation on this theme is provided by the fonts at Clawton and

Tetcott, whose bases are like these square bowls in reverse. Luppitt, the most ferociously carved of all Devon fonts, also belongs to this type. It has agitated scenes along the main surfaces between the faces. At Stoke Canon there are whole human figures along the angles, 11 crouching downwards, and caryatid figures on the shafts, an Italian motif. Less exotic is the common type of Purbeck marble font, found in many other counties as well, with a square shallow bowl like a heavy table-top, and plain shallow friezes of round-headed arches along the sides (Clyst Honiton, Crediton, Dodbrooke, Hemyock, Hennock, Kenn, Malborough, Southleigh, Talaton). The first of the series of bishops' MONUMENTS at Exeter Cathedral are also of Purbeck marble, the earliest late C12, the next, to Simon of Apulia † 1223, in the higher relief of the Gothic style of the early C13.

The EARLY ENGLISH PERIOD of the early C13 is not well represented in Devon. The most accomplished work is the lower part of the chapter house at Exeter of c. 1225, where the capitals have good stiff-leaf foliage. Frithelstock, founded in 1229, the only monastic church in the county with substantial standing remains, still conveys something of the nobility and austerity of the E.E. style. But in parish churches C13 Gothic detail remains rudimentary, characterized by simple lancet windows, sometimes tentatively grouped together, as at Sampford Peverell, Haccombe, Aveton Gifford (an interestingly complete C13 cruciform church), and Branscombe (where one can trace the gradual enlargement of the C12 church by early C13 transepts and a later C13 chancel).

The great landmark of the later C13 which inaugurated the DECORATED STYLE in Devon is the rebuilding campaign at EXETER CATHEDRAL, initiated by Bishop Branscombe around 1275, and continued under his successors into the mid C14. The design with its palm-tree-like sprouting and spreading piers and ribs is one of the most beautiful in English architecture, a mature flowering of the ideas developed earlier at Wells and Lincoln – though by the time the nave was carried out, still to the same design, it had become decidedly 20 conservative. Equally novel was the luxuriance of the carving of bosses, corbels, and capitals, matched by the sumptuous cathedral 17 furnishings of the early C14 in both stone and wood. The intricately detailed pulpitum (by *Thomas of Witney*), the delicate sedilia, and the 16, 19 towering timber bishop's throne are exceptional on a national level. 18 But in parish churches this new taste for variety of pattern and richly ornamented surfaces did not make itself felt until the C15, when it became an ingredient of the local Perp style. The spliced-up arch-mouldings of the cathedral are imitated only at Cheriton Fitzpaine; its sixteen-foil piers find an echo in the simpler mid C15 ones of Totnes.

Generally the masons of the cathedral workshop seem to have had little immediate impact on the countryside. The vagaries of Dec TRACERY, whose variety is demonstrated so well at the cathedral, 22 never became popular. Buckland Abbey has the remains of a large geometric Dec window in an unusual position above the chancel arch, but in parish churches elaborate designs are rare (Bampton, Bere Ferrers, Exbourne). Even ogee reticulation is uncommon (Clay-hanger, Dittisham, Milton Damerel, Mortehoe, Tavistock, West Down). This lack of interest in Dec tracery is a surprising aspect of the most ambitious C14 project after the cathedral, the collegiate church of Ottery St Mary, established by Bishop Grandison in 1337, for this is in 14

other respects a progressive building, clearly influenced by the
21 cathedral in the layout of its E end, and with a similar emphasis on rich
furnishings (the parclose screens are among the earliest surviving in
Devon). The elaborate vaults, partly with curved ribs, are indeed
more advanced in style than those of the cathedral and can be
associated with the work by *William Joy* at Wells.

However, Ottery was a collegiate foundation, and is exceptional;
most parish churches were much less ambitious. Instead of the
elaborate moulded piers and arches of the chancel of Ottery, arcades of
this period mostly have plain double-chamfered arches on simple
octagonal piers (as at Halberton). Some quite accomplished rebuilding
schemes continued the tradition of the unaisled cruciform plan (Tawstock, Bere Ferrers, the latter more elaborate than most, with two
contemporary tomb recesses). Where show was required, it was
concentrated on TOWERS and SPIRES. Two groups of these survive:
the one in the south-west, around Kingsbridge, has the C13 stone spire
of Modbury as its earliest example, and embraces Holbeton, Ermington, Diptford, and Buckfastleigh. The northern group includes Barnstaple, Ashford, Swimbridge, and Bishops Tawton. At Barnstaple the
tower is datable to 1388, and its lead-covered spire still retains its
medieval wooden frame. Bishops Tawton (a bishops' manor) is
exceptional in having a crocketed stone spire. The elaborately sculp-
23, 24 tured W front of Exeter Cathedral (not completed until the C15) has
no close imitations, although one can point to a few possible cases of
work by its sculptors (a large, odd, perhaps re-used figure at
Abbotskerswell; the ambitious decoration of the W tower at Upton
Pyne). But the loss of nearly all monastic buildings of this period
makes the picture very incomplete: there is tantalizing evidence that
Hartland had an early C14 cloister decorated with sculpture.

The outstanding MONUMENTS of the Dec period are the sequence
of bishops' effigies at Exeter, pre-eminent among them the exquisitely
15 carved and painted one of Bishop Branscombe (†1280). Bishop
Stapledon's tomb of 1328 is more elaborate, with a painting on the flat
canopy above the effigy, while that ascribed to his brother is uniquely
accompanied by figures of horse and groom. The growing C14 fashion
for a canopied structure above the effigy is illustrated by the monuments to Bishop Grandison's relations at Ottery (†1358 and 1374).
During the C14 the local gentry also begin to be commemorated by
effigies (rather later than elsewhere in England): two very similar
ladies exist at Axminster and Membury, and others at Bere Ferrers
and Littlehempston. Especially good C14 knights are to be found at
Atherington, at Bere Ferrers, and at Haccombe, where several of the
fine collection of monuments preserve their original gesso and paint. A
simpler tomb at Mortehoe (†1322) with incised figure is of special
interest because it includes tracery patterns.

So far, everything that has been mentioned is the exception rather
than the rule, for the great majority – perhaps 95 per cent – of pre-
Victorian Devon churches date predominantly from the PERPENDI-
CULAR PERIOD. Nationally, this is the style that developed in the
second half of the C14. In Devon, its earliest firmly dated manifes-
tation is at the cathedral, with the work of *Robert Lesyngham*. His S
portal of the W front, with its little up-to-date fan-vault, dates from
c. 1377 (he came from Gloucestershire, and the famous fan-vaulted
cloisters at Gloucester are attributed to him). In 1389–90 he remod-

elled the great E window, with its lights defined in the new manner by emphatic horizontal and vertical divisions. One is on less certain ground if one tries to give dates to the Perp work elsewhere in the county. Records of consecrations and of building activity may not relate to the existing fabric, as was pointed out by A. Hamilton Thompson in what is still the best available study of medieval church building in Devon,* and the C 14 dates traditionally associated with some Perp work are unconvincing (Dartmouth, Kenton, Tavistock). The piecemeal evidence that does exist (occasional references to work on new building in the Registers of Bishop Lacy, bequests in wills, building accounts, and heraldic evidence on the churches themselves) all points to much reconstruction and enlargement in the C 15 and early C 16. The town churches are the best recorded: Crediton, between 13 1413 and 1478; Bradninch tower, 1437; Okehampton, complete rebuilding, 1448; Totnes tower and other works, 1440s; Tavistock, aisle, 1440s; Plymouth, aisles, 1480s; Honiton, from c. 1480 to the 1520s; Cullompton, tower, as late as the 1540s. The most ostentatious work indeed all belongs to the early C 16: the fan-vaulted Dorset aisle at 30 Ottery St Mary is of after 1504; the S porch and Greenway aisle at 28 Tiverton of 1517; the Lane aisle at Cullompton of c. 1526, the last two also with stone vaults. The thinner evidence for village churches likewise suggests that most rebuilding is of the C 15 onwards (Hunt-shaw, 1439; Bridestowe, 1450; Spreyton, 1451; Powderham, 1480s), and a late date for Perp work in the remoter western areas is suggested by a study of churches of the Tavistock Deanery.‡

This golden age of church building, which coincides with Devon's increasing wealth as a result of the cloth trade, is impressive in bulk, impressive in occasional architectural details, impressive often in its furnishings, but standardized in much of its detail. Firstly the PLAN. The enlargement of existing churches took the form of adding aisles on either side of the nave – a process which had begun already in the C 12. But the special feature of the Perp period in Devon is that throughout the county – although most frequently in the richer south – the aisles were often carried through to flank the chancel, so as to form eastern chapels (often used as chantry chapels by the leading local families). In the most thorough rebuildings the older chancel arch was eliminated, so that division between chancel and nave was expressed only by the rood screen. Outside, where eastern chapels exist, a fine E view of the church results, so characteristic of the South West, with three parallel 26 gables and three large windows. In some cases the old transepts of the C 12 and C 13 were incorporated, as can be seen from the changes in masonry. But in the largest churches the Perp builders added new short transepts outside the new aisles; at Combe Martin this has resulted in a remarkable N show front with transept in the centre, symmetrically flanked by N porch and N vestry. Where money was available, the whole church, or at least the show front, was embattled (the most usual decorative motif), and if funds allowed, we find ornamentation (also of towers) with quatrefoil friezes and openwork battlements, as on the Greenway aisle and porch at Tiverton. 28 Generally, the extra money went on ornament, not (as e.g. in East Anglia) on making the churches more lofty (here perhaps one sees the long-term influence of the aesthetic character of the cathedral). The

* *Archaeological Journal*, vol. 70 (1913).
‡ C. Fryer Cornelius, *Trans. British Archaeol. Assoc.*, vol. 15 (1952).

great majority of churches are hall churches, i.e. with nave and aisles
of more or less the same height, so that the dominant impression of the
interior is of a comfortable, generous breadth. Apart from the
cathedral and Ottery St Mary, the more ambitious effect of a taller
13 nave with clerestory was attempted only at Crediton, Cullompton,
Culmstock, North Molton, North Petherwin, and Tiverton. (The
clerestories at Axminster and South Molton are C 19 additions.)

Perp TOWERS are generally at the w end, unless they are on older
27 foundations, as at Colyton, where a unique octagonal lantern crowns
the older crossing tower. w towers have buttresses of two main types:
set diagonally (type A), or set back from and at right angles to the
corners (type B). Type A, the older one, continued to co-exist with
type B, which became by far the most common form in churches of the
South West, especially on towers put up with the intention to impress
by a display of wealth.* John Harvey has suggested that the tower with
type B buttresses was introduced c. 1400, and derives from the late C 14
work of the great mason William Wynford at Wells. Such towers, like
their Dec predecessors (see above), were at first planned to have spires,
and in some cases we know that spires were built but have since
disappeared through fire, as at South Molton. But the design that soon
became the standard one was the straight top with corner pinnacles.

Some of the tallest towers are in North Devon: Hartland (130ft),
Chittlehampton (115ft), South Molton (107ft). Chittlehampton, like
Cullompton further E, illustrates the influence of the ornate Somerset
type, with the belfry windows (paired in the case of Chittlehampton)
filled with tracery, and pinnacles on the set-offs of the buttresses.
Somerset influence, strongest in the east of the county, is apparent also
in the applied sculpture on the exteriors of Broadclyst and Cullompton. But Hartland and South Molton are more characteristically
Devonian: austere compositions with tall pinnacles but relatively
small belfry windows. In the south-west there is a distinctive group
which has a polygonal stair-turret in the centre of the show front
instead of in the more usual corner position. This dour, castle-like
composition originated before 1449, when the tower of Ashburton was
chosen as the exemplar for Totnes. Totnes was embellished with
pinnacles, niches, and buttresses; other examples of the type are
25 plainer (Harberton, Ipplepen, Littlehempston, Thurlestone). Pinnacles on battlements are frequent but not universal. w and NW of
Dartmoor they are specially large, octagonal, castellated, and thickly
crocketed, as at Plymouth (under construction from 1460), Buckland
Monachorum, Sheepstor, Tavistock, and Walkhampton. Prominent
pinnacles are characteristic also of the secular Perp buildings in this
151 area: Tavistock abbey gateway, Morwell Barton (on which see further
below).

Some of the most distinctive regional differences in late medieval
churches are dictated by the different BUILDING MATERIALS available in Devon (see further on this the introduction on building stones,
above). Walls are of local stone, most often of rubble, but occasionally,
as granite became more widely used in the C15, of squared ashlar
(Widecombe-in-the-Moor, Peter Tavy). Inside, the more refined

*Examples of type A: Bideford, Chawleigh, Highweek (Newton Abbot),
Moretonhampstead, Northam, Weare Giffard; of type B: Ashburton, Chittle-
hampton, Chulmleigh, Combe Martin, Hartland, Holsworthy, Plymouth,
Tavistock, Totnes.

detail that became fashionable in the Perp period could not easily be produced in coarse material such as the local red sandstone, which had been adequate for simple octagonal piers. The most usual materials became the creamy white Beer stone, quarried in the east of the county, which could be finely carved. Further west, in the areas to which Beer stone could not be transported easily by sea or river, the harder granite from Dartmoor became the standard building stone, and dictated a much simpler treatment of detail.

A   B

The PIERS of Perp arcades are of two main types (not counting the older octagonal form which continued in use in the C15). The simpler one (called type A in this book) has four main shafts and hollows in the 29 diagonals. With broad hollows carried up into the arches without intervening capitals, it is found widely also in Somerset, Dorset, and Wiltshire. This was the type which could be most easily produced in granite (often as a monolith); the variety typical of the Devon and Cornwall granite areas has a narrow instead of a wide hollow. Type B is 32 more elaborate, and has, instead of a hollow between the shafts, a wave-moulding in the diagonal; in a few ambitious cases, several wave-mouldings and sharp arrises are combined to give the impression of clustered piers (Bradninch, Broadhembury, Woodbury). Capitals of both A and B type piers may be confined to the shafts, or may be bands running around the whole pier, sometimes moulded, but sometimes (especially when of Beer stone) carved with a frieze of large leaves. These leaf-frieze capitals are called Devon standard capitals in this 32 book. The arches of the arcades at their most logical have mouldings which follow the form either of the simple A or of the more complex B type piers (Crediton is a good example of the latter); but there are many deviations from this principle. The arch shapes range from quite sharply pointed to nearly semicircular and four-centred, the last two probably being most typical of the later examples.

Perp WINDOW TRACERY in Devon has been inadequately studied. It is relatively uniform, and often much restored and so of doubtful reliability. The only spectacular example apart from the cathedral is the W front of Colyton, an original design where a finely carved 27 doorway is combined with a huge, strictly rectilinear window. In the granite areas windows are simple and often uncusped. Elsewhere there 25 are a few local patterns that deserve a special mention. One is the device of intersecting round-headed arches (Atherington, Weare Giffard, and Monkleigh, where it is perhaps associated with the building work of c. 1423); another is the inclusion of a star shape in the tracery lights (Ipplepen, Newton Abbot, Plympton, Sherford, Staverton). Although seemingly a Dec motif, the examples are almost all in a decisively Perp context, and in the case of the window from the chapel at Newton Abbot (now re-used in St Mary Abbotsbury) can be dated by heraldic evidence to the mid C15.

With the exception of the sumptuous late Perp aisles already mentioned at Cullompton, Ottery, and Tiverton, stone vaults are not found in the chancels or naves of Devon's Perp churches, although they do occur in some specially ambitious PORCHES. Brixham and

42 Plympton have lierne-vaults, Berry Pomeroy a tierceron-vault, Holcombe Rogus and Torbryan small fan-vaults. Among other porches, the two-storey one at Kenton is an especially elaborately carved late Perp example. Generally, carved enrichment is chiefly a characteristic of early c16 work (Awliscombe, Broadhembury).

The almost universal covering of nave and aisles is the type of TIMBER ROOF known as the wagon or cradle roof. Its distinguishing feature is the existence of curved braces to every rafter. The effect is indeed like that of the canvas of a wagon, especially if the spaces between the timbers are plastered or ceiled (whether this was a medieval or a later practice remains uncertain). Most Devon wagon roofs have decorated bosses at the main intersections; several emphasize the bays above the rood screen felicitously by a 'celure', i.e. a boarding and cross-ribbing of the panels between the main timbers, further enriched by motifs such as suns and stars (Hatherleigh, Hennock, Ideford, Ilfracombe, Kings Nympton, Lapford, Swim-
43, 29 bridge, etc.). At Cullompton and Chawleigh the whole roof is treated in this splendid way, at Beaford and Ugborough a whole aisle, at Hartland a whole chancel chapel. Where there is no chancel arch, the wagon roofs run uninterrupted from w to E. In three churches –
41 Honiton (renewed), Ilsington, and Luppitt – the crossing is emphasized in a remarkably original way by semicircular braces thrown diagonally across the space at the E end of the nave. The result is a huge open cross-rib vault of timber. At Ilsington the effect is particularly intricate. Buckland Monachorum is exceptional in having a hammerbeam roof with angels; carved angels occur too in the Clothworkers' aisle at Tavistock.

Among LATE MEDIEVAL CHURCH FURNISHINGS in Devon, SCREENS take pride of place. They are rightly famed, and have been studied in greater detail than any other aspect of Devon churches (*see* Further Reading: Bond and Camm). When both good and complete, they are indeed dazzling. Including fragmentary survivals, well over a hundred remain, as well as numerous parclose screens dividing off eastern chapels. Their survival can be attributed to the remoteness of Devon from the reformers of the c16, and perhaps also to a reluctance to destroy work that in many cases can only recently have been completed. Their present condition, however, owes a good deal to assiduous and skilful restoration in the later c19 and c20 (see below, on c19 church restoration).

The tradition of lavishly decorated screens begins in Devon in the c14 at Exeter Cathedral and Ottery St Mary. These are of stone, as are the lesser screens in the Lady Chapel and other chapels of the cathedral, which date from the 1430s and, interestingly, combine Perp tracery with the favourite Dec motif of the nodding arch. The Lady Chapel screen design was imitated in the splendid mid c15 stone rood screen at Totnes and, still later, in an early c16 screen at Colyton.
34 Other stone screens are at Awliscombe, Bideford, Culmstock,
49 Dunsford, Marldon, and Paignton (Torbay), but several of these functioned as enclosures for chantry chapels, and must be mentioned again under monuments.

Stone screens are the exception. The most celebrated ROOD SCREENS are of timber, and in churches rebuilt in the Perp period with no structural division between the E and W parts, the most ambitious examples could run all through from N to S, across both aisles as well as the nave. The chronology of these screens is uncertain. What is clear (from Renaissance ornament and other evidence) is that many (perhaps the majority) are late C15 and C16, although there are a few examples with straightforward Perp detail which traditionally have been assigned to the earlier C15 (Bovey Tracey, Halberton, 37 Uffculme).

Most Devon rood screens carried a loft with parapet to W and E which was supported by a coving. The N section of the screen at Atherington is the only complete survival of this arrangement; the impressive reconstructed lofts at Kenton and Staverton are based on it. Marldon retains the E parapet. More often the coving remains but the parapet has gone. When screens cross the aisles near the piers, some provision had to be made for this encounter. At Swimbridge 33 openings are left for a small altar to be placed against the pier, and forward-curving panels above it serve as a reredos. At Bradninch, Broadhempston, Dunchideock, Harberton, Kenn, and Torbryan, the piers are encased by the screen.

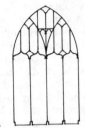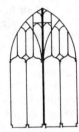

A   B

Rood-screen TRACERY at its simplest consists of narrow arched lights separated by mullions (Welcombe, perhaps C14, Parracombe, Tawstock). More commonly, the lights are grouped window-wise into four with conventional top tracery. This falls into two types: type A, where the central spandrel between the two sub-arches is treated as a single unit, and type B, less common, where the windows (like the doorway in the centre of the screen) are subdivided by a thick central mullion. Among outstanding examples of screens with type A tracery are: Bovey Tracey, Bradninch, Buckland-in-the-Moor, Chawleigh, 37 Chulmleigh, Dunchideock, Feniton, Harberton, Ipplepen, Kenn, Kentisbeare, Kenton, Kings Nympton, Manaton, Marwood, Paignton (Torbay), Pinhoe (Exeter), Plymtree (datable to c. 1470), 32 Staverton, Talaton, Uffculme. Some of these vary the design of the upper lights by including flamboyant tracery motifs (Kentisbeare, Pilton) or shields (Chulmleigh). Examples of type B are Atherington, Broadhempston, Burrington, Halberton, Hartland, Lapford, Pay- 39 hembury, Swimbridge, and Uffculme.   33

One of the greatest delights of Devon screens is their ribbed COVING above the arches, and above this, covering the cornice, friezes of densely carved foliage, sometimes with little figures of birds and men sitting or crawling in it. In the decoration, particularly of the coving, the transition from Perp to early Renaissance motifs can be studied with profit. The simplest coving has tracery patterns (Chawleigh, Halberton, Plymtree, Uffculme); others have stylized foliage or shields between the ribs (Hartland, Swimbridge). The appearance of such Italian devices as medallions, arabesques, and putti (Atherington, Lapford, Morchard Bishop, Warkleigh, Willand) suggests a date for these examples in the second quarter of the C16. Holbeton and Lustleigh, with their playful Italian motifs, must also be of this period. Yet East Allington is dated 1547, and its surviving parts show no Renaissance details whatsoever.

In addition to the standard type of screen, three special local types must be mentioned, all probably of the early Tudor period. One is confined to Dartmouth and the area to its w. The screen of St Saviour Dartmouth, made in 1496, may be the first; others are at Chivelstone, East Portlemouth, Rattery, Sherford, and South Pool. These screens have semicircular heads to their four main lights, each pair linked by a crocketed ogee gable. A second local variety of great charm is to be found at Holbeton and in a parclose screen at Ugborough (cf. also the bolder and perhaps earlier Stokeinteignhead). The four lights are again round-headed, but above them are shields and interlaced ogee arches, and in the spandrels charming openwork leaf, tendril, and scroll motifs. Finally there are the mid Devon group of early C16 parclose screens at Coldridge and Colebrooke and the rood screen at Brushford, which are distinguished by highly fanciful Flamboyant tracery with delicate filigree detail. They may have been made by foreign craftsmen: their closest parallels are in Brittany.

Wainscots of screens are decorated with tracery, occasionally with carved figures (Bridford, Lustleigh) or carved Renaissance ornament (Marwood, Warkleigh), but most commonly, and especially in South Devon, with painted figures. Bond and Camm recorded around forty screens with painting of this kind. The standard is by no means as high as that found in East Anglia, although recent cleaning has in several cases revealed unexpectedly good detail and lively colour which had been hidden by later overpainting (Bovey Tracey, Bridford, Chudleigh, Manaton). The early C16 paintings at Manaton are close in style to others at Alphington and Cheriton Bishop; the Bridford screen (which is datable to after 1508) has grisaille painting on the back which links it to the striking and unusual paintings at Ashton on the screens around a chantry chapel furnished in the early C16. These have bold half-figures with scrolls, very much in the style of early continental woodcuts. Most frequently the wainscots have rather dumpy little figures of saints; less often, scenes from the life of the Virgin, as at Ugborough, or painted Renaissance ornament, for example at South Pool, Blackawton, Chivelstone.

Compared with Devon screens, Perp PULPITS are often oddly coarse, though equally exuberant in decoration. The noteworthy ones are nearly all of stone. Only Pilton is of a type common to all England. The most frequent Devon variety once again illustrates the persistence of the Dec tradition: small figures (usually badly carved) are set under nodding ogee or triangularly projecting canopies, and between thickly foliated buttresses (Chittlehampton, Swimbridge, etc.) or within even more thickly foliated frames (Dartmouth, Dartington, Dittisham, Harberton, Torbryan, etc.). They are all grossly encrusted with leaf decoration; tracery plays only a minor part in their design.

Perp FONTS are dull on the whole, mostly octagonal, and very often with quatrefoil decoration (Chittlehampton, Kingsteignton, Woodbury).

Carved BENCH ENDS are frequent (more in North than in South Devon), and of the same type as in Cornwall: the ends are rectangular, without the sloping or pointed tops and poppyheads found elsewhere in England. (Poppyheads occur only at Ilsington.) Those that are dated are of the early C16 onwards. An exception is the pair of panels at Colebrooke with large, vigorous carvings of wild man and fool; they came from a prayer-desk in the Copplestone Chapel, and have been dated on heraldic evidence to before 1473. A noteworthy example is the bench end at Coldridge which has an inscription commemorating the date 1511, and the donor of much of the church furnishings, Sir John Evans. The largest assemblages of carved bench ends are at East Budleigh and High Bickington; backs and fronts of benches are preserved more occasionally (Braunton, Frithelstock, etc.).

South Devon bench ends usually have just tracery in two tiers; in 32 North Devon there are initials (mostly unexplained), shields with or without coats of arms, figures of saints, and symbols of the Passion, as well as much tracery and foliage, in which the arrival of the Italian fashion can be watched. It came late. Hartland of 1530 and Northlew of 1537 have no Renaissance motifs; Dowland of 1546 has. The Renaissance brings a typical new foliage, heads in roundels, and other familiar motifs. Benches, increasingly in demand as sermons became more important, were some of the few furnishings undisturbed by the liturgical upheavals of the mid C16. One can see the type continuing unchanged at Braunton (where dates between 1560 and 1593 are recorded) and at Alwington (1580). Early Renaissance carving can also be found in the excellent panelling which is now arranged around the font at Swimbridge, but perhaps once had some other purpose, and on 40 doors at Tiverton and Totnes.

As for other furnishings, a highly singular item is the PYX BOX at 47 Warkleigh, a wooden container for the Sacrament, still with its simple painted decoration. Another rare survival is the coarsely carved Golgotha base with skulls which once formed the foot of the rood at Cullompton. A few VESTMENTS are preserved (Brixham, Culmstock, Holcombe Burnell, Exeter St Petrock, Malborough, Woodland). There are interesting early CLOCKS at Exeter Cathedral and Ottery St Mary. Medieval STAINED GLASS in Devon is mostly a fragmentary story. The exception is the E window of the cathedral, a rewarding combination of outstanding early C14 panels with others of the later 44, 45 C14 and C15. The clumsy but engaging figure style of the most active C15 local school of stained glass artists is best studied at Doddis-combsleigh. Good individual figures are preserved at Abbots Bickington, Bere Ferrers, Bondleigh, Littleham near Exmouth, and Little-hempston. Haccombe has the most rewarding range of medieval TILES. Distinctive embossed tiles were produced in Barnstaple and 48 can be found in many North Devon churches; they are in the medieval tradition but appear to date largely from the C17. The bold decorative IRONWORK of the door at St Saviour Dartmouth, however, despite its 46 date of 1631, is essentially medieval.

Devon is not a county of BRASSES. The earliest with an effigy is at Stokeinteignhead (c. 1375). Easily the best are those to J. Hanley and wives at Dartmouth (1408) and to Sir Peter Courtenay at Exeter Cathedral (1409). Also in the cathedral is an early example of a kneeling figure (Canon William Langton †1413). Stone MONU-MENTS of the Perp period are more rewarding. The traditional type of full-length effigies on tomb-chests is represented at its grandest by the Courtenay tombs at Exeter Cathedral and Haccombe (late C14 and c. 1400, both much restored). The best of the other effigies are of alabaster, brought from outside the county: a charming late C14 miniature at Haccombe, the refined effigy of Bishop Stafford (†1419) in the cathedral, an unusually detailed mid C15 lady at Horwood. But the notable feature of most Perp monuments is not the sculpture (which is often poor) but the rich effect of the decorative architectural surround.

The taste for a tomb-chest with an elaborate surround is shown already in the Annery chapel at Monkleigh (1423). At Exeter Cathedral the splendid canopy over Bishop Branscombe's tomb was new in 1443; the one added above Stafford's tomb was probably made to match. This design with four-centred cusped arch is echoed in a monument at Ashwater of c.1442. At Colyton there is a miniature canopied tomb of 1449. The later C15 Kirkham chantry chapel at Paignton (Torbay) also has small-scale effigies, incorporated in a gloriously ornate, utterly unrestrained screen copiously decorated with statuettes (remarkably well preserved). The screen includes a relief with the Mass of St Gregory, an uncommon subject, found also in the later Oldham chantry at Exeter Cathedral (1519), but the quality of the decorative carving here, and likewise in the contemporary Speke chantry of 1518, is much poorer. Rather better are the canopied monuments to Sir Thomas Grenville at Bideford (1513) and to Thomas Andrew at St Mary Arches Exeter (1518).

Still more remarkable is the chantry of Precentor Sylke in the cathedral (†1508), of special interest not only for its enclosing screen, which combines a cadaver tomb with much small-scale sculpture of the Passion, but for the contemporary wall paintings of Resurrection and Entombment within the chapel, which suggest it functioned as an Easter Sepulchre enclosure. The popularity at this time of the tomb combined with Easter Sepulchre is demonstrated also by a number of varied canopied tomb-chests in the chancels of parish churches, generally without effigies: at Holcombe Burnell, South Pool, and Woodleigh (all with carved Resurrection scenes); at West Alvington (the Purbeck marble type, formerly with brasses); and at Bishops Nympton (†1540), Bondleigh, Heanton Punchardon (†1523), and Throwleigh.

The earliest monument with Renaissance ornament – if the date of 1522 assigned to it is correct – appears to be a tomb-chest at Bere Ferrers, decorated with simple wreaths. As in architecture, Perp forms continued strong in the later C16. The Cary monument at St Saviour Torquay of 1567 and the Whiddon tomb at Chagford of 1575 have intriguing mixtures of Perp and early Renaissance detail, but the Waldron tomb-chest at Tiverton of 1579 is still entirely in the medieval tradition.

Rebuilding and repair of CHURCHES continued in a traditional manner (St Budeaux, Plymouth, 1563; Drake aisle, Buckland Monachorum, c.1600, with an unusual stone barrel-vault, perhaps re-used; Great Torrington, 1651; St Stephen and St Thomas, Exeter, both of the 1650s–60s). The only entirely new church of importance, Charles Church, Plymouth, of 1640–58 (now reduced to a ruin), is also completely in the Gothic tradition, although its revival of Dec forms indicates a certain self-consciousness.

FITTINGS had to adapt to the changing liturgical needs of the post-Reformation Church, but the survival of so many medieval screens reveals how a conservative approach often prevailed; indeed, as has already been noted, PEWS with carved bench ends in the late medieval manner continued to be made in the later C16. To these were added FAMILY PEWS: Tawstock of *c*. 1540–50, notable for its early Renaissance ornament; Holcombe Rogus with remarkable early C17 carved 91 scenes. Alwington also has an elaborate one, although some of its woodwork comes from the hall at Portledge. The ornate mid C17 chancel panelling at North Molton is likewise of secular origin. PULPITS are numerous but difficult to date. The late C16 type continues unchanged into the C17: Clovelly (1634), Horwood (1635). Specially rich is the pulpit at Shebbear, with three tiers of barbaric little figures in blank arcades. The Laudian reforms of the early C17 briefly revived the significance of the chancel, and thus of seemly SCREENS. By far the most lavish example is the one at Washfield 92 (1624), with its lushly carved cornice above a Corinthian arcade. Colyton has a good early C17 screen of stone, and there are lesser wooden screens at Rose Ash (1618) and Whitestone (where there is also a gallery of 1621). Generally, the Jacobean style in WOODWORK continued into the mid C17 (Braunton chancel panelling 1653, Sandford W gallery 1657). Exminster has a rarity, a C17 plaster vault imitating the all-over effects of a ceiled roof, but decorative PLASTER-WORK, despite its proliferation in secular buildings, is uncommon. WALL PAINTING after the Reformation was generally confined to texts: well preserved C16 examples can be seen in the little chapel at Taddiport, Great Torrington; more unusual are the C17 Old Testament scene and figures at Bratton Clovelly.

In MONUMENTS of *c*. 1550–1650 Devon is prolific, but not as accomplished as the home counties. The first appearances of early Renaissance detail have already been noted. The Haydon monument at Ottery of 1587 is still in this tradition, but generally from the 1580s designs become more complex and ambitious, although execution – especially of the figures – is often crude, and some of the biggest monuments are of a baffling rawness (Berry Pomeroy, Holbeton). The first representative in the county of the grand free-standing tomb with columns and vault entirely in the classical manner is at Tawstock 73 (1589). The Carew monument at Exeter Cathedral, also †1589, is interesting in combining classical detail with a figure in consciously medievalizing armour. The Gilbert monument at Exeter Cathedral (†1596) and the Bampfylde one at Poltimore (†1604) still have recumbent figures behind low arches, but later examples of the columned tomb have the triumphal-arch form of canopy made popular by the royal tombs at Westminster: Wembury (†1608), Colyton (†1628), Marystow (†1629), Cadeleigh (†1637). The column and vault type was adapted for less bulky wall-monuments, e.g. with pilasters instead of columns, and with the vault reduced to an arch: Torquay (†1604), Crediton (†1605). Two of unusually good quality, closely related to each other, are at Holcombe Rogus (†1614) and 82 Tavistock (†1615); they are perhaps London work, for their design is similar to a monument of 1612 at Hayes, Middlesex. The elaborately decorated Acland monument at Broadclyst (†1613/14), which can be attributed to the Exeter mason *John Deymond*, shows how a local workshop might produce indifferent figure sculpture, but excelled in the rich, all-over strapwork ornament that was equally popular at the time in plasterwork and woodwork.

Such decoration is also found on lesser memorials. The most

common of these (as elsewhere in England) is the wall-monument with kneeling figures, often facing each other across a prayer desk. One of the most charming early examples is that to the musician Matthew Godwin at Exeter Cathedral (†1586). The kneeling figure was also adopted on a larger scale, as at Musbury, where the bold but crudely carved Drake monument (†1611) has six nearly life-size figures in this position on top of a table tomb. But the traditional type of tomb with recumbent effigy continued popular into the 1630s; among the most memorable is the accomplished monument at Holcombe Rogus to Sir John Bluett (†1634) and his wife, with their eight children kneeling along the tomb-chest, and the touchingly simple figure of the young Thomas Welshe at Alverdiscott (†1639). More complicated compositions also became popular at this time, executed with rustic vigour, although without the refinement of contemporary progressive London work. At North Molton, the Bamfylde monument (†1626) combines a recumbent effigy with kneeling figures both in front of and behind the tomb-chest, and includes also a seated mourning figure of the widow with head propped up on hand. This type of seated figure became a favourite and can be found, often as the main subject, in a series of monuments of the 1630s (Crediton, Kenton, Newton St Cyres, Plympton). Frontal demi-figures in niches or oval medallions are frequent, especially in North Devon (Alwington, Barnstaple, Combe Martin (specially good), East Down, Monkleigh, Swimbridge, West Down), and also occur in Exeter (St Petrock). They date from c. 1630– c.1665. Standing figures, interesting as precursors of an important C18 form of monument, are found at Eggesford (†1630), Newton St Cyres (†1632) and Ottery (†1652). At Tamerton Foliot, Plymouth, there is an unusual standing figure in a shroud which must be derived from John Donne's monument at St Paul's Cathedral, London, of 1631.

MAJOR SECULAR BUILDINGS:

MEDIEVAL TO MID SEVENTEENTH CENTURY

Devon is not perhaps famous for its CASTLES,* yet it is of interest to the student of castellology on account both of numbers and of varieties of design. Okehampton indeed ranks with all but the most spectacular, and Dartmouth is of national importance as the birthplace of English artillery fortresses. There are some fifteen earthwork castles of the late C11 and C12, and a further ten of similarly early foundation which have substantial buildings of stone. Of these, Totnes, Lydford, and Okehampton are important for the history of castle development from the late C11 to the early C14. The gatehouse at Exeter is among the earliest Norman architecture in England.

The location of the early castles established an interesting relationship with the general settlement pattern which was to persist for

*The paragraphs on castles are by Robert Higham.

several centuries. Some were founded in existing towns, as at Exeter, Lydford, Totnes, and Barnstaple; conversely, some actually gave rise to towns, as at Okehampton, Plympton, and Great Torrington. Other settlements near castles became small seigneurial boroughs – a prominent feature of medieval Devon and Cornwall. Places such as Winkleigh and Bampton, no bigger than nucleated villages elsewhere, had become boroughs by the C13. Some castles of all periods until the later Middle Ages, for example Okehampton (founded by 1086) and Berry Pomeroy (a C15 development of an earlier manor house), besides some less well known examples, stand well away from other human habitation – a reflection of the underlying settlement pattern of Devon, which with its mixture of highland and lowland zone characteristics produced small dispersed settlements more frequently than large nucleated ones. Castles often stood alone, as did manor houses, churches, and farmsteads. Except for the highland mass of Dartmoor, the sites are well distributed across the county; and even on Dartmoor, c. 1300, the lord of the manor of Gidleigh copied his Courtenay neighbours at Okehampton and built a small defended house.

Licences to crenellate are not a general guide to later medieval developments: frequently, as at Hemyock, they reflect the social ambitions of lesser men, and many of the seventeen places for which a licence is known have no substantial remains at all. In contrast, major works at Tiverton and Berry Pomeroy were carried out without formal sanction. At Compton the tradition of defensive building had a final 59 fling about 1500, but here the impressive façade is ostentatious rather than functional. The later buildings are, like the earlier establishments, marked by a strong sense of individuality, in both size and planning. By the time of Compton's final development, however, the appearance of a specialized artillery fort at Dartmouth marked the beginning of new trends and the division of the castle's residential and defensive roles.

The earliest UNFORTIFIED DOMESTIC BUILDINGS of which remains survive belonged to the bishops. Their palace at Exeter still has its grand entrance doorway of the early C13, besides fragmentary evidence for a major contemporary aisled hall with timber posts. Up to the Reformation the bishops held fourteen manors and had no fewer than twenty-two residences, but of these tantalizingly little remains – a vaulted fragment perhaps of c. 1300 at Chudleigh, two walls of a C14 building at Bishopsteignton, and a fortified curtain wall and angle tower at Paignton (Torbay). Of the dwellings of secular magnates before the C14 we know little in detail. Excavations within the castle precincts at Okehampton, however, have shown that the ambitious early C14 building campaign of the Courtenays provided for comfortable private chambers in addition to the great hall, and they also developed Tiverton to a high domestic standard. Investigation at other major sites has been less comprehensive, so that dates and sequences of building are not always clear. At Powderham, despite many later alterations, the shell of the large late C14 hall of a junior branch of the Courtenays is still recognizable, with its three service doorways, the kitchen beyond in line with the hall, and a fortified solar block at the other end. The outstanding example of a grand secular establishment of the late C14 is Dartington, the seat of the great magnate John Holand, Duke of Exeter, half-brother of Richard II. This was, perhaps surprisingly, an undefended site. It was laid out

57, 58 between 1388 and 1400. The vast great hall, with private rooms at either end and huge kitchen in line with the hall range, lies between two courtyards, a small one (known from excavations), which had private domestic quarters, and a much larger one, with the apartments of the duke's retainers; of this, one range is still clearly recognizable, with its separate entrances to chambers on each floor, and projections at the back for fireplaces and garderobes.

Double courtyards are found elsewhere, although in some cases may have reached their completed form only in the C16 – see e.g. Great Fulford, North Wyke, Old Newnham. In lesser manor houses farm buildings may take the place of retainers' lodgings, or an outer court might consist simply of a forecourt enclosed by a wall and gatehouse, as was the case at Bradley, Newton Abbot. Whether or not there was an outer court, by the C16 the main buildings were often arranged on a courtyard plan. No. 10 the Close, Exeter, and Littlehempston, both with four substantially medieval ranges, are especially attractive examples. Partial demolition, or roofing over of the courtyard (Poltimore; Portledge), has sometimes obscured such a plan, but the type can be recognized all over the county, remaining popular throughout the C17, and often preserved even in C18 and C19 62 rebuilding schemes (Werrington, Holcombe Court). The disposition of the different elements of the courtyard plan, however – hall, kitchen, service rooms, private apartments – is surprisingly varied, the result of successive partial rebuilding and alteration, so that each house is an individual and intriguing puzzle.

The focus of the medieval house was the great hall, where the main architectural display was the OPEN TIMBER ROOF, which by the C14 could be constructed in a single span, without the support of aisle posts. Up to the early C16, the open roof remained the accepted form both for the great hall and the main first-floor chamber. Devon is a remarkably rich area for the study of such roofs, which survive in large numbers (see also Farmhouse Introduction). The majority, including the most spectacularly decorated ones, date from the later Middle Ages, but they have some interesting predecessors.

The available evidence suggests that before the C15, among several experimental forms, the type commonest in the larger houses in Devon was the BASE-CRUCK, i.e. a roof where the crucks extend from below the tops of the walls to a collar or upper tie level only, the roof above being completed by a common rafter or crown-post structure. Such a roof existed over the early C14 hall at Okehampton Castle and over the C14 guest hall at Buckfast; lesser examples, perhaps of comparable date, survive in farmhouses which must once have been houses of higher standing, for example Bridford Barton, which has a very simple base-cruck roof with collared common rafters above. The lack of longitudinal upper bracing in such a roof could be made good by the introduction of CROWN-POSTS supporting a collar purlin – a solution that remained relatively rare in Devon, although it was known in England from the C12, and was used over the nave and transept vaults at Exeter in the mid C14. Crown-posts combined with base crucks occur at Youlston Park; Moorstone Barton, Halberton; Wood Barton, Kentisbeare; and also in the more easily visible entrance block at late C14 Dartington. (Crown-posts were also used 58 over the hammerbeam roof of the hall at Dartington – see below.) An alternative, probably slightly later combination of crown-posts with arch-braced principals also occurs occasionally (e.g. Parsonage Farm, Newton Ferrers).

Some hybrid types of roof are of pseudo-crown-post construction, with braced struts between collar and apex. Examples are the unusually ornate solar roof at Lustleigh; the Old Rectory, Cheriton Bishop; Clifford Barton, Dunsford; Home Farm, Hockworthy; and (without braces) Lower Bramble, Ashton. A different, also possibly early type is the arch-braced roof with upper purlin and spere truss with collared common rafters above, as at Bury Barton, Lapford (with square-set purlins, an early type); Rudge, Morchard Bishop; and Thorne, Clannaborough.

The most common roof in larger houses from *c.* 1400 was ARCH-BRACED, with a high, often cranked, collar. Longitudinal strengthening was provided by massive ridge pieces and by side purlins, sometimes in as many as three rows. The principal rafters, which frequently take the form of jointed crucks (the type of roof construction that became most widespread in Devon – see Farmhouse Introduction), have curved braces morticed into them, rising to meet below the collar. In smaller houses the arch-bracing is often confined to the central truss over the hall; in more important buildings, arch-braces are complemented by curved wind-braces below the purlins. Occasionally grandeur was achieved by combining arch-braces with common rafter roofs, in the manner of the wagon roofs of churches (Little Marland, Petrockstow; Woodbeer Court, Plymtree; Fishleigh Barton, Tawstock; Acland Barton), but this is surprisingly rare in secular buildings.

Easily visible arch-braced roofs range from the particularly grand one over a first-floor hall preserved in the Distillery, Southside Street, Plymouth, to the much plainer hall roof at Bradley Manor, Newton Abbot, datable to the early C 15. Others not concealed by later ceilings include the large upper chamber at Shute Barton, the hall roofs at Knightstone, Littlehempston, and Wortham, and – on a more modest scale – the roofs of the hall at Higher Harestone and the former hall at Sand. At their simplest, the arch-braces are chamfered, but they can be richly moulded, and are occasionally exceptionally ornate, as in the case of the hall roof at Lustleigh, where both main and intermediate trusses are emphatically cusped. By the early C 16 it was often the wind-braces which were exploited to form decorative patterns (Slade at Cornwood, and the late medieval hammerbeam roofs mentioned below) in an insistent diagonal network comparable to the contemporary celures of church roofs.

The HAMMERBEAM ROOF, which had evolved elsewhere in England in the C 13 and C 14 to span especially wide spaces, was used for really grand effects. It reached its apogee in the C 14 roof over Westminster Hall, and the influence of that building can perhaps be seen in the late C 14 roof of the hall at Dartington. The massive scale of 58 the Dartington roof can still be appreciated, even though the present hammerbeam construction is C 20, and omits the original arrangement of crown-posts above. There seem to be no immediate successors to this roof, but a modified type, the false hammerbeam, where an arch-brace rests on the hammerbeam and the hammerpost is omitted, occurs in the late C 15 and early C 16. In North Devon there are two excellent closely related examples, Weare Giffard and Orleigh Court, 60 both lavishly carved and decorated, with splendid heraldic beasts on the hammerbeams, and cross-bracing between the trusses. Bradfield House has another sumptuous example; Traymill, Thorverton, a more modest one. In Exeter there is the exceptional roof to Nos. 8–9 Cathedral Close, where the traceried spandrels once more recall the tradition of Westminster Hall. But other features of this roof, for example the coved apex, the use of intermediate trusses, and the braces with curved feet, are comparable to a group of richly moulded late medieval roofs in the Exeter region: at Cadhay and, in Exeter itself, at the Guildhall, the Deanery, and Bowhill. The Guildhall can be dated to the later C15; the others may be as late as the second quarter of the C16.

Of other INTERIOR FEATURES there is only fragmentary evidence – mostly late medieval – to indicate that they could be of high quality. External stone doorways could be carved as well as moulded (Weare Giffard). The best houses had traceried windows to the hall, either of stone (Old Newnham) or, more commonly, of wood (Little Hack-worthy, Tedburn St Mary; Stockwell Manor, Bradninch). Chimneypieces could also be showpieces for sculpture; easily the most flamboyant is the late C15 one with huge overmantel installed by Bishop Courtenay at his palace in Exeter. A popular type which continued into the later C16 has a simple arrangement of quatrefoils or roundels with shields on the lintel (Bindon, Cadhay, Tytherleigh Cott at Chardstock, Knightstone); hooded chimneypieces are less common, although C16 examples exist at Totnes. Humbler fireplaces, especially in the granite areas of the west, often have a simple flattened ogee arch. Externally, CHIMNEYS could be treated quite elaborately (Old Newnham; Stowford at Harford). The most notable medieval secular WALL PAINTING is the delicate Resurrection scene in the hall at Littlehempston. Among surviving WOODWORK is the elaborate but puzzling pinnacled SCREEN at Wortham, probably not made for its present position.

Also at Wortham is a finely carved inserted hall ceiling. Although the tradition of the open hall remained strong in Devon, the snugger, less draughty ground-floor hall begins to appear from the early C16, either created within an existing hall (as at Wortham) or built anew (the back ranges of No. 10 The Close and the Treasurer's House, Exeter). All three have fine framed ceilings still decorated entirely in the medieval tradition, as is another outstanding example (not *in situ*) at Holcombe Court. The C16 framed ceiling, a grid of heavily moulded timbers, sometimes has the joists in between 'counterchanged', i.e., placed in alternate directions in adjacent squares. Such ceilings were used not only for halls but for the ground-floor parlours that were treated with increasing consequence at this time (*see* e.g. Bowhill, Exeter St Thomas; Old Newnham). They are often a feature, too, of the small but well appointed medieval CLERGY HOUSES which survive in unusual numbers in the South West (Old Vicarage, Sampford Peverell; Bull House, Pilton; Vicarage, Colyton).

Now to PRIVATE APARTMENTS AND OTHER ROOMS. Before the C16, the solar, or main private apartment, was generally on an upper floor raised above an undercroft (e.g. at Lustleigh). Castles have some of the earliest survivals, for example Okehampton, already mentioned, and Tiverton, where something survives of the early C14 chamber block with an upper room with elaborate windows, fireplace, and garderobe. C15 upper apartments, well supplied with fireplaces and garderobes, remain at both ends of the hall of Compton Castle, where the solar, as so often, overlooks the chapel (cf. also Bradley, 61 Newton Abbot). At Holcombe Rogus in the early c 16 old and new fashions co-exist: the screens passage still echoes the pattern of the late c 14 Dartington – next to the three service doors, a fourth leads to stairs to apartments over tower porch and service rooms – but at the high end there was probably a ground-floor parlour as well as a grand first-floor chamber.

First-floor chambers surviving on their own have sometimes been interpreted as independent first-floor halls (Bradley Manor, Newton Abbot; Shute; Neadon, Manaton; Yeo, Chagford) or tower houses (Bindon), but the first three examples may simply have been the private apartments of houses where the contemporary ground-floor halls have disappeared. At Berry Pomeroy remains of both types of building can be seen within the castle precinct, the late medieval great hall, and an adjacent tower-like four-storey block with two upper storeys of heated chambers.

Arrangements of service rooms and particularly KITCHENS are by no means standard, very likely because what one sees now may be the result of successive alterations and rebuilding. By the c 16 kitchens were often in a range parallel to the hall (Littlehempston, Bowhill at Exeter, Youlston, Saltram). This arrangement is sometimes described as typical of the South West, but it is not universal, especially in larger houses: at Compton, Old Newnham, and North Wyke, the kitchen is in a range adjacent to the hall (at Newnham very oddly at the high rather than the low end), while at Dartington and Powderham it is in 57 line with the hall.

Accommodation for RETAINERS of the kind found at Dartington is necessarily less common in smaller establishments, and has been little investigated. At Bickleigh Castle there appear to have been chambers in the gatehouse and a c 15 hall lying at right angles. Intriguing remnants of apartments around outer courtyards survive at North Wyke and at Old Newnham. Similar arrangements existed in the late medieval country retreats of monasteries: both Morwell Barton, a possession of the abbots of Tavistock, and Leigh Barton, which belonged to Buckfast Abbey, preserve independent heated chambers above the gatehouse and in ranges around a courtyard.

Many medieval manor houses had PRIVATE CHAPELS. Evocative free-standing survivals are the little c 12 thatched building at Bickleigh, the handsome Perp chapel at Ayshford, and the more rustic structure at Bury Barton, Lapford. In later medieval houses, chapels were sometimes attached to the solar wing, as at Compton Castle, Bradley Manor at Newton Abbot, and Higher Harestone. At Bradley, most unusually, a late medieval corridor or anteroom was added alongside the hall to provide access to the chapel, making the main range two rooms deep. Occasionally there is evidence for small upper chapels, especially in buildings which belonged to the clergy (Place Court, Colaton Raleigh; Edge Barton; and in Exeter at the Bishop's Palace, the Deanery, and Nos. 9–10 the Close), but they also occur in other houses (e.g. Bindon). At Berry Pomeroy the chapel was in the gatehouse. It was unusually elaborate, with an arcade, and late medieval wall painting – a rare survival.

Medieval GATEHOUSES were often architectural showpieces: Bickleigh and Tiverton are especially impressive; Tawstock, Shute, and 63

Bradworthy show how the type lingered on into the Elizabethan and Jacobean period. An alternative by the C16 was an elaborately decorated GATEWAY in an enclosing wall, as at Elizabethan Collacombe, where classical detail replaces the longstanding local tradition of Tudor Gothic.

Other medieval buildings associated with the largest houses have been little studied. The present chapel at Powderham, with its good arch-braced roof, could have originated as a retainers' hall in the outer courtyard. Among OUTBUILDINGS those of ecclesiastical establishments are the most impressive: the C14 barn with base-cruck roof and C16 stables at Bishop's Court, one of the bishop of Exeter's country houses, and the great BARNS of the abbeys at Torre, Torquay (Torbay), and Buckland. A circular DOVECOTE, possibly medieval, remains at Pridhamsleigh, Staverton, another, probably later, at Holcombe Court.

One other late medieval building type should be mentioned: the CHURCH HOUSE, the predecessor of the village hall, usually sited on the edge of the churchyard and sometimes combined with living accommodation for the clergy. G. W. Copeland identified over sixty survivors in Devon (*see* Further Reading). The most common type is two-storeyed, often of ashlar, with an exterior stair to the upper floor; especially good examples are at Holcombe Rogus, South Tawton, Throwleigh, Walkhampton, and Widecombe.

EXTERIORS of houses of the MID C16 TO MID C17 were only gradually affected by the Renaissance. The adoption of classical detail at first made little difference to the tradition of adding to and improving houses piecemeal. As in churches, early Renaissance ornament of the early to mid C16 appears most commonly in woodwork (panelling at Great Fulford, a door at Bradley Manor, Newton Abbot), more occasionally in stone carving (entrance doorway at Great Fulford). The symmetrical classical exterior which became the norm for the great houses of the Elizabethan and Jacobean era elsewhere in England is rarely found in Devon. Nor do the rural houses emulate the decorative external display of contemporary urban timber-framed fronts (*see* Town House Introduction). The larger rural houses continued to be built of stone, although cob was also used widely. Timber was used for internal partitions, but exterior timber-framing occurs only very occasionally in less important parts of the building (Coaxdon Hall). The Ham Hill and Beer stone used in the eastern part of the county permitted more elaborate detail than the obdurate granite of the west, but the overriding impression throughout rural Devon during this prosperous century is of solidity and comfort rather than exterior ostentation.

A notable exception must have been Protector Somerset's ambitious new wing at Berry Pomeroy, added to an existing tower house within the castle precinct to serve as a demonstration of his power in the South West. This was probably the first house in the county to use fully understood Renaissance architectural forms. Only fragments and foundations remain of the classical loggia with rusticated piers and arched niches which stood in front of the new hall, but enough to suggest that it is unlikely to have been of local workmanship. Somerset's hall was of double height, with a floor above which may have been used for a long gallery. A similar arrangement with top-floor gallery occurs at Holcombe Court, remodelled probably from the 1560s, although the external architectural forms here are entirely in the local Tudor Perp tradition.

A characteristic feature of the great hall at this time, at Holcombe 62 Court and elsewhere, is a pair of broad, straight-headed, mullioned-and-transomed windows (often replacing narrower medieval openings); stylistic change here is confined to gradual replacement from the mid C16 of hollow-chamfered by ovolo-moulded mullions (although both types survive into the C17 and cannot be used as a simple dating criterion). At Collacombe Manor the windows retain their intricately 66 patterned leading. Here, the exterior has also been modernized by a classical doorway – a rarity, if it is of the same date as the interior plasterwork of 1574 (on which *see* below) – but the general impression is still of asymmetry, dictated by the functions of the different rooms. A more ambitious remodelling took place at Bradfield, where the wings were rebuilt in the late C16, and a regular front was achieved by the addition of an oriel room at the high end of the hall, balanced by a porch at the other end, although the classical details, particularly inside, are still very uncertain in their proportions. These examples all retained the traditional tall open hall. The earliest datable ground-floor hall on a really grand scale is at Buckland Abbey, remodelled by the Drakes in 1576.

Buckland, a highly eccentric recasting of a medieval abbey church, is *sui generis*. Elsewhere, the introduction of the ground-floor hall with windows the same height as those of other rooms made a symmetrical (or nearly symmetrical) treatment of an E-front exterior easier to achieve, with the traditional porch with upper floor as a central feature. Early C17 examples are Walronds, Cullompton, a rural house type, although in a town, and the more substantial Canonteign, with a plain exterior, but with windows carefully matched and graded in size from the eight lights on the ground floor of the wings to three and four lights on the floors above. Forde House, Newton Abbot, also with a symmetrical early C17 front, is smaller but more interesting, for it introduces a variety of forms – triangular and semicircular – for its blind gables (there is no attic floor), which, like its interior decoration, suggests some awareness of Jacobean stylistic trends outside the county. Mid C17 Sydenham is another handsome regular front, made more intricate by projections to the forecourt from the far-projecting side wings. But at Cadhay, quite exceptionally, early C17 architectural attention was concentrated on the internal courtyard, which is delight- 64 fully faced with chequerwork flint and stone in the East Devon manner, and decorated with four delicate aedicules with royal statues, no doubt by masons more often employed on church monuments. For a complete contrast one should look at Boringdon, near Plymouth, with its enjoyably barbaric versions of classical mouldings in granite, and a presumptuous five-storey tower-porch still in the late medieval tradition.

INTERIORS from the mid C16 onwards followed national trends. Greater emphasis on private rooms as the hall decreased in significance often led to the complete rebuilding of the wings at either end of the hall to provide new parlours and upper chambers, often on the occasion of a marriage, as is indicated by the coats of arms on interior decoration. More generously scaled staircases were provided to reach the upper rooms, sometimes fitted within existing walls (Forde House, Newton Abbot), but more often in a projection at the back of the hall

(Holcombe Court and Bradfield), or, less usually, at the end of a wing, approached by a corridor (Rashleigh Barton). The simpler type has a solid core of masonry, but in the C17 framed staircases of timber, sometimes around a small well, are more frequent; there are good examples at Forde House at Newton Abbot, Bradninch, Portledge, and Sydenham, the last especially ornately carved. Lesser houses such as Sand had simpler timber newel stairs around a central pole. None of these houses is on a really grand scale. Devon was far from London and the court, and there is no example of the great Elizabethan or Jacobean prodigy house with its separate state and family apartments. Forde House, where Richard Reynell entertained Charles I, simply has a succession of elaborately decorated first-floor chambers, and not even a long gallery. Indeed, long galleries are rare in Devon; the most

65 impressive example is at Holcombe Court, exceptional in having tiny rooms opening off it. Others are in wings, rather than above the hall, e.g. Cadhay, Widworthy, Portledge, the last fitted up in the second half of the C17 – remarkably late. But if most houses were relatively small, judged on a national scale, they made up for it in the sumptuousness of their interior fittings.

The high quality of JOINERY, in both large and small houses, was a tradition established already in the late medieval period. Even in lesser houses beams are massive, and timber doorcases elaborately stopped and moulded. In the larger houses carved and decorated screens, panelling, and overmantels are frequent from the later C16. Fine examples are the panelling at Buckland Abbey, and the delicate inlaid work in the dining room at Sydenham; the richest ensembles of the early C17 are the parlours at Bradfield and Bradninch, both with intricately decorated inner porches. Screens at their simplest are of the sturdy post-and-panel type common in farmhouses. More elaborate ones have small panels, as at Widworthy (where they have unusual *trompe l'oeil* painted decoration). By far the richest is the exceptional

75 example at Bowringsleigh, which is partly of ebony, and unlikely to be local work. But in and around Exeter there were undoubtedly craftsmen familiar with continental pattern books who were responsible for the vast quantity of richly ornamented woodwork to be found in both houses and churches. One speciality was the heavily studded and faceted door with fan motif, good examples of which survive in Exeter

76 at the Guildhall and No. 10 the Close, and at Forde House, Newton Abbot. Carved figurative panels are less common. Among the best is

68 the Job overmantel in the parlour at Bradninch, but the more rustic scenes in the muniment room at Holcombe Court also deserve a mention.

Even more remarkable than the woodwork is the quantity of PLASTERWORK of this period. The county's prosperity is expressed by the luxurious ornament that can be found in both large and small houses, to a degree unparalleled elsewhere in England. Plasterwork became fashionable in the great English country houses from the 1560s. The spread of the craft to the South West may have owed something to the men trained at Longleat; some of the geometric ceiling patterns are very similar to those used in Somerset and Dorset. A fascinating insight into how craftsmen could accumulate ideas is provided by a tiny notebook (a unique survival now in the Devon Record Office) which belonged in the later C17 to the Devon plasterer *John Abbot*. It includes both geometric ceiling patterns and a miscel-

lany of designs for figures and strapwork ornament derived from
Netherlandish Mannerist sources, of the type used for early c17
ceilings and overmantels, but, alas, there is no indication of dates or
executed works.

The earliest datable Devon ceiling belongs to the long gallery at 65
Holcombe Court. It bears the name of Roger Bluett, who died in 1566,
and is still very simple, with individual wreaths within a flowing
pattern of simple ribs, and a frieze with early Renaissance motifs. At
Totnes, dates in the 1570s are suggested by the initials on ceilings in
several merchants' houses. More sophisticated is the work for the
Tremaynes at Collacombe, dated 1574: a hall ceiling with the inter- 66
secting single ribs and pendants that became a standard type, with
more unusual individually modelled atlas brackets masking an internal jetty, and a pedimented overmantel with precociously overlapping
pilasters. The interior decoration of Buckland for Sir Richard
Grenville, dated 1576, is closely related. Single-rib ceilings with
geometric patterns, often embellished with angle scrolls, continued to
be popular into the early c17, when they co-existed with a richer type
with broad enriched double ribs. Both kinds appear in the sequence of
early c17 upper chambers at Forde, Newton Abbot, the grandest
room with a splendid barrel-vault with pendants and bracket-figures
(for the latter cf. two surviving figures at Widworthy). Such barrel-
vaults were the successors to the open timber roof; other fine examples
in upper chambers, all with dates in the 1620s, are at Hams Barton,
Chudleigh; Rashleigh Barton; and No. 62 Boutport Street, Barnstaple. The last two are particularly good examples of the c17 67
tendency for the ornament to spread over all available surfaces.
Figural subjects are uncommon on ceilings, although the one at
Barnstaple includes small religious scenes. More unusual is the
ceiling in the Butterwalk, Dartmouth, which is covered with a Tree
of Jesse.

OVERMANTELS could also have religious subjects (Butterwalk,
Dartmouth; Holcombe Court main chamber), but even more
frequently they had heraldic achievements, with supporters or surrounding garlands enmeshed in strapwork (see e.g. the upper chambers at Portledge). The heraldic overmantel of the Court Room at
Holcombe Court (1591) is one of the finest; the coarse but impressive
one in the hall at Boringdon shows that the type was still current
around 1640.

There must have been close contact between the craftsmen in
different materials, for the taste for elaborate Netherlandish-inspired
decoration displayed in both woodwork and plasterwork all over the
county can be found also in contemporary church monuments (for
good examples of intricate strapwork see the tomb of George Slee at
Tiverton, or the Gorges monument at St Budeaux, Plymouth).
However, with the exception of Cadhay, already mentioned, it made
surprisingly little impact on local architectural traditions. Among
PUBLIC BUILDINGS the only spectacular effort in the Renaissance
style is the forebuilding of Exeter Guildhall, of 1592, with its upper 74
orders of columns embellished by strapwork (although the arcade
below is highly eccentric). But Blundell's School, Tiverton, of 1604, 71
one of the most ambitious schools in England of its time, is traditionally Perp, apart from its round-headed doorways. Likewise, the
arcaded fronts that were popular for almshouses in the later c16 and

70 C17 (Tiverton, Barnstaple, and, most impressively, Moretonhampstead) assimilated the round-headed arch into the vernacular tradition
still based on late Perp forms.

RURAL BUILDING: 1400–1800

BY PETER BEACHAM

The pattern of settlement in the Devon countryside is dominated by
the thick scatter of individual farmsteads, the great majority on sites
already established by the late Middle Ages. Looking at the modest,
even humble, exterior of most Devon farmhouses it is difficult to
believe that they may have been built in the C15 or early C16 with
layers of subsequent alteration completely disguising their earlier
origin. Hundreds of farmhouses survive from this late medieval
period, when they originated as open-halled or partly floored houses.
Well before 1550 such halls began to be adapted by gradual flooring in
and partitioning, while new two-storey houses began to be constructed
on the same basic plans. As their owners demanded increasingly
sophisticated standards of privacy and comfort in the C17 and early
C18, such houses were often further altered and extended, eventually
resulting in the building of radically different house types. Many
houses show the complete evolutionary sequence from open hall to
two-storey house subdivided and extended into many specialist
rooms. The vast majority began life as farmhouses surrounded by their
own land, though the term 'farmhouse' encompasses a wide social
range, from little more than a cottage at one extreme, to the substantial
houses of very large farms or even minor estates (often suffixed
'barton' in Devon) at the other.

Devon farmhouses show particular affinities with the traditions of
South Somerset and Dorset. The cut-off westwards with Cornwall is
much more distinct. Late medieval houses are thickly concentrated in
central Devon and eastwards into Somerset, spreading throughout the
rest of the county to varying degrees but becoming less common
westwards. The same pattern can be observed in many other respects.
Farmhouse interiors display comparative sophistication in excellent
early roof carpentry and stud-and-panel screens, and in C17 internal
plasterwork and other decoration. Solid internal walls and more
straightforward carpentry become more characteristic westwards and
northwards, but the odd parish can always confound such generaliza-
tion. Dartmoor shows important variations, including a distinctive
house type, the longhouse, and good exterior features in granite,
especially in the C17. As one might expect in such a large and diverse
county there are many more local variations: an example is the
similarity in roof carpentry techniques of early houses in central
Devon, indicating localized schools of carpentry in the late medieval
period.

Externally, diverse BUILDING MATERIALS produce subtle and
visually interesting variations, nowhere better demonstrated than in
that quintessential Devon building material, COB. This earth walling

technique depends upon the coherence under compression of a mixture of clay or sand subsoils, straw or dung at the right moisture content. Because the cohesion of the material only lasts so long as the cob is kept dry (otherwise reverting to mud again), cob walls are usually given the threefold weather protection of an insulating stone plinth underneath, a continuous weather-coating to the wall surface in lime render or limewash, and a wide eaves overhang of slate or thatch or tile above. Mixing cob is a heavy and labour-intensive activity, and so is often done by cattle-treading. Straw is usually (but not always) added to assist drying out and to distribute shrinkage cracks throughout the wall. Walls are built without shuttering by pitching the soft but cohesive wet cob up on to the wall in layers or 'raises' about a foot deep, the surfaces being left rough until dry enough to be pared down.

Because the basic material is on-site subsoil, the truly local character of cob is expressed in marked variations of colour and texture, best seen in the usually unrendered walls of farm buildings. Colours change with the soils, from the strong reds of the Red Devon Sandstone to cream, yellow, buff, ochre, brown, and grey on the clays of the Culm Measures and the Devonian Slates and Shales. Variations in texture result from the interplay of the soils with localized methods of cob building, some of which are still alive today: the bus shelter at Down St Mary was new built in cob in 1978. Cob is found in the earliest farmhouses, and throughout the social and functional range in the humblest building of the farmyard as well as the most sophisticated farmhouse. It also infills timber-framed internal partitions and sometimes forms the entire chimneystack.

Cob gives way to rubble walls where stone is more freely available. But even in the granite stronghold of Dartmoor it is rarely completely absent, being used to heighten or repair stone walls even in high-quality granite houses such as Higher Shilstone, Throwleigh, and the 81 Church House, South Tawton. Granite is regularly used as a carefully 69 dressed walling material in large squared ashlar blocks externally or smaller squared blocks internally, and for door frames, windows, and fireplace surrounds, emphasizing the distinctive character of Dartmoor farmhouses. The many local building stones are used for important display features like the impressive lateral and axial stacks. 72 Towards the Dorset and Somerset border some C17 farmhouse exteriors display Beer or Ham stone mullioned windows and also patterned masonry using chequered flint and limestone. Elsewhere render, roughcast, daub, plaster, and limewash in traditional white–cream–buff colours often obscure any evidence of walling materials. Some new owners mistakenly remove these claddings to expose rubble walls behind, with disastrous visual as well as practical consequences.

BRICK is rare as a walling material even in the later C17 at farmhouse level, occurring then only E of Exeter. But it does crop up in C17 chimneystacks. Around Exeter are examples of early brick stacks comparable to those in Topsham houses (Church Cottage, East Budleigh; Perriton Farm, Whimple). It is rarely found elsewhere; an example is the modelled brick stack inserted into the former open hall at Westacott, North Tawton. In West and South West Devon, as in Cornwall, local slates are used for cladding walls as well as roofs; in contrast, red clay pantiles are common on roofs towards the Somerset border.

THATCH was the original roofing almost everywhere: surprisingly large amounts of smoke-blackened medieval thatch survive sometimes beneath later coverings. It is combed wheat-reed with a plain ridge that gives the gentle, unassuming finish to the traditional Devon roof, quite different from the much coarser finish of imported water-reed (and a world away from the contrived prettiness of many roofs crowned by the heavily patterned ridges now in vogue). Traditionally, water-reed was used only where locally available near the estuaries. In the earliest thatch levels other materials are found, especially rye thatch (e.g. Sheldon, Doddiscombsleigh; Lower Chilverton, Coldridge). There is also broom and heather, often on wattling instead of battens (East Down Farm, Dunsford).

Now for CONSTRUCTION. Outside walls are solid; external TIM-BER-FRAMING is used only for some C17 porches and rarely for small sections of C17 walling. In contrast, timber-framed internal partitions are common, infilled with wattle and daub, cob, and occasionally cob bricks (Acorn Cottage, Thorverton).

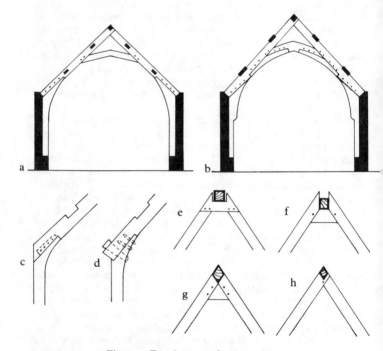

Figure 1. Farmhouse roof construction
a. Jointed cruck truss with through purlins and cranked collar
b. Jointed cruck truss with arch-braced cranked collar and trenched purlins
c. Mortice and tenon jointed cruck, side-pegged
d. Free (or slip) tenon jointed cruck, face-pegged
e. Early apex: saddle with square-set ridge
f. Early apex: yoke with square-set ridge
g. Apex with block, ridge set on edge
h. Jointed apex, ridge set on edge

ROOFS are often more historically informative than any external evidence. They survive from the C15 in large numbers, sometimes complete in every detail. In much of Devon the characteristic roof truss of the C15–17 is of cruck construction. There are massive true crucks (Chimsworthy, Bratton Clovelly; Leigh Barton, Coldridge; Pilliven, Witheridge) and substantial raised crucks (Westcombe, North Bovey; Higher Shilstone, Throwleigh).

But the commonest and most distinctive Devon type is the JOIN-TED CRUCK (Figure 1), which appears elsewhere in England only in neighbouring parts of Somerset and Dorset and is also found in South Wales. It consists of two timbers joined at eaves level, the lower timber a post of varying length set in the wall, the upper a principal rafter carrying to the ridge. The most common joint is formed by a long tenon on the wall post set into a correspondingly long mortice in the centre of the principal rafter pegged from the side, although a face-pegged variation with a slip tenon (usually considered earlier) is also known (Cleavehanger, Nymet Rowland). Other variations include the scarf joint (Rudge, Morchard Bishop) and the side-lapped joint. The height of the wall post varies from a full-length timber carrying to the ground (the massive examples in the barn at Ayshford, Burlescombe, rest on large timber pads) to vestigial short legs at the other extreme. Some trusses in the South Hams and North Devon have a single curved principal entering the wall as no more than a slightly curved foot. There is another C17 variation with a straight principal jointed on to a short straight wall post (Drascombe Barton and Nattonhall, Drewsteignton; Higher Rixdale, Dawlish). Devon cruck construction also includes the END CRUCK (Figure 2), a single curved timber carrying up from the end wall to the ridge.

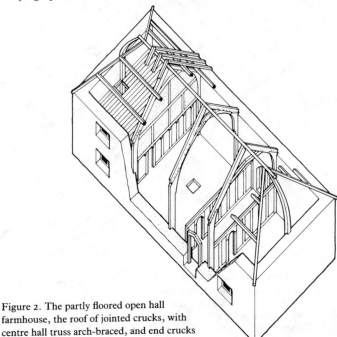

Figure 2. The partly floored open hall farmhouse, the roof of jointed crucks, with centre hall truss arch-braced, and end crucks

Many C15–17 roofs are of relatively straightforward carpentry. At Hole, Black Torrington, the smoke-blackened roof is a series of slight A-frame trusses on the back of which the original thatch is fastened directly to wide battens with no purlins or rafters, a widespread technique also found in some larger houses (e.g. Totleigh Barton, Sheepwash). Arch-bracing, usually confined to the central hall truss, is often used as a means of giving grandeur to the open hall, as in larger houses (Figure 2). Where more elaborate medieval roofs occur, they are generally indications that a farmhouse was originally of higher social status (*see* General Introduction). But some elaboration of earlier roofs is common, particularly in the areas of rich carpentry traditions. The roof principals, arch braces, purlins, and collars can be chamfered and stopped: decoration as elaborate as at South Yard, Rose Ash, where deep transverse channels run over truss, collar, and arch-bracing, is, however, exceptional. The farmhouse roof can also display wind-braces, though the more usual feature is the high-level curved or cranked collar. Rare examples of the clasped purlin are found (Bungsland, West Anstey; Bridford Barton; and Fernworthy, Lydford). The apex shows some evolution (Figure 1, e–h), from the LINKED APEX to the more common JOINTED APEX.

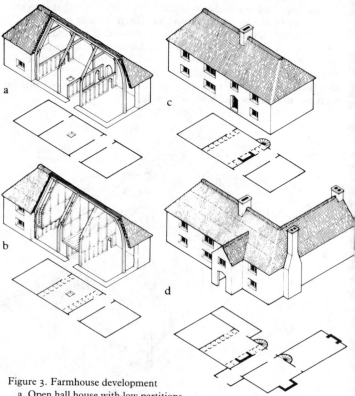

Figure 3. Farmhouse development
   a. Open hall house with low partitions
   b. Open hall house with jettied chambers
   c. Two-storeyed house with axial stack and staircase
   d. Two-storeyed house with porch, cross-wing, and outshot

As for PLANS, rural houses of the C15–17 are of single-room depth on a TWO- OR THREE-ROOM PLAN divided by a cross-passage. The three-room type is much the commonest. This basic plan is modified only gradually, and not seriously challenged by radically different arrangements until the late C17 and C18 (Figure 3). Only on Dartmoor is its pre-eminence overturned by the occurrence of the LONGHOUSE (Figure 4). Although similar in plan (the longhouse shippon for animal shelter replacing and elongating the third domestic room below the cross-passage), the two types evolved against the different agricultural environments of upland and lowland Devon. Other early house types are few and far between. Apart from the rare first-floor halls at Neadon, Manaton, and Yeo, Chagford, there are two- and three-room houses without a cross-passage (e.g. Chapple, Gidleigh, and Rose-bank, Britton Street Lane, Dunsford) and even single-cell houses of the C16 (Yeo, Chagford).

That the two- or three-room cross-passage plan is a lesser version of the major medieval house rather than an evolution from the longhouse is strongly supported by the Devon evidence. Not only is there a complete range of scale of this type, from the miniature, like Rose Bank, Britton Street Lane, Dunsford, through substantial houses such as Lower Lye, Stockland, to the grander examples with their chapels and other prestige features like Bury Barton, Lapford: there is also the distributional evidence that the longhouse belongs to Dartmoor and its surrounding countryside with only a handful of examples further afield.* The two traditions share many common features of later medieval and post-medieval domestic development. In both types the HALL (the room 'above' the cross-passage) is the principal living room usually throughout the period. It is the largest, the only heated room initially, and boasts the best of whatever decoration is going. 'Beyond' the hall lies the INNER ROOM, its greater privacy making it a private chamber, or parlour later on. 'Below' the cross-passage the LOWER ROOM of the three-room plan originally performed a service function: it too is unheated in the late medieval house, but often became a kitchen with the insertion of a large fireplace in the C17. The process of gradual subdivision of the open hall and extension of the building with extra rooms is common to both types.

Far from being a primitive survivor, the longhouse (Figure 5) is capable of the same degree of sophistication as the other house types throughout the period. Here is a perfectly functional building for hill-farming, providing house and cow byre under one roof. It is skilfully sited for shelter, recessed into the hillside, often incorporating huge site boulders, its long, low shape orientated down-slope. This enables easy clearance of dung from the central drain of the shippon via a square dung-hole in the lower gable end wall above the drain exit. Splayed slit windows give light and ventilation to the cow-house and the hayloft above while maintaining maximum weather protection. Nor is the shippon architecturally the poor relation to the house, for its walls are often of massive ashlar granite blockwork (Sanders, Letta-ford, and Westcombe, both at North Bovey; Hole, Chagford; Higher Shilstone, Throwleigh) and its doorway has moulded features (e.g. the pointed-head example at Whimington, Sampford Spiney, and the C17 door at Higher Shilstone, Throwleigh). The cows back on to the

*Two recent discoveries are on the foothills of Exmoor: Brinscott, Berrynarbor, and Inner Narracott, Bittadon.

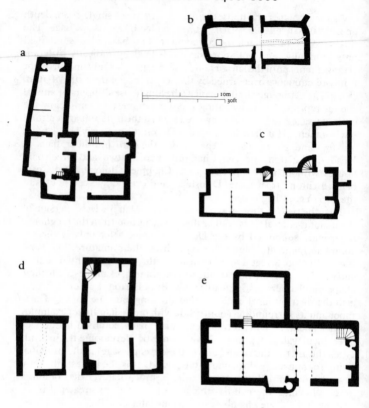

Figure 4. Farmhouse plans

a. Hill, Christow: two-room cross-passage plan with later kitchen cross-wing.

b. Houndtor, Manaton: excavated longhouse

c. Lower Lye, Stockland: three-room cross-passage plan with seventeenth-century cross-wing

d. West Chapple, Gidleigh: longhouse (shippon with transverse drain) with later cross-wing

e. Lower Chilverton, Coldridge: three-room cross-passage plan with lateral stack and staircase wing added

f. Chimsworthy, Bratton Clovelly: longhouse with integral shippon and late medieval cross-wing, with C17 staircase

g. Lower Allerton, Dartington: three-room cross-passage plan with seventeenth-century porch, staircase, rear wing, and later extensions

h. Whimington, Sampford Spiney: longhouse with remodelled upper section; kitchen wing (with smoking chamber) added to the rear of the cross-passage

i. Knoddy, Week, Dartington: transitional seventeenth-century plan with staircase to the rear of the cross-passage

j. Pennyhill, Stockland: early-eighteenth-century symmetrical plan, two rooms deep

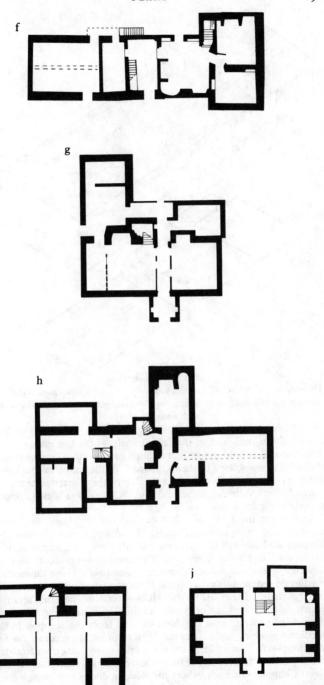

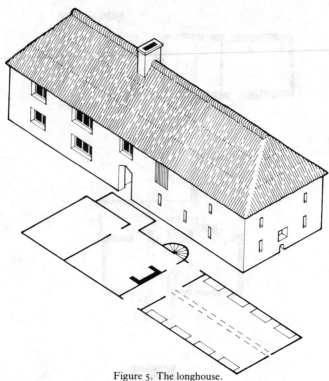

Figure 5. The longhouse.
The shippon is 'below' the cross-passage, with a central drain, and dung-hole
above in the end wall; the tethering-posts and mangers are along the side walls,
with a hayloft above

central drain, tethered to the lateral walls where the mangers and
drilled stones to hold the upright tethering stakes often survive even if
the cows have gone (Higher Uppacott, Widecombe-in-the-Moor;
Sanders, Lettaford, North Bovey). Rarely these arrangements are
transverse when the lie of the land thus dictates, as at West Chapple,
Gidleigh (Figure 4, d).

Finally, it must be said that the supposedly classic longhouse
arrangement of a common access through the cross-passage for
humans and animals is very rare indeed: hence the importance of
examples like Higher Uppacott, Widecombe-in-the-Moor, and the
deserted house at Chaddlehanger, Lamerton. Their immediate
medieval predecessors excavated at Houndtor (particularly instructive
for the visitor; Figure 4, b) and Meldon certainly had this arrangement, but the vast majority of standing longhouses show varying
degrees of separation of the domestic end from the shippon in the
medieval phase as well as later on. Most common is a separate door to
the shippon from outside, with or without a connecting door from the
cross-passage. While some of these are certainly later adaptations (e.g.
West Chapple, Gidleigh, where the shippon doorway is complemented by an inserted cross-wall on the lower side of the cross-passage),
other medieval examples were built from the start with such radical

separation. Outstanding in the latter category is perhaps the most sophisticated longhouse of all, Higher Shilstone, Throwleigh, with a 81 medieval arrangement of a solid full-height cross-wall at the lower side of the cross-passage and a connecting door to the shippon as well as a separate outside entrance. At Westcombe, North Bovey, the original shippon entrance is, uniquely, in the gable end wall of the shippon. There are yet other longhouses where the separation becomes complete with the creation of another heated room between cross-passage and shippon by annexing part of the shippon (again, Westcombe, North Bovey, and Nattonhall, Drewsteignton).

While many houses were built two-storeyed from the mid C16 onwards (e.g. Luggs Farm, Membury), large numbers built with OPEN HALLS and PARTLY FLOORED HOUSES underwent gradual MODERNIZATION to fully two-storeyed houses between the early C16 and the end of the C17: it is the visible evidence of this process in so many interiors that is the most remarkable feature of Devon houses (Figure 3). Many houses still have their medieval roofs intact. At Hill, Christow, two such roof levels, each with its own smoke-blackened thatch, survive, one above the other. The extent of SMOKE-BLACK-ENING is crucial evidence for the earliest building phase, when smoke from the chimneyless hearth rose uninterrupted to the roof to percolate out through the thatch: even where there are smoke louvres (Middle Clyst William, Plymtree; Leigh Barton, Coldridge; Rudge, Morchard Bishop) the degree of smoke-blackening is impressive. That so many smoke-blackened roofs survive is an indication of the substantial quality and lofty dimensions of the open halls, since they could accommodate the insertion of a first floor without much disturbance of the original roof structure: alterations, if necessary at all, are usually confined to a slight raising of the height of the walls, often in a layer of cob, which could accommodate a flatter roof pitch (frequently an C18 and C19 alteration to accord with a new front), and the cutting of the lower purlin or wall-plate to allow for upper chamber windows.

At least some of these open halls were originally only divided at ground-floor level by LOW PARTITIONS, the earliest probably framed wattle-and-daub or the like, replaced later by more substantial construction (Townsend, Stockland; see Figure 3, a). Some surviving stud-and-panel screens that relate awkwardly to later floor-levels and first-floor partition walls began as low partitions (Lower Lye, Stockland; Lower Chilverton, Coldridge). Not all open halls had even low 77 partitions: some may have been unsubdivided LONG HALLS (Pumpy Cottage, East Week, South Tawton). Some hall houses were very small (Rose Bank, Britton Street Lane, Dunsford); others had full-height partitions from the start, as examples of original closed trusses survive. At Middle Clyst William, Plymtree, and East Holm, Newton St Cyres, both sides of the closed trusses are smoke-blackened, demonstrating that there was an open hearth on either side (there seem to be three such hearths at Middle Clyst William), but more commonly such partitions must have divided the heated section of the house from the unheated part, since they and their roofs show smoke-blackening only on the hall side, as at Culm Davy, Hemyock.

Partial flooring-in began well before the end of the late medieval period as upper chambers were either incorporated into new-built hall houses, as at Livenhayes, Yarcombe, or inserted at one end or both ends of an existing open hall over the inner room and the cross-passage. If such chambers have been inserted, the partition will be smoke-blackened on the hall side, since the open hearth still continued in the hall, but clean on the inner chamber face, although the roof over the chamber will be smoke-blackened from the earlier phase. A remarkable Devon feature is the projection of these chambers forward over the ground-floor partitions into the still open hall, the joists and partition thus forming an INTERNAL JETTY comparable to the jettied front walls of many town buildings at this period and adding to the architectural distinction of the hall (Figures 2 and 3, b). They are impressive features, usually with chamfered edges and rounded ends, and sometimes (as at Westcombe, North Bovey) enriched with a moulded cap on which the upper partition is supported. Chambers were sometimes jettied into the hall from both ends, as at Sanders, Lettaford, North Bovey, though, as in this example, part of the cross-passage jetty was subsequently destroyed if an axial stack was inserted later. At Lambert, Cheriton Bishop, the chamber walls are carried on moulded bressumers, the one over the cross-passage bearing another stud-and-panel screen.

Some internal jetties are original features – the first-floor walls framed into a closed truss (at e.g. the Glebe House, Whitestone; Newhouse, Christow). Where they are insertions, the first-floor chamber wall will be a small distance away from an open truss. A jetty can be the only surviving evidence of the partially floored stage of a hall house, especially if the roof has later been replaced, as in the early C17 sections of Lower Ridge, Chardstock. In North Devon jetties are usually over the cross-passage, not the inner room, suggesting – since they also have solid cross-walls at the upper end of the hall – that such houses may have originated on a two-room plan to which the inner room was added later. An upper chamber projecting very far into the open hall may have the joists supported by a cross-beam instead of a jetty with a bressumer above the joists. At Higher Shilstone, Throwleigh, such part-flooring extended so far into the hall from over the cross-passage that when the massive axial stack was subsequently inserted it was easily accommodated behind the cross-beam of the chamber.

The hall often persisted open to the roof long after the insertion of such chambers, as the smoke-blackening of the inserted partitions on the hall side shows, and sometimes it even survived the insertion of chimneystacks. The Old Hall, Chulmleigh; Priesthall, Kentisbeare; Hill, Christow; and Hill, Loxhore, still with unceiled halls, provide rare opportunities to see the character of such a room in this transitional phase. When the flooring finally occurred, the continuing importance attached to the hall as the principal room is often demonstrated in the comparatively elaborate decoration of the cross-beams and joists. They can be richly chamfered and stopped, or set in intersecting grid patterns with very deep chamfers and large stops.

The addition of CHIMNEYSTACKS was one of the more important developments of the late C16 and C17. Timber hoods, stacks, and smoke bays are rare survivals (e.g. Middle Clyst William, Plymtree; Rudge, Morchard Bishop), although mortices or peg holes for such timber structures sometimes survive (e.g. in the roof at Luggs Farm, Membury). The hall stack is either AXIAL (Figure 3, c), backing on to the cross-passage (where it may sometimes be constructed in the cross-passage itself, thus creating a lobby entrance, as at South Yard, Rose

Ash), or LATERAL, on the side wall of the house, and usually the front wall for display. Higher Tor, Poundsgate, Widecombe-in-the-Moor affords a rare instance of the stack being set on the wall between the hall and the inner room. Both axial and lateral stacks are constructed with excellent masonry. On Dartmoor, such display work often includes ashlar granite blockwork and moulded bases and corbel stones to the cross-passage wall of the axial stack, with similar blockwork and moulded caps above ridge-level (e.g. an impressive crenellated cap at Aller, Christow). Lateral stacks, a special West Country feature, can be even more exuberantly decorated, with patterned masonry, set-backs and set-offs, and datestones. There are good groups in Otterton and in School Street, Sidford. Occasionally, the upper section of the stack can be round.

Later C16 and C17 chamber luxury is represented by the occasional garderobe (Hobhouse, Drewsteignton; Boycombe, Farway – a double) and especially by fireplaces, e.g. the prestigious decorated examples in Beer stone dated 1583 at Poltimore, Farway, and at New Inn House, Chardstock, where the date of 1594 is inscribed in one of three roundels. Large kitchen fireplaces were often inserted into the lower room, but kitchens can also be specially-constructed additional rooms or cross-wings: they can occupy the full width of the house (Scottishill, Dunsford) and incorporate ovens and walk-in smoking chambers. Ovens of brick or cloam (coarse North Devon pottery) become increasingly common from the C17 onwards. SMOKING CHAMBERS for curing food are located alongside the fireplace, as at Luggs Farm, Membury, and Whimington, Sampford Spiney (Figure 4, h), or offset behind the stack, as at Manor Farm, Strete, and Droridge, Dartington. There are rare examples of corn-drying kilns with perforated tiled floors and high-level access to an adjoining granary (Stallenge Thorne, Hockworthy).

The position of STAIRCASES is not always consistent. The partly floored house often had a ladder access to the upper chamber, and at Livenhayes, Yarcombe, the late medieval pointed-head door frame to the original jettied chamber survives in the centre of the first-floor partition wall. At Bishop's House, Lower Street, Chagford, and Barn Farm, Luppitt, the inner-room ceiling joists frame an original ladder access to the chamber above. Original or inserted spiral stairs, in solid timber steps as well as in stone, are often located in a characteristic bulge beyond the line of the lateral walls by the stack, but also at the inner-room junction with the hall and at the junction of the cross-wing with the main house. Some have double doors at their head to give separate access to the first-floor chambers. Staircases could be built in specially added rear wings, or incorporated as the principal feature of a cross-wing, as at Lower Chilverton, Coldridge. Two, three, or more staircases may be required by the C17 to give access to all the upper chambers in a complex farmhouse.

The demand for extra comfort necessitated EXTENSION AND REBUILDING as well as internal modernization. Among early examples, at Chimsworthy, Bratton Clovelly (Figure 4, f), the original medieval house has an open hall cross-wing and at Buddle, Broadwoodwidger, a second open hall was built on to the original house. Most cross-wings or additional rooms were constructed in the later C16 and C17; sometimes they became the smartest part of the house. At Lower Ridge, Chardstock, the upper part of the medieval house was rebuilt as a symmetrical front in the C17. At Westacott Barton, North Tawton, the later cross-wing to the medieval house has a ten-light mullioned window with a king mullion to the ground floor, a five-light window to the first floor culminating in a specially formed gable above, and exceptionally fine C17 plasterwork to both floors. At the other extreme, extensions provided more service rooms, and there are examples of the earlier house being demoted to a service wing (Higher Hele, Cornwood; Yarde, Silverton; Bagtor, Ilsington; Ashford, Burlescombe). Rooms were added longitudinally despite the practical difficulty of inter-connection. The most common extension is the OUTSHOT, a lean-to structure (which can be part of the original build), sometimes running the whole length of the building. In the C17 the hall was sometimes enlarged by a two-storey bay projecting beyond the front wall.

Two-storey PORCHES are often part of the C17 smartening-up process of earlier buildings, but some houses were built with integral porches (Figure 3, d). In Central and East Devon they are often timber-framed and open on the ground floor, as at Spencer's Cottage, Coleford, Colebrooke, where the timber-framing with its curved tension bracing has been exposed, or in high-quality masonry (e.g. in flint and limestone blocks at Luggs Farm, Membury). Townsend, Stockland, boasts two C17 porches on opposite sides of the house. Dartmoor longhouse porches are sometimes incorporated into porch wings wide enough to allow a room alongside the entrance passage as well as a chamber above (Middle Bonehill and Lake, Widecombe-in-the-Moor).

As a consequence of all these developments, there was no 'Great Rebuilding' of Devon's farmhouses during the later C16 and the first half of the C17. W. G. Hoskins himself pointed to the tendency for Devon houses to be modernized rather than rebuilt during this period, and later research has revealed that this was a historically continuous process from the late C15 to the early C18. A rare archaeological investigation of a non-moorland farmhouse site at Middlemoor, Sow-ton, found eleven major building episodes between the early C16 and the early C18.

Towards the end of this period, the basic plans show considerable evolution and variation. Many houses display a large number of rooms with specific functions, like parlour, kitchen, dairy, pantry, and buttery, and the privacy and comfort of the upper chambers, as well as their numbers, is increased: Welltown, Walkhampton, and Whiming-ton, Sampford Spiney (Figure 4, h), with their six-room ground-floor plans, and Poltimore, Farway, where four staircases serve the fully developed house, are examples at the upper end of the vernacular scale. Later C17 houses show the tension between traditional patterns and emerging national plan forms. In attempts at a more centralized arrangement, staircases were sometimes built at the rear end of the cross-passage, as at Woodcott and Knoddy (Figure 4, i), both at Week (Dartington), and Exton at Woodbury. Exton has the principal heated rooms at either end of the three-room plan, the central unheated room having a service function (cf. the similarly placed service room in the four-room Drascombe Barton, Drewsteignton). Another variant is the lobby-entry house (e.g. Brown's Farm, Woodbury Salterton). At Moxhayes, Membury, the builder incorporated an integral rear lean-to for staircase, service rooms, and upstairs corridor into a two-room cross-passage plan of 1683. Internal corridors became necessary to give separate access to the different specialist rooms: Higher Rixdale, Dawlish, has C17 corridors to both ground- and first-floor rooms.

From the late C17, symmetry, at least in the main elevation, becomes the hallmark of the new-built house, as at Gulliford, Woodbury, and Ford Farm, Dunsford. Ford has the service rooms in the cross-wings of a U-shaped plan. The double-pile house also makes its appearance; here, equally sized and windowed rooms, two deep in the larger houses, are placed either side of a central entrance hall from which the staircase rises, the symmetry emphasized by placing the stacks at the gable ends. Even a modest farm like Pennyhill, Stockland, displays a version of such a plan apparently as early as 1704 (Figure 4, j). Brick now makes its appearance in houses like the Old Manor, Talaton, with smart chequered brick walls added c. 1700 to the principal elevations of the L-shaped medieval house.

Gradually, the nationally familiar house types of the later C18 and C19 spread into the countryside, slowly displacing the county's own distinctive building traditions. Some houses were subdivided into cottages as the rural population rose. It is to this later period that most of the numerous smaller cottages belong: their predecessors in which the agricultural workforce of the C15–17 lived have not survived. Most Devon villages have cottages dating from this time, few as spectacular as the continuous C18 thatched terrace stepping gently downhill at Nos. 1–13 Fore Street, Morchard Bishop. Some of the small cottages of the late C17 and early C18 husbandmen survive, but many represent later C18 and C19 efforts to improve housing conditions for agricultural workers: typical examples are illustrated and described, with a plan, in Charles Vancouver's study of 1808 (*see* Further Reading). These early model cottages were given local character by their rubble or cob walls and hipped thatched roofs, a tradition continued even later in the local slate roofs of the Bedford Estate cottages in West Devon and the flint walls of the Rolle Estate cottages in the east of the 168 county. But many dwellings for the rural population continued to be very basic. The so-called squatters' cottages of the C19 were often only one-up and one-down: a good group survives, characteristically built right on the road junction, around Knowle Cross, Whimple. At Spanishlake Cottage, Doddiscombsleigh, a tiny cob dwelling of this basic type, attached to the upper end of the barn dated 1771, was still inhabited in the mid C20.

DECORATION is comparatively limited in range and style, and features tend to persist so long as to make precise dating impossible: a few plainly chamfered cross-beams and the odd fireplace lintel are all that some farmhouses and most cottages have to offer. But carpentry details and plasterwork, sometimes superseding earlier painted or stencilled decoration, give relative richness to many a farmhouse interior, echoing the tradition of classy roof carpentry.

Because most window and door frames were constructed in timber, many farmhouses have lost their original external decoration. The most impressive surviving external evidence is, consequently, found in C17 granite door frames and windows of some Dartmoor houses: a particularly characteristic door frame has a heavy roll moulding carried round the door and the spandrels, the latter often lugged and decorated with stylized foliage like the oak leaves at Lake, Widecombe-in-the-Moor, and Higher Shilstone, Throwleigh. Elsewhere 81

there is the occasional spectacular survivor in timber, like the mullioned-and-transomed fronts at Great Gutton, Shobrooke; Upcott
Barton, Cheriton Fitzpaine; Woodbeer Court, Plymtree; and Middle-
80 combe, Uplowman; more common is a single original window, usually
an ovolo-moulded example of the C17. Surviving window tracery,
even the cusped head, is exceptional: the rare examples (e.g. Little
Hackworthy, Tedburn St Mary; Keymelford, Crediton Hamlets) tend
to be the small windows in the back wall of the hall. Anything more
elaborate, like the traceried examples at Traymill, Thorverton, is a
sure sign of originally superior status, and the same applies to moulded
reveals or window-heads (Boycombe, Farway).

STUD-AND-PANEL SCREENS, separating the different rooms and
the cross-passage, are among the most impressive features of the
Devon farmhouse interior: many houses have two or three such
screens, and there are rare examples of their use at first-floor level
(Lambert, Cheriton Bishop; Lane End, Christow; Nos. 10–12 Fore
Street, Silverton). They are constructed of heavy upright studs
morticed into head and cill beams, the recessed panels filled with wide
planks; decoration can be as simple as chamfers and stops or enriched
with ornament along the head beam (The Old Hall, Chawleigh). The
chamfers stop at a higher level if there is (or was) an original bench
against the screen: rare is the carved bench end (the Old Rectory,
Cheriton Bishop; Clifford Barton, Dunsford; Coxtor, Peter Tavy).
Some are also decorated with paintings or stencilled patterns: there are
several good examples around Sidmouth (Tudor Cottage, Church
Street, Sidmouth; St Mary's, Station Road, Newton Poppleford; the
78 Old Manor, Talaton). At the Old Manor the painting of the screen to
the inner room is carried up over the joists of the internal jetty in
strapwork and stylized foliage. The mid C17 taste for geometrical
patterning is represented in the unusual screen at Higher Fursden,
Sandford. Other decorative panelling, including linenfold, is sometimes found as a prestige feature in hall or parlour (the George Inn,
Chardstock; Rudge, Morchard Bishop) and even in the chamber
(Middlecombe, Uplowman).

From the late C16, a particularly impressive feature, even in the
national context, is the insertion of PLASTER CEILINGS into these
relatively modest buildings. They show variations of single- and
double-rib forms in geometric and floral designs and range from the
79 simplicity of the ceilings in the C17 modernization at Hill, Christow,
and Home Living, Brampford Speke, where decorative centrepieces
are framed by cornice mouldings, to the elaborate ceilings in the C17
cross-wing at Westacott Barton, North Tawton, with its kite pattern
and central pendant, or the extensive range of plasterwork in many
rooms at Rixdale, Dawlish. There are also plaster panels and overmantels, like the sun overmantel from Great Moor, Sowton, now in Exeter
Museum, or the early C17 example at Bury Barton, Lapford, which
commemorates a marriage in 1614. A Devon speciality, despite its
impractical location, is BLACK AND WHITE (and occasionally RED)
DECORATION on the inner and back faces of the fireplace, in
geometric or floral designs and sometimes in SGRAFFITO PLASTER-
WORK. The moulding and painting of fireplace jambs and lintels is
also common in the late C16 and C17. Some fine examples are found,
often with embellishments and dates, in granite on and around SW
Dartmoor (e.g. Welltown, Walkhampton) and in Beer stone in East

Devon (e.g. Poltimore and Boycombe, both at Farway). The DATE STONES also plentiful at this period often help to corroborate structural and decorative evidence for the development of a house, but their significance is as likely to be social as structural, recording such events as a marriage or a change of ownership.

FARM BUILDINGS in Devon show the importance of animal husbandry with subsidiary degrees of arable. They are of careful construction, generally later than the house, though sometimes contemporary, as at Bury Barton, Lapford, where two ranges of C16 buildings survive in the inner courtyard. Occasionally farm buildings are converted from abandoned houses: on Dartmoor at Neadon, Manaton, at Yardworthy and Yeo, Chagford, and at Pizwell, Lydford, the present farmyards comprise several former medieval houses.

Farm buildings are usually grouped around the farmhouse and farmyard, although later on there is increasing separation of the house from the yard. Field outbuildings are comparatively unusual. A major exception is the unique group of thirty-five linhays on Braunton Marsh and Horsey Island on land lately reclaimed from the sea, with the farmhouses inland. The farmstead grouping tends to be relatively open, but there are C17 examples of enclosed courtyard plans, showing later development into the C19 double courtyard plan, as at Bury Barton, Lapford. The number and range of buildings and layout reflect regional differences and developments in farming practice: compare, for example, the complex farmsteads of lowland Devon (e.g. Poltimore, Farway) with the smaller range of buildings in a Dartmoor farming hamlet such as Lettaford, North Bovey. As agricultural practices improved, farm plans evolved from informal clusters around the yard to courtyard plans epitomized in the model farms of the C18 and C19. The BARN's centrally placed double doors for controlling the draught for threshing on either side of the oak-beamed threshing floor make it easy to recognize, and it is often the only building with early features (e.g. the C16 barn at Lower Chilverton, Coldridge). BANK BARNS are constructed into the hillside, giving a shippon at ground-floor level and ground-floor access to the barn above from the rear (e.g. the spectacular double barn at Lower Jurston, Chagford). The commonest building is the LINHAY or LINNEY, an open-fronted shelter for animals, usually with an upper floor for fodder storage, the roof supported on the open side on timber or stone columns. The cowhouse or SHIPPON, integral in the longhouse, can also be a separate structure in the yard.

Other farmyard buildings include POUND HOUSES, the specialist building for cider-making; ROUND HOUSES or HORSE ENGINE HOUSES often added to the barn, providing a circular walk for the horse which worked the machinery in the barn; MALT HOUSES, with their long low floors for the germination of malting barley; and GRANARIES, either as separate buildings or as upper storage rooms above cartsheds, subdivided into boxes for the different grains.

Some of the smaller buildings surrounding the house represent the combination of the domestic and farming economy. Occasionally a detached kitchen building or bakehouse can be found to the rear of the cross-passage, as at Little Hackworthy, Tedburn St Mary, and North Morte, Mortehoe. ASH HOUSES are a particular feature of eastern Dartmoor but also occur elsewhere. They are small circular or square buildings, often with a corbelled stone roof, in which ash from domestic fires was stored over winter to be used on the fields in spring. DOVECOTES can be purpose-built (e.g. the grand example at Prid-hamsleigh, Staverton) or incorporated in the upper part of the house or farm building.

Of minor structures, STADDLE STONES are worth mentioning. Now much more familiar as garden ornaments, they are straight columns with a mushroom-like capping-stone to deter vermin, used to support ricks or timber-framed granaries. Rarely, solid circular stone-built RICK STANDS occur, like the pair at Bullaton, Hennock, with moulded stone caps. BEE BOLES are curved or square apertures in a wall plastered internally for the straw bee-skeps; there are eight in the wall at Batworthy Mill, Chagford, three above one another at Northcote, East Down, and examples in the house walls at Heath Cottage, Bridford, and Scottishill, Dunsford.

Many Devon farmsteads still possess a complete range of such domestic buildings and farm buildings, impressive testimony of an ancient but now fast disappearing rural society and economy. Its C19 peak is perfectly symbolized by the chapel-like farm office standing proudly by the front door of Yeo Farm, Chagford, architect-designed (by *James Crocker* of Exeter, 1873) down to the last detail, including the office desk.

TOWN HOUSES:

MEDIEVAL TO MID SEVENTEENTH CENTURY

BY MICHAEL LAITHWAITE

Few houses earlier than the mid C16 are to be found in Devon towns. Open halls are rare, and so are medieval smoke-blackened roof-timbers. Fires, especially in the thatch-covered areas of East Devon, are partly to blame, but rebuilding from Elizabeth's reign onwards is the chief explanation. In spite of wartime bombing and post-war urban development, some exceptionally fine early post-medieval town houses, built largely with the proceeds of the overseas trade in cloth, tin, and Newfoundland fish, remain at Exeter, Plymouth and Barnstaple. Several of the smaller towns benefited architecturally in the same way: Dartmouth and Totnes in particular are rich in C16 and C17 merchants' houses.

The characteristic C15 to C17 Devon town house is timber-framed with stone side-walls, a fashion that reached, in a small way, even to the village-like Dartmoor towns such as Bovey Tracey and Moreton-hampstead. In equally sharp contrast to the countryside, three-storeyed houses were already being built in the late Middle Ages, and in Exeter, at least, four-storeyed ones by the mid C16. In the centre of the more important towns it is only the very grand houses, like those in the Close at Exeter, Yogge's House at Plymouth, and the Great House of St George at Tiverton, that are wholly stone-built. Brick is rare for anything but chimneys. It starts appearing as a major material towards the end of the C17, although Barnstaple has an earlier part-timber, part-brick house (No. 74 High Street). Barnstaple also seems to be unusual among the larger towns in having a significant amount of cob-building in the town centre, tucked away in boundary walls and back-street cottages. Externally, many of the houses may be recognizable only by their jettied upper storeys, as most have been plastered, covered with slate-hanging, or otherwise refronted in the C18 and C19, and the timber-framing that is exposed has often been considerably restored.

Earlier FRAMING is plain, with widely spaced vertical studs; the medieval examples (e.g. No. 13 Higher Street, Dartmouth, and The House that Moved, Exeter) also have big downward braces. No. 46 High Street, Exeter, with a coved third storey enriched with attached shafts and angels, is a rare decorative example of the mid C16: elaboration seems to have come in mostly in the early and mid C17. The basis of these later fronts is a series of small, rectangular moulded panels combined with carved oriel windows. The Butterwalk and 95 No. 4 The Quay at Dartmouth add enriched columns, while Nos. 223–225 High Street, Exeter, have panels of moulded plasterwork. The dramatic effect of these fronts was usually completed by a gabled roof (often now hipped back), a single gable for the narrower houses but two or more for the wider ones. The Manor House Hotel at Cullompton (1603) has no less than four gables, with jetties and oriels to 96 match. Exposed timber-framing survived until at least the 1660s, although the Tudor House at Exeter (c. 1660) was slate-hung from the first. The Tudor House illustrates another late feature, the unjettied, timber-framed front with small pentices at each floor-level. Nevertheless, old habits were not easily shaken off; at Totnes, No. 52 Fore Street of 1692 is still gabled and jettied (though the timber-framing was probably never exposed), while in the early C18 Nos. 26 and 28 High Street combined gables with classical cornices and pilasters.

The STONE FRONTS are usually plain, in the manner of rural houses, with simple mullioned windows: Yogge's House at Plymouth has a good oriel, and a house in The Square at North Tawton has a bay-window with attached shafts between the lights, but these are exceptions. The pilastered classical front of 1585 at No. 16 High Street, Totnes (probably also with a gable originally), is unique; remarkable also is the arcaded loggia to its ground storey, rare in a private house (cf. the late C16 and C17 almshouses at Barnstaple, Moretonhamp- 70 stead, and Tiverton, and Exeter Guildhall). Of the similar arcading of 74 market halls little survives; the fine granite columns of the fruit-market house (or Church Walk) at Totnes now stand in front of the Guildhall. BUTTERWALKS, or rows of houses built out over the pavement on columns, seem to have started rather earlier. No. 35 High Street, Totnes, has stone columns of late medieval character; the first 97 documentary reference to such houses in the town is in 1532. Other surviving examples are at Dartmouth (1635–40) and Plympton St 95 Maurice; two fine ranges at Crediton were destroyed by fire in the C18.

These street arcades provided a shelter for stalls, which, in Totnes at least, could be owned separately from the houses behind them. There were also shops in the ground-floor front rooms of the houses, but of these little structural evidence remains. The House that Moved at Exeter has large arcades with shouldered heads on the ground floor, apparently a form of medieval shopfront. At Nos. 37 and 38 New

Street, Plymouth, are more easily recognizable C17 examples with wide openings separated by ovolo-moulded wood mullions.

The best surviving examples of INTERNAL PLANNING are often to be found in the houses with the narrowest fronts, one room wide and one or two rooms deep. The streets of Exeter, Barnstaple, Dartmouth, and Totnes, and probably much of Plymouth, must have been lined with buildings like these. Surviving medieval examples are Nos. 1 and 2 Catherine Street (off the Close) and Nos. 11 and 12 and The House that Moved, West Street, all in Exeter; and No. 13 Higher Street, Dartmouth. Two good mid C16 examples are Nos. 46 High Street, Exeter, and 49 Wolborough Street, Newton Abbot. Some are two rooms deep on ground and second floors, but with a large hall on the first floor. The grander versions are mainly post-medieval.*

The houses that are two rooms deep (most numerous in Totnes) most often had a ground-floor shop at the front with a hall behind, both entered from a side-passage running the depth of the house. The staircase was usually a winding one built round a central newel-pole, the treads fitted into a hollow midway along one of the side-walls. Good examples remain in New Street, Plymouth. Behind the front block was a courtyard with, at the rear, a DETACHED KITCHEN BLOCK, occasionally (as at No. 68 Fore Street and Manor Cottage, Totnes) deepened to include a parlour or dining-room; there is evidence that in some cases (e.g. No. 70 Fore Street, Totnes) the kitchen was moved to a second detached block at the rear. The upper floors were mostly bedrooms, except perhaps for a study or counting chamber. Some houses had a combined parlour and bedroom at the front of the first floor, known (at least in Exeter and Totnes) as a fore hall. Linking the front and back block at first-floor level, and occasionally also on the second floor, was a narrow timber-framed GALLERY, a persistent local feature that survived in Devon towns until the beginning of Victoria's reign. A C17 variant appears in Barnstaple at Nos. 3 and 8 Cross Street, where the rear section of the front block is divided between a back room and a staircase with straight flights. It is in fact the forerunner (No. 8 is dated 1635) of the stock terrace house found in London from the Restoration onwards. The gallery-and-back-block design as a whole is rare in England outside Devon. Examples are known in Bristol, Chester, and Taunton, but the main parallels are on the Continent, particularly in France, where the plan was already in use for high-class buildings in the late Middle Ages.

Some houses are L-shaped. Examples one room wide with a narrower rear room (of which No. 33 St Andrew's Street, Plymouth, now a museum, is the best of the C16) are rare in Devon. No. 39 High Street, Barnstaple, probably had an open hall at the rear. Wider-fronted L-shaped plans could develop a rear wing of considerable length: the much-altered White Hart Hotel in South Street, Exeter, is one of the better medieval examples. No. 43 High Street, Totnes (costume museum), is a remarkably good mid C16 house of this type, its three-room rear wing with hall and kitchen extended twice in the late C16 and early C17.

Occasionally the full three-room-and-cross-passage rural plan appears with a rear wing, for example at the Manor House Hotel at Cullompton (1603) (kitchen wing behind the service-end), and at the

* At Exeter, a group of three-room-deep examples with an open hall in the centre was demolished in the 1960s and 1970s.

Great House of St George, Tiverton (a very long wing with stair-turret attached behind the parlour end). Walronds, Cullompton (c. 1605), is still more complex: a U-plan house, but with the right-hand cross-wing lying in front of the hall (presumably to fit in with the plot-width) and a rear wing at the service end.

Full courtyard houses, i.e. with ranges on four sides, are exceedingly rare. There are two fine medieval examples in the Close at Exeter, Nos. 8–9 and 10–11, the former with an open hall on the l. of

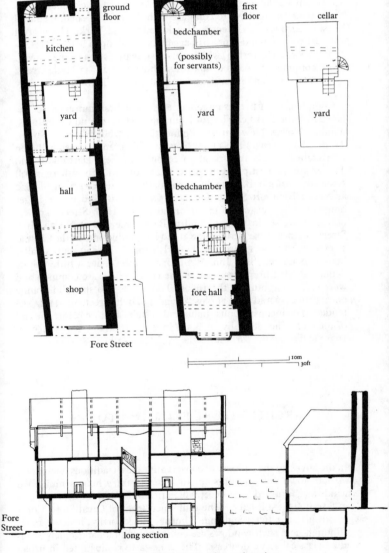

Totnes, No. 70 Fore Street, plan and section

the courtyard, the latter, following remodelling in the early C 16, with a two-storeyed hall range at the rear. Yogge's House at Plymouth (c. 1498) should also be mentioned, although it is quite unlike an ordinary house – fully three-storeyed, with no main hall and with galleries projecting into the courtyard.

Detached back blocks may have been more popular for the wider-fronted houses: at No. 7 The Close, Exeter, for example, the rearmost of three separate blocks survives. Coronet Place, Kingsbridge, preserves a late medieval domestic middle range and a contemporary warehouse or stable range at the back. At Totnes, Little Priory in Fore Street may be the remnant of a wide, late medieval back block.

There are no terraces to compare with the rows of small medieval houses identified in Coventry, Tewkesbury, and York. The nearest are the two-room-and-cross-passage houses with open halls at Nos. 8–12 Fore Street, Silverton (which only just qualifies as a former town). More common are pairs of houses such as Nos. 41–42 High Street, Exeter, of 1564, and Nos. 48 and 50 Fore Street, Totnes, of the early C 17.

Complete INTERIORS no longer exist. The best impression of the late C 16 to mid C 17 can be got from those which are now museums, notably No. 32 New Street, Plymouth, and No. 70 Fore Street, Totnes. Decorative PLASTERWORK on ceilings and, occasionally, on overmantels was a feature of merchants' houses. Dartmouth and Totnes are the best places to see it in any quantity, but there is still 67 some good work in Barnstaple, particularly the superb ceiling of 1620 at No. 62 Boutport Street. Of the PANELLING used in the larger houses the best examples *in situ* are at No. 10 High Street, Totnes; others are re-set in the guildhall at Barnstaple and at No. 32 High Street, Totnes. Apart from some grand late Gothic ones in the Close at Exeter, FIREPLACES are usually fairly simple: those in some smaller houses in Exeter (Ship Inn, White Hart Hotel) have a little Gothic detail. Hooded fireplaces, rare in the countryside, are common and were still being built in the 1660s. Totnes has two splendid granite ones (probably mid C 16) at Nos. 32 and 43 High Street. STAIRCASES tended to be inconspicuous. Balustraded stairs are rare before the end of the C 17. The oldest by far is at No. 8 Cross Street, Barnstaple, of 1635; at Totnes the earliest date is 1692 (No. 52 Fore Street).

ARCHITECTURE FROM 1660 TO 1800

In the later C 17 the strength of conservative local traditions is apparent in both town and countryside. In lesser country houses mullioned windows continued to be acceptable until well on in the century (and in farmhouses still later). The mullioned front of Great Stert, Corn-wood, is dated 1674; Stallenge Thorne, Hockworthy, is dated 1675, although here such windows are combined with a handsomely mod-elled classical stone doorcase. The same taste is illustrated in urban 98 buildings: the Gothic Charles Church at Plymouth, of 1640–58, has

already been mentioned; Plympton Grammar School of 1664 is still
Perp, and at Kingsbridge mullioned windows are found in both the
Grammar School of 1670 and the Shambles of 1685. But by this date
both Exeter and Plymouth had examples of more progressive styles.

Among TOWN BUILDINGS FROM THE LATER C17, the Custom
House at Exeter, of 1680–1, is a charmingly modest example of the 103
post-Restoration domestic brick idiom, the centre of an interesting
group designed around the improved quay. Earlier than this,
Plymouth received a much more ambitious showpiece in the decidedly
Franco-Flemish Baroque gateway to the Citadel, built after the 99
Restoration by *Bernard de Gomme*. Government patronage at
Plymouth produced other buildings on a grand scale. The new
Dockyard, planned in 1690 under *Edmund Dummer*, but perhaps
drawing on the ideas of *Robert Hooke*, included a long officers' terrace
(only one sad fragment survived the last war) which was a very early
example in England of a balanced composition made up of individual
houses. The group of houses at the nearby Ordnance Yard, of *c.* 1720,
fortunately still complete, is in the more abrupt and romantic mode of
Vanbrugh (although there is no direct evidence of his involvement).
Such groups remained exceptional and without local imitators. The
Exchange in Queen Anne's Walk at Barnstaple, built under Rolle 100
patronage in the early years of the C18, is another isolated example of
Baroque, of a different kind, on a more modest scale, but with quite
sumptuous details which associate it with work by *Talman*. Firmly
documented work by nationally known architects is rare: an exception
is St George at Tiverton, the county's only major church in the Wren 116
tradition, for which *John James* provided the design in 1714.

The Barnstaple Exchange, with its covered arcade for merchants
alongside the quays, reflects the town's importance as the chief port of
North Devon, and it is indeed the ports that have the most interesting
domestic buildings. Barnstaple High Street still has one proud frontage with decorated plaster cornice dated 1710. More survives at 105
Bideford, Barnstaple's rival further west. The most sumptuous example, now part of the Royal Hotel, is chiefly important for its interior 107
decoration, and must be mentioned again below. The most interesting
urban development at Bideford is Bridgeland Street, laid out on newly 102
reclaimed land in the 1690s. Despite alterations, the up-to-date

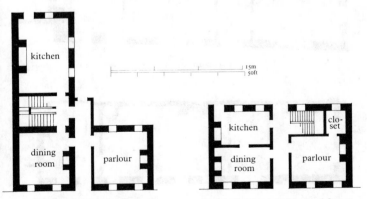

Bideford, No. 4 Bridgeland Street   Bideford, No. 31 Bridgeland Street

character of a notable sequence of brick houses remains recognizable; like the Barnstaple house, they have cornices and dormers instead of the older form of gables to the street, and many still have their original panelling and closed-string staircases. The broad frontages permitted generous plans. The most common type – a double pile, with the staircase at right angles to the central hall behind one of the front rooms – is found elsewhere too at this time, for example in the fine house of granite ashlar, built in 1685, which is now the Town Hall at Okehampton. The spread of brick building in North Devon is illustrated by a handsome example at Great Torrington, No. 28 South Street, dated 1701. A quite different type of urban house is found on the south coast, at Topsham at the mouth of the Exe, the port which was beginning to eclipse Exeter. Here there is a most attractive and unusual series of long, narrow houses of the later C17 to early C18. Each is at right angles to the Strand along the seafront, and each is only one room wide, with the short wall facing the street distinguished by a simple curved gable. The long side originally faced a yard with counting house. In and around Topsham, the distinctive small bricks used at this time, especially for chimneys, were imported from Holland; it is tempting to see some continental influence also in the layout of these merchants' houses. At Exeter little of note remains from this period. The best houses, somewhat altered, are No. 40 High Street, a rare case of a brick front with C17 artisan mannerist features, and No. 143 Fore Street, of chequered brick, dated 1716–17.

Among the inland towns, Tiverton was the most important, until the mid C20 with a large number of good C18 houses, the result of rebuilding after a particularly disastrous fire in 1731. Two specially good survivors with finely detailed brick fronts are Gotham House and Amory House. In other towns really elaborate C18 houses are rare. The Mansion House at Dartmouth has good interiors of c. 1730, Palmer House, Great Torrington, has a handsome brick front of 1752,

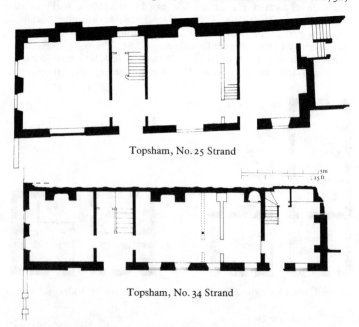

Topsham, No. 25 Strand

Topsham, No. 34 Strand

still in the Baroque tradition, and the mid C 18 pilastered stone front of
Leburn House, Bampton, also deserves a mention. Mid C 18 civic 117
buildings are few; the best of them is the Guildhall of South Molton 115
of 1739–41, which incorporates handsome C 18 features from Stow,
Cornwall.

Devon was slow to adopt the type of COUNTRY HOUSE that
became popular in court circles after the Restoration: the compact
gentleman's residence in brick or stone, with a hipped roof and
symmetrically disposed windows (at first mullioned-and-transomed,
later on sashed). The earliest cases where the new style appears are in
modernizations of older buildings. Great Potheridge, the family home
of General Monk, of which only a tantalizing fragment remains, was
refurbished in the 1660s; the wing adjoining the hall was rebuilt to a
double-pile plan, with hipped roof, modillioned eaves, and suites of
apartments reached by a grand staircase with heavy urn balusters in
the new manner. The stair-hall ceiling has the tight circular wreaths of
the court style framing paintings. Manadon, Plymouth, was refronted
in 1681, with modillioned eaves, and dormers with pediments of
alternating shape. Other examples of piecemeal remodelling are North
Wyke, where the rebuilt wing still has its handsome C 17 rectangular
mullioned-and-transomed windows, and on an even larger scale, Great
Fulford, where one side of the courtyard house was reconstructed to
provide a once magnificent first-floor state room approached by a new
staircase beside the remodelled hall.

The newly built country house on a compact plan begins to appear
only towards the end of the C 17. An early and important example,
burnt down in 1808, was Escot House, designed by *Robert Hooke c.*
1678, and illustrated in *Vitruvius Britannicus*. Some of its features, for
example the raised centre and giant pilasters, both motifs of Dutch
inspiration, are echoed in other houses of the period: Pynes, Upton
Pyne, somewhat altered, but still with a stately brick seven-bay front
on a massive scale; Nethway House, Kingswear, of 1699; and the
charming Mothecombe of c. 1710, which is of a more homely size, and 111
without a raised centre. Hayne, Plymtree, has more eccentric pilasters 114
with garlanded Ionic capitals (also a Dutch motif), Maristow an early
C 18 front with raised centre with oval windows. But apart from a few
exuberant doorcases (Langdon Court, Wembury; Franklyn House,
Cowick Lane, Exeter), exterior detail in the Baroque spirit of the early
C 18 is uncommon. Even well-proportioned pediments are rare:
among the few good pedimented fronts are Plympton House, with a
handsome stone front completed c. 1720, and the tall, brick Ebford
Manor, Woodbury. Other pediments are often steeply and unclassi-
cally angled (Bickham, Kenn; Treasurer's House, Exeter). These are
relatively small houses; large and grand frontages are not a feature of
Devon, although Poltimore, with its long eleven-bay entrance range
with channelled pilasters, must have been an impressive exception
when it was in its early C 18 state.

Brick buildings, never widespread, are most common in the eastern
part of the county. Some of the early ones are very simple, such as the
large but plain Pinbrook, Exeter (1679); Aunk, Clysthydon; or
Fordmore House, Plymtree, with its late C 17 flat front with a proud
display of nine wooden cross-windows. More sophisticated designs are
found among the smaller brick houses beginning to appear on the
outskirts of Exeter towards the end of the C 17, such as Little Duryard

(with another steep pediment), or the specially appealing Belair (now
part of County Hall), which combines brick with stone quoins and
pediment. Stedcombe, near Axmouth, of c.1697, also of brick with
stone dressings, is a more exceptional type, an attractive example of the
compact, four-square house with belvedere rising from its hipped roof.
113 The most sophisticated brick house of the early C18 is Puslinch, near
Plymouth, a harmonious, very restrained seven-bay composition with
centre breaking forward, its only ornaments the stone quoins, keystones, and pediment over the door.

Several of these early C18 houses have more than one show front;
other examples of this are Buckland-tout-Saints and Bowden, near
Totnes (both remodellings, with two adjacent formal fronts). The best
example of the type is Lyneham, near Yealmpton, with handsome
stone elevations on all four sides. No architects are known for these
buildings, although it is at this time that a few names of local builders
who could probably design begin to be recorded: *Richard Allen*,
103 builder of the Exeter Custom House in 1680–1, and *John Moyle*, an
Exeter builder and carpenter who was employed at Powderham from
1710 to 1727, and also at Antony House in Cornwall, close to
Plymouth, in 1718.

As for LATE C17 INTERIORS, the characteristic STAIRCASE has
a closed string from which rise stocky urn-shaped balusters. The
handling of the newels at half-landings is often clumsy (as at Great
Potheridge); local carpenters clearly took some time to adjust to the
new fashions. The grander closed-string baluster stairs are constructed round a well: notable examples are at Youlston Park, Pynes, and
the Royal Hotel, Bideford. At Combe, near Gittisham, an impressive
dog-leg stair was constructed within the area of the former hall. The
more-elaborate type of stair, using carved panels instead of balusters,
94 makes only one appearance in Devon, at Cross, near Great Torrington, and this is an import from the demolished Grenville mansion at
Stow, Cornwall. The new type of PANELLING with very large
bolection-moulded units can be seen for example in the refurbished
93 upper rooms at Sydenham (where the staircase hall was also given a
ceiling in the new style) and in the hall at Orleigh Court.

The joinery of this period is less memorable than the work of the
plasterers. By the later C17 they had mastered and developed the court
style of PLASTERWORK which had been introduced by Inigo Jones at
the beginning of the century, but was not widely disseminated
throughout the country until the time of Wren. The mid C17 stage of
the transformation of local traditions is well illustrated just over the
county border by the elaborate ceilings at Forde Abbey, Dorset. The
post-Restoration plasterwork at Bowringsleigh and Bovey House is
still in a transitional manner, with charmingly rustic renderings of
topical subjects fitted into the new formal circles and ovals. (Topical
subject matter continued popular on a rustic level into the C18 – see
Tackbeare Manor, and Smallacombe, Lifton.) By the 1680s the new
style was fully fledged, and the major works can hold their own with
contemporary plasterwork anywhere in England. The ceilings no
longer have the tight wreaths of the Jones style. Their details are in
daringly high relief (assisted by wire armatures beneath the plaster):
realistically modelled fruit and foliage, grotesque masks, writhing
serpents, and even small figures are characteristic motifs. Some of the
106 finest ceilings are those of the Exeter Custom House, the sole

documented work of *John Abbot* of Frithelstock; the virtuoso ceilings at Youlston Park and at the Royal Hotel, Bideford, are so similar in 107–10 their motifs and technique that one would like to attribute them to Abbot as well. There was similar work at Dunsland, now destroyed. Similar but slightly less elaborate ceilings can be found over the long gallery at Portledge, and over the staircases at Pynes and Downes (*see* below), while simpler versions in smaller houses (Cleeve House and Franklyn House, Exeter; Hensleigh, Tiverton; Shell House, Topsham) all show that while styles might change, the tradition of lavish plaster decoration continued as popular as ever.

Among interiors of the early c18, Puslinch and Plympton House have specially fine panelling and staircases (the early c18 type with thin balusters and open treads), and Plympton also has two quite Baroque stone overmantels. Kitley preserves from its early c18 phase an unusually sumptuous imperial stair, inserted into the former hall. In these houses of the south-west part of the county, lavish plasterwork is less common: the best examples are the similar ceilings at The Priory, Totnes, and at Gatcombe, Littlehempston, which have elegant centrepieces in high relief, perhaps of *c.* 1730.

Apart from St George Tiverton, already mentioned, there is little 116 CHURCH BUILDING OF THE LATE C17 TO MID C18. St Andrew Stoke Damerel was rebuilt as a mid c18 preaching box to cater for the expanding population of Plymouth Dock, but its original fittings do not survive. By this time there were rivals to Anglican places of worship. Chulmleigh has a well preserved Congregational chapel of 1710, and Exeter the impressive Nonconformist chapel known as George's Meeting, which dates from 1760. An even rarer survival is the Ashkenazi Synagogue at Plymouth of 1762, also still with original fittings. The few surviving rural chapels of this date are delightful in their domestic simplicity (Loughwood, Dalwood, perhaps of *c.* 1700; Salem Chapel, East Budleigh, of 1719).

The most ambitious of Anglican FURNISHINGS of this period is the fine organ, in its handsome case, erected on the pulpitum of Exeter Cathedral in 1665. In village churches all that need be singled out are the Corinthian screen at Cruwys Morchard, and the unusually grand royal arms of 1677 at Frithelstock, a special effort by the plasterer *John Abbot* for his native parish. On an endearingly humble level, the character of the Georgian village church, with its plastered interior and homely clutter of box pews and tall pulpit, is preserved especially well in the small and remote churches of Molland, Parracombe, and West 90 Ogwell; the first two retain a speciality of the period, a solid painted wooden tympanum filling the chancel arch (Satterleigh has another). A delightful minor feature, popular in North Devon from the mid c18, was the engraved slate sundial. Many of these are signed by *John Berry* of Barnstaple, the most elaborate of them at Tawstock (1757).

Late c17 and early c18 mural MONUMENTS with handsome architectural surrounds, often embellished by leaf scrolls, garlands, and putti in the Wren–Gibbons style, are a speciality of Exeter (St Mary Arches, St Petrock, St Stephen) but are also found in the north of the county, for example at Ilfracombe, Molland, and Clovelly (where there are as many as six dating from the 1670s–80s). A good cartouche at Tawstock of 1705 is signed by *Thomas Jewell* of Barnstaple. More ambitious monuments in the continental Baroque manner are extremely rare: Lady Narborough at Wembury, †1678,

fifth Earl of Bath at Tawstock, c. 1680. A typological exception is the
standing statue of Lady Fane †1680 at Tawstock, by *Balthazar
Burman*, a copy of an earlier statue by his father at Cambridge. The
most interesting local sculptor of the early C18 was *John Weston* of
Exeter. His speciality was the inclusion of a lively and unusual
Resurrection scene as part of a larger monument (St Petrock Exeter
†1717; Whitchurch †1722); other works by him are at Denbury and
Dartmouth. Outstanding monuments of the middle years of the C18
are few: the most eccentric is the entirely secular-looking standing
figure of William Pole at Shute (†1741). The restrained and accomplished architectural memorial in coloured marbles is well represented
at Eggesford (†1723). Portrait medallions continued popular throughout the C18 (Stowford †1726, †1770; Tawstock †1758; Georgeham
†1775), but the later examples really belong to the neo-classical
tradition of the second half of the C18.

As for HOUSES OF THE MID C18, just as the extremer forms of
English Baroque did not gain a hold in Devon, neither did PAL-
LADIANISM, the more controlled architectural style that developed in
reaction to it. The county had few landowners who were interested in
providing the grandest type of display, the spreading façade with far-
reaching wings or pavilions, and of those that were built, still fewer
exist now in their complete state. The earliest documented example of
a Palladian front in the grand manner is the remodelling of Castle Hill,
where the narrow hillside site determined straight links to the new end
pavilions. This was carried out for the Fortescues with the advice of
the arbiter of the new taste, *Lord Burlington*, with his protégé *Roger
Morris* as architect, in 1728–9. The exterior has been restored to its
characteristic Palladian plainness; the sumptuous interior which provided the contrast to this was destroyed by fire in the 1930s. More
imposing (but less Palladian) was Haldon, Kenn, built in the 1730s for
Sir George Chudleigh, but the tall cental range and quadrant links to
pavilions have gone, and only a back wing remains. On a smaller scale,
Rockbeare is still attractive; the main range has been altered, but two
elegant small pavilions survive from a handsome mid C18 stuccoed
composition. Lupton House, Brixham (Torbay), had a more compact
front, but has lost the pedimented attics to the end bays which gave it a
distinctive Palladian character. Elsewhere, more ambitious schemes
remained incomplete. The two accomplished detached brick and
stone garden pavilions (one with a library on the upper floor) built at
Stevenstone in the 1720s were perhaps the start of an intended
rebuilding programme. At Bicton a single quadrant wing of the 1730s
stood alone until the house was completed c. 1800. The appeal of
quadrants continued into the later C18: Stover Park of 1776–80 has a
single one, Shute House of 1787 a pair, but in other respects these two
houses belong to a later tradition. The spreading front of Downes is an
interesting composite creation: the stone facing and quadrants were
added only in 1794 by the local architect *Thomas Jones* to free-standing
brick pavilions probably built in the 1730s.

Generally, when new houses were required, the compact post-
Restoration type with double-pile plan and hipped roof remained
acceptable, brought up to date by the occasional Venetian window or
neat classical doorcase. A good example is Kelly House of 1742–3,
where we know the name of the architect: a local carpenter, *Abraham
Rundle* of Tavistock. Kingston House, Staverton, of 1743 similarly

continues the tradition of the four-square house, with a plain, unusually tall exterior, but with interesting fittings, including an ill-fitting but exceptionally lavish inlaid staircase. The more carefully composed proportions which are a hallmark of Palladianism are found less often. The house that lays best claim to the title of a Palladian villa is Kings Nympton Park of 1746–9 by the Dorset architect *Francis Cartwright*. Closely modelled on Roger Morris's Marble Hill, it was built for James Buller of Downes and his second wife, who was the daughter of Pope's patron Lord Bathurst of Cirencester Park in Gloucestershire.

Piecemeal remodellings are more common. They could take many different forms, at their simplest providing a polite, symmetrical face to an older house, as at East Down Manor or Cadhay. At Bowden a handsome early C18 range was added directly in front of the old hall, doubling the house in depth; more often, however, new or rebuilt wings continued the traditional plan of ranges only one room deep around a courtyard. A specially ambitious example is Saltram, where in the course of the C18 the main range was remodelled, the W wing recast as a Palladian composition, and a new E wing added. At 123 Werrington the new mid C18 range is across the courtyard from the old hall; it has the progressive features of a central canted bay and, behind the main rooms, a spacious corridor intended as a sculpture gallery. Sometimes an alternative entrance was provided in the polite symmetrical front of a rebuilt wing, as in the elegant new C18 S front of Maristow, and similarly in numerous smaller houses, such as the rectories as Alphington (Exeter) or Whitchurch.

The object of such alterations was to provide a sequence of elegant reception rooms on the ground floor, with spacious bedrooms above. The INTERIORS of the main rooms could be lavish. The tradition of busy plasterwork continued, the high relief of the late C17 tradition giving way in the second quarter of the C18 to a fashion for large central ceiling panels with classical figures in low relief (Bowden, 119 Saltram entrance hall, Dartmouth Mansion House), mixed up with 121 details and motifs in a variety of styles in a manner typical of provincial craftsmen eager to assimilate ideas from different sources. (Dartmouth Mansion House, a new building, unlike the others has its main reception room, in Palladian fashion, on the *piano nobile*.) The saloon at Poltimore, remodelled from the old hall c. 1750, is similarly eclectic: 120 splendid, with formal classical doorcases in the manner of William Kent, but with Rococo details appearing in the ceiling. Werrington has a comparable mixture: very Kentian fireplaces and much good plasterwork, the ceilings in the more delicate style of c. 1750–60. At Castle Hill some good Rococo chimneypieces remain. Of similar date are the charmingly light-hearted Rococo ceilings at Powderham, although even more memorable is the staggering exuberance of the Powderham staircase hall, created within the medieval hall in 1754–6 122 by three otherwise unknown craftsmen: *John Jenkins, William Brown*, and *Stephen Coney*. It was a last fling in the free tradition of Baroque ornament, for around this time more up-to-date pattern books became available. Instances of their use are the sophisticated Rococo wall decoration at Combe, near Gittisham, and an overmantel at Stedcombe, near Axmouth.

It is revealing that so many of the leading county families – the Courtenays of Powderham, the Bampfyldes of Poltimore, the Rolles of Stevenstone, the Parkers of Saltram – preferred to improve or add to their houses rather than rebuild them. But in the LATER C18 the younger John Parker, the first Lord Boringdon, was not content to employ a local architect-builder, for in 1768 he commissioned *Robert Adam* to create a new saloon in the C18 wing built at Saltram by his father. It is one of Adam's most impressive interiors, the best example of his refined neo-classical style in the South West, although not his first work in the county. This is at Ugbrooke, which he transformed into a trim battlemented castle (his first castle design) for Lord Clifford; but the interiors are simple, and cannot compare with the sequence at Saltram, where Adam did further work in the 1770s. By this time the Adam style had caught on, and Adamish plasterwork can be found at Stover (1776–80) and likewise at Shute (1787), with delightful, very un-Adam-like rustic scenes. The architects of both these houses are unknown, although Stover was perhaps designed by its enterprising owner, *James Templer*, a government contractor who had trained as an architect, and was at one time a partner of *Thomas Parlby*, who built the kitchen at Saltram. A more exotic alternative to plasterwork was imported Chinese wallpaper. Good examples of the later C18 are to be found at Saltram, Youlston, and Newnham.

There is little information available about local ARCHITECTS AND BUILDERS active in the later C18. Architects were not always employed: the 1760s work at Powderham was supervised by a Mr Spring, perhaps the same as *William Spring* who was clerk of the works at Ugbrooke. But there were also gentleman-architects such as *Philip Stowey*, who in partnership with *Thomas Jones* (and with the advice of *James Wyatt*) designed the handsome Palladian Law Courts at Exeter in 1773–5. His own house, Kenbury, Exminster (now demolished), had details similar to the eccentric quadrant-fronted Ashley House, Tiverton, perhaps also by him. The diarist *John Swete* designed his own house at Oxton, a rather plain affair with canted bays (1781) – but then his main interest was in landscape. In 1788 *William Jackson* of Exeter, a painter and musician, built Cowley House for his son, an elegant small mansion with the newly fashionable feature of two full-height rounded bows; he was probably also responsible for the bows added to Rougemont House, Exeter. (Bows were popular at this time, see also Shute, and Combe House, Combe Fishacre, Ipplepen of 1793.) Minor figures such as the Exeter builder *Joseph Rowe* designed the stables at Ugbrooke (1793), Kentisbury Rectory, Cornworthy Vicarage, and no doubt other small classical houses. But the designers of several good larger houses remain a mystery, among them Bridwell (1774–9), with its accomplished oval entrance hall and pretty ceilings and fireplaces, and Winslade Manor of the 1780s, with its surprisingly grand central galleried hall with eclectic Adamish neo-classical decoration.

From the 1760s onwards the names of architects from outside the county begin to appear more often, although buildings of really high quality on a national level remain few. *John Johnson*'s Killerton (1778–9) is refined but not especially exciting. Sharpham is another matter. This tautly designed neo-classical mansion by *Sir Robert Taylor*, begun in 1763 for a naval officer, has affinities with the architect's home counties villas, but unlike them is sited in a most dramatic position, high above the Dart. Its memorable interior has as its *tour de force* a breathtakingly bold cantilevered oval staircase. The neo-classical style in a different mould is provided by *James Wyatt*'s music room at

Powderham (1794–6); its sumptuous details include an excellent 130
chimneypiece by *Westmacott*. A lesser room in a similar spirit, no 131
doubt by provincial craftsmen, is the dining room added to Rock- 132
beare. The refined neo-classical work at Syon Abbey (Marley House)
also deserves a mention, as does the crisp mathematical-tiled envelope
of *S.P.Cockerell*'s Nutwell Court, Lympstone, of 1802.

The most interesting URBAN BUILDINGS of this period are at
Plymouth, the result of the growth of the Devonport Dockyard, which
gave rise to developments on an unparalleled scale. In the Dockyard
itself, the main survivors of this time are the C18 slipways (impres- 153
sively roofed over later) and the vast roperies built after the expansion 154
of the 1760s. The large barracks at Stonehouse are more impressive for
their size than for their minimal classical detail; of wider significance is
the spacious Naval Hospital, laid out in 1758–62 on an innovative
pavilion plan by *Alexander Rowehead*, a model for later hospital
buildings on the continent as well as in England. C18 town planning on
a more ambitious level appeared first at Exeter, with Bedford Circus,
an oval of houses by a local builder-carpenter, *Robert Stribling*, begun
in 1773 (demolished after war damage). More extensive development,
which has survived better, took place in Exeter from the 1780s, chiefly
by another builder, *Matthew Nosworthy*, whose brick houses with 133
Coade stone trimmings and elegant ironwork clearly take their cue
from London terraces. The style continued in vogue in the Exeter
suburbs into the first years of the C19, until it was overtaken by the
fashion for stuccoed fronts in a more neo-classical idiom.

The urban terrace also makes its appearance in the 1790s at the
burgeoning seaside resorts, although The Beacon, Exmouth, of 1792
onwards, is not really a unified group, and the much more ambitious
formal stuccoed crescent of Fortfield Terrace, Sidmouth, begun in the
same year by a London speculator, *Michael Novosielski*, was never
completed as planned. The first terraces of Torquay also date from the
1790s. Thereafter the story of seaside resort architecture, with only a
few exceptions, is one of villas and *cottages ornés*, and must be taken up
again later. But one of the first and most eccentric of the latter species
belongs to the C18: the charmingly quirky A la Ronde at Exmouth, 138
designed in 1798 by the Misses *Parminter*. They were inspired by San
Vitale, Ravenna.

So far, apart from A la Ronde and Adam's castle exterior at
Ugbrooke, the buildings mentioned have been in the classical tradition. The more frivolous GOTHIC OF THE C18 first makes an
occasional appearance in churches – as early as *c*. 1730 for the church at
Filleigh, rebuilt as an eyecatcher for Castle Hill but no longer in its
original state. Werrington church was rebuilt in Gothic in 1742; the
Gothic surround to *Sir Henry Cheere*'s monument at Shute dates from
1741; Teigngrace church of 1786 is an interesting Gothic-classical
hybrid. In secular buildings the style gained ground in the later C18:
windows with 'Gothick' heads appear at Powderham in 1769, and a
more coherent Gothic façade was created by *John Meadows*'s remodelling of Hartland Abbey (1779). Hartland may have influenced Tawstock Court, not far off, which was gothicized after 1787, apparently 127
to designs of the owner (although *Soane* was also involved, providing
details for the classical stair-hall). Elsewhere, pattern books could
provide the inspiration: those of *Batty Langley* were followed for a
fireplace at Hartland and for the hall doorway at Great Fulford, which

also has a series of Gothic-trimmed rooms of *c.* 1800. Gothic was also a favourite style for garden buildings (cf. below); it is demonstrated most flamboyantly by two triangular belvederes, at Powderham (1779) and Haldon (1788), the latter housing a remarkable *Coade* stone memorial to Stringer Lawrence. Notable church monuments of the later C18 are few. The best collections are the memorials to the Templers at Teigngrace and to the Wreys at Tawstock.

THE NINETEENTH AND TWENTIETH CENTURIES

During the Napoleonic wars, *c.* 1790–1815, the county was opened up to outside influences as never before. Travel was expedited by the new turnpike roads, and the rivers and estuaries were spanned by new bridges – fine survivals are Cowley Bridge over the Exe at Exeter by the county surveyor *James Green* (1813–14) and Totnes Bridge by *Charles Fowler* (1826–8). While John Swete travelled the county and extolled in his diaries the wild and romantic scenery, others took a more practical approach. Even inhospitable Dartmoor began to be exploited for its minerals, its granite, and its agricultural potential (see also Introduction to Industrial Devon). The leading figure here was Sir Thomas Tyrwhitt, who built his house at Tor Royal, Princetown, as early as 1785, established a railway to take granite and produce down to Sutton Pool at Plymouth, and in 1806, in order to provide manpower for these enterprises, set up the Princetown prisoner-of-war barracks, of which some of *Daniel Asher Alexander*'s original buildings still remain within the modern prison. A little later came the Haytor granite tramway (*see* Ilsington), built by the Templers of Stover in 1820 to link up with their earlier canal leading to the quays at Newton Abbot and Teignmouth.

The most direct surviving evidence of the war effort is the massive Napoleonic fort at Berry Head, Brixham, at the southern end of Tor Bay. But it was PLYMOUTH, the major naval centre, which changed most drastically. Here a significant shift in architectural taste, which gradually affected the whole of the county, was achieved almost entirely through the influence of one man, *John Foulston* (1772–1842). In 1811 this London-trained architect, who has been aptly described as 'the Soane, the Smirke and the Nash of the West Country',[*] won a competition promoted by the Mayor of Plymouth, Edmund Lockyer, for a group of public buildings that would do justice to the city's growing importance. His noble group of Royal Hotel, Theatre, and Assembly Rooms of 1811–13, followed by a Library in 1812 and an Athenaeum in 1818–19, were a confident demonstration both of the splendour of the Grecian temple front, still a relative novelty for public buildings, and of how Grecian detail could be elegantly employed for interiors. We can assess their quality now only from drawings, for all these buildings disappeared during and after the Second World War.

[*] J. M. Crook, 'Regency Architecture in the West Country, The Greek Revival', *J. Royal Soc. of Arts* (June 1971).

What remains of Foulston's work at Plymouth displays his versatility as a neo-classical designer: fragments of his grand stuccoed terraces around the Hoe; austerely Grecian villas and delightful, more 142 domestic suburban houses at Stoke, on the fringe of Stonehouse. Of Foulston's Union Street, the bold stroke of town planning which united the Three Towns of Plymouth, Stonehouse, and Dock (renamed Devonport), only the skeleton remains, although it still has as its *point de vue* the column which forms part of a little group of new 147 civic buildings for Devonport. They were an original concept, a deliberately picturesque combination of the architectural styles of antiquity – Egyptian, Grecian, Roman, and Hindu – although only representatives of the first two now remain. Gothic, not yet a scholarly style, is absent (although later on Foulston was to employ it at Tavistock and elsewhere, see below). Foulston's Grecian manner was not quite the exclusive style for public buildings at this time. His group at Plymouth was preceded by *David Laing*'s refined but less severe Custom House of 1810, while at Stonehouse, Royal William 148 Yard, *John Rennie*'s colossal Victualling Yard of 1825–33, is entered 146 through a monumental archway recalling the military grandeur of Rome.

DEVON TOWNS in the early C19, especially those on the coast, flourished as genteel places of residence. Several followed Plymouth in adopting the neo-classical style to dignify their centres. The seaside resorts of the south coast had begun to develop in the later C18, but became more noticeably urban only after 1800. The stately sweep of Den Crescent at Teignmouth with the Assembly Rooms as its centrepiece was built in 1826 by *Andrew Patey* of Exeter; at Exmouth (likewise on land reclaimed from the sea) a pleasure garden with Grecian temples was laid out around the same time. At Ilfracombe on the north coast, which developed a little later, neat Grecian baths were provided in 1836, as a focus for the residents of the new stuccoed terraces on the hills above the old town. At Exeter the Grecian baths of 1821 at Southernhay have disappeared, but the frontage of the Higher Market remains as one of the most magnificent examples anywhere in England of a Grecian temple front used for this purpose. It dates from 1834–8 and was designed by *George Dymond*. Grecian trimmings were still in vogue in the 1840s when the centre of Newton Abbot was improved, although for its new suburbs a picturesque free Italianate or 135 Jacobean was the choice. Similarly in the suburbs of other towns one can observe how the stuccoed neo-classical style takes over from around 1810–20, and was transformed into Italianate or Tudor in the early Victorian years. Exeter is a particularly rewarding hunting ground for both small villas and more ambitious terraces (some of them never completed), scattered piecemeal by optimistic developers over the hills overlooking the city. The most striking is the tall, austere group in a minimal Soanic style, probably by the local builder *John Brown*, which crowns the hill at Pennsylvania. Handsome stuccoed villas and terraces can also be found on the outskirts of Barnstaple, 134 Okehampton, and Tavistock, and, above all, on the steep hills of the Palk estate around Torquay, energetically developed by the *Harvey* family. Here the villa in its own grounds becomes the dominant type, 5 the earliest examples of the 1830s quite severely classical, the later ones embellished by bay-windows and Italianate trimmings. The influence of urban neo-classicism is also apparent on a humbler level, in the appealing C19 terraces of trim plastered cottages, adorned with simple classical doorcases, which crowd the slopes above the harbours of Appledore, Bideford, and Dartmouth.

Both TOWN AND COUNTRYSIDE in the C19 were affected by the spirit of improvement. The most common type of urban replanning involved the clearing of open markets from the main streets, and the

156 provision of separate covered market buildings. Many of these remain (see also under local architects below), although the most interesting of them, *Fowler*'s Lower Market at Exeter, was lost in the Second World War. Among the most ambitious of such schemes was the remodelling

151 of Tavistock from *c.* 1822–60, by *Foulston* and others, for the Dukes of Bedford. Their taste for battlemented Gothic, inspired by the abbey ruins, gives the town a pleasingly distinctive character. The Dukes, the most extensive landowners in the west of the county, were active builders in the countryside as well, providing model farms (as at Milton Abbot) and cottages for the working population which was expanding as a result of the mining boom in the area (*see* Tavistock and Morwellham). Another major Victorian landowner was the Hon. Mark Rolle, who embarked on a vigorous campaign to improve the buildings on the estates around the family seats of Stevenstone in the north and Bicton in the south. Plenty of his solid farmhouses of the 1850s–60s remain, with their courtyards of well-planned buildings (e.g. at Otterton), and still more numerous are the groups of flint and

168 brick cottages built from *c.* 1870, often decorated with diaper brickwork, initials, and date. Concern for the welfare of the rural populace was also shown by the building of VILLAGE SCHOOLS, often designed at this time as consciously picturesque adjuncts to the village: as examples ranging from 1820 to 1870 one could mention those at Beer,

169 Milton Abbot, Clyst St George, Woodbury Salterton, and Woodbury. Among urban schools of the same period, the most unusual is the one at Tiverton of 1841, built for the children of the laceworkers at the Heathcoat factory. The suburb of West Exe, which expanded around

136 the factory, includes St Paul's Street, with its generously laid out terraces in a pleasant late Georgian idiom. At Barnstaple, quite extensive C19 working-class housing (now mostly demolished) developed around the Derby factory, and the railway works had a similar effect in Newton Abbot. But industrial buildings which make an

155 impact on town centres, such as the Axminster carpet factory, are the exception; most of the remains of Devon's C19 industries are to be found in the countryside, especially on Dartmoor and in the Tamar valley (see further the Introduction to Industrial Devon).

The neo-classical ideal was not confined to the towns: it can be found as well in the COUNTRY HOUSES of the early C19. Buckland House, Buckland Filleigh is one of the earliest and most interesting in this manner, remodelled in 1810 by *James Green* (1781–1859), who had settled in Devon in 1808 when he became county surveyor. At Buckland Greek Doric is used not only for the grand portico, but also,

145 more unusually, as the lower order of a two-tier top-lit saloon. Green's main activity was bridge and canal building – his classical commitment is expressed in the fine aqueduct to the Rolle viaduct at Great Torrington – but he was also responsible for the library at Fursdon, and one would like to know more about his architectural activities. Two other houses with full temple porticoes (both Ionic) are Oaklands, Okehampton, of *c.* 1816–20 by *Charles Bacon*, completed by his

pupil *Charles Vokins*, and Follaton by *G.S.Repton* of 1826. Repton's
Widworthy Court of 1830 was also intended to have a portico. There
are others whose designers are unknown: Bydown in North Devon,
and, on a smaller scale, Woodville House, Bideford, and Honeylands,
Pinhoe Road, and Hoopern House, Pennsylvania, both at Exeter. On
a minor level, the lodges of Stover and Winslade must also be grouped   143
among the buildings dominated by the Greek column.

Not all houses adopted the temple front on a monumental scale.
Most often, neo-classical allegiance was expressed externally simply
by neat porches or one-storey colonnades, attached to plain, well
proportioned stuccoed buildings. *Foulston* set the pattern around as
well as in Plymouth; Parkwood, now Newton House, Kelly College,
Tavistock, is a good example. In this bracket one can also put Perridge
House, Holcombe Burnell, by *George Byfield*, *c.*1813, and the elegant
and refined Arlington, of 1820–3 by *Thomas Lee* of Barnstaple (1794–
1834), where the sequence of main rooms is well preserved. A top-lit
central staircase was often the grandest interior feature, as at Stonelands, Dawlish, and the plainer and coarser Parke, Bovey Tracey, of
1826. Trehill, Kenn, 1827 by *C.R.Ayers*, has a specially ambitious
and lofty stair-hall decorated with statuary. Canonteign House of   144
1828, also by *Ayers*, has a renewed interior, but was to a similar plan.
At Poltimore an imposing imperial stair was fitted into the central
courtyard of the older house. Often modernizations at this period were
less radical: bay-windows and colonnades were the most common
additions (Rockbeare House; Bickham, Kenn) and the two were often
linked together, as at Craddock House. A more exceptional style for
this date is the Italianate *villa rustica*, used by *John Nash* at Sandridge
in 1805, with a picturesque circular tower very similar to his better
known Cronkhill, Shropshire.

In the 1830s one can discern a taste for more ornamental and eclectic
exteriors: *Basevi*'s Bitton House, Teignmouth, is well studded with
Grecian trimmings, while *Edward Davis*, another pupil of Soane,
mixed Grecian with Gothic detail at Barcombe Hall, Paignton (Torbay). By the 1840s *Samuel Beazley*'s classical Hillersdon House shows
decidedly Italianate leanings in its enrichment. But before pursuing
the classical ideal further one should look at the chief early C19
alternative.

In the early C19 GOTHIC became a fashionable alternative style,
especially for the seaside summer villa, providing the romantic and
picturesque appeal lacking in the more austere versions of neo-
classicism. Luscombe, just outside the newly developing resort of   150
Dawlish, designed in 1800 by *John Nash* for the Hoare family, was an
important trendsetter for the C19: an ingeniously planned stone
castellated villa whose surrounding walls were intended to make it
look larger than it is. Houses on a grander scale, in a serious although
still pre-archaeological Gothic, are Haine and Lifton Park, both of
*c.*1810–20. Most seaside cottages of this period were much less
ambitious, adopting the light-hearted C18 approach to Gothic ornament which is used also for the occasional lodge and estate building
(for good examples of these see Mamhead, Tawstock, and Stuckeridge
at Oakford). Low whitewashed walls are enlivened by a delightfully whimsical mixture of pointed wooden windows, decorative
glazing, and pretty ironwork, often capped by picturesque thatched
roofs. Architects are generally unknown, although *John Rendle* of

Teignmouth was responsible for one of the most ambitious examples, the thatched rectory of Kingsteignton (1815) behind whose rustic exterior is a surprisingly sophisticated sequence of curved rooms. Sidmouth, already a fashionable visiting-place for the aristocracy in the last years of the C18, preserves a rich assortment of these early *cottages ornés*; others can be found at Budleigh Salterton, Dawlish, and Shaldon, across the river from Teignmouth. Endsleigh 'Cottage', built in 1810 by *Sir Jeffry Wyatville* for the Duke of Bedford on his estates near Tavistock, shows how fashionable the concept had become, for this is not a cottage but a substantial house, although ingeniously designed as a picturesque and informal composition in the midst of *Humphry Repton*'s splendid landscape.

The *cottage orné* of the 1820s onwards is usually in a more self-conscious pattern-book Tudor, with hoodmoulded windows and steep bargeboarded gables: Elysian Fields, Sidmouth has some choice examples. Tudor also became fashionable for larger houses. Eggesford (now a ruin) by *Thomas Lee*, Wiscombe Park, Southleigh, by *Joseph Power* of Colyton, Warleigh House, remodelled by *Foulston*, and *G. S. Repton*'s refacing of Peamore and Kitley all date from the 1820s, and so does the start of the improvements at Tavistock, where the town centre was remodelled for the Duke of Bedford in a battlemented Gothic, so as to be in keeping with the restored ruins of the abbey. Tavistock is of stone; for suburban villas and terraces local builders most frequently used stuccoed fronts enlivened by Tudor gables, a style which continued popular into the 1840s in the Exeter suburbs.

The change to a more studiously correct historical approach comes with Mamhead, designed in 1825 by the young *Anthony Salvin*, a country house where not only the exterior modelling and broken skyline aim at C16 authenticity, but where allegiance to Tudor is expressed also in the interior detail and decoration. The finishing touch is the stables, concealed in a convincingly Gothic sham castle. Culver, Holcombe Burnell, of 1835 by *George H. Smith*, has similarly serious Tudor interiors, while the additions to Powderham Castle by *Charles Fowler* illustrate how by the 1840s the castle style could express romantic appeal both with panache and with historical conviction.

So far nothing has been said about the evolution of the GROUNDS and GARDEN BUILDINGS which complemented country houses both of the C18 and of the C19. Bicton still gives a good impression of an early C18 formal layout, with its rectangular canal, although the gardens as we see them now are largely C19. Early C18 terraced gardens also survive at Langdon Court, Wembury. At Castle Hill the formal C18 water basin was remodelled later, but something remains of the long avenues laid out in the 1730s, stretching to distant *points de vue* on the horizon. The buildings at Castle Hill were in a variety of styles, including a sham castle (which gave the house its name) which was built probably in the 1740s under the influence of Sanderson Miller, a very early example of the type. Werrington also was ambitiously landscaped in the mid C18. Saltram has an interesting survival of the transitional approach of the mid C18: a woodland walk where more relaxed and romantic winding paths provide the links between artificial features. These include the C18 favourite: the grotto (to be found also at Tapeley Park and Haine). In the later C18 both the formal parterre and the straight avenue were abandoned in favour of the picturesque setting devised by *Capability Brown*, where an irregular lake is framed by judiciously composed clumps of trees and woodland, and undulating lawns sweep right up to the house. Ugbrooke is Brown's own chief achievement in the county; he also worked at Mamhead. Others soon copied his style: Saltram was remodelled by *Richmond*; Bridwell, Kitley, Sharpham, and Tapeley Park are other good examples of later C18 landscaping of this type; and C18 drawings tell a similar story of such remodelling elsewhere (Castle Hill, Hartland Abbey, Poltimore). Landscaping of this kind could incorporate garden buildings, as is shown by the examples at Stover and Saltram, the former classical, the latter including a more playful Gothic summer house, while *John Swete*, a great enthusiast for the picturesque and romantic, built a Gothic hermitage among the woods at Oxton. Delightful, well-preserved rustic hermitages of the early C19 remain at Bicton and at Killerton.

Around the turn of the century the taste for the dramatic and the exotic became more marked. This could simply be expressed by planting on a grand scale, as at Arlington and Killerton. But at Werrington there is an unusual Indian-influenced temple of *c.* 1800, while at Endsleigh, *Wyatville* provided in addition to a charming tiled dairy and shell-encrusted summer house, a 'Swiss cottage' recalling   139 the romance of Alpine travel to complement *Repton*'s skilful handling of the naturally sublime scenery of the Tamar valley. We meet Repton again at Luscombe, making the most of a gentler valley above Dawlish as the setting for Nash's castellated villa. In other places the growing appeal of allusions to a native historic past is reflected in the appearance of castellated walls and medievalizing detail, as in the embellishments at Hemyock Castle, or in Lord Rolle's more extensive landscaping around Great Torrington.

Among the functional buildings associated with country mansions, the most extensive are STABLES. At their grandest they are laid out around a courtyard, as at Killerton, Saltram, Stover, Sharpham, and Youlston. Those at Sydenham have especially well preserved interior fittings; those at Mount Tavy, Tavistock, are on an unusual semi-circular plan (*c.* 1800). WALLED GARDENS are frequent: see for example Bridwell, Combe, Holcombe Rogus, Rockbeare. Among the functional buildings of the early C19 the prize must go to the delectably curvaceous glasshouse at Bicton of the 1820s, a reflection of   137 the new theories of J. C. Loudon. Less common in Devon is the C18 MODEL FARM closely associated with the house; the best example is at Rockbeare. (For other model farms *see* p. 94.)

The styles adopted for EARLY C19 CHURCHES were as various as those for secular buildings. The best neo-classical examples have gone: at Exeter *Green*'s St David of 1816–17 and *Andrew Patey*'s St Leonard of 1831 were rebuilt later in the C19; at Plymouth *Foulston*'s St Catherine (1823), in a distinguished Soanic style, was destroyed only after the last war. The most original example of the spacious, minimal church Gothic of the Regency period is the centrally planned St James Teignmouth, by the Londoner *W. E. Rolfe*, 1817–21, for which *Patey*   160 was the executive architect. Patey used other styles as well: an eccentric neo-Norman at St Michael Teignmouth, 1823, and quite an impressive lofty version of Gothic for the rebuilding of both St Thomas Exeter, 1829, and Dawlish (much altered). At Exeter the remodelled interior of St Stephen (1827) is in an especially elegantly elongated Gothic (1827); St Petrock, more eccentrically reconstructed the following year by *Charles Hedgeland*, is more obviously Perp in its detail. In Plymouth, *Foulston* used a less inspired plain lancet style for St Paul Stonehouse (1830). In quite a different spirit are the robust neo-Norman basilica at Honiton by the versatile *Charles Fowler* (1838), and the more archaeologically self-conscious Norman chapel at Killerton by *C. R. Cockerell* (1840).

The common feature of these churches (with the exception of Killerton chapel) is that they were designed as preaching spaces with galleries, a fitting particularly detested and therefore removed by the Victorian High Church movement; as a result, the original spatial quality of these early C19 interiors is difficult to appreciate. For similar reasons other furnishings of these years have also largely disappeared; the most interesting survival is the enterprisingly Dec screen at Haccombe of 1822, probably by *John Kendall*. As mason to Exeter Cathedral he also did much to embellish that building, although little remains of his work apart from two west-front figures in a medievalizing style. The monuments of the early C19, especially in the seaside towns, are mostly chaste and rather repetitive wall tablets, often imported from outside the county; there are three versions of a cast-stone design by *Coade & Sealy* (at Holbeton, Plympton, and Teigngrace). In contrast to these, from the later C18 humbler folk began to be commemorated by the engaging, well-lettered slate tombstones which were a speciality of local masons, especially in North Devon.

Hundreds of simple rural NONCONFORMIST CHAPELS were built or rebuilt in the C19 (far more than can be mentioned in this book), the older denominations supplemented by the two sects which originated in Devon in the early C19, the Plymouth Brethren and the Bible Christians, the latter especially widespread in their homeland of North Devon. Their humble barn-like chapels are epitomized by the remote example at Cookbury of 1840. Other denominations, especially the Wesleyans, favoured a little more elegance. A late Georgian domestic style remained popular into the mid C19. It is seen at its most charming 167 at Pancrasweek (1838) or Rackenford (1848). Town frontages are occasionally in a more stylish Regency spirit (upswept parapets at Great Torrington, 1829, 1832; ogee-headed windows at Teignmouth Gospel Hall). The grand neo-classical front is rare: Ashburton Methodist chapel with its large Ionic portico of 1835 is an exception. Chapels were not subject to the same liturgical revolution as Anglican churches, and as a result some well preserved early C19 interiors have survived: good examples are Prescott Baptist chapel and Spiceland Friends Meeting House (both in the parish of Culmstock).

The influence of the Gothic revival on Nonconformity was gradual; rural buildings remained preaching-boxes, content with a few Gothic trimmings, but in towns the larger chapels began to be rebuilt with towers, in competition with their Anglican counterparts. Lavington Chapel, Bideford, with its odd twin spires, is as early as 1856 (by a local architect, *E. M. White*); the more accomplished Sherwell Congregational chapel, Plymouth (by an outside firm, *Paull & Ayliffe*), dates from 1864; the Congregational church at Exeter (of which only the tower and spire remain) is of 1868, by the Londoner *John Tarring*. But the grand Baptist chapel on Mutley Plain, Plymouth (1869 by *Ambrose*), is debased classical; and the Wesleyan chapel, Dartmouth, rebuilt in 1875, still has a classical front with big pediment. Gothic for urban chapels only becomes common from the 1870s; such buildings are disappearing fast, but among worthy surviving landmarks (at the time of writing) are *Bridgman*'s Methodist chapel at Torquay (1873) and United Reformed church at Paignton (1887), the Congregational church at Teignmouth (1882), and the Thorne Memorial chapel at Barnstaple (1891–2 by *W. C. Oliver*). The social importance of such C19 chapels is often evident from their extensive ancillary halls and school buildings (also now rapidly diminishing in number); Tiverton retains several such groups, the most impressive the large cluster of buildings of the Congregationalists in St Peter's Street.

The 1840s saw the beginning of the GOTHIC REVIVAL. The development of a scholarly interest in medieval architecture went hand in hand with the growth of the Anglican High Church Tractarian movement. The ideal, as advocated by Pugin and the Camden Society, was the C14 church in the 'second pointed' or Dec style.

Exeter, with a High Church bishop and residual High Church tradition, was one of the earliest dioceses to respond to the new religious and architectural ideals: the Exeter Diocesan Architectural Society, set up in 1841 to promote Camdenian principles, was the first such organization outside the universities. But rural Devon, already well supplied with medieval churches which, inconveniently, were mostly Perp, provided limited scope for the expression of the new principles. Only Plymouth and the seaside towns required a large number of new buildings, and Plymouth's strong evangelical tradition was resistant to innovations emanating from Exeter. Earnest patrons had to content themselves with remodelling and restoring, and with providing small chapels for remote hamlets. Among Dec building of the early 1840s is St Andrew Exwick by the local architect *John Hayward* (q.v. below); the chapel at Smallridge, Chardstock, built in 1840 by the energetic High Churchman Arthur Acland (later Arthur Troyte, *see* Huntsham); and the small Dec church at Woodbury Salterton (1843). *Benjamin Ferrey*'s competently Dec St John Plymouth, with its fine spire, and his chapel at Chevithorne also date from 1843.

Early 1840s refittings, of which there were a significant number in Devon, concentrated on the chancel: most of these were altered later in the century or have been lost since. One of the most complete survivals is the ambitious Dec refurbishment of the chancel of St Thomas Exeter, remodelled in 1842 to provide a setting for the monument to the vicar's wife, which was carved by her father, *John Bacon*. Less archaeologically accurate but equally High Anglican is the 1843 chancel of Uffculme, with its stone altar and kaleidoscopic E window. Stylistically more correct is the Dunsford chancel of 1844–5.

Further impetus to the Revival came a few years later, largely through the patronage of the Coleridges of Ottery St Mary. The restoration of Ottery parish church, one of the really ambitious C14 churches in the county, was a primary objective of the Diocesan Architectural Society as early as 1841. Work did not begin until 1847, the Lady Chapel under *Woodyer*, the chancel and nave under *Butter-field*. Butterfield's personal and original polychromatic style, so much at odds with correct archaeological restoration, is expressed more openly in his rebuilding of Yealmpton (1848). A purer historical rendering of the Dec ideal is the little church at Landscove, an early work by *J. L. Pearson* of 1849, provided by Louisa Champernowne of

Dartington in one of the hamlets of the parish; its influence is seen in the rather more eccentric St Barnabas Brooking, built by her brother a few years later.

161 The most notable demonstration of Dec in all its sculptural fecundity is the mausoleum at Bicton, designed in 1850 by *Pugin* for Lady Rolle, an intimate expression of piety in the medieval manner. In the same year a very different building was begun in Plymouth, St Dunstan's Abbey, an early example of pioneering social work by the Anglican church. *Butterfield*'s design is stylistically innovative as well, with its picturesque grouping inspired by continental Gothic. The abbey was not completed as intended, but the boldly composed refectory (now chapel) can hold its own. On a smaller scale *William White*'s early church, school, and parsonage at Hooe, Plymouth, of 1854–8 are also unconventional. But generally correct English C14 Gothic continued to be favoured in the 1850s; good examples are St John Bovey Tracey (1853 by *R.C. Carpenter*, for a vicar whose brother was the Earl of Devon), and the little R.C. church at Axminster designed by Pugin's pupil *William Wardell* in 1855. Earlier R.C. churches are at Tiverton, where the group of buildings of 1836–9 by the local architect *Gideon Boyce* are still in a more amateur Gothic, and at Barnstaple. Here the neo-Normam building begun in 1844 had Boyce as its executant architect, but documentary evidence suggests that the original design may have come from *Pugin*, who was experimenting with Romanesque in the early 1840s.

The other R.C. alternative to Gothic was Italian Baroque, and this is represented by the surprisingly lavish refurbishing of the chapel at Ugbrooke (1840 onwards). The most prolific C19 R.C. architect in Devon was *Joseph Hansom*. His first major work was the cathedral at Plymouth of 1856, in a minimally detailed yet spatially impressive lancet style. His mature manner, angular and intense, is strikingly demonstrated in the Priory at Abbotskerswell, with its extraordinary tower over the chancel, and by Our Lady, St Marychurch, Torquay (Torbay) of 1865, an ambitious group with presbytery and orphanage. Another impressive R.C. complex is *George Goldie*'s St Scholastica's Abbey, Teignmouth (1861–3).

By the 1860s, as the railways made communication easier, the contributions of architects from outside the county became more numerous and varied. *G.G. Scott*'s seriously Gothic work in Devon began with the chapel at Luscombe (1862) (one can hardly count his early lancet effort at Chudleigh Knighton of 1841), and was continued by major restorations at Barnstaple (1866), Totnes (1867), and Exeter Cathedral (from 1870). *Henry Clutton*, working for the Duke of Bedford, contributed the powerful and original church of St Mary Magdalene, Tavistock, in a version of early French Gothic. The C13 Gothic French cathedral with sculptured portals and soaring spire was the inspiration for St Michael Exeter, built by the little known *Rhode Hawkins* for that energetic patron William Gibbs of Tyntesfield, Somerset.

The best hunting-ground for Victorian churches by major architects is Torquay (Torbay), where the wealthy population of the expanding resort was not content with *Salvin*'s modest buildings of the 1840s. *G.E. Street* added the more intensely Gothic St John (1861–3), *Arthur Blomfield* the inventive St Luke (1863), while *Butterfield* contributed 162 the most remarkable building of all, All Saints Babbacombe (begun in

1865), its interior an extreme example of his emphatically wayward use of structural polychromy. Later on *Pearson* built All Saints (1883–9) and enlarged St Matthias (1881, 1894), and *Scott* improved St Mary Magdalene (1881–2).

Elsewhere it was a matter of remodelling village churches, not always sensitively: *Ferrey*'s rebuilding of Otterton of 1869–70 appears particularly brash. In the same year *Pearson* was given the task of rebuilding the church at Dartington on a new site; medieval remains were incorporated, but the handsome Perp result is much grander than the original. Other architects who left their mark as distinctive restorers are *Henry Woodyer* (Kenn 1863, Chudleigh 1869, Stoodleigh 1879–80) and *William White* (Cadbury 1856–9, Stockleigh Pomeroy 1861–3, West Down 1872, West Anstey 1887).

Both restored and new churches were not complete without FURNISHINGS AND FITTINGS.* The Torquay churches have some of the richest ensembles, while Down St Mary and Washford Pyne are village churches with specially evocative and well preserved Victorian interiors. Among individual works, *Butterfield*'s fresh and original coloured marble fonts at Ottery St Mary and Babbacombe, Torquay 163 (Torbay), are especially memorable. Among early Victorian craftsmen in the county mention should be made of *Simon Rowe* of Exeter, who worked on the w front of the cathedral in succession to *Kendall*: the altar and rederos at Exwick (1841) and the fonts of Broadclyst (1843) and Bicton (1850) show his tightly detailed, rather fragile Gothic at its best. By far the busiest carver and sculptor in the county, however, was *Harry Hems* (1842–1916). Hems arrived in Exeter in 1865 to work on the Albert Memorial Museum and stayed to establish one of the 152 most prolific ecclesiastical workshops in Victorian England. Paternalistic, High Church, an extrovert and expert self-publicist, Hems was a flamboyant figure: by the late 1880s he employed seventy men in Exeter, with staff in London, Oxford, and Ireland as well. The firm's well understood and carefully executed Gothic can be found in churches throughout the county. Outstanding examples are the screen restorations at Littleham (1883), Staverton (1889), and Kenn (1890). Within a traditional vocabulary Hems could produce work of great richness and variety, as in the fittings of Winkleigh (1871–2) and Revelstoke (1881–5), and in the alabaster reredoses – a speciality of the firm – provided for St Paul Honiton (1893) and Swimbridge (1894), to name just two examples. The firm also produced a large range of churchyard memorials and the occasional effigy (Harberton, 1895). Other effigies can be found at Powderham, 1868 by the Exeter sculptor *E. B. Stephens*; at Ottery St Mary, 1879 by *Thrupp*; and at St Michael Exeter, 1883 by *Armstead*, an elaborate founder's tomb. But monuments of this kind are exceptional, for in the C19 the most common form of memorial became the stained-glass window, so important to the Victorians for a re-creation of a medieval atmosphere of devotion. For varied collections of STAINED GLASS, including works by many of the major firms, one should visit Ottery St Mary, Holy Trinity Ilfracombe, St Peter Tiverton, and St Eustace Tavistock. The Index of Artists at the end of this book will lead the enthusiast to the work of many other exponents: *Wailes, Willement, Warrington, Hardman* (especially the Bicton Mausoleum, 1850), *Clayton & Bell, Lavers &*

*I owe most of this paragraph, and much information in the following ones, to Dr Chris Brooks.

Barraud, Heaton, Butler & Bayne, Shrigley & Hunt, and the *Kempe Studios* all produced good work in Devon. *Morris & Co.* executed notable windows for St John Torquay (Torbay) 1865, St Eustace Tavistock 1876, Emmanuel Plymouth 1881, and a complete set for Monkton from 1874; the distinctively mannered Pre-Raphaelite style of the lesser-known *W. F. Dixon* can be recognized at Barnstaple 1878, Shobrooke 1881, Dawlish 1876 and 1884, Challacombe, and Parracombe. An important aspect of c19 stained glass in Devon is the strength of local firms – as it is in almost all aspects of church building and fitting in the county. The earliest of importance was *Robert Beer* of Exeter, who favoured intensely coloured windows with stiff little figures in medallions (Axminster, Chudleigh, and Thorverton). The firm was continued after *c.* 1850 by Robert's son Alfred and later became *Beer & Driffield.* The most important Devon workshop from the 1860s was that of *Frederick Drake* (1838–1921) of Exeter, who had been articled to Beer. His windows, sometimes similar to those of Clayton & Bell, are distinguished by their visual clarity and by a distinctive blue/purple palette (St Michael Exeter 1868 and 1883, St Petrock Exeter 1881, St Michael Teignmouth 1880s and later). As *Drake & Sons* the firm produced windows clearly influenced by Aesthetic and Arts and Crafts design: outstanding is the w window of Holy Trinity Torquay (Torbay), 1907. Also important in the late century, and more markedly Aesthetic, were *Fouracre & Watson* of Plymouth (Emmanuel Plymouth 1880s and later, e window of Plymstock 1888).

An account of c19 church building in the county should not proceed further without examining the role of LOCAL ARCHITECTS of the Victorian period. Here churches and secular work must be considered together, for the public buildings of the towns are almost entirely by local men. The chief among them was JOHN HAYWARD (1808–91). He was a nephew and pupil of Charles Barry, but all his Devon work is enthusiastically Gothic. He was architect to the Diocesan Architectural Society from its foundation, and demonstrated his belief in the ecclesiologically correct spirit of the Camden Society already in his work of the 1840s. His first church, a small chapel at Tipton St John of 1839–40, was built for the Coleridges of Ottery, one of a series of important High Church patrons. St Andrew Exwick at Exeter of 1841, also small, with 'second pointed' nave and chancel, was a studious and, in national terms, notably early demonstration of Camdenian principles; so also was the rebuilding and refitting of Sowton for the Garratts of Bishop's Court in 1844–5, and the partial rebuilding of Uffculme in 1847–9. In 1850 came the commission from Lady Rolle for a new church at Bicton, where Pugin's contemporary mausoleum must have made a significant impact. Hayward's church is notable for its elaborate programme of sculptural decoration. His other new churches are relatively few – St James Ilfracombe (1856) and Beer (1876) are among the most ambitious. Crediton (from 1877) is the chief among his many church restorations; he also restored Holcombe Court in 1863 and, again in the 1860s, Bradfield, where most of his work is Jacobethan. For his major secular buildings he used Gothic: St Luke's College Exeter, 1851, and, most 'impressively, the Royal Albert Memorial Museum Exeter of 1865–6, the latter in an accomplished Ruskinian manner, with plenty of polychromy. His smaller buildings include numerous attractive vicarages (an early one is Bishops Tawton, 1841, and the best is Woodbury, 1849) and small schools (e.g. Brampford Speke, 1867–8). The more ambitious new buildings for Blundell's School, Tiverton (1882), were carried out when he was in partnership with his son *Pearson Barry Hayward* (1838–88).

EDWARD ASHWORTH (1815–96), who was articled to Robert Cornish of Exeter, and then to Charles Fowler, settled in Exeter in 1846. Like Hayward, he was an active member of the Diocesan Architectural Society. His church restorations (or rather, in some cases, rebuildings), like his antiquarian drawings, are painstaking and scholarly, respecting the Perp tradition of the county, although his preference for removing plaster from the walls can make his interiors unappealing. He worked at many of the major parish churches: Cullompton 1848–50, Tiverton 1853–6, Bideford 1862–5, Axminster 1870, Broadclyst 1882. His larger new churches are spacious but unexciting (Withycombe Raleigh 1862, Topsham 1874).

DAVID MACKINTOSH of Exeter was active chiefly in the 1840s–50s. Like Hayward and Ashworth a member of the Diocesan Architectural Society, his work is conservative and rather pedestrian (rebuilding of Heavitree, Exeter, 1844, restorations at Chudleigh 1847, Hartland 1848, Northam 1849). The tower of Holy Trinity Barnstaple of 1843–5 is his most notable new building.

ROBERT MEDLEY FULFORD (1845–1910), who was active especially in the 1880s, was a church architect of a very different character. The son of the vicar of Woodbury, he was articled to Hayward and, before setting up on his own, worked in the offices of William White and Ashworth. He gave up architecture when he was ordained in 1891; the firm then became *Fulford, Tait & Harvey*. In his restorations Fulford did not hesitate to leave the imprint of his own quirky style, and his inventive tracery and elaborate fittings give a distinctive Victorian flavour to many simple village churches – see for example Poltimore (1879–80), Washford Pyne (1882–4), and Bow (1889). Also worthy of note is his use of sgraffito for interior decoration: his scheme of 1873–5 at Colaton Raleigh is immediately contemporary with Henry Cole's pioneering schemes at South Kensington and may be the earliest in any English church. In his secular work he favoured picturesque effects, with tile-hanging in the Shaw tradition. Woodbury School (1870) is an early and attractive example; later ones are Maypool, Stoke Gabriel (1883), and the fanciful workshop at Exeter for the sculptor Harry Hems (1881).

Other local architects active in more limited areas were the GOULD family of North Devon (*Richard Davie Gould* (1817–1900) and his son *John Ford Gould*, who joined the practice in the 1860s and died prematurely in 1881). J. F. Gould was responsible for the best of their church work (Down St Mary and Winkleigh, both 1871–3, and the chancel of Sheepwash, 1879–80). R. D. Gould's most extensive and interesting work is at Barnstaple, where he was Borough Surveyor for forty-six years, and responsible for much replanning, including the new market buildings of 1855–6. His early secular work tends to be classical (Bridge Buildings Barnstaple 1844, Crediton Town Hall 1852), though he also collaborated with *P. C. Hardwick* on Hall (1844–7), in the Jacobethan manner, and designed Bideford Town Hall (1850) in an attractively handled Perp. West Buckland School of 1861 and Bridge Chambers Barnstaple of 1874 are both Gothic.

At Plymouth, growing to keep pace with the expanding Dock-yard, the neo-classical tradition established by Foulston and continued by Wightwick remained strong into the mid C19. The handsome Devonport Library and Mechanics Institute by ALFRED NORMAN is in the Italianate of Barry's London clubs. JAMES PIERS ST AUBYN (1818–95) used a more picturesque form of Italianate for the Devonport Market of 1852, but he could also deploy Gothic skilfully. His practice was in London, but he worked extensively in Devon and Cornwall, where his aristocratic family connections were undoubtedly good for business. His later churches, particularly Maristow Chapel, 1871, and Noss Mayo, 1882–5 (both designed for wealthy titled patrons), are remarkable for the lively polychromatic interiors gleaming with polished marble.

JAMES HINE (1830–1914) was the most active Goth in the Plymouth area from the 1860s. From 1869 he was in partnership with *Alfred Norman*; later the firm became *Hine & Odgers*, and *W.H.May* joined them in 1906. An early work is Western College, Plymouth, 1861, already with serious, well carved Gothic detail, but his triumph was the Plymouth Civic Buildings of 1870–4, which he won, together with Norman, in competition. The profusely ornamented exterior is still impressive, even though only half the group survived the war.

Torquay also grew fast in the C19, but it was essentially a conglomeration of comfortable suburbs for holiday visitors, and there were few public buildings of significance until the early C20. The plum church commissions went to major outside architects (*see* above). Among the local products is EDWARD APPLETON's little Masonic Hall of 1857, at the time a lone demonstration of support for Butterfieldian aesthetics among the stuccoed villas designed by JACOB HARVEY (1783–1867) and his sons. JOSEPH WILLIAM ROWELL (1827–1902) also was active in this area, settling in Newton Abbot in 1855. His work ranges from the attractive Italianate housing of the 1850s for the Courtenays at Newton Abbot to eclectic Tudor for Sir Lawrence Palk's new manor house on Lincombe Hill at Torquay (1861) and a more mature Victorian Gothic for the little church at Collaton St Mary, Paignton, Torbay (1864).

It is clear that by the 1870s local architects and patrons considered that Gothic was the proper style for major PUBLIC BUILDINGS. In addition to *Hayward*'s Exeter Museum and *Hine*'s Plymouth Guildhall there were the Town Hall at Bideford (1850 by *Gould*), *Edward Rundle*'s Town Hall at Tavistock of 1860 (although this is rather a special case, as it is a continuation of the Duke of Bedford's policy of providing a town centre in keeping with the remains of the abbey), and *William Harvey*'s Torquay Museum of 1876.

There are exceptions to the Gothic rule: the stolid classical Town Hall of Great Torrington of 1861 can simply be labelled old-fashioned, but the Town Hall at Tiverton of 1864, by *H.J.Lloyd* of Bristol, is a surprisingly showy effort in fashionable French Renaissance. Market buildings are different again: *Rundle*'s at Tavistock is a solid utilitarian structure hiding behind the more ornate Gothic shopfronts; *John Chudleigh*'s competition-winner for Newton Abbot of 1871 (of which only one building remains) is in a more old-fashioned chunky *villa rustica* style; but the buildings at South Molton of 1861 by *W.F.Cross* of Exeter consist of an elegantly lightweight market hall behind a handsomely decorated Italianate frontage. Cross, who left Exeter to establish a London practice in 1867, was skilled in designing buildings for complex functions. His Wonford Asylum at Exeter (1865–9) is imposingly laid out in the guise of a Jacobean country house, an interesting contrast to the plainer, still classically proportioned compositions of the large institutions of the 1840s. The most distinguished of these are *Fowler*'s well planned asylum at Exminster and *Scott & Moffat*'s workhouses at Tiverton and Bideford. The later C 19 desire to dress up such establishments is shown by *R. Stark Wilkinson*'s terracotta-trimmed Exeter Digby Asylum of 1885–6 and by the original free classical frontages to the eye hospitals of the turn of the century: at Plymouth of 1897 by the local firm *King & Lister*, at Exeter of 1898–1901 by the outsider *A. Brumwell Thomas*. On a lesser level, eccentric cases of the reaction against Gothic sometimes found among builders of board schools are the curiously neo-Norman examples by *Charles Pinn* of Exeter at Yeoford and South Zeal.

The most individual local architect working at the turn of the century was ALEXANDER LAUDER of Barnstaple, who was also a versatile designer and craftsman. His original style is illustrated by two Barnstaple buildings: the Gliddon & Squire showrooms of 1903, ornamented from his pottery works, and Ravelin Manor, his own idiosyncratically decorated house.

As for LATER C 19 URBAN DEVELOPMENT, Plymouth was the only great Victorian town of Devon, growing rapidly but haphazardly in the hinterland of the ever-expanding dockyards. Only fragments remain of its Victorian heart, but in the inner suburbs there are still plenty of proud public buldings, often in the distinctive local grey limestone. Their quality is, as one would expect, generally higher than in the smaller towns. *Hine*'s Gothic contributions have already been mentioned, but the classical tradition also remained strong, grandly demonstrated at Plymouth by barracks for the navy, by the Institute for the Blind (1876 by the local architect *H. J. Snell*), and, most prolifically, by the stuccoed suburban terraces and villas expanding up the hills. The new stylistic fashions of the later C 19 are also represented. Norman Shaw's picturesque urban style was exploited already by the appropriately named Queen Anne Terrace, North Hill, of the 1880s. *Snell*'s excellent Technical College at Stonehouse of 1897 is in a free Renaissance, while *Thornely & Rooke*'s Plymouth Museum and Library of 1907 is the only civic building in the county in full-blown Edwardian Baroque. Only Torquay could provide a few rivals: a large but slightly dull Town Hall of 1911, and the much more enjoyable frivolous Pavilion of the same year, a confection of *Doulton* faience and 173 Art Noveau ironwork by the Borough Surveyor, *H. A. Garrett*. Elsewhere, the only building to express the grandiloquence of the Edwardian period is *Aston Webb*'s Royal Naval College at Dartmouth, of 1905–9.

The other Devon towns which grew most spectacularly in the later C 19 were the late developers among the seaside resorts. Paignton (Torbay) and Ilfracombe both retain distinctive, little altered late Victorian centres that have considerable period charm. Ilfracombe, where *W. H. Gould* was one of the most active local architects, is memorable for its spiky terraces and hotels in the local pale yellow brick, profusely embellished with ironwork; Paignton, for long a poor relation of Torquay, burgeoned from the 1870s, its eclectic classical urbanity largely determined by the local architect *G.S.Bridgman*. Lynton and Lymouth, exploiting the dramatic scenery of the north coast, are more fancifully romantic, their mood caught by a gabled and turreted Town Hall (1898 by *Read & Macdonald*). At Dartmouth York House and its neighbours (1894) are in a comparable spirit, an extravagant riot of timber-framing and painted panels that would have made the sober-minded men of the vernacular revival blanch; the architect was the Borough Surveyor, *E.H.Back*. The urban emphasis of seaside resorts began to evaporate after the turn of the century. Architecturally, the negative results of this are only too apparent at Westward Ho! and Woolacombe, where embryonic Victorian centres have been swamped by indifferent C20 expansion. The positive side is represented by the return to the tradition of the more exclusive individual secluded cottage or villa, for example at Budleigh Salterton, Saunton, and Croyde, which must be considered under later Arts and Crafts architecture.

LATER C19 CHURCHES began to be influenced by the Arts and Crafts movement from the 1880s onwards. The more progressive buildings have broad instead of soaring spaces, and are eclectic in their stylistic sources. The general enthusiasm of this period for late Gothic is often combined with a greater deference to the local Perp tradition, but fittings are frequently quite untrammelled by medieval precedent.

The foremost architect is *J.D.Sedding* (1838–91), who started work with his elder brother *Edmund Sedding* of Penzance (1836–68). Among his most delightful works in Devon is the vicarage for All Saints Plymouth (1887), a skilful reinterpretation of a picturesque town house in the old English tradition. He also built a pretty lodge at Flete for the Mildmay family, who were the patrons of his most important church work. At Holbeton (1885–9) the flamboyant tracery of the screen takes its cue from the existing late medieval woodwork, though the vigorous naturalistic carving of the bench ends is less dependent on precedent; at Ermington (another Mildmay church) his charming free classical lychgate of *c.* 1890 is much more original, although equally at home in its setting. Lychgates could provide the only opportunity when a church had already been fully restored: the intricately crafted one of 1894 at Ilfracombe is by Sedding's pupil *Henry Wilson*, who took over the firm after his master's early death. The low screen in his fine new chancel at Salcombe has his typical glowing enamelwork; Lynton, also completed by Wilson, is an even richer treasure house of unusual Arts and Crafts furnishings. J.D.Sedding's architectural mantle was also assumed by his nephew *Edmund Harold Sedding* of Plymouth (1863–1921), who built two broad and airy churches with great traceried W windows, very much in his uncle's manner: St Mary Abbotsbury, Newton Abbot, and St Peter, Shaldon, Teignmouth, the latter dominated by its splendidly inventive furnishings. Also worth remarking is his excellent remodelling of Princetown church (1899) and the chunky church rooms of 1892 with which he complemented his uncle's vicarage at All Saints Plymouth.

Another striking interior ensemble is to be found at St Matthew, Chelston, Torquay (1895–1904), which has a remarkable well-head font designed by *Gerald Moira* and sculpture by *F.Lynn Jenkins*. The church itself, an early work by *Sir Charles Nicholson*, is interesting as a reinterpretation of the Devonian Perp tradition. His later church at Yelverton (1910–14), with its accomplished, reticently detailed interior, is less derivative. The influence of Sedding's broad buttressed w windows can be seen in *W. D. Caröe*'s major work, St David Exeter, begun in 1897. Its spacious nave, bound together by great transverse 166 arches, is a surprise after the busy exterior. Caröe's personal style is also well expressed at Woolacombe, and by two of the many churches built at this time in Plymouth: St Gabriel and St Boniface. Another worthwhile suburban Plymouth church, likewise in a free Perp, is the admirably detailed but unfortunately uncompleted St Mary Laira (1911), by the Plymouth architect *T. R. Kitsell*.

Leonard Stokes is represented by two R.C. churches, his very early Sacred Heart, Exeter, designed in 1883 when he was working with the Exeter architect *Charles Ware*, and his less derivative Holy Saviour, Lynton, of 1910.

The most prolific architect of local origin of this time was *G. H. Fellowes Prynne*, the son of the vicar of St Peter Plymouth, whose church he rebuilt in 1880–2, adding the powerful pinnacled tower in 1906. Prynne generally favoured a lofty version of late Gothic. Among his churches are Newton Ferrers 1885–6, Budleigh Salterton 1891–3, and the sensitively small-scale church of 1893 at Horrabridge; in 1905–7 he also enlarged and remodelled Holy Trinity Exmouth, adding a characteristic reredos in 1912. St Peter Ilfracombe, 1902–3, with its odd spiral columns, is a departure from his usual style. His restorations are memorable for their delicate, lyrically detailed woodwork: Payhembury (1895–7) and Loxhore (1900–3) are good examples. A similar taste is displayed in *Temple Moore*'s elaborate medievalizing screen at Littleham (near Bideford) of 1891–2.

By this time reaction had set in against ripping out earlier FURNISHINGS, for their Perp style was no longer felt to be incongruous. Around 1890 *Sabine Baring-Gould* of Lew Trenchard took the lead in rescuing discarded fittings at Staverton. His cousin *F. Bligh Bond*, the expert on medieval screens, assisted in the full-blooded restoration of the screens at Staverton and Lew Trenchard and elsewhere, modelling them on the complete medieval survival of Atherington. The carving of the screen at Lew Trenchard was carried out by the *Pinwells*, daughters of the rector of Ermington (where the largest display of their handicraft can be seen). Their workshop produced a considerable quantity of competent woodwork for churches, in the medieval tradition, but distinguished by a rather studied naturalism.

Hems, by now *Hems & Sons*, of course continued into the Edwardian period, but competition, along with new approaches, was growing. *Herbert Read*, who had worked for Hems since 1874, established his own business in Exeter in 1891 to carry out conservative restoration work. The firm still flourishes, and is responsible for the present complete appearance of much medieval woodwork. C20 examples of its tradition of skilled craftsmanship entirely based on medieval precedent can be seen at Ashprington, Exbourne, and Chagford (1935–8). Rather less derivative was the Crediton firm of *Dart & Francis*, whom *Caröe* chose as both contractors and executants for all his undertakings in the county: the firm's skills are on full display in Crediton church, where, among much else, they executed the extraordinary monument to Redvers Buller.

Interesting STAINED GLASS in the Arts and Crafts tradition, of the late C19 onwards, includes work by *Henry Holiday* (Arlington,

Mortehoe); *Heywood Sumner* (Holbeton, Oakford); *Selwyn Image* (Mortehoe); *Comper* (Clovelly); and *Christopher Whall* (Lynton). The oddest is the window by *Arild Rosencrantz* at Oakford, of 1908. The later work of the major local stained-glass workshops has already been mentioned.

VICTORIAN COUNTRY HOUSES continued the battle of styles which started in the earlier C19. Some followed the Tudor tradition but with a little more emphatic detail. Pitt House, Chudleigh Knighton, of 1841 by *Scott & Moffat*, is distinguished by Jacobean gables; Hall, designed by *P. C. Hardwick* and executed by *R. D. Gould* of Barnstaple (1843–7), mixes Jacobean with more overtly Gothic elements. Elsewhere Gothic continued to be used in the Regency manner for romantic or ornamental effect, as at Watermouth Castle, completed by *Wightwick* in the 1840s, or Lee Abbey, Lynton, of *c.*1850. (A curious counterpart is another seaside villa, Redcliffe Towers, Paignton, Torbay, of 1853, in Hindu style.)

The most fervent secular expressions of the Gothic ideal are not found before the 1860s: the chief among them are *William White*'s 158 remodelling of Bishop's Court (1860–4) and *William Burges*'s Knightshayes (1869–74). Their interiors make an interesting contrast: Bishop's Court, for the High Church Garratt family, sombre and serious, with its own lancet-lit chapel; Knightshayes, for the Heathcoats, the Tiverton mill-owners, in a more fanciful escapist mood (not quite as elaborate as Burges intended, but with much of his colourful decoration now restored to view). *Scott*'s additions to Hartland Abbey of 1862 and *Ferrey*'s mansion at Huntsham (1869) are further examples of the solid and earnest Gothic of this decade. A rather different case is Check House, Seaton, of 1865–6 by Ruskin's protégé *Benjamin Woodward*, an original adaptation of the principles of Gothic structural polychromy for a seaside villa. The most interesting later work by a Gothic architect is the enlargement of the Chanter's House, Ottery St Mary, of 1880–3, a rare example of a major secular work by *Butterfield*. *Waterhouse* made some additions to Culver House, Holcombe Burnell, in 1872–5, tactfully in keeping with the character of the early C19 Tudor work.

More frequent are the restorations or remodellings which were intended to reinstate (or invent) Gothic or Tudor character, often by eliminating later alterations. This approach gathered momentum during the C19. The indiscriminate accumulation of brought-in woodwork at Weare Giffard of the earlier C19, the *cottage orné* treatment of Knightstone, or *Ewan Christian*'s ruthless rebuilding of the Bishop's Palace at Exeter in the 1840s gave way around 1860 to a more serious and scholarly attitude. It is illustrated by the alterations and extensions to Bradfield, Bowringsleigh, and Holcombe Court, and by the occasional new house in straightforward Jacobean, such as Sidmouth Manor by *G. Somers Clarke*, of 1869. Yet the magpie approach remained popular with amateurs. The small house at Sidmouth built by the local antiquarian *Peter Orlando Hutchinson* in 1860–4 combines parts salvaged from the church with Gothic of his own creation, while *Sabine Baring-Gould*'s Lew Trenchard of the 1880s onwards is an even more daringly outré (and surprisingly successful) blend of invention, imported foreign features, and appropriations from local buildings. In this gallery of Gothic eccentrics one must also place the Manor House at Chelston, Torquay (Torbay), of *c.*1870, with its extraordinary flying stair, an engineer's dream realized, and Reeve Castle at Zeal Monachorum, the fantasy which *W. Carter Pedler* built for himself as late as 1900.

The alternative to Gothic was classical, with Italian or French Renaissance modulations when taste demanded something more florid. In the 1840s Foulston's pupil *George Wightwick* remained a stolid proponent of the neo-classical both in the Plymouth suburbs and in the country (Calverleigh Court, additions to Lupton House, Brixham, Torbay), although occasionally he also built in Tudor (Tristford, Harberton). *Blore*'s large additions of the 1840s and 1860s to the Palladian Castle Hill are suitably Italianate. A more flamboyant free Renaissance was used effectively by *David Brandon* at Sidbury Manor (1879), while at the same time the Rolle mansion of Stevenstone was heftily remodelled by *Charles Barry Jun.* in a showy French Renaissance – but this only survives as a ruin.

These later houses are contemporaries of an alternative mode, the picturesque 'Old English' inspired by English vernacular architecture of the C17. Among the major architects who led the way here, *Nesfield* is represented in Devon by Babbacombe Cliff, Torquay (Torbay), of 1878, *Devey* by Broomford Manor of *c.*1870 and by the minor buildings which remain from the demolished Membland. The largest [170] and most interesting example is *Norman Shaw*'s Flete (1878–85), an [157] older house ingeniously remodelled and extended to provide a grand mansion for the Mildmay family (neighbours and relations of the Barings of Membland). Flete, although with interiors in a sumptuous Jacobean, is all of stone, and quite dour and castle-like outside. The more obviously picturesque half-timbered and tile-hung effects of the Shavian tradition were adopted at Rousdon, *Ernest George*'s first major [159] country house (1874–8), built for the wealthy grocer Sir Henry Peek. Unlike Flete, this is a new building, fascinating for its intricate Victorian planning, and complemented by attractive estate buildings and lodges. Also by George, on a lesser scale but in a similar style, are Stoodleigh Court and Woodhouse, Uplyme. Other smaller essays in 'Old English' are High Bullen, Chittlehamholt, by *E. H. Harbottle*, 1879, and Twytchen, Mortehoe, *c.*1880, and Spurfield, Exminster, 1887–9, by *J. L. Pearson*. The revival of the early C18 red brick Queen Anne or Georgian style, in which Shaw was also a pioneer, is barely represented: *Ernest Newton*'s remodelling of Fremington, *c.*1880, is the best early example. Rather grander are the effects achieved by two refacing jobs: by *Belcher* at Tapeley Park (1898) and by *Tapper* at Bicton (1908–9).

Many of the grander C19 country houses were complemented by formal gardens, and by arboreta with specimen trees. The C19 planting at Bicton is among the best preserved; remains of other schemes, generally simplified in the C20, can be found e.g. at Arlington, Bradfield, Knightshayes, Lupton House Brixham (Torbay), Powderham, Tapeley Park, and Brunel Manor Torquay.

Neither the half-timbered house nor the grand red brick mansion fits easily into the traditional rural Devon scene. But some of the most interesting HOUSES OF THE 1890s ONWARDS are by architects working in the Arts and Crafts tradition, who displayed a conscious response to local building materials and traditions. An early landmark is The Barn, Exmouth, 1896 by *E. S. Prior*, with its idiosyncratic [172] textures of local stone, and (originally) a thatched roof over a butterfly plan. On a larger scale, *Daniel Gibson* and *T. H. Mawson* demonstrated a sensitivity to both site and local materials in the simply detailed house set in admirable formal gardens (the best of their kind in the county) at Wood (1900–5). Mawson also designed the gardens at Hannaford Manor, Widecombe-in-the-Moor, this time for a house by *A. Wickham Jarvis* of 1904. Smaller but significant original houses of 171 this period are Coxen, Budleigh Salterton, a specially appealing revival of cob building by *Ernest Gimson* (1910), and Penlee, Lydford, a free adaptation of the Dartmoor longhouse tradition by *Halsey Ricardo* (1908–11).

Other inventive architects demonstrated their own personal styles in the small commissions that came their way. The delightful Cottage Hospital of 1899 at Halwill is *C. F. A. Voysey* at his most characteristic. *Walter Cave* experimented with a variety of styles in his small buildings on the family estate at Sidbury Manor and elsewhere. For outsiders, the seaside resorts offered some of the best opportunities: *Harrison Townsend* provided a quirky show house for a new development of the 1890s at Salcombe; *Baillie Scott* (using local materials) built one of his characteristic gabled suburban houses at Sidmouth (1909).

In other towns the Arts and Crafts style made less impact, although 174 an interesting exception is Kingdon House Tavistock, an ingenious design for a printing works, by a local man, *Southcombe Parker*, of *c.* 1906. Some of the best urban buildings of this time are the banks, usually continuing the safe and sober style of C19 precedent, but sometimes a little more daring (see e.g. Bideford, Tavistock).

In the more select seaside resorts the Arts and Crafts tradition continued into the 1920s, particularly at Budleigh Salterton on the south coast, and at Saunton and Croyde on the north, the best houses tucked unassumingly into the landscape and hard to find. Monkswell Park, Ilsham (now on the N fringe of Torquay), 1924–5 by *H. L. North*, is a skilfully reticent example. At Torquay the most accomplished local practitioner was *Fred Harrild*, a pupil of Lutyens. His ravishing terraced garden of Castle Tor, Torquay (*c.* 1930–34), is very much in the Lutyens tradition, but he also favoured a picture-postcard thatched-cottage style, illustrated best by his two 1920s houses at Holne. The taste for this slightly twee and cosy type of revived *cottage orné* with vernacular allusions is found elsewhere (Cockrock, Croyde, and Higher Traine, Berrynarbor, both by *Oliver Hill*). The most famous example is the Drum Inn, Cockington (Torbay), 1935 by *Lutyens* himself, part of a more ambitious, unrealized scheme to preserve the traditional character of Cockington from encroaching Torquay. (A comparable concern is demonstrated by the efforts of the Hamlyns at Clovelly around the same time.)

Lutyens was of course far more than an architect of pretty cottages. Indeed, the Drum Inn, despite its traditional thatch and white walls, is not a cottage, but was intended as quite a substantial hotel. In 1909 he built some genuine cottages at Milton Abbot for the Bedford estate in his accomplished earlier vernacular style; his later sympathy with quiet, domestic Georgian is illustrated by his subtle additions to Mothecombe (1922–5) and his remodelling of Saunton Court, where he also created a delightful garden (1932). But his major work in 175 Devon is the sublimely romantic Castle Drogo for Julius Drewe of the Home and Colonial Stores, slowly achieved between 1910 and 1930. In this colossal scheme, of which only part was built, he shows his effortless mastery of the grand manner, especially in the highly original handling of the circulation spaces. There are only two 176 Edwardian mansions in Devon that can compete. One is the Manor House, North Bovey, which is in a stately but much less dramatic neo-Tudor, designed by *Detmar Blow* in 1906–7. The other is the extra-ordinary Oldway House, Paignton (Torbay), built by the millionaire Isaac Singer, and remodelled by his son Paris Singer in 1904–7 as a miniature Versailles.

AFTER 1918 the scale of country-house building was much diminished. Two examples worth singling out, where quiet vernacular elements in the Arts and Crafts tradition are handled with some originality, are Coleton Fishacre, Kingswear, 1926 by *Oswald Milne*, and Ashcombe Tower, 1935 by *Brian O'Rorke*, the latter with some hints of the architect's modern interests. Among the more ambitious GARDENS created at this time, those at Coleton Fishacre, Dartington and Flete are especially notable.

The best of the few CHURCHES of between the wars are at Paignton (Torbay), both of 1939 and completed only after 1945: *Maufe*'s St George and *Cachemaille Day*'s St Paul, each in their architect's personal version of minimal Gothic. More eccentric is St Luke Newton Abbot, with its Byzantine-Romanesque detail. The most remarkable church furnishings are those provided for the newly completed Buckfast Abbey: rich neo-Romanesque metalwork, mostly by *Bernhard Witte* of Aachen (1928–32), and a memorable Expression-ist bronze relief to Abbot Vonier by *Benno Elkan* (1938).

The most important INSTITUTIONAL BUILDINGS of between the wars are those begun after 1931 by *Vincent Harris* on Exeter University's new campus. They are in a gentlemanly neo-Tudor, rather clumsily sited. *Charles Holden*'s chapel at Torbay Hospital (1930) is more minimally detailed, but also traditional. New building types are sparsely represented: a few quite showy cinemas (Paignton (Torbay), Barnstaple), a hesitantly moderne garden-suburb model factory (Farley's at Plymouth, 1930). A much more abrupt challenge to convention was presented by some of the buildings put up by Leonard and Dorothy Elmhirst for their educational enterprises at Dartington Hall. They included a headmaster's house (1931–2) and, soon after, 177 boarding houses and some smaller houses, all by the Swiss-American 178 architect *William Lescaze*. Sophisticated designs entirely in the Inter-national Modern style, asymmetrical and flat-roofed, they remained a curiosity in Devon; the only consistent effort to continue the style was a housing estate which was planned by Lescaze at Churston Ferrers (Torbay). The simplified but traditional approach used for the low-cost housing at Dartington by *Louis de Soissons* proved more accept-able (see this firm's more affluent 1930s estates at Dittisham and Exeter).

These were all private enterprises. Both the county council schools and early C20 public housing in Devon are unremarkable, except at Plymouth, which has housing ranging from the replacements to the Barbican slums, which started before 1900, to the post-First-World-War cottage estate at Swilly laid out by *Adshead*.

The great opportunity for the local authorities came only after the Second World War, when devastating bomb damage made REBUILDING necessary at both Exeter and Plymouth. The two cities took different approaches. At Plymouth, where little was left of the Victorian centre, there was a clean sweep (the damaged Guildhall was only just reprieved) to make way for the new centre planned by *Abercrombie* and *Paton Watson*. Their bold plan, uncomfortably imposed on Plymouth's idiosyncratic topography, unfortunately paid little attention to the city's distinguished legacy of Regency planning and building. Exeter, following the recommendations of the more conservation-minded *Thomas Sharp*, preserved most of its historic plan, though here also there was a regrettable amount of post-war destruction. In both cities medieval and Tudor relics received disproportionate attention in comparison with buildings of later periods, and in both there is a disappointing lack of distinguished new architecture to compensate for what was lost. The main Plymouth buildings of the 1950s along Royal Parade are cumulatively quite impressive, and certainly better than the mediocrity of Exeter's widened High Street, but none deserve to be singled out here. Nor is there much that is architecturally worthwhile in the extensive new Plymouth suburbs, apart from a few churches that were quite daring in their time.

These more progressive Plymouth CHURCHES are the Ascension, by *Potter & Hare*, 1956; St Paul, Efford, by *Paul Pearn* of *Pearn & Procter*, 1962; and St Peter (R.C.), Crown Hill, 1967 by *John Evans* of *Evans & Powell*, the last with a central plan. The church rebuilding and refitting that took place in both cities as an immediate result of war damage is depressingly pedestrian, although as exceptions one should mention the careful restoration of the damaged parts of Exeter Cathedral, the work of *S. Dykes Bower* at St Mary Arches Exeter, and the rehabilitation of the gutted St Andrew Plymouth, with its arresting windows by *Piper* and *Reyntiens* (1958). Elsewhere, the most notable post-war church building is the eastern extension to Buckfast Abbey, by *Paul Pearn* (1965), a brave and successful departure from the pre-war Gothic of the rest of the abbey. The chapel provided the first large display of the brilliantly coloured slab-in-resin glass developed by Father *Charles Norris* of Buckfast, setting a trend that has been followed in many other Devon churches.

Other post-war CHURCH FITTINGS of note are few. Exeter has a mural of 1957 by *Hans Feibusch* at St Sidwell and stained glass by *John Hayward* of 1966 at St Mary Steps. The granite furnishings by *Louis Osman* and stained glass by *Frank Wilson* at Bickleigh near Plymouth (1964) and the fittings at Cornworthy of 1971 by *Alan Croft* are rarities in reflecting the tough architectural mood of the time. Good contributions of the eighties, less abrasive and refreshingly varied, are a glass screen at Bideford by *Peter Tysoe*, some robust ironwork in St Petrock Exeter by the *Harrison Sutton Partnership*, and a striking tapestry by *Bobbie Cox* at St Stephen Exeter.

The first major post-war INSTITUTIONAL BUILDINGS were traditional in style: *McMorran*'s Devon County Hall at Exeter of 1957–64 successfully combines quiet neo-Georgian detail with asymmetrical grouping of the main elements. At the university, building continued to a modified version of *Vincent Harris*'s unsatisfactory grand pre-war plan. His last building, the chapel, completed in 1958, is the most successful: simple but stately domestic neo-Tudor, with a harmonious, subtly lit interior. But by then the university had adopted *Sir William Holford*'s master plan, and the hilly campus began to be scattered with informally grouped inward-looking clusters, in an undemonstrative but quietly modern, slightly Swedish-inspired idiom. The general impression of the campus now is of a disappointing muddle, for the two conflicting successive master plans have been further compromised by the more crowded later additions which sprang up to cope with the rapid expansion of the 1960s–70s. They are mostly in a forceful and more aggressive style, the most prominent among them those by *Sir Basil Spence & Partners* and the *Playne Vallance Partnership*. The shift of taste around 1960 is only occasion-ally demonstrated elsewhere, for example in a few bold and vigorous school buildings such as the additions to Queen Elizabeth School, Crediton (by *R. N. Guy*, of the County Council's Architect's Depart-ment, 1965) and the more gaunt and dour Ilfracombe School, 1966–70 by *Stillman & Eastwick-Field*. However, the latter firm's pleasant school for children with little or no sight at Exeter, of the same date, is in a much gentler spirit.

The sixties saw the introduction of the SLAB and the TOWER BLOCK. The first major examples in Devon were at Plymouth: the tower of the Civic Centre (by *Jellicoe, Ballantyne & Coleridge*, 1961) and the answering office block over the station at the opposite end of Armada Way were deliberately intended to counter the blandness of the post-war central reconstruction. Plymouth is of a size where large buildings, if carefully placed, need not be disastrous to their surround-ings, as is shown also by a few more recent distinguished newcomers: the sleek offices for Moneycentre, by *Marshman Warren Taylor* (1975), and the powerful theatre by *Peter Moro*, completed in 1987. But elsewhere in Devon modern architecture is not easily assimilated; the intimate scale of most towns and villages, together with the preponderance of traditional local building materials, makes large modern structures appear alien. At Barnstaple the domineering slab-and-podium of the Civic Centre of 1968–70 looms as a totally inap-propriate adjunct to the tightly knit historic centre, while in Torquay the rash of insensitively sited and generally undistinguished hotels and flats, which started in the 1960s, has been disastrous to the balance of buildings and landscape which characterized the Victorian townscape. An exception, however, can be made for Torbay Hospital (sited beyond the older Torquay suburbs), with its striking crescent of ward blocks by *Fry Drew & Partners* of the 1960s, and a pleasantly stepped out canteen range by *Pearn & Procter* of 1982.

In the conservation-conscious 1970s and 1980s, the desire to fit in tactfully has become an overriding concern of the architect working in Devon. The buildings which achieve this best do so without sur-rendering their individuality. Interesting forerunners, ahead of their time in this respect, are the residential additions and the farm buildings of 1966 onwards at Lee Abbey, Lynton, by *Scarlett Burkett Associates*. The additions to King Edward VI School at Totnes (*Stillman & Eastwick-Field*, 1971) show the new taste for discreet white walls and pitched roofs applied to schools. Outstanding among additions to major country houses is the work by *Powell & Moya* of 1974–7 at Winslade Manor, which they sensitively restored and 180 converted to prestige offices for a national firm, with dignified but not overpowering buildings behind (the first transformation of this kind in the county). In an urban context, Plymouth Magistrates Court of 1979–80 by the *City Architect's Department* shows how a reticent but quite large and entirely modern building can appear acceptable in a sensitive area close to some of the city's few medieval houses. The most recent efforts to fit into a historic context combine bold modern detail with traditional massing and roofscapes; good examples are the Teignbridge District Offices at Forde House, Newton Abbot, by *Leonard Manasseh & Partners*, 1985–7, with gables paying homage to its C17 neighbour, and the tactful, barn-like visitor centre at Buckfast Abbey by *Richard Riley*, of 1983–4.

Unfortunately, paying lip service to preservation while cramming in too much, combined with lack of attention to detail, often leads to disappointing results. This is the case at Exeter with the grossly detailed mock-Georgian offices along Southernhay, or the Guildhall Shopping Centre with its jumble of historic façades, pastiche, and mediocre new buildings. A later and bolder mixture of old and new is the St Thomas development at Exeter, by *Marshman Warren Taylor*, 1974–86, a disparate but successful group made up of a handsome rehabilitated C19 station building, and new supermarket, library, and engagingly brash, Stirling-inspired swimming pool. The high-tech image made its first appearance in a few strident and colourful buildings at Belliver, Plymouth – the only industrial estate in the county of any architectural interest. The most impressive industrial engineering work is the Frigate Complex of the 1970s at Devonport, Plymouth, by Sir *Alexander Gibb & Partners*.

HOUSING is the most ubiquitous type of new structure. Among the few individual buildings of originality are houses by *Leonard Manasseh* at Beaford (1966–8), by *Peter Aldington* at Goodleigh (1970–1), and by *Peter Blundell Jones* at Stoke Canon (1976–7). As for groups, the early post-war public housing at Exeter and Plymouth is of little interest architecturally. The first of more individual distinction was a small development at Dartington: Hunters Moon, by *L. Manasseh & Partners*, 1968–72, simple white-walled houses with pitched roofs, quite tightly grouped, traditional in scale but modern in detail. The much larger private estate outside Dawlish in a similar mode by *Mervyn Seal*, 1971–6, endeavours, sometimes a little too trickily, to recreate the atmosphere of a densely knit seaside village. The style was imitated widely in the better housing developments (both public and private) of the 1970s, providing a welcome change from previous approaches: particularly satisfying are the straightforward simple terrace houses echoing the character of their older neighbours at Bull Hill, Bideford (1978–9 by *Torridge District Council*). The first more ambitious reflection of the national move in favour of low-rise urban housing and of vernacular imagery was the development of 1977–8 for Exeter City Council by *Marshman Warren Taylor* by the riverside at
179 Shilhay, a comfortable mixture of brick and tile-hanging on a humane scale, but dense enough to be appropriate for a city. Its influence can be seen in the more recent urban rebuilding in Plymouth, for example the uneventful but friendly terraces around Harwell Street, a noticeable change of heart from the drab early post-war blocks which were such dismal substitutes for the lost Regency terraces of Devonport and Stonehouse. Private housing of the 1970s, especially the mushroom growths of seaside flats and retirement homes, are often less discreet, and less than an asset to such intricate and small-scale towns as Dartmouth and Sidmouth. However, Plymouth Sound is a fitting setting for the boldest example: Ocean Court of 1976, a stepped

pyramid of flats overlooking a marina, once again by *Marshman Warren Taylor*. In the housing groups of the 1980s the influence of post-modernism has contributed to more flamboyant and expressive detail, with picturesque roof-lines and contrasting brickwork, although few go to such whimsical extremes as the group in Oke-hampton Road, Exeter (by *Cayley & Hutton*, completed in 1985). At their best, these buildings can fit happily into an older context, as is the case with groups of the early 1980s at East-the-Water, Bideford (*Torridge District Council*), Castle Quay, Barnstaple (*North Devon District Council*), and West Exe, Tiverton (*Mid-Devon District Council*).

A sympathetic approach to the setting of new buildings is paralleled by some imaginative conversions of problematic redundant ones such as Abbotskerswell Priory. But this introduction should not end on a complacent note. The pace of change in the county continues to accelerate, and as the Preface indicates, constant vigilance is needed not only to ensure that the best is preserved, but to encourage new buildings worthy of the legacy of past centuries.

FURTHER READING

Among GENERAL WORKS the best and most comprehensive account is *Devon*, by W. G. Hoskins (1954, reprinted 1974), which deals with far more than buildings. As it has an excellent bibliography, these notes can be brief on older sources. For the architectural historian, useful topographical surveys are R. Polwhele's *History of Devonshire* (3 vols., 1793–1806), incomplete and uneven, but quite informative on buildings; Daniel Lysons's invaluable *Devonshire*, vol. VI in his *Magna Britannia* (1822); and William White's thorough *History, Gazetteer and Directory of Devon* (1st ed. 1850; 2nd ed. 1878–9; 3rd ed. 1890). The impressions of early visitors to Devon, from Leland onwards, are gathered together in R. Pearse Chope's *Early Tours of Devon and Cornwall* (1918, reprinted 1967). Many Devon houses are depicted in the amateur but instructive early C18 topographical drawings by Edmund Prideaux, published by J. Harris in *Architectural History*, vol. 7 (1964). Extracts from John Swete's diaries of his Devon tours are included in *Devon's Age of Elegance*, ed. P. Hunt (1984), illustrated with C19 prints. T. Moore's *Devonshire* (3 vols., 1829–36) is useful for its contemporary illustrations, as is Britton and Brayley's *Devon and Cornwall Illustrated* (1832).

The first more specialized guide books for visitors also start in the early C19 (Butcher's *Beauties of Sidmouth*, Banfield's *Ilfracombe, A Stranger's Guide to Plymouth*, etc.). They are valuable for their accounts of contemporary building activity, as are the best of the older histories of individual towns, such as M. Dunsford, *Tiverton* (1790), W. F. Gardiner, *Barnstaple 1837–97*, R. N. Worth, *Plymouth* (1872), J. T. White, *Torquay* (1878). (Others will be found listed in Hoskins's *Devon*.) The local histories published since 1950 are far too numerous to list here: relatively few are very informative on architecture, but those useful in this respect include F. Pilkington, *Ashburton* (1978), R. Freeman, *Dartmouth* (1983), M. A. Reed, *Pilton* (2nd ed., 1985), P. Russell, *Torquay* (1960) and *Totnes* (2nd ed., 1984), *Uffculme* (Uffculme Local History Group, 1988), and U. Brighouse, *Woodbury* (1981). On Exeter there is W. G. Hoskins, *2000 Years in Exeter* (1960), *Discovering Exeter*, an excellent series of booklets on the suburbs published by the Exeter Civic Society (1981 onwards), and B. Little, *Portrait of Exeter* (1983); on Plymouth, C. Gill, *A New History of Plymouth* (2 vols., 1966, 1979) and *Sutton Harbour* (2nd ed., 1976).

Antiquarian and architectural matters began to be taken seriously with the publication from 1843 onwards of the *Transactions of the Exeter Diocesan Architectural Society* (*TEDAS*) (they are also informative, if biased, on contemporary ecclesiology). The principal local periodical is the *Transactions of the Devonshire Association* (*TDA*), which began in 1862; nuggets can also be discovered in *Devon* (later

Devon and Cornwall) Notes and Queries, from 1900. The *Proceedings of the Devon Archaeological Society (PDAS)* are chiefly concerned with prehistory, but its latest issues, and also the Society's agreeably produced recent series of booklets, *Devon Archaeology*, include some architectural studies. The accounts of individual buildings published in the *Archaeological Journal* on the occasions of the Royal Archaeological Institute's Summer Meetings (vol. 70, 1913; vol. 104, 1957) are still valuable. An overview of recent approaches is provided in three particularly helpful collections of essays published by Devon County Council: *Devon's Traditional Buildings*, ed. P. Beacham (1978), *The Archaeology of the Devon Landscape*, ed. S. Timms (1980), and *Devon Buildings*, ed. P. Beacham (1989). Exeter Museums Archaeological Field Unit has published useful *Reports* (from 1985) on buildings they have investigated, including the gatehouse at Rougemont Castle, Exeter, the Exeter Guildhall, and the Bishop's Palace. The newsletter of the Devon Buildings Group (established 1984) is instructive on buildings at risk.

For detailed architectural information on individual buildings one needs to consult the Department of the Environment's statutory *Lists of Buildings of Architectural and Historic Interest*. The resurvey of rural areas, begun in 1983 and at the time of writing nearly complete, is admirably thorough; the towns, resurveyed earlier, are less comprehensively covered. Major gardens are listed in the *Gardens Register* compiled by English Heritage in 1987.

General ARCHAEOLOGICAL introductions to Devon are A. Fox, *South-West England 3500 B.C.–A.D. 600* (2nd ed., 1973), S. M. Pearce, *The Archaeology of South West Britain* (London, 1981 ed.), and M. Todd, *The South West to A.D. 1000* (1987), which has a very full bibliography. As for PREHISTORY, a gazetteer of Devon barrows has been published by L. V. Grinsell in *PDAS*, vols. 28 (1970), 36 (1978), and 41 (1983). A sample of the 'invisible' cropmark sites of the Devon lowland may be seen in F. M. Griffith, *Proc. Prehist. Soc.*, vol. 51 (1985). The first publication of Dartmoor reaves is by E. Gawne and J. Somers Cocks in *TDA*, vol. 100 (1968). Subsequent work was published by A. Fleming in *Proc. Prehist. Soc.*, vols. 44 (1978), 97–124, and 49 (1983), 195–242 (reave systems and Holne excavations), and for south-west Dartmoor by G. J. Wainwright *et al.* in *ibid.*, vols. 45–8 (1979–82). The Dartmoor sites described in the gazetteer represent only a very small proportion of the landscape readily accessible to the visitor. Essential equipment is the Dartmoor 1:25,000 map in the Ordnance Survey's 'Outdoor Leisure' series, which gives much archaeological information. R. H. Worth's *Dartmoor*, ed. G. M. Spooner and F. S. Russell (1967), is still the single most informative companion to the Moor; for a different view, see T. Greeves, *The Archaeology of Dartmoor from the Air* (Exeter, 1985). J. Somers Cocks and T. Greeves, *A Dartmoor Century 1883–1983* (1983), includes old photographs of sites since destroyed. For Exmoor see L. V. Grinsell, *Archaeology of Exmoor* (1970).

The more recent surveys of ROMAN Devon, mainly from the military angle, are V. A. Maxfield in *Roman Frontier Studies 1979*, ed. W. S. Hanson and L. J. F. Keppie (*BAR* Int. Ser. No. 71), F. M. Griffith, 'Roman Military Sites in Devon: Some Recent Discoveries', *PDAS*, vol. 42 (1984), and P. T. Bidwell, *Roman Exeter, Fortress and Town* (1980). For Hembury see M. Todd, *Antiq. J.*, vol. 64 (1984).

The most recent POST-ROMAN survey is S. M. Pearce, *The Kingdom of Dumnonia* (1978).

For MEDIEVAL sites on Dartmoor see A. Fleming and N. Ralph in *Med. Archaeol.*, vol. 26 (1982), and D. Austin in *The Medieval Village*, ed. D. Hooke (1985).

Brief surveys of INDUSTRIAL DEVON are provided by W. Minchinton's *Devon's Industrial Past: A Guide* (1986) and *Devon at Work* (1974); more detailed studies of two areas can be found in F. Booker, *Industrial Archaeology of the Tamar Valley* (1967) and H. Harris, *Industrial Archaeology of Dartmoor* (3rd ed., 1986). For particular towns see M. Bone, *Barnstaple's Industrial Archaeology* (1973), M. Chitty, *Industrial Archaeology of Exeter* (1974), A. Patrick, 'The Growth and Decline of Morwellham', *TDA*, vol. 106 (1974), C. Gaskell Brown, *Industrial Archaeology of Plymouth: A Guide* (1980), and C. Edginton, *Tiverton's Industrial Archaeology* (1976). On particular aspects: C. Hadfield, *Canals of South West England* (1967), H. Harris, *The Grand Western Canal* (1973); J. Hall, *Railway Landmarks of Devon* (1982); J. Kanefsky, *Devon Tollhouses* (rev. ed., 1983); W. Minchinton, *Windmills of Devon* (1977); W. Minchinton, *A Limekiln Miscellany: The South-West and South Wales* (1984); W. Minchinton, *Life to the City: An Illustrated History of Exeter's Water Supply from the Romans to the Present Day* (1987); W. Minchinton and J. Perkins, *Tidemills of Devon and Cornwall* (1971); M. Atkinson *et al.*, *Dartmoor Mines: The Mines of the Granite Mass* (rev. ed., 1983), A. K. Hamilton Jenkin, *Mines of Devon: The Southern Area* (1974) and *Mines of Devon: North and East of Dartmoor* (1981), and T. Greeves, *Tin Mines and Miners of Dartmoor – A Photographic Record* (1986).

The most thorough account of EXETER CATHEDRAL, although now out of date in places, is H. E. Bishop and E. K. Prideaux, *The Building of the Cathedral Church in Exeter* (1922). A good recent summary is V. Hope and J. Lloyd, *Exeter Cathedral, A Short History and Description* (1973). On the Saxon minster see C. Henderson and P. Bidwell in *The Early Church in Western Britain and Ireland*, ed. S. M. Pearce (1982). A. Erskine (ed.), *The Fabric Rolls of Exeter Cathedral* (2 vols., 1981–2) provides important documentary evidence for the medieval building work. Nicholas Orme, *Exeter Cathedral As It Was* (1987), discusses the liturgical changes of later centuries. On particular topics: C. J. P. Cave, *Medieval Carvings in Exeter Cathedral* (1953); M. Glasscoe and M. Swanton, *Medieval Woodwork in Exeter Cathedral* (1978); M. Swanton, *Roof Bosses and Corbels of Exeter Cathedral* (1979); and C. Brooks and D. Evans, *The Great East Window . . . A Glazing History* (1988). For other new research, including J. Allan on the west front, see *Transactions of the British Archaeological Association Exeter Conference of 1985* (forthcoming).

For MONASTIC FOUNDATIONS see J. Stephen, *Buckfast Abbey* (1970), H. P. R. Finberg, *Tavistock Abbey* (1969), and D. Seymour, *Torre Abbey* (1978).

On MEDIEVAL CHURCHES and their furnishings less recent work has been done. The most succinct introduction is still A. Hamilton-Thompson in *Archaeol. J.*, vol. 70 (1913); see also B. Creswell, *Notes on the Churches in the Deanery of Kenn* (1912) and in *TEDAS*, 3rd ser., vol. 3 (1920), and, more recently, J. M. Slader, *The Churches of Devon* (1968), which has useful lists and illustrations. C19 studies include G. Oliver, *Ecclesiastical Antiquities of Devon* (3 vols., 1840–2) and

W. Spreat's *Picturesque Sketches of the Churches of Devon* (1832), valuable for its pre-restoration views. J. Stabb's *Some Old Devon Churches* (3 vols., 1909–16) and *Devon Church Antiquities* (1909) have numerous photographs.

Names to look for in local periodicals are C. F. Cornelius, on the Newton Abbot area in *TDA*, vols. 78 (1946) and 79 (1947), and on the Tavistock area in *J. Brit. Arch. Assoc.*, vol. 15 (1952); also G. W. Copeland in *Annual Reports and Trans. of the Plymouth Inst.*, vol. 17 (1935), on towers, and in vol. 21 (1947–9) on ancient chapels. Bishop Lacy's Registers, published by the *Canterbury and York Soc.* (2 vols., 1963, 1972), are useful for documentary evidence for the Perp period. J. Bony, *The English Decorated Style* (1979), and J. Harvey, *The Perpendicular Style* (1978), are essential background for an understanding of Devon churches in the light of recent approaches. On FURNISHINGS, for fonts see K. M. Clarke in *TDA*, vols. 45–54 (1913–24); for screens, vol. 2 of F. Bligh Bond and F. Camm, *Rood Screens and Rood Lofts* (1909), which is devoted entirely to Devon; for bench ends K. M. Clarke in *TEDAS*, 3rd ser., vol. 3 (1920); for 'Barnstaple' tiles L. Keen in *J. Brit. Archaeol. Assoc.*, 3rd ser., vol. 32 (1969); for monuments W. H. H. Rogers, *The Ancient Sepulchral Effigies of Devon* (1877), A. C. Fryer on Bristol craftsmen in *Archaeologia* (1923–4), C. F. Cornelius on the Newton Abbot area in *TDA*, vol. 83 (1951), on Haccombe A. W. Searley in *TDA*, vols. 50–5 (1918–23), and on Paignton G. M. Rushforth in *TEDAS*, 3rd ser., vol. 4 (1929–37).

Two general surveys of MEDIEVAL CASTLES are R. A. Higham, 'Early Castles in Devon, 1068–1201', *Château Gaillard*, vols. 9–10 (1982), and R. A. Higham, 'Castles in Devon', in *Archaeology of the Devon Landscape*, ed. S. Timms (1980). Also useful is R. A. Higham, 'Public and Private Defence in the Medieval South West: Town, Castle and Fort', in *Security and Defence in South West England before 1800* (Exeter Studies in History, 19), ed. R. A. Higham (1987). The most extensive archaeological work has been at Okehampton: see R. A. Higham, *PDAS*, vol. 35 (1977), R. A. Higham and J. P. Allan, *PDAS*, vol. 38 (1980), R. A. Higham, J. P. Allan, and S. R. Blaylock, *PDAS*, vol. 40 (1982), and R. A. Higham, *Okehampton Castle, Devon: Official Handbook* (HMSO, 1984). For other recently excavated sites see T. J. Miles on Barnstaple in *PDAS*, vol. 44 (1986), A. D. Saunders on Lydford in the HMSO guide (1982) and in *Med. Arch.*, vol. 24 (1980), and S. Rigold on Totnes in the HMSO guide (1952) and in *TDA*, vol. 81 (1954). Exeter is dealt with by H. M. Colvin, *The History of the King's Works*, vol. 2 (1963), and by E. T. Vatchell, 'Exeter Castle: Its Background and History', *TDA*, vol. 98 (1966). Accounts of other individual castles are given by A. W. Everett, 'The Rebuilding of the Hall of Compton Castle', *TDA*, vol. 88 (1956), and *Compton Castle, Devon* (National Trust, 1975); B. H. St J. O'Neil, 'Dartmouth Castle and Other Defences of Dartmouth Haven', *Archaeologia*, vol. 85 (1936), and A. D. Saunders, *Dartmouth Castle* (HMSO, 1965 etc.); E. T. Vatchell, 'Eggesford and Heywood Castles (Wembworthy)', *TDA*, vol. 95 (1963); F. W. Woodward, *Plymouth Citadel* (1987); R. A. Higham, S. Goddard, and M. Rouillard, 'Plympton Castle, Devon', *PDAS*, vol. 43 (1985); and D. and A. Woolner, 'Castle Dyke, High Week, Newton Abbot', *TDA*, vol. 85 (1953).

On HOUSES the best sources are the local periodicals, the accounts of the Royal Archaeological Institute's Summer Meetings (see above), and articles in *Country Life*. There is no single synthesis, but A. Emery's wide-ranging monograph on *Dartington Hall* (1970) has much comparative material on medieval buildings. For particular types of small medieval houses see W. A. Pantin, 'Medieval Priests' Houses in South West England', *Med. Archaeol.*, vol. 1 (1957), and on church houses, G. W. Copeland in *TDA*, vols. 92–7 (1960–7). More recent detailed studies have revealed the complexity of the historical development of even quite small buildings – see e.g. J. Lomas on Higher Harestone, *TDA*, vol. 106 (1974); B. Morley on Leigh Barton, Churchstow, *PDAS*, vol. 41 (1983), and J. R. L. Thorp on houses at Silverton, *PDAS*, vol. 40 (1982). Major country houses have been much less well studied, although several illuminating *Country Life* articles deserve special mention: M. Girouard on Powderham Castle in *CL*, 3 and 18 July 1963; J. Cornforth on Saltram in *CL*, 17 April, 11 May, and 14 September 1967; M. Binney on Sharpham in *CL*, 17 and 24 April 1969; and R. Haslam on Compton Castle in *CL*, 5 November 1981, and on Hartland Abbey in *CL*, 8 and 15 August 1983. Recent National Trust guides can also be recommended. Devon plasterwork of the C16 and C17 is listed and illustrated in K. and C. French, *TDA*, vol. 89 (1957), but deserves fuller investigation; on this subject see also M. Jourdain in *CL*, 2 April 1940, and B. Oliver in *TDA*, vol. 49 (1917). On West Country woodwork of the same period, A. Wells-Cole, 'An Oak Bed at Montacute', *Furniture History*, vol. 17 (1981), is broader in scope than its title suggests.

Only a selection from the great wealth of Devon's traditional FARMHOUSES is mentioned in the gazetteer: the reader is referred to the Department of the Environment's most recent statutory lists (see above) for more comprehensive surveys of the farmhouses and farm buildings in each parish.

Much of W. G. Hoskins's writing is relevant social and economic background to the study of rural Devon's building traditions. Some of his inspirational early essays on such subjects as 'The Study of Old Farmhouses' were brought together with other agrarian essays by him and H. P. R. Finberg in *Devonshire Studies* (1952), reprinted as *Old Devon* and *West Country Historical Studies* by their respective authors in 1966. R. H. Worth's early classification of longhouse development, *The Dartmoor House*, is reprinted in *Dartmoor* (1981). There is more background on the agrarian history of Dartmoor in Michael Havinden's and Freda Wilkinson's essay on farming in *Dartmoor, A New Study* (1970). C. Vancouver's *General View of the Agriculture of the County of Devon* (1808, reprinted 1969) includes a section on early-nineteenth-century rural buildings, including plans and illustrations of model cottages.

More recently, much material on vernacular building has been published at both local and national level. On cob there is little yet, except in J. R. Harrison, 'The Cob Wall in England', *Trans. Ancient Monument Society*, vol. 28 (1984). N. W. Alcock's early work, which stimulated much subsequent research, is well represented in the *TDA*, where a major series of articles on farmhouses mirrors the developing understanding of the subject: I, vol. 100 (1968); II, vol. 101 (1969); III, by S. R. Jones, vol. 103 (1971); IV, with C. Hulland, vol. 104 (1972); V, by C. Hulland, vol. 112 (1980). See also Alcock's articles on 'Sowton, Houses in an East Devon Parish', *TDA*, vol. 94 (1962); 'A Devon Farm – Bury Barton, Lapford', *TDA*, vol. 98 (1966); 'The Medieval Houses of Bishops Clyst', *Med. Arch.* (1965); 'The Medieval Buildings of Bishops Clyst', *TDA*, vol. 98 (1966); 'Devonshire Linhays – A Vernacular Tradition', *TDA*, vol. 95 (1963); and, with P. C. Child and J. M. W. Laithwaite, 'Sanders, Lettaford – A Devon Longhouse', *PDAS*, vol. 30 (1972). Alcock also edited the *Survey of Dartington Houses* (Exeter Papers in Industrial Archaeology, No. 3). See also P. C. Child and J. M. W. Laithwaite, 'Little Rull – A Late Medieval House near Cullompton', *PDAS*, vol. 33 (1973); Laithwaite's reassessment of Alcock's earlier study of 'Middle Moor, Sowton', *TDA*, vol. 103 (1971); and E. H. D. Williams, 'Poltimore Farmhouse, Farway', *TDA*, vol. 106 (1974).

The turning point in the understanding of c 15 to c 17 farmhouses is marked by Alcock and Laithwaite's 'Medieval Houses in Devon and their Modernisation', *Med. Arch.*, vol. 17 (1973). Of general surveys there is P. C. Child's pioneering essay, 'Farmhouse Building Traditions', in *Devon's Traditional Buildings*, ed. P. Beacham (1978); the same volume also has K. Coutin's 'Farm Buildings'. Further plans, illustrations, and references are in P. Beacham, 'Local Building Traditions in Devon from the Medieval Period to 1700', in *Archaeology of the Devon Landscape*, ed. S. Timms (1980). *Devon Buildings*, ed. P. Beacham (1989), includes specialist accounts of building construction: longhouses (P. Beacham); farmhouse building traditions and farm buildings (both P. Child); town houses to 1675 (M. Laithwaite); later c 17 and c 18 town houses, and wall painting and lime plaster decoration (both J. Thorp). E. Mercer's *English Vernacular Houses* (HMSO, 1973) and R. W. Brunskill's *Traditional Buildings of Britain* and *Traditional Farm Buildings of Britain* (1982) are national surveys with many Devonian examples; the same is true of *Cruck Construction*, ed. N. W. Alcock (CBA Research Report, No. 42) (1981).

On TOWN HOUSES up to *c.* 1700 the pioneer study is D. Portman, *Exeter Houses 1400–1700* (1966). M. Laithwaite's extensive research on Totnes is summarized in his article in *The Transformation of English Towns*, ed. P. Clark (1984). *Topsham, An Account of Its Streets and Buildings* (Topsham Society, 1971) is a useful illustrated account. Recent studies of individual buildings include James and Jennifer Barber in *TDA*, vol. 105 (1973) on Plymouth houses, and J. Thorp in *PDAS*, vol. 41 (1983) on No. 4 The Quay, Dartmouth.

Now to ARCHITECTURE OF THE C17 ONWARDS. The crucial national work on the documentation of architects of this period is H. M. Colvin's *Biographical Dictionary of British Architects, 1600–1840* (1978). A. E. Richardson and C. L. Gill, *Regional Architecture of the West of England* (1924), is a valuable, if vague, illustrated survey of lesser domestic architecture. On larger houses, *Country Life* articles remain the most useful source (see also above). Important articles reappraising the Regency period in Devon are F. Jenkins, 'John Foulston and His Public Buildings in Plymouth, Stonehouse and Devonport', *J. Soc. Archit. Historians*, vol. 27 (1968), J. M. Crook, 'Regency Architecture in the West Country, The Greek Revival', *J. Royal Soc. of Arts* (June 1971), and D. Watkin on Buckland Filleigh in *The Country Seat*, ed. H. Colvin and J. Harris (1970). For dockyard buildings see J. Coad, 'Historic Architecture of HM Naval Base Devonport, 1689–1850', *Mariner's Mirror*, vol. 69 (1983). For Exeter during the eighteenth and nineteenth centuries, consult J. V. White, *Provincialism, A Study in the Work of General Practitioner Architects, 1760–1840* (1963), and R. Newton, *Eighteenth Century Exeter* (1984) and *Victorian Exeter* (1968). On Tavistock in the C19 see C. E. Hicks in *TDA*, vol. 79 (1947), P. V. Denham in *TDA*, vol. 110 (1978), and M. Brayshaw (on the Duke of Bedford's cottages) in *TDA*, vol. 114 (1982). On Nonconformist chapels see A. Brockett, *Nonconformity in Exeter 1650–1875* (1962), R. Thorne in *Devon's Traditional Buildings* (1980) and in *TDA*, vol. 107 (1975), and C. Stell's forthcoming R. C. H. M. volume on chapels in South West England.

There are now monographs on many of the major C19 architects who worked in Devon (J. M. Crook's *Burges*, J. Summerson's *Nash*, A. Quiney's *Pearson*, A. Saint's *Shaw*, etc.). Otherwise for buildings of the last hundred and fifty years one is still often dependent on contemporary sources. Much information on C19 churches comes from the Devon Nineteenth-Century Churches Project's research in the diocesan archives. B. F. L. Clarke's notes at the Council for the Care of Churches are also a useful source. An excellent study on two Arts and Crafts buildings is G. Hoare and G. Pyne's *Prior's Barn and Gimson's Coxen, Two Arts and Crafts Houses* (1978). The restoration of Dartington is enjoyably covered by R. Snell, *William Weir at Dartington Hall* (1987), the development of Exeter University by B. W. Clapp, *The University of Exeter, A History* (1982).

For an understanding of the post-war planning of the two main cities, J. Paton Watson and P. Abercrombie's *Plan for Plymouth* (1943) and Thomas Sharp's *Exeter Phoenix* (1946) are essential reading. N. Venning, *Exeter, The Blitz and Rebirth of the City* (1988), chronicles the post-war rebuilding; R. Fortescue Faulkes, *Exeter, A City Saved?* (Exeter Civic Society, 1977), discusses what has happened since.

Finally, a conspectus with case histories of settlements of all types is provided by Frances Griffith's *Devon, An Aerial View* (1988).

DEVON

ABBOTS BICKINGTON

ST JAMES. Very small and quite on its own. Early aisleless plan with
s transept (unmoulded pointed arch to the nave), and early w
tower without buttresses or w door, and with minute round-
headed bell-openings to N and S. The small N windows of nave and
chancel pointed trefoiled, i.e. *c.* 1300. The S transept and S nave
windows of two lights with tracery of about the same date. Ceiled
wagon roof. Restoration 1868. – STAINED GLASS. C14–15 fragments in the E window, a St Christopher, a Christ crucified, a St
Anthony, etc. – TILES. Quite a number of the Barnstaple tiles
much used in this part of Devon. – MONUMENT. Minor wall-
monument to Thomas Pollard †1710, placed diagonally in the NE
corner of the church.

COURT BARTON, close to the church. The site of the manorial court
held by Hartland Abbey; later the seat of the Pollards.

ABBOTSHAM

ST HELEN. Quite unusual in that the broad, short tower of rough
brown rubble (buttresses only at the foot, no pinnacles) is placed in
a N transeptal position, forming a refreshing group with the low
chancel and higher nave. The plan of nave, s transept, and chancel
points to the C13; see the two lancet windows (nave and chancel s).
Other windows renewed. There were restorations in 1848
(chancel) and 1870–2 (nave). Inside, the exceptional feature of two
completely domestic-looking two-light windows of the late C16–17
in the upper E wall of the nave above the chancel arch. Late
medieval ceiled wagon roofs in nave, transept, and chancel, in the
nave moulded ribs and angels with shields, in the chancel large
bosses. – FONT. Circular, Norman, fluted bowl, cable-moulding
round waist (cf. Beaford, Bradworthy, Clayhanger, and Parkham
nearby). – BENCH ENDS. Of the usual type, with representations
of the Crucifixion, Christ carrying the Cross, saints, a kneeling
figure, and a tumbler, apart from the usual tracery, Perp leaves,
and Renaissance medallions. – PULPIT. 1896, with openwork
wooden tracery. – STAINED GLASS. Several good windows by
Hardman; s transept 1849 by *Beer*, w window 1909 by *P. Bacon.* –
MONUMENT. John Willett †1736, still the late C17 type so amply
represented at Clovelly. Architectural, with Corinthian columns
and putti.

REHEBOTH BAPTIST CHAPEL. 1852. Small, of rubble. Gabled,
with arched openings with Gothick glazing. A small railed yard in
front.

(ABBOTSHAM COURT. The ancient seat of the Shebbeares. Remodelled in the early C18 with two-storey-and-dormers five-bay front. Wing and tower behind of 1841 and 1872, added by the Beste family.)

(CORNBOROUGH. Irregular Georgian front, two storeys, projecting wings. Cliff-top watch-tower of 1750.)

(KENWITH. Castellated Regency Gothic front, older behind. The dower house of the Pine-Coffin family.)

KENWITH VIADUCT. Part of the Bideford by-pass. 1986–7 by *MRM Partnership*. An eight-span box-girder bridge on slender concrete columns.

ABBOTSKERSWELL

ST MARY. The great surprise is the more than life-size late medieval STATUE, probably of the Virgin and Child, which was discovered built into the S chancel window. It is unfortunately very seriously damaged, but was once of high quality – see the clasp of the cloak and the modelling of the neck. The chancel – see the N lancet – is C13. N aisle Perp with granite piers of A type with capitals connected by a horizontal leaf frieze. The W tower has diagonal buttresses and a stair-turret in the centre of one side. Restored uneventfully by *Butterfield*, 1881–3. – SCREEN. With standard tracery of A type, the upper parts restored, incorporating a good vine-leaf frieze. – PARCLOSE SCREEN. – STAINED GLASS. E window by *Gibbs*, 1883.

CHURCH HOUSE. Restored but picturesque two-storey C16 building of rubble; wooden window-frames with arched lights, all renewed. On one side an external stair; also an internal newel, now blocked. On the other, two wooden doorways leading to a large and a small downstairs room.

A pretty older village centre, with an attractive group of houses on a raised causeway running up the hill, swamped by post-war estate housing on the other side of the valley.

THE PRIORY, Priory Road. The former R.C. priory of St Augustine, converted to flats in 1986–7 by *Keith Proctor*, was established for a community of Augustinian canonesses which, founded in 1609 at Louvain, moved to England in 1795 and, encouraged by Bishop Vaughan of Plymouth, settled in an existing house here in 1860. *Joseph Hansom* added an ambitious church to its E and priory buildings to its W in 1860–3. They are in grey limestone banded with red, much less bald than his earlier R.C. cathedral in Plymouth, and have an interestingly varied outline, with a polygonal chapter house (now an activities room), N of the church, and a massive octagonal E tower capped by a Rhenish spirelet. Hansom's contemporary St Wilfrid at Ripon, Yorkshire, has a similar tower – an indication of the growing interest in continental Gothic at this time. The sources here are mixed, for the windows of the church are French C13 Gothic, with Hansom's favourite spherical triangles in the clerestory; roundels with trefoils below.

The domestic buildings face S, a long main range with a central projecting clock turret and flanking wings. The E wing is the original plain rendered early Victorian house – an odd contrast with the picturesquely finicky detail of the rest. Trefoil-headed ground-floor windows; two storeys of originally smaller windows lit forty-eight cells above; steep roofs of patterned slates. The interiors, with spine corridor on axis with the church, and main rooms leading off, are generously scaled, with plenty of simple, slightly churchy joinery.

The church has been retained as a communal area, opened up by a new cross axis and N entrance near the W end, with a glazed porch. The domestic buildings hardly prepare one for the gawky fervour of the church interior, the aisleless nave crowded with oversize angel busts supporting clusters of marble shafts, squat upper columns carrying the arch-braces of the roof. Even stranger is the top-lit octagonal sanctuary within the tower, narrower than the nave, and set apart from it by two tall and slender marble columns. They give the illusion of the beginning of a spacious ambulatory – an ingenious handling of space on so small a scale, hinting at the treatment of the E end of Hansom's much larger church of the Holy Name, Manchester, although here the ambulatory stops short at two angled side altars. The lofty character of the sanctuary is explained by its most spectacular feature, the towering tabernacle over the altar, a spiky affair liberally adorned with angels, designed by *Benjamin Bucknall*, a pupil of Pugin, for the rite of the Perpetual Adoration of the Sacrament which the priory was granted the right to celebrate in 1860. A winding stair at the back leads up to the level where the monstrance was displayed. Much coloured stencilling on the sanctuary walls.

CEMETERY, to the E. A small, atmospheric survival. Enclosure with simple openwork crosses for the canonesses; grander carved stone memorials for the clergy. Nearby, a rustic wayside shrine, lined in bark and clad in corrugated sheet.

LIMEKILN. *See* Kingskerswell.

ACLAND BARTON   5030
Landkey

The original home of the Acland family, of which a younger branch settled in South Devon in the mid C16 (*see* Killerton). Main range and W wing of an early Tudor manor house, now a farmhouse. Rendered rubble walls. Windows of the main range all altered. The doorway with the date 1591 probably marks a remodelling, when an upper floor was inserted in the hall. Staircase within the hall, quite generous in scale, a straight flight, with turned balusters. Hall screen partly of very thick timbers, partly the more usual Elizabethan square panels. Across the screens passage older paired doorways with shouldered heads which led to the service rooms. The W wing, now separate from the house and truncated at the S end, has two stone windows of three arched lights on the ground floor and an arched doorway in between. Wooden windows above. The first floor has a fine wagon roof (uncommon in a secular building); moulded principals and carved bosses to the S part; a former chapel? Painted spiral decoration on the moulded wall-plate – an unusual survival. The centre of the wing later partitioned off as a chamber, with remains of decorative plaster cornice and wall decoration.

ALFINGTON
Ottery St Mary

1090

ST JAMES. Roughcast brick in an unadorned E.E. 1849–51 by *Butterfield*, financed by the Coleridge family (*see* Ottery St Mary); nave and chancel intended as temporary, hence very plain. N vestry and massively buttressed W belfry added by *Butterfield* in 1879–83. The iron tie-rods inside date from 1849. – FONT, with square base chamfered into the bowl, by *Butterfield*. – STAINED GLASS. W lancets with evangelist symbols (probably by *Gibbs*, 1882; RH). – E triplet with Crucifixion and saints in small medallions by *Hardman*, to designs by *Pugin*. – MONUMENT. Bishop Patteson, murdered in Melanesia in 1871: inlaid marbles, surely also by *Butterfield*.

PARSONAGE AND SCHOOL. 1850 by *Butterfield*. Brick with half-timbering and tile-hanging; inventively varied gables. Some Gothic elements, but the whole remarkable in its anticipation of the English vernacular revival of twenty years later. Main room with fine tiled fireplace surround.

ALVERDISCOTT

5020

ALL SAINTS. Unbuttressed W tower with small pinnacles. N aisle 1579, but its arcade on slim octagonal granite piers with elementary capitals is early C19. The straight timber entablature (instead of arches) was described as 'recent' in 1848. Later C16 wagon roof in the aisle. 1863–6 restoration by *Gould*. – FONT. Norman, of block-capital shape, with a little rosette, fleur-de-lys, etc., decoration. – REREDOS. 1880 by *Hems*. – PULPIT. Made up from early Renaissance panels. – (Late medieval TILES in the porch. – STAINED GLASS. An early work by *Shrigley & Hunt* of Lancaster, 1881, a rarity in the South West. RH) – MONUMENT. Thomas Welshe †1639, ten years old; touching, life-size effigy in Van Dyck dress on a tomb-chest.

83

(WEBBERY MANOR. Early C19 Tudor; mullion-and-transom windows with dripstones. Built by the Cutcliffe family.)

(WEBBERY BARTON. The older manor house. Of medieval origin, now chiefly late C17. Windows with keystones; C18 oak panelling in one room.)

ALWINGTON

4020

ST ANDREW. A big church, though quite on its own next to a farm. Fine tall W tower with buttresses of B type, gargoyles, and big pinnacles. Nave, N transept, S aisle. Aisle arcade of five bays with granite monoliths of A type, capitals to the main shafts only, and depressed pointed arches. Ceiled wagon roofs. – Portledge FAMILY PEW, picturesquely raised at the E end of the S aisle. Its jolly Jacobean carvings, including tall balusters and strapwork tops, were brought from the hall at Portledge (q.v.). – The wood-work in the church is altogether a most interesting jumble. The PULPIT, with Coffin arms and Renaissance medallions, was made up from bench ends and wall-plates of the wagon roofs in 1792, the REREDOS from bench ends from Parkham church in 1806. – FONT. Octagonal, Perp, granite, with elementary patterns. – TILES. In the nave, of the usual Barnstaple type. – BENCH ENDS. Many; also bench fronts made up of ends, etc. Motifs include tracery, Renaissance heads, and monsters. One has the date 1580. Also many early C20 bench ends in the old tradition by *Reuben Arnold*, a local craftsman. – STAINED GLASS. S aisle E: heraldic fragments. – Chancel E and N, 1868. – Chancel S, 1937 by *White-friars Studios*: delicate drawing in the Comper tradition. – MONU-MENTS. Richard Coffin † 1617 and wife. Two frontal demi-figures in shallow relief, holding hands; fifteen children below. Erected 1651. – Minor memorials to the Morrisons of Yeo Vale in the N chapel.

YEO VALE. The house has been demolished. It belonged to the Morrisons in the C18, to Charles Bruton in 1850. On the hill above, parts of a Perp chapel from the house, re-erected as a folly.
See also Portledge.

APPLEDORE
Northam

4030

A little maritime settlement at the meeting of the Taw and Torridge estuaries, remarkably unspoilt, a welcome contrast to the indifferent seaside suburbia between Northam and Westward Ho! The shipbuild-ing industry, which flourished especially in the C18 and C19 as a result of North American trade, miraculously still continues.

The compact streets of simple white-walled C18 to C19 houses are a delight to explore, enhanced by their hillside setting rising gently from the estuary. First the QUAY, made in 1845 in place of private jetties, but widened and straightened (a pity) in 1938–9. Since then some inappropriate municipal planting has been undertaken. An informal array of houses of varying heights faces the water, several once provided with large upper-floor windows to light sail lofts (Nos. 15a, 19). Near the centre THE BETHEL, a seamen's mission chapel, pedimented and with round-arched windows; at the end the SEAGATE HOTEL, mid C19, two-storeyed, with rusticated ground floor. Down a lane behind this to MEETING STREET, lined with simple cottages, with others tucked away down alleyways. On the W side the BAPTIST CHAPEL of 1858, stone, Gothic; higher up a larger INDEPENDENT CHAPEL of 1816 (now United Reformed), relatively grand, with a rendered pedimented front, Doric doorway, rusticated window surrounds, and a bell cupola. Attractive vistas also down VERNONS LANE and along MARKET STREET, a very narrow lane parallel to the Quay, with low houses with plenty of unspoilt small C19 shop-windows. Among them No. 23, the GLOBE HOTEL, makes a show with vermiculated quoins and channelled stucco. The market of 1829 at the W end has alas been replaced by an unsympathetic restaurant.

The other streets running uphill from Market Street, ONE END STREET and BUDE STREET, have a similar mixture of terraced cottages, interspersed with the occasional larger house enjoyably embellished with classical trimmings in the late Georgian tradition. Bude Street is the grander, with several five-window fronts with the speciality of variously enriched string courses (Nos. 2, 16, 24). No. 33, near the top, has a good Doric porch and upper pilasters.

Above these streets the more spacious ODUN ROAD, with the wealthier houses overlooking the estuary, among them ODUN HOUSE, now the Maritime Museum, three storeys with Doric porch. Back towards the sea along MYRTLE STREET, where there is a particularly handsome group of late Georgian stuccoed houses on the E side facing Richmond Yard, for example BRADBOURNE HOUSE, with big porch and end pilasters with recessed panels. Nearby, set back from the road, the remains of DOCTON HOUSE, rubble stone with granite doorways, supposed to have originated as a monastic hostel, converted into the C17 mansion of the Docton family. Their coat of arms is in a scrolly cartouche on the exterior.

Myrtle Street faces the site of the creek which was Appledore's earliest quay. It was transformed by the construction of RICHMOND YARD, built in 1849–56 by William Yeo. The tall stone walls enclose an impressive stone-lined DRY DOCK, 330 ft long. The yard is named after the centre of the Yeo family's North American trade, Richmond Bay in Prince Edward Island, from where half completed wooden sailing ships were sent to be finished off and fitted out at Appledore.

Down NEW QUAY STREET (named from a new quay of 1745 built by the merchant James Benson) another dock with a rubble stone two-storey warehouse, now a grain store. Further on BIDNA WHARF, with the APPLEDORE SHIPYARD of 1969, one of the largest covered shipyards in Europe when built, with room for two ships of up to 5,000 tons each.

RICHMOND ROAD was constructed to provide access to the new dock. On its w side THE HOLT, built for the dock owner William Yeo c. 1850. Stuccoed, eight bays, recessed centre with Ionic columns *in antis*. The ground-floor windows round-headed, the upper ones segment-headed. Now flats, with the grounds built up. Also in Richmond Road, METHODIST CHAPEL, 1851, a pretty design with over-large pointed windows with Gothic glazing, and a large quatrefoil tablet over the entrance.

IRSHA originated as a separate settlement beyond the Point at the N end of the Quay. It consists almost entirely of the picturesque narrow, winding IRSHA STREET, following the line of the shore, with simple terraces of cottages continuing on both sides for nearly a mile.

Between Irsha and Appledore proper the church which replaced an older chapel of ease.

ST MARY. 1838 by *J. Williams*, tower and w end 1909 by *John J. Smith* of Bideford. The original building with an E front with bare pinnacles and a very large Perp window between, in the tradition of the Commissioners' churches. Interior with broad nave, narrow aisles, octagonal piers, low clerestory, and rib-vaults of plaster on little cherubs' heads with spread-out wings. – Much Victorian STAINED GLASS. S aisle E by *F. Spear*, 1951.

ARLINGTON

ARLINGTON COURT. 1820–3 by *Thomas Lee* of Barnstaple for Colonel J.P.Chichester. Built on a new site, some way E of the church, to replace a plain Georgian house of *c.*1790 by *John Meadows*, which itself replaced an earlier building. There were Chichesters at Arlington from the C16 until 1949, when the estate was bequeathed to the National Trust.

Lee's house has a severely plain exterior; cream-painted stone, with unmoulded window openings, and as its only external decorations, giant Tuscan angle pilasters and a one-storey semicircular Greek Doric porch, in the centre of the short three-bay front. Five-bay garden front, two storeys, with the service basement concealed by a stone terrace. Attached to the N side a somewhat over-dominant service wing with rusticated window surrounds, added in 1864. Behind this a lower range, perhaps older.

As so often in Devon, the plain exterior does not prepare one for the lavishness within. The entrance porch leads into the STAIR-CASE HALL, in its present form of 1865, when the rooms on the N side of the house were replaced by the grand staircase which starts in one flight and divides in two to reach the gallery or upper landing. Over the original, smaller, staircase hall a rectangular roof-light (earlier, brought from Buckland House); shallow segmental arches at either end of this space on both floors; the plasterwork (rosettes in coffering) perhaps redone in the C19. The chief of the original rooms are the BOUDOIR to the E, and the three interconnecting rooms along the S front. All have very delicately detailed plaster ceilings with neo-Grecian friezes; the one in the centre of the S front is an oval on shallow Soanian arches. Between the three S rooms pairs of yellow scagliola columns. In the SW room wallpaper with bold green scrollwork said to be original. Large C19 green marble fireplace in the SE room, with splendid steel grate. The boudoir has canted end walls, now with mirrors flanked by Raphaelesque pilasters (later C19 additions). Fine small Ashburton marble chimneypiece. In the adjacent MUSIC ROOM, the painted ceiling was regrettably destroyed when this part of the house was converted into staff flats *c.*1950. The room was restored in 1977–8. Original plain marble fireplace. In the DINING ROOM on the E front (formerly the library) a delicate late C18 marble fireplace, presumably re-used from the previous house. (The Victorian dining room N of the house has been demolished.) On the HALF LANDING, displayed against crude round-headed windows, some C19 heraldic stained glass.

STABLES, near the church. 1864, a noble L-shaped group with a cloister of rusticated arches, and a stone clock-turret over a pedimented central niche. Opposite the entrance a small GRANARY brought from Dunsland, the National Trust house tragically destroyed by fire in 1967.

GROUNDS. Landscaping largely of before 1850. Magnificently sublime planting taking advantage of the steep valley to the W of the house, around a LAKE with an island, created by damming the river Yeo. Near the water an urn in memory of Miss Rosalie Chichester †1949, an Adam design with an inscription cut by *Reynolds Stone*.

Across the lake, two stone TOWERS set romantically among trees, an unfinished project by *William Dredge*, of *c*. 1849, for a suspension bridge to take a drive from the main road. S and E of the house a C19 flower garden, a conservatory (rebuilt in 1983 incorporating parts of 1843), and a wilderness with pond. Beyond is an OBELISK of 1887.

ST JAMES. The church lies in the extensive, beautifully landscaped grounds of the house, with a magnificent yew tree on the S side. Rebuilt in 1846 by *R.D.Gould*: nave, N transept, chancel; Perp tracery. W tower of 1899, a copy of the old tower, with buttresses of type B and polygonal stair-turret. It has niches for images high in the buttresses. – Unusual chancel floor TILES, black with white scrollwork, executed by *Powell's*. – STAINED GLASS. E window by *Henry Holiday*, 1885; white figures against Morris-inspired scroll-work and plants. – MONUMENTS. Worn effigy of a lady, C14, in a N recess in the chancel. – Many minor examples of the changing taste of the C17–19. First in date is Gasgoigne Canham † 1667, architec-tural, with strapwork and putti on open pediment. – Edward Bampfield † 1720, small, but with pretty flower garlands. – John Meadows † 1791 (the architect of the previous house), inscription only: 'Nature had stamp'd upon his mien a smile/ That mark'd his mind insensitive of guile'. – Mary Ann Chichester † 1791, by *J.F. Moore* and *J. Smith* of London, handsome big wall-monument in white, pink, dark red, and grey marbles; a circular relief is the main motif. – Mary Anne Gertrude Chichester † 1858, by *Physick* of London, with an angel taking the young lady up to heaven. – Lieut. Louis Chichester † 1858, also by *Physick*, naval trophies. – Major George Chichester † 1876, Gothic, alabaster aedicule. – Rosalie Caroline Chichester † 1949, the last of the Chichesters of Arlington, by *John Piper*. Oval plaque in the early C19 manner, with urn above; fern and sea-shell decoration.

Near the church GLEBE HOUSE, the former rectory, with curved Greek Doric porch, bowed ends, and deep eaves, very elegant and restrained. Built soon after 1824 for the Rev. James Chichester. (Vaulted entrance hall, and a good staircase with wrought-iron balusters.)

5030   ASH BARTON
                        2 m. E of Braunton

Farmhouse incorporating fragments of quite a sizeable manor house, mostly C17, the seat of the Bellews. Courtyard plan. Gabled main range with symmetrical W front, the details still in the early C17 tradition although the main gable carries the date 1665. Doorway with hoodmoulds; mostly blocked or reduced C17 windows, orig-inally evidently of four lights or more. Two lower ranges behind, with smaller mullioned windows still preserved. In the main range two rooms with bolection-moulded panelling, and a good C17 dog-leg stair with turned balusters and moulded string. Several C17 doorways with stopped mouldings.

ASH HOUSE
Iddesleigh

5000

The seat of the Mallets from 1530 to 1881. An attractive early C18 front range, one room deep. Seven bays, two storeys, stuccoed, the centre with pediment on pilasters.

ASHBURTON

7060

Ashburton is a town of great charm, situated in a steep-sided green valley with the moor and the extensive woods of Holne Chase close at hand. There are few buildings of individual importance, but many modest C18–19 houses to delight the eye: gables, slate-hanging, and early Victorian fronts with quoins picked out in another colour. Unlike Totnes, there is surprisingly little earlier building in the main streets (apart from a few deeply buried C16 and C17 structures behind later fronts), despite the fact that the town, lying on the old Exeter–Plymouth road, was a borough from 1238, deriving its prosperity from both tin and cloth. In the later Middle Ages it was the most important of the four Devon stannary towns. Much rebuilding of the C18–19 was encouraged by the coaching trade (the town is halfway between Exeter and Plymouth). The town centre has survived remarkably unspoilt by the C20 (apart from some clearance for road widening in North Street, which destroyed some medieval houses, and mediocre rebuilding of the 1970s at the N end), helped by the bypass which takes the through traffic, and, more recently, benefiting from the careful planning control operating within the Dartmoor National Park.

St Andrew. Reached through the churchyard by means of a fine iron gate of c. 1700. The W tower is the most imposing feature, 92 ft high, an austere design in grey granite, with set-back buttresses and a powerful polygonal turret in the centre of the N face (the show side facing the town), flanked by narrow belfry windows. Octagonal pinnacles. The tower was chosen as the prototype for Totnes in 1449, and so is probably of the earlier C15. The rest of the church is of limestone rubble, rebuilt at around the same time. The N side is a beautifully varied composition: NW stair-turret, one bay of the aisle, N porch (originally two-storeyed), transept between two further aisle bays, chancel, and finally a very odd low room projecting beyond and slightly below the chancel (vaulted by a pointed tunnel-vault). Everything embattled. The S side also has a SW turret, battlements, and indeed everything as on the N, except that the porch no longer exists.

Inside, five-bay arcades, making no distinction between chancel chapels, transepts, and nave. Tall octagonal piers (with concave surfaces, an exceptional refinement); double-chamfered arches. Very elementary Perp tracery of the four-light aisle and the five-light transept and E windows. Fine long wagon roofs and aisle ceilings, the N aisle with carved decoration. In the S aisle appears the initial L, supposed to refer to Bishop Lacy (1420–56). In transepts and chancel chapels four re-used trefoil-headed PISCINAS. The interior is otherwise disappointing, the result of over-much restoration. Many of the older furnishings were stripped out in the later

C18.* Sanctuary restored 1840. Thoroughgoing restoration by *G.E. Street* in 1882–3 (walls scraped, chancel raised, E window reconstructed, screens added, tower arch and W windows rebuilt to new designs). – PAINTING. Crucifixion by *Legassick*, a local artist, part of a former reredos. – Two splendid C18 CANDELABRA.

OUR LADY AND ST PETROC (R.C.), Eastern Road. 1935 by *Edward Walters*, small, of grey stone; apsed sanctuary added 1976–7 by *Charles White*. – STAINED GLASS by Father *Charles Norris*: two W windows in C13 style, 1936; eight E lancets of St Stephen, St John, and silhouettes of saints, in slab glass set in epoxy resin, 1977.

UNITED REFORMED CHURCH, North Street. Formerly Congregational. Ashburton's earliest Nonconformist church, known as the 'Great Meeting' after enlargements in 1739; refronted, extended and regalleried in 1818; later alterations in 1892 and 1965. W front with a wide central doorway and two heights of window. E front with three windows, the central one formerly a door to the galleries. Interior with late C18 candle sconces, chandelier, and clock. – STAINED GLASS. E window large, early C17 Flemish, of the Presentation in the Temple, given in 1934, formerly in the chapel of the Royal Female Orphanage, Westminster.

METHODIST CHAPEL, West Street. 1835, enlarged 1908, with Sunday school in front. Unusually grand giant Ionic portico, with pediment.

ST LAWRENCE'S TOWER, St Lawrence's Lane. A survival from a chapel (said to be once part of a bishop's palace) given to the town in 1314 by Bishop Stapledon for the newly formed Guild of St Lawrence. The tower is probably early C16: lower two stages with set-back buttresses, NW turret, corner pinnacles; spire renewed in the C19. Roughcast in 1931. Perp W window lighting an upper room formerly used by the grammar school recorded from the mid C16. The body of the church rebuilt as schoolroom-cum-courtroom *c.* 1700, a single room with a good plaster cornice with large pendants, C18 benefactors' arms in relief below. Early C19 Gothic panelled benches. E extension 1911.

TOWN HALL, North Street. Built by Lord Clinton as a Market Hall, 1849–50 by *A. Norman*, Italianate, with an asymmetrically placed tower. The S end was insensitively truncated for road widening in the 1970s.

RAILWAY STATION (former), St Lawrence's Lane. Built for a branch line from Totnes in 1872. Now a garage and hardly recognizable. Nearby, the stucco-trimmed SILENT WHISTLE (named after the line was closed in 1962).

PERAMBULATION. The main street – East Street, West Street – winds its way down a hill and up again, with the broader North Street running off at its lowest point, and St Lawrence's Lane, not quite opposite, leading S. Starting near the parish church, WEST STREET has rewarding contributions from every century. Several good houses framing the vista downhill: No. 32 and MAPLETON HOUSE both with slate-hung upper floors, one with giant corner pilasters, the other with rusticated quoins; BANK HOUSE with handsome enriched dentilled cornice. Off to the S behind the Methodist church, St Andrew's Close, a C20 development worth a

---

*Pulpit and lectern are now at Bigbury.

detour: housing for the elderly by *Seagrim & Read*, 1974–6, for Teignbridge District Council. Pleasantly laid out, if a little mean in its details. An archway leads to white-rendered houses grouped loosely around a square. The low stone community room was converted from the town mill. Further downhill in West Street on the s side, a moulded Gothic archway leading to Church Path, then, facing down North Street, LLOYDS BANK, 1893, of red stone with shaped gables, nicely detailed, but modest in comparison with the handsome NATIONAL WESTMINSTER (formerly Devon and Cornwall) BANK of 1891 further on in East Street. This is the one grand classical front in Ashburton, all granite, the ground floor polished, the upper floor left rough; pedimented doors and upper windows. The rest of West Street is Georgian and earlier.

In NORTH STREET the notable buildings are the CARD HOUSE, with twin gable above two floors of slate-hanging with punched patterns of hearts, clubs, etc., apparently unique; the TOWN HALL (*see* above); and No. 4, with a medieval stone archway. On the w side, beside the Town Hall, KINGS BRIDGE, with a delightful view of the backs of old houses overlooking the River Ashburn and the town leat. No. 5 KINGSBRIDGE LANE is the best surviving example in the town of an C18 wool-weaver's house, with large first-floor windows and weatherboarded top-floor drying loft. (Nos. 81 and 83 North Street and 22 West Street are similar.)

Now back to the junction of the main roads and up EAST STREET. On the l. No. 33, with fish-scale slate-hanging. Further up the hill the GOLDEN LION, with a life-size lion on the porch, built as a private house *c.* 1790 for Nicholas Tripe, surgeon. Brick front with five windows to the street. Two full-height canted bays to the w; to the E an extension of *c.* 1820 with upper assembly room lit at either end by a pretty derivation of a Palladian window: a triplet of arches without intermediate pilasters. Immediately E a short early C19 three-storey terrace with delicate lattice balconies. Opposite the Golden Lion a handsome stone CONDUIT with domical roof, early C18 in style, although erected in 1791. Behind it, No. 65, formerly part of the Spread Eagle Inn, a plain front concealing fragmentary medieval fabric and some linenfold panelling. At the top of East Street an elaborately bargeboarded former coach-house on the s side. On the N, Ireland House (No. 83), earlier C19, given by the Dean of Westminster, John Ireland, to the grammar school which he had attended; restored and converted to flats in 1977. Beyond, in EASTERN STREET, THE HALL, a charming villa of 1803 on the edge of the town. Three bays, lower wings, with busts of Byron and Scott. (Polygonal entrance hall, with bust of the builder, Mr Tucker, by *P. Olivieri*, 1828. Staircase with one fluted and one twisted baluster to each tread.)

BELFORD MILL. Four storeys, with weatherboarded top drying floor. Probably an C18 woollen mill which became a corn mill before 1850.

DRUIDS MINE. Mid-C19 ruins of an engine house and separate conical chimney, stone with brick top.

In BORO' WOOD a well sited embanked ENCLOSURE of unknown date.

AUSEWELL WOOD. Traces of medieval and post-medieval MINES and charcoal burning.

5090

ASHBURY

ST MARY. Rebuilt by *J. F. Gould* in 1871–3 at the expense of Henry Woollcombe, Archdeacon of Barnstaple, whose family lived at Wadlands, the manor house (demolished *c.*1965). Plain, small, aisleless. Older w tower with diagonal buttresses and small pinnacles. Much re-used material. Simple whitewashed interior. Redundant 1977 but preserved by Woollcombe descendants.

STATION, now a private house. Built *c.*1873. Goods shed with wooden canopy.

WADLAND BARTON. Formerly a manor house, now a farmhouse. Simple timber four-light window, the date 1568 inside.

ASHBURY HOUSE. Demolished 1934. The porch is now at Churston House, West Putford.

9070

ASHCOMBE

ST NECTAN. A rare dedication, cf. Cornwall, and also Hartland, North Devon. Unbuttressed, markedly tapering w tower of early character, s transept, chancel with evidence of original lancet windows. There was a consecration in 1259. Exterior with harsh ribbon pointing, interior whitewashed. The Perp arches to chancel and s transept and the N aisle with B type piers added by the Kirkhams, lords of the manor – see the heraldry in the standard capitals. Ceiled roof with small bosses. The pretty panelling of the w wall l. and r. of the tower arch belongs to the restoration of 1824–6 by *Salvin*, then working at Mamhead. From this time also the chancel N and s windows, traceried s door, s porch, and the rebuilding of the N aisle. – BENCH ENDS. Mostly two-tier tracery; also Kirkham arms. – STAINED GLASS. E window with medieval fragments, two C17 Flemish roundels, and brightly coloured decorative glass of the 1820s. – N aisle E: quite a lively Ascension, 1885.

VICARAGE. Nice early C19 villa with veranda.

SCHOOL (former), at the crossroads, 1½ m. SE. Probably by *Salvin*. Very simple: cruciform, red sandstone, Perp doorway.

ASHCOMBE TOWER. *Brian O'Rorke*'s only major country house, built in 1935 for Sir Ralph Rayner, M.P., and interesting in showing how an architect with modernist leanings (O'Rorke was best known for his interiors for ocean liners) could find a pared-down Arts and Crafts tradition compatible. Long rendered exterior with gabled wings and slate roofs, sparing dressings of rough limestone to accentuate the verticals, the central windows on the garden side laced together. A squat older tower incorporated at one end. The interiors (still with their contemporary furnishings) are more boldly progressive.

LITTLE HALDON. On the heathland N of Teignmouth golf course some Bronze Age BARROWS and a prehistoric non-defensive circular EARTHWORK called Castle Dyke. The PORT WAY running NE–SW across Little Haldon is believed to be prehistoric in origin.

ASHE HOUSE
N of Musbury

A house of the Drake family from the late C15 to 1793. Damaged in the Civil War, and again in 1787 when a fire destroyed offices and stables. What remains is a long two-storey range, the l. part with C16 arched windows of four lights, the r. with mullioned-and-transomed windows below dripstones. Projecting behind this part is the southern of the two wings added in 1669. Separate CHAPEL with C16 straight-headed mullioned windows. Some building material was brought from Newenham Abbey, Axminster, after the Dissolution.

ASHFORD

ST PETER. Rebuilt by *R. D. Gould* of Barnstaple, 1854. The N tower with spire – Barnstaple parish church *en miniature* – was completed (or rebuilt) in 1798. Inside, a confusing jumble of old bits of WOODWORK re-used haphazardly, as at Weare Giffard and Alwington: bench ends in the pulpit, Elizabethan panelling in the bench ends and the vestry. – SCULPTURE. Small damaged C14 relief figure of St John (vestry). – STAINED GLASS. Bright E window by *Gibbs* (*Builder*, 1862).

GOSPEL HALL, by the roadside. 1835. Small, rubble, gabled (windows altered). In a small walled burial ground.

(ASHFORD HOUSE. Early C19 stucco, with veranda.)

ASHILL
Uffculme

ST STEPHEN. Combined church and schoolroom, 1882 by *R. M. Fulford* (cf. Avonwick). The schoolroom to the N of the nave divided off by movable shutters. Red-brick exterior, buff brick inside, enlivened by a stone chancel arch and tiling in the chancel. – Sturdy low wooden chancel SCREEN and other fittings. – STAINED GLASS. E window 1904; other windows with the original pattern glass of 1882 designed by *Fulford* and executed by *Drake*. Pretty stylized floral forms in the window-heads.

ASHPRINGTON

ST DAVID. Tall and very slim W tower, rising in four tapering stages without buttresses and with a low NE stair-turret, no doubt the earliest part of the church. S aisle with big red sandstone battlements; battlements also on the N side, which has a polygonal stair-turret. The porch has lost its upper floor. The piers tall, of B type, with capitals only to the four shafts. Ceiled wagon roof in nave and chancel. Extensively restored in 1845, including replacement of all windows. – FONT. Circular, Norman, with palmette frieze and a strip of cable-moulding above. – SCREEN. Two old doors remain, standard type A tracery, and remains of paintings of saints on the wainscoting. – The PARCLOSE SCREENS, PULPIT, LECTERN, REREDOS, and other chancel woodwork all done by *Herbert Read* between 1900 and 1930, an ensemble of good traditional craftsmanship. – LADY CHAPEL ALTAR. 1966 by *Herman Lewis*; artificial stone. – BRASS. Inscription and two shields to William Sumaster † 1589. – MONUMENTS. Sir John Kelland of Painsford † 1679. Nice scrolly decoration. – Henry Blackhaller of Sharpham † 1684. Architectural, with columns (in organ chamber). – Jane Pownall of Sharpham † 1778. Large standing figure bent over an urn. Unsigned.

In the village, pretty C19 Sharpham estate cottages, and a village school, all with bargeboarded gables and dormers and lattice window-panes; also ASHPRINGTON HOUSE, early C19, three-bay front with broad projecting eaves and a Tuscan porch.

PAINSFORD, I m. W. The seat of the Kellands in the C17, now reduced to an L-shaped farmhouse, with rendered Victorian garden front. Ruins of a loggia with octagonal piers remain from a wing projecting to the W. At the back, s and W walls of a separate chapel refounded by John Kelland in 1687. s doorway with remains of an inscription. Ruins of once substantial outbuildings. Some also of C17 date: E of the house a building with carriage arch and mullion-and-transom windows; close to it a later building with red-brick arches and circular windows.

See also Sharpham House.

ASHREIGNEY

6010

ST JAMES. The tower to the N of the nave in a transeptal position, as in some other North Devon churches (*see* Introduction). Buttresses of type B stopping at a moderate height; low obelisk pinnacles. s porch with an outer door whose outer moulding rests on angel corbels. Nave and s aisle of four bays, the arcade on B type piers with capitals only to the main shafts, the capitals of a concave octagonal form (cf. Chittlehampton). Open, unceiled wagon roofs in both, in the aisle on angel corbels. Restored in 1889 by *Samuel Hooper* of Hatherleigh. – ROYAL ARMS. 1713.

ZION METHODIST CHAPEL. Built in 1906 by the Bible Christians, replacing a former chapel whose graveyard remains in the valley below. Slated roof, rubble walls; corners and openings lavishly trimmed with the pale brick and terracotta typical of the period.

(WOODROW BARTON. Virtually intact late medieval roof. C. Hulland.)

ASHTON

8080

ST MICHAEL. The largest of the churches in the upper Teign valley, now surrounded only by a few houses on its rocky eminence. All Perp, the W tower with diagonal buttresses, plain granite windows, and obelisk pinnacles. W door with quatrefoil decoration in the spandrels. s doorway with trefoil-headed niche above. Tower arch with multi-shafted responds made up of colossal pieces of granite.

N aisle of five bays, Beer stone piers of an unusually elaborate profile (two shafts in the diagonals). Unceiled wagon roofs. Sensitively restored in 1881–3, and in 1899–1901 by *C. E. Ponting.* – FONT. Perp, with Chudleigh heraldry.

SCREENS. The rood screen runs right across. Tracery of standard type and three bands of cornice decoration plus cresting. The central band is substantially original with traces of early paint. The screen was restored in 1908, with a new rood loft, by *Herbert Read.* Wainscoting with thirty-two small painted figures of saints and doctors of the church, male and female alternating, on red and green grounds earlier than most. But the really remarkable figures at Ashton are those on the back of the screen, i.e. within the N 38 chapel (formerly the Chudleigh family chapel). Together with the fragmentary remains of glass and wall painting (*see* below), they indicate the elaborate nature of the late medieval decoration of such a chapel.* The paintings are mostly demi-figures of prophets with beautifully twisting scrolls, largely monochrome, of wholly convincing quality, perhaps because copied from woodcuts or blockbooks. Most of the inscriptions refer to the Incarnation and are taken from the services for Advent, the feast of the Annunciation, and (more unusually) the feast of the Transfiguration. In addition, the Annunciation appears on the E side of the doors, and the Visitation on the side of the parclose screen facing the chancel. The tracery of this screen is also out of the ordinary, with more bladder-like shapes than usual.

PULPIT. Very handsome, Jacobean, square, with the customary short blank arcades as adornment of the panels, and with a square sounding-board. – BENCH ENDS with two-tier tracery. – ALTAR RAILS. C17. – SOUTH DOOR. Late medieval, studded. – WALL PAINTING, N wall of N chapel, above the Chudleigh burial vault. C15; Christ with Emblems of the Passion. – STAINED GLASS. In the N chapel fragments of high quality including figures of Gabriel, St Sidwell with a scythe, a kneeling knight, and heraldic glass of the Chudleighs, Bishop Lacy (1420–55), and Bishop Courtenay (1478–86). – Chancel E window c. 1881 by *F. Drake.* – ROYAL ARMS. Painted; 1735. – BRASS. William Honnywell † 1614, with bones and skull. – MONUMENTS. Coffin-shaped Purbeck marble slab with cross (cf. Brixham, Crediton, Kingswear). – George Chudleigh † 1657. Painted wall-monument with much heraldry and symbols of mortality. No effigy.

The Chudleigh seat from the C14 to 1745 was at PLACE (later LOWER BARTON), abandoned after the family moved to their new mansion at Haldon near Dunchideock. By Polwhele's time the kitchens had been converted to two farmhouses. Much altered in the 1930s. The surviving range was part of a large courtyard house. The r. room, with kitchen fireplaces, has a ceiled wagon roof (probably of the 1930s) below a genuine medieval roof. Good arch-braced and wind-braced roofs over the other parts.

LOWER BRAMBLE. An unassuming stone house hidden away in a remote valley, now a farmhouse on the familiar tripartite plan, but once grander, as is shown by the scale of the hall (originally c. 22 ft wide) and the good medieval roof, perhaps early C15. The porch

---

*For further details see the excellent guide: *Ashton Church, Devon*, by Marion Glasscoe, 1984.

with stone archway, the inner doorway with a moulded wooden frame, the moulded beam to a former internal jetty over the cross-passage, and other unusually ornate doorways all date from an excellent remodelling of c. 1600. Above the plain plaster barrel ceiling to the chamber over the hall three bays survive of the smoke-blackened roof. Main and subsidiary chamfered trusses with arch-braced principals up to the upper collars. The more uncommon features are the lower cranked collars carrying king-posts halved on the upper collars, supporting a square-set ridge-piece. Lower wind-braces; two sets of purlins, butted to the main trusses, but clasped to the intermediate ones by small upright pieces.

ASHWATER

3090

ST PETER. The surprising thing about this church is the ancient piers between nave and S aisle (the arcade is of six bays). As they are at present, they alternate between an octagonal shape (buff stone) and a variety of the A type (granite) in which the main shafts towards the E and W are duplicated. The arches are all granite. The explanation is, no doubt, that a C14 arcade of octagonal piers was later replaced by the C15 A type arcade and that this had to duplicate the shafts to tally with the greater thickness of the octagonal piers. The church may have begun as an aisleless cruciform building, from which the N transept remains. The nave is uncommonly wide. Nave and S aisle, also wide, with wagon roofs; Perp windows of granite throughout. Chancel rebuilt in the 1880s, with wooden chancel arch. Above the priest's door on the S side a re-used C12 corbel. Unbuttressed W tower with obelisk pinnacles and a NE turret of odd plan (curve instead of angle to the W), rising higher than the tower. Tower arch tall and unmoulded on the simplest imposts.

FONT. Norman, of polyphant(?), with angle faces and on the main sides tendrils, scrolls, etc., and also on the W side a running animal in a frame with two symmetrical animal-heads. – BENCH ENDS. Some old, but much restored. – Lavish WOODWORK of c. 1882, including REREDOS with flamboyant canopy-work over a tile painting, STALLS, and TOWER SCREEN. Some older BENCH ENDS, much restored. – ROYAL ARMS, S wall. 1638, large, of plaster. – MONUMENT. To a member of the Carminow family, probably Thomas Carminow †1442. The most ambitious late medieval monument in north-west Devon. Recumbent effigy on a tomb-chest with elaborately cusped quatrefoils. Canopy with a depressed pointed arch, double-cusped. Top with leaf band and a row of quatrefoils. The design of the canopy is derived from those of Bishop Branscombe's and Bishop Stafford's tombs in Exeter Cathedral. Inside, the little vault is coffered with diagonally placed pointed quatrefoils. At the W end remains of a panel with the Trinity.

(OLD RECTORY. Attractive, irregular late Georgian rendered exterior; mid C17 core. Two and three storeys. Two Venetian windows at the back of the main range. On one rear wing an early

C19 bell-turret; the other wing has Gothick windows, said to be reset. Garden wall of cob with niche studded with stones.)

SANDYMOOR CROSS. Remains of a substantial Bronze Age BAR-ROW CEMETERY, much reduced by ploughing.

ATHERINGTON

5020

ST MARY. The W tower has diagonal buttresses only at the foot, but rises to an unusual height. No pinnacles. The stair-turret attached on the S side, not quite at the E corner, rises unusually high above the tower. W door with fleuron decoration. Nave, N aisle (four-bay arcade, A type piers with capitals to the main shafts, depressed pointed arches), S transept, lower chancel. Much restored by *J. L. Pearson* in 1882–4, when all the windows were renewed, but the curiously un-Devonian tracery pattern of full-height mullions crossed by intersecting round-headed sub-arches is apparently authentic. In the NE chapel two angel corbels on the E wall. Unceiled wagon roofs with bosses in nave, aisle, and chancel, restored.

SCREENS. The screen between nave and chancel is probably the one brought from Umberleigh chapel, demolished c. 1800. Three four-light panels, each narrow panel with crocketed and finialled ogees, with tracery below and above; square top (cf. Parracombe). – Between N aisle and N chapel a much richer screen. The almost complete preservation of the rood-loft gallery is unique in Devon (cf. Marwood), and much imitated by restorers of other screens. Tracery of B type, ribbed coving, the ribs rising from angel figures, and between the ribs partly Perp tracery and partly early Renaissance foliage and putti (cf. Lapford, Marwood). Cornice of three bands. Loft gallery with thick niches with elaborate and delicate openwork ribbing on the undersides of the little vaults of the niches. The back of the loft is patched with painted boards with post-Reformation inscriptions and coats of arms. – BENCH ENDS. Asymmetrical (a type more common in East Anglia than the West Country), with tracery patterns including the 'Atherington' intersecting arches. – STAINED GLASS. N chapel N made up in 1883 by *Clayton & Bell* from many C15 fragments; a Virgin and Child is recognizable. – E window also by *Clayton & Bell*.

MONUMENTS. Knight, perhaps Sir William de Champernowne, c. 1240, not well preserved, but of excellent quality. Around the tapering slab a band of stiff-leaf foliage, similar to (although a little more developed than) that on the Longespée effigy at Salisbury Cathedral (of c. 1230–40). The drapery is also comparable. The Atherington effigy is one of the earliest in the country with crossed legs (cf. also Shepton Mallet, Somerset), a fashion that may have started with the West Country sculptors who derived their style from the W front of Wells Cathedral. – Knight and Lady, possibly Sir Ralph Wylmington and wife. Later C14; see her hairstyle. Tomb-chest with quatrefoil decoration. – Sir John Basset, c. 1530. Brass on tomb-chest with quatrefoil decoration; knight and two wives, twelve children in two groups and shields above and below. Brought here in 1818, with other Bassett memorials, from the chapel of their house, Umberleigh. – Anthony Snell, yeoman, † 1707. Handsome architectural tablet with floral decoration.

BAPTIST CHAPEL. 1833. Tall, rubble, low-pitched gable, arched openings with intersecting glazing bars. Later Sunday School adjacent.

(ASHLEY MANOR. Stuccoed, c. 1830, with additions. Garden front with full-height bowed centre.)

UMBERLEIGH HOUSE. The seat of the Bassetts, much remodelled c. 1800. Some carved panels from the porch are at Watermouth Castle (q.v.). Unremarkable rendered exterior, five bays with extensions, concealing a medieval core with a heavily moulded roof of high quality: eleven arch-braced trusses with short, curved feet, three tiers of purlins, remains of wind-braces at two levels. The outbuildings behind incorporate remains of a C13 chapel (two lancet windows and a blocked doorway).

6040   AVETON GIFFORD

ST ANDREW. Reduced to a shell in the Second World War, but faithfully rebuilt in 1948–57. A spatially satisfying design of c. 1250, unusual in a county of widely standardized late medieval churches. Cruciform, with an aisleless nave and a dominating crossing tower with large SW corner turret. The arches of the crossing tower each rest on three strong shafts with moulded capitals. The N wall of the nave has single lancets high up, with inner nook-shafts. The E window and S transept windows also have nook-shafts, but in addition elaborate geometrical tracery with circles containing quatrefoils or cinquefoils, and even circles containing secondary foiled inner circles. The only trouble is that it has not been possible to verify whether these windows, the grandest in Devon (except for Exeter), are original or at least correctly renewed; Davidson in his manuscript notes of c. 1830–40 does not mention them at all. The porch, on the other hand, is unquestionably genuine. It possesses an outer doorway with three orders, an inner with two, its depressed pointed arch from inside partly blocked by the smaller, steeper pointed opening from outside. A specially interesting feature of crossing arches and porch arches is that the arch mouldings start direct on the moulded capitals with trunk-like shapes as big in diameter as the shafts below the capitals, but that the rest of the arch voussoirs consists of more finely moulded, thinner members dying into these strange trunks. The chancel was flanked by later chancel chapels with arcades whose piers are of A type, granite, with capitals only to the main shafts. The chapels have not been restored, but their Dec windows have been reset within the blocked arcades.

BRIDGE, on the road from Modbury to Kingsbridge. Causeway 1,200 ft long, with six arches of which five are still medieval. Eight more blocked arches.

(CHANTRY. C18 and early C19. Rendered, with veranda and an apsed music room.)

AVONWICK   7050

ST JAMES. 1878 by *R.M.Fulford*. Aisleless church-cum-schoolroom
(cf. Ashill). – Simple lancet-style open SCREENS between nave
and chancel by *Hems*.

Avonwick is a scattered settlement with several attractive late
Georgian frontages and a former MILL by the river some way to
the W.

BLACK HALL. *See* North Huish.

OLD BRIDGE (Devon Backbone). Single arch of 27-ft span, originally for packhorse use.

STATION, now a house. Built in 1893. Stone with limestone dressings. Three massive chimneys. A wooden canopy, now with side
walls, over the platform. Goods shed with large doors and a smaller
stone shed to the N. Signal finials on the gateposts.

AWLISCOMBE   1000

ST MICHAEL. Unbuttressed W tower with stair-turret. The pretty S
porch, with doorways with fleurons to the S and also to the W and
with niches above, was built by Thomas Chard, the last abbot of
Forde Abbey and a native of the parish. Remodelling of other parts
of the church probably also of the early C16, especially the S
transept, which has a S window of five lights (tracery renewed
1886–7) also with fleurons in the jambs. Inside, this window is
embellished by quatrefoil panelling set into the concave reveal, and
by niches for statues to l. and r. The arch into the transept is also
panelled (rather more neatly), and decorated with fleurons. Tower
arch likewise panelled, as is the arch into the N chancel chapel,
evidently an addition, as it appears behind the last bay of the
normal N arcade. This has the same enriched B section of piers as
at Broadhembury and Bradninch. Ceiled wagon roofs, the one in
the chancel dating mostly from *R.M.Fulford*'s restoration of
1886–7, painted by *Palfrey* of London. Organ chamber added at
the same time.

FONT. Plain, octagonal, Perp, with four-petalled flowers in the
panels. – SCREEN. Of stone, with angels as corbels at the foot of 34
the tracery. Bligh Bond thinks the screen was originally, like that
at Compton Bassett in Wiltshire, of veranda type, i.e. with two
walls behind each other and a vault below the rood-loft. The
central entrance is decorated with fleurons like the porch. The
cornice replaced by C19 battlements. – PULPIT, DESKS, and
LECTERN all of 1886–7 by *Fulford*, executed by *Hems*. – FONT
COVER. 1890 by *Hems*. – TILES in the chancel by *Godwin*. The
diapering of the chancel walls has been whitewashed. – Painted
ROYAL ARMS of Charles II over the S door. – (BELL. Exeter
foundry, *c.*1480, with coin impressions in the crown. JS) –
STAINED GLASS. In the S transept E window a few tiny medieval
fragments brought from Ivedon House, to where glass from the
chantry chapel had migrated. – MONUMENTS. John Pring of
Ivedon, who fought with Wellington, †1820. Neo-Grecian tablet

with medallion profile, by *Peter Rouw*. – Captain Daniel Pring
†1846. Bust in classical niche.

SCHOOL, dug into the hill S of the church. 1875, altered.

TRACEY. Derelict in 1988. Dramatically sited on a hillside terrace
1 m. E. The rendered exterior of *c.* 1790, with its once elegant Ionic
loggia along the main front, conceals an earlier C18 house, built for
the Charde family, which is shown on a drawing of 1763. The older
house had a regular five-bay front and lower recessed wings, like
the present house, but was of two instead of three storeys. At the
back a staircase window with stained glass, dated 1858. To the W a
neo-classical wall with honeysuckle decoration screens a service
court. STABLES beyond, with two oculi and a steep gable over the
central archway. To the E a steep drop to a woodland garden with a
fountain.

2090   AXMINSTER

ST MARY. Grey, with a tall strong tower over the crossing, a Dorset
rather than a Devon feature (but cf. Colyton, Crediton, Aveton
Gifford, Branscombe). The show-fronts are N towards the town
(quatrefoil parapet and two-storeyed porch) and W (five-light early
C15 window). The building history is complicated. From a Norman church there is only a former S doorway reset in the E wall of
the S chapel. Two orders, with small angle colonnettes. Two types
of chevron, with little cusp-like rolls decorating the soffit of the
inner order. Chevron also down the outer jamb. The piers of the
crossing tower and the W parts of the chancel masonry early C13,
likewise the squints into the chancel from both N and S. The
chancel windows and the stepped-up group of SEDILIA and
PISCINA early C14, the piscina especially pretty, with a very steep
gable on head corbels. Former transepts have disappeared.

The Yonge family added a chancel aisle on the S side *c.* 1480.
The N aisle and porch followed *c.* 1525–30, the S aisle only in 1800
('bald and tasteless carpenter's Gothic' according to Davidson),
replacing the S transept or Drake family chapel. The interior is
whitewashed in the taste of that date. The clerestory windows were
added in 1834, when the W window was reconstructed. In 1870
Edward Ashworth removed much of the early C19 work, provided
both aisles with new capitals, carved by *Hems* (those of the N aisle
had been hacked back), and installed correct but dull new fittings.
The N aisle roof dates from 1903, a facsimile of the medieval one.
Further restoration in 1923 by *William Weir*.

PULPIT and READING DESK. Both 1633, with the typical
round arches on squat pilasters as the recurrent motif in all panels.
– SCREEN to the Yonge (N chancel) chapel. – DONATIONS
BOARD (S chapel), framed, with a pediment, as grand as a reredos.
– ROYAL ARMS. 1767. – CANDELABRA. Brass, *c.* 1750. – MONU-
MENTS. Two C13 stone effigies in the chancel, badly preserved: a
priest; and a lady (Alice de Mohun †*c.* 1257?) holding an image of
the Virgin and Child, an unusual feature, imitated at Membury
(q.v.).

ST MARY (R.C.), Lyme Road. Designed by *Wardell* in 1855, erected
by *Goldie* in 1862. Dec, nave and chancel only, but quite a lively

exterior with red stone dressings and rather wild E window tracery. – STAINED GLASS. Large late C19 E window; Annunciation and saints. – Several memorial windows to the Knight family, the chief benefactors, one of 1938 by *Paul Woodroffe*. – Langran memorial window 1952 by *Charles Norris*; fused glass.

UNITED REFORMED CHURCH, Chard Street. Built by the Independents in the late 1820s. Three-bay ashlar front with slated roof. The Sunday School is on the site of the 1698 chapel.

STATION. 1859. One of a series between Salisbury and Exeter designed for the L.S.W.R. by *Sir William Tite* and *Edward N. Clifton*. Gothic, with asymmetrical gables of brick with stone dressings. Slate roof. Flat timber platform canopy on slender cast-iron columns with Gothic capitals.

The town lies to the N of the river Axe. An ancient settlement, with a market by the C12, it was burnt in the Civil War (although rebuilt by 1669, when there were 200 houses). The chief impression is of respectable houses of the C18–19, when prosperity came from the Axminster carpet works and the coaching trade. The main road – Lyme Road, Lyme Street, Victoria Place, Trinity Square, West Street – undulates pleasantly through the little town, past the twin foci of the George Hotel and the church and its churchyard, with minor streets leading off. E of the church, a house with a medieval Gothic arch (said to come from Newenham Abbey, *see* below) and C18 Gothic windows, then a stuccoed house with similar windows.

SILVER STREET curves around the church to the N. Here the Axminster carpet factory was established in 1755 by Thomas Whitty, and carpets were made 'by the pliant fingers of little children' (S. Shaw, 1788). The group of stone buildings dates from after a fire of 1827. Three storeys, of large dressed limestone blocks. Broad segmental windows with original small panes on two lower floors. Three doors with large entablatures and Tuscan pilasters. Curved corner. Alongside, Whitty's house (the Law Chambers), two storeys, cream mathematical tiles, with two-storey bow-windows and porticoed central door.

To the W the former REGISTER OFFICE, bold Victorian Gothic with traceried fanlight. Opposite, WEST STREET forms the third side of the widening around the church. Near the junction with Castle Street a pretty late C18 shop with Greek Doric columns and a nice doorway with incised pilasters. Then VICTORIA PLACE, a good terrace of *c.*1840 on a curve, once with a continuous first-floor balcony (now surviving only at the W end). Opposite, the GEORGE HOTEL, on an island site. Plain three-storey painted brick S front of the C18. Over a carriage arch a later C18 assembly room with Venetian windows either end and an attractive interior with Adamish ceiling and a tiny elegantly bowed minstrels' gallery on one side. Good fireplace with Ionic columns and a classical scene. The back parts of the hotel of stone, and older, but much has been demolished for a bleak car park. The surrounding streets have also suffered; the Co-op to the E is a particularly painful eyesore.

Up CHARD STREET, however, more worthwhile buildings: on the r. an early C19 shop with a handsome pair of bow-windows; further on a broader house with shallow curved windows on brackets on two floors, and a wooden doorcase with fluted columns; then

the United Reformed Church (q.v.). On the other side OAK
VIEW, a modest early C19 front with a Doric porch, and next to it
OAK HOUSE, the best house in Axminster, built in 1758 by Simon
Bunter, lawyer. Two storeys with dentilled cornice and parapet, in
diapered brick with blue headers. Stone quoins at the corners and
framing the three central bays; stone window surrounds. Central
Venetian window over a similarly tripartite group of door with two
windows. Irregular back elevation eight windows wide with two
projecting wings. Good open-well staircase with moulded soffits.

Returning S, CASTLE HILL HOUSE, set back in its own garden, is
another good later C18 house, faced with mathematical tiles, with
rusticated quoins, Venetian window, and good staircase. Opposite,
GLOUCESTER HOUSE, early C19, also mathematical-tiled, then
cottages running down the steep slope to the group of MILLS at
the bottom of Castle Hill. 'The old brush factory' is of five bays
and three storeys, stone with brick dressings under a pantiled roof,
with small-paned round-headed windows. Castle Mill, red brick
and of three storeys, has a flat roof behind a castellated parapet.
Another six-bay stone and brick mill with a pantiled roof.

In CASTLE STREET the AXMINSTER SALE ROOM of 1795-6, a
former Methodist Chapel, red brick, and in MARKET SQUARE
the former market building of 1830 (now showrooms), one-
storeyed, formerly open on one side, much altered.

Finally, a few outliers. To the SW in WEST STREET, towards the
station, a couple of tall late Georgian town houses. Up LYME
ROAD to the NE, LYME HOUSE, with two bowed windows, and
LOUP HOUSE, Victorian Gothic. In STONEY LANE, PIPPIN
CENTRE, a nice early C19 stuccoed surburban villa with Doric
portico *in antis* and arched first-floor window with intersecting
glazing bars.

TOLCIS. Tolcis Farmhouse and Tolcis House are both late medieval
hall-houses in origin.

SECTOR, E of the town, off Sector Lane, in its own small park. The
home of the C19 local antiquarian James Davidson. The irregular
rendered early C19 exterior with Tudor windows and porch dated
1838 no doubt conceals an older core. Pilasters with incised
decoration.

NEWENHAM ABBEY, Abbey Lane, 1 m. SW. A Cistercian abbey
was founded by William and Reginald Mohun in 1245-6. Lower
Abbey Farmhouse probably stands on the site of the W range, and
an outbuilding incorporates the N wall of the church. The church
was 280 ft long, the cloister 120 by 120 ft, but only minor fragments of masonry remain.

CLOAKHAM. Remodelled c. 1800. Three bays, two storeys. Pretty
canted porch with two paired and two single Corinthian columns,
quadrant returns, and iron balustrade. Canted bay-window.

SHAPWICK HILL. Some of the barrows are still upstanding in the
linear BARROW CEMETERY, others are visible only as soilmarks.

See also Coaxdon Hall *and* Weycroft.

AXMOUTH

ST MICHAEL. Norman walling in nave and chancel. The N doorway
the one more conspicuous piece of Norman date, with one order of
colonnettes (one capital scalloped, one with elementary upright
volutes, the ornament of the voussoirs zigzag and crenellations).
The s aisle added in the C13; see the circular piers. The chancel
windows, with pointed trefoil heads, may be contemporary or a
little later. Perp W tower with higher stair-turret. W door, tower
arch, chancel arch, and arch into the chancel chapel all without
capitals. Restoration 1882–9 by *Hayward & Son*, with carvings by
Hems. The nave roof and the NE vestry with its big chimney and
bold E windows are of 1889. – FONT. 1889 by *E. Hore* of Axmouth,
oddly pinched. – PULPIT. 1890 by *Hems*. – In a recess in the
chancel wall EFFIGY of a priest, C14. – PAINTINGS. C15, against
two piers: Christ showing his wounds, and St Peter. – STAINED
GLASS. In the s aisle, three windows by *Bell & Son* of Bristol,
c. 1890, with delightful rural detail.

Neat village with a neat street down the hill accompanied by a
stream. Several good C16 and C17 houses. The most externally
impressive is STEPPS, with two lateral stacks with set-offs and
moulded caps, four-centred arched doorway, and ovolo-moulded
mullioned windows. Inside, two stud-and-panel screens, and in a
first-floor room a C17 moulded plaster frieze with acanthus leaves.
Other pretty thatched cottages facing the church, whose tower
looks towards the wide, slow river Axe.

Axmouth was a Roman port, but the river silted up in medieval
times. Although a pier was built in the early C19, trade declined
after the railway came to Seaton in 1867.

SEATON BRIDGE, designed by *Philip Brannon* and built in 1877, is
the earliest surviving massed concrete bridge in Great Britain, the
concrete marked to look like masonry. Three segmental arches.
Toll house at the E end also of concrete.

HAWKESDOWN CAMP. A HILLFORT in a commanding position on
the E side of the Axe valley, above the town. Its eastern, least steep
side is protected by multiple defences.

See also Bindon *and* Stedcombe House.

AYLESBEARE

ST MARY. Conventional East Devon Perp, with W tower, N aisle,
and N chapel. Panelled chancel arch. Restored in 1896–9 by
E. H. Harbottle, tower restored 1924 by *Harbottle Reed*, chancel
roof bosses over-glossily repainted in the 1950s. – FONT. Perp,
octagonal, with C18 domed COVER. – ALTAR TABLE, COM-
MUNION RAIL, recutting of the PISCINA, and other chancel
fittings of the 1840s. – MONUMENT. Edward Kenyon †1843 by
E. B. Stephens. Neo-classical mourning figure and an urn within a
Gothic frame.

MINCHEN COTTAGE. A fragment of a manor house, with an attractive chequerwork hall chimneypiece dated 1589.

AYSHFORD
Burlescombe

The low, uneventful W front, rendered, and with all windows altered, conceals the remains of the medieval manor house of the Ayshfords (a farmhouse from the later C17). In the centre of the N–S range evidence for the earliest phase, the smoke-blackened jointed-cruck trusses of a two-bay hall. At the S end a closed truss with sturdy timbers and a round-arched wooden doorway. In the E wall a low two-light wooden window with cusped heads. At the S end a C17 wing extends E, of rubble, with hipped roof and ovolo-moulded three-light windows, rather handsome. On a chimney-stack: 'built 1607, restored 1910'. The upper room served by this stack has a plaster ceiling with enriched ribs and a fireplace with flattened arch with stopped mouldings. The adjacent upper chamber in the older part of the house has an excellent barrel-vaulted ceiling with single ribs and the usual decorative motifs in between. Ornamental arcading on the end walls, and the date 1631 over the fireplace. Later porch and stairs built into the re-entrant of the two wings.

To the E, outbuildings around a yard, including a large BARN of seven bays, the N side now open, other walls of cob. Huge jointed-cruck trusses extending down to stone bases (quite a rarity), three sets of purlins, lower wind-braces. Probably C16.

CHAPEL. Small free-standing Perp building with diagonal buttresses and a rebuilt bellcote. Two-light windows; also some tiny pierced quatrefoils set into the side walls. Wagon roof with carved bosses. Restored to use as a chapel in 1847. – SCREEN. Painted red, green, and blue. Cusped lights with straight heads, crenellated beam with fleurons. – Striking STAINED GLASS by *Willement*, of 1848, with texts on diagonal bands of yellow set in clear glass and small painted figures in the top lights. – MONUMENTS. Henry Ayshford †1666 aged one year. A small slate tomb-chest with incised arches. – John Ayshford †1689. Architectural wall-monument with cherubs' heads and flaming urns.

BAMPTON

ST MICHAEL. Quite a large church, the earliest part the nave S wall and the base of the tower, which has diagonal buttresses only at the front, a three-light window with intersecting tracery, and an unmoulded tower arch. The chancel looks early C14 – see its windows (all renewed) with cusped, intersecting, and also flowing tracery, and the ogee-headed piscina. The chancel is a good deal lower than the nave. The body of the church is C15: nave and N aisle, four-light windows with large, simple tracery (the N aisle cusping probably removed), panelled chancel arch, solid, plain S porch. The arcade piers inside standard B type with standard capitals. Wagon roofs old but repaired in restorations of 1872 and 1896–8 (the latter by *Sampson* of Taunton). – PULPIT. Mid C16 carving with green man. – SCREEN with standard type A tracery and ribbed coving with the Bourchier knot, restored by *Herbert*

Read in 1938, cresting renewed 1965. – SCULPTURE. Fragments of panels with small figures in niches, perhaps from a former stone pulpit. – REREDOS. Pedimented centre, pilasters flanking panels with texts. The centre (now empty) was intended for the painting of Christ carrying the Cross presented in 1812 by Richard Cosway, the miniaturist, who was a local man. – At the w end of the nave, PAINTING of the Flight into Egypt (with ferry and ferryman in red) attributed to *G. Ghezzi* of Rome (†1721). – STAINED GLASS. Nave SW, a collage made in 1921 by *M. Drake* of medieval pieces including an Ascension, Trinity, and Coronation of the Virgin, all of the same workmanship, and a figure of St George below. – MONUMENT. In the N wall of the chancel extensive fragments of a tomb-chest, possibly of Lady Thomasine Bourchier †1453, of Cornish catacleuse stone (cf. e.g. St Endellion, Cornwall).

CASTLE. To the N of the town a sizeable but incomplete motte and bailey, the bailey, roughly rectangular, surviving only on the s and E. The motte ditch (located in excavation) is now filled in. The castle belonged to Robert of Bampton, who held it against King Stephen in 1136.

The attractive small town, formerly more prosperous, with its wealthy C18 houses of local limestone, lies in a valley between the church to the SW and the castle to the NE. In CASTLE STREET to the E, CASTLE GROVE, late Georgian; on the W side, CASTLE HOUSE, with large doorcase with fluted Ionic columns, and No. 9 (Bampton Antiques), with C19 ogee-arched iron shop-window still with neo-classical motifs. BAMPTON STUDIO opposite is part of a grand three-storey composition of 3–1–3 bays, divided by pilasters, interrupted by later doors and shop-windows. The wider market place at the foot of the hill splits in two around some messed-about infilling (plaque of 1798 at the s end).

In FORE STREET, the l. fork, the WHITE HORSE, with a porch on thin iron columns and black stuccoed end pilasters, and No. 11 with a doorway with *Coade* stone keystones and vermiculated quoins (cf. Southernhay, Exeter), then Nos. 1–5 NEWTON SQUARE, with plain Georgian fronts. The best house is further up the hill in LUKE STREET: LEBURN HOUSE, built by Richard 117 Bowden, a cloth merchant, in 1766 – or rather rebuilt, for the massive stone stack of an older house, still with its fireplace at basement level, is embedded behind the handsome Georgian stone front. This is incorrectly classical, with its four bays and five pilasters to the upper floors, but very appealing. Details still in a Baroque idiom: deep coved cornice breaking forward over each pilaster; segment-headed windows with stone keystones. The back, visible from the churchyard, has two rusticated end pilasters. Inside, a similarly quirky dog-leg staircase, fitted in next to the old stack on the site of an older stone stair. It rises to the attics with a sharply ramped rail and three different types of balusters. Nice foliage plasterwork on the second-floor landing ceiling. The adjoining house, LOWER LEBURN may once have been a service wing.

THE SWAN, w of the church, much altered, was the C16 church house. From here the churchyard path is one of those back lanes so typical of shrunken towns. To the s the former VICARAGE, early C15 with C16 w wing, much altered in the early C19. Past

CHURCH TERRACE and BARNHAY HOUSE, late C18, via
MARY LANE, with its BIBLE CHRISTIAN CHAPEL of 1862 and
school of the same size, to BROOK STREET, a broad thoroughfare
running from the crossroads to the river. On the S side some fine
small-town C18 houses, especially No. 8, BROOK HOUSE. Across
the BRIDGE of 1827 the former workhouse on the r. and a few
substantial early C19 villas in BRITON STREET, e.g. No. 6 with
Doric doorcase. Former WATERMILL off Brook Street to the N.
BRIDGE. Late C19, 70ft span; of iron. It looks like a suspension
   bridge, but the rods and the decorative chains hung from granite
   piers have no structural function, and it is in fact of girder
   construction.
TOLL HOUSE. Built c. 1819–26. Square, two-storeyed, of stone,
   with a door at one side.
WONHAM HOUSE. 2m. W. A fragment of the large late C19
   mansion of the Kennards, spectacularly sited above the Exe valley.
   W wing and half-timbered top floor demolished c. 1960. E wing
   dated 1889. The N side still quite attractive, with canted porch
   with two Tudor arches with delicate Renaissance motifs, boldly
   mullioned window, and trim hipped-roofed pavilion at the end of
   the service wing. SE room with elaborate plaster ceiling.

5030   BARNSTAPLE

Barnstaple is the most important town in North Devon. Although the
approach through the indifferent western suburbs and around the
destructive inner ring road are not inviting, and the ugly civic tower
and extensive new shopping areas may be further deterrents to the
architecturally-minded visitor, the town still has much to offer the
explorer.

   Barnstaple grew up at the lowest crossing point over the Taw and,
until the estuary silted up in the C19, prospered both as a port with an
enviably sheltered harbour, and as the major market centre of North
Devon. Pilton, now a suburb to the N across the Yeo, a tributary of the
Taw, is recorded as a burh fortified under Alfred, and may have been
the older settlement, but by the late C10 Barnstaple had its own mint,
and a century later was one of the four Devon boroughs mentioned in
Domesday Book. It was granted a charter by Henry II. The early
medieval form of the town is still apparent from the street plan, with
the curve of Boutport Street following the line of the ditch outside the
walls. The wooded motte of the castle held by Judhael of Totnes in the
early C12 still rises above the roof-tops. But when Leland arrived in
the early C16, the town walls were 'almost clene faullen', and as a result
of later prosperity not much medieval fabric remains, apart from the
parish church, the core of the impressive bridge over the Taw, and a
few fragments of the Cluniac priory which Judhael had founded in the
early C12. The C16 and C17 were a golden age for the port, when trade
with America began to develop, although during the C18 Barnstaple
was eclipsed in this by her rival Bideford. Five ships from Barnstaple
joined Drake's fleet in 1588. Several groups of almshouses remain
from this time, founded by the wealthy merchants whose monuments
fill the church; their own well-appointed houses have survived less
well than for instance at Dartmouth, for a regrettable quantity of

demolition went on during the last century, yet a surprising number of buildings of the C16–17 remain concealed behind later polite front-ages, including one of the best plaster ceilings in Devon. In the early C18 Defoe called Barnstaple a 'large, spacious and well-built town'

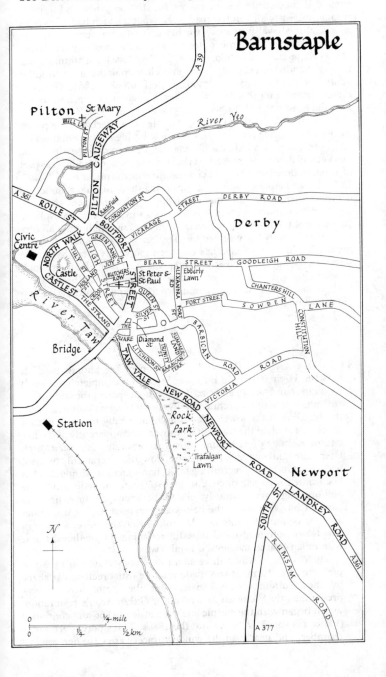

with houses of stone; in his day Irish wool and yarn were among the major imports, attracting the clothmakers of Tiverton and Exeter to the market.

The suburbs, already 'more than the town' in Leland's time, expanded considerably in the early C19; stuccoed villas and terraces sprang up, especially on the road to Newport, which had originated as a rival medieval settlement further downstream, founded by the Bishops of Exeter in a corner of their manor of Bishops Tawton. To the W a working-class suburb known as 'Derby' developed around a lace factory founded in 1825 (cf. Tiverton). The population grew steadily: 3,748 in 1801; 5,079 in 1821; 7,902 in 1841; 9,698 in 1901. The main increase came after this date, when a rash of suburbs began to spread over the hills to the W: 14,700 in 1931; 18,159 in 1981.

It is now difficult to appreciate the role of the harbour; the proud early C18 exchange remains, but the quay beside it has been filled in, and even the C19 warehouses lining the Yeo are disappearing. The market still flourishes, moved off the street to its own buildings as part of a well-planned series of C19 civic improvements under *R.D.Gould*. Indeed, Barnstaple's continuing appeal as a shopping and commercial centre – increased at the time of writing by the imminent arrival of the North Devon motorway – is a serious threat to the atmospheric character of the town, for an intricate mixture of buildings of all ages can only too easily be swamped by the sheer scale of modern developments. So far, the damage has not been too great; there have been demolitions, but the High Street still preserves much of interest, and, encouragingly, recent housing along the riverside has been tactful both in scale and in the way it has incorporated and found new uses for older buildings.

CHURCHES

ST PETER AND ST PAUL. The position of the church is ideal, between High Street and Boutport Street, yet completely screened by them. Nor has C19 and C20 development spoiled the scale of the surrounding houses. Architecturally the most remarkable feature of the building is the tower, placed asymmetrically to the S, not far from the E end, in the transeptal position, and apparently of the late C12 or early C13 (cf. Braunton) and incorporated into the church later. The lead-covered broach-spire, now idiosyncratically twisted, was added in 1388–9, according to the borough rolls, although it has been much repaired since, e.g. in 1636 (date on pediment). The bell-openings are curiously placed between the broaches and covered by pediments; the bells hang exposed higher up, under another pediment – like a little roof. Inside the spire, a maze of woodwork, often restored but still retaining the medieval frame with much-braced medieval central post.

The church in which three altars were consecrated in 1318 was probably cruciform. It was made into the usual rectangular shape by the addition of Perp aisles, but the atmosphere is now predominantly Victorian as a result of *Gilbert Scott*'s restoration, which began with the steeple and the S aisle in 1866 and continued (under his son *J.O.Scott*) into the 1880s. The S porch, NE organ chamber, and nearly all the window tracery are C19: one original

Perp window remains in the N chancel chapel. At the NE corner of the chancel the two-storey Bibliotheca Doddridgiana, added in 1667, with wooden mullioned windows (remains of a double-rib ceiling in the upper room, a late example). The large straight-headed and transomed windows of the N aisle are perhaps of the same date. Scott must have decided to leave them unaltered, as he also refused to comply with the proposal to demolish the tower.

Inside, Scott swept away the piers carrying straight beams, dating from repairs after a storm of 1810, and the galleries and chancel fittings of 1823–4, and rebuilt all the arcades in correct C14 fashion: A-type piers with finely moulded arches (carving by H. Hems). Two restored medieval PISCINAS. – Some reset Barnstaple TILES by the pulpit. – Most of the C19 FURNISHINGS are unremarkable, apart from a good ORGAN CASE by J. O. Scott, 1882. – SCULPTURE. Bust of Aaron, remains of a life-size statue removed in 1878. – Much Victorian STAINED GLASS, most notable the tower lancet by Clayton & Bell, and the N transept, 1878, and W window, colourful designs by W. F. Dixon, in a mannered Pre-Raphaelite style.

MONUMENTS. A large number, reflecting Barnstaple's C17 prosperity, but for the most part dingily displayed (although the crude repainting of the Tucker monument is not to be recommended either). Many more were lost in the C19. The best early ones are in the S aisle; later minor tablets are gathered together in the N chapel. – Elizabeth Delbridge † 1628. Kneeling figure. – Raleigh Clapham † 1636. Two kneeling figures facing each other, small kneeling figures below. – George Peard † 1644. Good frontal bust, head resting on one hand. – Richard Ferris † 1649. Semi-reclining effigy in relief between columns, broken pediment above. – Walter Tucker. Half-figure, head on hand, his daughter and her baby lying beneath. – In the S chancel aisle Nicholas Blake † 1634 (bust, head resting on one hand; in an oval recess), Richard Beaple † 1643 (demi-figure with book), and Richard Harris † 1688 (with standing and reclining allegories). – On the N transept W wall Thomas Horwood † 1658, a demi-figure with head on one hand, the elbow resting on a pile of books. – SUNDIAL, on the outside of the S chapel. 1732; an elongated octagon.

ST ANNE'S CHAPEL (now museum), in the churchyard. An early C14 chantry chapel raised above an undercroft, later used as the grammar school. Picturesque group with elevated doorway decorated with fleurons, later castellated two-storeyed porch, and a large three-light E window typical of its date. Good arch-braced roof. Undercroft with chamfered wooden piers, each with two braces supporting a central longitudinal beam. In the chapel, C16 school desks with turned legs.

ST JOHN BAPTIST, South Street, Newport. 1883 by G. R. Abbott, replacing a chapel of ease of 1820. Bath stone dressings. NE tower.

HOLY TRINITY, Barbican Terrace. Tall tower of fine proportions with large Somerset-type twin bell-openings from a church of 1843–5 by D. Mackintosh and G. Abbot, the rest of which proved unsound and was rebuilt by William White in 1867. Dull interior: quatrefoil piers, clerestory, quite an ambitious arch-braced roof; apsed chancel, with STAINED GLASS of 1875 by Powell.

IMMACULATE CONCEPTION (R.C.). Begun in 1844 largely at the expense of Sir Bourchier Palk Wrey of Tawstock Court for the benefit of his Catholic wife. According to *The Tablet*, by *Gideon Boyce* of Tiverton, but he may only have been the executive architect. The *North Devon News* reported in 1855, when the church was opened, that the designs had been supplied by *Pugin*, and it is known that Pugin visited Tiverton in 1844. A conscientious exercise in Romanesque revival – an unusual R.C. choice at this date. Tall, apsed, and aisleless; a w wheel-window, otherwise plain outside. Chancel arch with chevron, chancel with plaster rib-vault, neo-Norman PULPIT and FONT. Accompanying vestries, school, etc., all demolished; the church itself derelict.

The NEW CHURCH next door, of 1984, by *John Cooper* of *Friend, Kelly & Friend*, for which the old one has been abandoned, is in direct antithesis to it: a low, shallow-pitched, spreading roof of laminated timbers; no interior supports; seats fanwise; altar lit by a lantern. – STAINED GLASS. By *Charles Norris* of Buckfast: the Risen Christ behind the altar; in the side windows formalized (and more successful) angels in red, orange, and white.

BAPTIST CHAPEL, Boutport Street. 1860, lecture hall and class-rooms 1870, all by *R.D. Gould*. Rubble walls, round-headed windows.

CONGREGATIONAL CHURCH, Cross Street. By *R.D. & J. Gould*, 1870. Gabled Gothic.

GROSVENOR STREET CHAPEL. Built for the Plymouth Brethren in 1848.

NEWPORT METHODIST CHURCH. 1910. Gabled aisles, thin corner spirelet, with school of 1892 by *A. Lauder*.

THORNE MEMORIAL CHAPEL, Bear Street. An unusually ambitious building for the Bible Christians. Rebuilt in 1891–2, retaining part of the chapel of 1875–6, both phases by *W.C. Oliver*. Purple local stone, the tower banded in limestone. Plate tracery. Gable to the street. Impressive interior with cast-iron fittings and woodwork by *Hems*.

WESLEYAN METHODIST CHURCH, Boutport Street. Of the large, grossly Gothic building by *A. Lauder*, 1867, extended 1885 and 1905, only part of the outer walls remains.

PUBLIC BUILDINGS

CASTLE, at the w end of the town, between the rivers Taw and Yeo. Motte and bailey, the very large motte towards the town. The bailey, now occupied by Castle Green, is bounded by land reclaimed from the estuary in modern times. A second bailey on the town side, suggested from documentary references, has never been proven. Excavations in the 1920s showed that the defensive ditches received water direct from the estuary. On top of the motte, foundations of a circular stone tower, 65ft in diameter with walls 10ft thick, surrounded by an outer wall of lighter build.

The castle existed by the early C12, when it was associated with Judhael, formerly of Totnes (q.v.), created Lord of Barnstaple by Henry I. In 1136, Alfred, son of Judhael, abandoned it because it was weak. The walls may date from the time of Henry de Tracey, who was granted the castle by King Stephen. In 1228 the defensive walls were reduced to a height of 10ft on royal orders; but a hall, chamber, kitchen, and other buildings were mentioned in 1274, a chapel in 1333. The castle was in some disrepair by 1326, and in ruins by Leland's day.

CIVIC CENTRE, North Walk. By *E.H.Surgey* of *Devon County Council*, 1968–70. An alien imposition: a nine-storey tower of offices with projecting concrete floor-bands, an undistinguished but prominent landmark (cf. Plymouth). Low MAGISTRATES' COURT and POLICE STATION in front. Plain grey detailing, simple covered walks.

GUILDHALL, High Street. 1826 by *Thomas Lee* of Barnstaple, a pupil of Soane and Laing. Smoothly rusticated ground floor; upper floor with niches and Ionic pilasters; pediment with the town arms. Quite modest but dignified. Good original courtroom. In the adjoining first-floor room, very elaborate panelling with fluted pilasters and an overmantel of 1617 from Dodderidge's house, No. 10 Cross Street (demolished).

MARKET, behind the Guildhall. Impressive Pannier Market, 320ft 156 long, with glass and timber roof on iron columns, 1855–6 by *R.D.Gould*. On the opposite side of the new street, BUTCHERS ROW, linking the High Street and Boutport Street, a long row of one-storey butchers' stalls. At the W end of the market the Queen's Hall (*see* Boutport Street, Perambulation 2). Corn Exchange added in 1864.

LIBRARY, Tuly Street. 1986–7 by *Nigel Kirk* of *Devon County Council*. Three storeys; shallow brick arches to the ground floor.

QUEEN ANNE'S WALK. Built as an exchange, a single colonnade 100 which faced the quay along an inlet since filled in. Lavishly adorned. Tuscan columns, doubled at the angles, and, in the centre, pillars supporting a pedestal on which stands a statue of Queen Anne given in 1708 by Robert Rolle of Stevenstone (cf. the porticoes of Inigo Jones's St Paul's Cathedral and of All Saints Northampton). This is no doubt the date also of the superstructure, but the columns may be re-used from an earlier arcade. The parapet is decorated with garlands and coats of arms. The design has been attributed to *William Talman* on the basis of its close similarity to Talman's hall front at Drayton, Northants. Restored in 1986 by *Herbert Read*. In the colonnade the TOME STONE, an ancient stone on which merchants sealed their bargains, formerly in front of the Quay Hall, placed here in 1909. The baths and washhouses added behind at the time of a restoration in 1859 were converted to a freemasons' hall in 1868.

BRIDGE. Probably built originally in the C13 of masonry (never of wood). Sixteen stone arches, thirteen of them medieval, the three on the town side apparently replaced in 1589. 520ft long plus the original causeways, the W causeway 1500ft, the E one, up to the South Gate, 300ft. The bridge has been widened three times, the last time – in concrete faced with masonry – in the 1960s, when the cast-iron additions of 1834 (by *James Green*) were replaced in masonry. On the underside of the arches the medieval width of less than 10ft can still be seen.

TOWN STATION, Castle Street. *See* Perambulation 1.

BARNSTAPLE STATION. Built as Barnstaple Junction Station in 1854. Rubble with ashlar dressings. Single-storey station offices dwarfed by the tall, gabled stationmaster's house. The remaining platform canopies of curved corrugated-iron sheets supported on timber posts and beams with cast-iron brackets are similar to those found elsewhere on the line.

BUS STATION, The Strand. 1922 by *E.Y.Saunders*, Borough Surveyor. Designed to match Queen Anne's Walk on the N.

PERAMBULATIONS

1. W of the High Street

A tour of the town can start at the BRIDGE (q.v.). THE SQUARE, at the E end of the bridge, originated in the early C18 when the river was embanked. A few plain houses of this date remain on the N side, but piecemeal C19 improvements and, more disastrously, the needs of modern traffic have left the area with little cohesion. On the NW side BRIDGE BUILDINGS, 1844 by *R.D.Gould*, his first important work in the town. Stucco frontage, with Greek Doric columns on the ground floor, giant Corinthian pilasters, and balustraded parapet curving around to The Strand; still in the tradition of Regency urbanity. In contrast, *Gould*'s later BRIDGE CHAMBERS of 1874 takes its cue from the medieval bridge, a 'well grouped block of domestic fourteenth-century Gothic', as it is described in the town guide of 1886. Brick, with a steep roof with ventilator-flèche and Dec windows. Planned as a suite of offices with a public hall. There was a similar building on the S bridge approach. Both were built when the bridgehead was realigned for the now demolished railway bridge of 1873. To the S a substantial house of 1872, presented to the NORTH DEVON ATHENAEUM in 1888 by the Barnstaple benefactor W.F.Rock. Within The Square the ALBERT MEMORIAL CLOCK TOWER of 1862 by *R.D.Gould* and relics of a public garden laid out in 1875. At the NE corner of The Square and Boutport Street, the former West of England and South Wales District Bank of 1872 (now a bookshop); mansard roof added by the Devon and Cornwall Bank who occupied the building from about 1879 to 1906.

In BOUTPORT STREET immediately on the r. one of Barnstaple's best buildings, No.62, now the WOOLWICH BUILDING SOCIETY. Its perfectly proportioned early C19 front with Greek Doric doorcase and two shallow bow-windows through three storeys dates from when it was the Golden Lion Hotel. Earlier, it was a private house. The arms of the Company of Merchants trading with Spain suggest that it belonged to one of those merchants. Inside, excellent plasterwork of the early C17 to the first-floor rooms (now visible from the ground floor, as the first-floor structure has been removed). The middle room (dated 1620) has an elaborate barrel-vaulted ceiling with a curvaceous pattern of broad enriched ribs with cage-like open pendants, four biblical scenes, and the gayest display of exotic animals. On the end walls arms and strapwork. Another single-rib ceiling in the front of the house with winged horses. In a small back room a ceiling with broad ribs, large corbels, and figures. Frieze with prancing horses. Next door the ROYAL AND FORTESCUE HOTEL, also with an early C19 bowed front trimmed with ironwork, facing down the High Street, C18 parts behind, much altered.

The long, narrow HIGH STREET is the main thoroughfare through the old town. Apart from brash modern shopfronts and a few undistinguished c20 intrusions, the main impression is still of an attractive variety of stuccoed frontages of the c19, with a sprinkling of c18 brick. Gribble in his *Memorials of Barnstaple* (1830) refers to the 'spirit of liberality and emulation' among the inhabitants, who after the Improvement Act of 1811 'vied with each other in removing low antiquated fronts and ill contrived dwellings and replacing them by tasteful and commodious structures'. Out of sixty-eight houses in part of the High Street, he continues, twenty-four had been wholly rebuilt, and twenty-five refronted or modernized. So, as these revealing figures indicate, much of Barnstaple's older history still survived beside or behind the High Street's new genteel façades. Investigation has confirmed that this pattern was not radically altered by developments of the next century and a half.*

Taking a selection of the older survivals first, one can start mid-way down the w side of the High Street with the THREE TUNS, the best surviving example in the town of a gallery-and-back-block house, even though its timber-framed front is a pastiche of 1946 by *Bruce Oliver*. Tudor fireplace upstairs; moulded beams and panelling of *c.* 1600. Further N, No. 74 has a genuine timber jettied front with stone party wall on the l.; the rest of the building is of brick, earlier c17, a rare combination in the West of England. Two chimneystacks with pairs of diagonal shafts. Restored in 1974 when the adjoining Holland Walk was made (a pedestrian precinct with folksy gables). Opposite, No. 73, also c17 brick, the front rebuilt in 1986. Further down on the E side No. 38, a low-ceilinged c16 or c17 house behind its plain c19 front, and No. 39, with a good early c18 brick front with stone keystones and the remarkable survival of a rear wing with a substantial late medieval roof (of cruck type with early apex details). Near the N end No. 60 (CLARENCE HOTEL) on the w side, a low c17 structure behind a later front (timber framing exposed inside).

Returning s along the High Street, among the contributions of later centuries one cannot miss VICTORIA CHAMBERS, built in 1887 as the Victoria Temperance Hotel by *J. King James* of Birmingham, stone and tile-hanging with a show of balconies (cf. Ilfracombe hotels), and a cheerful corner turret overtopping the older roof-lines. Long striped brick flank to Gammon Lane. Across the lane No. 65, with a giant arch to the High Street (made in the early c20 for an art shop). The core is a late c17 house with rare detached back block. Then only frontages remain, rebuilt in 1986–7 as part of a major redevelopment scheme for Prudential Assurance by *Alec French Partnership* (job architect *Ted Nash*). Further s the upper parts of later brick fronts with a good assortment of detail can be picked out among the stucco: No. 71 (rusticated window heads); No. 75 (end pilasters and cornice); Nos. 81–82 (stepped keystones). By Cross Street No. 86 makes a special show: built as the National Provincial Bank in 1854: good carving, engaged columns. Further on, amid a nicely varied stucco group,

* Extensive redevelopment plans of 1983 were later reduced in scope so as to be less damaging to the High Street. On the w side, s of Gammon Lane, new building has taken place behind existing frontages; on the E side redevelopment has been deflected to the area around Joy Street and Green Street.

105   No. 82, dated 1710, which has a delightful coved plaster cornice
with a splash of trophies. Next door No. 91 has a central pedimented window with early C19 Grecian detail. No. 97 is early C18
again, with a swept parapet, Doric pilasters, mask keystones, and
urns. No. 98 has a late C18 stuccoed front to an earlier house. Now
within the shop (which has been extended backward) an early C17
broad-rib ceiling and contemporary fireplace, formerly in a
detached back block. There is a replica pendant of the single-rib
ceiling formerly on the upper floor. The s end of the street is
Victorian. No. 15, by Church Lane (S. Daw & Co.), is colourful
Ruskinian Venetian of c. 1890. Then Nos. 9–12 on the E side, a
specially grand seven-bay Italianate composition with alternating
first-floor window pediments. The two-window section with
rounded corner is an extension of as late as 1893.

CROSS STREET led from the High Street to the West Gate and St
Nicholas's chapel (removed in 1852). On the N side several interesting houses, concealed by later stucco fronts. From E to W:
No. 3, early to mid C17, altered; original window at the top of the
side all to PAIGE'S LANE (and doors and doorcases on the second
floor). Behind No. 4, a wing fronting Paige's Lane, formerly
belonging to a separate house, has a medieval arch-braced roof
(probably re-used). In No. 6, exposed within the shop, an early
C16 fireplace and trefoil-headed laver. No. 7, with an C18 front
with Doric pilasters, is a gallery-and-back-block house built
c. 1635 for Thomas Horwood, the merchant who founded the
almshouses. Fireplaces, overmantels, and a first-floor ceiling are
now at Stafford Barton, Dolton; the ground-floor ceiling is at
Shute gatehouse (qq.v.). No. 8 is a similar house of the same date,
the back block and gallery now demolished. Ground floor and
courtyard now all one shop, but excellent fittings remain: two
single-rib ceilings (one visible in the shop), and elsewhere contemporary fireplaces and good joinery. Larger later landmarks are
the POST OFFICE of 1901 in heavy C17 classical style, and the
Congregational chapel (q.v.) on the s side. The corner with The
Strand is dominated by the chapel's tall Gothic JUBILEE
SCHOOLROOMS, pale Marland brick trimmed with black and red,
1894 by *Lindley Bridgman*. Across the road Queen Anne's Walk
(*see* Public Buildings) by the site of the quays.

CASTLE STREET leading NW is now a busy traffic route. The oldest
house is on the E side: CASTLE CHAMBERS, C16–17, low, with
two gables, much altered inside, but with a good small well staircase with turned balusters. On the W side, QUEEN ANNE'S
COURT, 1879, quite dignified red brick, nicely converted to flats
in 1984, together with the adjoining warehouse (by *Gordon Bailey
Associates* for Spiral Housing Association). A little further on,
CASTLE QUAY COURT, 1983–6 by *Peter Ferguson* of North
Devon District Council (principal architect *John Laird*), two
gabled groups of flats overlooking the river, crisply detailed in pale
yellow and red brick. Between them the former TOWN STATION
of 1898 (now restaurant and wine bar) has been preserved as a
centrepiece, a low tripartite composition, stone with ashlar dressings, the platform side with canopies on cast-iron columns with
four-way brackets.

This part of the town, once with an attractive C18 promenade known as North Walk (cf. Exeter's Northernhay), was spoilt in the C19 by the Barnstaple–Ilfracombe railway, and, when that had disappeared, by the inner ring road and brutish tower of the Civic Centre (q.v.). Opposite are the PUBLIC GARDENS, the former grounds of Castle House, built in the precinct of the castle (q.v.) and demolished in 1976; a C19 LODGE remains. Now up TULY STREET past the Library (q.v.) towards the area of the cattle market behind Fore Street. Facing this, GLIDDON & SQUIRE'S large showrooms for farm machinery, 1903 by *Alexander Lauder*, with bold and colourful use of materials: white brick with blue brick arches framing upper show windows; end pediments with appropriate terracotta reliefs made by Lauder's Devon Art Pottery. Further on the GOLDEN FLEECE, with C19 stuccoed front with vermiculated keystones, surviving amidst extensive redevelopment of 1986.

See also Pilton.

2. E *of the High Street*

E of the High Street, opposite Cross Street, is the Guildhall with the market behind alongside Butchers Row (q.v., Public Buildings), the result of a successful and radical replanning of this part of the town in the mid C19. To the S of this a delightfully quiet enclave around St Peter's church, entered also by a gateway from the High Street made in 1829 by the Barnstaple Iron Foundry from a plan by Mr *Hooper*. Beyond the church the former St Anne's Chapel, now museum (q.v.); to its S, Church House, built as Sunday Schools, two storeys, Gothic, by *W.C.Oliver*, 1894–5. The narrow CHURCH LANE leads S, with the former PAIGE'S ALMSHOUSES (Nos. 1–2), 1656, and HORWOOD'S ALMSHOUSES AND SCHOOL, founded 1674 and 1659 respectively. The school is an L-shaped attachment round an angle of the street. Both sets of almshouses are simple two-storeyed cottages with wooden mullioned windows. Small oblong courtyard behind, with more dwellings on both sides, like another lane. The school is also two-storeyed, with original stopped door frame and upper mullioned windows; inside, the date 1659 above a fireplace.

Back now to the junction of High Street and BOUTPORT STREET, which curves NE along the line of the ditch of the medieval town. On the W side No. 75 is the former NORTH DEVON DISPENSARY, 1834–5, three bays, sedate, with giant Tuscan pilasters. Next door, the CINEMA of 1931 by *W.H.Watkins* of Bristol is more showy, but carefully designed to be in scale with its neighbours. Green glazed tiles, broad pilasters of red moulded brick, grotesque masks by *Eric Aumonier*. It replaced the Theatre Royal. Opposite, narrow late Georgian frontages above shops (No. 50 with the date 1790). On the W side mostly C19 stucco, up to No. 96, which forms a grander cornerpiece to Butchers Row, channelled stucco with arcaded ground floor. On the other side of Butchers Row the QUEEN'S HALL, similarly detailed, was also part of the market development by *Gould*, damaged in 1941 and rebuilt by *Bruce Oliver*. No. 128 (the North Country Inn) is a gallery-and-back-block house with galleries on both sides of the courtyard. Early C18 plaster ceiling with scallop shells.

On the E side of Boutport Street, here quite spacious, No. 37, SYMONS EMPORIUM, takes pride of place, a confident late Victorian refronting of 1899 by *F.W.Petter* of Barnstaple, with polychrome tile bands and an elaborate iron canopy over the large display windows (formerly with statues above). Some quieter late Georgian buildings follow. A diversion W down JOY STREET, past the site of the East Gate, can take in another late Victorian showpiece, built in 1896 by *Alexander Lauder* for the Barnstaple Cooperative Society. Of stone, with imposing canopied upper windows. To the N, GREEN LANE, an intriguingly narrow back street, where No. 3 (Red Cross Headquarters) is worth a look: a rubble stone warehouse, but with tiny Gothick windows with intersecting glazing on the first floor, and the date 1837. It will soon be a lone survivor in the comprehensive redevelopment of this area.

Back to Boutport Street and the desolation of the demolished Congregational Chapel. Then No. 11, set back, an attractive detached house of *c.* 1820, three windows wide, with a closed semicircular entrance porch and arched ground-floor windows. No. 10 has a five-bay front of *c.* 1710 with a pretty shell hood. PRIORY COTTAGE behind, in Coronation Street, possibly incorporates scanty remains of the Cluniac PRIORY of St Mary Magdalene, founded by Judhael of Totnes *c.* 1107. Two old walls are visible, a r.-hand gable with slit window, and buttresses, a N wall with two more buttresses.* At the end, RACKFIELD, an alley to the E, named from the racks of the clothing industry, later replaced by a C19 tannery and brewery. Some rubble stone buildings remain.

E along VICARAGE STREET. First THE PRIORY, formerly the vicarage, rebuilt by Martin Blake, vicar from 1628 to 1646, and much altered in 1865 when the street was widened. Stone and brick five-window front with battlemented two-storey porch and C19 Gothic bay-window. Other windows with wooden mullions; diagonal end stack. Vicarage Street continues E to the area known as DERBY, from the Derby connections of John Boden, a former partner of John Heathcoat of Tiverton. His DERBY LACE WORKS were opened in 1825. There were originally three factories, which by 1830 were employing 1,000 people. Only one remains: the main building, originally four-storeyed, the top floor and cupola removed after a fire in 1972. Windows all renewed. Of fireproof construction with cast-iron columns supporting the typical shallow brick arches. Additions of 1874 and later. Near the entrance, former evening institute for employees, 1900. The surrounding area, once densely built up with working-class streets, largely complete by 1837, has been much thinned out by piecemeal C20 clearance and rebuilding.

Further S, BEAR STREET was extended E from Boutport Street at the same time. Off Bear Street EBBERLY LAWN, a grander terrace of *c.* 1794 overlooking a private lawn, much altered. Stuccoed, with coupled pilasters at the ends. Houses of 1868 by *R.D.Gould* on the other side. Back by Bear Street, past Portland House, with a Gothic mason's shopfront (Youings & Son) of 1891, to Boutport Street.

*Remains of an aisleless church, 88 by 32 ft, were recorded in the C19.

3. SE of Boutport Street

The sector of the town s of the junction of Boutport Street and Queen Street has been horribly mauled by roadworks and clearance of the 1960s. SILVER STREET, w off Queen Street, still has a little character, but the better remaining group lies s of the ugly inner relief road, most easily approached from The Square by LITCH-DON STREET. This was formerly the main road s out of the town. The chief attraction is PENROSE'S ALMSHOUSES, founded in 1627, an ambitious symmetrical front with projecting centre and corners. The receding parts have one-storey colonnades of rudely hewn circular granite pillars in front, which are in line with the gabled projections. Four-centred doorways. The side parts have large 'posthumously Perp' windows to light the boardroom on the l. and the chapel on the r. Behind is an attractively spacious courtyard with a central pump, surrounded by more dwellings. Good chapel furnishings of the C17–18: panelled pews, desks with turned balusters, plaster pendant for a chandelier, with vine tendrils and grapes.

Also in Litchdon Street the POTTERY of the late C19 potter C. H. Brannam. Picturesque showrooms of 1886 by *W. C. Oliver*, cream and red striped brickwork with terracotta panels. Bottle kiln behind. Further along Litchdon Street several pleasant stucco houses, Nos. 21 and 22 of 1839 (good staircases in Nos. 21 and 23).

In TRINITY STREET to the w, SALEM ALMSHOUSES of 1834. Three ranges along three sides of an oblong court open to the street, two-storeyed, of stone, with Gothic timber casements to the broad windows.

TAW VALE, parallel to Litchdon Street, is a creation of the 1840s along the river bank where there were formerly shipyards. The handsome Coalbrookdale dolphin lamp-standards were added later. First the IMPERIAL HOTEL, stuccoed, much extended in 1902 from the C19 house incorporated at the w end. Then TAW VALE PARADE, starting with a stucco terrace with rusticated ground floor and continuous iron balcony, followed by UNION TERRACE, a symmetrical composition, the centre with Doric veranda and honeysuckle balcony, flanked by outer houses with covered balconies. Towards Newport, ROCK PARK, a riverside pleasure ground given by W. F. Rock and opened in 1879. Laid out by the Borough Surveyor, *R. D. Gould*, who perhaps designed the pretty LODGE. NEWPORT ROAD continues SE with pleasant early C19 suburban development. On the s side Nos. 94–96, a terrace with Doric doorcases; on the N side a grander group with three-storey centre with Ionic pilasters. At right angles, TRA-FALGAR LAWN, a group of linked terraces, incised pilasters 134 between the houses. The centre is a pedimented four-bay villa with Tuscan colonnade along the ground floor; the sides are of three houses, each with Tuscan porches. The whole faces a lawn (cf. Ebberly Lawn, Perambulation 2).

NEWPORT, part of the town from 1836, originated as a medieval borough within the parish of Bishops Tawton, founded in rivalry to Barnstaple by the Bishops of Exeter in the late C13. Few buildings indicate its antiquity, apart from the OLD DAIRY, a former farmhouse with a lateral stack and remains of mullioned windows, on the s side of the road. SOUTH STREET also is principally modest early C19: on the E side Nos. 1–7, a good stuccoed terrace; No. 24, with Gothick porch; CLARENCE PLACE, with Ionic doorcases; also the former Sunday Schools (Auction Rooms), 1841, quite grand rusticated stucco. In RUMSAM ROAD several separate villas and a few older cottages.

4. The E suburbs

Plenty of late C19 housing in the characteristic pale yellow Marland brick of North Devon, and much of the C20 beyond, enveloping the few older buildings. In GOODLEIGH ROAD, GORWELL HOUSE, early C19, five bays, long one-storey colonnade, and IVY LODGE, a battlemented lodge of c. 1800, enlarged c. 1880, which belonged to the demolished C18 mansion of the Incledons.

RAVELIN MANOR, Ravelin Gardens, off Constitution Hill. Built c. 1873 by *Alexander Lauder*, the local architect, artist, and potter, to whom Lethaby was articled. Lauder himself lived here in later life (†1922). A compact house, picturesque in the manner of 'artistic' houses of the 1870s; red brick with generous terracotta trim, decorative chimneystacks. The full-length terracotta figures supporting the porch hint at something extra. The rooms, grouped round a spacious staircase hall, have exposed beams downstairs, wooden barrel-vaults on the first floor. But the remarkable feature is Lauder's decoration. The stair-hall, lit by a large mullioned-and-transomed window, has four walls covered in low-relief sgraffito panels, with scenes from 'A Midsummer Night's Dream', in an accomplished, slightly Pre-Raphaelite style. Large Gothic fireplace of white terracotta. The bedrooms have four more exotic pottery fireplaces from Lauder's Devon Art Pottery (founded 1876). Three-dimensional tiles in brilliant glazes: bunches of grapes, lizards, and frogs, all in high relief. The most elaborate fireplace has two maidens standing in alcoves, with a variety of creatures along the lintel. Perhaps the inspiration was French C16 Pollisey ware, which was revived in England after the Great Exhibition.

Two houses nearby, THE FIRS and GARRON, both much altered, may also be by *Lauder*.

BEAFORD

ALL SAINTS AND ST GEORGE. Nave and two aisles. Short N tower (in a transeptal position) with short slated broach-spire. s porch with a niche over the entrance, openwork cresting and pinnacles. Inside, four-bay arcades of granite with A type piers, capitals only to the main shafts, simply decorated abaci, and depressed pointed arches. Fine wagon roof in the aisle with cross-ribbed panels. Undistinguished restoration of 1878–9 by *Price & Wooller* of Weston super Mare (chancel and N chapel rebuilt). Tower rebuilt 1908–9. – FONT. Norman, of goblet form, the bowl fluted and with cable-mouldings at the rim and between bowl and shaft. – (STAINED GLASS. A window by *Alice Erskine*, 1915. PC)

(OLD PARSONAGE. Of c. 1500, with stud and panel screen. C. Hulland)

ARTS CENTRE (a Dartington offshoot). Warden's house by *L. Man-asseh*, 1966–8, an attractively simple design, white-walled, with monopitch roof. Galleried living room, with an upper studio reached from the gallery.

The tradition of good modern building is continued by the VILLAGE HALL, by *John Simmons*, c. 1982, using traditional local forms: rendered walls, and a loggia with thick stone piers like a linhay.

WOOLLEIGH BARTON, 1¾ m. NW. Remains of a medieval manor house incorporated in a farmhouse: a very rich C15 wagon roof, a garderobe with original door, and an attached chapel now with C17 roof (C. Hulland).

CASTLE HILL, above the Torridge, is the site of a HILLFORT.

BEAWORTHY   4090

ST ALBAN. Low unbuttressed W tower with unmoulded pointed arch towards the nave. The body of the church aisleless; the masonry might be C12–13. S doorway with two Norman capitals with heads, the columns supporting them now built over. Restored in 1871 by *Samuel Hooper* of Hatherleigh.

WINSFORD COTTAGE HOSPITAL. *See* Halwill.

BRONZE AGE BARROWS. Substantial examples along the high land of the ridge running NW through Beaworthy and Halwill.

BROADBURY CASTLE, a rectangular earthwork adjacent to the transmitter station on Beaworthy Ridge, is a substantial half-acre enclosure in a commanding position which until the C19 stood to a greater height. It is plausibly interpreted as a Roman fortlet or signal station (a function analogous to the C20 one).

BEER   2080

ST MICHAEL. 1876–7 by *Hayward & Son*, paid for by Mark Rolle. Set into the steep slope above the town so that the chancel is raised above the nave. A show W front to the street: arcaded narthex, large W window, NW tower. Interior enriched by early French detail: polished marble shafts, foliage capitals (carved by *Hems*). Clerestory articulated by wall shafts supporting the arch-braced roof. – (CLOCK. Early C18, with later escapement. – BELL. Early C15. JS) – STAINED GLASS. E window by *Ward & Hughes*, 1889, in their pictorial High Renaissance manner. – N aisle window 1903, also by them, designed by *T. F. Curtis*.

CONGREGATIONAL CHURCH, opposite the parish church. Opened in 1866, enlarged in 1880. Tall and flint-faced.

PRIMARY SCHOOL. Prominently sited on the hill above the village. 1978–80 by *Lucas, Roberts & Brown*.

ALMSHOUSES AND CHARITY SCHOOL. Given by Lady Rolle in 1820. A pretty Gothic design, with deep eaves forming a continuous porch, and a patterned tiled roof.

CEMETERY. 1866. Another Rolle gift. A solid little Dec building with steeply pitched roof, craggily profiled bellcote, and good dripstone terminals of Youth and Age, carved by *Hems*.

FORE STREET, leading down from the crossroads to the beach, has an attractive mixture of cottages, including much built by the Rolle estate in the C19. A little stream runs down the street, in two places collected by square stone conduits of *c.* 1700, with pagoda tops and ball finials. Facing down the street, three-storey flint and rubble houses, dated 1664. Near the first conduit a pretty thatched U-shaped house with projecting wings to the road. Further on, to the r. of the Congregational Hall, an altered but once quite grand house: seven bays, the centre three advanced, four gables, windows with projecting keystones. Then DIAMOND HOUSE, three storeys, C17, with an especially effective mixture of flint and Beer stone. Two decorative lozenges in the centre. The DOLPHIN HOTEL is also of flint and stone, with four tall upper windows. At the end of Fore Street plenty of picturesque diversity, with No. 2 with stone mullions and patterned tile roofs, dated 1894; BEACH HOUSE, 1903, brasher, with spiky corner gable; and THE COTTAGE, with a very steep thatched roof, perhaps genuinely old, and its striking Arts and Crafts neighbour, a tall house with corbelled-out bay, clustered stack, and curved mullioned ground-floor window. Round the corner up COMMON LANE an especially appealing row of Rolle estate cottages, 1873, flint-faced and brick-trimmed, each with a gable with a spike and a little porch.

168

On the cliff slopes and along the road to Seaton are a sprinkling of more affluent early C20 seaside houses, mostly of stone, the later ones with mullioned windows and spreading roofs (see e.g. St Michael's Mount and Beer Haven, near the church), discreetly blending into the hillside – very different from the earlier tradition of stuccoed seaside villas (cf. Torquay).

Underground QUARRIES to the W of the village were much worked in the Middle Ages and later for high-quality limestone. The huge caverns created by the extraction of the stone are now open to visitors. The new quarry to the N of the road, opened in 1883, is now used only for the production of powdered lime, and there is an enormous modern LIMEKILN at the entrance to the underground quarries.

BEER HEAD. Traces of a Celtic FIELD SYSTEM show as lynchets both under existing hedges and as earthworks within the fields. Here also is mainland England's most westerly *in situ* flint deposit, exploited during the Neolithic period for use throughout the South West.

See also Bovey House.

6090   BELSTONE

ST MARY. Granite, ashlar, with two-stage W tower, unbuttressed and with obelisk pinnacles. Plain granite windows. Interior with low octagonal granite piers between nave and S aisle. Extensively restored and refitted by *Hayward & Son*, planned 1875, executed 1881–2.

BELSTONE COMMON is the site of HUT CIRCLES and CAIRNS, some of the cairns especially good, either with retaining kerbs or – like the Nine Stones – set within circles of orthostats.

BELSTONE CLEAVE. *See* South Tawton.

BERE ALSTON
Bere Ferrers

4060

Once an important centre, now chiefly bungalows and market gardens. The silver mines along the river Tamar were worked from the 1290s to the C15; a market existed by 1295, and a borough was created soon afterwards by Reginald de Ferrers. The mines were reopened in the C19. Quays on the Tamar remain at Weir Quay and Hole's Hole. The chief port was Morwellham (q.v.).

UNION SMELTING WORKS, Weir Quay. Established c. 1830. An assay house and count house project on either side of the smelter.

HOLY TRINITY. 1848.

MAYNARD SCHOOL. Granite doorway dated 1665, granite mullioned windows. C19 additions. The oldest known purpose-built school in Devon.

CALSTOCK VIADUCT. Designed by *Richard Church*, one of the two engineers for the railway line to Gunnislake, and completed in 1907. Constructed of about 12,000 concrete blocks. Twelve arches of 60 ft span carry a single track 118 ft above the Tamar.

BERE FERRERS

4060

ST ANDREW. Low down, close to the meeting of the rivers Tavy and Tamar. Of considerable interest because it belongs essentially to a period earlier than nearly all South Devon village churches. It consists of nave, long transepts, and chancel, plus S aisle, S porch, and S chapel. C. Fryer Cornelius suggests that the nave may be C12 in origin, the chancel and former N chapel mid C13. The transepts were built or rebuilt in the early C14; the principal recorded date is the foundation by William de Ferraris in 1333 of an archpresbytery with an arch-priest and four priests. The N transept arch and the recess in the N transept (both of blue Roborough stone) appear earliest. Of the windows, some are C13 (two-light cusped lancets with a pointed quatrefoil above, chancel N), others are clearly Dec, including the fine five-light E window with intersecting tracery, and the windows of great variety in the transepts. Three PISCINAS, C13 in the chapel, C14 in the transepts; double SEDILIA. W tower, thin and unbuttressed, perhaps C13. Only the S aisle and S chapel, with A type piers and depressed moulded arches, and the two-storeyed S porch with a handsome ribbed ceiling are Perp, of the late C15 or early C16.

FONT. Circular, Norman, of Hurdwick stone, in the form of two capitals, the top one with big volutes. – SCREEN. Only the wainscoting remains, with some original painting. – BENCHES. Many, and not only bench ends as usual. Decorated with large, i.e. one-tier, blank traceried arches. One front pew with shields, including arms of the Willoughby de Broke family. – STAINED GLASS. A specially precious possession of the church. In the E window part of the early C14 glass. Christ seated in the centre light, the Ferrers donor and his wife kneeling in the outer lights. Also figures of saints, less complete, and smaller fragments in the tracery.

The colouring still with the glow which later medieval English glass so often lacks.

MONUMENTS. Excellent original white limestone recess in the N chancel wall, with a big cusped arch under a crocketed gable – no ogee details. Under the arch in the recess the slender figures of a cross-legged knight and a lady wearing a wimple. The cusps end in fine heads; in the gable two censing angels. Such angels appear in St James's Chapel, Exeter Cathedral, about 1290, the head cusps in the Sir Robert Stapledon monument at Exeter Cathedral of c. 1320. The effigies at Bere Ferrers may represent Sir William de Ferraris and his wife Matilda, but could be older. They have been attributed to Bristol craftsmen, c. 1300. – In the N transept another original recess, the arch of Roborough stone, with the effigy of a cross-legged knight in a lively position with hands on sword (of the same type as the effigy at Dorchester, Oxon), probably early C14. – Also a free-standing tomb-chest of Purbeck marble with shields in early Renaissance wreaths, said to be for Lord Willoughby de Broke, † 1522. The curious Purbeck slab with rose tracery on a honeycomb ground may be the canopy of this or another early C16 tomb.

The crowded CHURCHYARD overlooks the river. Many C18 slate tablets, and some simply inscribed CHOLERA 1849. Under the E window, a worn Portland stone slab to C. A. Stothard the antiquarian † 1821, who fell to his death while recording the tomb in the chancel.

BERE BARTON. Licences to crenellate were granted to the de Ferrers family in 1337 and 1340, but only one or two medieval features remain in the rear of Bere Barton farm, which may incorporate parts of a medieval domestic range (ground-floor room with moulded beams; remains of stone newel stair and garderobe). Immediately behind are the remains of a battlemented wall which may originally have enclosed a courtyard. The rebuilding of the manor house reflects a period of prosperity in the early C14 (cf. the rebuilding of the parish church) based on the royal silver mines. The front of the house is C18, with projecting wings.

(RUMLEIGH HOUSE. Mid C18 brick front with canted bays, extended in the C19 and C20. Original staircase and one first-floor fireplace; a later C18 fireplace in Adam style.)

(WARD HOUSE (Chelfham Senior School). Rendered C18 three-bay front with central pediment and modillioned cornice. Pedimented doorcase with fluted pilasters. Front r. room with fielded panelling and a chimneypiece with carved frame. Good staircase with three different balusters to each tread.)

RAILWAY VIADUCT over the Tamar. 1904–7 by J. C. Lang and the engineers W. R. Galbraith and Richard Church. An early use of concrete blocks.

BERRYNARBOR

ST PETER. An impressive-looking church, thanks to its tower, and one of some architectural interest. The oldest visible part is the arch between N transept and nave, evidently Norman. The chancel follows, E.E., with lancet windows (E window C19) and a pointed

trefoil-headed PISCINA. The nave is wider than the chancel. Beer
stone arcade between nave and s aisle of four bays with A type piers
and standard leaf capitals. The last pier but one has two pretty
niches for images, one to the NW, the other to the SW. Red
sandstone w tower, 96 ft high, with buttresses of type B, a higher NE
stair-turret, a w door decorated with fleurons, a large four-light w
window with one transom, large niches for images high up on all
sides, and projected pinnacles. Tall arch towards the nave. Open,
unceiled wagon roofs in nave, aisle, and s porch. Restored in 1887–
9. – FONT. Square, Norman, with scalloped underside. – MONU-
MENTS. Kneeling figure of c. 1620, chancel N wall. – Richard Berry
† 1645. Wall-monument with the usual figures of parents and
children kneeling and facing each other. – Jane Spence † 1815, by
Stephens of Exeter, odd, with an oval inscription plate and an urn
side by side. – Joseph Bassett † 1846. Pink marble columns and urn.

MANOR HOUSE, just w of the church. It was the house of the Berry
family: HB on the label stops of the hoodmoulds of the four-light
early Tudor windows. Only a fragment remains, with ashlar-faced
front and symmetrically arranged windows. One wing was
demolished in 1889. The porch dated 1634 was transferred to
Westaway, Pilton, near Barnstaple.

Berrynarbor is an intricate little settlement in a steep valley close to the
sea. Near the church a long, low range of cottages and an inn dated
1675.

BRINSCOTT. A longhouse, a rarity in North Devon. The doorways to
house and shippon are blocked, but the shippon interior is well
preserved.

HIGHER TRAINE, 2 m. SW. Partly rebuilt by *Oliver Hill* in 1939.
Somewhat crazy, but after all no more fanciful than many much
admired early C 19 *cottages ornés*. Stepped gables, a row of triangular
bay-windows, and the garden walls interrupted by tall brick pylons
to frame main vistas. Formerly thatched. Altered in 1976, when the
hall was opened up to form a gallery.

BERRY DOWN. Sited on the high ground an extensive Bronze Age
cemetery of large ROUND BARROWS.

See also Watermouth Castle.

BERRY POMEROY   8060

There is no visual connexion between the village, dominated by its
church, and the castle, a mile away in the woods on a cliff overlooking
the Gatcombe Brook.

ST MARY. Architecturally, the interior disappoints after the exterior.
The w tower is tall and rendered, only of two stages (buttresses type
B). Both N and S aisles are embattled. In addition the N aisle has the
asymmetrical accent of a rood-stair turret, the S aisle of a two-
storeyed S porch. The windows are all Perp and large. Inside, the S
porch is vaulted in two bays with blank arcades to W and E walls (cf.
Crediton, Chagford). The church interior itself is very wide and
looks rather stripped, owing partly to the dull new roof. The Beer
stone arcades have B type piers and standard capitals. On some of
those on the S side are inscriptions commemorating benefactors of

the church building and their wives. The tower arch rests on responds similar to the arcade piers. Restoration 1878–9.

SCREEN. One of the most perfect in Devon, complete not only in that it extends from N to S wall but also in having preserved its original coving, its cornice (with only one band of decoration), and its cresting. The tracery is type A standard. On the wainscoting painted figures cut short at the knees. – ALTAR RAILS (W end of N aisle) and ALTAR TABLE early C18. – STAINED GLASS. In the S chapel E, old fragments reset, including three heraldic shields. – E window 1897, two chancel windows 1908 (Nativity and Christ and the Elders, in memory of the Rev. H. S. Prinsep), all by *Christopher Whall*. – N aisle E by *Veronica Whall*, 1926 (PC). – MONUMENTS. Sir Richard Pomeroy † 1496 and wife. Tomb-chest with two tiers of quatrefoils as decoration under a Tudor arch with handsomely carved ornamental band and cresting. – Seymour family, 1613 (Lord Edward † 1593, and Sir Edward and his wife and family). The effigies rather comically on three tiers above and behind each other and all three stiffly propped on their elbows, late examples of this posture. To head and feet of the lady a baby and a little girl sitting dead frontal in a chair. Against the wall of the tomb-chest kneel the children. The whole under a shallow coffered arch and flanked by black Corinthian columns (with shaft-rings). The figure carving astonishingly naïve. To think that the children and grandchildren of Lord Protector Somerset were satisfied with this!

BERRY HOUSE, close to the NE end of the church. C16–17, the windows georgianized. The house was the rectory before the Reformation and used also on the occasion of visits of the Priors of Moreton to whom the church belonged. (Inside, two doorways and a fireplace from the castle.)

CHURCH HOUSE. The rear to the churchyard least altered. Two lateral stacks. Moulded beams in a N ground-floor room.

TITHE BARN, close to this group.

LOVENTOR. The former seat of the Bakers. Now a hotel. Plain rendered C18 seven-bay, two-storey front with later porch. Earlier wing at right angles, with two-storey porch and a C17 doorway with moulded frame. C18 staircase.

CASTLE. The leafy approach gives no hint of the spectacularly romantic setting, half way up a wooded hillside looking out N over a deep ravine and river. The higher ground to the S does not make this an ideal defensive site, and it appears that although the de Pomeroys were here from the Norman Conquest to 1547, their fortifications date only from the later Middle Ages. A park was enclosed in 1207, but the castle is specifically referred to only in 1496, when gate, cellar, kitchen, and numerous chambers are mentioned. The gun-ports show that the surviving defences cannot be earlier than the late C14. In 1547 the castle was bought by Edward Seymour, Duke of Somerset, who was to become Protector under Edward VI. He embarked on substantial additions, left incomplete at his execution in 1552. His family retained the estates, and an inventory shows the castle to have been occupied in 1688, but by the time John Prince, vicar of Berry Pomeroy, described it in his *Worthies of Devon* (1701) it was an abandoned ruin.

The existing defences, of local rubble with a little red sandstone and granite dressings, consist of the gatehouse, two stretches of

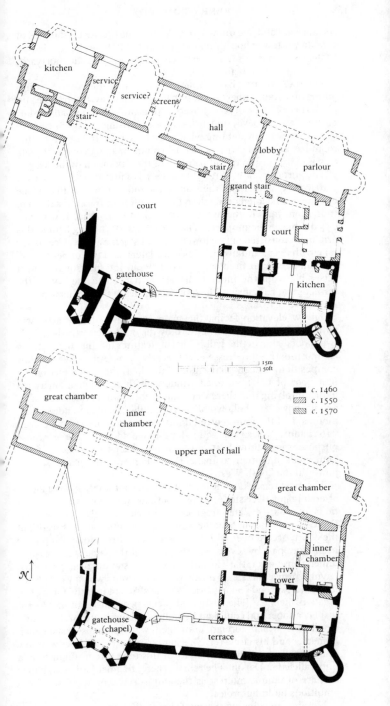

kitchen

service

service?

screens

stair

hall

lobby

parlour

stair

grand stair

court

court

kitchen

gatehouse

great chamber

inner chamber

upper part of hall

great chamber

inner chamber

privy tower

gatehouse (chapel)

terrace

N

15 m
50 ft

■ c. 1460
▨ c. 1550
▨ c. 1570

Berry Pomeroy Castle: plans of ground and first floors.

curtain wall, and one mural tower. Within the precinct is the shell of a medieval tower house, remodelled in the C16, and extended by Protector Somerset's grand new wing on the N side of the courtyard, of which only fragments remain.

The GATEHOUSE has two canted towers with gunports. Seatings for massive roof timbers suggest that there may have been stone gun platforms on top of the towers. Archway with portcullis slot, machicolation above, and below it a surprisingly large (i.e. non-defensive) window lighting what must have been the CHAPEL: the room has an arcade with octagonal columns, and a competent late C15 Flemish-inspired wall painting of the Adoration of the Magi.

The curtain wall W of the gatehouse has a first-floor passage (to a garderobe chamber and the stair to the roof) lit by tiny Beer stone openings. The longer stretch to the E, with faint traces of a ditch in front, continues to the MARGARET TOWER, D-shaped, with late C15 double œillet gunports. The TOWER HOUSE lying behind this originally consisted of two lower floors of storage and service rooms (one with ovens and fireplace inserted later), and two upper storeys of chambers with fireplaces, served by an internal square turret accessible from the inner courtyard. Attached to the NW is the former great hall; inside, the relieving arches of three of its windows are still recognizable.

The W elevation facing the main courtyard of the castle was entirely refaced in the earlier C16 by the de Pomeroys, who added two floors above the hall. Certain features of the three-storey composition are progressive: the nearly symmetrical five-window composition, the central position of the door, the appearance on the first floor of tall transomed windows with rectangular unarched lights (implying that there were important rooms at this level). The details, however – hollow-chamfered mullions, square-ended hood-moulds, and the four-centred doorways inside – are typical Devon C16 Tudor. Not so the 230-ft-long range added to the N, whose purpose was to provide state rooms on a scale that suggests it was Somerset's intention to make Berry Pomeroy his major seat of power in the South West.

The most remarkable feature of the NORTH RANGE was a loggia of crisply cut Beer stone, whose footings were exposed in excavations of 1982–5. The fragments discovered tally exactly with Prince's description: 'a noble walk whose length was the breadth of the court, arch'd over with curiously carv'd Free stone, supported in the fore part by several stately pillars of the same stone of great dimensions, after the Corinthian Order, standing on pedestals, having cornices or friezes finely wrought; behind which were placed in the wall several seats of Frieze-stone also, cut into the form of an escallop shell ...' The rusticated piers, pedestals, and mouldings display a sober and confident handling of Renaissance architectural detail, for which foreign craftsmen were perhaps responsible. Somerset and his circle (cf. Sharington at Lacock, Wilts) were the leading patrons of this new style, at this time rare in England and unparalleled in Devon. The remains here, fragmentary though they are, are of unique interest as the only survival of Somerset's own ambitious building projects.

Nothing remains of the interiors of the rooms behind, where Prince saw 'statues and figures cut in alabaster, chimneypieces of polished marble, rooms adorned with mouldings and fretwork ...'; whether all this was complete in Somerset's time is unknown. The layout can be deduced from the fragmentary outer walls: a traditional great hall rising through two storeys, with a bay-window looking N over the valley, kitchen and service rooms to the W with a separate suite of first-floor chambers, parlour to the E, with a great chamber above, equalling the hall in size and approached by a staircase inserted in the old hall. Above this there may have been a long gallery (no evidence of dividing walls), as at Broughton, Oxfordshire, or (a little later) at Holcombe Rogus. Further E is a later range of private apartments; the projected W wing completing the courtyard was never built.

BICKINGTON

7070

ST MARY. W tower with stair-turret in the centre of one side and low pinnacles. Early C16 priest's door in the S chancel wall. N aisle separated from the nave by a four-bay arcade on octagonal piers with double-chamfered arches. The rest, restoration of 1882–4 by *R.M.Fulford.* – Plain FONT with early C17 COVER.

(By the churchyard a picturesque group of cottages made from a former church house.)

COOMBE PARK. Three-bay rendered front with central pediment and moulded window surrounds.

BICKINGTON BARTON. Late Georgian front; Doric porch with stone columns.

BICKLEIGH
Near Plymouth

5060

ST MARY. Perp W tower with buttresses of B type and projecting polygonal pinnacles. The rest by *Charles Fowler*, 1838, with octagonal piers on tall bases (for box pews); alterations by *J.D.Sedding*, 1882. Chancel refurnished in 1964 by *Louis Osman* at the expense of the Lopes family (Lord and Lady Roborough). Granite ALTAR, COMMUNION RAIL, and PAVING. In sympathy with their hard, tough surfaces, an abstract Jackson-Pollockish REREDOS, and an E window with STAINED GLASS designed by *Frank Wilson*, made by *Edward Payne*, with a spiky pattern of yellow, grey and purple. – FONT. Perp, octagonal, crenellated, with large flat leaf pattern. – BENCH ENDS. With two-tier blank traceried arches. – SCULPTURAL FRAGMENTS. Old font (?), circular, with incised zigzag. – Base of a quatrefoil pier, presumably from the old church. – MONUMENTS. Sir Manasseh Lopes of Maristow † 1831, by *Westmacott Jun.* Seated mourning figure with anchor. – Three Lopes children † 1823–32. Small mourning putto, classical surround. – Sir Ralph Lopes † 1854 and his widow Dame Susan Gibbs Lopes † 1870. A pair of Gothic tablets with mourning angels.

The village has been much expanded by housing for the Royal Marines.

TAVY RAILWAY VIADUCT, carrying the line of the Plymouth, Devonport and South West Junction Railway over the confluence of the Tavy and the Tamar. Built *c.* 1889–90. Eight bow-string girders, each of 112 ft span, rest on masonry approaches at each end. *See also* Maristow, Warleigh.

BICKLEIGH
Near Tiverton

Church and village on the E side of the Exe valley, the castle, very picturesquely placed, on the W.

ST MARY. Tucked into the hillside above the village. Unbuttressed W tower with stair-turret not at the corner, probably C13. Late medieval S arcade with B type piers and standard capitals; the rest rebuilt in 1847–8 in a competent and robust Dec, progressive for its date. Varied window tracery. Hammerbeam roof. – Contemporary *Minton* TILES in the chancel. – REREDOS. 1881 by *Hems*; wall arcade with polished marble columns. – PULPIT. C18. – BENCH ENDS. Some with tracery, one with a man with a bundle of tools. – MONUMENTS to the Carews in the S chancel chapel. John Carew † 1588. Kneeling figure between columns. – Elizabeth Eriseys, née Carew, † 1618, reclining under an arch with fluted columns and elaborate top structure: putti reclining with hourglasses below the Carew arms, flanked by obelisks. In front of the tomb-chest a baby. – Peter Carew † 1654. Bad busts of husband and wife in niches (same hand as the Walronds at Uffculme). – Sir Henry Carew † 1681. A sadly jumbled-up composition in the E window of the family chapel. He lies on a tomb-chest and two children kneel to his head and feet. Behind and above him on the window-sill his wife reclining. The top decoration stands against the window. – Henry Blackmore Baker and his brother, † 1841 and 1849. Sophisticated traceried blind window in the form of a spherical triangle.

BICKLEIGH HOUSE (former rectory). Plain Regency stucco; Tuscan porch.

BICKLEIGH MILL. Watermill, now a craft centre.

STATION (former). Built *c.* 1885. Gables with zigzag patterned barge-boards and fancy roof cresting. Small goods shed, now a salt store. Wooden canopy on brackets.

BRIDGE over the Exe. Five arches with pointed cutwaters.

WILLIS FARMHOUSE. C16 and C17, of medieval origin, with original louvre arrangement in the roof.

At BURN, 1 m. S, a chain suspension FOOTBRIDGE. Two three-inch link chains with iron-rod supports and tie-bars suspending two rows of 1-ft-wide planks.

BICKLEIGH CASTLE. In an idyllic setting by the W bank of the river. Remnants of a defensible manor house rather than a castle, tidied up and renovated by successive owners from 1925, too much so to be easily interpreted. A grand gatehouse behind an incomplete water-course (presumably successor to a moat) which has been prettily laid out as a water garden. In front is a very handsome Italian C18 wrought-iron gate. The manor was held by a junior branch of the Courtenays from the early C15 (*see* Powderham; the senior branch was at Tiverton just up the river), succeeded by the Carews in the C16. The buildings were partly demolished in the Civil War. After the last male Carew died in 1681 they were used as a farm and stores until 1925.

GATEHOUSE of roughly coursed sandstone, much repointed and originally taller; it now ends abruptly above the second floor. C15 simple chamfered archway of three orders, two-bay passage with sexpartite vaults with thick chamfered ribs on polygonal responds; some upper windows with cusped lights below straight heads. Other windows renewed later. Some of the cusped one-light windows may be C20 additions. On either side of the archway rectangular projections. The l. one, much rebuilt, has a staircase in the upper part (the doorway and lower stair are later C20 insertions). On the S side remains of a larger newel stair which may have provided access to a demolished range as well as to the gatehouse. On the W, two large square projections, probably garderobe chutes for the upper rooms. A guard room on either side of the archway; on the first floor a large chamber, restored in the 1920s, and probably not originally a single room. The four doorways to garderobes and stairs suggest more than one apartment. The wooden screen and the overmantel with the Courtenay arms on the long wall brought in; smaller fireplace with depressed arch in the short N wall.

The original layout of the other buildings is unclear. Fragmentary foundations opposite the gatehouse may be those of a hall, but apart from the gatehouse, the most substantial medieval survival is the range on the S side of the courtyard called Old Court House, now in separate ownership (*see* below).

N of the courtyard a building used as a farmhouse until 1925. Much altered inside, with a brought-in staircase of *c.* 1600 (from Scotland) providing access to the gatehouse. At the W end a large kitchen fireplace with the remains of a smoking chamber. In the former dairy beyond, a remarkable reassembled overmantel from the castle with the arms of Carew and Mohun (marriage of 1626): a very large stone lintel, busily carved in low relief with a jumble of small figure scenes no doubt inspired by Netherlandish pattern books, including a windmill, a walled city, a stoning scene, Susannah and the elders, and other figures in early C17 dress. Was there a general theme? The Prayer Book rebellion of 1549, suppressed by the Carews, has been suggested. N of this range a former coach house and stables, with clock turret.

OLD COURT HOUSE, S of the courtyard. Originally part of the castle. In the S wall several cusped windows, some (and also one of the stone two-centred doorways) probably new or not *in situ*, as they accord with the later inserted floors and chimneystacks and not with the medieval open hall for which evidence is provided by the smoke-blackened roof. This roof is of some grandeur, originally with three sets of purlins and upper and lower wind-braces. Five jointed-cruck trusses remain (two of them arch-braced) with a ridge carried on a yoke. The building has been truncated at the E end. In the outbuilding to the W a wooden late medieval arched doorway.

CHAPEL, to the E, across the road in a cob-walled enclosure. An endearing little thatched building, of a date rare in Devon. Nave with plain C12 doorway of well laid tufa, with two unmoulded orders, chamfered hoodmould and imposts. Rubble walls, apart from the dressed quoins, plinth, and windows. C15 cusped three-light windows to the nave. Chancel with tall splayed round-arched E window and much restored C15 wagon roof. – STAINED GLASS (brought in). Late medieval Virgin and Child (chancel s). – The chapel presumably belonged to a C12 manor house, of which no trace is visible in the existing buildings. There is also no evidence that the steeply rising ground to the w was (as sometimes happened) used as a motte.

BICTON

BICTON COLLEGE OF AGRICULTURE. The vast mansion of the Rolles, who inherited the Bicton estate through marriage in the early C17, now appears entirely Edwardian, thanks to *Sir Walter Tapper*'s work of 1908–9. But this was only a neo-Georgian facelift. The essential form of the house, although without its rather frivolous roof balustrade, and with less regular fenestration, is identical to that shown in an engraving of 1831 (Moore's *Devonshire*). Large three-storey squarish main block, of red brick immaculately tuck-pointed; Tuscan colonnade along the front, central full-height bow. Lower wings run out behind, connected by quadrant corners, enclosing a generous service court. The archway to this with its neo-classical bell-turret must be early C19, dating from the completion of the house by *James Wyatt*, who began work *c*. 1800 for the Lord Rolle who succeeded in 1796 and died in 1842. Before that time there was only a two-storey range, the start of an ambitious but incomplete mid C18 building campaign.

The main ground-floor interiors are Edwardian (library and dining room to l. and r., billiard room in the wing beyond the library). Fine cornices throughout. Sumptuous imperial stair with Ionic columns on the landing, clumsily divided from the low entrance hall with its seated statue of John, Lord Rolle, 1844 by *E. B. Stephens*. Behind the house, post-war students' accommodation, tactfully sited.

EAST LODGE. Grand, channelled-stuccoed, two storeys, with central archway on eccentric capitals. Called the New Lodge on a map of 1809. The SOUTH LODGE is of one storey, with paired pilasters.

BICTON GARDENS. The grounds are now a separate concern from the college, and by approaching them from further s one misses the splendid effect of the view from the house of the lake, formal gardens, and obelisk beyond. The C18 layout with its axial vistas is said to date from *c*. 1735, after a design by *Le Nôtre*; late for such formal planning, although cf. the exactly contemporary work at Castle Hill. But the present appearance of the gardens is largely the work of John, Lord Rolle (†1842), and his second wife Louisa Trefusis, daughter of Lord Clinton. During their time the LAKE in front of the house was created (dug in 1812 by French prisoners of war), the arboretum (1830), pinetum (1839), and monkey-puzzle avenue (1842) planted, and most of the buildings erected.

137   The most exciting building is the PALM HOUSE, quite small (68 ft long, 29 ft high), but of a wonderfully swelling bulbous trefoil shape, placed against a straight wall. The side lobes are supported by thin iron columns, the glazing is by small overlapping panes between iron ribs. It dates possibly from *c*. 1820–30 (certainly

before 1838, when it appears on a plan), and its design must be inspired by the theories of J.C. Loudon, the advocate of curved glasshouse roofs. The maker was probably *W. & D. Bailey* of London, who designed similar early curved glasshouses to Loudon's design.

s of the palm house, the ORANGERY, at the head of the Italian gardens. Central open loggia with two Ionic columns. In the pediment a bust of the Duke of Wellington; in niches at the sides busts of Nelson and Sir Walter Raleigh, 1806 by *Coade & Sealy*. Lawns step down from here, plentifully scattered with urns and sculpture, to the C18 formal basin flanked by canals. The OBELISK on the horizon was erected in 1747.

SHELL HOUSE, in the American gardens. Of *c.* 1840. Circular, of large flinty chunks; cyclopic castellation. Collections of shells in cases, not on the walls.

HERMITAGE, beyond the pinetum, close to the lake. Dated 1839. All of wood and very charming, a late example of the type. Octagonal centre, low wings, shingled roofs. Complete with basketwork lining, rustic furniture, and deerbone floor (cf. Killerton).

ICE HOUSE and tunnel, near the lake, *c.* 1800.

RESTAURANT, 1982–5 by *Lucas, Roberts & Brown*, tucked away behind the orangery, and numerous other C20 tourist attractions; the grounds are fortunately large enough to absorb them.

Outside the grounds, NW of the house, the CHINA TOWER, in Baker's Brake. Built in 1839 by Lady Rolle as a gift to her husband, and named from a china collection kept there. Castellated octagonal lookout tower.

BICTON CHURCHES, at the corner of the gardens, close to the road. When in 1850 Lady Rolle decided to commemorate the death of her husband she commissioned both a new church from Hayward and a mausoleum from Pugin (he preferred to call it a mortuary chapel), to the NE of the old church, by then ruinous. From this medieval church there remain only the tiny w tower and the wall of the nave with Perp windows.

The MAUSOLEUM is a memorable building, among the most convincing which exist by *Pugin*. Severe, steeply roofed, heavily buttressed exterior. Inside, blue on yellow *Minton* tiles on the floor, a vaulted ceiling with square, prettily decorated panels, E and W windows also designed by *Pugin* (made by *Hardman*), and on the N wall the surprisingly elaborate Rolle monument carved by *George Myers*, a tomb-chest with ornate quatrefoil decoration and a foliated brass cross on the lid and behind the back wall, with angels and shields with supporters all in ogee arches. Opposite, the Baroque tomb of Denys Rolle † 1638, which Pugin must have hated. Two figures, she recumbent, he reclining, propped up on his elbow on a tomb-chest, and a baby lying on the ground below the chest. An arch behind. Black marble with white figures and ornamental dressings. Attributed plausibly by Mrs Esdaile to *William Wright* (cf. Eggesford).

ST MARY, the new church by *Hayward*, is a careful cruciform composition with s tower, N porch, and Dec tracery. It was an early demonstration in Devon of Camdenian ideals. The Diocesan Architectural Society commended the 'spirit of liberal zeal' and 'the judicious regard to ecclesiastical propriety in which the whole has been conceived and executed'. Much carving by *J. Dudley* of London: kings and queens on the dripstones, from Edward I to Victoria (and Albert), English divines in the nave, evangelists at the crossing. – FONT by *Simon Rowe*. – Unvarnished WOODWORK; colourful *Minton* TILES; STAINED GLASS by *Warrington*.

4020

BIDEFORD

Of the two chief North Devon ports, Bideford easily outbids Barnstaple in general attractiveness, if not in antiquity. It owes its modest charm to its position on the W side of the Torridge, a more awkward site than Barnstaple, so that the narrow streets of small white plastered houses have to climb steeply uphill, as at Dartmouth. As in so many Devon ports, the town expanded towards the river on reclaimed land. Most of the buildings facing the water are more recent than the rest, but there is nothing out of scale. The pretty group of Victorian and Edwardian public buildings near the bridge fits in happily, and the most recent new housing is commendably in character.

In the Middle Ages Bideford was an unimportant place, the property of the Grenvilles, notable only for its impressive bridge across the Torridge. It was a borough by 1217 and had a market by 1271, but never had its own Member of Parliament. Prosperity came with the growth of trade to the New World in the C16 and C17. The town was made a free borough in 1573; shipbuilding developed, and continued into the C20. A new quay was begun in 1663. By the late C17 Bideford was second only to Topsham among the Devon ports sending ships to the Newfoundland fisheries; the tobacco trade was also an important source of wealth up to the later C18. The grandest houses date from the end of the C17, with a particularly sumptuous example at East-the-Water, the settlement across the river, and a whole sequence of fine brick houses along the newly laid out Bridgeland Street, which attracted Defoe's special attention, and which are indeed among the best urban merchants' houses of this time anywhere in England. As the foreign trade of the port declined towards the end of the C18, later building in the town is on a much more modest scale, although there are several handsome early C19 suburban villas. The population was still only 2,987 in 1801; 5,775 in 1851, 8,754 in 1901, 12,210 in 1981.

ST MARY, Church Walk. Rebuilt by *Edward Ashworth* in 1862–5 except for the W tower (diagonal buttress, N E polygonal stair-turret, no pinnacles, unmoulded pointed tower arch). The church is large and wide, entirely in traditional Devon forms. All Saints Chapel on the N side, formerly the mayor and corporation's enclosure, was sensitively converted to a morning chapel in 1982 by *Lucas, Roberts & Brown*. It is divided off from the church by an engraved glass SCREEN by *Peter Tysoe*. – FONT. Large, circular, Norman, with thick rope-mouldings separating panels, three of them decorated, one with a Maltese cross. The whole type quite out of the ordinary. – TOWER SCREEN. Made up of early Renaissance and Elizabethan woodwork from the Grenville Chapel. – STAINED GLASS. A good Victorian collection: E window by *A. Gibbs*, 1865, very colourful, N window by *Dix*, and several other good examples. – MONUMENTS. Sir Thomas Grenville † 1513, between chancel and chancel chapel,

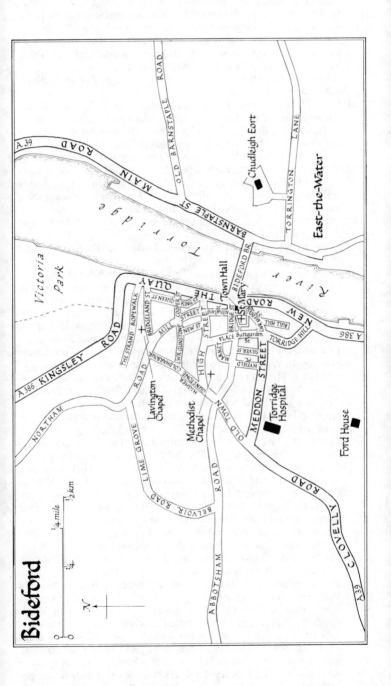

with a fine stone screen preserved from the old church. Sir Thomas in armour on a tomb-chest with three cusped quatrefoils (little pinnacled niches between them). Canopy with depressed arch with large leaves in the spandrels. – John Strange †1646, mayor, with moving inscription recording his labours during the plague of that year. Bust in strapwork surround. – Many minor tablets.

SACRED HEART (R.C.), Northam Road. 1892 by *Lethbridge*, baptistery and turret 1907.

LAVINGTON CHAPEL, Bridgeland Street. Named after its minister, Samuel Lavington, †1807. A tall gabled front with twin corner towers with twin tall spires, 1856–9 by *E. M. White* of Bideford, an early use of such a design by the Nonconformists. It replaced the Great Meeting House of 1696, contemporary with the street.

METHODIST CHAPEL, High Street. Built for the United Methodists in 1913 by *Beddoe Rees* of Cardiff, the final flowering of Methodist self-confidence before the First World War. Large, free-standing building with tall gabled front and octagonal corner turrets. – (STAINED GLASS. Two-light windows by *Arnold Robinson* and *Edward Woore*, 1938.)

For the TOWN HALL, LIBRARY, and other buildings in the town centre *see* perambulation.

GRENVILLE COLLEGE, Belvoir Road. Assembly hall 1982 by *Gundry Dyer Partnership* (project architect *Carole Trim*), a hexagon, with walls of attractive mottled greyish-buff brick, and a shallow-pitched laminated-timber roof with broadly splayed eaves (disappointingly covered in roofing felt). Two angled windows lighting side chapels, with STAINED GLASS by *Robinson*, 1985. Dining hall by the same firm with four pitched roofs with decorative ridge tiles, sensitively echoing the forms of nearby older buildings. *See also* Moreton.

TORRIDGE HOSPITAL, Meddon Street. Built as a workhouse in 1835–6 by *George Gilbert Scott* and similar to Scott's workhouses at Tiverton and Tavistock. One-storey entrance range, main three-storeyed block behind with octagonal centre and pediments to the diagonal sides. Central lantern. Two-storeyed flanking wings.

THE TOWN. The BRIDGE is the *raison d'être* of Bideford. It is said to have been first built by Sir Theobald Grenville in the C14, and the present structure is supposed to date from the C15. That, of course, as with most bridges, must be understood *cum grano salis*. Most of the present stonework belongs to repairs (e.g. 1638), and especially the widening of 1865. The bridge is 677 ft long and has twenty-four arches – a most impressive structure, whatever its age. It crosses the estuary of the river Torridge, as the similar bridge at Barnstaple crosses that of the Taw. Facing the bridge a trio of civic buildings. On the l. the TOWN HALL and LIBRARY, mostly of 1905 by *A. J. Dunn* of Birmingham in quite a playful free Tudor, red brick with stone dressings. The civic buildings are enlivened by a tower, a Perp oriel, and a corner balcony and turret. Behind, *R. D. Gould's* Town Hall of 1850. On the r., BRIDGE BUILDINGS by *W. R. Bryden*, 1882, tall, of stone, a little French in its details, built as a Library and School of Science and Art, to replace the older Grammar School building. From this, preserved in the staircase hall, royal arms, a cartouche with the bridge, and some other carvings. s of the Library TANTON'S HOTEL, a once handsome early C19 stucco front with a series of shallow bay-windows with curved sides, a favourite local type. Hidden behind this group, on the steep slopes around the church, a cluster of delightful streets and passages with terraces of small white-walled houses with minimal classical detail of the C18 to early C19: doorcases with brackets, painted raised bands around the windows. Good examples in CHURCH WALK, LOWER MEDDON STREET (a little grander, some houses of three storeys), and BULL HILL, at the end of which some very tactful replacements by *Torridge District Council* have been added in the same spirit (1978–80), a welcome change from earlier, less sensitive infilling elsewhere in the town. BRIDGE STREET, running steeply up from the bridge, would benefit from similar treatment in place of the gaping car parks created in the 1960s.

Further pleasant terraces remain higher up in BUTTGARDEN STREET, SILVER STREET, and HYFIELD PLACE, the last, like a number of Bideford's minor streets, approached through an archway. These three run s from the MARKET PLACE, a large sloping square filled by the extensive but not very distinguished market buildings of 1883–4 by *John Chudleigh* of Exeter. At the corner of Silver Street the NEW INN HOTEL, with a big porte-cochère with High Victorian naturalistic capitals. On the W side a restrained early C19 terrace, above a raised pavement with attractive railings with honeysuckle pattern. On the N side Nos. 13–14, earlier C19 stucco, with panelled pilasters, and next door the rarity of an Art Deco frontage, created for a building society. Original jazzy glazing; upstairs, an apsed panelled boardroom.

Back down Bridge Street to ALLHALLAND STREET, a narrow lane running parallel to The Quay, with a good sequence of C18 houses on its W (once river-facing) side. Nos. 6–7 have two first-floor Venetian windows, No. 8a, MERCHANT HOUSE, has a good C18 Doric doorcase. Between them, a passage through to the tiny CHAPEL STREET. At the corner of the HIGH STREET, LLOYDS BANK, 1892, with cheerful free Jacobethan detail in contrast to the sober classical banks opposite. The grander of these is the part of the NATIONAL WESTMINSTER BANK with vermiculation and Gibbsian blocking round the windows. The earlier part is of 1850 by *E.M. White*. The High Street winds attractively uphill with a medley of good C18 buildings (e.g. No. 65, red brick with two canted bays) interspersed with brasher C19 commercial offerings (Co-op, with jolly terracotta trimmings, 1886), and the Methodist church (q.v.) at the top.

Now along the waterfront. On THE QUAY (from s to N), after Bridge Buildings, a stuccoed early C19 frontage with pilasters, then the Rose of Torridge Café, much altered, but essentially a C16 jettied timber-framed building with later stuccoed front. Further on the KINGS ARMS, with three low storeys, also possibly older than its stucco frontage. Then the GAS SHOWROOMS, with a display of 1930s features, and a good C18 house at the corner of the High Street with dentilled cornice, and on each front four upper segment-headed windows with keystones. After KINGSLEY HOUSE (formerly a hotel) with its nice C18 Doric doorcase the frontages break back, marking the site of a late C17 quay. Several lanes converge on this: KING STREET with old rubble stone warehouses on both sides, COOPER STREET winding down the hill, and QUEEN

STREET, with a good C18 house, three storeys with two full-height bays.

Facing the river, further on, PROSPECT PLACE, an early C19 terrace. On the other side of Bridgeland Street the OLD CUSTOMS HOUSE, early C19, with a bowed staircase wing projecting at the back. Little to see further on apart from the BIDEFORD ARTS CENTRE, built as a Municipal and Technical School in 1896 by *G. Malam Wilson*, as we are told on a large plaque. Free Gothic, in brash red terracotta, with large windows to the N. KINGSLEY ROAD follows the line of the Pill stream (culverted in the C19). On its opposite side, VICTORIA PARK, reclaimed from swamps in 1912, and a statue of Charles Kingsley, 1906 by *Joseph Whitehead*.

BRIDGELAND STREET is the best street in Bideford, in Defoe's time 'well inhabited by considerable and wealthy merchants'. It was a speculative development of the 1690s on Bridge Trust Lands, by Nathaniel Gascoyne, at the time when the prosperity of the town was at its height as a result of the tobacco trade with the New World. Despite some later heightenings, altered ground floors, and added stucco and bay-windows, one can still recognize many of the broad-fronted two-storey-and-attic brick houses that lined the street on both sides – one of the first consistent uses of brick for urban building in the county. As so often at this period, the houses are not uniform in design. No. 28 on the S side, leased in 1692 to Jonathan Hooper, has the least altered exterior (apart from the pretty curved bay-window added over the doorway): a generous eight bays with segment-headed ground-floor windows, deep dentilled cornice, pedimented dormers (rebuilt), and the most splendid decorative rainwater-heads dated 1692 and 1693. In this house a broad central passage leads to a cobbled courtyard flanked by two back wings (one with a substantial kitchen). The more common type of plan is more compact, a tentative version of a double pile, with three rooms (two front, one back), and a dog-leg staircase at right angles to a broad central passage. In many such houses excellent original joinery and plasterwork remain, hidden behind the altered fronts: No. 31, for example (now two shops), described as 'well nigh finished' in 1692, has fielded panelling in one ground-floor room, and two plaster ceilings with quatrefoil and oval centrepieces on the floor above.* No. 26 (the Red House), refronted, like its neighbour, with late C19 mathematical tiles, likewise has excellent panelling on both floors, and a well preserved staircase with turned balusters and moulded string. The first lease dates from 1700.

No. 12 opposite, later known as the Great House (now a Masonic Lodge), has been altered and truncated, but is still the grandest house in Bridgeland Street. An attractive two-storey front covered in rusticated stucco; four bays, with segment-headed windows. The Ionic doorcase in the r. bay was probably once in the centre (the cornice upstairs indicates that the house extended further E). From the broad entrance hall an archway to the stair-hall, unusually sited in the front of the house. The late C17 stairs are in the grand manner, around a small well, with sturdy urn-shaped balusters and newels with balls. Plaster ceiling with central guilloche decoration, perhaps later. The room beyond, entered by another archway, has

---

*For plans of Nos. 4 and 31 Bridgeland Street *see* p. 83.

bolection-moulded panelling and an acanthus frieze around the cove of the ceiling. In the room above (much altered for Masonic purposes) a bold late C17 fireplace with eared surround (not *in situ*). Also on the N side several lesser houses with good features. No. 13 has an original staircase in the standard position; so has No. 8, where behind an unpromising front is concealed a house of *c*. 1700 remodelled in the early C19 (see upper and lower parts of the staircase). In an upper back room a good fireplace with an eared surround. No. 4 has a later C18 stair with oval roof-light and a quatrefoil ceiling on the first floor. There are only a few total rebuildings, the most notable near the top of the street, No. 23, early C19, with a pretty pair of shallow bows and an elegant contemporary staircase, opposite the more discordant spiky Gothic of the Lavington Chapel (q.v.).

Bridgeland Street runs into Mill Street; from here one can explore COLDHARBOUR and LOWER and HIGHER GUNSTONE, two narrow lanes which climb further uphill, delightful except for some poor C20 infilling which ignores the street-line, or turn N towards THE STRAND, which once faced the wharves along the Pill. At the E end, by the entrance to the ROPEWALK running back to the quay, No. 4, with a small but charming stuccoed Regency front with upswept gable and tented balcony, masking the bulk of BLACKMORE'S DEPOSITORY (built as a collar factory *c*. 1906). To the W, Nos. 15–16, perhaps C18, then, in ascending grandeur, classically trimmed stucco mansions of the C19, ending in No. 26 with an Italianate tower.

To the NW, wealthy villas once on the fringes of the town. Within the grounds of STELLA MARIS CONVENT in Northam Road, NORTHDOWN HOUSE, the home of Charles Kingsley, early C19. Its remarkable feature is a cantilevered wooden staircase rising in a swooping elongated spiral up to the first floor. Marble fireplace with busts in one of the front rooms. Additions by *Scoles & Raymond*, 1908. YORK HOUSE, also part of the convent, has three stuccoed canted bays to the garden, *c*. 1800, TORRIDGE LODGE a wing with rounded end. In NORTHAM ROAD, hidden in its own grounds, IFFIELD, an irregular *cottage orné* of *c*. 1840, still in the Regency tradition, possibly a remodelling of an older house. Elaborate bargeboards and Gothic windows with coloured glass; castellated conservatory wing.

Several other large houses in their own grounds off HEYWOOD ROAD on the way to Northam: WOODVILLE HOUSE, stuccoed neo-Grecian, with four Ionic columns *in antis* under a pediment, and a one-storey Ionic porch at the side; DURRANT HOTEL, with Greek Doric porch of 1810 and an earlier nice curved staircase with ogee-headed Venetian window; also PORTHILL, *c*. 1760, square, stuccoed, with Doric porch, and ROSEHILL, a little later, with a good staircase.

To the W, less ambitious suburban development. Some nice mid C19 small stucco villas in ABBOTSHAM ROAD. The notable buildings to the S are WOODAH, Torridge Hill, a five-bay stuccoed Regency front with deep eaves, right on the road, with a later C19 Gothic folly tower in its grounds; OLD FORD HOUSE, New Road, a much altered medieval stone hall-house; and FORD HOUSE, early C19, with trellis veranda, in its own grounds.

Across the bridge, EAST-THE-WATER, essentially an artisan district. The chief exception is the ROYAL HOTEL. This, opened in
1888, incorporates at its N end a remarkable house of 1688, the
mansion of the merchant John Davie. Average C19 stucco exterior.
Inside, a splendid late C17 staircase with turned and carved balusters, three flights around a well. Landing doorcases with open
pediments. Two first-floor rooms with bolection-moulded panel-
107, 110   ling and gorgeous plaster ceilings, among the best in Devon,
perhaps by *John Abbot* (although even more daring than his work on
the Custom House at Exeter). Reminiscent also of the ceilings at
Youlston Park (q.v.) and the destroyed plasterwork at Dunsland.
Both rooms have wreaths or garlands with flowers in the most daring
relief, entirely detached from their background; also writhing
serpents, bursting pomegranates, and grotesque masks.

On the hill directly behind the hotel, SPRINGFIELD TERRACE, mid
C19, with Corinthian pilasters and verandas, facing a narrow path
beside the railway. The former STATION (now Midland Bank)
dates from 1855, single-storeyed, with a small canopy over the yard
entrance. Further N, between Barnstaple Street and the river, and
prominent from The Quay opposite, crisp white groups of local
authority housing of 1980–4 with pitched roofs of interestingly
assorted heights, by *Heber, Percy, Parker, Perry Associates* (Phase
One) and *Torridge District Council* (Phase Two). Still more prominent in the view N towards the estuary is the massive but elegant
BRIDGE built for the by-pass in 1986–7 by the *MRM Partnership*,
very tall, with eight shallow arches of prestressed concrete sections,
the three central ones 300ft wide.

6040   BIGBURY

ST LAWRENCE. Early W tower with short spire. Diagonal buttresses
not reaching high up, plain, narrow, round-headed bell-openings,
battlements on the corbel-table, one tier of gabled dormer
windows. Tall, unmoulded tower arch. The church all but rebuilt
by *E. and J. D. Sedding* in 1868–72. But the fact that the N aisle
and S transept have arches with piers of B type and capitals only to
the shafts, not the hollows, may well go back to the medieval
building. The early C14 SEDILIA, PISCINA, and tomb recess in
the chancel also look confidence-inspiring. – PULPIT. From Ashburton; on a chalice foot, with low panels with big flat ogee arches
and shields beneath them, and a very broad cornice at the top.
– LECTERN. Eagle, timber, remarkably vigorous, also from Ashburton, said to have been made by one *Thomas Prideaux* as a
present from Bishop Oldham of Exeter (1505–19). The bird is said
to have originated as an owl (cf. Oldham's chantry chapel, Exeter
Cathedral). – STAINED GLASS. Some old heraldic fragments. –
MONUMENTS. Early C15 brasses to two sisters. – Slate to John
and Jane Pearse † 1612 and 1589 with incised figures.

BIGBURY COURT, W of the church. Large, plain late Georgian (?)
house; but to the E as an outbuilding remains of an earlier building
with a gabled S porch and a trefoiled window. Datestone, 1764. To
the S a circular dovecote.

(CEDAR HOUSE, Cleveland Drive. 1938 by *Felix Goldsmith*. Flat-roofed, timber-framed, and timber-clad seaside house, gently Early Modern.)

(BURGH ISLAND. Ruins of a medieval chapel. Luxury hotel of 1930, converted to flats 1984.)

BINDON
Axmouth

2090

Extensive C20 alterations have unfortunately detracted from the considerable interest of this unusual medieval house, formerly the seat of the Erle family. Its centre is a compact square block with a suite of apartments on the first floor, fitted up *c.* 1500, but perhaps within an older shell. Was this a self-sufficient tower-house, or did one of the irregular later wings replace a hall range? The entrance front to the W is unexceptional, the result of an early C17 remodelling: two gables, central porch, ovolo-moulded windows. On the N side, however, there are still square-headed two-light cusped windows, the larger ones at first-floor level.

The chapel, squeezed into the SW corner of the same floor, may be the one for which Roger Wyke obtained a licence in 1425, although its fittings look *c.* 1500. Three-light Perp window; within its jamb a little vaulted niche with pinnacled buttresses and angel supporters. Moulded ceiling beams, screen with pierced upper lights, the lower ramped to fit the adjoining staircase. In the room next door an elaborate fireplace of the late medieval Devon type: a row of five quatrefoils, also fleurons around the moulding. Stone doorway to the larger adjoining chamber, which has a four-centred fireplace in the end wall. The stair-turret next to it was built *c.* 1959. One truss remains of an arch-braced roof. Another fireplace with remains of fleurons in the room below. The doorway on its r. was moved from the end wall of the NW wing. Much good joinery of *c.* 1500, not all *in situ*. Long one-storeyed neo-1500 wing to the N added by *John Bellamy* in 1969. Overmantel with the Judgement of Solomon, brought from Barnstaple.

BISHOP'S COURT
Clyst Honiton

9090

An intensely Gothic mansion – a creation of 1860–4 for the High Anglican Garratt family (cf. Sowton) by *William White*, one of the most interesting of the Victorian Gothic revival architects. It is a transformation of a house of *c.* 1800 which itself incorporated remains of the most important medieval country residence of the bishops of Exeter (acquired in 1265 and used by them until 1546). The general disposition of the main hall range between the projecting wings must go back to the medieval house, although the only pre-C18 details now visible *in situ* are two small ground-floor rooms at the back of the S wing, each with a C16 ceiling with moulded beams, and with ovolo-moulded window mullions.

Drawings show that before White's time, the house remodelled by Admiral Graves in 1803 had a symmetrical white stuccoed front with pediment over three central projecting bays, Georgian

Gothick glazing, and projecting wings with Perp windows, the one on the l. probably lighting the medieval chapel, the one on the r. perhaps altered to match it (Swete shows this wing without Gothic detail). White kept the shell of this building, but did his best to destroy the symmetry, resiting the entrance at the r. end of the central range, adding a somewhat contrived composition of buttress, double chimneystack, and arched windows in the centre, and giving the wings different emphasis. The N wing, with a library, received a boldly corbelled out oriel, the s chapel wing was ennobled by thin lancets and a bell-turret with an open timber, rather continental-looking belfry. This inventiveness is damped down by the straight parapet around the main house, although the service wing added beyond the chapel has a more successfully romantic skyline of clustered chimneys and tall half-hipped patterned-slate roofs. On the garden side there is a mixture of double- and triple-arched windows on thin columns, two hefty flying buttresses, and a NW polygonal turret. Throughout, the mottled rubble walls are enlivened by a judicious use of dressed stone, no less than seven or eight varieties, as Eastlake noted in his *History of the Gothic Revival*.

The interior is a remarkably well preserved example of a serious mid C19 architect's conception of domestic Gothic. At the back of the hall an arcade of four pointed arches on thin black columns. Fireplace with stumpy green shafts; much stencilled wall decoration. The furniture is *White*'s own: mirrors, cupboard, table, coat-and-hatstand. In a blocked C16 window recess in the corridor behind, some medieval fragments, including a well carved head of a bishop. The corridor is screened from the stair-hall to the N by an odd grouping of one thick and two thin columns; another thick column and arch appear half-way up the stairs, purely for effect.

The library and drawing room, although rewindowed, are essentially early C19, with simple marble fireplaces; the drawing room has a stencilled ceiling, and a boudoir opening off in the little NW turret. In the dining room adjoining the hall, more sombre Gothic rere-arches to the windows. Another Gothic arch at the s end of the corridor, with an angel in a corner niche, as a prelude to the CHAPEL, entered through a doorway with carved hoodmould and painted angels above. Rather chilly imitation ashlar stencilling, and a lofty elaborate open timber roof. Many contemporary fittings: carved piscina and bookrest with bust of an angel, many metal candlesticks, candelabra, altar cross with semi-precious stones (all designed by *White*), stalls, and west gallery. Triptych by *Westlake*; good C13-style stained glass probably also by *Westlake*. Cross-shaped brass to John Garratt †1886. In the w wall the impost of a medieval arch, left exposed by White. Upstairs, the spine corridor with oval roof-light, and other details, survive from the pre-Victorian house.

The very large barn and stables SE of the house, at right angles to each other, date from the time of the bishops of Exeter. The BARN, now 90ft long, but originally perhaps 115ft, is of brown rubble sandstone. Impressive arch-braced base-cruck roof, with common rafters above the collars, and lower wind-braces, some curved. End truss with two vertical timbers supporting the middle purlins (cf. Dartington entrance block). An early C14 date seems most likely. The STABLES, 120ft long, of Heavitree ashlar, may be early C16. Originally floored at both ends (fireplace at first-floor level at the N end). Arch-braced roof. Discreetly adjoining the stables are the warehouses for Taylor's paints; they are invisible from the house, which is used in an exemplary way for the firm's offices.

BISHOPS NYMPTON   7020

The church lies back from the steep main street of the village, within a big churchyard.

ST MARY. One of the stateliest W towers in North Devon (cf. South Molton and Chittlehampton). Four stages, with large buttresses of type B and gargoyles beneath the battlements. The pinnacles were regrettably shortened in 1959. High plinth, square-headed W door, a small niche on the E side. Very tall Perp tower arch towards the nave. Thin, tall S arcade of six bays, A type piers, capitals only to the four main shafts. Large three-light Perp windows, the chancel E window of four lights. The ceiled wagon roofs of nave and S aisle contemporary with the arcades; both have good bosses. Restored in 1869 (by *Ashworth*) and again in 1877.

FONT. Norman, square, of table-top type, with four shallow blank arcades to each side of the top, on a transitional base. – SCULPTURE. Wooden figure of St James the Less, c. 4ft, C15 (?), an unusual survivor. Formerly on the tower; now in the wall above the vestry. – STAINED GLASS. E window and chancel S 1869, S chapel E by *Clayton & Bell*. – CHARITY BOARDS and a colourful painted wooden tablet to one of the donors (John Blackmore † 1733, with Father Time and skeletons), under the tower. – MONU-MENTS. In the chancel N wall a very remarkable ornate late Perp 51 wall-monument, probably doubling as an Easter Sepulchre, and probably to Sir Lewis Pollard † 1540, an eminent Devon lawyer. Tomb-chest with two tiers of quatrefoils surrounded by cable-mouldings. The chest in a recess under a depressed pointed arch, the jambs and arch with intertwined foliage; the spandrels also closely decorated. – Several C19 Gothic tablets, e.g. Edward Balman † 1818, with coloured marble shafts.

CROSS. A superior medieval farmhouse of c. 1500 on a three-room cross-passage plan. Roof of five trusses, the principals with short curved feet, smoke-blackened throughout. Inserted jettied cham-ber over the inner room. C17 hall ceiling; the screen earlier, with an integral bench end. Porch with plaque over: 1624 BHI. C18 cross-wing to the E.

WHITECHAPEL BARTON. A sizeable E-shaped two-storey manor house, originally of the Bassett family. Tactfully restored in the C20; some wooden-mullioned windows remain. Good interiors, including an early C17 hall screen, bolection-moulded panelling in the hall and in a first-floor room in the W wing, and a ground-floor room with C18 panelling and an earlier plaster ceiling.

GARLIFORD, 2m. N of the village. A well preserved HILLFORT overlooks the river Yeo.

ST JOHN BAPTIST. The church is small and approached usually from the E. It forms a singularly happy picture, with the various roof-heights, and the spire contrasted and set against the background of the grounds of Tawstock Court with mansion and church. Bishops Tawton is indeed in several ways a near relative of Tawstock. The tower, it is true, is not over the crossing, but on the N side. It is buttressed only at the foot and has a crocketed octagonal stone spire, a unique feature in Devon. On the ground floor a two-light E window of the early C14 which now looks into the vestry. The chancel arch is the feature most directly dependent on Tawstock. It is unmoulded, but has a moulded sub-arch on head corbels. The chancel itself was rebuilt in 1864–6 by *Gould*, the N aisle by the same firm in 1878. The tracery on the S side and the S porch are also C19. The aisle in its present form is Perp, with a three-bay arcade with piers of B type and standard leaf capitals. An additional half-bay butts against the tower and opens into it with a fine four-light Perp window. The windows have tall two-centred arches and Perp tracery. Perp also the W door and the frame of the W window of the nave. Wide original ceiled wagon roof in the nave. The chancel, raised up several steps in Victorian High Church fashion, has a REREDOS (concealed by a curtain) of glazed tiles in robust Victorian colours.

SCREEN, in the tower arch. Partially blocked, three bays, standard tracery, squarely framed, cornice with one strip of foliage. Arms of Chichester and Hall in the spandrels (Thomasine Hall, who married Richard Chichester, died in 1502). – BENCH ENDS. C19, imitated from those at Atherington. – STAINED GLASS. An interesting Victorian sequence. E and chancel S by *Lavers & Barraud*, 1860s, with rich mosaic patterning. Three in the N aisle by *Lavers, Barraud & Westlake*, 1870s, still quite bright colours, with a vivid red. S aisle window near the W end by the same firm, 1893. N aisle W a very unusual window in pale colours, of departed friends of the donor (†1895), with a background of leaves and acorns. – MONUMENTS. Lady Ursula Chichester †1635, with a kneeling figure. – Infant daughter of Charles Dart †1652. Tablet with a baby in swaddling clothes, 9 in. long, lying below the inscription plate. – John Chichester †1669. Tablet still with some strapwork, though with a cornice going classical. – Sir Francis Chichester †1698. A big, rich, and rather coarse wall-monument with caryatids, columns, and arms in a lunette above. – W. H. Law †1855. Marble, women and urn in a clumsy frame, by *Sartorelli*. – Two other Law tablets, †1883 and †1895, by *E. J. Physick*; draped Gothic arches.

SCHOOL, by the churchyard. 1841, simple mullioned windows, bell-gable.

OLD VICARAGE, W of the church. 1841; two shaped Jacobean gables, three storeys, mullioned windows, the ground-floor ones of four lights. Extension in the same style behind. By *Hayward*.

COURT FARMHOUSE, S of the church. A medieval residence of the bishops of Exeter. Medieval fabric may survive in the two-storeyed service wing to the S, but the three corner towers, battlements, and general tidying-up date from c. 1800.

LAW ALMSHOUSES, on the main road. Quite a striking group of 1885. Three pairs of gables, paired Gothic entrances.

The main road divides the village from the church. On the E side of the village street, ROSEHILL, a stuccoed Regency house with dentilled eaves and pilasters with incised Greek key, and two far-projecting full-height bow-windows with conical roofs, one carried round the corner rather in the manner of Nash (cf. Sandridge). STABLES with one Gothic window and two lunettes.

HALMPSTONE FARM. An attractive group of stone outbuildings and farmhouse, the latter of medieval origin (arch-braced roof), but remodelled in the late C17 with symmetrical garden front with five wooden cross-windows, and good contemporary fittings (stair-case and plasterwork).

MONUMENT, Codden Hill. An urn on a tapering cylinder to Caroline Thorpe † 1970, by *Clough Williams Ellis*.

See also Hall.

BISHOPSTEIGNTON

ST JOHN BAPTIST. Nave with Norman W portal, one of the best in Devon. Two orders of colonnettes with zigzag and scale patterns and the voussoirs decorated with zigzag, some kind of rudimentary fleur-de-lis, and, in the inner order, beakheads and a large bird at the S end. A Norman tympanum furthermore walled into the S wall, outside. This is strange indeed, showing the Three Magi marching along under arcades, and a figure (possibly the warning angel) dead frontal in a wide, pleated skirt. Everything rigidly stylized, of an unconcern with realism to which one is used only in tribal art. W tower of 1815 in front of the N aisle. Tall arcade between nave and N aisle with standard capitals but slender piers of unusual section (four shafts, and in the diagonals long shallow hollows with four inserted shafts; cf. East Ogwell). – FONT. Circular, Norman, with three bands of much reworked decoration.

The village, close to Teignmouth, attracted gentlemen's villas in the early C19. Several in FORDER ROAD; also, in FORE STREET, CROSS HOUSE, with an especially good delicate two-tier timber veranda on three sides (future uncertain).

BISHOP'S PALACE, ½m. NE. Two red sandstone walls survive of Bishop Grandison's summer palace. One has small ogee-headed windows as befits its date: 1332.

LYNDRIDGE, ½m. NW, was a notable large mansion, gutted by fire in 1963. The wings had been demolished in the C18. The centre, with a fine ballroom with a ceiling dated 1673 and other work of this date (all destroyed), was refaced in brick and given a Queen Anne appearance in 1916 by *James Ransome* for Lord Cable. The later C17 owner was Sir Peter Lear, followed by a branch of the Templer family in the mid C18. Grounds laid out in 1913–14 by *Ransome*, with *Robert Veitch* of Exeter and *Edward White*.

(THE MOORS. 1868 for John Robin by *J.A. Hansom*. DE)

BITTADON

ST PETER. Largely rebuilt in 1883. Aisleless, low, no more than a chapel in size. W tower stump with modern pyramid roof. – FONT. Square, on four round shafts. – MONUMENTS. Henry Ackland †1675. Corinthian columns, broken pediment. – Edward Pointz †1691. Similar, but with trophies above. – SUNDIAL. Of slate, very pretty, by *J. Berry*, 1764 (cf. Kentisbury, Marwood, Tawstock).

BITTADON BARTON. C18 five-bay front; C17 wing with stair-turret.

INNER NARRACOTT. An Exmoor longhouse, a rarity. C17 chimneystacks and lateral staircase.

ROUND BARROWS. 1 m. N, a good group of nine. Further N, on the S side of NORTH HILL CLEAVE, another three and an Iron Age earthwork enclosure.

BLACKAWTON

ST MICHAEL. Low W tower with diagonal buttresses. Polygonal stair-turret in the centre of one side. Battlements on a corbel-table and no pinnacles (cf. Ashburton). S porch attached to the S aisle. Windows mostly with four-centred arches and mullions only, no tracery. Beer stone arcades between nave and aisles with piers of B type and standard capitals; the arches moulded. The lower projecting chancel older, i.e. belonging to the church dedicated in 1333 – see the curiously adapted chancel arch, the blocked N windows, the fine double PISCINA with pointed trefoil arches and pointed quatrefoil above, and the SEDILIA. Restored in 1887–90 by *E. Sedding.* – FONT. Circular, Norman, the usual type with palmette frieze and cable-moulding above, but of unusually high quality. Domed FONT COVER. – PULPIT. Jacobean type, with the usual stumpy blank arcades. – SCREEN. Outer panels painted with Italian antique work, incorporating the cyphers of Henry VIII and Katharine of Aragon. Broad four-light sections of B type. The coving and most of the cornice gone. – WALL PANELLING. – MONUMENTS. Brass to Nicholas Forde †1582 and wife. – Richard Sparkes †1700, yet still the old tomb-chest type. Black lid with inscription only; no effigy.

OLDSTONE, ½ m. NE. The mansion of the Cholwich family, later the Dimes, burnt in 1893 and now in ruins and completely neglected. A Georgian seven-bay front with Tuscan doorway and behind it earlier fragments: a porch, and above it a tall Perp three-light window of church size (a neo-Gothic creation?). Older walls, in one case standing three storeys high. The grounds were once elaborate. There were three lakes, a grotto, and a hermitage (B. Jones).

WADSTRAY, 1 m. E. 'A neat small seat', built *c.*1787 by Andrew Pinson, a Dartmouth merchant, with 'extensive prospect of sea and land' (Polwhele). Two two-storey bow-windows, pedimented doorcase, rendered.

FUGE. Remodelled *c.*1725 by the Hayne family. Nine-bay, sash-windowed front with centre of five bays. Contemporary gatepiers.

BLACKBOROUGH

ALL SAINTS. On an impressively bleak height above the Culm valley. 1838 by *James Knowles Sen.* for the fourth Earl of Egremont, Knowles's first important patron. W tower, nave, and chancel, in an unhistorical but forceful E.E. Rendered exterior. The needle-spire and the roof date from *E.H.Harbottle*'s restoration of 1895. W gallery on iron piers. – Original plaster arcaded REREDOS, painted in 1895.

BLACKBOROUGH HOUSE. A car dump now surrounds the ruins of the palatial double villa built in 1838 by *Knowles* for the first Earl and the vicar of the new church. Italian Renaissance style with an arched colonnade around, and originally two towers.

SCHOOL. 1840 by *R.J.Marker* of Uffculme.

BLACK TORRINGTON

ST MARY. W tower with diagonal buttresses and obelisk pinnacles. Nave and wide S aisle, with straight-headed windows; N transept separated from the nave by an unmoulded pointed arch. Arcade of five bays between nave and aisle with granite piers of A type, capitals only to the main shafts, elementarily decorated abaci, and depressed pointed arches. Good unceiled wagon roof in the aisle. Restored in 1901–3 by *L.H.Reichel*; new roof, lengthened chancel. – FONT. C15, octagonal, of granite. – COMMUNION RAILS. Jacobean, now screening off the font. – (CHAMBER ORGAN by *Avery*, 1791. Gothic case. AC) – TILES. With the usual Barnstaple motifs, fleur-de-lis, rose, etc. – MONUMENTS. Very pretty slate plate to Benoni Bampfylde †1721. The inscription reads:

> Think not his pious Parts have here an End
> No! They to Heaven with his pure soul ascend
> His undissembl'd Love Discourse and Truth
> For Age a Pattern, and a Rule for Youth,
> Unto the Living Charity doth preach
> And Christian Courage to yᵉ Dying teach.

By the same hand other plates of 1722 and 1725.

BEARA COURT, 1m S. Mostly late C19, a clumsy effort in the Old English style with bargeboarded and half-timbered gables for (and perhaps by) the antiquarian *Lucius H. Reichel*. (Minstrels' gallery faced with C16 bench ends.)

(COHAM, 1m. NW. Seat of the Coham family. Gateway dated 1765. Gabled stone W front, rebuilt in 1872 in Elizabethan style by the Coham-Flemings. N wing with C18 bay-window and Venetian staircase window.)

EAST GRADDON, 1½m. SW. A late medieval longhouse with an original roof (a rarity in the area). Small early cross-wing off the hall.

HOLE, 1½m. SE. A farmhouse built longitudinally into a steep hillside; it may never have had a through passage to the rear. Unusually for Devon, with a baffle entry against an exceptionally wide stack inserted into an otherwise orthodox three-room house. Later stable and hayloft at the lower end. Primitive, smoke-blackened roof: slight A-frame trusses and thin collars, the thatch carried directly on wide battens on the backs of the principals, with no purlins or rafters.

BLEGBERRY
2½ m. NW of Hartland

2020

A remote L-shaped detached farmhouse, the courtyard wall with observation platform and loopholes, now unfortunately dominated on the landward side by large recent agricultural buildings. Dated 1634 on a chimneystack and 1627 on a former upstairs plaster overmantel incorporated into the later staircase hall. It may be on the site of the fortified house which Alan of Hartland built in 1202 as a result of the earliest known licence to crenellate in the county. The farm and adjacent fields were known as Castle Tenement in the C19.

BONDLEIGH
6000

ST JAMES. Norman S doorway with tympanum representing the lamb in a circle and symmetrical birds l. and r. A kind of basket-work decoration of the arch. Plain imposts. Built into the wall at the E end of the aisle two very finely wrought and well preserved Norman capitals with elementary volutes and plenty of small-scale decoration of squares with diagonals across and dots in the triangular cells between the diagonals. Norman also the FONT, square, of table-top type, with large elementary zigzag, four-lobed leaf, semicircle, and blank-arcade motifs. The rest of the church Perp. In the nave, tall window in the S wall, two lights, one transom. Arcade to the N aisle with piers of A type and standard Devon capitals. The N windows straight-headed with transoms, i.e. C16. (Some old roof beams, bosses, and carved wall plates.) The W tower with buttresses of type B and with pinnacles. – (TOWER SCREEN. Incorporates fragments of the rood screen.) – In the N wall of the chancel a fine TOMB RECESS. On the tomb-chest with quatrefoil decoration effigy of a priest. Above the depressed arch blank tracery of large matter-of-fact, not at all intricate forms. The whole monument self-assured, but not as luxurious as many of the period. It was no doubt put up at the same time as the chancel E window with its niches for images on the l. and r. – STAINED GLASS. Fragments of medieval glass in the chancel windows, probably also contemporary with the tomb recess; in the tracery of a S nave window a late C15 Annunciation. – BENCH ENDS. A few, with coarse tracery and some other motifs which seem to indicate a later C16 date.

BONDLEIGH BARTON. A larger than average four-room-and-cross-passage house with smoke-blackened medieval roof.

BORINGDON
Plymouth

The Boringdon heiress Frances Mayhew married John Parker in
1583. Their descendants moved to Saltram in the C18, and by the
later C18, so Polwhele records, the house was ruinous and rented
to a farmer. The part to the E of the porch was demolished c. 1800.
The rest remained habitable until after the Second World War,
then decay set in, and by the 1980s only the walls were standing.
Even in this state, the house was one of the most intriguing among
the major houses of the South West. Minor modifications of the
later C17 onwards had disappeared, leaving dour rubble walls with
dressings of intractable local granite, some in late Tudor style,
some determinedly fashioned into a semblance of classical forms,
the bones of a lengthy remodelling which took place from the C16
to the mid C17. The date 1640 was on the hall chimneypiece. In
1986–7, after total ruin had seemed almost certain, the building
was converted to a hotel.

The main front, facing S, is dominated by a five-storey tower-
porch. It ends oddly with two corner chimneys in the form of
Tuscan columns, and has a very undogmatic but in its way successful portal, probably later than the tower itself. Round-headed
archway with Tuscan columns flanked by shell-headed niches;
above these and running round the arch a frieze of little arches. To
the l. the two four-light two-transom windows of the double-height
hall, divided by a later buttress, and above this a slate-hung upper
storey (a gallery?; cf. Holcombe Rogus) with two four-light
windows. These, like nearly all the windows elsewhere, are of the
plain late Tudor type, with chamfered mullions and dripstones,
but above there is an attic storey with an unusual amount of
enrichment, which must be a later addition, perhaps mid C17: two
square openings with bolection mouldings ornamented with a
debased form of egg and dart; coarse carved heads in between.
Above these a string course with a band of eggs only, and battlements with coats of arms, some in scrolly cartouches. The string
course and battlements are carried round over a four-storey wing
projecting from the upper end of the hall. This has a four-light
window on the ground floor lighting a chamber opening off the hall
(cf. Bradfield). This room now provides a route from the hall to the
large wing added to the SW in order to house a great staircase – see
the irregular positions of the staircase windows on the W side.

The W front has three elements. On the r. is the staircase block
already mentioned. In the centre, a three-storey range with a six-
light window on the ground floor and two four-light windows
above, all with arched lights, unlike the windows elsewhere. This
may be the oldest part of the house. To its l., a C17 wing with on
two floors paired windows with a continuous hoodmould, and
originally with a parapet rising to form blind semicircular gables.
Adjoining this is a small wing to the N of the hall, corresponding to
the opposite area on the S side. At the screens-passage end of the
hall another projection for a staircase, with garderobe added later.
E of the screens passage the site of the service end has been
replaced by extensions for the hotel.

The interior was totally transformed in 1986–7. It is now the C20 counterpart to Weare Giffard, and equally irritating for the historian. A superficially convincing instant patina has been achieved by mixing the genuine with imported old materials. However, the splendid proportions of the double-height hall can now be appreciated again, with its chief feature, the great plaster chimneypiece of 1640, restored to its full glory. It stands against the back wall, with royal arms with supporters above strapwork, flanked by clumsy over-life-size caryatids of Peace and Plenty. The granite doorway incongruously placed in the centre of the screens was brought from the SW room, where it had been re-used as a fireplace. The hall woodwork is all new, as is the plaster ceiling – a very convincing C17 pastiche, although entirely un-Devonian in its repertoire. In the rooms at the SW end are several original granite doorways which mix Tudor arches with some attempt at classical ornament; the archway from the S oriel room to the stair-hall is especially elaborate. The staircase itself is a new but quite convincing creation in C17 style.

Extensive outbuildings to the E, also converted for the hotel: two long two-storey ranges at right angles, and a former barn.

BORINGDON ARCH. *See* Saltram.

BORINGDON CAMP. *See* Sparkwell.

2090   BOVEY HOUSE
                            Beer

An interesting and attractive house, now a hotel, in a secluded position between Beer and Branscombe. From the C13 to the C18 a seat of the Walronds (cf. Bradfield), in 1762 it passed by marriage to the Rolles. It was subsequently neglected and reduced in size, but restored in 1868. Facing E is the original hall range, now two-storeyed, and a projecting three-storey wing to its r., all of red sandstone in well laid ashlar, with a variety of straight-headed ovolo-moulded mullioned or mullion-and-transomed windows, all with dripstones. Hall windows each of six lights with a transom. At the back another wing facing S was added as a C17 show front (see the gatepiers), of rubble, three-storeyed, with three straight gables and a staircase projection in the re-entrant angle.

The present exterior appearance of the hall is presumably of 1592, the date on the very fine ornamental rainwater head (an early example). The entrance doorway, curiously set (or reset) in the side of the projecting wing, is the oldest visible part, with a moulded archway with very worn capitals to the inner order. Within the porch a more conventional late Perp doorway with the usual leaf spandrels. The hall interior (now subdivided by folding doors) has good late C17 panelling and simple fireplaces, and ceilings with ovals decorated with oak leaves and grapevine. (At the S end, remains of an earlier ceiling with moulded beams preserved above.)

On the r. of the former screens passage a C16 wooden doorway with animals in the spandrels, and beyond, in the three-storey wing, a room with complete C16 panelling: linenfold with a frieze of Renaissance medallions, overmantel with lozenges, architectural scenes and coats of arms, Dutch tiles in the fireplace. On the first floor the King Charles II Room with an interesting post-Restoration ceiling: the new type of central oval, but with old-fashioned, naive low-relief detail. It commemorates Charles's flight after the battle of Worcester: in the centre a large oak tree with a man's face, around the oval smaller trees and horsemen. Early C18 staircase.

In the front garden in a summer house two medieval STATUES of a king and a bishop, weathered but good-quality C14 style. The heads project forward, as if intended to be seen from below. In an outbuilding a 14ft diameter DONKEY WHEEL dated 1868, used to raise water from a well.

BOVEY TRACEY
8070

The medieval church lies uphill to the E of the town, with a wide view towards Dartmoor.

ST PETER, ST PAUL, AND ST THOMAS OF CANTERBURY. Tall tapering unbuttressed granite W tower, only the battlements and pinnacles of ashlar (re-used when the top stage was added). W window with intersecting tracery. The S side of the church and the S porch, with four-light windows, decorated battlements, and pinnacles, a stately sight. The interior rather low but spacious. Whitewashed walls with five-bay Beer stone N and S arcades on piers of B type with standard capitals. The outer N aisle was added by *Slater* in 1858, when the church was refitted (galleries and pews removed). Further restoration 1887–8. Aisleless sanctuary of one bay. Wagon roofs in nave and chancel, boarded with bosses. The S porch has a ribbed ceiling with a central boss showing four heads with their chins meeting in the centre.

FONT. Usual octagonal Perp type with quatrefoil panels. Late C17 COVER. – LECTERN. Brass, late C15, from the same, probably East Anglian, workshop which produced, with the same moulds, the lecterns of St Martin Salisbury, St Nicholas Bristol, and others. Preserved during the Commonwealth (together with the plate and registers) by the ejected royalist vicar James Forbes (*see* below). – SCREENS. Rood screen, said to date from 1427. Tracery type A 37 standard. Richly carved fourfold frieze in the cornice, with leaf scrolls, thick square individual leaves, and pomegranate. Restored in 1887–8. The fan-coving is new. The screen, and also the parclose screens (with panelling motifs in the pierced spandrels), have mostly Victorian colour, but the PAINTINGS of apostles and prophets on the wainscot of the main screen are original (restored by *Anna Hulbert*) and are dated by Croft-Murray to the early C16 and compared with Chudleigh. Below the figures, spaces for parchment or paper texts, now missing. – The stone PULPIT belongs to the screens in its style. It is uncommonly lavishly decorated with, in each panel, two figures above each other and bossy leaf strips up the angles between the panels. The workmanship of the ornament as usual much better than that of the figures. – CHANCEL STALLS. Three with misericords. – ROYAL ARMS. 1662.

MONUMENTS. Nicholas Eveleigh †1618, quite a sumptuous affair. Standing wall-monument of white stone with effigy propped up on one elbow. Corinthian columns l. and r. supporting a straight cornice with three small allegorical figures. Between the columns an arch as background to the effigy. In the spandrels naively carved angels. Under the arch a plain space with just 1620 I.D. on it, plausibly identified as *John Deymond* of Exeter.* – Elizeus Hele † 1636. Same type, but alabaster, and in front of the tomb-chest two kneeling wives and a son, quite large figures. The ornament still (in spite of the date) wholly strapwork and fruit hangings. – Outside in the churchyard by the s wall of the chancel a curious shrine of 1655 to Maria, wife of the Rev. James Forbes. (The sequestrators would not allow her a tomb inside the church.) It has the inscription 'Surgam–Vivam–Canam' and three odd acroteria of obelisk-like shape, the centre one looking like a mermaid.

sw of the churchyard a former CHURCH HOUSE, rendered. One old moulded doorcase and window. Projecting stair at the back.

The little town was founded by Henry de Tracey in the early c13, but there are few old houses in the centre to single out. The most interesting is Nos. 60–70 FORE STREET, a late example of a hall-house, with an original lateral stack, chambers at either end, and a two-storey porch. Inserted hall floor of the c17.

In EAST STREET Nos. 20–24 also began as an early c16 hall-house (original roof). TRACEY ALMSHOUSE is of 1910 in early c19 style; No. 21, the Manor House, is mid c19 in appearance, but with a late medieval core. (Large granite fireplace in the hall, evidence for an internal jetty.) The main road curves down to the BRIDGE over the river Bovey, dated 1642. Nearby the handsome mid c19 OLD MILL with central tower (built to pump water to a nearby house).

At the sw end of the town an atmospheric Victorian group of a wilfully gabled terrace, vicarage of 1851, church house of 1852, and church.

ST JOHN, 1853 by *R. C. Carpenter*, was built at the expense of the vicar of Bovey Tracey, Canon Charles Courtenay, a brother of the Earl of Devon. Chancel and aisled nave with w bell-gable, in a sensitive, well proportioned Dec. Simple interior with arcades on octagonal columns (N aisle added 1862 by *J. W. Rowell*), dominated by a rich clutter of Anglo-Catholic furnishings. – REREDOS for the high altar (now in a side chapel) by *C. F. Hansom*, delicately carved, mosaics by *Salviati*, and excellent STAINED GLASS by *Hardman* in the E window, all of 1874. – The low brass SCREEN and other metalwork and the FONT of Devon marble are part of the furnishings of 1853 enthusiastically commended by the *Ecclesiologist*. – ORGAN. Moved from the chancel to a new w gallery c. 1945. – In the churchyard elaborate MEMORIAL to Emily Gurney. Crucifixion with angels below.

BAPTIST CHURCH, Hind Street. 1824. Tall, with pedimented gable and round-arched windows. (Galleries on Doric columns.)

TOWN HALL. 1866. Rusticated basement; Gothic windows.

BOVEY TRACEY SCHOOL. 1879 by *E. H. Harbottle*.

STATION. Disused. Built c. 1866 of random stone, single-storey, with two chimneys. Wooden canopy over the entrance. Large goods shed to the N. Station yard gates with massive fluted cast-iron posts.

On BOVEY HEATHFIELD the Bovey–Newton road cuts through a massive earthen bank. On the N side of the road, lesser earthworks running E–W. All are believed to have formed part of the Civil War

* See A. Wells-Cole, 'An Oak Bed at Montacute', *Furniture History*, XVII (1981), 1–19.

defences of Bovey Tracey. The ball clay from the sediments under-lying the Heathfield has been mined for several centuries.

At BOVEY POTTERIES three 20-ft-high brick BOTTLE KILNS, two built in 1860 and oval in plan, one of 1902, and associated buildings (now used as stores) – a remarkable intrusion of the Staffordshire pottery industry into the landscape of South Devon.* There were once many more such kilns.

CANDY'S POTTERY, Heathfield, established in the mid C19, has lost its oldest buildings, but several later structures remain: a two-storey flat-roofed office block of cream brick with red brick dressings; a long two-storey cream brick workshop; a tall modern building of grey reeded metal; a 100-yd-long tunnel kiln; and associated structures.

MINES. There were several micaceous haematite mines to the N of Bovey Tracey. At KELLY a mine that existed in the 1790s was reopened in 1879–92 and 1900–46. Adits, a tramway, and a dressing shed containing major items of equipment still survive. Remains of other mines worked from the 1890s to c. 1911 can be seen near Hawkmoor Hospital (PLUMLEY, SHAPTOR, and HAWKMOOR MINES).

HAWKMOOR HOSPITAL. Established on the Hawkmoor estate in 1913 as one of the first chest sanatoria in the country. Staff housing near the main road, 1925. CHAPEL of 1928–9, given by Dame Violet Wills, with stained glass in the E window by *Arnold Robinson* and *Edward Woore*. On the hillside overlooking the valley the WARD BLOCK, 1939, in the modern style popular for such build-ings, a long, rendered, single-storey range, flat-roofed with broad eaves, with veranda and projecting bowed centre. In front, NUR-SES' HOME of 1946, three storeys with bowed glazed staircases at the ends, a ward block since the 1970s when the hospital was converted for use by the mentally handicapped.

DEVON HOUSE OF MERCY (former; now Devon House flats). 1865–74 by *Woodyer*. Extensive institutional buildings in an austere free Tudor, rubble stone, irregularly grouped gables, tall brick chimneys, and some wayward Gothic windows. The former chapel, originally with lancets and steep roof, now unrecognizable.

PARKE (Dartmoor National Park Headquarters), ½ m. w. A handsome white-rendered early C19 house of five by four bays, built by William Hole. Heavy central porch with two pairs of Greek Doric columns; entablature with guttae only. At the rear, four-centred doorway and door of c. 1600. Central top-lit staircase. In the C18 owned by Lord Ashburton (*see* Widecombe), who, according to John Swete, 'softened the harsh and rude features of the scene around him' by blowing up the granite masses in his best meadows, and planting the hills.

COLEHAYES PARK HOTEL (Field Studies Centre). Early C19. Two storeys, deep eaves, Greek Doric porch *in antis*. Later Italianate additions. BRIDGE and LODGE GATES early C19.

INDIO HOUSE. 1850 by *David Mackintosh* for Charles Aldenburg Bentinck. Austere Tudor relieved by romantic crenellated chimney-stacks.

The HAYTOR GRANITE TRAMWAY runs through the parish (*see* Ilsington).

* Future uncertain.

A main-road village which developed from 1259, when a market and fair were granted to Henry de Tracey, Lord of the Manor of Nymet, while the older settlements at Nymet Tracey and Broad Nymet declined. At the crossroads, BARAKEL and RIDDAWAY'S STORES are a former inn, early C16 with C17 additions.

CONGREGATIONAL CHAPEL. 1898 by *William Carter Pedler*, the local magnate. Brownstone with moulded red brick details, in a version of E.E.

ST BARTHOLOMEW. At Nymet Tracey, now a small hamlet, ¾m. SE. Unbuttressed W tower, with a tower arch older than Perp. Granite N arcade with A type piers: the nearness to Dartmoor is patent. Chancel rebuilt in 1859–62 and again during the 1889 restoration by *Fulford & Harvey*, when galleries and pews were removed and nearly all the windows were renewed in Hatherleigh stone. Inventively varied tracery, the S windows seemingly copies of C14 originals. Two windows at the E end of the N aisle original. The blocked arch in the chancel S wall was intended for an organ chamber. Medieval wagon roofs to nave and aisle, restored 1889. Chancel roof boarded, with large foliate bosses carved by *Hems*, forming a ceilure over the sanctuary.

FONT. C15, octagonal, with traceried panels with fleurons above. – REREDOS, designed as an integral part of Fulford's sanctuary ensemble, with vigorous carving by *Hems*; likewise the CHANCEL STALLS. – COMMUNION RAIL. C17; alternate plain and twisted balusters. – SCREENS. Rood screen with some original colour (overpaint recently removed), straight-headed four-light panels with pierced spandrels and the usual type A tracery, and N aisle screen also straight-headed panels but slightly different tracery details and with linenfold on the wainscot. – PULPIT. Plain C18. – STAINED GLASS. E window by *Drake*, 1890. – Two in the N aisle and one in the nave by *R.M.Driffield*, 1889–90, with his deliberately primitive figure drawing.

On the S side of the churchyard ST MARTIN'S is supposed to incorporate remains of a medieval chapel.

VICARAGE. Large, urbane, and prosperous-looking; 1837 by *William Bibbings*.

BROAD NYMET, 1 m. SW. A settlement consisting now only of the BARTON, C16 with a C19 front, and the tiny disused and derelict medieval parish church of ST MARTIN. C13 chancel and nave under one roof, W bellcote, later S porch. Trefoil-headed lancets, one triplet next to the porch, another in the E wall, with pierced spandrels. Wagon roofs; studded door in a round-headed archway. No furnishings remain.*

(GRATTANS MANOR. Early C19, 1–2–1 bays, plus a r. extension. Rendered, with rusticated quoins. Later veranda along the front. The two back wings with unusually careful rear elevations, each with a recess between windows on the upper floor.)

STATION (former), 1 m. S. Built *c.* 1865. Imposing two-storey station house of Dartmoor granite with lighter ashlar dressings and round-

---

*I am indebted to Angela Blaen's research on Broad Nymet and Nymet Tracey for details in this entry.

headed windows in pointed arches in groups of two and three.
Similar style single-storey waiting room and offices. Canopy with
attractive cast-iron brackets with creeper design.

COLLATONS. Three-bay rendered early C19 s block with Tuscan
porch. C18 rear wing.

BOWDEN HOUSE   8050
1 m. SE of Totnes

In the C16 owned by the Giles family, from the early C18 to c. 1800
by the Trists. It was Nicholas Trist who gave the house its present
handsome early Georgian E and S frontages (in 1722, according to
Polwhele). Red sandstone, coursed to look like brick. Two storeys
with stone cornice and blocking course. Georgian sashes in stone
surrounds. 2–5–2 bays on the S front, 2–3–2 on the E. The two end
bays on each front and the central bay on the S front are articulated
by giant pilasters. The pedimented S door is rather awkwardly
placed below thin central pilasters. But, as can be guessed from the
irregular back parts where a mullioned window is visible, the S and
E fronts conceal the complicated remains of an older house, with a
Tudor great hall lying in the angle of the two later wings.

The E front (new built in the C18 above brick vaulted cellars) has
in its centre a sumptuously decorated reception room, one of the
few examples in the county of an essay in Baroque taste, the details
rather better than the sum of the parts, as so often in provincial
work. An early C18 date seems likely for most of the decoration,
although some of the embellishments may be later, among them
the arms of the Adam family, owners of the house from c. 1800,
which appear on the ceiling. The room is an awkwardly long
rectangle with windows in the short side (perhaps the result of
extending an older E wing). On the wall opposite the windows,
giant pilasters flank arched niches with full-length grisaille figures;
central doorway with open pediment and bust. Rich cornice and
garlanded frieze. The long walls have niches with shells, and
medallions above of Charles I and Elizabeth I. On the S side a
broad coffered doorway with eagle and garlands above leads to the
stair-hall. The fireplace opposite, not centrally placed, has a grand
but quirky overmantel in two parts: Britannia (?) and a veiled
figure, below a voluted top with a large classical bust; above this a
quatrefoil with a mythological scene. Equally striking is the plaster
ceiling with its lively, very large low-relief figure of Mercury in a 119
central panel, trumpeting Victory and Pegasus in cartouches, putti
in roundels, and mythological scenes in rectangles. The disparate
scales of the different elements are reminiscent of the entrance hall
at Saltram.

In the S wing a good C18 staircase around a well, with fluted
balusters and newels and a ramped rail. In the adjoining room
re-used C16 panelling and a brought-in wooden overmantel
elaborately carved with the arms of the second Earl of Bedford
(†1585) and flanked by high-relief figures of Judith and Holo-
fernes. From here one reaches the earlier parts of the house by a
stone four-centred doorway leading into the former screens passage. Another doorway at the opposite end. Adjoining is the Old

Kitchen, i.e. the Tudor great hall, with a late C16 single-rib plaster ceiling and remains of a Pegasus frieze. In the W wall two oval openings (now blocked). The fabric of the hall is possibly older than the ceiling, as from this part of the house projects a much rebuilt N wing with an early Tudor wall painting on the upper floor. Further W part of a small staircase of c.1600 with robust turned balusters.

Upstairs, early C18 panelling in the central room on the E front, another panelled room and closet in the S range. The service wings (extended in brick in the later Georgian period) and the outbuildings have been much altered for holiday flats.

7040

BOWRINGSLEIGH
West Alvington

An estate of the Bowring family until the early C16, acquired by William Gilbert in 1543 and by William Ilbert in 1695. The present baronial appearance, with a castellated four-storey tower to the r. of the Tudor frontage of the mansion, is the result of *Richard Coad*'s restoration of 1868–73 for William Roope Ilbert, after the E wing had been damaged by fire in 1843 and the house let as a farmhouse. S front with three-storey porch, two storeys of regularly disposed mullion-and-transom four-light windows (all renewed), battlements, gables, and dormers (all added in 1873). The sturdy tower is a restrained version of a more ambitious project, embellished only by a polygonal turret on the W side and some Gothic windows for the chapel on its ground floor, one Dec, one Perp.

Inside, much remains of the Gilberts' remodelling of the later C16 to early C17. Hall to the l. of the porch with attractive C16 plaster ceiling with single-rib intersecting pattern and central pendant. Fireplace in the back wall with flattened ogee arch; overmantel made from a four-poster bed. The outstanding feature is 75 the magnificent screen, a very accomplished classical piece of the early C17, with six Corinthian columns, a rich cornice, doors with faceted panels in strapwork, and ebony inlay. Beyond the hall, the dining room, with an entertaining later C17 ceiling depicting war, with contemporary horsemen, guns, cannon, and victories. Despite the rustic detail, their arrangement around a central octagon displays an awareness of the new court style of the Restoration (cf. Bovey House). Bolection-moulded double doors to the study beyond.

On the other side of the screens passage, entered by a stone doorway, the library, refitted in the restoration. (It had a ceiling devoted to Peace, destroyed in 1843.) Beyond this, within the C19 tower, the galleried chapel, with a much restored screen brought from South Huish, arranged in two tiers. On the upper tier, five damaged painted panels with figures. Ceiling with bosses. Behind the tower, facing E, a large late C19 neo-Tudor drawing room, with two bay-windows and a quatrefoil-patterned ceiling, and a later billiard room. C19 main staircase beyond the screens passage; upstairs, fielded panelling in the room over the dining room.

The service rooms were largely rebuilt in the later C19 on old foundations. Older than these is the room known as the old kitchen, with hoodmoulded windows with arched lights, within a three-storey range built (in the C17?) against the hall. At the far end of the W service wing a lofty, square C19 kitchen; across the back courtyard, separate laundry with pretty wooden arcade.

Square stone SUMMER HOUSE, C17, in the garden to the E. Two sets of handsome rusticated GATEPIERS.

BRADFIELD
Uffculme

One of the largest mansions in Devon, the seat of the Walronds from the C13 to the early C20 (cf. Bovey House). It is deceptively C19 in appearance when approached from the S, but its core, visible from the E, is a major late medieval hall, re-windowed c. 1600, when a large new wing was added at the upper end. The Tudor character was reinstated in the restoration of c. 1860 carried out for Sir John Walrond, a conscientious effort for its date, by *John Hayward*, who published an account of the work in 1867.* At this time the entrance was moved to the reconstructed S front and a large service wing added further W.

The E front of grey limestone rubble overlooking the attractive but decaying C19 topiary gardens is nearly symmetrical: projecting gabled wings; porch and oriel room in the re-entrant angles (respectively dated 1604 and 1592). In the centre the large hall windows of four and three lights with transoms; before 1860 this was a single eight-light window, no doubt also an alteration of c. 1600, as during restoration traces of earlier windows were found. The porch was entered from the side by a doorway (now removed) which had quite a correct Doric surround whose composition is imitated (with some minor variations such as the projecting centre of the entablature) by the C19 S entrance.

Before 1860 the house had plain roughcast walls 'almost without buttresses cornices or stringcourse'. Such Devonian reticence clearly did not accord with the C19 taste for more boldly modelled exteriors. The roughcast was stripped, mullions were renewed, the panels with shields reset on canted bays added to the wings, two turrets added to the hall roof in place of 'square slate-covered boxes', and the roof-line was further enlivened by finials springing from octagonal corner buttresses (a feature of some early C16 Dorset houses – a C19 invention here?).‡ The larger buttresses on the N side are also additions. The new entrance side to the S was given consequence by a bay-window similar to the eastern ones, and a grand three-storey porch.

Inside, the spectacular feature of the hall is the early C16 hammerbeam roof, one of the most ornate in the county, repaired *in situ* c. 1860. Heavily moulded arch-braced trusses with apex pendants rest on beams with angel terminals. Subsidiary trusses

---

Transactions of the Exeter Diocesan Architectural Society, vol. I (1867), 79–84.

‡Photographs taken in 1852 however show slender corner pinnacles and what appear to be thin corner buttresses, so these may be original features. The projecting wings at this time were without bay-windows; the carved panels with shields appear between upper and lower sash-windows.

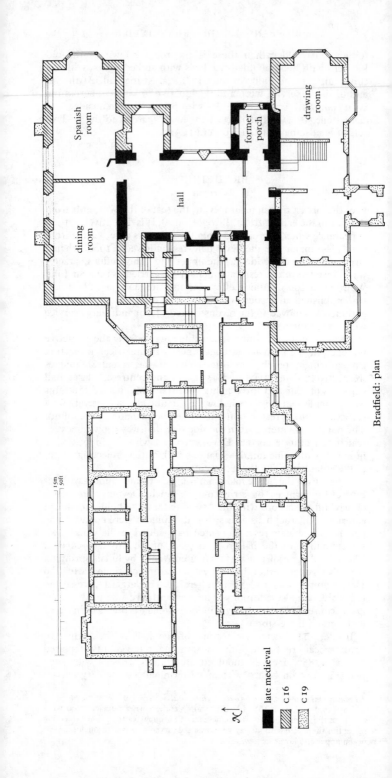

Bradfield: plan

late medieval

C 16

C 19

Spanish room

dining room

hall

former porch

drawing room

1.5m
5 0ft

also with pendants, and with angels at the junctions with the main purlins. Two lesser sets of purlins, all moulded, and wind-braces on three levels in the form of cusped tracery. On the walls linenfold panelling and a frieze of Renaissance heads in square panels, all much renewed when stripped of paint during restoration. N gable wall with the arms of James I and two crudely painted soldiers. S gable also with arms; below it a gallery with woodwork carved with bold strapwork above two openings with paired arches. The W doorway at gallery level is C19, replacing a single-light ogee-traceried window (copied in the S wall of the N staircase). The oriel room opens from the hall by a semicircular stone arch with typically early C16 panelled reveals and fleurons in the outer moulding: it must once have framed a shallower oriel window. In the oriel room a fireplace with stopped jambs and a renewed four-centred arch, and panelling similar to the hall. The stone doorway from hall to parlour is up some steps (the N wing is over a basement). It displays the still delightfully incorrect classical taste of the late C16: thin fluted Ionic columns on tall plinths, with long fluted strips above the capitals.

The parlour is decorated with the greatest panache: plaster ceiling with enriched double ribs and pendants and exceptionally elaborate woodwork; overmantel with arches and figures; similarly decorated inner porch, comparable to Bradninch. (The woodwork, stripped, restored, and repainted (after 1867), all boarded over at the time of writing.) Above the panelling, frieze of Spanish leather. The inner porch also leads to a later C19 dining room made out of two rooms. This has a ceiling in imitation of the parlour, and panelling of late C17 type. Opposite the oriel room another stone doorway to the staircase, with symmetrically turned balusters and decorated square newels of c.1600, rising two and a half storeys around a small well. The plan suggests that there was a garderobe opening off the stairs. The service rooms and kitchen at the lower end of the hall were reconstructed in the C19 as living room and entrance hall. A four-centred doorway survives; also a faceted door of c.1600 to the buttery service hatch. In the range opposite the hall a late C16 basement window survived the C19 rebuilding; another in the linking range to the N.

W of the house picturesque C19 STABLES with a three-storey part with a bell-turret and a clock in the gable.

ALL SAINTS CHAPEL, E of the house, close to the road. 1875 by *Hayward*. Modest but inventive – canted apsidal sanctuary, with a trefoiled lancet beneath a gable on each face. Grey, brown, and cream stone. Bellcote between nave and chancel. – STAINED GLASS by *Clayton & Bell*.

BRADFORD

ALL SAINTS. Norman S doorway with one order of colonnettes; no tympanum. The S windows renewed. Low W tower, unbuttressed, with pinnacles, an unmoulded pointed arch towards the nave, and W door and W window of C14 forms. It was repaired and heightened in 1550. Chancel S windows and chancel S door earlier

C14 or *c.* 1300. N aisle late Perp with several types of straight-headed three-light windows and the usual arcade with A type piers, capitals only to the main shafts, slightly decorated abaci, and low depressed pointed arches. Said to date from 1438. Restored by *Hooper* of Hatherleigh, 1871 (chancel rebuilt). – FONT. Circular, Norman, with small fluted bowl. – BENCH ENDS. A few. – CHEST. Of *c.* 1600. – TILES of Barnstaple type. – MONUMENTS. On the S wall an incised slate slab to the Maynards of Bovacott, 1666–8. – Many LEDGER STONES.

See also Dunsland House.

9000   BRADNINCH

A little town rather than a village. A borough was established in the late C12, a charter for market and fair granted in 1208, and there was a mayor from 1604. After the decay of the cloth industry, the town prospered again with the growth of the paper mills at Hele in the C18. Despite C20 expansion on the fringes, the centre remains attractively unspoilt.

From the crossroads near the top of the hill, PETER STREET leads to the S, with the BAPTIST CHURCH of 1832, with angular Gothick windows and recesses. To the W the HIGH STREET runs steeply downhill, with raised pavement with nice railings on either side. To the E, FORE STREET starts with the GUILDHALL, 1921, neo-Georgian, unappealingly rendered, then broadens into a sloping rectangle with a wide grass verge, bordered by roughcast cottages, a few dignified by late Georgian pedimented doorcases or fanlights. Halfway down, CHURCH STREET, with two-storey stone SUNDAY SCHOOLS at the corner, 1838, restored 1905. Tudor windows and rusticated quoins, and a view of the church tower through Gothic iron gates with overthrow.

Near the bottom of the hill, at the start of NEW STREET, COMFORT HOUSE, long and thatched, with large projecting two-storey porch dated 1681, when the C15 house was remodelled for Isaac Watts, wool merchant, and his wife Mary (initials on porch). Arch-braced medieval roof and good late C17 fittings inside. (In WEST END ROAD, No. 60, a Gothic *cottage orné*. Four ogee-headed windows.)

ST DISEN. A tall pink tower with buttresses of type B and a stair-turret. A two-year indulgence was granted in 1437 in return for funds for rebuilding the tower. N and S aisles both buttressed, with large three-light windows. S porch 1876. An interior of respectable size: six bays. The piers of an unusual variety – B type, but with two waves in each diagonal instead of one (cf. Broadhembury). In one of the N piers a niche for a statue. The arcades were taken down and re-erected in 1841, and the roof heightened, increasing the spaciousness of the interior. The fine arch-braced nave roof, however, dates from the 1889 restoration by *Hayward & Tait*.

ROOD SCREEN, running across nave and aisles, A type, with fan-vaulted coving to E and W; cornice with three strips of foliage scrolls. Where the aisle piers break the regularity of the composition there are wider solid uprights and two niches. Early C16 wainscot PAINTINGS of prophets and apostles, the four Latin doctors of the church, sibyls, Annunciation, Visitation, Adam and Eve, Expulsion from Paradise, etc. Restoration and recolouring of the screen, mooted in the 1840s, was carried out in 1853. Exuberant colours: red, green, white, and gilt on a blue ground, particularly successful on the coving. Also of 1853 eight male figures on the northernmost wainscot panels and the two statuettes in the niches, all the work of *Bradley* of Exeter (signature at the S end of the screen). – SOUTH PARCLOSE SCREEN. Simpler Perp tracery, and also painted figures.

Large stone PULPIT, designed by *E. L. Parsons*, executed by *Hems*, 1889; polygonal, on a squat stem, with vigorous foliage but insipid figure. – SANCTUARY FLOOR. An attractive design, 1889, in pink, grey, white, and green Devonshire marbles, by *Blackyer* of St Marychurch. – STAINED GLASS. In the nave, a complete set of pattern glass by *Drake*, last window 1872. – S aisle first from E by *Hardman & Co.*, c. 1880. – Sainthill MONUMENT in the chancel, 1679, white marble, with two black ovals, good, though cold; broad and competent, up-to-date decoration.

METHODIST CHURCH, Millway. 1832, large and ambitious, neither classical nor Gothic. Angular windows between pilasters linked by angular arches; pediment. Later entrance, but with original Tuscan door frame. Prettily panelled W gallery. – STAINED GLASSS in the entrance vestibule, good big memorial window to Hepburn † 1917.

BRADNINCH MANOR. The seat of the Sainthills. The first Peter Sainthill (a lawyer who was Recorder of Bradninch) leased the estate in 1547 and completed a new house in 1553. Most of the existing building is later, although the basic half-H-shaped plan may go back to this time. According to the *Gentleman's Magazine* of 1825 the house was formerly twice the size. What one sees now is a two-storey central hall range, symmetrically refronted in brick in the early C18, with Georgian sashes, eared upper window surrounds, and pedimented central doorcase, flanked by gabled stone wings with renewed wooden mullioned windows.

The interior suffered badly in the 1970s, when panelling and chimneypieces were unscrupulously removed, but the most important room remains intact. This is the JOB ROOM with its early C17 68 fittings, the front room in the wing to the l. of the hall. It has a splendid plaster ceiling with enriched double ribs and large central pendant with faces, a plaster frieze, and the most spectacular woodwork. Panelling with Corinthian pilasters enriched with musical instruments, animals, putti, etc. An even more elaborate internal porch (cf. Bradfield) with decorated free-standing columns with open niches below, and strapwork cresting between obelisks. The *pièce de résistance* is the fireplace overmantel, with three relief scenes with perspective backgrounds (Abraham and Isaac, the trials of Job, and Jacob and the angel). Rather lumpy Flemish-style figures. Caryatids at the sides, and below, clumsy representations of Ceres and Bacchus. There were formerly two other overmantels and panelling, in the library behind the Job Room, and in the King Charles Room on the first floor, all now removed.

In the angle between hall and library a grand STAIRCASE around a narrow well, early C17, with closely set turned balusters, the carved newels alas deprived of their heraldic finials. The C18 HALL is a restrained classical room with a handsome marble fireplace with a frieze of classical foliage, and a little pediment rising over the central panel. At the other end two Ionic columns mark the former position of the screens passage.

HELE PAPER MILLS (Wiggins Teape). Prominently sited in the valley, 1 m. SW. The paper mills were first established on the river Culm in 1762. The present buildings are C20: a tall, red-painted concrete structure and cluster of lower red brick and concrete buildings, and two tall metal chimneys.

STOCKWELL MANOR, Stockwell. A medieval house, drastically remodelled in the C19 and early C20, chiefly interesting for the survival of two Dec timber windows, both reset possibly as early as the C16, the ground-floor one with cusped trefoil heads, the first-floor one with intersecting tracery.

3080   BRADSTONE

ST NONNA (a Cornish saint, cf. Altarnun). Norman S door of one order with capitals which were once decorated, and a simply moulded arch. Within it a later pointed granite arch. Beside the doorway an extremely primitive holy-water stoup, triangular, made of three stones. All this of limestone. The nave masonry may also be Norman, the chancel masonry the same, but the windows here tiny trefoil-headed C13 lancets. Perp N arcade with granite piers of A type with slightly decorated capitals and castellated abaci; four-centred, simply moulded arches. Perp W tower of granite ashlar with diagonal buttresses and big panelled polygonal pinnacles. Ceiled roof with bosses.

BRADSTONE MANOR. The best part is the gatehouse, close to the church, early C17, three-storeyed, with the third storey in the gable. Canted projections at the sides, a staircase in the l. one. On top a lively display of many obelisk-like pinnacles. Doorway with flattened arch in a square head and large leaves in the spandrels. The house of the Cloberry family is now a much altered farmhouse of the usual three-room and cross-passage plan, with back wing and outshoot. Three-storey porch of ashlar (Hurdwick stone), with mullioned windows and Tudor arch, in line with the gatehouse. To the r. another mullioned window, to the l. the main living rooms remodelled with large Georgian sashes. Inside, these rooms have re-used C17 panelling. Painting of a rustic scene over the hall fireplace. The room above the end parlour with early C18 bolection-moulded panelling.

GREYSTONE BRIDGE. Eight spans, cutwaters. Partly paid for by Thomas Mede, Abbot of Tavistock, in 1439.

3010   BRADWORTHY

The church lies by the side of a townish square with several nice humble white-rendered houses of the C18 to early C19. The back wing of the inn close to the churchyard is possibly of medieval origin.

ST JOHN BAPTIST. Wide aisleless nave with S transept and very shallow N transept opening into the nave with unmoulded, i.e.

early, arches. The chancel of two dates. In the older part a late C13
S window and a N window supposed to have been the E window
originally. Chancel extension c. 1400. Of the same date the S
doorway and the nave windows. W tower of c. 1500 or later, with
pinnacles and W door with heavy square-headed label; rebuilt in
1884 after being struck by lightning. Restoration 1883. Wagon
roofs; the chancel roof ceiled. – FONT. Square, probably Norman;
undecorated. – PULPIT. c. 1700, with open baluster-work exposing
the parson's legs. – REREDOS. Tripartite, with handsome elaborate
pokerwork decoration; C18. – TILES. The usual Barnstaple designs
(fleur-de-lis, rose, etc.). – MONUMENTS. Good minor tablets. –
Ann Nichols † 1694. Voluted frame with open pediment and putti. –
Thomas Cholwill † 1714. Architectural, with urn. – Langdon
family, c. 1848. Elaborate Gothic tabernacle. – Ezekiel Rouse and
wife, † 1856, 1864. Also Gothic. – Many good slate tombstones in
the churchyard.

HIGHER ALFARDISWORTHY, 2 m. SW. Attractive group of farmhouse and extensive outbuildings, some of late medieval origin.
Former chapel N of the house, of stone heightened in cob, and with
later extension and inserted floor, but retaining two moulded arch-
braced trusses and a set of moulded purlins. L-shaped rendered
farmhouse, much altered, with some C18 panelling in the E wing.
Close to the house a small building formerly used as a school.

(BLATCHBOROUGH HOUSE, 2 m. W. Shooting lodge of 1822 built
by the Calmady family and attached to an C18 farmhouse. Gothic
windows, decorative bargeboards.)

BRAMPFORD SPEKE   9090

ST PETER. Rebuilt in 1853 by *Butcher*, except for the late medieval W
tower (diagonal buttresses, obelisk-like pinnacles on the battlements, straight-headed bell-openings) and the cusped arch of a
founder's tomb built into the S transept wall. The rest already High
Victorian in character: bold asymmetrical massing, Dec tracery,
double-chamfered arches. N arcade with octagonal piers. Interior
whitewashed and refitted later. – Some heraldic STAINED GLASS.

STATION, now a private house. Built c. 1884. Stone with cream ashlar
dressings. A gable at each end with wooden bargeboards; bay-
windows on to the platform; decorative cresting to the roof tiles.
Separate two-storey stationmaster's house. Approached from the
village square by a latticed iron FOOTBRIDGE with cast-iron posts
and arched braces.

Despite some unhappy modern infilling, the village centre can still
offer a typical range of local buildings, with many C18 and later
cottages, cob walls, and the C19 brick vicarage, chapel, and village
school (1867–8 by *Hayward*, red and black brick). Nearby,
BRAMPFORD HOUSE, with a handsome early C19 three-bay front
with incised pilasters and an Ionic porch. Also some disguised
earlier houses, like STOOKS, with smoke-blackened roof and end
cruck, and Taylors and Home Living, an outstanding pair of late
medieval farmhouses. TAYLORS presents an exceptionally long
thatched range to the street, with rear cross-wing, the upper end
with three gabled dormers and jointed-cruck roof trusses beneath,

the other end significantly lower, with simple massive cross-beams. HOME LIVING, hidden behind cob walls, is a medieval house of which three bays of the open hall roof survive with the remnant of an earlier jointed-cruck closed truss beneath. The house also has very good C17 fittings, including the hall fireplace with Beer stone mouldings. In the upper chamber a fireplace and a mid C17 plaster ceiling, with cornice mouldings framing a foliage centrepiece of oak-leaves and thistles. Another ceiling in the adjoining chamber has been dismantled, with sections re-used throughout the house, including a date plaque of 1656.

BARROWS. *See* Upton Pyne.

BRANSCOMBE

ST WINFRED. An important church in a charming sheltered position away from the village. It belonged in the Middle Ages to Exeter Cathedral, and bishops have evidently taken an interest in it. The dominant feature is the big, plain central tower, late Norman except for the very top, including the round stair-turret, as is shown by the windows and the bell-stage openings. Unmoulded pointed E and W crossing arches. Norman also the nave, as proved by its corbel-table. C13, perhaps of the time of Bishop Branscombe, i.e. *c.* 1250–60, the transepts, not branching out from the tower, but W of it. For the date see the triple-shafted arches from the nave and the lancet window in the N transept. The nave was lengthened at the same time. The chancel is early C14, judging by its windows and the cusped ogee arches of the four-stepped SEDILIA and PISCINA group in the S wall. Low side openings in the N as well as the S wall. The E window, replaced by Bishop Neville of Exeter (1458–64), is of five lights with usual Perp tracery. Open roofs to chancel, transepts, and nave, the latter distinguished by moulded principals and carved bosses. The church was carefully restored by *W.D.Caröe* in 1911.

FONT. Brought from East Teignmouth in 1911. Big, C15, with octagonal bowl with quatrefoil panels. Large leaves and a head to support the bowl. The pillar with blank tracery panels. – PULPIT. C18; excellent example of a three-decker, almost unique in Devonshire. – BOX PEWS in the N transept. – WEST GALLERY. Late C16 with turned balusters, approached by a charming exterior staircase. – SCREEN. Plain woodwork of *c.* 1660 on a medieval stone base. – ALTAR RAILS with twisted balusters probably also of the 1660s, on all four sides of the altar. The contemporary altar table now used as a credence table. – WALL PAINTINGS. Fragments on the N wall, perhaps of the late C15. Seven deadly sins (lust). – ARCHITECTURAL FRAGMENTS. One interesting early Norman pair of shafts with spur bases. – MONUMENTS. Remains of a C14 arcaded tomb-chest. – Ann Bartlett. Large stone monument with strapwork cartouches, etc., but no effigy (same hand as Southleigh). Dated 1608. – Joan Wadham (of Edge Barton) † 1583, perhaps erected by her son Sir Nicholas Wadham, founder of Wadham College Oxford. It portrays her two husbands, John Kellaway and Sir John Wadham, kneeling opposite each other; she had 'much issue' and 'several children' by them, as the monument shows.

BRANSCOMBE MOUTH. On the clifftops to the W lies BERRY

CASTLE, a substantial earthwork enclosure possibly of the Iron Age. Further w, the remains of BARROWS and a possibly prehistoric FIELD SYSTEM. More striking than these, however, are the extensive deep PITS immediately w of Branscombe Mouth where chalk was quarried on a large scale in the post-medieval period for limeburning, some of it in the limekilns in the immediate area, some shipped along the coast from the beach.

The village is scattered along a delightful valley winding down to the sea. Numerous thatched cottages, a single-storey thatched SMITHY, and some good farmhouses. They all look rather late, but some at least are probably of the C16–17, for example MARGELLS, dug into the hillside, only its lateral stack giving anything away outside. Its interior reveals a small and richly decorated late C16 house. Stud-and-panel screens to both sides of the cross-passage, substantial timber-framed partitions in squared panels with wattle-and-daub filling in upper chambers, and, above all, richly moulded intersecting ceiling beams in both the ground-floor rooms display the richness of local Devon carpentry in the late C16. In one upper chamber even a wall painting, typical of this period, with foliage pattern in several colours with chevron-patterned border and frieze.

Many other good houses. CHURCH LIVING and CHURCH LIVING COTTAGE are a substantial L-shaped medieval house, possibly a summer residence for Exeter canons. Main block with wind-braced, smoke-blackened roof and timber partitions. The cross-wing, built partly of ashlar, also has a late medieval roof but is probably older in origin – see the paired lancets in the front gable, perhaps for a first-floor hall. HOLE is a courtyard house, home of the Holcombe family in the C15–17. Chequer stone-and-flintwork of c. 1600 at the back (cf. Cadhay). GREAT SEASIDE, close to the beach, is a picturesque group of stone farmhouse and outbuildings round a courtyard.

See also Edge Barton.

BRATTON CLOVELLY

ST MARY. The church poses some architectural problems. The first centres round the w tower. Externally it appears late Perp, of granite, with a tall NW stair-turret and no pinnacles. But the absence of a w door and the obviously older masonry of the lower part of the w wall indicate two building periods.* Moreover, to the N is a large blocked pointed arch and a roof-line above, as if of a former N transept of the C12 or C13. Inside, similar traces can be seen more clearly on the s side of the tower, where the s aisle extends to the w side of the tower. A double-chamfered pointed arch on the plainest responds opens to connect tower and s aisle. It may be the remains of a s transept, but is not in line with the blocked N arch. The w window of the s aisle is tiny and pointed, with deep C12–13 embrasure. Very tall tower arch to the E, with imposts of the same design as the nave arcades but with double instead of single-wave mouldings. The nave is the second problem.

* Bishop Grandison acquired the patronage in 1336. A rebuilding project by him has been suggested, but the details at the w end look too early (although cf. Ottery St Mary).

The first impression is of exceeding height. Positions of N door and rood-stair door (but not the S door) might suggest a lowered floor. The Perp piers rest on square foundation blocks. Are they remnants of older arcades?

The chancel is the next part in time. Its windows look early C14. The aisles were added still later. The arcades are in the usual Devon Perp style: piers of grey polyphant stone of B type with standard capitals. The chancel arch is of the same B type and tallies in height with the arcades. The extremely barbaric head-keystones inside and outside the N aisle windows may look early, but are probably 'folk art' of the C15. The aisles are both covered with ceiled lean-to roofs, and the nave has a plastered ceiling of very flat pitch. Aisles and nave have old bosses. Externally the N aisle is (as usual) less ornate than the S aisle. The latter has battlements and an embattled W stair-turret (on the N side a similar turret, close to the mysterious earliest, blocked arch, has been broken off).

FONT. Circular, Norman, the Cornish type of St Stephen-by-Launceston, i.e. with faces at the angles and rosettes, etc., in the centres of the four sides. – SCREEN. Only part of the wainscoting of the old screen survives. – WALL PAINTINGS. In N and S aisles an extensive and unusual C17 scheme, uncovered and conserved in 1986 by *Anna Hulbert*. In the upper register a series of figures: Christ and the Apostles on the S, Prophets on the N. Below are texts in elaborate frames with architectural niches and much scroll-work. On the E wall of the S aisle a scene of a military encampment with David and Goliath, a prominent armoured figure. In a roundel above, extracts from Hebrews xi: 'who through faith sub-dued kingdoms and put to flight the armies of aliens'. Is a topical allusion intended? The quality of the paintings is not high, reflect-ing the lack of a strong C17 tradition for such work in churches. – STAINED GLASS. C15 heraldic glass in the vestry. – Two angels in the tracery of a S window. – Much Victorian glass by *Lavers & Westlake*, 1883–92.

CHIMSWORTHY.* A farmhouse of outstanding interest. Two major medieval phases with subsequent adaptation. The main range, which runs N–S, sloping downhill, is probably the earliest. Five cruck trusses of massive construction form the core, linked at their apexes with huge yokes on which an equally massive ridge is set square between the principals. At the lower end, the former hayloft above the shippon, floored by similar timbers of excep-tional size. Their contorted form suggests that they are tree-trunks used more or less as they came to hand, completely undecorated, though they become more regular at the upper end (where the E blade of the northernmost cruck is jointed). This is a long way from the rich carpentry traditions of mid Devon, and though the primitive appearance suggests an early date, the more likely explanation may be the conservative building tradition of the W part of the county. The cross-wing at the upper end was also an open hall, subsequently floored. Good late C16 and C17 details, above which the smoke-blackened roof survives, of arch-braced construction with cranked collars, lower wind-braces, and jointed apexes.

*For a plan of Chimsworthy *see* p. 69.

An interesting mix of farmhouses in this remote parish NW of Dartmoor. WEST BURROW is another longhouse. NORTH BREAZLE and WRIXHILL have late medieval three-room-and-cross-passage plans, with well preserved sequences of later alterations.
See also Orchard.

BRATTON FLEMING
6030

ST PETER. W tower with diagonal buttresses only at the foot, no pinnacles, and an unmoulded round-headed arch to the nave. Nave and N aisle rebuilt in 1702–3, possibly after the tower had collapsed, and reconstructed again in *Hayward*'s restoration of 1855–61. The N arcade has rather clumsy shallow pointed arches. The N chancel arcade however is apparently of the C14, that is unusually early: broadly handled continuous mouldings, the inner order with a hollow between two fillets. – MONUMENTS. All minor, the best to Bartholomew Wortley, rector, †1749, aged 97, with a handsome Latin epitaph with marble architectural surround.

CHURCH HOUSE. Much altered; restored in 1895. The usual two-storeyed C16 type with external stairs, now with three chimney-stacks.

BAPTIST CHAPEL. 1850. Long, low, partly rendered, with arched openings and hipped roof. Two-storey Sunday School behind.

METHODIST CHAPEL. 1854 for the Bible Christians, the Sunday School of 1891. Rubble, gabled, round-arched openings, date roundel. Sunday School rendered.

CASTLE. In Castle Field a truncated mound, almost certainly a former motte, and presumably part of the C11 or C12 manor house.

CHELFHAM RAILWAY VIADUCT. Designed by *Frank W. Chanter*, engineer, the major engineering work on the 1ft 11½in. gauge Lynton and Barnstaple Railway which operated from 1898 to 1935. Eight 24-ft-wide arches span the valley of the river Yeo 70ft below; the S end of the viaduct is built on a curve. Cream-coloured Marland brick with blue brick bands at the springing of the arches and at rail level; the taller piers with rusticated masonry bases. Parapets removed.

BRAUNTON
4030

ST BRANNOCK (a Celtic saint, tutor to the family of Brychan, King of Brecknock, who begat so many of the saints of Cornwall). An ambitious church, serving a very large parish. There was a priest here by 857. Architecturally the church is one of the most interesting, and also one of the most puzzling, in North Devon. Its most evident distinguishing feature is the massive S tower in a transeptal position, apparently of Norman date, with a tiny window in the W side and a set-off higher up (above the eaves level of the church). Visually its charm is the lead-covered broach-spire with pedimental or gabled bell-openings between the broaches, very similar to Barnstaple.

The church is built of uncoursed grey stone, with the exception of the chamfered pilaster buttresses of ashlar which rise from splayed plinths near the corners of the w front. These must belong, with the early Gothic w door, with double-chamfered arch, to the late C12 or perhaps the early C13, and so indicate a church already at that time of considerable size. Perhaps of the same date, or a little later, the three lancet windows on the N side of the chancel, the double-chamfered chancel arch, and the unmoulded pointed arch opening into the s tower. The N transept also opens into the nave with an unmoulded pointed arch (now blocked by the organ), no doubt also C13, as are the two lancet windows flanking the chancel arch. But these are a problem, for they suggest aisles, and the great surprise of the interior is that the nave is aisleless, despite its width of 34 ft. Were there arcades which were eliminated later? No other trace of them remains. The nave windows, although with renewed Perp tracery, could be early C14 in their shapes. From the Perp period the nave roof, the heavy buttresses added to take the increased thrust, the vestry N of the chancel with open timber roof, and the s chancel chapel with a two-bay arcade with B type piers, coarse thin capitals only to the main shafts, and double-chamfered arches. Ceiled wagon roof. The nave wagon roof is open (restored 1850), and is well supplied with bosses (sow and pigs over the font). General restoration 1887–9 by *White*, chancel restored 1872–3 by *Christian*.

FONT. Square bowl of Norman shape, with faces at the corners, but with tracery of c. 1300 (probably Norman and later reworked). – PULPIT. C17, octagonal; READING DESK dated 1636. – N transept GALLERY. 1619. – SCREEN. Across the chancel arch, four-light sections as usual, but thin shafts and the tracery more elementarily Perp than in most. No coving and probably not meant to have any. – REREDOS, or rather altar-back, of c. 1935 with panelling and central crowning segmental arch. – COMMUNION RAILS. Balusters of balls of equal size like beads, presumably early C17. – BENCH ENDS. A remarkable set, filling the whole nave, the E ones complete with frontals. Interesting also because parish records prove that the number was enlarged in 1560, 1568, 1578, 1579, 1583, and 1593. The representations include the usual instruments of the Passion, shields, initials, and some whole figures. There are no Renaissance details. – SCULPTURE. In the w wall of the s tower, re-used as a window lintel, pre-Conquest tomb slab. – CANDELABRA. Three with lovely elaborate wrought-iron stars above, dated 1833, the middle one with coats of arms. – STAINED GLASS. E and W windows by *Percy Bacon*, 1909.

MONUMENTS. Brass to Lady Elizabeth Bourchier †1548, a palimpsest with the head of a knight on the back. Small kneeling figure, separate inscription. – Late C16 relief with the initials RB and MB, against the s wall, panels flanked by three superimposed orders of short columns, no figures. – Sumptuous monument to the Incledon family, dates of death 1736 and 1746, with trophies along the sides and figures of angels by the achievement on top. – Frances Baker †1782. Pretty, with cherubs' heads, garlands, etc.; not signed.

CHAPEL OF ST MICHAEL, on a hill ½ m. NE, visible from far away on all sides. It is in ruins. The building was late Perp, with a w

porch, w bellcote, single-light N and s windows, and a larger E
window.

St Brannoc (R.C.) (Chapel of St Brannoc's Well). 1958 by
Joseph E. Walter.

Caen Primary School, Caen Street. 1873, enlarged 1883 and
1896.

Velator Bridge, over the river Caen. Built *c.* 1815, probaby by
James Green.

The main road bypasses the old route through the village, along
which there are many worthwhile houses. By the churchyard,
Church House, with a double covered stair to an upper four-
centred wooden doorway in the gable end. At the other end a
carriageway through to the churchyard. Two upper wooden
windows with pairs of arched lights and original iron bars.
Opposite is a house with a delightful two-storey early C19 veranda,
and No. 28, with a frieze made up of re-used medieval carving,
including Perp quatrefoils, said to come from the village cross.
Along East Street a pleasant mixture of stucco villas (e.g.
No. 3) and cottages; also the United Reformed Church
with large later C19 schools in front of an older chapel founded in
1662. Broadgate is a former manor house, now subdivided and
much altered, but with a fine medieval arch-braced roof with intermediate trusses, a first-floor chimneypiece dated 1626, and a plaster frieze.

Town Farm, North Street. A remarkable survival of a town farm.
Late C15 and C16 house, now subdivided, with a raised cruck truss
over the lower end of the hall with chamfered arch-braces, forming
a courtyard with C18 farm buildings.

Cobblestones, Willoways Lane. 1905 by *Francis Troup* in the
Arts and Crafts manner; rubble stone with canted bays, complete
with landscaped garden.

Fairlinch, 1m. NW. An early C17 house with a two-storeyed
crenellated porch, datestone 1629, and heraldic shield. On the
ground floor a panelled room with interwoven griffins in the cornice. Chimneypiece of 1635 incorporating figures and a heraldic
shield of the Burgoyne family. Enriched plaster mouldings on the
ceiling beams supported on Corinthian pilasters. Chamber above
with C17 plasterwork of geometrical strapwork design welling out
from truncated central pendant bosses and enriched with naturalistic scenes and animals, very similar to Rashleigh Barton (q.v.).
Late C18 extension with a staircase with turned balusters and a
large Venetian window, the main room with an eared chimneypiece decorated with swags.

Buckland Manor, ½m. NW. Symmetrical seven-bay Georgian
front of two storeys and dormers, the ground-floor windows with
keystones, added to an older house. U-shaped plan, the wings
projecting to the rear C17 and C18 in appearance (but remains of
an arch-braced roof in the r. wing). Porch with Tuscan columns;
sundial dated 1789 above. Another sundial of 1759, and a datestone of 1762 on the l. gable end. Main range with C18 panelling.

Peel Tower, ½m. E. Three-storeyed tower built *c.* 1846 by
Thomas Mortman to celebrate the repeal of the Corn Laws.

Braunton Great Field, to the w of the village, is one of the
very few open fields in the country still cultivated on the medieval

strip system. It is rivalled in size and completeness only by the field at Laxton, Notts. Furlongs, headlands, and the boundstones can all still be seen, although many of the strips have been amalgamated; there were over 600 in 1840, 140 in 1986.

s of the Great Field, BRAUNTON MARSH was reclaimed in 1811–15 by dint of constructing the GREAT SEA BANK with sluices to drain the area. *James Green*'s GREAT SLUICE of that date still survives, with three openings of massive ashlar blocks. Further s, HORSEY ISLAND, reclaimed by a further bank and drains in 1850–7. All the farmhouses, like Town Farm, are some distance away inland, but the fields are dotted with linhays for animal shelter and storage, about thirty-five altogether, a unique sight in a county where field outbuildings are so rare. They are often surrounded by a walled enclosure. The larger ones have circular stone columns to the open side and a hayloft above. (The small circular building alongside Marsh Road is probably earlier.)

See also Ash Barton *and* Saunton.

7040   BRENDON

ST BRENDAN. Far up in Exmoor, and accessible only on picturesque routes. Rebuilt in 1738, it is said, from materials brought over from Cheriton. The tower, rebuilt or renovated in 1828, is superficially of Devon type, but in its details clearly post-Gothic. Angle buttresses, obelisk pinnacles. N arcade (octagonal columns, stilted Dec arches) and windows of 1873. – FONT. Square, Norman, with curved lines towards the bottom of the bowl, a diagrammatical interpretation of the scallops of such fonts as Ilfracombe. – Also a small circular C12 STOUP(?) with zigzag band above foliage, birds, and a beaded wavy band, standing on a short piece of carved shaft (recut) with animals in lozenges. – REREDOS. C19. Carved wooden tracery; figures in niches. – STAINED GLASS. E window of 1884, with Crucifixion and grisaille panels. – SUNDIAL. 1707.

Restored LIMEKILN at Watersmeet on the East Lyn.

4080   BRENTOR

ST MICHAEL DE RUPE. An exciting sight for miles around. A small church (40 by 14 ft) with w tower on a steep cliff of volcanic stone, standing all alone with its w front not 3 ft from the precipice. The site must have been of importance long before, for the walls of an earthwork surround the rock.* The tower, 32 ft high, is embattled and unbuttressed. The body of the church has battlements on a corbel-table. Windows deeply splayed inside but only slightly outside, i.e. C13 at the latest, although some of the fabric may be C12. The earliest record of the church is of before 1150. It belonged to Tavistock Abbey, which in 1232 established an annual fair here. There was a consecration by Bishop Stapledon in 1319. Restored in 1889–90 at the expense of the Duke of Bedford.

CHRIST CHURCH, North Brentor. 1856 by *Richard Gosling* of

---

*Defensive banks and ditches survive to the N and E of the outcrop. Other surface disturbances are due to C19 manganese mining.

Torquay. Lancet style, with w tower. The CHURCH HALL is a former National School of 1832, extended later. Tudor details.

PROVIDENCE METHODIST CHAPEL, in North Brentor village. 1847 for the Bible Christians. Very plain: rendered rubble, gabled with small gabled porch, round-arched windows. Later Sunday School adjacent. Burying ground at the side.

LANGSTONE. E-shaped, with some late C16 granite mullioned windows, much rebuilt in 1907. Battlemented gateway; stables with cupola.

BRIDESTOWE   5080

ST BRIDGET. The scanty remains of a Norman arch of one order set up s of the church. There is a reference to rebuilding the church in 1450–1, but of that work little remains. w tower rebuilt 1828–30; unbuttressed, with crocketed pinnacles. Unmoulded tower arch. Arcades also rebuilt (repairs and reseating 1866–8 by *Gould*, general restoration from 1890 by *Fulford & Harvey*). – SCREEN. Some poor fragments of the old wainscoting. – MONUMENT. Honor Calmady † 1665. An architectural wall-monument.

CASTLE. In Burley Wood, within a later prehistoric enclosure. Well preserved remains of a motte with two baileys in an elevated position above the Okehampton–Launceston road. In the Norman period the manor of Bridestowe was held by the Pomeroy family of the lords of Okehampton.

FERNWORTHY. A farmhouse, perhaps once more important, with a medieval roof unusually combining a central true cruck with a base-cruck and spere-truss at either end of the hall.

GREAT BIDLAKE, 1 m. W. E-plan, with straight gables and mullioned windows; much restored. 1594 on a re-used mullion head; 1848 on the r. wing.

LEAWOOD. The manor house of the Shilstones, set in an C18 park. Plain front range of 1–2–1 bays concealing an older house with two-storey wings flanking a courtyard. At the back, very pretty Georgian Gothick windows, Doric porch, and a C16 or earlier doorway. Stables dated 1711 with the Calmady arms and well preserved interior. LODGE with Gothick glazing.

BRIDFORD   8080

ST THOMAS-A-BECKET. An all-granite church. Unbuttressed w tower of ashlar with unmoulded tower arch inside on the plainest responds. Ashlar-built N aisle, but earlier chancel, if the evidence of the Dec window detail (reticulated tracery) can be trusted. Ashlar again for the nave, with two fine Perp windows r. and l. of the s porch. N aisle piers of A type with four unmoulded capitals. Nave and aisle with wagon roofs; remains of a painted CELURE above the rood screen.

SCREENS.* Of exceptional interest. The ROOD SCREEN is datable by a board (now detached) with the initials of Walter South-

---

* This account is based on notes kindly contributed by Anna Hulbert.

cote, rector 1508–50. The coving has gone, although triangular
pieces from it, with leaf decoration, have been nailed on to the
spandrels of the panels, which have standard A type tracery. The
rich ornament includes pomegranates, gourds, and palm pillars
with lily-work capitals (could these refer to the Temple of
Solomon?). On the wainscoting charming small carved figures,
only 8 in. high (cf. Lustleigh), instead of the usual painted ones.
On the back, grisaille figures in exotic dress, one of the head-
dresses similar to Salome's at Ugborough. The back coving once
grisaille as well. – The PARCLOSE SCREEN (with tracery of a
different pattern) also has grisaille paintings (cf. Ashton): the subjects appear to be alternate wise and foolish men. Much of the
colour of both screens (revealed by cleaning by *Anna Hulbert* in
1974–81) is in excellent condition, the azurite blue and the streaky
marbling of the sill both rare survivals. It is revealing that less
expensive pigments were used on the back (e.g. red lead instead of
vermilion). On the second post from the N a ring, apparently
original, perhaps for a chained Bible, and evidence for some structure against the N bay.

PULPIT. Three-sided, coeval with the screen, although the top
band of decoration was perhaps originally part of the rood-screen
cornice. Painted arabesque panels inside. – BENCH ENDS with
two-tier tracery. – STAINED GLASS. Fragments and figures in the
tops of the N windows.

OLD RECTORY. Much remodelled in the C19 and C20, but with a
stud-and-panel hall screen, the panels decorated with six C16
figure paintings identified by E. Clive Rouse as the Nine Worthies.

BRIDFORD BARTON. The present farmhouse incorporates two bays
of a plain but massive roof possibly of the early C14 – a rare
survival. They are of base-cruck construction with heavy arcade
plates (as purlins), a spere-truss with aisle posts, and collared
common rafters. In the rear wing added in the C15 three arch-
braced trusses, diagonally set purlins, and a clasped, square-set
ridge.

LAPLOYDE BARTON. A superior mid C17 house of three ranges
around a narrow courtyard.

Many good C15–17 farms, including WOODLANDS, Heath Lane,
with a C17 threshing barn and an C18 cider house and ash house,
and NEADON, Neadon Lane, with a complete medieval roof.

BRIDGERULE

ST BRIDGET. On its own on a hill above the village. Perp W tower of
ashlar granite, unbuttressed, with big cusped pinnacles. Nave and
N transept (connected by a plain C13 arch) plus later S aisle with
three-light Perp windows and an arcade of five bays with granite
piers of A type, capitals only to the main shafts, and depressed
pointed arches. Good open wagon roofs. C13 chancel, with
remains of a low PISCINA. S porch with late Perp doorway,
square-headed, flanked by quatrefoils. In the porch a C12 PILLAR
PISCINA re-used as a stoup. Minimal volute decoration in low
relief. – FONT. Very crude Norman; eggcup-shaped bowl and

shaft of one piece without articulation. – Late Victorian SCREEN with painted figures on the dado, and REREDOS with highly coloured reliefs in Gothic niches. – TOWER SCREEN with crude painting of the Annunciation. – STAINED GLASS. S windows 1857. – On the N side a window framed by an unusual wooden niche. – Minor MONUMENTS include John Kingdon †1808, urn against an oval of grey marble, by *Emes & Stephens* of Exeter, and other Kingdon memorials.

BRIDWELL
Near Uffculme

0010

Built in 1774–9 for Richard Hall Clarke and owned by the Clarke family until 1980. Plain stuccoed mansion in a commanding position, facing S. Five bays, two and a half storeys above a basement, tactfully extended N by a back wing of the same height *c.* 1913. The centre projects slightly, with Venetian windows on the upper floors and a small open pediment above. Stone porch of *c.* 1913. The only external ornament is plain bands between the floors. The architect is unknown, and the exterior is indeed not specially distinguished in its proportions, so the interior comes as a surprise. It is exquisitely decorated, with plasterwork somewhat in the Adam manner, but with that mixture of neo-classical and personal motifs that is so characteristic of provincial work (cf. Shute, Stover).

Oval entrance hall; ceiling with fan ornament, fluted frieze. The blue and cream ceiling of the room on the l. includes within its arabesques panels with musical instruments, but also more homely beer barrels and barley, crossed guns and cartridges. In contrast, the excellent fireplace is a most sophisticated piece. Panels with classical sacrifices set in coloured marbles: Derbyshire bluejohn with a strip of 'landscape' Cotham marble below. Original grate engraved with sphinxes. On either side a niche with reeded capitals. The room to the r. of the hall has another good ceiling with more conventional honeysuckle ornament. A niche on either side of the door; unusual ogee Gothic fireplace in fossil marble, and between the windows an elegant oval mirror with sphinxes and husk garlands surmounted by the Clarke lark. Plain staircase, lit by a Venetian window and with another pretty ceiling, rising to an unexpectedly elaborate tripartite landing: an oval centre from which arches lead to small lobbies with elongated oval domes.

STABLES. Red brick, U-shaped, dated 1779, tucked neatly behind the house. Two blind arches and one small arch to each of the wings; stone keystones.

GROUNDS. A plan of 1779 shows the small landscaped park around the house, with a lake at the foot of the slope. N of the house the MUSEUM (derelict), built by Richard Hall Clarke in 1809, a stone building incorporating some black volcanic lumps, with Gothic windows and porch. It has a re-used medieval arch-braced and wind-braced roof brought from near Plymouth. Behind the stables a small MONUMENT, a lump of stalagmites on a triangular base set with knucklebones. Another pyramid of stalagmites in a field to the E, incorporating a trefoiled piscina. Near the

beginning of the W drive a WALLED GARDEN close to the site of
the old house: walls of cob, stone, and brick, late C17 coat of arms
above the entrance.

OLD BRIDWELL, close to the walled garden. Before disastrous alterations in 1986 the farmhouse of c. 1800 was surrounded by a large yard
of buildings, including two large BARNS with jointed crucks and
excellent wide entrances with depressed four-centred heads. In the
SW corner an attractive thatched L-shaped HOUSE of two main
periods. S range early, with smoke-blackened jointed cruck trusses.
Two rooms only (cross-passage and lower end probably destroyed);
what remains is divided by a stud-and-panel partition with shoulder-
headed doorway. The E room was the medieval hall, now with a
large stack inserted together with the later floor. The N range along
the road is problematic. Unheated, it is entered on the ground floor
by a four-centred doorway (reset?), with external stairs to the
first floor, but no internal access to the main house at ground level.

BRIXHAM see TORBAY

₅₀₅₀   BRIXTON

Now on the edge of Plymouth.

ST MARY. Early W tower with diagonal buttresses, corbel-table to
support the battlements, and no pinnacles. Interior with granite
arcade of A type with capitals only to the four shafts and depressed
moulded arches. Squints from the chancel aisles. Two-light window
in the vestry, said to come from Spriddlestone, a former Fortescue
mansion (cf. below). Restoration 1887, and 1894 by *Charles King* of
Plymouth. – STAINED GLASS. E window 1885 by *Clayton & Bell*. –
MONUMENT. Lucy Palmer † 1834 (kneeling female by an urn) by
Walker of Bristol.

CHURCH HOUSE (?), N of the church. Much altered. Two late C15
windows on the W side, the lower one with two cinquefoiled lights,
the upper with plain arched lights, possibly reset.

BRIXTON HOUSE. W front of 1835 by *George Wightwick* for Henry
Collins-Splatt, added to an earlier house. Five bays, cornice and
hipped roof. Central Venetian window above a large porte-cochère
added c. 1850. Other mid and later C19 alterations. Hall screen with
Corinthian columns.

SPRIDDLESTONE HOUSE. Late Georgian, stuccoed, three by three
bays, projecting eaves, Tuscan porch. Built by a branch of the
Fortescues whose ancient seat was at Spriddlestone Barton, from
which some material has been re-used in a barn and shippon.

WEST SHERFORD, 1 m. N. Former manor house granted to Francis
Drake after 1582. C16, the W part heightened and extended in the
C17. Four-centred doorway to a cross-passage, two-light granite
window above. Some ground-floor windows with arched lights.

See also Higher Harestone.

BROADCLYST

ST JOHN. A substantial church on which much money must have been expended. Tall w tower completed in the c16, with tall two-light bell-openings decorated as at Cullompton, where the tower is altogether very similar (cf., for example, the gargoyles under pinnacles carved on the buttresses). w door and top battlements generously decorated. The rest of the church probably an earlier Perp rebuilding. Exterior with embattled aisles and s porch; turrets at the w ends of the aisles. Large four-light Perp windows. Spacious interior: six bays with slender piers of B type, and standard capitals. On one capital the Stafford knot, perhaps in deference to Bishop Stafford († 1419). The arches have fleurons as a special decoration and spring from angel figures. All this is clearly c15. The N aisle, the E window, and the SEDILIA with tall crocketed gables must be earlier. They look mid c14. The tracery of the window is unusually fanciful for Devon. The ribbed plaster vault dates from 1832–3, when the church was reroofed, apparently with fireproof iron trusses. Flat aisle ceilings with lozenge-shaped panels and spidery metal bosses. Chancel restored, E window renewed, and stone REREDOS added in 1882 by *Ashworth*; rather dull.

FONT. Early Victorian Gothic; 1843 by *S. Rowe.* – PULPIT. 1895 by *E.H.Harbottle*, oak and polished granite. – FURNISHINGS. Much by *Herbert Read.* – STAINED GLASS. N aisle, Merry memorial window, 1910 by *Heaton, Butler & Bayne*, with their typically sombre, dramatically packed groups of figures. – S aisle E, First World War memorial window by *Clayton & Bell.* – N aisle E, kaleidoscopic Nativity by *Leonard Walker*, 1924. – MONUMENTS. Mid c14 knight under the sedilia, identified as Sir Roger de Nonant. – Sir John Acland † 1620, the first Acland to settle at Broadclyst. Erected in his lifetime; dated 1613 and 1614, with (bad) figure propped up on one elbow. To the l. and r. far-projecting pairs of columns and an elaborate strapwork cresting with obelisks and achievement. The whole overcrowded with cartouches, strapwork, fruit, and putti – one of the most sumptuous Jacobean monuments in Devon and the most splendid of a related group with foliate strapwork friezes, probably by an Exeter mason, *John Deymond* (cf. Eveleigh monument, Bovey Tracey; Jeffrey monument, Whit-church Canonicorum, Dorset; Leach monument, Talaton). – Edward Drew † 1622 and family. Recumbent figures under a canopy in the SE corner of the S aisle, the children kneeling in relief against the E wall. – Henry Burrough † 1605 and wife. The usual wall-monument with kneelers.

Because so much of this exceptionally large parish was in Acland ownership (and through Sir Richard's gift is now owned by the National Trust), Broadclyst remains one of the least altered of the great estates of Devon, affording models of estate buildings proper around the great house at Killerton (q.v.) and a typical range of village, hamlet, and farm buildings, all in a countryside remarkably (for its proximity to Exeter) uncompromised by modern develop-ment.

A tour of the centre should begin at the church, part of a classic village group with the RED LION INN (much altered c18 and later interior, but attractive tiled exterior), BROADCLYST HOUSE (over-large; mid C19), and the cottages and almshouses scattered around the green. Behind Broadclyst House, down by the river, CLYSTON MILL, the present C18 mill buildings with miller's house and undershot water-wheel on a much older site. Behind the Red Lion, QUEEN'S SQUARE, with C17 and C18 thatched cottages, Nos. 2, 3, and 4 with gothicky first floor surmounting the squatter ground floor of the original C16 building. Across the main road, past the thatched BUS SHELTER, by *Randall Wells*, 1925, into SCHOOL LANE, where the JUBILEE SCHOOL and schoolmaster's house of 1810 (see inscription) have Gothic windows set in Killerton stone surrounds contrasting well with the red sandstone walls. Here and in TOWNEND and TOWNHILL a typical range of C15–19 housing, the earlier structures mostly disguised by C19 details. COLLEGE, in BURROW ROAD, has a lateral stack, a late medieval roof, and a stud-and-panel screen with mural decoration of painted black foliage. At Townend, MARKER'S COTTAGE, another late medieval house, with remains of polychrome painted decoration on the screen between hall and inner room.

Back to the main road. GOULD'S COTTAGES, on the corner of CHURCH LANE, is a terrace of four (originally three) houses by *Benjamin Gould* of 1778. In Church Lane, BURROUGH'S ALMS-HOUSES, 1605, substantially reconstructed in 1883. Between the village centre and Dog Village, the long range of NEW BUILD-INGS, eight blocks of housing built after a fire in 1870, with interesting variations of detail on what at first sight seem exactly similar houses.

Of the many C15–19 farmhouses in the parish some have exceptionally early and good medieval features, among them OLD PARK (smoke louvre), NEW HALL (eight-bay roof with moulded arch braces), and PINN COURT (five medieval bays, wind-bracing, and arch-bracings, including an arch-braced end-cruck). Typical C15–17 development is evident in, for example, WEST CLYST, with its inserted framed C17 ceiling, richly moulded. The farmyard buildings include model C18 and C19 layouts, e.g. at NEW HALL, on a double courtyard plan with many specialist buildings including an integral dovecot, mostly early/mid C19. MOOREDGE COTTAGES in Moor Lane, once one large farmhouse, now subdivided into three cottages, had a medieval three-room cross-passage plan, with smoke-blackened roof, a section of stud-and-panel screen, and a C17 cross-wing off the upper end with initials and datestone HAD 1624.

ASHCLYST. A former manor house, once a court house of the canons of Torre. L-shaped, one wing probably C15, with original fireplaces.

SPRYDONCOTE, 1½m. N. Georgian brick front of five bays and two storeys with parapet.

WINDMILL, at Dog Village, ½m. S. Operational from 1786 to 1815. Stone tower with modern roof; no gear.

WATER TOWER. 1942. Concrete. Circular tank on a central column supported by eight slightly splayed legs.

DOLBURY. *See* Killerton.

See also Columbjohn, Killerton, *and* Westwood.

BROADHEMBURY

ST ANDREW. Broad, strong W tower with buttresses of type B and stair-turret; three-light bell-openings. Two-storey N porch (with niches for figures) cutting into one of the C14 windows of the nave. In addition, one unusually ambitious Perp window opened in the nave wall to give light to the pulpit, with figures sticking out at the springing points of the tracery; angels towards the nave, a man and a woman towards the outside (cf. the screen at Awliscombe). S aisle also Perp, with buttresses and large three-light windows. The porch has a panelled stone vault, a C17 wooden gate, and a richly decorated doorway with niche above. Chancel rebuilt 1843 by *Hayward* with a good Perp E window (a copy of the original?); the rest restored by him in 1853–5. Inside, four bays to the S aisle plus one to the chancel chapel, in which a Perp priest's door was opened up in 1974. Piers in which the waves of the type B section are duplicated (cf. Bradninch, Awliscombe). Unceiled wagon roofs, largely reconstructed by *Harbottle Reed* in 1930. – FONT. Perp, octagonal, with primitive tracery and surprisingly primitive figures. – STAINED GLASS. S aisle windows by *Heaton, Butler & Bayne*, of various dates and styles. – MONUMENTS. Francis Drewe + 1675, not yet classical in its forms. – Another Drewe, early C17, kneeling between double columns.

An uncommonly pretty village of thatched buff-washed cob with a remarkable number of medieval houses. Its careful preservation is largely due to the Drewe family: Julius Drewe bought half the village *c.* 1900, and many of the houses were restored and thatched by *Philip Tilden* for Sir Cedric Drewe in the 1950s.

DREWE ARMS (former church house). Two adjoining ranges, the entrance in the lower one to the N. In the two-storey S part a good late Perp stone window: five arched lights and carved spandrels.

THE GRANGE. The site of a grange of Dunkeswell Abbey, bought in 1602–3 by Edward Drewe (†1622), who built a large H-plan mansion which was completed by his son Thomas and considerably altered in the C18. The Drewes owned the house until *c.* 1890. Of the original house it is chiefly the back (NE) side that is recognizable: two symmetrical gables on projecting wings, mullioned-and-transomed windows. SE front refaced, refenestrated, and given a small pediment in the mid C18; at the same time the space between the wings on the SW front was filled in, and the whole house stuccoed. The best woodwork was exported to America soon after 1904, but one good ceiling, several large plaster overmantels, and some panelling (much restored) remain from the early C17. Excellent mid C18 staircase in the central range, with slender turned balusters and fluted newels. One ceiling with later C18 Adam-style plasterwork.

See also Kerswell Priory.

BROADHEMPSTON

ST PETER AND ST PAUL. The W tower, as so often, is the oldest part of the fabric: short and narrow, marked batter, no buttresses. Above the large later W window, thin lancets. No pinnacles. Low

NE corner stair-turret. The masonry of the door and window surrounds early too. Tower arch unmoulded on simple responds. The
next part in time is the chancel, much restored, but with bits of
C13 plate tracery in the side windows. An indulgence for rebuilding the nave was granted in 1402, but the present Beer stone
arcades are probably later C15, of five bays, B type piers with
standard capitals, four-light windows. S porch with original wagon
roof. Numerous restorations: 1777, 1842 (walls rendered), 1853–4
by *J. L. Pearson* (chancel, with new E window), 1876–7 by *John
Chudleigh* of Exeter, 1896–8 by *E. H. Sedding* (new roofs and flooring). – FONT. The usual octagonal Perp type of Devon, rather
plain. – SCREEN. Across nave and aisles and encasing the dividing
piers with triangular projections. The tracery of the panels of B
type, the top parts all of 1903. – STAINED GLASS. Old bits reset in
a S window: heraldry of the Rowe family. – MONUMENT. A
charming black stone plate decorated with naïve angels and the
names of Robert Warrying and his wife in circles with two hands
joined from one to the other. Their daughter is also commemorated: 'Mother and daughter both within this tomb/Enwrapt
doe lye in one earths comon womb/Expect ye day when twin in one
new birth/A resurrection shall bring them forth …' The date is
1654.

THE MONK'S RETREAT. A former church house, E of the church,
with a passage through from the village square and a two-light
stone transomed window above.

SALEM CHAPEL. An attractive, simple chapel within its own walled
ground, just one domestic Georgian window above a Tuscan
porch.

METHODIST CHAPEL. Now a house. An arched window above the
door with quite an elaborate classical surround.

Many good C17 to early C19 farmhouses in the parish, e.g. MANOR
FARMHOUSE, SNEYDHURST, FORDER GREEN FARMHOUSE.

BEASTON is interesting as a transitional type, *c.* 1740–50, for the
Rowe family (cf. Kingston House, Staverton). Stately, symmetrical five-bay ashlar front with coved cornice and hipped roof, but a
modest interior only one room deep with a corridor to the service
wing projecting on the l.

BROADWOOD KELLY

ALL HALLOWS. W tower with B type buttresses. S aisle with
straight-headed uncusped windows. Late Perp arcade with granite
piers of A type, capitals only to the main shafts, depressed pointed
arches. Unceiled wagon roofs to nave, aisle, and S porch. S door
dated 1695. Restoration and refitting of chancel 1868–9 by *Gould.*
– FONT. Octagonal, of granite, very elementary decoration, but
probably C16. – ORGAN CASE. Perhaps earlier C19. – STAINED
GLASS. Assembled in a N window, Virgin from a Crucifixion,
dated 1523, and a kneeling man and woman, above them in a
roundel a praying cleric; St Sidwell in the head of a window. –
TILES of Barnstaple type. – MONUMENT. Webber family, 1754,
of wood, with pilasters and broken pediment.

BROADWOODWIDGER   4080

St Nicholas. In a good position on a hill facing Dartmoor. The early C13 survives in the chancel arch, pointed, on plain slightly decorated imposts. The tall tower arch may be of the same date. Unbuttressed W tower with a rectangular NE stair-turret rising above the tower top. N transept (also an early feature), chancel, and S aisle; S chancel chapel added before the aisle (see the confusion between the various arches). The four-bay arcade between nave and aisle has granite piers of A type with capitals only to the main shafts and depressed pointed arches. Original wagon roofs. – FONT. Granite, octagonal, with rosette decoration. Restored in 1871. – SCREEN. With standard A tracery, no coving, and remains of two bands of ornament from the cornice. – BENCH ENDS. A large number of the usual Devon type of c. 1530, with instruments of the Passion, initials, etc., and also some with mid C16 heads. – MONUMENTS. Knight in armour, c. 1500. The legs of the figure are missing. The recess in the E wall of the S chapel where it is placed is obviously too low. The best part of the monument is the tomb-chest, with figures of mourners standing under nodding ogee canopies. The knight is supposed to be a member of the Upcott family. – Excellent C18-19 slate headstones in the churchyard.

School. Late C19. Stone, with pale brick bands and striped voussoirs. SCHOOL HOUSE attached.

Upcott, 1 m. NW. Remains (possibly the parlour wing) of a good early Tudor manor house. Two-storey porch. To its r., two storeys of granite mullioned windows; two more in the gable end, an early C16 heraldic shield in the lower one. Dog-leg stair of c. 1700. In the room beyond, behind an C18 china cupboard, an unusual small five-light window cut from a single stone. Another remarkable window upstairs, a single slab pierced with two plus two trefoil-headed lights.

Buddle, ¾ m. NW. A small late medieval farmhouse with two separate smoke-blackened roofs (cf. Chimsworthy at Bratton Clovelly).

Among the historic farmsteads demolished for the construction of the Roadford reservoir (begun 1985) in the remote valley of the River Wolf, Shop, with a C17 lobby-entrance farmhouse and a large bank barn with a continuous pentice roof to the yard, and Combepark, the most grievous loss, a rare early C18 example of a brick farmhouse on a double-pile plan.

BROOKING   7060
Tigley Cross, Dartington

Chapel of ease, parsonage, and school, begun by Henry Champernowne of Dartington († 1851), completed by his family – an interesting example of idiosyncratic Tractarian patronage.*

St Barnabas. 1850–5, built under the superintendence of Mr *Pennell* of Exeter. The designer is unknown. Long chancel, nave

---

*I am grateful to Mr C.J.Pickford for information in this entry. For further details on church and patrons see his article: 'A Devon Enigma, an account of St Barnabas Brooking', *Churchscape* 5, 1986.

with s aisle, s tower with slender broach-spire – a picturesque group, especially from the SW, reminiscent of the church at Landscove (q.v.) built a few years earlier for Henry Champernowne's sister by J.L.Pearson, although here the E.E. detail is skimpier. The interior is a surprise, dominated by two s arcade piers of polished marble, of massive girth, dramatically lit from behind by the upper windows of the open tower. The piers, of Madrepore marble quarried on the estate, were shown at the Great Exhibition as geological specimens. The rest of the interior of Caen stone. Chancel arch of short shafts with carved corbels; unusually, another similar but more ornate arch divides off the sanctuary. Simple original fittings – PISCINA, ALTAR, PULPIT, FONT – making use of local marble. – STAINED GLASS. E window by *Hardman*, 1886. – s aisle w 1873, possibly by *Clayton & Bell*.

BROOKING HOUSE, the former parsonage. A sturdy, simply detailed composition with boldly projecting porch.

5000   BROOMFORD MANOR
                                Jacobstowe

Colonel Sir Robert White-Thompson, who bought the estate in 1858, commissioned *George Devey* to design him a new Tudor manor house. It was built in 1871–3, of local stone roughly squared and laid in uneven courses, rock-faced up to ground-floor windowsill level, more smoothly cut above. The roof is tiled, but not all the decorative tile-hanging and half-timbering proposed in the designs was carried out. The house is of three storeys on an irregular plan which, combined with some of Devey's favourite architectural features, results in a highly picturesque effect. Entrance front with a wide Dutch gable above the front door to the l. To the r. two bays are set back, and the next two set back again; with each set-back the roof is lowered. Garden front with a two-storey tower-like bay with a conical roof in the centre, to the r. a gable and french windows, to the l. a substantial chimneybreast. On the rear front, to the r. a gable with an asymmetrically placed two-storey bay with a hipped roof, to the l. a couple of recessed and gabled bays linked to the offices by a two-storey quadrant bay. Mullioned windows with transoms to the ground-floor and staircase windows. Tall square chimneystacks rise in groups of two, three, and four. Over the kitchen a louvred cupola with a dinner-bell.

The OFFICES, which incorporate a fragment of an older building, are of two storeys next to the house, single-storey beyond. The adjoining buildings, all with gables of differing pitch and width imposed upon and intersecting each other, continue in the office elevations a measure of the picturesque irregularity of the main house. One of Devey's conical-roofed bread-ovens projects between the kitchen and the bakehouse. L-shaped LODGE. Stone-built ground floor with half-timbering above, and a boat-shaped multiple chimneystack – a Devey trademark.*

*I am grateful to Jill Allibone for this entry.

BRUSHFORD

6000

ST MARY. No bigger than a chapel, and not in a village – just by a farmstead. W tower stump with shingled top and low slated spire. Nave and chancel Norman, the chancel with one Norman N window, the nave with an undecorated Norman S door. The pride of the church is its ROOD SCREEN, very similar to the parclose screens at Colebrooke and Coldridge, i.e. with straight-topped panels and no coving, the panels filled up with un-English flamboyant tracery, and each of the main tracery forms again with the finest filigree of sub-tracery, the bars less than ¼ in. thick. Ogee-headed door frame with brackets for three figures. – PULPIT. Early C17, hexagonal. – On the floor of the nave two BELLS by *William Dawe* of London, *c.*1400.

BRUSHFORD BARTON. The seat of the Luxton family from the C16 to 1922. Georgian sashes; shallow porch on granite columns with iron balustrade and nice doorcase.

BRUSHFORD MILL. Polite three-bay front with late Georgian sashes.

BUCKERELL

1000

ST MARY AND ST GILES. Small and cemented outside. The plan seems early medieval, with transepts and no aisles. W tower also early (unbuttressed). Wagon roof in the nave. Some late medieval work indicated by a stone dated 1403. Restored from 1838, refloored and reseated 1906–11 by *R. W. Sampson*. – SCREEN. Brought from elsewhere. Restored by *Hems* in 1892. Grand, but narrow, with coving to E and W and very tall slim four-light openings; the tracery of B type. – WEST GALLERY and BOX PEWS plain C18. – PULPIT. 1910, but with three badly preserved old panels with figures of saints. – STAINED GLASS. Chancel N and S by *Warrington*, 1851. Tense little figure groups in medallions, and the Coleridge arms. – MONUMENTS. Several minor ones to the Smythes of Deer Park and the Graves of Hembury Fort. Only two are notable: Elizabeth Graves †1767. Neo-classical tablet with unusually well carved flower garlands. – Admiral Samuel Graves †1787 by *John Bacon*, 1792. Mourning female in relief seated in a roundel, an eagle above, the whole at the foot of a tall tapering back plate vaguely of the usual obelisk type.

SUNDAY SCHOOL, in the vicarage garden, SE of the church. Low, with Gothick lancets and lattice glazing in the gable, and a porch with a Perp window. Presumably early C19.

BUCKERELL HOUSE. A large *cottage orné* of *c.*1840 with bargeboards and Tudor dripmoulds.

DEER PARK HOTEL, ½ m. E. The large rambling mansion of the Smythes, in its own grounds. Built by Nicholas Fry probably in the early C18 (Polwhele), but much enlarged since. Early C19 stuccoed exterior. S front with two full-height bows and a parapet. On the E side a two-storeyed pedimented projection with the entrance.

HEMBURY FORT HOUSE. Formerly Cockenhays, now an old people's home. On a magnificent hilltop site. Enlarged by Admiral

Graves after *c.* 1750. Three storeys, rendered. Recessed three-bay centre between pedimented wings, probably additions to an older house, as they are without the plat-band in the centre. They have large round-arched French windows with tripartite casements above. Greek Doric porch with paired columns. Entrance hall with heraldic painted ceiling.

BUCKERELL KNAP and BUSHY KNAP. It has been suggested that these are fortified outworks of Hembury (*see* Payhembury), but in spite of their odd appearance no firm evidence has ever been found.

7060
BUCKFAST ABBEY
Buckfastleigh

Buckfast has an exceptional monastic history. The present Benedictine house, established here in 1882 by French monks from La Pierre-qui-vire and augmented soon after by German novices, stands on the site of the richest medieval Cistercian monastery of the South West. There was indeed a monastery before the Norman Conquest, established in 1018. It was granted by King Stephen in 1136 to the Abbot of Savigny and became Cistercian when the Savignac order affiliated to Cîteaux in 1147. After the Dissolution the buildings were sold to Sir Thomas Dennys of Holcombe Burnell, but remained ruinous and unoccupied until *c.* 1800, when they were acquired by Samuel Berry who, about six years later, built a romantic castellated Gothic mansion where the w range had stood, and levelled the rest of the site, leaving only a tower further s and a couple of outer gateways. To the w the guest hall and other ancillary buildings survived as farm buildings. The Benedictine monks first occupied the Berry mansion, but soon after excavated the medieval site, and largely followed its ancient plan for their new monastery.

Today, the visitor approaching the abbey from the w sees on the r. the temporary church put up in 1882 (now the chapter house), grey limestone with brick dressings and a Dec w window, projecting forward, then in the angle the so-called Abbot's Tower, c 14, but considerably restored. Four storeys, with taller battlemented stair-turret. Two-centred archway. Straight-headed two-light windows, the upper ones with ogee lights, those on the top floor larger, with transoms. One room with a garderobe on each floor. The tower is linked to the Berry house on the l. by the three-storeyed w range, one of the four built by *F.A. Walters* around the site of the medieval cloister, beginning in 1883. (Later monastic additions 1933, 1953, new E wing 1964 by *Walters & Kerr Bate*.) Walters's style is an austere Romanesque, an unusual choice for the date, but no doubt influenced by the history of the site. The w range has a carefully articulated wall: first-floor windows linked beneath round-headed arches and framed by pilaster buttresses and corbel-table. A low forebuilding in similar style masks the entrance to the Berry house, which, although deprived of its castellations, is still recognizable: canted centre, polygonal towers embellished with little quatrefoils. Two rooms inside with original simple classical fireplaces, one of white, the other of black marble.

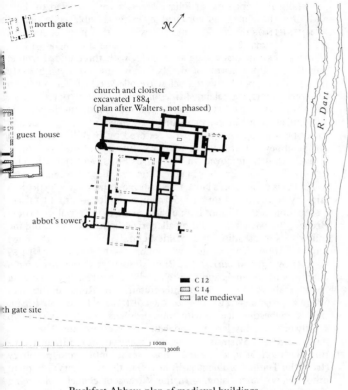

north gate

church and cloister
excavated 1884
(plan after Walters, not phased)

R. Dart

guest house

abbot's tower

■ C 12
▨ C 14
▧ late medieval

h gate site

100m
300ft

Buckfast Abbey: plan of medieval buildings

Beneath the house a medieval barrel-vaulted undercroft survives from the lay brothers' range. To the N is the church, also by *F. A. Walters*, begun in 1907, consecrated in 1932, and built almost entirely by a small group of monks working under a master mason – a remarkable achievement.

The CHURCH is large, 220 ft long, following the plan of the excavated C12 building, with aisles, one chapel to each transept, and originally a square end, although the extended E transept of Fountains type is a departure from the simpler excavated plan. This had a square E chapel, probably a later enlargement of the original E end. The general character is a mixture of English Cistercian and French early Gothic, with the exception of the tall tower over the crossing, a concession to Benedictine traditions. The proportions of the tower, with its tall pinnacles, are Perp, although the detail, disconcertingly, is transitional Gothic. The exterior is of local grey limestone with generous Ham Hill dressings; the interior is Bath stone, crisply cut, cool and rather mechanical, relieved by vaulting cells of red sandstone. A scholarly elevation, transitional Gothic, each bay with a tribune of two round-headed openings enclosing pointed arches (cf. Sens, Canterbury). Quadripartite rib-vaults to the nave, transverse tunnel-vaults to the aisles (as at Fountains).

Details are kept simple; foliage capitals are restricted to the E end. But the church is enriched by a remarkable collection of FURNISHINGS of 1928–32, mostly by *Bernhard Witte* of Aachen, inspired by masterpieces of German Romanesque metalwork. – HIGH ALTAR of black Belgian marble, with three gilded frontal panels and a RETABLE of the Pentecost, by *Witte*, with lively figures of the apostles seated below trefoiled arches, very much in the spirit of C12 Rhineland shrines and retables. – NORTH TRAN- SEPT ALTAR. STATUE of the Virgin and Child, the lower part with full swinging drapery a medieval fragment of *c.* 1400, found in the abbey ruins, the upper part, restored by *F.A.Walters*, based on the abbey's seal. – NAVE ALTARS. Fussy conventional Gothic revival, mostly removed in the 1970s. – STATIONS OF THE CROSS. By *Witte*. Enamel plaques, the drawing style reminiscent of Nicholas of Verdun's late C12 Klosterneuburg altar. – CORONA. Also by *Witte*, based on C12 German examples. – SCULPTURE. Coronation of the Virgin, high up in a niche in the E wall. – FONT. Bronze, the bowl supported by allegorical figures representing the four rivers of paradise, as at Hildesheim. The reliefs on the bowl include Abbot Vonier and two donors. – PASCHAL CANDLE- STICK. By *Fritz Mühler*, 1932. Brass. Four seated angels around a column with enamels and low-relief gilded figures. Free-standing apostles above. Freer in its interpretation of Romanesque than Witte's designs. – Two bronze CANDELABRA by *Benno Elkan*, free Romanesque again, with four prophets and four virtues in scrollwork (cf. his larger candelabra in Westminster Abbey). – PAVEMENTS. Lavish use of precious materials in the Italo-Byzan- tine tradition of *opus alexandrinum*: verde antico and porphyry (from the Temple of Diana at Ephesus) in the sanctuary; Egyptian onyx below the crossing. – In the N transept chapel a charming PAVEMENT designed at the abbey, with a leaf pattern inspired by C17 textiles. – CEILING PAINTING, below the crossing. By Father *Charles Norris* and *E.W.Tristram*, *c.* 1939. Tempera. Icon- like figures within a grid of lettering. – STAINED GLASS. Transept and sanctuary windows with prophets, W and porch windows, all in a late C12 style by *Harry Grylls*. – MONUMENTS. Abbot Anscar Vonier †1938. Bronze bust by *Benno Elkan*. – Also a bronze RELIEF by *Elkan* (N choir aisle), a remarkable Expressionist piece, with the kneeling abbot looking up to a half-figure of Christ, set against small scenes of his life in low relief. – PAINTING. Portrait of Abbot Vonier by *Simon Elwes*.

BLESSED SACRAMENT CHAPEL. Added at the E end in place of two of the E chapels, 1965 by *Paul Pearn* in a style radically different from the rest of the building; a bold decision with a successful result. Square, with four columns supporting a folded concrete vault. Slightly projecting E end. An effectively reticent casket for Father *Charles Norris*'s brilliant mosaic GLASS of 1967. The E window shows Christ at the Last Supper (the face set in resin, the rest in concrete). In the side windows, abstract patterns: red and yellow (N), blue and purple (S), yellow and grey (W). The S window frames a large wooden abstract SCULPTURE by *David Weeks*. The corresponding N panel has been left blank. ALTAR of Beer stone, STEPS and COMMUNION RAILS of Ashburton mar- ble. CRYPT below, now used as an exhibition centre. Tactful exterior, the concrete structure clad in grey limestone which blends well with the older buildings.

CROSS in front of the abbey. From Palstone, near South Brent. Incised crosses on each face.

W of the medieval church and monastic buildings was an outer court. Along its W edge are remains whose interest was recognized fully only after excavations began in 1982. They are an exceptional discovery, as little is known of the buildings on the fringes of medieval monastic sites. The principal structure is a massive hall running N–S, plausibly identified as the GUEST HALL and dated to the early C14. It stands on foundations of a C12 building. Much survives of its E wall, including the entrance doorway (robbed of dressed stone), and of the shell of the service rooms at the S end. The jamb of one of a pair of doorways to these survives, with a relieving arch above. Adjacent is a laver with a chase for a pipe at the back. Evidence was found for one hall window with a cusped ogee-arched light. At the N end foundations of a two-storey solar block with garderobe extension. The most remarkable features are the long, deep chases for roof timbers, one remaining in the E wall, another in the cross-wall beside the laver, and two more in the S gable wall. They imply a four-bay roof structure, most probably of base crucks, over the unaisled hall, heavily braced below the collars, with longitudinal end bracing to the purlins. At right angles to the S end of the guest house a wing added in the C14 or C15, formerly with a large heated first-floor room above three ground-floor storerooms. Converted to a farmhouse after the Dissolution. Restoration planned 1987, together with the S two bays of the guest house, including partial reconstruction of the roof.

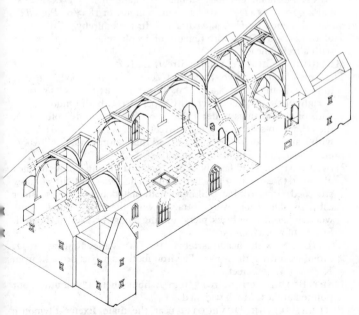

Buckfast Abbey: reconstruction of guest hall (Stewart Brown)

SHOP, N of the guest hall. 1983–4 by *Richard Riley*. Designed in the form of a large barn-like gatehouse, as the main approach to the abbey from the car park. (Buckfast is the third largest tourist attraction in the South West, with 400,000 visitors a year.) The shops are discreetly set back behind an arcaded walk. Pleasant use of local materials: limestone walls, Delabole roofs. Tricky triangular windows.

SCHOOL, N of the church. By *Brett & Pollen*, 1965–8 and, like the E chapel, a well-judged expression of confidence in the style of that decade. Low and well grouped, mostly grey brick with brown boarding above a limestone plinth, tied together horizontally by a continuous band below the windows.

At the N end of the outer court, remains of a C12 GATEWAY; three bays, traces of a groin-vault. At the S end a much enlarged and altered medieval GATEHOUSE, the archway rebuilt, but with re-used late medieval moulded granite jambs.

7060   BUCKFASTLEIGH

HOLY TRINITY. On a hill N of the town, overlooking Buckfast Abbey a little further N and Dartmoor behind. W tower of the C13, small and thin, with angle buttresses, a corbel-table at the top, a (later) spire, and an unmoulded tower arch. C13 W window; the same design in the chancel E window. The N and S windows of the chancel smaller and also E.E. C15 granite nave arcades of five bays, with octagonal piers and double-chamfered arches. N and S transepts. Restoration, including new roofs, by *Hayward*, 1844–5. – FONT. Norman, circular, similar to Paignton's. – BOX PEWS. Early C19. – STAINED GLASS. One window of 1873 by *Powell & Son*, designed by *H.E.Wooldridge*. – In the churchyard the ruins of a C13–14 CHAPEL with remains of deeply splayed windows, one with a trefoil head.

METHODIST CHAPEL, Chapel Street. Early C19.

The small market town became a centre of the woollen textile industry in the late C18 and C19. Two MILL BUILDINGS survive at right angles to each other off Chapel Street, both random stone with brick dressings under a slate roof, one four-storey plus attic, the other two-storey. In Chapel Street, four WEAVERS' COTTAGES with slatted wool loft over. Two- and three-storey stone millworkers' housing; also in Market Street.

HIGHER MILL, Buckfast. Now the Buckfast Plating Co. A complex of late C18/early C19 woollen mills. The two- and three-storey stuccoed stone rubble buildings with slated upper floors under asbestos slate roofs were cottages, with the mill behind. Long wooden launder on brick piers running along the back of the mill. Stump of a brick chimney.

STATION. Now the headquarters of the Dart Valley Railway. 1872. Stone with brick dressings. The iron footbridge was brought from Keynsham, Somerset.

DART BRIDGE, on the road from Ashburton to Plymouth. Four pointed arches. Much widened.

PRIDHAMSLEIGH DOVECOTE, near the main Exeter–Plymouth road. *See* Staverton.

HIGHER KILN QUARRY. Joint Mitnor Cave has yielded important Pleistocene faunal remains, but no human material.

BUCKFASTLEIGH MOOR is the site of Bronze Age cairns, settlements, and reaves; a major reave still forms the parish boundary on the top of Pupers Hill. To the NW some good medieval 'beamworks' – openworks for tin.

HEMBURY CASTLE. An Iron Age hillfort in the upper Dart valley. At the W end a small C11 or C12 motte with narrow bailey on two sides. The earlier hillfort may well have acted as an outer bailey.

See also Buckfast Abbey.

BUCKLAND ABBEY
Buckland Monachorum

4060

A museum since 1951, owned by the National Trust and administered by Plymouth City Museums. The abbey, founded in 1278 for Cistercians, was granted in 1541 to Sir Richard Grenville. He did not do much to convert the buildings to domestic use, but his grandson Sir Richard (of the 'Revenge') was responsible for more extensive alterations – the date 1576 appears on the hall fireplace. Sir Francis Drake bought the property in 1581 and it remained in his family until 1946.

What one sees now is an irregular Elizabethan mansion with a surprisingly tall and powerful tower. The explanation of this feature lies in the fact that Sir Richard kept the central tower over the crossing of the church (and the aisleless nave and chancel as well, although their roofs have been reduced in height and the transepts have been demolished; the N transept is still visible in an C18 view by Buck). It is this secular invasion of the church itself which makes Buckland Abbey remarkable – a sidelight on the attitude of Grenvilles and Drakes to the tradition of religion and piety. The church can be seen everywhere through the overlay of later walls and furnishings. Outside, the roof-line of the transepts and blocked C13 windows are visible; inside there is also plenty of medieval evidence, especially upstairs. In the conversion the entrance was originally on the N side, into the W end of the hall which was formed in part of the nave, extending into the area of the crossing. The present entrance through a porch formed from the former N transept chapel was made only in the C20. The chancel was divided off to become a service room, a large kitchen wing added to the S, and a wing for a grand staircase (the stairs rebuilt in the C19 and again in the C20) added S of the site of the S transept, utilizing its W wall. The planning is unconventional, with the service end away from the original entrance. Another significant innovation was that the hall was not open to the roof, an early instance in Devon in a major house. It is nevertheless quite tall, allowing for a mezzanine floor on either side.

A description of the interior has to be a curious mixture of medieval ecclesiastical details and later remodelling. The present N entrance porch, the former transept chapel, still has its complete vault with hollow-chamfered ribs on moulded capitals. The former chancel (restored and refurnished as a chapel in the 1920s) has triple-shafted responds and corner shafts at the E end for a vault (springers visible on the floor above; also remains of the great window, with nook-shafts). In the N wall an original aumbry; in the S wall fragments with two carved heads reconstructed as a PISCINA, and SEDILIA (on the site of the original one) made up from three little vaults with lierne-vaults and traceried ogee gables. Foundations of the ALTAR with some reset medieval tiles (similar to some found at Plympton); various other loose fragments.

In Grenville's GREAT HALL the medieval remains have been concealed. It now has an excellent plaster ceiling with interlocking single ribs, lozenges alternating with pendants; the pattern continues down a kind of cove on the N side where there are four large brackets with satyrs holding shields (cf. Collacombe Manor). At the W end, on the upper part of the wall, an allegorical frieze with knight and trees; over the fireplace in the N wall the date 1576 and shields in strapwork surrounds, flanked by figures of Justice, Temperance, Prudence, and Fortitude. On the E wall an elaborate strapwork cartouche. The plasterwork is some of the earliest in Devon with a firm date. The fireplace has the characteristic C16 granite arch with upturned centre. S wall with two large windows (four lights, two transoms), the stonework renewed. Handsome panelling with unusually large panels for the C16; arches flanked by fluted pilasters, frieze with red and white inlaid decoration.

The two floors above and W of the hall were damaged by fire in 1938. At the W end of the first floor the DRAKE DRAWING ROOM with good late C16 panelling, restored. Above the great hall a room

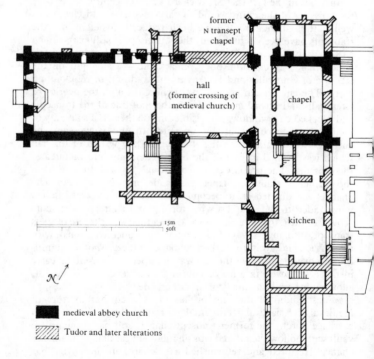

Buckland Abbey: plan

with panelling of 1772. At this level two medieval corbels of winged ox and eagle are visible. On the top floor a GALLERY made after 1938, occupying nearly the whole of the nave and crossing of the medieval church, of which many features remain, notably the great transverse arches and vaulting springers of the crossing. The most remarkable detail is the remains of a Dec window, with two encircled quatrefoils flanking a large sexfoil, which fills the space above the E crossing arch. It was originally glazed and external, although the chancel roof was raised above it at a later date. A door has been inserted below. The room was used as a chapel in the C17.

In the added S wing, an elegantly detailed C18 STAIRCASE with original dog gates. Beyond is the Tudor KITCHEN with huge fireplaces in S and W sides and plain mullioned windows high up.

SE of the house, and thus remarkably close to the medieval church, is the abbey's early C15 BARN, 154 ft long, one of the best surviving illustrations of the scale of building needed to cater for the revenue of a large monastic establishment (Buckland held 20,000 acres). Large E and W porches, formerly two-storeyed (both adapted as dovecotes), with handsomely chamfered archways. Small slit windows in the well-buttressed walls. Arch-braced roof with cambered collars and three sets of purlins. By the driveway near the barn a stretch of wall with slit openings, possibly the remains of another outbuilding or perhaps a defensive wall built after the abbey had obtained a licence to fortify its precincts in 1436.

E of the barn another very long outbuilding of medieval origin, possibly the guest house (cf. Buckfast). Shallow buttresses with one set-off (not unlike the tithe barn), but an upper-cruck roof. Remains of possibly original fireplaces. At either end an upper floor; many Tudor openings inserted later, one window with drip-stones with Grenville badges. Altered and extended in 1793–4 by *William Marshall*, the agricultural economist, who wrote *The Rural Economy of the West of England* at Buckland Abbey. To the N he added model farm buildings consisting of semi-octagonal oxen-sheds.

Little remains above ground of the domestic buildings which lay around the cloister to the N of the nave. The present boundary wall between abbey and cider house is in part the S wall of the N cloister range, with blocked windows and a fireplace.* Further N a building with battlemented tower, perhaps part of the abbot's lodgings. One Perp window, a decorated string with fleurons below the battlements; inside the tower a little ogee-headed stone doorway. Stable range adjoining. The house to the W was made in the 1940s by drastically altering another medieval building of unknown origin.

BUCKLAND BREWER   4020

ST MARY AND ST BENEDICT. Norman S door with one order of colonnettes (volute capitals), the decoration of the arch exactly

*Trial excavations in 1984 revealed substantial surviving foundations of the N cloister range.

identical with Shebbear and West Woolfardisworthy. NE (Orleigh) chapel of two bays with octagonal piers and double-chamfered arches. w tower with buttresses of type B, pinnacles, w door, and Perp w window. SE door with a pretty decoration of branches, leaves, and shields covering the main moulding of jambs and arch. The small rectangular room to which it leads appears to be a rebuilding of the Chapel of the Fraternity of St Michael (mentioned in 1547). Some original Perp windows.* The rest of the church 1879–80 by *Hooper* of Hatherleigh. – FONT. 1771 by *Thomas Jewell*. – MONUMENTS. Anthony Dennis †1643. The usual kneeling figures. – Philip Venning †1656. Small, with demi-figure, frontal, cheek in hand. – John and Mary Davie †1710 and 1709. Sumptuous big wall-monument. – Edward Lee †1819, by *J. Richards* of Exeter. Rather bad, with a small female figure and the inevitable urn against a pyramid.

CHANGE IN TIME, w of the churchyard. Possibly a former priest's house or church house. (The church was a possession of Torre Abbey.) L-shaped, with a medieval core.

SALEM METHODIST CHAPEL stands remote and windswept by the roadside on Thorne Moor, in a walled burying ground with many slate headstones. Suitably plain, with rendered walls, round-arched windows, and gabled porch. Built by the Bible Christians in 1830 and enlarged in 1863. The former Sunday School, a short distance away, is now a dwelling, and a new schoolroom has been built behind the chapel, out of sight, but a sign of the continuing dynamism of rural nonconformity.

BAPTIST CHAPEL, by the roadside, at Eckworthy, near Tythecott hamlet. Built c. 1840. Small, box-like, rendered and whitewashed, in a small burying ground. Modern porch.

ORLEIGH MILL. Four-storey grist mill rebuilt in 1884 (datestone) with pitch-back cast-iron wheel.

See also Orleigh Court.

HEMBURY. The Iron Age CONTOUR FORT on a spur 1 m. s of the village is preserved in field boundaries and as a ditch, in spite of erosion.

4000   BUCKLAND FILLEIGH

Church and house are exceptionally beautifully placed between undulating hills, luxuriantly wooded, and with views towards Dartmoor. In the grounds an appropriately placed serpentine lake, probably dating from the mid C18 landscaping for William Fortescue, Master of the Rolls, a friend of Alexander Pope. A branch of the Fortescues owned the estate from the C15 until 1834, then Lord Ashburton and, from c. 1870, the Brownes.

ST MARY. Very small, of rubble stone. Unbuttressed w tower with low pinnacles; unusual tower arch. Plain Norman s doorway. The church is castellated to s as well as N. Straight-headed three-light windows (heavily restored). Granite N arcade of three bays, A type piers, moulded strip capitals, nearly semicircular arches. Restored and refitted in 1886–7 at the expense of Thomas Fortescue, Lord

* Information from D. Seymour.

Clermont, and William J. Browne, the later owner of the estate. – PULPIT. With some re-used early Renaissance panels. – BENCH ENDS with initials, etc. – STAINED GLASS. Many good Victorian examples commemorating Brownes and Fortescues. – E window 1884, Crucifixion with pale figures against quarries. – s, third from E, by *Ward & Hughes*, a fussy design. – s fourth: old heraldic glass reset. – N aisle second: a dramatic scene with Moses, *c.*1886. – N aisle third: 1878. – MONUMENTS. Henry Fortescue †1691. Inscription framed by columns and putti. – Mary Spooner †1752. Handsome tablet of white and veined buff marble. – Ann, the wife of John Inglett Fortescue, builder of the mansion, †1815.

BUCKLAND HOUSE. The old Fortescue mansion, damaged by fire in 1798, was transformed in 1810 for John Inglett Fortescue by *James Green*, who had worked under Rennie and became the County Surveyor in 1808. His work here shows him to have been an accomplished and innovative practitioner in the neo-classical style which was just at this time becoming popular in Devon.

The drive sweeps up to the large one-storeyed Greek Doric porte-cochère on the N side, which Green made the main entrance front. A long range of 2, 2, 3, 2, 2, bays; ends and centre with pedimented gables. But the main showpiece is the E front of the rebuilt E wing, which has as its centrepiece a splendid, functionally pointless pedimented Greek Doric portico with four giant unfluted granite columns. On the s side something of the older house is recognizable: an asymmetrically placed projecting two-storey porch corresponds to the position of the old screens passage, with the hall to the r. Beyond this the rebuilt E wing comes forward to complete an F-shaped plan in ingenious deference to the owner's name. The s end of this wing has a canted bay with veranda above, relaxed Regency domestic, in contrast with the classical severity of the N and E sides. The exterior is rather unattractively covered in Roman cement, no doubt to mask the difference between the old and the new work.

The interior is inventive but odd. The chief curiosity of the plan is the sequence of grand top-lit spaces in the centre of the house (perhaps in part created by the roofing-over of an earlier courtyard). Staircase hall opening off the passage between N and s entrances with two fluted Greek Doric columns on both ground floor and landing (a daring innovation, the first known instance of Greek Doric used for the interior of a country house). Elegant wooden staircase, with a lozenge pattern between straight balusters around a top-lit well. Adjoining, a long narrow inner hall between N and s fronts, also top-lit, with a gallery on all four sides, leading into the saloon in the centre of the E wing, a double-height room with central 145 domed lantern. Greek Doric columns on the ground floor, Ionic ones above, cast-iron gallery balustrade on four sides. The spandrels around the dome with plaster rinceaux, the dome itself treated more soberly, with plain ribs. The ground-floor drawing room to the s of the saloon has Ionic columns at either end. Along the s front the old hall, low, with moulded beams, panelling with the Fortescue arms, and a good black marble Gothic fireplace of 1810. On the other side of the entrance passage the library, with a marble mantelpiece with putti. Another marble fireplace in the N E room. Excellent doorcases throughout, those on the ground floor with pediments with corner acroteria.

MODBURY. A thatched cottage formerly in the grounds of Buckland House, 1 m. SE, very perfect of its kind (in its position wholly *verwunschen*, Pevsner called it in 1952).

BUCKLAND IN THE MOOR

7070

One of the most attractive of the tiny moorland villages on the E edge of Dartmoor. The small church overlooks the splendidly wooded slopes of Holne Chase and the winding valley of the river Webburn.

ST PETER. Two-stage unbuttressed W tower with stair-turret in the middle of one side. The W window, if correctly restored, is of *c.* 1300. N aisle with three-bay arcade of A, i.e. Cornish, type. Wagon roofs, much renewed, in nave, chancel, and S porch. – FONT. Norman, goblet type, with palmette, rosette, and cable ornament. – SCREEN. Standard type A tracery, renewed coving, and a handsome three-frieze cornice. Coarsely painted figures in the wainscoting, the outer panels with the Adoration of the Magi and the Annunciation, early C16. On the chancel side some caricatures. – Medieval TILES reset under the W tower.

BUCKLAND BEACON. Two slabs of rock inscribed with the Ten Commandments in 1928 by Mr Whitley, to commemorate the defeat of the new Prayer Book.

BUCKLAND COMMON, besides forming part of the Rippon Tor parallel reave system (*see* Ilsington), provides other evidence of prehistoric settlement.

BUCKLAND MONACHORUM

4060

ST ANDREW. An ambitious church, almost all late Perp, a possession of Buckland Abbey (q.v.). The W tower (type B buttresses) is crowned by big polygonal pinnacles set on a polygonal projection which on the bell-stage replaces the buttresses. The pinnacles much crocketed. The W fronts of the N and S aisles are also pinnacled; so are the two-storeyed S porch and both transepts. Large windows, four-light in the W fronts of the aisles and the N and S fronts of the transepts, five-light at the E end of the chancel. The aisles are of five bays, the chancel aisles of two. Their arcades are lower than those of the nave and aisles. Slender piers of A type, moulded arches, excellent granite work. The transepts not in line with the arcade bays. They correspond to two bays. Arches on the line of the transept W walls spring from corbels above the arcade capitals. The meeting of the arches at the beginning of the chancel is confused. On the N it is clear that an earlier, simpler (double-chamfered) chancel arch was partly preserved. Ceiled wagon roof in the S chancel, but in the nave a hammerbeam roof with figures of music-playing angels; rather too much renewed, it seems. The church was restored in 1869 by *Roger Elliott* of Plymouth.

The pride of the church is the DRAKE AISLE, i.e. the S chancel aisle, supposed to date (like the N chancel aisle) from after the Reformation (*c.* 1590? *c.* 1610?). It is distinguished by a heavily ribbed tunnel-vault of granite (re-used material from Buckland

Abbey?). Three bays with a boss at each of the diagonal intersections, the kind of design more often found in wood. The MONU-
MENTS it contains also are remarkable. Two of them are by *John
Bacon*: that of Lord Heathfield, the Admiral, and that of Sir Francis
Henry Drake. The Heathfield monument, of 1795, is on a large
scale. Against a grey pointed-arched back plate an obelisk in relief
with the medallion of the hero of Gibraltar, to which an allegorical
female (Britannia?), larger than life-size, raises up the arms of
Gibraltar. A putto stands by her feet, a helmet on his head, and the
big key of the fortress in his hand. On either side reliefs of a sea and a
land battle, and above them lunettes showing a cannon on a movable
stand, and a kiln for making cannon balls. – The Drake monument
(†1794) is less important. – Monuments to the second Lord Heathfield †1813 by *Bacon Jun.*, and to Dame Eleanor Elliott Drake
†1841 by *Westmacott Jun.*

Of other furnishings in the church the following deserve notice.
FONT. Perp, big, octagonal. – Is the second FONT – heavy, eggcup-
shaped and undecorated – Norman, and has it always been a font? –
TOWER SCREEN. Three sections only of the screen which stood
originally in Sheepstor church. Standard type A tracery; only one
ornamental frieze in the cornice. – BENCH ENDS. With two tiers of
blank traceried arches. – STAINED GLASS. Chancel E: small
fragments of old glass; the rest by *Powell* of Whitefriars, probably
designed by *Holiday*, under the influence of Morris; see the foliage
backgrounds. – Sanctuary S 1870 by *Drake*. – N transept window by
Kempe Studios, 1880, with unusual pictorial scenes of missionaries.
– S transept window probably by *Fouracre & Watson*. – S aisle
window by *Kempe & Co.*, 1907. – MONUMENT (in the tower).
Joseph Rowe †1708. Incised slate slab.

SCHOOL, W of the church. Endowed in 1702 by Lady Modyford and
repaired in 1724, but possibly older, with its Tudor-type porch,
four-centred granite doorways, and two-light arched windows.
Taller centre window on the first floor, with a transom. The original
plan probably a single ground-floor schoolroom, subdivided in the
C18 to form a schoolhouse at the rear.

In the village several stone cottages, with stone arches presumably
from Buckland Abbey. The DRAKE MANOR INN, much altered,
is perhaps a former church house. Stair-turret on the E side. THE
GIFT HOUSE is reputedly the almshouse endowed in 1661 by Sir
Francis Drake, second baronet. Two-room plan with granite mullioned windows.

BICKHAM. A later C19, quite distinguished Queen Anne revival
house in its own grounds, built from roughly coursed grey limestone
rather than the homely red brick one more often associates with this
style. Built for William Morris's brother-in-law, the date said to be
1876. Five bays, with broad segmental arched recessed porch in the
centre. Shaped aprons below the windows; dentilled cornice and
hipped roof. Irregular sides, each with a shallow bay, one for the
drawing room, one for the dining room. The staircase which rises
from the spacious central hall is perhaps a genuine C18 import; it fits
oddly with the canted ceiling supported by tapering octagonal
columns. Some C18 fireplaces, brought from Maristow.

CRAPSTONE, 1 m. SE. Now a farmhouse. A C17 remodelling of an
older house: two-storey porch, two storeys of mullioned windows,

granite doorways. Date 1646 over the hall fireplace, with arms of the Crymes family, and other good contemporary internal features.

POUND, 1 m. E. A rainwater head is dated 1781, but the house was remodelled c. 1820 by Sir Anthony Buller. Two-storeyed late Georgian entrance front, an irregular five-bay centre with projecting two-bay wings, all slate-hung. On the garden side to the l. a pediment with lunette over the four centre bays. (C18 staircase.) Extensive outbuildings, including STABLES dated 1847.

DENHAM BRIDGE, 1 m. W, on the Bere Alston road. Rather fine, with one pointed arch across a deep ravine.

N of Berra Tor the remains of a possible circular Iron Age ENCLOSURE. Another, of two concentric earthworks of unknown date, lies on a gentle hilltop W of the A386 1 m. N of Roborough.

For MEMORIAL STONES from Buckland Monachorum, *see* Tavistock, Perambulation 1.

See also Buckland Abbey.

7040
BUCKLAND-TOUT-SAINTS

ST PETER. A tiny church, on its own. Largely rebuilt 1799, refitted 1874. Cruciform, with a small battlemented W tower and renewed Perp tracery. – REREDOS Perp and C17, STAINED GLASS C19 and early C20.

BUCKLAND-TOUT-SAINTS HOTEL. The house belonged in the C18 to John Henry Southcote, and from 1793 to William Clarke of Plymouth. It is handsome, of stone, with two regular five-windowed fronts to S and E, the early C18 type of Mothecombe and Lyneham. The chimneys, springing rather oddly from near the corners of the hipped roof, and the roof itself were reconstructed in the early C20. There was previously a balustraded parapet. Windows with stone surrounds and large keystones (sashes renewed), plat-bands above both basement windows, and a later porch with thin paired Doric columns. The ovolo-mullioned basement windows on the S side, the changes of levels inside, and the irregular W and N sides suggest an older core. Several simple but vigorous plaster ceilings in early C18 style (some perhaps early C20 restorations). The SE room, which doubles as an entrance hall, has scrollwork and heads with wreaths, the smaller central S room a ceiling with similar details on a square with projecting lunettes, and panelling of c. 1700. Ruined DOVECOTE, circular, of narrow coursed granite.

3020
BUCK'S MILLS
Parkham, near Woolfardisworthy, Bideford

A picturesque fishing village with a group of limekilns on the beach (the hearths now filled in) and another kiln perched in a dramatic position on a rocky platform with an inclined plane to the top of the cliff. In a wooded combe, the small, undistinguished church of St Anne.

BUDLEIGH SALTERTON   0080

Originally the hamlet of Salterton on the Rolle estates, Budleigh
Salterton developed as a resort in the early C19. It grew only slowly.
Despite its pretty situation, its shingle beach meant that it never
became as popular as Exmouth or Sidmouth. The large, flat, circular
pebbles are used extensively and attractively for walling. Apart from a
single late Georgian terrace there are no architectural set pieces, but a
pleasant assortment of *cottages ornés* and Victorian villas, the gaps
between filled by early C20 development, including one outstanding
Arts and Crafts house and others which show that the Arts and Crafts
tradition continued strongly among local architects into the 1920s and
30s.

ST PETER. 1891–3 by *G.Fellowes Prynne*, the gift of Mark Rolle,
built in place of a chapel of ease of 1811. Large and cruciform. Only
the lower stage of the intended NW tower and spire completed. Grey
limestone with Doulton stone trim. E.E. details. W end with three
paired lancets, asymmetrical E end with two apses and vestries.
Clustered arcade piers of Doulton stone and marble. The Lady
Chapel in the S transept has its own triple arch and ambulatory. –
PULPIT of sandstone with pierced panels of brass and iron, given by
Lady Gertrude Rolle. – SCREEN of Beer stone and marble with
dense metal cresting, both designed by *Prynne*. – Other furnishings
destroyed in the Second World War. – Of the STAINED GLASS only
the small windows of 1893 in the baptistery remain; by *Percy Bacon
Bros*.

TOWN HALL. 1925 by the local architect *Hatchard Smith*. Modest,
and quite domestic: stucco with red brick trim, circular windows,
dormers in the grey slate roof.

LIMEKILN, truncated, by the beach car park.

The best houses of the town centre are near the E end of FORE
STREET, whose widened end forms a little square before SOUTH
PARADE leads towards the beach. On the S side the ADMIRAL'S
HEAD and the OLD CLINK, both C19 stuccoed. The start of South
Parade is marked by a polygonal-ended house (where Millais stayed:
the nearby wall is said to be depicted in his 'Boyhood of Raleigh').
To the N, set back above a lawn, FAIRLYNCH, a delightful early 141
C19 *cottage orné*, now the museum. A neat, symmetrical front, with
arched windows with Gothick glazing flanking a pointed oval
window above the thatched porch. A tiny thatched belvedere rises
above the roof.

Beside Fairlynch, FORE STREET HILL climbs steeply, past
POPLAR COTTAGE (three windows, pedimented doorcase), to
EAST TERRACE, which lies along the side of the hill facing the sea.
Five houses of red brick, *c.* 1800, two storeys and basement, with
gently curving full-height bow-windows and doorcases with broken
pediments. Continuing up the steep lane further N, GREY GARTH,
1923 by *A. Leighton*, set into the side of the hill, roughcast with stone
dressings. An informal, carefully detailed back elevation with stone
mullioned windows, a corbelled-out bay, and well composed slate
roofs, with a big chimney breaking through. The front is more
severe, with a parapeted centre, and rather less successful. Nearby,
UMBRELLA COTTAGE and THE COTTAGE, a *cottage orné* converted *c.* 1805 from an earlier group. A very long thatched range,

with a trim thatched porch on the E side. (On the S side rustic
wooden posts, on the W a tented veranda and Gothick window.)
Behind, a path leads through the wooded slopes which still frame
the little town centre, past WATCHHILL, grand neo-Georgian of
1929 by *Hatchard Smith* (3–5–3 bays, canted at the ends).

Down to CHAPEL HILL, with a thatched house (No. 2) with nicely
curved corner. Along UPPER WEST TERRACE relics of a prominently sited early C19 villa development: PROSPECT HOUSE,
stuccoed and parapeted, three bays with central niche, and
UPLANDS, once similar. Further down CHAPEL STREET
Nos. 25–27, another *cottage orné* with elaborately glazed windows,
the central one a lozenge, and a pretty lattice balcony. EAST
TERRACE and WEST TERRACE, at right angles to Chapel Street,
were completed by detached villas only in the 1920s–30s. At the W
end, LAWN HOUSE, early C19, stuccoed, with bracketed eaves,
two projecting wings, and a balcony in between. From here THE
LAWN runs past the church, with an engaging mock-medieval
terrace stepping down the hill. A lively design of repeated asymmetrical units, in a picturesque mixture of materials: roughcast,
stone mullioned bay-window, half-timbering, and a large two-light
cusped wooden window, red tiled gables to add a touch of colour.
1935 by *A. C. Martin*.

In the HIGH STREET little to notice except for the Regency stuccoed
front of THE FEATHERS, and on the N side the Regency revival
POST OFFICE (*temp.* George V) with Gothick round-headed
windows in an effort to respect the *genius loci*. Between the High
Street and the cliffs above the sea, villas were laid out from the early
C19. The best are in CLIFF TERRACE, three-bay houses, with
incised end pilasters (No. 7 the least altered). Across the road,
private gardens stretching to the cliff edge; No. 6 has a thatched
circular gazebo. In CLIFF ROAD another villa of *c.* 1830, THE

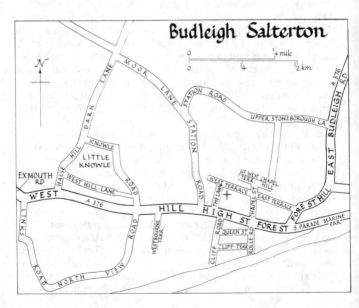

CLIFF, with an eccentric half-timbered Swiss-chalet extension of 1882, added for the local historian Dr T.N. Brushfield. Top-lit, with coloured glazing.

More villa development to the W, along WEST HILL, the continuation of the High Street. On the N side ARCH BROOK and THE BAYS, late Georgian stucco, their pilasters incised with volute capitals. On the S side WESTBOURNE COTTAGE, 1927 by *Rogers & Bone*, a pair in the Voysey tradition, roughcast with corner buttresses, then WESTBOURNE TERRACE running up to the cliff top, with tall Victorian houses with bargeboarded gables and Tudor hoodmoulds. Other similar examples on the N side of West Hill. Further on, near the turning to Little Knowle, THE COTTAGE, another precise early C19 composition, Gothick glazing bars in straight-headed windows, rustic porch, thatch, with bracketed gutter below (not a vernacular detail, although one copied by Gimson at Coxen, *see* below).

LITTLE KNOWLE, an old hamlet in a secluded valley, expanded in the C19 into a delightfully haphazard group of houses amidst greenery. The best of the earliest are LITTLE KNOWLE HOUSE, roughcast with channelled quoins, and KNOWLE COTTAGE, an early C19 pair. Close by, EBENEZER CHAPEL of 1844, altered 1887, with a dignified pedimented front with black channelled corner pilasters and two emphatic rusticated doorways. Good iron gateway with overthrow and lamp. A serpentine lane with Victorian evergreen planting (cf. Elysian Fields, Sidmouth) leads past other houses up to two tall gabled Victorian villas. Further W, off West Hill, LINKS ROAD, which starts with three pairs of houses by *Charles Bone*, 1907, in a quirky version of Arts and Crafts. Roughcast with playful angular tiled hoodmoulds; tiled roof above a prominent cornice. Further up nearer the golf course predictably opulent detached houses of between the wars, e.g. the DUTCH HOUSE in NORTH VIEW ROAD, a showy confection of L-shaped gables and black pantiles, by *Orphoot & Whiting*, 1924. No. 5 North View Road is a good quieter example, roughcast and gabled, with a corner entrance. Other large houses along the EXMOUTH ROAD, notably DOWNDERRY HOUSE, 1929 by *Rogers, Bone & Coles*, a late example of a butterfly plan (cf. The Barn, Exmouth), roughcast with brick trim. The small gable over the centre door is flanked by tall chimneys. Garage in the l. wing. The symmetry is not carried through at the back.

KNOWLE is a hamlet between Budleigh Salterton and East Budleigh, with several good houses on its fringes.

COXEN, N of the viaduct. One of the few houses designed by *Ernest* 171 *Gimson*. It was built in 1910 for Basil Young, Gimson's blacksmith. A remarkable and, it seems, unique example of a revival of cob construction by one of the leading members of the Arts and Crafts movement. *Young* designed the ironwork and acted as clerk of the works to the eight builders, only one of whom had any experience of cob building. The house is not a slavish copy of a Devon farmhouse but fits admirably into its setting. (The modern garage is an unfortunate addition.) Main range of three storeys, the attic windows (for nurseries) set deep into the steep slope of the originally plain thatched roof. A living room projects at right angles, and the front door is placed protectively in the angle, with a delightfully simple stone slab as a canopy. Leaded windows with traditional quadrant catches. Beneath the eaves the strange (and rather disruptive) feature of wooden gutters on delicate iron brackets. At the back, adjoining the kitchen end, a one-storey service wing. As a foil to the cob and thatch, three sturdy stone chimneys, and a mellow low stone garden wall with ball-topped piers. A circular thatched summer house at one end (originally unglazed). Inside, the kitchen has been stripped and the living room fireplace is later, but otherwise the interior is well preserved. No drama (apart from a single steep truss exposed at attic level), but plenty of solid, well crafted details which repay attention: good joinery, including plenty of fitted cupboards. The handling of the small staircase with its solid wooden steps and curved walls lit by a little landing window is especially satisfying. In the hall, carved panels with some Renaissance ornament and Old Testament scenes, probably foreign, c16 and c17.

FREWINS, Bedlands Lane. 1912 by *Cecil Hignett* of Letchworth. Another aspect of Arts and Crafts influence. A close of small artisan cottages, roughcast and patterned brick in alternation, with roofs of red pantiles. A passage through the end house to allotments beyond. Purpose as well as layout, with its variety of frontage lines, suggests the influence of Parker & Unwin's work at Letchworth.

SHERWOOD HOUSE, Bear Lane. By *A. C. Martin*, *c.* 1932, extended in 1939. An overblown c20 version of a thatched *cottage orné*, well detailed, but without Gimson's finesse.

LEEFORD. A small but handsome late Georgian white stucco house in a delightful park setting. Centre of three bays with a colonnade of six Tuscan columns, flanked by one-storey wings with urns on the corners. Gateposts with similar urns. Interior much altered in the early c20.

TIDWELL HOUSE. *See* East Budleigh.

3010   BULKWORTHY

ST MICHAEL. A picturesque and quite unusual composition: w front with two big buttresses and a bellcote (1873 presumably); s porch with chamber above, which is reached by an open staircase running up along the w part of the s wall; s aisle of only two bays built against the s porch. The church is tiny. It is said that an inscription which has now disappeared attributed the building of the church to Sir William Hankford, Chief Justice of the King's Bench (cf. Monkleigh), and the years 1414–22. There are few interior features worth mentioning. Arcade of granite piers (A type) with capitals only to the main shafts and depressed arches. E window of latish Perp design. Restoration 1873–4. – FONT. Octagonal, but made out of a Norman one of the same design as Abbots Bickington.

4000   BURDON
                        1 m. sw of Highampton

The front is a Georgianized farmhouse. At the back, the date 1569 and initials of the Burdons (who lived here till the mid c19) on the frame of one of the few surviving four-light windows. Two far-projecting wings enclose a narrow courtyard with a C16 gateway.

BURLESCOMBE

ST MARY. Grey rubble with yellow Ham Hill dressings. W tower with diagonal buttresses, rebuilt in 1637–8 (see the tablet). Late medieval nave arcades: N aisle of Beer stone, B type piers with standard leaf capitals; S aisle similar but with capitals only to the main shafts. Three original wagon roofs. Roof to the Ayshford Chapel (N aisle) with carved wall-plate and angels with arms. Three-light Perp windows, the tracery slightly more richly cusped on the N side. Reseated and restored in 1844. Eclectic ALTAR of that date. – FONT. Ham Hill stone. Octagonal with quatrefoils, moulded underside, unusual base with square shafts. – ROOD SCREEN. Tracery of A type with very thin mullions, ogee-headed doorway, renewed top parts. The cheerful painting dates from 1844. – STAINED GLASS. Old heraldic fragments in N aisle lights. – E window by *Powell*'s, 1858, nice small-scale scenes in the usual strident colours of the time. Nativity with angels and scrolls. – S aisle E in memory of Major Browne of Canonsleigh †1845. Diagonal scripts as in the chapel at Ayshford (q.v.). – MONUMENTS. Several to the Ayshfords of Ayshford. Nicholas Ayshford †1557. Late Perp tomb-chest with figures holding shields; no effigy. – Roger Ayshford †1610 and Elizabeth Ayshford †1630. Wall-monuments with the usual kneeling figures facing each other, the later one with a more elaborate surround with ribbonwork, open pediment, and achievement. – Henry Ayshford †1660. Table tomb.

TOWN HOUSE, opposite the church. Irregular, with stone quoins. Arched upper windows with Gibbsian surrounds.

See also Ayshford *and* Canonsleigh.

BURRINGTON

HOLY TRINITY. Tower on the N of the nave in a transeptal position, SW polygonal stair-turret, the pinnacles on top missing. Nave and S aisle. Arcade of five bays with granite piers of A type with capitals to the main shafts only, simply decorated abaci, and semi-circular arches. Old unceiled wagon roofs. Four granite-traceried windows in the S aisle. S door original with blank Perp tracery. Restoration 1869 by *Hayward*. – FONT. Norman, square, re-tooled. The bowl has a scalloped under-edge with four scallops to each side. – SCREEN. Complete with ribbed coving and cornice with three strips of ornament and cresting. The tracery of the open panels of B type. Between the ribs of the coving decoration with stalks and flowers. – COMMUNION RAILS. Of *c.* 1700, with alternating twisted and straight balusters.

GOSPEL HALL, by the roadside near the village. Small, white-washed and gabled, in a small burying ground. Slate tablet in the gable 'IHS AD 1846'.

NORTHCOTE MANOR. Now a hotel. L-shaped, neo-Tudor.

BUTTERLEIGH

St MATTHEW. The unbuttressed w tower and nave may be C 13 in origin. Much rebuilt by *Hayward* in 1861, when all the windows were given simple uncusped geometric tracery. The thin octagonal N arcade piers look early C 19. – POOR BOX. C 17, made from a single oak log, carved and painted, *c.* 4½ ft long, with triple locks. – STAINED GLASS. N aisle 1928 by *Morris & Co.*, still in the late Victorian manner. – Several Victorian windows. – Chancel N and s by *Lavers, Barraud & Westlake*, 1876.

BYDOWN
Swimbridge

A trim neo-Grecian mansion in a small park with two immaculate white stucco fronts. Entrance side to the s, the doorway framed by two full-height Ionic columns *in antis* carrying a pediment, flanked by tripartite windows with elongated brackets below their pediments. Some incised Grecian decoration around the windows. Four engaged columns at the centre of the w front. Paired corner pilasters to both fronts. The date must be *c.* 1820–30. The date-stone of 1789 in the hall, and another on the service wing of 1758, with the arms of the Nott family (who owned the estate to *c.* 1925), are obviously reset. Contemporary decoration in the handsome entrance hall and central stair-hall. The entrance hall has a shallow vault on Ionic columns and doorcases with anthemion friezes, pediments, and acroteria. The dome of the stair-hall is pierced by a circular lantern. Cantilevered stairs with turned wooden balusters. Landing doorcases with Greek-key frieze and incised capitals. In the sw ground-floor room an Adamish frieze and ceiling, rather out of date for the early C 19; in the s drawing room a cornice which must be Victorian.

CADBURY

St MICHAEL. A modest C 15 church set into the slope of a hill. Unbuttressed w tower with a square N turret rising above battlements; plain w door. Nave, N aisle, and chancel extensively restored in 1856–8 by *William White*; his unmistakable touch is seen in the asymmetrical lancet groups on the N side, all flush to the wall. Perp arcade with B type piers, continuous capitals, and flattened arches. White raised the E bay of the nave to form a longer chancel; the nave roof is also his. – REREDOS. Stone, *c.* 1842 by *George Wightwick*, a blind arcade flanked by tall Commandment panels in Gothic frames, embellished by marble work added in 1890–1 by *R.M.Fulford*, executed by *Hems*. On the N wall an angel bust supporting a bookstand (as in White's chapel at Bishop's Court). – FONT. Norman, square, with four big scallops on each side (cf. Nether Exe). – Elizabethan double LECTERN with bulbous foot, richly carved. – Two BENCH ENDS made into a

prayer-desk. – STAINED GLASS. N aisle E quite a rarity: a whole
C15 figure, Christ showing his wounds, carefully reset under a C19
canopy, and flanked by C19 vine scrolls. – N, centre, three lights
with Christ, Moses, and Aaron, 1863. – Complementary window
on the S side of Christ with angels, 1868. – MONUMENTS. Minor
tablets to the Fursdons of Fursdon (q.v.).

CADBURY HOUSE (former vicarage). Remodelled c. 1830. Picturesque asymmetrical Tudor, one wing with pierced bargeboards.

CADBURY CASTLE. The massive ramparts of the HILLFORT survive. A ritual shaft was excavated within it.

CADELEIGH

9000

ST BARTHOLOMEW. W tower with diagonal buttresses and NE
stair-turret and two ogee-headed recesses with small images of the
patron saint and of St Anthony. Nave and N aisle are separated by
an arcade with standard B type piers with standard capitals. The
walls provided with plain white plaster panelling probably in 1766,
when the low BOX PEWS were installed. Window tracery replaced
piecemeal, 1902–10. – PULPIT, CHOIR STALLS, and ALTAR
TABLE. 1890 by *Hems*. – COMMUNION RAIL. Of c. 1700. –
TILES. C13; in the N aisle floor. – MONUMENTS. Sir Simon
Leach, his second wife, his son and daughter-in-law. Erected
c. 1630, the largest of its type in any Devon parish church. Tomb-
chest with recumbent figures. The children kneel small against the
front of the chest. To head and feet two large kneeling figures,
behind coupled columns which carry a coffered arch on which rises
a broken pediment. The whole grand, but not sculpturally accomplished. The triumphal-arch form of canopy is derived from the
type introduced on the monuments of Elizabeth I and Mary Queen
of Scots at Westminster Abbey (cf. the Pole monument at Colyton). A specially attractive feature is the position against a large
window so that light falls on to the figures from behind. – Lady
Bridget Leach † 1691. Wall-monument with large urn.

CADHAY

0090

Ottery St Mary

An attractive small manor house on a courtyard plan, essentially of
the C16 and early C17. Tactfully restored and tidied up after 1910
by *H. M. Fletcher* for W. C. Dampier Whetham, after subdivision
into tenements. The significant earlier owners were John Haydon,
a lawyer, son of the steward of Bishop Veysey, who acquired the
manor in 1527, built 'a fair new house' according to Risdon, and
died in 1587, and his great-nephew and heir Robert Haydon, who
married a daughter of the Elizabethan Privy Councillor Sir Amias
Poulett and died in 1626. Their house is now concealed behind a
polite stone entrance front of the C18, added by the Peere-Wil-
liams family after the Haydons had sold up in 1736.

Front door with rusticated surrounds and pediment; regularly disposed Georgian sashes. The crow-stepped gables may be later, perhaps of after 1802, the date of the arms in the centre (Williams, Graves, and Hare families). Hoodmoulds over the windows, some cut back, and straight joins between the ground-floor hall windows and those above (l. of the door) hint at earlier phases, as do the little ovolo-moulded windows high up in the wings, and the large hall chimneybreast (the matching projection to the r. appears to have been added for symmetry). The w wing has service rooms (much altered). The E wing, facing the garden, is more overtly of the Haydons' time, although with some c20 help. The unarched ovolo-moulded mullioned windows to two floors and attics and the two bay-windows look c. 1600, although the broad central polygonal stair-turret rising to the attic may be mid c16. Its tiny medieval quatrefoil window could be re-used: perhaps from the College at Ottery St Mary, where John Haydon became one of the first governors of the church in 1545. On the gables carved bull and bear finials, Haydon supporters. The s range, with a long gallery on the upper floor, was added by Robert Haydon, closing the courtyard.

64   This internal courtyard is an exceedingly pretty feature of Cadhay. Its regular ornament is unique among Devon courtyard houses. It is entirely faced with chequerwork of sandstone and flint. This is a speciality of East Devon (cf. Great House, Colyton) although similar decoration is found elsewhere (the lost 'Holbein' gate at Whitehall). In the centre of each side a classical aedicule with a statue (Henry VIII and his three children), the figures crudely carved, although their surrounds are quite sophisticated: fluted shell niche, Corinthian columns, strapwork, comparable to the contemporary church monuments in the Exeter area. The date 1617 below the statue of Elizabeth.

The hall is now a ground-floor room with a high coved ceiling. Large fireplace still with the Gothic motif of shields in quatrefoils. The heraldry includes arms of the Pouletts and their connections and must have been carved on in Robert Haydon's time. On the first floor the fine original open timber roof is visible. The arch braces were cut back when the space was subdivided (partitions removed after 1910), apart from a fragment in one end truss, but the roof is clearly of the late medieval type peculiar to the Exeter area: heavily moulded principals with semicircular section above the collar; wind-braces with curved ends, evidence for intermediate trusses, as e.g. at Bowhill, Exeter. What is the date? It has been suggested that John Haydon took over and remodelled an earlier house, but it is equally possible, given the county's conservatism, that this late medieval roof type continued into the mid c16.

In the E range, ground-floor rooms with c18 panelling; a c16 fireplace in the first-floor room next to the hall. The long gallery is modest and narrow. Originally its only windows to the s were in the projecting central bay. Windows to the courtyard with hollow-chamfered mullions, a reminder that this older type was still in use in the c17 for less important parts of buildings.

The grounds were laid out after 1910; fine yew hedges s of the house. The fishponds may be older.

CALVERLEIGH
Tiverton

9010

ST MARY. Small, on a hillside. Unbuttressed W tower with polygonal NE stair-turret. No pinnacles. Nave and S aisle; Perp three-bay arcade (B type piers, standard leaf capitals); C14 S doorway (reset?); wagon roof. Chancel and N wall rebuilt in 1883–7. – SCREEN. Standard tracery (type A), round-headed arches in square frames, no coving, perhaps altered. Some re-used fragments in the tower arch. – STAINED GLASS. W window in the style of *Kempe*, 1904. – S aisle W pieced together by *Drake* in 1883: fragments from St Trémeur, Carhaix, in Brittany. – MONUMENTS. Mary Coleman † 1636. Kneeling figure between columns, three faces in medallions behind; crudely painted. – Joseph Nagle † 1813. Nice plain tablet with urn.

CALVERLEIGH COURT, up a drive to the W of the church. 1844–5 by *G. Wightwick* for Joseph Chichester Nagle. Handsome cream-stuccoed house of two storeys with deep projecting eaves. N front with three widely spaced bays and a one-storey Greek Doric portico. E front with a canted bay.

CANONSLEIGH
Burlescombe

0010

A C12 house of Augustinian Canons was transferred to Canonesses in 1284. The remains are very scanty. Parts of a C15 gatehouse with two small two-light windows with elaborately cusped ogee heads below straight hoodmoulds, over large blocked archways. The gatehouse has fleurons including Tudor roses. Much further E are taller fragments, the remains of the reredorter and what seems to be the S wall of the E range. The reredorter has diagonal buttresses and so probably dates from the time of the nuns.* Between gatehouse and reredorter stood an C18 house of which the two wings and the stables survive. Good solid stonework with quoins and keystones emphasized. Similarly detailed outbuildings close to the gatehouse.

CANONTEIGN
Christow

8080

Two mansions: on the hill the trim, white neo-classical house built for Captain Pellew, later second Viscount Exmouth, in 1828; by the road the large late Tudor seat of the Davie family, who had acquired the previously monastic estate after the Dissolution. The old house, already in decay in Polwhele's time, was subdivided as a farmhouse, and for many years provided an evocative scene of gentle decline. It was rescued by a radical restoration in 1972–5.

*I owe these details to Mr J. H. Small.

CANONTEIGN BARTON, the Tudor house, is substantial but plain,
of rubble stone with rather clumsy strainer arches over the
windows, probably all intended to be covered with plaster. The
main front faces E, on an E plan, two storeys with large straight-
gabled attics. The windows are disposed with the most careful
symmetry. Two ground-floor four-light transomed windows on
either side of the projecting porch, giving no hint of the position of
the hall. The wings have the exceptional feature of eight-light
ground-floor windows, reducing to six and four lights for the two
upper storeys. Ovolo mouldings throughout (except for a few
windows at the back). All this suggests a date not earlier than c. 1600
(cf. Walronds, Cullompton). N and S elevations are also nearly
symmetrical, apart from a broad chimneystack on the N side
probably indicating the site of the kitchen, and a small door, not
quite central, on the S side, perhaps later. The W side is very plain
(no plinth or string course) and less regular. The back of the house is
now close to the road (diverted when the Pellew house was built).
Possibly service buildings here were destroyed at this time and the
back tidied up later.

The interior also has been too altered to be interpreted easily.
Removal of later partitions has revealed the ground-floor hall to the
l. of the entrance, with fireplace on the back wall, and behind this a
plinth which must formerly have been external. Several stone
Tudor doorcases: one opposite the entrance, two leading to rooms in
the S wing. Another leads to the N wing, at the end of a corridor from
the hall. The stopped chamfered beams suggest that the small room
to the r. of the porch has always been separate from the corridor,
which runs alongside it. Two fireplaces in the N wing, now a single
large room. Upstairs there appears to have been a similar corridor,
for two original wooden doorcases remain, one on each side. The
area above the hall is now two rooms divided by interlocking
cupboards; in one of these cupboards (immediately S of the porch)
remains of a fireplace with plaster overmantel with the Davie arms
in strapwork, surrounded by garlands and bunches of fruit. The S
staircase, much rebuilt, incorporates some original turned balusters. The attics have traces of partitions, and five fireplaces.

Across the road, good two-storey stone FARM BUILDINGS
around a yard.

CANONTEIGN HOUSE. The architect for Captain Pellew's elegant
neo-classical house of 1828 was C. R. Ayers of London, who had the
year before built Trehill, Kenn (q.v.). Two storeys, plus a service
basement (visible only from the back). Five-bay front with central
portico with Ionic columns, side windows pedimented, centre
windows in blind arches with wreaths. Seven-bay flanks. The side
entrance with Baroque hood must date from c. 1910, when the
interior was reconstructed by Forbes & Tait after a fire. Plain top-lit
galleried central hall (repeating the original plan; cf. Trehill). The
rectangular roof-light was remade to a new design in the 1970s.

ENGINE HOUSE of Wheal Exmouth LEAD MINE, close to the Tudor
mansion. A roofless ruin; stone with dressed quoins, round-headed
openings, detached octagonal stone chimney.

CASTLE DROGO
Drewsteignton

7090

1910–30 by *Sir Edwin Lutyens* for Julius Drewe, successful tea mer- 175
chant and founder of the Home and Colonial Stores, who retired
early to establish himself as a country gentleman. A C20 baronial
stronghold, spectacularly sited on a granite outcrop above the
Teign gorge on the edge of Dartmoor, the territory of Drewe's
reputed medieval ancestors. It is one of Lutyens's most romantic
buildings, medieval in spirit, although not in detail – a total contrast in mood to his contemporary formal classical work at New
Delhi. Lutyens may have been recommended by Hudson of
Country Life (for whom he had earlier restored Lindisfarne Castle).
But it was Drewe, not Lutyens, who determined on a castle, and
insisted that the main range should have authentically solid granite
walls, 6 ft thick. Indeed the architect wrote in 1910, 'I do wish he
did not want a castle but a delicious lovely house with plenty of
good rooms in it.'

The site was bought in 1910. First plans included a variety of
fairly conventional courtyard layouts before the final scheme was
agreed in 1911: a U plan open to the N, with splayed outer wings
(cf. two of Lutyens's other houses, Papillon in Leicestershire and
Goddards at Abinger, Surrey) embracing a vast courtyard entered
by a gatehouse. Only a fraction of this was built: the E wing and the
splayed service wing to its N, and the foundations of the S range,
which was to have had the principal living rooms. In 1912 it was
agreed to transfer these to the E wing, and to omit the W wing
completely. The basement of the S range became the chapel. Work
continued until 1930, the year before Drewe's death.

The completed fragment has a compellingly abrupt sublimity
that would have been diluted in the more ample and even arrangement of the earlier plan. The exterior detail is minimal Tudor:
mullioned-and-transomed windows without dripstones set in vast
expanses of sheer ashlar walling of local granite, carried up without
interruption to an irregular crenellated parapet (cf. Shaw's Flete,
q.v.). Only the entrance is a little less austere, with moulded
plinths to the polygonal corner turrets, and a corbelled-out central
oriel with a large and striking relief of the Drewe lion below the
window.

The interior also has plenty of exposed granite. The planning is
complex, because the two ranges, as well as being at an odd angle
to each other, are on different levels (three and four storeys). This
gave Lutyens plenty of scope for unexpected spatial effects in the
handling of the circulation areas, and these are Drogo's greatest
triumph, the more so since they represent a compromise from the
original grander plan. A vaulted corridor (instead of the longer
intended gallery) leads to the magnificent stone staircase occupying 176
the whole width, providing a monumental approach to the dining
room, which had to be fitted into the ground floor after the change
of plan. The lofty stairs, ingeniously enclosing a smaller private
staircase, have shallow domes over the landings, and are lit by a
massive 24-ft-high window with no less than five transoms; the
subtle change of scale of the lights should be noted. The drawing

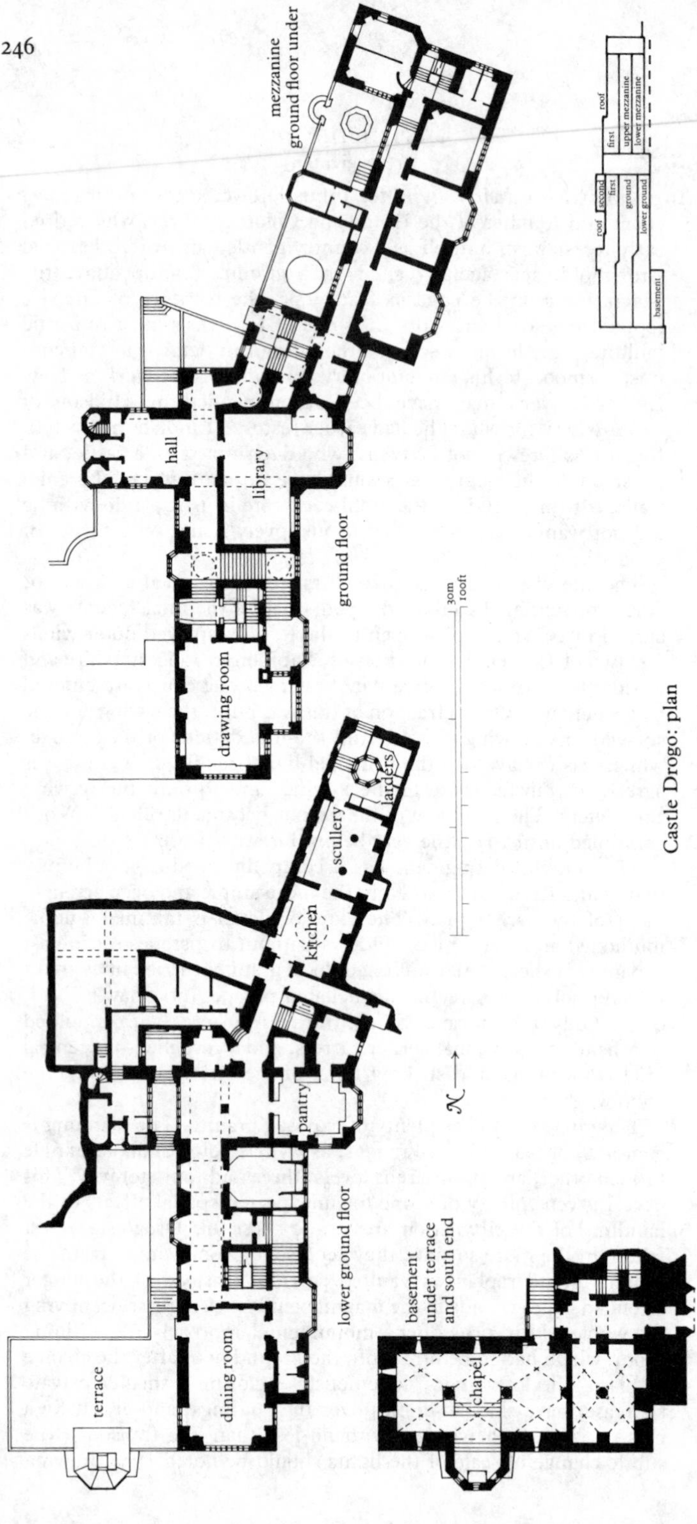

Castle Drogo: plan

mezzanine
ground floor under

roof
first
upper mezzanine
lower mezzanine

roof
second
first
ground
lower ground

basement

hall

library

drawing room

ground floor

30m
100ft

kitchen

scullery

larders

pantry

N →

lower ground floor

basement
under terrace
and south end

terrace

dining room

chapel

room, above the dining room, has an intriguing internal window looking out on the staircase, a typical Lutyens conceit. This room has painted wooden panelling; the library, on the other side of the staircase, is more austere, its L shape divided by a granite arch. Heavy oak coffered ceiling; bookcases designed by Lutyens.

The N wing is more intimate, with bedrooms on the upper floors, service rooms below. The axes of the two ranges meet ingeniously in a circular lobby to the N of the entrance hall. A stone stair leads down to the roof-lit kitchen (with round table and dresser to Lutyens's designs), the scullery with quasi-Romanesque columns, the larders neatly ranged round a hollow octagon. At the end of the wing the delightful N stair climbs five storeys to the tower top: cantilevered stone steps but an independently constructed oak cage of balusters. The foundations for the unbuilt great hall in the S wing were used for the CHAPEL, an effectively cave-like space with a polygonal-ended sunken chancel, lit by slit windows. Stained glass and fittings from Wadhurst, Drewe's former house in Sussex.

Lutyens was dissatisfied with the abrupt approach produced by the curtailment of the original plans, and designed a gatehouse and outer range to the N in 1916. Full-scale mock-ups of these were made, but not proceeded with. The only other buildings erected were the STABLE BLOCK, with stables and motor house, to the N, the CASTLE COTTAGE and LAUNDRY, $\frac{1}{2}$ m. N, and the TURBINE HOUSE (still operating) in the Teign gorge. The formal GARDENS NE of the house were laid out from 1920 (planting by *George Dillestone* of Tunbridge Wells) in place of earlier plans for more elaborate terraced gardens to the E. Their main features are an impressive circular lawn and a rectangular rose garden, surrounded by tall yew hedges. *Gertrude Jekyll* advised on natural planting for the long approach drive.

CASTLE HILL
Filleigh

6020

The formal cream-coloured house surveying its nobly landscaped grounds from its hillside terrace is one of the surprises of North Devon, a rare example in the county of an C18 country mansion on the grand scale. It is a disappointment to learn that although the long Palladian composition of *c.* 1730–40 was carefully restored to its pre-Victorian external appearance after a major fire in 1935, much of the interior had to be reconstructed.

The Filleigh estate belonged to the Fortescues from the C15, and in the later C17 replaced Weare Giffard as the family seat. An older house at Castle Hill was remodelled *c.* 1684 by Arthur Fortescue and his son Hugh (†1719). It was given its Palladian dress and its long nine-bay wings in line with the main range (the site allows for no other arrangement) by the second Hugh Fortescue, Lord Clinton (later first Baron Fortescue). A surviving letter proves that he consulted *Lord Burlington* and *Lord Herbert* on the design. A contract of 1728–9 with their protégé, *Roger Morris*, exists for the refacing of the house in Portland stone. The main interior feature was the remodelling of the old hall as a double-height saloon. There were later alterations, among them the creation of a circular library in the early C19, and in 1841 *Blore*'s enlargements for the second Earl, which included a large porte-cochère, on the N side, remodelling of the entrance hall and stairs, and the addition of a top storey under a mansard roof. Blore also added service wings and stables in 1861. But many of these additions were removed after the fire, when the interior was much simplified by *Gerald Wellesley* (1935–8). The present N entrance porch is of 1974 by *Raymond Erith*.

The plain rendered front of the main range has the minimum of emphasis: two storeys, 2–7–2 bays, with a pediment only to the central entrance, and a cupola on the roof (restored 1935). Straight wings to l. and r., each of nine bays, with pedimented and rusticated centre flanked by upper circular windows with busts (the surviving ones now all on the E wing). The W wing, originally a service wing with the kitchen, is now flats; the E wing contained an orangery and the estate office. The approach is from the E, through Blore's stable block, to the entrance in the main range, now restored to its C18 central position on the N side (Blore's porte-cochère had been at the E end).

Wellesley's interior has a hall with three coffered arches on either side and a generously proportioned staircase in C18 style to its E. Along the S front a very large drawing room and small library have replaced the shorter Palladian double-height saloon and library. In the drawing room fine doorcases with open pediment and arms, copies of the C18 ones, and the early C19 carpet from the former library. The best C18 fittings are in the rooms at the E end of the main block, with some Rococo furnishings from Pickwell Manor, Georgeham, brought here in the early C19. In the E corner room, an excellent Rococo overmantel with mirror frame with birds, and a fireplace with a charming panel of Aesop's owl and cockerel, with a central figure in armour. In the room behind a good fireplace of coloured marbles and a panel with putti. On the W side of the central range the dining room, with a very large fireplace with terms, formerly in the saloon. Upstairs in the SE bedroom yet another excellent overmantel, probably of the mid C18, with a painting with the Judgement of Solomon and very fanciful surrounds with wings, fronds, etc., and a broken pediment. In a back bedroom a minor marble fireplace with lions' masks.

Blore's STABLES extend in an L beyond the E wing, one range rusticated, with central clock-turret, the other with entrance arch and circular windows with busts, like the wings of the main house.

The GROUNDS are still splendid. Laid out by Lord Clinton from the 1730s, their formal landscaping was modified later by the second Earl Fortescue (1751–85). The immediate surroundings of the house were recreated in the C19. To the S a balustraded terrace with plenty of iron and lead figures, including lions, sphinxes (inspired by those at Chiswick House), greyhounds, and lion seats, many of them provided by *John Cheere*; also a fine marble urn. From here the grass terraces made in the C19 step downhill, originally flanked by avenues and obelisks. The formal basin at the end was later extended and converted to a more serpentine form (plan of 1763). The banks were designed to give the illusion of a port, with trees 'shredded and formed into masts' (1769); in 1772 there was even a 'great boat' in the paddock, and a wherry with an awning 'to give it the appearance of a gondola'.

On the same axis to the N is a castellated ruin (now covered by ivy), encircled by a wall, largely hidden by trees, but clearly intended to dominate the view to the N. It is an early example of a sham castle (inspired by Vanbrugh, it has been suggested) and was the feature that gave Castle Hill its name. Its exact date is unknown: there are references to it in 1752, and it probably existed in 1746, the year when Lord Clinton was made Baron Fortescue of Castle Hill, although a painting of before 1746 shows a temple in this position (an unexecuted project?). The castle must surely be associated with Sanderson Miller's at Hagley, of 1747, built for George Lyttelton, who was married to Lord Clinton's half-sister.

Visible in other directions from the house are (or were) a mixture of functional and decorative *points-de-vue*. To the SE, on the horizon at High Bray, a SHAM VILLAGE (now demolished) complete with church tower, and the MENAGERIE at Clatworthy (now obscured by trees), in fact a pair of Palladian cottages with wooden Ionic portico. To the SW at Filleigh (q.v.) the church was rebuilt in 1730 on a new site as a Gothic eyecatcher; in the same direction is SPA WOOD COTTAGE, with a façade in the form of an arch. Other embellishments to the grounds have disappeared, including a hermitage, a Chinese temple, and a Satyr's temple. UGLY BRIDGE, a single rocky arch E of the house, is close to the site of the Sybil's cave (now filled in). Later additions include a four-column Ionic temple of 1772 (another more elaborate temple built in memory of the first Earl survives only as a shell) and two small temples in the woods behind the house of 1831.

In the DEER PARK to the E, a pretty, rustic stone bridge. The drives from S and E have GATEPIERS with wreathed balls.

CHAGFORD   7080

High up above the river Teign, on the edge of Dartmoor, one of Devon's four medieval stannary towns, its centre pleasantly unspoilt by through traffic or undesirable development.

ST MICHAEL. All Dartmoor granite, ashlar built. Tall W tower with buttresses set back from the angles, originally with pinnacles. Two-storey embattled S porch vaulted inside in two bays on blank wall-arcades; three foliated bosses. Long, low, dark interior, restored in 1865 (plaster removed). Two five-bay aisles: monolithic granite octagonal columns, two-centred double-chamfered arches, perhaps c. 1400. – Perp FONT of 1857 by *John Aggett*, a local man. – Medieval PARCLOSE SCREENS with standard tracery and pierced spandrels. – The other embellishments reflect the changing tastes of the last hundred years. Sanctuary decorated in a totally un-Devonian way by *J. L. Pearson*, 1888. His REREDOS is a delightful piece, a triptych in Quattrocento style with crisply drawn Ascension and Saints. – On the E wall colourful embossed TILES with peacock and foliage frieze, now timidly curtained. – CHOIR STALLS. 1914, with demi-angels. – In contrast the ROOD SCREEN, 1925, PULPIT, 1928, and later PEWS, all by *Herbert Read*, are entirely traditional. – ORGAN CASE. By *S. Dykes-Bower*, *c.* 1961; colourful. – STAINED GLASS. E window probably by *Pearson*; small figure scenes, heavily outlined. – N aisle: three windows by *Clayton & Bell*, 1884–93, good colours. – S aisle: Suffer Little Children by *O'Connor*, 1877, pictorial. – MONUMENTS. Sir John Whiddon † 1575. Tomb-chest surmounted by two decorative arches framing armorial back panels. A remarkable document of its date, still entirely early Renaissance, except for some odd strapwork cusping. Otherwise plenty of motifs such as mermen and mermaids in the cresting, baluster columns with Ionic capitals, etc. A suspicion of Perp lingers in the foliage. – John Prouz † 1664. Wall-tablet with Corinthian columns, open pediment, and arms.

S of the church, down an avenue, CHAGFORD HOUSE, the rectory until 1887. Late Georgian, five bays with two added, rendered, with overhanging eaves and Tuscan porch.

To the W, in a row facing the W tower of the church, an exceptionally fine group. First, two thatched granite houses. The THREE CROWNS, the former town house of the Whiddons, is built of very large, regularly laid granite ashlar. Details of the early C16. Centrally placed two-storey porch with four-centred moulded arch, gable with finial; on each side two windows to each floor, all with chamfered mullions and square hoodmoulds. End chimneystacks (the l. one with original fireplace). To its S the former GUILD HOUSE of St Catherine, possibly built as a church house, less regular ashlar. Four-centred granite doorway with balls in the spandrels, later ovolo-moulded mullioned windows in two storeys. The interior now without an upper floor; altered in the C19, when the back extension was added. WHIDDONS and CHURCH STYLE COTTAGE follow, a picturesque and complex group with a projecting wing to the road and a passage through to a back lane with a good row of stone houses. Then the GLOBE HOTEL, a regular early C19 rendered front of five windows with two reeded doorcases.

N of the church the MARKET PLACE, a wedge-shaped area on a slope, partly infilled. The centrepiece, the gift of George Hayter-Hames, is the MARKET HOUSE of 1862, a robust octagonal Gothic structure with conical top (in the spirit of e.g. the kitchen of Glastonbury Abbey). On opposing sides coped stone gables with Dec window and doorway.

Simple white-plastered houses line the streets running out of the town centre for quite a distance, with many little courts of buildings behind. To the N, at the foot of the hill, MOORLANDS HOTEL, a large, rambling complex, part of it originally a warehouse for serges and blankets, a mixture of early Victorian Italianate details and Gothick glazing.

To the E, in LOWER STREET, BISHOPS HOUSE, rendered and thatched, with sturdy two-storey C17 porch. The house itself is late medieval.

CHAGFORD HOUSE. The seat of the Hayter-Hames family. Five-window rendered front of *c.* 1820. Tuscan porch.

RUSHFORD TOWER, 1 m. NE. A small sham castle, now hidden in woodland, built by the Hayter-Hames family. Round tower and lower square battlemented tower.

WHIDDON PARK, 1¾m. NE. A substantial remnant of the large manor house of the Whiddons. Three-storey s-facing range of granite ashlar, with chamfered mullioned windows. On the W side a porch with roll-moulded, round-headed arch; the date 1649 over the inner doorway. Was there once a hall to the N of this? E range with kitchen, and an impressive range of stone stacks. (Good wooden newel stair. Tudor fireplace in one ground-floor room.) To the N a large thatched barn. The deer park of Sir John Whiddon, a prominent Elizabethan lawyer, is bounded by a granite-block wall at the entrance to the Teign gorge.

HOLYSTREET MANOR, 1m. NW. A medieval core, but drastically rebuilt and extended in 1914. Partly of granite ashlar; picturesquely grouped chimneystacks, mullioned windows. Grandiose Edwardian hall with neo-Jacobean staircase, chapel, and contemporary outbuildings.

OUTER DOWN. 1911, restrained Tudor; stables with tall water tower.

CHAGFORD BRIDGE, over the Teign. Built c. 1600. Three arches of granite ashlar; small cutwaters.

The parish is particularly rich in C15–17 farmhouses. The outstanding example is HOLE, 1½m. SW, which, with Higher Shilstone, Throwleigh, represents the peak of the fully developed longhouse tradition of the C17. L-plan, the medieval house, cross-passage, and shippon oriented downslope, the cross-wing built into the hillside off the upper end. The development of the house was obviously more complex than this, as the curious set-backs to the walls of the main block and the cross-wing and the rebuilt rear wall of the medieval house blocking the cross-passage demonstrate. Spectacular front, all in large ashlar granite blocks. Two-storeyed porch and two four-light granite mullioned windows with roll-mouldings and king mullions. Timber cross-passage door with elongated fern leaves in the spandrels. Impressive shippon, rising tall from the road entrance, with splayed slit windows in the gable end and all round on the ground floor. Large hayloft door above. Central drain and tethering-posts remain inside. Separate exterior entrance and a solid wall to the cross-passage, as at Higher Shilstone. The house has been little altered since 1650: excellent interior features include a stud-and-panel screen, with a partially floored phase represented by upper-chamber joists projecting over the screen to bear on the cross-beam in the formerly open hall. Large stacks at the gable end of the cross-wing and backing on to the cross-passage. Granite farm buildings arranged to give the house an informal courtyard setting around a granite-lined dung pit in the centre of the yard.

LOWER JURSTON. A longhouse of the C15–18 with a room added at the upper end in the C17 and a kitchen wing built across the rear of the cross-passage (cf. Whimington, Sampford Spiney). Behind the shippon, the large bank barn at the upper end of the yard incorporates stone-lined cellars (for root storage?).

Other notable farmhouses in the parish include YELLAM, a medieval longhouse refurbished in the C17; YARDWORTHY, with remains of three former houses in the farmyard; and HIGHER HORSLAKE, a three-room-and-cross-passage house with a late medieval roof (one true cruck, and evidence for low partitions).

YEO. The farm of Wallace Perryman, one of the pioneers of hydroelectric power on Dartmoor in the early c20. The MILL is still driven by the original water-wheel. The farm buildings incorporate two former houses of types rare in Devon, one a single-cell late c16 building, the other an upper hall with a corbelled c16 fireplace. The FARM OFFICE outside the front door of the farmhouse, still with its architect-designed desk inside, is by *James Crocker* of Exeter, 1873.

MEACOMBE. Beside the road the remains of a Neolithic CHAMBERED TOMB.

KESTOR ROCK, Chagford Common. A series of fields, with scattered huts, forms part of a parallel reave system which continues in 'fossilized' form in the enclosed land immediately to the NE. Excavations demonstrated that the roofs of the huts were supported on an inner ring of posts, with the ends of the rafters seated on or in the stone walls. The huts may possibly have had timber-built predecessors (cf. Holne Moor and Shaugh Moor). For the house in the 'Round Pond', just over the parish boundary in Gidleigh, a roof open in the centre to give a 'light-well' has been suggested. Evidence of ironworking within the house is considered by the excavator, Lady Fox, to be contemporary and not a later re-use of the building, which she views as the dwelling of a smith of chiefly status, or similar personage.

On HURSTON RIDGE, further s, and on CHAGFORD COMMON itself are prehistoric parallel reaves, a remarkable double stone row, and cairns and settlements.

BUSH DOWN. Mining was carried out here for many centuries, ceasing only towards the turn of the c20.

CHALLACOMBE

6040

HOLY TRINITY, on the edge of Exmoor at Barton Town, close to a farm. Medieval w tower with diagonal buttresses. Perp belfry windows. Nave and chancel rebuilt 1850, restored 1874–5. Plain pink-washed interior with bold arch-braced roof. – REREDOS with marble columns. – PULPIT. Quaintly arranged with access from the vestry. – STAINED GLASS. E window with good figures under canopies, by *W. F. Dixon*, 1874.

SHOULSBARROW. An Iron Age HILLFORT in which hut circles have been recorded, in a strong position 1½ m. SE of the village, with fine views of the whole of North Devon.

On CHALLACOMBE COMMON some of Exmoor's finest groups of BARROWS, including the impressive linear Chapman group; also single STANDING STONES and stone settings. The massive WOOD BARROW lies on the Somerset boundary.

CHARDSTOCK

3000

ST ANDREW. The parish was in Dorset until 1896. c15 embattled s aisle and former porch, faced with small squared stones; the rest an overpowering and un-Devonian rebuilding by *J. M. Allen*, 1863–4. w tower with pierced parapet and conical-topped polygonal turret. Transept roof with patterned tiles. Over-elaborate interior: piers of Ham Hill stone of alternating shape; chancel arch with both capitals and corbels richly carved; black marble shafting in the chancel. The carving all by *Grassby*. A mixture of stone and marble also for REREDOS, low SCREEN, and FONT. – The PULPIT is more attractive, of enamelled brass and iron openwork. – STAINED GLASS. E window designed by *Allen* and executed by *O'Connor*: small figure scenes intensely coloured but overwhelmed by the varied colourful surrounds.

ST ANDREW'S SCHOOL, opposite the church. 1850, enlarged 1885. Centre with shaped gables; projecting wings, one with a pretty oriel. W of the church the OLD VICARAGE, C19 gabled Tudor with mullioned windows.

Near the crossroads the GEORGE INN, probably the former church house, a long thatched building of medieval origin (smoke-blackened jointed-cruck roof) with an early Tudor mullioned window with four arched lights on each side of the entrance, and a large lateral stack. In the room to the r. of the passage an internal jetty; linenfold panelling on the other side. In the room beyond a stud-and-panel partition, and beyond this again a massive fireplace, its lintel spanning the whole width of the house.

CHARDSTOCK COURT, facing the church. A former manor house of the bishops of Salisbury. L-shaped, basically late medieval, the E–W range perhaps the original open hall, the N–S range two-storeyed, with original features remaining: newel stair, doorways, a blocked cinquefoil oculus in the N gable, a trefoil-headed upper window, and a stud-and-panel partition on the upper floor. A long detached range with medieval roof was destroyed *c.* 1930.

CHARDSTOCK HOUSE. Long Georgian front.

TYTHERLEIGH COTT (formerly New Inn House). A medieval house with a later projecting front wing. Smoke-blackened roof, the principal truss of true cruck type with double chamfer running over the arch-bracing. The chamber over the hall has an exceptionally prestigious Beer stone fireplace decorated with three carved roundels, the central one dated 1594, another with initials AP.

WOONTON FARM. High up to the NW of the village. Late C17 SE front, facing away from the farm buildings behind. Once quite distinguished. Rubble stone with hipped roof, seven bays, the lower windows with stone mullions and transoms and flat-headed arches of dressed stone with large keystones. Upper windows with sashes.

LOWER RIDGE, 1 m. NW. A former farmhouse. Very smart, almost symmetrical C17 E end defined by a higher roof-level between Beer coping-stones. Walls in coursed squared blocks of flint with Beer stone dressings. Three- and four-light mullioned windows with ovolo and hollow mouldings. Inside, the late medieval joists of the upper floor, which jettied out into the originally open hall, were retained as a canopy in the C17 room, with squared panelling added beneath. In the lower room the massive fireplace almost the full width of the house is typical of this area. Good C17 fittings throughout, including many broadly chamfered cross-beams, and sgraffito plasterwork in two end-room fireplaces.

At SMALLRIDGE, a hamlet to the S, church, school, and Wesleyan Chapel.

ALL SAINTS was built through the efforts of Arthur Acland (later Troyte; cf. Huntsham) in 1840. Enlarged in 1890. Nave and chancel only, with a W bell-gable. The remarkable feature of the chancel is the vault with thin sexpartite ribs and carved corbels and bosses. The nave much less ambitious, with elementary scissor-braced roof. – STAINED GLASS. Good E window (the Day of Judgement) in memory of the Rev. T. A. Walrond, the first incumbent.

SCHOOL. E of the church.

WESLEYAN CHAPEL. Built c. 1800 on an irregular plan. Rendered walls and hipped roof, formerly thatched.

6030

CHARLES

ST JOHN BAPTIST. Tower (unbuttressed, without W door or pinnacles) and outer walls old; the rest rebuilt in 1875 and restored in 1890 by *Gould*. – Minor WALL MONUMENTS to members of the Gregory family, c. 1700.

TOLL HOUSE, Newtown Bridge, ½ m. SE. Single-storey, with overhanging eaves and a bay-window.

MOCKHAM DOWN is the site of a fine Iron Age HILLFORT, partly damaged by quarrying, with a small BARROW nearby.

7040

CHARLETON
Near Kingsbridge

ST MARY. Medieval tower with diagonal buttresses; NE octagonal stair-turret; S transept. Four-bay N arcade with A type piers. All much rebuilt in 1849–50; renewed windows with Dec tracery. – REREDOS. C19 Gothic frame with paintings of the Evangelists by *Cyril Worsley*, 1964. – SEDILIA. Moved to the N side of the chancel in 1891: two cusped arches. – STAINED GLASS. E window c. 1887. – MONUMENTS. T. Whinyates † 1783 and family. Gothic tablet by *Boulton*. – Captain Twysden † 1864. Bold shield and sword against grey marble.

PARISH ROOM AND SCHOOL. Built for Earl Compton by *F. J. Commin*, c. 1889. Mullioned windows, bargeboarded gables.

The Charleton SLATE QUARRIES were among the most important in Devon, conveniently close to the estuary for easy transport.

7010

CHAWLEIGH

ST JAMES. W tower with diagonal buttresses and small pinnacles. Embattled S porch, the base and battlements decorated with
29   quatrefoils. Nave and S aisle separated by a Perp granite arcade of four-plus-one bays, the piers of A type with capitals only to the main shafts, the arches semicircular. Ceiled wagon roofs with cross-ribbed panels, the chancel panelling and cross-ribbing on a much smaller scale (an excellent effect). The chancel roof was described as 'recently erected' in 1842 (of plaster?). – ROOD SCREEN with standard type A tracery. Elaborate cornice and much of the coving of 1910. The type as in the Exeter neighbourhood. – SOUTH PARCLOSE SCREEN. – MONUMENTS. Handsome wall-tablets to George Radford † 1667 (cf. West Worlington and South Molton) and Ambrose Radford † 1703.

By the church gate a former CHURCH HOUSE and the SCHOOL, a long, two-storeyed stone building of the early C19 with large windows with hexagonal glazing.

THE OLD HALL (former rectory). Early C16 core; many later additions. Irregular front with large full-height timber hall window, probably C19, but in C17 style with geometric leaded panes. The early C16 hall survives unfloored. Richly moulded stud-and-panel screen. Gallery above with a late C18 balustrade on the early C16 carved bressumer. Arch-braced roof with ogee curve at the top (cf. Sand) and wind-braces.

In the village is the METHODIST CHAPEL, built by the United Methodists in 1922. Popular contemporary L-plan, with gabled chapel and schoolroom separated by a folding screen. Rubble masonry with lavish trimmings of pale brick.

On the A377 at Chenson, an oddly shaped two-storey TOLL HOUSE with angled extension, dating from the 1830s.

CHELDON

7010

A remote hamlet on the slopes above the Little Dart.

ST MARY. Small medieval nave, chancel, and W tower, the top stage probably C17. Three-light Perp windows. Ceiled wagon roof to the chancel. – SCREEN made from two mace rests of 1737 and 1743. – BENCH ENDS with Perp tracery patterns. – Busts of Mary Connell and Alice Eliston from a lost MONUMENT of 1711.

CHERITON BISHOP

7090

Prettily situated in a hollow between hills, the church raised above the village lane and reached by steps.

ST MARY. Late C13 chancel with typical tracery in the E window and lancets in the S and N walls. The rest Perp (the S side rebuilt in 1884, with a porch). Roughcast W tower with diagonal buttresses. N aisle ashlar granite with traceried three-light windows. Inside, five bays with piers of A type with unadorned and unmoulded capitals. Ceiled wagon roofs, in the chancel with bosses. – FONT. Norman, circular, with four bands of ornament. – PULPIT. With C16 Renaissance panels, much restored. – ROOD SCREEN. The part to the N chancel chapel remains, with much original colour. Straight-headed panels with one strip of grapes, etc., in the cornice. The spandrels of the panels pierced, but odd triangular pieces stuck on (a replacement). The tracery of the four-light openings is of type A. Painted saints in the wainscoting, c. 1520, by the same hand as the N aisle screen at Manaton and the N and S aisle screens at Alphington, Exeter. Many of the figures are from the same cartoons. – Part of the CHOIR SCREEN now on the S wall, with remains of figure panels.* – BENCH ENDS. With two-tier tracery. – CHANCEL FITTINGS. 1869, of local workmanship, attractive. – SCULPTURE. Small fragment of C15 Nottingham alabaster. – ROYAL ARMS. A rare painted Elizabethan example over the S door. – STAINED GLASS. E window by *Hard-*

*Information from Anna Hulbert.

man. – BRASS. The Rev. R. L. Pennell †1872, with a scene of his death as a missionary in Zanzibar.

CHURCH COTTAGE. Probably a church house of c. 1600, of cob.

OLD RECTORY. Core of the late C14–15, remodelled in the C16–18, extended in the early C19, so that the plan is now two rooms deep. In the front range an almost complete medieval roof. Crucks and jointed crucks with square-set ridge. A central post rises from each collar to the saddle-piece. From its foot, longitudinal curved braces spring to support the ridge. This local version of the crown-post, relatively rare in Devon, is found also at Clifford Barton, Dunsford, and Uphill, Lustleigh.

TOLL HOUSE. Built c. 1838, of sandstone, a fine example. Original door, porch, and side windows.

The parish is rich in farmhouses, among them LAMBERT, a large and important farmstead showing Devon vernacular at its C15–17 best. In its C17 form it is comparable to Westacott, North Tawton: indeed, Lambert has the same cross-wing feature of first-floor window reducing to four lights from ground-floor width, and crowned by a special gable to accentuate the grandeur of the new parlour wing. Inside, the classic development, with chambers inserted over inner room and cross-passage in the C16, both jettied out into the hall over stud-and-panel screens. The chamber wall of the inner room has large framing on a moulded bressumer; the lower end chamber wall has a stud-and-panel screen on a similar moulded bressumer. The excellent fittings include a spit-rack over the hall fireplace and a spice-cupboard in the hall. Extensively restored and remodelled in 1983. TILLERTON is a cob and thatch farmhouse with an excellent C16–17 interior. Inner chamber jettied into the hall above a post-and-panel screen, on a moulded bressumer with carved brackets; early C17 moulded ceiling beams to the hall, and a carved wooden cornice of the same date on the lateral chimney-breast. GORWYN must have once have been a superior medieval house. It has an unusually elaborate pair of jointed crucks over the hall, arch-braced, with evidence for a boss; the posts have moulded false corbels on shafts. The smoke-blackened roof suggests that there were once only low partitions.

(WOODLEIGH HALL. A large house of 1896–8. Granite ashlar, bargeboarded gables.)

8000   CHERITON FITZPAINE

ST MATTHEW. Red sandstone. W tower with type B buttresses and central polygonal stair-turret, the upper part of the tower roughcast. Two-storey S porch, the front crowned by nice stepped-up battlements. Inside, a fan-vault on angel corbels, with bosses showing emblems of the Passion. Three-bay C15 arcades, with piers of an unusual profile, clearly influenced by Exeter Cathedral – four main shafts with thin triple shafts in the diagonals – separated by a red sandstone chancel arch from the two-bay chancel arcades which have demi-angels above the capitals. Apart from the chancel, all roofs renewed during *James Crocker*'s restoration of 1883–5, when galleries were removed, the stone REREDOS was enlarged, the PULPIT reconstructed, and TILES and other furnishings were added. – SCREEN. 1926 by *Caröe & Passmore*. Traditional, very lavish, the centre with coving. – Ancient CHEST, a hollowed-out tree-trunk. – ROYAL ARMS. 1665. – MONUMENTS. John Moore of Upcott Barton †1691. Painted architectural wall-monument. – Nicholas Hickes †1704 and wife. Grey marble, carved drapery, cherubs' heads and cartouche.

A pretty village, with many buff-washed and thatched cob cottages, its character diluted by the considerable quantity of post-Second-World-War building. By the churchyard, a former CHURCH HOUSE, long and thatched, altered for use as a school. The ALMS-HOUSES, founded in 1594, consist of plain one-room dwellings, with a row of five chimneys towards the street (the fifth house is an addition of 1853). POOLE BARTON, close to the church, is a complex of three houses of the C15–18, with prominent lateral stacks.

TANNERY, Upham. Now a house. Two-storey, of random stone, rendered.

(STOCKADON. Small farmhouse with alterations of the early C16 and later visible at the back: good moulded wooden hall window of six lights and moulded cross-beams to the inserted hall floor.)

UPCOTT BARTON. Once a manor house, now a farmhouse, in 1455 the scene of the notorious murder of its owner, Nicholas Radford, by retainers of the Courtenays. Handsome late C16 and C17 front, not quite symmetrical, with a rebuilt C17 porch. The windows all richly moulded, transomed, and mullioned. Over the service end a late medieval arch-braced roof. Hall, stair, and inner room were rebuilt in the early C17 and considerably enriched later in the same century. Of that period the staircase with turned balusters and panelled dog-gate, and much plasterwork. The finest ceiling is in the inner room, with geometric design, central pendant, and double-moulded ribs enriched with sprays and arabesques of foliage, fruit, and flowers. Bolection-moulded panelling, including a painted panel over the fireplace. Plasterwork also in the chambers over the hall and inner room, a coved ceiling with moulded cornice under the arch-braced roof. The moorcocks in the plasterwork allude to the Moores, who acquired the house by marriage to the Courtenays in 1620.

CHEVITHORNE
Tiverton

9010

ST THOMAS. Red sandstone, nave and chancel only. 1843 by *Benjamin Ferrey*, built through the exertions of the Rev. William Rayer †1866, as the inscription on his marble table-tomb in the churchyard explains. Dec windows with large naturalistically carved headstops. – In the W rose window and in other tracery lights good, richly coloured decorative STAINED GLASS; also as borders around the grisaille glass in the lights below. – MONUMENTS. Plain tablets to the Heathcoat-Amorys. – In the churchyard, one to Michael Heathcoat-Amory †1936 by *Eric Gill*.

VICARAGE, behind the church. By *William Burges*, c.1870 (cf. Knightshayes), in his unmistakable muscular Gothic. Three gables, central arched door, unmoulded mullion-and-transom windows, very large chimneys.

CHEVITHORNE BARTON. Gabled medium-sized manor house, the seat of the Francis family until 1664, when it passed by marriage to Edmund Prideaux of Forde Abbey, then to Francis Gwyn, and in the C19 to the Rev. J. F. Griffith. An attractive exterior of rendered rubble on a slope above the road. Two storeys and attics, full-height gabled porch in the centre, to the r. a large gabled projection. The service side on the l., rebuilt in the C19, was remodelled in 1930 by *Sir Albert Richardson* for the Heathcoat-Amorys, to create a large L-shaped living room. One genuine early C17 room in the E wing: the OAK ROOM, lined completely with Jacobean panelling divided by fluted pilasters. Plaster frieze with spindly grapevine; single-rib ceiling with lozenges and rosettes of the usual kind. Less usual the theme of the overmantel: in a central panel Orpheus seated beneath a tree playing his harp to the animals and birds, at the sides caryatid figures identified as Hope and Wisdom, all of engaging crudity. Behind this room a good later C17 staircase with sturdy turned newels with balls, continuing up around a small well to the attic floor. Upstairs, a four-centred doorway to the room above the hall.

CHITTLEHAMHOLT

6020

ST JOHN BAPTIST. 1838 by *R. D. Gould* for Lord Rolle of Stevenstone. Pre-ecclesiological Gothic. Aisleless, with lancet windows; lancet triplets at the W and E ends. On its own near the neglected manor house.

In contrast, the GOSPEL HALL, also of 1838, set in a large walled burial ground in the centre of the village, is a trim, partly rendered box with Gothick glazing.

HIGH BULLEN. Now a golf-course hotel. A good small late Victorian mansion with a belvedere tower with views of Exmoor and Dartmoor. 1879 by the local architect *E. H. Harbottle* for R. H. Moore. The exterior is in Shaw's Old English tradition, with plenty of gables, dormers, and tile-hanging, and appealing details such as the pentice seat to catch the afternoon sun set below the large staircase window with twelve leaded lights. Harbottle's ecclesiastical interests are given expression by the Gothic arch in Bath stone leading into the recessed porch. Other Gothic arches inside, plain apart from well carved dripstones, frame the staircase on both the ground floor and landing. The appeal of the garden elevation regrettably diminished by picture-glazing.

CHITTLEHAMPTON

6020

The large church faces the attractive village square and the valley broadside on, a vista created in the 1870s, when cottages surrounding the churchyard were removed. On either side of the square, thatched cottages; on the S side the WESLEYAN CHAPEL, papery Gothic, dated 1858 (doorway 1905).

ST HIERITHA (or Urith), a local saint, murdered by heathen

Devonians with their scythes in the C6. Her cult may explain the exceptionally ambitious church. The W tower is one of the most spectacular in Devon, though with its large double two-light ornamented bell-openings rather of Somerset than of Devon type. It is of four stages, 115 ft high, and has six type B buttresses. Pinnacles on all the set-offs of the buttresses give the tower a fine, gradually tapering outline. Quatrefoil and similar friezes at the base and at each stage. The battlements with openwork quatrefoil decoration. Eight openwork pinnacles are the crowning feature. Image niche low on the S side. The W door is square-headed and elaborately moulded.

Nave with aisles and transepts. S aisle embattled, with a quatre-foil band below the battlements. S and N transepts also embattled. In the N transept a blocked Perp doorway; is it connected with access to the shrine, which lay N of the chancel? Three- and four-light windows, all renewed in the C19, and more uniform than formerly (N aisle windows previously square-headed; E window previously with reticulated tracery). E of the church was a low vestry (could it have been on the site of an ancient chapel or shrine?), swept away in 1843 when the chancel was extended E. Elaborate Perp S porch: entrance with fleurons, a niche above, and a ceiling with cusped wooden panels and bosses. More fleurons on both sides of the S doorway; a broad foliage bracket above. The door itself contemporary, with blank tracery, pinnacles, and orig-inal ironwork.

The interior much affected by the 1871–4 restoration by *Hayward* (piers reconstructed, walls left unplastered). Nave of five bays between chancel and N and S chapels. Piers all of B type, the N side with concave octagonal capitals to the main shafts, the S side with standard Devon leaf capitals. On the N side of the chancel arch a niche for a statue. N of the chancel, another more elaborate one with a vaulted canopy which used to house one of the images of St Urith, known to have been removed by 1540. It stands by the entrance to a narrow chamber with an odd arched entrance, presumably the site of the shrine. The slab now within this cham-ber was moved from the N transept in 1954. Original timber ceil-ings with cross-ribbed panels to N and S transepts (Giffard and Rolle chapels).

FONT. Octagonal, C15, with panelled base and sides. – PULPIT. Stone, with little figures under nodding ogee canopies in narrow panels with leaf frames; St Urith on the N side. The figures barbarically carved (partly as a result of being scraped of paint). – CHEST. Medieval, with three locks. – STAINED GLASS. E window 1871, in the style of *Lavers, Barraud & Westlake*. – By *Hardman* the chancel S, 1872, and the ambitious Te Deum tower window, 1893 (with earlier tracery lights). – MONUMENTS. Three in the N transept, or Giffard Chapel. John Coblegh of Brightley with his two wives, c. 1480–90. Brass; small figures. – Grace Giffard † 1667. Fragment of a large monument, the figure semi-reclining. – John Giffard. A standing wall-monument with recumbent figure on a tomb-chest, elaborate, but not of high quality, erected after 1622 by his grandson, who, like his father († 1622), is represented by a kneeling figure. On the back wall two further generations com-memorated by two bearded profile heads in medallions. Open pediment with coat of arms and reclining putti above. – In the s transept, Samuel Rolle †1746 by *P. Scheemakers*. Marble, with relief of mourning putti, and two flaming urns. – In the church-yard, a number of good early C19 slate tombstones. – LYCHGATE c. 1880.

THE BELL INN was built in 1888 by the Rolle estate, which owned much of the parish in the C19.

BRIGHTLEY. A moated site with medieval retaining walls, a great rarity in North Devon. In the C16 and C17 the seat of the Giffards, it is now a C17–19 house with a five-bay front and a re-used C15 porch and doorway. Arms set on the porch.

(HUDSCOTT HOUSE. From the C18 a seat of the Rolles. C19 front with sashes and a Tuscan porch. Inside, a C17 plaster armorial overmantel. C18 orangery and stable block. Coachman's house of 1711, brick.)

HAWKRIDGE BARTON. Now a farmhouse. Inside, there is a plaster ceiling with the arms of Acland impaling Tremayne (marriage of 1615).

CHIVELSTONE

7030

ST SILVESTER. W tower of Totnes type; no pinnacles. s side with aisle front, porch, and rood stair-turret. Five-bay granite piers of A type and capitals only to the four shafts. Semicircular moulded arches. – PULPIT. The most rewarding object at Chivelstone, quite a different type from the usual Devon pulpits. It is hollowed out of one huge piece of wood and has consequently none of the far-projecting nodding ogee canopies of the others. The decoration keeps close to the body, and all the motifs are small and busy. Four friezes at the top, then small flat panels, with shields under blank ogee arches. Chalice-shaped foot. – SCREEN. Here also in the cornice there are only small motifs, no large leaves. The tracery of Dartmouth type. In the wainscoting, twelve figures in the nave, Renaissance arabesques (as at Blackawton and South Pool) in the aisle. – PARCLOSE SCREENS. Damaged, the tracery of Holbeton type. Panels painted with feigned brocade, c. 1530. – ALTAR RAILS. Late C17.

SOUTH ALLINGTON HOUSE. Built by *Thomas Ponsford* of Totnes for the Pitts family, c. 1840. Three bays with pedimented centre, one-bay wings, Doric porch with arched window above.

CONGREGATIONAL CHAPEL, set above the lane near Ford, 1 m. N, in its burial ground. Now roofless. Late C18. Slaty rubble walls, arched windows. A picturesque though melancholy evocation of rural dissent in gentle decay.

At EAST PRAWLE, 1½ m. s, the most southerly place of worship in the county, the METHODIST CHAPEL built by the Bible Christians in 1848. Low, with colour-washed rubble walls under a hipped slate roof. One of the last surviving unashamedly vernacular chapels in Devon.

CHRISTOW

ST JAMES. Granite is used for the ashlar-faced W tower, dated 1630, entirely late Gothic, with type B buttresses and obelisk pinnacles, and for the piers and arches of the two aisles, of A type, with four unmoulded capitals. Ceiled wagon roofs in nave and aisles. Restored unobtrusively in 1862 by *E. Ashworth*, who rebuilt the chancel, added the S porch and NE vestry, and repaired the tracery, etc. – FONT. Square, Norman, each side with three big scallops (cf. Cadbury, Nether Exe). – PULPIT. Incorporating a Flamboyant panel. – SCREEN. Uncoved, with solid spandrels and usual tracery. – BENCH ENDS. Some with two-tier tracery, some with leaf panels. – ROYAL ARMS of Charles II. Carved stone. – REREDOS. 1862. Blind arcade with painted metal panels. – STAINED GLASS. Small old fragments in S windows. – S aisle E 1862 by *Clayton & Bell*, illustrating the Ministry of Healing, dramatically grouped figures, with the synthesis of medievalizing formality with realism that characterizes the best of their mid-century windows. – MONUMENTS. Two to the Pellews, Viscounts Exmouth (of Canonteign), who both died in 1833. By *Gaffin*; uninspired. – Many minor tablets to other members of the family.

BETHESDA BAPTIST CHAPEL, behind a small yard in the village. 1856. Tall and gabled. Round-headed windows, two blocked. Small porch.

The parish is rich in medieval–C17 farmhouses. The large village now incorporates some farms, like SMITHHAY, where C20 external alterations almost completely disguise a large medieval house. Chambers jettied into the originally open hall from both ends. Stud-and-panel screens to the cross-passage of exceptional quality and size. Rich C17 mouldings in the hall. At the other end of the scale are small medieval houses later subdivided into cottages, like CARPENTER'S and LANE END: both have chambers over the inner room, jettied forward from stud-and-panel screens; Lane End also has part of a re-used stud-and-panel screen between ground- and first-floor level.

HILL* can stand as the archetypal farmhouse for the whole of Devon, so many of the traditions are represented in this remarkable but small-scale L-shaped structure. Beneath the typical, mostly C19 disguise lies a medieval house on a two-room cross-passage plan with early cross-wing off the upper end and two rear outshots. Cob wall construction on a stone rubble plinth. Internally the late medieval house is defined by a smoke-blackened roof carried on jointed crucks and end-crucks, but the core of an earlier medieval structure survives beneath as the present hall with its own true crucks and smoke-blackened thatch. This room is one of the most remarkable in Devon, for although it houses a later axial stack (with typical ashlar granite blocks and corbel to the cross-passage), it was never floored, and so offers a clear impression of the character of the medieval hall-house at farmhouse level. Typical later C16 and C17 adaptation and extensions include chambers inserted over the cross-passage and the lower room and a new two-room cross-wing subdivided by a stud-and-panel screen and

*For a plan of Hill *see* p. 68.

incorporating a kitchen with a large gable-end fireplace and ovens. In the parlour and first-floor chamber of the medieval part, early C17 plasterwork in single-rib patterns. Repaired in 1975–8 by *John Schofield*.

Immediately s of Hill is ALLER, a much altered late medieval house with a smoke-blackened arch-braced roof, stud-and-panel screens, and jettied chambers. Some of these features at the lower end were introduced from a demolished house nearby during recent restoration, but the screen between hall and inner room with painted decoration in foliage pattern is original. Plaster plaque above the door: WMM 1707. Unusual crenellated moulding to the cap of the axial stack.

NEWHOUSE. Late medieval, now subdivided: originally a three-room cross-passage plan. Stud-and-panel screen between hall and inner room, with hollow mouldings and step stops; jettied chamber above of the same period; first-floor wall framed into a closed truss with tie-beam.

RESERVOIRS. Near Christow, a complex supplying Torbay with water. TOTTIFORD DAM, 1861, an earthen embankment with a puddled clay core, is the oldest on Dartmoor and impounds 103 million gallons. The similarly constructed KENNICK DAM was built in 1881–4 to create the largest of the three reservoirs (195 million gallons). In 1907 TRENCHFORD DAM was completed, the longest of the three at 720 ft (171 million gallons).

See also Canonteign.

CHUDLEIGH

A small market town, now bypassed by the Exeter–Plymouth road, mostly rebuilt after a fire in 1807. A pleasant variety of early C19 houses and a plentiful supply of inns, notably the OLD COACHING INN, tall and rendered, with shallow Regency bows to the end bays. The BISHOP LACY INN has an excellent medieval roof with moulded arch-braces and wind-braces. s of the main street the late C19 gabled SCHOOL and the solid Italianate TOWN HALL, both in grey limestone (a mean C20 library and health centre in between). In WOODWAY STREET near the town hall a CHAPEL built by the Independents in 1830; a three-bay gabled front with a pedimented entrance behind a narrow railed yard. At the opposite end of the town near the church, the OLD GRAMMAR SCHOOL, a long, rendered range with a porch room on columns, dated 1668.

ST MARTIN AND ST MARY. The w tower looks C13, red and grey stone, with buttresses only at the foot, small windows, and battlements above a corbel-table. (Consecration 1259.) The church itself restored and refitted in 1847–9 by *David Mackintosh*, and restored again, with a new roof, emphatically buttressed on the outside, by *Henry Woodyer* in 1868–9. N transept also with renewed Dec tracery, but the chancel N windows, of red sandstone, look genuinely C14. Late Perp s aisle of seven bays. Type A granite piers with unmoulded capitals; three-light granite windows without tracery. E window with correctly ecclesiological Geometric tracery by *Mackintosh*, 1847–9. The dominant impression is of *Woodyer*'s roof, arch-braced, with a broad longitudinal rib broken by a big circular boss at the crossing. Transverse strainer arches in the aisles.

FONT. Plain, big, circular, of granite. – REREDOS. By *Woodyer*. Tracery designs in marble inlay. – SCREENS. Although the tracery pattern is standard (type A), the proportions are not: the sections are uncommonly broad and have depressed round-headed tops. Solid spandrels with large trefoil leaves. One decorated strip in the cornice, plus cresting. Wainscot paintings of alternate apostles and prophets in bright red and green drapery against a white background, exceptionally well preserved, restored in 1976 by *Anna Hulbert*. Inscribed scrolls below. – BENCH ENDS. With two-tier tracery. – WEST GALLERY. By *Mackintosh*, 1847, old-fashioned for its date; front with a thin blank arcade, on iron supports. The space below divided off in 1975 by sliding glass screens by *Peter Gundry*. – The new SOUTH DOOR re-uses a C16 granite archway and C19 studded doors. – CLOCK. Mid C18. – STAINED GLASS. E window 1847 by *Robert Beer*, one of his best, intense vibrant colours, small single-figure medallions on a grid of royal blue and crimson. – MONUMENTS. Sir Piers Courtenay and wife, 1607 (N side of chancel). Quite grandly conceived, but uncertain in its classical detail. Kneeling figures before a prayer desk, tomb-chest below, framed by a Gothic arch but set within paired Doric columns supporting a steep pediment with clumsy reclining figures. – Elizabeth Powney † 1782. Relief with mourning husband. – Other minor wall tablets.

REDEMPTORIST CONVENT (R.C.), Old Exeter Street. 1887. Limestone with brick dressings. Small, minimal-Gothic chapel, with two marble columns as screen between nave and sanctuary. – STAINED GLASS. Good pictorial Crucifixion, late C19. – Recent windows by *Charles Norris* of Buckfast: two in the nuns' choir, abstract with a cross, 1981, two in the nave, Annunciation, 1984.

PALACE FARM, Rock Road. In the garden, substantial remains of a medieval house of the bishops of Exeter: on the W side an enclosure wall with slits; fragments of three buildings, including one end of a formerly storeyed structure of *c*. 1300 – two stone-vaulted ground-floor rooms with a stair-turret attached to one corner.

TOWN MILL. Three storeys, of stone, plastered, with a lucarne on the front and a large (18 ft diameter) pitchback wheel. Two-storey plastered mill house and stone outbuildings round a courtyard, now housing craft workshops.

BRIDGE on the old Exeter Road. Reinforced concrete two-pinned arch of 150 ft span. Two side spans each of 90 ft.

On the side of the eastbound A38 at Harcombe a very large double LIMEKILN, known locally as the Tramps' Hotel.

HAMS BARTON, 1 m. NE. A rewarding fragment of a once larger manor house, the seat of the Hunt family in the C16–17. L-shaped, the long E wing to the road deceptively unrevealing. The W wing has disappeared. In the former central range, a stone doorway to the screens passage, a stud-and-panel screen, and a ground-floor hall (now subdivided) with a ceiling with moulded beams and joists and an end fireplace. A two-centred stone doorway led to the lost W wing; traces of a newel stair are visible externally. Bedrooms with original C16 partitions. Fine arch-braced roof with two sets of opposing wind-braces and chamfered lower purlins. The spectacular feature of the E wing is the sumptuous first-floor great chamber, one of the best of its date in the county. Splendid barrel plaster ceiling with enriched ribs and central pendant, the arms of James I on the end wall, and on the overmantel the date 1621 and the arms of Hunt and Meredith, in a strapwork surround. Hidden above the ceiling is an older three-bay smoke-blackened arch-braced roof, suggesting that this may once have been the hall range. The ground floor was later adapted to provide service rooms. One stone archway remains, between the buttery area and the former kitchen. A later kitchen to the S. On the reconstructed staircase some re-used linenfold panelling.

WHITEWAY. A large, handsome late C18 red brick mansion, built by the first Lord Boringdon (†1788), then the seat of his brother, Montague Edward Parker. Two show fronts: the entrance side of 2–3–2 bays, with a broken-off extension to the r. The service wings have been demolished. Three storeys, pediment with a scrolly oval with bust, and central porch with four wooden Tuscan columns. The garden front is longer, with a central full-height canted bay with stone surrounds to the windows, and Venetian windows to l. and r. Stone bands between floors and at sill level. Rainwater-head dated 1774. Good coloured marble neo-classical fireplaces in dining room and drawing room; simple elegant curving top-lit stair in the angle between the two wings. Excellent grounds with views over Dartmoor.

HARCOMBE HOUSE. Now a convalescent home. Gabled and mullioned neo-Jacobean, built in 1912 by *A.F.Woodman* and *J.A. Lucas* for Sir Edward Wills, who died in 1921. His tomb, enclosed by iron railings, is eccentrically sited on a mound to the SE.

See also Ugbrooke.

8070

CHUDLEIGH KNIGHTON

A C19 parish to the SE of Bovey Tracey.

ST PAUL. 1841–2 by *Scott & Moffat*. A trim pebble-faced exterior, cruciform, with lancet windows; no tower. – FITTINGS by *R.M.Fulford*, 1876: REREDOS with sgraffito panels, low wooden SCREEN combined with choir stalls. The sgraffito decoration of the chancel walls has been whitened. – Some Victorian STAINED GLASS, outshone by three E lancets by *H.J.Stammers*, 1961: Trinity with Christ in Majesty, surrounded by historic crowds. Good colours, stylized sketchy figures, not over-precious.

PITT HOUSE. 1841 by *Scott & Moffat* for the Incledon-Webber family. Compact neo-Jacobean, squared limestone, on an E-plan, with crenellated rounded bows to the wings, an oriel over the central door, and rather stylish shaped Dutch gables, not at all what one might expect from Scott. Back wing with first-floor ballroom, billiard room below, and gabled corner tower, added in 1880. The ballroom has large mullioned windows to the little central courtyard, and a coved, panelled ceiling. Oak-panelled stair-hall. Converted to flats 1985–6; the ballroom has been subdivided.

CHULMLEIGH

St Mary Magdalene. A collegiate church from the C13. Proud four-stage late Perp w tower, restored in 1879 by *Ashworth*. Buttresses of B type with pinnacles on each set-off (cf. Chittlehampton), big pinnacles on the battlements, a four-light main w window with a row of quatrefoils at its foot, and three-light bell-openings. w door of granite. The body of the church has Perp windows, the walls and window details renewed during the restoration by *J.F.Gould*, 1879–81. Embattled s porch, the battlements with capitals only to the main shafts. Ceiled wagon roofs throughout, the panels in the chancel smaller than in the nave and aisles. Nave and chancel with angel figures above the wall-plates. Tall granite tower arch, the imposts of A type. In the s porch a Norman stone with a figure of the Crucifixus in a roundel. Christ is shown as a crowned figure in a short tunic. The feet are nailed side by side with two nails, not on top of each other with one, i.e. the iconographically earlier type. Serpents on either side.

FONT. Panelled, octagonal, C15. – PULPIT. Designed by *R.M.Fulford*, executed by *Hems*, 1879. Open wooden tracery, delicately detailed, with figures in niches and St Mary Magdalene under a canopy below the bookrest. – SCREEN. Across nave and aisles, *c.* 50 ft, very complete, of the type common near Exeter. A type tracery with little shields in the lights, original ribbed coving on both sides, and tracery elements between the ribs (no Renaissance elements yet). Cornice with three bands of close ornament and cresting. Four evangelist figures above, apparently continental Baroque. – Plain panelled REREDOS, possibly *c.* 1840. – Robust Gothic STALLS and BENCHES by *Gould*, 1879–81; marble steps and elaborate SANCTUARY TILES probably of the same date. – STAINED GLASS. Many Victorian and later windows, the most notable the chancel E and s aisle E, *c.* 1859 by *Hardman*, with attractive scrollwork backgrounds. – s aisle second from E 1903, an early work by *Caroline Townshend*, three saints, charming scenes below, rich subtle colours. – In contrast the N aisle E window, 1859 by *Beer*, with its brightly coloured figures, appears very strident.

Chulmleigh is an attractive small town, until *c.* 1830 on the main road from Exeter to Barnstaple. It was a borough from 1253, and a centre of the cloth trade in the C17 and C18. The church lies near the w end of the town, with an unobstructed view to the s over the woods and hills beyond the Little Dart river. From the churchyard small streets and alleys lead to FORE STREET, mainly modest late Georgian. In the middle of the w side the MARKET HALL, 1894, classical, with ground floor of channelled stucco. At the N end a nicely pompous cast-iron pump-cum-lamppost occupies the centre of the road. Closing the vista, RAINBOW HOUSE, Georgian, with quoins and Gibbsian door surrounds with keystone heads. Adjoining to the l. a house with Gothick windows. In SOUTH MOLTON STREET the BARNSTAPLE INN with royal arms of 1633 and king-mullion window frame to the street.

CONGREGATIONAL CHAPEL, East Street, behind a railed burying ground. Rebuilt in 1710; subsequently repaired, altered, and enlarged. In 1836 the schoolroom was built up to the street. Rubble walls, hipped slate roof, gabled porch, and large pointed-arched windows. The interior is outstanding, to be compared with George's Meeting in Exeter. It has two galleries, one of them for singers, late C18 chandeliers, an early C18 clock with Gothic traceried case, and C18 monuments and shields of arms. The Communion table and octagonal pulpit with its canopy are early C18.

At COLLETON MILLS, a plastered single-storey rectangular TOLL HOUSE with one corner cut off for an observation window.

STONE BARTON. Above Stone Barton farm low earthworks forming an oval enclosure with W entrance, probably the foundations of a medieval manor house belonging to the Courtenays of Okehampton.

BROOKLANDS FARMHOUSE. Late C17, three storeys, with a three-room lobby-entrance plan, a three-storey porch, and a later stair-turret.

CADBURY BARTON CHAPEL. Probably C16, with a wagon roof. Now a farm building.

See also Colleton Barton.

CHURCHSTOW

ST MARY. The parent church of the borough of Kingsbridge (q.v.), prominently sited on a high ridge. W tower with stair-turret of South Hams type reaching higher than the unpinnacled tower (cf. Thurlestone nearby). The N transept is the oldest part of the present fabric (E window). S aisle and two-storeyed S porch later. Arcade of six bays with monolithic granite piers of A type, capitals only to the four shafts, and nearly semicircular moulded arches. The arch into the transept simply double-chamfered. Ceiled wagon roofs. The pulpit and the base of the screen incorporate some old carving.

PARSONAGE. 1838–48 by *William Railton*.

CHURCH HOUSE INN. The former church house, well built of ashlar, with a large chimneystack at the W end. Central round-headed doorway. Windows all renewed.

See also Leigh Barton.

CLANNABOROUGH

ST PETROCK. Plain early medieval plan with chancel, nave, and W tower. The tower is early, unbuttressed, with battlements with short pinnacles. Tower arch on the plainest imposts; the arch mouldings altered Perp. The rest simply restored in 1858–9, with new chancel arch and traceried windows, at the expense of the Wreford family, who were connected with the Hardmans. Hence the STAINED GLASS by *Hardman & Co.* (E window 1863, nave N 1867), the mural BRASS to Annie Hardman †1881 and Selina Wreford †1892, and the good chancel N window of 1900, with St Martin, another joint Wreford and Hardman memorial – MONUMENT. Grace Freke †1783. With marble vase and cherub.

OLD RECTORY. A long rendered house with two early C19 canted bays with their own thatched roofs – an endearing touch.

CLANNABOROUGH BARTON. A four-bay Georgian house built by

the Wreford family in 1801. Two centre bays recessed; colonnade of six granite Doric columns. Much original plasterwork and joinery. The back wings flank the farmyard.

APPLEDORE. Georgian, five bays, two storeys.

Among the farmhouses in the parish are COLTSFOOT, early C17, with an unmodernized interior, and THORNE, C14–17, with massive late medieval roof carpentry (unusual jointed crucks with face pegs and slip tenons; cf. Rudge, Morchard Bishop and Bury Barton, Lapford).

CLAWTON 3090

ST LEONARD. The oldest part is the chancel, with one Norman N window. The W tower probably C14; unbuttressed, with tall unmoulded arch towards the nave. Centrally placed polygonal stair-turret on the S side of the tower (an unusual feature in North Devon; but cf. Totnes, Ashburton, etc.). Obelisk pinnacles. Straight-headed N and S aisle windows, with cusped pointed lights. Arcades of four bays. Octagonal piers with castellated abaci and double-chamfered arches. The E bays different, of blue polyphant stone; four shafts in the main directions and four in the diagonals, elementarily decorated capitals and abaci. These bays were probably meant as transepts. Squint from the S aisle into the chancel. Good wagon roof in the N aisle.

FONT. Norman, circular, of polyphant stone, with one top band of cable. The base more elaborately decorated with four faces at the angles and half-rosettes on the main surfaces, as if it were a fragmentary re-used font itself, of the Cornish St Thomas-by-Launceston type (cf. Tetcott nearby). – TILES. Some of Barnstaple type with fleur-de-lis, lions, swans, roses; by the font. – ROYAL ARMS under the tower; large, undated, but cf. Ashwater. – Chancel decoration (now largely whitewashed), REREDOS, and STAINED GLASS in the E window all of 1891–7. – Late C18 ORGAN in Gothic organ case. – MONUMENTS. Tiny brass acquired by a former vicar at Oxford. – Christopher Osmond, 1631. A slate plate and above it in relief the life-size figure of a semi-reclining man with columns l. and r., carrying an entablature, two allegorical figures, and an achievement.

BLAGDON. A rambling stone and cob former manor house, much altered in the C19.

Among the farmhouses GUNNACOTT may be singled out, an isolated stone house of medieval origin, later remodelled, the C17 carpentry unusually rich for North Devon.

EASTCOMBE. Late C17 with mid C19 additions. On the front a sundial dated 1737, with the surprising inscription, 'the time is shown at all hours of the day at Jerusalem and Barbados, whilst noon tide only is shown at Goa, Isfahan' (and ten other places).

CLAYHANGER 0020

ST PETER. A small church, much renewed. The W tower the oldest part, with diagonal buttresses only at the foot. Nave without aisles,

E window with ogee reticulation, i.e. early C14. The chancel otherwise, and the fine chancel arch of Ham Hill and volcanic stone, of 1879–81 by *Hine & Odgers*. – REREDOS. Incorporating fragments of a Jacobean gallery and cresting from the medieval rood screen. – FONT. Small, the bowl fluted, *c.* 1200 (cf. Abbotsham). – BENCH ENDS. Many with ornamental and figure designs, the standard Devon and Cornwall type. – Double LECTERN, Jacobean, with moulded baluster post.

NUTCOMBE MANOR HOUSE. The present appearance is simply a rectangle with a symmetrical two-storeyed three-window front, the windows of four lights, on the ground floor with transoms, on the upper floor without. Originally the present centre had a porch, and the house extended farther to the l. and ended with a short projecting wing. Gables also have disappeared. Inside, ground-floor hall with an early C17 plaster overmantel with coarse caryatids, and a plaster ceiling with thin ribs and pendants. A later plaster ceiling upstairs, and a chimneypiece painted with a hunting scene.

OLD RECTORY. Much rebuilt in 1823. Rendered front with hipped roof.

CLAYHIDON

1010

ST ANDREW. Stuccoed tower. Late medieval nave with original roof. Five-bay S arcade with B type piers. W gallery possibly early C19; other fittings from the time of the restoration of 1846. – In the churchyard good MONUMENTS, and the two-storey rubble OLD SCHOOL, dated 1824.

WELLINGTON MONUMENT. Outlined against the sky on the Blackdown Hills to the N. By *Thomas Lee*, begun 1817, the obelisk (175 ft tall) completed 1854, the intended cast-iron statue never erected.

CORDWENTS. A late medieval farmhouse, built partly floored. Original upper chamber jettied out on shaped joists over the stud-and-panel screen. The typical later C16–17 adaptations include an exceptionally large inserted axial stack, the back to the cross-passage with very smart coursed squared flint blocks. Heated chamber above.

CLOVELLY

3020

Clovelly is one of the show villages of England, an extremely steep cobbled street with a few side alleys, leading down to a miniature harbour sheltered by a curved pier, with a large inn by its side and a small fortification nearby. It was the building of the pier by George Cary in 1587 that led to the growth of the village; its consciously picturesque preservation is the result of deliberate control by the Hamlyns, who succeeded the Carys as lords of the manor, particularly Mrs Christine Hamlyn (*née* Hamlyn-Fane, †1936). The general impression is still superficially genuine, but as the date plaques (mostly of 1914–25) reveal, many of the houses have been rehabilitated and altered. No cars are permitted. The houses are mostly whitewashed. Many from their style and their little segment-arched hoods on the doors may be dated late Georgian. The charm of the village is largely the intricacy of the overlapping of houses in all dimensions. It is quite beyond description.

At the top of the street MEMORIAL to Queen Victoria, 1901 by *Baroness Gleichen*. On the edge of the harbour a circular LIME-KILN.

The village is surrounded by wooded slopes. Much of the planting is early C19, due to Sir James Hamlyn Williams, who also, in 1829, built along the coast to the E a three-mile drive, known as the HOBBY DRIVE, a remarkable example of the new romantic appreciation of wild nature in her real wilderness, not trimmed to look wild, as had still been the ideal of improvers a short time before.

The church and mansion stand close together at the top of the hill, some half mile from the village.

ALL SAINTS. Evidence of a vanished Norman church is the arch moulding of the outer doorway into the S porch, with zigzag decoration. The low, unbuttressed and unpinnacled W tower also early medieval, its arch towards the nave round-headed and unmoulded. The rest is Perp. N aisle with granite arcade of four bays with type A piers; capitals only to the main shafts, and depressed pointed arches. Open wagon roofs, plastered behind. – FONT. Norman, of undecorated block capital shape. – PULPIT. Plain Jacobean, dated 1634. – BENCHES. Perp, undecorated. – STAINED GLASS. Chancel N: fragments of heraldic glass. – N aisle E: to James Hamlyn Williams †1861. Small figured medallions. – E window, with three tiers of small figures, 1885 by *Kempe Studios*. – W window, with three large figures, also by *Kempe Studios*, 1898. – S window 1905 by *Comper*, an Annunciation and St Mary of Bolsena, in memory of Mary Christine Manners. A good example of Comper's delicate early style.

MONUMENTS. Unusually many, mostly to Carys; none of the highest quality. Robert Cary †1540. Brass in armour, the figure *c.* 30 in. long. – Sir Robert Cary, 1586. An odd design, the solid superstructure with six engaged columns, the interstices between adorned with big strap cartouches. – Group of wall-monuments all by one workshop, with inscription framed by columns and various forms of pediment, no two identical. The date of the earliest is 1652, but it was probably made in the 1670s to match the others; the dates 1675, 1677, 1680, 1685, 1686. Another in the same tradition as late as 1728. – Of Hamlyns the following have monuments worth recording: Zachary †1759, of Clovelly Court and Lincoln's Inn, with portrait medallion against obelisk (the inscription says: 'Exemplarily modest, diligently capable, communicative, he acquired a handsome fortune, not only unenvied, but with the Esteem and Love of all who had the Pleasure of knowing him'). Very chaste, not at all Rococo. – Lady Hamlyn †1797, with standing woman by an urn, and Sir James †1811, with seated woman by an urn, both by *T. King & Sons* of Bath, and both rather busy in detail; not neo-classical. – Colonel Hamilton Fane †1868 and wife. Gothic tabernacle of veined marble with carved angels. – In the churchyard several unusual memorials. James Berriman †1903. Standing figure of Christ. – Mary Christine Manners †1904. A wooden cross with peacock decoration and medallion of the Virgin and Child (a re-used foreign piece?). Lettering on the concave stone base by *Eric Gill*. – Another wooden cross, with Crucifixion, to the Hamlyns. – Along the N churchyard wall several well lettered memorials in the Eric Gill tradition.

CLOVELLY COURT. The seat of the Carys, then of the Hamlyns. The part built about 1740 by Zachary Hamlyn with Gothic details, and elegantly classicized by Sir James about 1795, was burnt out in 1944. What remains is a fairly plain rendered two- and three-storeyed L-shaped house, the entrance with Gothic arched doorway between polygonal turrets with trefoiled lancets, a Perp window above. Early C18 STABLES, U-shaped, of red brick. LODGE of 1900. Handsome gatepiers with balls.

CLOVELLY DYKES, at the crossroads where the road to Clovelly village leaves the A39. A fine example of a HILLFORT with wide-spaced ramparts of 'South Western' type. The ramparts originally completed their circuit S of the A39; only soilmarks now survive.

See also Buck's Mills.

CLYST HONITON

ST MICHAEL. Much rebuilt by *William White* in 1876 (cf. Bishop's Court) except for the W tower (broad and short, with stair-turret and buttresses of type B) and the modest low N arcade (piers of B type with capitals only to the four shafts). By *White* the short S aisle with the porch leaning up against its W wall. – FONT. Square Norman bowl of table-top type, one side with the usual shallow blank arcades, another with a plain fluted zigzag motif, the other two reworked in the C16 or C17. – MONUMENT. John Yarde †1575. Recess with Tudor arch, but a few awkwardly applied classical motifs.

See also Bishop's Court.

CLYSTHYDON

ST ANDREW.* W tower of grey local sandstone, with buttresses of type B and stunted classical pinnacles on the battlements. It is as late as 1658 (datestone inside) but is probably a rebuilding. Good S aisle and porch of c. 1500, balanced by an embattled rood-stair turret. On the porch keystone the arms of St Clere supported by an angel; porch fan-vault with a central boss. S aisle with piers of A type, standard capitals. N aisle 1856, the arcade in imitation of the S aisle, but the windows still pre-archaeological. Plaster wagon roofs also of this date, the chancel (most unusually) with flat plaster ribs imitating wood, and small rosettes as bosses. – Well preserved contemporary fittings: tall BOX PEWS (also some C18 ones); Lord's Prayer and Creed on Gothic panels. – FONT. C15, recut; ogee octagonal oak FONT COVER. – STAINED GLASS of the 1840s and 1850s: two E windows by *E. Baillie*, with arms of the Huyshes in grisaille (there

---

* Based on an account by Francis Kelly.

were two Huyshe rectors in the C19). – One N window by *Clayton & Bell*, 1881.

CLYSTHYDON HOUSE. Small, two-storey late Georgian house with canted bays, the property of the Huyshes of Sand in the C19.

AUNK MANOR FARM. An C18 nine-bay brick front, unusual for Devon, very plain but well built in red brick with blue headers, the windows with flat arches of rubbed brick. Plat-band between the two floors; hipped roof with sprocketed eaves. Two wings extend back to form a U at the rear. This side is even plainer; in the main range just one window and a central door. Two ovolo-moulded windows in the W wing, probably re-used. Staircase with turned balusters.

RATCLYFFE. Two-storey white-stuccoed Regency house in its own grounds.

CLYST ST GEORGE   9080

ST GEORGE. Slim W tower of red sandstone with stair-turret. The tower arch panelled. The church, gutted in the Second World War and plainly rebuilt by *T. J. Rushton*, had been extensively restored in 1854–5 by the Rev. *H. T. Ellacombe*, a frequent correspondent to the *Ecclesiologist*. The pretty LYCHGATE dated 1867, with decorated bargeboards, was designed by him and paid for by William Gibbs.

LADY SEAWARD PRIMARY SCHOOL. Endowed by Lady (Hannah) 169 Seaward in 1705, rebuilt in 1859, perhaps also to the design of *Ellacombe*. An unspoilt picturesque L-shaped group of school and schoolhouse at the crossroads. Much surface patterning produced by roof tiles, limestone crazy-paving walls, and glazing bars. Unusual arcaded veranda with ironwork in the openings. Bell-turret at one end.

OLD RECTORY. Handsome C18 brick front, five windows with keystones.

PYTTE. A late Georgian house of the Gibbs family, probably with an older core. Extensively remodelled and enlarged by *S. Gambier Parry* in 1911, with a new long, asymmetrical rendered S front with gables and mullion-and-transom windows. Now six dwellings.

CLYST ST LAWRENCE   0000

ST LAWRENCE. Slim W tower, nave and porch, all of ashlar; chancel slightly narrower, of rubble, perhaps older. The tower quite tall, so that the church looks oddly like an appendix to it. Diagonal buttresses. Stair-turret with a figure of the Virgin in a niche halfway up, and two more figures higher up. W doorway two-centred, with fleurons continuing down the jambs. Panelled tower arch. The nave has Perp windows and an old wagon roof. – FONT. Norman, of the plainest and crudest. – The SCREEN has lost its tracery, but the fan coving to the W and two closely decorated cornice strips remain. – Medieval CROSS in the churchyard.

CLYST ST MARY

ST MARY. Rendered exterior. The present church is confusing.
Originally it was small, C13, probably on a cruciform plan, with a
W tower. Transepts enlarged 1818; further enlargement *c.* 1869 by
Ashworth (tracery replaced throughout and church re-aligned N–S);
fittings of the new chancel, i.e. the old N transept, 1895–7. –
FONT. 1818. Octagonal, on a baluster stem. – STAINED GLASS. E
and W by *Lavers, Barraud & Westlake*, 1874.

BRIDGE. The oldest surviving in Devon, mentioned in 1238. Raised
causeway, 600ft long. Five arches, the two westernmost probably
dating from 1310, when the bridge was substantially rebuilt.

See also Winslade Manor.

COAXDON HALL
2m. N of Axminster

A puzzling remnant of a larger house partly destroyed by fire in 1770.
Acquired in 1590 by Richard Symonds, a lawyer, in the C17 it was
the property of the Parliamentarian Symonds D'Ewes. Attractive
exterior of grey squared rubble limestone. Two wings of *c.* 1600,
facing S and W, with stone ovolo-moulded mullioned windows on
two floors, coped gables, and roofs with jointed-cruck trusses.
Simple post-fire N wing. The original hall has disappeared. The
present central entrance in the W wing leads into a double-height
hall, a C19 conversion from two storeys. In the SW corner a
parlour, with mullioned windows on two sides. Beyond this a
doorway to the S, then a very puzzling room with two mullioned
windows on the S side, but, against the clearly much later N wall,
two octagonal posts with pyramid stops supporting a chamfered
rail as if the room was once open to the courtyard. Above the rail a
timber-framed wall, now only visible internally at first-floor level,
with a very long eleven-light mullioned window, now blocked.
(Did it light a gallery?) Reset linenfold panelling below. The house
once continued further E, as the now external fireplace indicates.

COCKINGTON *see* TORBAY

COFFINSWELL

ST BARTHOLOMEW. The earliest part the austere W tower with
unmoulded tower arch and a strong batter, unbuttressed, two-
stage, now dark roughcast. Inside, a type B arcade between nave
and N aisle with standard capitals, except that the W piers display
heraldry as well as foliage (arms of John Holbeame †1473 and
related families). – FONT. Norman, circular, with palmettes and a
band of crosses saltire above and of cable below (same type at
Combeinteignhead nearby). – Traces of WALL PAINTING.

COURT BARTON. Manor house close to the church, partly C16 and
older. Two good five-light granite windows. The S wing was used

as a court house by Torre Abbey. Cobbled yard with granite archway.

COFTON
Dawlish

9080

ST MARY. A small church of the C13, in ruins in the C18, vastly restored in 1838–9 by *Charles Fowler* for the tenth Earl of Devon, a leader of the High Church revival. The stone altar remains from the fittings of this time – an early example. N aisle 1863. – REREDOS. 1886 by *Hems*, to the designs of the *Earl of Halifax*; unremarkable. – STAINED GLASS. W window 1886 by *Drake*.

COLATON RALEIGH

0080

ST JOHN THE BAPTIST. Apart from the unbuttressed early C16 W tower, much rebuilt in 1873–5 by *Fulford*. N aisle *c.* 1200 with very fat circular columns; S aisle with circular and multifoil capitals. Elaborately decorated E end, with carved capitals to the chancel arch, much sgraffito work (an early example of this technique), and an ornate wooden ALTAR FRONTAL with trefoiled arches. – Reset ancient PISCINA. – Norman FONT with cable moulding. – Pretty painted ORGAN CASE in the S transept. – STAINED GLASS. 1856–7. Christ with crown of thorns and angels.

NATIONAL SCHOOL, near the church. 1840, a simple white rendered building.

PLACE COURT. Remains of a small medieval house, the former 'rectory or mansion house' of the Deans of Exeter Cathedral. It stands not far W of the church, its large garden surrounded by a remarkably long thatched cob wall. Grey rubble. Two-storey ashlar porch, its two-centred archway moulded on both sides. The two-light Dec window above this and the single light at the side belong to the chapel, possibly the one mentioned in documents of 1307 and 1335. The hall lay to the l., but this part has been substantially rebuilt. Inside, the late medieval hall screen remains, with two four-centred arches, and a stone archway to the kitchen at the back of the cross-wing. (The second stone archway is C20.) The upper chamber in the front part of this wing has a fine roof with three moulded arch-braced trusses. A low stone arch leads to the chapel, which has the remains of a wagon roof, and a small piscina.*

On Colaton Raleigh Common a number of prehistoric ROUND BARROWS.

COLCOMBE
Near Colyton

2090

All that survives is part of a late medieval domestic range (now farm buildings) which belonged to a manor house of the Courtenays. Sir

---

*I am grateful to Canon J. P. Hoskins for details in this entry.

William Pole, the antiquary († 1635), rebuilt the house and made it his seat; it became a farmhouse after the Civil War, when the Poles moved to Shute, and was ruined in Polwhele's day. It is commonly called Colcombe Castle, but there is no visible evidence that the house was ever fortified. A stream runs around one side of the site – was it formerly moated? The present house occupies a terrace, perhaps re-used from earlier times.

6000

COLDRIDGE

St Matthew. High up to the N of Dartmoor. W tower with diagonal buttresses and polygonal NE stair-turret. The rest Perp, but incorporating a C12 building: see the chancel N window, with voussoirs of yellow and red stone, and the odd blocked pointed arch on the plainest imposts on the N side of the W bay of the nave (opening into a former tower?). To its E a clean quoined vertical joint against which is the half-hexagonal impost of the later arcade. The N aisle earlier than the S, which has a tall granite arcade with A type piers and capitals only to the main shafts. N chancel chapel early C16, with straight-headed windows and decorated imposts above the arcade capitals. Other windows with various but not unusual tracery patterns. Aisles with ceiled wagon roofs with good bosses. E window 1877, when the chancel was restored. The rest of the church conservatively restored in 1897. – FONT. Square, C12, table-top type, with seven flat blank arches on each side. – The remaining FITTINGS are early C16, probably largely given by John Evans, a park keeper of the Marquess of Dorset's deer park at Coldridge. His MONUMENT is in an ogee-arched recess in the N chancel chapel, no doubt his chantry chapel. The effigy must once have been of fine quality; a relaxed pose with the head slightly on one side. A shield gives Evans's name.

35　　PARCLOSE SCREEN dividing chapel from chancel. Of the same unusual type as at Brushford and Colebrooke, i.e. with Flamboyant, un-English tracery, each tracery opening finely subdivided by a lacework of tiny Flamboyant curves, the bars less than $\frac{1}{4}$ in. thick. Finials with remains of filigree cresting in between. – The ROOD SCREEN runs right across nave and aisles. It has standard type A Devon tracery, ribbed coving with tracery decoration between the ribs, and a cornice with two bands of ornament. – PULPIT. Timber; exceedingly fine in the carving. Flat niches for figures, but now without them. Nodding ogee canopies above and intricate tracery above these, but without any Flamboyant shapes. – BENCH ENDS. Also given by John Evans, for one bench has a (re-cut) inscription asking the reader to pray for him and calling him 'factor huius operis anno regni regis Henrici octavo tercio', i.e. 1511. These bench ends, with tracery, a head of St John (his patron saint) on a platter, and knobbly leaves still entirely unaffected by the Renaissance, should give a clue to the approximate dating of bench ends in other places. The inscribed bench end has linenfold panelling along the front (as has the inside of the parclose screen). – TILES. Of Barnstaple make, with roses, lions, pelicans, etc., reassembled in front of the altar. – STAINED GLASS. Early C16 figure of a king in the E window of the N aisle and a few other tiny fragments. – MONUMENT. Coffin-shaped slab with foliated cross, re-used with a C17 inscription.

CASTLE. Immediately w of Millsome Farm, on a knoll beside the river Taw, lies a probable medieval earthwork castle whose overall plan is difficult to appreciate. It has no known history.

TOLL HOUSE, Taw Bridge, on the B3220. Single-storey, with central bay and windows at each end.

LOWER CHILVERTON.* A late medieval farmhouse, clearly 77 illustrating a gradual late C15–18 evolution. The details are of exceptional quality. Medieval roof on four jointed cruck trusses, the hall section with arch-braces on the central truss, chamfered and pyramid-stopped threaded purlins, and wind-braces, each rafter of large, square-cut timber. The whole roof is smoke-blackened, surviving complete with original thatch and even impressively regular thatching battens and ties. Two stud-and-panel screens, between hall and inner room, and hall and cross-passage (the third, between cross-passage and lower room, has been removed), are probably examples of low partitions, over which two chambers were inserted before the mid C16, while the hall remained unceiled. When it was ceiled, it was richly detailed (see the moulded and stopped cross-beams) as well as being of exceptional height (reflecting the height of the medieval hall). To the w, early cob BARN with C16 doorway with shouldered head.

EAST LEIGH HOUSE. A C16 or earlier farmhouse in origin, remodelled in the C17 (plaques dated 1664, 1673) and later. The oldest part is the centre and w end of the main range: the former inner room beyond the hall was converted to an entrance hall in the late C17, and a staircase block added behind. Many features of c. 1600, including local mudstone-block hall fireplace with a later cloam oven.

EAST LEIGH BARTON. A late medieval house with an exceptional roof, perhaps as early as the late C14. Three huge true cruck trusses remain, with cambered collars with simple central bosses. Two of the trusses have yokes to carry the square-set ridge, one with a large saddle. Original smoke-louvre *in situ*, a very rare survival, complete with its pitched roof of louvred boards.

COLEBROOKE   7000

ST ANDREW. Isolated on top of a hill in a scattered parish. Porch and N aisle of ashlar, the chancel more roughly built. The oldest part must be the nave, see the blocked round-headed arches in its s wall, presumably a low Norman arcade to a vanished s aisle. Two heads now in the s transept were probably corbels of that nave. A transitional s arch suggests a predecessor to the present s transept, which has windows of the early C14 and two low ogee-headed tomb recesses. The chancel is of the same date. In fact it is known from records that the chancel was 'parvum, inhonestum, male fenestratum et male co-opertum' in 1281 and still in 1301, but 'competens' in 1330. A squint connects the transept (which served as Lady Chapel) with nave and chancel. The rest looks Perp. w

*For a plan of Lower Chilverton see p. 68.

tower quite big, with diagonal buttresses and three-light straight-headed bell-openings (against its s wall a pretty SUNDIAL of 1889 by *Hems* in C17 style). N aisle with thin type B piers and standard capitals. The NE (Copplestone) chapel, probably built *c*. 1460 (chantry to John Copplestone †1457), is singled out by an oddly Flamboyant window. It uses similar forms to windows at Staverton and Ipplepen. The fireplace (now blocked) was added in the C16 when the chapel became a family pew. The PRAYER DESK with the Copplestone and Gorges arms (marriage of 1472), now in the chancel, also came from the chapel. It has crudely vigorous over-size reliefs of a wild man and a fool.

FONT. Octagonal, Perp, with quatrefoil panels and shields, tracery on the broad pillar. Jacobean FONT COVER with two-sided terminal figure (wings added 1898). – REREDOS. 1896 by *Hems*, stone, with relief of the Descent of the Holy Spirit. – PULPIT. 1903. The former plain pulpit of 1805 now a LECTERN. – PAR-CLOSE SCREEN to the Copplestone Chapel. Very mannered but of great charm; not at all in the usual Devon tradition. Linenfold panelling in the wainscoting, graceful spiral-fluted colonnettes, and tracery partly ogee reticulated, partly of more complex Flamboyant forms, Franco-Flemish rather than English. A Breton workman has been suggested. Moreover, the main shapes are finely subdivided by a filigree of bladder-like or drop-like forms, of the kind which the French call *mouchettes*. The same carver must have worked at Brushford and Coldridge. The ogee heads in the N aisle must be an addition. – MONUMENTS. Slab with unfoliated cross, perhaps C13–14, outside the chancel s door. – Elizabeth Coryton †1667. Wall-monument with Corinthian columns and broken scrolly pediment. – CURIOSUM. Small translucent porcelain plaque of the Ascension, German, *c*. 1840, given *c*. 1925.

W of the church SCHOOL and CHURCH HOUSE of 1874 in bold and incongruous red brick, with large plate-tracery window.

The hamlets of the parish are now more substantial than Colebrooke itself. Lying in the richest part of mid Devon, the parish includes a large number of good farmhouses.

At COLEFORD groups of thatched red cob buildings typical of this area cluster round a crossroads. The two-storey projecting porch of SPENCER'S COTTAGE is an excellent example of how timber-framing occasionally appears in rural Devon on such porches added to earlier buildings. This one is open to the ground floor with a flat arched entrance; the first-floor framing is exposed to show curved tension braces.

At PENSTONE BARTON a fortress-like array of buttressed cob outbuildings around a rendered farmhouse. (Simple ceiling with the date 1737 and the initials of William Pidsley.)

At KNOWLE, an endearing chapel, ST BONIFACE, its C19 chancel with Dec window and patterned tiles attached to a nave with small domestic windows converted from an older schoolhouse.

COPPLESTONE. At the junction of the parishes of Colebrooke, Crediton, and Down St Mary, a CROSS SHAFT. The decoration is mostly interlacings, but also on one side two panels with crosses saltire. On the same side higher up a round-headed niche no doubt for an image. The date of the cross is probably late Saxon.

COPPLESTONE HOUSE. The seat of the Copplestones from the C13 to the late C16, bought in 1787 by Robert Madge, who rebuilt the house on a new site, incorporating some older fabric. Five bays, partly rendered; to the r. of the central door part of a blocked arch. Above the door an uncusped mullioned window of four lights, enriched with late medieval scrollwork. The window above is an imitation, added when the centre of the house was heightened to three storeys in the late C19. Other windows all regular Victorian sashes.

COOMBE HOUSE. The estate of the Snells was acquired through marriage by the Sillifants in 1677. They rebuilt the house in 1795, but it has been altered since. Small stuccoed mansion with C19 panelled pilasters. Two canted bays linked by a two-storey colonnade, the ground floor with Greek Doric columns.

WHELMSTONE BARTON. A former manor house, mostly early C17, with C18 additions. Good two-storey porch with ball finial on the gable. In a barn, old roof timbers possibly from a chapel licensed in 1374. Gateway with coped gable and ball finial. Good outbuildings.

(HORWELL BARTON. An early C19 front of 1–3–1 bays, the end bays set back.)

PASCHOE. Rebuilt c. 1850–60 in an attractive Tudor Gothic. Garden front with a central porch flanked by bay-windows; straight gables, mullioned windows. The seat of the Calmady-Hamlyn family from c. 1600 to c. 1963.

(GREAT HEALE. An early C17 cob farmhouse with a well preserved interior.)

COLLACOMBE MANOR
Lamerton

4070

The most interesting features of the house date from the later C16, the time of Edmund Tremayne (†1582), a clerk to the Privy Council and colleague of Cecil who had spent two years in Italy. His house demonstrates the extent to which new ideas in planning and decoration were beginning to be introduced into the county. The building had been owned by the Tremaynes from 1366, and remained their seat until c. 1700, when they moved to Sydenham (q.v.). It was let as a farm from 1810, when parts were demolished, and restored in the 1950s by Major Archibald Jack.

The entrance front makes a most attractive ensemble. Within the garden wall (with a rectangular gunloop, perhaps from the time of the Civil War) a broad depressed arch flanked by Doric columns carrying an entablature. In line with this the porch, its pedimented doorway (a modification of an older archway) harmonizing with the gateway, and on the l. the huge hall window (five mullions and two transoms) remarkably preserving its late C16 patterned glazing, with 3,400 criss-cross lozenge panes. This window is straight-headed; the little oriel of the porch and the other windows have arched lights. The porch must originally have been taller.

The main range was a remodelling rather than a rebuilding of the later C16 – see the early C16 stone doorway on the W side of the screens passage, with depressed arch and continuous moulding. But the special interest of the house is the hall, where the date 1574 66 appears above the Tremayne arms on the overmantel of the fireplace on the back wall. The hall is still double-height, in Devon's conservative way, but the overmantel is a remarkably precocious and sophisticated classical piece with overlapping pilasters and classically moulded pediment. Around the walls a contemporary plaster frieze (close to those at Trerice, Cornwall, of 1572 and Buckland Abbey (q.v.) of 1576). Ceiling with single ribs and openwork pendant, an early example of the type that became so popular all over Devon. E of the fireplace, level with the frieze, the surprising feature of three little arches, their tympana filled by plaster shells. They are internal windows from an upper room which lies above a small chamber tucked between the hall chimneystack and the solar. A C19 drawing shows this area open to the hall on the ground floor, an extension of the principle of the oriel as a private retreat (cf. Bradfield, q.v.). The E wall of the hall displays the arms of Elizabeth I in plaster, on a jettied-out upper wall supported by brackets decorated with five grotesque satyrs (cf. Buckland). The jetty is probably earlier than the plasterwork which covers it. Beyond this wall are a ground-floor parlour and a first-floor solar (now subdivided), with another good chimneypiece with Tuscan columns and a classically moulded lintel on brackets. Its overmantel, with male and female terms and arms in a strapwork cartouche, is now in the little parlour made in the E wing in the 1950s. The solar formerly had a plaster barrel-vault.

The E wing, set at an irregular angle to the main range, is older; the former chapel in the projecting part to the E may be the one licensed in 1448. In the centre of the wing, a staircase with symmetrical balusters rises around a core which contains a remarkable garderobe sluice with access from two upper levels. A stream flows along a paved channel beneath.

6010
COLLETON BARTON
Chulmleigh

A manor house of the Bury family until the early C19. Cellar windows on the W side and the back entrance to the screens passage indicate a pre-Reformation house. The present appearance tallies with the date 1612 in the hall. Front of E-shape, except that the E wing (a converted granary) is asymmetrically long and low. Main windows of up to six lights, with transoms. Hall with plain panelled screen and single-ribbed plaster ceiling with pendants. Parlour on the W side with rich and varied panelling and another plaster ceiling. S of the house, on axis with it, a GATEHOUSE with chapel on the upper floor (first licensed 1381).

9010
COLLIPRIEST
Tiverton

Main front built c. 1778 by Thomas Winsloe (Burke's *Seats*), five bays and three storeys, with parapet. Projecting one-bay wings, Doric porch. Plain and dignified. The S front belongs to an early C18 house originally of nine bays, the three middle ones emphasized by pediment and cupola. Arched windows to the ground floor. Now divided into flats. In the ground-floor flat two Ionic columns survive from the good Adamish interiors of the later building phase. The former STABLES are of six bays with blind arches, all stuccoed.

CRANMORE CASTLE, directly above the house. A large but not very strong Iron Age hillfort.

COLUMBJOHN
Near Broadclyst

9090

A younger branch of the Aclands of Acland Barton (q.v.) in North Devon established themselves here in the later C16, before they built Killerton 1 m. away in the mid C18. Of their earlier house of c. 1590 only the gate arch of the gatehouse survives, Renaissance in detail but still Gothic in conception.

¾ m. N of this, ST JOHN, on the site of the chapel to the house that preceded the one of c. 1590, a miniature church, prettily Romanesque with pantile roof. 1851, built largely through the exertions of Arthur Acland (later Arthur Troyte of Huntsham, q.v.).

COLYFORD
Colyton

2090

ST MICHAEL. 1888–9 by R.M. Fulford, originally intended as a private chapel. Flint exterior. Nave, chancel, S transept, S porch, N vestry. S side strongly composed around the broad face of the transept (cf. Washford Pyne). The church is entered through a screened W vestibule which is also the baptistery. Nave and chancel faced with buff and red brick. In the S transept a simple recess intended for the founder's tomb. – ROOD SCREEN. Large, strongly membered. – REREDOS. 1891, oak, with a relief of Bartolommeo's 'Entombment' in an elaborate surround, the minute detail crisply executed.

The suburban spread along the main road from Exeter to Dorchester originated as an early C13 new town founded by Thomas Bassett, Lord of Colyton. A bridge was built in the mid C13.

STATION. Notable for its C19 cast-iron urinal.

COLYTON
2090

ST ANDREW. The most characteristic feature of the church is the 27 octagonal top storey of its crossing tower. Crossing towers are rare in Devonshire (but cf. Crediton, Branscombe, Axminster) and connect Colyton with the area further E. The ground stage is late Norman; see the plain imposts to the narrow arches inside which separate the tower from nave, chancel and transepts. The arches are pointed and entirely unmoulded. From the visual point of view they divide the church completely. The nave is light and wide, C15, with aisles nearly the same width as the nave, and large four-light windows on N and S. To the W a most remarkable group of three windows, the side ones of four lights, the middle one of nine with two transoms, going down to about 4ft from the ground and incorporating the W door in its composition. Two-storeyed S porch. The upper parts of the nave and the aisles were renewed in 1769, and again in 1818, when they received their curiously classical, but diagonally placed capitals and round arches. Galleries were removed in 1897. After a fire in 1933 more renewing had to be done (roofs).

As for the E parts of the church, the transepts and the chancel keep the original Norman shape. But the five-light E window is evidently of the early C14, and the Perp style added two-bay chancel aisles with four-light windows. Their piers have standard capitals with thick, bulgy horizontal leaf friezes, their imposts three-petalled flowers. Panelled entrance arch from the transept to the N chapel. In the S (Pole) chapel a much restored PISCINA with two cusped gables and an angel with a shield.

SCREENS. Stone screen to the S chancel chapel, originally to the chantry of Thomas Brerewood, vicar of Colyton, 1522–44, with his initials and rebus. Six main arches, the fourth, ogee-headed, for the entrance, the others subdivided into two lights each with simple Perp tracery. The design is copied from the Exeter Lady Chapel screen of a hundred years earlier. – Jacobean stone screen to the N chancel chapel, i.e. the chapel of the Yonge family who owned the Great House. The motif of the scrolled oculus in the parapet is derived from Longleat. – Other furnishings post-1933, by *Harbottle Reed* at his blandest, apart from the FONT and PULPIT of 1886 by *A. Norman*. – CROSS. The best pre-Conquest sculpture in the county: well preserved fragments of a Saxon cross, found after the fire of 1933. The shaft has scrolls with a bird and a lion on the front and interlacings on the sides. The date is probably C10. – CANDELABRA. Brass; 1796. – STAINED GLASS. W window 1906 by *Hardman* (drawing in the church).

MONUMENTS. Margaret Beaufort Countess of Devon †1449 (originally in the N transept). A recumbent figure, no longer than 3ft, on a tomb-chest with niches, under a row of three crocketed canopies. The horizontal cornice above, with quatrefoil decoration, probably early C19, when the monument was moved. Small figure of the Virgin at the W end, censing angels at the sides, other angels at the apex of the lierne-vault, all with renewed heads. The head of the effigy carved by *Hems*, modelled on his granddaughter, in the mistaken belief that the monument was to a child. – William Pole †1587 and wife. Elaborate genealogical monument decorated with scrolled oculus (cf. Yonge screen) erected by his son Sir William Pole, the antiquary. – Sir John Pole †1658 and his wife †1628, still entirely in the Elizabethan tradition, free-standing between chancel and S chancel chapel, with an eight-column canopy, the centre part raised, arched, and supporting a crest; the figures propped up on their elbows and not good. – Other C17 monuments to the Poles (of Colcombe and Shute, qq.v.) in the S chancel chapel. – W. Westover †1617. Hanging wall-monument, the usual type with kneelers facing each other across a prayer-desk. Corinthian columns l. and r.; achievement at the top; strapwork and ribbonwork. Attributed to *John Deymond* of Exeter (cf. Broadclyst, Talaton). – Good cast-iron GATEPIERS, 1842.

UNITARIAN CHAPEL (former), Church Street. Built *c.*1746.

Round-headed windows. C18 MANSE (Coombe House) in Queen Street.

METHODIST CHURCH (formerly Congregational), King Street. 1814, small and stuccoed. Gable-end with ball finial.

METHODIST CHAPEL (former), Rosemary Lane. 1838.

The little town has an attractive centre: a triangular area on a slope. At the top, a cast-iron FOUNTAIN with lamp-standard, 1863. The main focus is the COLCOMBE CASTLE, an inn with Greek Doric fluted half-columns to the doorcase. On the S side the small TOWN HALL, a late case of Tudor revival, 1927 by *J. Archibald Lucas* for the feoffees of Colyton, who previously met in the Old Church House (*see* below), one of several substantial C16 and C17 stone buildings in the town.

OLD CHURCH HOUSE, by the churchyard. Dated 1612. Three storeys; not the usual type of church house. The short side facing the street has five-light mullioned windows to the two upper floors, their hoodmoulds continued as string courses which, with other strings below the windows, neatly divide the wall into five bands. (Inside, much brought-in woodwork and old glass. Some C18 wall painting upstairs.) Opposite, the LAW CHAMBERS and adjacent shop to the l. incorporate interesting remains of a C16 town house. The l. part has a ceiling with intersecting moulded beams and two stone doorways in the back wall. In the r. part a single-rib plaster ceiling in four compartments and a fireplace with a painted overmantel with four rustic female figures: Virtue, Truth, Good Reputation, and Bad Reputation. Large stone rear wing with end stack.

VICARAGE AND BREREWOOD HOUSE, W of the church. The house of Thomas Brerewood, Chancellor to Bishop Veysey in the early C16, is still recognizable, although altered and extended later and divided in two in the 1970s. Two-storey porch; above the door Brerewood's badge, a briar, the date 1529, and his motto of a convinced pedestrian, 'peditatio totum, meditatio totum', on oddly angled scrolls, perhaps altered when the porch room was heightened and given its crow-stepped gable. The core of the house older (smoke-blackened jointed cruck truss with yoke, above the hall). Large hall window with Victorian casements. The solar wing to the S much remodelled, but retaining (in the present hall of the vicarage) a nine-compartment framed ceiling to the former parlour, with thick, well moulded timbers, no doubt of 1529, as the porch has a similar ceiling. At the S end, a study with C18 fielded panelling, a fireplace flanked by Ionic pilasters, and fragments of stained and painted glass taken from the church in the C19. The wing behind built in 1902.

GREAT HOUSE, South Street. The family house of the Yonges, including the diarist Walter Yonge (†1649). An attractive but puzzling exterior, largely early C17. U-shaped plan, possibly the remnant of an older and larger house. The main entrance front is now in the SW wing, handsomely faced with flint chequerwork, a speciality of East Devon. Symmetrical, with mullioned windows; the central door and cusped window above may be C19 improvements. In this wing, two late Tudor fireplaces on each floor, and panelling of *c.* 1600 in the W ground-floor room, with inlaid lozenge-pattern frieze. Behind, facing SE, a long row of first-floor mullioned windows, perhaps for a long gallery now subdivided.

On the opposite side of this range a continuous dripstone is carried round over a side doorway with a moulded wooden arch, leading through a lobby into the SW wing. The NW wing has service rooms and a dovecote above. In the NE first-floor room, Stuart arms in plaster above a bolection-moulded fireplace. Was this a courtyard house with a hall range which has disappeared?

A few nice minor C18 houses. COLYTON HOUSE, behind the vicarage, red brick, late Georgian, is hidden in a walled garden. Three-bay front with added bay; Tuscan porch. OROOLAY HOUSE, Queen Street, has a long later C18 rendered front. Otherwise small cottages along the little streets, mostly rendered, too many unfortunately suffering from a 1980s fashion for stripped rubble stonework.

TANNERY. C18/19. One of only two in the country still tanning by the traditional oak bark method. Mainly three-storey painted stone buildings with wooden louvred shutters on top floors and slate and corrugated-iron roofs. Square brick chimneystack at the W end. On the approach road a DRYING SHED for cleaning and curing skins, of two storeys, C18/19 stone rubble with wooden-louvred first floor and thatched half-hipped roof.

STATION. Built c. 1868. Red brick, with yellow and black brick for the round-headed windows, the doorways, and as decorative bands. Single-storey station offices with large glazed sliding doors and two-storey station house.

See also Colcombe.

1090

COMBE
Near Gittisham

Romantically set below hanging beechwoods planted in the late C18, a sizeable house (now a hotel) of Elizabethan appearance, E-shaped, with gables and mullioned windows. The Tudor details belong to a restoration for the Rev. Thomas Putt after 1815, when the r. wing was rebuilt, the upper storey added to the main range, and the windows all renewed. But the fabric is essentially the house of the Beaumonts, bought by Nicholas Putt, a wealthy lawyer, in 1615, and remodelled internally by later Putts. A medieval ogee-headed doorway in a timber-framed wall was found behind panelling at the high end of the hall. The present hall is a handsome double-height room of the later C17 with grained pine panelling, broken-pedimented doorcases, bolection-moulded fireplace, and an overmantel flanked by pilasters carved with fruit. The grand staircase beyond is of the same date, with urn-shaped balusters and a closed string, around a narrow well. The landing window was renewed in the early C19 with tracery and heraldic glass.

In the l. cross-wing an early C19 drawing room (former dining room) with neo-Jacobean geometric ceiling. Dining room (former drawing room) with C20 wall painting, a good C18 plaster ceiling, and a later neo-classical marble fireplace with busts. The best interior is the adjoining smaller room, which has a most delicate Rococo overmantel of carved pine, with birds and flowers around an oval mirror; the fireplace surround has a scalloped lintel and S-

shaped side flourishes of the kind that appear in pattern books of
c. 1755–60. On the ceiling garlands of fruit, and flying birds in high
relief, clearly inspired by the fireplace. Two matching doorcases,
with broken pediment, birds in the centre. In the rebuilt service
end of the house brick vaulted cellars, and a large kitchen with
chamfered beams, probably re-used. Contemporary service courtyard behind on a generous scale, entered by a large archway.

N of the house a derelict ORANGERY, very plain; five bays with
central pediment. To the N and E is a series of WALLED
GARDENS, shown on a survey of 1787.

COMBEINTEIGNHEAD

CHURCH. Externally the church looks very new, owing to restorations (1851, 1887 by *Fulford*), even the W tower with diagonal
buttresses and later pinnacles (white, while all the rest is red). The
tower arch is unmoulded. The church has two C15 aisles with
octagonal piers and double-chamfered arches, earlier N and S transepts, and an aisleless chancel. Two squints into the chancel. In
the E wall of the N transept a recess with an ogee arch and in it a
tomb-chest with mixed Gothic and Renaissance motifs, with arms
and a brass plate against the back wall. It is the MONUMENT of
Alice Hockmore † 1613. – FONT. Circular, Norman, with palmette
decoration and above a band of crosses saltire and below one of
cable (just as at Coffinswell in the close neighbourhood). –
SCREEN across the chancel entrance. Restored by *Hems*, *c*. 1905.
Standard tracery of type A, the sections unusually narrow. Two
bands of decoration in the cornice. The coving is new. – BENCH
ENDS. Specially attractive, two with individual saints, two with
two saints each and below them two wild men, a fool, and an
archer. – CHOIR STALLS with triple-arched canopies by *Fulford*. –
PAINTING. Jael and Sisera; Italian (Neapolitan?) C17. – STAINED
GLASS. E window by *Drake*, 1905.
BOURCHIER ALMSHOUSES. Founded 1620, red sandstone, no
conscious façade composition, but with original timber window
casements and four-centred doorway still of Tudor style.
BUCKLAND BARTON. Now a farmhouse. Panelled room and plaster
ceiling of *c*. 1600, when it was the seat of the Hockmores.

COMBE MARTIN

The beauty of Combe Martin is decidedly its surroundings and not
the buildings of the long straggling village, running down the
combe to the beach, the Victorian houses nearer the sea with the
typical upper bay-windows of seaside boarding houses. Combe
Martin was once very wealthy: records of the reigns of Edward I,
Edward III, Henry V, and Elizabeth prove the existence of silver
and lead mines. Early C19 efforts to revive the industry failed.
Abandoned shafts and adits exist in many places. The only
upstanding relic, on the hill to the NE, is the chimney of KNAP
DOWN MINE, which worked until 1875. Noteworthy in the village only the PACK OF CARDS INN, a rare C18 folly, built on a

cruciform plan with a towering display of symmetrically grouped chimneys, eight altogether. Near the church, BROOKLANDS, three bays, early C19.

ST PETER AD VINCULA. One of the best churches of the neighbourhood. Proud W tower and proud N front, both in some ways unusual. The W tower is 99ft high. It has buttresses of type B, niches for images high up, two tiers of gargoyles, battlements, and tall, thin, crocketed pinnacles. The bell-openings are specially big (for Devon – perhaps under Somerset influence); three-light with Perp tracery. W door decorated with fleurons. Battered figures remain in five of the eight niches. On the W side a demi-figure of Christ. The N side is very remarkable, symmetrically composed, with projecting porch, transept, and NE vestry, the effect now marred by a deplorably insensitive additional vestry. Between these projections the aisle wall appears with two large four-light Perp windows. The whole of this side of the church is embattled and pinnacled. On the S side there is also a symmetrical composition of transept and porch (the latter built or rebuilt in 1725).

These Perp and later additions hide the C13 church, of which there remain the chancel with lancet windows and an E triplet, and the S transept with its unmoulded pointed arch to the nave – an indication that the W tower reckoned with a nave narrower than at present. As the chancel is also narrower than the nave, the pier at the junction of N aisle and N chancel chapel is thicker than the others, and the designer of the church has made use of this to insert into it two niches for images side by side, facing W. The niches have canopies and semi-octagonal pedestals. (The figures date from 1962.) They appear as if they were part of the rood screen. N aisle of three tall bays with piers of B type and standard leaf capitals. The N transept also has B type responds and little concave capitals. The N chancel chapel opens into the chancel with only one arch. Wagon roofs everywhere (ceiled in 1727). The church was restored c. 1858 by *Hayward*.

FONT. Octagonal, Perp, with faintly recessed blank arch designs. – ROOD SCREEN. Wainscoting with painted figures (the only preserved example in North Devon). Tracery of A type; coving and cornice restored by *Herbert Read*, 1911–12. On the side to the N chapel plaster coving of 1727; the remains of extensive C18 remodelling otherwise removed in 1912. – PARCLOSE SCREEN with type A tracery and a pretty cornice frieze. – BENCH ENDS of the usual Devon type; nothing special. – Much good C19 WOOD-WORK: reading desk with censing angel, eagle lectern, choir stalls, communion rail. – REREDOS with free Gothic tracery, 1972 by *Doris Downing*.* – STAINED GLASS. Much of the C19–20, not of high quality. Chancel SW: one old fragment of a seraph. – Chancel E: brightly coloured medallions, 1862. – N aisle centre and W: large, rather eccentric figures of 1855 and 1866. – MONUMENTS. Judith Hancock † 1634. Good frontal demi-figure between columns. On the entablature two standing putti. – George Ley † 1716. Much cruder, fruit and cherubs on a heavy surround. – Good slate TOMBSTONES in the churchyard.

*An early CLOCK by *John Coles*, 1735, with buckets of stones for weights, is now in Ilfracombe Museum.

STANDING STONE, Knap Down, ⅝m. NE. 5ft high, with squared sides.

PREHISTORIC AND MEDIEVAL REMAINS. The 'fossilized' remains of a medieval strip field system are clearly visible on the steep sides of the valley above the village. On the high hills overlooking the Bristol Channel, isolated barrows and standing stones.

COMBE RALEIGH   *1000*

ST NICHOLAS. Unbuttressed C14 W tower with the staircase turret attached in an unusual way. The Perp arcades inside, and also chancel arch and arch between chancel and chancel chapel, with the usual type A piers and capitals only for the four shafts. The robust chancel roof 1886.

CHANTRY HOUSE. Late medieval priest's house, possibly built in connection with a chantry founded in 1498. Two-part plan, similar to priests' houses at Trent in Dorset and Farleigh Hungerford in Somerset. Hall with framed ceiling with bosses; chamber or upper hall above; three-storey service end with newel staircase; a small room over the porch. Post-and-panel partitions.

COMBPYNE   *2090*

ST MARY. In size only a chapel. Low C13 W tower with big angle buttresses. The chancel, with a group of three C13 lancet windows at the E end and a saddleback roof, much restored in 1878 by *George & Peto* (cf. Rousdon). No aisles. – STAINED GLASS in the tower by *Jones & Willis*, 1878, badly faded.

See also Rousdon.

COMPTON CASTLE   *8060*
Marldon

The approach is unforgettable. So Pevsner wrote in 1952, and later 59 extensive restoration has done nothing to spoil the impression. Compton represents a final fling of the medieval castle-building tradition. The highly spectacular fortress front added by John Gilbert to his small manor house dates from *c.* 1520. As in many late medieval castles, the emphasis of the design lay in visual impression rather than functional defensibility. The appearance is symmetrical: a central entrance is flanked by towers with corbelled oriels. Fine windows with cinquefoil heads not only at the upper levels but also lower down. It is doubtful whether the crenellations, machicolations, and portcullis grooves were anything more than show, for access to the wall top was restricted, there is no wall-walk, and the higher ground beyond makes the site vulnerable. The wall itself is no thicker than those of the house, and its continuation around the sides and rear hardly constitutes an impressive defence. Its primary purpose, in fact, was to define the courtyard (note the internal buttress). There is only one corner tower, at the SE. Entry to the back courtyard was at the ends of the

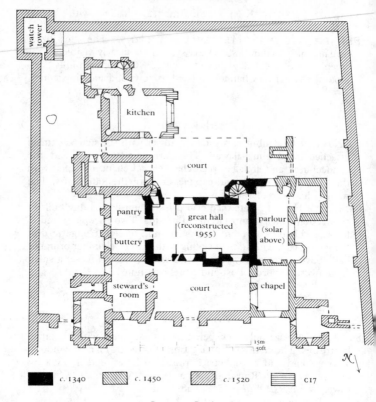

Compton Castle: plan

c. 1340   c. 1450   c. 1520   C17

façade beside the two front towers. These towers are to some extent genuinely defensive, for their barrel-vaults and loops at ground-floor level give a degree of cover to the adjacent walls.

The Gilbert family's undefended manor house consisted of a mid C14 hall, flanked by solar and service rooms at either end which were rebuilt in the later Middle Ages. The hall itself – in ruins from the C18 – was reconstructed in the 1950s, as faithfully as possible to what survived of the original. Oak arch-braced roof of four bays, covered in Delabole slate. The window tracery is of a greenstone from Oxfordshire similar in colour to the now unobtainable local medieval stone. Windows with shouldered arches below, ogee arches in the upper lights, and quatrefoils above. The fireplace in the side wall would however have been unlikely in the mid C14. The C15 first-floor solar at the w end, with its own fireplace and chimneystack, is reached by a (reconstructed) stair in the corner of the hall. The tower at the sw corner represents the first move towards defensibility (cf. Powderham). The fragmentary entrance at the rear must have been connected with a small s courtyard which preceded the present larger one. The ground-floor chapel, projecting beyond the solar at right angles to the hall range, is possibly older than the solar block (see the doorway to the

courtyard). Two large four-light Perp windows, one to the courtyard, one at the (liturgical) E end, level with the outer fortifications, and so protected by an iron grille. Well preserved ogee-
headed piscina, ground-floor squints (one of them original), upper-
floor cusped window of two lights, giving internal views from the
solar.

In the screens passage at the E end of the hall two simple hollow-
chamfered C14 doorways to buttery and pantry, and a third, smaller, to the stairs leading up to the upper chambers. Beyond these,
everything was rebuilt c. 1500, the accommodation interlocking
ingeniously with the outer fortifications. Upper chambers on two
floors, well supplied with fireplaces. The 'steward's room' projects
forward to balance the chapel, linked to the NE corner tower.
Another service room is in the tower midway along the E front,
with the large barrel-vaulted kitchen (massive open fireplace with
three flues, flanking ovens) and SE tower beyond. The W end of the
kitchen was rebuilt in the C17, the date of various windows
elsewhere.

The main building material is limestone rubble, with dressings
of red sandstone, white Beer stone, and granite.

COOKBURY   4000

ST JOHN AND THE SEVEN MACCABEES. Nearly the whole of the
Norman church survives. The W tower is small, narrower than the
nave, but with odd additions to N and S, almost like a dwarf W
transept, closed towards the nave so that the (unmoulded pointed)
tower arch is only as wide as the tower proper. Norman also the
masonry of the nave and chancel (some of the round-headed
windows may be C17 restorations). Three-light E window of
c. 1300 (if it is original in design). The N aisle arcade is a Perp
renewal: granite piers of A type with moulded capital strips and
depressed pointed arches. S transept also Perp. Restorations
c. 1870 (roofs renewed) and 1959. – ALTAR. Made up from Perp
panels. – FONT. C13, with corner shafts. – PULPIT. Jacobean,
altered, brought from Launceston church in Cornwall; the panels
re-used in a pew. – BENCH ENDS. Fourteen medieval, mostly very
plain. – TILES. Of the Barnstaple designs not unusual in this part
of Devon. – STAINED GLASS. E window by *Beer*.
METHODIST CHAPEL. Built by the Bible Christians in 1840. A rare
survival of the contemporary vernacular style adopted by this
denomination: rendered walls, half-hipped slate roof, like a plain
farm building, standing by an unmade track outside the village.
See also Dunsland House.

COOMBE BARTON   5010
1 m. NW of Roborough, near Great Torrington

Tudor manor house. The porch doorway has imposts of A type
(with capitals only to the main shafts), exactly as in Devon Perp
churches. Straight-headed two-light, three-light, and four-light
windows of early Tudor type. In the hall a large heraldic late

Tudor (or early C17) plaster overmantel. The fireplace immediately adjoins the porch.

CORNWOOD

The parish covers the southern parts of Dartmoor, where much evidence of prehistoric settlement survives. The shelter to the s of the moor has made the neighbourhood a favoured spot for good houses.

St Michael. Low, early, unbuttressed w tower with small bell-openings and a taller unembattled NE stair-turret. Nave and aisles, transepts, s porch. Perp arcades of five bays with monolithic granite A type piers and depressed arches. The entrance arches into the transepts of the same design. Restored in 1875. Chancel C13, with plain trefoiled SEDILIA and remains of lancet windows, refurbished in the C19, with alabaster REREDOS of 1867, much marble shafting, and C19 STAINED GLASS, including E windows with small, brightly coloured panels in the manner of *Beer*. – PULPIT. Jacobean, with panels covered with a simple carved all-over pattern. – MONUMENTS. R. Bellemaine † 1627. Wall-monument with kneeling figures beneath a steep pediment. – Another in the s (Slade) chapel with larger figures of Philip Cole † 1596 and his wife Joan, with an oculus of Longleat type above. – John Savery † 1696 as a child, a small figure reclining comfortably on a mat.

School. 1859, in granite and polychrome brick. Steeply pitched roofs, Gothic dormers.

Blatchford Park. Probably C16 in origin; remodelled in the C18 by the Rogers family. U-shaped, with a regular stone s front of 2–5–2 bays with Georgian sashes and parapet and an early C19 Tuscan porch. In the E wing, probably the main range of the older house, a good C17 dog-leg staircase with splat balusters. w wing added c. 1770. Landscaped grounds, with a lake created in 1827 by *James Green*.

Delamore. 1859 by *J. P. St Aubyn* for Admiral George Parker. 'A very handsome pointed mansion', wrote the *Ecclesiologist*, commending the architect for abstaining from 'needless irregularity and from superfluous turrets'. The garden front is indeed regular neo-Elizabethan, with canted bay-windows. The entrance side is in a more romantic asymmetrical Gothic, but with the main accents provided by strictly functional elements: a large traceried stair window, three-storey porch, and prominent chimneystacks. The material is granite ashlar. Two contemporary LODGES.

Fardel. Remains of a small medieval manor house, confusingly altered, owned by the Raleighs from the C14 and the Heles from the C17. An attractive ensemble from the w, glimpsed through garden gatepiers with large balls. On the l. the detached CHAPEL (licensed 1432). E window with two quatrefoils above three arched lights, side lancets, restored arch-braced roof, trefoiled aumbry, piscina and sedilia. An adjoining building, now a BARN, has straight-headed mullioned windows. The HOUSE is entered by the projecting lower wing, with two-centred archway and two-light arched traceried window above. Another traceried and transomed upper window to the solar wing. The lower end of the house has been much altered, and is without an upper floor. The medieval hall in the main range has a C16 inserted floor and a large end stack. In the room above, a plain barrel-vault and two three-light mullioned windows. In the upper cross-wing a ground-floor room with fielded panelling and C17 plasterwork (extended in the 1970s). Adjoining is a good, small C18 staircase, shifted so that it is no longer beneath its coved ceiling. Other extensions at the back, much altered.

SLADE. The seat of the Slades in the C13, the Coles from the C14 to the C17, then the Saverys. Modest exterior, the windows of the main s front alas uniformly Georgianized in the mid C20. The hall windows previously had Georgian Gothic sashes. Two-storey C16 porch, of large granite ashlar blocks, in contrast to the rubble of the rest. In the garden, fragments of the older parts of the overbearing upper cross-wing (demolished in the 1960s and externally late Georgian); others were used to make up the three-light mullioned windows above the garage in the truncated remnant.

The chief interest is the late medieval hall, still open to the roof, and the roof is indeed remarkable; five bays with enriched arch-braced trusses, two sets of purlins, and in between them intersecting curved wind-braces. At their junctions small lozenge-shaped bosses, sixty in all, mostly with foliage but one with a Tudor rose. Is all this original? The taste for overall patterning is comparable to the more spectacular North Devon roofs (Weare Giffard and Orleigh Court), although the carving here is less rich. A mixture of C16 panelling, with Flemish Flamboyant tracery reset above linenfold. C16 fireplace with upturned arch. Another granite fireplace upstairs in the remains of the W wing, in a room with C18 fielded panelling. Behind the hall a courtyard enclosed by outbuildings.

On a steep slope to the SW a fine BARN with a large basket-arched granite doorway and an old door. In the GARDENS an ancient hornbeam hedge reputedly of the time of Elizabeth I.

GREAT STERT. Symmetrical front with two-storey porch, three-light mullioned window, and four-centred doorway, dated 1674, typically conservative. Contemporary gatepiers with balls. Remains of a plaster frieze.

Moorland farmhouses include the following.

CHOLWICH TOWN. The home of the Cholwiches from the early C13 to the mid C19, a splendid granite group, its early manor origins stubbornly surviving in face of the encircling china-clay spoil heaps. Granite doorways with depressed arches and roll-mouldings; hollow-moulded mullioned windows. Similar door frames and windows, apparently re-used, in an adjoining outbuilding and adjacent farm buildings.

HANGER. One of the grander medieval farmhouses which evolved through to the early C18 without losing anything of its quality. Good granite doorways and windows. C17 hall ceiling with richly moulded joists and beams. Lower C18 cross-wing with contemporary panelling and staircase.

HIGHER HELE. An C18 farmhouse with a five-window symmetrical front built in front of an earlier house with a four-centred arched door frame with foliage decoration in the spandrels. Integral ash house. Barn and outbuildings form a courtyard to the side.

LOWER HELE. Remains of a large C16 farmhouse, the upper end largely remodelled in the C19, the lower, with granite mullioned windows, used as a store. Behind, through an archway, a courtyard of farm buildings.

BLATCHFORD VIADUCT. By *Sir James Inglis*, engineer, 1893. The longest of the five railway viaducts on the line through Devon. Rock-faced granite piers support ten round-headed arches of blue engineering brick, with granite spandrels and brick parapets. Granite piers of *Brunel*'s original timber bridge of 1848 alongside to the N.

SLADE VIADUCT, to the W of Blatchford, is similar, with seven *Brunel* piers beside it.

PREHISTORIC SETTLEMENTS. Prehistoric sites and reave systems abound on the moor, with particular concentrations on Penn Beacon, Stall Moor, at the head of the Yealm N of Dendles Waste, and all the way up the Erme valley. On PENN BEACON are stone rows, one single and one double, and spectacularly sited on STALDON (Stall Down) is a fine single row. On STALL MOOR is the longest row on Dartmoor (and, it is said, in the world). Single, it runs from a barrow with a retaining kerb at its S end for over 2 m. to a barrow on the top of Green Hill, Lydford, ascending a total of 333 ft, with a dip down to the Erme valley included. This, and the enclosures in the upper Erme valley (*see* Harford), make a most impressive expedition.

TIN WORKINGS. Medieval and post-medieval remains abound beside the Erme and the Yealm. A number of blowing-houses or tin mills survive, some still with their wheelpits still visible.

CORNWORTHY

PRIORY. S of the village remains of a house of Augustinian nuns, founded possibly in the C13. Only the GATEHOUSE of c. 1400 stands up, with a stair-turret on the r., and on the l. a separate entrance for pedestrians. Main vault of two bays, each with eight ribs and large, very worn bosses; the smaller passage barrel-vaulted, with transverse arches. Of the rest of the buildings only indistinct grass mounds can be seen. The church was only 70 ft long.

ST PETER. W tower of Ashburton type. The rest greatly redone c. 1820, see, for example, the windows with wooden intersecting tracery. S porch at the W end of the S aisle, entered from the W. On the N a two-storey vestry. Granite S doorway. In the porch a medieval image bracket. Nave and aisles of five bays. Granite piers of A type with capitals and arches of limestone. – Granite ALTAR of 1971, Lady Chapel ALTAR of 1969, both by *Alan Croft*. – FONT. Circular, Norman, of red sandstone. In the top frieze crosses saltire, in the main frieze palmettes (cf. Ashprington). – PULPIT. 1757, with large sounding-board with ogee top and trumpeting angel, given by John Seale of Mount Boone, Dartmouth. – SCREEN. Much renewed, the tracery standard, the coving gone. Traces of painted arabesques on the dado. – SCULPTURE. Legs of the crucified Christ, by *Robin Williams*. – CANDELABRA. Brass, C18. – Of the early C19 the BOX PEWS, with fat wooden posts at the W corners, and the partly preserved

WALL PANELLING with seats in the w window recesses. –
STAINED GLASS. Patterned quarries from the time of a restoration
of 1775–6, the coloured glass in the top lights perhaps early C19. –
MONUMENTS. Sir Thomas Harris and wife, 1610. Two recumbent
figures under a low tester decorated with strapwork (very
similar to the Carew monument at Exeter Cathedral), supported by
walls jutting out half-way from the back wall and three short
columns in front. Two kneeling figures against the tomb-chest
between fat volutes ending in big claw feet. The end volutes have
the delightful device of little lions thrusting their heads and front
paws through the scrolls. – John Seale of Mount Boone, Dartmouth,
†1777, by *William Pindar*. Architectural, with Corinthian
columns and some neo-classical decoration on top.

OLD VICARAGE, s of the church. Three-bay late Georgian front
with good doorcase, by *Joseph Rowe* of Exeter, 1784. By the
churchyard the former SCHOOL, 1866, coarse Gothic.

CORYTON   *4080*

ST ANDREW. Broad w tower with diagonal buttresses. Chancel with
lancet windows. The rest much rebuilt in 1885 by *Alfred Norman*
for the Newmans of Mamhead: chancel arch with Purbeck shafts,
two-bay N aisle replacing an older N transept. – STAINED GLASS
by *Kempe Studios* (nave, 1893) and *Kempe & Co.* (N aisle, 1910).

CORYTON HOUSE (former rectory). Built in 1836 for Richard Newman.
Tudor style, possibly by *Salvin*. Steep gables, diamond
stacks, mullioned windows.

In BRANDIS WOOD a HILLSLOPE ENCLOSURE of probable Iron
Age date.

COTLEIGH   *2000*

ST MICHAEL. The usual village church of the district: w tower with
diagonal buttresses, N aisle separated from the nave by piers of B
type with standard capitals. Chancel partly rebuilt 1867. Old ceiled
wagon roofs in nave and aisle. Square-headed N and s windows. –
FONT. Simple, Perp, octagonal quatrefoil panels.

COTLEIGH HOUSE (former rectory), E of the church. Early C19 and
attractively eclectic: stone quoins and hipped roof, a large round-
arched central porch with fanlight, but Gothick windows.

SOUTH WOOD FARMHOUSE. Medieval hall roof (early face-pegged
arched-brace jointed cruck truss) above a single-rib plaster ceiling.

COTTLES BARTON   *6000*
North Tawton

Small Elizabethan manor house, handsomely thatched; sympathetically
restored in the C19 (date plaque 1866). Main range of two

storeys with two rooms on either side of a central cross-passage, and a taller porch with the date 1567. The service end to the W reconstructed after a fire. In the hall to the E, plain fireplace in the front wall, also dated 1567. The parlour beyond (subdivided by a later corridor) has a good plaster ceiling, panelling, and a carved wooden overmantel with small caryatids. Behind this room a back extension of cob with a spacious staircase, rising around a solid core to the room above, with a branch off to serve a back wing. Stopped first-floor doorcases of c. 1600; the one to the main chamber is part of a former double doorway, so there was once a further room. An unusual inner porch to the remaining main chamber with fluted pilasters and panelled door. Overmantel with the Cottle initials (MC) and the date 1599. Plaster frieze and fine single-rib ceiling with a pendant, a design similar to the upper room at Westacott Barton, North Tawton (q.v.), added later, perhaps c. 1630. Evidence in the roof space indicates that there was once a total of four upstairs rooms with decorative plasterwork, three in the main range, one in the back wing. The most surprising survival is the remains of an oak-shingled roof, the shingles pegged to big oak boards (unique in Devon), now concealed beneath later thatch. On the ground floor of the back wing next to the stairs, a room with heavily moulded beams; in the other back wing C17 wooden mullioned windows.

COUNTISBURY

ST JOHN THE EVANGELIST. Very high up, with views on all sides, at the start of the path to Foreland Point. Tower rebuilt in 1835, with obelisks and balls instead of pinnacles. Nave 1796, chancel 1846. N arcade also 1846, with one octagonal pier and low arches. – FURNISHINGS still pre-ecclesiological, with texts under Perp arches on the E wall flanking a Perp E window with STAINED GLASS only as coloured borders. – One reset medieval BENCH END (chancel S wall) with crowned swan and arms. – The only other feature of real interest is the SCREEN with big long balusters, a fully developed cornice, and a broken pediment above, all well carved, about 1700.

GLENTHORNE. Built by the Rev. W. S. Halliday about 1830, in a wonderfully sheltered cove far below the Lynton–Porlock road and reached on a private road with serpentines as daring as in the Alps. The house was designed by Mr *Halliday* himself in an undistinguished neo-Tudor style. Pretty Gothick windows. (Library added in 1846.)

OLD BURROW. Visible as two concentric earthen banks, a Roman FORTLET overlooking the coast for a great distance. Excavation produced evidence for a date in the C1 A.D. The site clearly formed part of a system of military signal stations or watch towers along the Bristol Channel (cf. Martinhoe Beacon).

ROUND BARROWS. The A39 passes close by a number of ridge-sited examples.

WIND HILL. *See* Lynton.

COVE   9010
3 m. N of Tiverton

St John the Baptist. Chapel of ease, 1855 by *Edward Ashworth* on a medieval site. Nave, chancel, s porch, w bellcote. Tall, angular exterior, conventional Dec.

COWLEY   9090
Brampford Speke

St Leonard. A chapel of ease to Brampford Speke. 1867–8 by *Rhode Hawkins*, paid for by William Gibbs of Tyntesfield (cf. St Michael, Exeter). Nave, chancel, N porch, bellcote over the chancel arch. Simple unbuttressed exterior with paired lancets flush to the wall and three-light E window with large sexfoil. – Contemporary FITTINGS. – Bold stone PULPIT entered from the vestry.

Cowley House. Handsome front of two and a half storeys, stuccoed, with two full-height bow-windows. Built shortly after 1788 for William Jackson of Exeter to plans by his father, *William Jackson*, a musician and painter. The builder was 'Mr Hicks'. Restored for the Midland Bank c. 1980. (Good staircase with scrolled balusters.)

Cowley Bridge. Three-arched, ashlar, built in 1813–14 by *James Green*.

CRADDOCK HOUSE   0010
Near Uffculme

An attractive small Georgian mansion with an earlier back wing. Stuccoed, with a parapet. Main front with two canted two-storey bays linked by a colonnade with four elegant Ionic columns. The s side to the garden has a longer and larger Ionic colonnade, probably added in the early C19, extending across all eight bays. This and the regular fenestration behind conceal the difference in height of the back wing – see the false windows on the l., cunningly painted with blinds. In two downstairs rooms (NE and S) two very lavish marble fireplaces with vestal virgins as caryatids, said to have been brought from Italy in the early C19. The reeded doorcases and other fittings also look early C19. A spacious stair-hall fills the space between front and back wings, with Ionic columns at its entrance, and an imperial stair, plainly detailed. A curiosity of the house is the double walls (the result of a remodelling?), allowing for small closets in between on the s side. STABLES with Gothick windows and original panelled boxes; central archway blocked.

CREACOMBE   8010

St Michael. Rebuilt 1857, E.E. Nave, chancel, s porch, and bell-gable. – Plain early circular FONT. – STAINED GLASS. Perhaps by *Wailes* (RH).

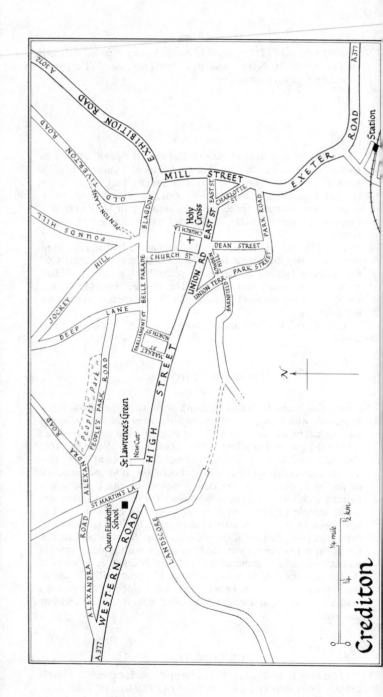

Crediton

CREDITON   8000

Crediton has an ancient tradition: it was the birthplace of St Boniface
and the seat of a bishop between 909 and 1050. The chief indication of
its early importance is the size of the church, which lies towards the E
end of the long, rather uneventful thoroughfare stretching for over a
mile from East Street to West Town. West Town, running from the
High Street to St Lawrence's Green, was a later development; for here,
in 1242, Bishop Jocelin endowed a hermitage adjoining the chapel of
St Lawrence in 'our new borough of Crediton'. The town prospered as
a centre of the woollen trade, especially from the C16 to the end of the
C18. Its early C18 appearance is known from a remarkably detailed
illustrated map (now in the Devon Record Office). The main
impression today is of brick and stuccoed houses of the later C18 and
C19, owing to several disastrous fires (the worst in 1743 when 460
houses were destroyed) and to road improvements, notably an
ambitious scheme of 1836 which removed the market from the High
Street and laid out Union Road and Charlotte Street in place of the
more tortuous older route which had connected East Street and West
Town. The population was c. 5,000 in 1801, and despite some C19
industry (leatherworking and malting) increased little until the 1970s,
when the town began to expand as a dormitory for Exeter.

CHURCHES

HOLY CROSS. No evidence remains for the pre-Conquest cathedral.
The church was collegiate from the early C12 until the Reformation;
hence its unusual plan, with an E part as long as the nave, and a   13
tower over the crossing as its main elevational feature. The lower
part of the tower is mid C12, as is apparent from the small windows
on N and S sides. The belfry has C13 pointed windows flanked by
trefoil-headed blind arches; battlements and pinnacles later. The
exterior otherwise, with its russet red castellated walls of sandstone,
is largely Perp in its general appearance, the result of rebuilding
from the early C15 onwards, although there is fabric of the C12 in
the transepts, and of the late C13 in the E Lady Chapel and SE
chapter house. The positions of these last two indicate that by the
time they were built the chancel was already its present size.
　　Inside, the lower Lady Chapel is separated from the chancel by a
solid wall, and the low arches of the crossing tower divide off
transepts, chancel, and nave. There is thus no unbroken vista
through the church. Its total length is 220 ft; the nave has six bays,
the chancel five. At the crossing appear the earliest parts of the
building: C12 piers with corner shafts with plainly decorated
capitals, scalloped or otherwise (scrolls, etc.), and pointed arches of
simple one-stepped moulding.
　　Next in date is the Lady Chapel, entered from the chancel aisles
by a straight ambulatory behind the altar wall – a rare feature in
Devon. It is a plain room with five later (Perp) windows. What there
is of capitals by the entrance and surviving in a fragmentary state
from the original windows is moulded and undecorated. The date
may be about 1300. The chapel was used as the grammar school
from the C16 to 1860 – hence the C16 door in the S wall, now blocked
– and restored in 1876–7 by *Hayward*. Double PISCINA, re-erected

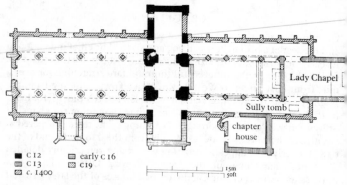

Crediton, Holy Cross: plan

Legend:
- ■ C12
- ▥ C13
- ▨ c. 1400
- ▢ early C16
- ▨ C19

Scale: 15m / 50ft

1921, with trefoil-headed arches under gables; a late C13 motif. It was formerly in the late C13 three-storeyed adjunct to the SE of the chancel, originally a chapel presumably open to the S aisle (see the blocked arches), with the collegiate chapter house, later the Governors' Room, on the top floor. The windows here all date from *Hayward*'s restoration of 1864.

The rest of the church – that is the chief impression the visitor gets of it – is Perp. Two-storeyed S porch with decorated battlements, vaulted inside, with foliage bosses; blank arches against the walls. The piers of nave and chancel of B type with capitals only to the main shafts and very broad wave-mouldings. Four-light aisle and chancel aisle windows. Clerestory (an unusual feature in Devon) with three-light windows in the nave, four-light in the chancel. Between the clerestory windows shafts rise to the roof from corbels right above the arcade capitals in the chancel, from corbels at the height of the fleuron-decorated cornice in the nave. Eight-light W window, imitated in the C19 in the E window. The date of all this is first half of the C15.

The church was called almost in ruins in 1413; in 1478 the beauty of the upper windows is praised by William of Worcester. However, the present appearance of the interior owes much to *John Hayward*'s restoration, which began in 1848 and continued to 1877. He renewed much dressed stone, exposed the blue–grey ashlar masonry of Thorverton stone, and reconstructed all the roofs. The nave roof has tie-beams with vertical struts, the chancel roof is ceiled. Chancel restored by *Hayward* and *Blomfield* in 1887–9. Further restoration in 1913 by *William Weir*.

FURNISHINGS. REREDOS. 1914 by *Fellowes Prynne*, stone, with carved frieze, dominating but rather pedestrian. – FONT. Norman, of table-top type, the FONT COVER by *Caröe*, 1904, in an energetic free Gothic. – Dec PISCINA in the altar wall, with multi-cusped head under a tall gable with sexfoil. – SEDILIA in the S chancel wall, early C15. Sadly mutilated remnants of three seats with elaborate if minute lierne-vaulting. Rounded backs with traceried panelling, and remains of good figure sculpture. Much original colour. The back of the structure, facing the aisle, includes a tomb-chest with vaulted recess above, set in panelling. It is traditionally called an Easter Sepulchre but is not in the usual place.

Above are the remains of a delicate figured frieze, also with much colour remaining. Annunciation at the E end; Nativity, Resurrection, Ascension (two scenes), and a soul carried by flying angels are also recognizable. – Oak CHEST with figure-carving of c. 1500. – Flemish MONEY BOX in the SE porch. – Other furnishings by *Hayward*: CHOIR STALLS 1877–87; NAVE BENCHES with traceried ends, and GOVERNORS' STALLS in the choir, 1900. – STAINED GLASS. Several good windows by *Lavers, Barraud & Westlake* (Lady Chapel E and S 1878, nave W 1884, chancel E 1897). – In the N aisle, window with West Country saints by *Hugh Arnold*, 1913, predominantly in cool blue. – S transept: armorial glass by *Horace Williamson*, 1926.

MONUMENTS. Three coffin-shaped slabs with foliated crosses. – Tomb-chest with panelled side embedded in a low stone wall S of the choir. – Sir John Sully † 1387 and wife, in armour and costume of the late C14, on a tomb-chest. – Sir William Perriam † 1605. Standing wall-monument, Sir William propped up on his elbow, his family kneeling in relief on the chest below. Pilasters l. and r., with ribbonwork, supporting a straight entablature and achievement. Pink marble, with good simple strapwork decoration at the back. – John and Elizabeth Tuckfield, 1630. Erected by the husband. His bust appears in a medallion at one side of her full-length seated figure, their son's at the other. The three parts are separated by black Ionic columns on very tiny plinths. The seated figure in black, too. The monument finishes with a broken pediment. An uncommonly satisfactory work of its date. – Redvers Buller Memorial. Mosaic and figure decoration on the E arch of the nave, 1911 by *Caröe*, executed (like much else in the church) by *Dart & Francis*.

ST LAWRENCE, West Town. A small chapel with lancet windows, all renewed. Restored (from a cottage) in 1920–1 by *Sir Charles Nicholson*.

ST BONIFACE (R.C.), Knowle Lane. *By Charles Ware & Partners*, 1870. Gothic. – SCULPTURE. Virgin and Child in cement and fibreglass, and relief of St Boniface felling the oak, both by *Kenneth Carter*. – STATIONS OF THE CROSS in mosaic, by *Arthur Goodwin*. – Abstract STAINED GLASS in the baptistery by *Charles Norris*.

CONGREGATIONAL CHAPEL, High Street. 1865, replacing the Broad Street Meeting House of 1757. Set behind a large forecourt, with manse adjoining. Quite a Baroque front, stone with Ionic pilasters, a pediment above, and arched entablature.

Also in the High Street the former BIBLE CHAPEL of 1860, enlarged in 1892, a simple brick building, three bays, pedimented, a contrast with the unprepossessing brick and stone WESLEYAN METHODIST CHAPEL in Union Street of 1892.

PUBLIC BUILDINGS

TOWN HALL and other public buildings. *See* Perambulations.

LIBRARY, Belle Parade. Nicely detailed, red brick with slate roof. One-storeyed, with boxed-out windows in the l. gable; c. 1980.

QUEEN ELIZABETH SCHOOL, St Lawrence's Green. Founded in 1547, rebuilt in 1860. A large complex. The original C19 neo-Tudor building faces the green, with parapeted schoolroom between two twin-gabled houses, red brick with stone dressings. C20 additions behind by the *County Council Architect's Department*; hall with arched windows and hipped roof of 1931–2 (*de Courcy Hague*); to the NW powerful classroom block of 1965 (*R. N. Guy*), three storeys built into the hill, the top floor oversailing, a good, unfussy design, the walls with pale blue spandrels articulated by black uprights.

SIR JOHN HAYWARD'S SCHOOLS (now Drama Centre), East Street. 1860 by *Hayward*. Purple stone with Bath stone dressings. Two large gables with small gabled dormers between mullioned windows.

PERAMBULATIONS

1. From West Town to the church

WEST TOWN has been least affected by C20 development. ST LAWRENCE'S GREEN is a pleasant start, laid out as a garden for Queen Victoria's Jubilee, and named from the chapel hidden behind the houses along the fork to the W. To the N the Queen Elizabeth School (q.v.). Nearby, WISTERIA, a cottage with an early C19 front with segmental arches. At the opposite end of the green another cottage with a cobbled alley beside it. From here the HIGH STREET leads down in a gentle curve, widening towards the town centre, at first with modest cottages, then with C18 and C19 terraces with ground floors converted to shops, with plenty of small alleys and courts behind reached through archways. Only a few individually notable houses: No. 52, C18, widely spaced windows with stone keystones and pedimented Doric doorcase; on the S side the LIBERAL CLUB, a tall three-storeyed house with a raised porch with stumpy granite columns. Set back up a lane, ERNEST JACKSON'S lozenge factory, plain C19 red brick, with the firm's offices of 1901 in front (No. 29). Further along on the S side the tall, emphatically late Victorian LLOYDS BANK and its neighbour, with hefty porch and over-sized window surrounds.

On the N side of the High Street the pedimented TOWN HALL of 1852 by *R. D. Gould*, built as public rooms for the Literary Society, DART AND FRANCIS's Ecclesiastical Art Works of 1884 (a few medieval touches to the façade), and the SHIP HOTEL, at the corner of MARKET STREET. This belongs to the improvements of the scheme of 1836. The urban Italianate of the hotel continues down the W side of Market Street with Nos. 2–6. The POST OFFICE of 1901, with broad striped stone and brick ground-floor arches, and the more demure two-storey CIVIC OFFICES make dignified neighbours. The covered market opposite has, alas, disappeared. It was built in 1836–9 at the expense of J. W. Buller of Downes (q.v.), one of the characteristic early C19 efforts to provide commodious market accommodation away from the busy main street (cf. Exeter, Tavistock). All that remains is two of the four corner buildings, on the N side of the site, with a row of contemporary shopfronts between: carefully composed red brick groups stepping down from three storeys to one, with windows under segmental arches. Between Market Street and North Street a row of contemporary shopfronts. On the site of the market itself an ineptly designed C20 FIRE STATION, sited with no sense of the civic order of the C19. In PARLIAMENT STREET, opposite the site of the main market entrance, OLD MARKET HOUSE, a red brick pub with rounded corner. Facing up North Street No. 4, specially handsome, stuccoed, with Tuscan porch and simple frieze below bracketed eaves, possibly incorporating much of the fabric of the manor house, shown on the great fire map as a three-storey Jacobean building. Further E, No. 7, GOTHIC HOUSE, early C19, with a battlemented part (now a screen wall) and Gothick windows.

Back up NORTH STREET to the High Street, which shortly afterwards splits in two. UNION ROAD of 1836 continues straight on towards the church. Its chief building is REDVERS HOUSE, built c. 1900 as a factory for Jackson's lozenges, a good solid red pile of three storeys with elaborate frieze and white brick window heads, converted to housing in 1984. Next door a MASONIC HALL of 1897. Further on the half-timbered CHURCH WORKERS' INSTITUTE and the WAR MEMORIAL in the form of a timber market cross have a more rustic air, standing on a terrace overlooking the playing fields in the valley (a view unfortunately marred by the ugly and prominent public lavatories).

One should now retrace one's steps to follow the older route uphill to the SE along UNION TERRACE. Nos. 1–5 are some of the best late Georgian houses in the town, set into the terraced slope. ST BREOCK has Soanian pilasters to the doorcase, No. 2 a rusticated stucco front with two full-height curved bays, a late C18 Doric doorcase, and a canopied balcony at the side, No. 4 a doorcase with Adamish capitals. The continuation is PARK STREET, with lesser cottages, and above the road level SPURWAYS ALMSHOUSES of 1557, cob and stone, with four lateral stacks, the original doors between them replaced by C19 Tudor casements. From here BOWDEN HILL descends towards East Town, an area now much cleared. But DEAN STREET, off to the S, still has a good continuous row of cottages, two with lateral stacks, suggesting that they are older than their C19 fronts, and a smaller group of buildings on the E side, one thatched, one C18.

2. Around the church and East Town

EAST TOWN, the more ancient but latterly the poorer part of the town, has suffered badly from piecemeal clearance. The church stands exposed to the main road since cottages here were pulled down in 1911, and there are only scattered houses to its N. In CHURCH STREET to the W, No. 1, C18, an ancient well with a stone arch tucked away beneath its cob garden wall. N of the church were the collegiate buildings, and presumably the pre-Conquest Bishop's Palace, of which there are no visible remains. The so-called OLD PALACE N of Church Lane incorporates medieval walls. Its front is pleasant early C18, red brick, with a trellis porch. Further N the VICARAGE, also hidden in large grounds, with a three-bay S front and a good late C18 doorcase. Close to its arched entrance from BLAGDON, PALACE COTTAGE, early C19 stucco with quoins and arched windows. Other older buildings in the neighbourhood include cottages at the foot of JOCKEY HILL and a long cob and thatched former MALTHOUSE, probably C18, behind in PENTON LANE, converted to houses in 1984; otherwise the slopes are covered by an indifferent spread of 1970s bungalows. In BELLE

PARADE a pair of early C19 houses and a large thatched cob cottage with a crinkle-crankle wall of rendered brick.

Earlier suburban development is more rewarding. Those interested should make a detour NW past the PEOPLE'S PARK (opened 1866) to ALEXANDRA ROAD, where there are some sizeable Edwardian houses including THE MOUNT, brick and half-timbering, and ST MARTIN'S, eccentric free Gothic, purple stone, half-timbering, oddly shaped windows.

Returning to the church, the final tour is to the E. CHARLOTTE STREET is the short cut to the Exeter Road of 1836. EAST STREET, the older route, has modest early C19 terraces, mostly only one window wide, and one grander house (now subdivided), THE LIMES, set back, a five-window front with later cement rendering and, inside, a massive C17 staircase with close-set turned balusters and square newels. E of the main Tiverton Road a nice group of thatched cottages around the small cobbled BULLER SQUARE. A few more scattered houses down the EXETER ROAD, especially CULVER HOUSE, early C19, plain red brick; WINS-WOOD COTTAGE and SPINNEY, a thatched range down PARK STREET; FAIR PARK on the hill above the road, with a plain C18 front and high enclosing walls; and further on towards the station, TAW VALE PARADE, an isolated, rather handsome development of C19 three-bay stucco houses, consisting of two pairs and the STATION HOTEL, with quoins and dentilled eaves. The STATION, opened in 1851, was built for the Exeter and Crediton Railway, a protégé of the G.W.R., possibly to designs by *Brunel*. It is a small, steeply gabled brick building with stone dressings and a slated roof, similar in type to G.W.R. wayside stations. Flat canopies on timber cantilevered brackets on both sides; on the platform side delicate cast-iron brackets give added support. At the W end a small timber SIGNAL BOX, typical of early designs by the L.S.W.R., which took over the line in 1862. Attractive FOOT-BRIDGE dated 1878.

See also Downes *and* Oldridge.

CREDITON HAMLETS

ST LUKE. Small Gothic chapel of 1835.

FORDTON. Overlooking the river with its old BRIDGE with cut-waters on one side, FORDTON HOUSE, with a late C18, stuccoed, five-window front with panelled corner pilasters and a low central pediment. Further up the lane, TROBRIDGE HOUSE, with a very good early C18 brick front: five bays, windows with segmental heads, stone keystones, and thick glazing-bars. Two-bay late C19 r. addition; wooden eaves cornice and pediment to the central door *c.* 1960. (Good early C18 staircase, panelling, and plaster ceilings with enriched ovals.)

EASTON BARTON. A medieval house with major C17 improvements (in 1644 it belonged to Philip Easton of Crediton). It makes a fine group with the adjoining courtyard of farm buildings, a rare C17 survival, little altered, reached through a gatehouse.

KEYMELFORD. A farmhouse of late C15 origin. Heavily smoke-blackened roof with louvre, and a contemporary hall window in the back wall: four lights with chamfered mullions and pointed heads – a rare survival. Altered in the C16–17, and extended in the C19 by a block in front of the service end and a cowshed and granary at the E end.

LITTLE HARFORD. A medieval farmhouse altered and extended in the C16–18. Original low partitions. The medieval roof is unusual: in addition to jointed crucks, a central post (smoke-blackened, although perhaps secondary) rises from the ground to the scarfed junction of two ridge sections, with a braced cross-piece carrying the purlin joints.

Other C15–17 farmhouses with good details are WOODLAND and EASTCHURCH; also No. 2 BARNSIDE VILLAGE and No. 16 UTON VILLAGE.

CREEDY PARK   8000
Sandford

The mansion built in 1846 by *William Burn* for Colonel H.R. Ferguson-Davie was destroyed by fire in 1915 and rebuilt in 1916–21 for Arthur Ferguson-Davie in a conservative Jacobean. Dark stone and rather forbidding. Main front with projecting wings, facing a terrace. Entrance at the back, with a two-storeyed balustraded porch and a big staircase window. Converted into thirteen units by *Lucas, Roberts & Brown, c.*1982. Earlier STABLES to the W, C18, two storeys, brick and rubble, central archway and oval windows.

CROCKERNWELL   7090
Near Cheriton Bishop

A hamlet on the Exeter–Okehampton Road. A chapel was licensed in 1390. The present church of HOLY TRINITY was converted from C17 cottages by *Edward Fennell* in the earlier C20. In the centre of the village one large roughcast house of five by five bays.

CROSS   4010
½m. N of Little Torrington

A splendid site on the S slope of the Torridge valley. An exterior of Regency appearance: 2–3–2 bays, roughcast, with rusticated quoins, two storeys with deep projecting eaves, and a Greek Doric porte-cochère. But this is an older house remodelled. The doorway is not central; and a top storey and a wing were removed in the C20.

The architectural importance of the house is its fitments acquired in the C18 by the Stevens family from Stow House near Bude in Cornwall, the Grenville mansion dismantled in 1720. (Other parts went to South Molton Guildhall, q.v.) Stow House was built in 1680–5. The grand staircase is 1685 at its most splendid, three flights around a square well, with splendid open-work carving in the Gibbons style: lush foliage, flowers, putti, etc. 94

The large Venetian window with fluted pilasters lighting the stair-case looks later. Other fragments from Stow in other rooms.

CROYDE

Quite a substantial hamlet in the parish of Georgeham, over-developed towards the sea.

ST MARY. Simple mission chapel of 1874, by the road. Plate tracery and lancets. No separate chancel. N aisle vaulted transversely. Original fittings.

COCKROCK. By *Oliver Hill*, *c*. 1925. Intended to be in the spirit of a Devon farmhouse, hence the thatched roofs and prominent stone chimneys, although the walls are of brick, whitened, with some weatherboarding. The effect is more of a cottage orné. Asymmetrical splayed wings, one of them ending in a circular workroom. Low mullioned windows in the Voysey tradition. Polygonal walled forecourt.

CRUWYS MORCHARD

House and church are close together, on their own.

HOLY CROSS. W tower with diagonal buttresses and pinnacles, and a brick top rebuilt in 1689 after a fire. C14 intersecting tracery to the tower and chancel windows. S aisle early C16 with straight-headed three-light windows and a five-bay arcade with the usual B type piers with standard leaf capitals. The unusual thing is the C18 alterations: white plaster panelling of nave, chancel, and aisle, plastering-over of the wagon roofs, insertion of the best early C18 SCREEN in Devon, in the grand classical manner with Corinthian columns with correct cornice and central pediment, addition of COMMUNION RAILS on three sides of the altar entirely with twisted balusters, simple BOX PEWS, simple PULPIT, and attractive bulbous FONT COVER with a dove. It would be interesting to know the date of the window tracery called with contempt in a report of 1855 'of Wardens' pattern'. Is the rain-water head of 1838 indicative? – STAINED GLASS. E window 1847. – MONUMENTS. John Avery †1695. Architectural, with Corinthian columns and angels flanking achievement. – William Stone †1852. Unusual small brass tablet: an angel with a scroll. – Good tombs in the churchyard, including an obelisk to Henry Shortridge Cruwys †1804, rector and last of the family's direct male line, recording that he 'lieth in a small house which he borrowed of his brethren the worms'. – Good early LYCHGATE of stone.

(SCHOOL. Small, dated 1844, in the Perp style.)

(OLD RECTORY. 1862, Tudor, unusually grand.)

CRUWYS MORCHARD HOUSE. The seat of the Cruwys family from the C12. The exterior now is of the late C17–18: seven-bay front with recessed three-bay centre with an C18 doorcase with Ionic pilasters. C19 parapet. One-bay E extension for a library, built in 1682. The W side rebuilt in 1732. C18 staircase from Enmore Castle, Somerset, installed in the C19; Ionic pilastered front doorcase from Bampton

House, Tiverton, added *c*. 1977. Inside, parlour with heavily moulded
C16 ceiling beams.

CULLOMPTON

ST ANDREW. As one cannot help approaching the church from the
W, the W tower will always be examined first. It is, however, the
last part in order of time, built only in the decade of the Reformation: 1545–9 (arms of Bishop Veysey of Exeter). It is 100 ft tall,
with stair-turret. The material is the local red sandstone, the
carved parts in Beer and Ham Hill stone. The quantity of decoration places it in the tradition of Somerset rather than of Devon
towers. Above the main W window three large panels with figures,
the Crucifixion, with the Virgin and St John, badly decayed in the
centre. The shafts flanking the panels, as over-decorated as the
Tiverton porch, display the beginning of an awareness of Renaissance motifs. Buttresses with three orders of gargoyles under pinnacles, pierced battlements, the top crowned by a good number of
pinnacles: at each angle five, and three more in the middle of each
side.

The other show side is the outer S aisle, the famous Lane aisle,
begun by John Lane, a cloth merchant, *c*. 1526. He died in 1529.
The S porch is in place of the W bay of the inner S aisle. An
inscription commemorating the donor runs at a comfortably low
level along the W wall of the Lane aisle so that everybody entering
the church should be able to read it and think of the donor. No
false modesty amongst the rich men of the late Middle Ages. The
Lane aisle has large windows (some probably re-used from the old
S aisle) separated by buttresses decorated with references to Lane's
sources of wealth: ships, cloth shears, teasel frames (for raising the
nap of the cloth), as well as the more usual monograms (cf. the
Greenway aisle at Tiverton). The battlements are decorated, as
indeed they are on the N side of the church too. Below the battlements of the Lane aisle a frieze with scenes from the life of Christ –
alas, now indecipherable.

On entering one finds a large, long, light interior: six bays of
nave with aisles, and the Lane aisle in addition. All the windows in
the aisles are of four lights, and there is a clerestory, a rarity in
Devon. No structural division interferes between nave and
chancel. In fact, the boarded wagon roof, on angel brackets and 43
with cross-ribs to all the panels (as it is usually done only for
'celures'), runs right through. The piers are tall and thin, of type
B, the capitals standard but with heads and figures besides leaves.
The Lane aisle is separated from the S aisle by curious piers,
buttressed towards the aisle. These buttresses have small figures of
saints in two tiers on their N, E, and W faces, sculpturally not
specially good (perhaps recarved). The aisle is fan-vaulted, a
gorgeous effect, inspired by the Dorset aisle at Ottery St Mary
which, in its turn, may reflect the Sherborne vault of *c*. 1475. The
unhappy position of the springers suggests that the vault may have
been an afterthought. The pendants have emblems of the Passion
of Christ and also cloth shears, teasel frames, and Lane's merchant's mark. On the floor is John Lane's tombstone, the brass

effigy lost. The church was restored tactfully in 1848–50 by *Edward Ashworth* (chancel rebuilt with grand Perp E window, chancel roof modelled on the nave, restored and strengthened with iron ties to counteract vibration from the railway).

SCREENS. The rood screen looks splendid right across the church, and glowing in warm sombre colours (renewed – who knows how often? In 1849 for example). It is coved to E and W, and has the original cornice and standard type A tracery. The rood beam high up also still exists, recorded as discarded in the churchyard in 1834, and later reinstated. – In the S aisle the curious GOLGOTHA, a unique survival, a massive oak base now in two pieces, carved roughly with rocks, skulls, and bones (original colour remains), with mortices for the rood figures. How it was fixed in position above the screen is unclear, except that the flat back suggests that it stood against a vertical surface. – The S parclose screen is similar to the rood screen but more cusped; the N parclose screen shows a curious straightening out of all the curves of Gothic arches, probably a very late attempt at putting reason into Gothic traditions. – BOX PEWS. Low, early C19; also SQUIRE'S PEW in the N chancel chapel. – WEST GALLERY. Jacobean on Ionic columns, like the screen as wide as nave and aisles together. The panels have the usual blank arches on stumpy pilasters and are separated by caryatids. – Other furnishings of 1849: elegant PULPIT with Perp tracery panels on slender wineglass stem, stone REREDOS, READING DESK. – CHEST. Iron-bound. – Among the mostly C19 STAINED GLASS, S aisle first from E by *Drake*, 1882; second from E 1930 by *Morris & Co*. – MONUMENT. Slab with foliated cross (S porch). An interesting design, growing like a tree, sun and moon on the sides.

UNITARIAN CHAPEL, Pound Square. 1912 by *R.M.Challice* of Exeter, the third on the site since 1698. Low red brick Gothic with adjoining schoolroom, in a walled burial ground.

CEMETERY, Tiverton Road. 1856. Two chapels, probably by *Ashworth*, well buttressed, with Dec tracery.

Cullompton consists essentially of one long main street, its length reflecting the town's prosperity as a centre of the cloth trade from the C16 to the C18. The exception is the area around the church, which, though prominent from afar, is tucked away down a lane, and stands in a pleasantly secluded churchyard with white-walled houses on two sides. To the NE the OLD VICARAGE, L-shaped with Tuscan porch, 1820 by *William Burgess* of Exeter, unfortunately pebbledashed. To the N, NORK HOUSE, 1888, carefully detailed in totally inappropriate harsh red brick and terracotta. Good contemporary interior fittings. To the S THE RETREAT, plastered cob, *c.* 1600, with good porch on timber posts (and a C17 black and white fireplace inside). QUEEN SQUARE and POUND SQUARE beyond, irregular spaces with rendered cottages (some C17) with Georgian doorcases, lie at the centre of an informal network of streets, suggesting the core of an old settlement predating the layout of Fore Street. LOWER BULL RING may be the site of one of the two cattle fairs. Now W from the church, past ST PATRICK'S, stuccoed, with heavy early Victorian window surrounds, pilasters, and bracketed eaves, to Fore Street.

FORE STREET has been too much rebuilt after fires (264 houses

destroyed in 1838) to be specially attractive, although the old street
pattern remains, with plenty of intriguing back courts reached by
archways through the houses. Up one of these, NEW CUT, the
METHODIST CHURCH. The inconspicuous location is typical of
C18 chapels (this one was rebuilt in 1872 to replace a chapel of
1764 destroyed by fire). The front has just a large arched doorway
and a tiny oval window below a hipped roof. On the W side of Fore
Street, behind later fronts, many houses with C16–17 features
remain, notably No. 26, with a screen visible in the alley leading to
the court, and No. 20 (the OLD TEA SHOPPE), a three-storeyed
C17 merchant's house with moulded ceiling beams and original
roof hidden below the present one. On the E side the WHITE
HART HOTEL, a dignified three-bay late Georgian stucco front
with Tuscan porch. Then on the W side the show houses of the
town. No. 8 has a broad timber-framed jettied front, unfortunately
shorn of its gables, but still with its C17 decoration of little Ionic
pilasters, brackets, and strapwork. Inside, ovolo-moulded axial
ceiling beams to the first-floor rooms and a rear newel stair.

Then, after a large four-centred archway (a C19 import),
WALRONDS, Fore Street's grandest mansion. Not at all urban in
character: a handsome, completely symmetrical rubble stone composition with large mullioned windows, the main range with three-
storey centre recessed between two far-projecting two-storey wings
(cf. Sydenham). Probably all of 1605, the date which appears on
the hall fireplace, with the initials of John Peter, a lawyer, who
acquired the property by marriage into the Parris family. The
association with the Walronds of Bradfield dates only from the
C18. The symmetry disguises a traditional plan with the ground-
floor hall divided from the entrance passage by a richly moulded
stud-and-panel screen, a superior version of the common vernacu-

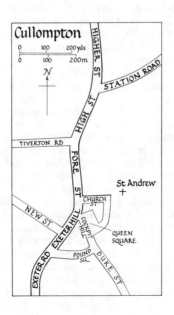

lar type of the South West. Good panelling in the NE room. Frieze with inlaid lozenges. The fireplace has pairs of crude Ionic columns and a band of four wooden arches over a large stone lintel. Contemporary decorative plaster ceiling; another in the room above. The staircase in this wing, remodelled with balustrading of c. 1700 around a solid core, projects at the back in a NW turret. The S end of the house has been altered on the ground floor, but in the upper SE room is the best ceiling, barrel-shaped, and another fireplace with the date 1605, served by a corbelled-out stack (the unheated room below was perhaps used for storage). On the garden side of this wing a small projecting stair with an octagonal wooden newel, in line with a large kitchen chimneystack. Beyond is a humbler wing extending S, built of cob, with a pair of jointed cruck trusses with posts extending down to a stone plinth.

96 A little further on Fore Street's third large house, the MANOR HOUSE HOTEL, an attractive mixture of 1603 (dated panel and initials TT for Thomas Trock) and 1718 (rainwater head at the back) when the house was remodelled for William Sellocke. Four-gabled jettied front between stone end walls, with upper windows on carved brackets. Bold hooded shell porch of the early C18, supported on pilasters. The back of the house also early C18, of red and blue brick, with windows with thick glazing bars, beneath a hipped roof with coved eaves. The front room on the l. was the former hall, with bolection-moulded panelling; staircase behind with closed string and twisted balusters. Part of an earlier newel stair survives above a back staircase. Opposite the Manor House No. 1, painted brick, with a late Georgian doorcase and windows with stone keystones.

N from here the road widens into a pleasant arc called HIGHER BULL RING (the characteristic shape for a cattle fair), where the best house is BARCLAYS BANK, red brick Regency, with two shallow full-height bows and a pedimented Doric doorcase. Opposite, the POLICE STATION of 1898, red brick, gable decorated with balls. On the edge of the town further N, much rebuilt former ALMSHOUSES founded in 1522, presumably the date of the four-centred stone archway.

SPORTS HALL, Meadow Lane. Designed by *G. W. Barrow* (District Architect *F. Rogers*). Striped brick, with recessed panels to enliven the blank walls.

LANGFORD COURT. A large house, originally late medieval, remodelled and enlarged in the C16–17, with one of the most complete displays of later C16 and C17 timber mullioned windows in Devon, and a pretty two-storeyed porch with pendants. The courtyard plan is of later date than the original hall block to the E (one closed truss with early yoked apex, smoke-blackened on the N side only). The long N service wing has seven pairs of jointed crucks, heavily smoke-blackened at the W end. In the S wing a common rafter roof, collar- and arched-braced, between pairs of jointed crucks, none of it smoke-blackened. Inside, stud-and-panel screens and a large end-stack with walk-in smoking chamber in the N wing, altered C17 staircase in the S wing. Massive cross-beams in the high-ceilinged hall block.

LANGFORD is an especially good hamlet of C15–17 houses, heavily disguised outside, on three-room cross-passage plans with classic

Devon house features and development. Was this an estate enter-prise associated with Langford Court?

(MOORHAYES. Farmhouse with plaster overmantel with arms of Elizabeth I.)

See also Hillersdon House.

CULMSTOCK

ALL SAINTS. Nicely placed just above the river Culm and its water meadows. The W tower would be quite ordinary, with buttresses of type B and a higher stair-turret, if there were not a yew tree growing out of its top at the meeting with the stair-turret. May it never be necessary to remove it! It may date from 1776, when the spire was taken away. The interior buff-washed and the whole extensively altered in 1825, when the roofs were raised, the rather awkward clerestory inserted, and the N aisle built, its windows ungainly Perp typical of the date, its arcade modelled on the medieval S arcade, its piers usual, of A type, with capitals only to the shafts. No chancel chapels; squint between S aisle and chancel. S aisle PISCINA with traces of paint, and graffito of Perp tracery on the credence shelf.* Shallow coved plaster nave ceiling and Perp-style chancel arch in plaster, both 1825. Decent wagon roof to chancel, and chancel fittings, 1879. – SCREEN. Stone, simple Perp, with a wide crocketed ogee arch for the entrance, re-erected for use as a REREDOS in 1835. – STAINED GLASS. S aisle E by *Wailes*, 1847, restored in 1897. – Also in the S aisle a good window by *Morris & Co.*, designed by *Burne-Jones*, 1896: Transfiguration and Angels. – COPE. The most valuable possession of the church, although cut about to convert it into an altar cloth. Restored in 1976–9. Late C15, and similar to the copes at Brixham (*see* Torbay) and Holcombe Burnell. The fifteen figures along the border orig-inally formed the orphreys. The main scene is the Assumption of the Virgin with angels and seraphim. The ground decorated with fleur-de-lys and pomegranates. A shield, formerly at the back, has the figure of Christ in Majesty. – SCULPTURE. Torso of a C15 draped figure, found in a cottage at Prescott.

BAPTIST CHAPEL, by the roadside at Prescott, in a walled burying ground. 1785, renovated 1892. Plain rendered rubble. Excellent interior with gallery, baptistery, and barrel-vaulted ceiling.

FRIENDS MEETING HOUSE, Spiceland. In an idyllic rural setting 1 m. outside the village. A meeting house stood here from the late C17. This one is of 1815, an outstanding survival, complete with its contemporary fittings. Rubble walls, hipped roof. S front with doorway and three windows, two for the large meeting house to the E, one for the smaller one and gallery to the W. In the main meeting house wood and metal CANDELABRA, four coffin stools, and the original SEATING: two tiers on an unpainted pine stand, and eighteen removable benches.

BARTONLANDS FARMHOUSE. Originally completely open to the roof. Jointed cruck trusses with yoke and saddle apexes. Good curing chamber.

*Information from Professor M. Swanton.

WOOLLEN MILL. Now dwellings. Three storeys, L-shaped, stone and brick. Of 1877–8, replacing an earlier mill. Until the 1930s water-powered; the metal frame of a 10ft diameter undershot wheel remains at the E end.

CULMSTOCK BEACON. On the summit a small 'beehive' HUT, much restored, possibly a rare surviving beacon hut of the C16.

DALWOOD

2000

ST PETER. Usual Perp in every way: the W tower, the arcade to the N aisle, the arch to the chancel chapel. N aisle with wagon roof. The other roofs and chancel arch are careful work by *Ferrey & Ferrey* of 1876–8. – In the E and NE windows fragments of medieval STAINED GLASS.

(TELEGRAPH COTTAGE, Stockland Hill Road. A former semaphore station of *c.* 1800.)

LOUGHWOOD BAPTIST CHAPEL. Virtually in the farmyard of Loughwood Farm. Rubble walls, thatched roof (restored by the National Trust). Probably of *c.* 1700. Simple interior, with early C19 BOX PEWS, octagonal PULPIT against the E wall (covered total immersion font in front), W gallery, and a nicely lettered tablet to the Rev. Isaac Hann, 'An Old Disciple', †1778 aged 88: 'Wit sparkled in his pleasing face: with Zeal his soul was fir'd: Few Ministers so humble were: Yet few so much admir'd.'

DARTINGTON

7060

ST MARY. Expensively rebuilt on a new site by the main road in 1878–80 by *J. L. Pearson*, re-using material and fittings from the old church near the Hall (*see* below). 'A good but not thrilling church; detail all in very good taste' (Goodhart-Rendel). Pearson copied the plan of the old church but increased the height by setting the old Beer stone arcades on Portland stone bases. Old stonework also in the chancel window, and notably in the S porch, with its handsome stone vault. The Perp tower is entirely new, of an un-Devonian elaboration, with tall crocketed pinnacles, figure carving by *Hems*, and a frieze of quatrefoils below the battlements. – HIGH ALTAR. From the old church, installed in 1836 by Archdeacon Froude, made from oak from the hall roof. – SCREEN. Centre medieval; coving and aisle sections by *Herbert Read*, 1913. – PULPIT. Of *c.* 1500, with the usual thick upright; the other details apparently confused at re-erection. – STAINED GLASS. Chancel and S chapel E by *Clayton & Bell*.

Dartington is famous for architecture of two periods. The medieval remains are among the most extensive surviving establishments of a great secular magnate; the 1930s buildings include some of the first examples in the country of the newly fledged International Modern style. The preservation and restoration of the first group and the creation of the second arose from the bold and successful reincarnation of Dartington under Leonard and Dorothy Elmhirst as a centre for experiments in rural reconstruction and progressive education. They

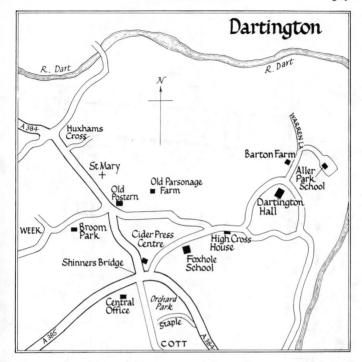

bought the estate in 1925 and began by restoring the largely derelict medieval buildings, adding new farm buildings and schools as the need arose. Economically the aim of the Dartington Trust was to establish that an estate managed on the latest scientific principles can pay. It started rural industries (notably spinning and tweed-weaving) and a company of builders (Staverton Builders, which later became independent of the Trust). Other early efforts (not all still operating) included a sawmill, a firm providing electrical services, a model farm for milk production, and a cider-making plant. Developments outside the estate included the large glassworks set up after the Second World War at Great Torrington in North Devon.

The buildings for these varied activities, the new housing for the estate workers, and the schools are scattered among the various older hamlets of the parish, to no single coherent plan or design – an interesting reflection on the pre-planning era when such haphazard rural development could be countenanced. More recent attempts to follow this pattern for new ventures have been resisted by the local planning authorities.

Medieval Dartington

DARTINGTON HALL, of the second half of the C14, vies for pre-eminence with Haddon Hall and Wingfield Manor in Derbyshire as the most spectacular domestic survival of late medieval England. Dartington belonged to the Martin family from the early C12 to the mid C14. It passed to the Crown in 1386, and in 1388 was granted by

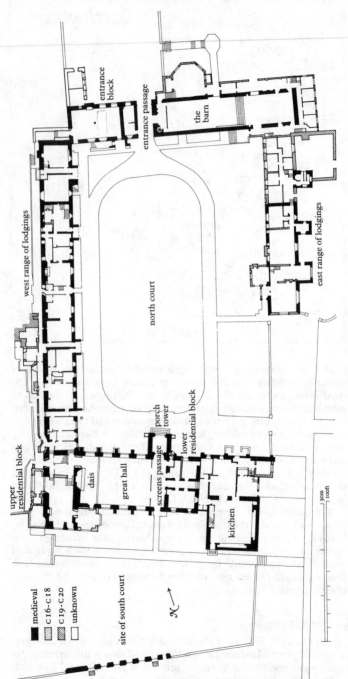

Dartington Hall: plan

upper residential block

west range of lodgings

entrance block

entrance passage

the barn

north court

east range of lodgings

porch tower

dais

great hall

screens passage

lower residential block

kitchen

medieval
C16–C18
C19–C20
unknown

site of south court

30 m
100 ft

N

Richard II to his half-brother John Holand, Earl of Huntingdon and later Duke of Exeter, who married John of Gaunt's second daughter. For a time he was a leading magnate, but he spent much of his later years in Devon, far from the court. He was executed in 1400 for plotting against Henry IV, but the family retained Dartington until the line ended with the death of Henry Holand, the fourth Duke, in 1475. Among later owners and tenants the most eminent were Margaret Beaufort, the mother of Henry VII, who lived here from 1487 to 1509, and Henry Courtenay, Earl of Devon, from 1525 to 1539. Sir Arthur Champernowne bought the estate in 1559, and it remained in his family until 1925, when it was sold to Leonard and Dorothy Elmhirst. The medieval buildings, by then much altered or derelict, were restored with meticulous craftsmanship by *William Weir* from 1926 to 1938.

Dartington illustrates one of the most dramatic of those sudden reversals of fortune encountered by buildings decaying after centuries of slow social decline. Pevsner's reaction of 1952 was: 'It may be objected that the C14 Dartington has re-emerged almost too perfect from under the hands of the careful and wealthy restorers. The setting and the buildings certainly combine the genuine with the comfortable and liveable-in to a degree which must appear even more ideal to the American than to the sloppier British.'

The buildings are grouped round a huge COURTYARD, 265 by 164 ft, the largest in a private residence before the C16. The hall range on the s side is the work of John Holand. The Chapter Act Book of Exeter Cathedral records activity shortly after he acquired the estate in 1388; the white hart of Richard II on the porch tower vault gives a *terminus ante quem* of 1399. Of the same date or slightly later the long two-storey ranges on E and W (the E side incomplete), still showing the occasional contemporary feature. The cruder N range with the entrance archway is more difficult to date, but the roof structure is probably of the second half of the C14. Holand was executed in 1400, apparently before he had time to build the grand gatehouse that one might expect for an establishment on this scale. Private apartments were provided at either end of the hall and in further buildings formerly grouped around a smaller courtyard to the s, which survived until the late C17.

Detailed examination should begin with the HALL RANGE. 57 Three-storey porch with a handsome two-centred archway with wave-moulded outer order and shafts below the soffit (the windows above are Champernowne alterations of the C16). Inside, an eight-rib vault with Richard II's white hart on the central boss surrounded by the wheat-ears of John Holand. The inner door, with two more finely moulded continuous orders, leads into the screens passage. On the l., the classic medieval arrangement of the three stone doorways which led to the buttery, pantry, and kitchen, and a fourth door to the stairs giving access to the apartments over the porch and service rooms.

The hall itself is on the grandest scale (*c.* 69 by 38 ft) and among 58 the finest of its date in the whole of England. Of the original fabric, apart from the walls, there remain the moulded two-centred rere-arches of the windows, the carved corbels for the roof timbers, the doorway in the sw corner formerly leading to the solar wing (cf. Compton Castle), and the huge fireplace (17 ft wide) with moulded flattened arch, directly behind the dais – a rare arrangement, for the open hearth remained popular in the grandest halls until the C16. The weak window tracery is, surprisingly, mid C18: it appears in late C18 views, whereas Buck's print of 1734 shows square-headed Tudor windows. *Weir*'s attractive post-and-panel screen was based on one in the Church House Inn at Torbryan, nearby – a vernacular rather than an aristocratic model. The banners with abstract patterns were designed by *Elizabeth Peacock* in the 1930s to represent the departments of the estate at that time.

The impressive five-bay open timber roof is entirely *Weir*'s, inspired by the shadow of the medieval timbers remaining on the end wall after the old roof had been taken down in 1813. Holand's roof, known from George Saunder's drawings of 1805 (only discovered after the restoration and now in Exeter City Library), made use of an interesting combination of the fashionable hammerbeam type with a crown-post system and lateral braces – an experimental stage in the development of the hammerbeam roof probably just preceding Herland's remarkable technical and aesthetic achievement at Westminster Hall for Richard II (begun 1394). Weir's reconstruction is more conventional, with a slightly wider span than once existed between the hammer-posts, with three tiers of wind-braces, and no crown-posts.

The first door in the screens passage opens on to a spiral stair leading to a small room over the porch and a larger one over the buttery and pantry, both with original fireplaces. The C16 Champernownes altered the larger room drastically when they put in the decorative plasterwork at the N end. Weir added the C16 panelling from Shepley, near Huddersfield, and plain solid beams. On the floor above is a similar pair of altered rooms. In the E gable wall above the ceiling the plaster reveals evidence of a crown-post roof supported on a cambered tie-beam over this part of the hall range. Beyond, slightly to the NW, with its own tiny court, screened from the main court by a buttressed wall, is the large free-standing KITCHEN (now refectory), 33 ft square in plan. It was a roofless ruin before Weir set to work. In adjoining walls, two massive fireplaces, their arches rebuilt, one with a reconstructed hood. Six tall windows (original in the E and S walls) with shouldered arches high up.

The PRIVATE HOUSE at the upper end of the hall range, probably always of three storeys and ostensibly neo-Elizabethan, is in origin late C14, with a twin stack of that date serving an upper room as well as the hall. The present approach from the hall may also be original. The block was much altered by the Champernownes, with a rebuilt gabled top floor and a C16 extension to the S. Some C18 alterations, including Venetian windows on the S side, were replaced when the house was Gothicized in 1846–51 according to proposals by Archdeacon Froude (a trustee during a Champernowne minority). More elaborate restoration schemes by *Pugin* came to nothing. Much of the C19 work disappeared in 1928–30, when *Weir* renewed all the S and W windows. The interior today is largely Georgian, with a mid C18 marble-paved hall, restrained plasterwork, a fine staircase with twisted and fluted balusters, and a suite of rooms on the first floor of the adjoining W range including a large panelled reception room with fluted pilasters.

The WEST RANGE is nationally one of the most notable survivals of a range of medieval lodgings. It is not precisely aligned with the hall range and may be a few years later – probably *c.* 1393–1400. Much of the detail is altered, but one can still recognize the division into five groups of lodgings, each of four rooms, two on each floor, reached from the projecting porches. The group at the N end is the best preserved, with its four-centred doorways within the porch, two-light shouldered windows with transoms, and exterior staircase to the upper rooms. Each chamber was self-contained, with plastered walls, a garderobe opposite the doorway within a (now destroyed) wooden structure on stone foundations, and a fireplace (see the row of stacks along the back wall). The upper chambers, divided by timber partitions, were open to the roof. The remaining lodgings lost their outer stairs and one porch in the C18. The interiors are much altered; in one, an interesting early C16 graffito of a ship.

The EAST RANGE (now offices, common rooms, etc.) was partly demolished in the early C19, when the remainder was converted to coach house and stables. C18 drawings show that it too once consisted of a series of lodgings extending to the hall range. The details (two-centred doorways, windows without transoms, larger garderobes in stone projections) suggest that it was slightly earlier than the W range. These two extended ranges, lining either side of the courtyard, provided ten pairs of lodgings on the W and probably fourteen pairs on the E – a total of forty-eight separate chambers, built to a high standard of comfort to accommodate Holand's household officers and retinue.

The ENTRANCE RANGE is not a proper gatehouse. The large carriage arch on the axis of the hall porch is curiously crude, round-headed, without dressed stone voussoirs; there is no other datable masonry as the windows have all been renewed, and the roof-lights inserted on the N side create a bad first impression. But the interior is rewarding. In the ground-floor room a sturdy central octagonal braced post, in the two upper rooms (now library) a much restored roof of complex type: base cruck trusses with a crown-post construction above. The short collar purlins tenoned in perhaps suggest construction by local carpenters unfamiliar with this type of roof. The intermediate trusses to the room over the gateway, and the end trusses with collars supported by two posts embedded in the wall, have similarities to the former roof at the lower end of the hall range, as does the crown-post construction with the upper part of the former roof of the great hall, so a date contemporary with the late C14 hall seems likely. Could this block have been a workshop and dormitory built by local masons immediately after Holand took possession of the site in 1388? (Cf. a similar structure of 1440 in this position at Wingfield Manor, Derbyshire.)

The courtyard is completed to the E by a low BARN of fourteen bays, perhaps late medieval or C16, which formerly had an opening on each side. It was converted to a theatre in 1933–8 by *Robert Hening* and *Walter Gropius*. To the N a polygonal C19 horse engine house.

S of the hall range is an isolated wall with seven four-centred arches which excavations of 1962 showed to have belonged to a medieval gallery, 84 ft long, part of a complex range linked by two wings with the rooms at either end of the hall. So here was a second COURTYARD, not very large and irregularly planned, with a two-room block to the SE and two chambers projecting from the W range. There is evidence to suggest that it was built in the late C14 and abandoned in the latter part of the C15. It may have provided private quarters for John Holand and his family. Dartington Hall, therefore, is not only an entirely unfortified mansion built in a defensive age, but marks an important stage in the development of the double courtyard house which became so popular with leading magnates and courtiers in the C15 and C16.

The GROUNDS to the S were laid out on the grandest scale by the Elmhirsts, assisted initially by *Avray Tipping* in 1927 (private garden), and more extensively by the American landscape architect *Beatrix Farrand* in 1932–5 (courtyard and woodlands) and *Percy Cane* in 1946–8 (flight of steps and vistas). The centrepiece is the so-called Tournament Ground (possibly a relic of C18 or early C19 landscaping), a wedge-shaped lawn surrounded by parallel grass terraces. Around it, winding paths and many magnificent specimen trees and shrubs. A few well sited SCULPTURES: the splendid Reclining Woman by *Henry Moore*, 1947, and two smaller works by *Willi Soukop*: Two Granite Swans, and Bronze Donkey, 1938.

The TOWER of the old church lies immediately to the N of the Hall. Within it several Champernowne MONUMENTS, the largest a wall-monument with Sir Arthur †1578, his wife and eight children kneeling before two prayer-desks; caryatids and strapwork on the base, frieze and cornice later. Also Henry Champernowne †1656, a plain architectural tablet of Ashburton marble; Rawlin Champernowne †1774, coloured marbles; and some minor slate tablets.

The Twentieth-Century Buildings

The variety of architectural styles of the new buildings resulted from an unusual combination of toleration and pragmatic innovation. 'The Trustees wished in every way to combine function, economy and delight, but since most of their needs were special, it was not easy to find architects who had specialised in the needs of children, or of cows, or chickens, or of wage earners or of factory buildings, between the years of 1928 and 1935.'[*] During those first years, architects were selected on the basis of their previous experience, and not for any stylistic qualities. The result was a curious mixture: *William Weir*'s painstaking restoration of the medieval buildings; versions of Arts and Crafts or Tudor for the first school and estate cottages; *Oswald Milne*'s less impressive watered-down neo-Georgian; *Louis de Soissons*'s simple, inexpensive groups of workers' cottages; and, at the same time, the first of the buildings by *William Lescaze* in the International Modern style that was to become the Trust's accepted mode in the 1930s. Although these rationally planned buildings did not set out to shock, they undoubtedly increased Dartington's reputation for the outré at the time.

After the Second World War there was more overall planning

[*] Letter from L. K. Elmhirst to N. Pevsner, 1952.

(*Elizabeth Chesterton*'s plan for Dartington and Totnes district, 1957, and others for Dartington Hall in 1965 and 1971). Nevertheless much of the post-war building is disappointing; indifferent speculative housing and school extensions which have compromised the clarity of the pre-war work. The exception is the refreshingly crisp group of houses at Hunters Moon (*Leonard Manasseh Partnership*). Plans of 1976 by *Tom Hancock* for the Trust for further clusters scattered over the parish were rejected by the local planning authorities.

ALLER PARK (Junior School). 1929–31 by *Ides van der Gracht* of the New York firm of *Delano & Aldrich* (architects of a student building at Cornell University built in memory of Dorothy Elmhirst's first husband). Aller Park was the first Dartington School, intended as a nursery school for the children of Dorothy Elmhirst and the estate families. Solidly and expensively built of dressed limestone, with large gables, tiled roofs, and sturdy chimneys, in a lavish Americanized Tudor. Pleasant symmetrical garden front with three coped gables, the centre one with a little oriel. In between them ground-floor classrooms with large arched orangery-type windows and roof terraces above, the l. one with an outdoor fireplace. Metal casements; surprisingly, they do not jar because of the generous reveals. On the upper floor at the back bedrooms and amazingly lush little tiled bathrooms.

The school turns its back on the three BOARDING HOUSES across the road, Blacklers (1933), Chimmels (1934), and Orchards (1935), their straightforward International Modern idiom a total contrast. Three rectangular blocks in staggered parallel, their gleaming white render set off by horizontal bands of windows divided by slate-grey panels. Blacklers was designed by *Lescaze*; the other two are to a similar design, slightly modified by *Robert Hening*, the executive architect (smaller recessed porches, with slightly thicker and less elegant pilotis). The group was at first romantically set among trees; the setting is now balder. Their floating quality has been diminished by an unsympathetic extension of 1964, cobbled on to Orchards, and by later fire escapes. At the far end of each block the house-parents' flat, divided from the rest by an entrance hall and staircase with a large window. The two later blocks have in addition balconies along their E sides. Beyond Blacklers, a large but undistinguished group of 1964 by *Acland, Barton & Smith*: a hexagonal DRAMA HALL with stridently purple brick walls, but a pitched roof with nicely graduated slates, and a rectangular sports hall, linked by a common foyer.

On the road to Aller Park School, four pairs of cottages. The two stone groups of 1926–7 (Nos. 1–4), well detailed, with big stacks and handsome slate roofs, were some of the first new buildings on the estate. By *A. Fincham*, clerk of the works (Nos. 1–2 with the assistance of L. K. Elmhirst and others). Nos. 5–8, in a different version of Arts and Crafts, roughcast, with the upper floors boarded, are of 1928–9 by *Rex Gardner*.

FOXHOLE (Senior School). 1931–2 by *Oswald P. Milne*, in a rather feeble, formal neo-Georgian. Plans for Foxhole had been begun before William Curry was appointed headmaster (*see* High Cross House, below), so nothing came of his protégé Lescaze's design for a progressive Junior School (a spine block with ranges running off at right angles). Milne's school is on a quadrangular plan, the front two-storey range with dining hall, the back with assembly hall, distinguished from the Georgian sashes of the rest by upper circular windows. The flanking lower buildings were originally library and art room. The classrooms (at first one-storeyed) are at the corners of the quadrangle, deliberately split up, and the living quarters in four (later two) houses in the side ranges (with separate bedrooms, and boys and girls not segregated, both revolutionary ideas at the time). At the back, partly hidden by later extensions of 1960–7 (*Barron & Smith*), a GYMNASIUM by *Lescaze*, 1934, very simple and functional, steel-framed and rendered, with a roof designed for outdoor recreation, and a slightly taller staircase tower. To the E a polygonal ART CENTRE, 1962, poorly detailed, its hexagonal module echoed quite pleasantly in the hard landscaping, and a DRAMA CENTRE of 1967, rendered, with pitched roof, both by *Michael Smith* of *Acland, Barton & Smith*.

177 HIGH CROSS HOUSE (Headmaster's House). 1931–2, the first essay in the International Modern Style at Dartington, and one of the first in England. *William Lescaze*, a Swiss architect who had settled in America, was commissioned by the newly appointed headmaster, William Curry, previously headmaster of the progressive Oak Lane County Day School, Philadelphia (1929), the building which had made Lescaze's reputation in America. A stark geometric composition, the smooth rendered exterior concealing a structure of brick cavity walls with steel beams for cantilevers and wide spans (instead of the reinforced concrete originally specified, which was beyond the local builders). Long two-storey range to the road (originally painted grey–blue in contrast to the impractical white of the rest); entrance between garage and servants' wing and kitchen. Metal casement windows, mostly in horizontal bands. The main rooms project irregularly into the garden. Here the composition is more interesting: low sw study with rounded end and generous terrace on its flat roof serving the guest rooms over the garage; taller se living room and adjoining dining room on a higher level. An ingenious mixture of outdoor and indoor spaces: inset open porch with thin steel supports, a sleeping balcony at the corner (marred by later glazing) next to the main bedrooms, and a second-floor terrace, shielded from the road by the top of the staircase.

The interior reflects the same aesthetic of abstract geometry: no mouldings – the smooth pressed steel doorcases were imported from America – the occasional curve, the play with different levels and with asymmetry, seen to good effect in the fireplaces with dark tiled surrounds, large marble lintels, and off-centre flues. The walls were originally painted in different tones (yellow and white in the hall, white and grey in the living room), not dead white throughout. The spaces are kept simple by concealed lighting (no overhead lamps) and well-made built-in furniture, for example the wall of two-way cupboards between dining room and kitchen.

WARREN LANE (formerly Park Road). At the corner by the approach to Aller Park, a pair of pre-Elmhirst estate cottages, of stone. The other houses in Warren Lane were built by *Lescaze*, with *Robert Hening* as executive architect, in 1934–8, in simplified versions of the style introduced at High Cross, in striking contrast to the earlier cottages of Aller Park. They form the most consistent International

Modern group at Dartington. Four pairs of workers' cottages were intended, but only Nos. 3–4, of 1934, were built to this plan. Apart from their stylistic innovations they departed from tradition by omitting the conventional little-used parlour and providing only a fitted kitchen facing the road and a large back living room facing w (so the breadwinner could enjoy the evening sun). Nos. 5–7, a similarly designed group of three, set closer to the road so as not to encroach on the agricultural land, date from 1935. Nos. 8–9, of 1938, painted brick instead of rendered, are larger four-bedroomed houses with garages to the road and balconies to the gardens, and have some extra touches of interior elegance: a curved wall to the living room and a circular skylight over the staircase.

No. 10, The Warren, is a more ambitious house, designed in 1935 for the dancer and choreographer Kurt Jooss, who taught and worked at Dartington from 1934. 'I am hoping that this house will give us an opportunity to make it a very distinctly "slick" house,' Lescaze wrote to Hening. As at High Cross, the best sides face the garden, with Lescaze's favourite motifs of recessed veranda adjoining the dining room (the free-standing steel support now enclosed in the later kitchen extension), a balcony over the projecting dance studio, and an upper roof terrace. The somewhat bleak front of two and three storeys, rising steeply above the road, has been altered tactfully by *Robert Hening*, in the spirit of the original, by the addition of a projecting garage and enlarged kitchen and utility room on the l. side (1969). The studio on the N side was subdivided *c.* 1964 when the house was used as students' rooms, regrettably with the loss of the original ribbon windows. Inside, the most notable feature is the serpentine wall between the spacious entrance hall and the living rooms, repeated on the generous first-floor landing, which serves all the bedrooms, including those of the servants, unlike High Cross. An opposing curved wall to a former bathroom has been removed. As at High Cross, the details are well finished: metal doorcases and skirtings, tiled fireplaces, staircase with flush panels and laminated rail, and much built-in furniture.

ARTS CENTRE, E of the Hall. A group of three buildings around a courtyard, much extended and added to over the years, and of no special merit. On the S side the DANCE SCHOOL, with a large hall, 1930–2 by *O.P. Milne*, enlarged 1934–8 by *Robert Hening*, and given a post-war foyer with large boarded gable in 1966. To its E the MUSIC ROOM, with bowed end and windows high up (1930–2), with extensions of 1966 by *Hening & Chitty*, and to the w the THEATRE SCHOOL, in utilitarian grey brick, by *Hening & Chitty*, 1967.

HIGHER CLOSE STUDENTS' CENTRE, across the road to the N of the Hall. 1963 by *Hening & Chitty*. Three sawtooth-fronted blocks linked by communal rooms, sited on a slope to take advantage of the views to the E, but distressingly ugly when one looks down on their flat roofs and poorly detailed backs from the car park above; not a good introduction to Dartington for the newcomer. (The intention was to preserve the distant views from the car park.) For the residents there are well contrived terraces and steps leading down to pleasantly planted courtyards and a pool.

BARTON FARM, near the road close to the Hall. House and farm buildings 1927–30 by the clerk of the works *Albert Fincham*; traditional buildings to house the farm previously within the Hall court-yard.

BARTON FARM COTTAGES, along the road. 1931 by *O.P.Milne*, white-painted walls, well detailed roofs (pairs of gables with swept eaves).

OLD PARSONAGE FARM. Built from 1931–2 as an experimental intensive dairy farm. Designed by *O.P.Milne* and the Danish farm manager *C.F. Nielsen* (with *J.R.Currie* and *G.F.Ventres*). Innovative T-shaped concrete-floored cowshed, with much attention to drainage, ventilation, and mechanical equipment. White-painted brick cottages by *Milne*, 1931; projecting hipped ends, wooden casements.

OLD POSTERN (former Parsonage). A substantial medieval hall-house converted for the Elmhirsts in 1927, when the restoration by *William White* of 1860 was much diluted. Rendered porch with corbelled-out oriel; two-centred inner archway. Hall with five-bay arch-braced roof with three sets of chamfered purlins, exposed after White had removed an inserted floor. Windows all renewed. Screens passage with moulded beams. The E wing rebuilt in the C19, the rest much remodelled, the courtyard beyond the hall roofed over. Unappealing brick hostel for students added behind in 1969 (*R. Hening*).

HUXHAMS CROSS. 1932 by *L. de Soissons*, invited to work at Dartington because of his experience in low-cost housing at Welwyn Garden City. A group of twenty-one houses for estate workers, cheaply built (*c.*£500 per house) of concrete blocks with asbestos roofs, but attractively laid out on three sides of a green, with just enough variety of grouping and roof-heights to give interest. One-storey houses at the ends. The elegantly reticent details – shallow-pitched roofs with broad eaves, rectangular-paned bay-windows neatly linked to the porch roofs – contrast favourably with the fussier 'executive houses' of the 1970s on the slopes beyond.

BROOM PARK, Week. 1932. Another group of *L. de Soissons*'s estate workers' houses, similar to Huxhams Cross but with a more formal symmetrical layout designed to take advantage of the view to the S. A central row of four pairs, with four more in each flanking cul-de-sac. The vista is ineptly blocked by a mediocre one-storey block added in the 1970s. Both Huxhams Cross and Broom Park were built by one of the first Dartington enterprises, Staverton Builders, under *A.E.Malbon*, previously general manager of Welwyn Builders.

CENTRAL OFFICE, Shinners Bridge. 1935 by *Lescaze*, an elegant white-rendered, horizontal-windowed, one-to-three-storey group on an asymmetrical H-plan. Planned with offices in the front range, lower laboratories and library behind (the upper end of the back range at first of one storey, raised, and extended by a boiler house, 1960–1). The buildings are neatly set on rising ground, so that the entrance (in the bar of the H) is at first-floor level. The lower end of the front range, originally on stilts with car-parking beneath, has been converted to further offices, as was envisaged in the plans. Spacious entrance hall with exposed steel supports. Well detailed staircases.

In the neighbourhood of Shinners Bridge several of the early buildings of the various Dartington enterprises. Near the central office the SAWMILL, 1931–2 by *O.P.Milne* (with *G.Turner* and *G.F.Ventres*). Straightforward wooden-boarded sheds, now disused. Further E the former TEXTILE MILLS, also by *Milne*, 1930–1, on the site of an older mill. By the side of the road at Shinners Bridge a double LIMEKILN with pointed arches.

CIDER PRESS CENTRE, Shinners Bridge. Two-storey shop and restaurant, designed to cope with the tourist masses, in the cider-house buildings, converted and extended in a vaguely vernacular idiom (1976 by *D.Ransom* and *R.Butler*). Pitched roofs, artificial-slate-hung walls, boarded interiors. Well concealed car parks.

STAPLE. A small hamlet of cottages on the slope of a hill. Above them, on a prominent hill-top site, ORCHARD PARK, Nos. 1–3, three large houses by *O.P.Milne*, 1931, for members of the Dartington staff. Designed as a formal group, the middle house with recessed centre and doorway flanked by circular windows, the end houses gabled. Rendered walls, swept eaves, large chimneys. No. 1 converted to flats in 1950.

HUNTERS MOON, Cott. By *Christopher Press* of *Leonard Manasseh Partnership*, 1968–72 and 1973–5. The most attractive of the post-war buildings put up by the Dartington Trust. Intended at first to be a mixture of local authority and low-cost private housing, but in the end all built for sale. Picturesque clusters of houses of different sizes linked by flat-roofed garages, arranged round two closes. Varied roof-lines, grey and black concrete tiles, white-rendered jettied fronts with some boarding; an early and skilful essay in the brand of neo-vernacular widely adopted since in Devon.

Nearby, the COTT INN, long and thatched.

Older Rural Buildings

The older rural buildings of the hamlets and farms (the subject of a published survey, *see* Further Reading) provide a good cross-section of C15–17 houses, mainly on the three-room cross-passage plan, but with interesting later C17 and C18 variations. Roof construction is dominated by the A-frame truss, some with short curved feet, one, COXLAKE, with short posts tenoned on to the feet of trusses, a C17 transitional form. Many excellent C16 door frames and stud-and-panel screens.

TIGLEY is late medieval, with an early stud-and-panel screen between hall and inner room, and a lateral stack.

LOWER ALLERTON,* also late medieval, has an inserted upper chamber jettied out over a narrow inner room projecting 4ft into the hall, and a two-storey porch. Good farm buildings, including a barn with a C16 shouldered-head timber door, a bank barn, and a roundhouse. LOWER VELWELL, C17, with stud-and-panel screen between hall and inner room, has a datestone 1731 on the kitchen stack. WOODCOTT and KNODDY,* at Week, are interesting examples of C17 remodelling, when staircases were made particular features of more centralized layouts. Knoddy has a floral plasterwork overmantel dated 1634 with the initials CGM. STEPS COTTAGE, Staple, is on a cross-passage plan, late medieval, with

*For plans of Lower Allerton and Knoddy *see* p. 69.

true cruck trusses. PETERS at Staple and WAILES at Week are small, late C17, on two-room plans without cross-passage; HORTIN at Staple is C18, on a one-room plan. YARNER is late medieval, with later C16–early C18 extensions producing a complex plan. DRORIDGE, C16, on a two-room cross-passage plan, has a C17 kitchen wing incorporating a large smoking chamber and ovens.

EARTHWORKS. In the North Wood, N of the Hall, a complex series of well preserved earthwork enclosures. Limited excavation has shown the westernmost one to be Roman. A smaller earthwork enclosure to the E in Staverton Ford Plantation may be medieval.

See also Brooking.

DARTMOUTH

Dartmouth is one of Devon's most ancient ports. Its sheltered position on the Dart made it a favoured harbour from the early Middle Ages, and it was the assembly point of the fleets which left for the second and third Crusades. But its chief interest from the C12 to the C15 was the wine trade with Bordeaux. The town was incorporated in 1341, and in 1346 furnished Edward III with thirty-one ships for the siege of Calais, i.e. more than any port but Fowey (forty-seven) and Yarmouth (forty-three). Chaucer says of his shipman: 'For aught I know he was of Derthemute.'

In the C16 the trade of the port was dominated by Totnes merchants exporting cloth and tin to France in return for linen and manufactured goods. Dartmouth men seem to have limited themselves to providing the shipping. From the end of the C16, however, and well into the C18, the town's merchants began to profit from the annual voyages to the Newfoundland fishery, using the proceeds to import luxury goods from the continent. In the 1720s Defoe found the town 'very large and populous ... though but meanly built', with 'some very flourishing merchants'. Later in the C18 a decline began, interrupted only for a brief period between 1871 and 1891 when it served fast steamships leaving for Australia and South Africa. The training of naval cadets began in 1863, but they are now in a college outside the town instead of in training ships by the harbour, and the population of the densely built up narrow streets has been dispersed to suburban estates. The old town centre exists for tourists; the historic town houses have become restaurants and antique shops (and are thus agreeably accessible to the visitor). On the whole the character of the place has been sensitively maintained, although it is beginning to be threatened by obtrusive summer flats along the riverside.

The best introduction is the enticing view from the ferry from Kingswear, with tier upon tier of streets of small houses along the hillside terraces. To understand the development of the town one has to appreciate that the streets closest to the waterside are late creations, reclaimed from the mudflats (cf. Bideford). Dartmouth originated as three riverside settlements. Hardnesse and Clifton, N and S of a deep tidal inlet, were already in the C13 linked by a causeway (now Foss Street), with a tide mill. South Town, S of Clifton, was annexed in a charter in 1463. Lower Street and Fairfax Place marked the waterfront of medieval Clifton, from which the New Quay (now known simply as

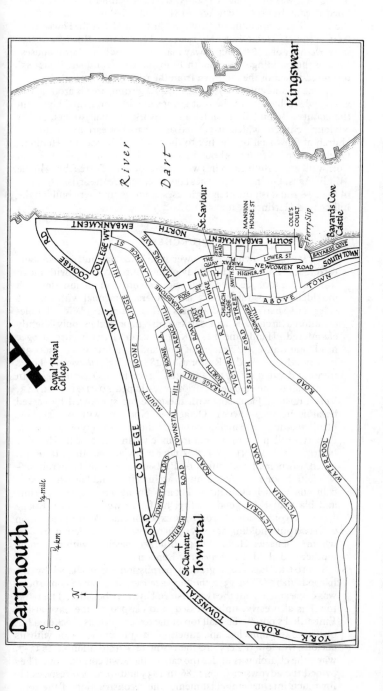

The Quay) was built out in 1584–5: the inlet behind Foss Street was filled after an Improvement Act of 1815, and the Market Place built on the site. The embankment between Clifton and South Town dates from 1833–7. Behind it the ramped Newcomen Road, a street improvement of 1865, swept away many of the best medieval houses. Finally the building of the South Embankment (completed in 1885) disguised much of the old town from the river.

For the architectural visitor the most rewarding area is around The Quay, which has one of the best groups of C17 merchants' houses in the county. Behind, in an intricate network of small streets, lies St Saviour's church, which originated as a chapel of ease to the mother church at Townstal on the hill to the W of Hardnesse (cf. Honiton, Okehampton, Newton Abbot in Devon, Launceston and Looe in Cornwall, etc.). Both churches were possessions of Torre Abbey in the Middle Ages. On the steep slopes above Clifton are the artisan terraces of the C18 and C19; the grander houses of the gentry were built on the hill behind Hardnesse, further N.

CHURCHES

St CLEMENT, Townstal. W tower with diagonal buttresses, stair-turret, and pinnacles. The body of the church is older, with much work of c. 1300; see the S door with one order of colonnettes with moulded capitals, and the N arcade piers, octagonal with concave sides and shafts in the diagonals (cf. St Saviour). Wide double-chamfered arches. N and S transepts, their arches only slightly chamfered. Handsome PISCINAS in chancel (with cusped ogee head) and transepts. Tracery of nave and transepts also c. 1300–30, if correctly restored. (Restoration 1881–5 by *Ashworth*.) The S transept divided off in 1983 (glazed screen by *S. G. Scardifield*). In the N wall of the chancel a curious eye-shaped SQUINT. – ALTAR. Very unusual. Jacobean, with the table top supported by carved heraldic beasts. – FONT. Octagonal, Norman, with two shallow blank arcades per panel, a variant of the table-top type. – BRASS. Robert Holland †1611. Figure in civilian dress with rhyming inscription. – MONUMENTS. Under a low arch in the S transept, much worn medieval effigy of Purbeck stone, in long robes. – William Roope †1666. Simple architectural tablet with Doric columns and achievement. – Thomas Boone, erected 1681. White and black marble, good quality, no figure work. – Mary Roope †1739, 'a young lady of promising expectations'. Portrait medallion with two putti holding drapery open to reveal it. Excellent work – by whom? – Charles Hayne †1842. Still neo-classical, with mourning mother and child, by *Denman* of London.

St SAVIOUR. Edward I granted permission for a chapel by the harbour in 1286. In 1372 the 'honesta capella de novo constructa' was consecrated, but the two western bays may be older. The tall W tower is also early, unbuttressed, and clasped by the nave aisles. Embattled S porch. The tall top of the tower, with its crocketed but obelisk-like pinnacles, and much of the present exterior with its curious window tracery are the result of a restoration of 1633–7, when the church was under the care of the town corporation. They owned the advowson from 1586 to 1835 and were also responsible for much interior embellishment. The reconstruction of the roofs and the replacement of some of the C17 work date from *Ashworth*'s restoration of 1891–3.

The very picturesque interior is better described topographically than systematically. One enters through the embattled s porch of 1620. Displayed next to the entrance is a DOOR with splendid 46 ironwork. The strap hinges consisting of two lions striding across a tree with large leaves are in the style of the C15, probably repaired in 1631 – see the date added in the centre. The s aisle (and the N aisle too) go as far w as the tower. The WEST GALLERY of 1633, with handsome carving still in the Elizabethan style, however, runs across the nave and aisles E of the tower, thus separating the first bays of N and s aisles. In the s one a fine early C18 staircase runs up to the w gallery, where the church keeps its large black former REREDOS with the Ten Commandments and between them a big carved Bible opened at Luke vii. Above the reredos a vast PAINT- ING by *William Brockedon* (1787–1854) of Totnes. It gained a 100- guinea prize of the British Institution in 1818. The nave arcades are not at all unified in design. The two w bays with octagonal piers with shafts in the diagonals and double-chamfered arches are the earliest. The next three bays are Perp, with normal B type piers with standard capitals; the arches are semicircular and decorated with fleurons, and in one case a continuous leaf scroll. But the N and s transepts behind the fourth bay are probably pre-Perp in their masonry. The problem is to relate all this to the known dates. 1372 would be uniquely early in Devon for the Perp work, uncomfortably late, stylistically, for the western piers. It seems most likely that the Perp arcades are a C15 remodelling, replacing work that was new in 1372, but which had been added to an earlier building of which the western bays still remain.

ROOD SCREEN, E of the fourth bay. Unusually complete and impressive, with tracery different from and less intricate than the standard, perfect coving, and splendidly carved friezes in the cornice. Accounts for its construction in 1496 exist. – The two PARCLOSE SCREENS are later (arms and initials of James Pelliton, mayor in 1567–8) and have standard tracery, but also several bands of cornice decoration, an uncommon enrichment.

PULPIT. Stone, encrusted with decoration. The panels, usually with painted figures or shields below ogee canopies, are here not wider than the thick uprights. The top is a frieze of enormous leaves, each about 10 in. wide; the foot a slender stem spreading into a palm-tree shape. – In the space at the E end of the nave close to the screen PEWS for members of the Corporation, typical neo-Dec of 1815, formerly in the chancel. – COMMUNION TABLE. 1588. The four carved figures of evangelists, placed on the front in 1893, were formerly the table legs. The chancel was restored by *E.H.Sedding* in 1887. He added the oak CHOIR STALLS. – ORGAN CASE. Rococo, by *Micheau* of Exeter, 1789. – SEDILIA and PISCINA. A combined composition with crocketed ogee tops. – Brass CAN- DELABRA in the nave, 1708. – STAINED GLASS. s chapel 1969 by *A.Attwood*, formalized pictorial, Christ and 'fishers of men'.

BRASSES. In the chancel to John Hawley, shipowner and three times Mayor of Dartmouth, † 1408, and his wives. He gave most of the money for the building of the church. He is shown as a knight. The three figures under tall ogee-shaped cusped canopies; very thin pinnacled buttresses (cf. Courtenay brass, Exeter Cathedral). The brass is one of the most important in Devon. – In the S chapel, C15 brass of a lady, date and name unrecorded. – MONUMENTS. Near the pulpit, the lower part of a medieval engraved slab with the figure of a priest in Eucharistic vestments, discovered in 1983. – Nicholas Hayman † 1606. Little wall-monument with ribbonwork on pilasters; emblems of mortality below. – Roger Vavasour † 1696 and son † 1727. Grey marble, broken segmental pediment with urn, two allegorical figures on pediment, putti below. Signed *Jo. Weston*.

54 ST PETROX. Close to the castle, i.e. right away from Dartmouth. An old foundation, but the present building largely 1641. Unbuttressed two-stage W tower. Low octagonal piers, N and S aisles, semicircular arches and elementary posthumous-Perp window tracery. Plain plastered barrel-vault. – FONT. Circular, Norman, with palmette frieze. – PULPIT. Dated 1641. Arches with Mannerist pediments. – Two large CHARITY BOARDS, early C19. – WAR MEMORIAL made up of woodwork from the C17 W gallery. – BOARDS with texts from a former reredos. – BRASS. John Roope † 1609. An unusually large figure for this date. – MONUMENTS. Elizabeth Roope. C17 inscribed oval, flanked by columns. – Good C17 and C18 LEDGER STONES.

ST BARNABAS (now an antique store). Very prominent from the river, with its small neo-Romanesque twin turrets linked by an open arcade (a feature borrowed from the Auvergne). In front of this a polygonal apse, also rather French; around it a strangely domestic wooden veranda sheltering the steps which lead up to the church from Newcomen Road. This E end is of 1884 by *George H. Birch*; it was added to a plain chapel of 1831 by *Joseph Lidstone*, built as a chapel of ease to St Petrox. The castellated W gable of this date survives.

ST JOHN BAPTIST (R.C.), Newcomen Road. Nave 1868–9, chancel 1873–6, in a minimal lancet Gothic, by *J. A. Hansom*.

BAPTIST CHAPEL (former), approached from Newcomen Road by the steep and narrow Chapel Lane. Late C18, enlarged 1847, when a school was added. Partly rendered; round-arched windows with Gothick glazing.

WESLEYAN CHAPEL.* The dominant building of the Market Square, large and ornate, 1816, rebuilt in 1875 by *John Wills*, still classical. Severely plain sides, with windows on three levels. Rendered front of five bays, central pediment, giant Ionic pilasters. The lower windows in the middle bays rise through two storeys.

FLAVEL MEMORIAL CHAPEL (United Reformed; formerly Congregational), North Embankment. 1895, grey limestone, Dec windows; built near the site of a C17 meeting formed by John Flavel, an ejected minister of St Saviour's. His memorial of 1691 is in the chapel.

CASTLE

54 The castle lies a mile S of the town facing Kingswear Castle in such a way that a chain could be passed in wartime between Dartmouth and a point below Kingswear Castle. The situation corresponds to

*Future uncertain.

that of Pendennis and St Mawes or the two ruinous castles at the mouth of the river Fowey. However, Dartmouth was in course of erection in 1481 and complete by 1494, and so it is earlier than these castles of Henry VIII. It consists of a rounded part begun first and a chief rectangular part with a polygonal lookout tower rising above the battlements. The rectangular basement room has seven openings for guns of a shape more advanced than used anywhere else in England at the time. They are rectangular openings, splayed internally, originally at floor level. In the rounded basement room, slits for muskets and later gun-openings. The ground-floor entrance is new but in the original position. The main ground-floor room has the same openings for muskets as below. In the rounded ground-floor room is the large opening with timber framing through which the chain went. On the first floor originally the living quarters, with fireplaces.

Visually the chief attraction of Dartmouth Castle is that it forms an indivisible group with the church of St Petrox, whose tower rises higher than that of the castle proper, but less high than the tower called GALLANTS BOWER (built in 1645). The bulwark above the bathing beach is C19 and C20 on the site of one of c. 1540. To the w of the artillery fortress the remains of a substantial stone curtain wall round an angle tower, surrounded by a ditch – the only surviving fabric from works recorded in the C14. In 1336, and again in 1388, 'a fortalice by the sea' was under construction.

PUBLIC BUILDINGS

ROYAL NAVAL COLLEGE. In the picture of C20 Dartmouth the dominant motif is no longer the castle or the harbour but *Sir Aston Webb*'s enormous college buildings stretching out along the hill of Townstal, N of Dartmouth. They are of brick and stone in a revised and vamped-up C18 tradition, not successful as an ensemble, because the Edwardian–Palladian motifs are not of sufficient bombast to fit the scale adopted. The tower is not high and broad enough for a distant view, and the side cupolas are niggling. The towers at the far ends are too small too – the same mistakes as made by Webb in the Victoria and Albert Museum and eighty years before by Wilkins when he designed the National Gallery to dominate Trafalgar Square. At the l. end of the main range the dining hall, at the r. end the chapel. In the middle, stretching out behind and at right angles to the front, the great hall. This has an open timber roof with transverse stone arches. The dining hall is tunnel-vaulted, the chapel provided with simplified Perp tracery and *Kempe Studios* windows of 1907–11. To the l. of the main range the sick quarters, friendlier and less pretentious; behind the chapel the headmaster's house. The date of the buildings is 1899–1905. (Inside, a bronze bust of George V when Prince of Wales; 1908 by *Hamo Thornycroft*.)

GUILDHALL, Victoria Road. 1849, plain, rubble, with mullioned-and-transomed windows.

HOSPITAL. Original gabled buildings of 1893, along the newly finished South Embankment. Extensions 1925, 1974, 1984.

PERAMBULATIONS

1. The Old Town Centre – South Town

THE QUAY, the present centre of Dartmouth, was created in 1584.
Little of that period is visible, yet nothing jars, and the total
impression is attractive. By the river is the low STATION PIER,
with glazed and valanced ramp down to the floating landing-stage,
opened in 1864 as the terminus for the Dartmouth and Torbay
railway, but used only by the steam passenger ferry from
Kingswear. At the s corner YORK HOUSE, a whacking big piece
of late Victorian half-timbering by the borough surveyor,
E. H. Back, dated 1894, built after this part of the embankment
replaced the old uneven line of jetties and creeks. Then a good
early C20 LLOYDS BANK, brick and stone Wrenaissance by
W. Couldrey of Paignton. No. 4, built for Robert Plumleigh,
mariner, in 1664, with a show front to FAIRFAX PLACE, is a good
introduction to Dartmouth's timber-framed houses, constructed in
traditional fashion, with stone party-walls containing the fireplaces
(serving also a demolished adjacent house).* Elaborate star-shaped
chimneystacks of imported 'Dutch' brick. Carved corner-posts to
first-floor jetty and oriel; the second jetty has a dragon beam supported by a figure of Samson (or Hercules?) and the lion. Originally, the house had a ground-floor shop or warehouse, with the
main domestic rooms above, and a courtyard and possibly a back
block behind (cf. Totnes, Exeter, etc.). Inside there is evidence for
three rooms on each floor and five attic rooms, nine of them
heated, and for a now vanished framed staircase instead of the
older newel type. Oak-hooded fireplaces remain on the second
floor, with traces of the sgraffito decoration popular in Devon at
the time.

The CASTLE HOTEL, the chief building of The Quay, has a genteel
façade of 1835 – battlements, two extremely shallow bows, doorway flanked by Doric columns – masking two houses built in 1639
by William Barnes and Joseph Cubitt, merchants (see the stone
party-walls, datestone, and modest first-floor plaster ceiling at the s
end) and two further blocks behind, all linked together by an
amazing top-lit staircase hall of 1835, filling the narrow space
between the two groups. Two jettied houses follow, then we reach
DUKE STREET leading W, with the BUTTERWALK, Dartmouth's pride: four timber-framed houses, lovingly restored after
serious damage in 1943. They were built in 1628–40, the most
ostentatious of their date in the town, on newly reclaimed land,
originally backing on to the river. One is dated 1640, another 1635,
with the initials MH for Mark Hawkins, the town receiver. Upper
floors built out over the pavement supported by granite piers,
forming covered walks, as at Totnes. The overhanging floors are
profusely carved. No. 6, nearest The Quay, has its timber-framing
exposed, No. 10 a splendidly rich oriel on carved brackets, ten
lights and two sidelights, No. 12, at the end, a corner bracket of
Samson and the lion, like the later one at No. 4 The Quay. Only
the two central houses preserve their gables, but enough survives

*This account is based on John Thorp's excellent analysis in *Devon Archaeologi-
cal Soc. Procs.*, 14 (1983), 107–22.

of the first-floor interiors to show the sumptuous standard of fittings. In No. 12 a quite exceptional ceiling, entirely covered by a tree of Jesse; evangelists in the corners. No. 10 has more standard ceilings (main room with single ribs and pendants, the room behind, next to the staircase, with central quatrefoil and cherub heads) but a remarkable overmantel depicting Pentecost, with Moses and David. Good moulded front doorcase and original door. The Museum (No. 6) preserves its newel stair with long post. Over the fireplace in a first-floor room the arms of Charles II, who was entertained here in 1671. Plaster ceiling and oak panelling. At the back of the house a small restored upper oriel.

Now up ANZAC STREET towards St Saviour's, built on higher ground, with small streets clustering around – the centre of the medieval settlement of Clifton–Dartmouth. In the small square NW of the church the ROYAL BRITISH LEGION, quite a tactful newcomer echoing traditional forms: stone arched ground floor, white render above, two-storey oriel, and three gables. In COLLA-FORD LANE, up steps to the S, No. 1a, with medieval stone arch to the basement, and typical stone party-walls framing the jettied front, and CHARITY HOUSE, next door, jetty with carved oriels above and below. A detour up SMITH STREET can take in a glimpse of the picturesquely steep CROWTHERS HILL, with one of Dartmouth's many conduits (1599, rebuilt 1847). From here ABOVE TOWN branches off to the l., parallel to the river, narrow streets of early C19 rendered terraces, nothing special except for No. 12 Above Town, with its flat doorhood supported by rearing horses. Then back down SMITH STREET, with another double-jettied house on the l. (No. 14) and late Georgian frontages opposite, to the SEVEN STARS, and via the narrow CHURCH CLOSE, past No. 7 with carved brackets, down to Fairfax Place.

In FAIRFAX PLACE an amazing Victorian creation of c. 1880: a row of shops with pargetting, slate-hanging in two colours, and iron cresting, far over-reaching any genuine C17 example. Note 'Chymist' engraved on the beam of the central house. From here Lower Street and Higher Street run S. LOWER STREET was close to the river before the embankment was built, with lanes running down to mooring-places. The most important older houses stood between the two streets. The best remaining group is at the start of HIGHER STREET. No. 1, The Shambles, has timbers exposed on two upper floors, the first floor with square framing, the upper one with simple uprights. Nos. 3–5 (Tudor House), with a timber-framed front of 1635, has two floors of oriels, the lower one of five plus five lights, carved corner-posts and beams as in the Butter-walk, and slate-hung gables. Single-rib ceiling in a first-floor room. The back of the house, with lower floor-levels, and the pole staircase are probably older. Then the CHERUB, the only complete medieval house in Dartmouth, a corner house, with two jetties to both front and side on simple upright timbers and dragon beams at the corners. Trefoil-headed windows (the front ones new), but no carved decoration. A single room on each floor; pole staircase. After this both Higher and Lower Streets are interrupted by the road-widening of 1864 which created NEWCOMEN ROAD with its mighty ramp snaking up the hill to provide easier access to the waterside, an impressive piece of engineering by *Bell* of London.

Near the start of the ramp, MANSION HOUSE STREET with the MANSION HOUSE of *c*. 1730. Later building abuts the rear, but this is still Dartmouth's best C18 house. Five-bay, three-storey brick front with arched ground-floor windows with heavy triple keystones; doorway treated like a Venetian window, with small side lights. Inside, much lavish decoration survives. Entrance hall with arch on Corinthian columns; ceiling with cartouches; fine well staircase with carved tread-ends, marquetry steps and landing. On the walls panels with the Labours of Hercules and zodiac roundels. In the main first-floor room an accomplished ceiling in low relief (cf. Bowden House and Saltram), the central panel with some rather light-hearted classical gods surrounded by bacchic figures and chained leopards. Shell niches in the end walls. The house was rented for civic functions in the C18.

Further s along LOWER STREET some older remnants: the rebuilt red sandstone medieval carriage arch to No. 6 (Speedwell House), and AGINCOURT HOUSE (No. 27), much restored, but preserving the shell of a probably C17 building (a re-used bargeboard of 1671 was found during restoration). The only house to mark the old width of Lower Street. Panelled timber-framing on the first floor, the plain centre probably replacing an oriel; corbelled party-walls; cobbled courtyard (glazed over) with galleries to a three-storey back block. Corbelled fireplaces on the upper floors, the first-floor one in the main block with sgraffito plasterwork. Towards the river a rewarding little group around FERRY SLIP, SUNDERLAND TERRACE, and, further on, BAYARDS COVE, a charming sequence of waterfront houses with a cobbled quay in front. Stone conduit of 1857. The only grand building is the OLD CUSTOM HOUSE, dated 1739, five bays with pediment and segment-headed doorhood. No. 5 has an unusual pattern-book doorcase of the early C19, and bracketed eaves. Then plain gabled and jettied houses with BAYARDS COVE FORT at the end, part of Henry VIII's defences of 1536–7, but probably built in 1509–10 to protect the harbour mouth. Rounded corners, eleven gunports at ground level, of similar type to those at Dartmouth Castle.

From this riverside level steps lead up to the higher line of NEW-COMEN ROAD, continuing as SOUTH TOWN. Houses with a pleasing assortment of bay-windows to take advantage of the view over the river. No. 22 Newcomen Road is especially handsome (dated 1792), with rusticated ground floor. No. 32 has an C18 doorcase, Nos. 20–21 South Town have low C18 doorcases with pediments on fat brackets, probably added to an older house, Nos. 24–25 attractive Regency bow-windows. The former Sunday School of St Petrox dates from 1823. Windows with straight dripstones (the unusual medievalizing tracery removed).

At WARFLEET, between South Town and the castle, two early C19 Gothic houses behind a battlemented wall above the road. WARFLEET MILLS, built as a brewery, is now potteries; C19, three storeys, central projection with gable.

2. *The Market Place to Hardnesse*

Starting at the Butterwalk, FOSS STREET leads N from Duke Street, with mostly rendered C18 and C19 frontages. It marks the line of the C13 dam constructed across the creek between Clifton and Hardnesse. The mill pool created from the creek to serve the tidal mill on the dam was filled in for the MARKET SQUARE in 1828–9. The Market is surrounded by nice unassuming terraces of the same period, No. 4 on the E side especially elegant, with a shallow bow the whole width of the house, lattice balconettes, and broad eaves. The MARKET itself is modest: a simple two-storey building in the centre with formerly open arched ground floor; one-storey open stalls around the perimeter. VICTORIA ROAD runs W, with early to mid C19 terraces and villas; N of the Market the lanes of Hardnesse climb steeply along the side of the hill.

First to the r., up BROADSTONE, for a good red brick C18 corner house, with three-storey canted bays and a pedimented doorcase. CLARENCE STREET, narrow and winding, has a former chapel of 1846 with thin Georgian Gothick windows, tall rendered C19 houses opposite, and No. 18, C18, with stepped keystones. Around the SHIP IN DOCK (rebuilt 1821), up RIDGE HILL to the picturesque NEWCOMEN LODGE, built by *T. Lidstone* in 1866 with much re-used material from the house in Lower Street where Newcomen, the inventor of the steam pump, lived. L-shaped, stone, with two gables and carved oriel window. Further on, ROCK HOUSE, solid, *c.* 1830, deep bracketed eaves. Higher up was MOUNT BOONE, demolished in 1905, the seat from 1724 of the Seales, one of the town's leading families. Castellated garden walls (now enclosing Edwardian houses). On the s slopes below off Clarence Hill, MOUNT GALPIN, the town house of the Seales' rivals, the Holdsworths, governors of Dartmouth Castle. C18, but much altered. Stuccoed, three storeys, central canted bay. In CLARENCE HILL Nos. 27–35, ST CLARA'S TERRACE, stand on the site of the medieval chapel of St Clare, overlooking the harbour. Ground-floor windows with segmental-headed arches with keystones. Further w No. 37, Victorian, with massive battlemented door surrounds, and other mid C19 houses. Then back by intricate steps and paths down to Foss Street.

E of Foss Street MAYORS AVENUE leads around the opening of the creek, filled in only in 1876–7. On the N side, long stone WAREHOUSES, possibly medieval ground-floor vaults, C19 above, small iron barred openings on the N side, wrought-iron jib hoist. In CORONATION PARK a 1725 Newcomen atmospheric engine from Griff Colliery, brought here in 1963 in Newcomen's tercentenary.

DAWLISH 9070

The old settlement was nearly a mile inland, around the parish church. The sheltered inlet of Dawlish Water, protected by hills on either side, began to attract visitors at the end of the C18. 'A bathing village' was how the *Gentleman's Magazine* described it in 1793, where 'summer lingers and spring pays her earliest visits'. John Swete described more censoriously, in 1795, how 'on the cliffs and over the Strand edifices of superior taste and higher expense crowd together – I wish I could have added, in some sort of symmetrical arrangement'. Some landscaping of the growing resort took place *c.* 1803; the stream was straightened so that it ran through a broad lawn, and The Strand and Brunswick Place

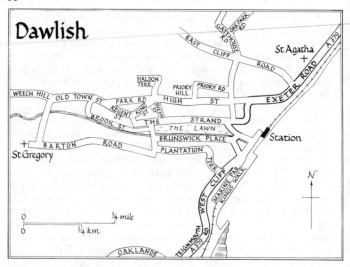

were laid out on either side. The interesting thing to us is that the
layout disregards the sea completely. A little later the terraces of
Brighton and Hove and the crescents of St Leonard's and Teignmouth
face the sea. Had the taste and the attitude to the restless, noisy,
terrifying sea changed just then? This pleasant pattern established by
the mid C19 has survived remarkably complete. Much remains also of
the modest commercial and artisan area which developed in the area
around the old route from the village to the beach (High Street – Park
Road – Old Town Street), parallel to The Strand, and there are still
plenty of C19 villas to be found on the hills above, their growth
encouraged by the arrival of the railway in 1846.

ST GREGORY. Rebuilt in 1824 by *Andrew Patey* (cf. Teignmouth),
  apart from the Perp red W tower with diagonal buttresses, stair-
  turret, and white pinnacles. Chancel and transepts rebuilt in 1874
  by *J.P.St Aubyn* (the start of an intended complete rebuilding),
  easily distinguishable by the use of grey limestone ashlar with Bath
  stone dressings and Dec detail. Patey's pinnacles, battlements, and
  roughcast were removed from the nave. His tall Perp windows
  remain, and inside, the B type piers with standard capitals, re-used
  from the medieval church, set on taller bases to allow for N, S, and W
  galleries (all removed in 1897). Chancel richly ornamented with
  polished marble shafts, with an *opus sectile* REREDOS by *Powell* of
  Whitefriars, added in 1899. (Patey's original reredos is now in the S
  chapel.) The W narthex, a two-storey internal division with glass
  screen, was made in 1984 by *Grant & Green* (project architect
  Michael Ford).
    ROYAL ARMS. Late Hanoverian. – STAINED GLASS. E window
  Resurrection scenes in an impressive seven-light composition, S
  chapel E a dramatic Transfiguration, both by *W.F.Dixon*, 1876. –
  MONUMENTS. Rev. John Trosse †1678. – Many chaste neo-
  Grecian tablets, the only figural ones two by *Flaxman*, both with
  mourning funereal figures and urns, one to Lady Pennyman †1801,
  the other to Mrs Hunter †1805. Among the others, Samuel Need-

ham †1797, of coloured marbles, by *M. Emes* of Exeter. – Rev. Charles Robinson †1805, again by *Flaxman*. Very austere, with two small amphorae and a chalice. – In the churchyard a large enclosure with polychrome Gothic arcading, by *G.G. Scott* for the Hoare family (cf. Luscombe), the earliest tomb of 1863.

St Agatha (R.C.), Exeter Road. 1909 by *Scoles & Raymond*. A good group, prominently sited on the cliff to the E of the town. Tall apsed church with a small turret with presbytery adjoining, all in red rubble stone with Bath stone plate tracery.

Methodist Church, Brunswick Place. 1861; simple lancets.

United Reformed Church, The Strand. More ambitious, with a bold broach-spire on one side. 1870 by *Tarring & Son*. (Schools added by *G.S. Bridgman*, 1884.)

The sea wall and station ruthlessly separating the valley from the coastline date from the opening of the South Devon Railway in 1846. The Station is typical of *Brunel*-designed stations of the period: a rendered two-storey block on the approach side, with impressive double-height entrance hall with coffered ceiling, segmental-arched tall sash-windows, and prominent keystones. Platforms at first-floor level with ridge-and-furrow awnings on broad latticed brackets. Some alterations c.1873 when the track was broadened. The Sea Wall (altered in 1855–76 when the line was doubled) forms part of the long railway embankment extending from Powderham on the Exe estuary to Teignmouth. Built of large limestone blocks for the most part with granite foundations and cappings, the wall at Dawlish has a curved profile to throw back the waves beating upon it.

Starting at the Station (*see* above), the first impression is misleadingly late Victorian, with the Royal Hotel, tall, denuded of much of its classical ornament, curving round a corner, and a Bank of 1890 opposite. Inland, this period is left behind as one passes down the narrow Beach Street (one low thatched house as a reminder of pre-resort days) to the start of The Lawn, the open stretch which gives Dawlish its special character. From the corner one can glance up Strand Hill, which climbs steeply upward to the N, starting with another thatched house with projecting wing to the road (over-restored) and continuing with minor early C19 terraced houses, only a few, alas, still with their original elegant windows (Nos. 4, 8, 15).

The Strand still has a spacious Regency to early Victorian flavour, with its simple two-storey stucco houses looking across the lawn to Brunswick Terrace. Near the end, Queen Street, part of the same layout, leads to the High Street; Regent Street continues straight on. Here and in the neighbouring Brook Street are terraces of stucco-trimmed cottages on a delightfully intricate scale, some only one window wide. Amidst them, two disguised country bumpkins surviving from the old village: Nos. 5 and 7 Regent Street, both with curved (staircase?) projections. More minor artisan terraces, some with purpose-built small mid C19 shops, in King Street, which forks back to the High Street. At the junction the former Town Hall of 1853, with rusticated ground floor and projecting centre pediment. The High Street is also on a small scale but has been brutally disrupted by a supermarket and car park. A detour uphill to the N should take in the early C19

HALDON TERRACE, the only really stylish group in Dawlish: nine three-storey stuccoed houses, the top storey unusually tall, divided by pilasters. Some attractive trellised verandas facing a communal garden. Further up the valley, THE MANOR (now council offices), in its own grounds running down to the stream. Built by 1811 but altered; two storeys, stuccoed, with veranda. (Good early C19 staircase.)

The most affluent part of C19 Dawlish was around the church. First, BARTON VILLAS, stately semi-detached houses of *c.* 1870. BARTON TERRACE has real villas in a pleasant variety of earlier C19 styles, from Grecian (No. 4) to Gothic (Nos. 5, 7), as well as hybrids such as No. 8 (doorway with ogee pediment on Doric columns). Back towards The Lawn, BROOKDALE, a very substantial early C19 *cottage orné* of the kind to be found in Sidmouth, thatched, with three Gothic bay-windows to the sea, and BROOKLANDS HOTEL, the end of a formal terrace looking down The Lawn. But in Dawlish there is no consistent formality. BRUNSWICK PLACE is haphazard and modest; good houses are No. 4, three storeys with Grecian decoration on its giant pilasters and bowed first-floor windows, and No. 5 with bowed windows, a Dawlish feature which recurs on No. 26. In between, indifferent recent housing on the site of St Mark's church,[*] and the remains of TORBAY MILLS, two and three storeys, roughcast stone, remodelled *c.* 1825, with massive external chimneystack and 30 ft cast iron pitchback waterwheel by *Bodley* of Exeter.

The fringes of Dawlish are also worth exploring. To the SW, MARINE PARADE, in the lee of the cliff, mostly later C19. Nos. 9–10 earlier, three storeys, with pretty honeysuckle balconies. Up a steep flight of steps to WEST CLIFF, the main coast road. Among the early C19 houses here, No. 22 with tented first-floor balcony and trellised balconettes, and No. 26 with a doorway with vermiculated rustication. Now inland along PLANTATION TERRACE to take in a scatter of pattern-book villas. No. 5 (an older house remodelled) has a Tudor doorway of the same model as No. 7 Barton Terrace. No. 7 is especially ornate, with tripartite Gothic windows with carved spandrels; Nos. 13–15 are a pair, with Greek Doric doorways.

Among the C20 suburbs spreading further S along the top of the cliff, the area worth a look is OAKLANDS, by *Mervyn Seal*, developed as the result of an open competition promoted by the County Council to encourage imaginative residential design. Thoughtfully grouped and landscaped houses, one of the first large-scale efforts (much copied since) to re-create the intimacy of the traditional seaside village. The earliest phase, 1971–6, makes effective use of narrow twisting and turning alleys and lanes opening off the main thoroughfare, enclosed by curving white garden and garage walls. The architectural details are in places a little arch (lumpy dormers, triangular windows) recalling the *cottage orné* rather than the true vernacular. Phase 2, off John Nash Way (1982 onwards), has clusters of larger houses with similar features, but more spaciously set out. Further on THE LINDENS, 1976–80, *Teignbridge District Council*'s own version of the same mode, but less carefully landscaped and detailed.

[*]Demolished in 1976. By *Hayward*, 1849–51, extended 1883–5.

The E suburbs of Dawlish have a different character. On the slopes
above the High Street, prominent from afar, THE PRIORY, Priory
Road, early C19 gabled Tudor, with a pretty drive and garden wall
of beach pebbles, and LAMMAS PARK HOTEL, elegant minimal
Regency, with a balcony on very thin supports. Further on the relics
of an affluent mid Victorian development of Italianate stuccoed
villas in large gardens. The best preserved survivals are RED-
CLIFFE, in East Cliff Road, and the especially grand OAK PARK
HOUSE, with a campanile, in Oak Park Road.

Outside the town, roughly from S to N

MINADAB, Teignmouth Road. An eccentrically shaped *cottage orné*,
thatched, with bowed projections and veranda on wooden posts;
unsympathetically extended.

HOLCOMBE. A delightful little hamlet now bypassed by the
Teignmouth Road, with HOLCOMBE COTTAGE, with Regency
Gothic windows, and ST GEORGE, a tiny, very plain C19 church
(nave 1867, chancel 1893) with a bell-turret.

STONELANDS, Weech Hill. Built *c.* 1820 as a dower house to
Luscombe (q.v.). Large, plain, two-storey stuccoed house with
hipped roofs, in its own well planted grounds. Entrance side with
broad Greek Doric porch. Garden side of 2–4–2 bays, the centre
recessed. Entrance hall with Ionic columns, with imperial stair
beyond.

RIXDALE, Lower Dawlish Water Road. An exceptionally large
farmhouse, C17, the lower end remodelled and extended in the C19.
A complex plan consisting of a main range now with five rooms in
line and three rear cross-wings. Two massive lateral stacks at the
front, one at the rear. The interior shows the later C17 farmhouse at
its smartest: the layout provides for a staircase, and connecting
passages at the rear – an interesting example of a transitional plan
form. Impressive plasterwork with double-rib mouldings with
geometric and floral patterns. Three ceilings, the richest in the
middle first-floor chamber, which also has an overmantel with the
armorial bearings of Thomas Tripe, dated 1669. Lower chamber
fireplace with squared sgraffito plasterwork. Large BARN below the
house: six bays, jointed cruck trusses.

EASTON HOUSE, Dawlish Warren Road. A small mansion in its own
grounds – a surprise amidst the chalet-land of Dawlish Warren.
Early C19 hipped-roofed centre, later extensions, including a water
tower of *c.* 1911.

DEAN PRIOR

ST GEORGE. Early W tower, unbuttressed and roughcast, of two
stages, with a central polygonal stair-turret on the S side, no pinnacles, and an unmoulded round-headed tower arch. Nave and
two aisles, divided by low octagonal granite piers with raw octagonal capitals and double-chamfered, fairly steep pointed arches. –
FONT. Norman, circular, of red sandstone, with a band of crosses
saltire and another broader band with two long distorted dragons.
– MONUMENTS. Sir Edward Giles †1642 and family, of Dean

Court. Kneelers of the usual, in 1642 already rather old-fashioned, kind. – Also a tablet to Herrick, vicar from 1654 to 1674, with a very rich, quite inappropriate strapwork surround, set up in 1857.

DEAN COURT, 1 m. N. With Tudor porch and a few Tudor C17 windows.

On DEAN MOOR, E and N of the Avon reservoir, many enclosed Bronze Age SETTLEMENTS. Before the reservoir was constructed a similar enclosed SETTLEMENT and a medieval FARMSTEAD were excavated. Nine prehistoric huts were found, and the enclosure wall sectioned. Finds pointing to a mixed economy included querns (for corn), a spindle whorl (for textiles), whetstones, and a little tin slag, suggesting the use of metal. The lump of iron ore built into one of the hut walls could indicate prospecting for metal by people without the technology for smelting iron. At the medieval settlement two buildings were found which were occupied c. 1250–1350. It has been suggested that they belonged to an outlying farm of Buckfast Abbey.

Also within the reservoir area, in the valley bottom, is a TIN BLOWING MILL which, with its mortar stones, can still be seen in extreme drought.

DENBURY

ST MARY. There was a consecration in 1318. The chancel could be of this date. It is unusually long. E window with intersecting tracery. Simple N and S windows: lancets subdivided into two lancet lights. Two-stage, unbuttressed W tower with three-light intersecting W window. Nave without aisles; N and S transepts. Repaired c. 1845; chancel restored in 1866 and under the S.P.A.B. in 1912 by *William Weir*. – FONT. Of pink sandstone, circular, Norman, with palmette decoration. – SCREEN, between nave and S transept. Panels with three-light openings and steeply pointed arches, much renewed. Said to have been brought from Dartington old church. – STAINED GLASS. E window by *Wailes*. – MONUMENT. John Taylor †1733, by *Weston* (cf. St Petrock, Exeter). Grey obelisk in relief with portrait medallion, gun-barrels lying apparently behind the obelisk. Sarcophagus below, and lower still, in the predella, relief of a naval battle. Two skulls as a tailpiece. Weston's receipt is dated 1736.

(GAIA HOUSE. Former rectory. Tudor front of 1847; gable with bell-turret. Late C17 rear range; wooden mullioned windows. Dog-leg stair with turned balusters.)

MANOR HOUSE. Possibly in origin a cell of the monks of Tavistock. The present house is C17, with a Georgian front, later medievalizations done by Hurrell Froude in 1825, and much, including the gatehouse, built in the earlier C20 for W. S. Curtis.

CONDUIT, at the crossroads. Now a war memorial. Stone, square, with a pyramidal top bearing the date 1771.

DENBURY CAMP. A strongly sited HILLFORT, a landmark visible for miles around. Presumably Iron Age, enclosing two substantial round barrows.

DIPTFORD

7050

ST MARY. Plain, small, early W tower with diagonal buttresses only at the foot, and unmoulded tower arch. No battlements. A broach-spire was added later. Low interior with N and S aisles of four bays, the piers low and octagonal, the capitals on the S side with some foliage ornament, the arches double-chamfered. Ceiled wagon roofs in nave and aisles. – SCREEN. Very little old; standard type A tracery and a usual design of the wainscoting. – MONUMENT. Nice largish wall-monument to Anne Taylor, †1763, sixteen years old. White and biscuit-coloured marble, no figures, but delicate decoration, not provincial.

CRABADON COURT. With porch and hoodmoulds of former mul-lioned windows. Old outbuildings – a good group.

BICKHAM BRIDGE. Three semicircular arches, not widened. The date may be early C17.

GARA BRIDGE. Originally for packhorse traffic only, but later widened. Single, obtusely pointed arch.

(BEENLEIGH. Late medieval, with C17 windows and gatehouse. Good screens doorways.)

CURTIS KNOWLE. Early Victorian, built by William Hare. Gables to the r. of the porch, dormers to the l. (MS).

DIPTFORD COURT. Fine stone gatepiers, but only a sash-windowed farmhouse at the end of the drive (MS).

BRADRIDGE HOUSE. A former farmhouse with attractive Regency additions: rendered, with a rounded end with veranda.

STERT. Small stone farmhouse, early C19, the property of the Heles until 1835.

DITTISHAM

8050

ST GEORGE. Of the church consecrated in 1333 the chancel may survive, with its ogee reticulation in the tracery of the E window. The other windows are Perp, as are the W tower (buttresses of B type, stair-turret and pinnacles) and the embattled N and S aisles, on the N with a rood-stair turret, on the S with a two-storeyed pinnacled porch. In the porch, two bays of lierne-vaults with big bosses; blank arcades against the W and E walls. Good Perp door-ways with traceried spandrels to both porch and church. The aisles are only of four bays, their piers of A type with capitals only to the four shafts. – FONT. Circular, Norman, with the same odd motif as at South Pool, perhaps meaning an arcade to which the columns were added in paint and into which figures were painted. – (SEDILIA with fragment of WALL PAINTING of a cleric in Eucharistic vestments.) – PULPIT. Painted stone, on a palm-like foot. The carving very crude *Volkskunst*, especially the figures. – SCREEN. Across nave and aisles. The painted panels in the wainscoting prove the early C15 as the time of its making. The sections of three lights in the aisles, of four in the nave. Tracery standard type A. – PARCLOSE SCREENS. Later, see the Flamboy-ant details of the large circles in the tracery. – STAINED GLASS. Chiefly coloured decorated borders rather like the glass one sees in

Victorian boarding-houses, but in the E window three panels with figures under canopies said to be by *Pugin*.

Dittisham is an intricate village perched on a steep slope above the river Dart. E of the church the start of a development by *L. de Soissons*, 1933–5 (cf. Churston Ferrers, Torbay), never completed as intended. Affluent houses with garages (the houses on the lower slopes ingeniously approached at first-floor level). The idiom is a restrained upmarket cottage vernacular: white walls, slate roofs, casement windows.

DITTISHAM MILL, 1 m. N. Close to the mill a tall stone house with quoins, three storeys over a basement. Broad windows with keystones.

BOZOMZEAL. The manor house, derelict for many years, was restored in 1988. C16 mullioned windows; single-storey porch.

7040

DODBROOKE
Near Kingsbridge

The church was the original parish church of Kingsbridge (q.v.). Dodbrooke had its own market in 1257 and was a borough in 1319, but never grew further.

ST THOMAS A BECKET. Low, broad W tower (with a spire which fell in 1785), diagonal buttresses, tall bell-openings with one transom. S aisle with S porch attached to its W end. Three- and four-light windows with four-centred arches, the individual lights with depressed arches; no tracery. The piers inside (six bays) of A type with capitals only for the shafts, and double-chamfered arches. The S aisle has a good wagon roof. Restored in 1878–86 by *Edmund Sedding*, who added the chancel and N aisle, re-using clustered columns from the S aisle at South Huish (q.v.). – FONT. Norman, flat and square, of table-top type, with five very shallow blank arches on each side of the top. – SCREEN. Restored by *Hems* in 1897 and extended across the N aisle. Paintings in the wainscoting re-done. Tracery much re-done. – PARCLOSE SCREEN with especially attractive Flamboyant tracery. – (MONUMENT. Elizabeth Coombe † 1666. Wall-monument with columns.)

RECTORY. 1837 by *J. Harrison* of London.

8080

DODDISCOMBSLEIGH

ST MICHAEL. The only place in Devon where one can get an impression of what the STAINED GLASS did to a Perp church. Five late C15 windows are preserved. The figures have the curious facial details characteristic of a local school of craftsmen whose work is also found at Exeter Cathedral, in Somerset (e.g. Winscombe), and in Wiltshire (e.g. Cradwell). In the N aisle the windows are of three lights, in each light a figure above a coat of arms, and above the figure plenty of white glass. So the colour of the windows is predominantly white and yellow, with little of blue, green, and red. The figures are saints (some restored) and the Virgin, the arms those of Chudleighs and Dodscombes. The E window represents the

Seven Sacraments and would have had a central figure of Christ as at Cadbury (q.v); the existing seated Christ was supplied during restoration by *Clayton & Bell* in 1879. Surrounding this figure are charming and most interesting scenes: l. light Eucharist, Marriage, Confirmation; centre light Penance; r. light Ordination, Baptism, Extreme Unction.

The church itself has piers with unusual sections: four main shafts, and in each of the diagonals two thin shafts with a hollow between (cf. Dunsford). Nave and chancel rebuilt by *Ashworth* in 1879; polychrome local stone. Roofs also 1879, in the N aisle incorporating medieval material. The W tower has a very odd buttress arrangement the N and S buttresses neither at the corners nor close to the corners, but in the centres of the sides. – REREDOS. 1917. Expressive relief of the Last Supper. – PULPIT. Nice late C18. – BENCH ENDS. C16, with shields in decorated circular panels above two small round-headed blank arcades. – Other STAINED GLASS. Chancel E by *M. Drake*; two S windows by *F. Drake*.

SHELDON. A late medieval farmhouse once important enough to have a small detached C15 chapel (as at Bury Barton, Lapford), with wagon roof, moulded ribs, and a ball-decorated wall-plate. Reconstructed by *John Deal*, using shuttered cob-wall techniques, in 1970. The house is of cob and thatch, with a C17 two-storey timber-framed porch. The lower end was rebuilt as a cross-wing in the C19. Stud-and-panel screen between hall and inner room: the inner room may have had a sleeping platform in its open hall phase, later partitioned off as a chamber. The hall chimney perhaps original. C16 dairy outshot to the rear. The hall later ceiled and a staircase inserted. The porch chamber had C17 plaster cornice decoration, of which only a fragment survives. The farm buildings have been sensitively converted into a residential training centre.

SPANISHLAKE COTTAGE. A typical cob barn, dated 1771 inside, with the rare survival of an exceptionally small cottage added in cob at the upper end: a primitive house-type which has almost completely disappeared from the Devon countryside. Yet it had a heated room on the ground floor (stack completely of cob) and an upper floor divided into two small chambers by a stud partition.

DOLTON   5010

ST EDMUND. Mostly rebuilt in 1848; restored in 1862 and 1874. The W tower old (diagonal buttresses only at the foot, no pinnacles). Upper part rendered. Good Perp W door of granite. The interior scraped and not attractive; all window tracery renewed. Octagonal piers between nave and aisle and slightly chamfered arches. S aisle roof with carved bosses and frieze. – The importance of the church is the FONT, not really a font at all, but two blocks from what must [9] have been a large Anglo-Saxon cross, one square with elaborate and well-preserved interlace on all sides, the other tapering with intertwisted symmetrical animals, a human head with moustaches growing into animals, and also interlace. – MONUMENTS. Barbara Lister †1696. Stone inscription plate surrounded by an elaborately carved wooden cartouche in the Gibbons style. – Three simple slate tablets to J. H. M. Furse and his two wives, †1950, 1887 and 1963, by *Lawrence Whistler*. – In the churchyard, tomb of Lawrence Whistler's wife, Jill Furse, by *Rex Whistler*.

Dolton is a large village in a remote part of Devon, with rendered and thatched houses. N of the church a little square with the ROYAL OAK; odd moulded blocked arches in the first floor.

CHAPPLE COTTAGE. A C15 and C16 house with good interiors. Roof with full cruck trusses, and a smoke louvre.

4 ASHWELL. A C17 cob farmhouse, probably of older origin, typical of the isolated settlements in this parish.

HALSDON HOUSE. The seat of the Furse family, and later of William Cory, poet (†1892). Early Victorian front with small central pediment between canted bays; the house behind late C17.

STAFFORD BARTON. The former manor house of the Staffords (1589–c. 1890), much altered. Castellated wing added in 1920, of old materials (elaborate early C17 plaster ceiling from No. 7 Cross Street Barnstaple). (Elsewhere, a plaster overmantel dated 1640; C17 joinery and Tudor screen from Looseden Barton, Winkleigh.)

DOWLAND

5010

ST PETER. Small church with W tower with thin diagonal buttresses and obelisk pinnacles; straight-headed nave and N aisle windows. External walls harshly roughcast in 1976. The unusual feature is the timber arcade; the piers are of the usual B type with elementary undecorated capital strips. Medieval ceiled wagon roofs. – FONT. Small octagonal bowl with ribs at the angles, perhaps C17. – Complete set of BENCH ENDS, mostly with tracery, but also Malchus's ear and the keys of St Peter. – STAINED GLASS by *Francis* of Crediton. – Some old pieces in a S window. – Good C17 LEDGER STONES.

CHURCH HOUSE. Large, thatched, somewhat restored, but with good stone stacks.

DOWN ST MARY

7000

ST MARY. Small and remote. Medieval W tower with buttresses of type B, no pinnacles, NE stair-turret. A remarkable triangular C12 tympanum over the S door. It illustrates Daniel in the lions' den. Norman window on the N side of the chancel. Perp N arcade with three low granite arches on A type piers, capitals only to the main shafts. The rest remodelled under the Rev. W. T. A. Radford, 1848–90: one of the richest Victorian ensembles in rural Devon. – REREDOS and sanctuary enrichments by *G. E. Street*, 1866, with carving by *Earp* and mosaics by *Salviati*. – Nave and aisle rebuilt in 1870–2 by *J. F. Gould*, who also designed the brass and iron PULPIT, and, in collaboration with Radford, the polychromy of the internal walls. – SCREEN of late medieval type by the village carpenters *William* and *Zachariah Bushell*. Begun in 1881. – BENCH ENDS. The current late medieval West Country type, unusually including monograms, profiles, a siren with a comb, a cherub with a scourge (cf. Lapford). – STAINED GLASS. E window 1854 by *Hardman*; the rest later, by *Clayton & Bell*. –

MONUMENTS. Several mosaic-enriched memorials of the Radford family.

OLD RECTORY. 1846 by *Hayward* for the Rev. Mr Radford. The usual nearly symmetrical gabled composition. Stone tracery in all the windows, two-storey porch, and a well preserved interior with Tudor doorcases and chimneypieces.

Evidence of Victorian Gothic activity in the village as well: VILLAGE HALL (former school), *c.* 1880, and a group of three cottages with bands of sgraffito decoration.

BUS SHELTER. A rare example of new building in cob, erected in 1978 by *A. Howard*, a local builder, whose object was to pass on the cob-building tradition. Walls in several 'lifts' or 'raises' on a rubble plinth, the cob built unshuttered.

DOWNES
Near Crediton

8090

Handsomely sited on a slight rise with fine views to the S. A two-storey, seven-bay, stone-faced S front with central pediment and parapet; curved links to one-storey pavilions with arched windows. The composition appears C18 Palladian, but the proportions of the main range suggest an earlier date. The explanation appears to be that to a house built by Moses Gould, who bought the Downes estate in 1692, considerable alterations were made by the Buller family, who inherited the house through the marriage of James Buller to Moses Gould's granddaughter Elizabeth.

The entrance is now on the W, through an Edwardian Baroque porch with Ionic pilasters created by *W. C. Marshall* in 1909–10 as part of a toning-down of obtrusive additions of 1866–74. The late Victorian character of the wing behind is still just recognizable. To the N were extensive service wings, now mostly demolished, partly of 1840 by *Henry Roberts*, partly older. The S range was originally only one room deep, with the staircase projecting at the back. The central hall and dining room to its r. were thrown into one in the later C19, and have heavy woodwork of that date. To the l. the bookroom has a simple ceiling of late C17 type with raised circle and quadrants, a re-used Jacobean fireplace dated 1604 (possibly from Dunscombe near Downes), and panelling of 1911.

The best feature of the house is the imposing staircase, entered from the hall by dog-gates. Three flights round a square well. The details are of a transitional type, still in the robust tradition of the late C17, but with the early C18 feature of an open string with carved tread-ends. Two sturdy balusters to each tread, with spirals issuing from carved urns. The ramped handrail is echoed by a dado with raised panelling. In the large arched landing window a C19 arrangement of stained glass including medieval fragments said to come from French monasteries. Splendid ceiling with daring high relief plasterwork still in the tradition of John Abbot's work of 1681 at the Custom House, Exeter. Central oval with foliage; side panels with fronds and rinceaux. Around the cove more light-hearted garlands and coats of arms, including those of James Buller and Elizabeth Gould, i.e. 1739–42, perhaps an addition. At the E end of the first floor a room with late C17 raised panelling and a painting of a biblical scene over the fireplace. At the w end a simple ceiling similar to the one in the bookroom.

The pavilions were perhaps also an addition of the 1730s (cf. James Buller's Palladian effort at Kings Nympton Park, q.v.). They are shown as existing on an estate map of 1784. The stone facing to the s front and the curved links with corridors behind were added in 1794 by *Thomas Jones* of Exeter. The E pavilion has a C19 Jacobean ceiling. Behind this is an E wing probably of 1794, with some good Georgian Gothic doorcases upstairs, two ostentatious Victorian marble fireplaces, and a former E-facing dining room with a shallow bow added in 1910.

Ambitious plans for rebuilding and remodelling in the 1820s–30s came to nothing. Plans for landscaping the grounds were made in 1831, with a formal terrace and flower beds on the s, and a vista of cedars and shrubs to the E.

8000

DOWRICH HOUSE
1½ m. N of Sandford

The house of the Dowrich family from the C12 to 1717. Fine embattled C16 gatehouse. The house drastically remodelled and extended in the C19. Original Tudor doorway. The l. part of the five-bay front also essentially Tudor.

7090

DREWSTEIGNTON

The village, with the church in its centre, is strikingly sited high on the edge of Dartmoor, with distant views on all sides. To the E is the Teign gorge, one of Devon's most picturesque (and popular) spots, with FINGLE BRIDGE, C16 or C17, of granite, with shallow arches and cutwaters.

HOLY TRINITY. Sizeable, all granite. w tower with diagonal buttresses. s aisle and two-storey s porch embattled. Large Perp windows in both aisles, more elaborate on the N side. Granite tracery in the s aisle. The arcades of five bays with piers of A type and the plainest granite capitals. Plain tower arch. Chancel rebuilt in 1862–3 by *Ashworth*. – BENCH ENDS. Two of the C16, traceried. – C17 CLOCK in the tower. – Nice WALL MONUMENT by *J. Kendall* of Exeter, 1807. – In the churchyard, granite MEMORIAL to Julius Drewe of Castle Drogo † 1931, by *Lutyens*.

The houses of the village are grouped round a square with the church at its centre. Many thatched cottages, like CHURCH COTTAGE, are of the C16 to C17, i.e. unusually early. The DREWE ARMS has a simple, unmodernized C19 interior.

CHURCH HOUSE. Given to the parish in 1546 (Hoskins). Solidly built of granite ashlar; two storeys. At the w end a large chimneystack, at the E end an exterior stair. Newel at the sw corner. Ground-floor room with chamfered beams, screen with turned balusters, and an arch-braced jointed-cruck roof.

OLD RECTORY. Late Georgian, with a pretty veranda to the garden.

SCHOOL (former). 1873–4 by *Charles Pinn* of Exeter.

There are many good farmhouses in the parish, including three off separate lanes on the Whiddon Down road. DRASCOMBE BARTON, C17, has an unusual four-room plan with two cross-passages; an unheated service room in the middle next to the hall. NATTONHALL is a C17 longhouse on a grand scale, with the upper-end chamber reached by separate doors from a staircase wing, one chamber with a lateral stack (cf. Westcombe, North Bovey). HOBHOUSE, C15–17, has a smoke-blackened roof throughout, a garderobe in the upper-end chamber, and in the modern porch a re-used two-light timber window with cusped head. Others include FLOOD, a longhouse mostly of cob, apparently all of the late C16 to early C17, the hall floored from the beginning; PRESTON, another C17 superior four-room-plan house with excellent fittings, the inner room end of three storeys; STONE, a former longhouse with its hall still open to the roof; and WEST FURSHAM, with intact late medieval roof and an elaborately decorated C17 hall ceiling. At SANDYPARK, PARFORD retains much of its original smoke louvre; at VENTON, MIDDLE VENTON is a longhouse with unconverted shippon.

STONE CROSS. A restrained earlier C20 design in keeping with Dartmoor traditions. White-rendered, with granite windows and swept slate roofs. Asymmetrical entrance front with a tall porch wing with a mullioned window above the entrance; big chimneys with set-offs.

LIMEKILNS. A massive bank of four, stone with flat arches, on a ridge above a quarry.

SPINSTER'S ROCK. A cromlech or burial chamber of Neolithic origin, possibly originally covered by a cairn of which no trace survives. The stones collapsed in 1862 and were 'restored' in incorrect positions, but the monument is still impressive, and publicly accessible in the field opposite Higher Shilstone Farm.

PRESTONBURY CASTLE. A fine Iron Age HILLFORT in a strong position overlooking the Teign valley 1 m. S of Drewsteignton. The site is protected by one complete rampart and, on the N and E sides not safeguarded by steep drops, two additional widely spaced ramparts. The fort looks directly across the wooded gorge to Cranbrook Castle, Moretonhampstead (q.v.).

See also Castle Drogo.

DUNCHIDEOCK 8080

There is no village proper; the church stands in the fields alone with a cluster of a few houses. The most remarkable of these, until its insensitive modernization *c.* 1966, was the later medieval CLERGY HOUSE (Rectory Cottages), the usual three-room plan, but of two storeys, with a hall with fireplace on each floor. Staircase in a lateral projection; garderobe opening off the inner room.

ST MICHAEL AND ALL ANGELS. Small, all red sandstone, with a very slim little W tower (with stair-turret) and a N aisle divided from the nave by red octagonal piers with moulded octagonal capitals and nearly round-headed two-centred arches; all this as usual in this part of the county (cf. e.g. Exminster). Double-chamfered chancel arch. Tracery and roofs largely C19. – FONT. Octagonal, Perp, with two small quatrefoil panels to each side and traceried pillar. – SCREENS. A complete rood screen across nave and aisle, very well restored by *Herbert Read* in 1893; doors, fancoving, and cornice decorated by four strips of scrolls and fruit and foliage-work. Between nave and aisle the three sides of the pier are encased as part of the screen. The tracery is standard (type A). Of the same type, but unvaulted, of course, and with only one cornice strip, the N parclose screen. – LECTERN. Intricately inventive free Gothic of the 1890s. – PULPIT. 1903 by *Read*, soapily textured. – BENCH ENDS with two-tier tracery. – MONUMENTS. Major-General Stringer Lawrence † 1775, by *William Tyler*, quite a grand, dignified affair with a portrait in profile in an oval medallion at the top of a grey marble obelisk, also in relief. The inscription says: 'The desperate state of affairs in India becoming prosperous by a series of victories endeared him to his country.' A legacy of £50,000 endeared him to his friend in India, Sir Robert Palk, the later owner of Haldon House, who erected this monument, referring in another inscription explicitly to the greater monument to Stringer Lawrence erected by the East India Company in Westminster Abbey.

BELVEDERE, Haldon Hill, above the site of Haldon House (*see* Kenn), and visible from afar. Built by Sir Robert Palk in 1788, and called LAWRENCE CASTLE to commemorate his friend and benefactor, General Stringer Lawrence (*see* above). Palk had had a successful career in India, becoming Paymaster to the Army and later Governor of Madras. The tower is triangular, with angle turrets and Gothic windows, like the earlier example at Powderham – both no doubt inspired by Isaac Ware's triangular belvedere, Shrub Hill Tower, built for the Duke of Cumberland in Windsor Great Park. Exterior of rubble stone, cement-rendered, at the time of writing in bad repair. Within, over-life-size *Coade* stone standing figure of General Lawrence, a copy of a Scheemakers portrait belonging to the former India Office. Lawrence is dressed as a Roman general, with one arm raised, a heavy cloak providing support for the figure in firing.* On the walls, three inscriptions recording his career, set behind shutters. (Gothic plasterwork in the upper room.) Cantilevered stone turret stair to the roof. The planting begun by Palk in 1772 nearly hides the tower from close up, but from its summit one can see far over Dartmoor, to Exmoor, and to the Isle of Portland in Dorset.

Close to the Belvedere a NEOLITHIC DOMESTIC SITE is known from excavations. It is one of the few so far discovered in the South West.

(In the woods between the tower and the site of Haldon House, a late C18 rustic flint BRIDGE.)

DUNCHIDEOCK HOUSE. A former Walrond house. The stuccoed late Georgian exterior incorporates an earlier building. Four-bay entrance front with Doric porch; garden side of 3–5–2 bays.

*Information from Miss Alison Kelly.

DUNKESWELL

ST NICHOLAS. The church built in 1818 by General Simcoe was rebuilt in 1868 by *C.F.Edwards* as an aisled cruciform structure. The tame W tower is a rebuilding of 1952. Whitewashed inside. Dec details; over-elaborate open roofs. – REREDOS. Stone blind arcade. – FONT. Norman, circular, with whole figures in an arcade of columns and very depressed arches. Among them a bishop, king, archer, and a beaked animal head. Very crude craftsmanship. – MONUMENT. Brass to *Henry Ezard*, sculptor, †1868, whose last works were the carved corbels of the church.

DUNKESWELL ABBEY, 2 m. N. In this remote spot William Brewer, Sheriff of Devon, founded a Cistercian abbey in 1201, a daughter house of Forde in Dorset. On part of the site of the abbey church, HOLY TRINITY, 1842, built partly of medieval materials in a puritanical lancet style by Mrs Simcoe of Wolford Lodge. Large, simple, chilly interior with over-scaled N arcade. – REREDOS like the one in St Nicholas. – Some scraps from the abbey displayed: fragments of C13 TILES with foliage and lions set in the chancel floor, and a COFFIN, one of two discovered, presumed to be those of William Brewer and his wife. The abbey church was 185 ft long; some traces of walls survive as the walls of the churchyard, and some ruins of the W range with the abbot's lodgings. Further W the remains of the Perp GATEHOUSE retain a little dressed stone. Earthworks in the vicinity include those of the abbey fishponds.

OLD SHELDON GRANGE, a C15–17 farmhouse, was a grange of the abbey. Unmodernized interior; original roof.

OLD SCHOOLHOUSE, close to the gatehouse. C19 Tudor, of stone probably re-used from the abbey.

CONNETS FARMHOUSE. C16, C17, and C19, with a four-room lobby-entrance plan created by the insertion of C17 fireplaces.

WOLFORD LODGE. 1928 by *Basil Oliver*, re-using material (including mathematical tiles) from the house built by General Simcoe, first Governor of Canada, c. 1800. Nice early Victorian LODGE and gates.

WOLFORD CHAPEL. Built by General Simcoe c. 1800. Gothic.

ROUND BARROWS. Two substantial ones on the S edge of the parish.

DUNSFORD

ST MARY. W tower with stair-turret, buttresses of B type, battlements, no pinnacles. N aisle separated from the nave by piers of unusual section: four main shafts and in each of the diagonals two minor shafts with a hollow between (cf. Doddiscombsleigh). Chancel 1844–5 by *J.Hayward*. Wagon roofs, the N aisle roof with pre-ecclesiological plaster panels prettily painted as vaulting. Tudor recess in the N wall. – Good ensemble of mid C19 FURNISHINGS: reredos, stone screen, font, chancel STAINED GLASS (also some small C15 figures in the tops of N windows). – LECTERN. Eagle book-rest. Base with painted panels by *H. Winsor*, 1846. – MONUMENTS. Sir Thomas Fulford (of Great Fulford) †1610. Standing wall-monument with recumbent figures on a tomb-chest. Three short Corinthian columns support a low tester. Against the back wall below the tester the kneeling figures of his seven children. – Francis Fulford †1700. Architectural, with flaming urns flanking an oval tablet. – Other minor Fulford monuments.

The village lies on a steep wooded slope above the Teign valley. Two ancient bridges, STEPS BRIDGE and CLIFFORD BRIDGE, both with segmental arches. Many C15–18 houses and cottages in the village centre (mostly cob and thatch, but some showy lateral stacks in ashlar granite), different in scale but all on the same basic plan. At the miniature end is the medieval ROSE BANK, Britton Street Lane, on the three-room plan but without a cross-passage; at the other extreme, LEWIS HILL, a long cob-and-thatch agglomeration of late medieval origin (arch-braced roof), with good C17 fittings including a chamber ceiling in rustic plasterwork with cherubs' heads, animals, and foliage and a ground-floor fireplace with chequered plaster.

Good C15–17 farmhouses include the following.

CLIFFORD BARTON. A substantial late medieval house with a C19 lower end wing giving an L-shaped plan. The medieval building phases are represented in the interesting roof carpentry: from the earliest phase are two arch-braced and wind-braced jointed cruck trusses with face pegs and buried double tenons surmounted (highly unusually) by a crown-post arrangement laterally braced only (cf. the Old Rectory, Cheriton Bishop). The hall survives almost completely in its developed early C17 form, including a stud-and-panel partition with integral bench and a very rare elaborate bench end.

DANDYLANDS. A mid C17 farmhouse, fully partitioned and chambered when built.

EAST DOWN. Much altered, but an important example of continuity in farmhouse development. The medieval roof over the core of the house, a two-bay open hall, has original wattling and broom below the later thatch: the extent of the earliest house is marked by end-crucks. The house was remodelled and extended in three directions in the C17: the upper end was rebuilt, a kitchen wing constructed at the rear, and an unheated room added at the lower end. Excellent carpentry details throughout. Adjacent a cob-and-thatch BARN with initials and date WT 1815 inside, and a round-house, imaginatively converted for use as a field study centre by *Stephen Emmanuel* in 1984.

FORD. A single-build late C17 farmhouse on a U-plan, the principal rooms either side of the central entrance with stair and through passage to the rear, the wings as service rooms. Plasterwork in the principal ground- and first-floor rooms (ovals of thistles and oak leaves on the ground floor, flowers on the first) and painted overmantels with landscape and hunting scenes.

SCOTTISHILL. A late medieval farmhouse now on a four-room plan. The front room was added at the upper end as a C17 kitchen whose fireplace occupies the full width of the house. Bee boles at ground- and first-floor level on the front of the house.

SOUTH HALSTOW. A remodelled late medieval house. A lease of 1539 refers to a parlour within the hall with chamber over. On the first floor, two painted legends. One reads: 'When thou art rich thou many friends shall find. If riches fail, friends soon will prove unkind.'

IRON MILLS, near the river, originally fed by a leat from Steps Bridge. An edge-tool factory which produced agricultural implements (cf. Sticklepath). A wheel and two trip-hammers survive.

COTLEY WOOD is the site of a substantial univallate HILLFORT on an irregular plan, in excellent condition, bisected by a road, and commanding wide views over Haldon and the lower Exe valley.

See also Great Fulford.

DUNSLAND HOUSE
Near Bradford

4000

Devon's most tragic loss since the last war. The seat of the Arscotts, Bickfords, Cohams, and Dickinsons, acquired by the National Trust in 1954, burnt down in 1967, when its restoration was nearly complete. The house had a Tudor S wing, with additions of 1660, and a substantial E wing of c. 1690 (seven bays, central pediment with giant pilasters). Inside were excellent woodwork and plasterwork and a ceiling of c. 1690 with the detached modelling of garlands and flowers characteristic of the supremely skilful plasterers working elsewhere in North Devon (Royal Hotel, Bideford; Youlston Park).

DUNTERTON

3070

ALL SAINTS. No village. Broad W tower with buttresses of type B and polygonal pinnacles. The attached church not longer than the tower is high. Arcade between nave and aisle of A type with a little decoration in the capitals and castellated abaci. The arches four-centred and slightly moulded. Restored 1889–90 by *O.B. Peter* of Launceston. – PULPIT. C18.

HILLTOP ENCLOSURES. Vestiges of two of the many on both sides of the Tamar valley in Dunterue Wood and W of Woodtown, corresponding to those on the Cornish side at Castle Park Hill and Carthamartha Wood. They may be of the first millennium B.C.

DURPLEY CASTLE
1 m. N of Ladford, near Shebbear

4010

A fine motte-and-bailey with well preserved earthworks. Traces of a double ramp and ditch around parts of the bailey. The motte had a concave profile, presumably reflecting a former tower within it. The origins of the site are obscure. Shebbear was a royal manor, but there is no record of a royal castle here.

EAST ALLINGTON

7040

ST ANDREW. W tower with corbel-table to support the battlements and no pinnacles. Buttresses of type B. Stair-turret not centrally placed. S porch at the W end of the aisle. The arcades of N and S aisles inside not all of one pattern: N piers 1 and 2 are octagonal, but have capitals of a type suitable only for piers of A type, as indeed are N 3–5 and S 1–4. Windows and roofs renewed in a restoration of 1873–5, paid for by William Cubitt of Fallapit. – PULPIT. On a chalice-shaped foot. The carving makes the C17 likely, though obviously in an attempt to do as the C15 had done. – SCREEN. Much re-done. The wainscoting now with oblong Elizabethan panels. The tracery type A standard, cornice of thin friezes of ornament, coving not preserved. Dated in one panel 1547. – STAINED GLASS. One old roundel in a N window. – MONUMENTS. Brass to John Fortescue †1595 and wife. – Unidentified brass of a kneeling woman, perhaps mid C16. – Edmund Fortescue †1624. Incised slab. High Sheriff, in civil dress. – John Fortescue †1649 and his wife †1628. Two poor kneeling figures in the usual composition. – Rev. Nath. Wells †1762. Nice simple wall-monument without figures and with very little ornament; by *Emes* of Exeter.

FALLAPIT. A seat of the Fortescues from the C15, acquired *c.* 1860 by William Cubitt. The exterior early C19 neo-Tudor, five bays with projecting centre bay (MS).

EAST ANSTEY

8020

ST MICHAEL. W tower with diagonal buttresses at the foot, no pinnacles, NE stair-turret. Aisleless nave. Much restored in 1871 by *E. Ashworth.* – (C18 PULPIT and COMMUNION RAILS; French REED ORGAN of 1870.)

EAST BUCKLAND

6030

ST MICHAEL. W tower with diagonal buttresses and no pinnacles. Nave pulled down when an austere new nave, in the place where one would expect a N aisle, was erected in 1862–3 by *R.D. Gould* for the use of the pupils of Devon County School (*see* West Buckland). – Gothic chamber ORGAN CASE (AC). – STAINED GLASS. Brightly coloured E window in the style typical of *Beer.* – *Berry* SUNDIAL on the porch.

EAST BUDLEIGH

0080

ALL SAINTS. Quite a tall tower (diagonal buttresses only half-way up), and quite a roomy interior (four bays, N and S aisles with piers of B section and capitals only to the four shafts; Perp windows). S aisle and tall S porch are embattled. S doorway with fleurons in the hollow moulding. Squint across the rood-loft staircase between S aisle and chancel. Some building work perhaps from the time of Bishop Lacy (1420–55), whose arms are in the glass of a N window. Ceiled roofs with bosses to both nave and chancel (repainted 1974). Chancel extended 1853 – hence the position of the C13 PISCINA, a simple pointed-trefoil recess. Further restoration in 1884 by

R.M.Fulford. - FONT. Panelled Perp. - PULPIT. 1894 by *Fellowes Prynne*, executed by *Hems*; figure panels in high relief and two tiers of angels. - SCREEN. Without fan-coving. Square-headed panels with Perp tracery and pierced spandrels (cf. Bow, Braunton, Calverleigh). - BENCH ENDS. Unusually numerous (sixty-three in all) and unusually varied: many motifs of large leaves, coats of arms (e.g. Raleigh), a ship, shears (cf. Cullompton), angels, faces in profile, etc. Not one Renaissance motif, although dated 1537. Additions of 1884 and 1902. - PAINTING. On the chancel N wall a Virgin and Child by *Edward Aveling Green*, brother of a former vicar and pupil of Burne-Jones. - STAINED GLASS. Chancel S 1929: peacock and tree of life. Unusual, bold colours. - MONUMENTS. Joan Raleigh, early C16, an incised floriated cross with the inscription backwards. - Among minor tablets, the Reade family, *c.*1866, an elaborate Gothic tabernacle.

SALEM CHAPEL. On the edge of the village, near the main road, an eye-catching little group of low white buildings around a walled yard, built by the Independents in 1719. Chapel with rendered walls, probably cob, and hipped slate roof. The original central entrance replaced in 1836 by two side doorways. Later vestry and Sunday School buildings. Inside the chapel, the vaulted ceiling is supported by an iron column. Original gallery and PEWS. C17 CLOCK on the gallery front, from Honiton.

East Budleigh was an important settlement until the Otter ceased to be navigable. The attractive village centre, with much cob and thatch, lies away from the main road, with some good houses, e.g. WYNARDS, with an early C19 red brick front and bracketed eaves below a hipped roof, but cob side walls. At the back an older BARN with small primitive wooden mullioned arched windows. VICARS MEAD, Hayes Lane, is of cob and thatch, with a later projecting wing with simple Venetian windows. It once had an exterior staircase, and may have been a late medieval church house. S of the bridge, on the W side, an ornate octagonal TOLL HOUSE attached to a thatched house.

In the parish several Rolle estate buildings (cf. Bicton), for example SAWMILL COTTAGE, built as two dwellings, dated 1876, with patterned brickwork. The estate sawmill was worked by a now vanished water mill.

At Yettington, YSHUAR is the former Bicton School House, 1847 'in the Swiss style of architecture' (White), built by Lady Rolle, converted into cottages in 1923 by *Rogers, Bone & Coles.*

PILLAR. Of brick, with a rectangular stone cap bearing religious inscriptions and a cross, erected in 1580 by the Sheriff of Devon who had to order the burning of a witch at the crossroads. In 1743 Lady Rolle added plaques naming the places to which each road leads.

TIDWELL HOUSE. A tall, plain, but well detailed red brick house built by one of the Walrond family who bought the estate *c.*1730. Five bays, the centre three set forward, parapet, rusticated brick quoins, straight-headed windows of rubbed brick. Ground-floor rooms with some fielded panelling; staircase hall centre back with three balusters to the tread (plain – twisted – plain) and a ceiling with good leafy cornice and centre quatrefoil with a griffin. The large arched staircase window probably a later alteration. Back stairs with turned balusters and closed string. Small reset Jacobean overmantel with arms and two flanking figures. U-shaped stables close to the house.

See also Hayes Barton.

6040   EAST DOWN

St John Baptist. The church stands secluded on the side of a hill, close to the manor house. According to Polwhele it was formerly the manorial chapel, enlarged after the church at Churchill was abandoned. As often in North Devon, the tower is in a transeptal position. This usually indicates an early date. Here the tower is on the N side, unbuttressed and unpinnacled and with a narrow, pointed, unmoulded arch towards the inside. The s aisle was added in the Perp style. Low arcade of five bays with piers of B type and standard leaf capitals; also figures and animals among the leaves. Unceiled wagon roofs. Everything much renewed in 1886–8 during *William White*'s restoration. – FONT. Its shaft is the most remarkable item in the church, a tapering hexagon, of wood, and with early Renaissance panels. Foot and bowl are additions of *c.* 1700. – SCREEN. Beautiful, but much restored by *Read* of Exeter in 1928. Wainscoting and tracery new. Ribbed coving with early Renaissance motifs between. Most of the cornice and cresting new. – ALTAR, s chapel. Made up from Elizabethan panelling. – STAINED GLASS. E window 1898 by *Kempe Studios*. – s chapel s signed by *L. L. Lubin* of Tours, 1891, pictorial, very un-English. – MONUMENTS. Edward Pine †1663. Wall-monument with two frontal faces in ovals; not good. – In the churchyard, Annie Arthur †1876, a late example of the neo-classical pedestal tomb, with mourning female and willow tree.

To the N, Church House Chamber, with tripartite windows and sunken crosses of *c.* 1800, although perhaps older in origin.

Methodist Chapel and School. 1901 by *Alexander Lauder*.

Manor House, just sw of the church. An attractive front, though badly proportioned on closer inspection – probably a rustic early C18 remodelling of an older house, which had belonged to the Pine family since the C13. Rough joins suggest that a projecting two-storey porch may have been removed. The centre is now defined by two wooden Doric pilasters on high plinths, with their own entablatures, and by a clumsily steep pediment. A pediment also to the Doric porch. Three C18 sashed windows on each side, not quite symmetrical. In the s-facing end wall a puzzling relieving archway of dressed stone above a bay-window, cut into by an upper window. Beyond this a Regency wing (former library). Large staircase hall between this and the C19 N wing. The entrance hall now has a single large room on each side. In the l. one reset Jacobean panelling and a later overmantel with finely carved hanging swags, now all painted. In the r. room a plaster ceiling with the Pine arms in a quatrefoil, and fielded panelling. The end bay is divided off by a shallow arch on two fluted Ionic columns. This, and the doorways and overmantel with broken pediment enclosing ball finials, perhaps *c.* 1760. On the first floor several rooms with panelling and coved ceilings. Stair-hall also with a coved ceiling; the stair itself renewed. The Pine-Coffins were here until 1866 (cf. Portledge). C18 STABLES, now cottages.

CHURCHILL. A farming hamlet, originally with its own church. Three houses, late-looking exteriors disguising C17 origins in at least two. A range of stone farm buildings shows the many specialist structures of the later traditional farmstead, including a spectacularly large bank barn, with an engine house to the rear, and a malthouse. Another barn has four bee boles set at an unusually high level in the S face of a cob wall.

NORTHCOTE was a Domesday manor of the Northcote family. The C17 farmhouse incorporates as a rear wing a fragment of the larger medieval house. A plaque with RR 1737 on a stack refers to major later alterations. Small upper chamber with one richly moulded raised cruck roof-truss with high cambered collar; a similar moulding on the fireplace. Courtyard of farm buildings, including a large stable block with hayloft above and adjoining granary; beyond, a walled garden with ash-house incorporating hen-roosts, and three bee boles one above another in an adjoining wall.

EAST OGWELL

The manor house stands so close to the church tower that the two appear almost as one.

ST BARTHOLOMEW. The plain W tower with completely plain tower arch may in its structure well belong to the early Middle Ages. Polygonal stair-turret, near one corner with tiny trefoiled and quatrefoiled windows. The chancel (S window) also looks E.E. S transept and S porch with a fireplace, much smaller than at Wolborough near by. The N aisle added Perp piers of an unusual moulding, the same as at Bishopsteignton; standard capitals; the arches nearly semicircular; the windows straight-headed. Restored by *R. M. Fulford* in 1884–5, when the chancel floor level was raised and the roofs rebuilt. Contemporary chancel fittings by *Fulford*. – SCREEN. Usual, except that the wainscoting has rather Flamboyant forms. – TOWER SCREEN. C17, not quite in its original condition. Two tiny caryatids; otherwise very plain panelling and a railing above similar to mid C17 altar rails. Is the whole assembled from various sources? – MONUMENTS. S transept: tomb-chest with a Tudor arch behind, flanked by small caryatids supporting an entablature with a steep pediment rising in the middle. Some of the leaf decoration still Perp in character, but mostly early Renaissance. Ascribed to Richard Reynell † 1585. The Reynell family (cf. Newton Abbot) built a burial chapel to the E of the transept, now a vestry, where some heraldic STAINED GLASS remains. On a wall high up, a tablet inscribed 'Golgotha R.L. 1633'. – Three tomb slabs of abbots of Torre, including an incised one to Thomas Dyare † 1523(?), presumably brought here after the Dissolution. – Built into the E and W gables of the N aisle, two halves of a C6 Early Christian BURIAL STONE with the Latin inscription CAOCI FILI POPLICI.

MANOR HOUSE. The seat of the Reynells until 1589, ruined by

Polwhele's time. S part rebuilt in the early C19. The three-storey L-shaped N part may be the parlour end of the medieval house. In the N gable a tall, partly blocked two-centred arch; in the W gable a blocked two-centred doorway.

JOLLY SAILOR INN. Called Church House Inn in the 1820s. Rendered and thatched.

OGWELL GRANGE (former rectory), Rectory Road. 1849. Interestingly irregular Tudor. Stone, with clustered brick chimneystacks and crested ridge tiles.

EAST PORTLEMOUTH

7030

ST WINWALOE (a Cornish-Breton dedication). Low W tower with type C buttresses and a low stair-turret. Two-storeyed N porch with straight outer stair. N and S aisles and N and S transepts. Arcades (five bays) of A, i.e. Cornish, type with capitals only to the four shafts and moulded arches. Restored 1881. – FONT. Perp, octagonal, plain. – SCREEN. Uncommonly small figures in the wainscoting, tracery of Dartmouth type, cornice, and three friezes of ornament. The spandrels altered. Lower panels with figure painting.

(HIGH HOUSE. C17 farmhouse with two-storey porch, within a walled forecourt.)

DECKLERS CLIFF, between Prawle Point and Kingsbridge estuary. On the downslope side some spectacularly well preserved lynchetted fields of prehistoric or later date.

EAST PUTFORD

3010

CHURCH (former). Rebuilt 1882. Now a farm building. – FONT. Circular, Norman, the bowl partly destroyed. Originally it was just like that at Harberton. – TILES. Of the usual Barnstaple type (fleur-de-lys, rose, lion, etc.) in the S porch.

EAST WORLINGTON

7010

ST MARY. Extensively and most oddly rebuilt in 1879 by *Clark & Holland* of Newmarket, architects to the Earl of Portsmouth, who paid for the work. Norman S doorway. The outer arch moulding with zigzag rests on a beast's head on the l.; three inner arch bands of saltire crosses. Norman also the masonry of the chancel, with a tiny window. This must have inspired the very unarchaeological Romanesque of the C19 W tower and S side.

EAST WORLINGTON HOUSE. Late C18 symmetrical rendered front of 1-5-1 bays. The centre is early C16, much altered (moulded arch-braced truss over the lower end). Parlour with late C17 plaster ceiling; good C18 fittings.

E of Burrow Cross a BARROW CEMETERY in variable condition.

See also West Worlington.

EBBERLY HOUSE
Roborough, near Great Torrington

5010

An unusual and attractive house, chiefly of *c.* 1816, rebuilt by Henry Hole, builder and wood-engraver of Liverpool, who inherited the estate from his uncle. Modest two-storey stuccoed main range, lined to look like ashlar, of 2–3–2 bays, divided by pilasters. Roman Doric porch with four fluted columns. Full-height bowed ends. These hint at the variety of room shapes inside; a provincial echo of the interests of contemporary architects such as Nash and Soane. *Thomas Lee* (*see* Arlington) would seem the most likely local architect, or was Hole his own designer? To the r. of the hall, an oval drawing room, tripartite, divided by shallow arches, and with an enriched cornice and marble fireplace. The hall itself is octagonal with the off-centre entrance neatly balanced by a niche. To its l. a small parlour and larger bow-ended room, now a kitchen. The large central chimneystack in this room as well as the general proportions of the range suggest an older house remodelled. Behind, Hole added a parallel range. In the N E part, above cellars, a large, handsome library, with the ingenious device of a fireplace below the window at the N end. Adjoining, a small oval stair-hall with elegantly cantilevered wooden staircase. Plain balusters, moulded soffits to the treads. Large room over the library with another fireplace under the window. The first-floor rooms in the main range, approached by a top-lit corridor, have coved ceilings and nicely detailed doorcases with triple shafts. The most intriguing puzzle is the room over the octagonal entrance hall, which has a low dome, but much too low to make a satisfactory space. Was the original plan a double-height hall with balconies? At the end of the drive, a charming miniature gate screen; two Ionic columns supporting a pediment.

EDGE BARTON
Near Branscombe

1080

A picturesque U-shaped group incorporating substantial remains of a medieval and Tudor house. The birthplace of Bishop Branscombe (†1280), from 1317 owned by the Wadhams, from 1618 let as a farmhouse. Much restored and added to after 1933 by *Frank Masters*, and again after 1951 (ground-floor openings all tactfully renewed). The hall in the central range, with an inserted floor and a large end fireplace, is approached on the E side through a C20 addition. Between the two a four-centred Perp doorway, perhaps not *in situ*, as it opens into the centre of the hall E wall. At the N E corner a newel stair with chamfered two-centred doorway, formerly external, providing access to the upper rooms of the three-storeyed N wing. This has Tudor two- and three-light uncusped windows. S of the hall and under the same (renewed) roof, an upper room with a large mullioned-and-transomed window below the S gable, and a Tudor fireplace, expressed externally by the large double stack next to the doorway in the W front. E of this room was a chapel (mentioned by Lysons) whose fabric is embed-

ded in later extensions. Remains of a fine early C14 circular
window with five trefoils visible in an attic. The piscina reset in the
C20 inner hall may also come from the chapel.

6010   EGGESFORD

The church lies on its own, near the site of the old Eggesford House.

ALL SAINTS. Small, much rebuilt in the restoration of 1867. W tower
older, low, with diagonal buttresses and no pinnacles. NE chapel
with a Perp arch of granite towards the chancel, the responds not
identical, the E one with four main shafts in the diagonals, the W one
with hollow diagonals instead of shafts, perhaps c. 1400. N arcade
rebuilt in 1867 when the church was restored at the expense of the
Earl of Portsmouth. – FONT. Norman, much restored. Bowl with
rosettes on each side and lower edge scalloped. – LAMPS. Victorian
ormolu hanging oil lamps of brass and iron. – STAINED GLASS. W
window with three small medieval heads, S aisle windows with old
armorial glass, including the arms of Reigny, the medieval lord of
the manor. – E window 1897 by *Clayton & Bell*. – N aisle, Marys at
the Sepulchre, by *Kempe Studios*, 1893.
    MONUMENTS. Sadly messed about, but an outstanding group.
Edward, Viscount Chichester, †1648, and wife. Prepared in his
lifetime. Alabaster, two excellent recumbent figures. – Arthur,
Viscount Chichester, †1674, with two wives. Erected in 1650.
Formerly in the N chapel together with the previous monument,
now in the nave. This must have been a remarkable composition,
with the life-size Viscount standing upright, the two wives slightly
smaller, lying on two sides of an open pediment, and a small
informal group of seven children below. Attributed by Mrs Esdaile
to *William Wright*. – William Fellowes †1723. A plain but noble
composition of varied marbles with severely straight sarcophagus
against pyramid and niche. Originally four kneeling figures at the
foot. – Henry Arthur Fellowes †1792. Urn against grey obelisk.
EGGESFORD HOUSE, ½m. W. An eminently picturesque large ruin
standing against the sky, surrounded by the woods of the Taw
valley, like the best of follies. Built on a new site in 1822 for Newton
Fellowes by the Barnstaple architect *Thomas Lee*, an early example
in the county of the use of an embattled Tudor style for a country
house. Dismantled in 1917.
(EGGESFORD BARTON. Mainly C18. Reset datestone of 1626.)
MEDLAND MANOR. By *W.C.* and *Bruce Oliver*, c. 1910. Mullioned
windows, hipped roof, and cupola.

3070   ENDSLEIGH
                           Milton Abbot

ENDSLEIGH COTTAGE, now a hotel run by a fishing syndicate, was
designed in 1810 by *Sir Jeffry Wyatville* for the sixth Duke of
Bedford, on a site chosen by the Duchess. The 'cottage' in the name
is significant: the house is one of the most revealing testimonies to
the strength of the Picturesque movement. It was intended as a

Endsleigh Cottage: engraving of the view from the south

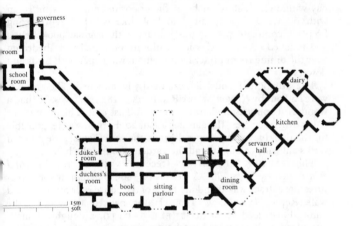

Endsleigh Cottage: plan

family residence, a convenient centre for visiting the extensive
Bedford estates in Devon and Cornwall. A long rhododendron-
enclosed drive leads to the entrance court. This is not especially
prepossessing: a haphazard composition made up of two wings
coming forward from the main range at an angle, slate roofs of
various heights, a plethora of chimneys, dormers, and gables, and
rendered walls artfully incised to give the impression of irregular
coursing. The STABLES opposite are less contrived; low stone
buildings around a courtyard containing a well with the foundation
stone of 1810 laid by the Duke's four sons.

From the garden side it is clear that the irregularity is the result of
a carefully controlled plan which takes full advantage of the stun-
ning views w and s over the Tamar. From here, the house appears as
a group of cottages. The E range, principally a service wing, recedes

behind the high wall of the kitchen court. The W wing, a pavilion intended as the 'children's cottage', is linked only by a low corridor and a veranda with rustic colonnade (although it is overlooked by the Duke and Duchess's own rooms at the side of the main range, a nicely human touch). The main living rooms face S, but the dining room, at the end of the angled service wing, has a bay-window looking SE along the line of Repton's terrace. The angle between this bay and the main range is neatly filled by another rustic loggia. Stone mullioned windows on the ground floor, a mixture of barge-boarded and coped gables, half-hipped roofs. The Duke and Duchess's rooms are singled out by bay-windows, and by a parapet with rounded merlons, flanked by non-identical angled chimneys (for corner fireplaces). The children's pavilion has similar chimneys but is embellished by a more light-hearted trellised corner veranda.

Well preserved interior. Sombre entrance hall with grained panelling simulating large panels. On the walls three long map rolls and a bust of the fifth Duke. Large stone fireplace with marble stippling with ingle-nooks within the Gothic arch. The dining room is Regency Gothick, with painted tracery above the panelling and plenty of Russell heraldry on the walls and in the stained glass of the bay-windows. Shallow niche at the opposite end. Drawing room with plastered dado painted to look like wood. Egyptianizing fireplace complete with grate. Library with original bookshelves and reduced copies of classical sculpture on top. In the bedroom over the dining room pretty hand-painted wallpaper with birds and flowers.

The situation of Endsleigh can hardly be matched. The grounds were laid out by *Repton*, whose Red Book of 1814 survives. He had a wonderful opportunity here and made full use of it. The plantations cover over 300 acres, the gardens about 20. Repton was responsible for the thickly wooded slopes down to the river Tamar, the miles of walks and rides along it, and the gardens around the house.

The GARDEN BUILDINGS (recently well restored by *Paul Pearn*) are by *Wyatville*. A design of 1809 by Repton for a picturesque cottage was abandoned. SW of the house is a broad terraced walk (Repton's view shows a conservatory between the walk and the bank above) leading to the SHELL GROTTO, a delightful shell-encrusted polygonal summerhouse overlooking the Tamar far below. Dim interior with opaque glazing; the tiny triangular windows high up have yellow glass with spider's-web leading. Further S, just visible from the house, the SWISS COTTAGE, perched on a bluff above the river, an early demonstration of the influence of the romance of Alpine travel. Restored with a thatched roof, as on old views, for the Landmark Trust. Two-storeyed, the timber frame clad with diagonal boarding, veranda posts with decorative notching. It originally functioned as a summerhouse above a labourer's cottage.

NW of the house the DAIRY DELL, another *Repton* creation, with POND COTTAGES next to a pool and nearby, the DAIRY, octagonal, surrounded by a loggia. Cool tiled interior with opaque glazing, fitted sinks and shelves. White tiles with ivy trails. There was a hydraulic system for washing down the table and slabs – see the hole in the central octagonal marble table. Further up the stream which feeds the pool, the HOLY WELL, a tiny rustic stone building incorporating some medieval fragments brought from Leigh Barton in the C19, with inscription declaring rather quaintly that it served as the baptismal font for the hunting seat of the abbots of Tavistock. Repton's picturesque setting extended to smoke rising on the horizon, for which purpose a fire was lit in an empty cottage, it is said, every day until 1940.

ERMINGTON

St Peter and St Paul. What most people remember about this church is its twisted spire, similar in outline to the more famous one at Chesterfield. But there is more to take an interest in. First of all, the whole steeple is C13–early C14: thin angle buttresses with only one set-off, small windows, small bell-openings, and battlements on a corbel-table. The design is similar to Holbeton. The chancel (see the s window with reticulated tracery, priest's door with curved ogee arch, and piscina) is C14. The s and N transept windows also go with that date. N and s aisles with granite piers of A type, the arches higher where the transepts were taken into consideration, lower for the chancel aisles. Inside, just two indications of a pre-C14 church: a re-used scalloped capital in the archway of the N vestry door, and a plain round-headed rere-arch, presumably Norman, behind the over-large square-labelled s doorway (in Perp style but more likely C19).

Extensive C19 fittings due to the restoration by *J. D. Sedding* for the Mildmays of Flete – see the initialled rainwater heads dated 1889 – although not as interesting as the work at Holbeton. Much of the woodwork designed and largely made by *Violet Pinwell* and her sisters, daughters of the rector: especially remarkable the huge REREDOS with wooden figured panels above a large alabaster scene of the Nativity (*c.* 10 ft long). Also by the *Pinwells* STALLS and BENCH ENDS, a smaller REREDOS in the s chapel (in memory of their mother, †1900), the openwork FONT COVER, and the ambitious PULPIT, with much figure carving, competent if not original. – SCREENS. The rood screen is mid C17 – see its ornament, just going gristly from the previous strapwork phase. The columns are a C19 replacement of balusters. – Parclose screen by *J. D. Sedding*, copied from Holbeton. – MONUMENTS. William Strashleigh †1583 and wife. Kneeling figures in brass below a thin arch. – Christopher Chudleigh(?) (son-in-law of the above) †1570. Tomb-chest with shields between fluted pilasters, Tudor arch, and above it florid early Renaissance decoration, well carved in limestone. Is it of several dates? – Margaret Rich †1675. Small tablet with putti heads and crowned skull. – Minor tablets, e.g. to the Swetes of Traine (*see* Modbury); also a banner with Swete arms and two helms.

LYCHGATE. By *J. D. Sedding*, *c.* 1890. Remarkably monumental, almost Lutyenesque. A double flight of steps from the road below the churchyard meets under the gate with twin round-headed stone arches on bulgy Arts and Crafts columns. At the sides big voluted buttresses.

The village centre, with its market place on a slope, has no remarkable buildings, but in the parish as a whole there are several good

farmhouses, some of them once more substantial manor houses –
STRASHLEIGH, Warren Lane, for example, the seat of the Strash-
leighs from the C13 to 1583, with remains of a C16 house with a
two-storey porch and an C18 wing, and HUNSDON FARM, with
several mullioned windows and the date 1629. COYTON has a
regular three-bay front, dated 1832, with the initials EPB,
HIGHER LUDBROOK an early C19 stuccoed front with corner
pilasters and pedimented windows and earlier back parts. At
LUDBROOK, a WATER MILL with mill house, early C19; undershot wheel and machinery survive. At PENSUIT, FILHAM MINE
ENGINE, the ruins of the engine house of the disused Ivybridge
Consols silver lead mine, 1856. At the junction of B3221 and 3211
a two-storey angle-fronted TOLL HOUSE with pointed windows
and a recessed central doorway.

ESCOT
Near Ottery St Mary

ESCOT HOUSE. 1837 by *Henry Roberts* for Sir John Kennaway,
replacing an earlier (and much more interesting) house built
c.1680 for Sir Walter Yonge by *Robert Hooke* and illustrated in
Vitruvius Britannicus. It was destroyed by fire in 1808. The present
building is a plain three-storeyed block of yellow brick with a
raised terrace to s and w at the level of the *piano nobile*. On the s
side a recessed central loggia. Greek Doric porch, central top-lit
staircase. Fine C18 PARK with lake.

ST PHILIP AND ST JAMES. Within the park. 1838–40, also by
Roberts. Simple nave and chancel with w bellcote. Late Georgian in
character, with lancets, prettily decorative flint masonry, and plaster-vaulted chancel. – Original BENCHES; chancel fittings later.

EXBOURNE

ST MARY. The outstanding feature of the church is its e window, of
three lights, early C14, fully cusped, with Dec tracery, but not of
the flowing kind (the principle is intersection cut short by a
depressed spheric quadrangle at the top). Inside, two nook-shafts;
on them two little niches for angel figures, and then above the
window a large, bold, cusped and crocketed ogee arch. The whole
composition may well be the work of an Exeter Cathedral mason.
The small chancel n window of the same date. Otherwise little of
special architectural interest. The w tower of ashlared granite with
buttresses of type B, hoodmoulded w door, and two niches against
the w buttresses. s aisle and s porch also of ashlared granite. The
arcade between the two granite, too: four bays, piers of A type,
moulded strips instead of capitals, and depressed arches. The s
aisle s windows straight-headed without tracery, the e window
with minimum tracery. The wagon roof of the s aisle unceiled. The
restoration of 1884–6 by *R.M.Fulford* included rebuilding the n
wall, the ingenious conversion of rood-stair turret to a passage
connecting pulpit, vestry, and organ chamber, and the partial
reconstruction of the chancel roof. Further restoration 1899 by

Tait & Harvey. – SCREEN. Much renewed, with standard type A tracery, no coving, two bands of ornament in the cornice, and cresting. – Other WOODWORK by *Herbert Read*, 1900–10; good Arts and Crafts pews. – STAINED GLASS. S aisle E 1886 by *C.H.Brewster*; elsewhere patterned glass designed by *Fulford*, made by *Drake*. – MONUMENT. Simon Westlake †1667. Rustic inscription with Ionic columns and segmental pediment.

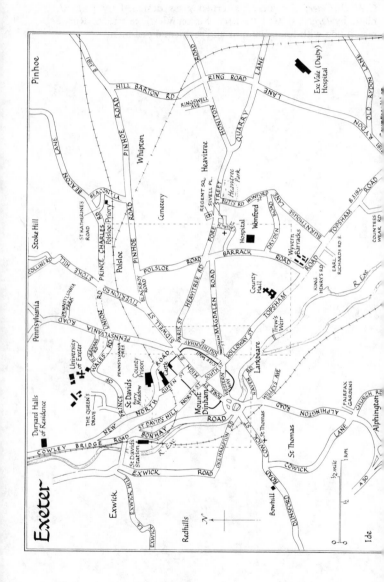

EXETER

INDEX OF STREETS

INTRODUCTION

The story begins c. A.D. 55–60 with the construction of a fortress for the Second Augustan Legion, the military headquarters for the South West of England. At the centre of the present town, on the hill commanding the lowest bridgeable crossing over the Exe, it was surrounded by an earth and timber rampart and ditch. Its most impressive building was a symmetrically planned stone bath house, whose foundations were exposed in the Cathedral Green excavation of 1971–3 and are now unimaginatively hidden again. Finds included fragments of the earliest figured mosaic in Britain. After the legion departed c. 75, most of the bath house was demolished; parts of its walls were incorporated in the basilica built on the NE side of the new forum laid out c. 80 across the present line of South Street as the civic centre of the town, with new public baths to its SE.

The Roman town took over much of the road plan of the fortress – the usual grid subdividing the land into *insulae* – and also retained the defences, until stone walls were built, taking in a much larger area, in the late C2. These are the existing city walls, although much rebuilt later. Evidence for remodelling of the basilica in the C3 and further alterations of the C4, together with very fragmentary discoveries of stone buildings elsewhere in the town, suggest that urban life continued to flourish, although not all the area within the walls was closely built up. But by the later C5 the basilica had disappeared, its site taken over by a possibly Christian cemetery, the forerunner of the one which may have been associated with the monastery at which St Boniface was educated in the C7.

Apart from the walls, the main topographical legacy of the Roman city is the line of the High Street, which in part follows the Roman main road. The four main medieval gates were also probably on or near the sites of Roman gates, and the line of Smythen Street and Stepcote Hill down to West Gate may reflect an early digression from the Roman grid.

In the late C9 the town re-emerged as one of the fortified Alfredian burhs after occupation by the Danish army in 877. The four main roads, traces of back streets (Waterbeer Street, Catherine Street), and possibly an intramural street (Bartholomew Street) date from this time (cf. Winchester and other late Saxon planned towns). The numerous churches and chapels within the walls (over twenty by the late C13) were mostly sited along the main streets or by the gates. Many may be late Saxon foundations, although only a few have any visible fabric of that period (St Olave, which may have originated as a chapel of a Saxon royal palace, St Martin, and the remains of St George).

The chief religious establishment at this time was the church later known as St Mary Major which survived in its C19 form within the cathedral close until the 1970s. Its Saxon plan is known from excavations. It was elevated to cathedral status when Exeter became a see in 1050, but became a parish church after the new, much larger Norman cathedral was built in the C12. This cathedral was served by secular clergy, who replaced some form of Saxon monastery. From the later C11 the only monastic foundation within the city was St Nicholas Priory, a Benedictine house. The vaulted undercroft of its surviving W range may date from not long after its foundation in the late C11. But

the most impressive early Norman building in the city is the gate-
6 house-keep of the castle, a powerful architectural statement of the
rude force of the Conqueror. The more refined and ornate style of C12
Romanesque is represented by the N and S towers of the cathedral,
which survived the later medieval rebuilding campaigns, by delicate
carved fragments from the cloister of St Nicholas, and by the spacious
7 aisled nave of St Mary Arches, an exception among the generally small
and cramped city churches.

Nothing remains either from the Cluniac priory of St James, S of the
town, founded before 1146, or from the two friaries (the Blackfriars
founded 1231–4 on the later site of Bedford Circus, and the Greyfriars,
at first at Friernhay near St Nicholas, then from the late C13 outside
the S gate). The parish churches, once closely (but no longer) hemmed
in by surrounding houses, were rebuilt and enlarged piecemeal in the
C14 and C15 in whatever way their awkward sites permitted. They are
characterized by their towers in odd positions (reflecting early plans?)
and by their red walls of crumbly Heavitree stone, in striking contrast
to the limestone of the cathedral. It is puzzling that there was no
attempt to rebuild any church on an ambitious scale comparable to
those in other prosperous late medieval towns such as Norwich.

As for domestic buildings, the wealth of the cathedral establishment
is demonstrated by the ample and richly decorated houses of the late
medieval clergy around the cathedral close, one of the best preserved
groups of this kind in the country. A comfortable standard of living is
also apparent from the later medieval guest halls in the W ranges of St
Nicholas Priory and the nunnery of Polsloe, to the N of the city.
Elsewhere, the best preserved late medieval house is the once rural
courtyard mansion of Bowhill in the suburb of St Thomas. Hardly any
of the surviving town houses are earlier than the later C16–C17. Few
are complete, but enough evidence remains to demonstrate the type
prevalent in the South West (cf. Totnes, Dartmouth): a tall, narrow,
timber-framed front, decorated with increasing bravura (see the
examples in the High Street), set between stone side walls, and with a
back block linked to the main building by a gallery beside a courtyard.

From the C15 Exeter became one of the chief cloth markets of the
South West. The guildhall, rebuilt in the late C15, with its flamboyant
74 free Renaissance forebuilding of a century later, and the more intimate
C15 Tuckers Hall in Fore Street remain as architectural expressions of
the corporate pride and wealth of that time. Throughout the C16 and
C17 Exeter continued as one of the richest of English towns. In the
later C17 Celia Fiennes found that 'the whole town and country is
employed for at least 30 miles round in spinning, weaving, dressing
and scouring, fulling and drying of serges. It turns the most money in a
week of anything in England.' Exeter's position as a port contributed
much to this wealth, although the silting-up of the river and the
development of larger ships gradually led to loss of trade to Topsham
further downstream, despite the construction of a canal in the mid
C16. The city's success in the later C17 in obtaining confirmation of its
customs rights over the whole estuary was marked by the erection of a
103 new custom house, a delightful building in the restrained brick style of
the Restoration, and by generous warehousing, of which much
survives around the reconstructed quay and improved canal. But this
came near the end of Exeter's golden period of prosperity.

By Defoe's time, although the serge market was still second only to that of Leeds, the city was noted not only for its trade and manufactures, but for being 'full of gentry and good company'. The neighbouring countryside began to be scattered with genteel mansions of which a few remain, embedded in the later suburbs (Belair, now attached to County Hall; Duryard House and Great Duryard, now university halls of residence; Cleeve House and Franklyn House, St Thomas). In the later c 18, as the cloth industry of the South West declined in the face of industrial competition, Exeter rose in importance as a centre for polite society. Assembly rooms were built in 1769, in a new French-styled 'hotel' (now the Royal Clarence) facing the Cathedral Green, the Exeter Bank was opened in the same year, and a new Sessions House in the Palladian manner was constructed in the castle precincts in 1773.

Around the same time the most ambitious residential development within the city, Bedford Circus, was begun. But this and much else of the c 18 in the city centre has gone, and apart from a few buildings near the castle and around Bartholomew Street, the character of the Georgian period can now best be appreciated in the suburban expansion just outside the walls. In Southernhay, where the Devon and Exeter Hospital, a handsome example of gentry philanthropy, had been established by Dean Clarke in 1743, the city determined on a development of a high-class residential quarter in the 1770s, although work did not begin until 1792. The style adopted for the new housing 133 was that of the brick terrace house, as built in London in the 1770s, introduced, it seems, by the local architect–builder *Matthew Nosworthy*. His use of *Coade* stone ornament perhaps owed something to the presence of members of the Coade family in Exeter. The fashion survived up to around 1810, as can be seen from scattered examples further out; after this the preferred type became the stuccoed neo-classical terrace or villa.

Plenty of these remain in the suburbs, which expanded fast as Exeter became increasingly popular as a place for inexpensive but civilized retirement for the families of military and naval men after the end of the Napoleonic wars. Large estates on the fringes of the town were released to the builder–speculator. The styles adopted must have been influenced by Foulston's work at Plymouth, but the designers appear to have been local builders; the *Hoopers* on the large Baring estates to the s w, *John Brown* in Pennsylvania Park, the most splendid of all the Regency developments, the *Wares* in the slightly later development of the northern suburbs stretching towards the railway. But clearly there was neither adequate capital nor demand to complete many of the schemes begun so grandly, and most of the early c 19 suburbs remain intriguing jigsaws of ambitious stuccoed fragments ending in c 20 bathos.

In the city centre the rebuilding of the markets was the chief civic enterprise of the 1830s; here, as a result of open competitions, the jobs went to outsiders: *George Dymond* of Bristol and *Charles Fowler*, Devon born but London trained. Only Dymond's monumental neo-Grecian Upper Market survives. It formed part of a larger scheme involving the creation of Queen Street as a new northern route out of the city. This too was not developed consistently; its proudest building is the Museum and Art Gallery, not built until 1865, by *Hayward*, the 152 most prolific and accomplished of the local Gothic revival architects. In the later c 19 the town continued to expand (population 1801, 17,412; 1842, 31,305; 1871, 41,467; 1911, 48,000), a steady but not dramatic growth, despite the arrival of the railway in 1844. No large industries developed, although the suburb of St Thomas grew to serve those that existed along the banks of the river.

This picture of Exeter as a quiet but prosperous regional centre altered in the late C20.* Firstly, the university became a significant feature as it expanded from the 1950s over the hilly NW suburbs. Secondly, after the motorway provided easier access in the 1970s, industry began to develop on a larger scale to the S and W of the city at Sowton and Marsh Barton. Neither development has so far produced much that is architecturally outstanding. Still more disappointing is what has happened in the city centre. Much was lost in the air raids of 1942, and although *Thomas Sharp's* plan, *Exeter Phoenix*, of 1946 displayed a sensitive appreciation of the best of the surviving older buildings, this did not prevent the N part of the High Street, where war destruction was worst, from being rebuilt in the undistinguished manner favoured by developers of the 1950s. The SW section, where slum clearance had begun in the 1930s, was savagely fragmented for an inner road (a departure from Sharp's original plan for a northern ring road), so that the river and its quays are no longer an integral part of the city centre. As if this was not enough, the Guildhall shopping centre, developed from 1969, involved the destruction of the best surviving medieval frontage, No. 38 North Street, the gutting of older buildings, replanning of back streets, and imposition of car parks. As a result the surviving historic buildings in the city centre can only occasionally (as in the Close, or in parts of Southernhay) be enjoyed as part of a visually satisfying townscape.

But one can end on a more positive note. After a few dismal examples, tall towers have been proscribed. Much in the suburbs is still a delight, and from the 1970s there has been both good conservation and some imaginative re-creation of urban intricacy in the town centre. The first scheme of this kind was the large housing develop-
179 ment of Shilhay, near the river, by *Marshman Warren Taylor*, planned from 1974, a refreshing departure from earlier public housing stereotypes. Later examples to explore are around Bartholomew Street.

THE CATHEDRAL

*Chief Planning Officers: from 1946, *Harold Gayton* followed by *M. Hewling*; after 1974, *R. Green*; City Architects: *H.B.Rowe* 1946–67, *Vinton Hall* to 1974, followed by *Jack Cross*.

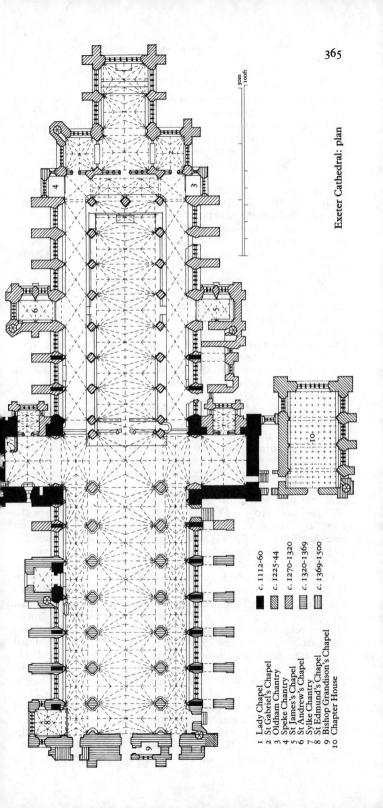

30m
100ft

Exeter Cathedral: plan

■ c. 1112-60
▨ c. 1225-44
▨ c. 1270-1320
▤ c. 1320-1369
▨ c. 1369-1500

1 Lady Chapel
2 St Gabriel's Chapel
3 Oldham Chantry
4 Speke Chantry
5 St James's Chapel
6 St Andrew's Chapel
7 Sylke Chantry
8 St Edmund's Chapel
9 Bishop Grandison's Chapel
10 Chapter House

INTRODUCTION

A Benedictine monastery dedicated to St Peter was founded here in the C7, refounded by Athelstan in the C10, destroyed by the Danes in 1003, and rebuilt by Cnut in 1018. The bishop's seat for the diocese of Devon and Cornwall was from 909 to 1050 at Crediton, a few miles N of Exeter, but in 1050 Leofric was installed as Bishop of Exeter in the presence of Edward the Confessor and his queen in the C11 monastery church, which served also for Leofric's successor. When the new cathedral went up, a little to the E, the minster became the parish church of St Mary Major. It was much rebuilt in the C12, and in 1864 *Ashworth* replaced the structure with a new church, which was itself demolished in 1971. Subsequent excavation revealed that the Saxon minster was a simple aisleless structure with later apse, a N W chapel or porticus, and, E of the apse, a half-sunken addition, possibly a burial crypt.

The Conqueror's nephew, William Warelwast, gained the see in 1107, and c. 1112 an entirely new cathedral was begun, on a far grander scale. Warelwast's E arm, up to the W end of a choir extending into the second bay of the nave, was consecrated in 1133. The unique towers flanking that choir are the most prominent survivals of this period. The rest of the nave was perhaps finished c. 1160. Then there was a pause. A chapter house was built after 1225, when Bishop Brewer reorganized the cathedral administration, but the choir remained unenlarged (unlike those of most other English major churches) until the late C13.

The rebuilding of the Norman cathedral was a major programme lasting from the 1270s to the 1380s, held up only by the Black Death of 1348–9 and its aftermath of economic depression. The chief building bishops were Branscombe 1258–80, Quinil 1280–91, Britton 1292–1307, Stapledon 1307–26, and Grandison 1327–69, the first especially celebrated for his initial impetus to the grand design, the last two of national importance as patrons of art.

Master masons included Master *Roger* from before 1297 to 1310, *William Luve* 1310–16, *Thomas of Witney* 1316–42 (thought to be the same as Thomas of Winton, active at Winchester, Wells, and elsewhere), *William Joy* 1342–52, previously of Wells and thought to be of Bristol origin, followed by *Richard Farleigh*, who had built the Salisbury spire, and from 1377 by *Robert Lesyngham* from Gloucestershire. The origins of the Exeter master who initiated the whole design in the 1270s are not known. More recently came pre-Victorian restoration work by *John Kendall*, c. 1805–29. The principal Victorian restoration, mainly inside, was that of 1870–7 by *Sir George Gilbert Scott*. A programme of external restoration had begun by 1899 (major reconstruction of W windows) and went on until 1913. Substantial repairs after war damage involved the rebuilding of the S E chapel of St James, gutted in 1942. An eye-opening stone-cleaning first of the interior and then of the exterior began in the 1970s and was largely complete in 1986.

Besides the yellow Salcombe stone of the walls and the unpolished Purbeck marble of the piers, local volcanic stone was used for vaulting-cells and, in the early C13, for the walls of the chapter house; in the early C14 the whiter Beer stone gradually replaced Salcombe for vaulting-ribs, tracery, bosses, etc. Some details of the choir are of

Portland stone. In the 1320s, eight quarries in Devon, one in Somerset, and one at Caen in Normandy were supplying stone. A quarry at Salcombe Regis was reopened for the cathedral in the late C20. Purbeck was also used for vaulting-shafts in the Lady Chapel, but not later, i.e. not after 1290, although it was kept for pier shafts throughout: the nave piers shaped at Corfe were paid for in 1333. Polished Purbeck marble was also used for the series of late C12/early C13 bishops' effigies. Much of the carved stonework was originally coloured, as recent cleaning has confirmed. Medieval paint is especially well preserved on the outstandingly fine late C13 monument to Bishop Branscombe, and on many of the vaulting bosses. The garish repainting of those begun in the 1970s fortunately gave way to a programme of more sensitive cleaning to reveal the original paint.

THE C12 CATHEDRAL

The major standing remains of the Norman cathedral are the two C12 N and S TOWERS which originally butted on to the Norman aisles in place of transepts – a unique arrangement. Late C12 parallels point to the Burgundian orbit (Lyon, Geneva), but the concept possibly derives from the C11 transeptal towers of Cluny III. The lower walls of the Exeter towers are severely unadorned, and indeed as inaccessible as keeps.

The N or St Paul's Tower is the earlier, with its lowest band of tall blank arcading only above the (presumed) height of the Norman nave and chancel roofs. The S or St John's Tower starts the first band lower down. Above the first (on the S second) stage of arcading is a frieze of intersected arches on the N, of blind oculi on the S. Also the S arcading on this stage has the new fashion of zigzag decoration. The next stage of blank arcading has zigzag N and S, the last stage with alternations of arched bell-openings and blank arcades. The whole top storey of the N tower was reconstructed in the C15 to house the great Peter bell given by Bishop Courtenay in 1484. The original C12 tops must be imagined with low pyramidal spires (see the roof-lines still visible against the turrets of the S tower).

As for the rest of the Norman building, we know that the cathedral had a five-sided main apse, according to remains of foundations seen during the restoration of 1870–7 in the presbytery bay nearest the choir, although no signs of such remains were found when the pavement was relaid in 1962. After the air raid of 1942 a circular scalloped capital of impressive girth was found among the ruins of St James's Chapel. This would seem to have come from a thick column, comparable to West Country examples of c. 1100–20 at Tewkesbury, Gloucester, and Hereford, apparently from the Norman chancel demolished before the late C13 construction began and, with other fragments, re-used in the new work. Fragments of capitals incorporating rib-springers suggestive of the Tewkesbury choir type are now in the cloisters. Other pieces preserved in the City Museum include three voussoirs with a large roll, clearly from a C12 rib-vault, and a small carved fragment, with faint painted patterns of addorsed birds, found embedded in the N porch stair-turret.

Norman walling still exists up to windowsill level in the nave and in the two bays E of the crossing. Flat buttresses remain outside the

N wall of the nave, and on the S side are the marks where they were cut back for the later cloisters. Inside the nave the lower walls have indications of responds with characteristic alternating red and white stonework. The Norman nave was probably as long as the present one, as is suggested by the early C13 work incorporated in the W front (q.v., below).

THE GOTHIC BUILDING CAMPAIGNS: CHRONOLOGY

In April 1258 Bishop Bronescombe (or Branscombe) was enthroned; in September that year he probably attended with great interest the consecration of the new cathedral of Salisbury. The 1260s must have been a time of scheming at Exeter. Before work could start on a longer E end, the Norman E arm was demolished and its materials used to level the ground E of it. This ground sloped considerably from N to S; St James's Chapel on the S side near a spring was consequently built above a crypt. Preparations may have begun by c. 1270, and actual building by c. 1275. St Andrew's and St James's Chapels flanking the site of the future chancel were ready for glazing in 1279, and the Lady Chapel at the E end, mentioned in 1280, was still under construction in 1289. From 1279 onwards the fabric rolls survive to document much of the work, though tantalizingly not all of it. Bishop Branscombe left instructions for his tomb between the Lady Chapel and the S aisle-end Chapel of St Gabriel, both part way up when he died in 1280.

Bishop Branscombe's successor, Bishop Quinil, is thought to have completed the Lady Chapel in time to be buried in it in 1291. By then the transepts had been remodelled. The fabric roll for 1285 records the throwing down of the wall of St Paul's Tower and in 1287 that of St John's Tower, opening them up by tall arches to what was then the Norman choir. The large S window with Dec tracery and an inserted transom is a later alteration. The high linking bays between the towers and what was to be the new crossing were probably completed later, at the time of the rebuilding of the crossing itself, i.e. in the early C14. To each transept was added an E chapel, of two shallow bays and one narrow window N and S as well as an E window. The two chapels were probably begun in the 1280s, when altars were removed from the transepts themselves, and the chapel vaults, like the Lady Chapel's in little, completed nearer 1300.

The Exeter presbytery, i.e. the beginning of the main vessel, may date from the 1280s and 1290s. The presbytery clerestory was glazed in 1301–2 and its vaults were painted in 1302. Bosses for the choir vaults, already being carved in the workshops in 1303, were being primed for painting on the ground in 1309. Structurally the whole E arm was complete by c. 1310, although there were afterthoughts in the presbytery in 1317 (see Tour, below). By this time the first bay of the nave, between the crossing and the Norman pulpitum, was being rebuilt, and splendid sanctuary and choir fittings were being made. The high altar was dedicated in December 1328 and the nave demolished down to windowsill level. New stone for the nave walls had been bought as early as 1324–5. Marble from workshops at Corfe for the main piers was paid for in 1332.

Work on a new W front began in 1329, and the W gable was complete by 1342. The N porch must date from the same period. The nave was roofed but (except for its E bay) we cannot be sure whether it was vaulted before interruption by the Black Death. No exact date for completion is known. The main work may have been ready when Bishop Grandison was buried in 1369 in his little chapel behind the W front, although the W screen was not finished. *John Pratt* was paid for carved work on the W front in 1375–6; the upper tier of figures was completed only in the C15.

TOUR OF THE GOTHIC CATHEDRAL

The plan from W to E, as the visitor usually travels, is this: nave of seven bays with aisles and N porch, crossing flanked by main transepts in the Norman towers, square-ended E arm consisting of one narrow bay for the pulpitum, then seven bays (three choir, four presbytery) with aisles, and flanking the middle bay to N and S the two chapels (St Andrew's and St James's) in E transeptal position. Beyond the high altar is a straight ambulatory one bay deep and the three-bay Lady Chapel flanked by aisle-end chapels. The E transeptal chapels, as well as all three E chapels and the ambulatory, are much lower than the clerestories of the E arm. Exeter's high vault runs straight through from E to W, supported by flying buttresses.

A detailed examination should start inside with the LADY CHAPEL. Stylistic evidence confirms the dates provided by the rolls. Stiff-leaf foliage is still used in the piscina and sedilia (and on one boss of the S transept chapel). Then we find at once everywhere bosses of enchanting realism in the rendering of foliage – vine, rose, hawthorn, oak, etc. – and on the elaborate corbels carrying the presbytery vaulting-shafts. The closest possible study of the Exeter bosses and corbels, preferably with glasses and a strong torch, will amply repay the effort wherever modern repainting does not obscure the carving. The Lady Chapel vault has longitudinal and transverse ridge ribs and two pairs of tierceron ribs in the N and S cells of each bay (one pair more than in Lincoln nave). The vaulting-shafts here consist of clusters of five slim shafts, three of Purbeck marble and the two in the angles filleted. Alternate shafts in entrances and archways of the E chapels are of Purbeck. The Lady Chapel is divided from the NE and SE chapels by two pairs of half-quatrefoil responds. In the retrochoir or ambulatory, the vaults of the three central bays also play minor variations on the tierceron theme. Outside, the battlements enclosing the low invisible roofs over the vaults of both Lady Chapel and retrochoir are early examples in the West Country of an initially royal decorative usage.

The TRACERY of Lady Chapel, NE and SE chapels, and presbytery aisles and clerestories (apart from the great E window which has been rebuilt) is essentially in advance of Westminster and Lincoln and Salisbury, although there are some similar elements in the E cloister walk, N end, at Westminster Abbey, presumably direct from France. But the Exeter tracery initiated before 1279 was entirely in keeping with contemporary London Court-style tracery, particularly that of Old St Paul's E arm, which reflected recent French work by the 1270s. Exeter was indeed ahead of St Etheldreda's Chapel in Ely Place, London (?1286 to after 1290), and London-influenced tracery such as that at Merton College choir (1289-94). At Exeter, apart from the usual trefoils, quatrefoils, and sexfoils in circles characteristic of geometrical tracery, are also trefoils, pointed cusping at the tops of individual window-lights, intersected mullions, spherical triangles and quadrangles – all in inexhaustible variations, with only the one limitation that corresponding windows (e.g. clerestory same bay N and S, NE chapel E window, and SE chapel E window) have the same patterns.

The internal elevation of the Lady Chapel and flanking chapels shows blank arcading (pointed trefoil heads) on the ground stage with pointed trefoils in the spandrels, and tomb recesses with cusped arcading have also cusped circles in the spandrels. A small S door is a replacement of 1437, with a nodding-ogee canopy conservative for that date, perhaps copying an earlier one; the motif usually appears in this cathedral only in fittings.

The four PRESBYTERY bays set the pier and vaulting pattern for the rest of the cathedral: piers of lozenge shape with sixteen close-set shafts (as already at St Paul's in London), correspondingly multiple arch mouldings, vaulting-shafts on corbels starting immediately above the piers but not connected with them, large clerestory windows, and comparatively low broad vaults with ridge ribs and three pairs of tiercerons (again more than anywhere before) in the N and S cells of each bay. The luxuriant palm-branch effect is unforgettable. In only one respect does the appearance today differ from that of c. 1300: for the first seventeen years of their existence these four bays had a two-storey elevation, with clerestory windowsills sloping like oblique aprons to the top of the main arcade. Two-tier chancels were rare in great C13 churches, though not unknown (Southwell, Pershore, and the not wholly similar, unaisled case of Rochester).

The three CHOIR bays next built were completed in 1309 with the same vaulting, but with elevations in three tiers, the triforium a low trefoil-headed intermittent arcade of four arches per bay, carrying a clerestory passage with a pierced-quatrefoil parapet. In the N and S TRANSEPTS, already opened up in the late C13, charming early C14 balconies were cantilevered into the old walls in place of a triforium, resting on little demi-vaults like the covings of later Devon screens. Each transept has a wooden ceiling originally painted to look like vaulting, and with oaken bosses (q.v. below).

As for the PRESBYTERY, soon the urge to homogeneity characteristic of this building was felt: in 1317–18 a shallow triforium with mock passage above was inserted in the four presbytery bays.* Some juggling with the relative position of choir and presbytery piers had already occurred to allow for the width of the choir passage, and signs of old clerestory mouldings at presbytery triforium level can be detected. But a consistent pattern was now ready to be continued in the nave. Another significant if slighter change in style occurs in progression from presbytery to choir in

---

* 'For thirty-eight marble columns ... for the galleries between the high altar and the quire £109s. at 5s. 6d. per column' (fabric rolls).

the design of the great corbels: leaves begin to lose freshness and tend to undulate or congeal into stylized knobbliness. This happened all over England. It marks the end of classic Gothic perfection and the coming sophistication of the Dec style. But Exeter on the whole, in its architecture though not in its fittings, avoided Dec vagaries.

In the NAVE the style set before 1300 remained valid, with the full sets of tiercerons and ridge-ribs already developed. Evolution can be seen only in details. The liernes of the little vault subsequently added to St Edmund's Chapel, at the W end of the nave and N aisle, appear elsewhere in the cathedral only in tiny vaults under the pulpitum of the 1320s (on both of which, *see* below). In the nave window tracery more complex motifs now occur, yet in consistent development from the E chapels. There are large spherical triangles filled with smaller ones, lozenges with two sides concave and two convex, circles with a wheel of curved fish-bladders (mouchettes), and various spoke motifs in circles. Ogee arches occur only sparingly, though elsewhere in England a standard early C14 motif.

The great W window and the great E window at opposite ends of the splendid tunnel demonstrate the changes of the C14. The W window, in a sense summarizing development all the way from the Lady Chapel, was probably designed by *Thomas of Witney* †1342 and completed by his successor *William Joy*, with nine lights, the centre one wider, under a big encircled star-cluster of cusped lozenges, etc. The upper part of the great E window of the 1290s, however, was rebuilt in 1389–90, keeping the mullions and main lights.* Originally there may have been a central roundel. The new Perp elements – centre panels rising straight to the arch – were presumably designed by *Robert Lesyngham*, the mason then in charge.

Change of style in the nave is also marked in bosses and corbels. There were many different hands busy on them. The best in the nave are as characteristic of the 1330s–40s as the best of the E arm had been of the 1290s. Two nave bosses may be singled out: second bay from the E, Christ in Majesty in the cross-legged pose of certain kings on the W front (*see* below); second bay from the W, the Murder of Thomas a Becket (Bishop Grandison was his biographer). Earlier than these, at the crossing, four great corbels were carved during 1309–13, possibly by *William Montacute*: the mason's head supporting St Catherine on the SE corbel is sometimes called his self-portrait, on grounds only of romanticism. But on the nave corbels of the 1330s cutting is shallower; there is graceful variety but less vitality.

The N entrance and PORCH belong to the same period as the W end of the nave (compare the treatment of the doorways). The exterior of the N porch, with three steep crocketed gables, was given seven sculptured figures in 1936–7.

ST EDMUND'S CHAPEL (re-ordered after 1918 as the Devon Regiment Memorial Chapel by *Guy Dawber*), just E of the W front, is a puzzle. Nothing fits exactly. Work may have been in progress in 1279 (there is a reference to glazing opposite the altar of a chapel of that dedication), implying an addition to the older nave, but there have been several subsequent changes of design. The W window has Y tracery (early, if of 1279), but the N window is a C14 replacement in keeping with the aisle windows. Neither is set symmetrically. The vault with lierne ribs (the only ones in the cathedral apart from the pulpitum) is not centred over the space, nor is it related to the neighbouring aisle bay, and the SE vaulting-shafts do not go down to the floor, but rest on a head corbel. Clearly the vault was the last afterthought of all.

A final note on parts of the interior not easily seen. Over the N porch are two rooms, one above the other, the lower with a large fireplace and adjacent oven and what seems to be a garderobe, the upper with a small fireplace. In the C19 this was the home of the cathedral dog-whipper. It shares a spiral staircase with the minstrels' gallery room over the corresponding nave aisle (*see* Furnishings: Nave and Crossing).

Also not publicly accessible are the TIMBER ROOFS above the vaults: an instructive sequence. The oldest, of *c.* 1290, is over the eight E bays, a scissor-braced roof with small raking struts supporting the side purlins. Nave and transept roofs have in addition the extra stabilizing feature of collar-purlins tenoned into crown-posts; the side purlins are held securely by intricately jointed vertical struts. In addition, the ingenuity of the early C14 carpenters is demonstrated by the construction of the timber vaults of the transepts. The wooden vaulting-ribs are attached to the contemporary ringers' floor by vertical planks; in the centre, where there is a hatch for raising bells, the ridge-ribs are secured by vertical iron bars.

THE GOTHIC INTERIOR: CONCLUSION

At Exeter, any symptoms of a style in advance of that initially adopted are unimportant. The main architectural design of the cathedral remained unaltered from its conception *c.* 1275 to the death of Grandison in 1369 – five active bishops later – and the completion of the building. It was a very personal design, of much character. One would wish to be able to ascribe its conception to a designer known by name and circumstance of life. The Master of Exeter felt driven to the *nec plus ultra* of an existing style, the style of 1250–60, rather than to the creation of a new style. Such artists exist at all times. In his vaults he used more tiercerons than anybody before, on his piers more shafts than anyone except the St Paul's master (but at St Paul's the vaults were less rich). This multiplication makes for richness, and the Exeter master handled it with a sense of luxuriance, the epitome of late C13 tendencies. His work makes even the Angel Choir at Lincoln appear restrained. (Had he worked at Lincoln? in London?) He did not abandon the accepted type of vault or pier. For his main vaults he did not conceive the next innovation after the tierceron, the lierne and the networks it led to, nor the pier leading up without complete break into the vaulting zone, nor the pier wholly or partially without capitals, nor curvilinear tracery.

The Exeter master's tracery is particularly personal, composed of motifs of immediate London derivation. The unencircled trefoil

and quatrefoil and spherical triangle and quadrangle and elemen- 22
tary mouchettes in spandrels were, indeed, the favourites of
French designers about and after 1250 (Sainte Chapelle, Notre
Dame s transept, etc.), and they became the main standby in
French cathedrals of the late C13 and early C14 (e.g. Nevers,
Carcassonne, Bordeaux). The Exeter master could have seen them
in France. But nearer home by the 1270s there had developed the
Court-style work of London and centres influenced by London.
He could see spherical triangles in the Westminster Abbey gallery,
Hereford N transept, Lichfield nave. He could see the sixteen-
shafted piers and the tracery at St Paul's. For he was emphatically
an Englishman. The proportions of his main vessel are utterly un- 20
French, generously broad, and the weight of the profuse palm-
branch ribs from l. and r. makes the interior appear decidedly low.
The proportionally short piers are also wholly against French
ideals, and the abundance of sculptured bosses has no parallel the 17
other side of the Channel.

Given these English characteristics of the building and its
impressive scale and richness of architectural conception, it is
surprising that it had so little direct influence in the diocese, either
in Devon or in Cornwall. The English parish church of the South
West is of great consistency of style, but its style, except in a few
instances, and in a general taste for richly decorated furnishings, is
not that of Exeter Cathedral.

THE WEST FRONT*

The W front is at first puzzling to the visitor. It consists of an image 23
screen in front of the lower half of the façade. This screen was an
afterthought, as is shown by the straight joints next to the inner
doorways. The original front of the late 1320s–40s appears to have
consisted of three grand doorways (the centre one under construction in 1330), with a large blind archway between the central and s
doors, now visible within Grandison's chapel. (Is there a corresponding archway concealed to the N of the central doorway?) A
crenellated course above the level of the doorways, now concealed
by the screen, was exposed during building work in the 1980s.

The elevation above the screen remains in its original form, with
the large central window already described, and steep lean-to aisle
fronts with rows of slender climbing arches crowned by raking
battlements. The battlements continue horizontally above the nave
window. Above and behind is the steep-pitched nave roof, the
space over the nave vault lit by a window of spherical–triangular
shape, with mouchette tracery, and with a niche crowning the
gable. A further puzzle should be mentioned before one turns to
the image screen. To its s is a massive buttress of exceptional
width, decorated with battlements and sunk quatrefoils, one of
which bends round an angle, a trick found on the early C13 W front
of Wells. It must belong to an earlier W front incorporated into the
C14 work.

The reredos-like IMAGE SCREEN is the most complete example
in England of a programme of C14 sculpture. It would have been

*This section owes much to the research carried out by John Allan during the
restoration of 1978–85.

even more spectacular in its original painted condition. Cleaning during restoration revealed plentiful traces of red and yellow garments, green leaves, purple grapes, etc., sometimes covered by post-medieval layers of limewash and red paint. There is no certain date for the two lower tiers of the screen but they can probably be associated with payments for porches in 1346. The design consists of demi-figures of angels, some playing musical instruments, supporting a single row of full-length figures. Except for the knight to the r. of the door, all these figures are seated kings; some formerly grasped some kind of rod or staff. They may represent the Tree of Jesse (the iconography has been confused by C19 additions; *see* below). The motif of seated cross-legged kings appears also in the w fronts of Lichfield and Lincoln, and was popular in early C14 manuscripts. The style of the Exeter figures is characteristic of *c.* 1330–50: stiffly tortuous attitudes, convoluted tubular folds of drapery, and long, rather solemn faces.

In the SOUTH PORCH the sculpture is considerably better preserved. Here an excellent Annunciation (s side) and Nativity (N side) occupy the upper tier, and the angel demi-figures are replaced by an ox and ass on the N side and Moses(?) on the s. Above the s doorway, niches with two lively demi-figures. The central doorway of the screen has spandrels with angels in low relief, the r. one possibly recut, giving it an oddly neo-classical feeling. The sculpture inside the central porch has disappeared.

In the r. wall of this porch is the door to the tiny CHAPEL OF BISHOP GRANDISON, filling the space between central and s porches. His burial there in 1369 suggests that at least this part of the screen was complete. The chapel has a pointed barrel-vault with an unusually large boss with a low-relief carving of Christ in Majesty, presumably directly above the lost tomb (cf. the painted tester of Walter Stapledon's tomb). On the E side, within the large blind arch with vine-scroll decoration once part of the older w front (*see* above), is a low arch, now blocked, through which the tomb would have been visible from inside the cathedral. On the s wall panels from a reredos. Arches to w and E without capitals, charming leaf-scrolls and fleurons in the arch mouldings (both motifs later popular in Devon churches).

The NORTH PORCH is of a design quite different from the other two, with a fan-vault, almost certainly by *Robert Lesyngham*, in charge at Exeter from *c.* 1377 after completing the E cloister at Gloucester. The group of figures of the central tier at this end may also be late C14. They are in a different style: quiet, dignified poses with simpler drapery with flat bands across the chest. They seem good candidates for the work 'ad frontem ecclesie' for which *John Pratt* 'ymaginator' was paid in 1375–6.

When the top tier was added to the image screen, the canopies of the kings were truncated; the C14 work survives at a lower level around the central doorway (was there a gable here?). This upper tier differs in all its details from the lower work. Its date is unknown, and the few distinctive details are simply Perp; it seems likely but unproveable that the niches and their sculptures are contemporary, *c.* 1460–80. The centre pair of figures, of which only the figure of Christ remains, are flanked by the twelve apostles, with the four evangelists on the buttresses. Of the other

figures only Noah (N buttress facing N) has been identified. All
except two of the figures have sharp, exaggerated, angular drapery
folds; there is a good range of C15 headgear and other costume
detail. Examination showed that all the upper canopies but one
have been replaced by a later Perp design of unknown date.

A few exceptions to the C14 and C15 pattern described above
can be noted: two C14 figures, one very worn, on the upper tier (N
buttress s face, and s sector) and a few C15 figures in inconspicuous
positions in the central register.

The tally of post-medieval repairs and additions to the W front is
a longer story. There are five main phases. *John Kendall* undertook
extensive repairs from 1805 to his death in 1829, including replacement of the lowest 3 ft of the image screen (modifying the medieval
design); new crenellations with angels on the N and s aisle sectors
(now largely replaced); the central figure of Richard II (1817); one
angel on the s return; the most southerly of the three angels s of the
s porch (bizarre pose, ruffled feathers*); heads of three of the four
figures on the lower register of the W faces of projecting buttresses;
the large figures of King Athelstan (1809) and Edward the Confessor (1810) high on these buttresses above the screen; and new
coping-stone, pinnacles, etc., all largely in Beer stone. Some of this
work is now in worse condition than the adjacent medieval stone.
After 1819 repairs continued, notably twelve new canopies to the
top of central figures by *Simon Rowe* (1838) in Beer stone, and the
openwork parapet in Bath stone above. *E.B.Stephens* added William the Conqueror (1865) on the s side of the N buttresses, and
James the Less on the N side of the s buttress, both in Bath stone.

Between 1899 and 1913 a major programme of masonry replacement was carried out under *Harbottle*, including the replacement
of the entire face of the W window in Doulting stone, perhaps
removing earlier *Coade*-stone repairs designed by *John Carter*
under the supervision of *Soane* (according to the *Gentleman's
Magazine*, 1817). There was also extensive renewal of crenellations, coping, finials, etc. On the image screen the figures were not
touched but there was much replacement of canopy-work,
parapets, etc., in Doulting and Ketton stone. (The new Ketton
canopies provoked bitter controversy between the S.P.A.B. and
the Dean and Chapter.)

Finally, repairs under *P. Gundry* from 1978 to 1985 included
replacement of the upper tier of canopies in the s sector, new shafts
and canopies at the SW corner, and consolidation of the medieval
figures by limewatering and sheltercoating with repairs in lime
mortar. One new demi-angel (replacing a shapeless lump), the
centre of a group of three s of the s porch, was added by *Simon
Verity* in 1982, and a new figure of St Peter, also by *Verity* (1985),
was placed in the empty niche high up in the upper gable, so
distant that its surprising C20 nudity does not appear as incongruous as one might expect.

---

*Although this may be a pre-Kendall replacement, as it appears on Carter's
drawings.

FURNISHINGS AND MONUMENTS

Choir and Presbytery

The early C14 fittings are characterized by far more fanciful treatment than the masons allowed themselves in the architecture itself. The exceptionally elaborate liturgical furnishings were perhaps seen as compensation for the lack of a major shrine. Reredos and stalls have been replaced, but *Thomas of Witney*'s PULPITUM (or rood screen), SEDILIA, and BISHOP'S THRONE remain from the rich ensemble created *c.* 1313–28 for Bishop Stapledon around the high altar, a group which cannot be paralleled in any other English cathedral.

16 PULPITUM. Completed 1324. Of triple-arcade veranda type (i.e. the front arches always open), originally with side altars against rear partitions that flanked a central archway and enclosed a pair of staircases to the loft (staircases removed and their walls opened up by *Scott*, who substituted his charming spiral stair in the s choir aisle; cf. Ely). The front arcade is of a novel type: three depressed ogee arches on piers with moulded capitals, the spandrels decorated with fantastically elongated quatrefoils packed with knobbly foliage. At the outer angles diagonal niches, a typically Dec conceit. Prominent parapet: cusped and crocketed blank arcade of thirteen ogee-topped compartments originally framing stone images, now with early C17 painted scenes from the Old and New Testaments, provincial versions of the taste for Venetian art. The parapet had elaborate cresting in wood, replaced with stonework by *Kendall* in 1819, with two compartments to each one below. The close relationship between the details of the C14 work and other major buildings in the West Country demonstrates Thomas of Witney's significance. Under the 'veranda' the little vaults with liernes are on a scheme somewhat similar to that of Bristol choir, and the central E bay (between the former stair-bays) is vaulted in miniature on the scheme of Tewkesbury nave (1322–6): indeed this small single bay at Exeter has been called a try-out for the Tewkesbury vault. The unusual angular plinths of the pulpitum's front piers are identical to those of the retrochoir piers at Wells, and the vaults relate also to those of the Wells ambulatory. There may have been an organ on the pulpitum as early as the C14. The present ORGAN CASE is of 1665 by *John Loosemore* (its side-towers of pipes removed from the NE and SE crossing piers in 1876, the case raised and deepened 1891). It is an important case, the central tower on its E face comparable in outline and position to that at Gloucester, and both probably modelled on Thomas Harris's then recently re-erected organ at Salisbury.

19 SEDILIA. Three canopied seats of Beer stone, the slender central pair of colonnettes (unusually) of brass or latten, one a renewal, the other said to be original. The whole was much restored both by *Kendall* and by *Scott*, who lengthened the pinnacles, and then again after war damage. The design of the sedilia – originally part of the larger composition of the great altar screen – has all the intricacy and unrestrained spatial play characteristic of the early C14, say at Ely or Bristol, but absent in the major architecture at Exeter. Here, as seen from the front, the seats have tall, plain, concave backs painted to

represent hanging cloth, with tiny heads on top; above these backs the sedilia are open to the s aisle. Each seat is crowned by a seven-sided canopy, two sides for the back, one each for the sides, and three for the front – the front unsupported, the back and sides borne by the pair of metal colonnettes and by outer walls (with matching but attached stone-shafted colonnettes). Minute star-vault inside each canopy. The gables ogee-shaped and sumptuously crocketed. (Three modern statues have been inserted.) On top of the canopies another set of tall, fragile three-sided canopies, with the point of the triangle towards the aisle. From the aisle one sees the elaborate shaft-work, with unexpected shafts and gables peeping through a gossamer of finely carved forms. The clue to the composition is that the gables towards the aisle are placed so that each shaft between them corresponds to the centre of a gable on the seat-front, as if playing the Lincoln arcaded counterpoint theme of over a century before. It is more easily seen than described.

BISHOP'S THRONE, or rather, architectural throne canopy, of 18 unprecedented grandeur, 1313–16, of oak from Bishop Stapledon's estates at Chudleigh and Newton St Cyres. The most exquisite piece of woodwork of its date in England and perhaps in Europe. Fortunately removed before the bombing of 1942. Thomas of Winchester, very likely Thomas from Winchester, i.e. *Thomas of Witney*, came for a month in 1313 to supervise selection of the timber, and his high wage of 3s. a week suggests that he was the designer and that the reputation of the Winchester choir stalls of 1308 was high. But the Exeter 'throne' is not a copy of them; it is rather an advance from them. On a basically square plan, the lowest and largest stage has big crocketed gables over cusped nodding-ogee arches (with finely carved human heads): these arches are some of the earliest nodding ogees in the country. The upper stages recede like an extended telescope, fantastically loftily pinnacled. The tall triangular aedicules on each side with tracery behind may originally have extended higher. Despite the difference in material, the aesthetic effect is much like that of the sedilia. Originally all painted and gilded.

CHOIR STALLS. The present grand set is *Scott*'s creation of the 1870s. The stalls made in 1309–10 for the new choir were replaced during the Civil War by pews for the Presbyterians. At the Restoration these in turn gave way to c17 Gothic stalls which became 'obscured by incongruous accompaniments' and were swept away by Scott in favour of the existing ones, carved by *Thomas Farmer* on the model of the early c14 Winchester choir stalls. That the Exeter stalls were of a more modest design is proved by a single surviving c14 back with openwork crocketed ogee arches re-used as the upper part of the door to the Sylke Chantry in the N transept.*

The c14 stalls apparently replaced a c13 set in the Norman choir, as is indicated by the style of the MISERICORDS originally attached to them and miraculously preserved through all these changes. They are the oldest set in England. In style forty-eight of them date from *c*. 1230–70, i.e. they were begun in Bishop Brewer's time; one other is of the early c14 and one of the c15. Some still have stiff-leaf foliage; in others the leaves are naturalistic. Figures include a lion, a

---

* Others, removed to St Lawrence's church in the c17, survived until the Second World War.

mermaid, a siren, a centaur, apocalyptic locusts, the Swan Knight, and an elephant. The elephant (N side) could have been carved from a drawing imperfectly made from life, for in 1255 Louis IX of France gave Henry III an elephant, which was kept in the Tower of London; sketches of it appear in the margins of Matthew Paris's contemporary chronicle of its arrival.

LECTERN, in the choir. A brass eagle, given to the cathedral in the C17, probably medieval. The C14 lectern from the cathedral is now in St Thomas (q.v.).

STAINED GLASS. See p. 384.

MONUMENTS. Described clockwise around the presbytery from the N. Bishop Marshall †1206. Purbeck marble coffin-shaped slab with effigy, transitional in type between those of 'Leofric' and Simon in the Lady Chapel. It rests on a Purbeck chest thought to be slightly later, with three seated figures in quatrefoils (Christ in Majesty, St Peter, St Paul); separate side-slabs propped up in the N aisle nearby are more likely to be part of Marshall's original tomb-chest. – Bishop Lacy †1453. Tomb-chest with a marble slab bearing the matrix of a brass. – Bishop Bradbridge †1578. Elizabethan tomb-chest; no effigy.

Bishop Stapledon †1326, next to the high altar and opposite the sedilia. Walter Stapledon founded Exeter College, Oxford. As Lord High Treasurer of England he was murdered by a London mob. The first of the canopied tombs, but only a low canopy. Remains of a stone superstructure were removed in 1805, when the present cornice on the S side replaced a wooden post-Reformation one. Below this, a depressed, cusped and crocketed ogee arch with trefoil spandrel tracery and fleurons in jambs and voussoirs. To the aisle three trefoiled openings with rather coarse foliage terminals and a frieze of hovering angels. The recumbent effigy looks up at a contemporary painting on the flat tester, of Christ displaying his wounds. At the E end, inside, a little carved figure of a king, reset (perhaps from the high altar reredos?), still with original paint. C18 railings to the aisle.

Bishop Woolton †1594, on the S side of the presbytery next to the sedilia. Elizabethan tomb-chest with strapwork pilasters, black marble slab on top, no effigy. (See also the wall-tablet to Bishop Woolton in the N transept, below.) – Bishop Berkeley †1327. Tomb-chest with a Purbeck marble slab bearing a matrix for brass demi-figures in a trefoil.

East Chapels and Choir Aisles, from E to W

LADY CHAPEL. REREDOS. A screen of niches, by *Kendall*. – SEDILIA. Three seats stepped up, with simple pointed-trefoil heads, and two-light PISCINA with sexfoiled circle on top. – WOOD CARVINGS. A small group of shepherds, one piping angel above, from an early C15 Nativity scene. Possibly from work discarded in the early C19; impressive even though fragmentary. – Virgin and Child with St Anne, possibly Flemish C19.

RETROCHOIR AND EAST CHAPELS. WALL PAINTING, S of the entrance to the Lady Chapel. Assumption and Coronation of the Virgin in the presence of the Trinity attended by the nine orders of angels, with the wall of the Celestial City below; once probably continuing down to the floor. Probably early C16 (cf. the painting in the N transept, below). Restored by *E.W.Tristram*, 1930. – Stone SCREEN to the Lady Chapel and its flanking chapels, *c*.1430. Identical in design to the transept chapel screens datable to *c*.1433, when the former wooden screens to these chapels were sold. Very slim four-light sections with standard Devon tracery and entrances headed by a boldly cusped arch with a soffit decorated with vine-scroll. On the mullions, small pinnacled niches and brackets for statues. The screen to the Lady Chapel was much restored after damage *c*.1657 when the chapel was used as a library. – STAINED GLASS. *See* p. 384.

CHOIR AISLES. C15 wooden SCREENS between choir and aisles at the 'E transept' bay, and at the W end of the choir aisles. Four-light doors with standard Devon screen tracery, the flanking sections of two lights only; pierced cresting of slender upright birds (pheasants?) between foliage. – The screen to St Andrew's Chapel (NE transept) has been reconstructed, that to St James's Chapel on the SE replaced.

ST ANDREW'S CHAPEL (NE transept). Early C14 CANOPY, not *in situ*, from a tomb or other furnishing. Three gabled compartments (empty) separated by three-quarter angels, with steep gables crocketed and pinnacled, and between the gables two well carved faces. The gables and their ogee-shaped pierced trefoils are on a similar though simpler pattern, and of the same overall width, as the aisle front of the high-altar sedilia. Was the canopy once part of the sanctuary furnishings?

STAINED GLASS in E chapels and choir stalls. *See* pp. 384–5.

MONUMENTS. E chapels and choir aisles, from E to w.

LADY CHAPEL. In the SE recess a coffin-shaped Purbeck marble slab to a bishop, probably of the 1170s–80s, when native Purbeck was supplanting imported Tournai marble. The slab is sometimes assigned to Bishop Bartholomeus Iscanus †1184, but it has also been suggested that it was retrospectively made for Leofric, the cathedral's first bishop, well after Warelwast translated Leofric's bones to the new Norman cathedral in 1133. However this may be, it is one of the earliest sculptures in Purbeck marble in the country: cf. the one at Salisbury (nave S aisle) assigned to Bishop Joscelin †1184, and the somewhat later abbots' effigies in local marble at Peterborough. The very flat relief is obtained by carving away the background between the figure and the framing arch, which is triangular and only slightly curved, with angels in spandrels. The draperies still with the few 'telescoped' folds usual in France fifty years before. – In the SW recess, Bishop Simon of Apulia †1223, also in Purbeck but now with the higher relief, easier attitude, and finer garment folds of the early C13. – Set in the floor, an incised marble slab with foliated cross to Bishop Quinil †1291, under whom the Lady Chapel was finished. – The N pair of recesses, in high contrast to the S pair, are occupied by Sir John and Lady Dodderidge †1628 and 1614, he in the scarlet gown of a judge in the Court of King's Bench, she in flowered brocade.

Bishop Branscombe †1280, between the Lady Chapel and St Gabriel's Chapel to the SE, as ordained in his will. Effigy of black stone, said to be basalt, still with its original painted decoration, an outstanding work, probably of London craftsmanship. The composition is similar to those of the earlier bishops' slabs, but no longer coffin-shaped. The still pre-naturalistic capitals and leaves of the framing arch, draperies with fewer, heavier folds, and the position of his hands should be compared to Simon of Apulia (above). The carving of the face is exceptionally sensitive. The quatrefoil tomb-chest, the separate angels at the foot of the effigy, and the canopy are additions of *c.* 1442 (reference in the fabric rolls to a 'new tomb'). The canopy is an example of the popular late Perp type with cusped four-centred arch, closely related to the tomb of John Holand from St Katharine's Hospital, London. It is decorated with a lively assortment of angels on frieze and cusps, their vigorous carving sadly obscured by C20 overpainting. – Opposite, Bishop Stafford †1419, with a delicate alabaster effigy with canopy around the head, comparable to others ascribed to carvers from Chellaston, Derbyshire, and a later chest and canopy, designed as a matching pair with those of Bishop Branscombe, but carved by a less able sculptor (compare the angels).

NE CHAPEL. On the floor beside Stafford's tomb a fine BRASS to his kinsman Canon William Langton †1413. Kneeling figure (an early example), with a scroll coming from his praying hands, and dressed in a cope, its form well represented, also the orphreys embroidered with his personal device, the Stafford knot. – Carew family monument, erected 1589. Proudly ambitious, with much heraldry (fifty-one families). Sir Gawen Carew and his wife are recumbent behind a low colonnade. Below, as in a truckle-bed, lies their nephew Sir Peter, wearing armour and ruff like his uncle, but also a C13 surcoat and shield, and – an early instance in sculpture of a conscious medieval revival – represented cross-legged.

RETROCHOIR. Flanking the Lady Chapel entrance, John Bidgood †1691 and James Raillard †1692, quite grand and sombre, a pair of black and gold wall-monuments of the type found in Exeter parish churches.

SPEKE AND OLDHAM CHANTRIES, at the N and S ends of the retrochoir, built out between the easternmost pairs of aisle buttresses. Sir John Speke died in 1518, Bishop Oldham – who founded Manchester Grammar School and (with his friend Bishop Fox of Winchester) Corpus Christi College, Oxford – in 1519. In design the two chapels are very similar outside, but quite different inside. The front walls of four sections have outer uprights decorated with small statuary (St Anne teaching the Virgin to read at the l. of the Speke Chantry entrance, much restored). Cornices with angels (cf. Branscombe and Stafford canopies, but a sad decline in quality). The large openings guarded by contemporary iron bars. Contemporary wooden door to the Oldham Chantry. Quatrefoil tomb-chests inside both. The Speke Chapel inside has fully panelled walls, figures of angels in niches above, and a gently vaulted ceiling with pendants; not an inch left unadorned. The Oldham Chapel has an unusually elaborate reredos with three figure scenes: Annunciation, Mass of St Gregory, Nativity (cf. Kirkham Chapel, Paignton), and a curved barrel-vault with a reticulated pattern of ogee quatrefoils, identical to the porch of St Peter, Tiverton. There is less decoration elsewhere, but the owls, Oldham's rebus, cannot be missed.

SOUTH PRESBYTERY AISLE AND CHOIR AISLE. In the bay W

of Bishop Berkeley's tomb-chest (*see* Choir and Presbytery, above), in arched recesses with carved label-stop heads between and at the ends, two recumbent cross-legged armoured knights: on the l. Sir Humphrey de Bohun, Earl of Hereford, †1322, on the r. probably Sir Henry de Raleigh †1303. – On the aisle floor, E end, one of the cathedral's two large medieval brasses (cf. Langton in the NE chapel, above): Sir Peter Courtenay †1409, formerly in the nave (cf. Courtenay tomb now in the S transept). Nearly life-size, much worn; said to be one of only six brasses representing Knights of the Garter, though he does not seem to be wearing the Order. The armour is a mixture of mail and plate, as on the effigy of the Black Prince at Canterbury. The border is mostly reconstruction, but in the upper corners are remnants of badges with falcons attacking a duck and a heron.

The other principal monuments in this aisle are post-Reformation, and are given chronologically. Bishop William Cotton †1621 (symmetrically opposite his successor Bishop Carey on the N side of the choir). Of alabaster, with a bearded recumbent figure in typical early C17 episcopal dress under an arched canopy on columns with symbols of fame, time, and death. – Nearby, wall-monument to Dr Edward Cotton †1675, cathedral treasurer. Restrained and with a good portrait bust (the sculptor deserves to be known). – Wall-monument to Dr Nicholas Hall †1709, cathedral treasurer. Less restrained, richly ornamented, with broken pediment, armorial cartouche, and winged cherub heads. – Near the W end of the aisle, Bishop Weston †1742 and his wife †1741 and daughter †1762 by *Thomas Ady*. Tablet with arms above and sarcophagus below. A kneeling angel points to the inscription. – Lt-Gen. John G. Simcoe †1806 by *John Flaxman*. Gothic wall-tablet with figures of a soldier with reversed musket and a Canadian Indian with tomahawk. Simcoe was the first Lieutenant Governor of Upper Canada, and founded Toronto.

NORTH PRESBYTERY AISLE AND CHOIR AISLE. On the N wall near the E end, opposite Bishop Stapledon, his brother Sir Robert Stapledon †1320. In an ogee-arched recess with angel heads as cusps of the arch lies the cross-legged effigy in contemporary mail armour, shown unusually between two enchanting figures, his squire and his groom, the latter holding a horse (damaged). If all this were in its original early C14 state, we should know better how exquisite English C14 carving could be. – Nearby, in a recess with a little forward-tipped vault, a shrouded C16 cadaver or emaciated corpse, perhaps *ex situ* but behind a grille of contemporary ironwork. Was it once the *memento mori* of Anthony Harvey †1564, whose tomb-chest, with mixed Gothic and classical details and no effigy, stands next to Sir Robert Stapledon's monument? – Bishop Valentine Carey †1626. As in the corresponding monument to Bishop Cotton on the S side of the choir, the bearded alabaster figure lies in early C17 episcopal dress under an arched canopy on columns, here simply with putti. – Wall-tablet to Robert Hall †1667, with broken pediment, coats of arms, and attached columns. – Wall-tablet to Rachel Charlotte, wife of Captain O'Brien, †1800 saving her child from fire. Coloured marbles; seated female figure with reversed torch. Signed *J. Kendall*, the cathedral surveyor.

North Transept

FURNISHINGS. CLOCK. Late C15 (traditionally given by Bishop
Peter Courtenay †1487), much restored and redecorated, notably
in 1760, the works now on view are a mixture of several centuries
in between (strike train c. 1485, quarters train late C17, going train
early C18). Large C15 dial with central globe round which revolves
the moon, also the sun, represented by a fleur-de-lys, with inscription 'Pereunt et imputantur' from Martial's Epigrams V.20.
References to earlier clocks in the cathedral records date from the
late C13 to the C15. – WALL PAINTING. On the N wall, Resurrection, early C16, like the painting in the retrochoir. Christ holding a
banner steps out of the tomb surrounded by sleeping soldiers. In
the distance on the l. three women, on the r. a contemporary
sexton and his wife carrying spade and lantern, in the background
Jerusalem, with a circular church. As accomplished, and with the
same 'woodcut' feeling, as prophets on a screen at Ashton, i.e. of
an important Devon school of late medieval painting. Traces of an
Entombment scene below. The paintings are enclosed by the
screens of the contemporary Sylke chantry chapel (see below).

MONUMENTS. Chantry of Precentor Sylke †1508. A Perp stone
screen with crisp tracery encloses the NE corner of the transept.
Tomb-chest with cadaver below a low arch, set within the screen.
On the uprights many small mutilated figure groups whose subject
matter suggests that they were conceived together with the paintings on the wall behind, and that the whole chapel (dedicated to
the Holy Cross) may have served for the Easter Sepulchre. Above
the tomb-chest on the s side the Trinity; at the sides the Mocking
of Christ, Crucifixion, Deposition, and Pietà; on the w screen the
Virgin with souls under her cloak, and saints including St Helena
and St James the Great.* The upper part of the wooden door is a
sole remnant of the early C14 choir stalls (see Choir and Presbytery,
above). – High up on the N wall, tablet to Bishop John Woolton
†1594, pedimented, with inscription between columns. Was it
originally part of his tomb in the presbytery (q.v., above)? – On
the w wall, Dr Edmund Davy †1692, bust in niche encircled by a
wreath. – E wall, Captain Benjamin Dollen †1700, portrait bust in
medallion and naval tail-piece scene. – Near the w wall, James
Northcote R.A. †1831 by his friend *Sir Francis Chantrey*, a life-
sized figure of the painter holding a palette, seated on a high
pedestal. – On the E wall, Crimean War memorial tablet to members of the 20th or East Devonshire Regiment †1854–5, flanked by
bronze figures of riflemen.

South Transept

MONUMENTS. In the SE corner, two slabs, one of Tournai marble,
one of Purbeck, rest on what may be a late C14 tomb-chest. One or
both slabs may relate to Bishop John 'the Chanter' †1191. – Hugh
Courtenay, second Earl of Devon, †1377 and his wife, Margaret
Bohun, †1391. Free-standing tomb-chest with effigies, heavily
restored (new heads and hands) after removal in the early C19 from

*I owe these identifications to Anna Hulbert.

a Courtenay chantry formerly in the nave (s arcade, between the piers of the second bay from the E). She has intertwined Bohun swans at her feet. – On the s wall, Sir Peter Carew †1575 with kneeling figure (see also his uncle's display in the NE chapel, above). – Sir John Gilbert †1596 and wife. Recumbent figures behind low arches (similar in this to the Bampfield monument at Poltimore). – Very Rev. Joseph Palmer, Dean of Cashel, †1829, by *Humphrey Hopper*. A female figure with reversed torch leaning on a draped urn. Cold.

Nave and Crossing

FURNISHINGS. Over the crossing a brass CHANDELIER, large, two-tiered, dated 1691.

MINSTRELS' GALLERY, above the N nave arcade at the bay corresponding to the N porch. Neither architecturally nor sculpturally of a high order. Presumably erected only after the removal of the scaffolds for the centering of the nave and vaults. The two corbels below, carrying the vaulting-shafts either side of this bay, differ in shape from all others in the nave. What is seen from the nave is the carved stone balcony of a hidden large, high room – big enough for an orchestra or antiphonal choir – over the N aisle. The pierced parapet takes the place of both triforium and clerestory parapet for this bay. Fourteen angels, including one at each end, in tiny flattish recesses, the twelve on the front with musical instruments: citole, bagpipe, recorder, viol, harp, jews' harp, trumpet, portative organ, gittern, shawm, timbrel, cymbals. Recent conservation has shown that the angels were trimmed to fit the recesses.

SCREEN to St Edmund's Chapel by the NW entrance. Possibly late C14 and contemporary with the vault within, this is the earliest in style of the cathedral's wooden screens. Simple and substantial, in solid oak, its only decoration is the pierced ornament along the top. Traces of bright red paint. – FONT, near the W end of the S arcade. Late C17, of Sicilian marble, with carved oak cover. First used in 1687. The pedestal of 1891. – The PULPIT designed by *Scott* was set up in 1877.

STAINED GLASS. See p. 385–6.

MONUMENTS. N aisle: Matthew Godwin †1586 aged eighteen, organist and master of the music at Canterbury and Exeter cathedrals, said to be the earliest monument to a musician in England. Kneeling in profile among instruments – organ, lute, theorbo, and trumpet; charming and full of feeling. – Also in the N aisle: officers and men of the Ninth Queen's Royal Lancers in India by *Marochetti*, erected 1860, flanked by bronze horsemen. – W wall of N aisle: Richard Doddridge Blackmore †1900, author of *Lorna Doone*. Portrait head in relief, signed by *Harry Hems*. – In the S aisle, tablets signed by London sculptors: to Saccharissa Hibbert †1828, roses within a sickle, by *Richard Westmacott Jun.* of Wilton Place; and to Sophia Charlotte Hennis †1834, seated female and draped urn, by *E. Gaffin* of Regent Street.

STAINED GLASS*

The GREAT EAST WINDOW was first glazed in 1304, when Master *Walter* was paid for the work. In 1391, after the masonry had been reconstructed, the window was reglazed by *Robert Lyen*. He incorporated much of the glass of 1304, including the three central top figures and the six outer figures of the lowest tier with their canopies and borders. The lively architectural canopies are comparable to those of Merton College Oxford: perhaps the original scheme here, as at Merton, had bands of figures alternating with clear glass. The figure-drawing is outstanding, and the facial detail of the upper three figures is particularly fine. The heads of the six lowest-tier figures are renewed, and the three central canopies of the tier, though doubtless originally of 1304 like the others, are now almost entirely restorations. From Lyen's reglazing of 1391 the four side figures in the middle tier survive. The central six figures and the canopies to the three in the middle tier were made *c.* 1470 by the same West Country workshop that produced the glass at Doddiscombsleigh: all this was brought from elsewhere in the cathedral and set into the E window in *Joseph Tucker*'s reglazing of 1750–1. Also of *c.* 1470 are the small canopies along the base, which, like most of the shields below them, were inserted in the 1760s. Much later restoration work was done in 1884–96 by *Frederick Drake*, to whom the relative visual coherence of the window is largely attributable. In 1948 the tracery openings were filled with shields and fragments gathered together from various parts of the cathedral. The whole window was renovated, and some new glass added, by *Alfred Fisher* in 1985–6.

The CLERESTORY window facing the bishop's throne was also glazed in 1304: grisaille, with a row of now-headless figures of saints under canopies. Though stylistically very close to the contemporary glass remaining in the E window, the figure-drawing seems to be by a different hand. The fragments in the tracery lights, totally impossible to see from ground level, were put in in 1948.

In the S window of ST GABRIEL'S CHAPEL (restored by *Drake* in 1878) some very neat geometrical grisaille dating from the first years of the C14, with the same naturalistic foliage – oak, hawthorn, ivy – as is found in the earliest bosses. Other remains of grisaille, incorporated with shields and heterogeneous fragments, in the E window of the chapel and, on the opposite side of the Lady Chapel, in the windows of ST JOHN'S CHAPEL, including three kneeling canons originally associated with the glass of *c.* 1470 now in the great E window. Various medieval shields, none in their original positions, in ST JOHN BAPTIST'S CHAPEL in the N tower and in the SPEKE CHANTRY. Some little C15 figures including a good angel's head in the E window of the OLDHAM CHANTRY.

Other medieval panels, brought in from elsewhere in the early 1950s, include the excellent mid C14 angel playing a harp now in the E window of the SPEKE CHANTRY, the late C15 Crucifixion panel of West Country workmanship in the E window of ST GABRIEL'S CHAPEL, and the C16 North European panels from

*By Chris Brooks.

Master Walter's glazing, 1304

Master Walter's glazing, largely restored

Robert Lyen's re-glazing, 1391

glass of *c.* 1470, inserted 1751

glass of *c.* 1470, inserted 1760s

Exeter Cathedral: great east window

the Costessey Collection in the two S windows of the LADY
CHAPEL: in the E one six Old Testament scenes, visually rather
aimless but in fact a typological sequence prefiguring the Passion;
in the W one a St Anne with Virgin and Child, flanked by scenes
representing the bribing of Judas and doubting Thomas.

The GREAT WEST WINDOW has been reglazed at least three
times since the Reformation. What was *William Peckitt*'s largest
window, designed in 1766, with figures under canopies and elaborate armorials, was removed in 1904 (heraldic panels, now
predominantly yellow as a result of fading, were leaded into
windows in the cloister room in the 1920s). Its replacement – the
Archbishop Temple memorial window, designed by *G.F. Bodley*

and executed by *Burlison & Grylls* – was destroyed in 1942; the present rather pedestrian window by *Reginald Bell & M.C. Farrer Bell* dates from the immediate post-war period.

Much major Victorian and Edwardian glass was also lost in the war, but in the S aisle there is still the Turner memorial by *Powell & Son*, the South African War memorial by *Clayton & Bell*, and the Tanner memorial by *Burlison & Grylls*, all competent, but none particularly exciting. Also, in the passage between S transept and chapter house a window of 1921 in memory of Frederick Drake designed by *Maurice Drake*, who portrayed his father as St James of Ulm, patron saint of glass-painters: a precisely similar window is in St Michael, Teignmouth.

The post-war windows of Exeter, carried out between the late 1940s and the mid 1950s, are a depressingly timid lot: the best are probably those by *A.F. Erridge* – the Courtenay window and the Nativity, both in the S aisle, and the Blackmore memorial in the N aisle. Also in the S aisle, the 1942 air-raid commemoration glass by *Christopher Webb* is worth a look. Windows by *G. Cooper Abbs* in the S aisle, *Hugh Easton* in St James's Chapel, *Ninian Comper* in St Andrew's Chapel, and *Reginald Bell* in St Edmund's Chapel are all more-or-less tired rehashes of tired conventions. The E window of the Lady Chapel, by *Marion D. Grant*, tries for a little originality, but incoherent design and anaemic colour sink it – depressing when one thinks of the glass Bazaine and Leger were designing for Audincourt in France at precisely the same time.

THE CATHEDRAL PRECINCTS

Exeter was a collegiate foundation, not a monastic one, but the reforms of Bishop Brewer (1224–44) provided a CHAPTER HOUSE for the use of the Canons, on a site previously part of the bishop's garden. It is a rectangular building in the traditional position S of the S transept, from which visitors now approach it. It was begun *c.*1225, as is suggested by its 'wind-blown' stiff-leaf sculpture. This appears on the capitals to the shafts of the finely moulded doorway from the cloisters.

Inside, the ground-floor stage is plain (and of red sandstone, as revealed by restoration in 1969) except for the main Purbeck marble vaulting shafts, groups of three with stiff-leaf capitals, meant for transverse arches and diagonal ribs, and with shaft-rings at sill-level of the next stage. On this stage blank arcades form two niches per bay, again with grouped shafts. The original blue lias columns of the arcades, replaced by Purbeck marble in 1970, showed the effects of a fire presumed to have destroyed the upper parts in 1413. Beginning in that year, the main shafts were replaced by shafts leading up to pretty niches for figure sculpture (not surviving) and then to the timber braces supporting the tie-beams of the low-pitched roof, charmingly decorated with a painted rendering of small fan-vault effects, of the time of Bishop Bothe (1465–78). The early C13 windows were replaced by four-light (E end seven-light) Perp windows with standard tracery. The C13 niches below had C15 wall paintings of feigned sculpture, but are now filled by large and horribly discordant fibreglass-and-aluminium sculptures on the theme of the Creation by *Kenneth Carter*, 1974.

The CLOISTERS may have been built originally by Bishop Brewer. The doorways to the chapter house and to the E end of the N aisle are of his time, but from 1377 building work was in progress under *Robert Lesyngham*. The cloisters were demolished in 1656–7, probably by the Exeter City Corporation, which set up the town serge market here. In 1887 the SE corner, with library above on the site of the C14 library, was rebuilt by *J. L. Pearson*, basing his cloister-bays on surviving fragments, with 'star vault' and large Perp windows. (For the STAINED GLASS, *see* above.) A screen and doors were added *c.* 1960 to form the 'cloister room' under the library.

For the C12 fragments displayed in the cloisters *see* p. 367.

For the Cathedral Close *see* p. 410.

CHURCHES

There were about fifteen medieval churches within the city walls, as well as numerous chapels. Only seven remain with fabric older than the C19: St Martin, St Mary Arches, St Mary Steps, St Olave, St 7 Pancras, St Petrock, and St Stephen. Among the later buildings, the most notable from the C18 is George's Meeting, an independent chapel of 1760, from the C19 the little church of St Andrew at Exwick, of 1841–2 by *Hayward*, very progressive for its date; St Michael Dinham Road, with its mighty spire, 1865–8 by *Rhode Hawkins*; and St David, 1897 by *Caröe*, especially inventive. Several city-centre churches were 166 destroyed in or after the last war (All Hallows Bartholomew Street, St John, St Mary Major), as were some suburban ones (St James, St Sidwell). Both replacements and new outer suburban churches are undistinguished.

ALL SAINTS, Whipton. 1861–2 by *Edward Ashworth*. A picturesque little building in volcanic stone with Bath stone dressings, Dec, with a steep bellcote with trefoiled opening. Chancel refurnished 1966. – Some STAINED GLASS of the 1870s. – BRASS. Anna Everard †1877, with angel.

EMMANUEL, Okehampton Road. 1896–7 by *Harold Brakspear*. Robust mixed Dec and Perp. Purple Pocombe stone with Bath dressings. The intended SW tower not built, but a polygonal SE vestry and shallow transepts add interest to the street scene. Inside, quatrefoil piers with carved capitals. Clerestory with stone shafts between the windows, supporting tie-beams. – STAINED GLASS. E window post-1918, colourful Te Deum; W window 1928. – In the screen dividing off the N aisle cross-shaped abstract glass windows by *Charles Norris* of Buckfast, *c.* 1970.

HOLY TRINITY, South Street. Now a social club. Rebuilt in 1820 by *Cornish & Sons*. Stucco front with tiny bell-turret. Interior with thin quatrefoil shafts and W gallery. Dec aisle windows. Chancel altered 1884 by *Ashworth*. Nice iron railings to the street.

ST ANDREW, Exwick. 1841–2 by *John Hayward*. A small but significant church built to serve the fringes of the working-class suburb of St Thomas. The *Ecclesiologist* described it as 'the best specimen of a modern church we have yet seen'. Built as a chapel of ease to St Thomas, whose vicar was the Rev. John Medley,

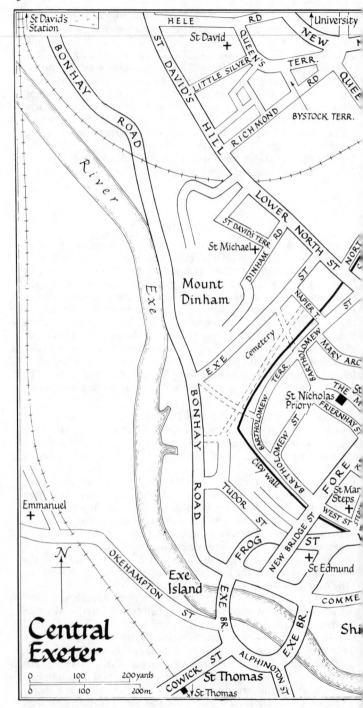

Central Exeter

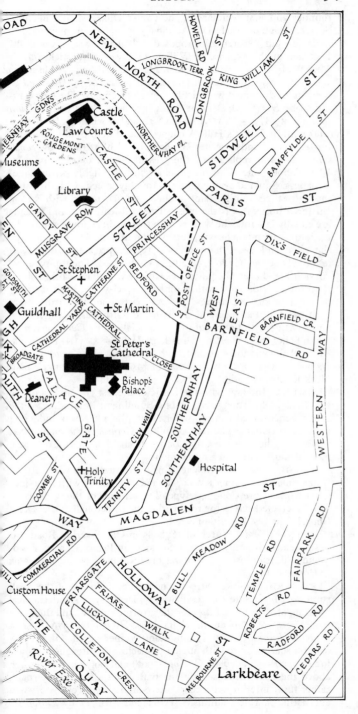

founder and first secretary of the Exeter Diocesan Architectural Society. Puginian early Dec, originally just chancel, nave with W bellcote, and S porch. A proposed NW tower was never built. Enlarged at the expense of William Gibbs of Tyntesfield (cf. St Michael) in 1873–5, when the N arcade with polished marble shafts was added and the chancel lengthened to the E, by *Hayward & Son*, and redecorated with richly stencilled ceilings. The new carving all by *Hems*. – REREDOS. 1841 by *Simon Rowe* with *Salviati* mosaics of 1875. – STAINED GLASS. E and W windows by *Beer*.

ST DAVID, St David's Hill. A chapel existed here by the late C12, but it was a handsome neo-Grecian chapel of 1816–17 by *James Green* that was replaced by the present church of 1897–1900 by *W.D.Caröe* – one of his finest achievements. Highly picturesque, if restless. Squared grey limestone, roughly tooled, with dressings in Bath stone and Portland stone. The NE tower with strong clustered buttresses is the most successful feature. E and W ends are equally fanciful, the W front with two turrets with spirelets, the E windows with two heavily buttressed mullions. The long sides of the nave and aisles have Caröe's typical projecting depressed arches above the windows to give shadow zones. The top parapets curve up, and even the buttresses have tops with concave gables.

166   Inside, a wide nave with a timber tunnel-vault, broken up by powerful transverse arches, and tall narrow aisles, hardly more than passages between and through the buttresses. – REREDOS, and STALLS with figures of the Annunciation, by *Caröe*, given by Sarah Thornton West of Streatham Hall. – STAINED GLASS. Many of the windows, including the E window, by *Kempe Studios*, 1900–4. – BRASS. Lady Duckworth †1902. Standing angel; bold black-letter inscription.

ST EDMUND. Integral with the fabric of the last two arches of the Exe Bridge of *c*.1200 (q.v., Public Buildings). Rebuilding of the tower is mentioned in 1448–9. The stump of a W tower and a C14 undercroft remain. The rest, rebuilt by *Cornish & Julian* in 1834, was demolished by the City Council to make a picturesque ruin incongruously sited on a roundabout.

ST GEORGE, South Street. War damage exposed walls with re-used Roman masonry, and a NW corner and W doorway with long-and-short work of pre-Conquest type. The remains of the W doorway were re-erected across the road within the ruined hall of the Vicars Choral. The rest has disappeared.

ST JAMES. *Fulford*'s church of 1878–85 in Old Tiverton Road was destroyed in the war. The new St James in Prince Charles Road, Stoke Hill, is uninspired post-war brick Gothic by *Gordon Jackson & Partners*, 1955.

ST LEONARD, Holloway Street. The medieval church of the small rural parish outside the town was replaced by a small classical building of 1831 by *A.Patey* for the growing suburb, and then by a large church of 1876–86, the chancel by *S.Robinson*, 1876, the rest by *R.M.Fulford*, 1883. The building is finely sited. On the SW tower a soaring spire with angled pinnacles. Picturesque E grouping of vestries (added by *C. Cole*, 1902) and polygonal apse high above the road. Limestone with Bath stone dressings. Ornate, rather fussy interior, with cusped rere-arches to the clerestory and alternating marble columns. – FONT and PULPIT by *Fulford*. –

STALLS. Free Gothic of 1914–15. – BRASS. William Miles † 1881, whose widow built the tower. Inscription flanked by saints, within a stone tabernacle. – Minor MONUMENTS from the old church, the best to Thomas Collins † 1761, a simple urn, by *Prince Hoare*. – Memorial to the Barings of Larkbeare and Mount Radford. Marble tablet with coat of arms; 1913.

ST MARK, Pinhoe Road. 1934–7 by *Ernest F. Hooper*. Pedestrian Gothic, red brick, the exterior display confined to the clustered stone pinnacles of the w tower. Pale brick interior, the arcades dying into the piers.

ST MARTIN, Cathedral Close. Typical of the crammed sites and odd plans of Exeter parish churches. Mostly red sandstone. Nave, chancel, and a tower forming a tiny N transept, with polygonal stair-turret. Ostensibly all Perp, with large transomed w window. But the NE corner of the nave has, high up, decayed but convincing long-and-short work in volcanic trap, which would fit the consecration recorded for 1065. Interior all plastered. Abaci of the chancel arch with fleurons, the arch above rebuilt: an unsatisfactory squashed shape to allow for an early C19 window above. Ceiled wagon roof.

The church is unusually rich in furnishings, but they are all minor in aesthetic value. – REREDOS. Of *c*. 1710 (arms of Bishop Blackall), stone, with two oval and two rectangular panels, formerly with Creed, Commandments, and Lord's Prayer, now painted over. – COMMUNION RAILS. Late C17, with twisted balusters, enclosing the altar on three sides. – PULPIT, BOX PEWS, and WEST GALLERY also of *c*. 1700, the w gallery with the arms of Bishop Trelawney (†1708). – STAINED GLASS. Medieval fragments (s window). – C15 heraldry and small pieces reset in margins. – MONUMENTS. Judith Wakeman † 1643, with small figures and ornaments partly of the gristly type characteristic of the mid C17. – Winifred Butler † 1673. Two cherubs above a panel. – Edward Seaward † 1703. With big clumsy cherubs and thick garlands. – Philip Hooper † 1715 by *Weston*. Grand, but not of high quality: kneeling bewigged figures flanked by two columns, two mourning cherubs, reclining angels on a broken pediment. – John Codrington † 1801. A mourning figure by a tomb. – Eliza Mortimer † 1826 by *Baily* of London. Ascending figure with angel.

ST MARY ARCHES (Diocesan Educational Resource Centre), Mary Arches Street. The least cramped of the medieval parish churches in its plan. Nave, two aisles, and shallow chancel originally probably larger. Unimpressive exterior; walls much patched (N wall rebuilt 1814). Disproportionately small w tower with semicircular N stair and parapet with balls, replacing a larger tower further w, from which the jambs of the tower arch can still be seen. The inside is a surprise, spacious, with four-bay arcades both of the C12 [7] (unique in Devon). Circular piers with square, many-scalloped capitals, square chamfered abaci, double-chamfered arches. Perp windows. Gutted in the war and restored in 1942–50 by *S. Dykes-Bower* with a plain plaster barrel-vault, cut into by a clerestory lunette on each side, in place of the late medieval wagon roof. More recently tactfully converted for weekday use as a library, with raised carpeted floor, discreet glazed NW office, and low bookshelves in the aisles.

REREDOS. By *John Legg*, *c.*1700, repaired by *Dykes-Bower*. Corinthian pilasters. Carved foliage around oval and arched panels formerly with the Commandments and the Lord's Prayer. – Twisted COMMUNION RAILS, part of the same refitting. – ALTAR FRONTAL. Made in the C18 from remains of a C15 cope and chasuble (Crucifixion and Saints). – Carved Hanoverian ROYAL ARMS above the S door. – FONT COVER with bracket made from sword rests.

MONUMENTS. Many to civic dignitaries, a proud display. – At the E end of the S aisle, formerly a chantry chapel with its own S door (now blocked), Thomas Andrew, twice mayor of Exeter, †1518. Recumbent effigy on a tomb-chest with four shield-holding angels, within an ogee-arched recess with elaborately undercut foliage around the moulding. In the spandrels four angels holding quatrefoils. Other little figures up the sides and along the straight top. – Robert Walker †1602. An upright oval between Corinthian columns; open pediment above. – John Davy †1611. With strapwork and naked putti, with original colour. – Thomas Walker and wife †1628 and 1622. Life-size kneeling figures facing each other in the usual way; simple architectural surround. – In the N aisle, Maria and Christopher Lethbridge †1659 and 1670. Architectural, with painted grey marbling and other original colours revealed by recent cleaning. – Five other wall-monuments of this Exeter type, with a variety of sober but inventive architectural frames (1666, 1673, and three of 1682).

ST MARY MAJOR, Cathedral Close. The unexciting church of 1864 by *Edward Ashworth* was demolished in 1971. Later excavation revealed that it stood on the site of an aisleless pre-Conquest church, identified as the minster replaced by the Norman cathedral (*see* Cathedral, Introduction, and Cathedral Close, Introduction).

ST MARY STEPS, West Street. Originally by the West Gate of Exeter. The small tunnel-vaulted room beneath the S chapel was built in 1600 as a porter's lodge. It is reached by a door in the S wall. Before New Bridge Street was built the main entrance into Exeter from the W passed the church and climbed steeply up to Fore Street. The church is mentioned in 1199, but the present building appears C15. Red Heavitree stone, in well cut ashlar blocks. In the E wall a blocked round-headed arch, perhaps for a priest's door. S aisle clearly later than the SW tower, see the junction inside. The tower opens into the church with two-centred N and E arches without capitals. Two-bay arcade with very depressed four-centred arches without capitals on A type piers. Ceiled wagon roofs. Restored in 1868–72 by *Ashworth*.

FONT. Norman, cylindrical, with crude palmette scroll, projecting cable-moulding lower down, and some other minor motifs. – SCREEN. The part across the S aisle C15, brought from St Mary Major after the old church was demolished in 1865. The painted panels in the wainscoting re-done; the tracery type A standard. The part across the nave, quite an accomplished copy, but with the arches more spread out, designed by *Ashworth* and made by *H. Hems*, with dado paintings by *G. B. Saunders*. – *Hems* also made the FONT COVER in Jacobean style (1870) and the carved wooden ALTAR (1888). – Another carved ALTAR in the S chapel. – The

ROOD FIGURES on the screen come from a *Hems* reredos of 1907, dismantled in 1966, when the chancel was reordered by *Lawrence King*. The floor was lowered to its medieval level (still remarkably high above the nave) and the E window given STAINED GLASS by *John Hayward*, Christ in Majesty, linear, muted Byzantine style, chiefly red, white, and yellow. – Painted TESTER also by *Hayward*. – CLOCK, outside on the tower wall (called Matthew the Miller and his Sons). Dial with seasons in the four spandrels, above three jolly, armed figures in an ogee-headed niche, one seated, the others standing. It was erected some time between 1603 and 1624.

ST MATTHEW, Newtown. 1881–90 by *Fulford & Harvey*. An urban mission church, built for the working-class parish of Newtown. Red brick with coloured banding. Ambitious plan, with transepts and chancel chapels. W tower never completed. Lofty interior with a display of polychromy: buff brick, coloured tiles, arcades with polished granite shafts and Corsehill and Pocombe stone voussoirs. – Terracotta and serpentine PULPIT, 1891. – Patterned GLASS by *Drake*.

ST MICHAEL, Dinham Road. Built as a chapel of ease to St David's in 1865–8 by *Rhode Hawkins*, financed by William Gibbs of Tyntesfield, an exemplar of Tractarian ideals in a poor district. A long and impressive church, with a massive spire, inspired by Salisbury, rising 220ft above the crossing, one of Exeter's chief landmarks. French Gothic detail, with some good carving by *Hurley* of Taunton. W front with a rose window and a row of archangels above the tripartite entrance. Five-bay nave with passage aisles. Naturalistic foliage and grotesque animals in the spandrels of the arcades. Chancel decorated 1883 by *Frederick Drake*, as a memorial to Gibbs. STAINED GLASS also by *Drake*. On the N side of the sanctuary a canopied niche with the founder's effigy, carved by *H.H.Armstead*, the clothes rendered with the elaboration of Baroque sculpture. – PULPIT. 1885 by *Arthur Blomfield*. – REREDOS. By *W.D.Caröe*, 1899, large, with stylized mosaic of Christ in Majesty framed by heads of the apostles.

ST MICHAEL AND ALL ANGELS, Church Street, Heavitree. The medieval church was rebuilt in 1844–6 by *David Mackintosh*. Tower 1890, chancel extended 1897, both by *E.H.Harbottle*. The late medieval nave piers were retained: six arches on B type piers with bold angel capitals without abaci. Arches with fleurons and foliage. Perp aisle windows with transoms. Harbottle's work was more ambitious: the E end of the chancel was raised up high above the vestries; the tower is a fine tall variant on the Somerset type, with pinnacles. – REREDOS. Part of *Scott*'s cathedral furnishings of the 1870s, brought here in 1939. An overpowering piece for a small church. Dramatic carving of the Ascension as a centrepiece, below canopies. – SCREEN. Part now used as the s parclose; standard tracery. – STAINED GLASS. Some grisaille panels with heraldry, one dated 1834. – MONUMENTS. Minor tablets from the old church. – Sebastian Isaac † 1685. Unusual carved oval tablet. – Thomas Gorges and wife † 1670 and 1671. Slab in front of the chancel steps with the often quoted inscription, 'The loving turtle having lost her mate / Begged shee might enter ere they shut the gate', etc. – (BRASS. Rev. A. Amerly † 1857.)

ST OLAVE (i.e. Olaf, a Viking king and martyr), Fore Street. A very
odd plan. On the S side, embraced by chancel and nave, a tiny
tower, built of large dressed stones, possibly a relic from an C11
palace chapel built for Gytha, the mother of King Harold. The S
wall of the nave was built out flush with the tower in 1815, when a
gallery was provided inside. The rest of the church late medieval.
N arcade with slender late C14 octagonal piers with double-chamfered arches. C15 short outer N aisle; Perp window tracery
(renewed). Restoration by *Gould & Son*, 1875. The tower has been
opened up to the church by a later arch, and the pulpit is squeezed
inside. – Victorian High Church fittings; good iron SCREEN
between chancel and N aisle; elaborate REREDOS and SANCTU-
ARY SCREEN of 1902. – SCULPTURE. Two late C12 fragments:
waterleaf capital; spirally moulded base. – Flagellation, C14, very
battered. – ROYAL ARMS of William III. – STAINED GLASS.
Reset figure of St Olaf (chancel S), C19. – Medieval BELL.

ST PANCRAS, Guildhall shopping precinct. The dedication suggests
an ancient origin, as did the medieval street pattern around the
church. Now the tiny building stands incongruously dished up on
a platter of municipal planting in the middle of a paved square.
The church is referred to only in 1191, but a possibly pre-Conquest S chancel doorway was found in the C19. Nave, chancel, and
W bell-gable only. The chancel, rebuilt stone by stone during
J. L. Pearson's restoration of 1887–9, has C13 details (cusped
piscina, lancet window, hollow-chamfered rere-arches), the nave
plain C16 windows and a late medieval wagon roof. Chancel arch
on corbels, in unsympathetic Bath stone, added by *Pearson*.

FONT. Elementary C12, circular, with thin beaded moulding. –
COMMUNION RAILS. Twisted; brought from St Stephen during
the re-ordering of 1977. – PULPIT. An attractive piece of *c.* 1600,
polygonal, with foliage around rectangular panels, the top supported by secular-looking caryatids with wreaths. Brought from
All Hallows (demolished 1906). – SCULPTURE. One C12 and one
C13 corbel reset in the chancel wall. – STAINED GLASS. 1899;
Crucifixion, St Pancras, and St Boniface, delicately drawn. –
MONUMENTS. Several tablets from All Hallows, the best the one
to I. Loveday Buller †1711, the border with flowers, fruit, and
skulls.

ST PETROCK. Exposed to the High Street only at the road-widening
of 1905, when the N door was made. Windows high up because of
its cramped position. The NW tower carries a tiny octagonal turret
of 1736. The interior is among the most confusing of any church in
the whole of England. The reason is that the present chancel
(added in 1881 by *Hayward*) turns round the whole direction of the
church. This chancel faces S, with a Dec window towards the
cathedral close; the original chancel, still there, but screened off,
faces E. To this original church a S aisle was added in the early C15,
and an outer S aisle was consecrated in 1573. A further enlargement S took place in 1587 and SW in 1828, part of a reconstruction
by *Charles Hedgeland*. The clerestory and skylights of different
shapes date from this time.

The octagonal skylight in the centre of the nave more than
anything else gives the church its peculiar secular character. Piers
of arcade and tower arch are of an unusual section derived from the

cathedral: four major shafts with three minor shafts in the diagonals. The long-fingered angels holding shields above the capitals
must date from 1828. – SCREEN, dividing off the medieval
chancel, now a Chapel of Unity; glass, with thin black uprights, a
large wooden cross as the main mullion, forceful without being
overpowering, by the *Harrison Sutton Partnership*, 1985; also by
them the attractive grille between Victorian chancel and vestry. –
Small carved ROYAL ARMS, C18. – STAINED GLASS. In the
medieval chancel by *Beer*, 1840s, in the later chancel by *Drake*.

MONUMENTS. A striking sequence of sombre architectural
wall-monuments of the late C17–18, in restrained polychromy. –
William and Mary Hooper †1683 and 1658. Large, with two   89
arches containing frontal busts, framed by Corinthian pilasters;
broken segmental pediment with urn. – Francis and Alexander
Worth †1675 and 1680. Swan-necked pediment on Corinthian
columns with putti; oval inscription within a wreath. – John and
Faith Mayne †1680 and 1679. Another oval, the pediment this
time segmental, with flaming urns and arms on top. – Jonathan
and Elizabeth Ivie †1717 and 1698. Brought from St Kerian
(demolished 1873). A less ponderous classical aedicule flanked by
angels with trumpets. Originally part of the monument, but now
displayed separately, is the graceful and vigorous oval relief of the
Last Judgement, a remarkable piece of carving by the Exeter
sculptor *Weston*. – Theodore Sheere †1782. Urn against a black
obelisk.

ST SIDWELL, Sidwell Street. The earliest church recorded in Exeter
(early C11), sited in the area of a Roman extramural cemetery, and
dedicated to a local martyr, so an origin as a mausoleum-shrine
would be a possibility. The immediate predecessor of the present
church, damaged in the war, was a Perp rebuilding by *W. Burgess*
of 1812, incorporating arcades of 1437. The building that we see
today is of 1957, by *Lucas, Roberts & Brown*. Brick. Single internal
space with transverse arches in concrete. – PAINTINGS on the E
wall by *Hans Feibusch*. – STAINED GLASS. W window by *James
Paterson* of Barnstaple. – (BRASS. Rev. John Galton †1878.)

ST STEPHEN, High Street. The distinguishing feature of the church
is the pretty E chapel (divided off in the reordering of 1972),
originally dedicated to St John the Baptist, raised above a single
arch under which a narrow street runs S. The plain chamfered
arch separating the church from the chapel is C13, and the crypt,
revealed in 1826 but sealed up and not now visible, is still older. It
had two short Norman columns with primitive capitals, one block-
shaped, one with an elementary honeysuckle motif. The outer
walls date from a rebuilding of 1664 after a fire; Perp tracery
within round-headed windows.

The charming interior comes as a surprise: inexpensive fragile
neo-Gothic of 1826, with thin quatrefoil piers and traceried openings in the ceiling (now blocked); cf. St Petrock. – TAPESTRY. By
Bobbie Cox, 1986. Triptych in a cross shape behind the altar,
whose darker frontal forms the base. Abstract pattern of asymmetrical chevrons and small squares, in subtle tones from deep
brown to lime green, chiefly yellows and ochres; confident without
being brash, unlike so many modern furnishings. – PAINTINGS.
Woman of Samaria, by *S. Bird*. – Crowning with Thorns,

attributed to a pupil of Van Dyck. – ROYAL ARMS. One of 1640; another over the E door, especially lively. – STAINED GLASS. 1946 by *Abbs*, unfortunately garish. – MONUMENTS. Two typical Exeter architectural wall-monuments of the late C17, to George Potter †1662, 'being a great benefactor toward the rebuilding of the church', and James Rodd †1678. – Thomas Bolithoe †1753. Mourning woman at an urn, landscape in low relief, against grey marble obelisk; by *Edward Coffin* of Exeter.

ST THOMAS, Cowick Street. By far the largest of the Exeter parish churches, but in origin not a city church at all. A chapel was founded in the C13 on the W side of the Exe Bridge by Cowick Priory, and later rebuilt on this site (consecration 1412) to serve the important settlement which grew up on the other side of the river from the city. Burnt in 1645 in the Civil War, rebuilt by 1657. C17 red W tower, with thin diagonal buttresses, polygonal stair-turret and pinnacles; Perp windows dating from *Hayward*'s restoration of 1871. The S aisle and the E end of the N aisle also C17; the rest of the N aisle and porch 1821. Chancel and transepts 1828–9 by *Patey*. Inner N door with Dec moulding, perhaps re-used. The arcades also probably medieval: simple double-cham-fered arches on octagonal piers with plain octagonal capitals. The E end of the N aisle, now a chapel, was fitted out as a family pew in 1838 for the Graves-Sawle family. Wooden vault with elaborate heraldic decoration. The lofty height and slightly eccentric tracery of Patey's chancel and transepts (designed for galleries) makes an effective contrast to the rest. – Sanctuary embellishments, REREDOS, and ALTAR 1842, Perp, incorporating the MONU-MENT of Christina Medley †1845, wife of the Rev. John Medley, and daughter of the London sculptor *John Bacon*, who designed the tomb. It is in the neo-Dec style, the effigy on a tomb-chest under an ogee recess. – FONT. 1842, also rich neo-Dec, part of Medley's programme of High Anglican adornment. – Eagle LEC-TERN of carved wood brought from the cathedral *c.*1840. A piece of great interest. The eagle is heavily restored, but the splendid three-sided stand is original, with its crocketed nodding ogee arches and three dogs on the base. Its close relationship to the bishop's throne and sedilia suggests that it was part of the early C14 cathedral choir furnishings (and thus the earliest known surviving English cathedral lectern). – ROYAL ARMS with abundance of carving, 1682. – MONUMENTS. Many wall-monu-ments, the largest to Sir Thomas Northmore †1713, large, archi-tectural, with standing allegorical figures and two more reclining on the pediment. – Over the N door another of 1740 (illegible), with similar figures.

BLESSED SACRAMENT (R.C.), Fore Street, Heavitree. Built *c.*1930. Classical miniature portico with green marble columns, against the large, rather clumsy red brick church. Apsed bap-tistery, also with columns.

SACRED HEART (R.C.), South Street. 1881–6 by *Leonard Stokes*, his first known design, when he was in partnership with C. E. Ware, and before his mature style developed under Bodley's influence. Unremarkable exterior of local limestone, mostly Dec, with a low NW tower (completed only in 1926). More rewarding inside, with quite dramatic contrasting spaces: low vaulted narthex, broad and lofty nave, with polished marble octagonal columns and triple inner arcades to the clerestory. Beyond the crossing a tall arch framing the apsed sanctuary, flanked by narrow side arches with statues in niches. – REREDOSES. Three, elaborately carved, by *Scoles*. – Coloured marble ALTARS, STEPS, and PULPIT. – PAINTING (N transept altar) by *Bernard Collier*, 1894, of West Country saints. – C17 painted PANEL of the Crucifixion. – Much STAINED GLASS. – (VESTMENT with medieval embroidered figures attached.)

ST BERNADETTE (R.C.), Galsworthy Square, Whipton. 1960 by *P. A. Byrne*; neo-Romanesque.

BAPTIST CHAPEL, South Street. Rebuilt in 1823, its gabled front obscured by a late C19 semi-octagonal addition and a lower C20 vestibule. Galleries on Ionic columns.

GEORGE'S MEETING, South Street. By far the most interesting of the Nonconformist churches, a testimony to the importance of Exeter as a centre of C18 dissent. Disused from 1983; sadly converted for commercial use in 1987. The church was erected in 1760, the first year of the reign of George I – hence its name. Tall red brick walls (the sides exposed only after post-war redevelopment). Three-bay front with round-arched windows and rendered quoins; moulded cornice and parapet overwhelmed by a tall hipped roof. Pedimented Tuscan porch. Sombre but magnificent contemporary interior. The galleries on three sides on fluted Ionic piers, the pulpit on a dais, and the W gallery with late C17 clock are being preserved; the organ of 1813 has been removed.

METHODIST CHURCH, Sidwell Street. 1905, in front of Sunday Schools of 1896, both by *F. J. Commin*, paid for by W. H. Reed. A fanciful and quite original design with raised octagonal centre with cupola on top. Façade with Baroque segmental pediment. Built in *Paul Cottincin*'s patent reinforced brickwork, with external decoration all in concrete.

MINT METHODIST CHURCH, Fore Street. Set well back. Rebuilt by *Cripps & Stewart* in 1969–70 on the site of the Wesleyan Chapel of 1813.

OLD CHAPEL, Bartholomew Street. Built in 1817 for Baptists seceding from South Street. Two street elevations, rendered, with central pediments, the three-bay E front divided by pilasters, with Doric porch.

SALVATION ARMY TEMPLE, Friars Walk. A startling contrast in styles: the older part a former Friends Meeting House of 1836, classical, with three-bay pedimented front, acquired in 1882 by the Salvation Army, who added a tall and ornate castellated and pedimented extension in dark red brick, 1890 by *W. Dunford*.

SYNAGOGUE, off Mary Arches Street. 1835, stuccoed, with Greek Doric entrance and well preserved interior fittings.

UNITED REFORMED CHURCH, Southernhay East. Tower and spire only remain of the church of 1868 by *J. Tarring*, polychrome, with Bath stone dressings and red bands. The rest rebuilt in 1956 by *R. M. Challice & Son*.

UNITED REFORMED CHURCH, Fore Street, Heavitree. 1902 by *F. J. Commin*. Free Gothic, with a gable at either end.

CITY CEMETERY AND CATACOMBS, Bartholomew Street. The old burial ground within the walls was opened in 1637. In 1837 it was extended on the other side of the wall with romantically sited catacombs in Egyptian style set into the slope of the hill. The demolished All Hallows church, 1843–5 by *Hayward*, stood close to the old burial ground.

CEMETERY, St Mark's Avenue, Heavitree. 1866. Two neat Dec chapels and a Gothic lodge by *Ashworth*. Heavitree stone, banded slate roofs.

MONASTIC BUILDINGS

ST NICHOLAS PRIORY, The Mint. The small Benedictine priory was established after 1087, when the church of St Olave was given by William II to Battle Abbey. Separate buildings, enclosed by a wall, were erected to the SW of the parish church. The priory at first had only six monks; indeed, it was never large. The surviving parts consist of the W range of the cloister, restored after 1913 by Exeter Corporation and accessible to the public as one of the Exeter City Museums, and – divided from it by the present road – part of the N range, much altered by conversion for domestic use. The tall blocked windows of the frater remain, together with two C15 windows of three and two lights in a projecting part to the N. The church lay to the S of the cloister; the rubble core of the W end of its N wall is visible inside the W range.

The walls of the W range are of red breccia and volcanic stone, largely Norman. The upper floor is a late medieval reconstruction. Norman undercroft with two short circular scalloped capitals, their abaci with a simple criss-cross band with drilled holes. Rough groin-vaults of volcanic stone, divided by unmoulded transverse arches of red and white stone; also diagonal arches connecting the piers with the outer corners of the room. S of the undercroft a room with a C14 barrel-vault; in its E wall a Norman doorway to the cloister. In the undercroft itself many C12 fragments. The water-leaf capitals and decorated arch voussoirs have been interpreted as part of a destroyed circular C12 lavatorium. There are also springers for small arches, each arch differently decorated. The intricate ornament relates to decorative work of c. 1160–70 at Wolvesey Palace, Winchester.

N of the undercroft is the Tudor Room (the first to be entered by the visitor), so called because of its late C16 plaster ceiling with Tudor roses and quatrefoils of single ribs. A similar ceiling in the ground floor of the adjoining tower to the W has the initials HM for the Mallet family, who acquired the priory buildings in the 1560s, and converted them to a dwelling. A handsome panelled four-centred arch connects the two rooms. From the tower room a comfortably bending staircase rises to the first floor, where there is a guest hall with chambers at either end (cf. Polsloe Priory, below). The whole range is covered by a handsome late medieval timber roof with arch-braced principals with short curved ends, and two tiers of wind-braces.

The chambers to the S are divided off by a sturdy post-and-panel screen with, at either end, an arched doorway with traceried spandrels. In the reveals of the hall windows traces of early C17 painted decoration. The N chamber is the grandest, with a later C16 plaster frieze to the bedchamber, a garderobe, and a small closet with a late medieval window in the adjoining W tower. Another small chamber in the top floor of the tower, approached by a tiny newel stair from the hall. At the N end of the range, the kitchen (its roof without wind-braces), with late medieval fireplaces in two walls. The upper walls are set back for a former upper floor.

ST KATHERINE'S PRIORY, Polsloe, off St Katherine's Road. A Benedictine nunnery was established shortly before 1160 by William de Brewer (whose son founded the abbeys of Torre (Torbay) and Dunkeswell, qq.v.). The W range, all that remains, is a rebuilding on older foundations, dating from c.1300, when cloister, S range, and SW kitchen were also reconstructed. Local red sandstone with volcanic stone dressings; much patched and altered during its later history as a farmhouse. Restored from 1980 after many years of dereliction. At the N end, a two-centred W doorway to the outer parlour. There was another doorway opposite leading into the cloister. On the first floor a three-bay guest hall, formerly approached by an external W stair. The stone fireplace in the W wall is probably C15. On the E side evidence for paired lancets within dormers.

The medieval roof was removed in 1862, but spere-post screens remain at either end, the S one especially remarkable, originally with five doorways (now three) with plain two-centred arches without capitals. From the centre doorway stairs led down to the detached kitchen; flanking doorways opened to buttery and pantry; and the end ones provided access to a stair to an upper room, and, via a gallery, to the frater in the S wing. At the N end the prioress's room, with garderobe and fireplace, and two carved corbels with male and female heads. A ceiling with moulded intersecting beams is part of the post-Dissolution conversion, when this room was extended with a jetty over the entrance below, and a N wing was added (demolished in the C18).

The church, a simple aisleless structure of the C12, is said to have been destroyed in the C17. The other domestic buildings were all pulled down soon after the Dissolution, when the priory was granted to Sir Arthur Champernowne, who exchanged it for Dartington.

PUBLIC BUILDINGS

ROUGEMONT CASTLE was established on Rougemont Hill in the N corner of the walled town after William the Conqueror had captured Exeter following a rebellion in 1068. There seems never to have been a keep within the inner bailey, whose ditch, rampart, and wall now encircle the law courts (q.v.). But beside the present entrance stands the formidable gate tower, the best preserved early 6 Norman gatehouse-keep in the country. The entrance archway (blocked in the later Middle Ages) was reached by a drawbridge across the moat. The approach is protected by two strongly projecting buttresses, linked at the top by an arch which supported a wooden platform reached through a door in the S wall at this level. The tower had three wooden floors above the entrance archway. The pair of triangular-headed windows lighting the second floor on the S, together with the use of square hoodmoulds and long-and-short quoins elsewhere, suggest the employment of Saxon masons, and a date in the late C11. The archway itself, however, is characteristic of the earliest Norman work in England, with its two unmoulded arches, simple cushion capitals, and demi-shafts to the inner order. Below the triangular window heads a billet-moulding runs through each window embrasure. The dressed stone is mostly East Devon sandstone (now very worn); the dark and rugged walls are of local volcanic trap. In the top floor of the tower was a N door to the wall-walk.

Of the stone walls on the mighty rampart which encircled the inner bailey by the time of King Stephen's siege in 1136 no features remain among the later repairs. At the W junction of the castle and city walls stands a simple rectangular tower, later pierced at ground-floor level. The polygonal tower at the E junction has been much reduced. Of the wall-tower near the gatehouse, and the second gatehouse on the NW, both shown in early illustrations, nothing survives. There were intermittent repairs to the castle from the C12 to the early C14, but none is recorded to the defences after 1352. Much of the area of the ditch survives as the gardens of Rougemont House (now museum, q.v.), landscaped in the early C18. The outer bailey occupied the area up to Bailey Street and Gandy Street. The present entrance to the inner bailey, an archway of re-used stone with sham portcullis dating from c. 1770, was built on the site of an entrance in existence by c. 1500.

C16 drawings show domestic buildings – of which nothing survives – on the site of the present law courts. A chapel once stood immediately N of the entrance lodge.

12 CITY WALLS (*see also* Perambulations). Nearly three-quarters of the circuit of the city walls survives. Although much patched and repaired, the core is Roman. In the late C2 the enlarged Roman town was given a stone wall, consisting of a rubble core faced with ashlar. The fabric visible today is principally the purple local volcanic trap (some of which may be Roman work), plentifully mixed with other materials: white East Devon sandstone, the crumbly bright red Heavitree stone used extensively from the late C14, and post-medieval brick. The stretches around the castle and on the vulnerable low-lying S side of the city were strengthened by mural towers, probably in the C13. There are records of considerable repairs in the later C14, but by the C15 the walls appear to have been neglected, although they briefly came into use again as an inner line of defence during the Civil War. The main gates (all probably on Roman foundations) survived until the C18.

The best stretch, up to 30 ft high, with several towers remaining, forms part of the castle defences (*see* above) at the N corner of the city, visible from Northernhay Gardens. S of Queen Street, the wall survives behind properties in Northernhay Street, and can be followed around All Hallows churchyard, overlooking the Longbrook valley, to the site of a corner tower which survived until the C19. Little remains of the SW stretch, which was breached by Fore Street in 1778, but beyond the site of West Gate the wall can be traced again, past the site of a watergate, stepping steeply up behind Quay Lane to where the South Gate stood at the start of South Street. Further on, behind the C18 terraces of Southernhay, the wall forms the boundary of the cathedral precinct. Here two towers survive. The northern one, 'Lollards Tower', was used as the bishop's prison until dismantled in 1469. It had three storeys of chambers, of which a vaulted ground-floor room and a C13 shouldered arch to the first floor remain. There was another tower on the site of the New Cut. Less well preserved stretches continue up to a pentagonal angle tower in Post Office Street.

LAW COURTS. Picturesquely sited within the leafy setting of the castle, directly opposite the new entrance. 1774, by *Philip Stowey* and *Thomas Jones* of Exeter, the designs improved on the advice of *James Wyatt*. Stone front, with a brick back towards Northernhay Gardens – a restrained classical composition of 3–3–3 bays with central pediment. Rusticated and arcaded ground floor, the centre three arches opening on to a vestibule, the others framing windows with channelled voussoirs. To the l. a quiet C20 extension in contrasting purple stone, to the r. a projecting wing of 1905, Italianate, in matching Bath stone but taller and fussier. In the court room, a large painting of the Acquittal of Susanna by *W. Brockedon* of Totnes (cf. St Saviour, Dartmouth), after 1815. In the courtyard, standing stone figure of Hugh, Earl Fortescue, 1863 by *E.B. Stephens*.

COUNTY HALL, Topsham Road. The formal approach from the W traverses the spacious grounds of two older houses, both preserved. COAVER, now a staff club, is an early Victorian stuccoed villa with pedimented bay-windows and curving balcony. Further E, now an adjunct of the new buildings, BELAIR, a delightful small house of *c.* 1700 built by John Vowler, an Exeter grocer, who married into the Baring family. Red brick, 1–3–1 bays, stone quoins and central pediment, bracketed central doorcase. Later Doric side porch. Inside, a fine staircase hall, the staircase with two thick twisted balusters to the tread, carved tread-ends, and moulded soffits, the ceiling with oval wreath, central cherub and trophies. The pilasters flanking the landing window have very odd capitals, quite clearly made from bunches of pistols. Upstairs, military trophies and the dates 1570 and 1641 reset over a door and a window.

The main buildings of County Hall consist of long ranges of buff brick in a pleasant, slightly bland, but well detailed semi-Georgian idiom, 1957–64 by *H.McMorran*, whose firm was one of the few to practise such a style at the time. The post-war hallmark is the asymmetrical composition. To the l. of the triple-arched open vaulted vestibule are the council chamber and committee rooms, with stone window surrounds and clock tower beyond as distinguishing accents. Sumptuously finished inside: Ionic columns on the staircase landing, shallow domes to the upstairs corridor. Council chamber and lofty committee rooms with moulded or boldly rusticated panelling; windows with bevelled panes. To the r. the plainer three-storey offices are grouped around two open courtyards with linking cloisters. Further E separate deep-plan block of 1984, tactfully in keeping, but lacking the finesse of the original buildings.

GUILDHALL, High Street. There was a Guildhall on this site already in the C14. The present front, built on granite columns across the 74 pavement of the High Street, replaced the medieval forebuilding in

1592–5. It is a design as picturesque as it is barbarous, with wildly detailed brackets above the fat Tuscan columns supporting the more elegant composite columns of the upper floor. Mullioned-and-transomed windows, the ornament chiefly strapwork, in Beer stone, originally coloured and gilded (as was discovered in a restoration of 1900 by *William Weir*). The present balustrade is not the original arrangement: a view on a map by Coles of 1709 shows a more elaborate balustrade (of which one tapering pilaster survives on the E flank), with taller corner columns, and a central pedimented frontispiece. This was removed in 1718.* The elaborate inner door was made in 1594 by *Nicholas Baggett*. It is carved on both sides, with a Doric doorway towards the hall which appears surprisingly classical and chaste after the orgies of the front.

The hall itself appears to be dated by building accounts to 1468–70. The impressive arch-braced roof of seven bays is particularly interesting as one of the best of a late medieval group in the Exeter area (cf. Law Library, Cathedral Close, and Bowhill, Exeter; and Cadhay). Their common feature is an upper coved section above the arch-braced trusses, and the use of bosses at the junctions of purlins, wind-braces, and intermediate trusses. At the Guildhall the principals rest on painted carved stone corbels. The roof was restored to view in 1863–4; at the same time a gallery was made in place of the magistrates' room. Side galleries were removed in a later restoration of 1887–8, when the Elizabethan panelling of the lower walls was restored, and the chimneypiece added with a bust of Queen Victoria by *Armstead*. Windows high up, with Victorian heraldic glass. Chandelier of 1789 by *Thomas Pyke*.

The medieval forebuilding had a chapel on the first floor. In the C16 building the main room was constructed as the council chamber; it became the mayor's parlour in 1901. It is reached by an original staircase to the l. of the entrance. At the back of the hall a block with cells (reconstructed in 1838), and a room above with Elizabethan panelling and carved frieze, restored in 1858.

CIVIC CENTRE (i.e. council offices), Dix's Field, Southernhay. 1965–72 by the City Architect, *Vinton Hall*. A clumsy affair faced with precast panels.

CUSTOM HOUSE, The Quay. *See* below, The Suburbs, Perambulation 1.

152 ROYAL ALBERT MEMORIAL MUSEUM, Queen Street. By *John Hayward*, 1865–6. In the E.E. style, an impressive symmetrical tripartite composition with the use of several types of coloured stone so favoured by Ruskin (chiefly reddish-purple Pocombe, with grey limestone plinth and buff Bath stone details). The tall central tower (like the University Museum at Oxford) of Hayward's original winning design was ruled out, and he substituted a gable with rose window. Recessed entrance with polished granite columns and early Gothic capitals. In the S wing the top-lit gallery for the museum; in the N wing the former library and reading room, with thin iron columns, and classrooms above. The entrance leads directly to the top-lit imperial stair; in an aedicule on the half-landing a statue of Prince Albert by *E.B. Stephens*. At the back a Venetian Gothic extension of 1894 by *R. Medley Fulford*.

*I owe these details to Stuart Blaylock.

ROUGEMONT HOUSE MUSEUM, Castle Street. Built *c.* 1768 by a surgeon, John Patch, the house and gardens improved after 1787 by Edmund Granger with advice from *William Jackson*. Facing the garden, two shallow bows with charming delicate tented balconies above. A canted corner bow on the entrance side. The delightful gardens cover the s slopes of the castle mound.

CENTRAL LIBRARY AND RECORD OFFICE, Castle Street, at the foot of the castle mound. Pre- and post-war taste side by side: the former library (now record office), 1931 by *Sydney K. Greenslade*, in unadventurous free Tudor, brown brick, mullioned windows, parapet; the present library, completed in 1965 by the City Architect, *H.B. Rowe*, an uneasy effort in the modern style: two mostly glazed upper storeys, with transparent view through the entrance to a garden behind, set on a base self-consciously faced with random stonework.

NORTHERNHAY GARDENS. Finely sited on the high, NW corner of the city, outside the castle and city walls. Like Southernhay, laid out as a walk in the early C17; fortified in the Civil War, replanted in the late C17, and remodelled again in the 1860s, when sculpture commemorating local worthies began to be introduced. By the N entrance the Deerstalker, 1875 by the local sculptor *E.B. Stephens*, an intense, rather awkward classical composition. Also by *Stephens* the duller seated stone figure of John Dinham, 1865. Thomas Dyke Acland, 1861, and Stafford Henry Northcote, 1st Earl of Iddesleigh, †1887, are standing stone figures. Small Renaissance pillar to the Devonshire Volunteer Force, 1895, with portrait relief of its originator, Sir John Bucknill. Dominating all these is a War Memorial in the heroic mould, with bronzes by *John Angel*, 1923: a flamboyant victory on a tall pedestal flanked by four seated figures. Through the city wall, of which a fine stretch is exposed here, one can enter the more secluded gardens of Rougemont House (*see also* Rougemont House *and* City Walls, above).

CLIFTON HILL SPORTS CENTRE. 1983–4 by *Nicholas Grimshaw*, a large, strident box of one and two storeys, clad with silver horizontally-reeded metal sheet. Porthole windows; orange and blue details.

LEISURE CENTRE, St Thomas. *See* below, The Suburbs, Perambulation 7.

EXETER UNIVERSITY developed from the Schools of Art and Science founded in 1855 and 1863 respectively, and from 1868 associated with the Albert Memorial Museum. The Royal Albert Memorial College, established in 1900 after the schools had merged with university extension classes, was based in the museum and in nearby buildings in Gandy Street. The Streatham estate, the nucleus of the present spectacular site to the N of the city, was acquired for the college in 1922. It expanded but slowly, for the college remained small and short of funds; indeed it was not granted a charter as an independent university until 1955. Until then degrees had been granted by London University.

The ample undulating grounds of the university now stretch E from New North Road to Pennsylvania Road and include a splendid wooded valley on the N fringe and much admirably preserved exotic late Victorian and Edwardian planting around the former Streatham Hall. The setting is indeed far more memorable than the individual C20 buildings awkwardly scattered over the hilly terrain. The topography does not lend itself to the gentlemanly symmetry proposed by *Vincent Harris*'s master plan of 1931, which envisaged a formal axis running up the steep slope to Reed Hall (the former Streatham Hall) with the main buildings fanning out from it to take advantage of the view over the city. The idea was given up after the war, when *Sir William Holford*, appointed planning consultant in 1953, devised a more relaxed layout of winding roads, with the principal centres as self-contained groups strung along The Queen's Drive. The more incoherent and crowded assortment of large buildings further N and E dates from the rapid university expansion of the 1960s–70s.

A tour starting from the W can take in the main landmarks roughly chronologically.

By NEW NORTH ROAD, a low C19 pedimented LODGE marks the entrance to the Streatham estate, acquired by Richard Thornton West, a retired Java merchant who died in 1878. His mansion, renamed REED HALL and used at first as a hall of residence, is now the university staff club, 1867, stately if clumsily detailed Italianate, with a campanile. Lofty rooms off a broad spine corridor; good cornices. Pretty Italian terrace gardens to S and E and many specimen trees on the slopes beyond. The planting was by the Exeter firm of *Robert Veitch*. N of Reed Hall, close to the drive, MARDON HALL, 1933, the first new hall of residence, by *Vincent Harris*, three storeys, very solid neo-Georgian, symmetrical with projecting wings.

Historically, one should now retrace one's steps to take in *Vincent Harris*'s other buildings, which are grouped together further S, off PRINCE OF WALES ROAD, tucked uncomfortably into the side of the hill. Individually they are impressive: WASHINGTON SINGER LABORATORIES (1931) and ROBOROUGH LIBRARY (1938–40) to the W; HATHERLEY LABORATORIES (1948–52) to the E, on a site originally intended for an arts building; and the CHAPEL (1958) in the centre of the intended triumphal way, which had by then been abandoned. But the hill makes the ingenious butterfly-plan of the layout impossible to appreciate, and the pattern is anyway disrupted by the intrusion of *Holford*'s LIBRARY of 1966 on the eastern site at first earmarked for biology laboratories. The earlier Harris buildings, although awkwardly bulky, are admirably detailed in a C17–Cotswold–Lutyens manner; reddish-buff brick with handsome steep slate roofs. The Washington Singer Laboratories have a long array of wooden cross-windows, contrasting oddly with the fussy classical stone trim of the tall staircase windows. In front of these are two pretty and very Lutyenesque open porches, square, with little hipped roofs. There is a similar incongruity in the Hatherley Building: austere post-war Georgian but for its over-heavy stone entrance.

The CHAPEL is the most successful composition, set broadside on to the central avenue. No superfluous detail, just three mighty stone mullioned-and-transomed bay-windows to articulate the plain brick walls – an entirely domestic idiom. Long, restrained interior with facing stalls in the conventional college arrangement, effectively lit by the bay-windows on both sides. Whitened walls, windowless, canted apse, the sole decoration the excellent CEIL-

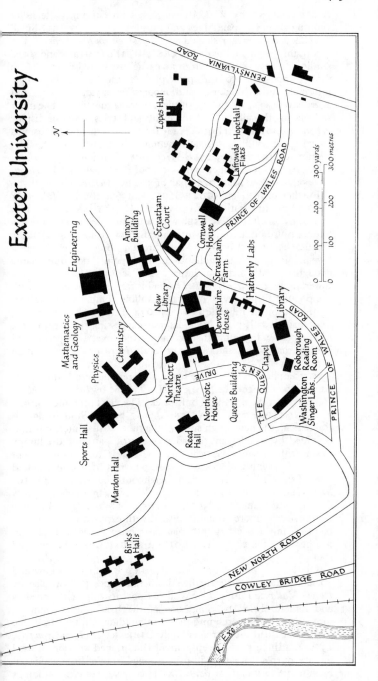

Exeter University

ING PAINTING by *W.T.Monnington*, with curving patterns of
vaulting shapes in pale blues and purples. – SCULPTURE. Small
Crucifixus on a dagger-shaped cross by *Moelwyn Merchant*.

N of this group *Holford*'s QUEEN'S BUILDING (arts and social
studies) of 1956–8. Apart from its partial use of red brick, it is in
direct opposition to the principles of the earlier buildings:
informal, inward-looking, and modern in style, although not
aggressively so. Two to four storeys around a courtyard. The inner
walls facing this all of different heights and styles. Exterior display
is confined to an open brick arcade facing the road and enclosing a
paved space with no special function. – SCULPTURE. Outside:
Figure for Landscape, by *B. Hepworth*; Tension, by *Moelwyn
Merchant*. In the entrance hall: Ascent of Forms, also by *Merchant*,
of wood; and End Maze 3, a small bronze by *Michael Ayrton*, 1970.

Further on, NORTHCOTE HOUSE, 1960, also by *Holford &
Partners*, administrative offices, with the GREAT HALL adjoining,
and DEVONSHIRE HOUSE, with students' common rooms; a
looser group, but also quite intimate and inward-looking. Delicate
details: lead-faced bay-windows through three storeys, and a
Swedish-inspired campanile as a focal point, not quite large
enough to make a distant impact. The sculptured heads on the
tower are by *Arthur J. Ayres*. The hall is treated more boldly, with
the popular fifties device of curtain-walling contained in a frame.
At the top of the hill, the NORTHCOTT THEATRE, 1967 by the
same firm, a tall, plain brick exterior expressing the form of the
fan-shaped auditorium. Inside, the curved foyer wrapped round
one end has a pleasant variety of levels. Very broad proscenium
arch.

NE from here are the more strident representatives of the 1960s.
At the top of the hill the SPORTS HALL, 1967 by *John Crowther &
Partners*, just plain walls of buff brick. The most prominent group
is CHEMISTRY and PHYSICS, 1963–7 by *Sir Basil Spence &
Partners*, in the new tough spirit of the time. Visual interest is now
provided by simpler and broader geometric patterns: the lumpy
tower with close-set vertical fins, the low lecture theatres kept
plain, the teaching blocks with walls punched by insistent dotted
lines of slit windows. In the same neighbourhood MATHEMATICS
AND GEOLOGY by *Louis de Soissons Partnership*, 1966–7, fussily
detailed and planned. ENGINEERING, 1968 by *Playne Vallance
Partnership*, is more straightforward, with exposed concrete floor
bands rising above a plinth planted with a glorious display of
heathers. At the end a trim BOILER HOUSE with a big pitched
roof.

The best of this group is the AMORY BUILDING (Law and
Social Studies), a little further down the slope, 1971–4, also by
Playne Vallance Partnership. Well composed, with canted corners
and forceful brick banding, one of the bands neatly running
forward to tie the porch into the main building. On the other side
of Stocker Road the extremely ugly LIBRARY by *John Crowther*,
1981–3, a three-storey deep-plan air-conditioned interior encased
in dark purple brick with ill-proportioned rows of little windows.
Next to it STREATHAM FARM, a C19 courtyard of farm buildings
(now works department), and opposite a low teaching building,
STREATHAM COURT, 1963.

The STUDENTS' RESIDENCES are clustered in two main groups, NW and E of the centre of the campus. The number of students in 1956 was 1,000, in 1980 nearly 5,000. The E group starts with CORNWALL HOUSE (*W. Holford*, 1971), low, well-proportioned common rooms, and most spectacularly, around the C19 LAFROWDA VILLA, the LAFROWDA FLATS (1971–6), also by *Holford*, built in recognition of the fact that organized hall life was no longer popular. Blocks of four storeys *en échelon*; grey brick. The sensitively landscaped setting is by *Sylvia Crowe*. Towards Pennsylvania Road HOPE HALL and LOPES HALL, both Victorian villas in their own grounds, with quiet extensions by *Vincent Harris*. Hope Hall is Italianate, brick and painted ashlar, Lopes Hall (formerly Highlands) has a long, symmetrical Gothic front. To its E RANSOM PICKARD HOUSE, an annexe of 1967.

To the N along Cowley Bridge Road, BIRKS HALLS, 1965–6, and DURYARD HALLS incorporating DURYARD HOUSE, an attractive brick house of *c.* 1700, five windows, central pediment, good staircase, linenfold panelling supposed to have come from the mayor's parlour in the Guildhall. THOMAS HALL further N is the former Great Duryard, a late C17 house built by Thomas Jefford, Mayor of Exeter; much altered in 1771 and in the C19. Stuccoed exterior; balustraded Doric porch. Music room of 1771. In a garden wall a porch hood with plaster reliefs of weapons, possibly from the front door.

ST LUKE'S TRAINING COLLEGE (now part of Exeter University), Heavitree Road. Founded in 1839, as a result of Sir Thomas Acland's campaign for training teachers for church schools. With St Mark's Chelsea, the first college of its kind. An extensive, picturesque Gothic group in random limestone; original buildings of 1852–4 by *John Hayward*, much rebuilt after war damage. Large free-standing chapel near the road, with Dec tracery, enlarged 1912.

For other University Buildings *see* Perambulations.

EXETER COLLEGE, Hele Road. The original buildings of Hele School 1849, grey limestone, modest. Extensions chiefly by *C. E. Ware & Sons*, 1908, gabled red brick with stone dressings. All swamped by the gauche slab-block of classrooms added for the college in the 1960s.

EXETER SCHOOL, Manston Terrace, off Magdalen Road. Begun on a new site in spacious grounds, in 1878, as Exeter Grammar School, by *William Butterfield*. Original buildings L-shaped, red brick with stone bands, a powerful six-storey tower in the angle, with masters' and matrons' rooms. Classrooms in the main N wing, with trefoil-headed windows under straight heads; dormitories on the second floor. Butterfield's intended great hall was not built, but his small free-standing chapel was added in 1885–6, brick with diaper patterning. The group does not add up to anything like Butterfield's Rugby; all the same, it is a pity that insensitive C20 additions crowd so closely: assembly hall 1965, science block 1969, by *Drury, Gundry & Dyer*; sixth-form modern languages block 1972 by *Charles E. Ware & Sons*; sports hall 1978 by *Staverton Construction Group*; classroom block 1985 by *Gilpin & Riley*. The exception is the music school near the entrance, 1975 by *Caroline*

Oboussier in association with *Gundry Dyer Partnership*, on a friendly scale, sympathetically echoing the materials of the C19 buildings.

ST PETER'S SCHOOL, Pennsylvania Road. Founded as Bishop Blackall's Middle Class School for Girls in 1709. 1888 by *James Jerman*. Red brick; an imposing but rather crowded front with Ionic pilasters; steeply pitched roof. Additions 1907, 1912, 1937.

WEST OF ENGLAND SCHOOL FOR CHILDREN WITH LITTLE OR NO SIGHT, off Topsham Road, Countess Wear. 1966 by *Stillman & Eastwick Field*. Low buildings on a humane scale, attractively grouped. An appealing mixture of textures: mottled brown brick, diagonal boarding, used both for buildings and garden walls.

BOARD SCHOOLS. The standard ingredients of early board schools – large schoolroom, classrooms in an attached wing, bell-turret – are deployed picturesquely in several surviving examples: ST THOMAS FIRST SCHOOL, Union Street, 1872 by *R. M. Fulford*, polychrome Gothic, plate tracery windows; ST SIDWELL'S SCHOOL, red brick with stone mullioned windows; and NEW-TOWN FIRST SCHOOL, Clifton Road, 1873 by *Pearson & Hayward*.

POST-WAR SCHOOLS. The STOKE HILL MIDDLE SCHOOL, 1953, with three-storey curtain-walled classroom block, and FIRST SCHOOL, 1954, both by the City Architect, *H. B. Rowe*, are good examples of the post-war school building campaign in the outer suburbs. Typical secondary schools of the same period are the informally grouped VINCENT THOMPSON HIGH SCHOOL, Ringswell Avenue, and PRIORY HIGH SCHOOL, Earl Richards Road South, built as Boys' and Girls' Secondary Moderns.

ROYAL DEVON AND EXETER HOSPITAL, Southernhay. Founded in 1741 by Dean Alured Clarke, who when a Canon of Winchester had established the Royal Hampshire Hospital. Many cities at this time became aware of the necessity of organized care for the sick (cf. the corresponding dates for London in John Summerson's *Georgian London*). Designed *gratis* by *John Richards*. The original plain brick building of 1741–3 with rusticated quoins and central cupola is still recognizable despite substantial additions: central windows brought forward, pediment added, 1772; Halford wing 1859; chapel 1869; Victoria wing 1894; Victory wing 1922.

WEST OF ENGLAND EYE INFIRMARY, Magdalen Street. 1898–1901 by *A. Brumwell Thomas*. Red brick and terracotta, quite a lively design. Founded in 1808 in Holloway Street, an early date for a specialized hospital.

WONFORD HOSPITAL, Dryden Road. Built as Wonford House for the Insane, a private institution, in 1865–9 by *W. F. Cross*. Neo-Jacobean, impressively set in spacious grounds. Long range of grey rubble with limestone dressings, attractively varied by a series of projecting gables and corner turrets. Central entrance up a steep flight of steps, with triple porch, bay-window, and shaped gables. Lodge to match.

EXE VALE (DIGBY) HOSPITAL, Old Rydon Lane. Built as the Exeter Hospital for the Insane in 1885–6 by *R. Stark Wilkinson*.* A vast spreading symmetrical composition in red brick, enlivened by

---

*Future uncertain at the time of writing.

liberal use of yellow terracotta dressings (Wilkinson was the architect of Doulton's London factories). Secluded in spacious grounds, and remarkably unspoilt by any later additions. An exotic touch is added by the tower at either end with bell-shaped dome, as if this were some Baroque palace in central Europe. Plainer towers elsewhere, and steep pyramid roofs to the entrance block, add further interest to the skyline. On the garden side the central wing is distinguished by large round-headed arches. Separate chapel, more conventionally Gothic, red brick with stone dressings. The self-conscious architectural features of this and the Wonford Hospital make an interesting contrast to Fowler's earlier and more pragmatic lunatic asylum at Exminster (q.v.).

REDHILLS HOSPITAL. Built as the St Thomas Union Workhouse, 1837. Utilitarian late Georgian, with radiating wings on a half-circle plan.

HONEYLANDS (Children's Therapy Centre), Pinhoe Road. An elegant early C19 Grecian villa in its own grounds, in a warm buff ashlar; 1–3–1 bays, the centre with pedimented Ionic four-column portico. Entablature carried round the sides. Later additions at the back.

WYVERN BARRACKS, Barrack Road. 1804, large, brick, with additions; the original part on the standard pattern of pedimented centre and cupola, used so often by the Georgians to make a utilitarian structure representational. The pediment here clumsily steep, with outsize royal arms of *Coade* stone.

TOWN BARRACKS, New North Road. Much of the cavalry barracks of 1792 survives. Red brick riding school, stables, and officers' quarters around a parade ground. Additions of 1867, including block with clock-tower.

DEVON COUNTY PRISON, New North Road, Mostly of 1853 by *Hayward*, replacing two earlier prisons: the County Gaol of 1789–95 by *William Blackburn*, and the House of Correction built in 1807–9 by *George Moneypenny*, an architect who specialized in prisons. His front gateway remains, the entrance with elaborate vermiculated rustication, the detail derived from the side doors of Burlington House. Hayward's building is of red brick with stone dressings, in a restrained classical style. Alterations and extensions by *E.H.Harbottle* before 1876.

ST DAVIDS STATION. The present stone-faced building is a major reconstruction and enlargement of 1910–12 by the G.W.R. of the 1864 station designed by *Henry Lloyd* and *Francis Fox* for the Bristol & Exeter Railway. This had replaced the original *Brunel* 'one-sided' station of 1844. Fox's overall roof of 132ft span disappeared during rebuilding, but his ornamented stone screen wall, which on the platform side has at first-floor level a tall elegant wooden clerestory lit by tall round-headed windows, can still be seen behind the later additions to the entrance frontage.

CENTRAL STATION, Queen Street. Opened by the Southern Railway in 1933 to replace the original Queen Street station of 1860. Faced in brown brick with stone dressings, a rectangular 'Wrenaissance' central block with arched entrances, heavily dentilled cornice, and roof-top lantern, flanked on either side by plainer curved wings containing shops with offices above.

ST THOMAS STATION. *See* below, The Suburbs, Perambulation 7.

St Thomas Railway Viaduct. 1846. Built of random coursed limestone with brick voussoirs, nearly ½m. long with sixty-two arches, to carry the single line of the South Devon Atmospheric Railway E from St Thomas station. When the line was doubled in 1861 a second viaduct was built abutting the first to form what appears to be, but is not, a single structure.

Pinhoe Railway Signal Box. A typical early L.S.W.R. design probably dating from the extension of the line to Exeter in 1860. A brick base carries horizontally boarded timber walls with sliding timber windows and a hipped slated roof.

Telephone Exchange, Castle Street. 1934, careful neo-Georgian, brick, arched ground-floor windows. Less careful post-war additions.

Telecommunications Centre, Shilhay. By the *Property Services Agency*, 1978–80. Traditional, brick with hipped roofs, in deference to local reaction against the prospect of a modern building on this prominent site near the old Exe bridge and the new roundabout.

Underground Passages. The sections open to the public (entrance from Princesshay) probably date from the C14 and C15. They brought water from wells in St Sidwell's parish to the Cathedral Close, the city, and probably the Blackfriars. The system originated in the late C12 as a buried pipe supplying water to the Cathedral Close.

Exe Bridges. The medieval bridge lay S of the Roman river crossing. Its remains – eight-and-a-half semicircular arches of *c.* 1200 revealed by war damage – are now exposed on the roundabout at the SW entrance to the city. Two of the arches are pointed but apparently of the same build. On the bridge are the ruins of St Edmund's church (q.v.). A new bridge begun in 1770 by *Joseph Dixon* was destroyed in 1775. Its replacement of 1776–8 by *John Goodwin* was superseded in 1905 by *Sir John Wolfe Barry* and *Cuthbert A. Brereton*'s steel bridge, itself replaced by the present road system in 1978.

Cowley Bridge. 1813–14 by *James Green*, County Surveyor. Three segmental arches; piers with niches.

THE CATHEDRAL CLOSE

The Cathedral Green, pleasantly quiet since the exclusion of traffic in the 1970s, can be entered by several narrow alleys off the High Street and South Street. The cathedral used to be more enclosed and sheltered than it is today. The green which now surrounds it on the N side dates partly from the C19, created after the treasurer's house attached to the N transept had been demolished in 1821. NW of the cathedral, seated figure of Richard Hooker, 1907 by *Alfred Drury*. The area to the W of the cathedral was opened up only in the later C20, when the C19 church of St Mary Major (on the site of the Saxon minster) was cleared away and replaced by shallow ceremonial steps, unfortunately focusing attention on the unworthy rebuilding of the war-damaged SW corner of the Close.

Detailed examination of the houses built for cathedral officials should start with the more attractive NE corner. Here the city wall is breached by the cobbled alley known as NEW CUT. The charming iron footbridge over it dates from 1814. On the N side, set back, the Archdeacon of Cornwall's house, a prim Tudor rebuilding of 1829–30 by *Charles Fowler*, in white stone, in contrast to the red Heavitree stone with later brick and stucco so distinctively characteristic of the other buildings. Opposite, close to the cathedral, No. 15, the former chancellor's house. The E front looks early C18. Seven bays, brick chequerwork, coved cornice, steep central pediment, hipped roof. In the room to the r. of the hall good bolection-moulded panelling and fireplace. Behind is a medieval range with at the present basement level the remains of a late medieval framed ceiling with moulded beams and fragments of bosses, and on the floor above a large room with the moulded jambs of a medieval fireplace.

Now along the N side of the Close. The medieval sequence starts with Nos. 12–13, the former Abbot of Buckfast's house. This was badly damaged in the war. The surviving wing to the Close formed the gatehouse. Then Nos. 10–11, now two houses, formerly the residence of the Archdeacon of Barnstaple, and the most appealing survival of the group. Front range, remodelled in the C17, of Heavitree stone, once extending further W, with an archway over a side passage. The main entrance is through a large round-headed archway with lozenge-shaped stops to the hoodmould, and the arms of Bishop Cotton (†1621) above. Splendid studded door with   76 faceted imitation-rustication and shell lunettes in high relief (cf. the similar door in the Guildhall). Through the archway one enters the exceedingly attractive little courtyard of a substantial medieval house. Before its C17 refurbishment the hall was in the front range (fragment of two-tier crown-post roof, smoke-blackened, a unique survival in Exeter, probably C14). Around 1500 the present back range was built, two-storeyed, with arch-braced roof. Two-centred doorway on the r. with traceried door, a lozenge above with the arms of Bishop Oldham (†1519), and another pretty cusped lozenge, possibly an insertion. Stone service range to the r. (now a separate house), much rebuilt after war damage. In the l. wing, with its picturesque but much altered timber-framing, a corridor to the front block. In the angle of l. wing and hall the tiny first-floor chapel with Dec SE window (three lights, upper lights hexagonal). Inside it has a wagon roof concealed by a C17 plaster barrel-vault. The porch below is a later alteration. In this porch, and also in half of the ground-floor room of the back range, the remains of a remarkable late medieval enriched timber ceiling. It is unclear how much is *in situ*; the present arrangement may be the result of antiquarian improvements by the artist and sculptor *John Gendall* who lived here in the mid C19. The ceiling has cusped quatrefoils in rectangular panels, carved bosses, and shields. In the living room it is divided from an C18 plaster ceiling by a mock-Gothic timber screen. The corridor to the front range, in a quite different mood, was decorated by Gendall with casts of Flaxman and Thorwaldsen reliefs.

Nos. 8–9a, now subdivided, originally formed another medieval courtyard house, but with the hall at right angles to the Close. It was a canon's house in the C14; later occupants are unknown. The hall (No. 8, known as the Law Library) is reached by a narrow open side passage through a four-centred archway to the l. of the front range. There was also a central carriageway (now blocked). Blocked opposed doorways near the s end of the hall (suggesting the service rooms were in the front range); the present entrance further N. The hall is cluttered up by partitions, but still open to the roof, a spectacular roof indeed, one of the most elaborate in Devon. Three bays with a louvre. Hammerbeams ending in horizontal angels; pierced tracery in the spandrels above the hammerbeams, and elsewhere. The main timbers, all heavily moulded, rest on carved stone corbels. The inspiration for this type of roof is the late C14 one over Westminster Hall, but the details, especially

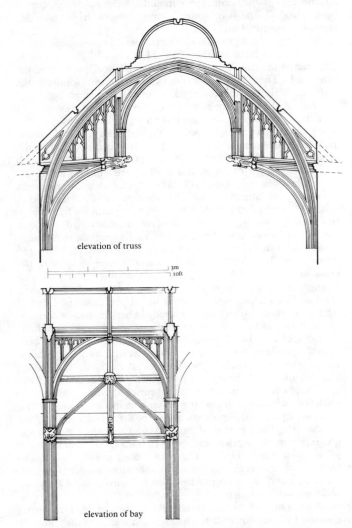

elevation of truss

3m
10ft

elevation of bay

Exeter, Nos. 8–9a The Close: section of roof

the coved section above the collar, are similar to others in and around Exeter, and suggest a date in the later C15. The lower end wall of the hall is timber-framed. Within it, visible from a small room between hall and front range, a timber doorway with elaborately cusped head. Next to it part of an early C16 wall painting. The front range, with stone ground floor, timber-framed first floor, and arch-braced roof, is probably contemporary with the hall; the E range also has an arch-braced roof but has been much remodelled. The solar range at the N end of the hall was rebuilt c. 1700 and refronted in the C19. Handsome red brick N front of three storeys, five windows wide, with very steep hipped roof, and an Ionic porch.

No. 7 was another courtyard house, leased from the Chapter by the Courtenays as their town house in the C17 and C18. From this time there survives a formerly separate back range with a small room with a single-rib plaster ceiling and a stone fireplace, and another ceiling with pendant upstairs. The rest was rebuilt in 1814 for the Devon and Exeter Institution for the Promotion of Science, Literature and Art, still in existence. The two main library rooms have charming oval roof-lights and galleries.

No. 6, the former subdeanery, has a pretty Georgian façade and a Roman Doric porch, probably dating from alterations of 1770–2. The stone wall is older. No. 5 has a front of c. 1700, red brick with broad windows, modillion frieze, and quoins with later channelled stucco, but the stone back wall and the L-shaped stone building behind with mullioned three-light windows are the remains of the house of the Annuellars (chantry priests saying annual masses) which was built as late as 1529. The property extended up to the corner of the Close, and from the later C16 was divided, sublet, and variously rebuilt, the result now being a nice assortment of white-stuccoed frontages concealing timber frames, with shops on the ground floor. No. 1, Mol's Coffee House in the C18, is the most flamboyant, with its curly Dutch gable, although this upper part is entirely an invention of c. 1885. Good later C16 features remain inside; rear newel with carved foliage on the post, C16 panelling on the first floor.

In MARTIN'S LANE, beyond, two more timber-framed houses. A little detour past St Martin's church and down CATHERINE STREET can take in a group of ruins in Heavitree stone, all that the war left of old Exeter in this area. They consist of part of the Annuellars' house: a kitchen with two large fireplaces and a spiral staircase on one side can be recognized. Adjoining, two outer walls of ST CATHERINE'S ALMSHOUSE, founded by Canon Stevens in 1450 and built in 1458. Two Gothic arches and a mixture of arched and straight-headed windows. Within the enclosure, close to the Annuellars' kitchen, the shell of a small free-standing chapel. Remains of a Perp E window and a piscina.

The W side of the Close, called CATHEDRAL YARD, starts to a different tune, with 'The Hotel', founded by William Praed in 1769, renewed and redecorated in 1827, and now called the ROYAL CLARENCE HOTEL. The original part is the plain four-storey stucco front with royal arms in the centre of the parapet. The busier three bays at the corner of Martin's Lane, with stucco added later, began as the Exeter Bank, also founded in 1769.

No. 16 is late C17, timber-framed with bay-windows, with later plaster; No. 17 also timber-framed; No. 18 rebuilt c. 1910, but with a charming staircase with inlaid treads, possibly genuinely C18, and an upper room very lavishly decorated in Louis Quinze style. Nos. 19–21 had late Georgian fronts which have been rebuilt in facsimile (good C18 staircase in No. 21).

Then the former premises of Wippell's, the church furnishers, continuing through to the High Street, large and strident, Gothic detail, 1883; the NATIONAL WESTMINSTER BANK is more discreet, with a stucco front, set back, and later banking hall in front. TINLEY'S café, a tall stucco corner building of c. 1825, was put up when the Broad Gate to the Close was demolished. Earlier stone back wall. On the other side of BROADGATE the excellent CITY BANK of 1875 by *Gibson*, a stately High Victorian palazzo, ashlar, channelled ground floor and quoins, sumptuous doorway with pairs of banded columns, heavy bracketed cornice.

Past the scrappy post-war w corner, the only older building of note on the sw side of the Close is Nos. 3–5 Little Style, a tall, isolated group of timber-framed houses with three gables facing away from the cathedral, probably late C17, on the site of a former workhouse. Close to this a post-war building for the Cathedral School, undistinguished, and behind, extending to South Street, the pathetic remains of the HALL OF THE VICARS CHORAL, preserved as a ruin after the war. Only the N wall of the hall remains. It was recorded as newly built by Bishop Brantyngham in 1388 and was an important example of late C14 secular architecture: two tall transomed two-light late Dec windows, deep embrasures with graceful cusped rere-arches. Doorway with continuous moulding. Amidst the ruins the pre-Conquest w doorway from St George's church (q.v.) has been disconcertingly re-erected.

Now back towards the cathedral. Close to the w front a group of houses on part of the site of the cloisters incorporating some medieval fabric. Nos. 1–2, dated 1762, have boldly rusticated C18 brick quoins; Church House has a seven-window front of Heavitree stone with fluted cornice, c. 1800. Behind is a two-storey building with formerly open ground floor, used as a market during the Commonwealth.

The DEANERY opposite lies in its own grounds, hidden behind a high wall. Apart from the Bishop's Palace, the Deanery is by far the largest and most complicated of the clergy houses in the Close, built for hospitality on a generous scale. Parts may go back to 1225, when the office of Dean was established by Bishop Brewer, or at least to 1301, when a visitation described the house as 'much improved', although little of these dates is easily recognizable. The buildings stretch out in a long irregular N–S line, with a w projection containing an upstairs chapel with a much restored Perp window, extended further w by a C19 addition with matching window. The main ranges, with exteriors too much altered to be specially attractive, are best viewed from the garden to the E. At the N end a much hacked about squarish block (with the present C18 entrance on the N side), mostly of purple volcanic trap and Beer stone, with later alterations in Heavitree stone. Flat clasping buttresses at the N corners; traces of tall windows in the E wall.

Possibly this was the C13 great hall (an C18 plan in the cathedral archives indeed describes this as an open hall). To its S a slightly projecting entrance with off-centre medieval archway blocked by a round-headed brick doorway. The two upper storeys here also a post-medieval rebuilding. Beyond is the long range which houses the best interiors (parlour and first-floor hall). C16 square-headed mullioned windows; above them tall round-headed windows with C18 sashes. The parlour was originally entered by another blocked medieval doorway which is cut into by the entrance already mentioned. At the S end a lower two-storey wing.

Inside, the N block of the Deanery is divided up into C18 rooms. A corridor with C19 trefoil-panelling leads from the front door in the N wall. (Concealed behind the panelling on the W wall, a late medieval fireplace similar to that in the parlour.) The former entrance through the E porch has a low medieval doorway in the opposite wall, leading to a room beneath the chapel (how the chapel itself was originally approached is unclear). The parlour to the S is a handsome room with a ceiling of moulded beams decorated at their intersections with bold fleurons now set against later plaster. The ceiling is probably of the same date as the elaborate fireplace in the W wall, which has the initials of John Veysey (Dean 1509, Bishop 1519) on its panelled jambs, and a lintel (damaged) decorated with quatrefoils, a type popular in Devon in the early C16. The new standards of civilized comfort which such a room represents were increased further c. 1600 by the addition of panelling topped by a pretty plaster frieze with putti with garlands. But the exceptionally thick wall in which the fireplace is set shows that this part of the house has older origins.

In the first-floor hall above, the W wall has a single-light trefoil-headed window, restored in the early C20, when evidence for three other windows, and a Dec fireplace, is said to have been uncovered. The small size of the window suggests that this wall may have belonged not to a hall, but to an earlier building with a different function. The present plain stone fireplace was installed in the 1970s in place of a medieval one previously in the Precentor's house.* The present appearance of the hall owes much to its C18 remodelling – minstrels' gallery with bulgy turned balusters, large sash-windows (set in the original embrasures) with heraldic glass of 1762 by *Peckitt*. But the excellent arch-braced collar roof is late medieval: originally six bays (the northernmost divided off in the C18), with coved centre and intermediate trusses with elegant curved projections, a simplified version of other late medieval roofs in the Exeter area. No bosses or wind-braces; stone corbels with heads or foliage as the only decoration.

The chapel in the W wing of the Deanery has a ceiled wagon roof with carved bosses (not of high quality), with angels at the ends of the principals. Remains of a fireplace in the S wall. Much restored in the C19 after having been used as a bedroom.

The wing to the S of the first-floor hall is now used by the Cathedral School. Good three-bay arch-braced roof with wind-braces, similar in construction to the hall roof. Also a first-floor fireplace with

*This fireplace, datable to 1496–9, is now in store (illustrated in M. Wood, *The Medieval House*, plate XLIII C). Evidence of wall painting was also found in the 1970s.

lintel carved with quatrefoils, and an adjoining warming cupboard.

The BISHOP'S PALACE stands in generous grounds stretching from the SE corner of the cathedral to the city walls. The medieval buildings were extensive, as early inventories show; truncated and remodelled from the C16 to the C18, they were given their present not very appealing exterior appearance largely by *Ewan Christian* in 1846–8, for Bishop Phillpotts. *Butterfield* carried out some further alterations in the 1870s for Bishop Temple, the first bishop to use the palace as a residence since the Middle Ages. The building is now in two parts. The W wing, which in the Middle Ages contained the bishop's private apartments and was originally larger, was almost entirely rebuilt by *Christian* in a dull neo-Tudor as the cathedral offices, retaining the medieval chapel at the back, and re-using some old material, e.g. in the SW turret.

The palace proper abuts the SE corner of this range. It is approached through a GATEHOUSE further W, with a C14 archway; upper parts renewed. No outbuildings remain. The main range is a compact block, two rooms deep. At first sight the S front looks largely C19, apart from the pretty bay-window, dating from 1500, which was transferred from Thomas Elyott's house next to St Petrock's when it was demolished in the C19, and, more significantly, the S porch. This has a C14 lower part – see the soffit shafts with moulded capitals in local volcanic stone – and an upper storey added in the early C16. The arms of Bishop Oldham († 1519) were moved in the C19 from this level to a new battlemented top storey. The inner doorway is the first visible evidence of a much older building. It is early C13, on a massive scale, of three orders, the middle one with heavily undercut Transitional-style zigzag, stiff-leaf capitals, keeled minor shafts, and a hoodmould with carved head-stops.

On the E side the general form of the palace appears C17, with its twin gables to the double roof. Windows all renewed. But on the ground floor the three large pointed arches, now with C20 glazing, also much renewed (the northernmost one in brick), may still reflect the original entrances from the screens passage to the now demolished service end. The service rooms were converted to chaplain's apartments in 1762–4 and demolished in 1812.

On the N side, two projecting buttresses may belong to the C13 work, indicating the line of the back wall of the great hall and its division into three bays. Near the E end of this side small blocked windows suggest a staircase preceding the present one. Otherwise the stone mullioned windows, as elsewhere, are C19, replacing the Georgian sashes dating from Bishop Keppel's remodelling of 1762–4.

Inside the palace there are only fragmentary remains of the earlier building phases. The most interesting is the large wooden pier of quatrefoil section now embedded in the spine wall between front and back rooms. It must have been part of a wooden arcade post of a large early C13 hall (cf. the C12 timber-arcaded halls of Hereford Bishop's Palace and Leicester Castle). Three more sections of similar posts were re-used to support the principals of the C17 roof over the back part of the building – two of them with necking and the beginnings of what could be stiff-leaf capitals. The post downstairs has been chopped short to take a beam for a low ceiling, part of a radical C17 remodelling which divided the hall by an axial wall, and (as evidence elsewhere shows) created four low floors within the shell of the medieval building. This work may date from the time of Bishop Seth Ward (1662–7), who restored the palace after the Restoration. His main living quarters were presumably in the now-demolished w range. Or could the low ceilings be part of a rough-and-ready Commonwealth remodelling for other uses? During this period the building was let to various tenants, including a sugar refiner.

The C18 alterations created much taller rooms on two floors only, of which the front two on the ground floor retain their original form. In the reception room the main feature is now an exceedingly ostentatious fireplace (repositioned in the C18 and again in 1952) which was installed by Bishop Courtenay originally in the parlour in the W wing. It is 12 ft high, with a display of family heraldry in three panels. The bishop's insignia in the central ogee-headed panel above, and the royal arms with the greyhounds of the Tudors, imply a date of c. 1485–6. In the reset bay-window in the dining room heraldic stained glass of various dates. In the hall several coats of arms, including a large one with a mitre from the time of Bishop Keppel, dated 1764, and two smaller ones with the arms of Henry VIII; also an angel bust, reset over the staircase.

The BISHOP'S CHAPEL on the first floor, behind the rebuilt W wing, lies close to the cathedral. E wall refaced in Heavitree stone, but with three C13 lancets (exterior stonework renewed perhaps in the early C19). Stiff-leaf capitals inside. The W part with a Perp window, added as an antechapel, has been divided off as a corridor to the cathedral. Remains of a spiral stair outside suggest there was an earlier link further E. The interior was restored by *Butterfield* in 1875; his wall decoration has been whitewashed, but some good Victorian stained glass remains (figures in medallions). Medieval wagon roof with small bosses.*

PALACE GATE runs from the palace gatehouse to South Street. The CONVENT SCHOOL of the Presentation of Mary, with plain rendered Georgian front and many later C19 additions, was formerly the house of the Archdeacon of Exeter. Opposite, Nos. 5–9, handsome red brick terrace houses of c. 1800 with *Coade* stone ornament similar to Southernhay (*see* The Suburbs: Perambulation 3). Behind them THE CHANTRY (Cathedral Choir School), tall, diapered brick, 1870 by *Ewan Christian*.

THE CITY CENTRE

The best place for an introduction to the town's topography is the crossroads at the old centre of the walled city. To the W Fore Street drops down steeply towards the river, although not as precipitately as Stepcote Hill to its s, which was the medieval route to the West Gate and the Old Exe Bridge. North and South Streets led from the crossroads to their respective gates (cleared away in 1769 and 1819), and the High Street, the route to the E from Roman times, leads NE, with the cathedral precinct on its s and the castle on the higher ground of Rougemont Hill to the N. This medieval pattern was little altered

* Three carved C14 bosses probably from Bishop Grandison's parlour are now in the Victoria and Albert Museum, London.

until the early C19, when Queen Street was created as an alternative route N. The network of small streets in between has been sadly blurred by the redevelopment of the last forty years, although rewarding fragments remain, particularly in the NW quarter, which was less damaged in the war than some other parts of the city. This perambulation starts with the High Street, then proceeds anticlockwise (E, NE, NW, SW) through the surrounding areas.

The crossroads are an unpromising start, architecturally. SW and SE corners have drab post-war replacements, NW is indifferent late Victorian. The NE has more character; No. 187 is an ambitious corner block in the Franco-Flemish style of c. 1885, with striped stonework and broad curlicued gables.* On the S side of the HIGH STREET No. 71, late C19, with a busy collection of late C17 motifs. On the other side of St Petrock, HALIFAX BUILDING SOCIETY, built for the Exeter Bank, a more sober early C20 front, with giant Ionic pilasters and a corner dome. Good banking hall inside with Ionic columns. On the opposite corner of Broadgate quite a sensitive later C20 contribution; 1978 by *Wilson & Womersley*, a slim canted oriel above an arcaded ground floor.

Then come a number of frontages whose narrow windows still reflect the size of medieval plots. No. 46 is visibly the oldest building, perhaps early C16, although truncated by a later cornice. Unusual coved upper jetty with little carved shafts; l. angle bracket with carved figure and demi-angel. The top window was originally of eight lights, across the whole width of the building. A blocked window in the E wall. The entrance was probably on the E side until No. 45 blocked a former alley. Several other houses have C16 fabric behind later fronts. No. 47 was built as a pair with No. 46, both originally with two-storey back blocks of the South Western type, that of No. 47 heightened in the later C17, when the surviving gallery connecting it to the front range was built. Nos. 41–42 are a pair of mirror-plan houses still basically intact above the ground-floor shop, well restored in 1983–4. Dated 1564 both externally and on an internal door head now in the Royal Albert Memorial Museum. Plain but complete timber front; three jetties, two gables, projecting oriels to all the upper floors. Fireplaces in the stone E wall. Each house had front and back rooms divided by a stone pier serving the back-room fireplace. Newel stairs survive at second-floor level; also, in the l. house, a second-floor garderobe alcove with seat. Extensive traces of late C16 wall painting, mostly now boarded over. No. 40 represents the later Stuart rather than the Tudor style, a rarity in Exeter. Narrow brick front, three bays with quoins, central projecting bay, big segmental pediment on the second floor, and a little brick decoration of an artisan mannerist kind.

On the opposite side, apart from the Guildhall (q.v.) with its C16 forebuilding projecting proudly into the street, less to single out, although the core of the TURKS HEAD is early C17, with three original fireplaces (one ground-floor, two first-floor). For Marks and Spencers at the corner of Queen Street *see* Guildhall Shopping Precinct below. The wealth of Exeter's C17 merchants is best

---

*The niche on one of these housed an early C16 wooden statue of St Peter from a former building on the site (now in the Royal Albert Museum). Early prints show this used as a cornerpost.

reflected by the group of spectacular show-fronts beyond, even though they have been much restored and totally rebuilt behind. Nos. 225–226 is five-storeyed, gabled, with plenty of carved decoration. A complex elevation, with windows running the whole width of the first floor, and the canted bays carried up to the floor above. Restored in 1907. No. 227 shows the timber front adapted to the taste of the later C17. The new motif is the 'Ipswich window' with its own pediment. Upper floors much restored in 1878. The C20 contributions on either side are instructive: on the l., the ruthlessly austere cubic corner block for C. & A., 1971, a classic example of the insensitive arrogance of urban design of the time; on the r. the more tactful No. 228, c. 1980 by *Alec French & Partners*, with a first-floor oriel over a ground-floor arcade with wooden piers. Then No. 229, which incorporates parts of a timber front (two canted bay-windows on carved brackets).

With the widening of the High Street one is plunged into a mediocre post-war world, long dull ranges on each side, brick with stone trim, horizontal emphasis rather than the verticals imposed by the old plots – a total break with the character of the old town. The buildings of the 1950s are neither confidently modern nor skilled in their use of the occasional pinched classical detail. On the N side LLOYDS, dignified by a giant archway and top cornice, by *E. Victor Beer*; adjoining blocks are by *Lucas, Roberts & Brown*. Opposite, and in the streets behind, a slightly more up-to-date idiom is used (boxed windows) by *L. H. Fewster & Partners*. BARCLAYS is redeemed by a nice top-lit circular banking hall. The central planting and partial traffic exclusion from the High Street date from the 1970s.

The pioneer pedestrian shopping street was PRINCESSHAY, running parallel to the High Street off Bedford Street to the S. It was laid out to command a vista of the cathedral in the manner recommended by *Thomas Sharp*'s post-war plan; to achieve this, the S side of Bedford Street was kept low. A worthy aim, but unhappy its execution, for the one-storey shops appear depressingly shack-like. It is all a poor compensation for the loss of the Georgian Bedford Circus.* At the end of BEDFORD STREET, STATUE of the 11th Earl of Devon by *E. B. Stephens*, erected 1880. This rebuilt quarter was intended to provide the city with a modern and conveniently central shopping area. It now seems very modest in comparison with the later shopping precinct behind the Guildhall (*see* below), and with the plans of 1988 for the redevelopment of the junction of the High Street, Sidwell Street, and Longbrook Street.

Before returning, one should explore the streets to the N of this part of the High Street. Past the sanitized back lanes behind the High Street shops and the seemly pre-war Telephone Exchange and Record Office (qq.v.) there is a steep and briefly picturesque climb to the castle, by way either of the narrow LITTLE CASTLE STREET, with slate-hung houses, a rubble stone warehouse, and, tucked away behind, the ample C19 premises of the British Legion (two storeys, Heavitree stone, round-arched windows), or of CASTLE STREET. Here there is a pleasant row of stuccoed late

*This was a handsome oval of houses, the N side built in 1773–5 by *Robert Stribling*, the S side completed in 1826, all demolished after serious but not irrevocable war damage. Bedford Circus replaced Bedford House, built by the Russells on the site of the medieval Dominican friary.

Georgian frontages (propped up by disconcertingly massive shoring) opposite the villa which is now the Rougemont House Museum (q.v.). Where the streets join, BRADNINCH HALL is set back on the r., a Georgian five-bay brick front with Tuscan porch of c. 1800. A detour can be made to the l. to take in NORTHERNHAY PLACE with a C19 stucco-trimmed terrace on the E approach to Northernhay Gardens (see Public Buildings, above).

To the W one skirts around the library set into the foot of the castle mound, an area clumsily refashioned after the war, with self-conscious stone plinths here and there as a nod towards the use of traditional materials, until one comes to GANDY STREET. This is an appealingly narrow old lane, the houses mostly early C19 stucco, rebuilt when Queen Street was laid out parallel to it. A few older buildings, e.g. No. 1 opposite the side of the museum, a substantial C18 house with straight-headed windows of rubbed brick. Across the road, behind a forecourt, the former University Building of 1907–9 by *Tait & Harvey* (now Exeter and Devon Arts Centre), a busy brick and stone baroque front with three pediments and paired windows with Gibbsian surrounds. In the middle of Gandy Street QUEEN'S WALK is a passage through to Queen Street past a delightful exterior stair with a cast-iron railing ending in a confident flourish.

QUEEN STREET has the best of Exeter's C19 buildings. It was laid out to connect the High Street with the New North Road, conveniently sweeping away some of the old streets where cholera had raged in 1832. The buildings show only a few traces of a coherent layout, but include plenty of robust individualists. For the first buildings on the W side see below. Starting on the E side at the corner of Musgrave Row and extending back to Gandy Street a bold later C19 four-storey Italianate building with rusticated quoins (the former Queen's Hotel), then a plainer and earlier terrace with some little Grecian touches. Nos. 83–84 (where Queen's Walk emerges) is the former Post Office of 1849, tall and narrow, with a very florid giant Corinthian order to the upper floors. After a lesser stuccoed stretch, the polychrome stone Gothic of the museum (q.v.), then No. 75, COUNTY CHAMBERS, also polychrome, but classical; and No. 74, the Post Office from 1864 to 1883, earlier and quieter Italianate, with alternating pediments to the upper windows. Still less flamboyant is the former DISPENSARY on the W side, 1841 by *S.A. Greig*, five bays, stuccoed, heavy doorcase with paired pilasters. This comes at the end of an innocuous C19 terrace, behind which HABITAT was neatly inserted in 1984–5. The main entrance is in Paul Street (see below).

The southern end of the W side of Queen Street is a more confusing story. The whole block from High Street to Paul Street now fronts the GUILDHALL SHOPPING PRECINCT, a creation mostly of 1969–76, with MARKS AND SPENCER at the corner of the High Street added in 1979–82 and the shops to the N of Paul Street in 1981–5. Plans for the redevelopment of this area were proposed as early as 1914 (by *T.H. Mawson*). The present scheme is a modification of a study by *Wilson & Womersley*; the buildings of 1969–76 are by *Alec C. French*, with *Lord Holford & Partners* as consultants. The whole is an example of the city centre package where a precinct with ample adjoining car parking is concealed behind old or pseudo-old frontages (cf. e.g. Salisbury, where it was done rather better). The drawback is that the window-dressing rarely extends to more than two sides, with disastrous results for the back streets, as will be clear if one enters the Exeter centre via the car parks along North Street and Paul Street. The main pedestrian entrances are through a discreet passage from the High Street, or more grandly through the HIGHER MARKET in Queen Street, designed in 1834 by *George Dymond* of Bristol, winner of an open competition, and executed after his death the following year, by *Charles Fowler*. It is one of the best market buildings of its date: a severely neo-classical frontage in Bath stone, with pedimented central entrance with four Greek Doric fluted columns.* The interior, originally aisled, has been converted to a two-storey shopping mall. On one side was a Civic Hall, which was demolished, as was the Fish Market behind.

The precinct itself is a crushing disappointment. The back of the market has lost its dignified steps beneath the raised ground level; the tiny church of St Pancras, deprived of its homely and historic setting of small streets, makes a pathetic and inappropriate centrepiece, its enforced preservation only too clearly conflicting with the developers' conception of interlocking squares surrounded by banal commercial building. In the square, bronze SCULPTURE by *Peter Thursby*, 1977, entitled 'Looking Forward'. The second phase had different aims, but there is little improvement in quality. The intention was, laudably, to blend old and new more subtly; the result is a pot-pourri of fakes, some more authentic than others. A scheme by *Powell & Moya* was rejected in favour of one by *Norman Jones & Rigby*. Facing the precinct is the classical stone arcade, an 'adapted replica' of a building from a site nearby, forming a curiously pompous prelude to the back entrance of Marks and Spencer. At the corner of the High Street and Queen Street the new building is allowed to express itself in a lumpily chamfered projection, topped by a ridiculously small lantern re-used from its early C20 predecessor. Along Queen Street it is concealed again behind quite an effective facsimile reproduction of the previously early Victorian stuccoed frontage. This has a little Grecian decoration on the parapet and on the attic a statue of the young Queen. Across PAUL STREET is the third stage, HARLEQUINS, by *Bruges Tozer*, 1985–7. In reaction to the previous developments, Exeter's first large-scale essay in post-modernism, jazzed up with plenty of colourful trimmings. Two storeys of shopping, with glazed mall and atrium in the latest fashion; spatially quite interesting. A discreet approach is provided through older Queen Street frontages; in Paul Street there is a more showy forecourt. The older car park is tucked away underneath, a considerable bonus.

NORTHERNHAY STREET, turning W off Queen Street beyond the commercial redevelopment, runs steeply downhill to the W quarter of the city centre, the least visited part, and full of surprises. On the S side the city wall (q.v.) is visible at the rear of back gardens. On the N, below the Rougemont Hotel, former TURKISH BATHS

Fowler's Lower Market at Exeter of 1835–7, destroyed in 1942, was an interesting contrast; not grandiose, but structurally innovative in its use of iron and laminated timber (cf. his Hungerford Market in London).

(now offices), 1891, three storeys, sturdily detailed in red brick. Opposite, ELIM PROVIDENCE CHAPEL, a former Plymouth Brethren Chapel built in 1839 and acquired for the Bible Christians in 1851, with a broad five-bay front with Ionic pilasters and central pediment and windows with quite fancifully classical surrounds. (Inside, tiered seats on three (once four) sides and a painted ceiling.) Then two massive granite gateposts with balls, relics of a stonemason's yard, and on the other side the delightful Nos. 4–7, three-storey early C18 houses with half-hipped gabled attic floors (cf. Topsham). At the bottom all is dominated by the former ST ANNE'S WELL BREWERY, now converted to miscellaneous workshops. Begun c. 1876; robustly detailed in a coarse version of rustic Italianate. Red brick with yellow brick dressings. Deep overhanging eaves; angular attic lighting. *James Jerman* was responsible for additions of 1886.

Northernhay Street ends in LOWER NORTH STREET, the main N access to the city until Queen Street was constructed. To improve it, the IRON BRIDGE was constructed in 1834–5 to oversail the awkward valley. Ironwork with nicely traceried spandrels; thin supports. Gothic cast-iron balustrades. By *Russell & Brown*, from the Blaina ironworks, Monmouthshire. On the S bridge approach, the CROWN AND SCEPTRE of the same date, solid, quietly Italianate.[*] Along the line of Lower North Street, NORTHGATE COURT, by *Christopher Roberts*, c. 1980, plain, rendered, in sympathy with the neighbouring Georgian houses remaining on the l. side of the bridge. There is even a rural-looking house of the C17 set back on the northern slope, with a projecting porch on wooden posts.

Beneath the Iron Bridge one reaches EXE STREET, running down to the river through an area once industrial but now almost entirely rebuilt. On the W side the stepped skyline of a large housing association development of 1979–86 by *M. W. T. Architects*. Quite an intricate use of levels, but harsh machine-made details when viewed close up. Above is the more genteel DINHAM CRESCENT, a Georgian travesty of 1979–84 by *David Young*. S of Exe Street NAPIER TERRACE, a single surviving C19 artisan group, steps deftly up the hill, facing the catacombs and cemetery (q.v.) laid out below the city walls in 1834.

Up to BARTHOLOMEW STREET, within the walls. On the l. a long low MALTINGS, later a pottery, with bottle kiln (now restaurant). First a glimpse up MARY ARCHES STREET, the beginning of the E side, all dereliction and car-parking, but with the church and the little synagogue beyond (qq.v.). On the W side St Olave's Court Hotel (*see* below) and a twin-gabled rendered front of the early C19. Back to Bartholomew Street, which continues W, making a dog-leg around the leafy former churchyard of All Hallows. This would be a delightful corner could the traffic be excluded, with its

---

[*] The timber-framed specialist will make a detour S to take in No. 18 NORTH STREET, where a C17 house, truncated by road widening in 1899, is concealed behind a front of c. 1930. Inside, a side through-passage with an oak-panelled screen with ovolo mouldings and scroll stops, an original rear door with moulded stops, and carved oriel brackets. Late C17 dog-leg stair and pedimented doorcases. Also the remains of a unique two-storeyed timber gallery connecting the main house to a three-storey rear block (now demolished).

group of Georgian terrace houses, at long last rescued from decay in 1984–6. The grandest is No. 32, C18, with an overscaled door-case with composite columns, and triple stone keystones to the windows.

The 1980s infilling is of mixed quality. ALL HALLOWS COURT, across the former churchyard, made a feeble and shoddy start; near the corner with The Mint, CARPENTER'S CLOSE, 1979–85 by *Lionel Aggett* of *R.C.A.Partnership*, is much better, ingeniously planned sheltered housing around intricate small courtyards, over-finicky in its detailing, but at least in the spirit of the intricacy of the old city, with its mixture of narrow lanes and intimate enclosed spaces. Another such contrast is round the corner where THE MINT cuts through the remains of St Nicholas Priory (q.v.). To its E is ST OLAVE'S COURT HOTEL, the former St Olave's rectory, hidden within its own grounds. A delicate Regency front, ashlar-lined stucco, a fringed band to the porch carried also across the house; shallow bow-window.

Parallel to and W of The Mint, FRIERNHAY STREET, another narrow lane running to Fore Street, largely rebuilt in 1981–4 by *McCarthy & Stone*; good courtyard layout, but deadening use of the roughened red bricks, so obviously factory made, that have been excessively favoured for later C20 Exeter redevelopment. Down towards Fore Street BEADLES TERRACE, simple white-walled housing, the alternative neo-vernacular mode, 1977–81 by *Jack Cross*, Chief City Architect. For a refreshing change, one can make a detour along BARTHOLOMEW TERRACE, a footpath around the NW corner of the city wall, with a delightful group of small early C19 stuccoed houses overlooking the slopes down to the river. The gem is No. 7, a very pretty Gothick *cottage orné*: canted bay, concave-arched windows, lattice balconies, vermiculated doorway.

In FORE STREET the most important survivals are on the N side. First, TUCKERS HALL, a remarkable survival, hiding behind the street front rebuilt in 1875–6 by *John Ware*. It began as a chapel, built c. 1471 for the Weavers, Tuckers (i.e. Fullers) and Shearmen, a medieval guild still in existence, and was converted to a hall after the Reformation, with inserted floor and fireplace. The original wagon roof survives, de-plastered in 1901–2, with moulded principals and purlins and carved bosses, once even richer, as slots show there must have been cusping along the principals, and carved figures below. The overmantel in the first-floor hall, and excellent panelling with pilasters and strapwork frieze, were added in 1634–8.

No. 143 Fore Street is the finest C18 house remaining in the city, probably built by Sir Thomas Bury. It is dated 1716 and 1717 on rainwater heads. Brick, in chequer pattern, with quoins, five bays, the centre one projecting, the lower parts hidden behind an Edwardian shopfront full of bulgy balusters, quite appealing in itself but regrettable here. No. 144, with an early C19 front, is older behind. One bay is visible of a three-bay C17 plaster ceiling on the first floor, a curious design with a circular table laid with plates in each bay, the middle one with a centrepiece with two dishes with massive fish-heads. In addition flowers, angel heads, and a menagerie of animals including unicorn, camel, monkey, dog, etc. No. 150 has a much altered front of *c.* 1800, corner pilasters, and a good *Coade* stone doorway hidden round the corner in Friernhay Street.

On the s side there are less ambitious stuccoed fronts to narrow houses (their widths still reflecting the late Saxon layout, *see* Introduction). The DEVONPORT INN is worth noting, with its panelled pilasters and bold Edwardian arched ground floor. Nearer South Street, as part of the post-war reconstruction, ST GEORGE'S MARKET, 1960 by the City Architect, *H.B.Rowe*, a now rather tatty effort in a belated Festival of Britain spirit.

The last sector of the city within the walls, between Fore Street and South Street, is the most disappointing, for here much was destroyed before and during the war, more was lost for the inner ring road, and rebuilding has been patchy and indifferent. Along SOUTH STREET there is at least a clear expression of post-war aesthetics. On the w side, maisonettes above shops; monopitch roofs with the prominent eaves that were used by progressive architects already in the 1930s. Less pretentious, and so more satisfactory than the rebuilding of the High Street. Opposite, the sad ruins of the Vicars Choral (*see* Cathedral Close) amidst mean low shops (cf. Bedford Street); further s just one good older group on the w side. The WHITE HART INN is the centrepiece, a late Georgian front, rendered, with rustic quoining; older behind, with a cobbled floor leading to the yard. The back bar is a good C16 parlour with a quadripartite ceiling with moulded beams, Heavitree stone fireplace, and framed wall. Next door No. 67, a twin-gabled timber-framed front of *c.* 1650, with continuous first-floor window (and original staircase).

But the photographer's delight (provided the camera is angled to omit the surroundings) is the steep cobbled view down STEPCOTE HILL, with at the bottom the cluster of St Mary Steps, and the late medieval building at the corner of West Street. Stone ground floor, two jettied floors above; on the side to Stepcote Hill windows with cusped lights. It contained three independent units, a good example of how intricate late medieval urban house planning could be: a ground-floor shop (facing WEST STREET), with heated chamber behind; and two first-floor shops(?), approached by an external stair from Stepcote Hill and entered by doors at first-floor level, one of which remains visible externally. From one of the shops there must have been access to the upper chambers. On the opposite side of West Street another small timber-framed house (the 'House that Moved'), much restored in 1961, when it was moved from Edmund Street; also a small group of mostly C18 brick fronts, close to the site of the medieval West Gate.

To complete the study of Exeter's remaining timber-framed houses one can make a detour to TUDOR STREET, on the former Exe Island NW of Fore Street, now dismally isolated beside the new road. The OLD TUDOR HOUSE, *c.* 1660, was restored in 1964–8 by *William Lord*. Four storeys, the first floor (and formerly other floors) hung with intricately carved slates; three heraldic features in wreaths. The side walls are of brick, the earliest surviving example in Exeter of brick used on a significant scale. Nearby a later brick warehouse with a crane, a relic of the industrial past of Exe Island.

THE SUBURBS

1. From South Street to the river

Beyond the site of the South Gate, demolished in 1819, and the bleak
wasteland of 1960s roundabouts, the line of South Street is continued s by HOLLOWAY STREET. On the s side much has been
swept away; of three remaining early C19 houses the centre one is
the most unusual: 'Egyptian' tapering windows and doorway,
combined with pediments on the first floor. Then No. 71, three
bays, red brick with upper pilasters, ground-floor windows and
door recessed behind a triplet of arches. On the N side, up GOOD
SHEPHERDS DRIVE, incorporated in a pleasantly laid out housing development of 1980–4 by *Charles E. Ware*, two older houses:
BISHOP WESTALL HOUSE, C18, red brick, three storeys and
five bays, with Ionic porch and C18 staircase; and BISHOP
PASTERFIELD HOUSE, on a slightly larger scale, with an early
C19 stuccoed exterior with pedimented Tuscan porch, but essentially of *c.* 1700 – see the bolection-moulded panelling in the hall
and the good staircase behind with sturdy turned balusters and
closed string, rising to the top floor. The ramped dado and
Venetian landing window are perhaps later alterations. Original
bracketed hood to the back door.

Back in Holloway Street the former HOLLOWAY STREET
SCHOOLS, 1875, raised up on a tall battered limestone terrace
above the road. Gabled, Gothic windows, polychrome brick trim.
At right angles, LANSDOWNE TERRACE, a decaying group of
ten stuccoed houses, some pediments remaining to ground-floor
windows. Holloway Street dips down towards the Larkbeare
Brook (now culverted; an early medieval bridge with two-centred
arch and chamfered ribs remains beneath the present road). On the
N side No. 28 is a fragment of LARKBEARE MANSION, once a
substantial C16 house, mostly demolished by C19 road widening.
One three-storey wing remains, of squared red sandstone (see the
side and back) with Georgian sashes and one older relieving arch.
In the ground-floor room a framed ceiling with counterchanged
joists. Garderobe at r. first-floor level. On the top floor, five trusses
visible of a good arched-braced roof, unusually, boarded with wide
planks. It was the home of the Baring family before they acquired
the adjacent Mount Radford estate (*see* below, Perambulation 2).
Further up the hill, hidden within well treed grounds, LARK-
BEARE HOUSE, built *c.* 1870 for J.C. Bowring, a solid pile in
random limestone with gables and mullioned windows. (Ruined
earlier GAZEBO in the grounds.)

Now s down MELBOURNE STREET to explore the rewarding area
of merchants' houses and villas on the slopes overlooking the river,
mostly built up after 1827. Minor early C19 terraces on both sides
of Melbourne Street; others stepping steeply down COLLETON
HILL to the river. At the corner the grander houses start: COL-
LETON HOUSE, five bays, Greek Doric side porch, and, at the
beginning of COLLETON CRESCENT, COLLETON LODGE,
three by four bays, but unattractively pebbledashed. The Crescent
itself is earlier than the surrounding streets, 1802–14 by *Matthew
Nosworthy*, in the same elegant late Georgian style as his earlier

terraces in Southernhay (*see* Perambulation 3, below) and elsewhere. Red brick, *Coade* stone surrounds, head keystones. A balanced design, with lower end houses, and the five centre houses of four storeys set slightly forward. The houses on either side of these have excellent tented balconies (not identical); the others have small lattice-work balconettes. The end house on the l. has been made neo-classical, with stuccoed flank wall and elaborate pilasters.

Beyond this, after a plain house rebuilt and extended in 1980, COL-LETON VILLA, where neo-classical detail still happily survives. It is a handsome end piece to FRIARS GATE, with pediment over all three bays, and palm-frond capitals to giant panelled pilasters. Along FRIARS WALK, past the Salvation Army Citadel (q.v.), a row of five pretty villas in the same spirit, 1833 by the builder *John Mitchell*, who developed the area. Incised corner pilasters of varying designs; hipped roofs on broad bracketed eaves; side entrances. Opposite, taller terraces, altered, and No. 17, an older house, now swamped by post-war development. The 1970s housing with its rendered upper walls (*Jack Cross*, Chief City Architect, 1976–81) attempts to be sympathetic; the 1960s tile-hung boxes of maisonettes make no such effort. To the w, the PARISH HALL, 1913 by *J. Archibald Lucas*, with a few Arts and Crafts free baroque touches, and LAWN HOUSE, another pre-suburban survival. Beyond this a path to QUAY LANE, leading down to the river.

THE QUAY, now divorced from the town by the new ring road, is still one of Exeter's most delightful spots, although in danger of being overdeveloped as a tourist trap. Its oldest buildings date from soon after 1676, when the Customs Port was reorganized, the Quay enlarged, and the Exeter Canal improved and lengthened to cope with the town's flourishing cloth trade. The CUSTOM HOUSE takes pride of place. It was built in 1680–1, a confident affirmation of Exeter's rights over Topsham, her longstanding rival downstream. The architect was *Richard Allen*. A very satisfying, homely brick front of two storeys and five bays, with a later extension on the r. Hipped roof above a wooden modillion cornice, central pediment. White-painted stone quoins, plat-band, and ground-floor arches. These were formerly open. Those on the r. were filled in already in 1685 to create an office for the Crown Customs Officer. The windows are later Georgian sashes, but original wooden mullion-and-transom ones survive at the back. The ground-floor rooms were used for storage; between them a massive staircase with bulbous urn-shaped balusters provides stately access to the Long Room along the front of the building, where captains presented their documents. This room, the smaller adjoining one, and the stair-hall all have spectacular ceilings, documented work by the plasterer *John Abbot* of Frithelstock. The Long Room has an oval with a wreath of flowers, masks, and snakes, all in the most daring high relief. Their closest parallels are the ceilings at Bideford and Youlston Park in North Devon (qq.v.). Painted royal arms at one end. The smaller room has a more delicate garlanded octagon.

Adjoining the Custom House to the l. a contemporary two-storey warehouse. To the r., first the little HARBOURMASTER'S

OFFICE, of 1778, with a curved parapet, and the PROSPECT INN, which partially encases another former WAREHOUSE. Although disguised by a new front in the C19, investigations in 1985–6 revealed that this is a remarkable C17 survival. It was built, probably in 1680, directly beside the C16 quay wall, and the front of the roof was cantilevered out over the water to provide a covered docking area 12ft wide. Seven of the massive oak posts which supported the front of the building still remain. The ground floor originally functioned as a covered quay, or transit shed, 100ft long; the upper floor was used for storage.

Opposite is the FISHMARKET, a late C19 open ironwork structure housing the KING'S BEAM (inscribed 'A. & W.C.Bodley, iron founders, Exeter, 1838') for weighing dutiable goods. Then, beside the cliff, two five-storey former WAREHOUSES of 1835, the one of white limestone by R.S.Cornish, the other of red stone with brick dressings by W.H. & W.W.Hooper. Beyond, late C19 BONDED STORES cut into the cliff. In this area, overmuch clutter of would-be-picturesque street furniture. The elaborate cast-iron lamp posts (by Macfarlane of Glasgow) flanking the cable ferry come from the Exe Bridge of 1904. On the opposite bank, more warehouses (some of them now the MARITIME MUSEUM), beside the CANAL constructed in 1564–6 by John Trew, with pound locks, their first use in Britain. Its present form dates from James Green's reconstruction of 1821–32. For other buildings across the water see Perambulation 7.

The industrial enthusiast can continue downstream to TREW'S WEIR, originally constructed in the 1560s. Wire pedestrian SUSPENSION BRIDGE of 1935. Two early FACTORIES. TREW'S WEIR PAPER MILL incorporates a two-storey stone and brick former cotton mill of 1780. It became a paper mill in 1834. The OLD MATCH FACTORY, 1774, two storeys, rendered brick, was formerly a flax mill, later a part of the paper mill.

Upstream from the Custom House a few more WAREHOUSES. Two were built for wine merchants, one of grey stone for Samuel Jones, 1878, another for Kennaway & Co., 1892. Further w two more buildings of the later C17. CRICKLEPIT MILL, brick, now colour-washed, with a large enclosed waterwheel, was built between 1659 and 1685. It was used for fulling and grist as well as for malting. Other adjoining buildings of this industrial complex have been demolished, but nearby is a remarkable survival – a TENTERING SHED, i.e. a cloth-drying shed, c.90ft long, originally open on both sides, with brick piers at ground-floor level, and wooden posts above. This was an area much used by the cloth industry: SHILHAY, the former island opposite, had open cloth racks until the early C19, and then timber yards. In 1977–8 it was developed by Marshman Warren Taylor for public housing. Their design was an important trend-setter in re-establishing a comfortably tradi- 179 tional densely knit urban idiom. 145 dwellings, mostly red brick with grey tile-hanging, grouped with plenty of variety. Staggered terraces along the street, broken by narrow alleys and well land-scaped garage courts. Towards the river the four main spine blocks project into a generous park-like lawn.

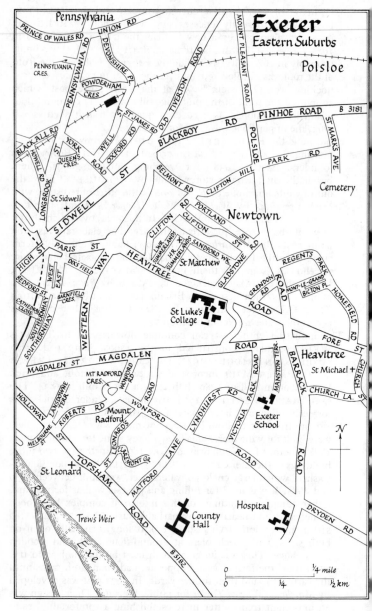

2. East: s of (and including) Magdalen Street

MAGDALEN STREET, which branches E from the South Street roundabout, has as its special attraction WYNARD'S HOSPITAL, former almshouses, founded in 1435, rebuilt and altered in the C17 and C18, and restored to a picturesque medieval appearance in 1863–4. It would be historical snobbery to deny their aesthetic

appeal. A charming cobbled courtyard with a wellhouse, surrounded by low cottages with tall chimneys; red Heavitree stone.
Along the road the CHAPEL, restored at the cost of Mark Kennaway, with glass by *Hardman*. Four-centred chancel arch with
elaborate imposts and luxuriant foliage scrolls in the voussoirs.
(Good portrait BRASS of G.G. Kennaway.) Further on in MAG-
DALEN ROAD, MAGDALEN ALMSHOUSES, Victorian Tudor of
1863, in brown volcanic stone. Among the early C19 stuccoed
villas opposite, Nos. 12 and 14 are especially rewarding, an unusually refined design, with recessed centre and chamfered angles;
trellis porches at the sides, nice fluted Doric gatepiers.

Other respectable villas of the same period, modest, but pleasingly
varied, can be found in the streets to N and S. They date from the
development of the MOUNT RADFORD estate which began in
1832. Mount Radford House itself, the C18 mansion of the Barings, survived until c. 1904. ST LEONARD'S ROAD, now fringed
with assorted houses hidden behind leafy front gardens, was the
former drive (one cedar tree remains). The style favoured by the
early C19 builders is mostly fairly plain neo-classical, embellished
by good verandas (see No. 28), although a few break into Regency
Tudor. No. 25 has cusped eaves and hoodmoulds, and similar
details occur also on the very pretty group of houses round the
corner in ST LEONARD'S PLACE, facing a lawn where Mount
Radford House stood. These were among the first to be built, as
was CLAREMONT GROVE to the E, where three more substantial
houses are hidden down a drive guarded by a little polygonal lodge
with curved porch. Their style is again decidedly Tudor, the first
with openwork bargeboards, the other two with castellations.

Now back to WONFORD ROAD, which has a scatter of small early
Victorian houses to E and W. To the W also a terrace, partly low,
partly tall and gabled, with patternbook Gothic detail (porches
with clustered shafts). No. 7, RICHMOND VILLA, is in an altogether grander mood, pedimented, although only two windows
wide, preparing one for the ambitious composition of the
QUADRANT, a curving group of 1–2–2–1 houses with low links;
giant pilasters, pediments to first-floor tripartite windows. It is
part of a strangely inchoate group around a circus; perhaps not
completed as first intended. On the W side five (formerly six) large
detached houses (MOUNT RADFORD CRESCENT) with full-
height canted bays; on the NE, instead of an answering quadrant,
just Wonford Road, with plain paired villas leading back to Magdalen Road.

A few detours can be made to take in some extra buildings. SW of
Mount Radford Crescent an abrupt change, a little enclave of
artisan terraces of c. 1900, crammed on to the steeply sloping site
(ROBERTS ROAD, etc.). Further E up MAGDALEN ROAD an Art
Deco FILLING STATION, surprisingly unaltered (No. 41).

Further out, for the connoisseur of suburbs, there are plenty of
interesting scattered houses, for here, as elsewhere around the city,
the suburbs did not spread consistently, but took advantage of the
best sites first. BARING CRESCENT, N of Magdalen Road, is a
spaciously set out group of detached stucco houses of c. 1820, until
after 1850 standing quite on their own overlooking the town across
the fields. They were built by *W. Hooper*, who was also responsible

for Nos. 151–155 MAGDALEN ROAD (BARING PLACE), orig-
inally two pairs with lower links (later altered), still in the red brick
late Georgian style of Colleton Crescent (c. 1810), although the
similar adjacent houses are stuccoed. Opposite, No. 78, a pleasant
brick villa; grander stuccoed examples down MANSTON TER-
RACE. Also s of Magdalen Road, VICTORIA PARK ROAD,
LYNDHURST ROAD, and the E end of WONFORD ROAD is the
area to explore for larger mid C19 Victorian houses in their own
grounds. The site of Exeter School (q.v.), just to the E, indicates
the extent of the built-up area by 1880. On the s side of Wonford
Road one early survival, OLD MATFORD, c. 1600, stone and cob,
with two-storey porch and moulded four-centred doorway, but
lacking any ancient patina.

A C20 excursion further s (*see* map p. 358) should be appended here
to take in the neighbourhood of Topsham Road. To the s the ST
JAMES' PRIORY ESTATE (KING HENRY'S ROAD, etc.), partly
by *L. de Soissons*, with some comfortable, well-built brick houses
of 1933 onwards in a late Arts and Crafts tradition. To the N, the
1920s BURNTHOUSE LANE ESTATE, Exeter's first major effort
at council housing. The most ambitious layout is a horseshoe with
closes off.

In TOPSHAM ROAD a little early C19 group, PROSPECT PLACE, a
red brick terrace (Nos. 187–189), and some individual houses
nearby. Further out, NEWPORT LODGE, a two-storey angle-
fronted former toll house.

3. *East:* N *of Magdalen Street*

SOUTHERNHAY is most pleasantly approached from the Cathedral
Close by the New Cut through the city wall (q.v.). It is the most
133   expansive layout of Georgian Exeter, still impressive, even though
the NW part was destroyed in the last war. The even and restrained
three-storeyed red brick terraces, following the line of the city
ditch, were designed by *Matthew Nosworthy* in 1789, his first
recorded work in Exeter, very much in the tradition of London
work of the 1770s: blank arcading framing the round-headed
ground-floor windows, white string courses, doorways with *Coade*
stone surrounds and pretty little faces in the keystones. Nos. 1–10a
were well restored when converted to offices in 1975–7 (by
P. E. Williams of *Richard Ellis*). Behind is a new landscaped walk
beside the city wall.

Opposite, in Southernhay East, development began a little earlier,
with the mid C18 Royal Devon and Exeter Hospital (q.v.) and
some individual late C18 houses, e.g. Nos. 27–28 with good doorcases, between others of the early C19, for example No. 36, with a
Roman Doric portico and, at the back, a nice trellised veranda,
visible now from SOUTHERNHAY GARDENS. Tucked behind,
but still disturbingly large by comparison, is LINACRE HOUSE,
an office development by *M.W.T.*, 1986–7, which expands over
former back gardens. To the N a grander, stucco terrace of c. 1820,
with a one-storeyed Greek Doric colonnade of twenty-one bays and
three pediments, and SOUTH HOUSE, with low wings and a one-
storey Roman Doric colonnade. The N end of Southernhay was
badly damaged in the war. On the w side the replacement is

BROADWALK HOUSE (*Leach, Rhodes & Walker*, 1974), an over-large office block uncomfortably dressed up to be slightly in keeping; red brick cladding between curtain-walled stair sections, top storey within a mansard, incongruous curly white balconies, all hopelessly failing to disguise its greedy bulk.

Off the middle of Southernhay East, BARNFIELD CRESCENT, the start of another *Nosworthy* development, planned 1792, built 1805, only five houses, details close to Southernhay, but no Coade stone. Delicate iron balconies. No. 1 was added in a similar style, *c.* 1840, but is of three storeys, not four, with a two-storey stone wing set back from the rest. Further N, DIX'S FIELD also leads off Southernhay; here, out of a long terrace, just three of *Nosworthy's* houses remain (*c.* 1808), opposite the dull Civic Centre, in an area otherwise entirely renewed.

The area just described is cut off sharply by the inner bypass (Western Way) from the suburbs stretching towards Heavitree. This area, like that to the S around Mount Radford, was developed from the early C19, but in a more piecemeal fashion. First a detour N to the small group of streets known as NEWTOWN, a working-class settlement developed from *c.* 1830, the first of its kind in Exeter. It was rehabilitated by the City Council in 1967–70, a pioneer effort of its type. CLIFTON ROAD (one side only remaining) has some of the earliest surviving terraces (just two rooms on each floor), with the CLIFTON INN at the S end, a nice rounded corner with minimal late Georgian detail. In HEAVITREE ROAD, LOWER SUMMERLANDS, the lesser part of a more classy development of after 1814; a two-storey red brick terrace of unusually broad houses with central doorways. The taller detached houses of HIGHER SUMMERLANDS were on the site of the Police Station. Further on, UPLANDS, a pair of houses of the late 1830s, much altered, the start of a stuccoed villa development by Exeter Municipal Charities, never completed, surprisingly by *Scott & Moffat*.

Then, on the S side of Heavitree Road a series of plain, well proportioned pairs of stucco villas, built by *W. Hooper* in the 1820s at the same time as Baring Crescent (*see* Perambulation 2, above). To the N, in GRENDON ROAD, ALMSHOUSES of 1880 by *R. W. Best*, gabled, Tudor; another group further on of 1892.

E of Polsloe Road is an area worth exploring: fragments of ambitious stuccoed layouts – over-ambitious, it would seem, for most were not completed as intended. Off Heavitree Road two large detached houses in their own grounds, SOUTHLANDS and CLYSTLANDS, the latter with central pediment and recessed Greek Doric porch. To their N MONT-LE-GRAND, 1840–1, with a single row of tall houses, the most elaborate with pediments; pediments also to the first-floor windows. BICTON PLACE has large houses around a rectangular green, Nos. 1 and 3 neo-classical, No. 2 castellated; the rest later and less ambitious. REGENTS PARK, begun in 1843, is also incomplete, just the beginnings of two elegant stuccoed terraces with round-headed ground-floor windows; pediment to the centre and E end of the N terrace.

POLSLOE ROAD itself illustrates the abandonment of the neo-classical style, starting with REGENTS TERRACE, but continuing with picturesque gables and bargeboarding, and ending with every extreme of Victorian ornament. This part of Exeter is indeed predominantly late Victorian, with only a few exceptions such as ST JOHN'S COTTAGE, near Jesmond Road, quite an elaborate *cottage orné* of *c.* 1840, and further S in BELMONT ROAD, SALUTARY PLACE, early C19, a very modest brick terrace on the N fringe of Newtown (q.v., above). From here one can return to investigate Heavitree (*see* below) or, on one's way back into Exeter down Blackboy Road and Sidwell Street, take in some further scattered examples of early suburban expansion.

In BLACKBOY ROAD Nos. 49–52, early C19 red brick; Nos. 39–40 and 31–34, stucco; and on either side of the road a few small early C19 closes (Salem Place, Spinning Path Lane). Nearby, an interesting contrast. KENDAL CLOSE is two ranges of planned working-class housing by the Improved Industrial Dwellings Company, 1876, striped brick. In the fork between Blackboy Road and Old Tiverton Road, ST ANNE'S ALMSHOUSES, a C16 L-shaped group of cottages, much restored in 1838, now attached to two houses rebuilt in free Tudor by *W. D. Caröe*, 1907–9. Caröe also restored the tiny CHAPEL, now used as an Eastern Orthodox church. It is a plain Perp single-cell building of Heavitree stone with volcanic dressings. Three-light E window, two-light side windows (with separate inner arches), ceiled wagon roof with some original bosses.

A detour can be made up OLD TIVERTON ROAD (the main route to North Devon until the New North Road was made in 1834) to include ST ANN'S TERRACE, 1821, ALBION PLACE off to the r., of the 1830s, and further up on the l. side ST JAMES'S TERRACE (Nos. 21–30), a grander stuccoed composition built before 1830: end houses slightly recessed, continuous balcony. To the N, in ST JAMES'S ROAD, was St James's church, built for this growing suburb in 1836, rebuilt in 1878–85 by *R. Medley Fulford*, and destroyed in the war. *Fulford's* picturesque VICARAGE remains, banded brick with some Gothic detail combined with vernacular-revival tile-hanging. S of St James's Road a pleasantly quiet oasis with humble C19 cottages and terraces in and around OXFORD ROAD and WELL STREET, and ST SIDWELL'S SCHOOL, mostly 1854 and 1895, with gable and bellcote.

The suburb of ST SIDWELL'S is now all C19 and C20, but was of considerable extent already in the Middle Ages, when it developed along the main street leading from the East Gate. It was named after the church dedicated to the local martyr, St Sativola or Sidwell (the English form early became associated with one of the many wells in the area which provided the city's water supply). The church itself (q.v.) may stand on a Roman cemetery site. The main road, SIDWELL STREET, was badly damaged in the war, and much of what remained was demolished in the 1960s. Among the indifferent commercial rebuilding of the Festival of Britain era, all that is memorable is VERNEY HOUSE on the s side, with its projecting circular kiosks in the tradition of Holden's pre-war London Transport buildings.*

---

*Radical plans for redevelopment of the N side and the junction with the High Street were under discussion in 1988.

4. East: Heavitree

The large parish of Heavitree, with its village centre on the main
London road, became joined to suburban Exeter during the C19,
although officially part of the city only from 1913. For the
approach, see Perambulation 3, above. At the junction of
HEAVITREE ROAD and Magdalen Road, the LIVERY DOLE
ALMSHOUSES, a medieval foundation. Simple gabled houses
rebuilt by Lord Rolle in 1849; low Perp CHAPEL of red Heavitree
stone at the E end, the E window with a spoke motif in the tracery.
On the S side of FORE STREET, SALUTARY MOUNT, a pretty
group of red brick houses in the *Nosworthy* manner, the oldest
dating from *c.* 1805, with *Coade* stone doorcases and keystones.
Opposite, HOMEFIELD PLACE, elegant neo-classical, the larger
corner house with nice gatepiers and overthrow, and an Ionic
porch. (For the other stucco development N from here see above,
Perambulation 3.) The rest of Fore Street has been indifferently
rebuilt. Up CHURCH STREET to the S, minor early C19 houses,
the best No. 19, with two shallow bows and deep projecting eaves.
Beyond was the HEAVITREE BREWERY, demolished in the
1980s, with a slightly Gothic gabled late C19 street frontage near
the churchyard, and further S, Heavitree House, embellished in
Moorish taste *c.* 1833, demolished 1949.

Off FORE STREET a few minor streets to explore: to the N REGENT
SQUARE, misleadingly named, with tight rows of artisan terraces
of 1883; to the S SIVELL PLACE, simple stucco of the 1830s, with
sunk panels over the windows as the sole decoration. Further on in
Fore Street a few late Georgian frontages, and DUCKE'S ALMS-
HOUSES, attractively rebuilt in 1853, with red brick Perp square-
headed cusped windows. Outside the village centre, HEAVITREE
PARK, 1825–9, a maltreated group of once exclusive villas with
their own drive and rustic lodge. To their S up BUTTS ROAD a
former independent chapel of the 1830s, with one domestic Gothic
window with intersecting glazing bars as a prominent feature; on
the hill above, MOWBRAY MATERNITY HOME, with a core of
1815.

S and E from here amorphous C20 suburbs enveloping a few older
sites. WONFORD, an ancient hamlet, is recalled only by a few C19
cottages in WONFORD STREET and DRYDEN ROAD; further E,
ruins of the medieval chapel of ST LOYE with C13 lancets, once
attached to a manor house; and E again, S of QUARRY LANE, the
site of the Heavitree quarries, first recorded in 1390, whose stone is
found all over Exeter.

5. North West: Pennsylvania

From the site of the East Gate at the end of the High Street, Longbrook Street leads NW, continued up the steep hill beyond by
Pennsylvania Road. The area was Exeter's most exclusive suburb
by the end of the C19 and, despite modern incursions, retains a
good cross-section of prosperous suburban housing, from late
Georgian to late Victorian. The beginnings are modest:
HAMPTON PLACE (Nos. 52–56 LONGBROOK STREET), two
storeys, and opposite a slightly grander three-storey frontage with

carriageway (rebuilt behind in 1971), in the local late Georgian idiom, red brick, ground-floor windows recessed under blind arches. Other early C19 houses follow; on the w, ELDON PLACE, built before 1830, a little more elaborate, with stucco trim. The domestic sequence is interrupted by YE LUCKIE HORSESHOE, the fanciful workshop of the successful Victorian sculptor *Harry Hems*, built in 1881 by *R. Medley Fulford*. A pair of tall Gothic arches under a gable, busily updated by Queen Anne tile-hanging; in the centre a niche with the figure of Art, above Hems's lucky horseshoe and motto. Opposite, FLATS for the elderly, 1984 by *P.D.Rowlands* for the City Council, red brick with blue bands, quite varied angles and roof-lines, in sympathy with the neighbouring Victorian terraces. Curving off to the r., QUEEN'S CRESCENT, 1898, with an attractive sequence of shaped gables; and YORK ROAD, with a more sober, still classically trimmed group of 1872.

Near the beginning of PENNSYLVANIA ROAD Nos. 8–10 (now linked as a nursing home), an enclave of *c.*1820–30; No. 8 four windows wide, end bays projecting; No. 10 a chapel-like front with giant Tuscan pilasters and pediment. In contrast, the houses of *c.*1880 in POWDERHAM CRESCENT, laid out a little further N around an oval green, proclaim their Ruskinian principles with a certain angular charm; vivid polychromy, spiky gables and porches, eaves with patterned brickwork. Only Nos. 6–11 are still in the stucco tradition. To the w, PENNSYLVANIA CRESCENT, *c.*1823, is pure Regency, one of the most delightful groups in Exeter; just five villas, the central one pedimented, all with pilasters with incised decoration. Two storeys over basements, side entrances, exquisitely delicate ironwork.

Further up Pennsylvania Road the gaps were filled in in the later C19 and after; No. 62 etc., tile-hung and gabled, are good examples of their kind. A detour to the E down UNION ROAD can take in DEVONSHIRE PLACE, a simple early terrace of 1826, and further on the LICENSED VICTUALLERS' ALMSHOUSES, 1872 by *A.H.Wills*, Tudor Gothic.

On the steeper slopes N of Union Road the ST GERMANS ESTATE, with large detached villas in their own grounds, is now mostly part of the university (q.v.). Beyond are a few early individual houses, e.g. PORTLAND LODGE, a small stuccoed villa by the road, 1824, originally with low wings, now heightened, perhaps built around an earlier core. Up a lane opposite, HOOPERN HOUSE, a larger regular neo-classical villa of five bays, built by 1831. Channelled ground floor with pedimented windows, Greek Doric porch, the stucco all an unfortunate drab grey. Edwardianized interior. Now part of the university.

On the brow of the hill, overlooking the city, PENNSYLVANIA PARK, the *pièce de résistance* of Regency Exeter, built in 1821 and apparently designed by *John Brown* of Exeter for Joseph Sparkes, a Quaker banker who lived in one of the houses, and named the terrace after William Penn's New England settlement. (The banknotes of Sparkes's Exeter Bank showed Benjamin West's painting of Penn's treaty of friendship with the Indians, used as a symbol of fair dealing.) A terrace of six very tall stucco houses with deep projecting eaves. Apart from the neat Ionic porches, almost astylar and very Soanian in the reduction of classical forms: just an incised pediment below the eaves; panelled projections on each side instead of pilasters. The chief adornment to each house is a delicate lattice balcony with roof supported on thin paired columns. The terrace, alas, is neither as intended, nor as built. Two further houses were planned; only Nos. 5–6 retain the original arrangement with the upper floors set back to create the illusion of houses almost detached, and only No. 1 has its original glazing bars. No. 3 has a sumptuous but inappropriate Italianate porch of c. 1890, with entrance hall and stair to match.

A few houses near the top of the hill: MOORVIEW LODGE, an 1824 thatched *cottage orné* with Gothick glazing; CUMBRE, well detailed free classical Edwardian, built for W. H. Reed; and RESERVOIR COTTAGE, limestone Gothic with pretty cusped gable, built for the Exeter Water Company's reservoir of 1873. NW from here, splendid panoramic views over the Duryard valley, but to the NE a dreary prospect of speculators' little red brick Monopoly-houses of the later C20. The only bright spot is towards the E end of COLLINS ROAD, where there are some more sensitively arranged groups, begun in 1977. White walls contrasted with brick and colour-washed surfaces; varied roof-heights and bracketed-out upper windows create some interesting vistas along the paths off the main roads.

6. North: St David's

Starting at the Iron Bridge (q.v., City Centre, above), Lower North Street leads up to ST DAVID'S HILL, the old, steep route N out of the city. To the W on MOUNT DINHAM, the edge of the bluff overlooking the river valley, the EXETER FREE COTTAGES, a delightful precinct of almshouses which, like St Michael's church (q.v.) and the school next to it, were paid for by the wealthy Exeter-born merchant William Gibbs. Built in 1862. Four parallel rows, the cottages in groups of four dwellings. Tudor details. The warden's house a little showier, with pretty cusped bargeboards.

Back to St David's Hill, which has a little ribbon development of soon after 1800, interspersed with later houses. The best of the former is on the W (St Wilfred's School), red brick with *Coade* stone detail in the Nosworthy manner. On the E some of Exeter's most wayward Victorian terraces, Nos. 16–20 with gross stone porches, Nos. 52–54 with coloured brickwork and crowstepped gables. Then on the W, at right angles to the road, WALNUT HOUSE, a pretty Regency villa, eclectically detailed, with one-storey colonnade and panelled pilasters but Tudor dripstones. Behind, discreetly set into the hill slope, studios for RADIO DEVON by *Marshman Warren Taylor*, 1985, coloured brick below a spreading tiled roof, jaunty lozenge-shaped windows. Near the roundabout below St David's church (q.v.), FARDEL LODGE, small, Gothic, stuccoed, on the edge of the large site of Exeter College.

From here one can turn back to the town towards the early Victorian streets laid out between St David's Hill and the new C19 route of Queen Street. Behind the church, LITTLE SILVER, a secluded enclave of terraced cottages (some replaced by a lawn), the end house possibly pre-C19, and RUSSELL TERRACE, red brick, well detailed, with round-headed doorways. s of these are grander efforts: SILVER TERRACE, facing E, stuccoed neo-classical, pediment and pilasters to the centre three houses; BYSTOCK TERRACE and QUEEN'S TERRACE of the 1840s, where classical balance is tempered by gables, dripstones, or decorative bargeboards; and RICHMOND ROAD of the 1860s, gabled, but with a severely classical ground floor of channelled stucco.

The most ambitious terrace is in QUEEN STREET itself, a proudly Italianate frontage, end and centre pediments, centre with attic as well, especially splendid since rehabilitation in 1984–5 by *Lucas, Roberts & Brown*. It faces an unworthy C20 miscellany along the E side of the street. Further s, the ROUGEMONT HOTEL, a tall, fussily detailed railway hotel opposite the Central Station, 1863, incorporating part of the city prison.

At the junction of Queen Street and New North Road, the CLOCK TOWER of 1897 by *T.H.Andrews* with top-heavy free Gothic superstructure; a little further N, bronze equestrian STATUE of Sir Redvers Buller (of Downes, near Crediton) by *Adrian Jones*, 1905. Nearby, BURY MEADOW COTTAGE, a former toll house. BURY MEADOW, opened to the public in 1846, with municipal limestone gatepiers matching those to the former Hele School (now Exeter College, q.v.) opposite, is overlooked by the pleasant paired villas of VELWELL ROAD, built by *John* and *Charles Ware* in the 1860s; others in ELMGROVE ROAD further s. Also by *Ware*, further E in NEW NORTH ROAD, CARLTON TERRACE and CLEVELAND VILLAS, 1867. N of the clock tower, beyond the college, ATTWILL'S ALMSHOUSES, 1839, two garden archways, then groups of six dwellings designed to look like semi-detached villas, volcanic stone, Tudor details, each with a marvellous array of brick chimneystacks. After this, houses in their own grounds. On the w side (with its original approach by the lodge on St David's Hill), the IMPERIAL HOTEL, its core a quiet late Georgian house of three by six bays. Ionic porch with four columns. Large curved-roof conservatory, brought from elsewhere. On the E, lodge to the Streatham estate (*see* University), on the w, further on, TADDYFORDE, an eccentric, slightly nightmarish late C19 mansion built by Kent Kingdon, a Unitarian woodcraftsman. Reddish brown stone, two canted sharply gabled bays to the w, Gothic porch to the N, and a corner tower, all hidden behind high castellated stone walls with a tall archway to the road. The theatrical effect is heightened by the contrast with the sleek modernistic flats which were built in the grounds in the 1930s.

7. West

ST THOMAS, across the Exe Bridge, was a separate medieval parish, largely rural until the C19. Several former country houses still remain on the fringes. Nearer the city there were a few early C19 aspirations towards gentility, now enveloped by the later artisan housing which developed as industry expanded along the riverside.

The immediate impact is of the C20: the complex near the roundabout consisting of leisure centre, Sainsbury's, small branch library, and the refurbished ST THOMAS STATION, grouped

round a car park and linked by covered passages. 1974–86 by
M.W.T. Architects, a cheerful and successful group, varied in scale
and texture, clearly inspired by the work of James Stirling (especially his gallery at Stuttgart). The former station of 1846 is in a
dignified stuccoed Italianate, with a frontage of round-arched
windows, and a delicate frieze between the two floors. The
LIBRARY has pale rendered walls enlivened by angular end
window and roof-lights; SAINSBURY'S is in banded brick. The
LEISURE CENTRE with the swimming pool has more startling
walls of glass with bright blue mullions, sloping and undulating on
the side to the roundabout in fit accompaniment to the swirl of C20
traffic, although an abrupt neighbour to the few sedate suburban
houses remaining along ALPHINGTON STREET. These are
HAMPDEN PLACE, a stuccoed terrace of five houses, with Greek-
key fret and first-floor pilasters with curious honeysuckle capitals,
and SYDNEY PLACE, a short red brick terrace with *Coade* keystones and lattice balconies. Another similar terrace of red brick
survives in CHURCH ROAD, amidst later artisan housing in the
small streets off COWICK STREET, the main suburban
thoroughfare.

SW of Alphington Street the INDUSTRIAL AREA near the river and
the canal, redeveloped from 1988 by *Halliday Mecham Partnership*,
incorporating older buildings, including the HAVEN BANKS
MALTHOUSE, rubble stone, much patched, part of a brewery in
existence by 1792. Nearby, former ELECTRICITY GENERAT-
ING STATION, 1903–5 by *Donald Cameron*, large and quite
showy, of dark red brick with yellow brick dressings. Three-storey
entrance bay with coat of arms flanked by recumbent female
figures. In WILLEY'S AVENUE the former WELL PARK
BREWERY, 1890, with former malthouse, a tall central red brick
block with yellow brick trim. Nearby in ISCA ROAD Exeter's first
council housing, ultra-plain terraces of forty-two dwellings, completed in 1907.

N of the line of Cowick Street and Dunsford Road indifferent C20
housing now stretches as far as the old settlement of Exwick on the
slope of the hill overlooking the water-meadows. The one development to catch the eye is in OKEHAMPTON ROAD, a whimsical
group for the Guinness Trust by *Cayley & Hutton*, 1977–85, a
flamboyant curved corner with inset entrance, stepped-out eaves,
upswept roof, blue and red brickwork, all in a frantic effort to
avoid monotony.

At EXWICK, past the little Victorian group of St Andrew's church
(q.v.) and SCHOOLS, the low stuccoed LAMB INN, and the
former POST OFFICE and BAKERY, by *Walter Cave*, given by
Anthony Gibbs, 1893, an eccentric corner composition with half-
timbered turret. To the W, up the steep EXWICK HILL, older
cottages, among them THE HERMITAGE, thatched, with
Gothick *cottage orné* trimmings.

BOWHILL, Dunsford Road. Substantial remains of a C15 manor
house which belonged to the Holland family (chapel licensed 1429)
and then to the Carews, who inherited it after 1509 and held it
until the later C17. After subsequent decline, rescued by the
Department of the Environment in 1978, stripped of later
unsightly alterations, and painstakingly restored. Originally a

courtyard house, as excavations showed. The surviving parts are
most of the E range, with the great hall; part of the W range
opposite, with the kitchen (a common Devon arrangement); and
the S range, alongside the main road, which has a ground-floor
parlour entered from the screens passage, with two service rooms
beyond, one containing a garderobe. Above were a great chamber
and two inner rooms. Set low down in the red sandstone walls of
the hall, tall square-headed Perp windows of Beer stone, each of
two lights, cusped and transomed. Between the windows on the E
side a Perp chimneystack. The entrance is through a two-centred
archway; there was until the C18 a porch with a later adjoining
stair-turret to which the small door on the l. led, and a projection
to the SE, perhaps for a stair and garderobe. The impressive hall
roof is probably late C15. According to recent investigations, it

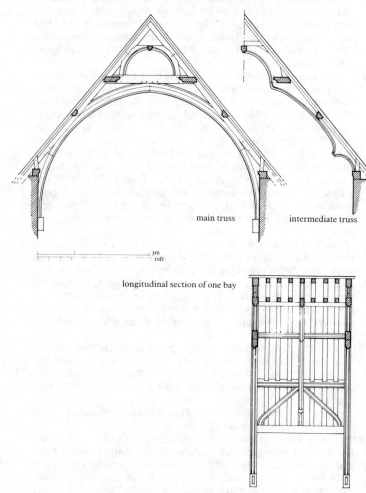

main truss   intermediate truss

longitudinal section of one bay

Exeter, Bowhill: section of roof

appears to be of the same date as the walls, although these, in a mixture of stone and cob, are curiously jerry-built in comparison with the sophistication of the roof design. The roof has jointed cruck trusses with heavily moulded arch-braces, alternating with lesser trusses. Above the level of the upper purlins, also moulded, is the distinctive coved top to be found in other late medieval roofs in the Exeter area (cf. Guildhall, Deanery, Exeter Law Library, Cadhay). The straight wind-braces with curved feet are also a local feature. s of the hall is a parlour (an early example of a parlour in the position where before one would expect service rooms) with a handsome framed ceiling, heavily moulded, probably of the same date as the hall roof. The roof of the great chamber above is a simpler version of the one in the hall. Beyond the inner rooms the rest of the s wing is separated by a cross wall from service or storage rooms beyond, later converted to a separate house. The kitchen in the w wing was originally open to the roof; good fireplace with joggled segmental stone arch. There is evidence that a pentice originally linked the kitchen to the screens passage.

COWICK BARTON, E of the N end of Cowick Lane. Possibly on the site of a small Benedictine priory founded in the C12. Stone, with three-storey central porch with four-centred archway. Stone ovolo-moulded mullioned windows. On each side, overlapping the end of the main range, a wing projects forward, probably additions of the late C16 or C17. Much altered inside. In the back wall of the hall remains of a late medieval fireplace with an overmantel dated 1657 above.

CLEEVE HOUSE, Exwick Lane. Still almost in the country. Much altered, especially at the back, but evidently a good late C17 house, seven windows wide, with a later C18 central Venetian window and Tuscan porch. Hall with black and white marble floor and bolection-moulded panelling. One room on each side, that on the l. with a robust plaster ceiling in the late *Abbot* manner: an oval in high relief with foliage, putti, etc. – even a horse. Flatter wreaths at either end. Small well staircase behind the hall, of the same date (balusters boarded over).

FRANKLYN HOUSE, Cowick Lane. Like Cleeve House, late C17: brick, dentilled cornice, plat-band, but with tuck-pointing and windows of the early C19. The best features a luscious swan-necked pediment and cartouche above the door, and one excellent ceiling. Staircase projection at the back. The stairs are on a large scale, but the balusters have been boarded over.

Near the Alphington roundabout a few early C19 villas: in COWICK LANE, THE VILLA, with a Greek Doric porch on the garden side, and the MANOR HOUSE, Georgian, with later stuccoed front (and one Rococo ceiling inside).

EXETER VILLAGES

ALPHINGTON

ST MICHAEL. All red, and quite an ambitious building. Tall w tower with diagonal buttresses, stair-turret, and limestone pinnacles. Two-storeyed N porch with niche above the entrance. Arms of the Courtenays of Powderham, who became patrons in 1403. All windows large Perp. Interior with N and S aisles, six bays, tall, thin piers of unusual section (four major shafts, four minor shafts and deep hollows separating them, i.e. two hollows to each of the four diagonals) and capitals with shield-holding angels. Extensively restored by *Hayward & Son* in 1876, when the E end was rebuilt and lengthened. Wagon roofs of the same date, with good carving by *Sendell*, including an angelic orchestra along the chancel wall-plate. Hayward also extended the nave arcades, widening the fifth bay and adding a narrower sixth, creating a powerful asymmetrical rhythm. – FONT. Norman, circular, and of high quality, with intersecting arches lower down, and above a band of scroll roundels with St Michael, the dragon, an archer, etc. – REREDOS. Wooden, of 1901. Elaborate canopy-work, free-standing figures and reliefs. Also of 1901, painted angels flanking the E window. – SCREENS. Rood screen originally with fan-vaulted coving. Tracery of usual (type A) design. Painted wainscot panels with much original colour, better than average, of *c.* 1520 according to Croft-Murray, showing some awareness of Netherlandish painting; by the same master who worked at Manaton and Cheriton Bishop. – Parclose screen with pierced spandrels and usual tracery; much restored. – W screen of 1875, made up from panels of 1625, with stumpy blank arcades, taken from a W gallery. – TILES. Two C19 types: E end floor tiles 1876–8, made by *Godwin*; S aisle window recesses with attractive memorial tiles by *Doulton*, 1898–1919. – STAINED GLASS by *Beer & Driffield*, 1878.

OLD RECTORY. The older part behind, with a good broad early C17 door, and a single-rib plaster ceiling to the room on the r., dated 1629. At r. angles a polite stuccoed wing with five-window front said to date from the time of the Rev. W. Ellicombe, 1780.

SCHOOL. 1876 by *J. W. Rowell* for the School Board. Attractive village group with separate master's house, slightly Gothic, with lancets.

Near the turning to Alphington from the main road, a little early C19 cluster: No. 1 CHURCH ROAD, with Ionic porch and bracketed eaves, and No. 2, with pretty Gothick glazing. Behind, in FAIR-FAX GARDENS, two low monopitch-roofed red brick houses by *Marshman Warren Taylor*, 1982, discreetly hiding behind curving garden walls.

See also Peamore House.

COUNTESS WEAR

The village is named after the Countess of Devon who constructed a weir across the Exe here in 1286. The BRIDGE dates from 1770. Near the river a double LIMEKILN set against a bank. The old village lies between the river and Topsham Road, around St Luke's church. Unpretentious grey limestone former SCHOOL near the church. No. 53 Countess Wear Road appears to be a substantial late C18 house revamped *c.* 1900. Large C17 doorway reset in a side porch; fan-shaped lunette with imitation studded rustication.

ST LUKE. 1837–8 by *Henry Lloyd* of Exeter. Appealingly pre-ecclesiological. Lancet style; plain grey limestone. Chancel 1895 by *E. H. Harbottle*, revved up by Bath stone dressings. – STAINED GLASS. E window *c.* 1895. – In the nave figures under elaborate canopies in a late Kempe manner. By *Wippells*: St Matthew, St Mark, Melchisedech *c.* 1911, St Luke 1937, St John 1945.

COUNTESS WEAR ESTATE, beyond the roundabout. Council housing of 1950–8, the stretch along the main road probably by *L. de Soissons*, a showpiece in the elegantly minimal tradition of Voysey.

WEAR HOUSE (Exeter Golf Club), N off Topsham Road. Plain late Georgian of *c.* 1804. Colonnade on the garden side; large mid C19 porte-cochère.

IDE

ST IDA. To a usual Perp red sandstone tower with stair-turret was added in 1834 by *Henry Hooper* a typical Devon church of that date (cf. Stoke Canon), i.e. castellated and looking from the outside as if it had aisles with lean-to roofs, but in fact aisleless. – BOX PEWS partly preserved. – Good TOMBS in the churchyard.

THE COLLEGE, at the lower end of Fore Street, by the stream. A much altered late medieval house, now cottages.

DRAKE'S FARM. C17 plasterwork in the parlour.

PINHOE

The church is a mile N of the village, very close to the RECTORY, a Queen Anne brick house with a medieval fragment at the back. Adjoining is a single-storey building with a cluster of large chimneystacks, possibly a former church house.

ST MICHAEL. W tower with type B buttresses and stair-turret. Nave and N aisle. The arcade of piers of B standard section, the capitals standard, individual fleurons in the arch voussoirs (cf. Broadclyst). Restored in 1879–80, the chancel by *Christian*, the rest by *Fulford*. Chancel and S porch were rebuilt, incorporating much old masonry. The fanciful wooden chancel arch is probably *Fulford*'s. – FONT. Plain Norman, with just two bands of elementary decoration. – PULPIT. Wood, late Perp, not specially ornate. – SCREEN. A rich specimen of A type, with four strips of scrollwork in the cornice. Like the pulpit, carefully restored by *Hems* in 1879–80. – POOR BOX with the small figure of a man (a beadle?) on it; Queen Anne costume. – STAINED GLASS. Pattern glass by *Drake*, 1880. – W window 1902, also by *Drake*.

PINBROOK, Beacon Heath. Dated 1679. An early example of a large brick merchant's house. Plain but stately: three storeys divided by plat-bands; seven bays of cross-windows; rear end wings with staircases. Built by Sir John Elwill, later sheriff of Devon. Former brick STABLES behind.

TOPSHAM

See main gazetteer in the normal alphabetical sequence (p. 820).

Exminster is a large village, now a SW dormitory for Exeter.

ST MARTIN. The exceptional thing about this all-red church is its
SE chapel, which received in 1633 a plastered wagon roof with
square and rectangular panels and in them lozenges with figures in
plaster of the apostles and evangelists. The work was due to a
member of the Tothill family of Peamore House. W tower of usual
type, with diagonal buttresses and stair-turret. The interior also
usual (for this part of Devon), with octagonal red sandstone piers
with moulded capitals and double-chamfered arches. Restoration
1841: from this time the thinly detailed S porch and the more
confident REREDOS. – FONT. Late C18, white marble. – PULPIT.
Good-quality work of c. 1700, with panels and some fruit and leaf
carving. – ALTAR RAILS. C17. – SCREENS. Rood screen with fan
coving and the usual tracery of type A. The cornice has three
bands of scroll, leaf, etc., decoration. – Parclose screen simple, but
with the same type of tracery. – (STAINED GLASS. Late window
by *Morris & Co.*, 1923; musical angels.) – MONUMENTS. In the
SE chapel a rather touching small alabaster wall-monument to
commemorate Mrs Grace Tothill who died in her eighteenth year
in 1623. Her reclining figure, propped on an elbow, appears in the
predella. – In the chancel the much more pretentious monument to
Otto Petre and his family, 1608, all white limestone, with kneeling
figures facing each other and columns and achievements. –
Another good big wall-monument to Philippa Cooke †1690, black
and gold. – (In the churchyard the elaborate High Victorian tomb-
chest of the Burrington family, debased classical.)

SPURFIELD. 1887–9 by *J. L. Pearson* for the Rev. S. Willoughby
Lawley. Rather prim Old English. Mullioned windows, tile-
hanging, and a half-timbered gable.

PRIEST HOUSE. Two two-centred archways.

CRAPLAKE FARM. A good group. Farmhouse with early C19 front.
Substantial C19 farm buildings, three ranges round a yard, the
barn dated 1845; coursed stone with granite dressings.

EXEVALE HOSPITAL. Set in vast grounds, and approached past
formal LODGES by a ceremonial avenue: the Victorian institution
at its most imposing. 1842–5 by *Charles Fowler*, built as the Devon
County Pauper Lunatic Asylum. Separate sanatorium 1877, further extensions 1906. The original buildings, remarkably complete, are an interesting example of Fowler's practical approach to
the asylum design of the time, combining a compact plan and ease
of supervision with reasonably spaced living quarters. Tall central
block with semicircular service range behind, from which six lower
wings radiate. Between them were exercise yards and gardens,
enclosed by perimeter walls with lodges (one NW lodge remains).
Plainly detailed, the main buildings of red brick with granite dressings, windows within round-headed arches. Floors and roof of
fireproof construction (laminated tiles on cast-iron bearers). Cruciform Gothic CHAPEL by *Joseph Neale*, 1877, red stone with Bath
dressings, lancet windows, bellcote over the crossing. Contemporary furnishings.

STATION. 1848 by *Brunel* for the South Devon Railway, and characteristic of his style: two-storey, Italianate, stuccoed, the twin gables formed by the double roof containing Venetian windows, moulded details to door and window openings. The large chimneys lack the solidity of smaller Brunel stations.

MILBURY BARTON. Transformed by *John Taylor* of *M.W.T.* from a neo-Georgian house into a 'modern version of the traditional Devon farmhouse', 1984.

EXMOUTH

Leland called Exmouth 'a fisher townlet'; its harbour lies just within the estuary, sheltered by Exmouth Point. By the mid C18 the excellent beaches had become a popular place for sea bathing, and the town was beginning to attract as residents 'some persons of condition', as Dr Richard Pococke noted in 1750. The first houses overlooking the sea (rather than the estuary) were begun in 1792; other modest new streets followed in the early C19. The most radical changes, from the 1860s, under the aegis of the Hon. Mark Rolle, the chief landowner, resulted in little of architectural consequence. The town is now buried in sprawling C20 suburbs which stretch as far as the older villages of Withycombe Raleigh and Littleham (qq.v.), in whose parishes the town remained until the later C19.

HOLY TRINITY, Rolle Road. 1905–7 by *G.H.Fellowes Prynne*, a total remodelling of a chapel of 1824 by *John Lethbridge* to which a chancel had been added in 1856 at the expense of Lady Rolle. A tall, proud building of grey limestone with Bath stone dressings. W tower of Somerset type; buttresses to both aisles and clerestory linked by shallow arches. Flamboyant tracery throughout. Tall arcades on clustered piers. E window high up above a very large carved stone REREDOS with relief of the Ascension. – Low CHANCEL SCREEN with slightly Art-Nouveau brass finials on top. – Apsed N chapel with MEMORIAL to Mark Rolle †1907.

ALL SAINTS, Exeter Road. 1896–7. Limestone with Bath stone dressings. Large, with apsed W baptistery and apsed SE Lady Chapel behind which rises the tower added in 1907, with rounded corner turret. – STAINED GLASS. Three windows in Lady Chapel and baptistery by *Veronica Whall*, 1926 (PC).

ST ANNE (R.C.), Brixington Lane. 1968 by *Keith Symmons*. Roof-lit and almost windowless. Semicircular seating round the altar.

HOLY GHOST (R.C.), Raddenstile Lane. 1915 by *Scoles & Raymond*. – STAINED GLASS. 1915 by *Scoles*.

GLENORCHY U.R. CHURCH, Exeter Road. Grey limestone, wooden octagonal turret, by *Habershon & Pite*, 1866.

FREE CHURCH OF ENGLAND, North Street. Classical, with triple-arched two-storey centrepiece.

METHODIST CHURCH, Tower Street. 1897. Gabled stone front flanked by two towers with spires and pinnacles (cf. Wesleyan Chapel, Ilfracombe, 1893).

Starting from the long seafront, the centerpiece is the JUBILEE CLOCK TOWER on the ESPLANADE, quite small, with pointed pyramid roof. Behind, the IMPERIAL HOTEL, a shadow of its former self since a fire in the 1970s. Plain, stuccoed; the centre is the l. end of the original building by *J.W.& E.M.Barry* of 1868. In the

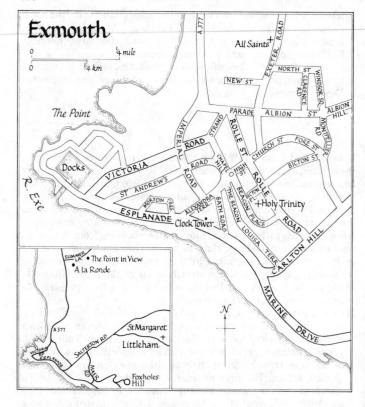

Exmouth

0   ¼ mile
0   ¼ km

All Saints

The Point

Docks

R. Exe

ESPLANADE

VICTORIA ROAD

IMPERIAL ROAD

ST ANDREW'S ROAD

MORTON CRES.

Clock Tower

ALEXANDRA TERR.

BATH ROAD

CHAPEL HILL

STRAND

ROLLE ST

PARADE

ALBION ST

NEW ST

EXETER ROAD

NORTH ST

CLARENCE RD

WINDSOR SQ

ALBION HILL

MONTPELIER RD

CHURCH ST

FORE ST

BICTON ST

HIGH ST

ROLLE ROAD

THE BEACON

BICTON PLACE

Holy Trinity

LOUISA TERR.

CARLTON HILL

MARINE DRIVE

N

SUMMER LA.

● The Point in View
● A la Ronde

A 377

St Margaret
Littleham

SALTERTON RD

VICTORIA RD

ESPLANADE

MAER RD

Foxholes Hill

grounds to the w, crudely converted to a house, the survivor of a pair of garden temples belonging to the pleasure gardens created *c*. 1824 on the land reclaimed from the sea. T-shaped, E portico with six Doric columns, porch on the w. After the building of *Smeaton*'s sea wall (1841–2) there was further development: ALEXANDRA TERRACE, running inland, and MORTON CRESCENT, a grand Italianate composition of the 1870s, originally more or less symmetrical, the centre with French mansard roof flanked by modillioned gables. On the point to the SW, the DOCKS, a financially unsuccessful venture of 1867, reconstructed in 1882. The LIFEBOAT STATION, of granite, with stepped gable, dates from 1903.

The older parts of Exmouth, as so often in Devon seaside towns, are further inland. Climbing up the wooded slopes behind the hotel one arrives at THE BEACON, a sea-view terrace, the earliest houses built from 1792 onwards. Not a unified group, just a pleasant mixture of red brick and stucco, late Georgian pedimented doorcases, porches with sturdy Ionic columns. Some original lamp standards of *c*. 1800, square tapered shafts with Greek-key pattern. LOUISA TERRACE of *c*. 1824 continues the line to the SE, with houses a little more spread out. In the neighbourhood of Holy Trinity more of the earlier C19, especially BICTON PLACE N of the church, with doorcases with Doric pilasters and steep open pediments above fanlights, and, in its simplest form, in the rather mutilated BICTON STREET. Respectable later C19 development continues up CARLTON HILL and along ROLLE ROAD, all the result of activity of the Rolle estate.

The centre of Exmouth is a disappointment. C19 rebuilding and C20 road engineering have left it with little character. As at Torquay (the town's chief rival as a seaside resort), the C19 commercial centre did not attract buildings on a grand scale. Along the main route continuing NE from Alexandra Terrace (High Street – Church Street – Fore Street) all that need be singled out is the COUNCIL OFFICES (corner of Chapel Hill), clumsy Italianate, much extended. W of this THOMAS TUCKER, at the corner of St Andrew's Road, an early C19 house with an enjoyable mid Victorian draper's front with iron columns and heads in the spandrels. Nearby, THE STRAND, the former quayside, as the name suggests, punctuated by a large bank at each end. The lawn and trees in the centre replaced the old market house in 1871. In PARADE to the N No. 2, early C18, with later stuccoed front with pilasters. W of Parade IMPERIAL ROAD with MANCHESTER HOUSE, late Georgian (see the back to Chapel Street), used from 1868 as a dispensary and much altered and enlarged as the Rolle estate office in 1899 by W. Palmer. Pedimented wooden doorcase.

The old EXETER ROAD (bypassed by the disruptive inner relief road further E) runs N from Parade. To its W, very simple early C19 artisan terraces built on reclaimed land: NEW STREET, the earliest, is especially complete. The LIBRARY in Exeter Road is the former Board School of 1877 by H. Lovegrove, picturesque, red brick, with patterned tiled roof, Gothic windows with surrounds of red and black brick, and a wooden belfry. The COUNTY PRIMARY SCHOOL opposite is a little plainer; tiled roof with half-hipped gables.

E of Exeter Road NORTH STREET climbs uphill, with some older houses including OLD MANOR HOUSE, seven bays with Georgian sashes, rendered, MANOR COTTAGE (No. 15), with Georgian doorcase, and its neighbour, with thatched roof and lower walls of stone. Further on and in the neighbouring streets minor terraces of the early C19, e.g. in George Street and Henrietta Street. CLARENCE ROAD has a more consciously elegant group, each house only of two bays, but with wooden porches with clustered columns, doorcases with reeded columns, and deep bracketed eaves. The alternative debased Tudor style also appears, in groups of tall gabled houses in North Street and in WINDSOR (formerly Brunswick) SQUARE.

S of this area ALBION STREET, running E from Parade. Its upper end has the most ambitious early C19 urban development, three-storey terraces, originally red brick, now mostly rendered. Doorcases with carved brackets on flat Ionic pilasters. In MONTPELLIER ROAD to the S, Nos. 14–22, an unusual villa design, the entrances in gabled projections, Tudor-arched doorways, no windows above. Further S around Church Street energetic C19 slum clearance is evident from the Rolle estate model cottages (some of the later ones by *Charles Bone*), for example the group in UPPER CHURCH STREET, red brick, with recessed entrance bays, generously scaled. In ROLLE STREET (cut through the old streets in 1866) the CHURCH

INSTITUTE and MEN'S CLUB, 1887 by *Medley Fulford*, with prominent star-shaped chimneys, quite picturesque.

By far the most interesting houses are two on the fringes of the town.

172 At the E end, overlooking the sea from Foxholes Hill, THE BARN (now a hotel), designed in 1896 for Major Weatherall by *E.S.Prior*, a brilliant exercise in Arts and Crafts design by a brilliant pupil of Norman Shaw, original equally as an architect and a scholar. An early example of the butterfly plan that became popular around the turn of the century. Centre with far-overhanging gables to N and S, and wings coming out diagonally from this centre so that the entrance as well as the garden side take comfortably embracing attitudes. The stonework highly odd, irregularly interspersed with large local red pebbles rounded by the sea, the chimneys of cyclopic thickness and roundness, the granite columns supporting the centre veranda on the garden side also deliberately shapeless. Prior welded these local materials and details into a most satisfactory whole. The roof, originally thatched, was rebuilt in slate after the house was gutted by fire in 1905. The interior has been totally remodelled. The six-sided entrance hall at first had a gallery leading to the bedrooms in the wings.

138 A LA RONDE, Summer Lane, W of the Exeter Road. A wholly delightful and unique creation, a sixteen-sided *cottage orné* built in 1798 by Miss *Jane Parminter* and her cousin *Mary Parminter*. Its plan was inspired by San Vitale at Ravenna, which they visited on their ten-year Grand Tour. Exterior of stone; lozenge-shaped windows at the angles. The rooms radiate from a top-lit central hall whose lantern rises above the steep roof, now tiled, but originally thatched. Below the lantern a gallery, reached by the most extraordinary feature in the house: a narrow shell-lined, grotto-like staircase. The gallery itself is decorated with the Parminters' designs in shells and feathers, a far cry from Byzantine mosaics, but very charming. (Unfortunately badly restored.) Feather-work decoration also in the drawing room, and elsewhere much skilful artwork in sand, seaweeds, shells, paper, etc.

POINT IN VIEW, further up the hill, is a diminutive Congregational Chapel built by the Parminters in 1811. Jane Parminter was buried there the same year. The 'point' of the name was the conversion of the Jews: in practice, it is a tiny chapel surrounded by four equally tiny one-storey almshouses with triangular-headed windows, and a former schoolroom, all stuccoed. The chapel is lit by triangular roof-lights in a pyramidal lantern. Nearby the former MANSE, added in 1829, with lattice glazing and a central diamond window still in the same happily eccentric spirit.

BYSTOCK. Edwardian neo-Baroque on a generous scale. Brick, with balustraded parapet. Doorway with Ionic columns. Hall with plasterwork in late C17 style.

KNAPPE CROSS, Brixington Lane. A substantial neo-Tudor brick mansion, gabled and with mullioned windows, in its own grounds. Built in 1908 for Dr S. Hoyle.

See also Withycombe Raleigh.

FARRINGDON   *0090*

ST PETROCK. Rebuilt in 1870–1 by *William White*, re-using some old masonry. W tower with older lower stage, and an un-Devonian broach-spire by White. White's personality is apparent also in the late C13 details, the boldly louvred belfry, and the wilfully asymmetric SW chimney to the nave. Interior faced with red brick, stencilled. N arcade of purple trap with Ham Hill shafts. Rerearches to all the windows. Simple fittings. – Recut Norman FONT, with geometric and scroll decoration (cf. St Mary Steps, Exeter).

FARRINGDON HOUSE. S front with an C18 core of 2–3–2 bays, two and a half storeys, with hipped roof and centre pediment. Much altered in 1897–1900 for the Johnson family by *E. H. Harbottle*, who added the gables, half-timbering, towers, casement windows, etc. C20 school additions.

UPHAM. Unassuming early C17 cob farmhouse with well preserved original joinery, and on the first floor a plaster overmantel with strapwork. Contemporary cob BARN.

DENBOW. Brick farmhouse of three irregular bays, *c.* 1700; modillioned cornice, hipped roof, diagonal chimneyshafts. The kitchen wing is earlier.

FARWAY   *1090*

ST MICHAEL. Charmingly tucked away. Three short circular Norman piers to the N aisle, with circular scalloped capitals. C13 double-chamfered arches, the E respond without a capital. At the W end a half-arch, cut into by the later tower. Chancel with single-chamfered S door and late C13 S window. Three-light C14 E window with ogee reticulation. All tracery much renewed in *C. F. Edwards*'s restoration of 1874–6, when the N aisle was rebuilt with vigorously spiky windows, and the N chapel added at the expense of Louisa Prideaux. Its wagon roof is prettily painted in the style of *c.* 1850. Arches to chapel and chancel embellished with marble columns. Unbuttressed Perp W tower of two stages only, with battlements and gargoyles. Stair-turret on the S side. Belfry windows (an extra one on the S side) with pierced stone filling. – Square FONT, with a little marble inlay, PULPIT, of rustic woodwork, and stone REREDOS, all by *Edwards*, 1874. – STAINED GLASS (E and W windows) all of 1876 by *F. Drake*. – COMMUNION TABLE. Elizabethan, used as an altar. – BUST to Humphrey Hutchins, 1628, in an oval niche in the N wall of the N aisle, to commemorate his rebuilding of this part of the church (only the forms of his N aisle E window survive); also an inscription to Richard Bucknoll † 1632: 'His zealous care was th' efficient cause/To build this fabrick for the use of Godes lawes ...' – MONUMENTS. Chiefly to the Prideaux of Netherton Hall (q.v.). Sir Edmund Prideaux † 1628. Recumbent figure in lawyer's robes under an arch, his son(?) reclining below on a projecting plinth. Pilasters with ribbonwork; simple strapwork. – Sir Peter Prideaux † 1705. Marble tablet with crude putto heads. – Sir John Wilmot Prideaux † 1826. Signed by *S. Manning Sen.* – Sir Edmund Saunderson Prideaux † 1875. Old-fashioned tablet by *G. G. Adams*, with two mourning figures. – In the chancel, two handsome restrained neo-classical tablets, with urns against a marble ground, to the Rev. Richard Blake †1788 and his relation Hannah Atkinson †1796.

BOYCOMBE. An attractive early to mid C16 stone rubble house, of the usual three-room-and-cross-passage plan, but uncommonly well appointed. The manor was owned by the Courtenays until the attainder of Lord Devon in 1538, then acquired by the Willoughbys. Front with two big stacks and three- and four-light windows with hollow-chamfered mullions and arched lights, the ground-floor windows with dripstones. Inside, both hall and parlour have carved wooden window lintels (in the parlour the decoration extends over the soffit as well) and ceilings with heavily moulded beams, arranged in the hall in a pattern of sixteen squares. At the back a large projection for a stair, unusually combined with a twin garderobe. Traces of a separate newel to the chamber over the parlour, which has its own fireplace. The mullioned window in the gable wall of this room was opened up in the 1920s. In the parlour, wall painting in a frame, with a sheep-shearing scene and a rustic verse, dated 1744.

POLTIMORE. An exceptionally appealing large C15–17 farmhouse with a complex history. Limestone rubble and cob walls under thatch, a long main range, two W cross-wings, and four staircases. The medieval house occupied the lower W end of the main range. It had an open hall and lower-end solar(?) divided by a cross-passage. Roof on jointed cruck trusses including a partially smoke-blackened arched-braced truss. Arch of a former window, in ashlar stonework, in the W gable end. During the substantial late C16 remodelling a chamber was created over the hall with a richly decorated fireplace in Beer stone, dated 1583, with initials including TH for Thomas Haydon. Later in the C17 a large fireplace with oven was added to the W gable-end, and the house was extended, at the upper end by another room, still with jointed cruck roof trusses, at the lower end by a partially timber-framed cross-wing. Excellent C16 and C17 features throughout, including three stud-and-panel screens and many ovolo-moulded mullioned windows, one with a king mullion. The second W cross-wing is C19. Large farmyard with specialist buildings, mostly C18 and C19 but including an earlier jointed cruck-roofed stable and ash house.

(Good lesser farmhouses are HORNSHAYNE, of c.1700 and c.1900, on three sides of a courtyard, and WOODBRIDGE, C16, with good joinery, and a plan with central service room.)

ROUND BARROW CEMETERY, between Broad Down and Gittisham Hill. One of the most extensive and impressive in Devon, classically sited along a long, commanding ridge. In contrast to most of those further W, the barrows here vary in structure in the same way as Wessex barrows do, and those that have been excavated have yielded grave goods of Wessex type, including fine shale cups now in Exeter Museum. FARWAY CASTLE has tentatively been interpreted as a ceremonial earthwork enclosure of the same date; it may, however, be later.

See also Netherton Hall.

FENITON

ST ANDREW. Low unbuttressed W tower with stair-turret. S aisle
added with large Perp windows. On an angle buttress a prominent
mass dial. Arcade with B type piers and standard capitals. The
arms on the capitals are Malherbe and Ferrers. Restored in 1877
by *R. M. Fulford*, who added the two-way credence table in the S
wall, readjusted the roof levels, and converted the S chapel into a
memorial chapel for Bishop Patteson, the Pacific Islands missionary martyr who died in 1871. On the E wall large brass inscription
to his father, Sir John Patteson, †1861. – SCREEN. Of A type, the
S part with coving to the E and W and a broad, densely decorated
cornice. – PARCLOSE SCREEN similar, though the tracery is not
quite identical. Both screens restored in 1877 by *Hems*. – BENCH
ENDS. A few with two tiers of tracery. – MONUMENT. 'Gisant',
i.e. corpse, in a low N recess, the shroud pulled away. Well carved
and well preserved (cf. Exeter Cathedral). The date must be
c. 1500.

FENITON COURT, close to the church. The seat of the Pattesons in
the C19. A plain late Georgian house with older parts incorporated.
Attractive S front with one-storey loggia with paired columns
between full-height canted bays.

FILLEIGH

ST PAUL. Rebuilt in 1732 by the Fortescues of Castle Hill (q.v.) as
an eyecatcher, but in its present form a curious effort in neo-
Norman, the result of a remodelling of 1876–7 by *Clark* of Newmarket.* The 1732 church was roughly cruciform, with a S transeptal porch, and a N transept with a turret with niches in its E face
which partly survives. Re-used medieval material in the two-stage
W tower and adjoining S wall. Clark added the S aisle and apsed
chancel. The interior is dominated by Fortescue memorial furnishings, the best of them to Countess Georgina, wife of the third Earl,
†1866. They include the coloured marble FONT, with realistic
foliage carving, and the good STAINED GLASS of the apse. The
chancel decoration, with blue and green painted panels with vine
scroll simulating mosaic, and the REREDOS date from after 1887
and 1906. Further elaborate foliage painting on the timbers of the
wagon roofs (the chancel roof painted by *Lady Susan Fortescue*
c. 1880). – Two small late C16 BRASSES, one to Richard Fortescue
†1570.

SCHOOL AND SCHOOLHOUSE. 1859–64 by *Butterfield*, a well composed group with bold chimneys and hipped dormers.

BREMRIDGE. A fragment of a larger house. Rubble stone, stone-
mullioned windows. Entrance arch dated 1624.

WEST CLATWORTHY. The farmhouse still has a section of a good
medieval roof with raised cruck truss (unusually, scarf-jointed near
the apex) and saddle ridge and evidence for an original smoke
louvre in the open hall.

See also Castle Hill.

* Although *Gilbert Scott* reported on the best means of restoring or rebuilding in
1864.

FLETE
Holbeton

157 A huge, romantically craggy and castellated mansion of rough grey rubble and granite, in its present form the creation of *Norman Shaw* for Henry Bingham Mildmay of Baring's Bank, 1878–85. The Flete estate was the ancestral home of Mildmay's wife, Georgiana Bulteel, until sold in 1863 by her brother to an Australian sheep-farmer. Mildmay bought it in 1876. Shaw must have been familiar to him through his work for C. L. Norman, another Baring partner. In typical Devonian fashion, the architect was not given a free hand, but had to rebuild piecemeal, incorporating parts of the earlier house. As a result the plan is not characteristic of Shaw or of the Victorian era, for the old courtyard layout survives, together with the shell of the Tudor main range with its five gables facing w – diminutive compared to the grand N entrance front. The Tudor house had been built by the Heles. The Bulteels inherited the estate in 1706 and undertook successive modernizations: two stuccoed pedimented fronts by the later C18, which have entirely disappeared, and a castellated Gothic remodelling of c. 1835 by *John Crocker Bulteel*, to his own designs.

The E and N ranges, although heightened and dramatized, follow the lines of this building. Shaw's lofty entrance tower, the dominant feature of the whole house, incorporates the earlier two-storey porte-cochère with its Gothic niches on either side housing two lively sculptures of the Falconer and the Huntsman (by *C. Raymond Smith*, 1842). Shaw simply closed up the archways, embellished the front with a two-storey oriel, and continued the tower upwards for a further two storeys to end in tall, irregular, jutting corner turrets. The rest of the entrance front received a third floor from which the crenellations rise sheer and dour, without any restraining horizontal cornice – a device Lutyens adopted later at Castle Drogo. To the r. is a long, lower range, also castellated, originally a riding school, rebuilt by Shaw as a kitchen wing with long gallery above. It was reconstructed, after partial demolition in the 1950s, when the house was converted into thirty-seven apartments for Mutual Households in 1961–8 by *Burn, Smith & Partners*.

The conversion left most of Shaw's main reception rooms intact, apart from the loss of the long gallery. They are generous in scale and enriched with much exuberant and intricate Jacobean-inspired ornament. In the large entrance hall the ample stairs around a double well take up only a quarter of the space. They are a typical Shavian spatial tour-de-force, with plenty of balustered landings at different levels to provide views of arriving guests. To the l. the library, with a large granite fireplace with quattrocento-style reliefs, original bookshelves, and Jacobean ceiling. In the bay-window two pairs of lights by *Morris & Co.*: four female figures in white drapery. To the r. the former dining room, with a large re-used late medieval fireplace. Arms and quatrefoils on the lintel; in front of it two quatrefoil columns, also apparently re-used medieval pieces. Beside the fireplace a broad, rounded bow-window (taken over from the earlier house) overlooking the cobbled forecourt of the Tudor house. The old hall of this house, lengthened through what must have been the solar wing, became the Victorian billiard room (now dining room). An ingenious double stair copes with the change of level from the entrance hall. The projecting SW wing (now altered) became a music room with organ (now removed) and a W gallery which opened also to the billiard room. A bow-window echoes the taller one of the dining room across the courtyard. In the S-facing range behind is the drawing room, with another bow-window, a very sumptuous Jacobean plasterwork ceiling, and an alabaster fireplace.

STABLES. Now converted to outbuildings.

LODGE. 1887 by *J.D.Sedding*, who restored Ermington and Holbeton churches (qq.v.) for the Mildmays. Picturesque composition, with a little bay-window between a timber porch and a kind of outdoor ingle-nook.

BULL AND BEAR LODGE. *See* Membland.

The GARDENS, admirably rescued by Mutual Households residents, include a water garden by *Russell Page* of 1925.

FOLLATON HOUSE
1 m. W of Totnes

7060

Now council offices, approached through an unsightly mess of car parks and temporary huts. A stately nine-bay late Georgian front of two storeys and attic, with a giant Ionic four-column portico and end pilasters. Built by *G.S.Repton* c.1826–7 for the Cary family, and illustrated in Ackermann's *Views of Seats* in 1830. Older rubble-built parts at the back. On the r. a long room with a C19 plaster ceiling in C17 style.

FOWELSCOMBE
1 m. SE of Ugborough

6050

A ruin standing alone in a field, overgrown by trees and nettles: the large mansion of the Fowels, sold by their descendants in 1759 and deserted about the middle of the C19. The building consisted of a tower to which a Tudor hall and porch were added. The hall fireplace was dated 1537. About 1800 this l. portion was supplemented by a castellated one on the r. to achieve pleasing balance.

FREMINGTON
5030

ST PAUL. Restored and largely rebuilt by *Sir G.G.Scott* in 1867. Early medieval N tower in the same position, close to the E end, as at Barnstaple and Pilton. Lancet windows on the N side; low pointed blocked arch on the W. – PULPIT. C15, stone, much restored, but with traces of colour. – Fragment of medieval WALL PAINTING on the S wall. – Elizabethan COMMUNION TABLE. – Minor WALL MONUMENTS.

FREMINGTON HOUSE. Remodelled c.1881 for the Yeo family by

Ernest Newton, whose unexecuted design for an elaborate terracotta w entrance front was published in *Building News* in 1882.
The s front facing the road is in quite a festive early-Georgian-
revival: red brick with stone trim, Baroque doorcase, central
parapet balustraded, with urns. This is a recasing of a genuine c18
wing standing on brick-vaulted cellars which had been added to an
older house (see the rubble walling at the N end). The E front has a
two-storey bow-window, probably early c19, but now ornamented
with later c19 terracotta. c19 dining room, service rooms beyond,
and stables around a courtyard. Inside, the s-facing rooms have
late c19 enriched panelling (cornices perhaps older); in the loftier
bow-fronted room some neo-Grecian ornament. Elsewhere, a jumble of re-used woodwork; upstairs, a c17 overmantel with large
figures in the room above the hall; two foreign c16 carved panels
with the Nativity and the Bathing of the Infant Jesus; and a fireplace with putti heads and acanthus, dated 1705. N of the house a
square brick GAZEBO with steep slated roof.

UNITED REFORMED CHAPEL. Above the main road through
Bickington village, behind a small graveyard. Built by the Congregationalists in 1835 as a result of mission preaching. Tall, with
rendered three-bay front. Continuous hoodmould carried round
the arched windows and arched door. Hipped roof. Interior much
altered. Semicircular lobby with curved doors.

NEWTON TRACEY GOSPEL HALL, Lower Loveacott. 1827. Tall,
rubble, gabled, with porch. Round-headed windows and a large
roundel in the gable. Low rubble Sunday School at the side. Both
behind a small railed yard.

(HIGHER ROOKABEARE. c17 strapwork overmantel with arms and
initials GSP, WP. Undistinguished painted brick exterior.)

(ELLERSLIE TOWER. Octagonal battlemented lookout tower;
pointed windows.)

At YELLAND, in the inter-tidal zone of the Taw estuary, a DOUBLE
STONE ROW can still be seen at low water. It probably dates from
the Late Neolithic or Early Bronze Age, when it would have stood
on dry land. Extensive flint scatters nearby point to activity in the
area from the Mesolithic period onwards.

4010

FRITHELSTOCK

PRIORY. An Augustinian priory was founded here by Robert
Beauchamp c.1229, colonized from Hartland Abbey. The church
– the only monastic church in the county of which substantial ruins
remain – must have been built soon after the foundation. It was
89ft long and 23½ft wide within its walls. The w front stands high
enough to show its three noble lancet windows, the centre one with
a trefoil head. The N and s walls had lancets high up, still clearly
visible on the N side. On the s side immediately in line with the w
front rose a tower, of which foundations and a blocked N arch
survive. The Lady Chapel, behind the E wall of the chancel and
connected with it only by two doors, was rectangular and as wide
as nave and chancel. The cloister was presumably N of the church,
as earthworks in the adjoining field indicate. The present Church
Farm to their w represents a post-Reformation replanning of the

former prior's dwelling, L-shaped, with square dripstones to the windows, and a C19 Gothic arched porch.

ST MARY AND ST GREGORY. The parish church lies so close that its E end touched the S tower of the priory church. Tall, tapering W tower with diagonal buttresses only at the foot, a N stair-turret, and C18 pinnacles. S aisle of three bays with quite sumptuous arcade piers of B type with elaborately canopied niches for images (the first facing NW, the second SW, the third again NW) and richly carved standard Devon leaf capitals. The chancel E window is unusually elaborate, early C14 in the Exeter Cathedral style, three lights, cusped heads, with a top circle containing three large cusped and three small uncusped spherical triangles. Two-bay S chapel with B type piers with concave capitals only to the shafts. The Dec E window (replacing a Perp one) dates from the restoration of 1885–6 by *Samuel Hooper* of Hatherleigh. Ceiled wagon roofs throughout. S porch castellated, with handsome openwork quatrefoil frieze. – FONT. On a circular Norman shaft with vertical zigzag decoration. – PULPIT. Jacobean. – BENCH ENDS. Some with profile heads, and (which is rarer) BENCH FRONTS with tracery. – TOWER SCREEN. Early C19, with painted frieze and simple Gothic doors. – TILES of Barnstaple type, in nave and aisle. – ROYAL ARMS. Plaster, 1677, very large and bold, under a pediment. Signed by *John Abbot* (1640–1727), the Devon plasterer who worked at the Custom House, Exeter.

FURSDON
Cadbury

9000

A pleasant, unassuming house of Georgian appearance, its older core concealed by successive modernizations by the Fursdons, who have been here since the C13. Two storeys with parapet, rendered S front with a centre of five bays and projecting two-bay wings, all with Georgian sashes (the upper ones thicker and older than those of the ground floor). Across the centre a one-storey Greek Doric colonnade with fluted columns, added in 1818; to the W, a two-bay extension with larger windows, for a library, *c.* 1813–15; both by *James Green*, the county surveyor.

Inside, several phases of remodelling. Of the early C19 the entrance hall, created in the l. part of the main range, small but elegant, with two Doric columns. An older fireplace in the W wall. The hall extends into the W wing, where there is a spacious staircase with two right-angled flights and plain balusters. In the front of this wing the dining room with reset panelling and overmantel of *c.* 1600, the mustard-yellow graining and painting perhaps also early C19. The library-cum-ballroom beyond has a black marble fireplace with two columns, a good cornice, and a modest number of recessed bookcases.

In the main range of the house, the position of the great hall is occupied by an C18 living room with a pretty carved fireplace, part of the work recorded for 1732, when the front of the house was refaced by a Minehead builder, *Richard Strong*, a new central entrance made (since removed), and the E wing enlarged. The upper part of the hall, however, was floored only in 1792. Behind is a good C18 staircase, with ramped handrail and two turned balusters to the tread, providing access to the N wing and to rooms later removed for the inner hall. In the E wing traces of older fabric, with beams visible by a side entrance. The wall here is a mixture of stone and cob. Behind the C19 entrance hall are service rooms, one (now used as a museum) with an angled fireplace. Other outbuildings around the backyard, one with a bellcote. Stables of 1845, simple U-plan.

GALMPTON
6040
South Huish

HOLY TRINITY. Built in 1866–7 to replace the old church at South Huish. The site was given by the Earl of Devon. The architect was *Richard Coad*, a pupil of Scott, who also worked at Bowringsleigh (and installed there the screen from South Huish). Straightforward, quite austere E.E., the chancel with lancets, the nave with plate tracery. Heavily buttressed w tower with pyramidal cap. – (FONT from the old church. C14 bowl, C13 quatrefoil base. – SCULPTURE. Parts of two alabaster retables found in 1867 in the old church at South Huish. C15. Annunciation and Adoration, both with donors; Betrayal, Scourging, Entombment, and Resurrection. – Chancel STAINED GLASS by *Lavers & Barraud*, 1868. – C18 WALL MONUMENT to the Lidstones.)

BOLT TAIL. *See* Malborough.

GEORGEHAM
4030

The church is set on a slight slope above the intimate little village street.

ST GEORGE. 1876–7 by *James Fowler* of Louth at the expense of the Hole family, a remodelling of a Georgian restoration of 1762, apart from the medieval w tower (buttresses of type B, embattled stairturret higher than the tower battlements, w doorway with continuous mouldings and fleurons) and the arcade of four bays between nave and s aisle (piers of B type with leaf capitals only to the main shafts). Another arch of the same design (doubled in the C19) to the s chapel. – SCREEN between aisle and chancel aisle of excellent Georgian design, with Ionic pilasters and a broken segmental pediment with achievement in the centre. It probably dates from 1762. – SCULPTURE. Unusually fine though badly damaged panel of the Crucifixion, *c.* 1300, *c.* 3 ft wide. The figure of Christ bent in suffering, as in contemporary manuscripts. John and Mary, two angels above, two kneeling figures l. and r. All heads knocked off. – REREDOS. 1876, with later (post-1918) sentimental painting. – PULPIT, TILES, and other furnishings of the same time. – STAINED GLASS. E window by *Lavers, Barraud & Westlake*, 1876. – Chancel N quatrefoil and w window by *Daniel Bell*, 1876–7 (RH). – MONUMENTS. In a recess in the s wall of the chancel chapel a cross-legged knight presumed to be Mauger of St Aubyn † 1294. Two angels supporting the head. Unusually complete, apparently

unrestored. Said to be not *in situ*. – Family of John Newcourt, later
C17, with six heads in roundels and a seventh smaller between them.
– John Harris, erected 1775, signed by *W. Tyler* and of the best
workmanship. Portrait bust at the top; below two putti, busy
around the profile medallion of Lady Dorothy Harris; inscription
below. Very well grouped, and displayed to advantage behind the
contemporary screen.

At Vention, a LIMEKILN and limeburner's cottage.

PICKWELL MANOR. 1902–5 for Sir Montague Style, a large gabled
mansion of rock-faced stone. Jacobean detail. Contemporary landscaped garden. Some medieval fabric in a rear wing and reset in an
outbuilding.

See also Croyde.

GEORGE NYMPTON 7020

ST GEORGE. Nave and N aisle with straight-headed windows. Three-
bay arcade with B type piers and standard leaf capitals. Old roof
bosses in N aisle and chancel. The W tower, rebuilt in brick, dated
1673. Restored 1882 by *E.H.Harbottle* (S and E walls of chancel
rebuilt). – FONT. Octagonal, Perp. – SEATS in the chancel
incorporate narrow panels with close Flamboyant tracery, no doubt
from a former screen. – STAINED GLASS. 1874 by *Hardman & Co.*
– MONUMENTS. Several to the Karslakes, including William
Karslake †1769 by *T. King* of Bath, very pretty, with a cherub
standing by a minute sarcophagus against an obelisk. – (Thomas
Gay †1802, by *I. Gould* of Barnstaple, with emerging butterflies, an
unusual motif.)

GERMANSWEEK 4090

ST GERMAN. The low unbuttressed W tower with rectangular NE
stair-turret is old. Tower arch to the nave completely unmoulded.
The masonry of the church walls, i.e. nave, S transept and chancel,
also looks older than Perp. Perp N aisle; low arcade of four bays
with piers of A type with capitals only to the main piers and
depressed pointed arches.

GIDLEIGH 6080

In a very romantic position in the E part of Dartmoor with woody
glens, rocks, and rushing streams, and the bare hill-tops around.
Church and castle lie close to each other.

HOLY TRINITY. All granite, all ashlar. Small, with two-stage W
tower now missing its pinnacles. Three-bay N aisle arcade with
octagonal piers and double-chamfered arches. C15, except for the
earlier S chancel wall. – SCREEN. Low and much pulled-about
tracery of type A, but the spandrels between the arches treated as
one field with a stem up the centre and intertwined leaf-decoration l.
and r. Cornice with two bands of decoration. All this *c.* 1530, but the

variously carved uprights are Jacobean replacements and the wainscot figures are transfers of 1853, as is the lovely, though inaccurate, colouring of the whole. – PULPIT and LECTERN both of 1853, both in granite, as is the three-bay REREDOS. – STAINED GLASS. Upper halves of the Virgin and St John in the E window of the S aisle, with flowered quarries, late C15, the quality not high. – Faith, Hope, and Charity by *A.L.Moore*, 1890.

CASTLE. Probably of the time of Sir William Prous, lord of the manor in the late C13 and early C14 (compare the architectural details with those of the rebuilding of Okehampton in this period, e.g. the use of aplite stone and the style of doorstops). Sir William must have been immediately imitating his richer Courtenay neighbours, perhaps employing one of the same masons.

Only an undercroft remains with solar above, to which there is both a fragmentary external newel stair and a narrow stair from the undercroft in the wall thickness. The ribbed vault which supports the solar encloses the undercroft, lit by a single window at the opposite end from the door. Both stairs have narrow windows of which one, recorded early this century, was cruciform. In the solar wall beside the external stair entrance a fireplace (note the supports for a hood) flanked by windows, one with window-seats. A square-headed door in the adjoining wall may indicate a former continuation of the building, as may the large stones projecting outside. Are we in fact looking at the stone-built solar end of a timber great hall, or at least a hall of flimsier stone construction which has not survived? Or did this door provide access to a garderobe? – in which case we have an individual structure, in fact a tower house of sorts. The solar has lost its roof, but there are traces of a wall-top parapet.

Gidleigh has been called a castle since the C17. In fact its only features of strength are its 6ft thick granite walls, with (originally two) buttresses, and the drawbar-slots in the doorways. Its terraced position on a slope is a weakness. It may have been part of a more extensive group: there is much stonework nearby, though not apparently related.

CHAPPLE. A typical Dartmoor hamlet of three early houses: a small C16 two-storeyed house probably of two-room plan, originally with no cross-passage; CHAPPLE, a large C16 farmhouse; and to the W, WEST CHAPPLE,* of particular interest because it illustrates the development of the longhouse. The shippon was converted into a dwelling during restoration in 1978. The medieval roof survives only over the cross-passage, with a closed truss with wattle-and-daub infill, and a fragmentary smoke-blackened cruck-truss. An upper chamber was jettied out over the inner room into the still open hall. The curious joist pattern of the hall suggests a timber smoke-hood, replaced by a permanent stack only after the hall was floored. Originally shippon and house were both entered from the cross-passage. The shippon has a dung hole above a central drain laid transversely according to the lie of the land. Off the upper end of the house a good late C16-early C17 cross-wing faced in ashlar granite blocks.

PRINSEPS FOLLY, Gidleigh Tor. A ruined building of *c.*1840 on a hilltop site.

---

*For a plan of West Chapple *see* p. 68.

GIDLEIGH PARK. The C19 Tudor house of the Whiphams, now a restaurant (MS).

PREHISTORIC SITES. The moor edge in Gidleigh parish is particularly rich in prehistoric ceremonial monuments. At SCORHILL, N of the North Teign river, is one of Dartmoor's finest stone circles (restored). To the W of BUTTERN HILL lies another circle, to the E a chambered cairn. Also in the area other simple and kerbed cairns. Easily accessible S of Batworthy at SHOVEL DOWN a fine complex of five stone rows, cairns, and a standing stone; peat shrinkage has permitted the identification of more stones in the rows than could be recorded by Worth and others. At the junction of two of the rows, and central to the whole complex, a fourfold circle of small stones, its overall diameter 28 ft. W of the stone rows on Shovel Down a good series of prehistoric fields and settlements provides clear evidence of multi-phase evolution. For the 'Round Pound' house, *see* Chagford.

GITTISHAM

1090

ST MICHAEL. Cemented outside, except for the S aisle, with pointed windows with tracery replaced by straight upright mullions in the late C17 or C18. The church, damaged in the Civil War, was repaired by William Putt (†1662) of Combe (q.v.) – see the ornamental gutter with his arms at the E end. Unbuttressed W tower. C14 chancel arch (restored) and inner N porch arch. Perp S aisle (B type piers), with the initials HB in the centre bay, probably for Henry Beaumont, *c.*1470. Behind the easternmost arch a panelled arch to the S chancel chapel (cf. Awliscombe), perhaps intended as a tomb recess. The arch has the Beaumont arms. Ceiled wagon roofs with bosses. Chancel restored in the C19, using the same colours as the floor tiles for the pretty painting of roof and communion rails. The rest retains an C18 character, with WEST GALLERY given by Sir Thomas Putt in 1701 (entered from external stairs S of the tower) and BOX PEWS of 1715, one with decorative carving in the S aisle. – ROYAL ARMS of Charles II. – PAINTING. Wooden panel with the Psalms and King David, in naive style, dated 1744. – STAINED GLASS. Chancel E 1873 by *Heaton, Butler & Bayne*, the Ascension, good colours and draughtsmanship. – Chancel N, some lively C16–17 Flemish roundels. – S chapel E heraldic, including the arms of Beaumont, *c.*1400, and Putt, *c.*1650.

MONUMENTS. Henry Beaumont †1591 and his wife, of alabaster and two types of marble; the typical composition with the kneeling figures in profile behind each other and flanked by columns. – Joane Beaumont †1627, with nice strapwork ornament and no figure work. – Lady (Ursula) Putt †1674 and Sir Thomas Putt †1686. A spectacular affair with a big tomb-chest in an arched recess of black marble. On the chest two oversized garlanded white marble urns. The back wall of the recess with blank architecture of pediment on brackets. The whole cold, competent, expensive, and metropolitan; variously attributed to *William Stanton* and *William Kidwell*. The urns could be by *Edward Pierce*. – Reymundo Putt †1812 by *Joseph Theakston*. – Rev. Thomas Putt †1844. Gothic mural brass by *Stephens* of Exeter.

Gittisham is an exceptionally attractive village. Spacious groups of thatched cottages off the main street, some with flint walling, some of cob. Up the hill the larger TOWN FARMHOUSE with projecting porch dated 1600, a fine set of late C17 timber cross-windows, W stack dated 1678, and good joinery. The cottages by the church were formerly the school founded by Sir Thomas Putt in 1720.

On GITTISHAM HILL lies Devon's largest BARROW CEMETERY. It continues into Farway parish (q.v.). The large STONE at the crossroads on the hill is probably originally of prehistoric ritual significance, but it has been moved twice in the last hundred years. *See also* Combe.

GOODLEIGH

5030

ST GREGORY. 1881 by *Ashworth*. Perp W tower with diagonal buttresses and pinnacles preserved. – MONUMENT. James Acland of Combe †1655. Small, rustic (Hoskins).

ARTS CENTRE (former chapel). Arched windows with linked hood-moulds (cf. Fremington). Nice railings in front.

YEOTOWN. An early C19 castellated lodge with two square towers and a crenellated bow-window survives from the seat of the Incledons.

At the SE edge of the village, a long low house by *Peter Aldington*, 1970–1. Hipped roof, walls partly glazed, partly of painted block-work – a deceptively simple envelope for an interior of considerable spatial ingenuity.

GREAT FULFORD
Dunsford

7090

The Fulford family have held the manor since the C12 or earlier. The house stands hidden away in its own grounds, a substantial court-yard mansion, larger than most in Devon though characteristic of the county in its reticent exterior and its patchy and undocumented history of rebuilding and remodelling from the Middle Ages to the early C19. Two-storey fronts to E and S, rendered, with Tudor windows mostly of four lights with transoms, some of them, e.g. the bays to the S, and probably also the battlements, dating from a Georgian Gothic tidying-up of c. 1800. Entrance archway in the E front, four-centred, early Renaissance dolphins in the spandrels, Fulford arms in strapwork above with Saracen supporters. On the first floor of this range two C16 plaster ceilings (one truncated); another in the S range, probably of the time of Sir John Fulford (†1580), confirms a Tudor date at the latest for these parts.

The hall range on the W side of the courtyard has a doorway with glazed roundels above an ogee arch, a direct quotation from Batty Langley's *Gothic Architecture Improved* of 1747. Clock turret of c. 1800 on the roof. The range is probably of medieval origin, see the two-centred archway in the opposite wall (behind a door), and the remains of a spiral stair to the S. The present appearance of the double-height hall with its coved ceiling and black and white marble paving is the result of the late C17 remodelling, probably begun

after 1689 by Colonel Francis Fulford. The interesting collection
of carved woodwork of various dates was probably installed at this
time: excellent linenfold panelling; parts of a Jacobean overmantel
with rustic scenes of Adam and Eve; three large C17 figures of Sir
Baldwin Fulford and Saracens; also some very good early Renaissance panels (one dated 1534).

The area N of the hall, and most of the N range, were also
ambitiously remodelled from the late C17. But in the C19 this wing
was left to decay, and most of the splendour has been lost. Grand
early C18 staircase (the lower flight renewed in 1919), twisted
balusters, carved tread-ends, two tall Gothic windows in the W
wall. At the top a fine door with a segmental scrolled pediment
leading into a very large first-floor room (a double cube?). Here
and elsewhere elaborate plasterwork and woodwork have gone,
save for a fragment of carved drops preserved in the hall. In the E
range, S of the entrance, former chapel on the ground floor with
late C17 panelling. Two other rooms in the E range with late C17
panelling and fireplaces. About 1800 the grand late C17 rooms
were abandoned in favour of a cosier suite in the S wing. Here,
several rooms remain with panelling with elegantly restrained
Gothic detail: on the first floor library and drawing room, on the
ground floor a dining room with coloured window glass and grey
marble Gothic fireplace. Adjoining this, an earlier C18 minor
staircase.

Behind the hall a SERVICE COURTYARD, the buildings mostly
one-storeyed. Bakery and brewhouse on the W (now a separate
dwelling), kitchen on the S. Landscaped GROUNDS, with a lake to
the S. Formerly the house was approached from this side, down the
beech avenue leading from the early C19 battlemented LODGE and
archway.

GREAT POTHERIDGE
Merton

5010

A puzzling and tantalizing fragment. The present farmhouse is the
remains of one of Devon's most ambitious later C17 houses, the
family mansion of General Monk, the chief engineer of the
Restoration. Its reconstruction must be assumed to date from after
1660, when he was created Duke of Albemarle, and may not have
been complete when he died in 1669. Much of the house was
demolished after the death of the second Duchess in 1734. What
remains is a part of a great hall, truncated to the N, probably of
pre-C17 origin, and a substantial S wing, a double pile with mighty
hipped roof, very much an innovation for Devon. This has a five-
bay, two-storey S front of irregularly coursed ashlar, with moulded
string course and carved wooden modillion cornice. C19 casements; the off-centre, over-scaled pedimented porch is also later,
perhaps moved from elsewhere when a door was made in this
front. (The door opens beneath the late C17 stairs.) To the W, this
S wing has just a blank wall and some blocked or altered windows;
then comes the hall and a section where the upper floor has been
destroyed. The parts further N have disappeared.

Directly opposite this W front, and linked to it by a low wall, are the remains of a facing range now only one storey high, with window openings which appear to correspond with those of the house. Could these be the 'magnificent stables' which Lysons described as still standing? Was the original entrance to the house on the other side, from the E? Lysons also mentions a chapel 'of Grecian architecture' (i.e. classical) taken down in 1770.

Inside the fragment of the hall reset early C17 panelling, two massive later C17 doorcases with fluted pilasters, segmental pediment, and cartouche, and a colossal overmantel with excellently carved putti and trophies around a flowery wreath enclosing a putto with a crown (an allusion to the Restoration, no doubt).

In the s range, a surprisingly grand late C17 staircase of two long flights. Heavy urn-shaped balusters decorated with acanthus and egg-and-dart, the two newels side by side on the half-landing suggesting that the carpenters were not yet easy with the type. The ceiling has three plasterwork wreaths enclosing paintings (in bad condition), one circle and two ovals. Elaborate egg-and-dart cornice. Upstairs to the E, a large N-facing room, now subdivided, and another to the s, with bolection-moulded dado panelling. On the w side of the stairs an attic stair leads up to the roof, whose structure suggests there were formerly dormers. The ground-floor rooms all altered; partly divided by a mezzanine floor inserted for the farmhouse.

GREAT TORRINGTON

4010

The chief attraction of the town is its position high above the river Torridge. The fall from Castle Hill down to the water is almost straight, providing some of the most dramatic views in North Devon. The hill-town character is most apparent from the sw approach by the old road from Exeter, which crosses the river at Taddiport (*see* below) and winds steeply up Mill Street. The more frequented route is from the SE, by the NEW BRIDGE built over the Torridge at the expense of Lord Rolle of Stevenstone (q.v.) by the county surveyor *Thomas Whitcher* in 1842–3. Lord Rolle was similarly responsible for the picturesque castellated appearance of the nearby TOWN MILLS, and for the re-evocation of the age of chivalry in the form of walls and arrow-slits at the castle site at the top of the hill. The road from the E is less enticing, with its straggle of urban growth, a reminder of the town's importance as a centre of glovemaking in the C19. Expansion elsewhere was fortunately prevented by the common lands along the Torridge valley to s and w.

ST MICHAEL. An explosion in the s transept tower in 1645 destroyed part of the church. The low SE vestry with thickly quatrefoiled battlements survived, also the E parts of the inner arcades. The w parts and some of the outer walls were rebuilt in 1651–5. The w tower and spire were added in 1828 by *W.B.Cock*. Masonry and composition of the C17 repairs are indistinguishable from the Perp past: nave, two aisles, and two transepts, placed surprisingly far w. The effect inside is of largeness (107 ft long) and bareness. The original piers were of B type with standard leaf capitals. In two of the s piers damaged niches for images. The renewed piers to the w are

shapelessly square with chamfered angles and carry double-chamfered arches. Restored *c.* 1861 by *William White*, who provided new
window tracery. – REREDOS. Stone relief of the Last Supper, by
H. Hems, 1878. – PULPIT. Late C17, with carved cherubs and
gilded lions' heads. The fine sounding-board was returned to the
church in 1960 after a sojourn in the V. and A. – STAINED GLASS.
Much of the C19, including four windows by *Lavers & Barraud*,
c. 1862. – MONUMENTS. Sarah Gooding † 1698. Wall-monument
with angels with shields; two caryatids flanking columns, ornate but
coarse. – Minor late wall-monuments by *Stephens* of Exeter and *Beal*
of Barnstaple. – For the churchyard *see* the perambulation below.

The town centre, pleasantly quiet, lies away from the main roads: an L
shape of two streets, High Street and Fore Street, both short but
quite urban. The focal points are the Town Hall and the Pannier
Market, as at South Molton, but here sited so that they complement
rather than compete with each other. The stuccoed and pedimented
front of the MARKET HOUSE, built in 1842 by the local mason
W. B. Cock, faces down the HIGH STREET from South Street.
Upper floor with Ionic pilasters between arched windows; ground
floor with rusticated arches with iron gates leading to a modest
arrangement of stalls supported by cast-iron Doric columns, flanking a narrow lane. A later glazed roof has been removed. The
TOWN HALL, rebuilt in 1861 on the site of a previous one, is a
sturdier building, still in the Georgian tradition. The pedimented
centre reaches out from the W side of the High Street with 'piazzas',
i.e. arched openings. Red brick upper part, stone pediments to the
windows. Upstairs a large assembly room with gallery (now
Museum).

Opposite, two low gables of the BLACK HORSE HOTEL, much
restored, the r. one with a genuine jettied timber front between
stone party-walls. The date 1681 on the fireplace lintel of the
downstairs room; a stud-and-panel screen in the passageway. On
the same side of the High Street the NATIONAL WESTMINSTER
BANK, formal C19 Italianate, with alternating window pediments.
Opposite, visible above ground-floor shops, a nice red brick C18
house with stone keystones to the windows. Round the corner in
FORE STREET other modest C18 and C19 frontages, the most
imposing that of the GLOBE HOTEL, 1830, with a three-storey
front with very tall first-floor windows within round-headed arched
recesses. Next door the PLOUGH, correct red brick neo-Georgian
of 1913, in chaste reproof to the cheerfully eclectic little POST
OFFICE opposite of 1903.

From the centre of the town excursions in several directions. First to
the NW. From the corner of High Street and Fore Street a narrow
passage leads to the spacious CHURCHYARD (a pleasant surprise),
the paths attractively paved with narrow North Devon cobbles
(*Cock*'s initials and the date 1813 in front of the church porch).
Simple white plastered houses with black paintwork to the S and E.
On the S side the SEXTON'S HOUSE, low, with Gothick windows.
To the N, NEW STREET cuts close by. On its N side the best house
in the town, PALMER HOUSE, built in 1752 by John Palmer, 118
mayor and attorney, and brother-in-law to Sir Joshua Reynolds,
who visited the house together with Dr Johnson. Red brick, two and
a half storeys, 1–3–1 bays, divided by giant Ionic pilasters with their

own entablatures, the cornice breaking forward above them. Good pedimented doorway. Flanking front-garden walls curving down to piers with vases. In the r. ground-floor room a nice plaster ceiling with octagonal centre and the Palmer arms; staircase with twisted balusters. At the back a later C18 wing, slate-hung. A shallow bow-window looks out on a ruinous octagonal gazebo in the remains of the garden. Nos. 6–8 New Street are converted stables and out-buildings of Palmer House.

Further w down New Street first the BAPTIST CHAPEL of 1829, set back, a charming front with concave upswept parapet and rusti-cated doorway; then the ROLLE ALMSHOUSES of 1843, a sym-metrical design with Gothic doorways in two gabled projections. PORCH HOUSE opposite has a seven-bay front with the early C18 type of flush-frame sashes, and a later altered Tuscan porch. Further on a long line of C19 artisan cottages, the earlier ones stuccoed, the later cottages of pale yellow Marland brick, becoming more genteel on the fringe of the town, with front gardens and bay-windows (Clinton Terrace, inscribed '1887, builder H.Labett'). Finally, a group of stuccoed villas with curious strapwork ornament around the windows.

s off New Street is WHITE'S LANE, with the oddest building in the town, William Vaughan & Sons' dominant chapel-like GLOVE FACTORY of 1884 by W.C.Medland. Quirkily detailed poly-chrome; red brick Gothic arches against Marland brick; stone plate tracery; fish-scale terracotta tympana. The hoodmoulds over the doorway are supported by carved hands; roundels display a pair of gloves and a glove press. Opposite, a BOARD SCHOOL of 1871 by Alexander Lauder, two gables with trefoiled lancets, the centre altered. Further on, a few stuccoed C19 villas: this was the affluent end of the town. One can return to the churchyard by CHURCH LANE, a back alley winding between high walls.

SOUTH STREET is the main artery of the old town. Near the E end No. 8, unassuming outside, has on the ground floor a handsome C16 ceiling with moulded beams framing nine panels containing Tudor roses. Further up on the s side is the lovely No. 28, dated 1701, an excellent example of its period. Two storeys, five bays, red brick with flush-frame sashes, hipped roof with pedimented dormers. The splendid hooded porch has trophies in relief inside the hood. In the l. ground-floor room a plaster ceiling with lobed centre with an exquisitely modelled group of musical instruments. Then, set back, CASTLE HOUSE HOTEL, plain early C19 stucco, with a nice cantilevered curving top-lit staircase inside, and romantically battlemented garden walls. After an ugly break for a car park, among smaller houses, No. 42, quite a grand three-storey early C19 front with rusticated window heads and a Tuscan doorway with fanlight. Opposite, a former chapel with three tall Gothic windows. After Windy Cross, at the top of the steep descent down MILL STREET, the WESLEYAN CHAPEL of 1832, with an upswept parapet similar to the parapet of the Baptist Chapel in New Street.

w of the town centre, modest C18–19 cottages down WELL STREET. Others to the SW in CASTLE STREET, interrupted by the late C19 gabled front of the HOWE UNITED REFORMED CHURCH. Near the end, CASTLE HOUSE, large, stuccoed, late C18, with an early C19 garden front with recessed Greek Doric porch (now closed in)

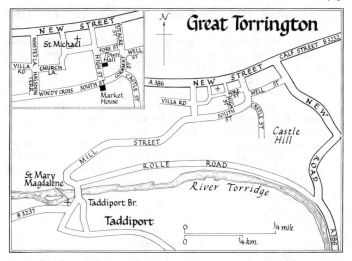

and a deep balcony with iron balustrade and canopy. The site of the CASTLE itself is occupied by the bowling green, surrounded by some more of Lord Rolle's mock battlements, with a little gazebo at one corner. The single earthwork fragment may have been part of the motte. There is a reference to the bailey in 1371. The castle is first documented in 1139, when it was captured from William FitzOdo by Henry Tracey. It was destroyed in 1228. The reputed site of the chapel, which survived until Leland's day, is occupied by the COMMUNITY CENTRE, i.e. the SCHOOLS rebuilt by Lord Rolle in 1834. Plain, two storeys, Georgian sashes. Nearby is a rectangular POUND with very substantial 8 ft random stone walls, no doubt re-used material. Along the walk above the river, halfway down the slope, a stone PYRAMID with two Gothic arched recesses on each face, 'erected in 1818 to commemorate the battle of Waterloo. Peace to the Souls of the Heroes'.

TADDIPORT. At the foot of MILL STREET the thatched TOR-RIDGE INN. The little TOLL HOUSE nearby, two storeys, rendered, with upper pilasters, stands at the entrance to ROLLE ROAD, which leads to the Town Mills along the route of the CANAL (closed in 1871 and filled in). The canal was constructed by Lord Rolle in 1822–4 to link Torrington to the navigable part of the Torridge below Weare Giffard. Across the road are some rubble stone warehouses from the time of the canal company; the rest of the site is covered by prominent C20 buildings for Torrington Creamery, which began as Torridge Vale Butter Factory in 1874. The medieval BRIDGE, with three arches with cutwaters, has been widened on the W side.

On the s bank ST MARY MAGDALENE, a tiny chapel, sole survivor of a leper hospital founded in 1344. Narrow unbuttressed w tower; nave only 30ft long. Above a blocked s doorway, a three-light straight-headed Perp window of oak. N chapel roof with sill plates carved with beaded scrolls. On E and s walls delightful C16 PAINTED TEXTS, restored in 1971. – STAINED GLASS. s window commemorating the leper hospital, a dense pattern of colourful figures, by *C. Sing*, 1972.

ROTHERN BRIDGE, W of the town. C15, widened by new arches springing from cutwaters. Original arches, slightly pointed. Bypassed by the ROLLE BRIDGE, built in 1928.

STATION (now a restaurant), close to the Rolle Bridge. 1872. Gabled two-storey house with one-storey waiting-rooms and offices. Platform canopy with attractive cast-iron brackets and columns. The track follows the line of the canal (*see* above), which Lord Rolle sold to the railway company in 1871.

BEAM AQUEDUCT, 1 m. N of the station, now carrying the private drive to Beam College. Built in 1824 by *James Green* to carry the canal over the river. A noble design of five arches between engaged Doric half-columns, the rounded bases forming cutwaters.

See also Stevenstone.

8070   HACCOMBE

HACCOMBE HOUSE, in its large grounds, is a nondescript Georgian structure of red sandstone now converted to flats. Centre of two and a half storeys, seven bays, with quoins, the three middle bays weakly stressed. One-storeyed Ionic four-column porch. A low six-bay l. wing of one and a half storeys projects at right angles, with a pediment over the central four bays. Tuscan porch and short pilasters above. No r. wing to correspond with it. Called 'lately erected' in 1803, but also 'built about fifty years ago' in 1872. It belonged to the Carews, who inherited it through marriage into the Courtenays in the C15.

ST BLAISE. The small church in the grounds of the house is of great interest both for its architecture and for its contents. Until the C20 it had special status as a peculiar of the Archbishop of Canterbury, with an archpriest who did not have to acknowledge the authority of the bishop. The church had a college with six chantry priests, established in 1335 and confirmed by Bishop Grandison in 1337. However, the fabric of the building is older. The pairs and triplets of lancet windows, though restored by *Hayward* in 1863–4, must be C13. The N arcade, with broad unmoulded two-centred arches with very elementary capitals (remade) on short sturdy red octagonal piers, was probably cut through the wall of an earlier aisleless building. The most curious feature of the church is two arms, in chancel and N aisle, presumably to hold candles or banners. – In the chancel and N chancel chapel medieval pavement, partly *in situ*, of red TILES inlaid with white clay with arms and other designs. Descendants of the series produced in Exeter from *c.* 1280, they must be dated after 1330 from the arms of the Archdeacon family who inherited the manor in that year, and presumably belong to a refurbishing for the newly founded college. The green-glazed white tiles are probably late medieval imports from Normandy. – STAINED GLASS. Several coloured figures, chiefly brown and green, of the original early C14 make.

More remarkable than these minor remains are the MONUMENTS. The earliest are three stone effigies of the later C13: a cross-legged knight, supposed to be Sir Stephen de Haccombe, remarkable for its unusually well preserved remains of painted gesso surface, stamped to indicate chain mail, the armour originally gilded, with a decorative pattern of flowing black lines; a lady wearing a wimple and holding a shield, and another wimpled lady holding a book, both with traces of colour. – Miniature alabaster effigy of a youth in civilian dress, 2 ft 2 in. long, late C14 (cf. the miniature effigies of Edward III's children at Westminster, 1376), with two lively angels at the head; an accomplished work. – On a renewed large tomb-chest with battlemented top, a much restored knight and lady, c. 1400, supposed to be Sir Hugh Courtenay and his wife, Philippa, the Archdeacon heiress. He rests on a tilting helm; she is supported by angels. – BRASSES. Sir Nicholas Carew † 1469, in spiky armour. – Thomas Carew † 1586 and Mary his wife † 1589; small. – Elizabeth, wife of John Carew, † 1611. – Unusually late floor brass to Thomas Carew † 1656 and his family, with kneeling figures and allegorical figures, of very rustic craftsmanship. – In 1821 *Kendall*, the architect to Exeter Cathedral, erected the stone SCREEN, a very neat neo-Dec piece, though not as imaginative and free as the probably contemporary, also Dec, REREDOS.

MILBER DOWN HILLFORT, SE of Newton Abbot, bisected by the road to Haccombe Cross. A classic hillfort of 'South Western' type. It has been suggested that its widely spaced ramparts (cf. Clovelly Dykes) provided secure accommodation for large herds of stock, indicating a predominantly pastoral economy. Of the original four complete circuits of ramparts only parts now survive, although the remainder can occasionally be seen as cropmarks. The site was occupied in the latest pre-Roman Iron Age and was last used defensively by William of Orange in 1688, shortly after he landed in Torbay. MILBER LITTLE CAMP immediately to the E, now largely destroyed, has been shown to be Roman in date.

HAINE
Stowford

The seat of the Harris family from the early C16 until 1865 (derelict at the time of writing) and an interesting example, early for the W of the county, of an ambitious but still entirely unarchaeological Gothic remodelling of the earlier C19. According to White, built c. 1810; with additions by the Blackburn family who bought the house c. 1864. Of rubble, battlemented. The main front to the E a tripartite composition with angled pinnacles to the projecting centre. Two tiers of pointed arched windows with tall traceried lights (cf. Nash's Luscombe); other windows straight-headed, some with stone, some with wooden tracery. At the SW corner a bay-window and a large end window between pairs of pinnacles, both lighting the first-floor ballroom in the W wing; at the NE corner a corbelled-out oriel. The service wing on the N side may incorporate the core of an older house, but there are no readily identifiable details.

Spacious entrance hall with Gothic fireplace with clustered shafts and a cornice with hanging Gothic arches. To the l. the staircase hall, with a roof-light of coloured glass, an imperial stair

with simple arched balustrade, and two openwork landing screens
of cusped Gothic arches (cf. Watermouth Castle). At the s end of
the E range the dining room, with a wooden panelled ceiling with
bosses. On the first floor of the s wing (at a lower level than the E
range) the remains of a ballroom and a grand reception room, both
with decorative ceilings with single ribs in the form of clumsily
designed tracery patterns, i.e. not yet seriously neo-Elizabethan.

STABLES, N of the house, with castellated clock-tower and
Tudor arches of brick on stone columns.

GROTTO. Cyclopic masonry, shallow gable, a rough entrance
arch. Inside, niches and vault faced with shells. Perhaps mid C18.

0010

HALBERTON

ST ANDREW. A large church of red sandstone, the tall tower similar
to Northam, diagonally buttressed only to the first stage; stair-
turret on the s face. The window beside it and the w window C14.
Aisle windows and battlements date from *Hayward*'s restoration of
1847–9. Much exterior refacing 1887. Inside, the arcades (rebuilt
by *Hayward*) are of two dates: the octagonal piers and double-
chamfered arches of the w bays C14, the taller E bays with fleurons
to the capitals C15. By *Hayward* too the unceiled wagon roofs to
nave and chancel. – REREDOS, polychrome chancel decoration,
and patterned sanctuary floor TILES of 1887. – FONT. Plain,
square, Norman, the bowl with three scallops on each side. –
PULPIT. Octagonal, with fin-like uprights to separate the panels.
In the panels flat arches with tracery below, but above, little diagonally placed buttresses, and behind them, but coming forward
between them, nodding ogee arches. The fact that this exquisite
play with spatial forms was still sought as late as the early C15
shows that Dec ideals continued to be cherished well into the Perp
period (cf. the stone screens in Exeter Cathedral). – SCREENS.
The early C15 rood screen runs right through nave and both aisles.
Eleven six-light bays, three of them doors. Tracery of B type. The
coving delicious: fan-vaulting with flying ribs, i.e. the panels
between the ribs openwork. – The N and s parclose screens have
Dec tracery and much cusping. Straight tops, no coving. The date
of the two screens may be identical, the designs are not. –
STAINED GLASS. N aisle Ascension by *Lavers & Westlake*, 1894. –
w window with four reset figures, C17(?). – MONUMENTS.
Richard Clark of Bridwell † 1728. Cherub heads and skulls. – John
Chave † 1796. Mourning woman by urn. – Henry Manley † 1819,
by *J. G. Bubb*.

METHODIST CHURCH. Built by the Wesleyans, 1816. Tall,
rendered, with curved gable and pediment. Tuscan porch.

SCHOOL. 1844. Tudor. Cross-wings with transomed windows with
lattice glazing.

VICARAGE, Lower Town. 1847 by *Hayward*.

HERNE PLACE. With plaster ceilings of c. 1600.

THE PRIORY. Late medieval cob house with lateral stone stack,
remodelled in the C19. Good original screen and exceptionally fine
hall ceiling, framed in squares, with joists running in alternate
directions. Twisted foliage scrolls along the main timbers. The

parlour also with moulded beams. The name of the house may come from the ownership of manor and church by the priory of St Augustine, Bristol.

ROCK HOUSE, close to the canal. Built for *Captain John Wisden*, an engineer to the Grand Western Canal Company (the canal was completed in 1838), of red sandstone, 2–1–2 bays, with rather eccentric heavy classical detailing, perhaps designed by himself. Porch with four Doric columns. Former outbuildings (Rock Cottage and Overock) in similar style.

ROCK BRIDGE. One of several elegant canal bridges in the parish.

(ROWRIDGE. Symmetrical late Georgian front, 1–3–1 bays, the centre recessed.)

(OBURNEFORD. Late Georgian farmhouse. Stables with Gothick glazing.)

MOORSTONE BARTON. Substantial remains of a major medieval house include a mid C14 range with a C15 S cross-wing (the original N cross-wing has been demolished). The hall range, on a three-room cross-passage plan, has a base-cruck roof of unusual stylistic interest, with arch-braces and cranked tie-beams with angle struts, surmounted by a crown-post with diagonal curved struts. It is of four bays, all heavily smoke-blackened. The two hall bays are defined by trusses closed above the tie-beams at either end. One has a smoke-window pierced through it. The arch-braces to the hall rest on carved corbels. One of the two central hall bosses survives, carved with vine leaves and grapes. The C15 solar wing, built two-storeyed with a lateral stack, has a roof on four pairs of jointed crucks. At the front end a blocked C15 window to each floor, of two wide lights with cinquefoil heads. The main range was probably built by Walter Ganson, whose family had connections with the court of Edward III. The solar may date from 1449, the time of the marriage of a daughter of John Ganson to John Walrond of Bradfield (q.v.) in the private chapel of Moorstone.

HALL
Bishops Tawton

5020

A sizeable neo-Jacobean house of 1844–7, splendidly sited on a high ridge looking S, designed for Robert Chichester by *P. C. Hardwick* with *R. D. Gould* of Barnstaple, as we are told by a Latin inscription in the baronial hall. This hall is the most eccentric feature of the house. At the W end of the main front, with its large and accomplished Dec window it looks like a chapel. Inside it is lofty, with an arch-braced roof, a W gallery, and atmospheric medieval detail including heraldic stained glass, a fireplace with motto, and a niche with a painted vault. The rest of the S front is austerely detailed, apart from three shaped gables and a low triple-arched porch with half-fluted columns. Ribbed ceiling in the entrance hall; another, and a neo-Jacobean fireplace, in the dining room to the l.

STABLES. A long range, partly C19, with a pretty clock-turret. To the W, a large stone BARN with two wagon-ways and buttresses, a relic of the outbuildings of the previous house.

ORANGERY, SW of the house. Rubble stone, three tall arched bays.

GATEPIERS with the Chichester herons. The present drive from the N was made in 1883; the older approach (shown on an estate survey of 1769) was from Herner to the S.

7050   HALWELL

ST LEONARD. The tall grey W tower with central S turret of Ashburton type is old: the rest is of 1879, except for the arcade between nave and N aisle, with granite piers of A type and nearly semicircular arches. The W bays were divided off by a glass and metal screen in the 1970s. – BOX PEWS. Early C19.

(STANBOROUGH HOUSE. Early C18 five-bay front of brick with stone quoins and a two-storey central porch projection. Earlier parts behind.)

STANBOROUGH CAMP AND HALWELL CAMP. Two very substantial earthwork enclosures. One of them is probably the burh described as Halwell in the Burghal Hidage, a Saxon document of c.910–20, but whether it was new built or established in a pre-existing hillfort is not known. 'Halwell' was the direct predecessor of the Saxon burh at Totnes. There is no actual dating evidence for either site. A short distance to the NE of Stanborough is a curious third earthwork, circular in form but wholly enigmatic in function. In the vicinity of both enclosures are a number of well preserved ROUND BARROWS. One of them lay within the defences of Stanborough.

GARA BRIDGE. See Diptford.

4090   HALWILL

ST PETER AND ST JAMES. The slim unbuttressed W tower with short pinnacles and the N nave wall medieval. The rest of the church rebuilt in 1876–9 by *Samuel Hooper* of Hatherleigh, simple, Dec. – In the churchyard a group of elegant early C19 slate TOMBSTONES, and the church LAUNDRY, close to the tower, also partly rebuilt by *Hooper*.

WINSFORD COTTAGE HOSPITAL, Beaworthy, by Halwill station. Built in 1899 by Mrs Maria Louise Medley of Winsford Tower in memory of her husband and designed by *Charles Annesley Voysey*, one of the best English architects of his time. One-storeyed, with Voysey's typical almost completely blank gables, a tall tapering chimneyshaft, window surrounds with irregular blocks of stone, the composition asymmetrical from the road but symmetrical to the garden, with two projecting wings and originally a veranda in between (extended as a rather ugly flat-roofed dayroom). Well preserved interior, full of delightful Voysey details: simple door furniture, ventilating grilles with a bird design. In the entrance hall a green-tiled fireplace with a copper hood.

BRONZE AGE BARROWS. See Beaworthy.

HARBERTON

St Andrew. A stately church with w tower of Ashburton type. Embattled s side with a two-storeyed s porch, handsomely vaulted in two bays on coupled blank w and e arcades, and with large four-light windows. The n side also embattled, with rood-stair turret. n and s aisles of six bays, large and light, with piers of A type and capitals only to the four shafts. Long ceiled wagon roofs. Restored 1861 and 1871–2. – FONT. Circular, red sandstone, Norman, with a frieze of rosettes, and below first a band of cable and then a frieze of upright petals. – SCREENS. Specially impressive rood screen. The wainscoting with rather touching paintings added in the restoration of 1870 (according to Baring Gould, contemporary portraits). Some of the old panels are displayed in the n aisles. Standard type A tracery; two friezes of ornament in the cornice. Cresting renewed. Round the piers of the arcade elaborate casing with canopy-work. – Also parclose screens. – PULPIT. Stone, with nodding ogee canopies and thickly carved uprights, exactly like Dittisham. The figures are clearly c17. – Good carved ROYAL ARMS of Queen Anne.

MONUMENTS. c17 tablet with wreathed oval to Thomas Risdon, the Devon topographer, a Trist connection. – A remarkable late Victorian and Edwardian sequence to members of the Harvey family. In the church Robert 'Tito' Harvey †1895 aged eleven by *Hems*, alabaster, the sleeping figure of the boy life-size and with a mortuary lily thrown across the body. – In the graveyard the Harvey mausoleum of 1895, again by *Hems*, and entirely in white marble; inside, life-sized recumbent figures, also in white marble, of 'Tito' once again, Alida Lady Harvey †1901, and Sir Robert Harvey †1930, all by the firm of *Toft* but of Italian workmanship; indeed, they would be entirely at home in Milan or Genoa, their stylistic genesis doubtless explained by Lady Harvey's Latin-American origins and Roman Catholicism.

Church House Inn, w of the church. Large and impressive. Restored, but still with several wooden window timbers, a round-headed oak doorway leading into the former brewhouse at the w end, and a good screen and other joinery inside.

Tristford. The seat of the Trists from the c18, after they had left Bowden House (q.v.). Now subdivided. A substantial neo-Tudor mansion of two dates. The centre is a symmetrical design with three straight gables, by *George Wightwick*, 1849, for Mrs Wynne Pendarves of the Trist family. Picturesquely enlarged c.1875 for J. F. Trist: a shaped gabled wing to the l. with a new entrance hall at the side; a steeply turreted polygonal tower to the r., once linked by a palm-house to the surviving clock tower with lead cupola. Original staircase, rich cornices, Gothic fireplaces. Behind is a much altered genuinely Tudor range, with large granite fireplace, its coat of arms in a scalloped recess with fat swags below probably carved on later.

EAST LODGE. Two-storeyed, Tudor, 1856.

Dundridge. The seat of the Harveys. Good late Georgian e front of five bays and two storeys, with pedimented Doric porch. Alterations of c.1893 by *W. H. Tollit*.

Arnold's, Luscombe. A farmhouse of longhouse type, the shippon not divided off from the passage. Front of finely coursed and jointed rubble with a roll-moulded string course. At the rear, outshots and a projecting stair-turret between hall and inner room.

HARBERTONFORD

A main-road hamlet of Harberton.

ST PETER. 1859 by *J. Nottidge*, endowed by Mrs Anthony of Great Engleford. Cruciform, with canted apse and central spirelet. Dec detail. Dramatic star-shaped scissor-braced roof over the crossing. Black marble shafts to the chancel windows. – STAINED GLASS. Life of St Peter (chancel).

PRIMITIVE METHODIST CHAPEL, Bow Road. A rare survival of this denomination. 1900. Street frontage decorated with red and yellow brick.

ZION CHAPEL, just outside the village. Built by the Baptists in 1795, small, of rubble, in its own burial ground.

CROWDY MILL. Built *c.*1800. Three-storey mill with two-storey mill house adjoining. Rubble stone with slate roof. Two overshot wheels on the N side.

HARFORD

ST PETROC. A humble church, with low unbuttressed W tower with short pinnacles. The staircase does not project. Nave, N transept, S aisle (of four bays with granite piers of A or Cornish type and semicircular arches), S porch. Ceiled wagon roofs. – MONUMENTS. Tomb-chest with pointed quatrefoil decoration. Brass effigy on top, supposed to represent Thomas Williams of Stowford, Speaker of the House of Commons, †1566; the armour still early C16. – John Prideaux and family, 1639, still the usual kneeling figures.

STOWFORD (Royal Agricultural Society). The present stuccoed entrance front facing S, three bays and three storeys, with a full-height bowed W end, is a late C18 rebuilding of the upper end of the much disguised and confused remains of the C16 mansion of the Williams family. This is recognizable from the courtyard behind, originally the entrance side, where a porch with round-headed archway with decorated keystone leads into the former hall, later used as a kitchen, with another range, much altered, at right angles. The large fireplace at the lower end of the hall still has a crenellated steeple capping to the stack (cf. Old Newnham). On the first floor two granite fireplaces with ogee arches.

LUKESLAND. Built in 1862 for a Mr Matthews from Plymouth. Two Jacobean gables flanking a bay-window, with a battlemented tower on the l., of red sandstone with limestone dressings, rising romantically above an idyllic water garden (made in the 1880s and 1930s). Inside, straightforward plan with good detail. Fan-vaulted axial corridor; staircase with hammerbeam roof and large Perp window (stained glass added after 1875). Entrance hall and stair-hall combined in the 1930s. In the grounds some masonry and a

Tudor arch from the old house which stood across the stream near the road, where the walled garden remains.

PREHISTORIC SITES. Harford parish occupies a long thin territory stretching into the heart of Dartmoor between Cornwood and Ugborough parishes, many of whose archaeological characteristics it shares. Harford has an unusually dense concentration of Bronze Age settlements all along the valley of the Erme. One of the largest, ERME POUND, much altered in post-prehistoric times, was used for annual drifts (stock musters) until the C20. Also in the valley are many relics of medieval tinworking. On BURFORD DOWN is a fine stone row amidst cairns, and s of Erme Pound another, double one. Part of the Stall Moor stone row (*see* Cornwood) also lies in the parish.

See also Ivybridge.

HARPFORD

An intimate cob and thatch cluster along a lane above the river Sid.

ST GREGORY. Much rebuilt in 1883–4 by *Hayward & Son*, but apparently faithfully, as a drawing in the church shows. Walls of reddish rubble, with a variety of windows, including some C13 lancets. N aisle with octagonal piers (much scraped) and simple chamfered arches, perhaps C14, with square-headed two-light windows. Unbuttressed W tower. – ALTAR RAIL. Late C17; heavy fluted balusters. – STAINED GLASS. E window *c.* 1870, the Ascension, good colours. – S aisle 1884 by *Kempe Studios*, St George and St Anne. – CHURCHYARD CROSS. Restored in memory of the Rev. Augustus Toplady †1778, Vicar of Harpford and author of the hymn 'Rock of Ages'.

BRONZE AGE BARROWS. *See* Newton Poppleford.

HARRACOTT
Tawstock

A small North Devon hamlet with a cluster of cob-walled thatched houses. Further s, on its own at the crossroads, the former church of HOLY TRINITY, 1844, with W bell-turret, substantial N and s porches, and Dec tracery, converted to a house in 1982, not very sensitively.

HARTLAND

ST NECTAN. The parish church lies higher up than the abbey, which, as usual, had chosen a well-watered valley site. The tower of St Nectan, at 130ft the highest in North Devon, commands the landscape to the W of the house and looks across a mile of fields towards America. The tower is late Perp, four stages, buttresses of type B, gargoyles below the battlements, and tall thin pinnacles. In the E wall a large recess with a statue of St Nectan, contemporary except for the head. The body of the church, in spite of its size

(137ft long), the crenellation of N as well as S aisle, and the addition of N and S transepts, does not look impressive from outside, chiefly owing to the consistently renewed windows, all reconstructed during the restoration of 1848 by *D. Mackintosh* of Exeter. The chancel was extended E at the same time.

The interior is large and tall, the sense of generous space helped by the uncommonly tall tower arch (responds of B type with concave octagonal capitals) and the width of the arches between nave and aisles. They suggest a date in the late C14, i.e. earlier than the usual Perp Devon church. The arcades are not yet of granite: the piers, though already of A section, are of buff limestone, short, and with simple moulded capitals. Arches of blue (catacleuse?) stone, double-chamfered. There are four bays to the nave, one to the transept, and one more to the chancel chapels. A great asset is the well-kept wagon roofs, of all kinds, in all parts: nave unceiled in the W part, ceiled and painted with delicious large stars in the panels (renewed 1982) in the E part. N aisle partly unceiled, partly ceiled, S aisle boarded with pitch pine, N transept plastered ceiling, S transept boarded panels with carved bosses, N chancel boarded and cross-ribbed in the rich way usual for 'celures'. In the chancel S wall a trefoil-headed PISCINA. N and S porches, the S doorway with fleuron decoration. W doorway with angel-head stops.

FONT. Norman, square, highly decorated, the bowl with scalloped lower edge and intersecting arches above, the shafts with vertical zigzags, the foot with intersected arches upside down. – REREDOS. 1931 by *Herbert Read*. – PULPIT. 1848. The pulpit bought in 1609 for 33 shillings (with lozenge panels fitted with arabesques) is now kept in a fragmentary state in the so-called Pope's Chamber. – SCREEN. One of the finest in North Devon, the wainscoting as usual, the tracery of B type, coving with unusually many ribs (seven, not counting the wall arches), four bands of ornament in the cornice, and a cresting of iron. Between the ribs decoration with flowers and also shields (which is unique). Coving at the back as well (five ribs). – PARCLOSE SCREENS of 1848. – ALTAR in the NE chapel with some Belgian Flamboyant tracery panels. Above this a wooden altar canopy introduced into the church as a memorial in the 1920s, made up of apparently genuine medieval pieces of *c.* 1300 also from Belgium: three cusped and sub-cusped arches within ogee crocketed gables separated by pinnacles. – PEWS. Nice plain C18 work. – BENCH ENDS in the S chancel chapel given by Hugh Prust in 1530. His initials occur on the usual shields; the tracery also is not out of the ordinary. No sign of Renaissance ornament yet.

SCULPTURE. In the S chancel chapel remains of small later C14 figure scenes, perhaps from the back of a chantry altar. – In the N chancel chapel two small standing figures above the broken-off top of an ogee niche, all rather crude. Probably pieces excavated *c.* 1828 by Lady Stucley in the Abbey grounds. – In Pope's Chamber (over the N porch) other miscellaneous fragments including C17 PANELLING and a HELMET from a monument to the Abbott family. – STAINED GLASS. E and W windows by *Christopher Webb*; the rest by *Caroline Townshend* and *Joan Howson*, 1931–3, over-obtrusive. – Three Flemish roundels in the S chancel chapel.

MONUMENTS. Perp tomb-chest of catacleuse stone (cf. St Endellion, etc., in Cornwall) brought from Hartland Abbey and used as the high altar until the 1920s. Very good and elaborate. Quatrefoil base, main panels with elaborately cusped and traceried quatrefoils, roundels, etc., separated by stone double buttresses with little ogee niches between. Cornice with fleuron decoration. – Brass to Ann Abbott †1610. Small kneeling figure and inscription. – Thomas Docton †1618. Lid of tomb; stone with metal inlay. – Among the wall-monuments of the late C17 and early C18: John Vetty †1694. Large painted architectural tablet with two mourning women and angels. – Paul Orchard †1740 and wife †1763, pretty wall-monument by *Kendall* of Exeter. – Nicholas Wolferstan †1763 and others, by *Tyley* of Bristol, with Father Time at the top. – Paul Orchard †1812, by *Rouw* of London, marble, very Grecian. – In the churchyard a plain, well lettered slate slab to the publishers John Lane †1925 and Allen Lane †1970, by *Will Carter*. The family came from Hartland.

ST JOHN. In the little town. No longer used as a church. Built in 1837–9 as a chapel of ease on the site of the former town hall. Rubble stone porch, with turret on the E side; the altar faces N instead of E. Typical of the date are the two-light lancet windows, the few remaining simple box pews, the unlearned Gothic reredos, and the curious pane of stained glass in the S window. The clock dates back to the town hall days. It was made by *John Morcombe* of Barnstaple in 1622, remade by the same in 1657, and altered again in the C18, when an anchor or recoil escapement and a pendulum were added.

NONCONFORMIST CHAPELS. Once there were seven Methodist chapels in town and parish. One survives at EDISTONE, 1878, built by the Bible Christians to replace a thatched chapel, its simplicity typical of many in this sparsely populated part of Devon. White rendered walls, slate roof, white-painted boundary wall.

HARTLAND ABBEY. The pre-Conquest foundation of secular canons attached to the church of St Nectan had by 1169 been re-established as a house of Augustinian canons, following the Arrouasian rule, through the agency of Geoffrey of Dinam. New abbey buildings were erected in a sheltered valley some way from the exposed site of the parish church; a building grant is mentioned in 1171. The existing house, as so often, occupies the site of the W range with the abbot's quarters.

Of the medieval buildings little is evident, although drawings show that, in addition to the W range, the massive C12 W tower of the church, N of the present house, and part of the range S of the cloister existed until the late C18. The cloister itself had been rebuilt in the C14 by Abbot John Buckerell (1308–29), as is known from a surviving Latin inscription reset in the E wall of the present house, together with fragments of the trefoiled arcades and their Purbeck marble columns. A drawing of 1769 shows these arcades in their original position, with figure sculpture in the spandrels: quite a rarity. But only a few carved fragments survive, excavated in 1928 (*see* St Nectan).

At the time of the Dissolution there were only four canons. In 1546 the abbey was granted to William Abbott, Sergeant to the

King's Cellar, whose descendants are still the owners. They adapted the W range as their house. The abbot's chamber, with fine Dec windows, and an adjoining hall with C16-looking windows and a large chimney are still recognizable in the 1769 drawings. By then a S wing had been added on the W side, dated 1705 (some original windows remain), balancing a medieval N wing which no doubt had the abbot's private rooms. But in 1779 the house was transformed for the then owner, Paul Orchard, by the architect *John Meadows*. On the W side he added a corridor on each floor to service the main rooms (a typical C18 improvement), so that the centre now has a sober C18 front, the windows with Gothic glazing-bars. On the E side he created a happy gimcrack Gothic composition: nine bays with pointed windows and a castellated parapet rising to a central pediment (cf. Tawstock Court). One-storey bay-windows, also crenellated. It is interesting to contrast this with the N porch and remodelled N wing, solid and serious Gothic of a century later by *G. G. Scott*.

Inside, first impressions are of Scott's work of 1862: an outer and inner entrance hall with a diagonal link, a strong trefoiled doorway with plenty of carved detail, and painted vaulting added to the ground-floor corridor. In the inner hall, reset late C16 panelling. The main reception rooms were refurbished a little earlier, c. 1845, in a rich neo-Jacobean taste influenced by the House of Lords. Squared beamed ceilings with bosses; sumptuous overmantels and panelling. Only the library is still in the more light-hearted Gothick of *Meadows*, with its arched bookcases and fabulous ogee-arched fireplace directly inspired by *Batty Langley*. In the S wing of 1705 two contemporary panelled rooms, an L-shaped lobby with pretty plaster ceiling with fruit, foliage, and cherubs' heads, and a staircase with twisted balusters. But at basement level one is back in the Middle Ages: thick walls, and several archways of the C13 or C14 are visible.

GROUNDS. The formal gardens E and W of the house shown on a survey of 1702 were replaced by lawns in the later C18. WALLED GARDEN further up the valley; WATER GARDEN, planted with the advice of *Gertrude Jekyll*.

Near St Nectan there are only a few cottages, among them, SE of the church, a former CHURCH HOUSE, two storeys, stone, with gabled projection with upper slit window (garderobe?) on the S side, and on the N a stair projection and segment-headed archway.

The little town is some distance away. It consists chiefly of a long winding street of white- and cream-walled cottages, widening into a MARKET SQUARE with the former chapel of St John in the centre. In NORTH STREET two facets of architect-enriched-vernacular of the later C20: the HARTLAND CLUB by *C. G. Metters*, 1979, white, with quirky angle windows, and the VICARAGE by *Anthony Hollow*, 1982, yellow brick with crested ridge tiles.

LIMEKILN, Moulds Mill. On the edge of the beach. Unusually, with a wall protecting the earth.

(BROWNSHAM FARM. Early C17 plaster ceiling on the first floor with fruit and vine-scroll ornament.)

(LOWER VALLEY FARM. A simple eyecatcher arch.)

EMBURY BEACON, NE of Welcombe. Much of the Iron Age PROMONTORY FORT on the cliff top has been lost through erosion.

Excavation has produced evidence for Late Iron Age occupation. On BURSDON MOOR and WELSFORD MOOR a large BARROW CEMETERY with a variety of different barrow types. *See also* Blegberry.

HATHERLEIGH

5000

Hatherleigh is a quiet, declining market town in a remote part of North Devon. The church lies at the upper end of the town, which climbs up the hillside. In the market place below the church a featureless MARKET HOUSE of 1840 (the town suffered from fires in 1840 and 1846). The best individual house is the GEORGE HOTEL, late medieval, possibly the court house of the abbots of Tavistock with courtyard behind. By the little square (with misconceived C20 chic improvement in the centre) the NATIONAL SCHOOLS, Tudor, 1838, two-storeyed. At the corner of SOUTH STREET an C18 stucco front with a broad Doric porch. Several nice houses around the churchyard, including the former rectory with a big hipped roof.

ST JOHN THE BAPTIST. W tower with type B buttresses, a polygonal NE stair-turret, battlements, and a shingled spire. Nave and aisles, the arcades of five bays with granite piers of A type, capitals only to the main shafts, and depressed pointed arches. No division between nave and chancel. Aisle windows of three lights, straightheaded, without tracery; N aisle E window of five lights with minimum tracery; S chancel chapel and chancel windows with Perp tracery. Ceiled wagon roofs, and CELURE of one bay. – (REREDOS. Of *c.*1840.) – FONT. Square, Norman, with graceful ogee-cupola cover (C18?). – PULPIT and READER'S DESK incorporate bits from the former SCREEN. – At the W end of the S aisle a PEW incorporating Jacobean panels. – BENCH ENDS with the usual foliage decoration. – COMMUNION RAILS with alternating fluted and twisted balusters. – STAINED GLASS. Flemish C17 bits in the S aisle W window. – (W window, N aisle E and W windows by *Clayton & Bell*; E window and one S window by *Powell's*.) – MONUMENT. Incised slab to John Yeo † 1662, a kneeling figure in armour, with his wife. – At the S entrance, former PRIEST'S HOUSE, now two houses, the SE one preserving medieval fabric.

OBELISK, 1 m. W. Erected in 1860 to commemorate Lieutenant-Colonel Morris. (Bronze relief of Balaclava by *E.B. Stephens*.)

DECKPORT. Former Elizabethan and Jacobean manor house of the Lethbridge family. Asymmetrically placed porch. Three-room lobby-entrance plan. Two- to six-mullioned windows. Two plaster overmantels.

HAWKCHURCH

3000

Close to the county boundary; in Dorset until the C19.

ST JOHN. A surprise, considering the statement 'church rebuilt' in the *Little Guide* and *Kelly's Directory*, for the rebuilding of 1859–61 by *John Hicks* of Dorchester,[*] directed and financed by the Rev. E. Cary Adams, was not a total reconstruction: the C12 and C13 work in the body of the church was preserved and re-erected and a clerestory added in a transitional Norman style, with the C12 corbel table with carved heads reset above it. The chancel and all the nave windows were reconstructed in correct C13 geometric. The new work is obtrusive only in the clumsy shafts and corbels of the nave roof. Very low medieval arcades, to the N aisle C12, one circular column with square scalloped capital corner heads, and a base with simple spurs, and one pier with space left towards the nave to allow for a screen. Chancel arch probably altered in the C13, but with well preserved C12 N respond: soffit shaft and two angle shafts. Main capital with three flat interlaced snakes and a head; carved abacus; remarkable, deeply undercut pair of dragons around the base. S arcade *c*. 1200, except for the later carving of the E respond and the heads to the E hoodmould. Round-headed arches on uncommonly fine capitals, with stiff-leaf foliage interspersed with musical animals, fabulous beasts, a man with bagpipes, etc. Elaborate base spurs. S door of similar date, with E.E. shafts and stiff-leaf capitals supporting a Caernarvon arch. Perp W tower with Ham Hill dressings. Pierced stone panels in the belfry windows, and a W door with a frieze of quatrefoils above.

Stone PULPIT, 1861, carved by *Henry Burge*. – STAINED GLASS. Chancel E 1862 by *Ward & Hughes*, side windows painted with quarries and scrolls by Mrs *Adams*, the rector's wife. – MONUMENTS. Thomas Moore †1695 and two wives. Baroque wall-monument. – Sir William Domett, 1829 by *John Chislett* of Beaminster, 'chaste and elegant' (*Gentleman's Magazine*).

OLD RECTORY. C19, reputedly by *Thomas Hardy*. Picturesquely set in its own grounds. Rubble stone. Trefoiled lights to a two-storey bay-window with its own stone roof.

Opposite the church an attractive group of houses along the main street, including the OLD INN with datestone BEHOLD AD 1547.

WYLD COURT. A small manor house owned in the C16 by the Moores, later by the Wyndhams and the Arundells of Wardour. Restored in the late C19 after division into cottages. Main range with four gables. Projecting cross-wing to the r., Victorian wing behind. The fenestration of two-, three-, and four-light stone ovolo-moulded windows with dripstones fits the date 1593 RM on the guttering to the r. of the porch; it is probably a remodelling of an older house. Four-centred doorway; coat of arms in a square panel above.

Good features inside, not all *in situ* (e.g. the stud-and-panel screen in the cloakroom off the hall). Two rooms l. of the hall, each with panelling, four-centred fireplace arch, and carved overmantel of *c*. 1600. In the further room a wooden doorway with cambered arch leads to a substantial staircase projection behind. A blocked three-light wooden-mullioned window shows that this projection was an addition of *c*. 1600 to the older main range. The stairs rise around a solid core; handsome dog-gate with two tiers of turned balusters (cf. Rashleigh Barton). Three upstairs rooms in the main range and one in the cross-wing have stone Tudor fireplaces; the one nearest the

[*] His principal assistant at the time was *Thomas Hardy*.

stairs has an especially grand overmantel with painted graining and three shields within shallow arches divided by hefty volutes.

HAYES BARTON
Near East Budleigh

The birthplace of Raleigh in 1552. Quite a substantial farmhouse built of cob, E-plan, thatched, with a stone chimney at the back dated 1627. Windows much renewed.

HEANTON PUNCHARDON

The church lies quite impressively along the hillside overlooking the estuary of the river Taw.

ST AUGUSTINE. Tall w tower of ashlar, with buttresses of type B, pinnacles, and unusual Dec three-light bell-openings. All the windows on the s side renewed, also the E window, probably when *White* restored the church in 1889–90. The N aisle, like the tower, is of ashlar, with straight-headed late Perp windows without tracery, the rough N porch obviously later, i.e. presumably post-Reformation (cf. other undatable porches of this kind, e.g. Morte-hoe). The w window of the N aisle, with its odd uncusped light, perhaps also post-Reformation. The feature of the interior that will be remembered is the arcade between nave and N aisle, with the usual Devon piers of B type placed not diagonally but so that they are square, on square blocks. Very thin cornices rather than capitals, and depressed arches, all painted. Is it a remanagement of Perp parts in the C18 or early C19? Aisle and nave with ceiled wagon roofs with bosses. – FONT. Octagonal, without datable features, on five shafts. – SCREEN. Clumsily restored, especially in the coving. The heavy type A standard.

MONUMENTS. Richard Coffin †1523, a Sheriff of Devon. An 52 extremely elaborate yet somewhat rustically decorated recess in the chancel N wall, without an effigy, probably intended to serve as an Easter Sepulchre. The decoration almost exclusively Perp foliage – no tracery or similar geometrical elements. Even the two tiers of quatrefoils on the tomb-chest have frames of leaves in the spandrels. The usual depressed pointed arch covers the recess. Cresting again with foliage, and a centrally placed little figure of an angel bearing a shield. Coffin's intertwined initials in the spandrels. – In the NE (Bassett) chapel: Elizabeth Bassett †1635, with the usual kneeling figure. – Arthur Bassett †1672. A good example of its date, architectural, with urn and putti on broken pediment. – John Bassett †1683. Oval in architectural frame, with angels, putti, etc. – Also Thomas Ballantine †1693. Black and marble oval on a shelf with putti, skull, and wreath. – Elizabeth Hart †1695. Medallion with plump cherubim. – (In the churchyard, the gravestone of Edward Capern, the postman poet, †1894, with his postman's bell, and verses by Alfred Austin, Poet Laureate.)

HEANTON COURT. The home of the Bassetts from the C15 to 1802. With its battlements and Georgian windows with heavy keystones, apparently an C18 reworking of an older building. Eleven bays, only one room deep, projecting three-storey end bays. The back windowless, with rubble walls. The house lies below the village, squeezed between the main road and the estuary.

HEMYOCK

A large but not very attractive village, apart from the delightful cast-iron PUMP of 1902, with a superstructure of balusters and finials, and the METHODIST CHURCH, a restrained rendered front with tall arched windows and a tiny porthole in the gable.

ST MARY. The masonry of the church and the low unbuttressed tower are perhaps C12 in origin. The tower seems originally to have been central – see the blocked round-headed arches to N and S. Extensively reconstructed by *Richard Carver* of Taunton in 1846–7, when the arcades with octagonal piers, the S aisle, and the roof were all rebuilt. (The arcades had already been rebuilt in 1768.) A cinque-foil-headed PISCINA remains in the S wall. W gallery and prominent PEWS with tall ends also of 1847. – FONT. Late C12, Purbeck marble, square, with scalloped sides. The base, with four shafts and similarly scalloped capitals, was discovered in 1847. It surely belongs to the font and not, as has been supposed, to a former S arcade. – Brass CANDELABRA. 1773. – STAINED GLASS. E window by *Hardman*, given in 1876; scenes under canopies. – Chancel S 1896 by *Gibbs*. – S aisle E, coloured lights given by the Misses Simcoe in 1847. – CHURCHYARD GATES. A welcome survival: made in the village in 1813, when the gates cost £17 14s 6d, the overthrow of £5 1s 3d, and the terminal balls to the piers £3 16s 10½d.

HEMYOCK CASTLE. An unimpressive flat site in the middle of the little town, immediately W of the church, still partly surrounded by a moat which was fed by an adjacent stream. In its present form the result of a licence to crenellate granted to William Asthorpe in 1380, although the moat may be older, and the ashlar work on the inner face of the gateway (barely visible) may represent the front face of the pre-1380 entrance (a straight joint revealed in conservation work in 1984 has been almost obscured by concrete facing). The additions of c. 1380 are two circular towers flanking the gateway and the enclosing wall with similar corner and intermediate towers, of which several survive in part. The wholly rubble defences are, however, largely a sham. The towers had no proper access, and the best preserved (the southernmost in the gatehouse) has no clear evidence of floors. The rubble portcullis groove could not have functioned properly, and lacks an upper operating chamber. William Asthorpe was a newcomer to Devon society who married into the local Dynham family. He clearly wanted his manor house to look impressive, and dressed it up in traditional castellated form.

Some further Gothicizing took place in the early C19, it seems, when the buildings which remained after the Civil War (when the castle had been used as a garrison) were a farm owned by the Simcoes of Dunkeswell. Arched wooden windows were inserted in some of the rubble outbuildings around the enclosing wall, and also in the S end of the farmhouse within the precinct, which was given a bowed end (used for a cider press) with little arched niches below the eaves (opened up as windows in the 1980s). The Perp granite doorway in line with the gatehouse is also an addition, brought, it is said, from Cornwall, perhaps by Henry Addington Simcoe, curate of Egloskerry (†1868). The house has been much altered, but is basically medieval, preserving a roof with two arched-braced trusses and evidence for wind-braces.

CULM DAVY, 1 m. N. Small C15 chapel of nave and chancel with W bellcote, heavily restored in 1860.

CULM DAVY FARM. Farm buildings of local stone surround a rendered, late-looking house. But this is a medieval hall-house, with the exceptionally good carpentry typical of the area near the Somerset border. Medieval roof on jointed crucks with an arch-braced central truss over the hall and massive lower wind-braces. The open hall was always subdivided from the unheated room at the upper end by the original full-height timber-framed partition with pointed-head door frame. The usual sequence of gradual flooring-in: first the well-carpentered floor of the inner room, then the lower room with a large end stack, suggesting a kitchen, and finally the hall, with its inserted stack and low ceiling.

CULMBRIDGE MANOR. Probably mid C17, extended in the later C17. Plan with two cross-passages, the r. one possibly added as part of the later C17 rebuilding of the higher end. The upper chamber at this end has simple plasterwork with the monogram CR and a crown, and the date 1678. In the hall, facing the fireplace, an original bench end with turned legs.

HENNOCK

ST MARY. Granite, ashlar-built W tower, unbuttressed. Embattled S porch. Windows all Perp. N and S aisles of four bays with granite piers of B type with undecorated capitals. Restored by *John Chudleigh*, 1874–5. Porch with centre boss of 1908 by *Hems*, designed by *R.M.Fulford*, the incumbent from 1898 to 1910. Ceiled wagon roofs to nave and aisles, with preserved CELURE or glory above the rood screen; panels of this transverse band across the roof decorated with suns and stars, recoloured by *Herbert Read* in 1975–82, in sympathy with the SCREEN. This has wainscoting with early C16 paintings of apostles (N aisle) and saints (choir). The original colour is especially well preserved where the screen was concealed by box pews; other over-painting was removed in 1975–82. S aisle screen coeval, but by a different carver and painter.* – FONT. Square, Norman, one side with the blank arcade of the table-top fonts, the others with elementary leaf motifs. – STAINED GLASS. In the tracery of one N window four quite good figures of seraphim.

VICARAGE. Late medieval, U-plan, with additions of 1906 by the Rev. *R.M.Fulford*. The original house mostly of cob, thatched, but the l. wing with close-studded timber-framing to the courtyard (filled with early C19 brick-nogging), a rarity in Devon. Shut off from the street by a high wall, barn, and gatehouse (now village hall).

*I owe these notes to the restorer, *Anna Hulbert*.

WARMHILL. A farmhouse, now subdivided. Good joinery of
c. 1600, including moulded door frame and front door, hall ceiling
beams and screens.

TEIGN VILLAGE is a street of two-storey dressed stone terraces
built *c.* 1912 to house workers in the local mines.

GREAT ROCK was the last working mine on Dartmoor (micaceous
haematite), still active in the 1930s.

BULLATON. A late medieval farmhouse, with the former open hall
and late C16 cross-wing at the upper end. Lower end rebuilt in the
C19. Exceptionally narrow inner room, subdivided from the hall
by a stud-and-panel screen with ship graffiti and original bench.
The farm buildings, all carefully sited to take maximum advantage
of the difficult hillside site, include barn, shippons, ash house, and
two circular rick stands of solid stone.

HERNER
Bishops Tawton

5020

ST JAMES. Built by the Chichesters of Hall in the 1880s. Nave,
chancel, and N tower with battlements and pinnacles. Geometric
and Dec tracery. (Some late medieval carving said to come from
Barnstaple Guildhall. Two C16 bench ends. Three screen panels. S
aisle window by *Kempe Studios*, 1895.)

HIGHAMPTON

4000

HOLY CROSS. Outside the village. Norman S door with one order of
colonnettes with very curious, somewhat dubious capitals. Unbuttressed, pinnacled W tower; nave and N aisle with straight-headed
windows, the individual lights pointed and cusped. The aisle is
separated from the nave by two tall shapeless granite columns of
1834 carrying the wall-plate of the old nave wagon roof. The
chancel also of 1834. – FONT. Norman, of the Cornish Fowey
type, with a small bowl adorned at the top by a broad band of
simple motifs such as crosses saltire, stars, etc.

CHURCH HOUSE, N of the church. With an old stone doorway, the
head renewed, and the date 1834, probably a restoration.

See also Burdon.

HIGH BICKINGTON

6020

ST MARY. Of the Norman church the S door remains (with moderate zigzag decoration of the arches, one beast's-head corbel, and
one order of colonnettes in the jambs) and the lower storeys of a
former S tower in a transeptal position. The arch into the nave is
pointed and unmoulded. A W tower was built instead in the Perp
style, tall, of three stages, with diagonal buttresses and short pinnacles. The rest of the church Dec and Perp. Nave and N aisle.
The arcade of four plus two bays, the two easternmost piers octagonal, the arches simply moulded. The four W piers of A type, with

1. Dartmoor from north of Iddesleigh

2. The South Hams coast:
Blackpool Sands, looking towards Dartmouth
3. Dartmoor, hut circles and part of a large parallel reave
system at Mountsland Common, Ilsington, second millennium B.C.
4. Dolton, Ashwell, seventeenth century
5. Torquay, the early nineteenth century resort

6. Exeter, Rougemont Castle, gate tower, early Norman
7. Exeter, St Mary Arches, nave, twelfth century

8. Bondleigh, St James, capital, Norman
9. Dolton, St Edmund, font made from parts
   of an Anglo-Saxon cross shaft
10. Buckland in the Moor, St Peter, font, Norman
11. Stoke Canon, St Mary Magdalene, font, Norman

8 | 10
9 | 11

12. Exeter, aerial view showing the cathedral precinct
in the south-east sector of the walled city
13. Crediton, Holy Cross, twelfth-century cruciform church
largely rebuilt in the fifteenth century
14. Ottery St Mary, St Mary, refounded 1337

15. Exeter Cathedral, monument to Bishop Branscombe †1280, detail
16. Exeter Cathedral, pulpitum, by Thomas of Witney,
completed 1324
17. Exeter Cathedral, nave, vaulting boss, c. 1330–40
18. Exeter Cathedral, bishop's throne,
by Thomas of Witney, 1313–16, canopy
19. Exeter Cathedral, sedilia,
probably by Thomas of Witney, c. 1313–28

15 | 17 18
16 | 19

20. Exeter Cathedral, nave, *c.* 1310–40
21. Ottery St Mary, St Mary, choir, mid fourteenth century

22. Exeter Cathedral, south nave windows, *c.* 1310–40
23. Exeter Cathedral, west front, begun 1329
24. Exeter Cathedral, west front screen, seated kings
to the north of the central doorway, *c.* 1330–40

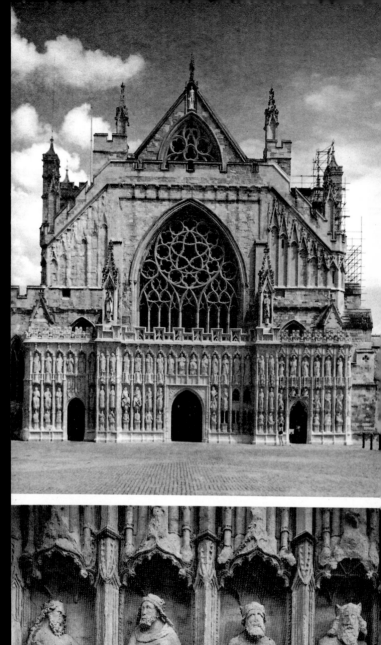

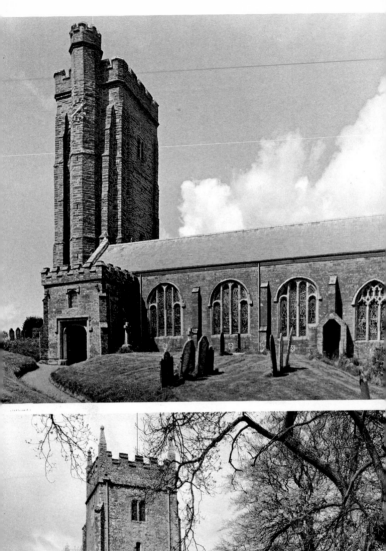

25. Thurlestone, All Saints, west tower and south aisle,
late medieval
26. Cockington (Torbay), St George and St Mary, chancel, aisles,
and west tower, late medieval
27. Colyton, St Andrew, west window and crossing tower,
fifteenth century
28. Tiverton, St Peter, south porch and Greenway Chapel 1517

29. Chawleigh, St James, largely late medieval,
chancel ceiling *c.* 1842
30. Ottery St Mary, St Mary, Dorset aisle, begun *c.* 1504
31. Honeychurch, St Mary, probably twelfth century,
chancel arch late medieval, fittings seventeenth/eighteenth century
32. Plymtree, St John, arcade fifteenth century,
screen and bench ends late medieval

33. Swimbridge, St James, screen, late medieval
34. Awliscombe, St Michael, screen, probably early sixteenth century
35. Coldridge, St Matthew, parclose screen, early sixteenth century
36. Colebrooke, St Andrew, parclose screen, early sixteenth century

33 | 35
34 | 36

37. Bovey Tracey, St Peter, St Paul, and St Thomas of Canterbury,
rood screen and pulpit fifteenth century,
screen paintings early sixteenth century
38. Ashton, St Michael, rood screen,
east side with wainscot paintings, late medieval
39. Lapford, St Thomas of Canterbury, detail of rood screen,
probably second quarter of the sixteenth century
40. Swimbridge, St James, font in early eighteenth-century casing,
incorporating carved work of the second quarter of the sixteenth century

41. Luppitt, St Mary, crossing, late medieval
42. Plympton, St Mary, south porch, vault, *c.* 1400
43. Cullompton, St Andrew, nave roof, late medieval

44. Exeter Cathedral, great east window, Isaiah,
by Master Walter, 1304
45. Exeter Cathedral, great east window, Old Testament prophet,
by Master Walter, 1304
46. Dartmouth, St Saviour, door, fifteenth century and 1631
47. Warkleigh, St John the Evangelist, pyx case, late medieval
48. Tawstock, St Peter, tiles, sixteenth century

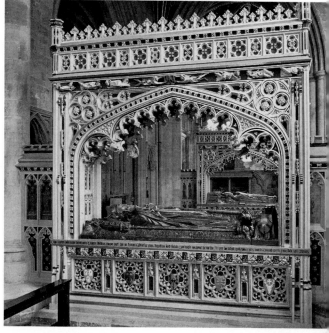

49. Paignton (Torbay), St John, Kirkham Chantry,
late fifteenth century
50. Exeter Cathedral, monument to Bishop Branscombe †1280,
canopy and tomb-chest *c.* 1442
51. Bishops Nympton, St Mary, monument
probably to Sir Lewis Pollard †1540
52. Heanton Punchardon, St Augustine, monument
to Richard Coffin †1523

53. Okehampton Castle, late eleventh and late twelfth centuries, reconstructed in the early fourteenth century
54. Dartmouth Castle, *c.* 1480–1494, with St Petrox, largely 1641
55. Buckland Abbey, barn, early fifteenth century
56. Torquay (Torbay), Torre Abbey, gatehouse, fourteenth century

57. Dartington Hall, hall range from the north-east,
late fourteenth century
58. Dartington Hall, hall, late fourteenth century,
roof by William Weir, 1926–38
59. Compton Castle, outer walls *c.* 1520
60. Weare Giffard Hall, hall roof, late fifteenth century

61. Newton Abbot, Bradley Manor, hall range from the east,
fifteenth century
62. Holcombe Rogus, Holcombe Court, early and late sixteenth century
63. Shute, gatehouse, late sixteenth century
64. Cadhay, courtyard, *c.* 1617

61 | 63
62 | 64

65. Holcombe Rogus, Holcombe Court, gallery,
probably before 1566
66. Collacombe Manor, hall, 1574
67. Barnstaple, 62 Boutport Street, ceiling, 1620
68. Bradninch Manor, Job Room, early seventeenth century

69. South Tawton, Church House, early sixteenth century
70. Moretonhampstead, almshouses, 1637
71. Tiverton, Old Blundells (former school), 1604
72. Sidford, houses in School Street, early seventeenth century

73. Tawstock, St Peter, monument to Frances Lady Fitzwarren, 1589
74. Exeter, Guildhall, forebuilding, 1592–5
75. Bowringsleigh, hall screen, early seventeenth century
76. Exeter, 10–11 Cathedral Close, door,
early seventeenth century

73 | 75
74 | 76

77. Coldridge, Lower Chilverton, hall, screen late medieval,
replace and ceiling seventeenth century
78. Talaton, Old Manor, jetty over inner-room screen,
ate medieval, with sixteenth-century painted decoration
79. Christow, Hill, chamber ceiling, early seventeenth century
0. Uplowman, Middlecombe, seventeenth-century farmhouse
1. Throwleigh, Higher Shilstone, late medieval longhouse,
emodelled in the seventeenth century

82. Holcombe Rogus, All Saints, monument
to Richard Bluett †1614 and wife
83. Alverdiscott, All Saints, monument to Thomas Welshe †1639
84. Holcombe Rogus, All Saints, monument
to Sir John Bluett †1634 and wife (detail)

85. Crediton, Holy Cross, monument
to John and Elizabeth Tuckfield, 1630
86. North Molton, All Saints, monument to Sir Amyas Bamfylde †1626
87. Newton St Cyres, St Cyriac and St Julitta, monument
to John Northcote †1632

ELIZABETH daught'r of S'r
ANTHONY ROVSE Knight.

SVSANNA daughter of S'r
HVGH POLLARD Knight.

88. Newton St Cyres, St Cyriac and St Julitta, monument
to Sherland Shore †1632
89. Exeter, St Petrock, monument
to William and Mary Hooper †1683 and 1658
90. Molland, St Mary, with Courtenay monuments †1724 and †1732

91. Holcombe Rogus, All Saints, Bluett pew, Jacobean
92. Washfield, St Mary, screen, 1624
93. Sydenham, staircase, earlier seventeenth century
94. Cross, staircase brought from Stow House, Cornwall, *c.* 1685

91 | 93
92 | 94

95. Dartmouth, Butterwalk, 1628–40
96. Cullompton, Manor House Hotel, 1603 and 1718
97. Totnes, High Street, Butterwalk,
sixteenth and seventeenth centuries, with later slate-hanging

95 | 96
97

98. Plymouth, Charles Church, 1640–58, tower completed 1708
99. Plymouth, Citadel, gate, by Sir Bernard de Gomme, 1670
100. Barnstaple, Queen Anne's Walk, perhaps by William Talman, 1708

101. Topsham, Strand, houses of the late seventeenth century
102. Bideford, 28 Bridgeland Street, 1692
103. Exeter, Custom House, by Richard Allen, 1680–1
104. Great Torrington, 28 South Street, 1701, doorway
105. Barnstaple, 82 High Street, 1710, cornice

106. Exeter, Custom House, detail of ceiling in the Long Room, by John Abbot, 1680–1
107. Bideford, Royal Hotel, East-the-Water, first-floor ceiling, 1688
108. Youlston Park, ceiling in end room of west wing, late seventeenth century
109. Youlston Park, detail of saloon ceiling, late seventeenth century
110. Bideford, Royal Hotel, East-the-Water, detail of first-floor ceiling, 1688

111. Mothecombe, *c.* 1720
112. Stevenstone, library pavilion, *c.* 1726–30
113. Puslinch, *c.* 1720–6
114. Plymtree Manor (Hayne House), *c.* 1710

111 | 113
112 | 114

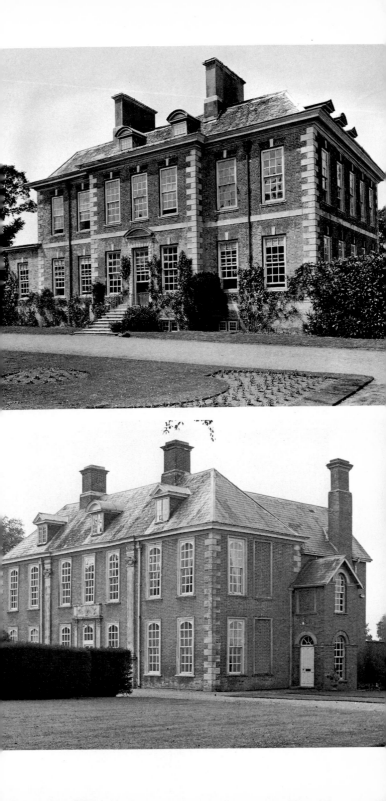

115. South Molton, Guildhall, by Cullen, 1739–41
116. Tiverton, St George, by John James, 1714–16 and 1727–33
117. Bampton, Leburn House, Luke Street, rebuilt in 1766
118. Great Torrington, Palmer House, 1752

115 | 117
116 | 118

119. Bowden House, ceiling, early eighteenth century
120. Poltimore House, saloon, mid eighteenth century
121. Saltram, entrance hall, mid eighteenth century
122. Powderham Castle, grand staircase, 1754–6

119 | 121
120 | 122

123. Saltram, west front, mid eighteenth century
124. Saltram, dining room, by Robert Adam, 1770–2, altered 1780–1
125. Saltram, saloon, by Robert Adam, 1770–2

123
124 | 125

126. Powderham Castle, east front, medieval,
with additions mostly of the eighteenth century
127. Tawstock Court, after 1787
128. Sharpham House, by Sir Robert Taylor, begun *c.* 1770,
staircase hall
129. Winslade Manor, staircase hall, late eighteenth century

130. Powderham Castle, music room, by James Wyatt, 1794–6
131. Powderham Castle, music room 1794–6,
detail of chimneypiece by Richard Westmacott the elder
132. Rockbeare Manor, dining room, late eighteenth century

130 | 131
132

133. Exeter, Southernhay West, by Matthew Nosworthy, 1789
134. Barnstaple, Trafalgar Lawn, *c.* 1805
135. Newton Abbot, Courtenay Park Road, by J. W. Rowell, *c.* 1840–60
136. Tiverton, St Paul's Street, *c.* 1850, with St Paul,
by Manners & Gill, 1854–6

133 | 135
134 | 136

137. Bicton Gardens, palm house, *c.* 1820–30
138. Exmouth, A la Ronde, by Jane and Mary Parminter, 1798
139. Endsleigh Cottage, by Sir Jeffry Wyatville, 1810, shell grotto
140. Sidmouth, Royal Glen Hotel, early nineteenth century
141. Budleigh Salterton, Fairlynch, early nineteenth century

137 | 139
138 | 140
       | 141

142. Plymouth, Belmont, Devonport Road, by John Foulston, *c.* 1825
143. Stover House, lodges, *c.* 1830
144. Kenn, Trehill, by C. R. Ayers, 1827, stair hall
145. Buckland Filleigh, Buckland House,
rebuilt by James Green, 1810, saloon

146. Stonehouse (Plymouth), Royal William Yard,
by Sir John Rennie and Philip Richards, 1825–33, entrance
147. Devonport (Plymouth), Column, 1824, and Institution, 1823,
by John Foulston
148. Plymouth, Custom House, the Parade, by David Laing, 1810

146 | 147
148

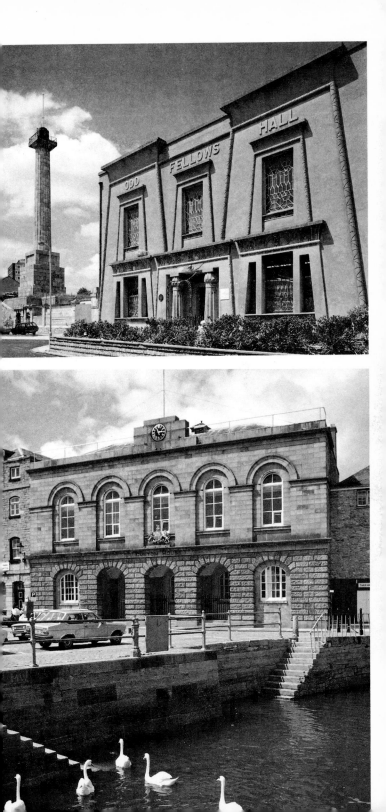

149. Mamhead, by Anthony Salvin, 1826
150. Luscombe, by John Nash, 1800
151. Tavistock, Town Hall, by Edward Rundle, 1860, and abbey gateho
late twelfth century, restored by John Foulston, 1824
152. Exeter, Royal Albert Memorial Museum, by John Hayward, 1865–

149 | 151
150 | 152

153. Devonport (Plymouth), Royal Naval Base, slipway, eighteenth century, roof 1814
154. Devonport (Plymouth), Royal Naval Base, ropery, 1772
155. Axminster, former carpet factory, after 1827
156. Barnstaple, pannier market, by R. D. Gould, 1855–6

153 | 155
154 | 156

157. Flete, by R. Norman Shaw, 1878–85
158. Knightshayes, by William Burges, 1869–74
159. Rousdon (All Hallows School), by Ernest George, 1874–8

160. Teignmouth, St James, designed by W. E. Rolfe,
built by Andrew Patey, 1817–21
161. Bicton, mausoleum, Rolle monument,
designed by A. W. N. Pugin, carved by George Myers, 1850
162. Torquay (Torbay), All Saints, Babbacombe,
by William Butterfield, nave 1865–7, chancel 1872–4
163. Torquay (Torbay), All Saints, Babbacombe,
font, by William Butterfield

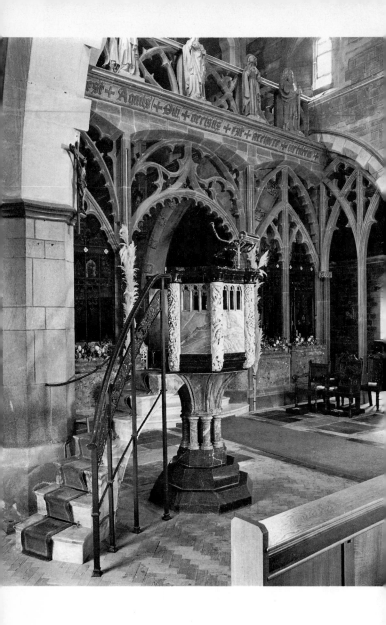

164. Teignmouth, St Peter, Shaldon, by E. H. Sedding, 1893–1902,
pulpit *c.* 1910
165. Torquay (Torbay), St Matthew, Chelston, by Nicholson
& Corlette, 1895–1904, font structure by Gerald Moira,
figure groups by F. Lynn Jenkins
166. Exeter, St David, by W. D. Caröe, 1897–1900

167. Pancrasweek, Lana Wesleyan Chapel, 1838
168. Beer, Rolle estate cottages, Common Lane, 1873
169. Clyst St George, Lady Seaward Primary School, 1859
170. Membland, Bull and Bear Lodge, perhaps by George Devey, c. 1880

167 | 169
168 | 170

171. Budleigh Salterton, Coxen, by Ernest Gimson, 1910
172. Exmouth, The Barn, by E. S. Prior, 1896
173. Torquay (Torbay), Pavilion, by H. A. Garrett, 1911
174. Tavistock, Kingdon House, by Southcombe Parker, *c.* 1906

175. Castle Drogo, by Sir Edwin Lutyens, 1910–30
176. Castle Drogo, by Sir Edwin Lutyens, 1910–30, main staircase
177. Dartington, High Cross House (Headmaster's House),
by William Lescaze, 1931–2
178. Dartington, Blacklers, by William Lescaze, 1933

175 | 177
176 | 178

179. Exeter, Shilhay, housing by Marshman Warren Taylor, 1977–8
180. Winslade Manor, late eighteenth century,
additions by Powell & Moya, 1974–7

179
180

capitals only to the main shafts. The SEDILIA with ogee arches point to the early C14, which may also be the date of the octagonal piers. Nave, N aisle, and W tower all Perp. Original ceiled wagon roofs. – FONT. Norman, square, like a large block capital. The semicircular surfaces decorated with large wheels, rosettes, and crosses, two motifs to each side. – BENCH ENDS. About seventy, a collection of a size unique in North Devon. They can easily be divided into different types: tracery, pairs of saints or prophets, instruments of the Passion, initials in shields, Renaissance foliage, Renaissance profiles in medallions, putti blowing trumpets. – STAINED GLASS. E window 1895 by *Ward & Hughes*. – Chancel s 1903, also by them, but designed by *T.F.Curtis*.

HIGH BRAY

₆₀₃₀

High up in an exposed position with beautiful views to the s and N (towards Exmoor).

ALL SAINTS. Broad, not tall, W tower with buttresses of type B, gargoyles and human heads below the battlements, and short obelisk pinnacles. NE polygonal stair-turret. N and s windows straight-headed. Low arcade of four bays between nave and s aisle. B piers and standard leaf capitals. Ceiled wagon roofs with crenellated wall-plates; no bosses. Restored in 1873 by *Ashworth*. – FONT. Norman, circular, with one shallow zigzag frieze, and on the collar palmettes. – SCREEN. Only three sections remain (in the tower arch), with standard type A tracery.

(CHURCH HOUSE. Two storeys, with staircase projection.)

BRAYFORD lies to the N by the river, with two churches.

ST JOHN. Unbuttressed W tower, largely rebuilt in 1620. Chancel and nave much restored in 1885. Ceiled wagon roofs. – FONT. 1727. Fluted bowl on baluster shaft. – Wall MONUMENT to George Gregorie † 1719. Broken pediment and cherubs.

BAPTIST CHURCH. The oldest in North Devon: 1820 (enlarged in 1924). Very simple, with round-headed windows.

ROUND BARROWS. The Somerset boundary runs along the watershed on BRAY COMMON. Along the summit marches a range of very fine round barrows, from the Five Barrows group in North Molton parish (where in fact seventeen barrows are known) to SETTA BARROW. There are also some STANDING STONES and stone settings.

SHOULSBARROW. *See* Challacombe.

HIGHER HARESTONE
Brixton

₅₀₅₀

The well preserved N and E wings of a small Tudor manor house, the home of the Wood and then the Wood-Winter family until the early C19, radically but sympathetically restored by *J. Lomas* of *Pearn & Procter*, 1972–3. Hall range with two-storey battlemented porch; solar wing to the N, with a small chapel projecting at a slight angle. The details in granite – straight-headed doorways with emphatic square dripstones, cable-moulded string below the battlements, windows with shallow arched lights – belong to a late C16 or early C17 remodelling of an older house. There was a chapel here already in 1378. Inside, much solid late medieval carpentry revealed by the restoration. In the hall (cleared of its later inserted floor), roof with arch-braced trusses with lower wind-braces, all with simple chamfers. At the lower end an internal jetty; later C16 screen beneath with rectangular panels, and one original door. Timber partition also at the upper end of the hall. Small circular squint high up. In the rooms over the screens passage a late medieval wooden ogee-headed doorway and a fireplace on large corbels. In the S wing a fireplace with the small central ogee popular locally in the C16.

9000

HILLERSDON HOUSE
Cullompton

Rebuilt in 1848–9 for William Grant by *Samuel Beazley*, better known as a theatre architect. The plans and specifications of 1847 survive. Essentially in the late Georgian tradition, but with the beginnings of the grander scale and florid and eclectic detail of the Victorian period. Red brick with stone dressings. SE garden front with the favourite Devonian composition of a one-storey colonnade between canted bays; NE entrance front with balustraded Tuscan porte-cochère and a pediment with a coat of arms. An unusual plan with much circulation space. The porch leads, via a triple arch of the squeezed proportions characteristic of the 1840s, to a sequence of top-lit vestibules (now glazed at first-floor level) on axis with the entrance. Only the rectangular centre one (intended as a billiard room) is shown open on the plans, but the two oval wells of the flanking octagonal rooms must have been added during building, as they all have the same robust cast-iron landing balustrades. Flat roof-lights above. The staircase at right angles to the furthest hall has twisted cast-iron balusters to its two long flights, a curved end and corner niches, and formerly an open arcade to a first-floor corridor. Service rooms to the NW; also a 'museum' (with good cornice).

The formal living rooms face SE, approached by a pedimented door in the first vestibule which leads to an anteroom. Main rooms *en suite*; grand double doors with architraves carved in a somewhat Rococo manner. In the anteroom and adjoining drawing room, windows with stained armorial glass and painted figure scenes. Drawing-room ceiling with a thin octagonal pattern with rosettes. Library beyond with original bookcases and grey marble fireplace with angled columns. Service yard at the back; one of its two back entrance lodges remains.

STABLES nearby, half-H-plan, with lunette windows. The GROUNDS with walled garden and lake date from the earlier house which stood a little to the N.

SUMMER HOUSE, SSW of the house. Five-bay front; tripartite entrance with Ionic pilasters.

HITTISLEIGH

ST ANDREW. High up, with only a farm near. A simple church of Dartmoor character. W tower of granite ashlar with diagonal buttresses. Windows all straight-headed, of the most elementary granite shapes. The N aisle E window has a pointed arch with three lights. Granite A type piers; four-centred arches. Ceiled wagon roofs in nave and aisle, the aisle roof more elaborate, with bosses and carved wall-plate. Unusual diagonally framed ceiling to the tower. – FONT. Norman, Purbeck, square, with simple incised zigzag. – SQUIRE'S PEW, at the E end of the aisle. 1619 for Thomas Furze of Eastchurch, quite plain panels, just with fluted framing, none of the usual Jacobean over-decoration.

SCHOOL. Late C19 Gothic, red brick, with half-hipped roofs.

HOCKWORTHY

ST SIMON AND ST JUDE. Stumpy W tower rebuilt in 1848. The rest – nave, N aisle, chancel, S porch – 1864 by the otherwise unknown *Charles D. Greenway*, who died in 1870 aged only 31. The angular massing and severe detailing give the church an aggressively muscular character: tunnel-like chancel almost as long as the nave. – PULPIT, CHANCEL WALL, and REREDOS are all of a piece, stone, simplified Gothic forms, bold marble polychromy. – (STAINED GLASS. E and SE windows by *Hardman*. RH)

HOME FARMHOUSE. Probably a church house. C14–17 and C19. Late C14 roof of devolved crown-post type (cf. Clifford Barton, Dunsford, and the Old Rectory, Cheriton Bishop).

COURT HALL. Dated 1659, much altered, but good C18 plasterwork in the room to the l. of the entrance.

STALLENGE THORNE. A minor manor house of the Troyte family of Huntsham, now a farmhouse. Delightful C17 gatepiers with very large balls. Two-storey porch, the doorway with an accomplished classical frame with broad convex moulding and pediment, all of Ham Hill stone, and so Somerset rather than Devon in feeling. In the gable the date 1675, probably marking the final stages of a lengthy remodelling. From the older house a fragment of stud-and-panel partition to the r. of the entrance passage. S front windows all with hollow-chamfered mullions, perhaps earlier C17; the porch cuts into one of them. The larger, lower window on the l. indicates the importance of the parlour by the C17. Behind this room, in a N wing, a complete later C17 panelled room – large panels of oak with bolection mouldings of deal (i.e. a transitional type). Overmantel with an elaborate pattern of raised rectangles. A parallel adjoining back range of the same date was perhaps built for the staircase (later replaced by the present stair in the front entrance hall). Bolection-moulded fireplace in a bedroom over the hall. Adjoining what was formerly the high end of the hall another back range, possibly pre-C17 living accommodation, later converted to service rooms and outbuildings. Next to the hall fireplace an C18 corn-drying kiln with perforated tiled floor, similar to examples in South Somerset.

HOLBETON

A pretty village with a haphazard cluster of cottages below the church. Close to the churchyard a former early C19 SCHOOL with a symmetrical one-storey front with wooden mullion-and-transom windows and a central archway. E of the crossroads a row of low ALMSHOUSES of the 1890s; slate roofs with broad eaves and little dormers.

ALL SAINTS. An unusually impressive church, with its E end high up above the street and its sumptuously (and tastefully) decorated interior which owes much to the C19 restorations, especially that of 1885–9 by J.D.Sedding, paid for by Henry Bingham Mildmay of Flete. The W tower and spire C13 to early C14 and exactly as at Ermington. Low rectangular NE stair-turret. Total height of the steeple 113ft. S porch of 1885 with angels and figure of Christ over the entrance and an excellent iron gate. The S door, in the Arts and Crafts spirit with its lozenge-work framing, and the W door with carved frieze and openwork iron plaques, are a foretaste of the furnishings inside. Wide nave with N and S aisles, quite exceptionally roomy. Five bays, arcades with piers of A type, capitals only to the four shafts, and depressed arches. Window tracery partly replaced and roofs renewed throughout in 1885–6. – FONTS. The first is Norman, square, with a flat bowl. On two sides blank arches with block capitals between upright and arch, on the two others two lions and a tree between, and a pattern of two leaf panels. – The second font is a fine example of the Victorian use of highly polished Devonshire marbles; a round bowl with tracery patterns with four tall angle shafts.

SCREEN. Extensively and excellently renewed by Sedding. The wainscoting of the N and S aisles is original. It has close, slim blank tracery. The upper parts are straight-headed, without trace of coving or rood-loft, but with a fine cornice and cresting. The main frieze of the cornice with a symmetrically arranged pattern with recurrent ornamental faces, obviously already under Renaissance influence, say c. 1535 or later. The tracery of the screen goes well with such a date: intersected ogee arches, luxuriantly crocketed, and in the upper part with suspended-looking motifs to fill the spaces between the main tracery bars. The cusping of the rounded tops of the individual lights (four within each section), for example, consists of intertwined blossoms. The motifs include Tudor badges (pomegranate, Tudor rose, portcullis). The parclose screens of the same design. The initials I E above the doorway. The centre part of the screen, by Sedding, has heart-shaped motifs enclosing shields.

Much carefully designed and well carved C19 WOODWORK; for example, the stalls, with delightful ends with oak-leaves and animals (in the manner of the choir stalls of Winchester Cathedral), the wooden sedilia, the bench ends of the nave pews, and the reredos, which encloses a PAINTING, Ecce Homo (Italian?), in a carved frame. Carved bosses on Sedding's roof over the chancel. – Other work of the same time: the fine ALTAR of marble with silver panels of the evangelists, and the marble chancel floor. – PULPIT. Of stone, with oak-leaves.

STAINED GLASS. E window with an excellent and unusual pictorial Ascension, with well-managed drapery and much slate-blue, dated 1886, by *Heywood Sumner*. – Three side windows of more conventional type dating from the restoration of 1865. – In the N aisle two very flamboyant windows by *Hugh Easton*, 1947 and 1950. – In the S transept (Membland) S window to Hillersdons of Membland, 1870, two angels on a geometric background.

MONUMENTS. Nave S: Andrew Fir(?). Architectural wall-monument with an oval panel; 1692. – Chancel: Elizabeth Bulteel †1835. Mourning figure with sarcophagus at an angle. – N chapel: Hele family. Three generations, with kneeling figures on four tiers and one central semi-reclining figure (Sir Thomas Hele †1670), making a total of twenty-three. Very old-fashioned, apart from the cherubs on top of the flanking Corinthian columns (could the kneeling figures be re-used from earlier monuments?). – Bulteel family, 1801 by *Coade & Sealy* in their artificial stone, with the same seated cherub weeping and hiding his face as at Teigngrace and Plympton. – Handsome LYCHGATE with a flight of steps up to the churchyard.

BULL AND BEAR LODGE. *See* Membland.

PAMFLETE. Late C18, stuccoed, much remodelled.

See also Flete.

HOLCOMBE BURNELL

ST JOHN. Rebuilt by *Hayward* of Exeter, 1843, but the W tower (red sandstone, with diagonal buttresses, plain granite bell-openings, and no pinnacles) and the arcade (low octagonal granite piers with double-chamfered arches) must be old. – ALTAR. A carved oak chest from Culver House. – SCREEN. Eight panels with painted figures made into the reader's desk: Annunciation and six Saints. – ORGAN, in simple case by *Waterhouse*, from Culver House. – SCULPTURE. Headless alabaster saint; good. – MONUMENTS. An interesting example of a late Easter-Sepulchre-cum-tomb (cf. Woodleigh). Mid C16 tomb-chest with shields in lozenges. Although the recess is framed by a Gothic arch with crockets, there are also rustic, but classical, putti. The large carving of the Resurrection at the back also shows Renaissance influence. – Richard Stephens †1831. A metropolitan piece. Draped broken column with inverted torches, all very sharply cut.

HOLCOMBE BURNELL BARTON. Manor house, mostly early C17, but possibly incorporating parts of a house built by Sir Thomas Dennis (†1561). Three-bay front with ovolo-moulded mullioned windows (hall window of the 1930s). Central cross-passage leading to a small rear courtyard flanked by kitchen wing and parlour wing. The parlour wing, also with stone mullioned windows, has traces of a stair-turret at the end. Hall with late C17 bolection panelling and two remarkable early C16 beams carved with vine scroll and foliage, possibly re-used. Parlour with good ceiling of *c.*1600. In a first-floor room a later allegorical plaster overmantel showing God and Mammon, surrounded by scrolly arabesques.

PERRIDGE HOUSE. Built by *George Byfield* for Josiah White, *c.*1813 (rainwater heads). A neat stuccoed Regency front of 1–3–1 bays, two-storeyed, the centre with pediment over a blind attic rising above the cornice. Full-width Ionic loggia (renewed, and the outer bays filled in, 1962). E wing 1906 in matching style. Staircase with iron balusters.

CULVER HOUSE. 1835 by *George H. Smith* for the Rev. Richard Stephens, with alterations and additions of 1872–5 for Edward Byrom by *Alfred Waterhouse*. Neo-Tudor, a relatively early example (Smith was a pupil of T. F. Hunt, author of *Exemplars of Tudor Architecture* and other pattern books). Gables with elaborate bargeboards, mullioned windows. Waterhouse altered some of the windows and extended the house at the r. end of the entrance to provide a larger dining room, in a style entirely in sympathy with the original, using the same purple volcanic stone. Richly decorated interior. The reception rooms, facing W over the garden, still have the 'panelled ceilings enriched with gilding and colours' as described in a sale catalogue of 1868. The broad spine corridor on to which these rooms open (cf. Mamhead) has Tudor doorcases (the initials of Edward Byrom must be later additions) and a heavily cusped ceiling of square panels. The Waterhouse dining room has a much plainer ribbed ceiling, brought-in Jacobean overmantel, and linenfold panelling. Staircase, also in its present form probably of the 1870s, with ceiled hammerbeam roof decorated with painted foliage panels. The organ now in the church was on the half-landing.

STABLES and COACH HOUSE, to the E. 1872–5 by *Waterhouse*. Simply detailed purple stone gabled front. LODGE of 1879. Fine grounds. In front of the house, balustrading from the Exe Bridge of 1776.

·

HOLCOMBE ROGUS

Holcombe Court and the church form an uncommonly attractive group on the hill, close together yet separated by a wall with a circular dovecote. The village climbs up to house and church.

ALL SAINTS. Perp throughout. Nave and two aisles, chancel and two chancel chapels. W tower with buttresses of type B. Three-light windows, except for the five-light window of the N chancel chapel, which is the Bluett family chapel. The Bluetts built Holcombe Court and held the manor to the middle of the C18. The nave arcades with piers of standard B type, on the S with capitals only to the four main shafts, on the N with standard Devon leaf capitals. One S pier with a diagonally placed niche for an image. The N aisle with wagon roof unceiled, the S aisle ceiled. S porch with graceful fan-vault and graceful arcading outside above the entrance. The body of the church was restored by *John Hayward* in 1858–9, when the arcades were cleared of plaster and the present seating installed. Further restoration in 1881. Chancel restoration 1875 by *J. Mountford Allen*, including the poppy-headed choir stalls.

REREDOS. 1875, designed by *Allen*, executed by *Hems*. – SOUTH PARCLOSE SCREEN to match the NORTH PARCLOSE SCREEN brought from St Peter, Tiverton, in 1854. B type, unusual in the pretty motif of scrolls or ribbons in the head lozenges of the tracery.

– BLUETT PEW. A rare example of a completely preserved

Jacobean family pew. Balusters, and on top small relief medallions with scenes from the early parts of Genesis and other Old Testament subjects. – PAINTING. Venetian, c. 1600, with the Virgin surrounded by saints and Venetian nobility. – STAINED GLASS. Chancel E, N, and S windows and W window all by *Hardman & Co.*, 1892, a characteristic set of the date.

MONUMENTS. Richard Bluett †1614 and his wife. Alabaster, 82 under a shallow coffered arch surmounted by lions, strapwork scrolls and achievement. The woman is recumbent, the man behind her, a little higher, semi-reclining on one elbow. Elaborate strapwork panel beneath the arch. Small allegorical figures on the cornice above the flanking columns. One of a group of early C17 monuments of very similar design, probably London work; cf. Judge Glanville †1615 at Tavistock and Sir Edmund Fenner, 1611–12, at Hayes, Greater London (formerly Middlesex).* – Sir John Bluett †1634 and wife. Also alabaster, under a heavy pediment, both figures 84 recumbent, she behind and a little higher. Eight children kneel against the front of the tomb-chest. – Rev. Robert Bluett †1749. Excellent, grand and sober, very metropolitan-looking, with urn in aedicule high up. On the pedestal of the urn a large relief of the Good Samaritan (by whom?). – Robert and Kerenhappuch Bluett, erected 1783, by *Mauge & Co.* of Bath (an early case no doubt of the use of '& Co.' for a sculptor's workshop). Two seated allegories by an urn high above an inscription plate. – Several minor C18 monuments.

CHURCH HOUSE (now called The Priest House). Between Court and church, an essential ingredient in the appealing view up the village street to the churchyard. Rubble stone, two storeys, some timber-mullioned windows. The special feature is the framed ceiling with moulded beams in the centre of the ground floor, originally divided by stud-and-panel partitions from the end rooms. A fireplace in the centre room, another, exceptionally wide, with two flues, at the S end. The details suggest that the building may have been adapted for domestic use in the early C16, perhaps for the priest, at the same time that the walls were raised to create a single large room on the upper floor. Restored by *C. R. Ashbee* in 1906, converted by the Landmark Trust in 1984–5.

HOLCOMBE COURT. The S entrance front is the most spectacular 62 example of the Tudor style in Devon. To acknowledge that is to admit also that Devon has no Tudor buildings of the scale to be found, for example, in the Midlands. In most respects Holcombe Court is a house on the compact courtyard plan usual in the county, only on a slightly more generous scale. The exception is the big buttressed tower over the entrance, with a broad and high stair-turret to its l. (not the more formal arrangement with symmetrical angle turrets of Hampton Court and so many other Tudor gate-houses). The concept is still in the tradition of the fortified manor house, but the tower is a showpiece not intended for defence; above the four-centred entrance archway a handsome corbelled-out bay-window with arched uncusped lights is carried up through all three of the upper floors. This work for the Bluett family belongs to the earlier C16; the hall to the r., with two massive six-light transomed

*I owe these comparisons to Adam White.

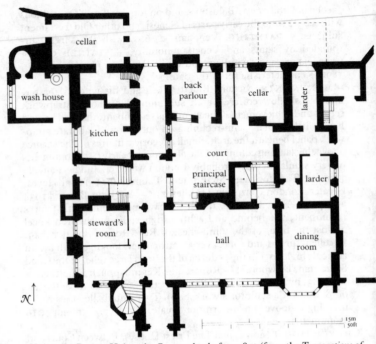

Holcombe Rogus, Holcombe Court: plan before 1859 (from the *Transactions of the Exeter Diocesan Architectural Society*)

windows, the gallery floor above it with two straight gables, and many interior fittings date from a remodelling which was begun before 1566 and probably completed in the 1590s (see the evidence of the plasterwork inside). The N and W ranges were rebuilt in solid Victorian Tudor *c.*1859–68 by *John Hayward* for the Rev. W. Rayer, who was also responsible for other alterations, re-using old materials, which has somewhat confused the history of the building.

Inside, the SCREENS PASSAGE is an impressive early C16 survival; not three, but four stone archways, the fourth one to the turret stair which leads to a suite of rooms in the tower and above the service rooms (cf. Dartington). The HALL itself is Victorian Tudor, with C19 screen, fireplace, and thin ribbed ceiling with the Rayer crest. The Rayer arms at the lower end are said to replace those of Protector Somerset. An oval window at the screens end survives as evidence for a late C17 remodelling. From the inner courtyard it can be seen that there was once a large window on the N side in addition to the two on the S.

To the E is the DINING ROOM, approached circuitously through the later C16 stair projection (the door in the E wall of the hall is C19), and through a lobby with four stone doorways (the E one C19). The dining room was fitted up in the later C16 with good panelling with Ionic pilasters, and a restrained wooden overmantel with paired columns and pedimented aedicules with little urns (a motif found also in panelling at Portledge). Plaster ceiling of square panels (probably applied over earlier moulded beams); in each panel a star shape of thin ribs with small foliate bosses. The bay-window of *c.* 1975 replaces a Victorian one. The MAIN STAIR is of the later Tudor type with broad steps around a solid core of masonry. Simple ribbed plaster ceiling. Lamp bracket in the outer wall. Between first and second floors a splendid door with three tiers of turned balusters.

The remarkable GALLERY to which the stair leads extends nearly the whole length of the front of the house, the best example of a C16 long gallery in Devon, although at 65 ft it is modest in comparison with such giants as the Queen's Gallery at Hampton Court, which was 180 ft, or Hardwick (166 ft). Its position above the great hall could have been inspired by Protector Somerset's Berry Pomeroy, the *nec plus ultra* of ambitious mid Tudor building in the county, but it can also be paralleled by leading houses elsewhere of the third quarter of the century (Broughton, Oxon, and Cecil's Theobalds, Herts). The gallery here presumably dates from before 1566, for on its flat plaster ceiling are wreathed initials spelling the name of Sir Roger Bluett, who died in that year. The simple style of the ceiling would fit such a date, making it the earliest datable plasterwork in Devon. The thin longitudinal ribs do not intersect in the usual manner, but split intermittently to form pointed ovals enclosing the initials or small foliage devices. The frieze has tightly curled arabesques and dolphins, still in the early Renaissance tradition. On the S side the gallery is lit by two large bays. In between these, and all along the N side, are a series of tiny rooms, nine in all, each with a plank door and a little window. They appear to be an original feature, although some may have been subdivided later (see the positions of windows and partitions on the S side). Who slept in such rooms? They do not seem to be paralleled in other Elizabethan houses, although Polwhele describes as a curiosity what seems to have been a similar arrangement at Annery near Monkleigh, North Devon, a large Tudor mansion demolished *c.* 1800. Near the top of the staircase on the N side is a larger room distinguished by a central ceiling motif, and with a timber framework for beds (or cupboards?).

From the gallery the roof over the lower E wing is visible, four arch-braced trusses, i.e. belonging to the earlier C16 building phase. Also from this period a few features on the first floor of the E wing: a fireplace, and a puzzling timber four-centred arch. The MAIN BEDCHAMBER over the dining room was remodelled in the later C16. Ceiling with intersecting single ribs, the fleur-de-lys terminals still of the small early type, the frieze similar to the gallery one, though more ornate. The plaster overmantel may be a little later, probably of *c.* 1591, the date of the one in the Court Room described below. It has a relief of Moses and the brazen serpent, crudely executed but quite a sophisticated design, in a strapwork surround flanked by pairs of terms with central bands and tassels. In the anteroom created in the C19, doors made up from elaborate late C16 woodwork.

At the opposite end of the house, over the service rooms, and now approached by a C19 staircase N of the screens passage, the DRAWING ROOM, or former COURT ROOM. This is dominated by an exceptionally fine large plaster overmantel: two exotic and spirited caryatids flank a coat of arms in a strapwork surround; the date 1591 appears on the geometric frieze above. The ceiling again may be earlier than the overmantel; it has intersecting ribs, at the sides descending to corbels, small bosses, and a modest central pendant. Later C17 sumptuous bolection-moulded panelling and double doors to a gallery overlooking the hall. In the NW corner a small staircase projection, perhaps originally a garderobe. In the SW corner, access to the tower, which contains the MUNIMENT ROOM, with unusually rich panelling of c. 1600: scenes of harvesting, the five senses, and floral motifs, and delightful hidden cupboards with drawers with simple marquetry. The room above has simpler panelling and an overmantel with the Chichester arms, for Elizabeth Chichester, who married Richard Bluett. He inherited in 1585 and died in 1614, and must have been responsible for the late C16 improvements.

The area below the Court Room is a puzzle. One simple stud-and-panel partition remains, but two of the screens-passage entrances (one with an intriguing folding door) now open into a narrow corridor which has a later C16 plaster frieze. Beyond this is a small steward's room (?), also with late C16 plasterwork, the overmantel pathetically obscured by later C17 panelling. N of this, in the rebuilt C19 W wing, the LIBRARY, with a spectacular early C16 ceiling, said to come from the N range, an excellent example of the type of heavy framed ceiling that preceded the fashion for plasterwork. Twelve main squares with carved bosses at the intersections are each divided into four further squares: forty-eight compartments in all, each beam moulded and enriched with beaded scrollwork.

The approach to the house from the Victorian entrance archway is given a pleasant informality by the attractive circular DOVECOTE to the E. Beyond this the STABLES, mostly C19, but incorporating older work; on the hill slope above, a WALLED GARDEN (the wall dated 1748, and partly lined with brick inside), entered between gatepiers with pineapples. W of the house a C19 balustraded TERRACE with steps down to a small lake.

FREATHINGCOTT FARMHOUSE. C17 and C19. A transitional plan: parlour below the cross-passage, service room beyond the hall (with a stack at the upper end of the hall); the kitchen in a wing behind. Good farm buildings, some C17.

See also Canonsleigh.

3000   HOLLACOMBE

ST PETROCK. Impressively sited on an exposed hill-top, the wind broken only by a row of pines. An aisleless church; the W tower low, unbuttressed, with saddleback roof; no W door (i.e. all early features). The S side of the nave has a lancet window and a very plain Norman doorway, the lintel stone, with a sloping pediment-like top, decorated with three big rosettes, such as often appear on fonts. Above it the badly preserved top of a lantern cross. Chancel E window of two lights with a circle above each cusped head. During extensive restorations in 1880-2 the tower was partly rebuilt (the saddleback roof – an unusual feature in Devon – apparently copies the medieval original), window masonry was replaced, new double-chamfered tower and chancel arches were built, and the church was re-roofed throughout. – FONTS. An octagonal font inside the church. – Outside the porch, another, square, Norman, on five shafts. – READING DESK with some re-used balusters.

HOLLOCOMBE
2 m. N of Winkleigh

6010

ST MICHAEL AND ALL ANGELS. Now a house. Delightfully composed small, unaisled church with an Arts and Crafts flavour, by *Edward Keenor* of Winkleigh, 1890–1. SW tower no higher than the nave roof, the shingled top stage with timber bell-openings; concave-sided pyramid spire.*

HOLNE

7060

ST MARY. Of the early medieval church the W tower still recognizable: unbuttressed, with a marked batter. Later the nave and two aisles of five bays, divided by low octagonal granite piers carrying depressed double-chamfered arches. The old wagon roofs in the nave unceiled, in the aisles ceiled. Reseating 1909 by *C. E. Ponting*. – SCREEN. Separate screens across S aisle, nave, and N aisle, all of the same design, with paintings (of no merit) in the wainscoting, standard type A tracery, no coving, and two bands of decoration in the cornice. – The PULPIT unusual in design, on a goblet (not a palm-tree) foot. The panels low, with just a gable above a shield, and then a broad cornice of four strips. Among the arms displayed are those of Bishop Oldham (1504–19).

VICARAGE. 1832. Charles Kingsley was born here.

The parish lies on the edge of Dartmoor, with some of the best scenery in the county. Two medieval bridges over the River Dart.

HOLNE OLD BRIDGE, ½m. N of Holne Park. Rebuilt in 1413, of four arches, three semicircular, the fourth segmental.

HOLNE NEW BRIDGE, ½m. NE of Hannaford House. Of the same date as the Old Bridge, with one small and two large semicircular granite arches.

BROOK FARM. The home farm of the large estate, later C18 and C19, the house slate-hung, on a symmetrical double-pile plan. Excellent range of farm buildings around the courtyard, including a first-floor barn with shippon below, and a roundhouse.

PIXIE'S HILL, NW of the village. 1928 by *F. Harrild*, a pupil of Lutyens. Picturesque vernacular. Rubble stone, heavily thatched, with deep eaves and eyebrow dormers; rendered chimneys with slate set-offs. Symmetrical front with two slightly angled wings, reminiscent of a butterfly plan. Well preserved details: leaded casements, plank doors, moulded beams.

TUMBLY. Also by *Harrild*, 1926, a similarly detailed thatched cottage. Originally just a tall, steeply roofed two-storey range with off-centre stone stack, and a lower S wing. One-storey E and W

*Contributed by Geoffrey K. Brandwood.

wings added in the 1930s, w wing extended 1952, all in the same
style. A spectacular site overlooking Dartmoor.

HOLNE MOOR, w of Venford reservoir, offers a fine view of one of
Dartmoor's most extensive PARALLEL REAVE SYSTEMS, a series
of linear banks of the second millennium B.C. The DARTMEET
system runs N from the terminal reave on Holne Moor, down into
the valley of the Dart, up over YAR TOR and CORNDON DOWN
and onward to the N side, covering some 8 sq.m. in all. In its
present form, it appears to date from the Middle Bronze Age. It is
dotted with small settlements and isolated huts. A particularly
good view can be had from Combestone Tor. Immediately s of the
terminal reave, a STONE ROW and a number of isolated BAR-
ROWS, and to the s and w of Venford reservoir a complex medieval
FIELD SYSTEM. Extensive medieval and later tinworking remains
are also apparent on the moor.

HOLNE CHASE WOOD. A well preserved Iron Age HILLFORT can
be seen in the wood, as well as more recent remains of the iron-
mining and charcoal-burning industries.

₃₀₀₀   HOLSWORTHY

Holsworthy has singularly little to appeal to the architectural visitor.
A market town already in the C12, it grew until the later C19. The
WHITE HART HOTEL in the High Street is early C19, a rendered
three-storey, three-window front, with ball finials on the parapet.
MARKET HOUSE of 1858. The square is still used for a weekly
market, although the cattle market was moved out in 1906. The
church lies at the E end of the town, a little away from the centre,
its N side still as close to the fields as if it were a village church.

ST PETER AND ST PAUL. Stately w tower of a type familiar in
Devon: ashlar granite, with buttresses of C type, pinnacles on their
off-sets (cf. Chittlehampton, etc.), and hefty crocketed pinnacles.
The rest of the church restored in 1858, 1865, and – heavily, by
Otho B. Peter – in 1881–2. Evidence of a Norman church is
afforded by two stones in the s porch, one a capital of a colonnette,
the other the centre of a tympanum showing the lamb carrying the
cross. Octagonal piers, double-chamfered arches. The chancel
dates from 1880–2; the N aisle was rebuilt in 1884. The general
impression throughout is of the Victorian work which replaced the
Georgian round-headed sashes and plastered and ceiled roofs. –
Old bits incorporated in several pieces of furniture: fragments of
COMMUNION RAILS with twisted balusters, an openwork carved
PANEL of c. 1710, BENCH ENDS. – ORGAN and ORGAN CASE
renovated in 1884, but in origin late C17 (the organ by *Renatus
Harris*) from Chelsea Old Church; sold to Bideford in 1723 and
brought to Holsworthy in 1865. – STAINED GLASS. N aisle w
window by *Bell* of Great Russell Street, 1876. – E window by
Lavers & Westlake, c. 1882 – MONUMENT. Richard Kingdom
†1816 by *J. Kendall* of Exeter.

RAILWAY VIADUCTS. To the SE, a graceful stone viaduct of
c. 1879, eight 50-ft arches carrying the branch line from Okehampton into the station. The parapets have been replaced by
concrete capping. To the SW, a ten-arched viaduct of 1898 which

carried the extension to Bude. The corbels provided at the springing to support the timber centering and shuttering during the
casting of the arches, which are of concrete marked to simulate
masonry blocks, remain as part of the design. The line closed in
1964.

SOLDEN MANOR. Now a farmhouse, but in the C17 a manor house
of the Prideaux family, illustrated in an early C18 Prideaux drawing which shows a long range with projecting two-storey wings and
a central two-storey porch. On either side of the porch two mullioned windows. The larger hall windows on the r. of four lights.
Gabled dormers above. Extension on the r. beyond the cross-wing.

THORNE. Remains of a medieval chapel – two lancet windows and
an arched doorway – now inside the farmhouse.

HONEYCHURCH   6000

ST MARY. An endearing little church on the N fringe of Dartmoor.
Two Norman beast heads (from a corbel-table?) in the S wall of the
nave indicate the existence of a Norman church of which the two-
cell plan remains unchanged, except for the Perp W tower with
type B buttresses, a low rectangular NE stair-turret, and pinnacles.
The nave now has straight-headed three-light windows. A niche in
the N wall appears to be a re-used Norman window. The chancel is
lower than the nave. Perp chancel arch with imposts of A type. 31
The triple E window replaced a Georgianized window in the
restoration of 1914 by *A. H. Powell* of Stroud. Wagon roof in the
nave. – FONT. Norman, circular, coarse zigzag and cable decoration. – BENCH ENDS. Elementarily decorated. – PULPIT. Rough,
hexagonal, C17. – Rustic BOX PEWS. – COMMUNION RAILS.
Baluster type. – Elizabethan ROYAL ARMS painted on the N wall.
– (ACOUSTIC POTS(?). Found in the blocked priest's doorway.)

SLADE. Now a farmhouse, but once a late medieval house of high
quality. Moulded Perp doorway of granite to the screens passage;
carved four-centred wooden doorway from hall to staircase projection; inner room with moulded beams.

HONITON   1000

Honiton prospered as a centre first of the wool and cloth trade, then of
the lace industry (until machines took over; *see* Tiverton). Defoe
describes it in the early C18 as 'a large and beautiful market town, very
populous and well built'. Its history goes back to *c.* 1200, when a
borough was founded by the fifth Earl of Devon. Like other new
towns, it developed along the main road, away from the older church
on the hill to the SE, on a typical medieval plan with generously laid
out main street and a back lane still evident on the S side. The long
broad High Street, disencumbered of shambles in 1823, and relieved
of through traffic by a C20 bypass, now reflects the final phase of
Honiton's prosperity, mostly pleasant homely two-storey Georgian,
the result of rebuilding after two fires (1747 and 1765). Plenty of gently
outcurving windows, punctuated by several former coaching inns and
the surprising neo-Norman tower of St Paul's church in the centre of

the N side. The general impression is not quite as unspoilt as in 1950, but there are still only a few jarring notes.

St Michael, se of the town centre. The old parish church, right outside the town on the hill (as are so many churches dedicated to St Michael). After a fire in 1911, of old parts only the outer walls and the tower remain. The rest rebuilt by *C.E.Ponting*, very faithfully. It was a remarkable church in its former state, a perfect rectangle, as the Perp style liked them, large and light, with wide windows and very wide aisles and with transepts about centrally placed and not projecting, marked only by the wider arches in the arcade and four-light instead of three-light windows. w of these wide arches the nave of two bays, e the chancel chapels of two bays. The chancel itself does not project to the e beyond them. So all that reaches out of the rectangle is the w tower with buttresses of type B and a w door with a vine frieze along jambs and voussoirs. The whole is late Perp, the w parts paid for by Bishop Courtenay of Exeter, Lord of the Manor of Honiton, *c.* 1480, the e parts, according to the inscriptions on the capitals of the arcade piers, by John and Joan Takell, who died in 1506 and 1529. Her will refers to a 'new ile'. Inside, the piers all of B type with standard capitals. The dominating feature is the wagon roofs (reconstructed after the fire) meeting at the crossing in an intersection of gorgeous wide-space semicircular timbers (cf. Luppitt, where the original roofs remain). The church was restored by *E.H.Harbottle* in 1896, and again after the fire of 1911. – SCREENS. 1926 by *Herbert Read*; traditional.

St Paul, the town church, replaces an older chapel of ease. 1835–8 by *Charles Fowler*, engaged as a result of his work on the Exeter markets. Well built and competently designed in the Norman style, or at least with plenty of Norman motifs. Only the w tower, providing an important accent in the High Street, is one that no Norman church could ever boast of – even with Norman pinnacles. Inside, seven bays with tall Norman columns, a clerestory, and an e apse similar to Early Christian basilicas – a fine, monumental interior, unfortunately rearranged and subdivided in 1986. The galleries have been divided off. The experimental iron roof originally provided by Fowler proved faulty almost immediately and was replaced by *Carver & Giles* in 1848. Reseating 1904 by *Edward G.Warren*.

REREDOS. 1893, an expensive piece designed by *E.L.Parsons* and executed by *Hems*, marble and alabaster, with a central panel of the Crucifixion. The high quality of the detail and cutting is worth noting. – ALTAR PAINTING. Descent from the Cross by *Salter*, 1838. – ROYAL ARMS in a relief roundel over the chancel arch, painted white. – STAINED GLASS. Several apse windows by *Powell & Sons*, with medallions, *c.* 1860–2. – MONUMENT. Rev. Richard Lewis † 1843, Master of the Grammar School, with a scene of him teaching, suitably, within a Norman arch, by *E.B.Stephens*.

Congregational Church, High Street. Attractively set back above the road, in its own burial ground. Built in 1836 on the site of a former meeting house. Italianate-Romanesque front, red brick, rendered quoins. Wide two-storey gabled porch added in 1862.

All Hallows Chapel (now museum), close to St Paul. Probably the remains of the chapel of ease; later used as a schoolroom by All

Hallows School, then as a school chapel until the school moved to Rousdon in 1938. E window C15, circular W window dated 1614, side windows four-light Tudor. Much rebuilt in the mid C18. E of the chapel the austere C19 Tudor school building, much rebuilt when converted to flats.

PERAMBULATION. Starting at the E end of the HIGH STREET, MARWOOD HOUSE, originally outside the town, is one of the few older houses, built by the son of Queen Elizabeth's physician. Symmetrical three-bay front with stone-framed windows and a two-storey central porch with four-centred archway. Fireplace dated 1619. On the N side, the first house of some pretension is No. 53, C18, five bays, three storeys, stuccoed, with parapet. (Contemporary features inside.) No. 59, Plympton House, has a lower irregular front with a late C18 pedimented doorcase. SILVER STREET runs off at an angle to the N here; one can return to the High Street past tightly packed cottages, via CHURCH STREET, a narrow alley leading past the old school buildings and chapel (*see* above). At the corner, Nos. 95–99, a good early C18 brick group (now painted).

Opposite, on the S side of the High Street, No. 62, one of the best C18 houses, red brick, five windows, stone quoins and keystones, and an open pedimented doorcase. Then, after two mid C20 eyesores, the two buildings which catch the eye are No. 68, handsome early C19 stucco, with a long iron balcony with Grecian motifs, and No. 94, now NATIONAL WESTMINSTER BANK, one of the few Victorian efforts: a dignified banker's front of 1877, with rusticated pilasters. Another Grecian balcony on No. 107, above a channelled stuccoed ground floor. W of the church the ANGEL HOTEL, a tall, three-storey Victorian front, with archway, and long ranges behind on the traditional inn plan. A detour N can take in ALL HALLOWS COURT, an essay in tightly knit urban design of 1980, houses grouped round a pleasant paved court, but disappointing in its use of harsh red mottled brick.

Back in the High Street the NEW DOLPHIN HOTEL, once grand, but with its early C19 character much reduced, and the former PANNIER MARKET with assembly rooms above, *c.* 1823, a modest stone front, the former ground-floor arcades now filled in, a pretty cast-iron balcony to the tripartite centre window. Then CENTRAL PLACE, a well preserved example of a side alley with early C19 cottages reached through an archway.

The MANOR HOUSE (No. 143), once the grandest house in the town, has an ambitious early C17 stone front, altered in the early C19. The rest – sadly – almost completely reconstructed when converted to offices in the 1970s. Ample three-bay centre with broad central entrance, two projecting full-height square bays with straight-headed windows with original hollow-chamfered mullions; five lights plus side lights. Early C19 the other windows (four lights, casements below rusticated heads), the plain parapet, and the Tuscan porch.

On the S side, at the corner of New Street, the most assertive Victorian building, LLOYDS BANK, *c.* 1870, with polished granite columns carrying heavy sandstone pediments over the two porches. Further on No. 128, early C19, Greek Doric porch, and No. 136 with Ionic pilasters on the first floor, one perversely incorporating a clock.

NEW STREET, running S from the town centre, has humble cottages, the best Nos. 39–41, thatched, with three bay-windows. Near the crossroads a little SHOPPING PRECINCT of c. 1980, a bold if not entirely satisfying marriage of materials: an iron-and-glass roof over rugged walls of re-used stone; commendably discreet in its approach from the High Street.

MILL to the S, with machinery.

At the W end, BRAMBLE HILL HOUSE, red brick Georgian, and some large C19 stucco villas, then suburban housing. Finally, on the N side of the road ST MARGARET'S HOSPITAL, founded as a leper hospital, rebuilt as almshouses by Thomas Chard, c. 1530, and now a pretty group of thatched cottages with Gothick glazing; on the S, a CHAPEL (now Pentecostal Church), single-cell, with late Perp windows.

COPPER CASTLE, Axminster Road. An engaging castellated toll house, still with its early C19 iron road gates.

Another TOLL HOUSE 1 m. W of the town centre.

HORRABRIDGE

5060

ST JOHN BAPTIST. 1893 by *G. H. Fellowes Prynne*, in his usual free Gothic, a simple chapel with a long sweeping roof and Dec and Perp tracery. It replaced a church of 1835.

METHODIST CHURCH. More ambitious than the Anglican church, with elaborate Dec windows.

BRIDGE. Medieval – probably the oldest in this part of Devon. Three obtusely pointed arches; refuge for pedestrians.

SORTRIDGE. *See* Whitchurch.

HORWOOD

5020

ST MICHAEL. The plan as usual in North Devon, one side aisleless (S), the other with an added Perp aisle (N). The chancel belongs to the earlier period (cf. the piscina with an odd horn-shaped drain). Arcade of five bays, low piers of B type with varied capitals, one with flying figures and shields, and depressed pointed arches. Bosses and wall-plates of the aisle roof original. Pieces of carved wall-plates reset in the S wall. S door dated 1669. W tower low, unbuttressed, with small pinnacles, and an unmoulded round-headed arch to the nave. Restored in 1889 by *Hayward & Tait*. – FONT. Norman, square, with scalloped under edge; much recut. – PULPIT. 1635, with tall, slim, restrained panels (blank arcades with lozenges, etc., in them); early Renaissance in spirit. – BENCH ENDS. Shields, etc., as usual; also two with saints, and others with the instruments of the Passion; not yet any Renaissance features. – COMMUNION RAIL (chancel chapel). Jacobean. – TILES. A good display of the Barnstaple type, reset in the chancel. – STAINED GLASS. N chapel E: four medieval figures in the lights. – Chancel S by *Mayer & Co.*, 1863, pictorial, bright colours. – In the N aisle two windows of c. 1899 by *A. L. Moore*, greenish. – CURIOSUM. Half-wheel bell frame, for a bell dated 1664, displayed in the church. – MONUMENT. Mid C15 alabaster monument to a lady, perhaps Elizabeth Pollard †1430. Horned headdress. Small figures of children under her cloak, on the pattern of representations of the Virgin of Misericord. Not very well preserved; *c*. 4 ft long.

HORWOOD HOUSE. The seat of the Dene family from the C17 to 1920. Georgianized rendered front with a two-storey porch on wooden posts and a mixture of sash and mullioned windows.

HOOPERS COTTAGE. A small stone house of *c*. 1600. To the r. of the entrance a lateral stack and a large projecting double garderobe. Inside, a stone spiral stair and good joinery.

EAST BARTON. A seat of the Pollard family, now a farmhouse. The main range rebuilt in brick in the late C17 – an early example in this area. Georgian sashes. (Good full-height dog-leg stair with thick turned balusters.) Earlier E wing (remains of early C17 plaster-work). Surprisingly ostentatious outbuildings: coach house with crow-stepped gable; barn with castellated end wall.

HUISH

ST JAMES THE LESS. Old, small, unbuttressed W tower. The rest of the church 1873 by *Street*, not of his best. – (STAINED GLASS all by *Clayton & Bell*.)

HEANTON SATCHVILLE. Rebuilt after a fire by *Sir Walter & Michael Tapper* for Lord Clinton, 1937. Late C17 style; H-shaped, with modillion cornice and sash-windows. Interior to match.

HUNTSHAM

Huntsham is a tiny village in a remote mid-Devon valley, energetically improved by Arthur Acland Troyte (cf. Columbjohn and Chardstock) in the few years before his early death. He took the name of Troyte on inheriting the neglected estate in 1852.

ALL SAINTS. Small, down a green lane, approached through a sturdy LYCHGATE of 1856. Slim unbuttressed W tower with round-headed tower arch. The rest largely C19. Restoration work began in 1854 under *Benjamin Ferrey*. The S side is a varied composition with chapel and vestry; Dec windows of Ham Hill stone. One old Dec window in the chancel N wall. N aisle 1871, with angular arches on octagonal columns and boldly carved respond capitals. Sanctuary with C19 stencilling under the wall-plate and prettily painted organ pipes. – REREDOS incorporating vine-scroll frieze from a screen. – PULPIT made up of bench ends. – Perp FONT in memory of Fanny Troyte † 1856. – Fine enamelled CANDELABRUM given in memory of her husband Arthur Troyte † 1857. – STAINED GLASS. Quarries and inscriptions, by *Wailes*. – In the churchyard very modest GRAVE MARKERS to Arthur Troyte and his family.

HUNTSHAM COURT. A grand mansion of 1868–70 by *Ferrey* for Arthur Troyte's son Charles, who married into the Walronds of Bradfield. In a rather forbidding Tudor Gothic, asymmetrical, with two projecting wings, but given a little romance by an angled stair-turret. Hall with an arcade of marble columns with lushly carved capitals.

In the village several solid stone cottages from the time of the Troytes.

The centrepiece is the POST OFFICE (formerly the smithy), with picturesquely angled slate roofs. Near the lodge the former SCHOOL (much altered) and adjoining SCHOOLTEACHER'S HOUSE with robust porch.

HUNTSHAW

5020

ST MARY MAGDALENE. Handsome arcade between nave and N aisle. Piers of B type with standard capitals, with figures (e.g. a tumbler in an unseemly posture) between the leaves, and with niches for images on the first pier facing SW, on the second NW, on the third again SW (cf. Frithelstock). Wagon roof in the nave. W tower with diagonal buttresses and no pinnacles. All this may be connected with the indulgence of 1439 to those who would help in the rebuilding of Huntshaw church. Only the chancel is considerably older (S window c. 1300). N aisle rebuilt 1862. Restored in 1876 by J. F. Gould, who was also responsible for the chancel fittings with carved work by Hems. – TILES in the chancel of the usual Barnstaple patterns. – (STAINED GLASS. One Kempe Studios window, the Annunciation, 1879.) – MONUMENT. Rich wall-monument to Thomas Saltren †1700.

LIMEKILN, Hallspill. Early C18, shaped like a figure of eight, with two kilns.

BERRY CASTLE, in a plantation above Huntshaw Mill Bridge. A spur-sited Iron Age defensive work.

HUXHAM

9090

ST MARY. A small church, much rebuilt; nave 1865 by Hayward, the rest by Ferrey, 1871. – FONT. Norman, with diagonally fluted circular bowl, a cable moulding below, a frieze of little circles, and symmetrically arranged spots on top. – SCREEN. Three bays only; the middle one is the entrance (with large leaves in the spandrels). The sides without arches, straight-headed, the tracery elementary ogee reticulation. The screen looks exceptionally early.

IDDESLEIGH

5000

The church stands with a group of thatched houses on a slope, looking towards Dartmoor.

ST JAMES. W tower with diagonal buttresses, a W door with elaborate though badly preserved leaf decoration, gargoyles, granite battlements, and tiny pinnacles. Nave, N aisle, lower chancel, and S porch. Tall arcade of four bays with piers of A type and capitals only to the main shafts. Unceiled wagon roofs. Partly rebuilt in 1720 and again in 1816–18; thoroughly renewed in 1878–9 by Charles S. Adye of Bradford on Avon (reseating, new roofs and windows). – FONT. Octagonal, Perp, with very plain decoration. Jacobean cover. – PULPIT. C17, panelled, with strapwork. – SCREEN. Only three divisions remain, with tracery of B type; no coving or cornice. –

MONUMENTS. Cross-legged knight in low arched recess in the N chancel chapel. Mid C13. – Slate plate to Wilmot Veale †1681.

WEEK COTTAGES. Nos. 1–2 were formerly a farmhouse. Many C17 timber windows, rare survivals, all ovolo-moulded, two with king mullions and timber hoodmoulds and labels.

See also Ash House.

IDEFORD   *8070*

ST MARY. W tower with plain granite windows. Evidence of a former Norman church is a gabled lintel with a serpent, a rudimentary 'tree of life', and a cock(?). The church was much rebuilt in 1850 by *Wightwick* and *Damont* but the piers are old: octagonal, red sandstone, with double-chamfered arches, the type usual on the Exe estuary (cf. e.g. Exminster). Medieval wagon roof. In the middle bay, above the site of the rood screen, the original celure or 'glory', with richer panelling and applied stars. S side rebuilt in 1852, including the porch. Chancel added in 1883 to designs by *Edward J. Dampier* of Colchester. – FONT. The usual octagonal Perp, possibly recut. – PULPIT and CHAIRS made up from pieces of rood screen. – Several windows incorporate medieval armorial STAINED GLASS.

UNDERHAYES. In the Middle Ages a possession of Torre Abbey; now mostly of the C17, on a four-room-and-cross-passage plan, with good C17 joinery in the hall.

WELL. Symmetrical five-bay front with mid C19 windows and a Doric porch, but a well preserved interior of *c.*1700 with a transitional plan: panelled entrance hall with rear fireplace; stairs with splat balusters in the rear wing; kitchen on the r. Good panelling in the first-floor rooms.

ILFRACOMBE   *5040*

In the C19 Ilfracombe became the most popular seaside resort of North Devon. Up to the end of the Georgian era it was a small fishing town, prosperous already in the Middle Ages because of its good natural harbour, by the C18 'a town of good trade, populous and rich', according to Defoe. Efforts to attract seaside visitors seem to have begun around 1830. Neat neo-classical public baths were built in 1836; the guidebooks which began to appear in the 1830s mention Coronation, Hillsborough, and Montpelier Terraces, sited above the town overlooking the sea, and Capstone Parade along the seafront was laid out in 1843. By 1860 there was a new town church to supplement the medieval one on a hill over half a mile away. But success on a grand scale came only in High Victorian days, especially after the branch railway line from Barnstaple opened in 1874, and the architecture of Ilfracombe is dominated by the tall houses and hotels of the last third of the C19, their gaunt brickwork relieved by surprisingly various iron balcony designs. *W.H.Gould* was the most prolific local architect.

The population rose from 1,838 in 1801 to 3,677 in 1851 and then to 8,550 in 1901, but since then growth has been much slower (10,133 in 1981). The resort began to decline in the 1930s; the railway has gone, and so have the largest Victorian hotel and the winter gardens. The

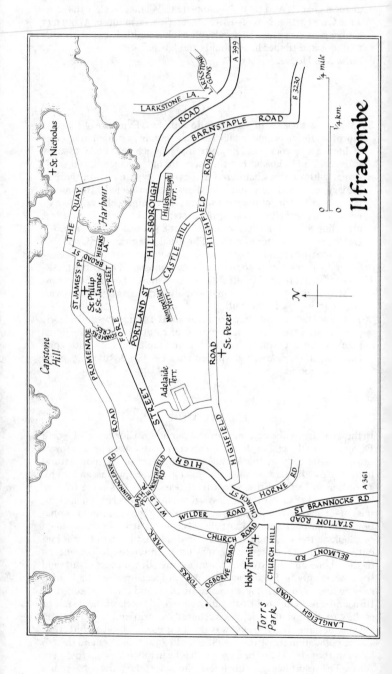

Ilfracombe

once handsome older neo-classical terraces are shabby and subdivided. Yet, nestling in its romantically rocky setting, the town has
much charm, and is still blessedly free from the ungainly C20
developments which have so spoilt Torquay. May it stay that way.

CHURCHES

HOLY TRINITY. The oldest part is the tower, in the N transeptal
position frequent in early North Devon churches. Low and unbuttressed, it has a simple pointed N door, a lancet window to the N, and
a low unmoulded pointed arch to the S into the church. Then, in
1321, Bishop Stapledon commanded that the church should be
enlarged, by a lengthening of the nave and the addition of aisles.
The present N and S aisle arcades of four bays to the tower do in fact
go well with a date in the second quarter of the C14: low octagonal
piers and simply chamfered arches. Of the same date the PISCINA
in the chancel. In the early C15 a N chancel was added with piers of B
type and simple, fairly big moulded capitals only to the main shafts.
The aisle windows, and probably the whole widening of the aisles to
their present size, appear to be later Perp still, though most of the
outer walls was rebuilt during the 1861 restoration by *Hayward*.
The arcade of the S chancel chapel is entirely of this date, as is the E
part of the N chancel chapel. The windows with their tracery were
also renewed. The chancel E window was formerly Perp, like the E
windows to the N and S aisles, as is shown in old illustrations. These
windows are of four lights, and so are those of the N and S sides, i.e.
the church was on an ambitious scale all round.

The wagon roofs are specially rewarding at Holy Trinity. They
are all ceiled. In the nave the beams rest on angel figures. Below
them are unusual corbels in the form of mythical beasts, possibly
older than the roof. At the E end of the nave, i.e. above the former
rood screen, is a splendid celure or 'glory', three bays enriched by
cross-ribs and much decoration. The two dormer windows, one N,
one S, that light this and the screen were remade in 1899 (*Fellowes
Prynne*), but they must have existed at least as early as the mid C18,
and so probably are an original feature. The chancel roof with its
own celure (cf. Swimbridge) dates from 1899 (coloured in 1961).
The N porch alone has an open wagon roof. Vestry added by
H. Wilson in 1894.

FONT. Square, Norman, with scalloped underside and a decoration of three rosettes on each side, much recut. – PULPIT.
Elizabethan, with two tiers of the characteristic arched panels on
short columns; flowers with stalks and leaves as the motif within
each panel. – Perp SOUTH DOOR with its original knocker. –
CHOIR STALLS by *Fellowes Prynne*, 1900. – STAINED GLASS. An
instructively varied sequence of the 1860s onwards. Clockwise from
the E: chancel E by *Hardman*, 1861. Crucifixion and other scenes,
excellent blue backgrounds, angels in the trefoiled lights. – S,
easternmost, *Willement*, much harder colours and drawing style,
also 1861. – S chapel SE, Stabb Memorial, 1896 by *Ballantyne* in an
old-fashioned painterly technique. – S second, St John Baptist, with
a lively floral background. – S aisle W, 1908 by *Kempe & Co.*, typical
pale colours, saints, etc. and many charming angels. – Then nothing
of much note until the N aisle third from W, 1893, a vision of the

Trinity, three angels, realistically depicted forest. – N, E of tower, 1861 by *Lavers & Barraud*, Resurrection scene, excellent colours. – N, first from E, 1860, crude but colourful. – N chapel E by *O'Connor*, 1862, memorably virulent purples and blues.

MONUMENTS. C12 tapered tomb slab with incised cross, very worn. – Marie Selwood †1634, a small crude tomb slab with interlace, still in the medieval tradition. – Many minor wall-monuments, including good architectural tablets in the N aisle, e.g. one of 1677 with an oval centre and a segmental pediment with arms. – Richard Bowen †1797 by *Regnart*, large, with sarcophagus and big trophy above. – LYCHGATE. By *Henry Wilson*, 1894. A delightfully inventive Arts and Crafts design. The roof with small graduated slates and pierced lead parapet. Frond-like iron bars set in a wooden frame.

St NICHOLAS. Situated highly picturesquely on a rock between sea and harbour. In existence by the early C15, and by the time of Henry VIII used as a lighthouse. Small, with an undatable rugged weatherbeaten exterior, rubble, partly plastered. Lantern over the W end; fish weathervane dated 1819; sash-windows. Entrance at the E end.

St PETER, Highfield Road. 1902–3 by *G. Fellowes Prynne*, for the growing suburbs. Exterior of grey limestone; inside, grey Combe Martin stone above red sandstone. Eclectic Arts and Crafts detail. Chancel with lancets high up, E window Dec, nave windows Perp. Unfinished NW tower-porch, with stone figures of angels support-ing the porch roof. Unexpected interior with spiral columns and quadrant arches over the aisles. Fittings also by *Prynne*.

St PHILIP AND St JAMES, St James's Place. 1856 by *Hayward*. Correct Geometric Dec. Prominent NE tower with a short spire of patterned slates, built instead of a more ambitious intended stone spire. Even so, the *Ecclesiologist* in 1860 considered it the 'finest new church in North Devon'. The CHURCH CENTRE nearby is a 1970s conversion of a former church school.

OUR LADY STAR OF THE SEA (R.C.), Runnacleave Road. 1893 by *Scoles*, rebuilt in 1929. Dec windows. – Two lavish REREDOSES, one wood, one stone.

BAPTIST CHURCH, High Street. 1891 by *W. H. Gould*. Red sand-stone. Perp polished marble shafts to the doorway.

UNITED REFORMED CHURCH, High Street. Broad polychrome Gothic front, tripartite side openings, the doorways flanked by iron columns. 1818, enlarged 1884.

METHODIST CHURCH, Wilder Road. 1898 by *W. H. Gould*. Random-coursed limestone. Bath stone dressings. Corner tower and spire. Church at first-floor level with schoolrooms beneath.

SALVATION ARMY, Oxford Grove. 1873. Large paired Gothic windows to an upper hall.

PUBLIC BUILDINGS

HARBOUR AND QUAY. The pier was built by the Bourchiers, Earls of Bath (*see* Tawstock), partly rebuilt and enlarged in 1760, and enlarged again in 1824–9. Low-water jetty added in 1873. Slightly frivolous entrance at the far end of the main quay, 1952, the style still 1930s moderne: flat roofs balanced between granite fins; porthole windows. Beyond, an incongruous group of Ionic pilastered public conveniences, a prettily bargeboarded lifeboat station, and a mean 1930s café. More could be made of this dramatic site below St Nicholas, with its excellent views of both coast and harbourside.

SCHOOL AND COMMUNITY COLLEGE, Worth Road. By *Stillman & Eastwick Field*, 1966–70. Boldly sited above the town, extensive two- and four-storey buildings of exposed concrete. Ruthlessly simple; projecting boardmarked uprights, concrete block cladding below red-painted window frames. Redeemed by its good proportions. Separate sports block down the hill. SCULPTURE. Three steel forms with white, 1969 by *Justin Knowles*.

GASWORKS, Hele. Handsome buildings of 1905, of grey rubble, with round-arched openings in yellow brick.

PERAMBULATIONS

1. From the harbour to the High Street, and back through the Victorian resort

A picturesque row of small houses lines THE QUAY on the N, ending with the HARBOURMASTER'S OFFICE and its neighbour, probably C17 behind their rendered and altered fronts. (Good joinery inside.) The other houses are Victorian, with the first-floor bays and varied cast-iron balconies characteristic of the later C19 parts of the town. On the W side the ROYAL BRITANNIA HOTEL, a stuccoed Regency exterior with three shallow bow-windows, concealing a structure of many earlier phases. On the Broad Street side two royal coats of arms. S of the harbour the C18 MANOR HOUSE, said to be the town house of the Wreys of Tawstock, an imposing front, yet only one room deep, built into the side of the hill. Red brick with red sandstone bands and keystones. Central canted bay flanked by two windows on each side, and lower wings beyond. High above, CASTLE HOUSE displays an early C19 Gothic front to the sea, a rarity in Ilfracombe.

BROAD STREET runs behind the buildings W of the harbour. After the Royal Britannia, No. 3, a chemist's, a low C19 stuccoed frontage with gable on the r., and Grecian touches to the pilasters framing the shopfront. Then relics of the pre-Victorian fishing port: Nos. 8–9, quite a tall group at the corner of Hierns Lane, *c.* 1700, colour-washed rubble with Georgian sash-windows, formerly with coved eaves (now boarded over), followed by the SHIP AND PILOT (marred by an unsuitable recent roof and dormers), and No. 12, a low two-storey cottage. No. 13, in contrast, is a tall early C19 stuccoed house facing up Fore Street.

FORE STREET, shabby and unspoilt, runs uphill from the harbour to the High Street and Holy Trinity church. Among the group at the bottom of the N side, No. 78, set back a little, with a pair of doors below road level, the l. one with its moulded and stopped frame suggesting a house of C17 date, although the rest of the exterior appears C19. Opposite, the PRINCE OF WALES, a low early C19 front with good moulded cornices and parapet, and the GEORGE AND DRAGON, with another C17 doorcase and renewed wooden casements. Plenty of good C19 shopfronts: No. 72 with a curved window and inset entrance, No. 8 opposite, a shop-window with consoles, No. 9 with original four-pane glazing, No. 10 with a smaller Georgian shop-window flanked by fluted pilasters. Further on, past a cleared area on the N side, BEVERLEY, a carefully designed small house built in 1873 as the police station by *H. W. Farley* of Exeter, and opposite, attractively tucked away above a raised and railed pavement, COBURG TERRACE, five late Georgian stuccoed houses, Nos. 3–4 with linked doorways. Other minor terraces of similar date follow on the slopes further up the hill: ROCK TERRACE and WATERLOO TERRACE (No. 27 with a nice Doric doorcase). Opposite, the scale of the later C19 begins to take over. This is the period which gives Ilfracombe its special character. First comes the CLIFTON HOTEL, then the even taller MONTEBELLO, all bay-windows and tiers of iron balconies. It faces down the similarly attired SOMMERS CRESCENT, where the E terrace is of 1874–6 by *J. H. Huxtable*, the w side of the late 1880s. At the area where Fore Street and Portland Street join the High Street, a former department store with two storeys of iron-framed shop-windows.

The HIGH STREET starts modestly with the PRINCE ALBERT, three storeys, dignified Italianate, with dentilled cornice and pediment over the central first-floor windows, and No. 4 also early Victorian. Much of the rest of the street has plainer stuccoed early C19 fronts, mostly of three storeys, some of two, with shops below. On the N side Nos. 18–19, probably C18, then the MARKET HOUSE, a handsome stone front of 1860 with two tiers of Doric columns with an Ionic order above. Three archways, the narrow central one for pedestrians, lead through vaulted passages to the former open market area beyond, awkwardly sited on steeply falling ground, with a two-storey market building of 1901. Further on, Nos. 41–42, the Old Post Office, is by *W. C. Oliver*, red and cream brick and stone. This part of the High Street is chiefly High Victorian, enlivened by touches of polychrome brickwork and punctuated by hotels. On the N side the CLARENCE, an eccentric design with pretty lettered iron balconies and small gables over the top windows; this was the oldest hotel in Ilfracombe, 'recently rebuilt' in 1886. On the s side further on the QUEEN'S HOTEL, early C19 stucco (but with ground-floor rustication removed). Other good late Victorian buildings are No. 99 (Ilfracombe Bookshop), with arcaded ground floor, and Nos. 141–143 of 1888, its upper floor with Romanesque window built as a Masonic Hall. OXFORD GROVE, off the High Street, is all polychrome brick of 1872–4, the corner building with clock tower by *W. H. Gould*. Near the w end of the High Street the WELLINGTON, a low inn, is a reminder of the pre-Victorian scale of the town.

NORTHFIELD ROAD connects the High Street to the area developed *c.* 1830 when Ilfracombe became a resort. Several attractive houses of this period, especially No. 3, a three-bay stuccoed villa with Doric porch. Opposite, an eccentric interloper, a MASONIC TEMPLE of 1899 by *H. M. Gardner* of Ilfracombe, with a quaint display of four classical orders. BATH PLACE at the bottom of the hill has as its focus the TUNNEL BATHS of 1836, an elegant one-storey channelled stuccoed building with a pedimented Greek Doric entrance *in antis*. It provided hot and cold baths, with a tunnel behind leading through the cliffs to secluded sea-bathing.

To the w, Nos. 1–2, with a combined Greek Doric entrance, most incorrectly designed; to the E, RUNNYMEDE, in the alternative, more romantic style of the time, with Gothic windows and barge-boarded gables.

From here, the TORRS PARK estate, laid out c. 1880 by *W. C. Oliver* of Barnstaple, stretches uphill to the w, with cliff walks and large detached villas (*the* beauty spot of the neighbourhood according to the 1905 guide). The earlier houses are stuccoed, the later ones mostly in the local pale yellow Marland brick, quite picturesquely grouped when seen from a distance against the hillside. Returning E towards the harbour one passes a good sample of those towering hotels which illustrate the somewhat grim styles of High Victorian pleasure architecture, for example the RUNNACLEAVE in Wilder Road, 1891 by *W. H. Gould*, a three- to four-storey terrace of rock-faced stone with yellow brick trim, pointed windows, and gables; the GRANVILLE, also built in 1891, prominent on the cliffs above, of the same materials, with a battlemented tower; and the GROSVENOR, brick with galleries. The most ambitious hotel, the Ilfracombe of 1867–71 by *Hayward*, was demolished in the 1970s.★ Further E the PROMENADE, an interesting example of a purpose-built parade of small shops dating from 1880. Two storeys; round-arched verandas with balconies above. Decorative tile bands. At the end a small theatre was added in 1911. The iron and glass winter garden opposite has, alas, been demolished, but the Victorian mood is continued by plenty of balconied houses in CHURCH ROAD and ST BRANNOCKS ROAD. Then, after the church of St Philip and St James (q.v.), built for the growing C19 population, one is back in Georgian Ilfracombe and the area around the harbour.

2. South and east of the High Street

As at Torquay and Teignmouth, spasmodic efforts were made in the earlier C19 to provide formal terraces overlooking the sea. The predominant impression is now of dilapidation rather than of grandeur. From w to E, the first is ADELAIDE TERRACE, c. 1840, on a raised terrace overlooking an open slope above the High Street, once a handsome balanced design of three storeys, stuccoed, with a rhythm of 1–2–2–2–1, the ends and centre projecting. Greek Doric porches with balconies above. The parapet rises to a small centre pediment in which there is an oval window. Further E, overlooking Portland Street, MONTPELIER TERRACE of the same period, less uniform, considerably altered, but better preserved. The w part consists of twelve tall houses, the E end has a lower group of six with the centre two houses of three bays, the others of two, and a further pair at the end with a very ill proportioned Greek Doric porch over a pair of doorways. The rest have pedimented Tuscan porches with deeply inset front doors, and for the most part later bay-windows and balconies added in a variety of styles. Only a few flat fronts (Nos. 8–12) remain to indicate the original restrained appearance. E again, HILLS-BOROUGH TERRACE of c. 1835, much messed about, originally

★It lay E of Runnymede Gardens and the museum and was of multicoloured brick with Gothic windows and French pavilion roof.

quite a sophisticated composition of fourteen houses (2–3–1–3–1–3–2), the centre part with two breaks forward. Stuccoed, with rusticated ground floor, Greek Doric porches. Finally the later LARKSTONE GARDENS, N of Hillsborough Road, which displays the total dissolution of Georgian proportions: five storeys, with bay-windows stretching up through four of them, three tiers of balconies, and Tudor dripmoulds to the top-floor windows.

E of Portland Street a few individual houses worth noting along HILLSBOROUGH ROAD. First, ST JAMES'S VICARAGE, a solid Tudor Gothic mansion, stone with brick trim, with touches of polychrome to the relieving arches over the windows. LASTON HOUSE is a plain, elegant, two-storey stuccoed villa built c. 1830 by James Copner, a Barnstaple surgeon. Greek Doric porch to the W, a bow-window to the S overlooking the sea. Tiny thatched circular summerhouse by the road. Further on the THATCHED INN, adapted as a *cottage orné* in the Repton manner, with tree-trunk veranda and a lunette in the thatched roof. Picturesque thatched garden buildings; all rather too prettified for modern tourists. To the N HILLSBOROUGH COTTAGE, an attractive mid C19 gabled house with scalloped bargeboards and fish-scale tiles, with a small octagonal Gothic BELVEDERE TOWER in its grounds. Banks cutting off the promontory at Hillsborough may be partly natural, enhanced with ditches to fortify the enclosed area. The siting is typical of a later Iron Age promontory fort.

3. West of the town centre, around Holy Trinity

The VICARAGE, of 1889, incorporates a good late medieval framed ceiling with carved bosses. The old settlement just to the N of the parish church attracted a few C19 villas, notably OSBORNE HOUSE in OSBORNE ROAD, c. 1850, and RUSSELL HOUSE, No. 11 CHURCH ROAD, c. 1830, with a central canted bay facing a spacious garden. Nearby, just below the churchyard, the former SCHOOLS of 1859 by *Foster & Wood* of Bristol, L-shaped, half-hipped roof, simple Gothic plate tracery in grey-green rubble walls – a sober, excellently massed building. S of the church, in BELMONT ROAD, Gothic in a totally different spirit: THE GABLES, a mid C19 villa, elaborately bargeboarded.

A little more of the pre-Victorian period to the S along ST BRAN-NOCKS ROAD: Nos. 5–8, stuccoed, with some Doric porches, and in HORNE ROAD, running parallel to the E, No. 37, BROOK VILLA, early C19, Nos. 35–36, three-storey terrace houses, and some older, much altered houses further on. Further S, among later suburban development, a few detached early C19 stucco villas in their own grounds: BROAD PARK HOUSE, Belmont Road, and LANGLEIGH HOUSE, Langleigh Road.

4. Outside the town centre

GOLDEN COAST HOLIDAY CENTRE, Worth Road. A substantial stone house of the 1850s at the top of the hill. Victorian Gothic traceried windows in the gables.

CHAMBERCOMBE MANOR, Chambercombe Road. Some C16–17 features, with a C15 core, but much altered and restored.

HELE, 1 M. E, is a hamlet with an attractive, informal cluster of houses in the dip of the road. C18 MILL, whitewashed rubble, with an 18 ft iron overshot wheel on a gable end.

BEARA FARM, E of Hele. Simple painted rubble exterior, but good C16–17 work inside: arch-braced hall roof with wind-braces; excellent C17 joinery; three rooms with decorative plasterwork.

LIMEKILN, W of the town, on the path to the cliffs. With a wooden lintel.

PALL EUROPE PAPER FILTER PLANT, Station Road. By *W. H. Saunders & Son*, 1977, a large, flexible steel-framed factory, given character by its exterior stanchions and kept tactfully low. Well landscaped.

See also Lee.

ILSINGTON

7070

The church makes a handsome group with the LYCHGATE (of 1908 by *T. H. Lyon*), which stands on granite piers adjoining the remains of the church house, now incorporated in ST MICHAEL'S COTTAGES. Traces of old windows; two arched granite doorways, one with carved spandrels. Walls partly of ashlar. Prominent lateral stack.

ST MICHAEL. W tower roughcast, unbuttressed, with stair-turret. The S side with a late Perp two-storey porch and S aisle, all embattled. Above the entrance into the porch, three niches. The chancel and S transept (see their windows), and also the N transept, belong to a Dec church, of cruciform plan. N aisle also Perp, with NW turret. Restoration 1884, the chancel by *E. Christian*, the rest by *E. H. Harbottle*. The interior offers a great surprise. Nave and chancel have a wagon roof. The arcades of the five-bay aisles take no notice of the N and S transepts; but these transepts also have wagon roofs, and in order to make the meeting of the longitudinal and the transverse wagon roofs possible in that spectacular fashion which is to be found at Honiton and Luppitt, the upper wall between the arcades and the nave roof is in the fourth bay simply left out. Only a bridge remains. The large semicircular diagonal timber arches of the crossing rest on little niches with figures. In the N wall of the N transept, a two-centred, almost straight-sided recess. In it a much earlier EFFIGY of a lady (*c.*1300; badly preserved). – SCREEN. Across nave and aisles. Standard type A tracery; cornice with three friezes of leaf, etc., decoration. – CHOIR STALLS. Designed by *Christian*, executed by *Hems*. – STALL ENDS. The only old ones in Devon which have poppyheads. The tracery decoration on some of them also uncommon. – STAINED GLASS. Divett window (S transept), 1888, in a Crane–Arts-and-Crafts style.

MANOR HOUSE, N of the church. C17; in ruins. A stone barn belonging to it opposite the Carpenter's Arms.

APPLEWOODS FACTORY, Liverton. Bottle kiln.

BAGTOR HOUSE. A substantial stone house, the seven-window front, with coved eaves, remodelled *c.*1700, the C16 house retained as a service wing behind. Ground-floor rooms and one upper-chamber closet all with good bolection-moulded panelling and contemporary doorcases. Central stair projection at the back; C18 well staircase with turned balusters.

BAGTOR MILL. Overshot waterwheel.

BAGTOR MINE. Tin mine, worked in the 1860s. Remains of dressing floors and a large wheelpit. The waterwheel installed in 1862 for pumping the mine was probably the largest on Dartmoor.

HAYTOR VALE. A row of houses built in 1825 for workers in the Haytor quarries. The hostel for single workers is now the ROCK INN.

HAYTOR GRANITE TRAMWAY. Built c. 1820 by George Templer of Stover House (q.v.) to carry granite from the Haytor and Holwell quarries to the terminus of the Stover canal at Ventiford Wharf (see Teigngrace). 8½ miles long, descending 1,300ft. The rails for horse-drawn iron wagons are made of flanged granite blocks, with a gauge of 4ft 3in. The best preserved remains of lines and points are near the quarries.

3 REAVE SYSTEM. The moorland areas of the parish, comprising RIPPON TOR, BAGTOR DOWN, and MOUNTSLAND COMMON, form part of one of Dartmoor's largest and most impressive parallel reave systems, which can be seen continuing into the present-day enclosed fields. Dotted throughout are dispersed prehistoric settlements and fields.

INSTOW

ST JOHN BAPTIST. S transept and chancel probably the oldest parts. In the chancel, windows of c. 1300, all renewed (the same design as at Westleigh nearby). N aisle with straight-headed three-light windows (each light with a flat ogee top), dated 1547 by an inscription on two of the piers of the arcade. It says that Richard Waterman and his wife Emma erected the aisle. The arcade has piers of A type (not of granite) with capitals of B type. Ceiled wagon roof in the aisle. W tower with diagonal buttresses, tall rectangular NE stair-turret, and no pinnacles. Restored in 1875 by W. White. – FONT. Plain, Norman, of block-capital shape. – TILES. Of the usual Barnstaple designs, in the chancel. – STAINED GLASS. N chapel E by Hardman. – MONUMENTS. (John Downe †1640, in a gown, with a book, leaning on a skull.) – Humphrey Sibthorp, the celebrated botanist of the Flora Graeca, †1797, and buried with a very Grecian monument at Bath Abbey. At Instow only a nicely executed oval inscription tablet by Kendall of Exeter. – Slate HEADSTONES in the churchyard.

RAILWAY SIGNAL BOX. Probably c. 1855; typical early L.S.W.R., with horizontally boarded walls, horizontally sliding timber windows, and a hipped slate roof. The signalman stood on the platform above the rail level to exchange the tokens necessary for single-line operation. Signal levers, wheel, and gearing preserved, for operating the adjoining level crossing (gates removed).

Overlooking the Torridge estuary some nice minor terraces and early Victorian semi-detached seaside villas, the result of a mid C19 effort to create a watering place here. The RECTORY in Glebe Lane is Regency, stuccoed, with Gothick glazing.

Methodist Chapel, Anstey Way. 1838, modest; two round-arched windows.

Massive fortress-like stone LIMEKILN by the estuary.

Remains of a WINDMILL on the hill near the church.

INWARDLEIGH
5090

St Petrock. Architecturally uninteresting. Low w tower with diagonal buttresses, nave and N aisle (four-bay arcade of granite piers of A type with capitals only to the main shafts and depressed pointed arches). Windows straight-headed. Restored in 1898 by *Tait & Harvey*, who partly rebuilt the nave wall, reseated throughout, and reconstructed the roof. – FONT. Norman, of block-capital shape. Shaft and foot with rosette, etc., decoration, the semicircular surfaces of the bowl re-cut probably in the C16. – STAINED GLASS. C14 angels in the tracery of the N aisle E window. – TILES. Of Barnstaple make: a few.

IPPLEPEN
8060

St Andrew. The w tower big, 91 ft high, of Ashburton type, the only one in the area with eight pinnacles, all very low, and an unmoulded tower arch. The s side of the church, with sw turret and two-storeyed s porch, all embattled, the N side with NW turret also embattled. Red sandstone tops to the battlements. In a small doorway in the N aisle a Norman tympanum, the representation chiselled off, but indications of a cross and a bird. The window tracery Perp and mostly renewed. Interesting E window of the s aisle (if it represents the original), with a star-shaped motif at the top as at Staverton and Littlehempston. s porch with plain tunnel-vault. Aisles of six bays on octagonal red sandstone piers with white capitals decorated with fleurons (many left in the block, unchiselled) and double-chamfered arches. s porch with barrel-vault and lancet window (re-used?). Restored in 1892 (by *Fulford, Tait & Harvey*) and 1924 (w window renewed). – FONT. The usual octagonal C15 type with quatrefoils and shields, and with three statuettes on pillar and bowl. One of the shields shows the arms of Bishop Lacy of Exeter (1420–55). – SCREEN. Wainscoting with painted figures including sybils, in style *c.* 1450 (restored by *Anna Hulbert*). Tracery of type A, the coving new. Cornice with handsome carving of leaves, grapes, and birds. – PULPIT. Approached by a delightful Georgian stair. C15, on a palm-tree foot. Carving in the same style as the screen, but sparser. – STAINED GLASS. E window 1906 (incorporating late C15 glass in the tracery lights), chancel N 1906, chancel s 1904, all by *Kempe Studios*. – s aisle E by *Drake*, 1897. – CHANDELIER (from Stone, Staffordshire). Probably made by *T. Shrimpton* of London *c.* 1765. – MONUMENT. Neyle family, erected 1727. Cartouche.

In Fore Street, PENLEE, Regency stuccoed; in East Street, THE ELMS, a mid C19 classical villa. Opposite the Wellington, a WATER PUMP dated 1868.

THE PRIORY. Mostly mid C19, but on the site of an Augustinian alien priory founded in 1143.

GREAT AMBROOK. Two-storey Georgian front of 2–3–2–plus–1 bays, with parapet. Older parts behind. (Undercroft with two monolithic granite piers.)

COMBE HOUSE, Combe Fishacre. Dated 1793. Three storeys, with two full-height bows and open-pedimented doorcase. Reeded eaves cornice.

COMBEFISHACRE HOUSE. Early C19, a handsome three-bay stucco front divided by pilasters; deep eaves on paired brackets. Good original interiors.

DAINTON. Large late C16 farmhouse, with C17 front and later cross-wing. Unusual roof carpentry: ten bays with twelve small purlin-rafters (i.e. horizontally laid) to each roof slope. At the upper end, an early C17 kite-pattern single-rib plaster ceiling to the ground-floor room and a plaster cornice to the first-floor chamber.

DORNAFIELD. Massive porch with a broad archway; the date 1664 on a shield marks the remodelling of a large medieval house for the Crossing family. Possibly originally a courtyard plan. Two sections of medieval roof remain over the hall and kitchen wings, and a later C16 roof in the rear range. Good late C17 fittings.

PREHISTORIC SITE. NE of Dainton village remains of an Iron Age settlement and earthwork enclosure, mostly destroyed by quarrying since the mid C20.

IVYBRIDGE

6050

The small town on the boundaries of four ancient parishes grew in the C19 around the paper mill. What gives it character is the RAILWAY VIADUCT across the wooded valley. The present structure of 1893, eight arches of granite and brick (engineer *Sir James Inglis*), replaces the earlier *Brunel* timber viaduct whose granite piers can be seen alongside. Lower down, a small high-arched BRIDGE over the Erme just opposite the plain stuccoed early Victorian LONDON HOTEL. Nearby are the STOWFORD PAPER MILLS, 1862, still in the masculine, dignified fashion of early C19 factories. Six storeys, three of brick upon three of granite. Engine house 1914, with tall brick chimney. STOWFORD LODGE, behind, is of two storeys with a tower; round-arched windows. (For Stowford, *see also* Harford.)

The best part of the town is the row of early C19 houses along ERME ROAD, overlooking the river, especially ERMESIDE, with a pedimented doorcase. In HIGHLAND STREET, slate-hung cottages climb up the hill.

ST JOHN. 1882 by *Hine & Odgers*, nave and chancel; N aisle with marble columns 1887. Local limestone with Bath and Portland dressings. – STAINED GLASS. E window 1890 by *Fouracre*. – SCREEN. 1911 by *Herbert Read*. – MONUMENT. Sarah Morris †1907, with marble angel, by *Romanelli*.

Uphill from the church an 1890ish villa, TREMORRAN, with jettied top storey, gables and tower.

METHODIST CHURCH, Fore Street. 1874–6. Plate tracery. SW

tower turning octagonal, with a short spire. Lavish interior fittings: statues, tiled pulpit, iron trelliswork. A good contrast with the former WESLEYAN CHAPEL opposite of 1867, now offices, set back from the road. Simple pedimented front with round-arched windows and Doric doorcase. Cheerfully colour-washed.

WATERSIDE HOUSE, Keaton Road. 1977 by *M.W.T. Architects* for South Hams District Council. A well-composed group of flats, two- and three-storey, for the elderly, on the edge of the town. A good example of how concrete blockwork can be quite appealing when combined with pleasantly proportioned windows and half-hipped roofs.

HENLAKE DOWN. On the edge of the down, above Ivybridge town, an embanked EARTHWORK ENCLOSURE of unknown function, almost certainly post-prehistoric. On the summit, ruinous HUT CIRCLES and CAIRNS.

JACOBSTOWE   5000

ST JAMES. W tower with diagonal buttresses and pinnacles. Aisleless nave. S doorway round-headed. Much restored in 1902. – FONT. Square, with chamfered angles; featureless. – MONUMENT. Lady Madden †1849, by *J. Ternouth* of Pimlico, London, with two large allegorical females.

Pretty wooden Gothic fencing around the churchyard and the former VICARAGE, a low building with early C19 Gothick glazing and Tudor dripmoulds to the windows.

CROFT. A remarkably complete C15–18 farmstead with farm buildings of the C17 and C18 in a courtyard in front of the house.

See also Broomford Manor.

KELLY   3080

ST MARY. W tower rebuilt in 1835 after being struck by lightning: granite ashlar, type B buttresses, polygonal pinnacles. Chancel 'done by *John Bollon* 1710' (plaque on E wall); odd posthumously Perp round-headed windows on the S side with dated dripstones. Inside, the earliest feature is the S jamb of the chancel arch, with a C14 capital with head (cf. Lifton). The arch itself was rebuilt when the Perp N aisle and N chapel were added. Five-bay arcade on A type piers with decoration in the abaci and simply moulded four-centred arches. – STAINED GLASS. N chapel E (formerly chancel E) late C15, extensively restored and redesigned by *Baillie & Son*, 1879. Crucifixion, Virgin, St John, and Edward the Confessor. Angels with shields in the tracery. – N aisle W probably by *Lavers, Barraud & Westlake*, mosaic style. – Others by *Lavers & Westlake*. – MONUMENTS. Flanked by the C18 Perp windows of the chancel, Richard Edgcumbe, rector, †1710. Pedimented wall-monument with an oval inscription which tells us he rebuilt the chancel 'a fundamentis'. – Rev. John Darke †1823, by *Shepherd* of Plymouth. Grecian sarcophagus. – Good, modest incised slate slabs to the Kellys: 1594, 1605, 1627.

KELLY HOUSE. A rare case in Devon of a well documented build-

ing history (the specifications survive), revealing in showing what a
local architect was capable of in the mid C18. Built in 1742–3 for
Arthur Kelly, to designs by *Abraham Rundle*, joiner and architect
of Tavistock. A competent, regularly planned house of five by five
bays with hipped roof, the usual early C18 type. Two storeys on a
basement (now filled in, so that the house appears squatter than
intended). Rendered walls, dignified by rusticated quoins, a pediment to the slightly projecting former W-facing entrance front, a
dentilled cornice (W and S sides only), and stone plat-band and
keystones. Entrance with Doric pilasters and entablature. The
back, with a bold Venetian window to the staircase landing, was
made the entrance in the C19, with the addition of an off-centre
porch and a low butler's passage leading to the service wing which
incorporates part of the older house on the site (medieval roof with
moulded arch-braced trusses).

In the C18 house good contemporary fittings: cornices; columned marble fireplace with overmantel with carved coats of arms
in the NW parlour; SW drawing room with a pedimented doorway
on Corinthian pilasters. Handsome stair-hall, the Venetian
window with a heavy broken pediment. Decorative plaster ceiling.
Stairs with twisted balusters and carved tread-ends. In the NE
first-floor room C16 and C17 panelling re-used (exactly as instruc-
ted in the specification). N of the house a low billiard and organ
room, added in 1877.

Two-storey STABLES with a central pediment, hipped roof, and
little cupola. Some of the window openings with perforated panes
of slate. Brick GRANARY on staddle-stones, unusual for the area.

₉₀₈₀   KENN

ST ANDREW. All red, and all embattled. The E window early C14:
five lights, intersected tracery, with pointed quatrefoils. The other
windows Perp. The piers separating nave from aisles also red; tall,
octagonal, and carrying double-chamfered arches, as usual in this
part of the county (cf. e.g. Exminster). Inside, the church is essentially Victorian, the product of some forty years of restoration
under the Rev. Reginald Porter (1858–94). Chancel restoration
1863 by *Henry Woodyer* (renovation of the roof, new flooring and
floor levels, new choir stalls, stone reredos with stone panelling).
Nave and aisles restored in 1866–9, again by *Woodyer*: reseating on
the pattern of remaining medieval benches, new nave roof, opening of the tower arch. Tower restoration 1882 by *R.M.Fulford*. In
1887–90, *Fulford & Harvey* restored the screen, provided a new
reredos, and inserted the mosaic angels in the E wall panelling, all
executed by *Hems*.

FONT. Norman, of the not unusual table-top type. – SCREEN.
Right across nave and both aisles. Fan-coving renewed; tracery of
type A, piers encased; wainscoting with bad paintings of saints,
evidently early C16. – PAINTING under the tower arch in similar
style, but about 5 ft tall: two female saints, and below heads of two
other figures; evidently not in its original state or setting. Croft-
Murray suggests some influence of Antwerp Mannerism in the
richer-than-usual costume details. – BENCH ENDS with two-tier

tracery. – PULPIT by *Fulford*, 1875. – STAINED GLASS. Four small figures in a vestry window, two of the early C14, two more of the late C15 in silver stain on white glass. – Several medieval shields in the S window of the S chancel chapel. – But the unforgettable glass is the series by *Hardman & Co.*: E window Christ in Majesty, 1867; the small W windows of the aisles with the Annunciation and the Nativity, both 1869; then the W window of the tower, 1880, and seven scenes from the Life of Christ in the big Perp windows of the aisles, 1880–92.

Kenn is a rich parish with several large houses. By far the most important was HALDON HOUSE, begun *c.*1735 by Sir George Chudleigh, enlarged in the later C18 by Sir Robert Palk, demolished in 1920. It was one of the few mansions in the county on a grand scale, according to an C18 tradition modelled on Buckingham House, London; this presumably referred to the pavilions connected to the main blocks by quadrant links, a feature of Buckingham House by 1715. All that survives now (apart from the BELVEDERE built by Sir Robert on Haldon Hill above; *see* Dunchideock) is a pair of cuboid lodges and a linking screen with Doric columns flanking an archway formerly opening to the stable court. Plain rendered three-storey wing behind, now the LORD HALDON HOTEL. The C18 house lay to the l. Beyond to the S is a C20 house apparently made from a C19 chapel – see the window in the end gable.

BICKHAM. A small mansion attractively set in its own park, the early C18 house of the Short family, disguised by early C19 asymmetrical additions to the entrance front: a colonnaded veranda running around two sides of the house, and a large projecting bowed dining room, with service wing beyond. At the back the early C18 house appears, three bays, rendered, with a steep pediment over the central projecting staircase bay. Large arched landing window with small panes; oval window in the pediment; coved cornice. One would suggest a late C17 date were it not for the good early C18 staircase with turned balusters. Nice neo-Grecian black marble fireplace in the later dining room.

TREHILL. A distinguished small neo-classical house, built in 1827 for J.H. Ley by *C.R. Ayers*, the London architect who designed Canonteign (q.v.) in the following year. Stuccoed, two storeys above a high rusticated basement, five bays, the centre one recessed behind a four-column Greek Doric porch. Parapet with intermittent balustrading. Niches with pineapples within the porch. On the S side a full-height central bow. The most striking feature is the top-lit central stair hall with curving stone cantilevered staircase 144 rising on three sides with only one intermediate landing. In the upper walls round-headed recesses with classical statues, originally open at the back to a first-floor corridor, giving a sense of depth to the fairly confined space. Flat glass-coffered ceiling with painted rosettes. The main rooms have good neo-classical cornices and fireplaces, the one in the library of black marble with brass insets. Original bookcases as well, in an Adamish style. To the W a low kitchen wing. In the grounds an ORANGERY, five bays with central pediment.

WOODLANDS. Improved in 1836 for W. Ley by *Anthony Salvin* and now reduced in size: a plain stone two-storey range. Salvin's hand is visible in the two-storey porch with Perp doorway and coat of arms above.

TOLL HOUSE, on the old Plymouth road, near the entrance to Woodlands. 1842. Two-storey, angle-fronted, with large buttresses, arched windows, and a large recessed porch.

HALDON. The site of the Neolithic settlement mentioned in the Introduction (q.v.) lies near Lawrence Castle (*see* Dunchideock), but there are no traces above ground.

KENNERLEIGH

8000

ST JOHN BAPTIST. Small, and much restored in 1847–8. Oblong unbuttressed w tower with small pyramid-covered pinnacles and C19 pyramid roof. Low nave and one aisle, the four-bay arcade with piers of type A section with capitals only to the main shafts. Old ceiled wagon roof in the chancel. – SCREEN. Small fragments of cornice used in the partition walls of the vestry.

KENTISBEARE

0000

ST MARY. The chief pleasure of the exterior is the w tower whose buttresses and stair-turret have a chequer pattern of blocks of pink and grey stone. The same in the buttresses of the chancel. Both parts are C14. The nave has different (earlier?) masonry. The windows, however, are Perp, as also is the s aisle. On the N side the easternmost of the nave windows is enriched by fleurons around the arch, and has large busts as head-stops. Similar fleurons to arch and jambs of the N doorway, with a canopied niche above. Inside, the arch of the enriched NE window also has fleurons; was there once a chapel or chantry here? The early C16 s aisle, as wide and grand as the nave, has the usual B type piers with standard capitals. One has a carving of ship and woolpack. Wagon roofs, the one in the chancel plastered in 1757. Restoration 1865–6 by *Hayward* (reseating, reflooring, and new vestry).

SCREEN. With A type tracery and coving to E and W, but a touch of the Flamboyant in the tracery at the top of each panel (cf. Kenton, Pilton). Fourfold cornice. – The S PARCLOSE SCREEN simpler. – PULPIT and READER'S DESK. Plain C18. The pulpit was originally signed *Isaac Bonifant* and dated 1736. – WEST GALLERY. 1632, the parapet painted with figures and texts, carved strapwork below. – Elizabethan PANELLING in the SE chapel, from Bradfield. – STAINED GLASS. E window by *Clayton & Bell*, 1882. – Chancel N 1889, in similar good drawing style. – Others in the chancel with stamped quarries by *Powell*'s of Whitefriars. – Two nave windows of 1887. – MONUMENTS. In the SE chapel John Whyting, merchant venturer, †1529. He gave the money for the building of the s aisle, and his arms are on the screen too. Elaborately panelled tomb-chest with subdivided cusped lozenges. Matrices of two brasses. – Another simple Purbeck tomb-chest, not *in situ*. – William Eveleigh and family †1697, 1700. Architectural, with open segmental pediment and putti heads. – Rev. G. W. Scott †1830. Marble, with a poem by his cousin, Sir Walter

Scott, on a scroll draped over an urn, attended by a putto. – Cleeve family. The usual ogee Gothic niche of the 1840s.

SAINT HILL BAPTIST CHAPEL, near the end of a quiet lane. 1830, rendered, with three pointed windows overlooking the burial ground.

PRIEST HALL. Picturesquely sited on a slope close to the church. Cob and thatch, the big stone lateral stack a later addition to this late medieval priest's house. Converted to cottages in the C19; restored with open hall in the 1950s. An ogee-headed wooden doorway is the only visible medieval sign in front, but at the back of the hall is the rare survival of a wooden window of four lights with trefoiled heads (top obscured). Two round-headed doorways in the screens passage: one may have led to stairs to an upper chamber. Another chamber existed over the screens passage, jettied out far into the hall. At the other end a parlour with four-light window, and a stone stair in the rear projection, probably a later addition.

KENTISBEARE HOUSE. 1841 by *J. T. Knowles*. Built as the rectory by the fourth Earl of Egremont for his brother (*see* Blackborough). Plain Regency style; deep eaves.

SCHOOL. Red brick, 1873–4, additions 1894.

COURT BARTON. Good C17 farmhouse with a symmetrical front. Two-room and cross-passage plan. Remains of a plaster ceiling in the main ground-floor room.

WOOD BARTON. Now a farmhouse, but incorporating a major medieval house which in 1336 was granted by John de Cogan to William de Seincler with the service of a carpenter called Walter atte Parke. It is tempting to associate the surviving roof with this date; it is the most sophisticated of a small group of early Devon roofs with base crucks and crown-posts (cf. Moorstone Barton, Halberton). Three bays survive, including a spere truss. The main trusses have chamfered arch-braces and remains of carved bosses. The upper section is cusped, as are the intermediate trusses, which have slots for further decoration, and the arcade plates are moulded. A simpler cusped base cruck remains from a later building phase (of uncertain date, but without smoke-blackening).

KENTISBURY   6040

No village; just church and farmhouse in a dip on the NW edge of Kentisbury Down.

ST THOMAS. W tower tall, with a NE stair-turret; no pinnacles. Tudor roses on the type B buttresses. The rest of the church entirely rebuilt, with a new N aisle and extended chancel, by *E. Dolby* of Abingdon, 1873–4, for the Rev. Thomas Openshaw, absentee rector and patron 1863–77 (he lived near Manchester). Some old material re-used, e.g. the Perp S porch and earlier S doorway with intricate continuous mouldings. N aisle with three-bay arcade of Bath stone and an elaborate but incomplete E end serving as the Openshaw Chapel: wall arcading on marble shafts, plate tracery windows. – Lavish C19 FURNISHINGS throughout: PULPIT with painted openwork panels, ceiled chancel roof painted with stars and musical angels, TILES of increasing elaboration in chancel and sanctuary. – STAINED GLASS. Many windows to Openshaw relatives: E window to the rector's brother † 1861, by *Clayton & Bell*, N aisle E to his parents-in-law, with attractively coloured archangels, and two more in the N aisle. – CURIOSA. Two C18 slate tablets with long eulogies to the Richards family, patrons and rectors from 1598 to 1773. – MONUMENT. Modest brass with Celtic cross to the Rev. Thomas Openshaw † 1877. – On the porch, one of *Berry*'s slate SUNDIALS, dated 1762. – Good slate GRAVESTONES.

CHURCH HOUSE. Two storeys, very small and simple.

KENTISBURY BARTON, W of the church. A large farmhouse with one three-light mullioned window remaining to the r. of the doorway. Datestone of 1672.

KENTISBURY GRANGE, 1 m. SE. A solid stone mansion of 1894 with Gothic doorway and mullioned-and-transomed windows. Built by a Mr Openshaw, a Manchester cotton merchant, a relation of the rector. (Excellent fittings; staircase window with stained glass by *Born* of Birmingham.) Now the centre of a caravan park.

WISTLANDPOUND FARMHOUSE. House of *c.* 1840, with across the road an impressive courtyard of model farm buildings of the same date (converted 1988). Built by the Fortescues of Castle Hill. N range with stone entrance gateway with pilasters, and a bell-turret. E range with bank barn and attached mill house with breastshot millwheel.

BAPTIST CHAPEL, beside the A399. 1851. Gabled, rendered, and colour-washed, with arched windows. All very plain. Sunday School of 1881, rubble with brick dressings, behind a small yard.

On MATTOCKS DOWN and KENTISBURY DOWN are round barrows and isolated standing stones.

KENTON

ALL SAINTS. The most ambitious church in this neighbourhood. A document of 1379 says that William Slighe wished to be buried in the aisle which he had built ('de novo construxi'). But that must refer to an earlier building than the present one, which is all late Perp. The W tower and S porch were the last additions and look early C16. The tower is of ashlar, 120 ft high, with buttresses of B type, large three-light bell-openings with one transom, four-light main W window, pinnacles with niches for figures below. The two-storeyed embattled S porch has a big ornate niche above the entrance and little niches above the gargoyles. Square-headed outer and inner porch doorways, elaborately carved, the outer one with dripstone heads. They, and the mullions above, are of Beer stone; the masonry otherwise is red sandstone, much patched with grey and white, perhaps re-used older material (see also the older stone footings of the chancel). Embattled S aisle with rood-loft turret, embattled N aisle with NW turret. All aisle windows of four lights with tracery of the usual A pattern of Devon screens. Six-light E window, the tracery correctly renewed.

The interior is spacious, though not as strikingly so as, for example, Tiverton or Cullompton. Total length 140 ft. Seven bays with piers of B type and standard capitals. Panelled tower arch. All roofs renewed in 1854 by *David Mackintosh*. Conscientious restoration in 1861–5 by *J. W. Rowell* of Newton Abbot (nave and chancel roofs, repairs to masonry, reseating). – PULPIT. C15. Much restored in 1882 by *Bligh Bond* from pieces rescued by Baring-Gould. New paintings under the nodding arches, between the thickly carved, very bossy leaves. – SCREEN. The wainscoting here with original painted panels, but in quality mere village craft; no comparison with the skill of the woodwork. The tracery of the panels is of the usual type, the fan-coving and cornice (with three decorated bands) much renewed. Rood loft new, the result of careful restoration by *Herbert Read* with the advice of *Bligh Bond* (centre 1899, aisles 1935–6). The heraldry includes Bishop Peter Courtenay of Exeter (1478–86). On the top of the screen, large silver cross by *Henry Wilson*, 1923, made for Exeter Cathedral. – DOOR into the NE chapel made up of bench ends with whole figures of angels with shields. – PARCLOSE SCREEN to the N chapel. Delicate tracery with odd multiform capitals to the thin mullions.

TRIPTYCH. 1893 by *Kempe Studios*, executed by *Zwinke* of Oberammergau; painted wooden panels in high relief. – STAINED GLASS. E window by *Clayton & Bell*. – Sanctuary N and s by *Drake*. – W and NE windows by *Ballantyne*. – A few ancient quarries in the N aisle windows. – SCULPTURE. Large relief in the chancel (Raising of the Widow's Son) by *Stephens* of Exeter, 1868; still classical in feeling. – MONUMENTS. Dulcebella Hodges †1628. A whole figure, seated, her head resting on her hand, the elbow on a table, just like the Tuckfield monument at Crediton. – Nicholas Martyn †1653. Open pediment and strapwork. – John Swete the diarist (*see* Oxton) †1821, by *Kendall*. Two urns and a long epitaph recording his 'love of literature and thirst for knowledge' and 'strong relish for liberal and elegant studies'. – Joshua and Emily Neale †1919 and 1923. Unusual carved slates with small birds and two linked garlands.

ALMSHOUSES. A good late C19 red brick group s of the church, symmetrical, gabled, with fat chimneys corbelled out at each end.

LIMEKILN with two circular kilns by the side of the road at Cockwood.

KERSWELL PRIORY
Broadhembury

0000

Founded between 1119 and 1129 as a cell of the Cluniac priory of Montacute; always very small. All that remains now is a farmhouse, which appears to be on the site of the church, and whose thick walls may incorporate some medieval fabric. The only clearly datable medieval feature is in the E cross-wing: a C12 doorway, its arch probably reset, the voussoirs with shallow zigzag decoration with small foliage decoration in the outer triangles, the jamb shafts with crude capitals. The door perhaps opened into the s transept from the cloister. The main range of the farmhouse has a hall with moulded beams and an adjoining parlour with an early C17 plaster ceiling divided into four compartments, each with a geometric pattern with small central bosses. Beyond this an C18 addition with a centrally placed front door facing w. To the s of the farmhouse was a large late medieval structure, latterly a farm building but no doubt once part of the domestic monastic buildings. It was demolished in 1985. Its roof timbers (six trusses, two of them arch-braced, with wind-braces) are stored at Buckfast Abbey for possible re-erection.

KILLERTON
Broadclyst

The grounds rather than the house are what count at Killerton. They were given to the National Trust by the Aclands in 1944. House and grounds were planned together by Sir Thomas Acland from 1770. The Aclands, who had been at Columbjohn nearby (q.v.) from the late C16, owned Killerton from the early C17, but did not make it their main seat until after 1672. A dated stone of 1680 is all that remains from that time.

The house is one of the rare cases in the county of a complete rebuilding. The new house, built in 1778–9 apparently as a 'temporary residence' (a more elaborate design by *James Wyatt* was rejected), dignified but by no means grand, is by *John Johnson* of Leicester. It is a plain two-storey Georgian box, five by seven bays, the former entrance side to the S distinguished by a slightly projecting centre and pedimented Tuscan doorcase. Extensions to the N were made by the tenth baronet, Sir Thomas, in the earlier C19, and after 1898 the W side was considerably altered and made the main entrance in a programme of aggrandizement carried out by *Protheroe & Phillips* of Cheltenham for the twelfth baronet. The porch of this time was replaced after a fire of 1924 by a more tactful entrance: a low entrance hall by *Randall Wells* in the angle of the house and the earlier Edwardian billiard room. Large round-arched doorway in the splayed side; spacious hall interior with chunky piers. It makes a nice contrast with the main survival of Johnson's house, the elegant corridor from the S entrance, with shallow domes on pendentives. The doorway with fluted pilasters and the plaster frieze of the dining room are also of Johnson's time, although the ceiling itself is Edwardian, as is much of the other decoration of the main rooms: Adamish plasterwork by *Jackson & Co.*, scagliola columns in the drawing room (made from two earlier rooms), and the heavy carved main staircase. Upstairs, Johnson's work is still recognizable in the domed upper corridor.

STABLES, near the entrance. 1778–80 by *Johnson*. Handsome stone Palladian design on a quadrangular plan. Blind arcade with lunettes flanking a pedimented archway; pediments also to the courtyard. Clock-turret and bellcote.

GROUNDS. The original layout of the 1770s was by the young *Robert Veitch*, who continued to work for the tenth baronet, establishing his nursery garden at Budlake, near Killerton, before moving it to Exeter. 500 acres were enclosed for the new park. The original surviving planting includes the Beech Grove, and the Spanish chestnuts and tulip trees in the chapel enclosure. The gardens close to the house are Edwardian, laid out with the advice of *William Robinson*, with terrace, herbaceous border, and rockery. On the terrace two large neo-classical urns signed *Coade & Sealy*, 1805.

BEAR HUT, NW of the house. (Not its original name.) A quaint thatched log summerhouse, in existence by 1831. Three chambers, the inner one furnished as an artfully rustic hermitage chapel, with wooden 'chancel arch', vaulting of deerskin, floor of knuckle-bones, and a lancet window with fragments of old glass (cf. the slightly later hermitage at Bicton). Octagonal central chamber roofed with matting and pine cones. Entrance room with cobbled floor, lined with wickerwork.

CHAPEL, NE of the house, in its own enclosure. 1838–41 by *C. R. Cockerell*, inspired by the Lady Chapel at Glastonbury, which was considered an exemplar for the neo-Norman style popular at that moment. Ashlar, with fish-scale slate roof and corner turrets; archaeologically very correct (although the W wheel-window with its zigzag is based on Barfreston in Kent, not Glastonbury). Timber barrel-vault, stall-wise seating. – ALTAR TABLE carved in Norman style by *Arthur Acland-Troyte*. – Side windows with patterned GLASS designed by Dean *Liddell*.

ICE HOUSE, built in a former quarry, completed in 1808. Stone façade added when the rock garden was made *c*. 1900.

CROSS, NW of the house. Of Celtic type, erected in memory of Sir Thomas Dyke Acland, tenth baronet, in 1878.

LODGES. The main lodge 1825 by *Cockerell*; Sprydon Drive lodge also by him.

DOLBURY. An Iron Age EARTHWORK within the grounds.

KILMINGTON

2090

ST GILES. Square W tower; four-centred doorway, stair-turret, battlements, and gargoyles. The rest of 1862 by *C. F. Edwards* of Axminster; dull. N and S arcades with octagonal piers. Brash wooden S porch. – STAINED GLASS. E window 1863 by *Horwood Brothers* of Wells, badly faded. – S aisle 1893 by *Ward & Hughes*. – N aisle window 1903 by *A. L. & C. E. Moore*. – MONUMENTS. Thomas Southcott †1715. Architectural, grey veined marble, two angels above the pediment. – Agnes Tucker of Coryton †1788. By *Charles Harris*. Elegant neo-classical tablet with a draped urn against a black marble obelisk. – Charles Tucker †1885. Brass with the four evangelists within niches, by *Frank Smith & Co.*

VICARAGE. 1911 by *Caröe & Passmore*.

CORYTON PARK. The park remains, but only one plain Italianate wing of the mansion built by the Tuckers in 1756. Its excellent Rococo fittings were sold in 1951.

KINGSBRIDGE

7040

ST EDMUND. The distinguishing feature is the C13 crossing tower on steep, slightly chamfered pointed arches and with corbel-table, battlements, and spire (one tier of dormers, bell-openings *c*. 1300 or later). Otherwise the exterior is much altered, chiefly by the addition in 1849 of a large chapel w of the s transept. Medieval s chancel chapel with three-light window without tracery; the priest's door cuts into a buttress (cf. Sherford, Thurlestone, Ugborough). Embattled s porch. Nave of three bays with octagonal piers, rebuilt in the later c19. s chancel chapel of two bays, and N chancel chapel of one bay with type A piers with capitals only for the four shafts. The arches leading from the w and E into the transepts are of the same type. All these arches are moulded, that from chancel into N chapel more finely than the others. A consecration is recorded for 1414. – FONT. Octagonal, of flat shape, c13? With two very shallow pointed arches in each panel. – ROOD SCREEN. Parts used in pulpit and reader's desk, with blank, completely Flamboyant arcading. – PARCLOSE SCREENS also Flamboyant and of a design different from any other in Devon. – MONUMENTS. Rev. George Hughes †1667. Architectural wall-monument. – Frances Schutz Drury †1817, by *Flaxman*. A young woman, very slender, rises up, helped by a small girl, and another young woman hovering slightly higher – a smooth composition of shallow curves. The design is a version of an earlier Flaxman monument at Milton, Cambridgeshire.

METHODIST CHAPEL, Fore Street. Built by the Wesleyans in 1814, enlarged in 1870. Charming colour-washed rendered three-bay front with pediment, set back behind a forecourt. Doorway with fanlight.

GOSPEL HALL, Fore Street. Also set back and partly hidden. Tall, of stone, with a hipped roof and an open veranda with stone columns.

The town's name comes from a bridge linking the royal estates of West Alvington and Chillington, mentioned in 962. The oldest settlement was at Dodbrooke (q.v.), but in 1219 Buckfast Abbey established a market at Kingsbridge on the E edge of Churchstow, a manor in their possession (cf. Newton Abbot). The little town consists chiefly of Fore Street, winding steeply uphill from the quay, starting with two stuccoed inns, the SHIP AND PLOUGH and THE QUAY.

FORE STREET itself is attractive, with c18–19 slate-hung fronts to the houses, their narrow frontages indicative of their medieval sites and of older fabric behind. The focal point is the small Italianate TOWN HALL close to the church, of 1850, with outsize slated turret with four-dial clock dated 1875. Nearby is the best group of buildings: the SHAMBLES, with granite piers of 1585 forming a loggia (cf. Dartmouth and Totnes). Upper floor altered in 1796 (the date when the feoffees 'improved' the town, repairing the streets and removing the central water conduits and butchers' stalls). Lower down, set back, the METHODIST CHAPEL (q.v.); higher up, the former GRAMMAR SCHOOL, founded by Thomas Crispin in 1670, a three-bay, two-storey front with wooden mullioned windows, emphatically pre-classical. To the r. the schoolmaster's house, rebuilt in 1840 with an extra floor. Now a museum devoted to Thomas Cookworthy, discoverer of kaolin. In the first-floor schoolroom a canopied master's desk and royal arms of 1671. Also worth noting in Fore Street, No. 66, with Corinthian porch and good Victorian shopfront; the KINGS ARMS opposite, with four sets of bay-windows; No. 49a (Myrtle House), C18 front, C17 parts behind; and the Roman Catholic church, with an early C19 Gothick front. E of Fore Street, an unspoilt back street with rows of modest rendered houses leads back to the river.

THE RIVERSIDE. Overlooking the end of the creek, now silted up and partly filled by an uninspiring car park on the site of the mill pool of a former tide mill, QUAY HOUSE (council offices), good late C18 (1789: DOE), three storeys, of stone, with a porch with thin wooden Doric columns. Nearby, grey brick LIBRARY and HEALTH CENTRE of the 1970s. Along the road E of the creek a nice neo-classical stucco terrace of four houses, c. 1830, with incised pilasters and contemporary railings with large bold motifs. Further on a pair of villas of the same period; then later detached houses. In contrast, on the W side of the water there is only thoughtlessly scrappy C20 development.

WAREHOUSE, Ebrington Street. 1802. Three storeys, of coursed rubble. To the r. on each floor doorways with a gantry above a louvred bellcote.

Three good separate LIMEKILNS on the Creek.

A bypass to the W now cuts off the western suburbs. Beyond lies UNION ROAD, with REDFORD COURT (The Retreat) and the remains of the WORKHOUSE, two extremes of the same date (1837), the one fanciful and sentimental, a villa with barge-boarding breaking forth into grapes, with grapes also in the cast-iron gate, the other grim, utilitarian, and classical.

On the edge of the town, among much recent housing, an estate by *Pritchard & Bull*, 1977. Nicely staggered terraces, simply detailed, rendered walls with timber-framed porches: a good and relatively early example of the type.

WELLE HOUSE, Wallingford Road. Two-storeyed gateway with a large round-headed moulded arch of c. 1600, incorporated into a once larger house of complex date.

KINGSKERSWELL

ST MARY. Unbuttressed W tower with stair-turret. The S side looks C19. Shallow S transept, low, with battlements, possibly (with the chancel) remaining from a cruciform church (Fryer Cornelius). S chapel and S aisle C14 or early C15, with red sandstone octagonal piers with red double-chamfered arches but limestone moulded capitals. Late Perp N arcade, the piers of B type with standard Devon capitals and moulded arches. In the S wall of the S transept a recess with elaborate, much cusped early Perp blank arcading, cut into by the present S window. Restored c. 1856 by *Hugall* and in 1875 by *Rowell*. – SCREEN. Parts of the wainscoting of the former screen used for chancel stalls. – STAINED GLASS. Fragments in the tracery of the E window. – MONUMENTS. Three badly preserved effigies of c. 1400 now in the N aisle: knight with angels supporting his head, one side of a table tomb incorporated in the wall below, possibly Sir John Dinham; and two ladies in modish dress, possibly his two wives, one with angels at the head, the other (unusually) with angels at the knees and a dragon at the feet.

Close to the church the scanty, ivy-clad remains of the MANOR HOUSE of the Dinhams.

ST GREGORY, Coles Lane. 1962 by *Evans, Powell & Powell*, rebuilt after a fire in 1977. Neo-Romanesque; apsidal E end, NW campanile.

SCHOOLS. 1856 by *Hugall*.

BARTON HALL. Red sandstone Tudor mansion built *c.* 1840 for H. Langford Brown, rebuilt after a fire in 1863.

ROSE HILL HOUSE. Of *c.* 1830, stuccoed, the garden front with a central pediment and lunette.

ROSEHILL RAILWAY VIADUCT. Seven brick arches on limestone piers. 1846–8 by *Brunel*.

LIMEKILNS. A small one, well preserved, at Decoy Brake, Abbotskerswell; another at North Whilborough, with a low parapet wall; a third at South Whilborough.

WINDMILL, North Whilborough. Tapering tower; no gear.

6010   KINGS NYMPTON

ST JAMES. Low, unbuttressed W tower with very small openings and recently renewed spire, the tower arch pointed and unmoulded. N transept also early, with a pointed and unmoulded arch towards the nave. S aisle Perp, embattled, with a tall five-bay arcade with piers of A type and capitals only to the main shafts. A coffin-shaped doorway and door in the chancel N wall. S porch with cross-ribbed unceiled wagon roof. Wagon roofs in the church as well. Celure, i.e. specially decorated wagon roof, panelled and with cross-ribs and carved bosses, above the rood screen. The chancel roof was plastered in 1755 to paint a picture on it of sky, clouds, and a large cross, the work of the incumbent, the Rev. *Lewis Southcombe* (cf. Honiton Barton, South Molton). – REREDOS. Early C18, big, with Ionic pilasters. – COMMUNION RAILS with alternating twisted balusters and columns also early C18. – FONT with baluster shaft and fluted bowl probably of the same date. – Jacobean PANELLING in the S aisle E (Pollard) chapel. – SCREEN. Complete with ribbed coving and cornice (three bands of ornament). The tracery type A standard. The panels between the ribs of the coving have, in the nave tracery, in the aisle leaf, head, etc., motifs. – BOX PEWS. – PULPIT. C18, with Gothick banister.

KINGS NYMPTON PARK. A rarity in Devon: a Palladian villa. Built in 1746–9 as New Place by James Buller of Downes (q.v.) after his second marriage to Lady Jane Bathurst. The contract was with *Francis Cartwright*, a master-builder and architect from near Blandford in Dorset.[*] The design is based on that influential prototype for English Palladianism, Roger Morris's Marble Hill, Twickenham (1724–9). The house is of two storeys and attics, with a hipped roof. The main elevation to the garden of five bays, the centre three with pediment and Ionic order above a rusticated ground floor. This follows Marble Hill as built, and not the designs published in *Vitruvius Britannicus*. Other differences are instruc-

---

[*]I am grateful to Nicholas Thompson for details about the contract.

tive: the residue of provincial Baroque traditions is seen in the emphatic keystones to the ground-floor windows and in the use of columns rather than pilasters for the centrepiece. The chief contrast is in materials; instead of a chaste white, the walls of Kings Nympton are red brick, and at the sides and back rubble stone. But the contract indicates that they were to have been plastered. The entrance front is very plain, with neither pediment nor window surrounds; the low Tuscan porch was added after the house was sold to the Tanner family in 1842. Snell (1907) states that the house had remained incomplete for a hundred years.

The planning (although not the interior details) also echoes Marble Hill. Low entrance hall on the garden side with four columns; staircase behind. This is of stone, with an iron balustrade, around three sides of a well, a light and elegant creation. Library in the SW corner with fitted bookcases and pretty marble fireplace. Morning room behind. Over the hall a large but plain billiard room, apparently a change of plan, as references to a cube room suggest that the intention was to create a double-height saloon as at Marble Hill. In the spacious cellars two re-used medieval stone doorways, probably from the old mansion, which stood on a different site. The kitchen, also at this level, below the library, has handsome brick groin-vaults on square piers. E of the house is a separate laundry: two storeys, rubble, with stone bands below the windows.

On the layout of the grounds Buller consulted his father-in-law Lord Bathurst of Cirencester Park, patron of Pope and keen horticulturalist. Planting continued into the 1760s. The house is now entirely hidden in the heavily wooded park.

BROOMHAM. A rare example in North Devon of a former longhouse, probably early C16, remodelled in 1638.

CAPELCOMBE. A C15–17 farmhouse with rich internal fittings. The two-storey cob projection was probably a corn-drying chamber.

KINGSTEIGNTON

Now mostly a sprawling suburb E of Newton Abbot. The older part lies further E along the road to Teignmouth.

ST MICHAEL. Tall grey W tower, buttresses of type B, W window with crude plate tracery, probably all C17. The rest of the exterior of squared red sandstone with Perp windows, renewed in 1824 and again in 1865. Nave and two aisles of five bays, B type piers, standard capitals. S door prettily decorated with a leaf scroll all along jambs and voussoirs, very similar in style to the leaf-work on the uncommonly richly decorated C15 FONT: the tracery pattern on the pillar is especially striking (blank ogee arches set horizontally). – SCREEN. Only the wainscoting survives: badly overpainted panels. Part of the screen was removed to the rectory in 1865. – STAINED GLASS. E and S aisle E windows by *Hardman*. – MONUMENTS. C18–19 minor marble memorials including S. Whiteway † 1847 by *S. Nixon*. – LEDGER STONES. The earliest is of 1670 (note the inscription).

THE CHANTRY AND ELMFIELD. Vicarage Hill, E of the church. A most surprising house (now divided in two): a *cottage orné* built in

1815 as a parsonage for Thomas Whipham by *John Rendle* of Teignmouth, otherwise unknown, but whose work, on this evidence, may well have included some of the gentlemen's cottages that were springing up along the coast at this time. Rendered and thatched, with an undulating garden front with thatched veranda originally on rustic posts (partly replaced) and a patterned pebble floor. Plainer entrance side with thatched canted bays. The porch altered. The interior is as ambitiously planned as any neo-classical villa: central top-lit hall with cantilevered stone stair; connecting suite of three rooms on the garden side, the end ones oval. But the details – stair balustrade, marble fireplaces, panelled doors – are all Gothick. The windows are particularly pretty, with arched lights, complicated cast-iron patterns, and coloured glass at the top. In the hall, two bays of the medieval rood screen from the church, re-used as double doors.

BABCOMBE MANOR. Mid C16, remodelled in the mid C17, now subdivided. Some granite windows from the earlier phase. In the back wall of the hall (now divided off in a corridor) an unusual C17 window with an elaborate plaster surround.

BELLAMARSH BARTON. A notable roof suggests that this began as a superior medieval hall house (seven closely spaced major and minor arch-braced trusses, all smoke-blackened). C16 lower-end solar wing, C17 porch with good enriched-rib ceiling to the upper room.

SAMPSON'S, Preston. A large late medieval former farmhouse, now a restaurant, with three stud-and-panel screens, the studs of the screen between hall and inner room exceptionally broad; it may be a low partition, since the upper chamber is jettied out into the hall over it.

WHITEWAY BARTON. Late C17 asymmetrical front, with a fine show of seven regular mullion-and-cross windows with leaded panes.

In NEWTON ROAD, alongside the site of the Hackney canal, CELLARS built *c.* 1843 by Lord Clifford for storing the ball clay exported from Teignmouth.

KINGSTON

ST JAMES. A pre-Perp church with a Perp N aisle. W tower with diagonal buttresses not reaching high up, battlements on the corbel-table, and the same arrangement for the rectangular NE stair-turret, which is higher than the tower. Separate trefoil-headed bell-openings. Early round-headed S doorway. S transept with plate tracery; two lights with a quatrefoil – late C13? There was a dedication in 1422, perhaps relating to the S side rather than to the Perp four-bay N arcade with its A type piers, capitals only to the four shafts, the arches with a double-concave chamfer. Three-light windows without tracery. The whole thoroughly restored by *E.H.Sedding* in 1892, work on the S (Wonwell) transept completed 1905. – FONT. Perp, octagonal, with quatrefoil. – One old BENCH END, and a piece of carved wall-plate in the chancel.

WONWELL COURT. A courtyard house of the C16–18, now a farmhouse, formerly a seat of the Ayshfords, inherited by the Wise family *c.* 1750. Georgian five-window front with shell hood over the doorway.

LIMEKILN, at the N end of Wonwell Beach.

KINGSWEAR

The best thing about the little town opposite Dartmouth is its position, with its houses rising steeply above the river, dominated by the ROYAL DART HOTEL, asymmetrical Italianate of the 1860s by *Edward Appleton*, built also as premises for the Royal Dart Yacht Club. Nearby is the STATION built *c.* 1864 for the Dartmouth and Torbay line. Timber, with canopies over the road approach and the goods line behind. Linked to the hotel by an archway which also gives access to the covered gangway to the floating landing-stage for the ferry. (The line was never carried across the river, although a station was built for it at Dartmouth, q.v., Perambulation 1.)

ST THOMAS. Medieval tower; the rest rebuilt by *Hayward* in 1847.

CASTLE. Much restored square battlemented tower of *c.* 1491–4, built at the same time as Dartmouth Castle, to guard the entrance to the river. Three storeys, with NW circular stair. Original gunports to both ground and first floors. Floor levels altered, and the top floor much rebuilt by *Thomas Lidstone* in 1855 when converted to a house for Charles Hayne Seale-Hayne M.P. To the NW a small circular vaulted tower, perhaps a magazine, connected to the castle by a later vaulted passage.

DAY MARK. A tapering 80ft column erected in the 1860s by the Dartmouth Harbour Commissioners as an aid to navigators.

On INNER FROWARD POINT a Second World War gun battery.

COLETON FISHACRE. 1926 by *Oswald Milne* for Rupert D'Oyly Carte, on a secluded site overlooking Pudcombe Cove. A long irregular building of local rubble, the polygonal porch neatly tucked between the main range and an angled wing with the principal living room. On the garden side a bow-window with conical roof as the chief accent, a loggia at one end. Tiled roofs, simple casement windows; the details all very understated, but still in the Arts and Crafts tradition. Inside, overmantel with painted map of the Dart estuary by *Spencer Hoffman*, and an ingenious windvane. Fine terraced gardens, with drive down to the beach.

GREENWAY HOUSE. Tall, late Georgian, stuccoed, five bays, with one-storey loggia on each side, overlooking the Dart.

NETHWAY HOUSE. Built by John Fownes in 1699, so a plaque records. A compact brick post-Restoration house, seven by five bays, three storeys, the centre emphasized by plain pilasters and a raised cornice (cf. Pynes, Upton Pyne; Mothecombe). (Good closed-string staircase; ceiling with simple oval and leaf sprays.)

KITLEY
Yealmpton

The seat of the Bastards, inherited through marriage to the Pollex-fens in 1710. The house is set in beautifully landscaped grounds, close to the creek, overlooking a lake divided off by a dam. Its present appearance is due to a remodelling of *c.* 1820–5 by *G.S. Repton* for Edward Pollexfen Bastard, an early example of a sympathetic approach to the Tudor style. The treatment is still symmetrical, although a picturesque outline is achieved by gables, pinnacles, and chimneys. Granite ashlar, the flat surfaces relieved by slightly projecting battlemented panels and a canted oriel on the S side, details borrowed not locally but from East Anglia (where Repton had worked previously), much as in the case of Salvin's more accomplished Tudor at Mamhead a few years later.

Repton's Tudor details were applied to a house which had earlier been Georgianized, as his plans and drawings show, but whose foundations go back to the C16. The complex history is best seen on the W side, where the H shape of the original house is still visible, its courtyard largely filled by a low wing added by Repton, behind which is the large window (now mullioned but previously Georgian) of the staircase added in the C18 within the great hall. The story is complicated by a change of levels, the ground floor of the Tudor house becoming the basement of the Georgian one. Several four-centred Tudor doorways survive at basement level, as well as an older one with a two-centred hollow-chamfered arch (re-used?) now leading down to cellars below the S range. Repton provided a terrace to conceal the basement level on the S side where the ground drops. On the E side, where an C18 saloon had been added in the E forecourt against the hall, and on the N side, where the Georgian entrance was, Repton did little more than replace the hipped roofs and sashes by gables and mullions and enliven the plain parapet by pinnacles.

Inside, the Tudor spirit extends only as far as the entrance hall in the N wing, with its grained panelling and coats of arms. From here one enters the early C18 stair-hall. The magnificently generous imperial stair (most unusual for Devon) fills the whole space of the former hall. Excellent craftsmanship: one fluted and two spiral balusters to each tread, inlaid steps, lower walls with fielded panelling, arched doorways flanked by fluted Ionic pilasters. The one opposite the stair leads into the C18 saloon, made into the dining room by Repton, preserving its bolection-moulded dado panelling and good cornice. The spacious library in the S range is all Repton, a tripartite interior divided by Ionic columns of yellow scagliola, with inset bookcases. Double doors lead to the morning room in the SE corner. In the low W range a small circular boudoir with a shallow dome acts as anteroom to a drawing room.

GARDEN LODGE. Square, thatched, one-storeyed, with rustic veranda and Gothic window.

KNIGHTSHAYES
Tiverton

9010

158 An eloquent expression of High Victorian ideals in a country house of moderate size. Built in 1869–74 by the arch-Goth *William Burges* for Sir John Heathcoat-Amory M.P., grandson of John Heathcoat who established the lace factory at Tiverton (q.v.). Owned by the National Trust from 1973. Proudly set on a terrace overlooking the

gardens to the s. The general impression is not as wildly medieval as Burges's work at Cardiff Castle or Castell Coch. Here, his favourite early French Gothic has been domesticated and applied to a nearly symmetrical composition of the standard neo-Tudor type: a main block flanked by projecting gabled wings, a low service range discreetly attached on the r. The creepers, part of the original planting, soften the powerful, even harsh contrast of the local reddish Hensley stone and crisply cut Ham Hill dressings.

Close up, the typically bold and wilful Burgesian details have plenty of impact: plate-tracery windows with thick chamfered mullions and transoms, steep gables and dormers, weighty crenellated chimneys and thrusting gargoyles. In the l. angle, lively carving below the corbelled-out first-floor oriel, the most obvious of the few asymmetrical touches on this side. The entrance front to the N is L-shaped, with a one-storey projecting billiard room at the NE corner. At the W end only the base was built of a massive tower over the staircase. It would have given the house a more overtly romantic silhouette. The low addition beyond (now shop) was built as a smoking room in 1902 by *Ernest George*.

Burges concentrated his energies on a flamboyantly imaginative scheme of interior decoration, prepared in 1873 (the drawings are in the house), but the family lost their nerve, and in 1875, when only a small part of his designs had been executed, Burges was replaced by the tamer decorator *J.D.Crace*. The Victorian interiors were subsequently toned down and altered, but something of their character has been recovered and restored by the National Trust from 1973.

The N porch, with a carved figure over the door, leads into the GREAT HALL, traditionally medieval, with an arch-braced roof and originally a screen (removed in 1914). It was intended for ceremonial occasions: at the high end is a gallery with a pierced stone balcony (for addressing the tenantry) supported by four hefty Devonshire marble columns. The staircase (by Burges apart from the finials) leads up behind. Large chimneypiece, less elaborate than Burges intended, but many excellent carved corbels belonging to the original scheme, the work of *Thomas Nicholls*, like other carving in the house. The main ones show figures engaged in various occupations (harvester, scholar, soldier, stonemason, etc.). Smaller corbels with animals below the stairs. The large bookcase with painted scenes of Christian and pagan art is not original to the house, but is by *Burges*, from his London house, made c. 1860.

The main living rooms face s. From E to W: DINING ROOM, with decoration mostly by *Crace*: painted ceiling, much restored, original frieze with quotations from Burns, wallpaper introduced by the National Trust (a Crace design for the House of Lords), simple chimneypiece with Latin mottoes. The octagonal MORNING ROOM has a beamed ceiling (repainted). Burges's wall decoration has gone (a frieze and stained glass with heroes and heroines of fairy-tales were intended). The LIBRARY also has been much altered; the Gothic bookcases have been cut down, and Burges's elaborate chimneypiece was never executed. The ceiling, however, has been restored to Crace's painted design. The DRAWING ROOM was to have been the climax of the Burges interiors, dedicated to Chivalry. The amazingly whimsical chimneypiece illustrating the 'Assault on the Castle of Love', a theme inspired by a C14 ivory, was never made, but the secret passage was prepared which was to enable the ladies of the house to look out over the mock battlements. Crace's plainer chimneypiece, removed in 1946, in turn was replaced in 1981 by a marble one by *Burges*, which had been cast out of Worcester College Oxford in 1966. The sparkling ceiling, with painted beams and Burges's favourite motif of Sicilian-inspired 'jellymould domelets', was uncovered in 1981. It had been boarded up already in 1889.

Upstairs, little of the original decoration remains apart from some Crace stencilling in a bedroom corridor, and the basic design of the boudoir ceiling (zodiac roundels repainted in 1981). The BILLIARD ROOM at the back of the house was, with characteristic Victorian humour, to have a display of Virtues in painted medallions (never executed) and Vices on carved corbels. The Vices are represented by vigorously carved animals, with an eighth corbel with an owl for wisdom.

STABLES, N of the house. A very Burgesian composition, with conical-topped turret to the Gothic entrance archway, red-painted dormers, and a picturesquely gabled hayloft on the courtyard side.

The WALLED KITCHEN GARDEN with turreted corners (their caps have gone) is also by *Burges*, as is the LODGE with bold gable and chimney.

GROUNDS. The gardens were largely created in the 1950s–70s. The fine formal gardens and terraces in front of the house have been much simplified. They were originally laid out by *Edward Kemp* (1818–91), who was a pupil of Paxton and had made his reputation designing Birkenhead Park. To the E the woodland gardens, begun in the 1950s. In two SUMMERHOUSES, wooden corbels by *Burges*, with animals and foliage, formerly in the hall.

See also Tiverton, Perambulation 3: Bolham.

1090

KNIGHTSTONE
Ottery St Mary

A medieval and Tudor house, rediscovered and improved in the C19 and C20. The C19 improver was Dr Drury, headmaster of Harrow. His family owned the house from 1803 to 1886, and were responsible for the fretted bargeboards to end and porch gables which give the impression of an overblown *cottage orné*. The lushly planted yew-hedged gardens in which the house is set, entered through wrought-iron gates with ball-topped piers, were created by Colonel Reginald Cooper in the 1940s.

Long, low exterior of brownish rubble, single-storey hall, two-storey cross-wings, a S wing beyond. Two late Tudor, or more likely early C17, hall windows, each of four lights with two transoms, ovolo-moulded and linked by a hoodmould. Porch with ample richly moulded inner and outer doorways of the same period, the inner one straight-headed, with well carved urn-shaped stops, and an original door, heavily studded in front and sturdily cross-braced at the back. Panelled hall screen of *c.* 1600 with later bolection-moulded central door. The hall fireplace, a conservative piece with a row of quatrefoils along the lintel, has the date 1567 and the initials of William Sherman, the Ottery merchant who acquired the house from the Bonville estate. It was formerly flanked by three-light transomed windows (see exterior wall). The structure of the hall is older than these improvements of the Sherman family, as is clear from the massive timbers of the roof; two and a half bays, the main trusses arch-braced and slightly moulded, the ridge carried on a yoke; two tiers of wind-braces. The use of arch-braces without crown-posts suggests an early C15 date. The plaster corbels with heads which mask the feet of the principals belonged with an elaborate plaster ceiling, probably of the early C17, of which only the frieze remains, vigorously decorated with mermen and with splendidly jocular monsters at the corners.

The solar wing was remodelled in the early C19; two four-centred doorways of that date lead from the hall, one to a simple early C19 stair-hall, the other to a parlour with a pretty flowered cornice. One Tudor fireplace remains in a bedroom. The service end was much altered in the late C17, with a dining room in the front part and behind it a good small staircase around a narrow well. The s wing beyond is medieval: in an upper room an arched-braced roof, at ground level a rough octagonal post (cf. the solar wing at Lustleigh) and a simple two-light wooden window. This work must, like the hall, date from the ownership of the Bittlesgate family. Their chapel was licensed in 1381 but its position is unknown. Behind the house, two wings of outbuildings; to the s, over a stream, a separate three-seated garderobe.

KNOWSTONE 8020

ST PETER. Rendered w tower with diagonal buttresses and polygonal NE stair-turret; no pinnacles. Most windows straight-headed. The interest of the church is its plain Norman s door, and the pre-ecclesiological interior, with an odd three-bay arcade between nave and N aisle: unmoulded round-headed arches on square piers with three-part abaci instead of capitals. It must be an C18 rebuilding. Coved ceiled roofs to nave and chancel, all whitewashed. Medieval wagon roof to the N aisle. – PULPIT. One panel of a former screen re-used. – MONUMENT. John Culme †1691. Two figures rest on the broken pediment.

The church lies on a slope above the secluded village, overlooking a long thatched range of cottages and the MASONS' ARMS, a former church house of the C16.

SHAPCOTT BARTON, 2 m. E. The former manor house of the Shapcotts, now a farmhouse. Mostly early C17. Porch with four-centred doorway. Good joinery and plasterwork inside. In the hall an early C17 ceiling apparently covering moulded beams – a grid, with the usual devices in panels. On the first floor another ceiling in a back room and a front room with frieze with winged horses, a popular motif.

LUCKETT. Plain stone exterior; elaborate C17 joinery inside.

LAMERTON

ST PETER. Rebuilt after a fire in 1877. Only the W tower older: diagonal buttresses, polygonal stair-turret, crocketed pinnacles (the W ones angled). – Jacobean FONT COVER. – Two MONU-MENTS were saved and restored: Hugh Fortescue † 1650 and wife, busts in arched niches holding hands; not good; and the Tremayne brothers of Collacombe, erected 1588, re-erected 1707, and characteristic of that date: a large standing wall-monument with columns and segmental pediment with reclining allegorical figures. The five brothers in a row, lively little figures, surprisingly small, on a platform at the foot of the columns.

The church is up a little lane from the village street, with the large C19 Tudor VICARAGE on the side facing the CHURCH HOUSE, a rebuilding with old material, restored in 1934. Round-headed central doorway of granite. Several substantial houses in the parish, including COLLACOMBE MANOR (q.v.).

HURLDITCH COURT. A C19 rebuilding on an older site. Traditionalist Tudor two-storey main range, porch, and long cross-wing.

VENN. An older house Gothicized by Richard Parsons in the early C19. Substantial entrance-tower of three storeys, battlemented. Pretty Gothick windows; bell-turret. Projecting porch with two granite columns. The main range is only one room in depth; fireplace dated 1635.

CHADDLEHANGER. A former longhouse (now a farm building) and an important example of the most primitive type, quite a distance from the moor, with the shippon only partly subdivided from the cross-passage by a later and flimsy timber partition. Original shippon fittings. A C15 two-centred granite door frame to the cross-passage and a pair of cruck-trusses survive from the early phase of the building.

(CAPELTOR. A cottage enlarged in the mid C19 as a house for the mine captain of the Devon Great United Mine.)

LANDCROSS
Near Bideford

HOLY TRINITY. Small, aisleless, basically medieval, with a projecting slate-hung wall turret replacing a tower destroyed by lightning c. 1820. – PULPIT with early Renaissance panels similar to those usual on bench ends. – BENCH ENDS. Some with shields, profile heads, and Perp leaves, two with tumblers in characteristically Elizabethan little arcades.

METHODIST CHAPEL. Long, low, and colour-washed, built by the Wesleyans in 1854 and enlarged in 1881. Its rural charm is heightened by the square-headed openings and two inscriptions.

(PILLMOUTH. C17 stone mullioned window and two-storey porch; C18 sundial. Said to be the birthplace of General Monk.)

(HALLSANNERY. Georgian front of five bays and two storeys.)

LIMEKILN, Hallsannery. C19. Large, two-walled, with crenellations and Gothic arches, complete with railed slipway from the river and charging ramp behind.

LANDKEY

5030

St Paul. The stately church, set high above the village street, overlooks a depressing quantity of Barnstaple dormitory housing; the group opposite is particularly unworthy. W tower with type B buttresses, polygonal NE stair-turret higher than the tower battlements, gargoyles below the battlements, and no pinnacles. Nave and N aisle, N and S transepts, both embattled and with gargoyles. Attached to the S transept a S porch with fleuron-decorated outer and inner doorways. Evidence of the pre-Perp church is the small lancet in the N chancel wall. The chancel was restored in 1868–9 by *William White* (stonework renewed, new roof). Squint from the S transept into the chancel.

The arcade between nave and N aisle is Perp, three bays with slender piers of B section, but plain capitals only to the main shafts. Also Perp the arches to the S and N transepts. Ceiled wagon roofs in nave, aisle, and S porch; the beams of the nave roof rest on head-corbels. (Head-corbels also as stops of hoodmoulds of windows; the Perp mason at Landkey must have been specially fond of figure sculpture.) – FONT. Octagonal, Perp, with tracery panels on the shaft, quatrefoil decoration on the bowl. – STAINED GLASS. Chancel E by *Shrigley & Hunt* (R. Hubbuck). – C18 SUNDIAL.

MONUMENTS. Three effigies of the Beaupel family. The cross-legged knight and lady wearing a wimple, *c.* 1300, must originally have been very fine. The knight has the upper part of his body turned so that his cheek lies on the pillow, no doubt to look at his slim young wife. Her drapery especially lively. – C14 effigy of a lady, stiffer than the earlier couple. – Sir Arthur Acland of Acland Barton (q.v.) †1610 and wife. Big standing wall-monument, Lady Acland recumbent, Sir Arthur behind her and a little higher up, semi-reclining. To her head and feet smaller kneeling figures. Simple decoration of the back wall. Figure sculpture of good quality but, at the time of writing, all poorly painted.

WILLESLEIGH. Georgian three-bay, three-storey front of stone, painted; projecting centre with pedimented Doric porch, Venetian ground-floor windows, bracketed eaves.

See also Acland Barton.

LANDSCOVE

7060

Staverton

St Matthew. An early work by *J. L. Pearson*, 1849–51. A church on a new site, paid for by Miss Louisa Champernowne of Dartington. Not at all Devonian. Conscientious Second Pointed; well grouped, especially from the W, where one sees the SE tower with broached spire rising behind the grey rubble-stone gables of nave and S aisle. Inside, alternating columns and roof with trefoiled wind-braces. – REREDOS carved by *Hems* in 1895 to *Pearson's* design of 1851. – Attractive LYCHGATE, strongly buttressed.

PARSONAGE. Also by *Pearson*, 1851. Good and solid, with mullioned windows, irregular gables, and large chimneys.

LANGTREE

CHURCH. The W tower has its stair-turret (reaching above the battlements of the tower) in the middle of the S side (a feature not unusual in South Devon, but very exceptional in this part of the county). Buttresses only at the foot; no pinnacles. Wide nave, N aisle with arcade of four plus two bays, the piers of granite, type A, with capitals only to the main shafts, and depressed arches. The N windows straight-headed, the chancel E window of a rare Perp tracery design. Restored in 1865–6 (chancel S wall rebuilt). – FONT. Octagonal, Perp, with simple patterns in the panels. – PULPIT. Late C17 with carved garlands, cherubs' heads, etc. – Two CHAIRS in the chancel with re-used Flemish C16 reliefs of Christ carrying the Cross and Christ crucified. – ROYAL ARMS. Large, of plaster, with strapwork decoration, very much as usual in North Cornwall.

LAPFORD

ST THOMAS OF CANTERBURY. W tower with diagonal buttresses, polygonal stair-turret at the SE angle (unusual), no pinnacles. Low on the S side a recess for an image (cf. North and South Molton). Nave and N aisle, separated by a rather tall granite arcade with A type piers, probably C16 – see the straight-headed, uncusped aisle windows. Other windows much restored and replaced by *Ashworth* during the 1888 restoration, when the E wall was rebuilt, the interior walls scraped, and the wagon roofs to nave and N aisle exposed. Fine nave roof with angel corbels at the foot of each principal, decorated bosses, foliated wall plate. Splendid CELURE with cross-ribs and roses-en-soleil.

The ROOD SCREEN is the best in the neighbourhood, probably of the second quarter of the C16, with type B tracery, ribbed coving with Renaissance detail between the seven ribs, and a very complete cornice with four strips of decoration and cresting. In type similar to Atherington. The empty rectangular panel in the screen was presumably for a reredos to a nave altar. – PARCLOSE SCREEN simpler. – SOUTH DOOR supposed to be Norman; in a Norman doorway. The door-knocker also old. – BENCH ENDS. Numerous, with initials, monograms (St John family), profile heads, Renaissance and late Flamboyant ornament; also figure with scourge (cf. Down St Mary) and heart, feet, and hands, symbolizing Christ's Passion. – STAINED GLASS. E window by *Beer & Driffield*, 1882–9. – N lancet perhaps by *Hardman*.

Lapford is quite a large village, recently expanded.

OLD RECTORY. L-shaped.

CONGREGATIONAL CHAPEL, by the roadside, at the edge of the village. Built c. 1847. Gabled, rubble, with buttresses and lancets. Battlemented porch. In a large walled burying ground with slate gravestones from the 1850s. Overthrow over the gate.

SUNDAY SCHOOL, in the village. Former Bible Christian Methodist chapel of 1861.

MILL. Three storeys, with overshot wheel and machinery. Two-storey mill house, plastered, with a tile roof. Also a former barn.

BURY BARTON. An extensive farmstead displaying classic continuity of development.* It lies in the SW corner of the large rectangular earthwork of a Roman fort.‡ The farmhouse stands in a large courtyard inside an outer court. Other detached buildings and detached chapel by the farm pond. The house has a medieval core, originally with a three-bay open hall possibly with cross-wings at both ends. Massive jointed-cruck roof trusses, arch- and wind-braced with yoked apex; one original truss of unusually sophisticated carpentry. Later lateral hall stack, and a floor inserted together with an early C16 stud-and-panel partition. Early C17 plaster overmantel with floral, figured, and heraldic reliefs and the initials JB and MB, probably commemorating the marriage of John Bury and Mary Arscott of Tetcott in 1614. Kitchen of this period, with another stud-and-panel partition. Slightly later, two more service rooms E of the kitchen. The many farm buildings include two C16 ranges with jointed-cruck trusses and a later round house in the inner courtyard. In the outer courtyard, largely of the C19, a spectacular range of linhays.

CHAPEL, visible on the hilltop site from some distance. Attractive exterior of thatch over local ironstone rubble walls with earth mortar, the recessed joints giving a delightful texture. Round-headed timber door frame. Granite E window with remnants of early C15 tracery; simple S window. Roof of typical Devon wagon type with every fourth truss enlarged with a chamfered rib. There was a consecration in 1434.

LEE   4040
Ilfracombe

A small settlement along a combe down to the sea, vaunted as a romantic 'smugglers' village' from the C19, when (as White's Directory tells us) Robert Smith bought the Warecombe estate, remodelled the village, and built himself a large house called The Elms overlooking Lee Bay.

ST MATTHEW. A chapel of ease of 1833, restored in 1860 by *Hayward*. Nave, chancel, w bellcote; plate-tracery window (glass by *Hardman*).

Close by is the SCHOOL, also of 1860, opposite the VILLAGE HALL, 1923, still careful Arts and Crafts, with small pyramid-roofed tower. The THREE MAIDS COTTAGE, supposed to date from 1653, is a show cottage, white and thatched, perhaps improved in looks around 1800 or later.

Close to the beach another group: the OLD MILL, an attractive cluster of stone buildings; THE SMUGGLERS, over-prettified, with the date 1627 (not original) and two large diagonally set stacks; and the WHITE HOUSE, still simple and appealing. The much extended LEE MANOR HOTEL is not an asset to the scene.

*The subject of a meticulous study by N. W. Alcock in 1967; *see* Further Reading.

‡Identified by Professor J. K. St Joseph, and used apparently from the C1 to the C3. The earthwork gives the *burh* name to the site.

LEIGH BARTON
Churchstow

A remarkable group, all on its own in a remote valley. It consists of an imposing late medieval gatehouse of institutional character, with a fragment of curtain wall, a farmhouse behind, and attached to this a formerly ruinous L-shaped range of lodgings (restored in 1984–6 by English Heritage). It was described from the C17 as a grange of Buckfast Abbey, although documentary evidence indicates that a family named Leigh were in occupation as freeholders already before the Dissolution: possibly they occupied only the farmhouse. The gatehouse is two-storeyed, with a nearly round-headed arch. The single upper chamber with fireplace and garderobe (cf. Morwell Barton) is approached by a newel stair on the E side and lit by a mullioned-and-transomed window at back and front. The L-shaped range is probably of the same period, built of the same local grey stone. Outer walls with single (W) and double (S) garderobe projections. The straight-headed upper windows with cinquefoil lights serve a series of first-floor chambers. Two are in the S range above the large kitchen, approached by an external stone stair and gallery with open timber arcade (renewed c. 1500?). A smaller chamber was in the W range, otherwise used as a storage area, reached rather awkwardly from the external gallery by means of a broad internal gallery along the E wall.

The farmhouse has a service end of medieval origin, but was mostly rebuilt in the C17. Fragments remain of a richly decorated early C16 screen, with spirally ornamented mouldings to former door openings, and enriched beam and upper rail.

LEW TRENCHARD

ST PETER. In a wooded valley close to Lew Manor. The masonry indicates several different builds. W tower unbuttressed with obelisk pinnacles, ashlar granite to the top stage only. Inside, arcade to N aisle on octagonal piers with concave sides (cf. Ashburton, Plymstock). The real character of the church, particularly the interior, was determined by the formidable *Sabine Baring-Gould*, antiquarian, hagiographer, novelist, expert on folklore and folksong, who was squire here 1877–1924 and rector 1881–1924. The structural work of his period probably includes the oddly detailed wagon roofs to S porch, nave, and chancel; the vestry; and the reconstructed five-light Perp S chancel window.

The interior is dominated by the ROOD SCREEN, complete with full loft, tabernacle work, and cresting. The original medieval screen had been broken up by Baring-Gould's grandfather in 1833, but enough remained to form the basis of the present screen, which was designed with the advice of Baring-Gould's cousin, *Bligh Bond*, and made under his supervision between 1889 and 1915 by the Misses *Pinwell*. Paintings in the centre part by *Margaret Rowe* (née Baring-Gould); those in the N aisle by *Branscombe*.

Other fittings eclectic in style and origin. – PULPIT. Modelled on the reconstructed medieval pulpit at Kenton, again made by the *Pinwells*, 1900. – BENCH ENDS. A few from the C16 attached to C19 benches: figures of Christ and St Michael, instruments of the Passion, medallion with bust of a woman and figure of a fool below. These may have come from the seating destroyed in 1833; others in the church are C19 copies. – LECTERN. C16 timber eagle from Brittany. – CHANCEL STALLS. Made up of panels, some with Flamboyant tracery, some with early Renaissance arabesques; good poppyheads that could be C19. Where were the different pieces from originally? – CHANDELIER. Late medieval, from Mechelen, installed in 1880.

STAINED GLASS. C16 Evangelists' heads inserted in the late C19 chancel window. – For a bit more variety, the E window in C16 style, 1914 by *Carl de Bouché* of Munich. – TRIPTYCH over the Lady Chapel altar. Flemish, early C16, probably by *Cornelius Engelbert*. – PAINTING. Over the altar, Adoration of the Magi by *Paul Deschwanden*, a duplicate of a painting at Fribourg in Switzerland. – MONUMENTS. A number of slate tablets and brasses to members of the Baring-Gould family, some of them brought from Staverton, some of them C17, some of them antiquarian forgeries. – Recumbent figure of Beatrice Gracieuse Baring-Gould, 1879 by *Knittel* of Fribourg. – The originator of the whole medley, Sabine Baring-Gould, has a plain headstone in the churchyard.

LEW MANOR. An attractive but not specially Devonian house. It is indeed not the genuine article but an intriguing confection by *Sabine Baring-Gould*. When he settled here with his large family in 1881 (after inheriting the estate in 1872), the house was a simple rectangle with a porch and plain rendered walls. Its gradual transformation into a rubble-stone-faced, E-shaped Jacobean manor house was achieved, without an architect, with the aid of local Baring-Gould-trained craftsmen. The sources are eclectic. The frontispiece to the porch, with Tuscan columns, small paired columns flanking panels above, and the date 1620, is a genuine local import, brought from Orchard (q.v.), but the tile-hung gabled w wing, with its moulded eaves and cornice, might be more at home in Surrey. At the back there is a picturesque little kitchen courtyard overlooked by a battlemented bay-window, which faces a miniature granite cloister perhaps inspired by the almshouses at Moretonhampstead. Nearby a very French-looking DOVECOTE with half-conical roof and obelisk-bedecked dormer. Near the front of the house, square GARDEN PAVILION with steep slated roof.

The interior is a similar mixture of the exotic with more homely Jacobean revival. In the former category is the ballroom in the w wing, with elaborate plaster ceiling with roundels, and a lavish overmantel brought from Germany, with spiral columns and realistically carved flowers and foliage. Elsewhere, plenty of neo-Jacobean ceilings, the most convincing re-creation the one in the long gallery on the first floor, with pendants and floral and animal motifs. It incorporates parts from No. 38 North Street Exeter. Much panelling, some genuine, some copied e.g. from Dunsland, the home of a Baring-Gould son-in-law. In the parlour to the r. of the hall, painted panels by a daughter, *Margaret Rowe*, with the Virtues and other allegorical figures including Investigatio and

Gaudium Vitae. Renaissance profile heads over the fireplace. In the morning room at the back, heraldic glass in the bay-window.

In the GROUNDS a lake made from a former quarry. *Gertrude Jekyll* advised on the garden in 1928.

In the parish several houses affected by *Baring-Gould* influence: THE RAMPS, picturesquely sited above the flooded quarry, partly slate-hung, was designed by him, likewise the OLD RECTORY, 1906, and probably the BLUE LION.

COOMBE TRENCHARD. Built by Baring-Gould's friend Henry Sperling, 1906, in a similar spirit, mixing tile-hung vernacular with an Italianate tower.

DOWER HOUSE. An early C16 house with a late C17 S wing. Late C19 interior alterations by *Baring-Gould*, who erected the medieval CROSS SHAFT nearby.

HAYNE BRIDGE, 3 m. W. Four semicircular granite arches; good.

3080   LIFTON

ST MARY. The biggest church in this comparatively uninteresting neighbourhood of West Devon. W tower (type B buttresses) with big polygonal pinnacles and three-light bell-openings, two-storeyed embattled N porch. Late Perp arcades of six bays (the two belonging to the chancel are lower) with A type piers, simply moulded capitals, castellated abaci, and simply moulded arches. The chancel arch with a capital with primitively carved faces (cf. Kelly). Old ceiled wagon roof in the nave. Restored 1871. – FONT. Square, Norman, of a type more Cornish than Devonian (but cf. Marystow): corner heads and between them simply ornamented intersecting arches. – BENCH ENDS. Four panels specially displayed, with arabesques in shields, i.e. c. 1550. – MONUMENTS. Large monument to Sir William, Sir Arthur, and Lady Harris, †1590, 1618, 1630. Three life-size kneeling alabaster figures all in a row, not good. – Large cartouche to John Dynham †1641.

LIFTON PARK. Built c. 1815 for William Arundel of Kenegle, Cornwall, who inherited the estate in 1775. A large mansion, derelict apart from the eight-bay W entrance wing. The style is an unarchaeological but quite demonstrative Gothic, with crudely traceried windows, embattled parapets, and shaped or crow-stepped gables. Large porte-cochère. Inside, to the l. of the large hall, a spacious stone staircase with cast-iron Gothic balustrade. Two decorative Victorian LODGES: HOME PARK, Duntz Hill, 1867, and SOUTH LODGE. Coloured brickwork, fanciful bargeboards, patterned slate roofs.

In the village the ARUNDEL ARMS; to its N an octagonal C18 stone COCKPIT, an exceptional survival.

SMALLACOMBE. A minor delight. Trim Georgian front with three sashed windows, behind neat brick garden walls. The rear to the farmyard displays craggy remains of an older rubble-walled house; good late Perp granite doorway with carved spandrels and a large spiral at the base of one jamb. An upper room has a remarkable coved ceiling with lively rustic C18 plasterwork, supposed to celebrate Marlborough's victories. Wreaths, trophies, and cherubs' heads, but also three doll-like figures modelled entirely in the round. Central Victory with wreath, and two soldiers with guns at opposite corners. Early C18 brick GRANARY with DOVE-COTE, a rarity in West Devon.

Lifton was the centre of an important Saxon royal estate. On TINHAY DOWN the lyncheted remains of a medieval strip field system.

See also Wortham.

LITTLEHAM
Near Bideford

4020

ST SWITHIN. An early plan is preserved on the N side, with transept and also two lancet windows. W tower with big buttresses covering the angles; no pinnacles. Perp S aisle with low arcade on A type piers and standard capitals. 'Substantially and ornamentally repaired in 1874' (White), and again by *Temple Moore* in 1891–2. He designed the magnificent ROOD SCREEN based on that of Partrishow, Breconshire (Powys). Square-headed tympanum behind filling the chancel arch; the whole painted and gilt. – FONT. Perp, granite, coarse. – BENCH ENDS with unusually bold, broad early Renaissance scrolls. – STAINED GLASS by *Kempe Studios*. – PAINTING. In the N transept Christ of the Trades, with scales, *c.*1300, according to Tristram. – MONUMENT. Lt Gen. H. H. Greacock †1891, also by *Temple Moore*. Recumbent figure with angels on a super-Gothic big and tall tomb-chest.

(LITTLEHAM COURT. Early C19; three windows, Doric staircase.)

TOLL HOUSE, on the old Bideford–Buckland Brewer road, at Yeo Vale. A fine two-storey example with half-octagonal projections at both ends.

LITTLEHAM
Near Exmouth

0080

On the edge of the built-up area around Exmouth. The church is raised up high in a churchyard above the remains of the village.

ST MARGARET AND ST ANDREW. The bulk of the church Perp: W tower with diagonal buttresses, nave and N aisle (begun 1528) with straight-headed three-light windows, piers of B type with standard capitals. S windows of the nave enlarged 1911. No S aisle, but a S chapel lower than the chancel arch and connected to it by two plain double-chamfered arches on very stunted piers without capitals, which look C14. The chancel must be still older, see the C13 trefoil-headed PISCINA in the E wall. A lancet window was discovered in the S wall but covered up again. The roofs date from *R. Medley Fulford*'s restoration of 1883–4 (the wagon roof of the chancel re-uses the old bosses). At the same time the church was re-seated and the N aisle and chancel arch were partly rebuilt. There are several features characteristic of Fulford's inventiveness: see, for instance, the priest's door encased by buttressing, and the combination of the tower screen with an intricate font canopy and cover.

ROOD SCREEN. Much restored (by *Hems*, 1883–4). Tracery of type A. Very lively and varied patterns in the original wainscoting. Coving C19. – Good PARCLOSE SCREENS, with linenfold wainscoting. – ALTAR RAILS of *c.* 1700. – STAINED GLASS. In the main lights of a N aisle window three late C15 figures, Christ showing his wounds, St Roche, and St Michael, by the same workshop that produced the contemporary glass at Doddiscombsleigh and in the E window of Exeter Cathedral. Restored by *Drake* in 1883. – E window 1883 by *Clayton & Bell*. – Windows either side of the S porch, with opulently draped figures in the main lights, 1911, designed by *G. Fellowes Prynne*, made by *Percy Bacon Bros.* – Three windows by *Kempe Studios*: 1893 (N); 1906, 1910 (S). – MONUMENTS. The residents of early C19 Exmouth were buried here: many minor tablets; also Major-General Elliot † 1803 by *Emes* of Exeter, decent plain urn against grey marble; Mary Peel † 1875 by *Kendall*, very large Grecian sarcophagus; and Viscountess Nelson, Lord Nelson's widow, † 1831 by *Turnerelli*, mourning woman at a sarcophagus.

8060

LITTLEHEMPSTON

ST JOHN. W tower of Ashburton type. Chancel of rubble, perhaps C13. Late C15 N and S aisles of ashlar, embattled, as is the two-storey S porch with pretty upper window. Rood-stair turret on the N side. The tracery mostly fancifully renewed during the restoration of 1863 by *T. Lidstone*,* but the E windows of the chancel chapels and the N chancel window are probably original. They have the 'star' design found also at Staverton, Ipplepen, and Torbryan, a Dec motif which in this area continued to be used in the C15. Good Perp S doorway with traceried spandrels and dripstone heads. Arcades of five bays, the usual Perp type, except that the W bay is narrower than the others.

FONT. Norman, red sandstone, seven-sided, with a rib design. – SCREEN. Right across nave and aisles. The tracery type A standard, the coving missing. In the cornice, bands with leaves, grapes, and birds, as frequently found. Some C18 colour survives. – STAINED GLASS, chancel N. From Marldon, unusually much: two whole large C15 figures (St Stephen and St Christopher), both with shield; two kneeling donors below. Restored in 1863. – MONUMENTS. Three worn effigies, supposed to be members of the Stretch family, C14 lords of the manor: a cross-legged knight in mail, early C14; a knight of the later C14 with good details of armour, no weapons, quatrefoil panels from a table-tomb incorporated below; and a lady, perhaps early C14.

Tiny, retiring village. Former SCHOOL of 1875, with polychrome brick lancets and bargeboarding.

OLD MANOR. A small late medieval house in a beautifully secluded position, in the C15 the property of Canonsleigh nunnery. Irregular courtyard plan on a miniature scale, with a large barn to the l. as one approaches the hall range. The kitchen perhaps always in the

---

* Some of the drawings are however signed by *E. W. Godwin*.

parallel wing behind the hall. The l. linking range used to contain the dairy, but the age of these parts is uncertain. The hall is entered by a plain pointed doorway without a special porch, perhaps *c.* 1400. Well-preserved open hall, with a simple moulded arch-braced roof of three bays; later plastering above the arch-braces. The most exceptional feature is the fine mid C15 WALL PAINTING on the dais wall: Christ rising from the tomb and displaying his wounds, between two censing angels, elegantly drawn. The fireplace below is an addition of the 1920s. In the back wall a Perp window, straight-headed, of two cusped lights with transom, probably a later insertion, and a doorway to a spiral stair, from the top of which there is a little window looking down on the hall. The screen has not survived, but in the screens passage an original timber partition remains, with a pair of plain arched doorways to the service rooms. These are at a lower level (a later alteration, together with their timber mullioned windows?). The room above the service rooms is made from two chambers, one at a higher level over the screens passage (see the remains of timber partitions). The house was well restored according to SPAB principles in the 1920s; later alterations to the back wings have been less sensitive.

GATCOMBE HOUSE. A neat white-rendered house (now subdivided) on a compact courtyard plan, of early C19 appearance, but incorporating work from the late Tudor period onwards. Entrance range of *c.* 1830, with deep Tuscan porch and Ionic pilasters above, two windows on each side. The parallel back wing is the hall range of the Tudor house of the Bogans. Ground-floor room with simple late C17 ceiling with three moulded ovals added between older beams. On the upper floor, a vaulted geometric plaster ceiling of *c.* 1600. Early C18 staircase. The wing linking the Tudor and C19 ranges has a fine early C18 reception room. Ceiling with a large oval: a big sunburst and relief of Jupiter riding on an eagle (details reminiscent of The Priory, Totnes); musical instruments and trophies of war in the corners.

LITTLE TORRINGTON

4010

ST GILES. Roughcast narrow w tower with thin diagonal buttresses and pinnacles. There was an indulgence for the rebuilding of the belfry after it had been struck by lightning in 1438. The tower was restored in 1899 by *Harbottle Reed*. Nave and s aisle, the arcade of four bays with granite piers of A type with capitals only to the main shafts, elementarily decorated abaci, and depressed pointed arches. – FONT. Circular, very primitive, with projected ribbed corners; what date? Jacobean COVER. – MONUMENTS. Henry Stevens of Cross † 1802, by *Peter Rouw Jun.* of London. Large, with mourning female bent over an urn. – Sarah Fortescue † 1821, simple, by *Baily*. – Thomas Stevens † 1832 by *Gould* of Barnstaple.

WOODLANDS. The mid C15 manor house of the Coplestones. Unrevealing exterior apart from the wooden ogee-headed door within the two-storey porch. Chamber over the hall with C17 plaster coat of arms of Joseph Coplestone.

See also Cross.

LODDISWELL

ST MICHAEL. C13 W tower with the typical diagonal buttresses not reaching high up, a broad rectangular stair-turret not going up to the top either, and the battlements on a corbel-table as at Woodleigh. Unmoulded tower arch. Also early the nave, N transept, and chancel with chapels: see the style of the PISCINA and SEDILIA, and the simple double-chamfered arches opening from transept and chancel, with half-octagonal responds in the chancel. From a S transept only an E respond remains; the rest replaced by the late Perp S aisle, with minimal uncusped tracery, piers of A type, capitals only to the shafts, and nearly semicircular moulded arches. Porch at the W end of the aisle. – FONT. Small, Norman, circular, with a frieze of elementary voluted palmettes and a narrow band of saltire crosses above. – PULPIT. Of coloured marbles; c. 1867. – STAINED GLASS. Early C16 heraldic glass, perhaps *in situ* in the lights, reset below. – Pre-ecclesiological E window by *Baillie*, a version of West's painting of Christ blessing children. – MONUMENT. Slate slab with black-letter inscription of 1616, remarkably late.

Loddiswell is quite a complex village, on the slope of a hill. Its most surprising feature is the CONGREGATIONAL CHAPEL of 1864, with two small towers with conical caps flanking the E gable, together with the SCHOOL. Paid for by Richard Peek of Hazelwood.

HAZELWOOD. Remodelled by Richard Peek in the 1830s, with additions of 1867. The roof was raised, with slate replacing thatch, in 1913. Grey stone, gabled, with clustered chimneys, romantically set on the side of a steep and remote valley. Wooden two-light arched windows with brick surrounds. Ceilings of the 1830s inside.

Close to Hazelwood, Richard Peek also built a cluster of estate buildings with picturesque pointed arches, including a Congregational Chapel with catacomb beneath for family burials, and a minister's cottage. By the river a BOATHOUSE; between fields and river, five pairs of solid GATEPIERS.

BLACKDOWN RINGS. At the W end of an Iron Age HILLFORT a substantial motte-and-bailey CASTLE commanding the Avon valley, with extensive views in all directions. The medieval bailey is above the level of the earlier enclosure; the motte is deeply concave, probably indicating a former tower rising up out of its centre. Loddiswell Manor was part of the honour of Totnes. The castle has no known history. It may have been founded at the Norman Conquest: the large outer enclosure would have been invaluable as a defence for an occupying army.

HATCH BRIDGE, 1 m. S. An old packhorse bridge, widened later.

LOXBEARE

CHURCH. Tiny, with an unbuttressed N tower stump, nave and lower chancel. S door Norman, with outer zigzag moulding of jambs and arch. The Norman E window was inserted c. 1850, when the chancel was largely rebuilt. Further restoration in 1896 by *E. H. Harbottle*, who designed the seating, incorporating earlier woodwork into the frontals. – CLERGY DESK. Brought here in 1970 from Exeter Cathedral, an excellent piece from the restoration of 1870–7, designed by *Scott*, executed by *Farmer & Brindley*. – PULPIT. With sounding-board; simple, probably *c.* 1660. – COMMUNION RAIL. Jacobean balusters, perhaps re-used. – WEST GALLERY. Jacobean; fragments re-used in the chancel seats. – The BELLS (not usually mentioned in these volumes) are of special interest here: three by *J.T.*, a C15 Exeter bellfounder. The *Little Guide* calls the bell-chamber 'a perfect example of the medieval period'. – MONUMENTS to members of the Cudmore family; minor.

CALVERLEIGH MILL. Watermill and cottages.

LOXHORE

A church of great charm, tucked away down a lane past some good farmhouses.

ST MICHAEL. Nave, chancel, N aisle. W tower with diagonal buttresses and no pinnacles. Chancel and nave tracery all renewed in a series of restorations (before 1844; chancel 1882 by *E. Dolby*; nave *c.* 1900 by *G. Fellowes Prynne*). The C19 chancel windows are quite original: the E window unusually narrow, two lights with transom, the S side with two lights lighting the SEDILIA, a pair of arches on a marble shaft. The interior is a surprise. The N arcade of three bays has wooden piers with a straight entablature. The section of the piers is quite exceptional. Kingpost roof with four-way struts over the chancel, wagon roof with old ribs and bosses in the N aisle, nave roof with very large bosses *c.* 1900.

FONT. Plain, square, Norman, with a very handsome C16 FONT COVER with elegantly concave outline and crocketed top; no Elizabethan features. Traces of painting with fleurs-de-lys. – PULPIT. Openwork wooden tracery over a base with fat marble columns; *c.* 1882. – LECTERN. 1903. Book-rest upheld by a well carved wooden angel. – The original tympanum between chancel and nave (cf. Molland, Parracombe) was removed *c.* 1903 and replaced by a ROOD BEAM supported by two very large carved angels, accomplished work in a late medieval German style. – SCREEN. Plain, C19, single lights. – STAINED GLASS. In the W window three figures below canopies, *c.* 1924, late for this pleasant Kempe-derived style. – MONUMENTS. Small brass plate with long inscription to Richard Carpenter † 1627, the lettering in many different types. – Similar plate to Mary Weber † 1671. – Edward Hammond † 1653 and Philip Hammond † 1704. Both architectural, the first restrained, with urn in open pediment, the second embellished with flowers, skulls, etc.

HILL. A small late medieval house with later shippon attached. Cob walls under a slate roof. The original layout has been obscured: the house is now of three-room plan without cross-passage. Probably early C16 the true cruck trusses raised on templates. Surprisingly, the unfloored hall remains (as, curiously, also at Hill, Christow). C17 semicircular stair. Across the courtyard a small C17 building, perhaps a detached kitchen.

ROBOROUGH CASTLE. A small motte with a concave top, in a high position with extensive views. No known history. The manor of Loxhore was held by the Lords of Okehampton.

LUFFINCOTT

ST JAMES. A remote church on the W edge of the county, close to Luffincott Barton, finely placed with a view towards the wooded slopes of the river Tamar. Perp nave and chancel in one. W tower rebuilt in 1791 by *Richard Sillifant*, mason, as is testified by an inscription. If it were not, the style would not show it. Old materials must have been re-used. Unbuttressed, with obelisk pinnacles. What, however, is disarmingly C18 is the panelled S door and the sash-windows put in on the N side of the nave in 1761. Above them, a carved Perp wall-plate, re-used. The nave has a nice boarded wagon roof with carved bosses. – FONT. Granite, octagonal, badly preserved.

LUFFINCOTT BARTON. Solid farmhouse, threshing-barn, and out-buildings of *c.* 1850 for the Tetcott estate.

LUNDY

The island lies 12 m. NNW of Hartland Point. It is about three miles long and half a mile wide, a precipitous rock with only one safe anchorage, on the E side close to the S end. It is now visited mostly by naturalists attracted by its rich flora and fauna, seabirds, and marine life but it has been inhabited since earliest times. Field systems of the later prehistoric period can be seen, particularly at Middle Park and Beacon Hill. N of the Threequarter Wall are several hut circles, and E of Shutter Point a cist has been found. In the old burial ground (by the Old Light) no less than four C6–7 inscribed memorial stones can be seen.

From the middle of the C12 to 1321 the de Marisco family were masters of Lundy, more than once in open opposition to the Crown. Then and later the island was frequently used as a base for piratical expeditions into the Bristol Channel. The final flourish of this lawless existence was the time about the middle of the C18 when Lundy was leased to the notorious Thomas Benson M.P., a Bideford merchant and smuggler. Under the ownership of the Heaven family, who bought the island in 1834, many improvements were made, and these were consolidated by the Harman family who bought Lundy in 1925. In 1969 it passed to the National Trust. They immediately leased it to the Landmark Trust, who have adapted many of its buildings for holiday use (architect *Philip Jebb*).

CASTLE, S of the village. Built by Henry III in 1243. Remains of outer walls and moat. Inside the fine square keep two holiday cottages around a cobbled yard.

ST HELENA. 1896 by *J. Norton* for the Rev. H. G. Heaven, the then owner of Lundy. Nave, chancel, and solid NW tower in native granite; the interior of nave and chancel in polychrome brick. Furnishings mainly by the indefatigable *Hems* of Exeter. Of the ancient church of St Elen the outline walls can still be traced inside the old burial ground.

OLD LIGHT. The lighthouse built for Trinity House in 1819 and designed by *Daniel Asher Alexander* is a beautifully proportioned granite structure 90 ft high, and at 567 ft above sea level the highest in Britain. It was replaced in 1897 by the new North and South Lights.

THE BATTERY. Built for Trinity House as a fog signal station, with granite steps down to cottages, magazine, and gun-station facing the Atlantic. Cannons are still in position, but the site was otherwise abandoned when the North and South Lights were completed.

TIBBETTS. A granite lookout on the second highest point of the island, built by the Admiralty in 1909. Now a holiday cottage.

MANOR FARM. A former hotel, restored to its delightful Georgian appearance in 1981 when Victorian and later additions were removed. Now holiday flats.

MILLCOMBE. Now a hotel. A plain classical house in a perfectly sheltered position, built for himself by W. H. Heaven shortly after he had bought the island, and surrounded by a garden with shrubs and trees – the only place where Lundy can be seen in so gentle a mood.*

LUPPITT

ST MARY. Architecturally the roofs of St Mary are a triumph. The late medieval wagon roofs of nave and transepts lead at the crossing to a magnificent climax: long, broad, semicircular timbers from the 41 corners of the crossing thrown diagonally from NW to SE and SW to NE, with a boss in the middle, a tent-like effect on a generous, most spacious scale (cf. Honiton and Ilsington). The chancel is late C13 or early C14 with a separate arch, the W tower Perp (with diagonal buttresses, stair-turret, and a proud panelled tower arch). Restorations in 1870–1 (nave) and 1880–1 (chancel rebuilt) both by *C. F. Edwards*, S transept repaired 1884, upper part of tower 1905 (*J. Houghton Spencer*); reseating and reflooring 1923 by *Harbottle Reed*. – The FONT is the fame of Luppitt, Norman of the most barbaric 'native' kind. A square bowl with heads at the corners and representations of a centaur fighting two dragons, a martyrdom with two men driving a nail into a detached human head, a group of dachshund-like animals, and a tree with dishevelled foliage (tree of life treated by an exceptionally unconventional carver?). – Norman PILLAR PISCINA in the chancel. – BRASS. Fragment of a palimpsest with part of a female figure, c. 1430–40.

MILL. Of stone, with ashlar quoins, dated 1875. Overshot iron and wood wheel of 11 ft diameter. Machinery survives. The adjacent MILL HOUSE is probably earlier.

MOHUNS OTTERY. A seat of the Carews. The house was rebuilt after a fire in 1868. Remains of a C16 gatehouse with four-centred archways with Renaissance detail in the spandrels.

BARN FARMHOUSE. A late medieval open hall house, its internal development typical of the later C16 and C17. Smoke-blackened

*I am grateful to Mr A. F. Langham for help with the entry on Lundy.

roof on jointed crucks with some original thatch. In the inner room the joists frame a square opening, now filled in, which probably originally admitted the ladder to the upper chamber.

Many other good C15–17 farmhouses, including GREENWAY, especially large, with cross-wings to front and rear, and POUND, an unusual late C17 farmhouse of brick; regular four-window front.

DUMPDON HILL. On the summit a commandingly sited Iron Age HILLFORT. The defences survive in excellent condition. The N side, the easiest of approach, is protected by a double rampart. Complex entrance in the NE corner.

LUSCOMBE
Dawlish

9070

The house lies in an idyllic spot, at the end of a long sheltered combe looking towards Dawlish. The site was acquired in 1797 by the banker Charles Hoare to suit his delicate wife. The setting was landscaped by *Humphry Repton* (Red Book 1799), the house designed by *John Nash* in 1800, during their brief partnership. It is an early example of the completely freely grouped, not at all symmetrical castellated mansion, one of Nash's first essays in this idiom. At first a plain villa was proposed, but Repton advocated the castle style, not only because it would be more picturesque, but because 'its very irregularity will give it consequence, while the offices and mere walls, which in a modern building it would be essential to conceal, in partaking of the character of the Castle will extend the site and make it an apparently considerable pile of building'. The service wing and walled courts behind indeed take up as much space as the house itself, which is no more than a small villa.

150

The house is ingeniously planned, with the main rooms of different shapes opening off a small circular central lobby. Externally the chief feature is the octagonal tower, of grey limestone rubble like the rest of the house, which rises above the S-facing drawing room of the same shape. The canted and castellated bay-window in front of it was added soon after the house was finished. To its r. is the conservatory, originally an open veranda. Ground-floor windows all with coarse Gothic tracery. On the N side a tower porch, with large Gothic-arched entrances serving as a porte-cochère, a device that became a favourite with Nash. Simple interiors, neo-classical apart from the Gothic windows, which originally had coloured glass in their top lights (some remains in the library). In the central lobby, pedestals with busts; staircase to its w with elegant S-shaped iron balustrades. In the octagonal drawing room a marble fireplace with classical figures, ascribed to *Flaxman*, who received payments in 1802–3. The large rectangular room to the E, planned as an eating room, was furnished as a library in 1851, the handsome bookcases topped by 'Etruscan Urns' possibly moved from the former smaller library on the w side. This was made into a dining room after the Second World War; the C19 dining room is now the kitchen (alterations by *Philip Tilden*).

CHAPEL of St Alban, close to the house. An incongruous addition of 1862 by *G.G.Scott* for Peter Richard Hoare, who had succeeded in 1856. Plain outside; inside, Scott's solid early Gothic, with apsidal E end and sexpartite vault, and a N arcade sumptuously adorned with marble shafts to the piers and carved capitals. Good STAINED GLASS.

GROUNDS. A formal garden W of the house; *Repton*'s open lawns to the E, with individual trees scattered over the parkland beyond. Repton's landscaping includes the belts of trees on the edges of the estate.

See also Harberton.

LUSTLEIGH

An attractively intricate village on the E edge of Dartmoor.

ST JOHN. The chancel is the earliest remaining part. It has a small lancet window, a recess with a two-centred head, SEDILIA with a pointed-trefoil head, and a double PISCINA with a blank quatrefoil at the head instead of tracery. All that is clearly C13, and not too late. The date of the W tower (unbuttressed, of two stages, with obelisk pinnacles) is hard to decide. In the S transept (access by a plain double-chamfered arch) is a recess with the badly preserved EFFIGY of a cross-legged knight, with angels supporting his pillow. The N aisle came last, with straight-headed windows and an arcade of A type, with capitals only to the four shafts and depressed arches with moulded section. In the N aisle also two recesses in which much earlier EFFIGIES have been placed: a knight and a lady of *c.* 1300. The faces are not what they originally were, but the design of the lady's draperies shows competent handling. There is also another knight, probably later in date, supposed to be a member of the Prous family.

FONT. The primitive Norman font forms the centre of an imitation-Norman font. – SCREEN. Luxuriantly carved, with carved statuettes in the wainscoting instead of painted figures (cf. Bridford). They represent prophets (see their scrolls) and look like scholars. At the apexes of the arches (with type A tracery) are evil-looking faces. The spandrels of the arches have scroll decoration. In the cornice one frieze of decoration. The date certainly C16. – PULPIT. 1903 by *Herbert Read*, designed to harmonize with the screen. – STAINED GLASS. Fragments in N windows. – INSCRIBED STONE. One of a group of early examples in Devon. A date of *c.* 550–600 is proposed. The inscription reads DATUIDOCI CONHINOCI FILIUS (the stone of Datwidoc, son of Conhinoc). – The CHURCHYARD resembles in shape a Cornish *lan*, or Early Christian enclosure. This and the inscribed stone may indicate that the church occupies a very early religious site.

SCHOOL. A tiny building of 1825 on the edge of the churchyard. Master's house on the ground floor, schoolroom above.

CHURCH HOUSE. Much restored in 1888.

BAPTIST CHAPEL. Mid C19. Small, gabled, of granite, with arched openings. A small burying ground at the front.

UPHILL AND GREAT HALL, Mapstone Hill. A major medieval house preserving two fine roofs, the property of the Wadham family of Ilminster in the C15, used as a rectory after 1601, enlarged in the C19, and subdivided in the C20. An attractively haphazard exterior. In the long, low wing to the l. the original hall and service end. The solar cross wing is on the r., concealed on the entrance side by a taller gabled extension with matching parallel range. Rendered exterior with Gothick windows and doors, the entrance in a battlemented addition in the angle between hall and solar wing. The Gothick parts are due to Samuel Whiddon, curate of Lustleigh, who restored the house in 1833–8. At the back the medieval phase is more evident, with a simple chamfered stone archway between two buttresses (probably stubs of a porch), indicating the site of the screens passage, and a two-light wooden trefoiled window set (or reset) as a dormer over the service end.

The hall range is now open to the roof throughout, with a gallery at either end – not the original arrangement. The lower end is much restored (see the truss dated 1888). Eight-bay roof, jointed-cruck intermediate trusses; the principals also jointed crucks, but springing from wooden wall-shafts with moulded capitals. The prominent ogee-trefoiled arch-braces, attached to both major and minor trusses by short struts, produce a specially lively effect. The braces meet below cranked collars; the major collars carry curved queenposts. Three sets of purlins, and lower curved wind-braces. The date may be c.1400. The unusual three-bay solar roof, perhaps constructed at the same time, has a still more complex play of trefoiled shapes, used for the arch-braces of the main trusses, for two tiers of wind-braces, for the lighter bracing of the minor trusses, and even for lateral bracing between the collars carrying kingposts, as if in imitation of crown-posts. The former rectory at Queen Camel in Somerset has a similar roof; cf. also the Old Rectory at Cheriton Bishop, which has similarly braced kingposts.

Between hall and solar a chimneystack with granite fireplaces on both sides. Beneath the solar are storerooms, with one original sturdy wooden post and tapered bracket. The good late Georgian joinery of the entrance hall makes an interesting effort to be sympathetic to the medieval work: doorcases with moulded shafts, and a front door with trefoiled panels.

SANDUCK. Good farmhouse and model farm buildings with the dates 1891 and 1901.

HUNTER'S TOR. The hillfort is strongly sited at the NW end of Lustleigh Cleave. In the rough ground around it the faint remains of a field system which appears to pre-date the fort, itself probably of Iron Age date.

LYDFORD

This peaceful village, formerly a small town, thanks to the absence of later development offers an unparalleled view of Devon's medieval past. Here we have two Norman castles, the defences and street plan of a late Saxon burh, and a church and graveyard site whose origins are no doubt earlier still. The promontory site overlooking the famous gorge of the river Lyd undoubtedly explains why Lydford became a fortified centre, and certainly adds to its present-day attractions. It was fortified by the later C9, when it appears in a list of West Saxon burhs;

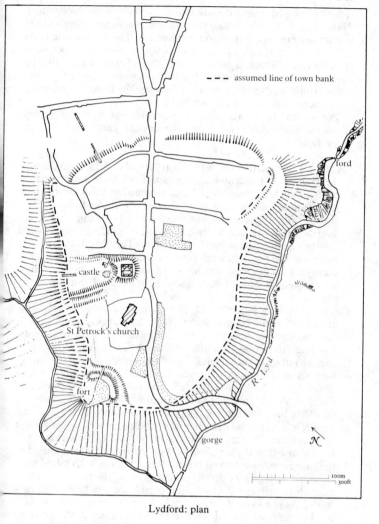

--- assumed line of town bank

ford

castle

St Petrock's church

fort

R. Lyd

gorge

N

100m
300ft

Lydford: plan

a century later it had a royal mint. In 1086 Domesday Book recorded it as one of five towns in Devon: one of Roman origin (Exeter), two others, like Lydford, of later foundation (Barnstaple, Totnes), and one a new Norman creation (Okehampton). It remained a royal borough until 1239, when it became part of the earldom (later duchy) of Cornwall. The administration of stannary law (for the tin-mining districts of Devon) was based here, and the later of the two castles had an important role as court and prison.

The churchyard is a large embanked area of a type whose origins probably lie in the early Christian centuries. The church is dedicated to St Petrock, a famous Celtic saint, but the surviving fabric is much later (*see* below). The defensive bank of the burh girdled the entire perimeter (it was discovered beneath the earthworks of both castles); it is best preserved where it runs across the neck of the promontory. There is a good view of it from the road. Excavations revealed an earth and timber rampart with a later stone phase. The narrow side lanes, still unsurfaced, running from the main streets towards the perimeter afford a rare glimpse of undeveloped Anglo-Saxon streets. Further streets may have been obliterated by the two castles, whose chronology is doubtful: there seems to be a gap between the latest occupation of the earlier and the foundation of the later.

The present-day village occupies only a fraction of the walled town whose ruins were described in 1795 as 'wretched remains' consisting of 'a few hovels'.

CASTLE (1). The earlier castle stands at the end of the spur to the W of the church. A crescent-shaped rampart cut from a surrounding rock-cut ditch encloses a small area defended on the W by the steep natural slopes of the spur itself. Excavation showed that the site overlay the Anglo-Saxon burh defences. The rampart had an internal timber revetment, and five timber buildings were spaced closely together immediately behind it. The date may be early Norman. The building work perhaps created the forty waste house sites recorded in Domesday Book. The castle probably went out of use in the mid C12, to be replaced by the second castle N of the church.

CASTLE (2). The larger of the two castle sites is one of the most impressive in the county. As at Totnes and Okehampton (qq.v.), excavations have revealed a complex history. The earliest known building (moorstone rubble, Hurdwick stone dressings), now enclosed deep in the mound, was a free-standing keep-like structure, about 50 ft square, with 10 ft thick walls, spine wall, well, and probably first-floor entry (there is no evidence for one at ground level). Its deeply splayed round-headed windows are still visible. It may have been built in 1194–5, when expenditure is recorded on a 'strong house' for the detention of royal prisoners. It is not known what its superstructure was like, for in the mid C13 it was ruined to a level at or below the first floor and the remaining masonry used as the foundations for two additional storeys whose walls were better endowed with granite dressings, but thinner (the thicker masonry beneath is visible both inside and outside the SW face of the new work). At the same time the original ground-floor windows were blocked and the mound, dug from an encircling ditch, piled up around to cover the earlier work. The original ground floor was filled in, except in the N corner, where a cellar was created by building a retaining wall across the smaller of the two parts of the original plan. At the same time the rectangular bailey running away from the building on the NW went up.

The final result was a castle with the somewhat misleading appearance of a motte and bailey with a stone tower on top of the motte – an illusion destroyed only by the modern excavations. It is interesting, nevertheless, that in the C13 this aspect was held to be of importance. Entered from a single door, the new building retained some of the features of the traditional keep: staircases and garderobes in the wall-thicknesses (emptying on top of the mound), the better accommodation in the upper storey (larger windows and fireplace), spine wall and battlemented wall top (hardly surviving).

Several architectural fragments, including round window arches, were perhaps re-used from the earlier building. The spine wall, fireplace, and several windows are a post-medieval rebuild.

The C13 work was probably ordered by Richard Earl of Cornwall, who also rebuilt Launceston Castle in Cornwall. He received Lydford in 1239 and obtained a market and fair for the town in 1267. By the early C14 and perhaps earlier the castle was being used as the Devon stannary-law prison. On the death of Richard's son Edmund in 1299, the building was already partly ruinous, though some repairs were carried out in the following century. It had its second heyday later, continuing in use as a prison into the C17 and as a courthouse as late as the C18.

St Petrock. Excavations have shown that an early oratory stood on the site of the church. As it now stands, the oldest parts – the PISCINA and N chancel window – are E.E. The rest is Perp. Low W tower of granite ashlar with type B buttresses and big crocketed pinnacles. S side also of ashlar. S arcade of three bays, the piers of A type with two-centred, simply moulded arches. Tower arch with panelled jambs. N aisle and vestry 1889–90 by *S. Hooper* of Hatherleigh; the old windows were re-used, and a granite arcade added in sympathy with the S aisle. At the same time the walls were scraped. – FONT. Simple, early Norman, tub-shaped. – The other furnishings are of after 1890. – SCREEN. 1904, designed by *Bligh Bond* and carved by the *Pinwells*. – BENCH ENDS. Sixty-nine, variously carved with saints, prophets, etc., in animal and plant surrounds; accomplished work of 1923–6 by *Herbert Read*. – STAINED GLASS. E window 1889 by *Fouracre*. – W window designed by *Fellowes Prynne* for Princetown, installed here in 1902. – Small C15–16 bits in the N aisle E and in a chancel window. – MONUMENT in the churchyard to George Routledge, watch-maker, †1802, with a memorable inscription: '... Integrity was the mainspring/And prudence the regulator/of all the actions of his life ...' (and much more in the same vein).

(BAYFIELD HOUSE, overlooking Lydford Gorge. The former vicarage, 1870 by *G. E. Street*. Picturesque Gothic: steep gables, conical corner turrets. GAZEBO, also with conical roof.)

MARY EMMA MINE, on the Okehampton–Tavistock road close to the Dartmoor Inn. Remains include buddles and wheel-pit.

The parish of Lydford is by far the largest in Devon; the grant of the manor to the Duchy of Cornwall in 1239 included the vast forest of DARTMOOR to its E, much of it still in the parish. The moor abounds in prehistoric sites and in evidence of the tin mining that encouraged the development of settlements on the fringes from the late C12 onwards. At CROCKERN TOR near Two Bridges the boundaries of Devon's four stannaries met, and here the Stannary Parliament of the tinners' representatives was held until 1730.

Only a few PREHISTORIC SITES can be mentioned here (*see* Further Reading for more detailed information). On the high NORTH MOOR cairns crown many of the hills, but evidence of prehistoric occupation is comparatively slight, and blanket bog prevails. Elsewhere, prehistoric settlements and field systems abound. At one of the largest, the unenclosed settlement at WATERN OKE on the Tavy, there are nearly a hundred huts, of which no less than ninety-four were excavated between 5 June and 27 July 1905 by the

Rev. I. Anderson and his eight workmen; by the following year a report running to thirteen pages was in print. He found some Bronze Age pottery (now lost). Other settlement sites are at HUNTINGDON WARREN (mixed with later pillow mounds), BELLEVER, WILLSWORTHY, SWINCOMBE, and pounds at HUCCABY and BROADUN RING. Small settlements and reaves may be encountered anywhere off the high moor. There are stone rows and other ritual features at LAUGHTER TOR, CONIES DOWN, 2½ m. NE of Two Bridges, LAKEHEAD HILL, HIGHER WHITE TOR, 2 m. W of Postbridge, and within the modern Fernworthy Plantation (at FROGGYMEAD and ASSYCOMBE), while the Green Hill row (see Cornwood) terminates in the parish. At FERNWORTHY are stone circles, cairns, retaining circles, and hut circles, and just outside the forest to the W lie the heavily restored but impressive GREY WETHERS stone circles. Some 200 yds to the S an earthwork cut by a leat has recently been tentatively reinterpreted as a Class II henge. At SHERBERTON, another good stone circle.

MEDIEVAL REMAINS include many wayside CROSSES, some of them perhaps set up as boundary markers in the C13. Of the same period perhaps the CLAPPER BRIDGES of flat granite slabs, for example at POSTBRIDGE, BELLEVER, and DARTMEET.

DUNNABRIDGE POUND, E of Two Bridges. A roughly circular 5½ ft drystone wall with gated entry, enclosing about 2 acres. Dartmoor cattle were gathered here from medieval times.

PIZWELL, near Postbridge. A hamlet of no less than four longhouses, on the edge of the open moor. One relatively unaltered one still has its distinctive shippon, cross-passage, and domestic end (roof raised in the C19). The upper ends of the other longhouses were also considerably modified in the C19, but the shippons remain virtually unaltered, with slit windows and central drainage holes visible outside, and central drains within.

LOWER MERRIPIT. A longhouse with shippon intact – an important survival, though even here the roof was raised over the domestic upper end in the later C19. The plan is original: the shippon, with separate entrance, adjoins the lower end, and the cross-passage, hall, and inner room are built into the hillside.

NUNSCROSS FARM, S of Princetown. The last smallholding to be taken from the moor. Foundations of a farmhouse built in 1870; beside it, an abandoned later farm.

TIN MINES. There are extensive field remains of the tin industry in many parts of the parish, with large areas of streamworking spoil heaps, and openworks, dating from medieval times onwards. Most of the visible mine sites date from the C19 boom. At WHITE-WORKS, S of Princetown, worked intermittently from the 1820s to 1876, pits, tips, and shafts remain. Further E, near Hexworthy, GOBBET MINE, worked from the 1830s, has a dressing area on the Swincombe valley with wheelpit and the remains of a crazing mill. HEXWORTHY MINE, active 1889–97 and 1908–12, has a stone-built wheelpit for a 36 ft waterwheel, a stone aqueduct, and a tramway.

POWDERMILLS FARM, Two Bridges. Former workers' cottages for the GUNPOWDER MILLS in operation from 1844 to the 1890s. A proving mortar remains on the drive. Three substantial granite-block GRINDING HOUSES in two sections on either side of a wheelpit; also two small chimneys and the ruins of other buildings.

PENLEE, Postbridge. 1901–11 by *Halsey Ricardo*, built as a holiday house for Arthur B. Rendel, a London surgeon. A free but appropriately austere Arts and Crafts version of a Dartmoor farmhouse. Long slate-roofed range with granite ground floor, rendered above; windows a mixture of casements and sashes. Large projecting porch with off-centre Tudor doorway. Exposed granite also inside: three sturdy doorways off the cross-passage, the centre one leading to a panelled staircase. Two original fireplaces with coloured tiles remain, one of granite, the other of marble. At right angles to the house, large music room added in 1911, with a gargantuan granite fireplace signed by the architect.

ST GABRIEL, Postbridge. Possibly the church-cum-schoolroom built by *Fulford* in 1868. Very simple: nave, chancel, bellcote, of granite.

See also Princetown.

LYMPSTONE

The old centre with its little harbour overlooks the Exe estuary; the fine views encouraged some early Georgian building on the slopes above, but the 'pretty townlet' with 'a great trade of ships', as Leland described it, declined as Exmouth grew from the late C18.

ST MARY. Medieval W tower: red sandstone, stair-turret, type B buttresses; small two-light windows above each other, as at Woodbury nearby. The rest is one of *Ashworth*'s conscientious but dull rebuildings: re-used chancel arch and Perp five-bay N arcade, new matching S arcade, with more emphatic foliage decoration. Vestry, organ chamber, and raising of the chancel roof by *R. M. Fulford*, 1889; chancel lengthened and S chapel added by *Harold C. King*, 1928. – STAINED GLASS. A representative late C19 collection. Good contrasts between S aisle E (1867, *Clayton & Bell*), N aisle W (1864, *Heaton, Butler & Bayne*), and one N and two S aisle windows (1889, 1884, 1900, by *Jennings* of Lambeth). – MONUMENT. Nicholas Lee †1759. Good quality, with lively portrait busts.

ST BONIFACE (R.C.). 1956 by *Joseph E. Walter*. Red sandstone.

Above the beach the main landmark is PETERS TOWER, an austere red and yellow brick clock tower with short spire, built in 1885 by W. H. Peters in memory of his wife. Its face to the sea was to tell fishermen the times of the tides. On the beach two stone LIMEKILNS, their hearths blocked.

Along the STRAND a pleasant sequence of Georgianized cottages; also BRIDGETHORPE, with two full-height canted bays, QUEEN ANNE HOUSE, with a five-bay brick front, and Nos. 1–3 BRIDGE COTTAGES, a former early C18 brick house of six bays. UNDERHILL has a group of three brick Regency houses, all with tripartite windows, the taller two with pedimented and fanlighted doorways. Up BURGMAN'S HILL some notable Georgian houses, especially GREENHILL, brick, three storeys, battlemented parapet, and THE MANOR HOUSE, with brick five-window front (ground floor altered). Further on, BELVEDERE, the dower house to Nutwell Court (*see* below), stuccoed and castellated, with three-storey

Italianate tower and a canted bay at one end. Nearby a one-storey
LODGE with an eccentric castle-shaped terracotta chimneypot.

NUTWELL COURT. Hidden in its own grounds. Transformed into an
exquisitely precise and austere neo-classical mansion in 1802 for the
second Lord Heathfield by *S. P. Cockerell*. The sharpness of line is
enhanced by the pale grey mathematical tiles which cover N, W, and
S walls. Entrance to the N: five bays, two storeys above a basement,
balustraded parapet, and a recessed entrance with two Ionic columns and entablature, set back below a broad segmental arch, a
motif reminiscent of Dance. The W front to the garden is taller, as
the basement level is exposed. 1–3–1 bays, centre with attic floor, all
very plain, and because of the loss of glazing-bars to the windows,
misleadingly dour. The composition is relieved only by the slightly
set back end bays, which have tripartite windows above basement
lunettes, an original inversion of the more usual Palladian elevation.

From the E side it is clear that all this is a remodelling of an older
house, whose red brick rear elevation and SW wing look C18, but
whose SE wing is still older: stone first-floor CHAPEL, with Perp
windows, boldly crocketed gable, and projecting corner pinnacles,
one with a statue of St George. This and some of the stonework are
very likely C19, but the building may be on the site of the chapel
licensed here in 1371.* The house which it accompanied (called a
castle by Risdon) was remodelled twice before Lord Heathfield's
time; after 1699 by Sir Henry Pollexfen, and again after 1754 by his
collateral heir Sir Francis Drake (collector of Drake memorabilia,
including Drake's drum now at Buckland Abbey). He converted the
chapel to a library. From his nephew Lord Heathfield's time is the
good stone half-oval cantilevered stair in a top-lit stairwell at the rear
of the main range, and the sequence of reception rooms. The rich
ceiling decoration of these and of the SW basement ballroom may in
part be later.

STABLES and servants' quarters in a long, castellated, two-storey
range E of the house, of red brick in English bond, and with some
diagonally set chimneys. Probably later C18 picturesque in its
present form, but perhaps incorporating earlier work.

RIDING SCHOOL, near Nutwell Home Farm. Built *c.* 1800. Very
large, of brick, with projecting eaves and pedimented gable-ends
with lunettes.

ST PETER'S SCHOOL (formerly Harefield House). By *William
Burgess* of Exeter, *c.* 1830. Stuccoed, slightly Soanian neo-Grecian
front of 1–3–1 bays, the centre deprived of its one-storey portico.
End bays panelled between pilasters. Parapet with acroteria. (Entrance hall with two Ionic columns; cantilevered stair with cast-iron
balustrade.)

ROYAL MARINE COMMANDO TRAINING CENTRE. A prominent
group of buildings of the 1960s when seen across the water. 'Both
Arms', SCULPTURE of 1969 by *Kenneth Armitage*, in the Command-
ant's Court.

LOWER HAREFIELD LODGE. One-storeyed. Good cast-iron piers
and railings.

---

*In the chapel anteroom, three STAINED GLASS figures of the C14.

LYNEHAM
Yealmpton

5050

A classic example of the compact gentleman's house, beautifully sited by a lake. Seven by five bays, stone, the two main storeys of ashlar, with raised quoins and plat-band, raised up above a rubble basement, and crowned by a hipped roof with top balustrade. Built c. 1700 for the Crocker family; inherited in 1740 by the Bulteels. The set-back windows with their glazing bars are later Georgian, perhaps of 1768, the date on the rainwater heads. Main entrance on the S side, with pedimented doorcase, leading into a broad panelled entrance hall with generously proportioned staircase beyond taking up the centre of the N side. Fluted and turned balusters, bolection-moulded panelling. Good panelling also in the back rooms and upstairs, its impeccable appearance and careful decoration dating from an exceptionally sumptuous modernization of the house in the 1960s. The front rooms refitted in the C18: former library to the r. of the hall, drawing room to the l., with marble fireplaces. Between front and back rooms a corridor (now partly blocked) originally leading to another doorway in the E front. Beside the main stairs a lesser one leads up to the attics.

The basement, at ground level on the W side, has a Tudor doorway flanked by two-light windows with chamfered mullions, *in situ* or (more probably) re-used, no doubt relics of the older house on the site, the seat of the Crockers from the C15. Within the basement, a lavish and rather gloomy dining room, created in the 1960s, with brought-in panelling of c. 1600; overmantel with strapwork over remains of a moulded fireplace surround. Modern kitchen next door: no trace of any vaults of the type popular in the other local houses of this date (Plympton House and Mothecombe).

Outbuilding to the W: a wall with old archway, and at the end the puzzling shell of a two-storey arrangement – early C18 doorway with fine swan-neck pediment, four windows with chamfered and moulded sills, tiny Ionic columns. What is their history?

LYNMOUTH

7040

The chief attraction is, of course, scenic. Architecturally the QUAY has on the W a pretty terrace of climbing-up cottages, called MARS HILL, the original route to the harbour. Characteristic of c. 1840–60 the few small early Victorian houses with Gothic detail and the bargeboarded villas (some built as hotels) that surround the harbour. Shelley had a cottage at Lynmouth as early as 1812, and Southey wrote enthusiastically about the village which, he said, was the finest spot he ever saw, except for Cintra and the Arrabida. Among the pre-Victorian houses are two facing a lush lawn right down by the stony harbour: ROCK HOUSE, with a thatched veranda on tree-trunks and a mildly Gothic front, and the MANOR HOUSE, plain and square (with additions). Above Lynmouth on the E the TORS HOTEL, a characteristic example of how the bargeboarded villa was later, in Lynmouth's heyday, enlarged by grossly half-timbered gables, etc.

On the ESPLANADE, LIMEKILNS, now furnished with seats, and the

RHENISH TOWER, rebuilt after the flood damage of 1951, erected originally about 1860 by one General Rawdon to store salt water for indoor baths. The tower is small and none too Rhenish-looking, but the allusion to Germany is appropriate, for the popularity of Lynmouth and its environs coincides with that of journeys up the Rhine to the Black Forest. The Zahnradbahn up to Lynton (the longest in Britain, opened 1890), the tidy footpaths through the woods, the frequency of conifers, all give a decidedly German flavour.

ST JOHN THE BAPTIST. 1869–70 by *E. Dolby*; enlarged in 1908. Apsed, French Gothic in style, in the manner of Street. Low embattled tower added in 1921.

BRIDGE over the High Street. Built in 1954 after the flood. Pre-stressed concrete: thirteen T-shaped beams, 95 ft long, set at a skew to give maximum opening at time of flood.

WIND HILL. *See* Lynton.

7040

LYNTON

ST MARY. Perched on the cliffs overlooking the sea. Unbuttressed, unpinnacled tower at the SW end. Nave S wall of 1741. New chancel in E.E. style by *E. Dolby*, 1868–9, re-used as the E end to the N aisle at a larger-scale rebuilding of 1893–1905. In 1893–4 *J. D. Sedding* with his pupil *Henry Wilson* began to build a new, broad nave with wagon roof and broad, fine Dec W window, and N and S aisles with octagonal arcade piers. Wilson exhibited a design for a tower in 1892. This came to nothing, but in 1905 he built a new chancel, oddly enough in the Romanesque style; not one of his best designs.

The FITTINGS of the remodelled church are characteristic of *Wilson*'s inventiveness and constitute one of the best collections of their date in Devon. – LECTERN. A delightful piece, in different coloured woods, with naturalistic foliage and openwork frieze. – COMMUNION RAILS. Openwork roundels with birds and trees. – PULPIT. 1896. Highly original. Octagonal, with low-relief oval panels with signs of the zodiac, art nouveau tendrils, and animals in between. Convex base with flowers; octagonal stem. – NORTH CHAPEL ALTAR. Beaten copper, with tree of life and bird motif in central vesica. – STAINED GLASS. Mostly plain with pretty art nouveau leaded patterns, typical of Sedding, but in the N chapel a N lancet by *Christopher Whall*, c. 1907: St Anne and the Virgin, a fine composition of blues, purples and greens. – W window also by *Whall*. – N aisle fourth from E by *Shrigley & Hunt*, designed by *Wilson*: four virtues. – FONT. Octagonal, with two shallow blank round-headed arches on each side; renewed c. 1870. The FONT COVER Elizabethan, with semicircular arches and turned finials. – MONUMENTS. Thomas Grose †1734. Of wood, painted with a choir of angels by *Phelps* of Porlock. – Several small beaten copper plaques of 1903, 1906, etc. – Excellent CHURCHYARD GATES of c. 1900.

HOLY SAVIOUR. Roman Catholic church and convent of the Poor Clares, designed in 1907 by *Leonard Stokes*, built to a simplified final design in 1908–10. The upper storey of the N range was added in 1924 by *Stokes & Drysdale*, the S part and the façade of the church were completed by *George Drysdale* in 1929–31. The church has a plain gabled façade and an Italian-looking bellcote by the side of a gable. Very odd neo-Perp windows. Interior white and Italian, tunnel-vaulted. W gallery on two Ionic columns. Raised choir, with cancelli of coloured marbles. The convent is decently and honestly utilitarian.

METHODIST CHURCH. 1910 by *Latrobe & Weston*, with fanciful art nouveau stone front.

CONGREGATIONAL CHURCH. 1904, with half-timbered gable, and NW tower-porch. Paid for by Sir George and Lady Newnes, and similar in style to the following.

TOWN HALL. 1898–1900 by *Read & Macdonald*. Small, but certainly an attempt at municipal architecture in a holiday spirit. Rough and dressed stone, wooden balconies, two short castellated turrets and gaily half-timbered gables. Utterly un-Devonian.

Lynton was no more than a hamlet before Queen Victoria's time. The railway reached it only in 1898 and has since deserted it again. The former station of the narrow-gauge Lynton and Barnstaple railway (1897 by *R. Jones* of Lynton) is now a house. Chalet style, with deep overhanging eaves. A nice example of earlier architecture is the ROYAL CASTLE HOTEL of 1810, in a glorious position high above and overlooking the sea. Slate-hung first floor, Gothick glazing, castellated porch. Similar modest long white houses in various places. The hotel style is High to Late Victorian, i.e. from the grimness of some of Ilfracombe and Westward Ho! to the heavy-handed gaiety of fancy tile-hanging and turrets and gables with woodwork painted white, e.g. the VALLEY OF ROCKS HOTEL, by *R. Plumbe*, 1888.

LEE ABBEY. 'Lee was never the site of a monastic foundation. It is only a melodramatic abbey' (Murray's guide book, 1872). The mansion, in sumptuous ham-fisted Gothic, was built *c.* 1850 for Charles Frederick Bailey, incorporating an older manor house of the Wichelhalse family. Sensitively adapted and extended as a conference and residential centre for the Lee Abbey Fellowship by *Scarlett, Burkett Associates*, from 1966.

Facing N is the old house, trimmed with red brick and remodelled as C19 service rooms. At the NW corner a big C19 porch with stained glass leads into the added W wing. Lofty staircase around a well with delicate cast-iron balustrade. C20 chapel on the top floor of the N wing. In the W wing, the C19 living rooms, taking advantage of the sea views, and a broad glazed corridor with transverse arches with pierced spandrels and good patterned tiles, leading to a big octagonal music room with odd fancy shield-shaped tracery in the large windows. Interior with bold timber ribs and a timber pendant. To the S a projecting bedroom wing of 1968 with a stubby entrance tower of reeded concrete, a praiseworthy effort of its time: in keeping with the spirit of the place, yet in a modern idiom. It stands in line with a C19 gatehouse with brick Gothic arch. Also from the mid C19 attempts at buttressed monastic garden walls, and a tower on the E side.

Attractive C19 outbuildings to the E with lattice windows, converted to a meeting hall in 1982. Further N, farm buildings of 1971, large, but discreetly designed to fit into the landscape; low sloping roofs, boarded walls. The unobtrusive sports hall of 1984 is similarly detailed. The road around the site was made in 1966; exemplary landscaping and planting.

Pretty C19 estate cottages and lodges.

WOOLHANGER MANOR, S of Martinhoe Cross. An eccentric octagonal MUSIC ROOM was added to the house in 1894 by Sir Henry Palk Carew. Mullioned windows, tall central lantern, two heavy hooded fireplaces. There was originally an organ powered by a waterwheel.

WIND HILL. The massive cross-ridge dyke defending a large spur, probably Iron Age in origin, has sometimes been identified as the Arx Cynuit where the Saxons fought the Danes in 878.

STOCK CASTLE, S of Barbrook. A small earthwork, possibly of the Iron Age.

ROBOROUGH CASTLE, above Hoaroak Water. A similar earthwork to that at Stock Castle, though slightly larger.

On CHERITON RIDGE and FURZEHILL COMMON, Bronze Age ceremonial monuments – barrows, standing stones, and stone settings – as well as hut circles and vestigial field systems, which are far less common on Exmoor than on Dartmoor.

MALBOROUGH

The parish boasts a splendid coastline, which encouraged the building of seaside villas from the C18 – *see* Salcombe.

ALL SAINTS. Very low cemented W tower with broach-spire and no battlements. Diagonal buttresses only at the foot. Low, unmoulded, steeply pointed tower arch, i.e. C13. S side with two-storeyed S porch and rood-stair turret. The windows mainly four-centred and of three or four lights without tracery. The S porch vaulted in two bays, the centre boss with four heads meeting at the chins (cf. Exeter Cathedral, Berry Pomeroy, Thorverton). The interior long and somewhat chilly. N and S aisles of six bays. Piers of A type with capitals only to the shafts and nearly semicircular arches. Restored in 1870 by *Richard Coad*. – FONT. Norman, square, not high, of the familiar table-top type, with five very shallow blank arches on each side of the top. – PARCLOSE SCREENS. – ALTAR CLOTH. Made up of late medieval parts of vestments; gold embroidered figures of saints and flowers and seraphim as decoration of the wine-coloured background.

BAPTIST CHAPEL. 1815, enlarged in 1872. Rendered, with a hipped roof, segmental-arched openings, and a small gabled porch. In a burying ground with an overthrow at the entrance.

INNER HOPE LIFEBOAT STATION. 1875. Surprisingly elaborate Gothic.

At LOWER TOWN, DYERS COTTAGES and, almost opposite, DAIRY COTTAGE are C18, with close similarities to the model cottage plans described by Vancouver (*see* Further Reading).

YARDE. A courtyard house with a five-window front dated 1718; older parts behind.

At BOLT TAIL a classic example of a PROMONTORY FORT or cliff castle where a projecting peninsula is fortified by a rampart to defend it on the landward side. It is probably of the later Iron Age. The mounds within the fort appear to be natural outcrops of rock rather than barrows.

MAMHEAD

Mamhead established *Anthony Salvin* as the chief architect of his time [149] for large country houses in the Tudor style. It was his first important job; the commission came to him in 1826, when he was only twenty-six. The Mamhead estate had been bought in 1823 by R. W. Newman, a Dartmouth merchant who became M.P. for Exeter and was knighted in 1836. The site is superb, with a view of the Exe estuary beyond the park which had been landscaped by *Capability Brown* in the 1770s. Above rise the Haldon Hills, thickly wooded as a result of energetic afforesting by a previous owner, Peter Ball, in the early C18. The old mansion of the Ball family, taken over in the later C18 by the Vaughans, Earls of Lisburne, stood lower down the hill, closer to the church.

Within this C18 landscape Salvin created a picturesque group evoking earlier ages. His neo-Tudor mansion is on a generous scale, with a symmetrical nine-bay gabled and battlemented E front in meticulously worked Bath stone. A little higher up the hill, a romantic castle of local red sandstone is a highly effective accent. It housed stables, laundry, and brewhouse (the beer brought by gravity to the cellars of the house). The castle courtyard is entered through a portcullised gateway between two gaunt square towers; on the show side to the E is a taller tower of striking outline with corbelled-out and machicolated turrets, based on Belsay, Northumberland (Salvin grew up in County Durham).

The novelty of the house lies in its knowledgeable use of Tudor domestic detail – elaborate finials and chimneys, and a triple oriel in the projecting centre of the E front, derived from Hengrave Hall in Suffolk. Greater freedom appears in the low adjunct to the s, successfully completing the composition: a cloister-like conservatory or camellia house which projects from the back wing and ends in a two-storey bay-windowed pavilion. The busier details suggest a slightly later date than the main house. The conservatory has four-centred arches with narrow close-set white-painted mullions with arched heads. In the spandrels, accomplished naturalistic flower-carving (precocious for the 1830s); on the parapet an ingeniously apt quotation in Gothic script from Chaucer's *Romaunt of the Rose*: '... Flouris yelowe white and rede/Such plente grewe there ner in mede'. In the angle of the house and conservatory a flower garden with a sundial decorated with strapwork.

The planning of the house is conservative. The main rooms face E and are served by a broad axial N–S corridor or gallery. The service rooms lie behind, across an internal courtyard – a version of the traditional Devonian courtyard plan (cf. Werrington) which Salvin took over from an earlier project by *Charles Fowler* relating to modernization of the original house. It is revealing that the patron rejected Fowler's daring Italianate elevations, preferring the neo-Tudor that was beginning to gain ground in the county in the 1820s (cf. Eggesford, Kitley, Tavistock town centre).

The main entrance on the N leads into a traditionally arranged screens passage (a legacy of the plan of the old house?). Beyond the unpainted openwork wooden screen the hall or billiard room, with a single-rib plaster ceiling, coloured glass in the upper lights of the bay-window, and a handsomely carved and painted heraldic overmantel, designed in 1835, showing Salvin's increasingly mature grasp of period detail.

From the screens passage one enters the broad fan-vaulted gallery, the main showpiece of the house. Here the Tudor mood was enhanced by five pairs of life-size sculptures by *Charles Raymond Smith* of monarchs and historic figures, of which only two remain (Cardinal Wolsey and a Bishop).* The statues appear in a sketch made by Mrs Salvin probably on her visit in 1838; two of them were exhibited at the Royal Academy in 1842 and 1844. The use of a sculpture gallery to display figures from English history instead of classical statues is unprecedented in country houses; it is revealing that it is exactly contemporary with the historical decorative schemes for the Houses of Parliament of which Newman, as an M.P., must have known.‡

In other main rooms more Tudor features (designed in 1832–3). In the dining room a painted and embattled chimneypiece with figures of Edward the Confessor and the Pilgrim, and an original buffet with strapwork legs. The drawing room has a strapwork ceiling with flowery medallions. More flowers on the fireplace and in the upper lights of the windows. The stained glass here and elsewhere in the house is all by *Thomas Willement*. Library in the SE corner with a ribbed ceiling grained to look like wood, and original bookcases. In an adjoining room to the S, octagonal with niches, a similar ceiling.

The grand staircase, projecting from the gallery into the inner courtyard, has Gothic balustrading painted to look like stone, embellished with red and blue, and a colourful large heraldic glass landing window. The interior decoration is in the bright colours of the Regency tradition, not yet the more sober tones of the Victorians. Upstairs, roof-lit spine corridor and bedrooms with simple Gothic fireplaces.

GARDEN BUILDING (now a house). C18, with a domed circular centre.

ICE HOUSE, circular (roof destroyed), S of the church, near the site of the old house, probably C18.

LODGES. Two very pretty examples, one thatched, with rustic veranda, another with decorative bargeboards – *Salvin* trimmings added to plain C18 boxes.

OBELISK, on the hill above the house. A red sandstone needle erected in 1742 by Sir Thomas Ball as a daymark for shipping.

St THOMAS. All red, small and on its own. The chancel with small lancet window on the S side, the W tower low, with diagonal buttresses. The nave has a N aisle (octagonal red piers and semicircular arches), a S transept, and a S porch. Extensive renovations

---

*The others were sold in 1985. They were of Lord and Lady Daubeny, Henry VII and Elizabeth of York, Henry VIII and Jane Seymour, Elizabeth I and Sir Walter Raleigh. The first four are now at Allerton Park, North Yorkshire.

‡But cf. the earlier staircase hall with founders and benefactors at Ashridge, Herts (by James Wyatt and Sir Jeffry Wyatville).

took place in 1830–1: E windowsill lowered, vestry and plaster roof added, piers cased in cement. The curious tooling of the aisle piers and capitals dates from this time. Plaster and cement were removed from the walls in 1914–15. The reseating dates from a restoration of 1854 by *D. Mackintosh*. – Oak REREDOS, 1908 by *Herbert Read*; Passion scenes, with quite expressive figure carving. – PULPIT. 1914, also by *Herbert Read*. – Heraldic STAINED GLASS by *Willement*, *c.* 1831, mostly presented by the Newman and Vaughan families. – MONUMENTS. Vaughan family, 1831. Inscription within two cusped arches. – Sir Robert L. Newman †1854 at Inkerman. Pink marble with white marble portrait medallion, framed in a cusped arch. Both by *Salvin*.

MANATON

7080

An exposed village near the high hills and granite outcrops. The church lies close to an unexpected green flanked by avenues of trees.

ST WINIFRED. W tower unbuttressed with stair-turret and obelisk pinnacles, much restored after storm damage in 1779. The S side of the church all embattled and all granite ashlar, with vaulted two-storey porch (cf. Berry Pomeroy, Chagford). N and S aisles of four bays, granite piers of A type, depressed arches. Ceiled wagon roofs. – REREDOS. Quattrocento style; figures on a gold background within wooden nichework. – SCREEN across nave and aisles, with much polychromy. Restored by *Sedding* in 1893. Standard four-light tracery (type A), coving much renewed, two decorated cornice bands. Central doorway with the charming and exceptional motif of small statuettes above each other in jambs and voussoirs (cf. North Bovey). In the wainscoting early C16 painted panels of saints (their faces savagely gouged out at the Reformation). Black outlines, lively colours. Restored by *Anna Hulbert*, 1980–2. – STAINED GLASS. Four C15 figures in the top of a N aisle window. – In the S aisle a striking window to Esmond Moore Hunt †1927 by *Frank Brangwyn*; large, rather disturbing figures of surpliced choirboys amid profuse, richly coloured foliage. – Many LEDGER STONES.

Close to the E end and the lychgate, a thatched two-storey granite house, probably the CHURCH HOUSE. At the back an upper window with two shallow arched lights.

(RECTORY (former). 1825 by *Charles Hedgeland*, much enlarged *c.* 1875.)

NEADON. A small hamlet which in the C17 had three substantial houses. Opposite Neadon Farm (a rebuild) UPPER HALL, a small but remarkable late C15 first-floor house. The only comparable building known in Devon is at Yeo, Chagford. The nearest parallels are perhaps precisely similar first-floor halls in Brittany.* The impressive granite ashlar blockwork at both gable-ends is curiously disrupted in the lateral walls, indicating substantial remodelling, although the evidence of first floor and roof suggests that the original form has been preserved. That the ground floor was used for storage and later as a shippon is demonstrated by the slit windows, central drain, and wide timber door, possibly moved from the centre of the

*Information from Professor G. Meirion Jones.

building (where there is a blocked doorway). First floor on massive square cross-beams with neatly chamfered joists: hall reached by an external (reconstructed) timber staircase through another timber-arched door. The puzzling double door, now partially blocked, is probably contemporary with the later subdivision of the once completely open first-floor space. At the W end of the hall a good garderobe, lavabo, gable-end fireplace with narrow dais, and large windows; at the E end a four-light timber window with cusped tracery and evidence for a sleeping platform above a partition. The roof accentuates this distinction: though the carpentry techniques are consistent (raised crucks with cranked collars), the two W bays are half the length of the two E bays, and the W end is slightly decorated and has wall plates. During repair and restoration in 1982–3 by *Vernon Hunt* and the *Harrison Sutton Partnership* several internal features were reconstructed on surviving evidence. The house may have been part of a larger complex, as is tantalizingly suggested by the continuation of granite blockwork along the wall fronting the courtyard into the lowest courses of the gable wall of the parallel building: this also has a similar roof truss and re-used cross-beams and joists. It incorporates a stone pigsty right on the roadside.

GRIMSPOUND, one of Dartmoor's most famous prehistoric sites, lies in a saddle at the N end of the Hameldown Ridge. It was quite vigorously reconstructed after excavation at the end of the C19. Within a massive enclosure wall lies a group of substantial Bronze Age HUT CIRCLES. The siting is not defensively strong, and the fact that Grimspound is more massively built than most Dartmoor enclosed settlements may be due simply to the ready availability of materials.

HAMEL DOWN, running S, is crowned by a fine series of massive ROUND BARROWS which dominate the skyline. In between are ring cairns and lesser barrows from one of which came the 'Hamel Down pommel', of amber studded with thousands of minute gold pins, found in the C19 attached to a dagger of Wessex type and destroyed in the bombing of Plymouth in the Second World War.

On both sides of the valley W of Hamel Down, in which the road runs, is a field system of well preserved STRIP LYNCHETS running right round the S end of CHALLACOMBE DOWN. It belonged to the hamlet of Challacombe, now reduced to a single farm. (For tin working in the valley bottom, *see* North Bovey.)

E of the hamlet of Water a small Iron Age PROMONTORY FORT, on the E end of the Houndtor Wood spur overlooking Lustleigh Cleave. A once extensive charcoal-burning industry has left its traces in the many circular banks surrounding slight depressions – the former hearths – in the woods running down to the river Bovey.

HOUNDTOR. The deserted hamlet lies immediately SE of the great outcrop of Hound Tor, 2 m. S of Manaton. Excavations have revealed a sequence of turf-built houses. Longhouses, some with drains at the lower (shippon) end and barns with corn-drying kilns and ovens, can be clearly seen. A 'cornditch' runs through the site – an asymmetrical walled bank to keep out deer – suggesting that the original settlement was the house downslope, within the cornditch. The excavations seemed to indicate that the first buildings could go back to mid Saxon times, but a more recent interpretation is that the settlement represents a shorter incursion into the uncultivated moor during relatively favourable conditions lasting from the C12 or C13 to the mid C14. Around can be seen fields – some of them prehistoric but remodelled in the medieval period – with numerous clearance cairns. The narrow ridge-and-furrow is probably C18/19.

HOUNDTOR II, to the N of the main settlement, consists of a single farmstead occupying a prehistoric enclosure. The basis for the barn is a HUT CIRCLE.

Not far from the deserted hamlet, GREAT HOUNDTOR,* a late C17 three-room and cross-passage-plan farmhouse with good contemporary fittings including panelling and an unusual patterned stone floor to the passage. In the yard an older longhouse remains.

MARIANSLEIGH

7020

ST MARY. After gutting by fire in 1932 some interesting remains of a C13 church were discovered in the S wall of the nave. They consist of two arches and two rough circular piers of a former S aisle. W tower with buttresses only at the foot. The tower arch narrow and low, completely unmoulded. N aisle Perp, the piers of B type with standard capitals, the windows straight-headed; the E wall of the aisle, with a piscina, is older. – (STAINED GLASS. E window by *Ken Baynes*, 1954, unusually good for its date.)

MARISTOW
Roborough

4060

A large house in an idyllic setting overlooking the Tavy estuary. Sir Massey Lopes (†1831) established himself here in 1798, and the house remained the family seat until the early C20. Three recent fires, the latest in 1982, left the top floor gutted and much else damaged. The W front, unappealingly clad in a drab roughcast, is a remodelling of 1907–9 by *George & Yeates*, but comparison with earlier engravings shows that all they did was add a central two-storey porch and lengthen the wings of an existing U-shaped house. The wings (with dining room l. and library r.) have steep pedimented gable-ends with lunettes; niches with classical statues below. (The shorter C18 wings each had a Venetian window with lunette and two oculi above).

The S front still reveals the C18 house of the Heywood family (they entertained the royal family at Maristow in 1789). Seven bays, the centre three projecting slightly, with a raised attic floor with oval windows. Central Doric pedimented doorcase. This wing has the most elaborate interior: a tall central saloon with Rococo-style plaster wall panels and ceiling, predating the early C20 (see the way the library door breaks into a wall panel). The entrance hall may well be the core of a pre-C18 building, but it has no visible old features. Three arches to the stair-hall to its S. Fine C18 well staircase with turned balusters, carved tread-ends, and moulded soffits. Two Ionic columns on the landing. At the N end an

---

*For a plan of Great Houndtor see p. 68.

agglomeration of service and other rooms. Above the kitchen a room with quite an elaborate plaster ceiling, perhaps early C19.

CHAPEL, projecting from the house to the E. A vigorously Gothic addition of 1871 by *St Aubyn*, crazy-paving limestone with yellow stone dressings, a big Dec E window, and a S tower with broach-spire, all ambitious enough for a village church. Sumptuous interior. Polished marble shafts; white marble reredos set in a streaky marbled dado; sanctuary roof enriched by gilded bosses.

FOLLY. Made up of architectural fragments from the previous chapel, demolished by St Aubyn; also two Ionic columns, perhaps from the front door of the house.

LODGES. A handsome pair, two-storeyed, with rusticated ground floor, triple-arched first-floor windows, and pyramid roofs. 1839 by *Charles Fowler* (cf. Bickleigh).

MARLDON

ST JOHN. A big church for the village to which it belongs. Early W tower with marked batter and no buttresses. Castellated N and S aisles, the N one with a castellated rood-loft turret, the S one with a two-storeyed porch. The porch is vaulted. Window masonry mostly from *Fulford*'s restoration of 1884. Aisles of five bays separated from the nave by tall type B piers with standard capitals. In addition, on the S side a two-bay chancel chapel erected by the Gilberts *c*.1520. The shelf-piscina is considerably older and must have been transferred from the chancel wall when this was opened up. – The stone SCREEN has gone (fragments kept in the upper-floor room of the porch), but its beginnings by the N and S piers can still be seen, combined in an original way with cenotaphs to Otho Gilbert †1492 and his wife under arches open to N and S. In one of them an effigy in armour far below life-size. The Gilberts owned Compton Castle near by. – FONT. The usual octagonal Perp type. – (STAINED GLASS. Window by *Mary Lowndes*, *c*.1920.)

CHURCH HOUSE INN. No doubt old below its somewhat fancifully gothicized front, with windows with concave instead of convex sides to the arched tops. The same in the post office next door. But the entrance doorway to the inn may be C15, approached by a double flight of stairs.

LIMEKILN, in the garden of Strainytor Bungalow. Large, round, and well preserved.

See also Compton Castle.

MARTINHOE

ST MARTIN. Small, unbuttressed, unpinnacled W tower, narrower than the nave. Low, depressed pointed opening of the tower to the nave: a very primitive form (cf. Parracombe). Nave and lower chancel, the chancel of *c*.1300 (E window Victorian). The early C19 restoration (flat ceilings, semicircular chancel arch) was swept away in 1866–7 by *S.S.Teulon*: new chancel arch, reconstruction of porch and roofs, and reseating; not as idiosyncratic as some of

his work. – Gorgeous stiff-leaf-decorated FONT of 1864 in polychrome marble, executed by *Pulsford* of Barnstaple. – SCREEN.
Very little of the tracery of the wainscoting is all that remains.

CHURCH HOUSE, SE of the church, much altered.

BRONZE AGE BARROWS. A good group SE of the village.

On MARTINHOE BEACON a defensive earthwork site shown by
excavation to be a Roman FORTLET, probably part of a Bristol
Channel signalling system (cf. Old Burrow, Countisbury).

MARWOOD

The church stands in an attractive position. The tall W tower points
out of the village across green hills and woods; the E end faces the
pretty late Georgian stuccoed front of MARWOOD HOUSE.

ST MICHAEL. W tower with buttresses only at the foot; no pinnacles.
Embattled S porch. The S transept is older, of the C13 (see the single
lancet on the E side and the unmoulded pointed arch to the nave).
The chancel also is C13, remodelled in the C14 (E window tracery
C19). The S door, judging by its moulding and small corbels, must
also be C14. Late Perp N aisle, replacing a former N transept (see the
foundations outside). So this was once a cruciform church. The aisle
has uncusped straight-headed windows and the usual Devon
arcade, five bays with B type piers and standard leaf capitals.
Unceiled wagon roofs, in the N aisle with moulded ribs and bosses.
Chancel largely rebuilt by *Hayward*, 1858–9, very correct Dec.
General restoration 1903 by *E. H. Sedding*.

The chief interest of the church is its SCREEN. Only the aisle
sections are preserved. It has standard type A tracery but unusual
wainscoting, with panels full of early Renaissance decoration motifs
between the ribs, just as at Atherington. Also as at Atherington the
fact that the coving at the back has only tracery between the ribs.
The back of the rood loft is preserved – a rarity. It has rude, broad,
elementary Perp motifs. On the wainscoting panels of the door is
recorded the donation of the screen by a parson of Marwood called
Sir John Beaupel. All that is definitely known is that Beaupel was
rector in 1520, but as no other name or date appears in records until
1561, he may have continued in office after 1520 and the screen may
well be rather later. – BENCH ENDS. Of Devon/Cornwall type with
the usual initials, shields, etc.; also a few figures of saints.
– PULPIT. Plain mid C17, with baluster legs. – REREDOS. Made up
from old panelling. – ROYAL ARMS. Big, plaster, *temp.* George III.
– STAINED GLASS. E window 1910 and S transept window 1916,
both by *Percy Bacon Bros*. Colourful archangels. – MONUMENTS.
William and Anthony Peard † 1652. A small rustic tablet with busts
of two youths, each with head on hand. – William Parminter † 1737.
Large, architectural, of white and grey marble, with two cherubs. –
SUNDIAL. By *John Berry*, 1762 (cf. Tawstock). – CHURCHYARD.
Slate gravestones, e.g. by *Knill* of Pilton. – Large angel by *Hems*,
1898.

WESTCOTT BARTON. A seat of the Chichesters in the C17; now a
farmhouse.

WHITEFIELD BARTON. A large farmhouse; the date 1771 over the door, but probably with an older core. Wings with pedimented gables with blocked lunettes.

MARYSTOW

ST MARY. s doorway with Norman remains of an arch. Simple billet and saltire-cross ornament. Chancel early C14, as is proved by the tracery of its s window and its trefoil-headed double SEDILIA. Perp six-bay N arcade with A type piers and arches. Perp w tower of granite ashlar with diagonal buttresses, partially rebuilt in 1824. In the s porch a fireplace (cf. e.g. Wolborough, Newton Abbot). Scraped interior, over-restored in 1866. – FONT. Norman, square, almost exactly as at Lifton; intersecting arches, corner heads. – SCREEN. Three sections only remain, under the tower arch; wainscoting and tracery of type A standard, no decoration of the spandrels, and nothing above. – MONUMENT. Sir Thomas Wyse (*see* Sydenham) †1629. One of the most ambitious monuments in Devonshire, a late example of the free-standing type with four pairs of columns supporting a coffered arch (cf. Colyton, Cadeleigh) and obelisks and an achievement on top. Two recumbent effigies, children against the high base (two kneeling, a little girl sitting in a chair (cf. Wembury), and two babies), all obviously not in their right positions now. Helm and gauntlets above.

See also Sydenham.

MARY TAVY

ST MARY. w tower of granite ashlar, unbuttressed, with a high stair-turret and obelisk pinnacles. s porch also of ashlar, with old wagon roof. s transept 1893. Perp s aisle with A type arcade with depressed moulded arches. At its E end in the E jamb of the last s window a niche for an image. – SCREEN. By *E.H. Sedding*, 1893. – STAINED GLASS. All by *Kempe Studios*, 1893–5.

METHODIST CHAPEL. 1836. Simple, rendered, with two round-headed windows.

The village lies in a fold of the moor, with evidence all around of the mines that were once so important. WHEAL FRIENDSHIP, at one end of the village, was one of the most productive copper mines, opened *c.*1796, with transport provided by the canal opened in 1803, linking Tavistock to the port of Morwellham on the river Tamar. Spoil heaps, wheel pits, and leats remain; also ruins of the arched condensing chambers and a flue of the later arsenic works which operated until 1925. The count house, with its overhanging storey in the centre, served also as the mine captain's house.

HORNDON COTTAGES, a small settlement originally called Miners' Town, was built by John Taylor in the early C19 to house miners from Wheal Friendship.

WHEAL BETSY. The remains of this ancient mine, reopened in 1806 and worked for silver lead until 1877, rise spectacularly to the E of the Okehampton–Tavistock road. The main feature is the shell of the ENGINE HOUSE built in 1867, together with shafts, spoil heaps, and tracks.

MEAVY

ST PETER. Sheltered in a fold of the moor. Part of the building goes back to Norman times, and if Loudon in his *Arboretum* is right, then the old battered wreck of an oak tree in front of the church is as old. The proof of the date of the church is the N respond of the chancel arch: a Norman moulding, with two rams' heads at its corners and an alternation of red and white stone as at Paignton and Plympton Priory. The chancel E window and the repositioned windows of the chancel chapel are C13. Unbuttressed W tower with large rectangular stair-turret; the plinth is granite, so the tower is probably all C15, despite its early look. Low angle pinnacles similar to Milton Abbot. S arcade also Perp, with A type piers and depressed arches whose mouldings suggest that the arcade is later than the S transept and chancel aisle. Wagon roofs, open in the nave, the others ceiled. Restorations in 1873–4 by *Hine & Odgers*, 1884 by *J.D.Sedding*. – REREDOS and ALTAR. 1884 by *J.D. Sedding* (the altar executed in 1896), of Devonshire marble, alabaster, and Caen stone. – STALLS of 1892. – STAINED GLASS by *Burlison & Grylls*, *Westlake*, and *Bacon*.

CHURCH HOUSE, on the village green. Now the Royal Oak Inn. Rendered, with lateral stack. At the back a staircase projection and a granite mullioned window overlooking the churchyard.

GOODAMEAVY BARTON AND MANOR HOUSE. Originally a single courtyard house. The Manor House at the front is early C19, with a C17 kitchen range at the W end, with granite mullioned windows. The Barton at the rear is a former barn; the r. hand range was possibly stables.

MEAVY BARTON. A small manor house of early C16 origin (remains of an arch-braced roof) much altered in the mid C17, when the service end to the r. of the entrance was demolished and the house made two rooms deep. Well preserved C17 features: granite mullioned windows and internal doorways; an open-well staircase with turned balusters and ball-topped newels. Good outbuildings.

GREENWELL. C16 and late Georgian. Porch with granite doorway.

On WIGFORD DOWN, extensive prehistoric fields, hut circles, enclosures, and cairns.

DEWERSTONE. A strongly sited FORT overlooking the river Plym, with an unusual double rampart, conventionally believed to be of Iron Age date, but possibly Neolithic.

MEETH

ST MICHAEL. Plain Norman S doorway with only the smallest amount of decoration in the outer moulding of the arch. Norman windows also in the N side of the nave and the rectangular NE stair-turret of the unbuttressed W tower. The absence of a W door also is usually evidence of an early date. The tower arch towards the nave is pointed but unmoulded. – FONT. Norman, square, on five shafts, undecorated. – Plain C18 SEATS. – ROYAL ARMS. Uncommonly swagger; dated 1704. Could they be by *John Abbot* (*see* Frithelstock)? – MONUMENT. Prudence Lamb †1843, by *J. Ternouth* of Pimlico. An angel carries the young woman up to heaven.

OLD RECTORY. 1825 by *William Burgess* of Exeter. Quite an elegant Regency design of three rendered bays below deep eaves, with plain pilasters between the windows, the outer bays with full-height segmental recesses.

WOLLADON. A rare single-phase farmhouse of 1666; a staircase gives separate access to individual chambers. No later additions.

5040

MEMBLAND
Newton and Noss

The house has gone, but the outbuildings remain as an impressive reminder of the self-sufficiency of the large Victorian estate. Membland was acquired *c.*1877 by the banker Edward Baring, later Lord Revelstoke, who married Georgiana Bulteel of Flete (q.v.). He transformed the c18 house, commissioning from *George Devey* large additions including a tower for a hydraulic organ. But the Barings suffered a financial crisis in the 1890s, and the estate was sold in 1916. By 1939 the house was derelict; it was demolished after the war, and replaced by a much smaller dwelling in 1966–8. Around it, remains of the Victorian outbuildings. To the E, a tennis-court enclosure with derelict cricket pavilion behind. To the W, STABLES, attractively converted to houses and flats after the Second World War, an irregular U-shaped layout, c18, the shaped gables at the ends probably a *Devey* improvement. The small Dutch-gabled building to the w housed the electricity supply. Opposite, the smaller group of HUNTING STABLES and FORGE. Further W, down the road, Membland Villa is the former GASWORKS, and Lone Pine, on the windy brow of the hill, the LAUNDRY, with a clock tower.

Around the estate many other lodges, farm buildings, and cottages, mostly in a distinctively spiky romantic style of continental derivation, with deep bracketed eaves and picturesque roof-lines (*see also* Noss Mayo). Good examples are EAST LODGE, WEST LODGE, and especially ROWDEN FARM, with a polygonal-ended farm building and projecting gabled porches to the upper doors. WARREN COTTAGE, on the cliff top, was built as a warrener's cottage. Polygonal glazed summer house in front (where Edward VII was entertained by Lord Revelstoke). The BULL AND BEAR LODGE, in a similar style to the other estate buildings, gets its name from its gatepiers with supporters of the Bulteel and Baring families; it stands at the boundary between their two estates. (The stock-market terms bull and bear come from the two related families.) *Devey* was perhaps responsible for these minor buildings, although there is no firm evidence. The details are rather different from his more usual Wealden-inspired cottage style.

170

2000

MEMBURY

ST JOHN. W tower with stair-turret, taller and slimmer than usual in East Devon. Buttresses of B type; lively goat gargoyles. The chancel is C13, see the group of three lancets in the E wall (with nook-shafts in the interior) and one N lancet. N nave windows early Perp, similar to those in the belfry: two cusped lights, with a quatrefoil in a straight-sided hexagon. In the N transept N wall more developed Perp windows: three lights with two groups of four narrow lights above. The N transept appears to be a rebuilding on old foundations. The further evidence of older building on the S side – fourteen reset animal heads biting a roll moulding, mostly re-used as label stops – presumably came from a C12 door destroyed when the later Perp embattled S aisle, chapel, and porch were added. S arcade with A type piers and capitals only to the shafts. (Also C12 a pier with scalloped capitals in the nave S wall.) S chapel with a squint. Chancel arch of the restoration of 1892 by *George Vialls*, who also rebuilt the N wall and S arcade.

FONT. Perp, octagonal, with pointed quatrefoil panels. – SCREEN to the S chapel. Tripartite, the sides of four lights each, with A type Perp tracery and traces of red paint. Linenfold panelling below. – STAINED GLASS. N transept N: canopy fragment. – MONUMENTS. In the N transept, in a wall recess, a lady of *c.*1300, almost identical to the monument at Axminster. – In the S (Yarty) chapel, monuments to the Fry family of Yarty. Nicholas Fry †1632 and wife. Wall-monument with kneeling figures beneath an arch. – Robert Fry †1725. – Frances Fry †1723, seventeen years old. Bust, with inscription starting 'Stop Passenger and view ys mournful shrine/which holds ye Reliques of a Form Divine/Oh she was all perfection, Heav'nly Fair!/And Chast and Innocent as Vestals are.' – In the S aisle: Shilston Calmady †1645. Architectural, with Corinthian columns.

The church lies a little above the single village street. The former SCHOOL has minimally Gothic windows.

MEMBURY COURT. At the back, remains of a late C13 chapel, with an E window of high quality. Three cusped lights below a sexfoil and lobed trefoils. Hoodmould with head-stops. The W end of the chapel was of two storeys, divided off by a timber screen. (Elsewhere in the house the date 1568 and a good oak ceiling.)

YARTY. The E-shaped manor house of the Frys, much rebuilt by Nicholas Fry, sheriff of Devon in 1626.

LUGGS FARM. The farmhouse is perfectly at home in the landscape: long and low, running gently downslope, with a vast sweep of thatch over limestone and flint walls. A late C16 house, built two-storeyed, but on the older cross-passage plan with outshots, to which the C17 added a two-storey porch and a rear cross-wing. Later barn at the lower end. The lower room is of particular interest: it was the kitchen, with a massive fireplace and a large smoking chamber alongside, double doors to the outshots, and a spiral staircase. Cross-wing with a remade staircase with flat balusters. In the roof, mortices of the original timber stack over the hall.

MOXHAYES. A small late C17 house, showing the vernacular in transition. Two-room cross-passage plan, but with end entry and integral lean-to incorporating service rooms and stairs. Excellent later C17 fittings, including plaster and painted decoration.

MEMBURY CASTLE. An Iron Age HILLFORT with irregular univallate defences enclosing some 3 acres and a complex entrance structure.

5010
                              MERTON

ALL SAINTS. W tower with buttresses leaving the angles free;
obelisk pinnacles. Nave and N aisle, the five-bay arcade with piers
of A type (capitals only to the main shafts), primitively decorated
abaci, and depressed pointed arches. S transept with S recess for a
monument (not preserved). Restored in 1872–5 by *R.M.Fulford*
(N aisle rebuilt, new chancel roof). – FONT. Square, Norman, the
under edge with three scallops to each side; Jacobean cover.
– REREDOS. 1864; of Caen stone. – STAINED GLASS. In the N
chapel E window extensive late medieval fragments including
figures of St Christopher, St Margaret, St Edward the Confessor,
and St Anthony. – E window by *Kempe Studios*, 1898.
See also Great Potheridge.

7010
                              MESHAW

ST JOHN BAPTIST. W tower of 1691. The rest a lancet box with
ruggedly Gothic masonry, still entirely pre-Ecclesiological, 1838
by *R.D.Gould*. Shallow sanctuary added in 1878. – MONUMENT.
James Courtenay †1685. Architectural.
(MESHAW BARTON. Much remodelled in the C17: good joinery;
dog-leg staircase.)

4070
                           MILTON ABBOT

ST CONSTANTINE AND ST AEGIDIUS. Granite ashlar W tower
with diagonal buttresses and a rectangular stair-turret. The church
is one of the few in the area with both N and S Perp arcades, also
granite, with A type piers and nearly round-headed arches. Their
oddest feature is the corbels above the capitals (for a rood beam?).
Wagon roof with bosses. – MONUMENT. Arthur Edgcumbe
†1815 by *Henwood* of Plymouth. Obelisk and urn. – Many C18
TOMBSTONES with rustic carved symbols.
The village is more interesting than the church because of the buildings put up under the aegis of the Dukes of Bedford, whose Devon
country seat was at Endsleigh. S of the church the VICARAGE,
1837 by *Blore*, a substantial Tudor mansion of ashlar, with tall
groups of diagonally set chimneys, and mullioned windows with
dripstones. Gothic marble fireplaces. E of the church some distinguished cottages, Nos. 3–8 VENN HILL; by *Lutyens*, 1909, an
irregular group of four, the centre two set back from the road, the S
one on the downhill slope with a shop tucked in beneath. Slate
roofs with typically Lutyenesque upswept eaves and chimneys
with set-back corners. The windows are either shallow bays dying
into the wall, or set back in deep reveals. Four-centred central
archway to the back gardens, with niche above. W of the church
two similar groups without the subtlety of detail, perhaps executed
by *Cannon*, architect to the Bedford estate. VILLAGE HALL of
1840.
SCHOOL, at Milton Green, on the main road S of the village. 1820 by

Wyatville, Tudor Gothic, a long range with two entrances within a single archway.

In the parish several Bedford estate farms, e.g. LEIGH BARTON, *c.*1865, a very complete layout around a small farmyard, and BEARA FARM, 1856, with a small planned farmyard with rubble outbuildings.

(HIGHER CHILLATON. An ambitious Gothic farmhouse of the 1860s.)

EDGCUMBE HOUSE. The seat of the Edgcumbes from the C13 to 1840. Irregular, of the C16, much altered; originally on a quadrangular plan. Refronted in 1719 (date over the shell-hooded porch), probably when the hall was subdivided. (Inside, a granite lintel dated 1592, and an overmantel with a plaster coat of arms dated 1675. Early C18 staircase.)

METHODIST CHAPEL, on the A384. Pretty rendered front, gabled, with arched openings, and a gabled porch. Built by the Wesleyans in 1835.

See also Endsleigh.

MILTON DAMEREL

3010

HOLY TRINITY. W tower rebuilt with the old materials in 1892: small, slim, narrower than the nave, without buttresses, W door, or pinnacles, i.e. early medieval. The chancel followed about 1300–1330, judging by the tracery: S window still geometrical (cinque-foils), though with pointed trefoil lights (cf. the piscina), but E window with ogee reticulation. The N aisle and the nave S windows latest Perp (straight-headed, no tracery). Inside, an unusually wide nave, but the usual arcade (three plus two bays) with A type piers, rudely decorated capitals, and depressed arches. – PULPIT. Rustic late C17 work. – ROYAL ARMS. Of plaster, 1664, very much as in North Cornwall churches. – TILES in nave and aisle of the usual Barnstaple type.

METHODIST CHAPEL. Set in a burial ground. Built by the Bible Christians in 1837, enlarged in 1892. Adjoining SUNDAY SCHOOLS and former BRITISH SCHOOL of 1840.

EARTHWORK, on the W bank of the Torridge, near Woodford Bridge. Possibly an Iron Age enclosure converted into an earthwork castle by the addition of another bank at its W end, so forming a crude motte and bailey. It has no known history. Milton Damerel manor was held of the lords of Plympton.

MODBURY

6050

ST GEORGE. Quite a remarkable church, above the town, the characteristic silhouette of its steeple visible from far afield. It consists of a tower with angle buttresses with many set-offs which do not reach very high up, and then, without any intermediate battlements, a spire with one tier of small dormers. It is said to have been struck by lightning in 1621 and rebuilt; if so, it represents its early C14 predecessor accurately. Much of the body

of the church also goes back to the early C14, notably the masonry
of the walls of the nave, the arches between nave and aisles with
their thick and short piers with odd bevelled capitals without
necking (cf. Haccombe) and similar arches, and the transepts
(datable by the tomb recesses in their outer walls). In the s
(Champernowne) transept, two recesses in the style of *c.*1300 with
five cusps and trefoiled subcusps. A head at the apex of each main
arch. Within are a shapeless lump and one later effigy of alabaster,
a knight in armour with a collar of roses, of *c.*1460. In the N
(Prideaux) transept a single, more elaborate C14 recess, deep
enough for two effigies (now hardly recognizable). Ogee arch with
crockets, flanked by flat pinnacles resting on atlas figures. The
aisles were altered in the late Perp style. Their windows with
depressed arches and mullions without tracery are characteristic of
the granite idiom of that style. Of the same date the arches into the
transepts and the chancel aisles with granite piers of A type and
capitals only to the four shafts, decorated abaci, and moulded
arches. Beneath the chancel a vestry of the same date, with small
two-light granite windows to E and S. Sanctuary restored *c.*1860 by
W.White.

REREDOS, at the W end of the S aisle. Victorian, of geometric
inlaid marbles, no doubt of the same date as the restored Dec E
window with its STAINED GLASS by *Lavers & Barraud.* –
PULPIT. Made up of parts of the wainscot panels of the former
screen; Flamboyant blank tracery. – Other MONUMENTS. In the
N chapel a remarkable, very large inscribed slab to Oliver Hylle
†1573, with a long poem still in black letter, but with Roman
capitals. – High up above the S nave arcade a small C17 monument
with several kneeling figures, of good quality, inscription illegible.
– In the N aisle John Swete of Traine †1690, a small architectural
tablet with an oval surrounded by a wreath.

BAPTIST CHAPEL, Church Street, set back behind a yard. 1807.
Rubble walls, partly slate-hung. The front gable is pedimented.

The town is small and picturesque, its good features well preserved.
It was prosperous already in the Middle Ages, when it had two
fairs and a market. The two main roads, Church Street and Brownston Street, run down a hill and up again, meeting at right angles
in the centre. Few buildings of special note, but nothing inappropriate among the appealing mixture of slate-hung and rendered
fronts, with a good variety of Georgian doorcases, and small Victorian shop-windows.

In CHURCH STREET, near the crossroads where the market buildings stood until removed for road improvements of 1827, the little
EXETER INN (much altered, but licensed already in 1563). Opposite, the WHITE HART HOTEL and ASSEMBLY ROOMS,
built in 1827 by Sir John Bulteel of Flete, each with a broad
pediment, the hotel distinguished by a slightly grander doorcase
with incised Greek key pattern. Further up on the same side, No.9
has an elaborately Baroque C18 doorcase with a scrolled open
pediment. On the other side an especially attractive group starts
with Nos. 30 and 29, slate-hung, with segmental pedimented doorcase, then No.28, with slates arranged in lozenge patterns high up,
at the start of a raised footpath. Set into the footpath the inscribed
stone from one of the conduits given to the town in 1708, this one

by Nicholas Trist. On the s side, set back, the BAPTIST CHAPEL of 1806, with a pediment crowned by a voluted top piece, and DENBURY HOUSE, tall, with doorcase in late C18 style; fluted columns with Tower of the Winds capitals.

N of the church at the top of the hill was the Court House, the Champernowne mansion destroyed in the Civil War and sold for building material in 1705. It stood on or near the site of a small alien priory. N of this at the beginning of Barracks Road the MANOR HOUSE, C16 or C17, with a two-storeyed porch, much disguised by rendering and Georgian windows. Beyond it the SCHOOL of 1881, a sturdy stone structure with a little Gothic detail and a square tower which has lost the top of its cupola. BARRACKS ROAD owes its name to the Napoleonic barracks. Further down, a large walled enclosure remains, with attached one-storey guard houses and sheds, probably of 1802.

The other main street, BROWNSTON STREET, has its grander houses at the top of the hill. TRAINE, built in 1780, has a long early Victorian one-storey balustraded colonnade along the street and a matching intermittent balustraded parapet, with raised centre. NORTH TRAINE, next to it, must also be early Victorian, with a handsome channelled stucco front with quoins and hood-moulded windows. Opposite is one of the CONDUITS given in 1708, still in the C17 tradition, with its bulbous top and obelisk pinnacles. Its donor was Adrian Swete, whose house, OLD TRAINE, is at the end of the cobbled path behind the nearby archway. A Georgian front, but C16–17 behind, with an archway through to a central courtyard. (Carved slab with the arms of Adrian Swete and the date 1708; a re-used fragment of a medieval tomb slab with part of a canopied niche with a bishop on the back.)

Down the hill the most noticeable houses are No. 45, tall and narrow, with a three-storey canted bay, a late Georgian brick front with nicely variegated headers, and No. 8, CHAIN HOUSE, the best early C18 example, four bays, with modillion cornice and pedimented dormers. Opposite, set back, KINGSLAND HOUSE, the former SCIENTIFIC AND LITERARY INSTITUTE, founded in 1840 by Richard King, a native of Modbury who settled in New York. It has an absurdly heavy Tuscan porch and rustic attached Ionic columns on the floor above.

Turning E at the foot of Brownston Street one reaches GALPIN STREET, the old main road, with another handsome C18 house, BROOK HOUSE, two storeys over a tall basement, and a third conduit of 1708, pyramidal-roofed with ball finial. NEW ROAD (made in 1827) turns S. Round the corner is the METHODIST CHAPEL, a neat stuccoed box of 1835 in the Georgian tradition; schoolroom next door of 1874. Finally, in the town centre s of the main crossroads, POUNDWELL HOUSE, with a substantial plain early C18 three-storey front, seven windows wide, Doric corner pilasters, and keystones above ground-floor windows. Earlier parts behind.

TOLL HOUSE, on the A379 at Stoliford. Two storeys, angle-fronted, with porch.

BROWNSTON. The hamlet has a simple E.E. chapel of ease of 1844 by *George Wightwick*; side chapel added in 1900.

HIGHER BROWNSTON. Late medieval to C17 farmhouse, of stone

and cob under a slate roof. Early c16 front range; two later cross-wings. The core is a longhouse with inner room, hall, and shippon, but without separate cross-passage and with no evidence of a separate shippon entrance. Smoke-blackened cruck roof, stud-and-panel partition, and floor inserted in the late c16. The excellent early c17 s wing has a spiral staircase with central newel post, stone risers, and solid treads. Fine carpentry features, including several ovolo-moulded mullioned windows. c18 N wing: parlour and dairy with access from the hall.

EARTHWORK, s of Oldaport Farm. A tongue of land projects between two streams. The neck is cut off by cross ramparts, and there are traces of ramparts around the top. An enigmatic site: excavation has produced a little Roman material, and the foundations of two 'towers' were reportedly found in the 1840s. Suggested interpretations have varied from an Iron Age defended site to a deerpark.

MOLLAND

A tiny village on a slope above Exmoor.

ST MARY. W tower with diagonal buttresses, gargoyles, and carved figures at parapet level; polygonal stair-turret. Chancel E and s walls rebuilt in the c19. Set into the s porch a fragment of a c12 arch moulding. But the interior is what counts. It is one of the most memorable in Devon, very completely preserved in its pre-Victorian form (sensitive restoration by *W. A. Forsyth*, 1935–9). Small, with Perp N arcade of B type piers with standard capitals and depressed arches. Low against one pier a niche with a broken image of a saint. – FONT. Norman, square, with a scalloped under-edge. – REREDOS. Part of a former screen. Crocketed, with tiny Renaissance details. – COMMUNION RAILS of *c.*1700. – BOX PEWS in nave and aisle. – PULPIT of the three-decker type, the sounding-board with a marquetry star, and a trumpeting angel on top (cf. North Molton). – SCREEN with a solid 'tympanum' with Royal Arms and Ten Commandments painted in 1808. – STAINED GLASS. E window 1893 by *Drake*. – Some window-heads with pre-Ecclesiological geometric patterns. – MONUMENTS. Fragments of a late Perp tomb-chest with quatrefoils and the Courtenay arms. – John Courtenay † 1660. Architectural; angels with urns. – David Berry † 1664. Architectural, stone coloured to look like marble, large but clumsy. – John Courtenay † 1724. Two putti and an open pediment with reclining angels. – John Courtenay † 1732, similar, plus an oval panel beneath with relief of the Ascension (by *Weston*?; cf. St Petrock, Exeter). – Francis and William Dovell † 1850, with a scene of their shipwreck, by *J. Thomas* of Bristol. – In the churchyard, good slate TOMBSTONES of the first half of the c19; a wide variety of lettering, e.g. by *J. Honey* of South Molton.

WEST MOLLAND. The former Courtenay manor house, partly rebuilt *c.*1720. Seven-window front.

GREAT CHAMPSON. Late medieval; porch with Tudor arch.

MONKLEIGH

St George. An all-Perp church. w tower with buttresses of B type and pinnacles. Some of the s aisle windows are of the same unusual design as at Weare Giffard and Atherington nearby: intersecting round-headed arches cut by mullions. They are presumably of the same date as the s arcade, for whose completion Sir William Hankford left money in 1423. The arcade is of five bays with granite piers of A type with capitals only to the main shafts, decorated abaci, and depressed pointed arches. Ceiled aisle wagon roof with bosses. The most important part of the church is the se chapel, or Annery chapel, with the monument to Sir William Hankford †1423, Chief Justice of the King's Bench. The tomb-chest is placed in a recess with a depressed pointed arch, exceptionally finely cusped and with exceptionally finely carved cresting, in high relief. The tomb-chest is decorated with seven pinnacled, ogee-arched niches, the centre one with a double arch, projecting more than the others. There is no effigy on the lid. – The screen between aisle and chapel is also among the most remarkable of the many Devon screens. Its tracery is of the standard A type, but the carving in the spandrels, especially on the E side, is superb: mostly leaves, but there is also a pelican. There are similar spandrels on the hall screen at Weare Giffard. – The parclose screen of the same pattern between aisle and chancel is of 1879, designed by *Fulford* and executed by *Hems*. – The benches in the chapel, a jumble of the usual Devon panels and Elizabethan bits, were also put together at this time. Was the Perp doorcase in the chapel brought in as well? The rest of the church reseated by *W. R. Bryden* in 1879. – Lock box (s door). Carved with monster and tracery; made up from a bench end.

Font. Norman, circular, of a very uncommon design. The bowl is fluted, and at the top of the shaft there is also fluting, pleated outward and then again inward, a little like a Chinese lantern. – Communion rails. C17. – Stained glass. Many Renaissance bits in the E window of the s aisle. – Tiles. Groups in chancel and se chapel, Barnstaple patterns. – Monuments. Brass of a kneeling knight, C16, on the N wall of the chancel, placed in a patchwork of bits from some C16 monument, tops of twisted columns, carrying the springings of little vaults, etc. – Two little slate plates, one to Henry Hurding †1627 and family, the other to Jane Coffin †1646, a reclining figure with baby, very delicately drawn. – William Gaye †1631. Two frontal demi-figures in niches, both with cheek leaning against hand. Below, it says:

> Since Epitaphs have given speach to stones
> Their rhetorick extorted Sighs, Tears, Groans,
> Some teach divinitye, but this commends
> Dry tears, stop sighs, and strangleth groans of friends

because of William Gaye's 'temp'rance, prudence, candour, pietye'. – John Saltren of Petticombe †1794. Woman, urn, and sarcophagus; by *J. Richards* of Exeter.

The Chantry, facing the church. Gothick, C18 windows, projecting centre bay.

Annery. Demolished in 1957. The neo-classical house of c. 1800, with giant pilasters and a full-height bow to the garden, replaced an older house, originally the seat of the Hankfords, to which a notable long gallery had been added, described by Polwhele (cf. Holcombe Rogus). The DOWER HOUSE remains, badly treated, but once an attractive Regency building: two storeys, stuccoed, with Doric veranda.

PETTICOMBE. Rebuilt by John Saltren *c.* 1796. Stucco, five-bay front with projecting centre; porch with paired Greek Doric columns. Gothick hermitage, rustic bridge, and small lake.

MONK OKEHAMPTON

5000

ALL SAINTS. Low, unbuttressed medieval W tower with big pinnacles. The rest (nave, chancel, S porch, NE vestry) rebuilt in a quiet Perp, 1855 by *F. Harper*. Unmoulded chancel arch; pulpit entered through the vestry. In the chancel, a cusped arch retained from an old tomb recess. – STAINED GLASS. E window by *Beer*, exhibited at the Crystal Palace in 1851. – Nave S window by *A. L. Moore & Son*, 1914.

BEER. A C16–17 farmhouse with a first-floor ribbed plaster ceiling with vine-scroll frieze. Some early C18 plasterwork in the W wing.

LAKE. A complete C17 farmhouse – a rarity in Devon.

MILL. Three storeys, of stone, C19. Two pitchback wheels each driving two pairs of stones; operating.

MONKTON

1000

ST MARY MAGDALENE. Medieval W tower, much renewed. The rest rebuilt by *Hayward*, 1863, a characteristically austere design: windows with flush tracery, no buttresses on the S side. The E truss of the nave roof effectively forms the arch into the narrower stepped-up chancel. – STAINED GLASS. E window of 1874 by *Morris & Co.*, designed by *Burne-Jones*: Christ, the Virgin, and St John, erected in memory of the Gard family. – Four N windows and three S windows in the nave, of 1879, and tower window of 1892 also by *Morris & Co.* – There was also *Morris* STENCILLING on the walls, now lamentably hidden by colour wash.

MORCHARD BISHOP

7000

ST MARY. High up, with a dominating W tower rising to 95 ft; type B buttresses, short pinnacles, polygonal NE stair-turret. W window of four lights in the style of Exeter Cathedral. N and S aisles, both embattled. An indulgence of 1451 suggests that building work was in progress. The Perp windows may date from this time; the Dec designs are of the restoration by *George Vickery*, clerk of the works to the Earl of Portsmouth, in 1887–91, when the walls of the aisles, apart from the SE corner, were taken down to ground level. Chancel C18 with round-headed windows; panelling inside, below of timber, above of stucco. The arcades between nave and aisles are of three bays, the piers and arches of red sandstone (piers of B type with capitals only to the main shafts). Walls scraped in 1887–91 (but a SE

pier retains its marbling from the C18 work on the chancel). The
fourth bay opens from the chancel into the chancel chapels. Piers of
limestone, the arch on the s side with Perp panelling. The chapel
here was probably the Eyston family chapel. Tomb recess with a
MONUMENT, two recumbent figures supposed to be William
Eyston †1505, in civilian clothes, and his wife, who paid for the
completion of the aisle. The carving must originally have been of
respectable quality. – SCREEN. Reconstructed from original parts
which indicate tracery of B type and ribbed coving with Renaissance
detail between ribs as at Lapford. The restoration was by *Herbert
Read*; N part 1928–30, centre 1940. – Fine C18 REREDOS with
Corinthian pilasters. – COMMUNION RAIL. 1768 by *W. Stribling*.

SCHOOL. Substantial, in volcanic trap, with a patterned slate roof; a
bold C19 composition, with large Gothic windows in the gables.

Much cob and thatch in the village centre, late exteriors usually
disguising C16–18 buildings. Even for Devon, Nos. 1–13 FORE
STREET are exceptional, a long, continuous range of small C18
thatched cottages stepping gently downhill, with simple casement
windows, the odd sliding sash, and brick stacks.

BARTON HOUSE. Stuccoed early C19. Two-storey, three-window
centre with deep eaves, lower wings, and later ornamental brick
stacks. Very pretty Gothic LODGE, thatched, with knobbly tree-
trunk veranda.

EASTON BARTON. The substantial stone manor of the Eastons (or
Eystons), of late medieval origin. Perp doorway; one- and two-light
Perp windows to the hall. Projecting two-storey solar wing with later
windows; a stair-turret in the angle, with a small cusped window.
First-floor chapel.

Two early farmhouses – Rudge and Middle Ash – have unusual and
experimental roofs, probably earlier than most.

RUDGE. The handsome gentleman-farmer's s front with two
entrances, added in 1852 by a new owner, Philip Saunder, disguises
a substantial medieval house of stone on a three-room cross-passage
plan with C17 rear cross-wing and outshot extensions in cob, the
home of the Leigh or Rudge family from the C14 to the C18.
Beneath the C19 roof an almost complete early C15 roof similar to
Bury Barton, Lapford. Devon carpentry at its best: five massive
jointed cruck-trusses with scarfed joint and unpinned tenon, the
wall-post bearing on to a template, each truss with a heavy three-
quarter-round moulding. Early apex type: arch-braced collars,
wind-braces, threaded purlins, and the rare feature of additional
collars to each pair of common rafters. A smoke louvre survives over
the hall. In a ground-floor room square panelling dated 1776 and
decorated with stars, the emblem of the Leigh family.

MIDDLE ASH. Originally a late medieval three-room cross-passage
farmhouse with an early barn adjoining to the w. Instructive
sections remain of the early C15 jointed cruck roof, including an
intermediate truss of unusual two-stage construction.

MOREBATH

ST GEORGE. The lower part of the w tower unbuttressed, probably
C13, the upper part with saddleback roof obviously belonging to

Butterfield's restoration of 1875–82, as do the carefully asymmetrical s windows of one, two, and three cusped lights. Perp N arcade of five bays; A type piers with capitals only to the shafts. N aisle with wagon roof. N windows with ogee-hexagon tracery, still more Dec than Perp, and deep curved inner reveals. The chancel roof dates from an earlier restoration of 1849–50. – FURNISHINGS. Seating, pulpit, and altar rails all by *Butterfield*, as is the specially good FONT, a plain polished black quatrefoil on red columns. – STAINED GLASS. E window to Montague Baker Bere †1858 and N aisle E window to the Rev. Richard Bere †1875, rather crude colouring by *O'Connor & Taylor*. – MONUMENTS. Nicholas Sayer †1713 and family. Small; Corinthian pilasters and putti with achievement. – Anne Bere †1802. Mourning allegorical female. – Several pretty late C18 Bere tablets in coloured marbles.

MOREBATH MANOR. The former seat of the Beres, rebuilt in 1892–4 for Charles Digby Harrod, son of the founder of the London store. The long rhododendron-lined drive curves up to a large mansion with vaguely Jacobean gables: a weedy late C19 frontage in pale yellow brick with incongruous red brick chimneys sprouting from the slate roof. Pretty conservatory porch. (Sumptuous interior with elegant woodwork and plasterwork by *Jackson's*.)

TIMEWELL HOUSE. Handsomely sited with fine views s. Early C19, five bays, rendered, two storeys with parapet. Porch with paired Greek Doric columns.

7050

MORELEIGH

ALL SAINTS. Unbuttressed, unpinnacled, low early w tower. A small church; nave and s aisle of three bays with piers of Cornish (A) type and plain capitals only to the four shafts. Chancel roof simply but nicely plastered in the C17. – FONT. Circular, Norman, with one frieze of two intertwined wavy lines. – PULPIT. Stately, C18, with sounding-board. – SCREEN. The foot of one section used as a reader's desk.

(MORELEIGH HOUSE. The former rectory, built *c.* 1840. Three-bay front; bracketed eaves.)

4020

MORETON

½ m. w of Bideford

Now part of Grenville College (*see* Bideford). The house is of 1824, eight bays wide, two and a half storeys high, with a hipped roof and a one-storey, four-column porch. In the same style on the same estate HIGHER WINSFORD.

7080

MORETONHAMPSTEAD

ST ANDREW. At the higher (E) end of the little town, quite on its own, with a commanding w tower of four stages, under construction by 1418. Granite ashlar-built, with diagonal buttresses, a polygonal stair-turret, and short obelisk pinnacles. Two-storeyed granite porch, battlemented; the body of the church roughcast. N aisle of five bays, the arcade on octagonal granite piers with octagonal capitals and double-chamfered arches. Aisleless chancel of two bays. All windows Perp, of usual design. A singular absence of fitments of interest; most date from the restoration of 1904–5, when the church was heavily scraped. – Wood and glass TOWER SCREEN, 1980. – MONUMENT. Captain John Newcombe †1855. Flags and broken column. By *Stephens*; still classical.

ALMSHOUSES. The most remarkable building at Moretonhampstead. Two-storeyed, the ground floor opened in a loggia of eleven bays of which the middle one is distinguished as the entrance. All built of very large granite blocks. The crudely turned columns quite primeval-looking, yet the whole dated 1637. The continuous dripmould over the whole arcade, ending in square dripstones, still remotely in the Tudor tradition. On the first floor, low wide windows above the second, sixth, and tenth bays.

The distinctive feature of the town centre is the way in which seven narrow streets converge from all directions on to the irregular space called THE SQUARE, confusingly filled by a central group of shops and houses. The varied accents at the corners include the BOWRING LIBRARY, 1901, with a display of yellow terracotta (cf. Newton Abbot); MORETON HOUSE, demure rendered late Georgian, thatched, as is its neighbour; the WHITE HART, rendered, with Greek Doric porch, next to HOMELANDS, early C19, with Doric porch and bracketed eaves; and the WHITE HORSE (the town was at one time an important stopping-place for coaches; there were once many more inns). At the corner of Ford Street a much disguised pair of early C17 town houses with timber-framed jettied fronts, with one wall of a former three-storey back block surviving behind. Further down FORD STREET, FORDER HOUSE, with a pretty three-bay late Georgian front with reeded cornice and Tuscan porch, and PITT HOUSE of the same date.

Between The Square and the church the two parallel streets, FORE STREET and CROSS STREET, probably developed from a single broad market place. A fire in 1845 destroyed most of the older houses here. In CROSS STREET the former WESLEYAN CHAPEL, dated 1817, sideways to the road; further on, MEARSDON MANOR, late medieval in origin, with a lateral stack and a good screen inside; CROSS TREE HOUSE, the former London Inn, with irregular Georgian windows; and the UNITARIAN CHAPEL, a former Presbyterian meeting house, rebuilt in 1802. The Almshouses (*see* above) lie beyond, on the edge of the town.

WRAY BARTON. A neo-Tudor manor house of *c.* 1840. Symmetrical garden front with canted bays. Ruins of the late medieval house in the grounds.

Three relics from different transport eras: a TOLL HOUSE, S of the town on the A382, two-storeyed, with a canted front with deep porch; the former STATION, in Station Road, from which remain the engine shed with round-headed windows, the goods shed, and some octagonal cast-iron gateposts; and the former BUS GARAGE in Pound Street, an inter-war period piece with a plain, formal rendered front with porthole windows.

WADE MINE. Remains of three buddles, with wheelpit and dressing floors, and the ruins of associated buildings. Adits to the hillside above.

PREHISTORIC REMAINS. On BUTTERDON DOWN and on MARDON DOWN – islands of unimproved land – cairns, hut circles, and a stone circle survive. The stone circle, on Mardon Down, apparently of Bronze Age date, has recently been re-discovered; it was last heard of in the C18. Twenty stones survive, many recumbent. More impressive is the cairn circle or 'embanked stone circle' on the N summit. On the tops overlooking the steep sides of the Teign valley are two fine hillforts. CRANBROOK CASTLE, overlying an earlier reave- or field-system, faces across the river to Prestonbury Castle, Drewsteignton. From here panoramic views can be obtained over much of mid Devon. WOOSTON CASTLE has massive and complex earthwork defences still in excellent condition under woodland.

MORTEHOE

_4040_

Despite its closeness to Woolacombe, still a snug cliff village with slate-hung houses, the church high up in a commanding position close to Morte Point.

ST MARY MAGDALENE. Unbuttressed and unpinnacled N tower, with a rough pointed N doorway, crudely built of large stones and difficult to date. The earlier low round-headed doorway between tower and nave, and the S doorway, also round-headed, perhaps of _c._ 1170, when William de Tracey is supposed to have founded the church. C13 chancel with two lancet windows, unmoulded chancel arch on plain imposts; S transept perhaps also C13. A simple Perp N aisle was added E of the tower: two bays with rough octagonal piers, no capitals, two-centred chamfered arches. A more surprising addition is the arcade of one and a half bays between nave and S transept. One slender octagonal pier (with the date 1618) stands in line with the W wall of the transept, but behind it a diagonal connexion has been created between that wall and the nave S wall. It is vaulted and has two (new) two-light windows. What was its purpose, and what is its date? Ceiled wagon roof in the S transept, open in the nave. Restored in 1857–60 by _R.D.Gould_, and again in 1885. All the window tracery has been renewed.

BENCH ENDS. Forty-eight of the usual Devon type and designs – Instruments of the Passion, saints, coats of arms, many initials, profile heads in roundels. – MOSAIC. On the chancel arch, large figures in the Pre-Raphaelite tradition, oddly incongruous in their place; 1903 by _Selwyn Image_, given by Dr G. B. Longstaffe of Twytchen in memory of his wife. – ALTAR FRONTALS. Embroidered, also to _Image_'s designs (shortly before 1903). – STAINED GLASS. Two chancel S windows by _Hardman_, one commemorating the architect Thomas Lee, drowned off Mortehoe in 1834. – N transept E 1886 by _H.Holiday_, Christ stilling the waters, good colours, a fine dramatic work. – Four archangels in the diagonal transept windows by _Selwyn Image_. – Other glass mostly by _Beer_ of Exeter. – MONUMENTS. Tomb-chest in the S transept, probably to William de Tracey, rector of Mortehoe, who founded the chantry of St Mary Magdalene in 1308 and died in 1322. Incised figure of a priest with a chalice on the lid. The sides of the tomb show the Crucifixion, two saints, and otherwise only tracery, but tracery of considerable historical importance in so far as it can here be dated safely. That should help in the dating of much window tracery. The designs are of two- and three-light blank arches, the lights cusped and pointed, and besides cinquefoiled circles, pointed quatrefoils, and also ogee reticulation. – Mary Newell † 1700. Rustic cartouche. – Mary Heddon † 1889. Designed by *A. Lauder*, made by *H. Hems*. Angels and an ascending figure in a classical coloured marble frame.

METHODIST CHURCH. A robust and informal group of church and hall, Perp, contrasting purple and Bath stone, of 1878 and 1901 by *W. H. Gould*.

SPREACOMBE MANOR. At the end of a remote drive; early C19 stucco, two full-height bows, Doric two-column porch.

TWYTCHEN. A large, studiously Old English house, a surprise in the centre of a caravan park. Advertised for sale in 1878; rainwater heads dated 1881, with the initials G. B. L. for the owner, a Dr Longstaffe. Much variety of materials, a little too precisely organized to be as convincingly picturesque as Shaw or Ernest George could be. Lower walls of stone, with large asymmetrically grouped mullioned windows; upper parts slate-hung, with some half-timbering in the gables; tall red brick star-shaped stacks. Divided into flats, but much remains of the sumptuous contemporary fittings in a Morris-inspired style: spacious stair-hall with quarried glass in the landing window, library with painted inscriptions and stencilling above panelling, and an impressive reception room with embossed gilded leather panels, decorative plaster ceiling, and stained glass by *Selwyn Image*: four figures of musicians.

NORTH MORTE. A late-looking farmhouse, perhaps disguising an earlier building. At the rear a rare example of a detached kitchen block (cf. Little Hackworthy, Tedburn St Mary), a small, square building of stone rubble walls under a pyramid filled by a massive chimney/oven complex with several other flues blocked and reduced in height.

DAMMAGE BARTON. Very picturesque grey stone farmhouse, windows and chimneys C17, but remains of an earlier structure incorporated. 1656 datestone on a stable building. Barn with semicircular addition.

MORWELL BARTON

4070

The country residence of the abbots of Tavistock. A chapel was licensed here in 1391. Considerable parts of the medieval establishment remain, sympathetically but confusingly improved and altered by the Bedford estate in the C19 and later. An ambitious plan: four ranges round a generous courtyard, the front range with a central gatehouse reminiscent of the one at Tavistock, castellated and pinnacled, with a broad depressed arch under a square head with a boldly moulded dripstone. Rib-vaulted carriageway.

The hall range lies opposite; in the two-storeyed r. range three small two-centred doorways (now blocked) which must once have led to separate lodgings (interiors all altered). Another doorway in the entrance range to a stair leading to the gatehouse chamber, which survives little altered, with fireplace and garderobe. An adjoining heated upper chamber is reached by steps branching off the stair. The l. range is mostly taken up by a barn, but this is a later rebuilding – see the straight join between it and a moulded doorway remaining at the far end. The large porch in the right angle of the hall range is a C19 addition (shown on a plan of 1867), and the hall itself has been subdivided, but four partially smoke-blackened arch-braced trusses and an embattled wall plate clearly indicate its late medieval origin. Some of the windows with cusped heads may be C15, but much of the fenestration is due to C19 re-ordering, as is the central gable on the garden front of the hall range.

MORWELLHAM

4060

A river port on the Tamar, established at the highest navigable point for vessels of 10ft draught. The port existed as early as 1238, when it belonged to the abbey of Tavistock. In the C16 it passed, with the other possessions of the abbey, to Lord John Russell, and so to the Bedford estate, which had much to do with its later development when it had to cope with the rapidly expanding exports from the mines in the Tamar valley. The present road to the quay was made in 1744; the 4½m. canal from Tavistock, including a tunnel 1½m. long, was begun in 1803 and completed in 1817. The port's greatest activity came after 1844, with the discovery of important copper deposits at Blanchdown, above Gunnislake in Cornwall, only 5m. N of Morwellham, followed by the production of arsenic and other minerals from the late 1860s. The existing quays were expanded W and a new dock 290ft long was begun in 1859. But in the same year the railway arrived in Tavistock, the canal was abandoned, and as mining production declined by the end of the C19, the port fell into disuse. Its relics began to be restored by the enterprising Dart Amenity Research Trust from 1970 as an open-air museum.

The most striking landmark is the WATERWHEEL, 32ft in diameter, the present one brought from china-clay workings on Dartmoor in 1975 and re-erected by the remains of a manganese ore grinding works. The wheel was worked by a leat from the canal. Near the quay the SHIP INN, a CHAPEL of 1859, workshops, and cottages, among them a group built by the Bedford estate in 1856, similar to others built in and around Tavistock. Downstream are LIME-KILNS; on the slopes above, the remains of the Tavistock Canal INCLINED PLANE RAILWAY, between the dock and the canal 250ft above. Trucks were raised and lowered by a chain running from a drum operated by a waterwheel. Also on view are the farm buildings of MORWELLHAM FARM (with a good set of granite staddlestones and a threshing-box worked by a waterwheel), and higher up the entrance to the Tavistock Canal TUNNEL, constructed by the mining engineer *John Taylor* from 1803.

MOTHECOMBE

The house makes a delightful picture behind its white wooden palings at the end of the village street. The date is *c.*1720 but the house is still of the classic English post-Restoration type: five-bay front, two storeys over a basement, attics with dormers set in a big hipped roof above broad eaves. Built of roughly coursed stone, with plain angle pilasters, the central window picked out by quoins, the others with very flat segmental heads. The glazing bars were restored in the 1920s. The doorway has a flat hood on brackets supported by granite columns on high plinths. The effect is simpler and more homely than that of earlier and grander pilastered fronts such as Pynes, Upton Pyne. The builder was John Pollexfen, who referred in his will to the 'new house by me erected'. Conservative plan, with the doorway opening into one end of an entrance hall. The staircase lies beyond, and a secondary stair behind it. All the rooms, including the upstairs ones, have handsome bolection-moulded panelling. Some original fireplaces of plain marble with mirror-glass in narrow panels above the lintel. Stairs with three thick spiral balusters to the tread. Even the cellars are handsome, with brick groin-vaults on square piers (as at Plympton House, Newnham, and Puslinch).

The Victorian additions made at the back by Henry Bingham Mildmay (*see* Flete), who acquired Mothecombe in 1872, were partly removed by *Lutyens* in 1922–5 and replaced by a more sympathetic dining-room wing projecting from the s front, with a low hipped roof echoing the main house. It is approached by a groin-vaulted corridor along the back of the house, wittily contrived to create a *trompe l'oeil* impression of greater length by the arrangement of narrowing arches and a changing floor pattern. Anteroom panelled in plain pine, divided from the dining room by black fluted columns. Outside is a raised terrace, overlooking the C18 walled gardens. Lutyens also created the small back courtyard by adding a link to the remaining C19 service wing. His more playful details appear here: little casements over an arch in the s range, an oval bathroom window on the opposite side.

MUSBURY

St Michael. w tower C15, the rest much restored in the C19: chancel 1865; s aisle C15 with A type piers, but windows of 1867; N aisle and arcade, s porch, and the E part of the s arcade all rebuilt by *Hayward* in 1874–6. – REREDOS. Mosaic; 1878. – SCREEN, in the tower arch. Of iron and glass, designed by Major *A.J.Wright*, 1968. – STAINED GLASS. E window, pictorial, 1875 by *Gibbs & Moore*. – MONUMENTS. John Anning †1793. Marble inscription in wooden frame. – The church will be visited chiefly because of the Drake monument, erected in 1611 by John Drake to three generations of his family. There are three couples in this large standing wall-monument, kneeling before prayer-desks, each behind the other and all facing E. The pairs are separated by projecting pillars pierced in a W–E direction by two-light openings for the second and third couples to look through. Rustic figure carving. The top of the monument is missing.

MUSBURY CASTLE, an Iron Age hillfort covering 6 acres, overlooks the village.

See also Ashe House.

NETHER EXE
1½ m. N of Stoke Canon

CHURCH. On its own in a field near the site of a lost manor house. Small, Perp, nave and chancel in one, w bellcote (cf. Up Exe). Restored in 1890 and 1906 (new roof). PISCINA with trefoil arch. – FONT. Norman, square bowl with scalloped underside (cf. Cadbury, Christow), on short round shafts on a square base with scalloped top. – MONUMENT. Mary Young †1771. Cartouche and obelisk.

NETHEREXE BARTON. C16 and C17. First-floor chamber with a plaster ceiling with central pendant and floral motifs.

NETHERTON HALL
Farway

The property of Canonsleigh nunnery, acquired by the Prideaux family after the Dissolution and rebuilt in the early C17 by Sir Edmund Prideaux (dated 1607 on the w front). An C18 Prideaux drawing shows the house with the entrance front much as it is now, with a two-storey porch with a semicircular gable and four-light mullioned windows on either side. The house was 'a picture of ruin' in the later C18. The projecting s wing, formerly with a chapel, was partly demolished during restoration in 1836–44.

NEWNHAM
Plympton

Now within the Plymouth boundaries and nearly swamped by the Newnham industrial estate.

OLD NEWNHAM. Substantial remains of the major late medieval house of the Strodes, now a farmhouse. Hall range with a long irregular wing at its w end, projecting s. As one approaches the grey rubble stone group with its appealingly varied roof heights, the telling details are the garderobe attached to the gable end of the s wing, with its small quatrefoil side window, picturesquely corbelled out over a stream, and two massive chimneystacks, crenellated and pinnacled, which serve the kitchen and the tallest section of the same wing. This s wing appears to be early C16, providing accommodation of various types – see the irregular arrangement of four-centred doorways and straight-headed windows with depressed lights on the courtyard side (some perhaps reset). An upper doorway suggests there was once another range at right angles, enclosing an inner courtyard. Close to the hall range, the three-storeyed section is treated more grandly, with two pairs of three-light windows to ground and first floor, the lower ones (now partly altered) singled out by more delicate ogee heads.

The hall range is earlier than the S wing, as is clear from the remains of a fine canted oriel window at its W end, perhaps early C15: two cusped lights and a transom to each face (the side ones visible indoors). The wave-moulded two-centred entrance doorway to the hall could be of the same date. The main hall window of six unarched transomed lights and the two-storey porch must be later C16 additions. The porch has a broad doorway with carved spandrels, and an upper window with heavy square-ended dripstones. The part E of the porch was rebuilt later still.

The interior is full of puzzles. The oldest features are two stone arches in the W wall of the hall, discovered only in the C20, not of granite, and two-centred. They look as if they should be in a screens passage. Was the direction of the hall reversed before the oriel window was added; has the window been reset? A former screens passage here could explain the position of the kitchen, whose site near the high end of the hall is most unusual. The hall has a C16 fireplace in the back wall, with typical upswept ogee arch. Opposite the present hall entrance, a four-centred doorway to a wing supposed to be the former chapel (licensed 1432), now subdivided. The evidence for this is its roof with two moulded arch-braces and two tiers of wind-braces.

In the S wing, the two rooms with the three-light windows have excellent, well preserved early C16 ceilings, the lower one with moulded beams carved with foliage trails, the wall plates also carved. In the upper room a framed ceiling with carved bosses and a fireplace with upturned arch. Off the adjoining room a projection to the W, probably for a garderobe. The other rooms in this range, now used for storage, were once part of the extensive domestic accommodation, as the garderobe at the end indicates.

The entrance to the house may originally have been through this S range – see the large (rebuilt) archway in the W wall. The present approach from the S breaches the remains of an apparently defensive wall with arrow-slits, running alongside a stream. The whole site deserves further investigation.

NEWNHAM PARK. The new mansion of the Strodes, built c. 1700 on high ground, with a fine parapet, is one of the handsome compact gentlemen's mansions that were becoming the fashion in the Plymouth area at this time. Five by five bays, a little smaller than Plympton or Lyneham; hipped roof, dormer windows with alternating triangular and segmental pediments. The basement is of granite, the upper walls are now rendered. Central doorcase with segmental pediment and fluted pilasters, connected by an inappropriately grand porch of c. 1900. Interior of regular plan, with a good staircase at the back leading to a square central landing. Three balusters to the tread. The two front rooms refitted later, the drawing room on the l. with C18 Chinese wallpaper, the room on the r. with plaster painted to simulate panelling. Front basement rooms with groin-vaults on square piers (cf. Plympton, Mothecombe). Also one re-used doorway with a chamfered arch and several two-light windows, possibly from the old mansion of Loughtor, inherited by the Strodes from a branch of the Courtenays, which probably lay a little to the W (see the old drain beneath the front lawn).

NEWTON ABBOT

The town began as two settlements at the head of the Teign estuary: Newton Abbot, founded by Torre Abbey in a corner of the parish of Wolborough soon after the abbey itself was founded in 1196, and Newton Bushel to its N, on the other side of the river Lemon, established by the lord of the manor of Highweek, with a market by 1246. The river has been culverted (Sherborne Road marks the old boundary), and the two markets were combined in 1633 on the Newton Abbot site, so that the dual origin of the town is no longer easy to perceive.

But the two medieval churches still exist on the N and S fringes of the town, as do the two manor houses, Bradley Manor, replacing the earlier castle site at Highweek, and Forde House, to the E of the town, some way from its parish church on Wolborough Hill. In the late C17 Forde passed by marriage to the Courtenays of Powderham, who in the C19 initiated both the rebuilding of the town centre, and the attractive Italianate suburban expansion to the E, towards the new railway station of 1846. The town grew rapidly in the later C19, together with the railway works, although it never became heavily industrial, and the general impression of the suburbs is still of genteel villas scattered up the surrounding hills. In the C20 the large council estate of Milber was added to the E, and the built-up area has since expanded N to Kingsteignton.

The centre is a disappointment, for the traces of the unusual dual medieval origins of the town and the once distinguished C19 development have both been brutally disregarded by mid-C20 planners; the N end of Newton Abbot is one of the worst examples in the county of callous road engineering (cf. Teignmouth and Barnstaple). Here and elsewhere painful gaps cry out for sensitive new buildings which could help to relieve the mediocrity of the commercial development of the last twenty-five years.

CHURCHES

ALL SAINTS, Highweek. On a hill NW of the town. One of the two main medieval churches although until 1864 a chapel of ease to Kingsteignton. Consecrated in 1428, and provided with a burial ground. W tower with diagonal buttresses; no pinnacles. Unmoulded tower arch. Aisles with arcades of B type and low pointed arches. N aisle windows Perp; S aisle three-light windows very plain, of granite. The S porch forms the W bay of the S aisle. Old wagon roof. E end 1892. – FONT. With tracery panels on pillar and bowl; contemporary with the rest. – STAINED GLASS. A little in the top of a N window.

ST LEONARD, Wolborough Street. 1835 by *R. Millard*. Rubble limestone. W gable with octagonal turrets and (later?) traceried windows. Gallery on iron columns. Chancel added in 1876 by *J. W. Rowell*.

ST LUKE, Milber. Begun in 1936 to serve the housing estate E of the

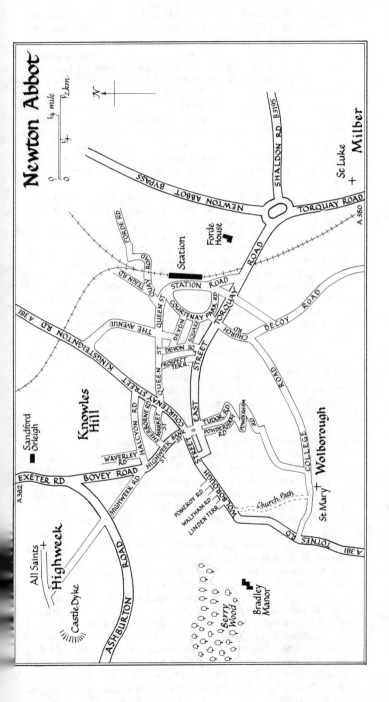

town. An extraordinary plan: a St Andrew's cross imposed on a long nave with apsed chancel so that three naves focus on the altar from different angles (a remarkable precursor of later liturgical planning). The plan is an interpretation of a church revealed in a dream in 1931 to the vicar, *J.Keble Martin* (better known for his *British Flora*). The architect was his brother, *Arthur Martin*. The building was completed only in 1963. Width, length, and height are all 1000 inches. The style is a pared-down Byzantine-Romanesque. Squat crossing tower with copper-clad pyramid roof. Rather dull rendered walls outside, but the interior of considerable interest spatially. Arcading on granite columns between the three naves. In the angular spaces between them, baptistery (N) and Oratory of Our Lady (S). NE Lady Chapel with stone altar, 1936, the first part to be built. The main altar also of stone.

ST MARY ABBOTSBURY, Waverley Road. 1904–8 by *E.H.Sedding*. Long flying-buttressed nave, wild W window with the swirling tracery divided by two strong mullions in the manner made popular by the architect's uncle, J. D. Sedding. The intended SW tower and spire never built. Passage aisles with detached shafts, with shaft-rings when one would expect capitals. Central E window, piscina, and pulpit re-used from St Mary's Chapel in Highweek Street (*see* Perambulation 2). The E window is unusually elaborate. It has the curvilinear star shape found in other local churches (Staverton, Ipplepen, etc.) and is surrounded by crocketed niches and badges of the Yarde and Ferrers families (*see* Bradley Manor, Public Buildings, below) – a useful indication of the C15 date of this tracery design (Richard Yarde died in 1467). – Elaborate SCREEN and REREDOS.

ST MARY, Wolborough. The parish church of the Wolborough section of the town, on a hill to the SW. Early W tower of two stages, unbuttressed, unpinnacled, with unmoulded tower arch. Nave and N and S aisles of six bays. Very shallow N and S transeptal chapels (with windows altered perhaps in 1710). The chancel of rubble projects beyond the aisles and is connected with them by two squints. The interior with piers of B type, but with the nice refinement of polygonal concave main shafts. The capitals Devon standard. S porch with fireplace and pretty doorway, decorated with leaves in the spandrels and fleurons in the jambs and lintel. The date of the S aisle (and presumably the S porch) is 1516.

FONT. Norman, circular, red sandstone with palmette decoration. – SCREENS. Rood screen across nave and aisles, and parclose screens to the transeptal chapels, all with mediocre painting of figures in the wainscoting. The tracery is type A, the coving missing. But there are specially fine friezes in the cornice. – LECTERN. Brass eagle on a heavily moulded pillar. Late C15, probably made in East Anglia. There are lecterns made from the same moulds at, e.g., Urbino and Oxburgh, Norfolk. – SCULPTURE. Fragments of a C15 alabaster panel of the Resurrection in the S porch. – PAINTINGS. Four Evangelists, C18; village art. – BELL in the church, with contemporary headstock and ironwork and two inscribed bands, early C15, by *John Bird* of London. – STAINED GLASS. Very small old bits in some window-tops. – C19 windows in the N aisle by *Kempe Studios*, an especially good one of 1890 of the Evangelists.

MONUMENTS. S chancel chapel: canopied table tomb, no effigy, inscription to William Balcall †1516. – Sir Richard Reynell (who built Forde House, q.v. below), quite grand, though the back wall is not in its original state. Erected in 1634. The two recumbent figures rest on a veined marble slab supported on coupled Ionic columns. Below, propped up on her elbow, Sir Richard's daughter, and right on the ground one baby. To Sir Richard's head and feet tall black Corinthian columns carrying an arch studded with putti heads, small allegorical figures, and an achievement on the entablature. Behind the columns two large standing figures: Justice (Sir Richard was a lawyer) and Time.

ST MICHAEL AND ALL ANGELS, Decoy. 1910. Red brick with stone dressings.

ST PAUL, Devon Square. 1859–61 by *J. W. Rowell*. Cruciform, with canted apse, lancet windows, and wooden bell-turret, rather awkward in its relation to the square.

ST JOSEPH (R.C.), Queen Street. W front with turrets and lancets, very old-fashioned. 1915 by *Scoles & Raymond*. Interior sensitively remodelled in 1976.

BAPTIST CHURCH, East Street. Two-storey turreted front decorated with bands of quatrefoils added in 1893 to a chapel of 1860 with lancet windows.

SPIRITUALIST HALL, East Street. The older Baptist Chapel, built in 1819, set behind a small burial ground.

UNITED REFORMED CHURCH, Queen Street. 1875. Redundant. A good solid W tower with crocketed balustrade and banded spire.

MAJOR HOUSES

BRADLEY MANOR. A remarkable medieval house still with many of its original features, given to the National Trust in 1938. In the C13 Bradley appears to have replaced Highweek Castle as the chief residence of the manor, which was granted to Theobald de Englishville in 1237, and passed to his nephew Robert Bushel. After 1402 the owners were Richard and Joan Yarde, the Bushel heiress. Much of the existing house is their creation. The Yardes moved to Sharpham in the C18, and Bradley was sold in 1751. Later owners included the Rev. Richard Lane from 1827, who made minor Gothic additions, and the Rev. Frederick Wall from 1841, responsible for less sympathetic Victorian alterations. Many of these were removed by Cecil Firth, who bought the house in 1909.

The house lies low in the wooded valley of the river Lemon, approached by a winding drive laid out *c*. 1830, which passes over the mill leat, and formerly arrived at an enclosing wall and gatehouse (demolished *c*. 1843). The delightfully varied composition of the late C15 E front makes a memorable impression: roughcast 61 walls with three uneven gables, a fourth gable set back on the l., the lower chapel coming forward on the r., all with Perp windows, and the long roof-line of the early C15 hall just visible behind. The central gabled section is an unusual addition: it provides an anteroom connecting porch and chapel, making the hall range two rooms deep – an exceptional arrangement for the C15. Within each gable is a tall corbelled-out first-floor window, cusped and tran-

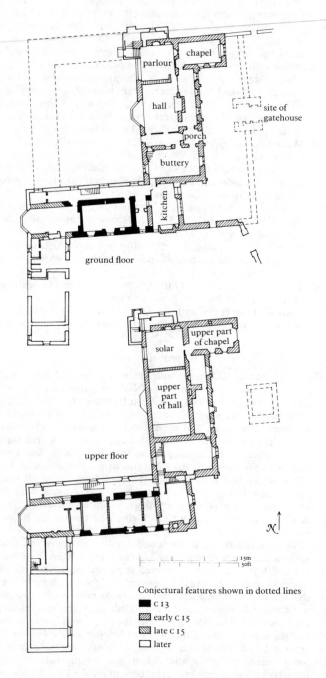

Newton Abbot, Bradley Manor: plan

somed. The little battlements are C19 embellishments, but the large carved head-stops to both upper and lower windows are largely original. The s gable and its window are C19 reconstructions. The chapel, licensed in 1428 and built up against the solar end of the slightly earlier hall range, has quite an elaborate Perp three-light window and straight-headed side windows of two lights.

On the w side the details are simpler: the hall unfortunately has a Victorian canted bay, but the two-centred chamfered doorway of granite is original. To the s is a range with an outer wall of the C19 which conceals an older – possibly C13 – two-storeyed building, whose upper room was originally approached by an external stair. Formerly, stable ranges to the N and W completed a small courtyard. The existing service wing projecting further s was added in the C17.

The hall survives open to the roof, of plain arch-brace-and-collar construction, datable to the early C15 from the arms of Yarde and Ferrers in the NE corner. In the C16 the parlour to the N was enlarged at the expense of the hall. Tudor arms are painted on the dividing wall. Between hall and antechapel, in place of the oriel window, a fine wooden screen of c.1530–40, with Renaissance ornament above linenfold. The CHAPEL has a wagon roof with carved bosses. In the w wall an early C15 window, formerly an external window of the parlour. Above there was formerly a w gallery which could be approached from the solar. (Fragment of a C15 alabaster angel with chalice at the foot of the cross.)

The service rooms s of the hall have been altered, but one original archway from the screens passage remains. The buttery is now a single room, probably once subdivided. S of it the former kitchen, with a large granite fireplace.

In the s range, within the C19 corridor, the former outside wall and traces of the external stair which led up to a pair of first-floor doors. The w one led into an upper chamber created in the C15, when this range was lengthened and re-roofed. The room has been subdivided, but in its E part the late medieval decoration is preserved, discovered behind C19 plaster in 1975: a striking pattern of black stencilled fleur-de-lys, with feigned drapery. On the E partition an IHS monogram with symbols of the Passion, possibly later. In the SW corner fragments of C16 painted decoration with Renaissance detail and pilasters. The adjoining chamber to the E was fitted up in the late C17, with panelling and a ceiling with delightful high-relief plasterwork garlands and shells. Above the buttery a large chamber with a coved ceiling and a plaster overmantel with the coat of arms of Yarde and Hele, c.1600.

CASTLE DYKE, Highweek, W of the church. A small motte and bailey commanding a clear view of the Teign estuary, probably a manorial residence of the C11–13, later succeeded by Bradley Manor (q.v. above).

FORDE HOUSE (Teignbridge District Council). The Wolborough manor house lies E of the town in its own grounds, stranded between railway and bypass. Its relatively modest early C17 exterior gives no clue to the surprise in store inside: a quite exceptionally rich display of wood-carving and – especially – plasterwork.

The manor belonging to Torre Abbey was bought in 1545 by John Gaverocke. The house in its present form is however the creation of Sir Richard Reynell, a lawyer, who had acquired the manor by the early C17 (the date 1610 appears on a rainwater head). By the time he entertained King Charles I in 1625 the decoration of the suite of first-floor rooms was probably complete. There are no major later alterations, for when the house passed by descent to the Courtenays it ceased to be a family seat.

Above the rendered E-shaped s front with its far-projecting wings rise five blind semicircular gables. Below them are two storeys of symmetrically arranged mullioned windows, the upper ones largely renewed, the lower ones with hoodmoulds forming a continuous string. The back has no projections. Here the blind gables are alternately semicircular and triangular. But the irregularity of the three storeys of windows on this side, like the differing floor levels inside, point to an older building remodelled. The low rear kitchen wing may also pre-date the existing house.*

The little plaster vault of the front porch, with its pendant, and the good studded door in a moulded frame give a foretaste of the craftsmanship to be found within. The ground-floor hall is entered in the traditional way at one end. It is not large, but comfortably fitted up with good panelling with a frieze, a carved overmantel, and a plaster ceiling with single ribs and angle sprays. At the high end two splendid faceted doors (cf. the early C17 examples in Exeter) reminiscent of Serlian designs. At the lower end another similar door. At the restoration of 1981–3 the woodwork was painted brown and cream in accordance with known contemporary colour schemes.

The main staircase, with sturdy carved newels and octagonal balusters, is fitted into a fairly tight space behind the hall. It leads up to the great chamber, by this time clearly a more important room than the hall, for it occupies the whole length of the w wing. The shallow barrel-vault is decorated with some of the most spectacular plasterwork in Devon. It is a little narrower than the total width of the room, no doubt owing to the form of the roof concealed above. At the sides are brackets bearing delicately modelled figures (cf. Widworthy), and a frieze. In the centre, broad enriched ribs enclose large square panels with winged horses – a favourite motif in Devon plasterwork. Cherubs' heads on the pendants. Arms in strapwork at the ends.

The other first-floor ceilings along the front of the house provide a delightful survey of the early C17 plasterer's repertoire. King Charles's Room, opening off the great chamber, has the popular pattern of intersecting single ribs and angle scrolls, and an elaborate tympanum with strapwork enclosing a roundel with a mermaid. Then comes a smaller room with a double-ribbed ceiling and frieze. Two barrel-vaults follow, the second unusually decorated with isolated small strapwork cartouches. At the end is a taller room in the E wing with single ribs and fat bosses. Behind it lies a

___

*Discoveries during repairs confirmed that Reynell remodelled rather than rebuilt. The evidence found for an older house includes remains of a N doorway to the screens passage, part of a turret stair by the hall chimneystack, and the ends of two cruck blades for trusses over the main range. Blocked mullion-and-transom windows were also found in W and E walls of the wings.

secondary stair. Plaster ceilings also to the two ground-floor parlours in W and E wings, the W one grander, with double ribs and a frieze made from the same moulds used for the small strapwork cartouches on the upstairs ceiling. (This design is also found in No. 10 The Close, Exeter.) Both rooms have contemporary wooden overmantels. The columned screen in the W room is clearly a later alteration. Some of the details of the plasterwork at Forde, for example the Netherlandish strapwork and some of the panel motifs, tally closely with designs assembled in the Abbot sketchbook at the Devon Record Office. The plasterers and woodcarvers responsible for disseminating this up-to-date style in C17 Devon may have been influenced by the work of the Dorset architect-mason *William Arnold* (cf. e.g. Montacute, Somerset), although this ornate decorative taste at Forde was not matched in the architecture itself.

Other features to note in the house include a corridor behind the hall, unusual in the C17 and perhaps a remnant of an earlier building phase; in the back wall at first-floor level the remains of a former newel stair; and, half-way up the main stair, a small mezzanine room (created in the C17, as it cuts across an earlier doorway). It is prettily painted with floral scrolls, renewed in the 1930s.

Good vermiculated C18 GATEPIERS with balls.

PUBLIC BUILDINGS

TEIGNBRIDGE DISTRICT COUNCIL OFFICES, to the E of Forde House, at a tactful distance. 1985–7, the original design by *L. Manasseh & Partners*, completed by the *District Council Architect's Department*. The elevations constitute an ingenious paraphrase in modern materials of C17 motifs: a rectilinear pattern of mullions is suggested by a free-standing green-painted grid supporting oriel windows on two floors, and the variety of the C17 roof-line is echoed by the alternation of steep gables with the small glazed semicircles of the top-lit corridors. The lift towers of uneven height, capped by little pitched roofs, are less successful. The entrance, from the N, is frankly of the late C20, through a big canted greenhouse porch.

LIBRARY AND TECHNICAL SCHOOLS, Bank Street. 1901–4 by the Cornish architect *Silvanus Trevail*, a proud statement after the town had become a single local authority in 1901. Grey limestone lavishly decorated with yellow terracotta. Below the corner gable, spandrel figures in relief.

SEALE-HAYNE AGRICULTURAL COLLEGE, 2m. NW. Founded by Charles Seale-Hayne M.P. A large complex on a hill, 1909–14 by *Gutteridge & Gutteridge*, with some later additions by *Beare & Claydon* and, more recently, by *Lucas, Roberts & Brown*. Large quadrangle with red brick and stone buildings in a rather fussy free Tudor. The gatehouse entrance with stripey turrets and broad segmental arch is the best feature.

COMPREHENSIVE SCHOOL, The Dyrons, Wain Lane. By *Stillman & Eastwick-Field*, c. 1973–6.

HOSPITAL, East Street. The dignified stucco entrance block (now Outpatients) with large archway and links to pavilions (one

heightened 1901) dates from the workhouse built in 1836–9 by
Scott & Moffat (cf. Tiverton, Bideford). Round-headed rusticated
windows. The District Finance Office on the l., also stuccoed, was
the old Poor Law Offices. The rest much rebuilt, an uphill straggle
of buildings in grey limestone with brick dressings, 1871 onwards.
To the r. the formerly separate hospital and dispensary, with a N-
facing wing in pretty cottage-hospital style, with mullioned
windows and half-timbered gables, by *Samuel Segar*, 1897.

MARKET HALL. 1871 by *John Chudleigh*. His adjoining Corn
Exchange, with tower over the entrance, has been converted into
the ALEXANDRA THEATRE. Solid chunky Italianate, grey
limestone.

STATION. 1924–5. Rectangular three-storey neo-classical block of
red brick with pilasters and stone dressings. Central dentilled pediment, flanked by mansard-roofed pavilions.

PERAMBULATIONS

1. To the south and east

The tower of ST LEONARD at the central crossroads is all that
remains of the medieval chapel of ease to Wolborough in the
Newton Bushel part of the town. Two stages, unbuttressed, grey
limestone. The rest of the church was rebuilt a little further down
the road in 1835 (*see* Churches, above). In front of the tower the
octagonal PLINTH of the market cross, with inscription commemorating the 'first declaration of William Prince of Orange of
the Protestant Religion and Liberties of England' in 1688. S of the
tower a few relics of the pre-C19 town: the low stretch of Nos. 1–11
WOLBOROUGH STREET, Nos. 1–3 with three gables, a timber-
framed structure, No. 9, the SHIP INN, also timber-framed, disguised behind later stucco. They make an odd contrast with the
other three corners, which aim at Regency urbanity. The grandest
effort is made by Nos. 2–6 COURTENAY STREET, stuccoed, with
paired pilasters, a few neo-Grecian trimmings (mostly stripped
off), a pair of fluted Greek Doric columns at the rounded corner,
and another pair to a shop in Courtenay Street. Opposite is the
GLOBE HOTEL, built by the Earl of Devon in 1842, stuccoed,
with channelled quoins, four-column Tuscan porch across the
pavement, and a side elevation of five bays embellished by a central
balcony. To the E an adjacent block of similar size, with large
arched first-floor windows for the former assembly rooms. Then
remnants of stucco terraces, much rebuilt and interrupted by the
undistinguished shopping precinct of 1975–9 (*Taylor Woodrow
Architects' Department*) on the site of the town hall and market
(q.v.). At the end, the Edwardian LLOYDS BANK, a busy classical display with paired Corinthian columns of white stone set
against red sandstone.

Now E along QUEEN STREET, which starts with a C20 horror, but
is essentially early Victorian; neatly detailed stucco terraces with
dentilled cornices. Shops below, upper floors at first two windows
wide, then only one, all with decorative surrounds. On the S side a
later three-storey range, where No. 58 has a well preserved former
chemist's shop of *c.* 1900, complete with pub-style engraved glass

and Baroque mahogany fittings. s of Queen Street the artisan houses of PROSPECT TERRACE (stuccoed on the w, later striped brick opposite) are worth a glance, as a contrast to the classier (and strictly segregated) streets parallel to it. The prelude is DEVON VILLA, set at an angle at the junction of Queen Street and St Paul's Road opposite the WAR MEMORIAL, an elaborate bronze affair of 1922.

ST PAUL'S ROAD leads to DEVON SQUARE, the centre of the development carried out for the Courtenays c. 1840–60 by the local architect *J. W. Rowell*. He adopted a provincial version of the type of *villa rustica* advocated by J. C. Loudon, ingeniously adapted to the demands of the site. At the level top of the square, the s side has a three-storeyed stuccoed palace frontage: projecting ends, shallow gabled centre, boldly rusticated doorways. Along the sloping w sides a terrace of villas steps smartly up the hill, each with a projecting centre with a pair of narrow arched windows above the door. The N side had both types, on a less ambitious scale. Immediately to the E, the back of COURTENAY PARK ROAD, 135 which forms an irregular crescent around the park overlooking the station; large semi-detached villas, mostly variously gabled, although one has deep eaves and a tower.

The s end of the Devon Square development is TORQUAY ROAD, with lesser stuccoed houses, from which EAST STREET leads back into the town centre. At the start of East Street, groups of mid C19 ALMSHOUSES, first Hayman's (Nos. 133–147) of 1840, still in an angular Regency Gothic, stuccoed and bargeboarded, then Reynell's (Nos. 109–115) of 1845, granite, with more correct Perp windows and central archway. Opposite, the former workhouse (q.v.: Hospital). Further along a few bitty remains of older houses. Cottages along an alley glimpsed through an archway in No. 55; No. 53, with nice C18 wooden doorcase and door, a carriage arch at the side; Nos. 35–37 (LOCOMOTIVE INN), low, two-storeyed, perhaps C17 in origin, with large chimneystacks behind; and, on the s side, the ABBOT'S LARDER, with a stuccoed-over jetty.

On the slopes of Wolborough Hill to the s, a lesser version of the Devon Square development: large villages along POWDERHAM ROAD, climbing steeply around a green; minor stuccoed terraces behind in TUDOR ROAD. Near the top, HIGHWOOD HOUSE, large, with a tower, in its own grounds.

Finally along WOLBOROUGH STREET. The beginning is a dismal mess of roundabouts and car parks. But on the s side an attractive cluster of older houses has been preserved: the 'Manor House', three-storeyed, with massive end stacks; several stucco fronts concealing older houses; the early C19 BIRCHINGTON HOUSE, with broad vermiculated archway; and No. 83, stone, with neo-Grecian Doric porch to its projecting centre. Then the long range of MACKREL ALMSHOUSES, 1874 by *Rowell*, extended 1894, all eighteen houses in crazy-paving limestone, with a continuous veranda and a little gabled stone entrance to each house. Off to the N terraces in similar limestone (with red-brick dressings) in POMEROY ROAD and WALTHAM ROAD, although LINDEN TERRACE is in the earlier stucco village style. A few more individual villas up CHURCH PATH, the short cut leading to St

Mary Wolborough. In Bradley Valley, neo-vernacular housing by *Ted Levy Benjamin*, 1978, a quite nicely grouped roofscape.

2. To the north

At the Highweek end of the town less of interest survives. From St Leonard's tower N up BANK STREET, past a tall, busily Italianate frontage (a former Post Office). Beyond Bearns Lane a much altered but once attractive lower terrace (pilasters with Egyptian capitals). The GOLDEN LION has a quiet early C19 corner frontage, easily missed behind the ugly lorry park. At the road junction, the proud terracotta Library (q.v.), and to the r. down MARKET STREET the more demure LIBERAL CLUB, a large C19 villa with triple-arched loggia on the first floor (a later alteration?). To the l., up the widened HIGHWEEK STREET, pathetic remnants only. No. 2 is the best later C18 house in the town, red brick with blue headers, elegantly compact. Pedimented projecting cornice; shallow bow-windows through two storeys; pedimented doorcase with columns. Tactful late C19 extension in similar brick, with a Shavian oriel window. An early C19 brick house opposite; porch with granite columns.

Further up the hill the gables and tower of the former ST MARY'S HALL and SCHOOLS, a picturesque but sadly derelict group, preserved as the *raison d'être* of all the demolition opposite when the road was widened, but scandalously left to decay for many years.* The hall was formerly a medieval chapel of ease to Highweek. The pinnacled Perp tower dates from a mid C15 enlargement by the Yardes of Bradley Manor; the two-and-a-bit crenellated gables clasping the tower belong to a remodelling of 1826, when the medieval arcade between nave and S aisle was removed. Further alterations were made in 1870 by *J. W. Rowell*. In 1904–6 the mid C15 E window of the S aisle and other features were removed to St Mary Abbotsbury (q.v.).

Nothing else remains in this area except for Nos. 1–3 at the start of HIGHWEEK ROAD, an early C19 stone pair with the two front doors neatly set beneath a single elliptical arch with glazed fanlight. Pilasters and moulded band. Along Highweek Road a few individual C19 villas (No. 10, in its own grounds, and No. 30); No. 16 has a quaint early C19 chapel-like front (a conversion?).

SANDFORD ORLEIGH, Exeter Road. Built *c.*1830 by George Templer after he had sold Stover House (q.v.), and subsequently the house of Samuel Baker (of the Nile). Rambling, stuccoed, with slightly eccentric Tudor detail: battlemented bay-windows and sash-windows with quatrefoil entablatures and dripstones. Similarly eclectic inside: E room with an arcade with (re-used?) A type piers with carved capitals, crowned by clumsy cusped arches, and a neo-Jacobean ribbed ceiling. NE (former billiard) room with brought-in early C17 overmantel.

3. To the north-east

This part of the town grew only in the later C19. THE AVENUE, built in 1888, running N from Queen Street opposite the Devon

---

*Repairs were begun in 1988.

Square development, shows how Rowell's villa style responded to the High Victorian taste for more colour and texture: at first the groups of houses are stuccoed, then of yellow brick trimmed with red, and, even more jazzily, of crazy-paving limestone with red brick and Bath stone. KNOWLES HILL beyond is picturesquely sprinkled with more affluent detached later C19 villas in their own grounds, one castellated, but most with gables.

E and NE of The Avenue are the flat marshes around the Teign estuary, mostly C20 industrial, but with intermittent remains of earlier rubble stone warehouses, dating from when this was an important transhipment centre. At JETTY MARSH, further N, remains of the QUAY of the Stover Canal (*see* Teigngrace), with a commemorative stone to George Templer, 1824, and parts of the lock gates. Another jetty at the end of Forde Road. By TEIGN ROAD, alongside the railway line, an impressive range of later C19 warehouses and maltings; rubble with red brick dressings. Two half-hipped gables projecting over loading bays; two pyramid-roofed malting kilns. QUAY ROAD, with humble stuccoed artisan terraces, leads back up to Queen Street. Beyond the railway line remnants of extensive G.W.R. locomotive and carriage building workshops.

BERRY WOOD HILLFORT. On a limestone hill with steep sides. Limited excavation of the interior has produced evidence of circular houses, with finds datable to the C1 B.C. and A.D.

NEWTON FERRERS

5040

HOLY CROSS. Perp w tower and N and S arcades with piers of A type. The rest rebuilt in 1885–6 by *G. Fellowes Prynne*. In the chancel early C14 Cornish polyphant PISCINA and sandstone SEDILIA. – The interior is dominated by Prynne's rich WOODWORK, all carved by *Hems*. – Alabaster and marble REREDOS by *J. D. Sedding*. – STAINED GLASS. E, S aisle E, and nave NW windows by *Clayton & Bell*.

GNATON HALL. A former seat of the Heles, partly rebuilt for Henry Roe 'in a neat and substantial manner' (Polwhele 1806), but apparently rebuilt again for H. R. Roe by *J. Birch* (villa about to be erected, drawing exhibited 1826). Courtyard plan. Rendered seven-bay entrance front, the centre with rusticated quoins, pediment, and a large Doric porch. S front with central bow-window. Inside, C19 floral ceiling painting.

PARSONAGE FARM, Parsonage Road. An example of the superior medieval house which later became a modest farmhouse. Its C19 exterior with sash-windows to the front is a total disguise, although it looks of this date because of its width, which could indicate double-room depth: in fact, it is an exceptionally large medieval building, as the prestigious stone door at the rear with early C15 mouldings indicates. But it is the roof which is most remarkable: of crown-post type, the crown-posts surmounting arch-braced collar trusses, with curved wind-braces. One jointed cruck truss to the cross-wing. Large stacks in the rear wall.

NEWTON POPPLEFORD

0080

ST LUKE. A medieval chapel, a chantry chapel in the C14, later
dependent on Aylesbeare, of which the small rubble W tower
remains, with Dec W windows, square-headed belfry windows,
and a N turret rising above the parapet (restored 1936). The rest
reconstructed in 1826, when the S aisle was added, a broad space
divided off by cylindrical wooden posts. Brick chancel with lancet
windows of 1875 by *R.M.Fulford*, who also added the octagonal
wooden posts close to the N wall to give the illusion of a N aisle. –
SCREEN. 1903.

Newton Poppleford was one of Devon's medieval new towns. A
market was granted in 1226 to William Brewer, Lord of
Aylesbeare. The pattern of the original layout is still evident in the
long street of cottages which runs E downhill from the widening
near the church. Several demonstrably old houses, including the
EXETER INN (a former church house, with a long rear room with
outside stairs), a house with a two-storey porch, and others with
lateral stacks, especially a group on the S side where the stacks in
Beer and Salcombe stone show various decorative devices. Other
early structures are heavily disguised, as in the terrace opposite.
Here ST MARY'S and the adjoining cottage, convincingly early
C19 in appearance, incorporate the hall and two-storeyed upper
end of a late medieval hall house (cross-passage and lower end
destroyed). The stud-and-panel screen preserves its original painted decoration: panels with repeating stencilled patterns of fleur-
de-lys, crowned M, five-leaved motif, and flower head, all with
zigzag decoration on the chamfers and the studs.

TOLL HOUSE. The oldest in Devon, built in 1758, a small rectangular thatched cottage at the junction of the A35 and the A376.

BRONZE AGE BARROWS. A good group on VENN OTTERY
COMMON, W of Venn Ottery.

NEWTON ST CYRES

8090

ST CYRIAC AND ST JULITTA. Up a steep slope W of the main road.
W tower short and strong, with low diagonal buttresses and stair-
turret. S porch of ashlar with wave-moulded doorway. Ambitious
Perp N aisle with three-light windows, their hoodmoulds on
animals and figures, buttresses between them, and little figure
niches above them; battlements and pinnacles, renovated in 1830–1
by *R.Cornish*. Inside, the N windows have shafts descending to low
sills. Arcade with piers of B type, standard capitals, two-centred
arches. N chancel chapel with panelled arch and ogee PISCINA. Old
wagon roofs in nave, aisle, chancel, and S porch. Older than all this
the chamfered round-headed rere-arch of the S doorway – evidence
for an aisleless C12 church. Restored 1913 by *E.H.Harbottle*.
– REREDOS. C19 Dec panels. – FONT. C18, of marble; also the late
C12 base for a four-columned font. – PULPIT. Good, plain late C18,
of mahogany, with a large sounding-board. – Painted ROYAL ARMS
of James II, 1685, a rarity. – CLOCK. Restored working mechanism, by *Lewis Pridham* of Sandford, 1711. – WOODWORK. Two
carved panels (Flemish?) incorporated in lectern and aumbry.

MONUMENTS. The church will be chiefly visited because of the
Northcote monument. In the middle John Northcote †1632, a 87
whole figure in high boots with sword and baton. To his l. and r. in
medallions the busts of his two wives with the following inscriptions: the first, 'My fruite was small/One Sonne was all/That not at
all'; the second, 'My Jacob had by mee/As many sonnes as hee/
Daughters twice three'. Below, the kneeling figures of his son, wife,
and children (original colouring), and two babies placed on the
ground. Plenty of inscriptions in which certain letters singled out in
red read as Roman numerals and confirm the date. – Another (tiny)
monument: to Sherland Shore, †1632 at the age of seventeen, seen 88
sitting by the table with his books, one elbow on the table, his cheek
on his hand, the attitude of the Tuckfield monument at Crediton 85
(and by the same carver?). – A good series of monuments to the
Quicke family. Thomas Quicke †1701. Tablet with broken voluted
pediment. – John Quicke †1704 and wife †1706. Oval, framed by
swags held up by cherubs. – John Quicke †1776. Coloured marbles
and urn. – Andrew Quicke †1793 by *Kendall* of Exeter. Urn and
tablet against a grey slab.

GLEBE HOUSE (former rectory). The usual dignified rendered early
C19 house.

NEWTON HOUSE (now flats). The former seat of the Quickes. Dull
rebuilding of 1909 after a fire. Rendered, with mullioned windows.
The grounds linked to the churchyard by a bridge (renewed) made
over the new turnpike road in the early C19.

(SHERWOOD HOUSE. By *Walter Cave*, 1918, for his cousin Adrian
Cave. Square plan with small central courtyard.)

(HORWILL DOWN. Regency, five windows, rusticated quoins.)

Much good C15–18 cob and thatch in the village centre, despite a
1960s road widening which was accompanied by an unusually
simple and sensitive local authority redevelopment: one- and two-
storey houses grouped around a village green alongside the new road
– a principle that could with benefit have been imitated elsewhere.

Many C15–17 farmhouses in the parish, the best EAST HOLME and
EAST HOLME COTTAGE at WEST TOWN, a long cob and thatch
farmhouse, now subdivided. Basic three-room cross-passage plan;
C16 extension at the service end. The C15 roof survives complete on
jointed-cruck trusses with chamfered arch-bracing and wind-
braces. The remarkable feature is the survival of original framed
closed trusses over stud-and-panel screens at each end of the hall,
subdividing the smoke-blackened roof and demonstrating that
there were always two separate halls heated by separate open-hearth
fires. Good subsequent additions: two lateral stacks in local volcanic
stone, a gabled stair-turret at the rear, a C16 stone fireplace, and
C16–17 cross-beams.

STATION. A wooden building apparently incorporating a signal box;
probably of 1851.

NEWTON ST PETROCK

4010

ST PETROCK. The oldest part no doubt the W tower, unbuttressed,
with an unmoulded pointed arch towards the nave. The rest all
Perp, N windows as well as S (chancel 1887), and the arcade between

nave and s aisle (four bays with granite piers of A type, capitals only
to the main shafts, and depressed pointed arches). – FONT. Norman; a shapeless big circular bowl on a short shaft. – PULPIT. C19
but with old panels of the Instruments of the Passion. – BENCH
ENDS. A large coherent set, with initials, coats of arms, Renaissance
scrolls, etc. – COMMUNION TABLE. Elizabethan.

NEWTON TRACEY

5020

ST THOMAS OF CANTERBURY. A modest church with several C13
windows preserved. w tower unbuttressed and unpinnacled, the
arch towards the nave round-headed and unmoulded. Perp w door
with arms identified as those of Pollard, Bourchier, and St Leger. N
aisle with a clumsy, round pier with a shapeless capital, perhaps
C13, no doubt hewn out of an older wall, discovered when the
present aisle was built during the restoration of 1867 by
R.D.Gould. – FONT. Early C13, still in the shape of a cushion
capital, and with cable mouldings at the waist, but with recognizably stiff-leaf foliage in low relief at the angles. – s and w doors with
good IRONWORK: straps with fleur-de-lys.
(NEWTON BARTON. A former manor house with the remains of a
frieze and a coat of arms of c. 1600 inside.)

NORTHAM

4020

ST MARGARET. A big church. Tall w tower, a landmark for shipping in Barnstaple Bay. Diagonal buttresses and pinnacles; polygonal stair-turret on the s side near the E angle. w door with
fleurons. N aisles, s transept. Extensively restored in 1849–65 by
David Mackintosh (the E window of five lights is modelled on
Houghton-le-Spring, County Durham). Wide nave with wagon
roof on angels; wagon roofs also in the transept; all much renewed.
In the nave, apart from the usual foliage bosses, some with those
symbols of the Passion which usually appear on bench ends. The N
aisle was added as late as 1593, as marked on one of the piers ('This
yele was made anno 1593'): five bays, octagonal piers with raw
capitals, double-chamfered arches. Chancel rebuilt 1865. – FONT.
C13, octagonal, with the flat blank arches of the table-top type (but
pointed). – Good Victorian STAINED GLASS. Two s windows by
Hardman; w window by Lavers & Westlake. – ORGAN CASE by
Cross of Exeter, the pipes decorated by the heraldic expert the Rev.
Charles Boutell and his daughter. – Several minor MONUMENTS of
the late C18/early C19 by such sculptors as Kendall of Exeter,
R.D.Gould of Barnstaple, J.Osborne of Bath, and Johnson of New
Road, London. – Sir Charles Chalmers † 1834 and his wife † 1840.
Oval inscription plate with lovely scrolly black-letter script.
The church lies back from a little square at the end of FORE
STREET, behind a much rebuilt CHURCH HOUSE with C19
cusped windows on two floors. The gabled front of the UNITED
REFORMED CHURCH provides another stone accent among the
white-rendered cottages. At the corner of Cross Street an engaging

BANK, an early C19 house with upper pilasters on inverted capitals. Further up the street one older house with a large lateral stack. In CROSS STREET, a long lane of white-walled cottages, the WESLEYAN CHURCH, 1878, Gothic, and Nos. 50–54, an odd building with giant pilasters and an attic floor with narrow little windows set into a high hipped roof. Beyond this, by NORTH EAST STREET with a few irregular older houses to NORTH STREET, which leads back to the square past a house with a pretty balcony.

To the S, up the hill, several larger houses, e.g. by the crossroads NORTHAM HOUSE, with Gothic glazing, and CROSS HOUSE. For houses off Heywood Road *see* Bideford.

See also Appledore *and* Westward Ho!

NORTH BOVEY

High up close to the E parts of Dartmoor, with a village green with old oak trees.

ST JOHN. All granite, the tower unbuttressed, of huge ashlar blocks, with a stair-turret, the body of the church roughcast. Perp window tracery, somewhat renewed. Buttressed aisles. Wide, low interior; arcades of five bays on octagonal granite piers with double-chamfered arches (cf. Chagford). Ceiled wagon roofs in aisles and chancel. Early C20 restoration by *Sir Charles Nicholson*. – FONT. Simple, octagonal, of granite. – SCREEN. Across nave and aisles. Tracery of A type, the coving gone; solid spandrels with blank tracery, the cornice with a single band. The most remarkable motif is the small statuettes above one another in the door surround (cf. Manaton). Parclose screens with three-light tracery. – BENCH ENDS. Partly two-tier tracery, partly larger leaf motifs. – STAINED GLASS. N aisle, first from E, four C15 evangelist symbols in the upper lights; third from E, remains of finials.

W of the green, at a tactful distance from the village centre, a compact group of white-walled houses with linking garages around a fore-court. By the *Michael Jaquiss Partnership*, 1977–8.

THE MANOR HOUSE HOTEL. The estate was bought by W. H. Smith († 1891), the lavish neo-Elizabethan mansion built in 1906–7 for W. F. D. Smith, later second Viscount Hambleden, by *Detmar Blow*, with *Walter C. Mills* as site architect. Comparable to Castle Drogo in scale, but without the sparkle of Lutyens. Restrained garden front of irregularly coursed granite with Bath stone dressings, magnificently set above terraces overlooking lake and river. The main part of the house is dignified by a triple-arched central loggia below a shaped gable; the domestic wing to the S, of equal length, rather boringly continues the line of the main roof. Additions to N and E in more rudimentary Tudor (1935). Eclectic interiors. The entrance hall, with a plastered barrel-vault, leads to a spine corridor with many Perp stone archways and a large Jacobean staircase. Facing the garden, the drawing room, with a good plaster ceiling and a wooden overmantel, and the great hall, formerly open to a splendid timber roof, with minstrels' gallery and huge stone fireplace; a floor was inserted (quite tactfully) in 1984. Service courtyard with stone archway between attractive diagonally set towers with hipped roofs. Jacobean LODGES.

The parish has several outstanding longhouses, especially at Lettaford and Westcombe.

LETTAFORD is a typical Dartmoor hamlet of three longhouses and associated farm buildings, and a former Methodist Chapel, converted to holiday accommodation. Of the longhouses, one has a lower end rebuilt in the C19; SOUTHMEAD still preserves its shippon as a store; but SANDERS is one of the best surviving examples anywhere on the moor. Repaired in 1975–7 by *Paul Pearn* for the Landmark Trust. The gable end of the shippon has walls of huge square ashlar granite blocks graduating into rubble masonry elsewhere: this, loss of the original shippon roof, and the higher roof levels over the house suggest considerable rebuilding. The separate shippon entrance looks inserted (surrounding stonework disturbed). Inside, it displays the classic features of splayed slit windows, central drain, stones drilled for tethering stakes along lateral walls, and early hayloft cross-beams. Later insubstantial timber partition to the cross-passage. At the upper end of the house, three late medieval roof-trusses survive, two on short raised crucks. The chamber jettied into the hall from the upper end has an original closed truss carried out on joists with rounded ends over the solid cross-wall of the inner room. Of the second chamber jettied out over the cross-passage at the lower end of the hall only a few joists survive (the rest were destroyed by the inserted axial stack and staircase). At the rear, an outshot and linhay. Opposite the rear cross-passage door, a good small barn of little squared granite blocks.

WESTCOMBE. A hamlet of two houses and farm buildings, including a circular ASH HOUSE with a stone-corbelled turf roof. The surviving longhouse is comparable in quality to Higher Shilstone at Throwleigh and Hole at Chagford. As at Lettaford, the shippon is of huge squared granite ashlar, but here with a round-headed granite doorway, unique in this gable-end position. Part of the shippon was later incorporated into the house with its own stack and a higher roof, though the original roof survives, on huge raised crucks; yoked apex, with smoke-blackening extending even to the upper part of the shippon truss, suggesting that the house and shippon were not originally separated by a solid full-height partition, as they were at Higher Shilstone. Upper chamber jettied out over the solid cross-wall of the inner room: nine massive joists, all chamfered and rounded, surmounted by square moulded bases to carry the bottom rail of the chamber wall. The C17 hall ceiling is of equal quality.

BLACKALLER HOTEL. A long range of two-storey white-painted buildings under a slate roof, once a WOOLLEN MILL. Opposite, one of the circular conical-capped ASH HOUSES (to store ashes for use as fertilizer) to be found around the village; there is another good example, recently restored by the Dartmoor National Park, at Westcombe (*see* above).

TIN MINING was carried out in the parish from medieval times to the C20. VITIFER and BIRCH TOR, opposite the Warren House Inn on the B3212, are the largest tin mines on Dartmoor. There are remains of intensive activity including tin-streaming, beamworks, shafts, and modern opencast mining; also leats and the remains of mine buildings.

PREHISTORIC REMAINS. The fine triple STONE ROW running up the hillside S of Headland Warren Farm was vigorously restored in the C19; its earlier form is not known. Large BARROWS crown many of the hills. On SHAPLEY COMMON is a particularly interesting BRONZE AGE SETTLEMENT of subtle features.

The square stone-walled ENCLOSURES on the hillsides were for the rabbits of HEADLAND WARREN.

NORTHCOTT   3090

A hamlet of Boyton, across the Cornish border.

BOYTON MILL. Early C19, three storeys, of rubble stone, with machinery and overshot waterwheel.

EARTHWORK, S of the mill in Northcott Wood, overlooking the Tamar. A defended enclosure, probably of the Iron Age.

NORTH HUISH   7050

ST MARY. Low early W tower with corbel-table below the battlements, diagonal buttresses only at the foot, a low stair-turret, a narrow undecorated doorway, and an unmoulded tower arch. The upper part is now slate-hung, and a spire added (when?). N transept, S aisle. The S aisle arcade with piers of A type and raw capitals to the four shafts. The S tracery is supposed to be of 1880, but the patterns are very singular for that date. A radical reordering took place in 1984, when the S aisle was divided off by a concrete wall and the ROOD SCREEN was removed and re-erected as an entrance screen. It has three-light panels, spandrels with thick canopy-work, and thin strips of decoration in the cornice. Pierced wainscoting (not original?). Old wagon roofs, also in the S porch. C13 PISCINA.

BLACK HALL. The C17 seat of the Fowells, improved in the C18 (according to Polwhele), with fine grounds, altered and enlarged for Hubert Cornish in the early C19. Five-bay front, paired pilasters at the ends, pediments to the ground-floor windows.

NORTHLEIGH   1090

ST GILES. Perp W tower with stair-turret, plain Norman S doorway, low Perp N arcade, Perp N chancel chapel with panelled arch to the chancel. Extensively restored: chancel rebuilt 1858, the rest given new windows and roofs in 1868–9 by *C.F.Edwards* of Axminster. – PULPIT. Jacobean. – SCREENS. One to the chancel with three arches of the same width, the central one for the entrance, the l. and r. ones with four lights each and Perp tracery. The coving original. – Another to the N chancel chapel, very simple, with late Perp tracery. – BENCH ENDS. Quite a number in the nave. – STAINED GLASS. Three complete late C15 figures in the N chapel E window (heads removed), clearly from the same workshop responsible for the Doddiscombsleigh glass. – E window, Christ in Majesty, 1872 by *Hardman*.

NORTHLEW

ST THOMAS OF CANTERBURY. A small but aisled church with some interesting remains of the Norman period, namely the lower parts of the unbuttressed W tower (windows on S and N sides), the W doorway with one order of colonnettes and a pointed arch, and the low inner tower arch, also pointed. The rest Perp: the pinnacles of the tower, the aisles with their four-bay granite arcades (piers of A type with capitals only to the main shafts and depressed pointed arches) and their windows (S side four lights and Perp tracery, set into a wall of ashlared granite; N side straight-headed without tracery), and the unceiled wagon roofs. In the S aisle and the N chancel chapel the roof has angels against the wall plate; in the N chancel chapel in addition outstandingly exuberant bosses spreading out big leaves in four directions. Restoration 1884–5 by *R. M. Fulford*. – FONT. Norman, a square bowl with saltire crosses and rosettes, on five columns; much restored. – SCREEN. Mostly new; only the wainscoting original. – BENCH ENDS. One of the set dated 1537. The date is interesting, as there is no Renaissance ornament anywhere, only tracery (some with Flamboyant forms), initials on shields, and the like. Repaired by *Hems*, who was also responsible for the new PULPIT, LECTERN, and ALTAR.

In the smaller of the two village squares, a CROSS with an ancient base, restored in 1849.

NORTH MOLTON

ALL SAINTS. Tall three-stage tower with type B buttresses, a niche with a (bad, though original) figure of the Virgin on the S side, a high plinth, an arched W door, and battlements decorated with quatrefoils. The tall pinnacles have, alas, been removed. Three-light aisle windows, and a three-light E window with an ornamental transom and dripstone with angel stops. The church was restored from the 1870s, chiefly in 1884–5 by *Ashworth*. The five-bay arcades inside have piers of A type with capitals only to the four main shafts. Above the arcade the un-Devonian motif of a clerestory. Its windows are low, of two lights, with decorated spandrels. Wagon roofs with bosses, that to the nave with cresting on the tie-beams and a celure over the screen.

FONT. Octagonal, Perp, with small figures against the shaft, and pointed quatrefoils and panelling against the shallow bowl. – PULPIT. Timber, but otherwise of exactly the same type as South Molton, with figures added by *Hems*. The sounding-board of *c.* 1700 has a trumpeting angel on the top. – SCREENS. Perp rood screen, of standard A design, all across nave and aisles. Reconstructed; the coving and spandrels have gone. – The two parclose screens differ in design: one has sixteen narrowly set, ungrouped lights with tall crocketed ogee tops, the other three panels of four lights each. – CHANCEL PANELLING. 'Jacobean', though probably as late as the middle of the C17; of domestic origin, brought from Court House in the 1840s (arms of the Parker family and their connexions). Obelisks as crowning motifs. The whole quite exceptionally ornate. – CLOCK. Of *c.* 1720. –

STAINED GLASS. N chapel E, painted lights with the four evangelists, perhaps C18. – Chancel *c.*1862, in the style of *Lavers & Barraud*.

MONUMENTS. Sir Amyas Bamfylde †1626. Big standing wall- 86
monument of alabaster, Sir Amyas recumbent, his wife seated at his feet, her hand against her cheek, the whole flanked by columns and crowned by an open segmental pediment. Their seventeen children shown kneeling against the tomb-chest and against the back. Original railings. – John Burgess †1758 and his wife †1772. Coloured marbles; inscription and urn set against a large marble oval; gracefully done by *King* of Bath. – In the churchyard, good inscribed slate tombs of the earlier C19, e.g. by *Honey* and *Roberts* of South Molton.

The church stands proudly above an irregular square. The village was at one time more important; a centre of the woollen industry until the C18, it prospered also from the mines in the parish, worked from the C16 to the C19. On the E side of the square, the SCHOOL, the former church house, enlarged 1875, with two storeys of large Tudor windows. To the W, in a more secluded position, COURT HOUSE, a former seat of the Parkers, later owned by the Bamfyldes. Built in 1553. Long two-storey stone front, the r. side with square-headed Tudor windows, the porch with an outer Tudor doorway. On the l. side later C17 windows with mullions and transoms. One room has Tudor panelling and a fireplace surround of 1692 (the latter from Poltimore House, q.v.). (Elsewhere, good bolection-moulded panelling, and, in a projecting rear addition, an open string staircase with twisted balusters.) E of the church was COURT HALL, now demolished, the Bamfylde house, chiefly late Georgian.

MINING REMAINS are visible on both sides of the Mole valley N of the village. Iron, copper, and even a little gold were mined from the C16 to the C19.

BARROWS. Excellent groups can be seen on Exmoor, from North Molton ridge on along the ridge from Two Barrows, past the Five Barrows group (actually containing seventeen extant or destroyed barrows) and on into High Bray parish (q.v.).

NORTH PETHERWIN   2080
In Cornwall since 1974

ST PATERNUS. Its chief architectural features connect the church with Cornwall more than with Devon: N aisle with thick circular Norman piers with many-scalloped capitals. Double-chamfered pointed arches. Clerestory windows (a rarity both in Cornwall and Devon) not above the apexes of the arches below, but above the piers. This oddity appears to be Norman at St Germans and later at Lostwithiel and Fowey. The style of the small Petherwin clerestory windows (and the aisle windows) is *c.*1300. The rest of the church Perp. W tower with diagonal buttresses, gargoyles below the battlements, and big cusped pinnacles. S aisle with Perp windows and granite arcade of five bays with piers of A type and capitals only to the main shafts. The Norman piers are followed on the N side by a chancel chapel of two more bays identical with the s arcade. C15 roofs to aisles and S porch. – SCREEN. Only part of the wainscoting of the screen survives. – COMMUNION RAILS. Now under the tower arch, with big balusters and other ornamental motifs which make the initially surprising date 1685 quite convincing. – BENCH ENDS. Only a few, with Instruments of the Passion. – BRASS. Leonard Yeo †1621. Inscription and two shields. – INCISED SLABS. Dorothy Killigrew †1634. – Three daughters of Edmund Yeo †1638.

(THE GLEBE. Regency stucco with Gothick windows.)

NORTH TAWTON

ST PETER. Much of the outside is of granite ashlar. E.E. W tower, low and unbuttressed, the shingle spire renovated in 1900. Nave and two aisles. Arcades of six bays with granite piers of A type with capitals only to the main shafts. The arches are nearly semi-circular. No structural division at all between nave and chancel. Sanctuary added in 1832. Unceiled wagon roofs to nave and aisles. W gallery on iron posts, 1829 by *Charles Hedgeland*, altered 1900. – FONT. Shell bowl on stem, 1832, still late Georgian in character. – BENCH ENDS. Some in the nave; others re-used behind the altar (tracery panels with pretty roses in leaves in the spandrels). – STAINED GLASS. C15 angels with shields in the tracery of one N window, including the Champernowne arms, as on one of the nave benches. – S aisle E, and a pair at the E end of the aisles, by *Drake*, 1877, 1879; adjacent S aisle window by *R. M. Driffield*, 1893.

EARTHWORK, in the village centre. Much denuded; regarded variously as a small moated site or a low motte. It has no known history. North Tawton manor was held of the lords of Plympton.

There was a market at North Tawton in 1270, but the town has declined to a village. In the square a former MARKET HOUSE, built in 1849 in an attempt to revive trade, plain, of stone, with two gables. Triangular market place, with a mean Jubilee clock tower of brick, plain early C19 stuccoed houses (replacements after several fires), and the remains of one notable older house of stone, BROAD HALL. Gable-end with late medieval six-light projecting bay-window, with a doorway on the l. Arched lights, the mullions (where not replaced) enriched with finely carved Perp foliage. A large chimneystack on the l. also belongs. Later parts with the date 1680.

STATION. Built c. 1865. Two-storey station house and single-storey offices of Dartmoor granite with lighter ashlar dressings; round-headed windows in pointed arches. Canopy with decorated brackets.

BURTON HALL, to the N. A C19 villa with weatherboarded walls, rather trim, very Victorian, yet curiously outlandish in detail. The explanation is that the building was brought from Norway by Fulford Vicary, the owner of the woollen mill, in 1870.

WESTACOTT BARTON. An example of the larger farmhouse, cob and stone under thatch, with an extensive range of cob farm buildings. The complex plan illustrates development from a simple late medieval hall to a later C17 house of some quality. The late medieval smoke-blackened roof survives complete with its original thatch, with evidence for a partially floored stage before a fully two-storeyed development. But the most important period was the late C16 and early C17, when the house was substantially extended both to the W and by a good two-storey E cross-wing. Another cross-wing was added in the C18, running S from the front range. The E cross-wing presents rural sophistication at its richest: ground-floor room with ten-light oak window with king mullion, upper chamber with similar five-light window, the unusually symmetrical architectural composition crowned by a gable roof over these windows to emphasize their importance. Early C17 plaster ceilings on both floors (the original joists beneath are moulded as well). The upper ceiling is particularly elaborate, of kite pattern, with a central pendant. It was repaired in 1984, after virtual collapse, by *Paul Pearn*. The design is very similar to that of Cottles Barton (q.v.). A final touch of C17 display is the modelled brick stack to the original range. Interior with C17 and C18 panelling, door frames, and built-in settle.

At ASHRIDGE BARTON and CROOKE, remains of medieval houses with chapels. UPCOTT FARMHOUSE has a medieval roof (entirely smoke-blackened, and with a smoke vent), a lower wing dated 1609, and good C17 joinery.

BURSTON. Plasterwork has been moved to Marston Hall near Grantham, Lincolnshire.

WOOLLEN MILL (former). A complex of stone buildings round a courtyard. The works were powered first by water and later by steam.

ROMAN FORT. A site of strategic importance, controlling the crossing over the Taw of the main routeway into Cornwall. The remains, which stood some 6 ft high until ploughing during the Second World War, lie S of the railway, adjacent to the river. Aerial photography revealed a complex of other Roman military works nearby.

BROAD NYMET. *See* Bow.

See also Cottles Barton.

NORTH WYKE
South Tawton

6090

Now the Grassland Research Institute. The substantial and interesting mansion of the Wykes or Weekes family, who lived here from the early C13 to 1714. The improvements and reconstruction carried out by *G. H. Fellowes Prynne* in 1904 for the Rev. Mr Wykes-Finch have tended to obscure the fact that the house is basically medieval, on a courtyard plan, with late C17 modernization.

The main courtyard, with buildings on three sides, is now approached from the W, through a wall with sturdy gatepiers with ball finials, on the site of a lost W range. Historically one should begin with the medieval gatehouse in the S range. It is two-storeyed, with a broad four-centred entrance arch and windows with unarched lights. Over the archway the arms of Edward VI. On the courtyard side three small arched openings to apartments. The E arch leads to the former chapel, possibly the one licensed in 1438. It had a chamber over its W end (rebuilt in 1904). The

adjoining crenellated E range is entirely of 1904, on old foundations. The N range has a handsome later C17 seven-bay front, with
tall mullion-and-cross-windows (of stone on the ground floor,
unusual in Devon), and a hipped roof, with original, very sturdy
double-A-frame trusses, above deep eaves continuing round the W
front. However, the irregularly placed doorway in the old screens-
passage position, the inner and outer basket-arched N doorways,
and the windows of the N wall suggest a C16 origin for this range.
It is one room deep, with staircase projections to the N (the stairs
reconstructed in 1904). W of the passage the former dining room,
with an Edwardian ceiling and the Wykes arms over the fireplace.

To the N a service courtyard with former stables and a long E
range with brewhouse and kitchen, C16 or older. Well preserved
interior features on the first floor: chamber above the kitchen (the
armoury) with C16 panelling and cupboards (one concealing a
trap-door to a hiding-place next to the brewery fireplace); adjoining room with plaster arabesque frieze; and stud-and-panel partitions elsewhere, partly reset, although the solid steps up to the
attics look authentic.

NOSS MAYO

A market was established here in 1286, and Noss was called a borough
in the C14; it is now only a small fishing village beside a creek of the
river Yealm, facing the older settlement of Newton Ferrers across the
water. Several quirky Baring estate cottages of the 1880s (see Membland).

ST PETER. Built by the Barings to replace a chapel of ease (the ancient
parish church is at Revelstoke, q.v.). A proud Perp church of 1882
by *J.P. St Aubyn*. W tower of red sandstone in a commanding
position. Arcades with Devonian piers but steeply pointed arches.
Richly decorated: chancel with marble facing and stencilling with
angels in quatrefoils; stencilling also in the nave; elaborate
REREDOS (triptych and wall frieze) and other contemporary
furnishings by *Hems*; STAINED GLASS by *Fouracre & Watson*.
LIMEKILN, set into a bank on Bridgend Quay. Early C19, massive
and semicircular, the hearth now enclosed by an outbuilding.
S of Noss Mayo, along the coast inland from Warren Beach, a massive
WARREN (or VERMIN) WALL built to keep rabbits in their place on
the cliffs. Nearby is the former Warrener's Cottage.

NYMET ROWLAND

ST BARTHOLOMEW. A small church, modest Perp apart from the
Norman S door (undecorated arch, no tympanum, a little decoration
on the imposts of the arch). The arcade between nave and N aisle (of
three bays, with type A piers and capitals only to the main shafts) is
of interest because it is of timber. Large round-headed window on
the S side dated 1636. In the N aisle an original wagon roof. Chancel
restored in 1874 by *Samuel Hooper* of Hatherleigh (new E wall);
general restoration 1889. – FONT. Norman, of cup shape, with

cable and concentric semicircles as decoration of the shaft; the bowl completely plain. – STAINED GLASS. Partridge memorial window, by *Veronica Whall*, c. 1927.

CLEAVEHANGER. Behind the late Georgian front block a medieval house with hall, cross-passage, and attached shippon. Smoke-blackened C15 roof of exceptional carpentry: jointed crucks with wall-posts to ground-floor level; early yoked apex. Wind-braces over the hall, and arch-bracing to the central truss. Early C16 stud-and-panel screen with full-height upper partition.

OAKFORD

ST PETER. Medieval tower with diagonal buttresses and later obelisk-pinnacles. The rest rebuilt in 1838 by *R.S.Pope*. Long, broad, unaisled interior, formerly with galleries; tall triple lancet windows. Chancel with chancel arch and Perp windows inserted 1903 by *E.Buckle*. – Minor MONUMENTS to the Spurways, the earliest to Margaret Spurway †1691, and children. Small, with painted drapery and rustic reclining figure. – STAINED GLASS. Some interesting contrasts. Among the traditional designs, e.g. W tower 1905 by *Heaton, Butler & Bayne*. – Exceptional chancel S window with Arts and Crafts patterns of inverted red heart-shaped flowers, by *Heywood Sumner*, 1891. – Nave NE to John Spurway, 1908: Art Nouveau figures with delicately toned faces strangely contrasted with brightly coloured formalized drapery, set within clear glass. By *Arild Rosencrantz*, the Danish designer who was responsible for the first English window made by Tiffany's (at Wickhambreux, Kent).

Oakford is a tiny, unspoilt village on a hillslope. Village shop in the former Melhuish Memorial Chapel (*T.Baker*, builder, 1838). Further down the former SCHOOL, c. 1840, with Tudor windows and a shaped gable.

OAKFORD MANOR, next to the church. Owned by the Spurways since 1613, remodelled in modern Georgian style by the Rev. William Spurway (†1837), retaining the earlier staircase.

STUCKERIDGE. A beautiful site on a hill S of the Exe valley. Rendered Regency house of two storeys with broad eaves; a trellised one-storey veranda on two sides. S front of five bays with arched ground-floor windows. At Stuckeridge Cross a pretty thatched and whitewashed Gothick LODGE. Windows with intersecting glazing-bars. Another similar but larger lodge close to the CHAIN BRIDGE over the Exe that leads to the N drive.

OFFWELL

ST MARY. W tower with stair-tower and diagonal buttresses; outer S doorway Dec, with ballflower, rebuilt in the C19. But the core of the church is of c. 1200: see the S chancel window and the plain semicircular chamfered chancel arch. Perp N arcade with A type piers, the easternmost capital with naked figures. Late Perp panelled arch between chancel and N chapel. The WOODWORK repays a good look. Pieces of different dates, some assembled by the Coplestones. – PULPIT. Erected 1724; carved figures of the evangelists added 1784. – READER'S DESK, made up in 1935, incorporating a richly carved Flemish panel of the Last Supper. – PANELLING from a former W gallery. – BOX PEWS of 1798, altered 1853. – TOWER SCREEN. Two bays from the medieval rood screen brought from St Mary Major Exeter in 1970. Perp tracery of four lights with small paired lights above, like a separate window. Dado with four painted saints on the r. Rich cresting with angels and foliage (the same design as the cornice of St Andrew's Chapel in Exeter Cathedral). – PAINTINGS. On the N wall, Lord's Prayer and Creed with Royal Arms in between (repainted 1974). – Texts over the N arcade. – STAINED GLASS. E window of c.1850, pre-Ecclesiological. – N chapel E with Flemish roundels in the top lights. – MONUMENT. Joanna Southcott †1696. Well proportioned Baroque tablet with broken voluted pediment.

OFFWELL HOUSE. Stuccoed, two-storeyed, with projecting eaves and tented verandas. Built in 1828 for Edward Coplestone, Bishop of Llandaff.

BISHOP'S TOWER, Honiton Hill. Crazy Italianate campanile, 80ft high, with machicolation and cast-iron trim, built in 1843 by Bishop Coplestone (†1849) as a water tower, to provide work for the unemployed and, reputedly, a view towards his diocese of Llandaff. The nearby house, rendered, with two square bay-windows, dates from 1847. LOWER LODGE with pretty decorated bargeboards.

The village is somewhat spoilt by C20 expansion. Bishop Coplestone was responsible for the COTTAGES with rustic porches, the little SCHOOL in Tudor style, and the former RECTORY, solid Elizabethan of 1845.

OKEHAMPTON

ALL SAINTS. The medieval parish church lies outside the town on a hill to the W in a large churchyard. There is a reference to the rebuilding of the whole church in 1448. It was rebuilt again, accurately, in 1842–4 by *Hayward* after a fire. He retained the tall three-stage Perp W tower of granite ashlar with B type buttresses and crocketed pinnacles, and also the Perp piers of A type with capitals only to the shafts. Interior embellished in the late C19: large REREDOS, of stone, 1891 by *Hems*; STALLS and ALTAR RAILS 1892; PULPIT 1872. Remains of the old REREDOS against the W wall of the S aisle. – STAINED GLASS. One S window by *Morris & Co.*, 1898, St Cecilia and angels. – N window by *Kempe Studios*, 1900. – Others by *Ward & Hughes.*

Downhill to the N the former VICARAGE, many-gabled and chimneyed C19 Tudor, possibly around an older core.

ST JAMES. Chapel of ease in the town, dominating the E end of Fore Street. Medieval granite W tower, B type buttresses, obelisk pinnacles. Blocked three-bay N arcade on octagonal granite piers. Restored in 1862 by *Ashworth*. Dull interior, apart from Perp, Tudor, and C18 WOODWORK worked into reader's desk and pulpit, the latter dated 1662.

BAPTIST CHAPEL. 1889, enlarged 1901. Minimal Gothic, but with a tall doorway with rusticated quoins.

EBENEZER CHAPEL, North Street. Now in industrial use. Once

quite elegant; a plain rendered early C19 front with pilasters, side niches, and an oval recess above the doorway.

UNITED REFORMED CHURCH, St James Lane. 1903, crazy-paving limestone, a spirelet on one side.

OKEHAMPTON SCHOOL, Mill Road. Good 1930s work of the County Council. Rendered walls and grey slate roofs; quadrangular layout. Additions of the 1960s.

The town was founded in the late C11 by Baldwin de Brionne, sheriff of Devon, on a site between the East and West Okement rivers, some way from the church on the hill to the w, and Baldwin's castle to the sw. Domesday Book refers to a market and four burgesses. The town is chiefly one main street: High Street, West Street, Fore Street, East Street, much of it widened and rebuilt in the C19, and suffering from the lack of a bypass for too long in the C20.

The best buildings are in WEST STREET and FORE STREET, between the two rivers. On the N side the TOWN HALL, with a fine ashlar granite five-window front of 1685, built as John Northmore's house and owned by the Luxmores from 1740 to 1821. Bold moulded stone string courses between the three full storeys. Hipped roof above a wooden modillioned cornice, which rises as a pediment over a coat of arms (perhaps a later alteration). Later canted bay above the entrance. The back parts earlier. Well preserved late C17 interior features: bolection-moulded panelling in the front r. room; an adjoining closet, fitted in the space behind the stairs (cf. Bridgeland Street, Bideford), which rise at r. angles to the central passage and continue through three storeys. Sturdy newels with pendant acorns. The first-floor front room was adapted as a council chamber after 1821 (when the Guildhall in the centre of the main street was cleared away). Across Market Street, LLOYDS BANK by *Horace Field*, 1908, neo-Georgian, with alternating pediments, tactfully picking up some of the details of the Town Hall. Opposite, the WHITE HART, looking early C19 with its four-column Tuscan porch with nice lattice balcony above, but also a late C17 house of five bays – see the three-storey stair rising around a small well, in an otherwise much altered interior. Georgian upper assembly room on the l.

Behind the Town Hall RED LION YARD, a shopping precinct of c. 1980; agreeable spaces, crudely mechanical pseudo-vernacular detail. The more confident Victorian equivalent is the ARCADES of West Street, still with its original shopfronts. Main entrance from St James's Street, dated 1900, embellished with plenty of terracotta and a cast-iron entrance veranda. In this area a few older houses around St James's chapel, notably Nos. 1–3 ST JAMES'S STREET, low, with massive stone stack, next to the stuccoed C19 KING'S ARMS. Off to the s PARK ROW, a complete street of simple early C19 stuccoed artisan terraces. The slightly grander ones in KEMPLEY ROAD lead to MILL ROAD, with remains of an industrial miscellany including the three-storeyed OLD MILL with waterwheel.

SIMMONS PARK, s of Mill Road, alongside the East Okement, was opened in 1907. Prettily laid out, with gatepiers with iron overthrows, boulder-studded walks, half-timbered lodges, and at the end a large, frilly-bargeboarded Swiss chalet.

STATION ROAD, running steeply uphill from Mill Road, has a progression of C19 suburban villas. The earliest (Nos. 26–38) are of c. 1840 (well before the railway arrived in 1876), an unusual design reminiscent of Plymouth neo-classical. Stuccoed pairs, each with a large central tripartite pedimented staircase window. Side entrances, tapering Egyptian gatepiers. Back towards the town centre, Nos. 14–16 come as a surprise, a daring attempt to be modern by the Okehampton Building Co. in 1936. Progressive cantilevered porches and balconies, flat-roofed stair-towers at the ends, but all arranged in traditional symmetry. Then the medley of a MASONIC LODGE, 1900 by *A. Lucas*, in a C17 classical manner, No. 2, with an early C19 five-bay front with heavy classical doorcase, and KENT HOUSE, a solid tile-hung villa of the 1890s in its own grounds.

NORTH STREET has a good late C19 BOARD SCHOOL with picturesquely varied gables and plate-tracery windows, and the MILL HOUSE, a rustically handsome late Georgian front with broad gable, central window below an arch with triple keystone, and a doorcase with a bold egg and dart cornice.

EAST STREET leads uphill out of the town. Nos. 11–13 are early C19 stucco, with an arched carriageway (a former inn?). Then, fragmented by too many garages, a sequence of mid C19 pairs and terraces with overscaled bracketed stone doorcases.

OAKLANDS, Oaklands Drive, on a hill N of the town. A large mansion with an exquisitely chaste neo-Grecian exterior, built for Albany Savile M.P. Begun c. 1816 by *Charles Bacon*, completed by his pupil *Charles Vokins* in 1820, illustrated in Ackermann's *Repository*, 1826. Two show fronts of finely laid ashlar. Seven-bay S front with an entrance porch of four plain giant Ionic columns, with capitals derived from the Erechtheum in Athens. W front with two Ionic columns in a recessed three-bay centre, flanked by single bays with paired giant Doric pilasters. Roof concealed by cornice and tall parapet. Alas, only pathetic remnants survive of a once magnificent but no doubt impractical interior after hamfisted conversion to flats in the 1930s. Octagonal entrance hall with corner niches, flanked by library and breakfast room, each with a simple marble fireplace. Of the central toplit stair-hall, with imperial stair and ten scagliola columns, only a couple of columns remain walled up in a cloakroom. Pretty octagonal LODGE with rustic veranda. Another LODGE of similar date in Ranelagh Road further W.

53 CASTLE. In a remarkably picturesque situation on a spur of shale above the rushing West Okement river. Higher woods to the sides; the knoll itself also so well wooded that the craggy fragments of walls tend to disappear when the trees are in leaf. Yet the castle is one of the largest in Devon, and of considerable architectural interest. The story of its development from the C12 onwards has been much clarified by Dr R. Higham's excavations of 1972–80.

The castle built at the Norman Conquest by Baldwin de Brionne passed in the 1170s to the Courtenays, who held it (with a brief interruption in the C15) until 1538. It is mainly of the native shale, with dressings largely of aplite, a type of granite quarried near Meldon close by from the C12.* Of the early castle, the large motte and the defensive bank to its W are the most obvious survivals. The

*The date of a fine carved head, probably from the top of an archway (cf. Parkham), found in the excavations.

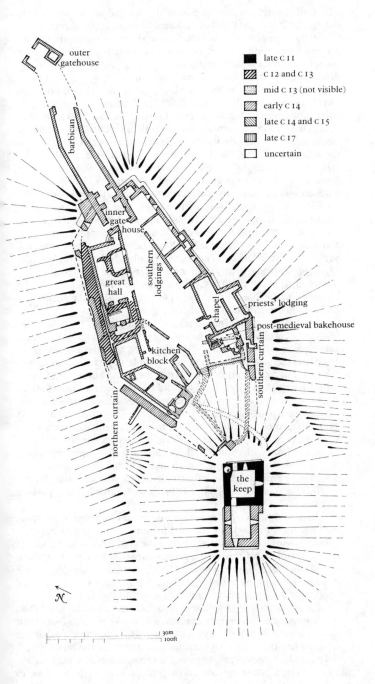

Okehampton Castle: plan

only visible early masonry is part of the original motte tower, now incorporated into the E half of the keep. Starting in the later C12, the Courtenays seem to have developed the site into something like its present form, with a bailey defended by a curtain wall containing ranges of domestic buildings, but by 1274 (when it was briefly described) the castle had become dilapidated.

The complete rebuilding by Hugh Courtenay II (who died in 1340) retained the traditional defended framework but added a sumptuous series of residences.* BARBICAN and GATEHOUSE, connected by a long, narrow passage, both have first-floor chambers (the inner one formerly vaulted). So does the ANTECHAMBER to the great hall, immediately N of the inner gatehouse, of which the stair in the corner gave access to the great hall itself (built on higher ground), to its own upper room, and to the upper chamber of the gatehouse. The roof of the GREAT HALL, supported by base-crucks set high in the walls, was of five bays: one for the two-storey chamber block, one for the screens, and three for the open hall. The positions of the end timbers can be seen in the gable ends. The stairway on the N probably led to the curtain wall. At the W end, the passage to the kitchens. The upper chamber has the fireplace and garderobe arrangements common throughout the castle. The detached KITCHEN BLOCK, with a large hearth in the E part of the kitchen and notable ovens in the W, was extended S and into the base of the motte in the later Middle Ages.

The N range of buildings enclosed by the CURTAIN WALL was originally continuous from motte to gatehouse. Buildings in the S range are as follows, from W to E. First a C17 bakehouse converted from a LODGING built c. 1400 in a space left open in the design of c. 1300. Then a CHAPEL, collapsed at the W end but intact at the E, with tracery of shortly after 1300 and on the S wall imitation ashlar joints painted on plaster. Between it and the adjacent short stretch of curtain a small (priest's?) LODGING. The three LODGINGS between chapel and gatehouse have basements with garderobes – so they must have been residential – but openings simpler than the large windows with shouldered arches at first-floor level, where the accommodation was grander, with fireplaces and lavish garderobes: a four-unit projecting block for two lodgings, a separate one for the third. The upper rooms enjoyed fine views over the hunting park on Dartmoor.

The MOTTE, on a rocky outcrop at the highest point of the spur, still has its W ditch (the E one was filled in and built over c. 1300). Norman work remains in the E half of the ground floor of the KEEP; the rest, of Hugh Courtenay's time, consists of basements without garderobes and upper lodgings‡ with windows, fireplaces, and garderobes as in the bailey buildings. A staircase rises from the NE angle into a projecting turret giving access to the wall-top.

In OKEHAMPTON PARK, close to the army camp, lie the fields, trackways, and well preserved remains of the longhouses (with their outbuildings) of a MEDIEVAL SETTLEMENT deserted perhaps in 1292, when the Courtenays created a deerpark for the castle. Other farmsteads were excavated before the expansion of Meldon Quarry. At HALSTOCK, SE of the town, on a spur overlooking the steep valley

---

*For further details, see the DOE handbook (H.M.S.O., 1984).

‡Or perhaps a greater and lesser chamber.

of the East Okement river, is a good PROMONTORY FORT defended by a circular inner enclosure and by a now incomplete outer bank and ditch of substantial proportions.

MELDON VIADUCT. Engineered for the L.S.W.R. by *W. R. Galbraith* and *R. F. Church*. Six Warren girders, supported on lattice piers (the tallest 120ft high), span 540ft. Constructed of wrought iron for single-line working in 1874, and doubled in steel to match in 1879.

Close to the viaduct, two large LIMEKILNS.

TOLL HOUSE, on the A386, ¼m. N of the town. One of the most attractive in Devon, single-storey, with a circular end, a high-pitched tiled roof (originally thatched), and a tall chimney.

OLDRIDGE

8090

Crediton

CHAPEL, on its own in a field. 1841–3 by *John Medley*, leader of the High Church party in Exeter, unpretentious but serious. Perp nave, chancel, and s transept; contemporary fittings. On the site of a medieval chapel rebuilt in 1789.

ORCHARD

4080

Thrushelton

Farmhouse incorporating the remains of a manor house. Much stonework, together with a datestone of 1620, was removed by Sabine Baring-Gould to his house at Lew Trenchard (q.v.).

ORLEIGH COURT

4020

N of Buckland Brewer

Tucked away down a Victorian drive. A substantial late medieval hall is preserved within a complex whose later history is not easy to unravel. The manor, an early possession of Tavistock Abbey, was held by the Dennis family from the C13 to the C17 (a licence for a chapel is recorded in 1416); in 1684 sold to John Davie, a Bideford merchant, whose family made additions in the early C18; in 1807 bought by Major E. Lee, whose nephew built Watermouth Castle (q.v.); and in 1869 bought by Thomas Rogers, who employed *J. H. Hakewill* to carry out extensive remodelling. After the Second World War, the house, by then in multi-occupation, was left to decay. It was eventually converted to flats in 1982–3.

The low rambling building of rubble stone has ranges grouped round a very small internal courtyard, with a long wing projecting s. Service buildings and stables form further courtyards to w and N. First impressions are predominantly Victorian, as Hakewill renewed nearly all the windows, and added the square gabled bays to the drawing room (s), dining room (N), and servants' hall (w). But the central feature of the main front to the s is still the attractive two-storey late medieval PORCH with outer two-centred archway with continuous mouldings with foliage trail, and inner archway with plain mouldings and sturdy original door. The room above the porch has a C19 corbelled-out oriel and a plain barrel-vaulted ceiling. It is now approached off a later stair by a slanting flight, probably an adaptation from an original newel stair.

The porch leads directly into the HALL, a lofty room of about 20 by 30ft. The showpiece is the four-bay late medieval hammerbeam roof. It is of a similar type to Weare Giffard, but less elaborately decorated (no cusping, and a plain wall-plate). The short hammer-beams are supported by small, well carved stone corbels with busts and half-figures (one bust with the Dennis arms: three battleaxes). Beneath the hammerbeams and the ends of the sub-principals are crocketed pendants, and on the hammerbeams a splendid series of sinuously elegant seated heraldic beasts.* Two sets of purlins, the spaces in between divided up into rectangles (as at Weare Giffard), with braces arranged alternately cross- and saltire-wise.

The lower parts of the hall have been remodelled. Against the E wall Elizabethan panelling with flat shell-arched tops, brought from elsewhere in the building in the 1920s. In the N wall a central fireplace with bold bolection surround, flanked by large round-arched double doors – modernizations by the Davie family (after 1684). There were formerly fire buckets in the hall with the Davie arms and the date 1721. In the S wall the large plain window, six rectangular lights with king mullion and transom, must be a late Tudor insertion (a relieving arch of a former tall N window is visible in a cupboard on the adjoining landing). To the W of the hall, in the area where one would expect the service rooms, there is a late C17 staircase with urn-shaped balusters, probably of the same time as the hall fireplace.

The doors E of the fireplace lead to an inner hall in a wing completed in the early C18 (the excellent rainwater heads on the six-bay E front are datable from the Davie and Pryce arms to c. 1720). Fine early C18 staircase, three twisted balusters to the tread, lit by a grand Venetian window, plain brick outside, but with square Corinthian pilasters of stone (or stucco?) inside. Landing and upstairs rooms on the E front with good fielded panelling. Downstairs, facing N, adjacent to the stairs, a panelled dining room formed in 1870. The rest of the N range is now Victorian service rooms and has been enlarged by corridors, but the roof timbers suggest that the core of this wing, plus the oddly aligned W range that completes the courtyard, and the wing projecting to the S, may in origin go back at least to the C17. Traces of a large chimneystack in the servants' hall (SW corner) suggest the site of the medieval kitchen.

Two LODGES of c. 1870, gabled Tudor, no doubt by *Hakewill*. ORLEIGH MILL. *See* Buckland Brewer.

OTTERTON

ST MICHAEL. Aloof above the village street. Rebuilt in 1869–71 by *Benjamin Ferrey* at the expense of Lady Rolle. The tower, tall and unbuttressed, is a survivor from the medieval church. It originally

---

*Nine out of ten survive.

stood between the parochial nave and the E end used by a small Benedictine priory. Adorned with Ferrey's French-looking gargoyles, it is now above the S chapel, composing awkwardly with the proud, rather urban Dec church of grey limestone with Ham Hill dressings. Wide, chilly nave with gross polished marble columns; foliage capitals carved by *Hems*; roof with cusped wind-braces. – STAINED GLASS. E window, good pictorial Crucifixion by *Ward & Hughes*.

THE PRIORY, N of the church. Remains of the house of the Duke family, incorporating masonry from the medieval priory (a dependency of Mont Saint-Michel, in existence by the late C11, suppressed in 1414, and later given to Syon Abbey). Two-storey porch with arched doorway; coat of arms above. Doors and windows much renewed. In the l. gable wall a large arched four-light mullioned window with transom and a two-light one above, both blocked. Some other old windows r. of the porch. The house was once larger. A sale description of 1777 quoted by Polwhele refers to buildings around a quadrangle called the nuns' court (perhaps the medieval cloister), and to an E front of 1696.

The village centre is an instructive example of local building from the C16 onwards, the farms and cottages pleasantly situated along the broad street with its open stream, although there is already a tendency towards prettying-up. Otterton, like the surrounding villages and countryside, is a good place to study C17 lateral stacks in the farmhouses, here built right on the road and showing off the different display techniques of the period such as set-backs, set-offs, decorative ashlar and patterned masonry, moulded caps and date-stones. In OTTERY STREET, THE BARN, RYDON, and ANCHORING all have rear cross-wings and later farmyard buildings, Rydon with date-stone 1707 and simple contemporary moulded plasterwork in upper chambers. In FORE STREET more lateral stacks, including BASCLOSE (date-stone 1697); other house types, including WATERING, a good example of a later symmetrical farmhouse; then, towards the E end of the village, a long terrace of cob-and-thatch cottages distinguished by surprisingly sophisticated classical doorcases, No. 6 particularly exuberant, with finials and castellations. The MILL has two undershot water wheels still working. Over the bridge, the former STATION, now a house, a model of simple restrained conversion. Also several typical examples of Mark Rolle's estate cottages of the 1870s onwards, especially good a group in flint and patterned brick at the E end of the village, dated 1877; note the low pigsties and woodsheds behind.

C19 Rolle estate buildings abound indeed all over the neighbourhood, not only cottages, but more substantial farmhouses and farm buildings. LOWER PINN, with a farmyard layout of 1851, is one of the earliest examples of the Rolle rebuilding campaign. Two-storeyed buildings of brick and stone, with black weatherboarded upper storeys, regularly arranged: stable and wagon shed opposite the house, cattle sheds on either side. The handsome flint and brick farmhouse is of 1864 by *J. W. Rowell*, still with traditional Georgian sashes. Other farms along the E side of the Otter valley include PITSON FARM, with outbuildings dated 1885, the farmhouse older, with lateral stack, and NORTHMOSTOWN FARM, rebuilt in 1864, with two-storeyed buildings around a courtyard and a brick farmhouse of similar type to Lower Pinn. The most ambitious group is SOUTH FARM, 1¾m. S of the village, down a lane with more estate cottages, its especially large farmyard entered by a grand archway dated 1869.

MONKSWELL, SE of the village. 1929, Arts and Crafts, with big chimneys, tiled hipped roof, and veranda between projecting wings.

HIGH PEAK. A major defensive site on the cliff-top, 1½m. NE of the village. Excavations in the 1950s and 1960s established that it was occupied in Neolithic, Iron Age, and post-Roman times. Now virtually lost through erosion.

MUTTERS MOOR to the N has produced flint scatters indicative of intense prehistoric occupation. Barrows and a stone circle could once be seen; the stone circle was taken away in the C19 by Lord Rolle to make a rockery.

OTTERY ST MARY

14 ST MARY. The church is large and important, yet does not dominate the little town. It lies stretched out, long and low, on a ridge just above the town centre. In historical importance it vies with Crediton for second place in Devon, although visually it is curiously unsatisfactory: no strong vertical accent, only two squat transeptal towers. The total length is 164ft, with an E end longer than the nave, for this was a collegiate foundation with forty members. It was established in 1337 by Bishop Grandison, who acquired the church from the cathedral of Rouen, owners of the manor from 1061 to 1325.

Some of the existing fabric may belong to a church consecrated in 1259, but it is not easy to distinguish, and the overall impression is of unified work of the mid C14. Possibly Grandison used the outer walls of an existing church for his collegiate choir, adding to it a Lady Chapel, flanking E chapels at the ends of the aisles, and two-storey vestries, and extending the church W by a new nave. The most surprising feature is the pair of transept towers, an archaic feature by the C14. The inspiration must have been the transept towers of Exeter Cathedral, and indeed the whole plan of the E end is a reduced version of that of the cathedral.

The details of the exterior are, however, curiously old-fashioned and quite unlike the cathedral; possibly they are influenced by surviving parts of the C13 church. Dec tracery is entirely eschewed. The windows are confined to austere groups of lancets, although these would once have been complemented by sculpture. In the E wall of the Lady Chapel, eight lancets, an unusual number, are flanked by niches, with another group of niches above. The aisles have single lancets, very plain on the outside, but with shafted rere-arches inside which could be of the C13. The clerestory and Lady Chapel N and S windows have triple lights below steep angular arches. The W end is of humble design, with a vaulted recessed entrance with splayed sides (cf. the cathedral W front), flanked by niches, a group of five lancets, and above these, a niche retaining the lower half of a statue, flanked by narrow windows.

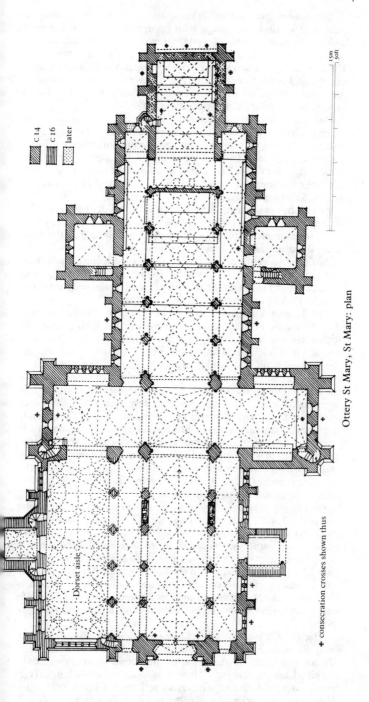

C 14
C 16
later

Ottery St Mary, St Mary: plan

Dorset aisle

+ consecration crosses shown thus

15 m
50 ft

The towers have narrow lancets, and on their E sides shallow gabled projections for altars, with groups of five lancets, rather awkwardly related to the B type buttresses. A similar plain projection on the W side of the S tower and formerly also the N tower (see the arch inside). The pierced Perp battlements are a replacement of 1872 of a restoration of 1826. The N tower is crowned by a short lead spire with an ancient (medieval?) weathercock fitted with two trumpets to produce a whistle (now silent).

Building must have proceeded quickly. No detailed dates are recorded, but shields on the reredos point to a time between 1342 and 1345, and the bosses and the nave monuments refer to Bishop Grandison (†1369) and to members of his family, the chief benefactors: Sir Otho, his brother, buried in the nave in 1359, and his sister Katharine (†1349), who married William of Montacute, Earl of Salisbury (†1344).

The stonework outside is pinkish-brown; inside it is grey. The six-bay chancel has piers of a complex and unusual section, taken up, though much simplified, in the nave. Capitals only on the main axes: the diagonal members run up into arches without any. The arches are two-centred, the small ogee-headed niches above their apexes conjectural restorations by *Butterfield* (the originals had been cut back flush with the wall). The chancel clerestory windows are also heavily restored.

But the most interesting parts are the vaults and the furnishings. The vaults are of great variety, comparable not with Exeter but with Wells and Bristol. They may be the work of *William Joy*, who was active at Wells, and at Exeter in 1347. In boldness of design, the chancel vault is of a high order. It represents one of the few cases in England in which the curvilinear spirit had penetrated into the vault. For while the early C14 delighted in ogee arches and even nodding, i.e. three-dimensional, ogee arches, it hardly ever attempted the effects of curves in vaulting, as the late Gothic style did (much later) in Germany and Spain. At Ottery the pattern is one of plain transverse arches, and between each pair a large central motif of a four-petalled pointed rosette. The two petals to N and S are connected by liernes with the wall-shafts supporting the transverse arches. The whole rib system is purely decorative, applied to a solid tunnel-vault of masonry.

In contrast to this pattern of predominant curves are the vaults of Lady Chapel, transepts, crossing, and nave, all consisting of thin, straight lines forming crosses and stars. The transept vaults preserve the same section for their whole height by the use of a continuous ridge rib forming a horizontal diamond in the centre of each bay. As no distinction in thickness is made between primary and secondary ribs, an effect of grid and trellis results, decidedly Perp in character. The same contrast between curved and straight can incidentally be noticed in the section of the chancel and nave piers.

The figured roof bosses deserve special study (Bishop Grandison, St John Baptist, St Anne and the Virgin, Annunciation, Virgin and Child, Assumption of the Virgin, Coronation of the Virgin, Last Judgement). They are probably the work of carvers also recognizable in the nave vault at Exeter. (Above the vaults, Hewitt records, original scissor-braced roofs remain.)

The main later additions to the church are the two porches and the DORSET AISLE or outer N aisle, apparently built for the use of the parishioners. It dates from the time of Bishops Oldham and Veysey (see arms in the N porch and on a corbel), i.e. between 1504 and the Reformation. A major benefactor was Cicely, Countess of Wiltshire, the owner of the manor of Knightstone, just outside the town. She married Henry Lord Stafford in 1503 and died in 1530. The Stafford knot appears on the moulding below the parapet. The aisle is fan-vaulted (cf. Sherborne Abbey, Dorset, and the Lane aisle at Cullompton). Its remarkable feature is the pendants of openwork bars, the end ones straight, but the three in the centre of spiral shape. The piers have multiple shafts (i.e. more elaborate than usual) and carved capitals. W window of six lights (renewed 1843).

The NORTH PORCH, the main parochial entrance, is of two storeys. It has a fan-vault inside. The S porch is also C16, but probably on older foundations. Tudor roses and Stafford knots on the string course; battlements decorated with quatrefoils. Above the corner doorway a niche with spiral columns. The door itself has ironwork dated 1575.

The architecture of Bishop Grandison's church was of course only the framework for what must have been a most luxuriant display of furnishings (as the C16 inventory makes clear). They were badly treated after the Reformation, and successive well-intentioned restorations of the C19 and C20 have not helped matters. This work began with *Blore*'s repair of the reredos in 1833; the Lady Chapel was restored by *Woodyer* in 1847–50, and at the same time a general restoration (one of the first objectives of the new Diocesan Architectural Association) was carried out by *Butterfield* under the aegis of the Coleridges. He lowered the floor levels of transepts, crossing, and W bays of the chancel to that of the nave, and provided new seating and much redecoration. In 1919, in reaction against the Victorian embellishments, plaster was regrettably removed from all the walls (except the S transept, tiled by *Butterfield* in 1878). The Victorian decoration of the nave vaults was concealed by gaudy recolouring in 1977. Despite all these distractions, what remains of the medieval furnishings is of exceptional interest.

The FURNISHINGS are described here topographically, starting with the LADY CHAPEL. – REREDOS. 1881. – SEDILIA. Mid C14, simple, supports without capitals, cusped arches. – WEST GALLERY (no doubt a singing gallery for the choristers) much restored by *Woodyer*, on three broad cusped and subcusped arches (cf. the Exeter rood screen), with finely carved corbel heads of a bishop and a lady against N and S walls. E parapet with three tiers of openwork quatrefoils. – LECTERN, a gilded wooden eagle, given by Grandison, one of the earliest eagle lecterns in England. – STALLS (formerly in the chancel) with misericords including Grandison's arms. – The EAST CHAPELS at the end of the chancel aisles retain their pretty decoration by *R. H. Podmore*, 1850. – In the RETROCHOIR some original TILES. – On the E face of the REREDOS behind the high altar, graceful subdued ogee decoration and traces of wall painting. The side facing the chancel is also of Grandison's time, but much restored by *Blore*. Only the general arrangement of the arches is authentic. All the projecting work had been hacked off in the C16, and the flat surface plastered. The arches when uncovered in 1829 still had original paint and gilding. Blore added the four pinnacled buttresses and the nodding ogee arches with steep cusped gables. The Exeter Diocesan Society called it 'a conjectural and far from happy restoration', an unnecessarily harsh judgement. The sculptured figures were added by *Herbert Read* in the 1930s. The top is straight and heavy, with ten shields and massive mouldings. The heraldry (royal arms and Grandison relations) was carved on in the C19, replacing earlier painted arms. – SEDILIA with curiously broken steep gables and ogee cusping. No solid back wall (cf. Exeter). – The ROOD SCREEN survived into the early C19 but has now gone. – PARCLOSE SCREENS (not *in situ*) mid C14; among the earliest wooden screens preserved in Devon. They have straight tops and cusped ogee arches; above each of them is a circle with an ogee trefoil.

In the SOUTH TRANSEPT *Butterfield*'s WALL DECORATION dominates, given in 1878 by Lord Coleridge in memory of his parents. Harsh tile mosaics with thin, dark patterns, executed by *Simpson* of Westminster. – CLOCK. Possibly C14 in origin, but in its present form later. The clock face, probably C15, shows the phases of the moon as well as the time.

NAVE. FONT. 1850, a square bowl on marble columns, a beautiful example of *Butterfield*'s brilliant polychrome inlaid work, using local marbles. – PULPIT. 1722 by *W. Culme*, with well carved little figures of the evangelists. – BENCH ENDS, in the Dorset aisle. C16. – WEST ARCADING. 1901–3 by *E. T. Rogers*, inspired by the E face of the reredos.

STAINED GLASS. Much of 1850–60, as part of the restoration. Especially good the Lady Chapel E, E chapels, and clerestory windows by *Hardman* to designs by *Pugin*. – Two Lady Chapel S windows by *O'Connor* (one of them of Christ and little children after Overbeck). – Dorset aisle W by *Wailes* (early: of 1843). – Nave W by *Warrington*. – S transept 1878 by *A. Gibbs*. – W window with Solomon c. 1856 by *Frederick Preedy*.

MONUMENTS. Otho de Grandison † 1358 and his wife Beatrice † 1374 in two richly canopied tombs opposite each other under the fourth N and S arcades of the nave. They are among the best South West English works of their date, still purely Decorated, with large, heavy ogee arches with thick crocketing and large finials. The arches themselves have trefoil cusping without ogee detail. All foliage is heavy and humpy. – At the E end of the S aisle, three brasses (two dated: 1542, 1583) to members of the Sherman family of Knightstone. – Between chancel and N aisle, John Haydon of Cadhay † 1587, first governor of the church after the Dissolution, probably adapted from an older Easter sepulchre (or is it a late example?). Tomb-chest with quatrefoil panels separated by fluted pilasters. Low canopy with pediment. No effigy.

In the S chapel, John Sherman † 1617, the wife of Gideon Sherman † 1618, and Dorothy Sherman † 1620, all with long rhyming epitaphs. – In the NE chapel a delicate aedicule with Corinthian columns reminiscent of those in the Cadhay courtyard (no inscription). – John Coke † 1632. Life-size standing figure in armour in a classical aedicule at the E end of the Dorset aisle. – William Peere-

Williams of Cadhay, by *John Bacon*, 1794, modest but refined (N transept). – Also in the N transept, in a Butterfieldian setting, Jane Fortescue Baroness Coleridge, signed *Fred. Thrupp*, 1879, recumbent, with two angels at her head, accurate dress in flowing folds, still in the Chantrey tradition. – Many minor Coleridge memorials.

THE COLLEGE. The collegiate buildings appear to have consisted of a small cloister to the S of the nave, with chapter house to its E, library, and gatehouses, which have all disappeared, and houses of the individual canons grouped loosely around the churchyard, of which some remnants survive, but too much altered for their medieval nature to be understood. S of the churchyard the WARDEN'S HOUSE, once larger, now of C18 appearance, with C17 staircase inside. A Perp fireplace is now in the Chanter's House. The VICARAGE nearby is mostly C19: E of it the Choristers' House and School survived into the C19. N of the churchyard the MANOR HOUSE remains, reduced in size in 1860, but with an C18 brick front and some older parts with mullioned windows.

The CHANTER'S HOUSE, NW of the church, is the most interesting, although not for its medieval remains. The S front, red brick, of five bays, apart from the added top storey, was built by the Heath family in the C18. The rest, of boldly diapered brick with half-timbering, dates from 1880–3, when *Butterfield* extensively remodelled the house for his friend, Sir John Duke Coleridge, first Baron Coleridge, Lord Chief Justice, who was a leading High Churchman. It cost £16,724, and is one of the architect's most ambitious domestic works. A new entrance porch was added on the E side, a long service wing to the N, and a tall gabled wing was built, with two full-height bay-windows overlooking the terrace to the W, for Lord Coleridge's huge library.

The interior preserves an atmospheric mixture of late C19 decoration and fittings, mixed with older materials discovered during the building work. In the porch some re-used stencilled beams and a wooden window with Ionic pilasters and brackets. The entrance hall has as its main feature a huge transomed and mullioned window, and a large wall painting with a coat of arms. The inner hall has been altered: the lower part of Butterfield's staircase has been replaced, the walls are no longer the original red, and the large genuine Perp fireplace (from the Warden's House) is a later insertion. It has shafted buttresses at the sides, and a lintel with a row of elaborately carved quatrefoils below a crested frieze.

But Butterfield's library remains in all its splendour, a long, sober, two-storeyed room almost on the scale of a college library, for Lord Coleridge's 18,000 books. Bookcases projecting between the bay-windows, incorporating some old woodwork: linking windows above; a gallery along the opposite side. Two marble fireplaces set in Butterfieldian surrounds of church woodwork, each with charming small reliefs by *Frederick Thrupp*, one with mothers and babies, after Flaxman. Reached from the gallery, a tiny recess in which is hidden an effigy of Lady Coleridge († 1878), also by *Thrupp*, another version of the one in the church.

Beyond the library, Butterfield constructed a delightful aviary, which survives, although of the adjoining conservatory only the foundations remain.

The older rooms along the S front include a great parlour,

known as the Cromwell Room (Cromwell and Fairfax met here in 1645). It has very broad panelling and three niches. To the w is the drawing room, and an early C19 room in a one-storey extension: coved ceiling, coloured marble fireplace.

METHODIST CHAPEL, Mill Street. Built by the Wesleyans in 1829. Tall, three-bay, gabled brick front.

UNITED REFORMED CHURCH. Built in the late C17; altered since, and Sunday school buildings added. Interior 50ft square, the ceiling supported by four timber posts. Seen from the road, behind its small burial ground, the chapel has preserved its meeting-house character, with brick walls and hipped slated roof. Porch flanked by large segment-headed windows; a small C18 window above to light the former gallery.

THE TOWN. The best houses lie to the E of the church, in CORN-HILL and PATERNOSTER ROW, a nice C18 group, especially THE PRIORY, red brick, five bays, central pediment (rainwater heads, 1759, 1779). S of the church the sloping town square, with a C19 brick Gothic building in the centre, and a WAR MEMORIAL by *Walter Cave*. To the w along MILL STREET more C18 houses on a modest scale, and Nos. 96–99, a curiosity, as a partly timber-framed house. By the river is the MILL, four storeys, red brick, with MILL HOUSE attached, and the substantial SERGE FAC-TORY built in 1788–90 by Sir George Young. Brick, with flat-arched windows and domestic-looking porch. It had the largest waterwheel in England. Behind this is an unusual circular TUM-BLING WEIR taking water not required to drive the mill water-wheel through a tunnel under the building to rejoin the river.

ST SAVIOUR'S BRIDGE is of 1851, Gothic, with five arched cast-iron girders of 83ft span, supporting cast-iron trays carrying the road surface; cast-iron railings above. Built by *Joseph Butter & Co.*, Stanningley Ironworks, Leeds, to replace an earlier bridge.

PATTESON'S CROSS. Brick, 1873 by *Butterfield*, commemorating Bishop Patteson of Melanesia (1827–71).

SALSTON HOTEL. Approached past two white stucco LODGES, one of the C18, one dated 1844. The house, with a low C18 wing, was enlarged into a pedestrian red brick neo-Tudor mansion by William Hart Coleridge (†1849). Symmetrical, with gables. Later C19 ballroom wing to the l., containing a C16 fireplace moved from the older part of the house, probably originally from the collegiate buildings at Ottery. Worn lintel with three quatrefoils, two angels, and three coats of arms, the central one of Henry VIII.

See also Alfington, Cadhay, Knightstone, Tipton St John, Westhill.

9080   OXTON HOUSE

Oxton was the home of the Rev. *John Swete*, the indefatigable Devon diarist and traveller, whose special enthusiasm was picturesque landscape. The estate had been acquired by his father in 1767. Swete's own sketch of the old mansion of the Martyn family shows a rambling house with the usual two-storey porch and mullioned windows. He demolished this in 1781 and built, apparently to his own design, a plain stuccoed two-storey mansion with two canted bay-windows now linked by a later Greek Doric one-storey portico. Interior much altered, apart from the central stair-hall lit by an oval lantern. Staircase with delicate iron balusters. Converted to flats in 1983.

The house stands in an exquisite sheltered position. Swete described in volume two of his diary (1792) how he built his new house on the same site as the old one because, 'though environ'd by garden walls, by an artificial terrace, where old Yews form'd an Avenue of Pyramids, by orchards and intersecting hedges, I saw that by the removal of these if I accommodated my plans to what nature herself had done, a sweet valley would be found, gently descending between old woods of oak through which a rivulet crept in and where every object visible was not only discriminated but rural and picturesque'. Swete continued to improve the grounds, adding a gatehouse and a thatched Gothic hermitage in 1792 (described in the *Gentleman's Magazine* for 1793). The drive crosses the lake by a charmingly eccentric cast-iron BRIDGE probably of the early C19. It has short Greek Doric columns as main posts, topped by vases, and a segmental arch treated as a Doric entablature.

PAIGNTON *see* TORBAY

PANCRASWEEK 2000

ST PANCRAS. Isolated on a hill. The N side of the church appears Norman, aisleless, with transept; in the chancel one small blocked window. The S aisle is obviously a Perp addition, with three- and four-light Perp windows and an arcade of five bays with granite piers of A type, capitals only to the main shafts, and depressed pointed arches. Richly carved wagon roofs. Squint from the N transept into the chancel. It cuts into an unexplained blocked, tall, round-headed arch. Unbuttressed W tower with big cusped pinnacles. Restored 1894–1910. Chancel stencilled 1909–10. – Rough octagonal FONT, surrounded by C17 RAILINGS. – PULPIT. Jacobean. – STAINED GLASS. Bits in the E window, said to come from Muchelney in Somerset. – The rest by *Burlison & Grylls* (Clarke).

GLEBE COTTAGE. Restored medieval (former priest's?) house.

LANA WESLEYAN CHAPEL. There is no more attractive chapel in 167 Devon. Built by the Wesleyans in 1838. Seen from the burial ground, looking across the slate headstones with a background of trees, it is quintessential chapel architecture. The walls are of rubble, with round-headed windows; the roof hipped and slated. Semicircular porch with columns. Inside there is a small panelled gallery. The adjacent buildings of 1894 once housed a Methodist day school.

THORNE. Farmhouse with remains of a manorial chapel, licensed in 1377, 1381, and 1400. Doorway, tall two-light window, and the hoodmould of another window of the same size.

VIRWORTHY WHARF. Wharfinger's cottage and small storehouses near the end of the now filled-in Bude Canal (begun in 1819, completed as far as Holsworthy in 1826).

PARKHAM

ST JAMES. Norman S door, similar to West Woolfardisworthy and Shebbear, with one order of colonnettes and decorated arch. The rest Perp. w tower with thin diagonal buttresses and big polygonal pinnacles, nave and S aisle with arcade of six bays (granite piers of A type, concave octagonal capitals, decorated abaci, and nearly semicircular arches). N chancel chapel of three bays of the same design, except that the arches are more pointed. Restored 1875 by *R.W.Drew.* – FONT. Plain, Norman. – COMMUNION RAILS. All balusters twisted. – MONUMENT. Thomas Saltren †1753 by *J.R. Veale.*

HALSBURY BARTON. Now a farmhouse. Owned by the Giffards until c.1740. Mid C16; panelled rooms.

See also Buck's Mills.

PARRACOMBE

ST PETROCK (old church). Small, away from the village, and now cared for by the Redundant Churches Fund. Early medieval W tower; low, with small pinnacles, diagonal buttresses only at the foot, no W door, and narrow round-headed bell-openings. It was struck by lightning and restored in 1808. The exceptional charm of the interior of the church is that it has never been restored. It is still much as it was two hundred years ago, a rare example of the usual furnishing of a modest village church, poor perhaps, but seemly. When the new church was decided upon, the old was in danger of demolition, but it was saved by protests and contributions. Ruskin headed the list.

The body of the church consists of a C13 chancel (see the E window, a pair of lancets) and a Perp nave and S aisle (arcade of four bays with piers of A type, but standard leaf capitals, and depressed pointed arches) with straight-headed windows. The division between nave and chancel is by a SCREEN of the same early type as at Molland, i.e. with no grouping of the mullions of the openings into sections (simply a number of narrow identical lights, each with its own cusped ogee arch), and a straight top to the whole screen. Above it a solid TYMPANUM, such as the post-Reformation Anglican church liked, but as only here and there survives (cf. Molland). The tympanum was repainted in 1758 with the Royal Arms, Commandments, Creed, and Lord's Prayer. – COMMUNION RAILS on three sides, with trefoiled openings.

PULPIT. Simply panelled, and still with sounding-board and attached reader's and clerk's pews. – Old, completely plain PEWS (C16?); added C18 BOX PEWS rising theatrically at the W end. – HATPEGS on N and S walls. – FONT. Plain, small, circular bowl, perhaps Norman, said to come from another parish. – Two oval TABLETS with texts on N and S walls. – MONUMENTS. Walter Lock †1667, and other Locks, including David Lock †1786. Slate tablets with painted wooden surrounds. – Samuel Flamant †1755. Classical recess above the vestry door. – In the churchyard a rich assortment of chest tombs and old slabs.

CHRIST CHURCH. Built in the village in 1878 by *W.C.Oliver.* W tower, nave and chancel, rather harsh randomly coursed stone-work. Dull inside, except for the STAINED GLASS. Excellent E and SE windows, attributed to *W. F. Dixon* (cf. his work at Challa-combe), probably *c.* 1878 (R. Hubbuck). Dramatic figures with swirling drapery in pinks and browns. – N aisle NE by *Heaton, Butler & Bayne*.

HEDDON HALL. The former rectory. Three-window Regency stuc-coed front; full-height bow on the garden side.

WOODY BAY STATION, now a house, at Martinhoe Cross. One of the Lynton–Barnstaple stations, 1898 by *Jones* of Lynton, in a similar style to Lynton Town Hall.

HOLWELL CASTLE. A fine motte-and-bailey earthwork on a spur S of the village. Strongly defended; part of the motte ditch cut through rock. Its history is unknown. Parracombe was held after the Conquest by William of Falaise, a powerful tenant-in-chief in Devon and Somerset.

VOLEY CASTLE and BEACON CASTLE. Small earthwork enclos-ures, probably of Iron Age date, facing one another E and W of the gorge of the river Heddon.

On Parracombe Common a number of well preserved BARROWS including a ring cairn and the linear group of the Chapman Barrows (*see* Challacombe).

PAYHEMBURY

oooo

ST MARY. Early unbuttressed W tower; Dec W doorway with fleurons in jambs and voussoirs. S porch with similarly enriched outer doorway but a Perp inner doorway. C18 porch gate. N aisle Perp, of Beer stone, with the usual windows and B type piers and capitals, one with the arms of Bourchier, Courtenay, Ferrers, and Malherbe. One window outside has the initials of Thomas Chard, the last abbot of Forde. The church was restored in 1895–7 (outer walls extensively rebuilt, nave roof reconstructed) by *G. Fellowes Prynne*, who was responsible for the splendid colour and rich textures of the interior. The painting of the ceiled wagon roof of the chancel, with square panels decorated with diagonal ribs, may date from an earlier embellishment of 1851, as do the chancel tiles and stained glass. These were incorporated in Prynne's scheme. He repainted and regilded the ROOD SCREEN and CELURE, and added angel musicians to the wall-plate of the chancel roof. The screen (B type tracery) is complete with E and W coving, cornice, and cresting. – *Prynne* also designed the LECTERN, FONT COVER, and PRAYER DESK with canopy, delicate work inspired by filigree Flamboyant tracery. – In the N aisle a carved stone niche with the Virgin and Child. – PAINTINGS. Three small panels for an uncompleted altarpiece, 1897 by *Edward Fellowes Prynne*.

Earlier furnishings. FONT. Plain, octagonal, Perp, with quatre-foil panels. – PULPIT. C18, with sounding-board. – BENCH ENDS. With two tiers of tracery (cf. Feniton, Plymtree). – Painted ROYAL ARMS of 1740, handsomely framed. – STAINED GLASS. C15 saints in N aisle lights. – MONUMENTS. Dorothy Goswell †1745 and her son, Rev. Timothy Terry, †1736. Large, of black and white marble, with two medallion portraits held up by cherubs, under a baldacchino with looped-up curtains. – Nice churchyard GATEPIERS dated 1831, with neo-Grecian gates, and an overthrow of 1911.

LEYHILL. The tantalizing fragment of a mansion which belonged to the Willoughbys from the late C16, passed by marriage to the Trevelyans in 1655, and then declined into a farmhouse. The E half very handsome: red brick with blue headers, apparently an early C18 rebuilding. Three bays, windows with thick glazing-bars, moulded stone surrounds, aprons, and keystones. A rough E wall suggests that the house once extended further. No main entrance survives. Older irregular W part of stone; N wing with date-stone 1657. Within the E part, bolection-moulded panelling and marble fireplace to the ground-floor room, two good stone fireplaces upstairs, and an early C18 staircase, with possibly re-used C17 columns and balusters on the landing. Over the kitchen at the W end a room with a plaster frieze with shields in strapwork.

HEMBURY FORT HOUSE. *See* Buckerell.

HEMBURY is one of the most striking and informative hillforts in the county. An impressive series of high ramparts and ditches, intensifying the already strong position on the S end of a greensand spur, dates from the later Iron Age, although excavations in the 1930s showed that the tip of the spur has an older history: after brief spells of Mesolithic usage, it was defended by a substantial palisade and causewayed ditch in the earlier Neolithic (radiocarbon evidence suggests dates between 3300 and 3100 bc). The finds and pottery from Hembury played an important part in the development of the study of Neolithic settlement. The Iron Age fortifications enclosed a larger area, and survive to a great height. Evidence of intensive use of the interior was found, and piles of slingstones were found at the gateways. More recent excavations have demonstrated that the ready-made defences were used by the Roman army in the very early stages of their campaign in South West England (before A.D. 50). Evidence for barrack blocks and a possible *fabrica* have been found.

PEAMORE HOUSE
Alphington

9080

A large and confusing house, now divided into four dwellings. Its neo-Tudor appearance is due to *G.S. Repton*'s modernization of *c*. 1825–30 for S.T. Kekewich. One's first impression is of the regular rendered S front of eight bays and two storeys; sash-windows with dripstones, many star-shaped brick chimneys. But to the W the two-storey porch, with inner doorway of red sandstone leading into a double-height hall, is evidence of an older house. The C19 entrance is on the E side, through a porch leading into the S range. From the early C19 there remains an entrance hall with stone Tudor fireplace, lit by a lantern with coloured glazing; behind the reception rooms a staircase with cast-iron balusters rising in a long flight curving awkwardly over the entrance doorway; and between the stair-hall and the old hall, a small square lobby with a shallow groin-vault. The great hall was lavishly panelled in the early C20. Kekewich arms over the fireplace, and the date 1620. *Henry Roberts* is supposed to have worked here in the mid C19.

PETERS MARLAND

St Peter. Old w tower with buttresses only at the foot; obelisk pinnacles. The rest of 1868, rebuilt by the More-Stevens family of Winscott. – (Several STAINED GLASS windows by *Beer*.)
(MARLAND HOUSE HOTEL. Former vicarage, early C19 stuccoed. Doric portico, symmetrical wings.)

PETER TAVY

St Peter. Quite a stately w tower of granite ashlar with buttresses of type B and big polygonal pinnacles. Perp w door. The whole s side is of granite ashlar, too. N aisle with arcade of A type, the arches double-chamfered. So is the arch into the s transept. – FONT. Octagonal, with simply carved tracery, etc., in the panels; late Perp. – SCREEN in the tower arch made up of bench ends with human heads in profile. – MONUMENTS. Well carved wall-monument to Thomas Pocock †1722. – Good slate gravestones of the C18.
CHURCH HOUSE (now cottages). Granite doorways back and front; small granite window to the churchyard.
WILLSWORTHY. A window with trefoiled head in an outbuilding may come from the chapel of the former manor house.
COXTOR. C16, altered 1837 and later. Surprisingly rich C17 hall with framed ceiling, panelling, and a fixed settle dated 1650 with integral carved bench ends.
PREHISTORIC REMAINS. There are in the parish, readily accessible on the w slopes of Dartmoor, many extensive Bronze Age settlements, enclosed and unenclosed. One of the largest and most complex is on STANDON DOWN above Tavy Cleave, where over forty huts have been recorded. Traces of intensive tinworking remain along the banks of the Tavy and its tributary streams. Amidst hut circles and cairns on the summit of WHITTOR (White Tor) lies a camp of Iron Age or earlier date, defended by two substantial ramprarts of stone. $\frac{1}{2}$ m. E a stone row runs N–S.

PETROCKSTOW

St Petrock. Of little architectural interest. Mostly rebuilt in 1879 by *J.F.Gould* (GR). Old w tower with diagonal buttresses and obelisk pinnacles. Old N aisle arcade of three bays with octagonal piers and double-chamfered arches. – FONT. Norman, a variety of the table-top type, but one side with two rosettes instead of the blank arcades. Nice Jacobean cover. – PULPIT. Also Jacobean. – STAINED GLASS. Some late medieval fragments. – Two s windows by *Kempe Studios*, 1891 and 1896. – MONUMENTS. Two brass tablets to commemorate Sir John Rolle of Stevenstone †1648 and his ten sons, and Lady Rolle †1591 and her eight daughters.

HEANTON WINDMILL. Remains of the mill built in 1756 include the keystone of a doorway. No gear.

LITTLE MARLAND. Stone farmhouse with C18 windows and the date 1799. It preserves a most unusual late medieval roof, in the form of a round-arched wagon vault as found in churches, with chip-carving on ribs, purlins, and wall-plate.

PETTON

CHAPEL. Neo-Norman, 1846–8 by *Gideon Boyce* of Tiverton. Nave, apsidal chancel, W bellcote. A miniature show W front with wheel window. Plenty of enjoyable detail, including Commandment boards in Romanesque frames.

PILTON

Now a suburb of Barnstaple on the slopes N of the Taw, but once a town in its own right, possibly older than Barnstaple itself. The church, which stands at the top of a broad street climbing up the hill from the river crossing, formerly belonged to a Benedictine priory, a cell of Malmesbury, founded in the C12. One enters the churchyard through pretty imitation-Tudor ALMSHOUSES of 1849.

ST MARY. On the N side the roof-line of adjoining monastic buildings can still be seen, the cloister running along the nave (hence the high sills of the N aisle windows), and other taller buildings butting against the N tower. For the tower is not on the W as usual, but on the N, in a position close to the E end, characteristic of this part of North Devon (e.g. Barnstaple) and of an early date. On the ground floor it exhibits large blocked pointed arches to N and E and a stair-turret. To the chancel it opens in a narrow pointed arch with a pretty rib-vault, to the N aisle in a tall pointed double-chamfered arch. The whole of this part of the church cannot now be examined, because of the organ. The ground-floor chamber was vaulted, or meant to be vaulted (see the shafts in the corners). On the upper floor the tower has an octagonal storey, a proof that it continued originally or was meant to continue in an octagonal spire. The whole tower was much restored in 1696 and the upper stages largely reconstructed in 1845–50. The N aisle also belongs to the early buildings. It is separated from the nave by unmoulded pointed arches which look as if they were cut out of the solid wall. The S aisle, on the other hand, is clearly Perp, with piers of A type, leaf capitals only to the main shafts, and arches almost semicircular. The four-light windows are renewed; their tracery is exactly as at Barnstaple. Chancel roof open-timbered; N aisle wagon roof now boarded but formerly plastered, said to date from 1639. Wagon roofs also in S aisle and nave.

FONT COVER. Very handsome, with concave sides, crocketed and finialed, possibly put together in Elizabethan times, with re-used early Renaissance panels and bits from a screen at the back, and a projecting tester. – PULPIT. Stone, late Perp, on panelled shaft with panelled body, reticent in taste as against, for example, the Dartmouth type. Jacobean sounding-board, and an iron hand holding an hourglass. – ROOD SCREEN. Across the nave and S aisle. The tracery is A type standard, except that in the central spandrels of each four-light section there is a different tracery pattern, including three mouchettes in a circle. Coving and cresting gone. The spandrels, where the coving should start, are filled with a jumble of Flamboyant bits. – Later PARCLOSE SCREEN of three bays with beautifully carved foliage in the spandrels and also an initial R for Raleigh. The chancel chapel is that of the Chichesters of Raleigh, who acquired the priory after the Dissolution. – COMMUNION RAIL across nave and chancel chapel: Elizabethan with arches, every second resting on a short column.

MONUMENTS. Sir John Chichester †1569. Big standing wall-monument of good quality, without any figures. Base articulated by short bulgy columns; main storey also with big columns with fine strapwork cartouches between. – Sir Robert Chichester †1627. Also a standing wall-monument, this one with life-size kneeling figures of Sir Robert, two wives, daughter, and two smaller children; good-quality detail. The odd feature is that besides a column on the l. and one on the r. there is one in the centre in front of the prie-dieu towards which the figures kneel. It comes farther forward than the side columns and leads to awkward consequences in the entablature above. The base, with detached marble shafts, is also eccentric. – Big and sumptuous wall-monument to Christopher Lethbridge †1713 and family, with rather crude putto heads and elaborate achievement. – Many later minor tablets. – Outside the church a *Berry* SUNDIAL of 1780.

BULL HOUSE, SW of the church. An excellent example of the comfortable standards achieved in superior small houses by the early C16. This well preserved and sympathetically restored C15 house with C16 solar wing was originally part of the priory, probably the prior's lodging or guesthouse. It may have replaced the earlier priory buildings as the main domestic structure by the early C16, as the community only numbered three at the Dissolution. The part one sees from the road is the solar wing, with Perp two- and three-light windows to the upper floor, the central one with the initials R B for Robert Bret, steward of the priory, who acquired it at the Dissolution and died in 1540. Adjoining to the E is a battlemented two-storey porch, perhaps originally a free-standing gatehouse, with an C18 room behind. The older hall range lies beyond, at an odd angle, its end truncated by the later wing.

The hall range has an arch-braced roof of seven bays (three of them over the open hall), two sets of purlins, and lower wind-braces. The two-storeyed ends to the range, divided off by timber partitions, may be late medieval adaptations. From the upper NW room a small quatrefoil peephole looks down on the hall. The SE ground-floor room has its own fireplace (now blocked), and a garderobe opening into the stream which runs through the under-croft below, also a separate entrance. This now opens into a short corridor on the SW side, added together with a stone stair to provide access to the solar wing. In this wing the most sumptuous room is the parlour, with a ceiling with heavily moulded beams with counterchanged joists. Traces of painted decoration on the beams. The inner room has a fireplace and garderobe over the older undercroft. Great chamber above, divided in two in the later C16 –

hence the two fireplaces, with a garderobe added at the W end, against the side of an earlier window.

SW of the church a tightly knit cluster of buildings. Opposite Bull House, PILTON ABBEY (a C19 name), large and plain, now flats, and PILTON COTTAGE, a gentleman's residence behind pretty iron gates of 1805 and 1824. The OLD RECTORY, down a drive, is of 1837, plain and stuccoed, with a pediment. W of the church the SCHOOL, L-shaped with mullioned windows, 1840, enlarged 1874, and close by it a tall stone GLOVE FACTORY. Further N, BELL-AIRE HOUSE and WYNARDS, once a single house, with Georgian front and C17 rear wing; also FAIRFIELD HOUSE, 1827, much altered (but good elliptical staircase inside).

PILTON STREET winds gently downhill from the church to the river, a well-cared-for sequence of cottages with Victorian fronts or Regency bows hiding older structures. The best groups are near the top. On the E side Nos. 78–83, several substantial houses later subdivided, probably C16–17 – see the arched doorway to the passageway in Nos. 81a–82. No. 83, with Tudor doorway, was formerly the Unicorn Inn. Opposite, Nos. 36 and 37 each have single-rib plaster ceilings of the early C17. Set back on the E side, PILTON HOUSE, C18, large, unadorned, two storeys and seven bays with parapet. Pedimented Doric porch. Further down on the W side the line is pleasantly interrupted by ALMSHOUSES of 1860, at right angles to the street. Nearer the river more of the C19, although YEO DALE, near Pilton Bridge, has back parts of the C17 behind its 1810 front range. Close to PILTON QUAY, artisan housing in FAIR VIEW and ROLLE STREET. The C19 warehouses along the quay have mostly disappeared, although a quiet domestic terrace overlooking the water (by *M.J.Smith* for the Spiral Housing Association, 1985) recalls their form, and incorporates some older fabric.

WESTAWAY, ½ m. NW of the church. A neo-Tudorized C18 house, the porch, dated 1634, brought from Berrynarbor Manor by C.H. Bassett of Watermouth Castle.

UPCOTT HOUSE, 1½ m. NE. Prominently sited overlooking the Taw estuary. White stuccoed mansion of the Harris family, dated 1752 on a rainwater head. S front of two plus seven bays and two storeys. Niches between the central three windows, and a three-bay pediment rather awkwardly containing a Venetian window. Deep one-storey Tuscan four-column porch. Much altered inside. At the back, service ranges round a courtyard. Converted to flats *c.* 1980. Lower down the Taw estuary a FOLLY – an eyecatcher in the form of a castellated sham gatehouse.

PLYMOUTH

INDEX OF STREETS

For localities within Plymouth, *see* Index of Places at the end of the book.

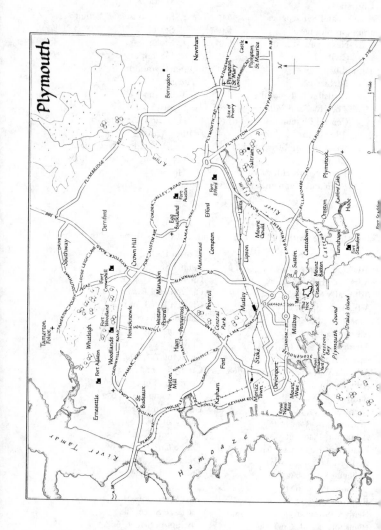

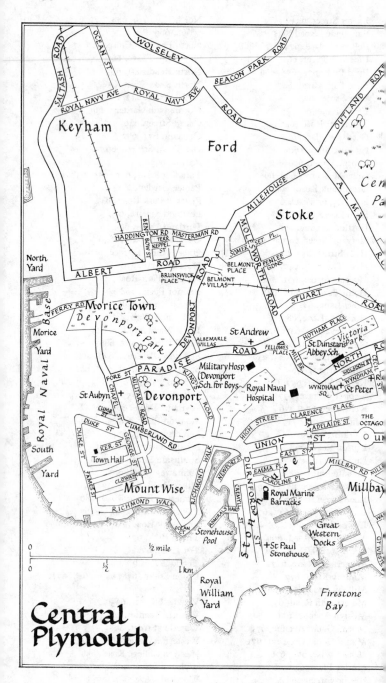

Central Plymouth

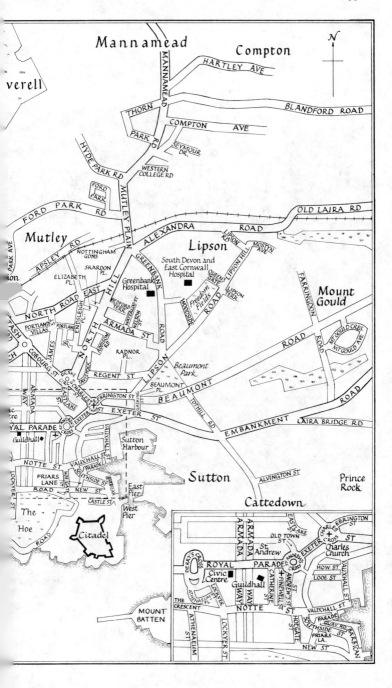

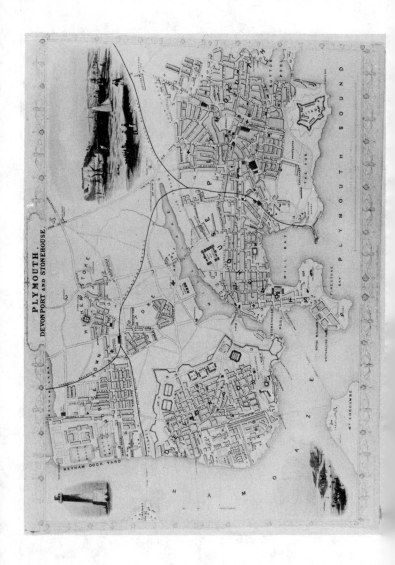

INTRODUCTION

Plymouth is the largest city in Devon – indeed, in the whole south-western peninsula. Its population in 1985 was 243,811, twice that of its nearest rival, Torbay. In many respects it seems an anomaly in the county, the grandly planned naval and military accents of its docks and harbours and the cordon of suburbs built for its labour force the very antithesis of the isolated habitations only a few miles N on the fringe of Dartmoor. It is not an easy place to grasp. During the C19 the three separate settlements of Plymouth, Stonehouse, and Devonport grew together. Then, in the Second World War, bombing devastated much of the area, and the replanning that went forward in its wake swept away the street pattern of the Victorian heart of the city. As a result, the civic and commercial centre is now almost entirely of the mid C20 onwards.

The position of the three towns is superb – indeed, it is surpassed hardly anywhere in England. From a hilly and frequently rocky expanse between the estuaries of the rivers Tamar and Plym – known here as Hamoaze and Cattewater – the city looks out over the vastness of the Sound, its islands and peninsulas. The southern coastline is broken by Stonehouse Creek, the Millbay Docks, and Sutton Pool. To the W lie the leafy grounds of Mount Edgcumbe in Cornwall; to the E, the woods of Saltram descend to the Plym, and further S the sheer cliff towards Staddon Point runs out to Great Mew Stone.

Mount Batten, the peninsula S of the entrance to the Cattewater, was a trading point from prehistoric times, but the most important centre in the early Middle Ages was Plympton, higher up the Plym, with its priory and castle. By the C15 the smaller dependent settlements around Sutton Harbour were growing in importance (cf. Dartmouth), and in 1439 the chief of them, Sutton Prior, was incorporated together with parts of Sutton Valletort and Sutton Ralf as Plymouth, and thus became the nucleus of the modern town. The naval significance of the area was already established. There had been several threats of French landings during the Hundred Years War, and in 1355 the Black Prince sailed from the Sound on his last French campaign. Even earlier, in 1287, 325 ships had been assembled here against Guienne, and on a more famous occasion in 1588 the Navy lay in the Cattewater while on the Hoe the captains awaited the first sighting of the Armada. It was from here in 1596 that the expedition set sail against Cadiz. But a wider world beckoned across the Atlantic, and Atlantic voyages were the foundation of Plymouth's fortunes. In 1620 the 'Mayflower' set out for the New World with 101 Puritans on board, and the explorers and buccaneers who put out from Plymouth numbered among their ranks the resounding names of Drake, Raleigh, Grenville, Gilbert, Frobisher, Hawkins, and in later times Cook and Darwin.

In the later C16 and early C17 the town expanded along the W side of Sutton Harbour around the site of the medieval Barbican – now the best place to appreciate something of the character of the Tudor and early Stuart port. Further W, but still quite separate, was Stonehouse, the property of the Mount Edgcumbes, with its own little port at Stonehouse Pool. W of Stonehouse Creek towards the Hamoaze were only isolated farms. This pattern changed from the later C17, as the

government began to realize Plymouth's military and naval importance. First came Charles II's Citadel, still towering above Sutton
Harbour, for the city had been staunchly Parliamentarian in the Civil
War and both invaders and potential regicides had to be kept at bay.
Then in 1692 William III established the Dockyard on the Hamoaze,
and the town of Dock, later to become Devonport, which began to
grow around it was given its own fortifications in the C18. Barracks,
progressively planned hospitals, and, in the early C19, *Rennie*'s
magnificent Victualling Yard were built (and still survive) at Stonehouse, and the little town developed into a popular residential area for
naval officers, with Durnford Street as its main artery, still with well
preserved modest late C18 terraces. The *raison d'être* for all this, the
Dockyard, was vastly expanded and rebuilt from the 1760s onwards.
Its C18 layout survived virtually complete until the Second World
War.

Civic developments caught up only in the early C19. In 1811 a
competition for public buildings, promoted by the Mayor of
Plymouth, Edmund Lockyer, was won by a young London architect,
John Foulston, who subsequently settled in the city. His hotel,
ballroom, and theatre, supplemented in 1812 by a library and in 1818
by an Athenaeum, gave Plymouth her first neo-Grecian buildings,
establishing a style that was to be widely imitated in the South West.
Alas, in the C20 much of this grandeur was wrecked by bombing, and
what was spared was given the *coup de grâce* by civic vandalism. Some
fragments remain of the streets of elegant stuccoed houses built up at
the same time around the Hoe by Foulston and his pupil *George
Wightwick*, and at Stonehouse rather less of similar but more modest
developments around Foulston's greatest planning achievement,
Union Street, laid out to unite the three towns in 1812–20. The newly
named Devonport also was given its own group of public buildings,
still partly extant, although sadly (and quite unnecessarily) deprived of
their surrounding terraces after the war. The failure to appreciate
Plymouth's unique neo-classical legacy is one of the most depressing
aspects of the post-war reconstruction. It was fuelled no doubt by
long-standing prejudice: Worth, the Plymouth historian, wrote in
1890 of 'the dreary wastes of stucco which replaced the honest slated
fronts of earlier Georgian days'.

Although so much has been destroyed in the centres of the three
towns, the elegance of Regency neo-classicism at its best can still be
appreciated in the suburbs. The best hunting-ground is Stoke, once a
village on the rising ground above Stonehouse Lake, where there are
several handsome villas by *Foulston*, and further N, where a grid of
stucco terraces (now sadly maltreated) was laid out around St Peter
and the R.C. Cathedral. Elsewhere, to the N and E of the modern town
centre, for example at Ford Park, there are still enjoyably imposing
houses in the heavier Italianate adopted by the mid C19.

The city grew rapidly in the second half of the C19 (population in
1851: 114,091; in 1901: 211,177). At this time the skyline was
transformed by the readoption of local limestone for churches and
public buildings. Many have disappeared (both in the war and later),
but the townscape is still memorably punctuated by sturdy grey walls
towering above smooth iridescent pavements that glisten when the
fine rain blows in from the Atlantic. The earliest of these new
landmarks were by Gothic Revival architects from outside (*Butterfield*

at St Dunstan's Abbey School, 1848; *Ferrey* at St John, 1851; the *Hansoms* at the R.C. Cathedral, 1856), but later the local practitioners took over. *James Hine* built Western College in 1861, the Guildhall (with *Alfred Norman*) in 1870–4, and later on St Jude and St Matthias. *H. J. Snell* was a Renaissance classicist, responsible for the Institute for the Blind on North Hill (1876), and the fine Technical College at Stoke (1897); Edwardian Baroque is represented by the Library and Museum by *Thornely & Rooke*. Less spectacular, but in some cases excellently detailed, are the churches of the early C20 built for the expanding suburbs (e.g. St Gabriel by *W. D. Caröe*, St Mary, Laira, by *T. R. Kitsell*).

By 1939 Plymouth had a population of 220,800; the area around Sutton Harbour and parts of Devonport suffered from overcrowding worse than in Liverpool or the East End of London, and the road junction at St Andrew's Cross was the busiest in the South West. The built-up area had expanded around the C19 docks up the Hamoaze as far as St Budeaux, and C20 council housing stretched NE from Ford towards Weston Peverell. But Manadon, the barracks at Crown Hill, and the other mid C19 forts which had been built in a ring around the city still stood in open country.

The devastation of the war (3,754 houses destroyed, 68,348 damaged, virtually the whole of the shopping centres of Plymouth and Devonport flattened) provided the opportunity for a radically new scheme. The Plan for Plymouth by *J. Paton Watson*, the city engineer, and Professor *Patrick Abercrombie*, published in 1943, proposed total rebuilding of the commercial area, with a new street layout designed to eliminate through traffic – a progressive concept for the time, although not quite as daringly innovative as the slightly earlier, war-time plan for the pedestrian centre of Coventry. But Plymouth, too, was to have its pedestrian way: a broad avenue sweeping through the shopping area from the Hoe to the station. All this was carried out rapidly and, apart from the treatment of the public buildings, more or less as envisaged. The Barbican area around the harbour, which the plan proposed to preserve as an old foil to the new centre, was left to crumble until the later 1950s, when it was threatened by wholesale renewal. Then, through the efforts of the Old Plymouth Society and the Barbican Association, renovation and conversion began. The rebuilding of Stonehouse was already under way, with industry and new housing segregated, but reconstruction was slow and bitty. At Devonport the blitzed shopping centre was absorbed into the expanded Dockyard, and, as at Stonehouse, there was little interest in retaining the grid of early C19 streets and what remained of their stuccoed terraces.

As the maximum density settled on for the inner areas was only 100 p.p.a., and most of the inner-city housing was not built above four storeys, additional accommodation had to be provided elsewhere. New neighbourhoods were therefore created on the edge of the city, of which the first to be completed were Ernesettle and Whitleigh. That was in the late 1950s, and the policy has remained in force, so that Plymouth now has a ring of outer suburbs embracing the old villages of Tamerton Foliot and Roborough to the N, and to the E the larger – and further expanded – settlements of Plympton and Plymstock. The first post-war industry, intended to provide some alternative to dockyard employment, was also sited at Ernesettle and Whitleigh; later industrial estates have developed at Estover and, most recently and flamboyantly, at Belliver.

The big disappointments in comparing the paper plan with what was carried forward with such energy and enthusiasm in the 1950s are the dominance of the roads and the mediocrity of most of the architecture – the inner ring roads slice pitilessly through old neighbourhoods, while the post-war buildings make little impact either on the broad, windswept streets of the city centre, or on the endless avenues winding over the suburban hills. Most of the taller city-centre additions put up in the 1960s–70s to try to improve matters appear pathetically crude, especially the hotels by the Hoe and the domineering car parks, and it was only in the 1980s that a few more distinguished newcomers began to appear, such as the deftly sited Magistrates Court and the justifiably prominent new Theatre. They were followed by pedestrianization and bolder landscaping (1987–8) in an effort to make the central area more acceptable. But the days of the modest mid C20 centre would appear to be numbered. Large-scale commercial developments (already beginning to appear on the fringes of the central area in the 1970s) now also threaten to overwhelm the heart of Plymouth. It remains to be seen whether the refurbishing proposed by the new City Planning Officer, *C.J.Shepley*, and the redevelopment under discussion in 1988 for parts of the post-war centre will succeed in creating a visually satisfying townscape.*
Meanwhile the deplorable record of neglect of worthwhile older buildings still continues, coupled with a lack of will to find appropriate new uses.‡

CHURCHES

ASCENSION, Crown Hill. 1956 by *Potter & Hare*. One of the most interesting of the new suburban churches. The exterior is slightly self-conscious, with its mixture of stone E and W and rendered side walls, and its avoidance of right angles, echoed by the untraditional window shapes. Porch-campanile with butterfly roof. The most striking feature is the pattern created in the E wall by the small hexagonal windows with coloured glass, whose frames project externally to cast interesting shadows. Light and spacious clerestory-lit interior; larger windows in the broad transepts opening off the sanctuary. Tapering concrete piers, folded roof. Progressive contemporary FURNISHINGS: free-standing altar under a baldacchino with paintings by *Robert Medley*; abstract stained glass in the E wall by *Geoffrey Clarke*;§ against the E wall, semi-abstract Crucifixion of stainless steel and glass by *Charles Norris*, 1976.

*City Planning Officers since the war: *J.Paton Watson* (1936–58), *J.Ackroyd* (1959–65) (both also City Engineers and Surveyors); *C.C.Gimmingham* (1965–74); *D.E.Winfield* (1974–85); *C.J.Shepley* (1985–). City Architects: *E.G.Catchpole* (1937–50); *H.J.W.Stirling* (1950–70); *C.J.Weeks* (1970–4); *E.H.Surgey* (1974–87).

‡A recent major loss (1986) was *E.M.Barry*'s fine Royal Naval Engineering College at Keyham. The Wesleyan Methodist Chapel in Union Street was demolished in 1987. Warehouses at Millbay are disappearing at the time of writing; *Foulston*'s Egyptian institution at Devonport and *Sedding*'s All Saints clergy house in Harwell Street still await repair.

§Designs by *Epstein* were not carried out.

CHARLES CHURCH, Charles Cross. Gutted in the Second World [98] War and preserved as an eloquent ruin in the centre of the roundabout at the E approach to the city centre. A rarity: built for a new parish created in the C17. The dates are 1640–58, but in spite of this it is wholly Gothic in character, and largely in detail – much more so than, for example, the Charles Church of 1662–5 at Falmouth, further west. The W tower, of limestone and granite, completed only in 1708, has type B buttresses; the bell-openings are round-headed, but with three pointed lights. Pineapple finials on the tower top. The present stone spire replaced a wooden one in 1766. W door with outsize leaves in the spandrels. Some Perp and some fancy-Perp window tracery, but the E window decidedly Dec in inspiration, with a large roundel filled by cusped circles and spherical triangles. Piers still as in St Andrew. Of the interior refitted in 1828–9 by *J. H. Ball* nothing remains.

EMMANUEL, Tavistock Road, Mannamead. 1870 by *W. H. Reid*, extended 1881 by *Hine & Odgers*. Cruciform, with nave and aisles of random limestone, tower and transepts of irregularly coursed ashlar. Dec tracery. Incomplete SW tower by *T. C. Rogers*, 1897; it was intended to have a spire. Spacious but dull interior (quatrefoil piers, plastered walls) redeemed by the excellent STAINED GLASS. E window of five lights by *Morris & Co.* to designs by *Burne-Jones*, 1881: two tiers of figures and lively small scenes of the life of Christ, in splendid colours. – Chancel N and S 1883–4, each with six musical angels, typical of *William Morris*'s own more static figures, against foliage backgrounds. – W and N aisle W windows by *Fouracre*.

HOLY SPIRIT, Clittaford Road, Southway. 1960. Plain, pale brick, with a small spirelet. NW extension 1985. – STAINED GLASS. Two windows by *Charles Norris*, 1985: Day of Pentecost and Gifts of the Holy Spirit.

ST AIDAN, Ernesettle Green. Very dull red brick combined church and hall, 1953 by *Body, Son & Fleury*. – Three STAINED GLASS windows of saints by *Osborne*'s of Plymouth. – Ancient FONT bowl, found in the local creek. – ORGAN CASE of 1884.

ST ANDREW, Catherine Street. Plymouth's medieval parish church, the largest in Devon, a typical example of the main church of a thriving C15 town. The E view a proud display, with six-light chancel windows and five-light chancel-aisle windows. The tower, 136 ft high, with buttresses of type B and big polygonal pinnacles, was paid for by Thomas Yogge, a merchant, in 1460, although probably completed somewhat later. Other dates point to building activity *c.* 1430–90. (*John Dew*, mason, was employed in building the S aisle in 1481–2; *John Andrew* worked on St John's aisle in 1487–8.) Length 185 ft, width 96 ft – typical C15 proportions. Nave and aisles of six bays plus two-bay outer aisles; chancel arch; chancel and chancel aisles of three bays, the arcades lower than the nave. All arcades with A-type piers with capitals only to the shafts, the most common West Country type. Decorated abaci, depressed arches. Window tracery renewed in the C19 (restorations of 1875 by *Scott* and 1826 by *Foulston*); other work of this century was destroyed when the church was badly damaged in the Second World War. Post-war restoration with entirely new roofs, 1949–57 by *Frederick Etchells*. The interior now rather dull, apart from the

powerful STAINED GLASS of the six E and W windows designed by
John Piper and made by *Patrick Reyntiens*, 1958, with bold deep
colours flowing across separate lights. – Good ALTAR FURNISH-
INGS by *Colin Shewring*. – MONUMENTS. Very rubbed-off monument to a civilian, C12–13, his head on a diagonally placed pillow
– John Sparke and wife, 1635, with kneeling figures in the Tudor
and Jacobean tradition. – Jane Barker †1769, bust by *Chantrey*
1829. – Mrs Risdew †1818, also by *Chantrey*. – Dr Woolcombe
†1822, by *Westmacott*, with two standing allegorical figures, Medi-
cine and Charity. – Other monuments perished in the war, but
many minor memorials remain.

ST ANDREW, Paradise Road. The village church of Stoke Damerel,
on the N fringe of Devonport. C15 W tower with diagonal buttresses and polygonal pinnacles, and some possibly medieval fabric in
the N wall; otherwise almost entirely rebuilt in 1751 to cater for the
growing population of the docks. Arcades with oak Tuscan columns on high bases; round-headed windows. A preaching box
wider than it is long, but the box pews, galleries, etc., all removed
in C19 restorations which also added tracery to most of the
windows (original Y-tracery remains, however, in the W tower and
two N aisle windows, and the oval gable windows are also C18).
Chancel rebuilt 1868, shortened in 1904, after a scheme to rebuild
the church as a cathedral for Devonport had been abandoned. The
only executed part of this project, a Lady Chapel E of the chancel,
1902 by *Caröe*, was demolished in 1967. Chancel E wall, rendering,
and S aisle windows all of 1904 by *Charles Cheverton*. – Perp FONT
and PULPIT, of plaster, the latter shown in the 1851 exhibition. –
Chancel refitted 1934. – STAINED GLASS. N aisle E 1863; rich
colours. – S aisle E 1873. – CLOCK on the W tower 1811. – MONU-
MENTS. An evocative collection of minor tablets of the C18–19 to
army and navy men.

ST AUBYN, Chapel Street, Devonport. 1771–2. The first new
church for the expanding docks. W front with tower and somewhat
Baroque octagonal spire now, alas, truncated. The tower sinks half
into the colossal pediment of the rectangular church itself. Heavily
detailed main windows with segmental tops. Interior with gallery
half-way up with giant Doric columns. Barrel-vaulted ceiling. C19
chancel.

ST AUGUSTINE, Alexandra Road, Lipson Vale. Built as part of the
Three Towns Church Extension Scheme, 1898–1904, by *C. King*
of *King & Lister*; W end completed only in the 1920s. Badly damaged in the war, reopened in 1954. Aisled, no tower, Perp windows
and battlements. The dormer windows above omitted in the
rebuilding. – Post-war STAINED GLASS in the chancel. – Carved
Lady Chapel ALTAR by *V. Pinwell*.

ST BARNABAS, Stuart Road, Devonport. By *J. P. St Aubyn*.

ST BARTHOLOMEW, Tavistock Road. 1958 by *A. C. Luxton*.
Uninspiring, red brick.

ST BONIFACE, Victoria Road, St Budeaux. Begun in 1911 to
designs by *Caröe*. 'An abundance of ugly and eccentric outlines'
(Goodhart-Rendel). Completed in 1965, with, in the NW corner
above the font, a striking STAINED GLASS window with the
Ascension, by *Charles Norris*.

ST BUDEAUX, Victoria Road. Now in the outer suburbs and close to a busy road, yet still clearly the village church of St Budeaux, built on a spur high above the Tamar valley. Unbuttressed w tower of early-looking masonry. Low pinnacles. The rest apparently rebuilt in 1563, an unusual date. Four-bay N and S arcades with depressed arches on A type piers; short sanctuary. Typically chunky West Devon granite Tudor windows, in the S aisle an arched one between two with straight heads. Re-roofed and refitted in the extensive restoration of 1876 by *James Hine*. – MONUMENTS. Roger Budockshead and family and Sir William Gorges and family, 1600. Tomb-chest with slate top and elaborate slate back-plate, with the same kind of lively strapwork ornament found in contemporary Devon plasterwork. – John Fownes † 1669. Plain, architectural. – Lewis Stanley † 1693, cartouche with drapery, and Charles Fortescue † 1715, architectural, both with well carved angels' heads as the main decoration.

ST CHAD, Whitleigh Green. 1955–6 by *Body, Son & Fleury*. Plain orange brick, a rather dull focal point for the post-war neighbour-hood. In the minimal Romanesque of between the wars: sanctuary lit by a squat tower, passage aisles with round-headed arches; moulded cornice. – Carved hanging ROOD.

ST EDWARD, Egg Buckland. A medieval church. W tower with buttresses and pinnacles of Plymouth type. S aisle of four bays with A type piers and depressed arches. Perp S porch. Chancel and N aisle of after 1864. Reordered, with new two-storeyed NE vestry, by *T.R.Kitsell*, 1907. – FONT. Octagonal, Perp, the bowl decorated with shields only, the pillar with simplest blank arches.

ST GABRIEL, Hyde Park Road, Peverell. One of the seven new churches planned for the Plymouth suburbs in 1906. By *W.D.Caröe*; nave 1909–10, chancel completed 1924, NE chapel 1954–5 (of stone from St George, Stonehouse). Free Dec, with the typical Caröe feature of relieving arches over shallow segment-headed aisle windows. Short chancel with blank E wall to the road, with a figure of St Gabriel (added in 1960). The composition of the chancel 'piquant but naughty' (GR). Long nave with tall octagonal piers, very flat arches and low wagon roofs; a window over the chancel arch. – REREDOS with low reliefs by *R.Pinwell*. Carved Christ in Majesty above, 1949. – Good *Caröe* FONT, with tapering sides and free stiff-leaf decoration. – ALTAR RAILS. C17; from St Bartholomew, Lostwithiel, Cornwall. – STAINED GLASS. *Caröe* devised a scheme with English saints. In the S aisle, St Oswald, war memorial window of 1918 by *Kempe & Co.* – Above the chancel arch five small figures by *Duncan Dearle* of *Morris & Co.*, 1946.

ST JAMES THE LESS, Ham Drive, Ham. 1958. Red brick, Georgian windows, deep eaves, and a rather Swedish bell-turret.

ST JOHN THE EVANGELIST, Exeter Street, Sutton-on-Plym. 1851–5 by *B. Ferrey*. The fine slender broach-spire with little lucarnes is a prominent landmark as one enters Plymouth from the E. The widened main road runs brutally close. Accomplished E.E., with plate-tracery windows. Inside, octagonal columns and simple scissor-braced open roofs. N Lady Chapel 1883, rebuilt 1955. The plain interior has been embellished by rich furnishings, mostly of c. 1900 onwards. – REREDOSES. High altar 1869, with carved figures; S chapel 1914. – SOUTH CHAPEL painted 1915. – FONT of polished limestones, 1912. – PULPIT. 1869, painted *c.* 1900 with scenes in Quattrocento style. – The SCREEN in the Lady Chapel was formerly the chancel screen; 1872, of ironwork on a wooden base. – Much STAINED GLASS, especially good the E window with Evangelists by *Hardman*, 1865, and three S aisle windows (1867–70). – The previous E window of 1862 is now also in the S aisle. – SW window 1979, from the garrison church of St Alban; formalized figures.

ST JUDE, Beaumont Road, Tothill Road. 1875–6 by *James Hine*. A church for the prosperous western suburbs, with a very prominent NW tower with spire completed 1881. Corner pinnacles with coloured marble shafts. Large Dec W window; aisles with trefoiled lancets. Large transepts. – Corbels and capitals all carved by *Hems*, as also the CHOIR STALLS. – (STAINED GLASS patterned leading by *Fouracre & Sons*; S aisle W with figures, 1895 by the same firm.) – To the E are the HALLS and the SUNDAY SCHOOLS.

ST LUKE, Tavistock Place. 1828 by *J. H. Ball*. Built as Charles Chapel; now used as a store by the library. Rather starved stucco front with arched windows, pediment, and bell-turret. The external pulpit with sounding-board was added in 1913.

ST MARY, Laira. Begun in 1911, replacing a mission church of 1874, on an awkward sloping site (given by Lucy Clark of Efford Manor). The architect not Caröe, as one might have guessed, but *T. R. Kitsell* of Plymouth. A fine fragment, unfortunately never completed. Chancel, unfinished SE tower over a chapel, nave of two bays only. Exterior of granite, interior of Bath stone, distinguished by some excellent carving by *J. B. Hunt* of Plymouth: gargoyles outside, angels and dolphins inside, cavorting among the playful late Gothic detail of the arcade arches. A light interior, lit by large windows with flamboyant tracery of great variety, clear glass with patterned leading, apart from some richly coloured top lights. – Some excellent original FITTINGS, also by *J. B. Hunt*, include the following (except for the reredos). CRUCIFIXION on the E wall. – SEDILIA. Nodding-ogee arch to the first seat; two more seats below trefoil-headed windows. – FONT. A delightful Arts and Crafts piece: a grey polyphant bowl, with slightly Art Nouveau carving at the corners, on a green marble central shaft and spirally decorated corner shafts. – COVER with crocketed spirelet supported by big volutes. – The REREDOS in the SE chapel is by one of the *Pinwells*.

ST MARY AND ST MARY MAGDALENE, Alvington Street, Cattedown. Closed in 1956, and converted to a church hall in 1988. Original building of 1899, red brick, at right angles to a larger church of 1910 by *Sir Charles Nicholson* (cf. St Paul, Yelverton), completed except for the W bay. Thick square piers with battlemented tops, the S aisle now divided off. Narrow N passage aisle; ceiled roof with black and white painted decoration.

ST MATTHIAS, North Hill. 1887 by *Hine & Odgers*. Perp, with a big square tower and large bell-openings, a distinctive element on the Plymouth skyline. Paid for by Mrs Watts in memory of her husband, Matthias Watts. Colourful materials: exterior of limestone and Portland; interior of yellow Bath and red Mansfield stone. – Fittings executed by *Hems*; PULPIT and FONT of Devon marble. – REREDOS by *Fellowes Prynne*, 1891. – Much STAINED

GLASS by *Fouracre & Watson*, the earliest the E window, 1890. – PARISH HALL of 1912.

ST MICHAEL, Albert Road, Morice Town. 1843–5 by *B. Ferrey*, repaired in 1874. Limestone; paired lancets, quatrefoiled clerestory, no tower. One of the first churches to have a neo-Baroque display of furnishings: two exotic altars were installed *c.* 1913.

ST PANCRAS, Pennycross, Weston Peverell. On a prominent hillside site, the churchyard with fine yew trees and old tombstones – a surprise in this new suburb. An old church, once a manorial chapel only, but much extended. Chancel medieval, simple Dec details; transepts and nave *c.* 1820, altered in 1870. Small W bellcote. N extension of 1984–5, providing a link to the church hall.

ST PAUL, Durnford Street, Stonehouse. 1830–1 by *Foulston*. Stone, of the narrow lancet style of the date, with a low W tower carrying spindly pinnacles. Chancel added in 1890 by *Hine & Odgers*.

ST PAUL, Torridge Road, Efford. 1963 by *Pearn & Procter*, a bold effort for its date. Large, unfussy flat-roofed rectangle in pale brick with a big S window with slab-in-resin coloured glass by *Charles Norris*. Campanile; linking passage to an older church hall. (Cf. St Margaret Mary (R.C.), Plymstock, below.)

ST PETER, Wyndham Square, Stoke. A complicated history. The church began as a Nonconformist chapel called Eldad, of 1830. It was licensed as an Anglican church in 1848, and a small chancel was added in 1849–50 by *G. E. Street*. The rest was ambitiously rebuilt in 1880–2 by *G. Fellowes Prynne*, whose father was the vicar. The huge tower of 1906, with its copper roofs and pinnacles, is visible throughout Plymouth. Dec detail. The interior, badly damaged in the war, was given a pure but chilly restoration by *F. Etchells*. – STATIONS OF THE CROSS by *Charles Stapleton*. – STAINED GLASS by *James Paterson*.

ST PHILIP, Weston Mill. 1912–13 by *N. Alton Bezeley*. Limestone, Perp. Tower porch not completed. The interior dominated by the large E window of the apse added in 1963; STAINED GLASS with standing figure of St Philip, in a mosaic style, by *Charles Norris*.

ST SIMON, Farringdon Road, Mount Gould. 1903–5 by *Harbottle Reed*, in the tradition of Caröe (see the segmental relieving arches above the windows with Flamboyant tracery). E end with corner turrets and a large window with thin mullions. Incomplete nave, finished off with a tame Perp front of 1956. Limestone exterior, purple-grey Dulverton stone inside, ceiled wagon roof. – PULPIT. 1908, of uncarved coloured marbles. – Rich chancel furnishings with *Pinwell* WOODWORK. – Some *Kempe & Co.* STAINED GLASS.

ST THOMAS, Royal Navy Avenue, Keyham. 1907 by *Hine, Odgers & May*; unfinished. Limestone. Uninspired Perp exterior, but a good nave roof.

CATHEDRAL OF ST MARY AND ST BONIFACE (R.C.), Cecil Street. By *J. A.* and *C. F. Hansom*, 1856–8, for Bishop Vaughan; the first of the Hansoms' many churches in the South West. Imposing but inexpensive. Dominated by an extra-slim spire added to the NW tower in 1866. Cruciform plan. A spare interior; E.E. paired lancets, clerestory, tall, thin octagonal columns, of granite in the nave, of marble in the choir. Restored in 1920–7 by *F. A. Walters*, who fitted up the colourful Blessed Sacrament chapel in the s transept, and in 1956–7 by *Hugh Bankart*. – Much late *Hardman* STAINED GLASS. – MONUMENT. Bishop William Vaughan †1902. Brass with recumbent figure, by *Hardman & Co.*

CHRIST THE KING (R.C.), Armada Way. 1961–2, a posthumous work by *Giles Gilbert Scott*. Brick, Gothic, small but lofty, with saddleback-roofed tower. – FURNISHINGS still in the Arts and Crafts tradition.

HOLY CROSS (R.C.), Beaumont Road. Erected at Teignmouth in 1854 to designs by *C. Hansom*; moved here in 1881. Nave extended 1888–9, chancel added, aisles 1907 by *Scoles & Raymond*.

HOLY FAMILY (R.C.), Beacon Park Road, Pennycross. 1955 by *E. W. T. Elford*. Austere; reinforced concrete portal frame with rendered brick. Finished and furnished in 1961 by *L. de Soissons & Partners*, who also designed the presbytery.

OUR MOST HOLY REDEEMER (R.C.), Ocean Street, Keyham. 1902 by *A. J. C. Scoles*. Built of unevenly coursed limestone, with lancets and plate tracery; no tower. Severely damaged in 1941, rebuilt in 1954.

ST EDWARD THE CONFESSOR (R.C.), Home Park Avenue, Peverell. N aisle with chapel, presbytery, 1911 by *Scoles & Raymond*; nave, sanctuary, s aisle, and baptistery, 1934 by *Wilfrid C. Mangan*.

ST MARGARET MARY (R.C.), Quarry Park Road, Plymstock. 1956–61 by *Paul Pearn*, a straightforward rectangle, faced in limestone, with side windows high up and a large colourful STAINED GLASS window by *Charles Norris* of Buckfast Abbey, the first example in Devon of the French slab-in-concrete technique which he had earlier used at Harlow in Essex. The subjects are St Gregory and St Margaret Mary. Over the entrance porch another window of the same type in the shape of a cross. Small bell-turret; covered link to the small church of St Gregory of 1933.

ST MICHAEL AND ST JOSEPH (R.C.), James Street, Devonport. Nave and s aisle 1861 by *J. A. Hansom*; chancel, N aisle, and Lady Chapel 1884 by *H. A. K. Gribble*. Limestone, with small dormers. W wall with two Dec windows and a SW turret.

ST PETER (R.C.), Tavistock Road, Crown Hill. 1967–70 by *John Evans* of *Evans & Powell*. The most interesting of the post-war R.C. churches. A corona for the hilltop: a centrally planned polygon, the design obviously inspired by Gibberd's cathedral at Liverpool. Pale concrete exterior; narrow windows alternating with buttresses rising above the parapet in mock crenellation to echo the spike of the central lantern. The church is divided segmentally, with chapels, vestries and confessionals fitted behind the main worship area. Behind the altar, a window for the display of the Sacrament, visible also from the chapel. – STAINED GLASS by *Charles Norris*: W and baptistery windows in fixed concrete frames, the latter most effective, with undulating lines of grey, blue, and green. Elsewhere, thinner panels of glass-in-resin set against the windows: abstract patterns in blue and red.

ST TERESA (R.C.), Blandford Road, Efford. 1958 by *Louis de Soissons & Partners*. Small rectangle with boldly projecting eaves and shallow-pitched roof. E clerestory-tower with a lozenge window lighting the altar. Outer walls of disappointingly coarse red brickwork; exposed concrete inside.

ST THOMAS (R.C.), Bampfylde Way, Southway. 1964 by *Evans & Powell*. Rectangular, with a large s clerestory window.

CONVENT OF NOTRE DAME, Looseleigh Lane, Derriford. Chapel of 1971 by *Lane*. – CRUCIFIX and sixteen windows with STAINED GLASS by *Charles Norris*.

CHAPELS AND SYNAGOGUE

BAPTIST CHAPEL, Mutley Plain. 1869 by *J. Ambrose* of Plymouth. This great limestone pile is almost the last survivor in Devon of the large auditory chapels of Nonconformity – a witness to contemporary confidence and means amongst Plymouth Baptists. Quirky debased classical elevation with huge central niche with Corinthian columns and pediment, between turrets with tall hipped roofs. Severe but imposing three-storey side elevations.

GOSPEL HALL, Ford Park Road, Mutley. Probably of the 1840s. Plymouth's best surviving building of the Plymouth Brethren, on a corner site at the end of a terrace. Rendered and colour-washed. Seven-bay side, with tall narrow windows with rectangular mouldings. Three-bay front with central projecting bay, open at first-floor level. Cornice and flat roof.

KING STREET METHODIST CHURCH, The Crescent. 1957 by *Sir Percy Thomas & Son*. The largest post-war chapel in Plymouth. A brick frontage following a curved building line, with hall and extensive premises. The chapel itself is very tall; the exterior has a few spare classical touches. It replaces a very large limestone building in King Street, whose site is now occupied by the pannier market.

METHODIST CENTRAL HALL, Eastlake Street. The wide, rendered three-storey front of 1940 disguises the 'Ebenezer' Wesleyan chapel of 1815, whose tall limestone walls can be seen from the side. One of the last of the plain, earlier C20 Methodist centres, without traditional ecclesiastical overtones, designed to provide for social and evangelical work in the major cities. Matter-of-fact interior with rostrum, tip-up seats, and a gallery. In the early 1970s the adjacent limestone school premises were replaced by the present three-storey brick building, partly supported on pillars, and the rather uneasily sited prayer chapel.

METHODIST CHAPEL, Peverell Park Road. Built for the Wesleyans in 1905. Tall and gabled, of limestone.

MILLBRIDGE METHODIST CHURCH, Hotham Place, Stoke. Limestone, with a large Dec window in the w gable. Later church hall of 1895.

OLD GEORGE STREET CHAPEL, Catherine Street. 1958 by *L. de Soissons* for the Baptists. A careful interpretation of the needs of a post-war city-centre congregation. Chapel with pedimented gable and thin spire, linked to the hall by covered walkways around a courtyard.

NOTTE STREET UNITARIAN CHAPEL. 1958 by *Louis de Soissons*. A crisp design. Small and square, with a portico and hipped roof surmounted by a slender central spire. In the side wall the 1831 plaque from the former Treville Street chapel.

SHERWELL UNITED REFORMED CHAPEL, North Hill. Prominently placed. Built for the Congregationalists in 1864 by *Paull &*

Ayliffe of Manchester and much criticized at the time because it was said to be the first Nonconformist chapel in the West Country to be designed in the Gothic style. Limestone rubble with a 135-ft-high tower with spire. Interior divided by arcades with paired iron columns, with a gallery around three sides.

STONEHOUSE MISSION, Union Street. An inner-city chapel spared by blitz and bulldozer, only to be demolished in 1987. Built for the Wesleyans in 1813. Rendered, with a three-bay front.

SYNAGOGUE, Catherine Street. 1762, the oldest English Ashkenazi synagogue. Plain rendered exterior with arched windows, the two in the E wall added after 1874; the W front also C19. The C18 interior is remarkably well preserved. Women's galleries on thin iron columns (extended along N and S sides in 1862). Original deal benches. ARK against the E wall, lavishly decorated and gilded. Two fluted Corinthian columns flanking an arch filled with a coffered pattern. Large urns on the entablature; the Tablets of the Law above, crowned by an open pediment. Enclosure with turned C18 balusters. In the centre the BIMAH, another enclosure with turned balusters, surmounted by eight original large brass candlesticks.

PUBLIC BUILDINGS

1. *Naval and Military*

CITADEL, Plymouth. Begun in 1666 by Charles II as a stronghold which might have to prove its worth in attack by enemies from within as well as from without (Plymouth had been a Parliamentary stronghold). A castle had existed close to the Citadel since the early C15. Leland called it a 'castle quadrate', with four round corner towers. Parts of one rounded bastion, about 12 ft high, remain by Lambhay Street. Another fort with angle bastions, built in 1592 to the design of *Robert Adams*, occupied the SE corner of the present fortress. In 1665 *Sir Bernard de Gomme*, engineer-general of the king's fortifications, was commissioned to build the new Citadel. His first plans – for a regular five-bastion fort adjacent to the old one – had by 1668 been modified so as to incorporate the Elizabethan fort; hence the irregular plan. The three N bastions and entrance were completed by 1670, and in 1698 Celia Fiennes reported that all was in good repair and 'looks nobly ... all marble full of towers with stone balls on the tops and gilt on the top'. Improvements to the S bulwarks were made in 1752–9. The Citadel remained the military headquarters of Plymouth until new buildings were provided at Devonport in the C18. The outworks were levelled in the 1880s, but the buildings inside continued in use as barracks, much rebuilt in the 1890s.

99   The chief architectural feature is the PORTAL, dated 1670. The style is French in derivation, but handled in a more Baroque way, although by no means as Baroque as the Italians would have made it. It was originally approached across a drawbridge, and defended by an outwork called the north ravelin with another drawbridge. Below, the portal has paired Ionic pilasters with niches between them and garlands between the capitals; above, a centre narrower than the arch below and very bulgy unfluted Corinthian columns.

Large trophies in the flanking bays. Top with a big, heavy segmental pediment. The armour and statues were originally gilded. The massive WALLS of the Citadel are of limestone with granite dressings. Facing the E end of The Hoe, the WEST SALLY PORT, with a framing round-headed arch, and a semi-hexagonal pediment with the royal arms. A third entrance to the s has a semicircular arch with a rectangular frame, with foliage in the spandrels.

Within the walls, a neat array of plain grey limestone buildings ranged loosely around a parade ground. The older ones are of rubble or rendered, the larger gabled additions of the 1890s of more precisely coursed ashlar. By the entrance the GUARD ROOM (shown on a view of 1737), rendered, one-storeyed, with a separately roofed sturdy colonnade. Then, anti-clockwise, first the former GOVERNOR'S HOUSE, late C17, doubled in size shortly after completion, and remodelled as offices in 1903. It is of three storeys, with prominent string-courses and a modillioned cornice, paired windows, two re-used granite doorways with star-pattern spandrel reliefs, and shaped end-gables. Opposite the gateway, on the site of the powder magazine, the OFFICERS' MESS of 1897, expressing its superiority by its height and mullioned windows (the main rooms on the top floor). Within the entrance the studded door from the governor's house, with square and oval panels.

ST KATHERINE'S CHAPEL, 1845, cruciform, in the lancet style, is a rebuilding of a smaller late C17 chapel which had replaced a yet older one on a different site. C17 granite N doorway. Simple iron-railed galleries, some later C19 stained glass, chancel wall and ceiling painting of 1914–18. Nearby, the former STOREHOUSE (now Accommodation Training), three storeys, rubble, with another re-used granite doorway, and further on a plain rendered building of five bays with a hipped roof. The rest is of the 1890s: ACCOMMODATION BLOCK of 1899, tall, gabled, and lower SERGEANTS' MESS and CONFERENCE ROOM.

In front of the officers' mess a lead STATUE of George II, 1728, moved here in 1903, and too small for its position. The king is dressed as a Roman warrior, with arm pointing forward.

FORTS. An interesting sequence. The earliest defences were on the site of the Citadel (see above). Henry VIII added to them by constructing four ARTILLERY TOWERS in 1537–9: Fisher's Nose protecting the Cattewater, Eastern King Point, Firestone Bay, and Devil's Point protecting Stonehouse Pool. FIRESTONE BAY (restored and converted to a restaurant) is the best preserved: seven-sided, with embrasures, loopholes, and a doorway surviving. In the later C16 the position at Fisher's Nose was protected further by a new fort which was absorbed into Charles II's Citadel (see above), and Charles also built the three-storey castellated tower for ten guns at MOUNT BATTEN, on the other side of the Cattewater. In the C18 attention turned to the defences of the expanding docks: the Devonport Lines were laid out in 1758, with rampart, ditch, and attendant barracks, and a group of redoubts on Maker Heights above Stoke were added from 1785, of which some traces survive. West King's Battery at Stonehouse and Staddon Point at Plymstock also originated in the late C18. STADDON POINT still has its tall, plain enclosing walls with casemates; it was converted to barracks after 1860.

By the mid C19 the existing defences had been rendered obsolete by the development of long-range artillery, and after the invasion scare of 1859, the Royal Commission on the Defences of the United Kingdom recommended an entirely new system: a ring around the town of strong detached forts, each capable of containing a small garrison. Sited about a mile apart (bombardment range was estimated at the time at *c.* 8000 yards), they were intended to offer protection from attack by land as well as by sea, and were the most ambitious British C19 land defences to be built, even more extensive than the smaller ring built at the same time around Portsmouth. The land forts start to the w of the Sound with Tregantle and Scraesdon (in Cornwall), and the sequence can still be traced through the C20 northern suburbs: Ernesettle, Agaton, Knowles, Woodlands, Crown Hill, Bowden, Egg Buckland Keep, Forder, Austin, Efford, Laira. They are completed at Plymstock by Staddon, Stamford, and Brownhill. Outer sea defences were provided by Bovisand at Plymstock, by Picklecombe, Polham, and Cawsand on the Cornish side, and by Breakwater, in the centre of the harbour approach. Mount Edgcumbe Gardens, East and West King's Battery at Stonehouse, and Drake's Island provided additional defence within the Sound.

Unlike the contemporary Portsmouth land ports, which are uniformly of brick, the Plymouth ones are of stone, and of considerable variety. The chief designer was Captain *Du Cane*, responsible for all the northern group. Of these, CROWN HILL, of 1868, seven-sided, with bastions and a grand neo-Norman entrance, is the most elaborate and best preserved. It was used as barracks until the 1980s and still has its original buildings inside. Most of the others were abandoned in the earlier C20, although in many cases all or part of their enclosing walls remains. More survives at Plymstock. STAMFORD, of 1865, also by *Du Cane*, is now a country club. It is an extraordinary design, with a frontage like a giant's Tudor manor house, with a massive four-centred archway, and four openings grouped together as if to form huge mullioned-and-transomed windows. BOVISAND (now an underwater research centre) is different again, 1861–70 by Major *Porter*, built of mighty granite blocks. Seaward-facing casemates in two tiers, the lower ones recessed below segmental arches, for 68- and 110-pounder guns. They are protected by iron shields, a modification made (under Captain *Siborne*) during building, to take account of the rapid advance in artillery power that threatened to make the forts obsolete before they were complete. *Siborne* also designed BREAKWATER (now a signal station), a two-tiered fort of iron on masonry foundations, on an oval plan, built in 1867–79 for the purpose of attacking ships at close range. The walls are of four thicknesses of iron plate separated by iron concrete.

ROYAL NAVAL BASE, Devonport. The dockyard at Plymouth, as at Portsmouth, developed to cope with the challenge of the Atlantic. Founded by William III, it is sited along the Hamoaze, the sheltered estuary of the Tamar. Plans for a dry dock, wet dock, officers' terrace, ropery, and storehouses were made by *Edmund Dummer*, Surveyor to the Navy, in 1692. The original dockyard, in what is now South Yard, was nearly doubled in size from 1763, by levelling the rocky hill to the s and replacing all the original buildings except the officers' houses. The contractors were *Templer* and *Parlby*. Meanwhile, in 1719–24, the Ordnance Yard had been laid out to the N by the Board of Ordnance to provide guns for the navy. Further N is North Yard, linked to the older areas by a tunnel. First known as the Government Steam Yard, it was opened in 1848 and extended in 1865. The vast expansion to the N at Keyham, now the site of the most extensive C20 activity, took place from 1899. In 1765 the dockyard had less than 500 employees. The figure rose to over 1,000 in 1800 and 12,000 in 1910.

SOUTH YARD. In the C19 White could write 'the neatness and order everywhere apparent excite the admiration of the stranger'. No longer so. The C18 dockyard survived virtually complete until the war, but much was totally lost in the devastation of 1941 – for example the dock offices, and the large double quadrangle of storehouses of the 1760s – and haphazard clearance and reconstruction since have surrounded the surviving buildings with confusion and clutter, so that Devonport no longer has the coherence of Chatham or parts of Portsmouth. But buildings of great interest remain, enough to convey something of the main phases of development, from the late C17 to the replanning of the 1760s and the improvements of the earlier C19.

The DOCK WALLS, pushed outwards after the Second World War, now enclose part of the former town centre of Devonport, so that the old entrance buildings are some way from the gates.

The NAVAL BASE MUSEUM is the former Pay Office of *c*. 1780, a three-storey, seven-bay limestone building in the plain style characteristic of the major reconstruction that took place in the later C18. Tripartite central window to the first floor. The ground-floor vaults on iron columns are a later insertion.

THE TERRACE to the S is a sad fragment. In 1692 a grand three-storey range of houses was built for the Commissioner and twelve senior dockyard officers, with offices at the ends, the first example in any of the English dockyards of a unified approach for officers' housing. It was a remarkably early date for a terrace of individual houses treated as a long palace front. The centre had a segmental pediment and cupola, balanced by end pavilions with triangular pediments. Of this, all that survived the war is the N pavilion, three houses in 2–5–2 bays with later Greek Doric porches, and the lower office wing coming forward, with a S-facing broad segmental pediment. Coats of arms in both pediments. The walls, now rendered were originally of brick with stone quoins, i.e. in the tradition of Wren's domestic manner, although as a whole the design is closest in style to the work of *Robert Hooke* (cf. especially the composition of his Bethlehem Hospital in London). Other buildings contemporary with The Terrace which disappeared in the late C18 replanning consisted of a low ropery running E–W, and a large storehouse by the waterfront, to the S of the single dry dock (which remains, now deepened).

The new ROPERIES are the most notable survival of the replanning of 1763–72, no longer complete, but still an impressive group of plain stone buildings on an imposing scale. The HEMPHOUSE of 1763 is of two storeys with arched windows. The three-storey MASTER ROPEMAKER'S OFFICES are dignified by a pediment and arched windows to the first floor; on the l. an extension with large Tuscan columns. The MASTER ROPEMAKER'S HOUSE, 1772, a simple three-storey house looking N over its own garden, has a blank wall to the W because the long three-storey ROPERY buildings once extended further. Originally, as at Chatham until the 1780s, there was a pair of buildings, a spinning house and a laying house (i.e. the building where the tarred yarn was twisted into strands and then into rope), each 1200ft long. The laying house was entirely destroyed in the war; two-thirds of the SPINNING HOUSE survived. Gutted by fire in 1812, it was reconstructed by *Edward Holl* in 1813–17 with an interesting fireproof interior consisting of iron columns down the centre carrying iron joists on which stone slabs were laid. The roof also is of iron: cast-iron principals and purlins, wrought-iron tie rods. At first spinning was carried out on each floor; later the building was used also for laying – hence the iron track and wheels suspended from the ceiling for transmitting power to the laying machines. The TARRED YARN STORES, two very wide buildings connected by beams and rollers, were used for hanging the tarred yarn. Windlasses remain in the roof, and in one building the original boarded lining to the walls. The entrance at the S end was, unfortunately, widened in 1968. Gable end with stepped top.

GAZEBO. A delightful retreat, erected on Bunker's Hill in 1822 to commemorate a visit from George III, who apparently had requested that this rocky outcrop should not be levelled with the rest of the dockyard. Approached by a winding pebbled path with seats in grotto-like alcoves, it is a circular ogee-roofed summer house with eight wooden Greek Doric columns and four concave sides, so that the interior is a concave square.

SLIPS. Most impressive is the C18 slipway covered by a vast strutted gambrel roof of 1814, now covered in aluminium (originally probably copper or zinc). On the S side the roof projects over the outer wall of the dockyard. By the water a figurehead from the Royal William. The SCRIVE BOARD is an adaptation of another slip for use as a moulding floor. The later slip roof is on an immense scale, also of *c.* 1820 and of similar construction, overhanging on the N side and hipped at one end. The walls are now clad in corrugated iron.

Of the other buildings in South Yard, the W part of the SMITHERY is of the 1760s, the E part of 1797. The SAWMILLS (still in use) are C19: two storeys with segment-headed windows. Over an inlet a SWING BRIDGE dated 1838, in elegant ironwork. A RAILWAY TUNNEL of 1840 leads to North Yard. C20 BRIDGE to Morice Yard.

DEVONPORT MARKET HOUSE is now stranded within the dockyard precincts. It is of 1852 by *St Aubyn*, limestone, with a slim Italianate tower at an angle, rising from a battered plinth. Elegant interior with three parallel iron-trussed roofs, and iron lattice balconies supported on slender iron columns with palm-leaf capitals.

MORICE YARD. The yard laid out in 1719–24 for the Board of Ordnance is still remarkably complete. The plans were by Colonel *Christian Lilly*, engineer, with *Andrews Jelfe* as clerk of the works from 1720. High up, overlooking the storehouses, is the OFFICERS' TERRACE, a distinctively wilful and rather fortress-like composition with a broken skyline, perhaps influenced by Vanbrugh, who was working for the Board at this time (cf. the Arsenal, Woolwich, London), although there is no proof of his direct involvement. The five houses are of local rubble stone with granite dressings, two to four storeys, with two tall accents with arched attic windows, and in between them a lower centre with pediment. The proportions of the windows are carefully calculated, as is best seen in the least altered house at the r. end. From the terrace a steep double flight of steps leads down the sheer face of rock to the gun wharves. The ARMOURERS' SHOP, 1776, is of two storeys in roughly dressed stone. The two original STORES are of brown rubble stone (the N one with a later upper floor); the later ones, of c. 1840–50, in grey limestone ashlar, fill the former open space in the centre. On the E boundary, small one-storey GUARD HOUSES with curved porches and porthole windows. Away to the N, replacing an earlier building in the centre of the yard, the POWDER MAGAZINE, 1744, a very plain brick front with four brick pilasters and pediment, rubble-built, with double-skin walls and a barrel-vault. Carved arms of the Duke of Montagu, Master General of the Ordnance. This was the last powder store to be built within the Ordnance Yard. Later ones were sited in a more safely isolated position upstream at Keyham.

NORTH YARD, opened in 1848, developed from S to N to cater for C19 and C20 warships, with buildings on an increasingly gigantic scale, housing a variety of functions under one roof. Among the earliest is the large QUADRANGLE BUILDING of 1853 by E. M. Barry. Two storeys, the main front to the harbour of 11–9–11 bays, each section with a central pediment, giant pilasters between the windows, pepperpot turrets at the ends. On the terrace above, plain stone OFFICES with pedimented ends, of 1910.

Further N at KEYHAM major redevelopment to serve modern warships took place in the 1970s. The FRIGATE COMPLEX, by the engineers Sir Alexander Gibb & Partners, is impressive both in its chillingly colossal scale and in its well-managed detail. The dominant feature is the row of six tall concrete piers on the seaward side which house the mechanism for the vertical sliding doors. Reinforced concrete construction, steel roofs, walls with crisp ribbed cladding and upper glazing. The FLEET MAINTENANCE BASE and SUBMARINE REFIT COMPLEX, 1971–80 by HKPA with Sir Alexander Gibb & Partners, consist of two older dry docks enclosed by new specialist workshops, stores, offices, and amenities. Cranes designed integrally with the buildings. The varied heights and shapes are neatly unified by rectangular cream-coloured precast concrete cladding panels. At one corner the NAAFI building, distinguished by a large canted glazed wall overlooking the water.

ROYAL WILLIAM YARD, Stonehouse. By far the most impressive single architectural group in Plymouth. It was constructed in 1825–33 by the young Sir John Rennie (who had been working on the breakwater), with Philip Richards, on fourteen acres at the S end of the Cremyll peninsula, six of them reclaimed from the sea. The first and most grandiloquent of the monumental compositions created by the Victualling Board of the Navy after the Napoleonic wars, the Yard is also among the most remarkable examples of an early C19 planned layout of industrial buildings anywhere in England. The main buildings are all of local limestone, impeccably dressed ashlar, with Cornish granite used for plinths and cornices.

146   The approach is from Cremyll Street, through a GATEWAY on the grandest scale, crowned by a statue of William IV 13 ft tall. Severe banded rustication, bulls' heads on the main pilasters, crossed anchors over the side entrances, good studded doors. Just within the Yard, a line of monolithic unfluted Doric columns of granite: on the S side the low POLICE BUILDING, on the N side the SLAUGHTERHOUSE, both with narrow channelled stonework in contrast to the broader lines of the gatehouse. The main group faces S across the water. In the centre MELVILLE SQUARE, with a tall central cupola, begun in 1829. Four ranges of storehouses around a courtyard; central archway flanked by big channelled pilasters. Three storeys of windows with plain stone surrounds, varied by segment heads to ground and top floors. The windows themselves are renewed, except at the back of the front block, where there are offices with domestic-looking wooden sashes. Iron columns inside; also iron trusses to the roofs. Plain, elegant cantilevered stair in the front range.

Flanking Melville Square, on either side of the basin, and conveniently close to the water for loading, the BAKERY and MILL (E) and BREWERY (W), each with a prominent chimney with entasis. They have the motif of giant arches framing the windows of their tall central buildings. The bakery is the only building on the site which is partly of up-to-date fireproof construction, with iron columns, beams, and stone floors, no doubt also to cope with the weight of the grain (cf. the dockyard ropery building). S of the brewery the COOPERAGE, originally a square building within a square of open arcaded ranges (cf. West India Docks, London). Lunette windows on the first floor, tripartite windows on the ground floor. Between the cooperage and the water, CLARENCE BUILDING, the first to be completed, with a seven-bay raised and projecting centre. Nearby the WATER ENTRANCE, with a grand double flight of steps, and gatepiers with vermiculated plinths. Near the E edge of the site two elegantly restrained OFFICERS' HOUSES, each with a five-window front, side entrance, and a hipped roof behind a parapet. Between them and Melville Square a tactful C20 COOPERAGE, in the area formerly used for open storage.

ROYAL NAVAL HOSPITAL, High Street, Stonehouse. Built to the S of Stonehouse Creek (now filled in) so that patients could be brought directly by water to a landing jetty on the N side of the site, and surrounded by high stone walls so that the sailors recruited by press gangs could not escape. 1758–62 by *Alexander Rowehead*, probably with *William Robinson* as consultant. A layout of remarkable interest, the earliest example of a hospital on a pavilion plan, with ward blocks kept small and separated by a one-storey Tuscan colonnade, to avoid the spread of disease. Jacques Tenon and Charles Auguste Columb on their tour of European hospitals in 1787 praised this hospital above all others, and it was a crucial influence on the French hospital reformers. The pattern of eleven blocks on three sides of a large courtyard is still clear, even though one block was destroyed in the war, the colonnade has been glazed and in some places given an extra floor, and an operating theatre has been added on the N side. The blocks are of three storeys, very plain, of rubble with ashlar dressings. Trafalgar Block, the central one on the far side of the courtyard, is dignified by a cupola, a central Venetian window, and an open arcade. It originally housed chapel, dispensary, and dispenser's quarters. On the opposite side, four official residences with central pediment. Good entrance gates to the courtyard, 1806. Outside them, two facing ranges by *Edward Holl*, early C19, the N one with a nice semicircular Tuscan porch. Near the remains of the jetty to the N, the low Admiral's Office and Pay Office. E of the main courtyard, two small octagonal buildings, the large octagonal water-tower with circular windows, and a small mortuary with pyramid roof, all of grey limestone. Later additions are mostly in yellow brick.

CHAPEL. 1883. Unusually ornate engineer's Gothic. Crazy-paving exterior walls, continuous wooden clerestory with trefoiled windows alternating with taller dormers. Broad nave with wooden piers supporting a hammerbeam roof full of notched and carved timbers. Apse with lushly carved capitals to the seven windows. Handsome quatrefoil marble font in a little baptistery beneath the SW tower.

MILITARY HOSPITAL, Paradise Road, Stoke. Now Devonport School for Boys. Clearly influenced by the Naval Hospital sited on the other side of the former Stonehouse Creek, and likewise originally accessible by water and hidden behind a high stone wall. Many later additions on the N side, but to the S the layout of 1797 is intact: four three-storey blocks of roughly coursed limestone connected by an arcaded ground floor, with small one-storey buildings in between, and a lower fifth block at the E end.

ROYAL MARINE BARRACKS, Durnford Street, Stonehouse. 1779–85. The 'fine pile of buildings erected by Messrs *Templer & Parlby*' (Copper Plate Magazine) still survive on three sides of a courtyard now closed by mid C19 additions. Facing Durnford Street behind substantial railings, the mid C19 Archway Block, a dignified composition with a pedimented centre with five tall round-arched windows above the entrance-ways. Pedimented end pavilions of three storeys; two-storey links with arcaded ground floor. The other three ranges around the courtyard are plainest classical of the later C18, of rubble limestone with ashlar dressings. The East Block is a three-storey range, forty-five windows long, with a slightly projecting pedimented centre; N and S ranges similar but shorter and without pediments. Dining hall at the SE corner with tall round-arched side windows. Mid C19 officers' residences at the SW corner. Also on the site the GLOBE THEATRE, converted and extended in the C19 from a bowls court. (Small circular auditorium, shallow domed ceiling, and circle supported on cast-iron columns.) The LONG ROOM was built as an assembly room in 1756. Brick with rusticated quoins, two storeys, pedimented Tuscan porch at one end, arched doorway with fanlight. One long room on each floor (much altered inside).

ROYAL NAVAL BARRACKS (H.M.S. 'DRAKE), Saltash Road, Keyham. Begun in 1879, the first permanent buildings of their type, much enlarged since. An impressive formal composition in free Italianate. The WARDROOM consists of three main blocks of three storeys, the basement rusticated, the side blocks embellished with stone balustraded balconies. In the centre a tower with handsome domed cupola, above an Ionic porch approached by an imperial stair. Inside, the staircase hall and main rooms have scagliola columns. The DRILL HALL is also treated monumentally, its stone walls generously columned and pedimented. The CLOCK TOWER is more eccentric: six diminishing stages, with two massively corbelled out iron balconies above the clock face. RALEIGH, GRENVILLE, and EXETER are survivals of the original C19 barrack blocks among many additions of the C20. ST NICHOLAS' CHURCH is long, rather Southern French in its inspiration, with faceted buttresses and a tall apsed sanctuary above an undercroft. There is no tower, but a belfry over the chancel arch. Aisles with quadrant vaults. (Stained glass by *Kempe Studios* of 1912–28.) MAIN GATES between two heavy pedimented pedestrian entrances.

RAGLAN BARRACKS, Military Road. *See* Inner Plymouth 6: Devonport.

ROYAL NAVAL ENGINEERING COLLEGE, Tavistock Road, Manadon. Prominently sited on a hill in the northern suburbs, the bland, pitched-roof buildings of the late 1950s onwards (by the *Ministry of Works* under *E. Bedford*) fill the park of MANADON. The mansion was owned by the Hall family in the C18 and by the Parlbys from 1792. It is now used as the administrative headquarters. The late C17 exterior (dated 1681) conceals an older core. Coursed rubble with granite dressings, seven-window front, deep eaves with carved brackets, dormers with alternate segmental and triangular pediments. Sash windows (replacing mullions-and-transoms). Earlier arched doorway, and inside, a mixture of early and late C17 features. Three back wings, an early C17 stair in the central one. CHAPEL to the N, converted from an outbuilding. Circular stone piers on each side, the openings between them glazed and slate-hung. The main residential block is of four storeys, brick above Portland stone, with end walls of local limestone rubble. Manadon replaced *E. M. Barry's* fine college buildings at Keyham, which survived until 1986.

BREAKWATER, across the Sound, 2m. s of the Citadel. By the great engineer *John Rennie*, with *William Knight* as resident architect. Begun in 1811; finally completed, with the lighthouse at the end, in 1841. A remarkable feat of engineering. It is 5,100ft long, and is said to have needed four and a half million tons of stone.

EDDYSTONE LIGHTHOUSE. The first structure on the Eddystone Rocks, 14m. s of the shore, was a somewhat fanciful-looking design by a gentleman-amateur-engineer, *Henry Winstanley*, built in 1696–1700 and swept away in 1703. Its plainer wooden successor, by *John Rudyerd*, a silk-merchant, lasted from 1709 until it was burnt down in 1755. It was replaced by *John Smeaton's* celebrated tower of 1756–9, a slender tapering column which, apart from the cast-iron lantern, was entirely of stone, meticulously strengthened by dovetails and cramps. The top stage of this is now on The Hoe (*see* Central Plymouth 2: The Hoe). It was taken down because the foundations were undermined, and replaced in 1879–82 by a taller tower by *Sir James Douglass*.

2. Civil

GUILDHALL, Royal Parade. 1870–4 by *Norman & Hine*, the local firm, but with *E. Godwin* as consultant. He had established himself for such jobs with his Northampton Town Hall of 1861–4. Only half the complex survives (reopened in 1959). The N block, with council chamber and municipal offices, was demolished after war damage. The remaining S block, built as Great Hall and Assize Courts, has as its main accent at the SW corner a tall campanile, damaged in the war, and given a lightweight Swedish-looking cap, quite out of keeping with the serious Gothic of the original conception. The new post-war W entrance, with wavy Festival-style canopied porch, is equally dated. N front with earnest reliefs at ground-floor level by *H. Hems*, tourelles and early Gothic plate tracery on the upper floor. The hall was remodelled after the war to provide a small lower hall and an upper main hall, with a false ceiling added above the arcades. Post-war stained glass.

CIVIC CENTRE, Royal Parade. 1961 by *Jellicoe, Ballantyne & Coleridge*. A disturbingly prominent lopsided imposition on the N vista from The Hoe, but more effective when one approaches from the E, where it becomes one of a series of civic landmarks, following St Andrew's church and the Guildhall. A twelve-storey slab of offices with forceful cantilevered butterfly roof, rising above lower ranges on stilts grouped around a courtyard. Both the height and the straightforward modern detailing were deliberate reactions against the indifferent low-key buildings of the first post-war years.

MAGISTRATES COURT, St Andrew's Street. 1979–80. A showpiece of the *City Architect's Department* on a challenging site, close to St Andrew, and cheek by jowl with the only two surviving ancient houses in the central area. In deference to them, a stone-faced ground floor, with a stepped-back upper part to reduce the bulk. The N entrance side is an attractive geometric black-and-white composition, relieved by the angled balconies in front of the upper offices. Straightforward plan with lofty entrance lobby, and corridors and waiting area around the courts in the centre.

REGISTER OFFICE, Lockyer Street. By the *City Architect's Department*, 1984. Small and low, of red brick, tiled roofs of shallow pitch, with overhanging eaves, the materials alien to the city, but neatly detailed.

LAW COURTS, opposite the Civic Centre. A bland box of 1963.

PUBLIC DISPENSARY, behind the Law Courts, facing Catherine Street. Now clinics. 1835 by *George Wightwick*. Ashlar, very plain; two storeys and five windows. Later porch.

CUSTOM HOUSES. *See* Central Plymouth 1: Barbican.

MUSEUM AND LIBRARY, Drake Circus. 1907 by *Thornely & Rooke*. Edwardian Imperial Baroque. The museum is one-storeyed, with composite columns and aediculed windows. The library has as its centrepiece a large Venetian window under an open pediment, and an interior restored in 1954, after being gutted in the war, by the *City Architect's Department*. Cantilevered staircase with light metal balustrade. Stained glass celebrating literary figures by *Morris & Co.*, 1925.

POLYTECHNIC, Drake Circus. Expanded after 1945 near the site of the Plymouth Technical Schools (*c*. 1887 by *Snell*, destroyed in the war), on the fringes of the redeveloped town centre. An over-crowded muddle. On the W part of the site a timidly modern block of 1955 by the City Architect, *H.J.W.Stirling*, for BUILDING AND ENGINEERING; steel-framed, with brick facing above Portland stone, and a grid of windows in a boxed frame. Indifferent slab blocks of the 1960s followed. To the N, a group of three blocks for the SCHOOL OF NAVIGATION (*H.J.W. Stirling*), with a small domed PLANETARIUM at the corner. Then the LIBRARY, 1971–4 by the *County Architect's Department*, more humane, of yellow blockwork, with terraces. The GENERAL TEACHING block, 1979 by the *County Architect's Department* (project architect *E.F.Blake*), is a crudely detailed massive cube with precast cladding panels of glass-reinforced plastic, some with relief projections forming a random pattern.

COLLEGE OF FURTHER EDUCATION, occupying several older institutional buildings. In central Plymouth, the old SOUTH DEVON AND CORNWALL INSTITUTE FOR THE BLIND, North Hill, is a pleasing composition of 1876 by *H.J.Snell*, limestone with sandstone trim around the windows. Five-bay giant-arched centre, lower four-bay wings. The S end, with a tower, was demolished after war damage. The former CORPORATION GRAMMAR SCHOOL, North Road West, is of 1896, gabled Tudor, with an impressive hall with louvre. The former SUTTON SCHOOL FOR BOYS, Regent Street, 1894, is a plain but dignified four-storey urban school, of limestone, with dressings in yellow brick. (*See also* Ford Park, Inner Plymouth Perambulation 2). In Paradise Road, Devonport, boldly inscribed with its name, is the former Devonport Municipal Science Art and Technical School. It deserves its prominent position on Stoke Hill. 1897 by *H.J.Snell*, in free Netherlandish Renaissance. Limestone with Bath stone dressings; gables with little shell-niched aedicules; central clock turret turning octagonal at the top. The new buildings are in the valley below the road, on the site of King's Road Station, closed in 1965. The flat roofs and gawky roof-lights of the workshops are unappealingly prominent. Eight-storey teaching slab. The hipped-roofed block behind is a little easier on the eye.

WESTERN COLLEGE, Western College Road, Mannamead. Now Cooperative Training Centre. Built in 1861 by *Hine* for the Congregational Theological College, founded in 1752, which settled at Plymouth in 1845. A landmark in this hilly suburb and a reminder of the long tradition of dissenting academics in the South West. Large, impressive, gabled high-Gothic range, of limestone with Bath stone dressings. Polygonal central bay with open porch, plate-tracery windows, and high pitched roof. Symmetrical two-storey wings, decorated with accomplished naturalistic foliage carving. In the entrance hall one traceried window; the rest modernized. The grounds were built up after the college closed in 1901.

PLYMOUTH COLLEGE, Ford Park and Hyde Park Road, Mutley. Founded in 1876; the main school buildings erected in 1878–80. Long, battlemented limestone range with mullioned windows. The asymmetrically placed, taller tower-porch has a window to the present library (the original assembly hall), which is distinguished from the other utilitarian interiors by moulded beams and some armorial glass. Additions of 1953–6 behind. To the l. a laboratory wing of 1927, on the site intended for a grand hall which was never built.

STOKE DAMEREL SCHOOL FOR GIRLS (former), Keppel Street, Morice Town. 1908 by *Thornely & Rooke*. Massive, limestone, with some giant arches at the N end and a rusticated plinth and cornice.

DEVONPORT SCHOOL FOR BOYS, Paradise Road, Stoke. *See* Military Hospital (Public Buildings 1).

SUTTON HIGH SCHOOL FOR BOYS, Albert Road, Morice Town. 1878; rendered, gabled Tudor.

ST DUNSTAN'S ABBEY SCHOOL, North Road, Stonehouse. Built for one of the first Anglican religious communities, founded in 1848 by Priscilla Lydia Sellon, the daughter of a naval officer, with the support of Dr Pusey, after Bishop Phillpotts had drawn attention to conditions in Plymouth following the cholera epidemic. The sisterhood rapidly set up an orphanage, schools, refuges, and other charitable works. The foundation stone of the abbey was laid in 1850, and building on a grand scale began to plans by *Butterfield*, with the intention of making the abbey the mother house for all Anglican religious orders. This never came about, and the buildings were less ambitious than planned. The large chapel was not built, and the refectory was converted for this purpose instead. The abbey was taken over by the community of St Mary Wantage in 1906, and continued as a church school after the sisters left in 1956.

The original buildings even in their incomplete state bear witness to Butterfield's skill at varied and original massing. They consist of the low range with the gateway, the refectory (now chapel) opposite, and a dormitory range to the W. The chapel was to have closed the courtyard on the E. Eastlake drew attention to the way in which Butterfield gave the 'generally dull and formal' local limestone life and interest by breaking it up into irregular courses. Plain domestic wing, with lancet windows to the nuns' cells, the elevation enlivened only by a little plate tracery and one gable with a Dec window above a buttress. The irregular fenestration, together with the contrasting roof heights of this range and of the lower link to the gatehouse, make an effective composition. Above the gateway a Gothic window to 'Pusey's room'.

The former refectory is more dramatic: a mighty chimney on the l., a tall steeply pitched roof, a tower with a corbelled window springing from a long buttress, and a drum staircase at the W end in a romantic Germanic mood. Dec windows in framing arches, the W one added after the building was converted to a chapel. The small cloister arcade along the S wall, with dying arches, is an addition of 1935, far from Butterfield's muscular spirit. Alabaster reredos. Two carved wooden angel corbels at the W end, C14 German Gothic in style. Further W a three-storey C19 school building and lower blocks, of less distinguished design. The cruder crazy-paving masonry, also used for the long two-storey enclosing wall along the street, contrasts with Butterfield's work. W of the chapel a refectory added in 1909 (with a chimneypiece from the original refectory), and other buildings, linked by an engagingly informal timber-framed covered walk.

BOARD SCHOOLS. Once a prominent feature of the Victorian

townscape: tall, sturdy institutions of grey limestone, towering above neighbouring houses. Among those built in Plymouth by 1885, the survivors are now mostly appendages to colleges, e.g. those in WOLSDON STREET and CASTLE STREET, now part of the School of Art; also PALACE COURT of 1880 (altered after the war), where a fragment of the early C16 mansion on the site remains. HOW STREET SCHOOL is now the Plymouth W.E.A. headquarters, with two possibly C17 archways from a demolished town house in the courtyard. EAST STREET SCHOOLS, Stonehouse, of 1887, is a lone survivor in the blitzed area s of Union Street.

PILGRIM PRIMARY SCHOOL, Harwell Street. In an area of new housing. Three low white pavilions with pyramid roofs. 1985. Most regrettably, it replaced the OXFORD STREET BOARD SCHOOL, which was an excellent, solid building, Gothic, with variegated slate roof, by the Cornish architect *Silvanus Trevail*, c. 1880.

DISTRICT HOSPITAL, Derriford. The first phase of the large new hospital buildings on the N edge of the city, planned in 1971, was completed in 1981. In the CHAPEL, two windows by *Charles Norris*. The subjects are pain and suffering, and healing hands.

SOUTH DEVON AND EAST CORNWALL HOSPITAL, Greenbank Road, Lipson. A sprawling complex of diverse origin and uncertain future. The hospital is to be transferred to the District Hospital at Derriford. The original hospital buildings were of 1881–4 by *H.E.Coe*, much extended later. Austere symmetrical grey limestone frontage to Hospital Road; tall centre and low detached pavilions with octagonal corner towers. Forecourt with lodge and chapel. Across the road to the E the former WORKHOUSE of 1851 by *Arthur & Dwelly*, undistinguished. At the end of the Greenbank terrace, FREEDOM HOUSE, the former Board of Guardians' offices, 1909, in a friendlier domestic Edwardian Baroque, brick with stone dressings, dentilled cornice and pediment. Also partly used by the hospital, the former BOROUGH PRISONS to the N, limestone and granite, 1849 by *Fuller & Gingell*.

EYE INFIRMARY, Apsley Road, Mutley. 1897 by *Charles King* and *E.W.Lister*. An original design, breaking with the local limestone tradition. Brick with stone dressings. Centre with arched entrance and oriel; two bulgy bows on either side ending in steep conical tiled roofs. All the windows with the odd feature of sashes set behind stone transoms.

PEARN CONVALESCENT HOME, Hartley Avenue, Compton. In its own grounds. An attractive long garden frontage with verandas and two copper domes over projecting bay-windows. The site was given by E.A.Pearn in 1892. His own house, Compton Leigh, was used for the superintendent and nurses.

NORTH ROAD STATION. Rebuilt as Plymouth's main station in 1960–2 by *British Rail Western Region* (architects *H.P.B. Cavanagh, R.L.Moorcroft*). An early example of a station incorporating an office block: INTER CITY HOUSE, a ten-storey slab with white spandrel panels. It was intended to correspond with the contemporary new focus of the Civic Centre across the valley at the opposite end of Armada Way.

ROYAL ALBERT BRIDGE, the railway bridge from St Budeaux to Saltash over the Tamar. By *Isambard Kingdom Brunel*. The bridge was an engineering feat for its date: 1857–9. It is a combined suspension and arched bridge. The technical reason for the two by no means elegant sausage-shaped tubular arches is that their outward thrust on to the abutments counteracts the inward drag of the chains. The oval section of the arches increases their stiffness and gives enough width for the roadway between the vertical chains hanging from the arches: not a handsome, but a safe and sound solution. The high granite shafts on the other hand are, from the Cornish side, a superb effect in the Doré sense.

ROAD BRIDGE over the Tamar. By *Mott, Hay & Anderson*, opened in 1961. A suspension bridge with a central span of 1100ft and side spans of 374ft. The reinforced concrete towers have legs at 50ft centres.

PERAMBULATIONS

1. Barbican

The houses of medieval Plymouth were clustered about the church of St Andrew. When the port grew in importance in the C16 and C17, the town expanded around Sutton Harbour. Post-war replanning makes this relationship difficult to appreciate. In the vicinity of St Andrew there are still two early houses, but they stand in isolation, separated from the rest of old Plymouth by a main road. Both now function as museums.

YOGGE'S HOUSE, Finewell Street. An interesting if considerably restored example of a substantial late medieval merchant's house, built soon after 1498 by Thomas Yogge, who died in 1509. (It was erroneously identified in the C19 as the Prysten or Priest's House, and hence preserved.) Limestone with granite dressings. Three storeys with galleried wings flanking a back courtyard. The back block to the W was replaced in the 1920s by Abbey Hall. The entrance has a slight projection with an arched doorway with carved spandrels. Windows with ogee-headed lights, the bay-window above the entrance especially grand (1–4–1 lights, with transoms). Inside, two stone newels and granite fireplaces.

MERCHANT'S HOUSE, St Andrew's Street. Now Local History Museum. The more usual type of late Tudor town house. C16, remodelled in the early C17 by William Parker. Excellent show front of timber between stone walls. Two jetties, with attics in a double gable above. Doorway to one side. The windows of the first and second floors run the whole width of the house. Pole staircase; granite fireplaces.

To the S, NOTTE STREET, widened after the war, with little of interest apart from a view of the white-rendered old people's flats and offices for Age Concern tucked away up HOEGATE STREET (1982 by *Marshman Warren Taylor*), more sensitive to the character of the old town than the first post-war efforts in this neighbourhood.

In SOUTHSIDE STREET one at last reaches an area of some coherence. Near the beginning is a late medieval building now incorporated in THE DISTILLERY (now a pub and restaurant).

Ground floor, probably used for storage, with a large four-centred archway. First-floor hall with fine arch-braced roof, seven out of eight trusses surviving, the braces, main purlin and collar purlin all with mouldings. Three tiers of wind-braces. The building's original function is unknown. In the C17 it belonged to the Hele family; in later times it became a debtors' prison, a Congregational meeting house, and part of Coates's gin distillery (two C19 stills remain).

Southside Street, running parallel to the harbour (which can be glimpsed intriguingly down the narrow 'Opes'), and New Street, higher up, were laid out in the later C16, after the building of a new quay in 1572. New Street, the best preserved part of old Plymouth, should be investigated first. It can be reached by FRIARS LANE, past TRINITY HOUSE, a handsome C18 house of three storeys, the sashes with unusually small panes (twelve plus twelve). Later C18 pedimented doorcase; two panelled rooms and a good staircase inside. It was later the vicarage of Holy Trinity (built in 1840–2, destroyed in the war), whose ruins remain opposite.

NEW STREET, narrow and winding, cut into the side of the hill, is an evocative mixture of tall limestone rubble warehouses of c. 1800 and lower buildings, many of them in origin timber-fronted merchants' houses of the C16–17. First, warehouses on both sides, rubble with brick dressings. Then on the s side two larger ones of the early C19, with well built stone arches and original ironwork (note the small arched ventilators). On the N side sadly inappropriate infilling (Hanover Court), but, opposite, a group of C16–17 houses (Nos. 34–40). Their proposed destruction as part of the post-war clearance schemes inspired the formation in 1957 of the Barbican Association, which bought and restored them, together with other houses in the area. The fronts of Nos. 34–40 are notable for the excellent timber joinery of their ground floors: No. 38 with door and row of ovolo-moulded windows framed as a single unit, No. 35 with handsomely carved stops to the jambs, and No. 34 with a pretty double-ogee-arched head and putti heads in the spandrels. Their C16 rubble backs, with massive chimneystacks, are visible from the 'Elizabethan Gardens' ingeniously created on the sites of later backland cottages in 1969–70 (architect *Alan Miller-Williams*). In the gardens a doorway of 1630 brought from the Hospital of Poor's Portion, and a reset tympanum with carved ship.

Further down New Street PALACE VAULTS, huge and rather military-looking warehouses dated 1809, reputedly for booty from the Napoleonic wars; expensively finished with stone lintels and a rounded string course. No. 32 is another Elizabethan house, restored in 1926 – over-restored one may now think, but pioneer work at a time when the whole area was threatened by slum clearance. Two jetties, with bracketed oriels to both upper floors. The interior (another museum) retains its original plan with through passage with wooden screen, two rooms on each floor, and an excellent example of a pole stair (or newel stair round a timber post) built out at the back. (Similar pole stairs survive in other houses in New Street.) Upstairs, carved architectural woodwork from demolished houses. Another jettied house opposite, with central doorway and oriel on carved brackets, between rubble warehouses.

At the end, the road divides around ISLAND HOUSE, which has two rendered jettied fronts facing the BARBICAN, i.e. the quay named from the now demolished medieval Barbican watergate. At its end WEST and EAST PIERS, built out to protect the harbour entrance in 1791–9, with the memorial to the Pilgrim Fathers erected in 1891, a sober Doric aedicule. In the same decade the Sutton Harbour Improvement Company, in fierce competition with Millbay, was responsible for the widening of the quay and the building of the FISHMARKET in 1896 on reclaimed land above new sewage tanks, at the entrance to Sutton Pool. An engaging building, resembling a railway station with its cast-iron columns and elegant fringed eaves boards. Designed by *Sir James Inglis*, engineer to the G.W.R. Opposite, No. 12, a tall C18 brick house of three storeys.

Now along SOUTHSIDE STREET, where more good large houses of the late C17 to C18 can still be recognized, despite later alterations. On the harbour side Nos. 23–24, seven windows, dentilled eaves, and Nos. 22 and 20–21, smaller, with end pilasters. Opposite, by Pin Lane, an older double-gabled house with a moulded doorway leading to a back court. No. 53 has a very attractive rendered white front with black-painted early C18 sash windows in three pairs, no doubt a modernization of an older building. Pedimented doorcase. Now down one of the Opes to the PARADE, a wedge-shaped area reclaimed from the sea by the C14, used later by the Royal Marines as a parade ground before their barracks were built at Stonehouse. On the s side the OLD CUSTOM HOUSE, a sturdy rubble building with heavy relieving arches over its openings, and two Tudor doorways. Once with a gabled top storey. Opposite, the refined and elegant NEW CUSTOM HOUSE, 1810 by *David Laing*, his 148 first job as Surveyor to the Customs. Finely dressed ashlar, with rock-faced rustication to the ground floor, and the upper windows recessed in blank arches. Recessed porch with groin-vault. The rear elevation is of rubble, but dignified by a little pediment. Its neighbours are a good warehouse dated 1847, and the THREE CROWNS, with nicely proportioned Georgian sashes.

Along the northern quays of Sutton Pool more warehouses survive, many now converted to new uses (with varying degrees of sympathy). On SUTTON WHARF a specially well detailed example of 1842 (arched windows); also a former COOPERAGE with neo-Tudor archway and battlements. Further on to the E, the former LOWER STREET BAPTIST MISSION (now offices), 1882, with shaped central gable. Behind the quay in VAUXHALL STREET the late C19 former MORTUARY (nicely lettered cornice), now a shop. The front incorporates two cast-iron columns salvaged from the Winter Villa at Stonehouse. No. 2 is the sole survivor of the prosperous houses that once existed here, a brick front of *c.*1800 with *Coade* stone doorway with vigorous head keystone (cf. Southernhay, Exeter).* Much of this neighbourhood, like other parts of the Barbican, was a slum by the later C19, hence the early municipal housing opposite: three-storey flats in

---

*Its neighbour, No. 4, demolished in 1963, was a grand C17 house on the South Western plan of back block connected by galleries; the front remodelled in the C18.

Vauxhall Street (1898, *James Paton*, Borough Engineer), and terraces of two-storey cottage flats running up Looe Street and How Street (exterior staircases at the back). The s side of LOOE STREET survived the clearance, and thanks to post-war efforts by the Barbican Association has a well-cared-for variety of brick, stucco, and timber fronts: highlights are No. 29, four storeys, early C18 brick; No. 30, late C18 stuccoed; Nos. 31–32, the Minerva, with two jettied upper floors; No. 33, rubble stone with oriels; No. 36 with another oriel; No. 38, early C18 brick; and the Plymouth Arts Centre, early C19, with an attractive undulating fascia (originally with bow-windows below).

2. *Foulston's Plymouth, The Hoe, and Millbay*

The activities which suddenly pushed Plymouth into the centre of architectural interest in England started shortly after 1810. They are chiefly concerned with *John Foulston* (1772–1842), a pupil of Thomas Hardwick who decided to leave London and settle in Plymouth when at the age of thirty-nine he had won the competition for the Royal Hotel and Theatre, a large and noble building, erected between 1811 and 1818, and swept away entirely before and during the Second World War. The Royal Hotel was followed a little further w by the Athenaeum (1818–19), gutted in the war and demolished afterwards. It was of a most unorthodox Greek Doric, asymmetrical, in a spirit of stout self-reliance and far from respectful to Greek precedent. A chapel nearby (later St Catherine) built by Foulston in 1823 has fared no better: it was demolished in 1958. In the neighbourhood of these public buildings Foulston with the help of his pupil *George Wightwick* laid out a regular grid of streets, with Lockyer Street and Athenaeum Street as the main N–S axes. The excellent stuccoed neo-classical terraces and villas they built along them have been much depleted by war damage and the gaps insensitively filled; much more could have been preserved and restored had the area attracted the same kind of concern as the Barbican did.

THE CRESCENT was the grandest effort. Twelve out of eighteen three-storey houses remain, divided by pilasters with honeysuckle decoration. The larger end house, No. 1, is embellished by five giant arches on Ionic half-columns. (Well restored interior, with oval staircase well with saucer dome; friezes with incised key decoration.) In LOCKYER STREET, WINDSOR VILLAS, six detached houses, each of three bays with slightly projecting centre, and two fragments of three-storey terraces: Nos. 22–24 with heavy Tuscan porches stepping up the hill, and Nos. 9–15, much rebuilt apart from Nos. 14–15. ATHENAEUM STREET is more modest and more complete, with stepped terraces of two-storey pairs, their doorways neatly placed together in the centre below shallow arches on elegantly incised pilaster-jambs, their ground-floor channelling relieved by segmental arches over the windows.

THE HOE, to the SE of this area, has a much older history. In the Middle Ages it is known to have possessed an odd adornment, Gog Magog, two giants holding clubs, cut into the turf (cf. Cerne Abbas, Dorset). They survived until the building of the Citadel in the C17 (*see* Public Buildings 1). Hoe Park was laid out in 1817 and extended in the 1880s, after the outworks of the Citadel had been abandoned. Around this time and later the seaward slopes were furnished with delightful shelters and seats set into the side of the hill, some with rather frivolous Art-Nouveau ironwork. The HOE DOME visitors' centre by the *City Architect's Department* dates from 1988. In front of the Citadel, MARINE BIOLOGICAL LABORATORY, 1888. The flat top of The Hoe is still occupied by a parade ground, uninspiringly asphalted, and by a string of unrelated and rather pompous MONUMENTS: STATUE of Drake by *Boehm*, 1884 (the same as at Tavistock); ARMADA MEMORIAL, 1888 by *N.A.Gribble*, with bronze relief and figures of Britannia and lion by *W.Charles May*; MEMORIAL to Prince Christian Victor who died in the Boer War, a red marble obelisk of 1902–3 by *F.W.Marks*, with bronze plaques by *E.Fuchs* and *G.O.Whiting*; MEMORIAL to the Royal Marines, *c.* 1920, stone figures of soldier and sailor, bronze figure killing an eagle, by *W.C.Storr Barber*. The largest is the WAR MEMORIAL to naval men, chosen as the axis for the layout of the post-war town in the valley below. 1920–4, designed by *Sir Robert Lorimer* with sculpture by *W.C.Storr Barber*. Tall obelisk with sculptured ships' prows and a copper globe supported by bronze atlantes, and with four lions at the base (cf. Portsmouth). The low exedra facing the city was added after the Second World War by *Maufe*, with two bronze groups by *William McMillan*. But the best of the monuments is the top part of *Smeaton*'s EDDYSTONE LIGHTHOUSE of 1756–9, re-erected here in 1882 (*see* Public Buildings: 1). It was an epoch-making achievement at the time, cosy as its scale looks now.

The NW side of The Hoe is closed by quite grand terraces: THE ESPLANADE, 1836 by *Wightwick*, of nineteen bays, and ELLIOT TERRACE and the GRAND HOTEL, in a fussier mid C19 Italianate. Much of West Hoe was used as a stone quarry until the later C19. The first housing in the area was the mid C19 terrace facing the sea in GREAT WESTERN ROAD, with a central pediment on the seaward side. N of this the break with the stucco tradition came with the DUKE OF CORNWALL HOTEL, Millbay Road, built to cater for the G.W.R. passengers to Millbay (*see* below). 1865 by *C. Forster Hayward*, confident High Victorian Gothic, much decorated with *Blashfield*'s terracotta, its skyline a multitude of gables, turrets, and chimneys. The tactlessly tall slab of the MAYFLOWER POST HOUSE not far off, of a century later (by *Nelson Foley* of Trusthouse Forte's Architect's Department, completed 1970), is no less assertive, but without any compensating individual character. Still worse is the HOLIDAY INN, intruding on the view towards the city centre. In contrast, the flats at EDDYSTONE TERRACE, 1979–80 by *Marshman Warren Taylor*, are a good example of tactful infilling in a mid Victorian stuccoed context.

MILLBAY, between The Hoe and Stonehouse, developed after its docks were built in 1840. The arrival of *Brunel*'s Great Western Railway in Plymouth, and the opening of the Millbay station in 1849, turned these into the main docks for ocean-going liners; closure of the station in 1941 led to their decline. A few dock buildings remained until 1988: an octagonal limestone LODGE, with ground-floor windows in round-headed arches; and some three-storey WAREHOUSES of c. 1857, of limestone rubble, with round-headed doorways on each floor, and interiors with cast-iron columns.* Multi-storey car parks to serve the city centre were added from 1987. A LEISURE CENTRE (by *Module 2*) is planned on the site of the station.

3. *Central Plymouth*

The rebuilding of the centre of Plymouth after its virtually total destruction in the Second World War is an interesting episode in the history of planning, radical in conception, speedy in execution. But the layout is more impressive on paper than on the ground, and the buildings themselves are almost without exception devoid of any local character and dismally unmemorable. So some of the proposals in the city's plan, *Tomorrow's Plymouth* (1987), are welcome. They include covered pedestrian shopping arcades, and bolder landscaping to counter the bleakness of the 1940s.

The Victorian town centre spread in crowded and haphazard fashion from the area around St Andrew's church northwards over the valley which The Hoe cuts off from the sea. The new plan, conceived in 1943 by *J. Paton Watson*, the City Engineer, together with *Professor Patrick Abercrombie* as consultant, abandoned the old street patterns. Within an inner ring road a snaking zigzag of shopping streets was created (originally intended for vehicles, pedestrianized in 1987), cut through by a grandiose pedestrian avenue, ARMADA WAY, running for 1,000 yards from The Hoe to the rebuilt station at North Road, a 'garden vista' in the Beaux-Arts tradition, although in its discrepancy of scale between large-scale landscape and modest buildings more reminiscent of the centre of Welwyn Garden City than of Paris.

The first new buildings were not more than four to six storeys in height. The most aspiring are around St Andrew's Cross and along ROYAL PARADE, which forms a windswept *via triumphalis* past the church and the remodelled Guildhall to the tall tower of the Civic Centre. The tower, however, was an afterthought, imposed on the original plan about 1960 in an attempt to provide a central focus. The sequence starts at ST ANDREW'S CROSS with the NATIONAL WESTMINSTER BANK (*B. C. Sherren, c.* 1960), with the favourite fifties motif of an inset frame to the centre. The best of the earlier buildings are on the N side. Ironically, it is this group, of c. 1951, the most worthwhile of the early 1950s rebuilding, that is one of the first to be threatened with redevelopment.‡ It starts with a well proportioned block of offices and shops by *Douglas Hamilton Wakeford & Partners* with a long, slightly curved side towards Old Town Street. Next to this BOOTS by *C. St Clair Oakes*, staff architect, with portholes to enliven the upper walls at one end. Further along Royal Parade, at the crossing of Armada Way, DINGLES, the first department store in the country to be rebuilt after the war, 1950 by *Sir John Burnet, Tait & Partners*, and opposite, PEARL ASSURANCE by *Alec C. French & Partners*. Both have symmetrical set-backs at the corner with a higher block

---

* Demolished to make way for new housing.

‡ The proposal (1988) is for a three-storey shopping mall with atrium, by *Chapman Taylor Partners* for Burton Property Trust.

at the re-entrant angle, and are conventional in their formal massing, although classical detail has been abandoned. To the w the PLYMOUTH CO-OPERATIVE SOCIETY by *W.J. Reed*, with Festival trimmings. Further s, at the corner of NOTTE STREET and Armada Way, BARCLAYS BANK, by *W. Curtis Green*, in a more traditional academic style, with large round-arched windows, and the HOE CENTRE services club by Messrs *Joseph*, of brick, in a vaguely Dudok manner, *c.* 1951.*

Other buildings need not be singled out. The co-ordinating architect from 1945 to 1951 was *William Crabtree*. The lesser shops (sixty-eight open by 1954) are mostly of three storeys, reducing to two as one progresses along the less important streets to the N. Most have as their common feature disappointingly bland frontages of Portland stone (instead of the beautiful local grey limestone and marbles of Victorian Plymouth). The fenestration is not identical, but the impression is of bittiness rather than interesting variety. From the viewpoint of The Hoe the most depressing feature is the dreary flat roofscape.‡

Around this dull but coherent centre, larger and glossier buildings of the seventies onwards jostle stranded Victorian fragments. At the w end of Royal Parade, near DERRY'S CROSS, a CLOCK TOWER of 1862, once a pivot of the Victorian centre, stands awkwardly in a triangular pedestrian space next to the former BANK of 1889, a handsome Italianate building with a bowed end designed to fit a street corner that no longer exists. The bank is now a pub, with a post-modern greenhouse-type extension of 1986 at the back. Close by is the THEATRE ROYAL, a welcome new focus, proposed in the post-war plan but built only after long delays. Designed in 1977, completed in 1982, by the *Peter Moro Partnership*. It is the latest in a series of notable theatres designed by this firm, but lacks the dynamism of their earlier designs. A smoothly elegant, slightly bland polygonal structure with a cluster of concrete fly towers above the sleek curtain-walling. Pleasantly irregular foyer space on several levels. Steeply raked auditorium with two galleries, the lower one descending on one side in place of boxes. No proscenium arch. Behind the theatre is the inevitable multi-storey car park; not far off is a pathetic replacement of the Athenaeum. The inner ring road here has been particularly brutal to Foulston's Plymouth (*see* Perambulation 2, above). Road engineering is even more dominant at CHARLES CROSS, at the other end of Royal Parade beyond St Andrew's Cross (*see* Inner Plymouth, Perambulation 1).

From the later 1970s the commercial centre of gravity began to shift to more recent buildings around the fringe of the post-war rebuilding. The first landmark was MONEYCENTRE at DRAKE CIRCUS, 1975 by *Marshman Warren Taylor*, the usual block-and-podium combination, but elegantly handled: eight storeys with bands of tinted windows alternating with cream unbonded tiles; the lower parts clad with the same material. Spacious pedestrian ramps up to first-floor level help to give the building a human

*The future of much of the area between Old Town Street and New George Street is uncertain at the time of writing.

‡Redevelopment of the w part of this area (between Derry's Cross, Western Approach, and Frankfurt Gate) was under discussion in 1988.

scale. At the N end of ARMADA WAY near the station the trailblazer is the ARMADA CENTRE, a covered shopping precinct for Sainsburys and others (1984–6). It has been kept low, with a taller hotel behind (*M.P. Design Group* with *Igal Yawetz & Associates*). By the same firm, SAINSBURY'S HOME BASE (1987–8), further W at the junction of Western Avenue and Union Street.

INNER PLYMOUTH

1. N of Cobourg Street and Charles Street

CHARLES CROSS, with its overbearing and exceptionally ugly car park dominating the ruined church on the roundabout, is an unpromising start. The C17 church (*see* Charles Church) was built to serve the suburbs which developed to the N of Sutton Harbour, and which are now fragmented by the ring road.

At the E corner of the roundabout LANYON ALMSHOUSES, with a reset plaque of 1679; the present Tudor buildings with crow-stepped gables are of 1868 by *Robert Hodges*. The earliest remaining houses in this area are on the S side of EBRINGTON STREET, running E from here, a stuccoed nine-bay terrace partly obscured by built-out shops, with keystones to the upper windows and a rainwater head dated 1784. Opposite, the TRAFALGAR, a jolly pub of 1897, of brick, with a shaped gable. Further on, GASKING STREET curves uphill to become LIPSON ROAD, the old route to Exeter before Laira Bridge was built. On the W side GASCOYNE PLACE, a reticent slate-hung three-storey terrace and pairs of houses with arched ground-floor windows, early C19, set back behind large front gardens. Some gatepiers with pineapples. Opposite, a busier later C19 stuccoed terrace with channelled quoins and keystones.

Lesser stuccoed terraces in the minor streets nearby, e.g. BEAUMONT PLACE, complete on both sides. E of this BEAUMONT PARK, the grounds of Beaumont House, the seat of the Bewes family, made into a public park in 1890. The house, which is now a clinic, has an C18 five-window, three-storey wing with two nice Venetian windows at the back, and a Regency E wing and porch, all stuccoed. Further N, SEVEN STARS, a villa still in its own grounds. Other early C19 villas in this area were gradually engulfed by the irregular grid of small C19 streets climbing uphill. Good houses in RADNOR PLACE N of Regent Street, with a terrace with bowed fronts (unusual in Plymouth). N of Armada Street plainer, humbler early C19 terraces remain in WATERLOO STREET and NELSON STREET, flat stuccoed fronts with arched doorways. Just to the N the grander BEDFORD TERRACE (a private cul-de-sac reached from the rear of the crest of North Hill), with ST JOHN'S TERRACE proudly overlooking the harbour, stuccoed, with rusticated ground floor with arched windows. At the W end a detached castellated villa, and opposite it another, BEDFORD VILLA, with pedimented wing and a porch in the angle.

Down NORTH HILL towards Drake Circus there was little building on the E side until the later C19. Coherent suburban development here started with SHERWELL HOUSE of 1883 (on the site of an older villa), and then QUEEN ANNE TERRACE, dated 1884 and 1885, its name as well as its style proclaiming its allegiance to Norman Shaw, a rarity in Plymouth. An excellent composition, three storeys, with alternating red-brick and slate-hung gables, oriel windows, and balconies. Lesser terraces in the same style behind in MARLBOROUGH ROAD and ADDISON ROAD, and more, with purpose-built shops, further s and towards the library.

On the w side of North Hill remains of a similar mixture of earlier C19 terraces and villas, those at the s end mostly swallowed up by the Polytechnic (q.v.). PORTLAND SQUARE was laid out in 1811, but little remains. To its w PORTLAND VILLAS, nicely grouped mid C19 stucco terraces with lower linking wings, and several detached houses. N of this NORTH ROAD EAST leads back to North Hill, with good terraces on both sides, on the N three storeys, on the s lower, with the popular mid C19 motif of triple arched windows. Behind these, off Endsleigh Place, ELIZABETH PLACE, a cul-de-sac with a glimpse of RESERVOIR HOUSE at the end, a handsome stuccoed villa with canted bay and veranda. In the garden a tiny Gothic summer house overlooking the reservoir. The unobtrusive main entrance to the house is in SKARDON PLACE, a small but varied street off North Hill, which also has a castellated end house, and RESERVOIR COTTAGE, with decorative bargeboards. Another detached villa, also with bargeboards, somewhat altered, close to North Hill. The RESERVOIRS themselves date from the C18. Around them remains of inscriptions etc. recording the water supply first brought to Plymouth in the later C16.

2. From North Hill to Mutley Plain and Mannamead

At the top of NORTH HILL, N of the Institute for the Blind (*see* Public Buildings: College of Further Education), a handsome mid C19 palace frontage raised above the road, with pedimented ends and neo-classical detail of a coarse kind over the end and the centre windows. Simpler stuccoed terraces along NOTTINGHAM GARDENS to the w. From North Hill the road drops down to MUTLEY PLAIN, where the late C19 suburban shopping arcades (concealing earlier terraces) are dominated by the mighty Baptist chapel at one end (q.v.), and at the other by the former automobile showrooms of 1930, one of the town's few major buildings of between the wars. Three storeys of large windows with original marginal glazing; rendered walls with giant pilasters. To the w, FORD PARK, a well preserved L-shaped layout of particularly lavish mid C19 villas with busy Italianate stucco detail, in close-set groups of two and three. Another pair in larger grounds in the angle of the L. A low limestone lodge with round-headed windows by the entrance (illustrated in *George Wightwick*'s album; did he also design the houses?). Now all part of the College of Further Education (q.v.).

From the N end of Mutley Plain MANNAMEAD ROAD climbs steeply uphill. Near the bend was the site of *Foulston*'s much advertised Athenian villa. The area became the most affluent of Plymouth's Victorian suburbs, developed after Mannamead Fields were sold in 1851. The most imposing houses lie along the ridge in SEYMOUR

DRIVE, large, detached Italianate mansions in their own grounds, still happily complete with their main gatepiers and garden walls to the s and service entrances from the N (cf. Torquay). The best houses are Kempton Lodge and Whitleigh.

A little further N COMPTON, with a few isolated buildings remaining from the older settlement of this name. No. 80 COMPTON AVENUE is the former vicarage of Emmanuel (q.v.), a delightful Arts and Crafts design dated 1906, an irregular roughcast composition with gables, long horizontal casement windows, and a stone-mullioned bay. Flat porch roof suspended from twisted iron brackets. Some way NE in LOCKINGTON AVENUE, among a varied selection of earlier C20 houses, the present vicarage, built by a priest from St Gabriel's as a private house, on a butterfly plan, with eccentric angled porch with inscription. Larger C19 houses at the s end of Lockington Avenue, e.g. No. 152 at the corner, with a grand campanile with decorative panels. The streets w of Mannamead Road are later and less ambitious. The best is THORN PARK, with terraces of after 1877 (still with Doric porches) surrounding a pleasant open space whose notable feature is an early C20 ovoid cast-iron urinal with decorative panels, by *Macfarlane* of Glasgow.

CENTRAL PARK, some way E of Thorn Park, was laid out on the open land remaining between the expanding suburbs of Plymouth and Stoke. At its N end, POUNDS HOUSE, a pleasant mid C19 classical villa. To its s, in CENTRAL PARK AVENUE, an isolated curiosity: Nos. 5–7 RUSSELL PLACE, a picturesque asymmetrical Gothic stone group with cusped lancets and a battlemented and machicolated tower, formerly the gatehouse to Devonport Prison (now demolished), built in 1849.

FARLEY'S, Tor Lane. The original buildings for Farley's Rusks are of 1930 by *A. V. Rooke* of Plymouth, a stylish model factory built on what was then a garden suburb site on the edge of the city. Four-storey main block, steel-framed, rendered brick, the detail classical-modernistic. Contemporary gates and loading doors. The car park at the back was formerly laid out as a garden; a wooden pavilion remains. Doubled in size in 1938–40 by *F. R. Fairmanor*; many post-war extensions by *Bazeley & Miller-Williams*.

3. To the E: Lipson, Laira, Mount Gould

The most interesting developments are around FREEDOM FIELDS, an open space with a sturdy granite monument commemorating the victory of the Parliamentary forces over the besieging Royalists in 1643. Off to the w WOODSIDE, a mixed group of small early C19 houses, date plaque 1810; No. 8, the grandest, stuccoed, with Tuscan porch. Along the N edge of the Fields, set back behind a private drive, QUEEN'S GATE, a confident yellow and red brick terrace of the 1890s, with all the trimmings of the old English style, half-timbered and tiled gables, decorative bargeboards, a conscious contrast to the restrained early C19 neo-classical stucco of LIPSON TERRACE across Lipson Road to the E. This also has a private drive, guarded by two charming little octagonal lodges. Each house of three bays with central porch and end pilasters, the centre of the terrace with anthemion on upswept parapet. Further

N, by MOSTYN AVENUE, MOUNT LIPSON COTTAGE, built
c. 1834–5 as a dower house to the now demolished Mount Lipson,
seat of the Govett family: a delightful small stuccoed villa with
canted bay looking N over Lipson Vale.

In LAIRA AVENUE, S of Old Laira Road, CLEEVE VILLA, with
trellis veranda and lattice glazing, THE GLEN, with pretty bargeboards, and No. 17, tall, with plain overhanging eaves, all belong
to a little development of *cottages ornés* which before the railway
blocked their view in the 1840s overlooked the broad expanse of
the Laira Water. They are now surrounded by a nicely haphazard
group of artisan cottages of c. 1900. Planned working-class housing
was provided in LAIRA BRIDGE ROAD, Prince Rock. The two-
storeyed flats and houses of 1893–6 by *Hine & Odgers*, built by the
City Council to house people cleared from Looe Street, were
among the first to be erected following the Housing Act of 1890.
Red brick with timbered gables, a conscious adoption of the Old
English vernacular idiom, as used, for example, for contemporary
London County Council housing. A little further out, two further
blocks of two-storey flats, of 1897 by *Wibling & De Boinville* for
the Plymouth Charitable Trusts; fancy wooden balconies to the
first-floor entrances.*

MOUNT GOULD AVENUE and MOUNT GOULD CRESCENT have
a later group of early C20 model cottages, begun by the Astors and
continued by the local authority (c. 1919), complete with institute.‡ Simple roughcast houses, their informal layout owing something to Parker & Unwin. Finally, back towards the centre,
SOUTH DEVON PLACE, on the N side of EMBANKMENT ROAD,
a good earlier C19 terrace, the central houses taller, with a
pediment.

4. Stonehouse and Union Street

Stonehouse was the smallest of the three towns, bounded on the N by
Stonehouse Creek and Lake, a long inlet which until the C20
stretched as far as Mill Bridge, W of Victoria Park. There was a
medieval settlement around Newport Street, by Stonehouse Pool,
with two churches and a manor house which belonged by the C16
to the Mount Edgcumbes. A defensive wall was built in the 1550s.
By the mid C18 this nucleus had begun to expand. An assembly
room was built in 1756 (the Long Room, later incorporated in the
Royal Marine Barracks of 1779–85); the Royal Naval Hospital was
established in 1758–62; and in 1773 the Mount Edgcumbes laid
out Durnford Street and Emma Place, which became a fashionable
residential area for naval officers. The most spectacular growth
came in the early C19, after *Foulston*'s grand design of Union
Street, laid out from 1812 to 1820, had united Plymouth and
Devonport, and *Rennie*'s great new Victualling Yard had been
created on reclaimed land at the tip of the peninsula. Grids of neat
stuccoed terraces were laid out N and S of Union Street, which was
punctuated mid way by an octagon. Public baths were provided S
of The Octagon (later removed for the Millbay Railway), and in
1850 a town hall at the end of Emma Place. Little of all this

*I owe these details to Chris Brooks.
‡Future uncertain.

survived the last war. The bombs wiped out the entire shopping centre, the town hall, most of Union Street, and much else. A section of the early C16 town wall survives near the site of the manor house, crenellated, with blocked gunport. Otherwise only Durnford Street remains virtually intact, Plymouth's most complete C18 street. Further N, the Naval Hospital is an important survival, but elsewhere the plan of 1943 envisaged total rebuilding, with an industrial zone S of Union Street and a new layout of residential neighbourhoods to the N, shopping to be provided by the rebuilt Plymouth central area. Building began but was never completed as first intended. The result is depressing: no focal point, here and there battered stucco terraces, between them vacant sites and the meanly detailed brick maisonettes of the post-war years of austerity.

DURNFORD STREET. On the E side the long set piece of the Royal Marine Barracks (*see* Public Buildings 1). Elsewhere, a satisfying sequence of quite modest late C18 three-storeyed terrace houses, stuccoed or slate-hung, with slate-hung backs. Some good doorcases with open pediments. Near the S end, by St Paul (q.v.), a grander corner building attributed to *Foulston*, with giant Ionic three-quarter columns above a rusticated ground floor. In ADMIRALTY STREET to the E a pleasantly unspoilt minor early C19 enclave of terraces. Off to the W, at the S end of CREMYLL STREET, MOUNT STONE, tucked away in the bowl of a former quarry. All slate-hung. Old, irregular N parts, much altered; S wing rebuilt *c*. 1780 after a fire, and improved in 1830 by *Foulston*, who moved the main entrance from the W to the S, with two columns *in antis* set into an otherwise blank wall. W rooms with good cornices. Near the S end of Durnford Street, overlooking Firestone Bay, was the Mount Edgcumbe family's WINTER VILLA, a lavish mid C19 Italianate creation with glazed arcaded loggias, replaced, alas, in 1978 by the more prosaic buildings of Nazareth House. W of Durnford Street ADMIRAL'S HARD, with BYRON HOUSE, a small stuccoed house with battered walls and bracketed cornice, picturesquely sited on the edge of the creek where the ferry crosses to Mount Edgcumbe.

UNION STREET is a mere ghost of the once bustling dockland artery. At the W end at the time of writing, now that the large WESLEYAN METHODIST CHURCH of 1813 has been demolished, only a few plain stucco terraces faintly recall the original character of the street. The Octagon has been smoothed away. The only remarkable building left is the former GREAT WESTERN HOTEL and PALACE THEATRE (now the ACADEMY) towards the E end. 1898 by *Wimperis & Arbour*. Four storeys with turrets, brown cast stone with ginger maiolica, Armada pictures on tiles, and Art Nouveau detail. Good original auditorium with two lavishly decorated curved balconies on iron columns. Generously scaled foyer, imperial stair, and upper restaurant in Cinquecento style. Opposite, one original terrace, and to its W the THEATRE, a tiled pub commemorating another theatre, now vanished. To N and S only pathetic relics of the smaller streets and dignified stuccoed terraces. To the N is the HIGH STREET, with the Royal Naval Hospital to its N (*see* Public Buildings 1), and to its S a fragment of the old grid around ADELAIDE STREET, *c*. 1820 by

Foulston, pedestrianized and half-heartedly restored in the 1970s. Low stucco terraces, generously provided with corner pubs, in a simpler version of Foulston's work around The Hoe. Ground-floor arched windows, end bays with pediments. CLARENCE PLACE, parallel to the N, has instead of parapets deep projecting eaves. Similar contrasts are to be found in the even more fragmentary terraces S of Union Street: Emma Place and Caroline Place. The blocks on the S side of EMMA PLACE (all that survive) have end and (formerly) central pediments; each house has a solid porch and giant pilaster with fancy capital. The end houses are larger, with side entrances and bowed back projections. Along CAROLINE PLACE are two terraces with deep eaves, one (Nos. 5–9) with the attractive motif of windows framed by shallow arcades on pilasters with incised decoration. Are these the five houses which were designed *c.*1835 for Caroline Place by *Charles Chapple*, a local architect?

5. Stoke

The old village of Stoke Damerel, with its parish church (St Andrew, Paradise Road), was gradually absorbed as a suburb of the Three Towns during the C19. The Military Hospital on the edge of Stonehouse Lake (*see* Public Buildings 1) dates from 1797. The first scattered groups of villas and terraces occupying choice positions on elevated sites overlooking Stonehouse Creek and the Docks appeared *c.*1825. They display the same neo-classical spirit as the new urban centres of Plymouth and Devonport. The best group is near the junction of Paradise Road and Devonport Road: ALBEMARLE VILLAS, by *Foulston*, a string of eight neat detached stucco houses set *en échelon*, two or three bays wide, with side entrances and a pretty variety of Grecian ironwork for verandas, garden gates, and railings (no longer, alas, complete). No. 3 was plainly rebuilt after war damage. No. 1 has a Doric entrance grander than the rest, facing Devonport Road. Opposite, ST MICHAEL'S LODGE, a larger house by *Foulston*. Entrance side of three bays with closed porch, heavy cornice, and tapering end pilasters; on the S side a full-height pilastered bow-window. Elegantly detailed hall with four Greek Doric columns and segmental arches, and one original fireplace.

Further up DEVONPORT ROAD, No. 157, typical of later, more Italianate houses. Then BELMONT PLACE and BELMONT VILLAS, the S side with pedimented projecting porches. At the end, in its own grounds, BELMONT, the best surviving of *Foulston*'s 142 villas, now a youth hostel. Built *c.*1825 for John Norman. Very pure neo-Grecian. Two stuccoed show fronts; the other two of brick. The entrance has a tetrastyle portico, the garden front two columns *in antis*. Well preserved interiors, complete with their mahogany doors, and several handsome marble fireplaces; the small library in the centre of the garden front has original inset bookcases with a Greek-key cornice. Restrained entrance hall, with shallow segmental arched ceiling and pairs of Doric columns, leading to the central hall with an imperial stair. The surprise is the room opening off the half-landing; a very Soanian picture gallery, now used rather inappropriately as a dormitory. It is top-lit, with

oval saucer dome and lantern. At either end a shallow barrel-vault
on paired pilasters with incised ornament.

Further E, along SOMERSET PLACE, with minor stuccoed terraces,
to PENLEE GARDENS, a shallow crescent of paired villas spaciously set out along a private drive with its own lodge. The central
pair is pedimented, but other details, e.g. the varied side
entrances, are not consistent. Set-back neo-classical screen walls
conceal the back gardens, an unusual feature. Opposite the lodge,
PENLEE COTTAGE, gabled Victorian Tudor. Elsewhere along
MOLESWORTH ROAD versions of the classical tradition: an
Italianate terrace with pedimented first-floor windows, and PARK
PLACE (Nos. 102–108), pairs with a nice variety of tripartite
entrances and bay-windows. The exception is Nos. 44–70, a High
Victorian Gothic terrace, of brick, with corbelled-out stone oriels.
Near the foot of the hill FELLOWES PLACE, with groups of two
and three stuccoed houses once overlooking Stonehouse Creek.
The water used to extend as far as MILL BRIDGE. To the E of this
HOTHAM PLACE, Tudor cottages with bargeboarded gables.

Further S another early piece of planned development around
WYNDHAM SQUARE, c. 1815, attributed to *Foulston*, an outlier of
expanding Stonehouse (*see* Inner Plymouth 4). Around the square
with St Peter's church (q.v.) a lively grouping of three-storeyed
terraces making full use of projecting pedimented pavilions. Further E, first a Gothic interlude: the ruin of a C19 SCHOOL, a long
limestone wall with Gothic windows, the R.C. Cathedral (q.v.),
and BISHOP'S HOUSE to its S (1859, enlarged 1899). In the grid
of neighbouring streets (WYNDHAM STREET, CECIL STREET)
quite a number of lesser stucco terraces have survived the reaction
against this kind of urban layout. DENSHAM TERRACE, on the S
side of NORTH ROAD WEST, is less spoilt than many. In WYND-
HAM STREET EAST a former CHAPEL, with tall, stuccoed,
pedimented front. The post-war ideals are illustrated nearby: the
star-shaped clusters of four-storey flats of c. 1954 by the City
Architect, *H. J. W. Stirling*.

The area between Wyndham Square and the centre of Plymouth was
fragmented first by the Millbay branch of the G.W.R., and then by
the post-war inner relief road further E. Since then, much rebuilding of 1980–5 by the *City Architect's Department*, with innocuous
rendered and tile-hung terraces replacing the old stucco streets.
The one group that deserves to be sought out is in HARWELL
STREET, where a tight triangular site was filled by All Saints
church (demolished), a church hall, and a remarkably original and
impressive CLERGY HOUSE by *J. D. Sedding*, 1887, a free Arts
and Crafts interpretation of a town house in the old English tradition, in a well handled mixture of materials: limestone ground
floor, roughcast above, mullioned windows of both timber and
stone, picturesquely grouped stair-turret and brick chimneys.
Neglected for many years, and still awaiting conversion in 1988.

6. Devonport

Devonport today is the saddest of the three towns. At first simply
called Dock, it began to develop in the C18 around the naval
dockyards and the navy buildings on Mount Wise. The parish

church of St Aubyn dates from 1771, a Unitarian chapel was built
in 1790, St John's proprietary chapel in 1799. Polwhele already
describes it as a 'town of elegance', with 2,400 houses. Civic
pride insisted on the establishment of a town in its own right, and the
name Devonport was bestowed by the king in 1824. The event was
immortalized by the erection of a column, together with a town
hall close by as the set piece of *Foulston's* formal layout around Ker
Street. Other public buildings followed; in 1841 the *Stranger's
Handbook* wrote of 'well-constructed houses in commodious
streets paved with marble'. This unique urban centre has until
very recently been treated with scant respect. Much that survived
the war has been demolished, and the replacements are of the
drabbest kind. Furthermore, the dockyards have encroached still
further, so that much of Fore Street, the former shopping centre
with its elegant Market House, is now within their bounds (*see*
Public Buildings 1: Royal Naval Base).

In the earlier C19 the town was still ringed by fortifications: the
Devonport lines, constructed in 1756, were enlarged in 1783 and
1810 (Devonport Park is on part of their site), and suburban
development was slow, hindered by the leasehold system of the St
Aubyn estate. Morice Town grew from 1791, when the ferry to
Torpoint began, with Albert Road (formerly Navy Row) as its
main thoroughfare, but other areas to the N expanded only from
the mid C19: Keyham after the opening of the Steam Yard (now
North Yard) in 1848, Ford from *c.* 1856, developed by the Devon
and Cornwall Freehold Land Society.

Foulston's group of civic buildings of 1821–4 at the end of KER 147
STREET stands pathetically isolated amid drab post-war
reconstruction. They deserve to be cherished, for they are among
the most remarkable of their date. As originally conceived, the
fledgling town of Devonport was provided with an idiosyncratic
demonstration of successive styles of architecture: Egyptian
institution, 'Hindoo' chapel, Grecian town hall, approached up a
street with classical terraces, and with a commemorative column
appearing off centre in the background. Today, only town hall,
institution, and column survive: the chapel was demolished
c. 1925, and the terraces were destroyed after the Second World
War.

COLUMN. Greek Doric; on the wall below, a plate inscribed Devonport Jan. 1st 1824. Aligned on Union Street, which Foulston had
laid out a few years earlier – hence its odd position in relation to the
town hall.

TOWN HALL. Austere and massive, facing down the street. 1821.
Restored in 1986–7 and now in community use. Four-column
Greek Doric portico with wide central intercolumniation; no
triglyphs or pediment, but a heavy cornice with blocking course
stepping up to a central figure of Britannia (*Coade* stone, modelled
by *J. Panzetta*), added in 1835. Two-storey addition of *c.* 1840 at
the back. The original building contains a single room with a coved
ceiling for assembly hall-cum-courtroom, with cells in the basement beneath.

INSTITUTION, to the r. of the town hall. 1823, At first a classical
and mathematical school, then a library, now a club, and shock-
ingly ill cared for at the time of writing (compare the careful

restoration of the Egyptian house at Penzance in Cornwall). The Egyptian style became fashionable after Napoleon's campaign: the best known example was P. F. Robinson's Egyptian Hall in Piccadilly of 1811–12. Stuccoed front of two storeys, with recessed central entrance with bulgy Egyptian columns and capitals, the windows with tapering frames, further outlined by a decorative giant frame of the same shape. The elaborate patterned glazing survives. Inside, the ground floor has been drastically altered, but the grand upper room could still be rescued. It retains its original window surrounds and doors with Egyptian motifs in relief.

The dignified terrace along the s side of Ker Street was torn down after the war and replaced by depressingly drab grey rendered flats, just a little more elaborately detailed (see the gutter brackets) than the indifferent housing in the neighbouring streets. To the N some early C19 remnants in CUMBERLAND STREET: on the s side Nos. 8–14, windows with neo-classical surrounds, channelled pilasters between each house. No. 7 is especially grand, with Corinthian pilasters to the upper floors, a pediment, and niches with urns in the side bays. Opposite, the CROWN HOTEL, stuccoed Italianate of 1880.

In DUKE STREET, w of Cumberland Street, mostly housing of the 1950s–60s, some of it attempting a little variety in the elevations (undulating balconies); also, breaking up the street pattern, three indifferent point blocks of 1963 (by *Wakeford, Jerram & Harris*). The one important survival is the LIBRARY and MECHANICS' INSTITUTE. The earlier part is of 1844 by *A. Norman*, with a central entrance facing w, three storeys with modillioned eaves, and originally with pediments to the windows, that is quite progressively Italianate for its date. Adjoining is the taller, more florid addition of 1852 by the same architect, with large first-floor Venetian windows to Duke Street. Both parts, in style and relation to each other, are clearly derived from Barry's Travellers' and Reform clubs, except that the later part has Venetian Cinquecento features absent in the Reform Club. Tragically little remains of the once fine interiors, designed by *Wightwick*. On the Duke Street front a tripartite ground-floor room survives, divided by shallow arches. The first floor has been split up; the Venetian windows once lit a long galleried hall with slim iron columns and bulging balconies.

At the N end of GEORGE STREET the rubble-fronted OLD CHAPEL, built for Unitarians in 1790, converted to a pub by 1801. It is an appealingly naive mixture of simple shapes: a broad gable with oval window, two circular windows below, and a lower projection with a lunette window in a pediment. George Street is the main N–S axis of Devonport. Near the N end the KING'S ARMS, striped brick with turrets and good glazed tiles, *c.* 1900. The rest mostly bitty post-war building, the better additions of 1980–2 by the *City Architect's Department* around CLOWANCE CLOSE, rendered and tile-hung; nothing over four storeys. Near the s end a few simple early C19 stuccoed terraces on both sides.

At the s end the urban mood dissolves, and one reaches MOUNT WISE, with its detached official residences overlooking the Sound. First the house built as the PORT ADMIRAL'S HOUSE, 1808–10, now used by the Royal Marines: three storeys, six windows, stuccoed; ground floor with segmental arches. Opposite, HAMOAZE HOUSE, built for the Duke of Richmond in 1795. Ashlar; five-window, three-storey centre. Later verandas and balcony. ADMIRALTY HOUSE (formerly Government House) is a grander composition of c. 1789–93: 3–3–3 bays, with three-storey projecting centre, lower side parts, and beyond these one-storey pedimented corner pavilions with Venetian windows.

Below the houses, RICHMOND WALK, constructed in 1787 to provide access to the sea, winds romantically around the cliff, past the SCOTT MEMORIAL, a bronze winged figure and reliefs, by *Albert H. Hodge*, 1913. OCEAN COURT is a sleek white stepped pyramid of luxury flats with balconies overlooking a marina, 1976 by *Marshman Warren Taylor*, the first development of its kind in Plymouth.

RAGLAN BARRACKS, Military Road. The GATEWAY remains of the barracks built in 1853–5 by Captain *Fowke* to replace the C18 barracks that had been laid out in a ring around Plymouth Dock. The gateway has a four-column Tuscan portico; royal arms in the pediment; central domed turret. Two flanking lodges. The DEVONPORT MATERNITY HOME, a plain limestone building of five by three bays, also belonged to the barracks. On the rest of the site two-storey maisonettes of the 1970s, grouped around cul-de-sacs. To the S, by Cumberland Road, RAGLAN GARDENS, an attractive stepped crescent of 1978–81 by the *City Architect's Department*; spreading eaves, entrances away from the street.

DEVONPORT PARK also marks the line of the C18 defences. It was laid out in 1858. Pretty contemporary LODGE with bargeboarded gables, decorated with glazed tiles and inscription. REFRESHMENT HOUSE with two-storey verandas with filigree decoration, rather Indian.* Terracotta FOUNTAIN to Admiral Napier, 1885. *Lanterne-des-morts* WAR MEMORIAL.

MORICE TOWN, to the N of the park, which developed with the expanding dockyard, was (like Devonport) badly damaged in the war. The earliest surviving area is the group of streets around ALBERT ROAD (previously Navy Row). In Albert Road itself quite modest early C19 terraces straight on to the road, some slate-hung. Other groups in KEPPEL STREET, KEPPEL TERRACE, and BRUNSWICK PLACE: simple stucco, two storeys, parapets. BENBOW STREET is worth a look, with more elaborate details: vermiculated keystones, pilasters between houses, original doors. The slightly later HADDINGTON ROAD, parallel to Albert Road, is especially impressive: a long straight sweep down to Keyham Yard. On the N side near the top of the hill, large houses, three bays, central doors with Doric porches. E from here up MASTERMAN ROAD to the remains of MOUNT PLEASANT BLOCKHOUSE, known as 'the pattypan'. Brick with granite paving. Spectacular views in all directions.

Further N, FORD, developed with an uninspiring grid of small houses from the 1850s. N of Wolseley Road, SWILLY, an early Plymouth City housing scheme, laid out by *S. D. Adshead* c. 1920, with pairs of houses originally in a very simple neo-Georgian style around NORTH PROSPECT CRESCENT.

*To be converted to an old people's home.

OUTER PLYMOUTH

By 1939 the built-up area stretched N of Devonport along the Hamoaze as far as the Tamar Bridge, taking in the old settlement of St Budeaux, but E of this around Honicknowle and Weston Peverell there was still open country, and Crown Hill and the other mid C19 forts stood on their own. The post-war plan pushed the boundaries outward to accommodate the population dispersed from the centre in new low-density neighbourhoods. Architecturally there is little of note: the schools are neat but repetitive, the housing lacks distinction, shopping centres are few and mean, the churches, often given key sites, are depressingly mediocre, and little is made of the few older buildings. The one redeeming feature (as in some of the contemporary post-war new towns) is the preservation of plenty of wooded open space and even of country paths, in the valleys dividing the different neighbourhoods.

Architectural highlights other than churches and public buildings (q.v.) can be summarized briefly (roughly clockwise from the w).

HAM, just to the N of the pre-war Swilly estate, has a generously laid out main thoroughfare, HAM DRIVE. To its N, across a wooded valley, HAM HOUSE, H-shaped, built for Robert Trelawney in 1639, altered in 1739 and later. Granite entrance archway and mullioned windows. Unattractively rendered exterior. Now converted to flats.

At ST BUDEAUX, by the old church at the top of the hill, GRAY CROFT, 1953 by *Sydney R. Edwards*, a well designed house still in a traditional Arts and Crafts style, on the site of the former rectory, rendered, Tudor doorway of re-used granite, hipped roofs. To the N, BUDSHEAD, with a few outer walls and granite arches of the mansion of the Gorges, demolished in the early C19. N from here, the first two post-war neighbourhoods: ERNESETTLE to the W, with a sadly inchoate circular green with church, school, and pub; WHITLEIGH to the E, with a long green beside Budshead Road along the side of the hill, but as usual, with church and shops failing to live up to the site. Over the valley to the S an elegant pre-stressed concrete FOOTBRIDGE on slender splayed supports: 1963 by *Drake & Lasdun*. Between Whitleigh and Crown Hill an area of industry, where the most prominent structure is CLARKS, the first large post-war factory in Plymouth. Two buildings: MAYFLOWER of 1956–7; and MERLIN of 1960–2 with some architectural pretensions: administrative block on stilts, blue spandrel panels, Festivalish detail. Both by *Power Clark Hiscock & Partners*.

N of Whitleigh, along LOOSELEIGH LANE, some large Victorian villas remain along the undulating lane between Crown Hill and Tamerton Foliot. Also LOOSELEIGH HOUSE, disguised by a heavy C19 bay-windowed front, but older behind. N elevation of c. 1800, with a rounded bow. Inside, a good C18 staircase, three flights, fluted and turned balusters, moulded soffits. Venetian window to the landing. Room on the r. with C18 enriched doorcases. Service wing with bell-turret (bell dated 1799); and, decaying behind, a pretty stable block of the same period, with two lunette windows, approached by an entrance with curved walls and gatepiers with balls.

The area N of Crown Hill was developed only from the 1970s. Apart from the village of Tamerton Foliot (*see* below), the one patch which catches the attention is the industrial estate of BELLIVER. The flamboyant building with brilliant green cladding panels was built for WELLWORTHY by the *Staverton Construction Group*, 1979. Crisp warehousing behind with overhanging roofs. Further on, BECTON DICKINSON by *Peter Legge & Associates*, 1980–2, a huge shed with bronze mirror glass to the semicircular projections for cafeteria and offices. Double-height corridors inside, with red structural piers. By the roundabout at ROBOROUGH, PLESSEY SEMICONDUCTORS, 1987 by the *Building Design Partnership*, a huge high-tech steel box, all silver grey,* for the manufacture of silicon chips. Three storeys, divided by a glazed internal 'street' housing cafeteria and rest areas.

More industry at ESTOVER to the E, but of no architectural interest: WRIGLEYS of 1973 is a particularly dreary concrete hulk. To the S a demonstration of the facilities demanded by later neighbourhoods: a large ASDA shopping centre by *Holder & Mathias*, 1976–7, with a small church as an adjunct, brick with hipped roofs, insulated by ample car parks from the surrounding housing. Further N, at WOOLWELL, an even larger shopping centre (TESCO), 1986–7 by *Kyle Stewart*, discreetly hidden behind grass banks. The boxy private housing beyond stretches to the fringes of the Dartmoor National Park.

VILLAGES

TAMERTON FOLIOT

On the N fringe of Plymouth, still recognizably a village, with older houses scattered among C20 infilling.

ST MARY. Perp W tower. The rest of the exterior also Perp, but heavily restored. Three E gables, the roofs made uniform in the C19. S aisle and S porch originally of *c.* 1500, rebuilt in 1851, when the early Perp E window was repaired. N aisle widened and rebuilt in 1894–5, in unsympathetic dressed limestone (eliminating evidence of an early N door). Inside, nave and chancel in one; five-bay N and S aisles with A type piers and moulded arches, the earlier N piers of granite, the S ones of Roborough stone. Nave wagon roof with carved bosses. – FONT. Octagonal, Perp, decorated with shields only. Pillar with the simplest blank arches. – PULPIT. C17, made up from older linenfold panels and carved Renaissance bits. – Nave reseated 1851; TOWER SCREEN (replacing a gallery) 1888; chancel fittings 1894–5. – STAINED GLASS. E window 1865. – MONUMENTS. An interesting collection. Tomb-chest with knight and lady, members of the Gorges family (Sir Thomas Gorges and wife?). Mid C14. – Sir John Coplestone and his wife Susannah. 1617, repaired and re-erected 1894. Standing wall-monument with large kneeling figures in the usual position, each under its own arch; the arches meet above the prayer desk in a corbel in the shape of a pelican. Kneeling children in relief against the base of the monu-

---

* The strident red trimmings were repainted grey after unfavourable royal notice.

ment. – Susannah Calmady †1617. She stands up in her shroud against a black shell-like background, with two seated women to l. and r. The figures are of alabaster. The motif of the standing figure in a shroud was made a funeral fashion by the monument to John Donne in St Paul's Cathedral, London (1631), so this can hardly have been erected as early as 1617. – Coplestone Bampfylde †1669, aged ten. A little scholar, dressed like a man, sits at a table, his elbow resting on it, and thinks about his reading (cf. Newton St Cyres). Inscription in Latin and Greek. – Minor monuments to the Radcliffes of Warleigh.

Along the road near the church, a pale colour-washed group: the VICARAGE of 1775 with C19 additions, and two late Georgian houses: KEMPS, with pedimented doorcase, fluted eaves cornice, and central pediment, and WADLANDS, a symmetrical front with windows in round-arched recesses. Further W, in the village centre, a rendered terrace of three small cottages dated 1805 with the same surprisingly sophisticated detail of a fluted eaves cornice as Kemps, and HILLSIDE, with C17 central projecting porch, but much altered. Up the hill several stuccoed early to mid C19 villas in their own grounds, e.g. DENMARK in Horsham Lane and, further on, MILFORD HOUSE, plain early C19, with good contemporary interior, built for the Hull family, market gardeners. The village prospered in the C19 from the market gardens supplying Plymouth.

CANN HOUSE, Tamerton Foliot Road. Now a Cheshire home. A good, asymmetrical Gothic villa in substantial grounds, dated 1863, built for the Grigg family. Local grey limestone; roof of variegated tiles. Expensively detailed. Entrance side with oriel above a canted open porch, prettily flanked by rustic Gothic seats. Back extension of 1937; less tactful later additions. Inside, the hall has moulded ceiling beams; the staircase behind a hammerbeam roof; and the drawing room a neo-Jacobean ceiling, two marble fireplaces, and two elaborately framed bay-windows. They face a terrace with quatrefoiled balustrade overlooking the secluded valley. Lower down a walled garden. LODGE, handsome Gothic gatepiers and gate to the former drive.

See also Warleigh House.

PLYMSTOCK

ST MARY AND ALL SAINTS, Church Road. W tower with buttresses of type B leading right up to the corbel-table on which stand the battlements. Higher rectangular embattled stair-turret. Nave and two aisles with granite arcades of four bays, on the S with octagonal piers, the sides concave (cf. Ashburton), and double-chamfered arches, on the N later, with the usual A type piers with depressed moulded arches. – FONT. Norman, red sandstone, circular, with a palmette frieze, the motif upside down as compared with the usual Devon practice. – PULPIT. 1666, with sounding-board with open-work obelisk and cresting. – SCREEN. Re-erected in the C19. Standard tracery, the coving not preserved. Cornice with one frieze of the usual decoration; bits from the others fill the spandrels. – CHEST. Made up with early C16 carved panels (German?) formerly part of a font cover. – STAINED GLASS. Chancel E: excellent Pre-Raphaelite Te Deum by *Fouracre & Watson*, c. 1880, their *magnum opus.* – In the s aisle, attractive clear patterned leading of *c.* 1900. – MONUMENTS. Several to the Harris family of Radford. The earliest is mid C17, the usual kneeling figures, but placed in a corner, so that one is against the E, one against the s wall of the s chancel chapel (cf. Pendarves monument, St Gluvias, Cornwall). The cornice, however, runs across the corner and rests on three columns of which the second is supported by a corbel coming out of the corner like a ship's figurehead. – John Harris †1677. Large, decorative wall-monument with a small kneeling figure in front. Big undercarriage, an oval inscription plate surrounded by a wreath, and a segmental pediment. – Harris monument, C18. Black and white marble, with segmental pediment and fluted pilasters. – Hare family (of The Retreat; *see* Hooe, below), 1852 and later. Four white ovals on a black background.

The old village is engulfed in a monotonous C20 suburb. In CHURCH ROAD, BURROW LODGE, a cottage dated 1835, built from timbers of the 'Bellerophon' (broken up in 1832) by the ship's surgeon, Dr Bellamy, and a few older houses. Others in FURZEHATT ROAD and STENTAWAY ROAD. DOWN HORN FARM in Horn Lane has a C17 two-storey porch with moulded granite archway.

Along RADFORD PARK ROAD it is a pleasant surprise to come upon RADFORD PARK, with its views over Hooe Lake. The Harris mansion (C16, modernized in the C18) was demolished in 1937, but a small, square early C19 LODGE remains, each side with a pediment over a segmental-arched recess. L-shaped addition behind of 1985. Octagonal gatepiers with large iron balls. Across the lake, the eyecatchers of BRIDGE and CASTLE, a small embattled gatehouse with wooden Gothick casements. Further on a more substantial sham ruin including a boathouse.

WAR MEMORIAL. Sited on the remains of a Bronze Age barrow.

GOOD SHEPHERD, Orestone. By *May* (of *Hine, Odgers & May*), *c.* 1886.

HOOE AND TURNCHAPEL

In CHURCH HILL ROAD, Lower Hooe, church, school, and vicarage form an instructive group of the 1850s by the young *William White*, built on the initiative of Sir Frederick Rogers, a keen Tractarian. Skilfully handled simple grey rubble limestone buildings set into the slope above Hooe Lake. To the N the L-shape of SCHOOL and schoolmaster's house, 1855, the former with bold timber dormers; to the s a handsomely proportioned lychgate. The church of ST JOHN, 1854, has a long chancel, nave, s aisle, and porch. Windows with paired lancets and a quatrefoil. Inside, a memorably elemental s arcade of unmoulded pointed arches on black marble octagonal piers with the simplest of capitals. – FONT. In the same spirit, red marble on a slightly tapering limestone base. – Very complete CHANCEL FURNISHINGS, also of coloured marble, in a more precise early Dec: REREDOS with gabled arcading and pierced tracery, CREDENCE SHELF with little Gothic aedicule, COMMUNION RAILS with trefoiled arches; but the SEDILIA just a plain marble back to a low window seat. – ALTAR FRONTAL with carved and painted wooden tracery (the chancel roof trusses also painted). – The CHOIR STALLS were moved to the W end of the church (together with the organ) during the reordering by *Frank Crowe* of 1968, when a nave altar was added. – SCREEN of 1907. – Nave cosified by linenfold PANELLING by *Violet Pinwell*, 1916. – STAINED GLASS. Mostly post-war; some by *G. Cooper Abbs*. – MONUMENTS. Two Gothic tablets to the Rev. J. Tapson † 1904 and his family.

Opposite the church an ugly grey 1960s housing estate built for the *Ministry of Defence*, of the type inspired by Middle Eastern flat-roofed hill villages, hardly appropriate for the wet Plymouth climate. Beyond, ST ANNE'S HOUSE by *White*, 1858, built as the vicarage. Two and three storeys, in a rendered and slate-hung vernacular, with casement windows and prominent chimneys.

At HIGHER HOOE, in an unpromising setting in BELLEVUE ROAD, first THE RETREAT, a small late C18 rendered house with quoins, cornice, and paired windows. Then, somewhat hemmed in, HOOE MANOR (formerly Belle Vue; now local authority housing), built in 1777 for Christopher Harris, younger son of John Harris of Radford. A very elegant small mansion: three-storey, five-window centre, two-storey wings, all of exquisite fine-jointed ashlar, the quoins picked out by delicate tooled decoration. Central windows with surrounds, others with raised keystones; cornice on stone bracket, Roman Doric porch. (Good interior with contemporary staircase, plasterwork, and fireplaces.) Gatepiers with the same tooling as the quoins. Attractive garden with pond surrounded by balustrade.

TURNCHAPEL. The first Earl of Morley built a dock here in 1800. Of the early C19, BORINGDON TERRACE, stuccoed, with pedimented doorcases, raised above the road. Along the steep lane leading down to Clovelly Bay on the Cattewater an attractively haphazard huddle of stuccoed and whitewashed houses. Overlooking them a CHAPEL, 'restored 1879', the date probably of the clumsy tracery filling the round-arched windows.

MOUNT BATTEN. Excavations have shown that this was an important trading point with the Continent from the late Bronze Age to the Roman period, and probably the earliest port of Plymouth. To the S lay a late prehistoric cemetery.

FORTS on the headlands. *See* Public Buildings 1.

OTHER AREAS

See Boringdon, Newnham, Plympton, Saltram, *and* Warleigh House.

5050

PLYMPTON
Plymouth

Plympton, lying at the E end of a creek of the river Plym, was once a port in its own right. Although now engulfed in a sprawling outer suburb of Plymouth, it was in the early Middle Ages a town far superior in importance to its offshoot Sutton, the core of modern Plymouth. At the Norman Conquest it was a royal rural manor with a small community of secular canons. Henry I granted the manor (together with Tiverton) to Richard de Redvers (†1107), and in his lifetime and that of his son Baldwin, medieval Plympton was created. Richard established the castle, Bishop Warelwast of Exeter founded an Augustinian priory in 1121 in place of the earlier religious house, and the borough had emerged by Baldwin's time, if not earlier. The borough indeed nestles so neatly with the castle that the overall plan gives the impression of a planted castle town. It prospered, becoming a stannary town in 1328, until its industries declined in the C19, and it was disenfranchised in 1832.

The part of Plympton known as Plympton St Maurice, with Fore Street tightly circling the s side of the motte and St Maurice's church close by, still has much appeal. In contrast, the low-lying site of the priory and St Mary's church is to be found in an unprepossessing, much rebuilt industrial area ½m. NW off Market Road. N of this, Ridgeway Road and Station Road may be the site of a medieval settlement established by the priory; another early centre lay further s along Underwood Road, which winds from E to W with a long line of C17–18 cottages.

ST MAURICE (or ST THOMAS), Church Road, just E of the castle. An indulgence refers to the rebuilding of the W tower, dated 1446. Buttresses of B type, polygonal stair-turret with conical roof, large three-light bell-openings. Two-storey s porch. N and s aisles with A type piers with depressed moulded arches. Built together with the second s pier from the E, the stone steps and base of a medieval pulpit. Restoration 1878 by *E. H. Sedding*; new nave roof based on the medieval one, 1905 by *Hine & Odgers*. – Small wooden FONT on tall pedestal. – C17 octagonal PULPIT. – C19 WALL PAINTINGS (St Thomas a Becket and St Maurice). – MONUMENT to Joshua Reynolds by *James Hine*, with portrait medallion by *F. Derwent Wood*, erected 1904.

CASTLE. A large motte with sub-rectangular bailey. On top of the motte the remains of a roughly circular building with rubble walls about 10ft thick. No architectural details survive except for putlog holes and, more interesting, substantial slots for reinforcing timbers running longitudinally around the structure on two levels (the only castle in the county known to have employed this device, perhaps intended to counteract the effect of building on a motte with an unconsolidated top). In 1136 the castle was besieged and razed by King Stephen, and the present remains may date from a rebuilding in the 1140s, when Baldwin de Redvers recovered his estates and was made Earl of Devon by the Empress Matilda. An inner circular tower may have been added in the late C12 or C13 (cf. Launceston, Cornwall). (Foundations in the centre of the motte are confirmed by a C16 view.) The castle was again besieged in 1224, when it was in the hands of Fawkes de Bréauté. In 1297 Plympton and its estates were inherited by Hugh II Courtenay of Okehampton. There are medieval references to a hall, chapel, and other buildings, but the bailey has been landscaped in modern times and there are no structural remains. The s entrance is probably modern; the N one corresponds with a medieval gatehouse. A further tower once stood at the W end or 'Barbican' (now built over).

PLYMPTON GRAMMAR SCHOOL, Stone Barton Road. By *Stillman & Eastwick-Field*, c. 1968–70.

BRIDGE. *Brunel's* railway line of 1849 crosses the road with a remarkably oblique bridge.

THE TOWN. The best groups of houses are along the narrow FORE STREET; irregular, mostly rendered Georgian frontages, some probably earlier behind, still reflecting the pattern of the medieval burgage plots. On the N side a few with their upper floors resting on columns (e.g. No. 18, supposed to be the former lock-up) or on piers (e.g. No. 20, earlier C17) (cf. Dartmouth, Totnes). The former GUILDHALL (No. 42), dated 1696, also has an upper floor resting on an arcade, but is a classical building with keystones to the arches, the three upper windows in line with them, and a wooden modillioned eaves cornice. It was given by the two local families, the Trebys and the Strodes. On the S side, No. 9, the RECTORY, early C18, also with a modillioned cornice to its seven-window front, and decorated aprons below the windows. (Good contemporary staircase and fittings.) Further on the steeply roofed TUDOR LODGE, late C17, with a timber-framed and plastered upper floor below broad eaves, and a carriageway on the r. (Late C17 dog-leg staircase.) Also PLYMPTON ST MAURICE HOUSE, later C18, four windows wide with projecting centre, and two full-height bows on the garden side.

In GEORGE LANE, a few C18 houses, and the former GRAMMAR SCHOOL, founded in 1658 and dated 1664, but in its tenor still entirely pre-classical. T-shaped, the main wing with the schoolroom above arcades on granite columns. Perp mullioned windows, perhaps re-used. It was here that Sir Joshua Reynolds received his schooling. His father was the master.

PLYMPTON HOUSE (St Peter's Convent), Longcaus. Close to St Maurice's church, hidden behind high garden walls. Begun by Sir George Treby, Lord Chief Justice (†1700), completed by his son, another George, c. 1715–20. Building accounts for 1720 mention *William Veale*, mason. Still in the comfortable, unostentatious William-and-Mary tradition, although rather grander than for example Mothecombe or Puslinch. The main front of Portland stone with rusticated quoins, seven bays with three-bay pediment, sashes with thick glazing-bars. Two tall storeys over a basement, which the lie of the land exposes as a third storey on the W side, where the upper walls are more humbly of brick with segment-headed windows. Large entrance hall leading to an E–W corridor. The staircase fills the whole of the SE corner of the house, exceptionally rich, with four graduated balusters to each tread, the handrail ending in a virtuoso roll, and the landing with Corinthian-column newels. Much bolection-moulded panelling, corner fireplaces, two fine Baroque marble chimneypieces with oval centres, the one in the hall flanked by fluted pilasters, the drawing-room one with scrolly volutes. The spacious service rooms in the basement have elegant groin-vaults on piers, as at Puslinch and Mothecombe. Many additions for the convent. Much of the walled garden remains, although not the tiled C18 dairy in the stables.

ST MARY, Market Road. This, although originally only a parish chapel attached to the priory, is the more important of the town's two churches. The granite ashlar W tower with its big polygonal pinnacles is prominent from far away. The bell-openings also are bigger than usual (three lights). The church has two aisles and two shorter outer aisles. The S side is the prouder, all embattled and pinnacled, with a two-storeyed porch adorned by three niches. The central one above the window holds a statue of the Trinity, the others, l. and r. of the window, have figures of the Annunciation. Below the window the crest of the Strode family, who settled at Newnham near Plympton in 1394. In the porch a complicated lierne-vault with three ridge-ribs and three transverse ribs. The springers are supported on angel corbels. On the N side of the church a simple one-storeyed porch and battlements only on the inner aisle. In fact the outer N aisle is the oldest part of the church and may originally have been a separate chapel. Its windows and piscina are clearly of the early C14. A dedication of Plympton parish church is recorded for 1311, but would parish church have been the term used in the case of a chapel such as St Mary's? Moreover, the present chancel and E end of the inner N aisle do not differ much in date; see the fine SEDILIA and PISCINA, the N and S chancel doors, and the lavish five-light E window with a six-pointed star in a circle. The rest of the church is Perp, probably early C15, with the exception of the outer S aisle, which must be later than 1452. The existence of the outer aisles makes the interior of the church appear very roomy, if somewhat confusing. Arcades of seven bays, the piers of Roborough stone and A type, the arches four-centred. The piers of the outer S aisle are of granite.

FONT. Perp, octagonal, of the usual type. – REREDOS. Designed by *J. D. Sedding*. – STAINED GLASS. Small odd bits in window tops. – By *Burlison & Grylls* outer S aisle E, outer N aisle E, S aisle W. – By *Clayton & Bell* N aisle W. – MONUMENTS. Medieval tomb slab with cross in the outer N aisle. – Also in the outer N aisle, in a recess, tomb-chest to Richard Strode †1464 with the little figures of mourners still complete (what has saved them from the iconoclasts of the C16 and C17?), effigy in armour, top with ogee arches and horizontal cresting. – Simpler recess with effigy probably to William Courtenay of Loughtor (S chancel aisle). – Sir William Strode †1637. Large tripartite wall-monument, he in the centre kneeling frontally, l. and r. his two wives kneeling with their elbows on prayer-desks and one cheek resting on a hand. Below, the busts of ten children crowded together to the l. of the inscription plate, and to the r. the relief of a skeleton rising. – W. Seymour †1801. By *Coade & Sealy*, cast stone, with the same weeping putto as at Holbeton and Teigngrace. – Viscount Boringdon †1817 in Paris, eleven years old. By *F. N. Delaistre*, 1819. A classical composition with two white putti leaning against an obelisk with the portrait of the boy; the whole on a black base. – Richard Rosdew †1837 by *Chantrey*, with portrait head in profile. – In the S porch, ALTAR SLAB from the priory.

PRIORY, Market Road. Little remains to be seen of the Augustinian priory founded in 1121, which at the Dissolution was one of the five richest Augustinian houses in the country. The site adjoins the S side of the churchyard of St Mary (originally a parochial chapel belonging to the priory). The W end and nave of the priory church were determined in excavations in 1958–9. The aisled nave, probably built in the C12, was 131 ft long and *c.* 33 ft wide. The domestic buildings lay to the S. From them remain some walls with medieval fabric in PRIORY ROW, and TOWER HOUSE, of four storeys. In its N wall a C12 gateway survives, with one order of colonnettes and voussoirs of alternating dark and light stone (cf. Paignton, Torbay). The upper late medieval windows were originally in the undercroft of the refectory. In 1872 undercroft, refectory, and kitchen could still be described as in good condition, but they have since all disappeared. Carved stones from the priory buildings can be found re-used elsewhere in Plympton (e.g. behind Alma Cottage in Station Road); others are in Plymouth Museum.

CHADDLEWOOD, Glen Road, off Ridgeway. A battered mansion, now subdivided and surrounded by new housing. Early C19 stuccoed S front of three plus one windows, porch with paired Doric columns, tripartite window above, added by the Symons family at the end of an older range. This has to the W a centre of 2–3–2 bays, with raised quoins. On the road to Sparkwell a small triangular rubble stone FOLLY TOWER with pointed archway.

At HARDWICK FARM, Drunken Bridge Hill, a medieval or C16 DOVECOTE, rectangular, with domical roof of oversailing courses of stone slabs.

LIMEKILNS, Haye Road. Two squat semicircular kilns linked by an elliptical arch, built into a bank SE of Haye Farmhouse.

PLYM BRIDGE. C18 on earlier piers; five round arches.

See also Newnham.

0000

PLYMTREE

ST JOHN. Nave and chancel seem the oldest parts. Blocked Norman N door. The W tower and S aisle Perp, the former with diagonal buttresses and a low stair-turret with decorated top. Restored by *G. Fellowes Prynne*, 1895. On the W front a statue of the Virgin. Decorated parapet also on the S porch, and flowers in the doorway jambs and voussoirs. The S windows of three lights, large, with nook-shafts on the inside. The interior is one of the most attractive in Devon, with its excellent late medieval woodwork. Sensitive restoration in 1910 by *William Weir*. S arcade with quite steeply pointed arches on piers of standard B section. The capitals also standard. Chancel arch with foliage ornament and the remains of a niche, hacked back for the later screen. The nave vault, with simple coffering over its E part, dates from the extensive restorations of 1827–9 by *Samuel Henson*, when parts of walls and arcades were rebuilt. The chancel roof is ceiled, with small bosses.

FONT. Plain, octagonal, Perp, with quatrefoil panels. – PULPIT. Plain C18. – SCREEN. One of the most splendid, with much colour; exceptionally well preserved. The Bourchier and Stafford emblems indicate it was the gift of Isabel, widow of Humphrey Stafford, Earl of Devon, who was beheaded in 1470. Wainscoting painted with figures, the first panels on the l. very coarse, the rest obviously different and better, but of no high aesthetic value either. Croft-Murray dates both hands to the early C16. Standard A type tracery. Coving on the E side as well. Broad, fourfold cornice, very compactly decorated. – ALTAR RAILS. C17. – Back wall around the altar with PANELLING with late C17 relief. – ALTAR TABLE. Plain and nice C18 wood panelling. – BENCH ENDS fill the whole nave. They have two tiers of tracery. – Small Flemish alabaster RELIEF, *c.* 1600, of the Resurrection, of remarkably high quality, with much delicate detail. – STAINED GLASS. Old fragments in the top lights of the E window and of one in the S aisle.

There are three major houses in the parish: Fordmore, Plymtree Manor, and Woodbeer Court.

FORDMORE has a simple but attractive two-storey front of the mid to later C17, of red brick in English bond (marred only by a crude C20 extension on the l.), proudly displaying the novelty of tall wooden mullion-and-cross leaded windows, remarkably not replaced by later sashes. Two end windows now blocked; originally there were no less than nine on each floor, the lower ones segment-headed. Only one window to each room made to open, by a small casement in one of the quarters. Hipped roof above a restored cornice. Central entrance hall containing a robust open-well staircase with urn-shaped balusters and a closed string, continuing up to attic level. Room on the r. with large moulded panels and bolection-moulded fireplace with panelled overmantel. Similar plainer chimneypiece to the room above, which has a ceiling with a simple foliage wreath. Older back parts of the house have been demolished. It was the seat of the Ford family from the C12 to 1702.

PLYMTREE MANOR (HAYNE HOUSE). The house of the Harwood family. An impressive seven-bay brick front of c. 1710, with good classical features applied with engaging provincial naïveté. Stone quoins and window surrounds, a door framed by delicately carved Corinthian pilasters, and two giant garlanded Ionic pilasters with their own entablatures, their high plinths quite unrelated to the window heights. Hipped roof above wooden eaves cornice; three dormers, one segment-headed, two triangular. This show front was originally only one room deep – see the blocked windows at the back at attic level. The back rooms at a different level from the front are C19, probably infilling between older back wings rebuilt at the same time. Interior much altered. The present N porch and staircase date from the early C20, when the original staircase was removed from the former central hall, now a drawing room. Good fielded panelling in the SE dining room.

WOODBEER COURT. A large medieval house which has declined to a farmhouse. Plain rendered exterior. The C15 centre of the S range recognizable by the door frame to the cross-passage, and by the roof over the W part of the hall and W chamber: a rare secular example of common rafter roof construction, the arch-braces and collar-braces to each rafter forming a barrel roof, all smoke-blackened. The flooring-in of the hall is possibly contemporary with the hollow-moulded hall window and inserted stack. The upper part of the front wall of the hall is a later rebuilding. The extensive C17 additions include a staircase block behind the hall range and the prestigious E wing with mullioned-and-transomed windows to both floors; the ground-floor parlour window boasts a splendid scrolled bracket at mid span. The N part of this range was probably a kitchen, with two very large stacks close together. The present courtyard plan was completed by early C18 N and W ranges of brick, mostly for farm rather than domestic use (e.g. the first-floor granary): the brickwork is similar to Fordmore (see above) and the Old Manor at Talaton (q.v.). A brick range continues W to include further agricultural buildings which once enclosed a large yard.

MIDDLE CLYST WILLIAM. Farmhouse originally on a four-unit
cross-passage plan; further rooms added longitudinally. Interesting evidence of its earliest medieval phase is the roof on arch-
braced jointed-cruck trusses with slip-tenons and saddle apexes,
with a single tier of curved wind-braces and a smoke louvre. Two
smoke-blackened closed trusses suggest that the house was divided
into sections from the beginning, each with its own open hearth.

CONGREGATIONAL CHAPEL, at the crossroads at Norman's
Green. 1850. A surprisingly large gabled stone chapel in a walled
burial ground. Lancets, buttresses, gabled porch.

9090

POLTIMORE

ST MARY. Red sandstone with dressings of volcanic trap. Unbuttressed W tower with C14 door and window, and semicircular stair-
turret. The rest much altered by *R. Medley Fulford*, who in the
restoration of 1879–82 repaired the chancel arch, opened up
squints, and added the arched stone canopies in the chancel (a
typical Fulford touch). In 1884 he added the two-bay S arcade (re-
using the doorway into the S transept) and doubled the number of
small high-up clerestory windows – an odd feature. – REREDOS.
1885, with tiled ALTAR SURROUND with two rather pretty angels
(which stylistically look *c.* 1850). – FONT. Plainest Norman. –
SCREEN. Of type A, with fan-vaulted coving to E and W, and a
cornice with three strips of foliage scrollwork. – SQUIRE'S PEW.
A low little bridge across the S transept which is decorated with a
Gothic plaster ceiling. – SEATING by *Hems*, 1882. – STAINED
GLASS. Sanctuary S, fragment of an excellent C14 Crucifixion,
found during restoration of the screen. – Chancel N and S,
Fortescue memorial windows, 1875 by *O'Connor*. – MONU-
MENTS. Richard Bampfield and wife, 1604. Recumbent figures
under a low canopy, the canopy not simply on columns as customary but squat arched openings between the columns (cf. Gilbert
monument, Exeter Cathedral). – Charlotte Buller, by *R.J. Wyatt*,
Rome, 1831, the young woman on a couch with two mourning
figures in attendance. – CHURCHYARD with cobbled path and the
date 1743.

Poltimore is a pretty village, with a mixture of white thatched houses
and C19 Bampfylde estate cottages in red brick and stone.

ALMSHOUSES, just N of the church, with an elaborate little relief
commemorating the foundation by Elizabeth and John Bampfylde
in 1631 and showing their portraits in medallions.

POLTIMORE HOUSE. A prominent sight on the main road into
Exeter. The former seat of the Bampfyldes, converted in the C20
to a hospital, then to an old people's home, and at the time of
writing badly in need of a sympathetic new use. The substantial
mansion stands in a spacious parkland setting (may it not be
despoiled by future development). The plain white stuccoed S
front conceals a characteristically Devonian piecemeal development of considerable complexity, best described chronologically.
The house is on a quadrangular plan, with the courtyard filled in at
a later stage. The oldest visible part is at the back, where the N
range still has three Tudor gables and some mullioned windows

Poltimore House: plan

visible on the N side, and two gables on the S, together with a big kitchen chimneystack. The adjoining E range had the hall, entirely transformed in the C18. The shape of the screens passage remains, and in the angle between the two wings a stair-turret of *c.*1600, with four-centred stone doorways leading off, although the stair itself, with its turned balusters, is later C17, a continuous flight around a little well.

The next stage was the addition by Sir Coplestone Bampfylde in the early C18 of the S entrance range, still much as shown in a Prideaux drawing: eleven bays divided into a rhythm of 4–3–4 by banded pilasters, two storeys above basements, with attics behind a parapet. The ground-floor interiors of this range have been altered, but some panelling remains on the first floor. In the mid C18 the old hall was remodelled as an up-to-date saloon, one of the 120 finest rooms of its kind in the county. The decoration is good, but in an odd mixture of styles, suggesting a combination of pattern-book sources. At either end handsome overdoors with open pediments flanked by niches, in a rather Kentian manner. On the upper walls quite florid garlands with vases of flowers: between the windows more Rococo plasterwork around oval mirrors, and on the ceiling, stringier skittish flourishes around a sunburst. Marble fireplace with dogs' heads and two hunting horns. The later rooms are a come-down after this. One upstairs room with a late C18 fireplace with *Wedgwood* plaques.

When Sir G. W. Bampfylde became Lord Poltimore in 1831, the S range was given a new porch, and the entrance hall altered to the present arrangement, with two pairs of Ionic columns dividing it from a new spacious imperial staircase, with cast-iron neo-classical balustrade, built out into the central courtyard. Flat roof above, with clerestory lighting. The decoration of the SW room, with its two composite columns, is also of this date. In the SE room an Adamish ceiling probably of *c.* 1908, when a W extension with ballroom with elaborate Italian marble fireplace was added beyond an already existing W range.* Extensive C19 service wings at the back (some demolished) possibly by *Ferrey*, whose obituary claimed that he worked here.

LODGE. Small and stuccoed.

GATEPOSTS with huge balls on slender pillars, dated 1681, repositioned (and awkwardly buttressed) near the main road. Another pair to the N, near the village.

3020

PORTLEDGE
Alwington

Hidden away between wooded hills, close to the N coast. The seat of the Coffins from the C11, and of the Pine-Coffins from 1796. Now a hotel. A major house on a courtyard plan, with the usual complicated and intriguing history of piecemeal growth and alterations. The present entrance is on the W side, but the oldest part is the E range, formerly approached through a gatehouse and outer court. The hall, now floored, and with the ground floor converted to a kitchen, is still recognizable. The two-storey battlemented porch with moulded round-headed archway looks Tudor, but within the screens passage is an older medieval low two-centred arch to a service room. Adjoining the porch to the N is an extension built out flush with it, with late C17 mullion-and-cross windows to its upper floor. The hall and floor above have large Gothick windows of *c.* 1800, likewise the solar wing to the S, where the ground-floor dining room has a ceiling with Pine-Coffin heraldry – i.e. after 1796. This wing once extended further E, as a survey plan of 1767 shows, possibly with a chapel. The long S extension, said to have housed the library of Sir Richard Coffin (Sheriff in 1687), now looks C19 Tudor, but an early C18 Prideaux drawing confirms that it was already in existence, with a plain open loggia at the S end.

To the W the main S range, two storeys with an attic floor with straight gables, still looks much as it did on the Prideaux drawing,

---

*After years of neglect, the ballroom was extensively damaged by fire in 1987.

apart from the disappearance of a mysterious large cupola. Two bays of late Tudor four-light windows with dripstones (the mullions replaced), with the odd feature of single-light windows in between (for closets?). The third bay on the r. has larger staircase windows at different levels, the bottom one unlike all the others, with stone mullions with arched ogee lights – perhaps an older window re-used. On the shorter w front the windows look early C19 Tudor, as does the large porch with rusticated Gothic arch, plaster vault, and pastiche Jacobean doorway.

The w porch leads into a large top-lit hall, an elongated octagon, created by roofing over the former courtyard. The Gothic doors on the ground floor and the neo-classical fireplace look early C19, but the gallery with its cusped wooden balustrade, and the glazed lantern supported by heavy timber trusses, must be a later Victorian remodelling. In the main s range, C17 work of high quality. Spacious early C17 dog-leg staircase with turned balusters, somewhat altered, but in its original position, as is shown by the C17 moulded and stopped doorways leading to the upper chambers, and the plaster ceiling, a single-rib pattern. Heraldic cartouches on the side walls. Good heraldic overmantels of the same date in the two first-floor chambers of the s range, the one in the sw room also with birds with foliage sprays and figures of peace and plenty. In the room over the dining room (i.e. the solar at the s end of the hall range) especially elaborate panelling of c. 1600, a series of identical architectural panels (cf. Holcombe Court), now painted white, probably rearranged when this wing was truncated and the Gothick window added. On the top floor of the s range a long gallery, now subdivided, with plasterwork in the Court style of the later C17: three circular wreaths, the outer two with quite tight foliage, the inner one with flowers, treated more freely, and with grotesque masks, very reminiscent of the work in the Royal Hotel, Bideford. On the gable wall a delightful flower spray; on the overmantel, arms in a scrolly wreath.

The service end of the house has a highly confusing history. The first-floor room N of the porch, later a nursery, has good early C18 panelling. The old kitchen, in the traditional position down a corridor from the former hall, has a C17 doorway; a similar door to a wing to the W. To the E, up some steps, a curious wooden loggia with coarse but ornate C16 decoration: square Ionic pillars, heavy brackets, arches with central pendants. Clearly not made for this position, and traditionally said to have been brought from one of the Armada ships wrecked off the N coast. It leads to a former chapel (now subdivided) with tall C18 Gothic windows.

Minor outbuildings to the N; further off, a walled garden. To the E the former stables, now converted to a house.

POUGHILL

8000

ST MICHAEL. Unbuttressed, unpinnacled w tower. Perp N arcade with B type piers and standard capitals, apart from the w respond with a green man. Three bays plus a fourth from chancel to chancel chapel, the latter panelled and decorated with fleurons (all extremely renewed). Old wagon roofs. Chancel rebuilt in the

restoration of 1855–6, with REREDOS and painted roof of the same
date. – Old BOX PEWS in the aisle. – Barnstaple TILES in the
tower. – STAINED GLASS. E window by *Drake*, 1875. – MONU-
MENT. Gertrude Pyncombe †1730. Draped marble urn with
cherubs, on a black marble base.

VICARAGE. Built *c.* 1840, still in the Regency manner, with deep
eaves and Gothick glazing.

SOUTH YEO. Early C16 farmhouse with good interior details; several
stud-and-panel screens.

9080

POWDERHAM

ST CLEMENT. Small and red, close to the river, quite away from the
castle grounds, to which it is connected by an ilex avenue. Small W
tower without stair-turret. Nave and two aisles of five bays, the B
type piers with standard capitals, at the E end with the arms of Sir
William Courtenay (†1485) and his wife, useful evidence, as this
common type of Perp arcade is so rarely datable. Wagon roof of
1857–8 by *J. W. Rowell* of Newton Abbot, who did much work for
the Courtenays. Chancel extended in 1861, probably also by him;
masonry of nave windows renewed 1864–80. The E bay of the N
aisle is screened off as the Courtenay family pew, still with its
Victorian upholstery, a rare survival.

SCREEN. Largely of 1853, incorporating medieval parts (fragmentary already in the early C19). – Old DOOR in the S porch. –
PAINTING of the Last Supper by *Cosway* (N wall; formerly over
the altar). – STAINED GLASS. C15 fragments in a N aisle window.
– In the Courtenay Memorial Chapel in the S aisle, E window 1844
by *Wailes*, S window 1870 by *Clayton & Bell*, instructive to compare. – Chancel E also 1870 by *Clayton & Bell*. – Tower W 1867 by
A. & E. Beer of Exeter. – Patterned glass in the aisles also by *Beer*,
1864–73. – Two S aisle windows 1876 by *Drake*. – N aisle W window
1935 by *Hubert Blanchford*. – MONUMENTS. Elizabeth de Bohun
†1378(?), whose daughter married the third Earl of Devon. Effigy
with the queer headgear of that period. – Harriet Countess of
Devon †1839 and family, a replica of the C15 Courtenay memorial
at Colyton. Originally in the N aisle; now chancel S. – Elizabeth
Countess of Devon †1867. Recumbent figure by *Stephens* of
Exeter, placed in the screened-off memorial chapel at the E end of
the S aisle (with good contemporary floor tiles, glass (*see* above),
and stencilled roof, all now, alas, blocked by the organ).

POWDERHAM CASTLE. Until its major transformations by *Charles
Fowler* for William Courtenay, tenth Earl of Devon, in 1845–7, Powderham was more a fortified manor house than a castle, although it
was strong enough to withstand an attack by the Bonvilles, the
Courtenays' rivals, in 1455, and was still defensible in 1645.

Before Fowler's alterations the building faced E towards the
river Exe (see the Buck view of 1734). A walled courtyard with
gatehouse (perhaps the barbican or bulwark mentioned by Leland)
was removed in the mid C18 for the landscaping of the gardens.
The visitor now approaches from the W over a bridge, through
Fowler's robust baronial gate-tower which leads into an operatic
forecourt enclosed by a curtain wall. To the l. of the main entrance

is Fowler's dining hall, with two-light transomed and traceried windows, but the rest is older. Behind the entrance tower, the high, gaunt range of limestone rubble with renewed battlements 126 probably dates from the time of Sir Philip Courtenay (†1419), who founded a junior branch of the powerful Courtenay family of Oke-hampton. It consists of the shell of the medieval hall, with service rooms and kitchen to the S, private rooms to the N, all in a single line, just as in a late medieval minor Devon manor house, although at the N end there are in addition a large tower with a chamber, and a smaller tower now partly embedded in additions to the E. The larger tower has a window with a single cusped light, and another restored one of two lights, possibly the window opened up by Fowler and made, on the Earl's instructions, 'an exact counterpart of the old one'. The corbelled-out oriel over the entrance, however, is Fowler's invention, added to a four-storey tower which may date from work carried out in 1539–40. There is another tower, of uncertain date, over the former E entrance.

The medieval remains visible inside can be quickly summed up: three stone service doors with two-centred arches and double-chamfered mouldings at the low end of the hall, and a flatter arched doorway above them, presumably to a lost hall gallery; a fireplace in the first-floor solar and a turret stair in the adjoining tower; remains of another staircase near the kitchen; and plenty of walls of great thickness. The chapel mentioned in 1450 projected E from the solar end and survived until remodelled in the C18.

The exterior, with its lumpy skyline and awkward mixture of rough stonework and rendered surfaces, is not particularly attrac-tive. The interior is also an unsatisfactory muddle: the medieval bones of the building made it impossible for the various C18 mod-ernization campaigns to achieve an effective sequence of spaces,

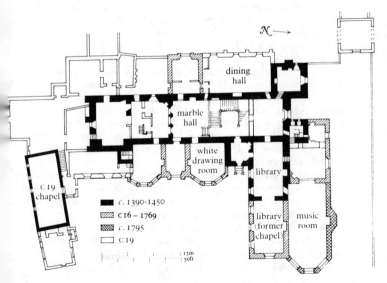

Powderham Castle: plan

although they introduced some craftsmanship of the highest order. Until *James Wyatt* added his splendid music room, no architects appear to have been involved; the accounts for 1710–27 refer only to *John Moyle*, the Exeter master-builder and bricklayer, and to supervisors called *Dalton* and *Spring* in the 1760s.

The following account follows the route in which rooms are shown to visitors. *Fowler*'s large single-storey DINING HALL in late medieval style, begun *c.* 1847 but not completely fitted up until 1860, has as its *pièce de résistance* a somewhat gross heraldic chimneypiece, copied from the one installed by Bishop Courtenay *c.* 1485 in the Bishop's Palace at Exeter. The adjoining anteroom was the medieval parlour or withdrawing room, refitted in the C19. The two remarkable bookcases with flamboyantly Baroque pediments, signed *J. Channon* 1740, deserve a mention; they belong to the first phase of C18 improvements and were formerly in the first-floor library created in the E wing over the medieval chapel. A matching overmantel and double doorcase remain *in situ* (not shown to the public). A little later the chapel was converted into a drawing room, now the LIBRARY, with a good mid C18 marble fireplace with terms, and bookcases added *c.* 1820. The delicate Rococo ceiling probably dates from the 1760s, when the Gothick windows were put in (extra payments to *William Jones* in 1769–70 for 'turning the heads Gothic'). Second LIBRARY in the room beyond.

130 Adjoining the libraries is the large apsidal-ended MUSIC ROOM added by *James Wyatt* in 1794–6 for the third Viscount, who inherited in 1788 and came of age in 1791. Wyatt had worked for his friend, the notorious William Beckford, at Fonthill. The music room is in a totally different spirit from the rest of Powderham, a sumptuous yet disciplined neo-classical interior in metropolitan taste, with the detail all under architectural control. Ceiling with central coffered dome, walls with marbled Corinthian pilasters, and niches with alabaster urns (the roundels above painted by the young Viscount and his thirteen sisters). Organ by *Seede* at one 131 end. Accomplished chimneypiece by *R. Westmacott Sen.* with large figures of musical shepherd and shepherdess flanking a relief frieze. It had a fine grate of ormolu by the French bronzeworker *P.P. Thomire*, dated 1788.* The furniture also contemporary.

Back in the medieval core of the building, one returns to the mid C18 improvements. The most radical was the vertical subdivision of the medieval GREAT HALL. The N end became the GRAND 122 STAIRCASE. It dates from 1754–6 and is the most spectacular space of its date in Devon. Three huge flights, spiral balusters, carved tread-ends; made by the Exeter joiner *James Garrett*. But the amazing feature is the superb plasterwork by the otherwise unknown *John Jenkins* and his assistants *William Brown* and *Stephen Coney*. Its diverse motifs, including trophies and pendant garlands of flowers and fruit, are mixed with an untrammelled exuberance which still recalls the traditions of English Baroque. The other half of the great hall, with the medieval service doors already referred to, had a ceiling inserted in the C18 and was fitted with panelling in the C19. Opening off it are a sequence of later

---

*It was sold in 1987 to the Victoria and Albert Museum.

C18 rooms facing E, incorporating the earlier E tower. An elegantly light-hearted Rococo ceiling in the drawing room, another in the upper room of the E tower (not shown).

CHAPEL. Fitted up in 1861 in an outbuilding to the SE. Its position, at an angle to the main range, marks the line of the outer court, and its superior roof with arch-braces and wind-braces suggests it was a late medieval building of some importance. C16 BENCH ENDS, possibly those from the old church at South Huish, which were given to the Earl of Devon in 1874.

BELVEDERE. Triangular tower of 1773, one of several modelled on the triangular tower at Shrub Hill, Windsor (cf. Haldon Belvedere, Dunchideock). Rendered brick. Hexagonal corner turrets.

DOVECOTE, Pigeon Vale. Now a cottage. Large, circular, of brick.

PRINCETOWN   5070

Unquestionably the bleakest place in Devon – not only because of the jail. Princetown lies 1,430ft high and exposed from all sides. Sir Thomas Tyrwhitt, Lord Warden of the Stannaries and a friend of the then Prince of Wales, determined to cultivate Dartmoor. He drained land, planted flax, and built himself a house here in 1785 (*see* below). In 1805, he conceived the idea of building in the neighbourhood a large group of barracks for the prisoners of war who were at that time mostly kept in hulks. They could, he suggested, be used to greater advantage to build roads and generally to help in opening up Dartmoor. Tyrwhitt also promoted a railway (*see* Roborough) for transporting granite and produce, from Princetown to Sutton Pool.

H.M. PRISON. Tyrwhitt's barracks for French prisoners of war were begun in 1806 on a 15 acre site to the designs of *Daniel Asher Alexander*. After 1850 they became a convict prison, and were extended and altered by *Hayward*. Some of Alexander's buildings remain,[*] and his layout is still recognizable. It was radial, in accordance with the ideal plan for hospitals and prisons advocated on the continent from the late C18 and put into practice already in England at the jails of Ipswich, Liverpool, and Dorchester. At Princetown, five blocks (increased to seven in 1812) were laid out like the spokes of half a wheel. They were supervised not from the centre, as elsewhere, but by troops stationed on the circular perimeter wall.

No. 1 block opposite the gate and No. 4 to the l. of the gate are original. No. 6 to the r. is the ground floor of one of the blocks added in 1812. In the early days, before subdivision into convict cells, the two main floors of each building had hammocks slung several deep between iron stanchions, with paved stone passages in between. The upper floor rested on a central row of granite pillars. As many as 500 men occupied each floor. No. 4 block still has its cockloft, lit by small clerestory windows, intended for indoor recreation but soon invaded by more hammocks. At one end of each block was a lean-to

---

[*] I am most grateful to Mr R. J. Joy of H.M. Prison Service for details about the surviving buildings.

latrine over an open leat, at the other a small cookhouse with a fireplace – the only source of heat in the building.

Also original within the walls are the three-storeyed former Infirmary and Petty Officers' Prison to l. and r. of the gate. The entrance wall, with a cyclopean granite arch inscribed 'Parcere Subjectis' (a quotation from Virgil), forms one side of a square. The others consist of the Surgeon's House (l.), the Agent's House (r.), and, across the road, the reservoir and water tower. The troops were quartered in a separate walled enclosure outside the prison. Of their barracks the guardroom (now Ladies' Club) remains near the walls; also a block now used for staff housing (Grosvenor Flats) and a guardhouse (now Dart Cottage). The church also dates from this time.

St Michael. 1813 by *Alexander*. w tower unbuttressed, with Perp battlements and pinnacles. The quatrefoil windows are as characteristic of the date of the church as the elementary two-light windows of the nave. The sanctuary was improved by *R.M. Fulford* in 1898, the nave excellently remodelled in 1908 by *E.H. Sedding*, who inserted the arcades with rectangular piers and dying arches, creating very narrow passage-aisles. – PULPIT. C18, with carved evangelists, brought from St Sidwell, Exeter.

The small TOWN which grew up around the prison prospered from the new granite quarries. Some early C19 houses remain, with heavy rustication. The DUCHY HOTEL was rebuilt in the early C20 by *Sir Albert Richardson*. By him also two pairs of houses at the s end of the town in his favourite vernacular Regency style, with slate-hung upper floors and projecting wings with quasi-Venetian windows.

TOR ROYAL. Remotely sited on the edge of Dartmoor, s of the town. The modest house begun by Sir Thomas Tyrwhitt in 1785 and completed in 1798 consists of the simple, solid E-facing main range, three bays wide, with a N service wing. Its Gothick dormers date from a tidying up by *Sir Albert Richardson* in 1912. About 1815–20 Tyrwhitt added a large one-storey s wing, with a new entrance with Doric porch, approached through the large walled yard. In this wing a top-lit entrance hall with frieze with railway wagons and corn sheaves to illustrate Tyrwhitt's plans for Dartmoor, and, between two reception rooms, elaborately ornamented neo-classical double doors, brought from the Prince Regent's Carlton House, London, after its demolition. To the w a sturdy water-cum-clock-tower. One-storeyed LODGE with Gothick windows.

PRINCE HALL. Much rebuilt from the late 1780s by Sir Francis Buller as a country villa. Rendered exterior; well-preserved features inside.

PUDDINGTON

St Thomas a Becket. Largely rebuilt in 1837 by *W. Bowden*, with new s porch and N aisle in Perp style, the latter reconstructed in 1880. The round-headed NE window of 1837 remains. – FITTINGS of 1837: woodwork with tracery ornament and heavy fleur-de-lys cresting. The Gothic choir stalls incorporate a C17 oak bench. The nave benches have some of the usual Cornwall–Devon BENCH ENDS.

(Former VICARAGE, *c.* 1840. Tudor hoodmoulds.)

PUDDINGTON LODGE. Attractive early Victorian Tudor. Wings with bargeboarded gables and ogee-headed windows.

PUSLINCH
Newton and Noss

5050

A perfect example of the medium-size early Georgian country house, [113] still in the Queen Anne tradition – nothing spectacular, but structure as well as decoration sound and comfortable. The father, grandfather, and great-grandfather of James Yonge, the C18 owner, had been Plymouth surgeons, and in the pursuit of their profession accumulated much wealth. James Yonge acquired the estate through his marriage with Mary Upton. The house dates probably from *c.* 1720–6, and appears – a rarity in Devon – to be a new building rather than a remodelling; the old house, originally on a quadrangular plan but now much reduced, lay to the w. Yonge's house is of brick with stone dressings, one of the earliest uses of brick in this area (although cf. Plympton House). Handsome seven-bay front, two storeys and attics over basements, the centre breaking forward and emphasized by quoins. Mansard roof with dormer windows, still with the alternating pediments of the late C17. The central door is up a steep flight of steps; doorcase with pediment and Corinthian columns on the entrance side (N), segmental pediment on the garden side opposite.

The plan is regular, with fine contemporary interiors. Entrance hall with four doorways symmetrically disposed at the corners; staircase hall beyond. Elegant stair with three balusters to the tread (two types of spirals). Raised and fielded panelling throughout. Dining room to the r., drawing room beyond. To their w a later extension, partly blocking the pedimented central window of the w side. The spacious basement, visible as a ground floor on the E side, with mullioned-and-transomed windows and two re-used granite Tudor doorcases, extends with groined vaults on square piers under the s and E parts of the house, much as at Plympton House and Mothecombe. In the garden wall next to the w extension, a small window with C20 engraved glass commemorating a tree, set in a coloured surround, by *Frank Wotton*.

Good BARN with some re-used stonework (two narrow round-arched windows).

PUSLINCH BRIDGE. *See* Yealmpton.

PYWORTHY

3000

ST SWITHUN. Out of the ordinary run of North Devon churches in several ways. First of all the church has a clerestory (cf. North Molton, Tiverton). Secondly the nave is separated from the s aisle by an arcade of octagonal piers and double-chamfered arches. This arcade, and also the clerestory windows and the chancel windows, is no doubt C14, the latter early in the century. The s aisle windows are obviously late Perp. The slim w tower is again unusual in that it is strengthened at the foot by angle buttresses. The unceiled wagon roofs inside are original. Restored in 1859 by *R. Medley Fulford* (windows renewed). – FONT. Plain, octagonal. – Victorian STAINED GLASS.

RECTORY. Early C19; Doric portico.

PARNACOTT. Similar to the Rectory.

CHAPELS. In Derril hamlet, two contrasting village chapels. The Methodist chapel built by the Bible Christians in 1843 as part of a little terrace, possibly converted from two cottages, is now the Sunday school. Its successor of 1904, on a large site almost directly opposite, is a tall, partly slate-hung building distinguished by an elaborate gabled porch with arched door and windows, carved bargeboards, and turned finials. The interior is calm and plain, with a central pulpit in front of a shallow arched recess.

8010   RACKENFORD

ALL SAINTS. W tower with diagonal buttresses and NE stair-turret. W door with renewed Dec window above. Nave and N aisle of four bays, the piers of the arcade of A type with crude standard capitals, the ornament mainly abstract. The nave has a ceiled wagon roof supported by crude figures holding shields. S side and porch rebuilt 1827; general restoration 1877–1902 by *A. Blomfield*. – FONT. Big, octagonal, Perp, with tracery motifs. – STAINED GLASS. E window by *A. L. Moore*. – MONUMENT. Arthur Chamberlain † 1941. Large carved wooden coat of arms; good.

RACKENFORD MANOR (formerly Cruwyshaye). Plain five-bay, two-storey Georgian house, enlarged in 1928–32 by *Allan Walton*. He added wings and re-designed the interior almost entirely. The style is neo-Georgian.

Rackenford, now a straggling village, was once more important. It had a market in the C13. The most appealing house is the STAG INN opposite the church, plastered and thatched, with a big projecting front porch.

OLD RECTORY. Early C19, the usual type with deep eaves.

EBENEZER CHAPEL, attached to a farm N of the village. Built by the Bible Christians in 1848. Typical rural chapel, rendered, with Gothick glazing, in its own little railed enclosure, with red brick SCHOOLROOM of 1891 on one side.

TOLL HOUSE, on the B3221. Curiously shaped, single-storey, with a round central projection with a door now bricked up.

6010   RASHLEIGH BARTON
                          Wembworthy

An unassuming exterior: plastered main range of cob, two crosswings, C19 and C20 windows (apart from remains of C17 hood-moulds and a panel on the N wing). As so often, the main range is late medieval (arch-braced roof with wind-braces, now concealed). But the chief interest is the unusually lavish modernization carried out in the earlier C17 for the Clotworthys, who inherited the house through marriage with the Rashleighs in the C16. The dates 1631 and 1633 appear on the plasterwork upstairs. The house declined into a tenanted farmhouse after it had passed by marriage to the Tremaynes in 1682.

In the hall, a C17 inserted floor with four-panel beamed ceiling, and a plasterwork frieze with shields. Fireplace with four-centred arch; later double oven, of cloam. But the main early C17 effort was concentrated on the N wing, a good example of how by this time the hall was no longer the main showpiece. Much good joinery throughout, and outstanding plasterwork, some of the best of its date in Devon. The parlour ceiling, of three bays, has a delightful free-flowing scrolly pattern inhabited by a wide variety of plants, insects, and animals, from dogs, cats, pigs, and cocks, to elephant, griffin, and Pegasus. Behind the parlour a panelled corridor leads to the comfortably large staircase, sited in a projection N of the cross-wing. The stairs, rising around a solid core, are divided off by a handsome dog-gate with two tiers of turned balusters; at the top a balustrade (reset) also with turned balusters.

The most spectacular room is the great chamber above the parlour, with a sumptuously decorated barrel-vaulted ceiling with pendants, the centre one with an openwork cage (cf. Boutport Street, Barnstaple). Within the enriched intersecting double ribs, birds, animals, and sprays of foliage. Scrollwork frieze with Pegasus figures. On the end wall the Clotworthy arms flanked by strapwork with small figures in medallions, and larger reclining figures. The back room of the N wing (now subdivided) has remains of a more conventional single-rib ceiling and end walls with arms amidst intricate strapwork threaded with bunches of fruit held up by two putti; also the initials I and MC and the date 1633. Opening off the room is a closet with original door. More C17 joinery in the rooms over the hall, and in an upper room in the S wing a chimneybreast with plaster arms and the date 1631.

Good OUTBUILDINGS: C17 cob BARN and CARTSHED, altered in the C19; late C18 rubble-walled STABLES.

RATTERY   7060

ST MARY. With wide views over rolling country on all sides. The small, two-stage, very tapering W tower, with diagonal buttresses only on the ground floor, battlements set on a corbel-table, and an unmoulded tower arch inside, is clearly of the C13. Nave and two aisles, the arcades on octagonal granite piers with double-chamfered arches. N and S transepts. Projecting chancel, presumably rebuilt after 1426, when it was described as too small and dark for services. The interior walls decorated with a complete sgraffito scheme of c.1870. – SCREEN. Restored by the Misses *Pinwell*, 1911. – STAINED GLASS. S chapel E by *Dix & Williams* of Bristol, 1843, one of several interesting windows of similar date.

(CHURCH HOUSE. Now an inn on the village green. Long and rendered; stone newel stair.)

MARLEY HEAD VIADUCT. Built for the G.W.R. in the 1850s; doubled c.1892. Partly of smooth stone piers in pairs joined by tall cross-arches, partly of granite with rusticated piers and brick-lined arches.

MARLEY HEAD TUNNEL. Double-bore as a result of doubling the

line. At the E, the N arch is of stone with a slightly decorated parapet, the S, at a lower level, of plain red brick.
See also Syon Abbey.

REVELSTOKE
Newton and Noss

ST PETER THE POOR FISHERMAN. On its own, romantically set
on the edge of the cliff overlooking Stoke Bay. Abandoned after
1882, when the Barings of Membland built a new church at Noss
Mayo (qq.v.), rescued in the 1960s by local effort, and in 1982
vested in the Redundant Churches Fund. Small NW tower with
saddleback top. Attractively restored as a part-ruin; the nave is
open to the sky, apart from the S aisle, which has an arcade with A
type piers and a rafter roof with bosses. Three-light windows
without tracery. Dec window to the N transept. The chancel, its
roof renewed, is divided off by glazing in the chancel arch.

REWE

ST MARY. Two-stage W tower, the top rebuilt by *E.H.Harbottle* in
1914. Battlemented N transept (Wadham Chantry) of the end of
the C15, now obscured by the organ. Chancel with late Perp
straight-headed N and S windows to the chancel, but a cinquefoiled
PISCINA which may be earlier. Perp S arcade; angels with shields
on the capitals. Much reconstructed in 1867–8: chancel restored by
Edmund Sedding, nave S wall and porch rebuilt by *Ashworth*, who
also provided a new roof and seating incorporating thirty-two late
C15 BENCH ENDS, mostly with tracery motifs, with heraldry
referring to Sir Nicholas Wadham. – SCREEN with type A tracery;
no coving. In the spandrels, scrolls with inscriptions (Jesu Maria,
Ego sum ostium). – Screen and PULPIT were painted in 1870, to
go with Sedding's colourful redecoration of the chancel. His painted roof (rebuilt with old materials) remains, but his stencilling of
the chancel walls has been whitewashed. – ALMSBOX on a fluted
column, dated 1632. – MONUMENT (behind the organ) to Paul
Draper †1689. Oval in architectural surround; steep broken
pediment.

THORNDON. The former rectory, attributed to *James Knowles*
(P. Metcalf), built in 1844 to replace the old rectory destroyed for
the Bristol and Exeter Railway. Stuccoed Italianate, with heavy
bracketed cornice and striking chimneys. Three-bay porch. Good
interior with impressive arcaded hall and staircase with glazed
dome, original cast-iron fireplaces, and huge arched cellars.

Rewe is a main-road village N of Exeter. Along the road a picturesque
series of late C19 estate buildings, beginning with a former FIRE
ENGINE HOUSE opposite the church. Brick with stone dressings;
covered outside staircase. It adjoins four pairs of ESTATE COT-
TAGES, the end pair with the village store. Patterned tiles, red and
yellow brick. Further on, REWE BARTON, a good group of C19
model farm buildings, the range facing the road of two storeys with

central archway of stone, other ranges one-storeyed, of brick, around a courtyard.

RINGMORE

6040

ALL HALLOWS. An early church with no Perp work – an exception in Devon. C13 steeple standing S of the nave. Low, with lancet windows exclusively, diagonal buttresses not reaching high up, battlements, and a tiny spire. The S porch with a pointed tunnel-vault inside. Nave, two transepts, and chancel. Some of the windows renewed. No window details later than *c.*1300, i.e. lancets with plain-pointed or pointed-trefoil heads. No tracery proper at all. Restored in 1862–3 and later under the Rev. F. C. Hingeston-Randolph, incumbent for over fifty years. He personally removed several layers of plaster over the chancel arch to reveal medieval WALL PAINTING, a scalloped diaper with a repeated pattern of stylized plant forms in red, green, and black, still preserved in good condition. The other walls were covered in the C19 with colourfully painted tin panels, since replaced by horrible rendering. – ROOD SCREEN and ORGAN CASE with pretty Victorian painting, probably of 1862–3.

ROBOROUGH

5010

5 m. SE of Great Torrington

ST PETER. W tower with diagonal buttresses and pinnacles. S arcade with granite piers of B type and four-centred arches. N wall and chancel rebuilt in a thorough restoration of 1868. The chancel in E.E. style, enriched with marble shafts. – MONUMENTS. Two little slate tablets with rustic strapwork, 1648 and 1652, to two Fortescue daughters.

METHODIST CHAPEL, Ebberly Lodge. One of a pair of lodges of *c.*1815, at an entrance to the drive to Ebberly House (q.v.). The drive is now cut by a new road. Taken over by the Bible Christians in 1839 as chapel and caretaker's house. Sunday school added in 1913. Both lodges squarish, rendered and slated. Pyramid roofs replaced by gables.

ROBOROUGH GRANGE. Gabled Victorian Tudor of 1842.

See also Coombe Barton *and* Ebberly House.

ROBOROUGH

4060

Near Plymouth

The WHARF built by Sir Thomas Tyrwhitt (*see* Princetown) at the end of the Plymouth and Dartmoor Railway still has the stable and hayloft for the horses which pulled the trucks: a stone building of *c.*1820 with a low-pitched hipped slate roof with a wide door at the NW end, wide double doors on one side, and blank walls on another.

PLESSEY SEMICONDUCTORS. *See* Plymouth: Outer Plymouth.

See also Maristow.

ROCKBEARE

St Mary. Much rebuilt in 1887–9 by *Hayward & Tait*. w tower, with diagonal buttresses and stair-turret, medieval, of grey ashlar, as are the N aisle wall and aisle arcade. s wall of red sandstone. Good Perp w doorway with fleurons around the arch. Piers of an unusual section, A type, with two hollows in the diagonals. Wagon roofs with bosses. – WEST GALLERY with Elizabethan parapet. – STAINED GLASS. E window: Virgin and angels, against clear glass, by *Louis Davis*, 1928. – MONUMENTS to the Porters of Rockbeare Manor. Thomas Porter †1815, with elegant Latin inscription, Grecian altar and urn, by *R. Blore*. – William Porter †1820, neoclassical, with draped altar. – Thomas Porter †1857, Gothic tabernacle. – In the churchyard a handsome Grecian urn to the Duntze family, 1795. – Nicely sited LYCHGATE of 1890.

OLD RECTORY. 1836. Three-window rendered front with tented veranda. On the E side a chapel, vaulted, with timber ribs.

ROCKBEARE COURT, immediately N of the church. Two storeys, with Georgian windows, a broad Doric porch, and a full-height bow, from the E, from the time of the Bidgood family. Older parts behind.

ROCKBEARE MANOR. A substantial country house in its own grounds, owned by Sir John Duntze in the later C18 and sold by his son to Thomas Porter *c*. 1815. The drive is entered between two handsome stuccoed gatepiers inspired by an Inigo Jones design. Each has two Roman Doric vermiculated columns framing a niche, with a pediment above. They must belong with the mid C18 Palladian house, whose original design is now partly obscured by Regency additions of *c*. 1820. White stucco front of three storeys: three central bays with a porch with paired columns, two fullheight bow-windows. The top floor, the porch, and the bowwindows date from *c*. 1820. A painting in the house shows a lower mid C18 building, with a pediment over the three central bays, and a cupola. The existing one-storey pavilions, pedimented, with Venetian windows, belong to this first Palladian phase. They are linked to the house by straight walls, each with a large archway. The house extends back with two long wings on either side of a central courtyard. The l. range has a bow-window for the kitchen; the r. one ends with a shallow two-storey bow to the garden, part of a dining room added *c*. 1770.

The interiors at the front of the house date from the remodelling of *c*. 1820. Central hall with early C19 black marble fireplace; staircase hall behind, with a window with Gothic glazing, and early C19 reeded cornice. The staircase around three sides of a well, mid C18 in style, is oddly proportioned and perhaps re-used. The S wing facing the garden was considerably remodelled in the 1920s for the Follett family by *Morley Horder*, who made the passage to the garden door. In the room to its w, a mid C18 fireplace and enriched panelling; in the room to its E another fireplace, probably not *in situ*.

Beyond this is the late C18 dining room, the best room in the house, bowed at either end and richly and colourfully decorated, with furniture and Axminster carpet to match. Orange Ionic scagliola columns at the corners, the colour repeated along the cornice; fireplace with Ionic columns in pink and orange inlaid marble and a scene of a sacrifice. Above the mantelpiece is a very large plaster oval with a classical scene tied up in an Adamish bow, and on the other walls plaster reliefs of large hanging lamps with dolphins incorporating lamp brackets. Ceiling with foliage scrolls in panels. The room recalls decorators such as James Wyatt, but the engaging boldness of detail and the slightly clumsy handling of the columns suggest competent provincial imitation rather than a London workshop. Above the dining room a bedroom with a fine blue-john fireplace. Over the hall the drawing room of 1820 has a yellow marble fireplace with an urn in relief, and modillioned doorcases; walls with *trompe l'oeil* architectural decoration (added in the 1920s).

The pavilions were originally billiard room and orangery, the latter once with a Venetian window at the side as well as the front. Behind and on axis with the house very handsome C18 red brick STABLES, H-shaped, with an arch on either side leading to a courtyard with two-storey coach houses in the far corners. In the centre, steps leading up to a formally laid out MODEL FARMYARD which has as its centrepiece a large barn, and on each side lower buildings with stalls, and a two-storey cottage. The grounds include a walled garden and a serpentine lake.

ROMANSLEIGH 7020

ST RUMON. Nave and chancel rebuilt in 1868 by *Ashworth*; the w tower added in 1887, with buttresses only at the foot. – (STAINED GLASS. Two chancel windows by *Clayton & Bell*. – Nave N and S 1953 and 1959 by *James Paterson* of Bideford.) – N of the church, scanty remains of St Rumon's HOLY WELL.

ST RUMON'S. The former rectory. 1860, but still of the wide-eaved Regency type.

HIGHER THORNHAM and LOWER KINGSTREE are good farmhouses with the usual three-room-and-cross-passage plan, both with well preserved C17 joinery.

WEST ROWLEY. A C17 lobby-entry house. Two-storey porch with sundial dated 1708. Wooden mullioned windows.

ROSE ASH 7020

ST PETER. Heavily restored by *Ashworth* in 1874, then largely rebuilt by *St Aubyn & Wadling* in 1882–92, apart from the w tower (low, unbuttressed, unpinnacled) and probably the N arcade (A type piers, capitals only to the main shafts). – SCREENS. Rood screen Perp; B type tracery, coving and cresting renewed. – N chapel parclose screens Jacobean, dated 1618, the solid lower panels with half-wheel motifs, the upper parts with plain long balusters and the arms of Anne of Denmark and Prince Henry above. – COMMUNION RAILS. Graceful, *c*. 1700–10. – Plenty of traditional Gothic WOODWORK of the 1890s. – STAINED GLASS. E window 1892 by *Drake*; others by the *Hardman* firm, including several late examples in pictorial style (chancel N and S 1925, nave

SE 1934). – MONUMENTS. Minor memorials to the Southcombes, who held the living from 1675 to 1949.

(OLD RECTORY. Built by the fourth Southcombe rector in 1718. Plastered ranges around a small courtyard.)

SOUTH YARD. A disguised late medieval house on a three-room cross-passage plan, the (later) hall stack creating a lobby entrance. In the hall, a mid C16 ceiling with deeply moulded intersecting beams and an unusual C17 panelled screen with integral bench and moulded bench ends. Late C15 roof on four jointed cruck trusses of large timbers ending in capitals, threaded double ridge, three tiers of wind-braces. But the most remarkable feature is the ornament on the E face of the main truss, cut through truss, collar, and arch-bracing. It consists of simple panelled tracery, but has only been roughed out in the upper parts. Were the timbers rejects from a grander house?

2090

ROUSDON
Combpyne Rousdon

159 A mansion on the grand scale (since 1938 All Hallows School), built in 1874–8 for Sir Henry Peek by *Ernest George* (of *George & Vaughan*, later *George & Peto*), the firm's first major country house, and the first important occasion where George was chiefly responsible. Henry Peek, M.P. for Wimbledon from 1868, knighted in 1874, was of Devon extraction (cf. Loddiswell). The family made its fortune by importing tea, then by expanding into groceries and Peek Frean biscuits. Peek bought the estate – consisting of the entire parish of Rousdon – *c.* 1868, and began by providing a combined parish church and private chapel (*see* below).

The house stands on the exposed cliff above Lyme Regis, a long, spreading composition, solidly built with 3 ft walls of a special waterproof construction (asphalt-covered brick, faced with local flint and Purbeck dressings). Sober Tudor mullioned windows, sturdy Gothic porch, enlivened by irregularly grouped timbered and tile-hung gables in Shaw and Nesfield's Old English manner, and by some free Gothic and Renaissance carving by the local sculptor *Harry Hems*. The dominating feature is the decidedly continental-looking tower, focusing attention on the grand end of the establishment. (George had published his *Sketches German and Swiss* in 1870.) The tower housed Sir Henry's Justice Room, with a separate entrance, a strongroom below, and a dressing room, museum, and astronomer's lookout above. Lady Peek's province was the SE corner, where her upstairs boudoir is distinguished by a decorative corner turret.

The irregular, picturesque effects disguise a straightforward plan with rooms grouped around two courtyards, with ingenious use of different levels for family and servants. The service court-yard is approached by a descending ramp which passes in a tunnel beneath the drive from porte-cochère to stables. The main court-yard, also at basement level, has a cloister arcade providing dis-creet access to the dairy (with pictorial tiles) sited beneath the library, and to the servants' and estate hall (which doubled as American bowling alley and rifle range) below the great hall. In the

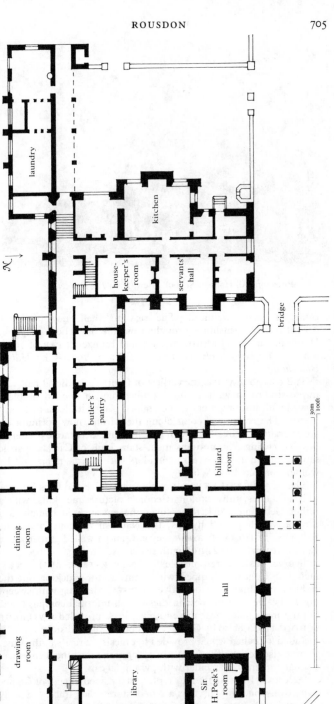

Rousdon (All Hallows School): plan

THE BUILDING NEWS JUNE 26.1874.

Rousdon, Devon... now erecting for
Sir Henry W. Peek, Bart. M.P.
George E. Vaughan, Architects.

Rousdon (All Hallows School): view (from *The Builder*)

centre a pretty wellhead. The servants' hall, now SCHOOL
CHAPEL, has furnishings brought from the old school chapel at
Honiton: carved REREDOS of 1921 and bronze ALTAR of 1928,
both by *Herbert Read*; STAINED GLASS of 1924–5 by *Hubert
Blanchford*.

The GREAT HALL is the earliest of George's medieval halls, an
impressive room with an open timber roof, a hooded fireplace
carved with hunting scenes, and stained glass with local historical
events. The reception rooms along the S front (now dormitories)
are restrained Jacobethan, with panelling and decorative plaster or
beamed ceilings. Sumptuous main stair, built of Carrara marble
salvaged from a local wreck; corridors with mosaic floors laid by
women convicts from Woking.

The STABLE COURTYARD, with estate office and fives court as
well as stables, fully exploits George's picturesque skills, with a
rather Germanic clock tower over the entrance (it contained a
carillon which played hymns, the National Anthem, and Rule
Britannia). BILLIARD ROOM beyond, and a walled garden (now
games area) with GAZEBOS with sea views.

George was also responsible for many ESTATE BUILDINGS,
including a farm (equipped with tramway for mucking out the
stables) and three very attractive LODGES, tile-hung with sweeping roofs. He is at his best in these small informal compositions.
On the main road, near the entrance, Peek provided a VILLAGE
SCHOOL (1876), also by George, with boldly massed steep roofs. It
included a kitchen which provided hot meals – a rarity at the time.
George also designed the MILEPOST opposite the school entrance,
a squat, square ashlar pillar with pyramidal cap.

ST PANCRAS. Built in 1872 to replace the ruined chapel of Comb-
pyne Rousdon. Now used as a school store. Plate tracery. Sturdy
pyramid-roofed W tower housing a vestry; playful taller octagonal
turret. Triple-arcaded porch, combined with entrance to the Peek
family vault. – STAINED GLASS by *Lavers, Barraud & Westlake*.

ST GILES IN THE WOOD

ST GILES. Perp w tower with diagonal buttresses at the foot only, short pinnacles; the side walls also partly medieval. The rest a dull, earnest Victorian rebuilding and refitting at the expense of the Hon. Mark Rolle of Stevenstone (q.v.); 1862–3 by *Hayward*. N and S arcades with five hefty Dec arches on polished marble columns with moulded capitals. Painted texts around the windows. Organ chamber and vestry added 1879. – Marble and alabaster PULPIT given by Mark Rolle. – STAINED GLASS. Several good windows (attributed to *Clayton & Bell*; RH): E window with Crucifixion; chancel s, a circular memorial window to John, Lord Rolle, †1842; and S aisle E. – BRASSES. Alenora Pollard †1430 (lower half of figure only). – Margaret Rolle †1592. Larger figure in Elizabethan costume. – Joanna Risdon †1610. Small kneeling figure beside inscription. – Other brasses with only heraldry and inscriptions. – MONUMENTS. Semi-reclining gentleman, bearded, c. 1630; a fragment of a larger monument. – Illegible C17 architectural tablet with oval wreath. – John Rolle †1842 and ancestors. Marble Gothic tablet.

Much C19 Rolle ESTATE HOUSING in the village. In the row facing the churchyard the earlier cottages have pretty trellis porches; those of the 1870s have more self-conscious Gothic detail – barge-boarded gables, pointed openings, and solid porches with fish-scale slates.

WINSCOTT HOUSE, a cheerless Gothic mansion of 1858–64 by *W. White*, has been demolished.

At KINGSCOTT, overlooking a burying ground, a BAPTIST CHAPEL of 1833 adjoining a late C19 SCHOOL, both gabled and rendered, with arched windows.

WAY BARTON, 2m. SE. A farmhouse, the former manor house of the Pollards. Set into the front wall, reset carvings (corbels?) with heads of two ladies wearing wimples (c. 1300) and the smaller head of a man.

ST GILES ON THE HEATH

ST GILES. Chancel with a small C13 window. Five-bay S arcade with granite piers of A type; capitals only to the main shafts, decorated abaci, low pointed arches. Chancel restored and church reseated in 1868 by *J. D. Sedding*; the rest restored in 1878 by *J. P. St Aubyn*, who rebuilt the S wall re-using the medieval windows, provided new roofs with decorative slate bargeboards, and added the low unbuttressed w tower with slate pyramid spire. – FONT. Circular, Norman, of polyphant. – Former REREDOS. Of slate, with texts and minimal decoration on pedimented and segment-headed panels, c. 1840 by *R. Reddicliffe* of Lew Down. – SCREEN. Only the cut-down wainscot survives. – BENCH ENDS. Rather broader in shape than usual. Elementary decoration of two blank cusped arches with roundel; the roundels have a rose, fleur-de-lys, and a frontal head. – MONUMENTS. Two C18 slate wall-monuments with simple ornament. – Slate memorials also in the churchyard.

The Bedford estate provided a substantial VICARAGE in 1869, and was also responsible for two model farms in the parish: NETHER-BRIDGE, dated 1869, and PINSLOW, 1863, both with farmhouses of the same date. Pinslow has an especially complete planned farmyard, making good use of the sloping site. s range with open cartsheds, haybarn, adjoining two-storey range with (formerly) water-turbine powered threshing loft, fattening shed, and two-storey E range with access to a dunghouse at a lower level.

NETHER BRIDGE, over the Tamar. Medieval, but much rebuilt, of local granite ashlar. Two tall cutwaters and refuges.

DRUXTON BRIDGE, over the Tamar. C18; three semicircular arches with granite keystones.

SALCOMBE

Until the mid C19 Salcombe was a small maritime settlement, where shipbuilding flourished until the coming of steam power. But already in the C18 a few gentlemen's residences were built on the cliff slopes overlooking the estuary, and in the C19 the unparalleled scenery and mild climate encouraged the growth of small villas and lodging houses. The pace of development increased when the railway arrived at Kingsbridge in 1893, and the Devon estate on the crown of the hill was sold as building plots. Since then there has been gradual undistinguished infilling with flats, and the inevitable tarting up of the old quayside centre, but no large-scale eyesores.

HOLY TRINITY. In a fine position overlooking Batson Creek. A chapel of ease to Malborough was consecrated in 1395, rebuilt in 1801, and rebuilt again on a new site in 1843 by *J.H.Ball* of Plymouth. Lancet style, with an elegant E.E. arcade with granite quatrefoil piers and muti-moulded arches. Elaborate timber roofs. Chancel 1889 by *J.D.Sedding*; a broad E window with geometric tracery, and dying arches to chapel and organ chamber. – FONT. Octagonal, of the usual Perp type, the ornamentation perhaps C17. – Low stone SCREEN with elaborate ironwork and lovely Arts and Crafts beaten bronze DOORS with enamelling. – Painted ALTAR FRONTAL with Quattrocento angels within trefoiled arches.

The centre of Salcombe is still an intimate cluster of small streets, with low slate-hung houses remaining in FORE STREET amidst tourist and boating shops, and clusters of early C19 stone warehouses in the short alleys leading down to the water. In ORESTONE the four-storey OLD WATCH HOUSE, perhaps C18. On WHITESTRAND QUAY, off Clifton Place, four warehouses, of two and three storeys. There is another, dated 1827, in UNION STREET. Here too the stone CUSTOM HOUSE of c.1820. N of Union Street THE ISLAND, built on reclaimed land, with nice modest C19 terraces. The stuccoed ISLAND PLACE, facing the water and set back behind iron railings, is especially appealing. In SHADYCOMBE ROAD, W of the church, PORCH HOUSE, one older house of rural type.

Further s along FORE STREET, CLIFF HOUSE, late C19, tile-hung, with prominent belvedere, and an esplanade across the road continuing that of the MARINE HOTEL. The core of this was 'a handsome modern marine villa', as White described it, built by

Lord Kinsale c. 1839, enlarged and opened as a hotel in 1895, and much altered since.

On the steep slopes above, mid C19 pairs of tall gabled villas curve around DEVON ROAD, overlooking Courtenay Park. Still higher up are the streets laid out by the South Devon Land Company from 1894, starting with Allenhayes Road and Herbert Road. Most of the houses were by local builders and are of no special interest, but at the s end of the estate, in FORTESCUE ROAD, off St Dunstan's Road, one enticing show house was built: LA TOURELLE, an early work by the highly original Arts and Crafts architect *C. Harrison Townsend*. Substantial, with roughcast walls and slate roofs. On the entrance side a bold, semicircular, partly slate-hung stair-turret, and a porch canopy suspended from decorative brackets. Carefully placed windows leaving large areas of plain walling. On the seaward side an open arcade supported by battered piers and a curved balcony respond to the view. The windows alas spoilt by picture glazing. From the foot of St Dunstan's Road one can descend by the steeply winding SANDHILLS, a later suburban development above a much extended mid C19 Tudor villa of the same name, down to NORTH SANDS.

CASTLE, at the N corner of the North Sands Bay. As at Dartmouth and Kingswear, part of the Tudor fortifications of the south coast. Remains of a curved bastion commanding the harbour entrance. Destroyed after its capture in 1646 from the Royalists.

THE MOULT, hidden below the road, tucked into a cliff terrace between North and South Sands. The present appearance is early C19 picturesque: a slightly irregular E plan, rendered, with barge-boarded Tudor gables, and Gothick glazing on the entrance side. The core is a house built in 1764 by Mr A. Hawkins, said to be the first gentleman's seaside residence in the area. Pretty trellised and thatched SUMMER HOUSE; former STABLES with shaped gable; one-storey former LODGE with Gothick glazing on the drive from North Sands.

FALCONERS, off Collaton Road, North Sands. An inappropriate curiosity; a mock-Wealden timber-framed house, complete with open hall and inglenook, erected at the Wembley Exhibition of 1925 by the Federated Home-grown Timber Merchants Association and reconstructed here in 1926 by Lady Moore.

LIFEBOAT HOUSE, on the beach at South Sands. Given by R. Durant of Sharpham, 1867. An attractive building of red sandstone with shaped gables and finials.

Beyond South Sands the cliff road ascends steeply through the wooded slopes to OVERBECKS, a splendidly sited large Italianate villa (now youth hostel), and the semi-tropical gardens of Sharpitor. On the lower road, BAR LODGE, an austere balconied house on the cliff edge built for himself c. 1890 by the Methodist architect *John Wills* (†1906).

N of Salcombe, BATSON CREEK, with an appealingly unspoilt hamlet of cottages around the water. To the N, SNAPES MANOR, or Ilbertstow, with a three-window, three-storey part of 1784; older behind.

SALCOMBE REGIS

ST MARY AND ST PETER. Of the Norman church the circular piers
of the N arcade with circular scalloped capitals and the mangled
remains of a doorway in the S wall of the chancel. Small bits of
Norman ornament rearranged inside. To the C13 belong the N
arcade arches and the S aisle (W window), and to *c.* 1300 the chancel
windows. Can the S arcade (with double-chamfered arches not
separated by capitals from the piers) and the chancel arch belong to
the same time? A dedication date of 1259 is recorded. The W tower
is Perp. A two-storeyed little late Perp addition containing vestry
and charnel house extends W of the N aisle further W than the line
of the tower. Unemphatic chancel restoration 1869 by *E. Christian*;
tactful general restoration 1924 by *W. Weir.* – TOWER SCREEN.
Plain C18. – PULPIT. Plain C18. – STAINED GLASS. C15 fragments in a N window. – Chancel windows by *Clayton & Bell.* –
LECTERN of wood, probably C15. – MONUMENT. Slate tablet to
Joanna Avant †1695, with inscription in Hebrew, Greek, Latin,
and English.

The parish includes much of Sidmouth, but the church still has an
idyllic rural setting, nestling in a tight little valley running down to the
sea, with just a few houses for company.

THORN. Used for the manor court. A late medieval farmhouse, much
altered. Good moulded beams in one ground-floor room.
ILAM HOUSE. A picturesque stucco villa with decorative bracketed
eaves; *c.* 1840 with mid C19 extensions.
The quarries at DUNSCOMBE were an important source for stone in
the Middle Ages. They were reopened in the 1970s for repair of
Exeter Cathedral.

SALTRAM
Plymouth

Saltram is the most impressive country house in Devon. The chaste
white mansion (kept in beautiful order by the National Trust)
stands in grounds rising gently above the E bank of the river Plym, a
welcome buffer to expanding Plymouth. Exceptional both in its
scale and the lavishness of its C18 interior decoration, its story is
nevertheless that of other Devon houses writ large: an older house
expanded piecemeal, and with an interior far more sumptuous than
the plain exteriors would lead one to expect.
    The estate belonged in the C16 to the Bagg family, then after the
Civil War to the Carterets. They sold it in 1712 to George Parker of
Boringdon (q.v.), who died in 1743. His son John Parker and his
wife Catherine Poulett (daughter of Queen Anne's minister) made
Saltram their chief seat, and – perhaps influenced by Lord Clinton's
work at Castle Hill – embarked on an extensive building programme, although not quite as ambitious as had been suggested by
some preliminary designs. Their connoisseur son, another John
Parker (later Lord Boringdon), who succeeded in 1768, employed
Robert Adam in 1768–72 and 1779–82 to complete or remodel the
interiors, and with the advice of his friend *Sir Joshua Reynolds* (*see*

Saltram: plan

Plympton) provided Saltram with a notable collection of paintings
as well as much excellent furniture (outside the scope of this book).
The next John Parker, first Earl of Morley, did little except enlarge
the library and add the porch, works carried out by *John Foulston* in
1818 and 1820. The Earl's engineering projects around the river
Plym left the estate encumbered by debts; Saltram was let until
1884, when the third Earl and his successors began a gradual
programme of restoration. Since 1957 there has been extensive
restoration by the National Trust.

The exterior is essentially the mid C18 house of John and Catherine Parker. They were responsible for the present s front (apart from the later porch), a seven-window range with slightly projecting three-bay pedimented centre (coat of arms by *Coade & Sealy*, 1812), flanked by full-height canted bays. This may incorporate older fabric – a Tudor four-storey mullion-windowed staircase tower adjoins behind. The E range was new in the C18 (see the brick-vaulted cellars), built to provide a suite of reception rooms. It is very plain, embellished only by rusticated quoins, pediments to the slightly recessed ends, and by Adam's later Venetian window to the central saloon. The W range, different again, is an C18 regularization of older parts into a vaguely Palladian rhythm of 2–3–5–3–2 bays; the intermediate sections consist of lower two-storey links. The centrepiece has the appearance of a later C17 block, but this is not borne out by the plan. The space enclosed by these three ranges is filled by small courtyards and tantalizing remnants of the Tudor house.

The interiors are described in the order seen by visitors. The ENTRANCE HALL is mid C18, low-ceilinged but richly decorated. The stylistic medley is characteristic of provincial work. Sober Palladian Doric entablature and pedimented chimneypiece with terms and classical bust. The chimneypiece, by *Carter*, 1753, has a delightful small scene of Androcles and the lion. More progressive Rococo curlicues at the corners of the ceiling, but in the centre an old-fashioned rectangle with curved ends framing a large low-relief figure of Mercury. Excellent overdoors representing the four elements. In the MORNING ROOM to the E a charmingly light-hearted ceiling with a musical centrepiece: fat putti with trumpets. Fireplace of coloured marbles attributed to *Cheere* (paid for work at Saltram in 1753). Contemporary red velvet wall-hangings. The VELVET DRAWING ROOM (SE corner) has another elaborate ceiling and frieze, and a later chimneypiece attributed to *T. Carter Jun.* Much enriched joinery, and an unusual carved and gilded fillet around dado, fireplace, and doorways.

At the W end a screen with columns and double doors to the SALOON. This huge room (perhaps never completed in the campaign of the 1750s) was refashioned by *Robert Adam* in 1770–2, and is one of his most splendid creations. Tall coved ceiling boldly decorated with painted roundels within lozenges, blue damask walls (restored in 1950), neo-classical doorcases with capitals derived from Diocletian's palace at Split. Adam also designed the large mirrors and supervised the other furnishings. Another excellent chimneypiece by *T. Carter Jun.*, with Doric columns and metopes in red Brescia marble, a relief of the Labours of Hercules, and a contemporary neo-classical grate. The notable carpet echoing the tripartite ceiling division was provided by *Thomas Whitty* of Axminster in 1770.

Beyond the saloon the DINING ROOM, first fitted up as a library by Adam, and converted to its later use in 1780–1, when a sideboard was added in the bowed end, and the side windows of the bay were converted to niches for urns. A cool green and stone colour scheme, with ceilings and overdoors painted by *Zucchi* with literary subjects. The plaster-framed pictures were added in place of the bookcases; the small roundels high up belong to the original decoration.

Another Axminster carpet, with a design echoing the circular pattern of the ceiling.

In the inner angle of S and E wings the main STAIR HALL, with ceremonial flights around three sides; one fluted and two spiral balusters to each tread, but other details something of a puzzle, the neo-classical newels and Greek-key fret on the landing suggesting later reconstruction. Top-lit, with lively mid C18 plasterwork with putti and garlands on the cove and around the lantern.

The FIRST FLOOR ROOMS shown to the public are in the SE part of the house. Their notable features are two Chinese wallpapers, the one in the dressing room a rare early C18 example with large pale elongated figures on a buff ground, the SE bedroom with the more common smaller figures in a landscape. Good minor C18 fireplaces in these rooms; an early C19 one in the adjacent boudoir.

Downstairs again, W of the entrance hall, the family rooms. The LIBRARY was remodelled by *Foulston* to take in the former music room; the division is marked by Ionic scagliola columns. Handsome Foulston fireplaces with brass inlay; mahogany bookcases of 1788 (pediment and cornices early C20). Adjoining, in the W wing, a room with rehung Chinese wallpaper and an C18 fireplace, then, down some steps (marking the junction of different building phases), the GARDEN ROOM, formerly used as a billiard room.

E of this range the inner courtyard, where the disparate character of the fabric of the house is most easily visible. Adjoining the back wall of the S range a tower with Tudor windows (behind this, alongside the library, an elegant C18 corridor with saucer dome and sinuous little back staircase), and parallel to the S range the Tudor service block, with chamfered mullioned windows and two round-headed stone doorways, the W one leading into the former kitchen with its two fireplaces side by side in the back wall. The back door W of the kitchen is also C16, but probably not *in situ*. N of this range the larger Kitchen Court (recent colonnade on the E side) and the GREAT KITCHEN built after a fire in 1778, a fine lofty room with a coved ceiling, designed by *Parlby*, its original fittings preserved.

STABLES. On a courtyard plan, and an attractive C18 brick composition: the range facing the entrance of chequered brick, and perhaps earlier than the rest; the other three plain. C19 gables on the W range. Granite entrance arch; pediment and bell-turret above.

The C18 layout of the GROUNDS exploited the views over the Plym estuary; alas, these are no longer an asset, so the recent planting has been designed to conceal the eyesores. The first scheme, dating from the 1750s and typical of the transitional style of landscaping of the period, included formal features linked by winding paths. The main survival of this is the WOODLAND WALK behind the orangery, which leads down to the river past a series of romantically placed urns with rockwork bases studded with marble and quartz (now only partly surviving). Beside the water the AMPHITHEATRE, with three rusticated granite arches, originally with urns on the parapet. Three small GROTTOES are dug into the cliff.

The replanning of the grounds in the 1770s in the new informal manner was undertaken by Mr *Richmond*, who was also employed by the Parkers' friends the Pelhams at Stanmer, Sussex. Several buildings were added at this time. W of the house the ORANGERY, built in 1773–4 by *Stockman*, to a design by *Richmond*; of wood, with seven very large sashed windows, a pediment over the central three. Nearby, the former CHAPEL, converted from a barn in 1776. Battlemented parapet; four Gothick windows. Interior altered. Also a small GARDEN TEMPLE, pedimented, with Tuscan columns, and the delightful CASTLE. An octagonal summer house with ogee windows and embattled parapet; the main room, raised over a basement, has a Kentian fireplace.

At Saltram Point, a BATH SEAT, a large granite slab on the edge of the beach. Off Plymouth Road the BORINGDON ARCH, flanked by pilasters, built in 1783 as an eyecatcher; small lodge and out-house concealed behind.

STAG LODGE. An early C19 pair, one-storeyed, of ashlar, with cornice and fluted frieze; central chimneystacks. Contemporary GATEPIERS. Other GATEPIERS SE and NE of the house, the former, large and rusticated, of the C17, brought from Boringdon.

SAMPFORD COURTENAY

An attractive village with many rendered cob houses, and quite a spacious area opposite the Church House on the W edge of the churchyard.

ST ANDREW. A proud church with W tower and S side all of ashlar (Culm measures sandstone) and all embattled. The tower has the usual late Perp buttresses of type B and big pinnacles, a broad hoodmoulded W door, and a four-light W window. The S side makes a handsome composition with porch, stair-turret at the W end of the S aisle, and a lower chancel. The S aisle windows of three lights with pointed arches and Perp tracery are C19; simpler straight-headed windows without tracery to chancel and unembattled N aisle. The chancel E window of five lights has the most elementary panel tracery, possibly restoration after damage in the Prayer Book Rebellion of 1549, which started in this village. E of the chancel a one-storeyed embattled extension.

Inside, a quite exceptionally wide nave, and wide, open aisles. N arcade of four plus one bays with A type granite piers and slightly decorated capitals; S arcade of four plus two bays, only the last two identical to those of the N arcade; the others are of beautiful grey Cornish polyphant stone (more amenable to carving) and have B type piers with capitals adorned with fleurons. Good wagon roofs throughout. Among the bosses a wheel of three rabbits and a sow and piglets may be noted (cf. Branscombe). Some of the bosses and wall-plate angels date from the careful restoration by *G. Fellowes Prynne* in 1889. He also inserted the S aisle windows already mentioned, and raised the chancel and sanctuary floors.

FONT. Norman, table top with canted sides and scalloping. – SCREEN to S chapel. 1923 by *Herbert Read*, incorporating old fragments (hooded, not coved). – PULPIT. Plain C18. – Former COMMUNION RAILS, re-used for choir stalls. C18, with twisted balusters throughout. – STAINED GLASS. Late medieval two shields in the E window and three seraphim and one shield in the tracery of the N aisle E window. – Also in the N aisle, fragments of the

Virgin and of a Golgotha with silver-stain borders and Renaissance detail, i.e. only just pre-Reformation, a rarity in Devon.

CHURCH HOUSE. Much altered in the C19, when the ground floor was used as a school, with schoolmaster's house adjoining, but inside the s end essentially of *c.*1500. Ground-floor room with stopped chamfered beams. Roof with jointed crucks with steeply cambered collars. In the upstairs room long table and simple fitted benches from when this room was used as a court room.

LOWER CLISTON. A late medieval two-room-and-cross-passage house, with C17 inner room and rear wing with dairy and parlour. Wooden mullioned windows; good C17 joinery.

SOUTH TOWN. A mid C17 farmhouse on an unusual plan: a heated room at each end and a small unheated central room, with passage and projecting newel stair behind.

SAMPFORD PEVERELL

ST MARY. Uncommonly instructive architecturally. Two periods are clearly discernible and both are dated. The church was consecrated in 1318. Of that period the well-built low w tower of big blocks of reddish ashlar with diagonal buttresses and no stair-turret. Bell-openings with simple plate tracery. Rebuilt of old material in 1815, when a shingled spire was removed. C13 nave and chancel; lancet windows grouped in pairs by quatrefoils above, but not made into real tracery compositions yet. The E window has three lancets under a hoodmould. N door with a very flat arch on shafts with shaft-rings. The N nave windows have tall nook-shafts towards the interior with typically E.E. moulded capitals; the shafts rest on a roll-moulded string course which is carried around the N door. The window arches are low, with almost straight arches. In the chancel a PISCINA with paired arches, and in the N wall a pair of trefoil-headed arches, rebated for a door. All the detail looks if anything earlier than 1318, say mid C13, and indeed we know of another dedication in 1259. The N wall was rebuilt in the restoration of 1861–4 by *Ashworth*, but rebuilt correctly. Ashworth also reconstructed the nave and chancel roofs. In 1498 the Lady Margaret Beaufort, Henry VII's mother, who owned the manor, added the s aisle. This has a decorative w gable with quatrefoil panelling, three-light Perp windows, and an arcade towards the nave with tall type A piers with capitals only to the shafts. Lady Margaret did not spend as much money on Sampford as John Lane on Cullompton and John Greenway on Tiverton. To the w of the s aisle a curious addition in much rougher masonry with a bold, tall chimneystack.

FONT. Norman, circular, with simple bands of decoration at top and bottom of bowl and bottom of pillar. – SOUTH DOOR. Late medieval, mullioned. – STAINED GLASS. A complete set of C19 windows, of the time of the restoration of 1861–4. Scenes from the life of Christ, against deep blue backgrounds. Of high quality. All by *Lavers, Barraud & Westlake*. – Also two later windows: s aisle third and fourth from E to the Rev. Mr Ireland †1908, who paid for the restoration of the chancel, and Bishop Phillpotts †1869, both with scenes under canopies. – MONUMENTS. Cross-legged knight, very badly preserved. – Lady Margaret Poulett †1602. Horizontal brass plate with kneeling figures above a black inscription tablet, between finely decorated pilasters. – Margaret Collins †1655. Much cruder, with elaborately painted and carved putti heads and skulls.

OLD RECTORY. A late medieval priest's house, said to have been built by the Lady Margaret Beaufort in the early C16. Hall with large upper cross-wing; a lower wing was demolished for the canal opened in 1838. Restored in 1850. Large lateral stack to the one-storey hall (the floor above was added only in the C19). Both hall and parlour have framed ceilings with richly moulded beams and joists in alternate directions. Above the parlour a solar (subdivided later) with wagon roof and a fireplace. Stone four-centred doorway; windows renewed in the C19.

The RECTORY opposite, with Tudor windows, was built in 1841 by the canal company in recompense.

The medieval CASTLE of the Peverells, demolished in the C18, was near Sampford Barton. A mound remains.

EAST PITT. A C15–17 farmhouse with superior carpentry, including a hall truss collar decorated with chamfers and a carved boss.

SAMPFORD SPINEY

Church and manor house lie hidden in a remote fold of western Dartmoor.

ST MARY. Perp w tower of granite ashlar, with tall pinnacles. S aisle with straight-headed three-light windows, also Perp. The N transept and chancel C14 – see the piscina, also the arch from nave into N transept, with a fine carved head corbel on the W side. Simple Dec tracery in the N wall of the N transept, with tomb recess below. S arcade of granite with A type piers and double-chamfered arches. Sanctuary rebuilt in the restoration of 1867 by *Alfred Norman*. – FONT. Perp, octagonal, with shields.

SCHOOL. Small C19 building in a field below the church. Two half-hipped gables over the windows. According to his album, by *George Wightwick*.

MANOR HOUSE of the Hall family, now a farmhouse. Long and low. Jacobean gateway to the front garden. Simple late Perp front doorway with the date 1607 and initials RH, GH. Mullioned windows to ground floor and formerly to attic floor, no doubt inserted into an older building. Ruinous range to the l. with a two-centred doorway. (Other two-centred archways inside the main range.) Barn and granary flank the front garden.

MOORTOWN. Long, irregular seven-bay front with Georgian segment-headed sash windows and rusticated quoins.

HUCKWORTHY BRIDGE. Very narrow, with cutwaters.

WHIMINGTON.* Large late medieval longhouse with later C16 and C17 additions and alterations: consequently a relatively complex plan and a confusing front elevation, which now has three gables above a cross-passage. The longhouse was originally of the usual plan, with C15 granite doorways between porch and cross-passage,

*For a plan of Whimington see p. 69.

hall and inner room, and in the separate shippon entrance (the shippon was converted to domestic use in 1986). In the late C16 the upper end was remodelled to form an extensive cross-wing, with hollow-chamfered mouldings to fireplace and windows, and a two-storeyed porch, and the later rear cross-wing blocking the passage was added as a kitchen: fireplace with oven-and-smoking-chamber complex, exceptionally large. At the rear upper end a dairy outshot with original fittings. The final six-room plan is comparable to the C17 layout of the nearby Welltown, Walkhampton (q.v.). In 1983–6, after virtual collapse, the house was comprehensively but carefully repaired by *R.Meadows*.

SAND
Sidford

A small stone manor house, the seat of the Huyshes from *c.*1560. Mostly of the later C16 (Burke's *Seats* records window glass dated 1594) but with an outbuilding which was once part of a late medieval house. The late Tudor building is of random rubble, the main range with a gabled two-storeyed porch and a ground-floor hall to the l. with two six-light mullioned windows with transoms. Above the first-floor windows the roof-line is enlivened by small blind coped gables, with flat tops and little finials. Cross-gabled wings, the NW one tactfully rebuilt and the SE one remodelled internally as part of the extensive renovations carried out for Rowland Huyshe in 1908–9 by *E.H.Harbottle & Son*. At the same time the exterior rendering was removed, the upper porch window added, and the house extended by lengthening the SE wing and providing corridor and extra rooms in a range parallel to the hall. So, apart from the lower two-storey N wing with its large double chimneystack, the back of the house is chiefly of 1909, although the re-use of old materials makes this difficult to guess.

Inside, much robust late Tudor work. The front door is original, and so are the wooden partitions flanking the screens passage, the one on the service side of the Devon stud-and-panel type common in vernacular buildings, the one to the hall with more sophisticated rectangular panelling, surmounted by five blind arches with Jacobean enrichment. In the hall, a four-centred fireplace in the back wall, and some heraldic stained glass. Spacious wooden newel stair, with heraldic beast crowning the single post, and sturdy turned landing balusters. On the way up a good Tudor doorway with carved stops, leading to the upper room of the N wing. Here there is a fireplace of late Perp type: a four-centred arch with four large quatrefoils on the lintel.

In the remodelled SE wing a staircase and other impressively solid, well-made joinery of 1909, modelled on the C16 work. In the original back wall a large kitchen fireplace with bread oven.

Early C19 views show, at an angle between the Tudor house and the thatched outbuilding, a small gabled building with a Dec window, perhaps the chapel for which a licence was granted in 1419. How this was connected with the two existing buildings is unclear. It disappeared after a C19 fire, which also left the NW wing of the house derelict.

The outbuilding, of which the w end (Sand Lodge) was converted to a dwelling *c.* 1909, preserves a late medieval roof, now six and a half bays long (both gable walls rebuilt). The two bays nearest the E end formed an open hall. The central arch-braced truss is delicately moulded, with an ogee apex below the cranked collar, moulded purlins, and curved upper and lower wind-braces. No smoke-blackening; perhaps there was a chimney in the original end wall. The two-storeyed third bay, once divided off by a studded partition, has moulded ground-floor beams and a roof with wind-braces and moulded purlins. The other bays simpler, with jointed-cruck trusses.

SUMMER HOUSE, s of the courtyard. A pretty thatched building with a porch with Tuscan columns, the arms of Rowland and Anne Huyshe (*c.* 1600), and an inscription in Greek and Latin. Windows and a recess made up from medieval material.

SANDFORD

ST SWITHUN. Originally a chapel belonging to Crediton. Nave and aisles late Perp, probably of 1523–4, when the chapel was reopened with a licence for a burial ground. Nave and two aisles of five bays, the two E ones originally housing the chancel (see the rood-stair doorways). B type piers with standard capitals; on a N pier a carving of two fighting boys; diagonally in one pier a niche for an image. Good ceiled wagon roofs to the aisles, with carved wall-plates and bosses. The nave roof partly old, but raised and given tie-beams when the clerestory was added in the restoration by *Hayward* of 1847–8. Chancel also of this date, as well as some fittings, although these have been messed about in recent years and the Gothic reredos of 1848 has been destroyed.

FONT by *Hayward*, executed by *S. Rowe*, with a cluster of lively angels beneath the octagonal bowl. – War Memorial SCREEN designed by *Caröe*, 1921–2. – BENCH ENDS. C16, with the usual rich assortment of South Western motifs, early Renaissance ornament, profile heads, etc. – WEST GALLERY. Unusually lush. 1657, yet the forms still purely Jacobean. Carved arcaded front, fluted columns. – CHEST. Mid C17, with arcading and marquetry. – Of the chancel E window STAINED GLASS by *Merrick* of Bristol, only small figures in medallions remain. – N and S aisle E windows by *Warrington*, 1886, 1890. – MONUMENTS. Mary Dowrich † 1604. Small brass plate with inscription; recumbent figure on tomb-chest, kneeling figures l. and r. – Sir John Davie of Creedy Park † 1692. Architectural, without figures, quite grand. – Sir Humphrey P. Davie † 1846. Relief of the Good Samaritan by *E. B. Stephens*. – Other minor Davie memorials.

SCHOOL, Church Street. Surprisingly grand; built by Sir Humphrey Davie. Stuccoed, with *Coade* stone detail. Big pediment, heavy Doric columns (originally an open colonnade), the windows of the front also pedimented. Dated in large figures MDCCCXXV.

Sandford is a large and attractive village, with C18 houses round THE SQUARE; also the LAMB INN, of C16 origin, as are other late-looking houses. In SHUTE, CORONATION PUMP of 1838 in a curved alcove.

BREMRIDGE. An early to mid C15 house, its medieval roof virtually intact.

HIGHER FURZELAND. A C16 three-room-and-cross-passage house enlarged and remodelled in the C17. Cob walls; lateral hall stack of ashlar. Good joinery of the mid to later C17: hall screen with geometric frieze; stairs with turned balusters in a rear stair-projection with an original wooden-mullioned window with leaded glass.

MIDDLE HENSTILL. Unusual ASH HOUSE in cob with a thatched roof.

PROWSE. A superior farmhouse of the early C15. Late medieval hall roof with jointed crucks and early apex (ridge square-set on saddle). In the two-storey E cross-wing a roof on massive jointed crucks with cranked collars and lower wind-braces. Later W cross-wing. In the cross-passage a patterned cobbled floor, and inserted decorated intersecting ceiling beams, as in the hall. Excellent door frames and other timber details throughout the building. Early barn with jointed crucks.

RUXFORD BARTON. Projecting cross-wings. The core is probably medieval, but the oldest visible parts are early C17 – see the gabled porch with fine moulded inner doorway and original door. In a first-floor room of the parlour wing a strapwork cartouche with Chichester arms and initials, dated 1608.

WHITEROSE. A small three-room-and-cross-passage farmhouse, notable for its good C16 screens, the one at the upper end of the hall with traces of painted figures of saints. The hall was floored in the early C17, when the rear newel stair was added.

See also Creedy Park *and* Dowrich House.

SANDRIDGE
Stoke Gabriel

8050

Hidden away above the E bank of the river Dart. Built in 1805 by *John Nash* for the widowed Lady Ashburton; an excellent example of his informal *villa rustica* style. Stuccoed, with deep eaves. The rounded bay at one end carried up as a tower, with three *œil-de-bœuf* top windows, is very reminiscent of his slightly earlier Cronkhill in Shropshire. Picturesque effects are achieved with a minimum of features; the curved tower acts as a foil both to the stockier square tower over the original entrance, and to the more fanciful ogee-spired turret over the service wing at the back. The impression is of a distant architectural composition in a Claude painting. Arched windows with thin glazing-bars. Between square and round towers a shallow one-storeyed bow with trellis columns and balcony. To the r. the arrangement is not original, for Nash's long conservatory has gone. Behind the site of this a new side entrance to the house was made in the 1950s, and a large archway formed to the service court, with new rooms above, discreetly detailed.

Well preserved interiors, elegant and restrained. Former entrance hall with corner niches, and wall arches carried on fluted corbels. Good acanthus cornices in drawing room and dining room; original panelled doors and recesses. In the dining room, which extends into the round tower, a bold grey marble Egyptian fireplace with tapering pilasters and original grate. Vaulted spine corridor, on the first floor with two oval roof-lights.

OLD COACH HOUSE. Another Claudian eyecatcher. Converted to flats in the 1970s. Now rendered instead of the original exposed stone. Symmetrical, with a tall centre accent of pyramid-roofed tower; hipped roofs, paired brackets. The end bays on the l. have been left unaltered; they have two large arches. The upper windows on the garden side are insertions.

SATTERLEIGH

6020

ST PETER. Tiny C15 church, aisleless, with low weatherboarded bell-cote. The nave without any N windows. S door original in original wooden frame. The nave is separated from the chancel by a 'tympanum', i.e. a cross-wall originally standing on the (demolished) screen (cf. Molland and Parracombe). The inscriptions on the tympanum late Georgian. CELURE above this part of the roof. No visible wagon roofs otherwise. – FONT. Octagonal, Perp, with quatrefoil panels. – PULPIT. 'Jacobean', but probably mid C17. – BENCH ENDS. A few, with simple tracery.

SAUNTON
Braunton

4030

ST ANNE. 1897 by *F. J. Commin*; minute, intended as a chancel of a larger church. It replaced a lost chapel S of Braunton Burrows. Stone exterior; pale local brick inside. – STAINED GLASS. Good E window of 1903 by *Mary Lowndes*, three lancets with saints, landscape backgrounds, much purple and blue.

SAUNTON COURT. Small late medieval rubble stone manor house with cross-wings and two-storeyed porch, owned by Sir Robert Chichester in 1545 and by Sir John Luttrell in the C17, unassumingly remodelled and extended in 1932 for G. Rankin by *Sir Edwin Lutyens* in an informal neo-Georgian style. All low-key, no tricks and fancies. Lutyens retained the old porch with its round-headed arch and the tall twelve-pane sash windows to the hall. To the l. of the main range he added a little service court with kitchen wing and master bedroom suite above. The small windows with sliding sashes in this part add a vernacular touch. The open hall was recreated by the removal of a later ceiling, and fitted up in C18 style with pilastered panelling and a painted ceiling medallion (attributed to *Cipriani*, c. 1740). Much Lutyens panelling elsewhere. C18 marble fireplace in the dining room. Behind the hall a broad corridor leading to the bookroom, which has shell niches in C18 style. Generous staircase, oddly detailed, with thin turned balusters on a closed string. (Of the medieval house, evidence remains for a smoke-blackened hall roof with arch-braced collars, and most of the roof of the upper cross-wing, with purlins and wind-braces.)

The terraced GARDEN is a delight. Lutyens made the best of a constricted site, laying out a lawn in front of the house, with a higher terrace at the side, reached by his favourite convex–concave steps. Overlooking the lower lane, an outbuilding was converted to a two-storey gazebo with clock. On axis with the porch, gatepiers with balls flank steps down to a lower terrace with a water channel flowing from a semicircular grotto with a goat's-head gargoyle; beyond this a circular pool. Wooden garden gates with turned balusters.

Below the road between Saunton and Croyde a long line of early C20 villas taking advantage of the panoramic views across the estuary. Several in a decent quiet Arts and Crafts style, e.g. SAUNTON HEATH and SAUNTON DOWN, roughcast, with Voyseyesque touches.

SAUNTON SANDS HOTEL. By *Alwyn Underdown*, *c.*1937. Modernistic, i.e. flat-roofed, not genuinely modern – even that a rarity among larger English hotels of that date. Considerably altered.

SEATON

2090

ST GREGORY, Colyford Road. In a large churchyard on high ground ½ m. from the seafront, with a low Perp W tower facing towards the river Axe. Much pulled about, and now highly confusing. A late C13 window with intersecting tracery in the E end of the N transept. Dec windows in S transept and N aisle. Squint between N transept and chancel. The arcades and chancel arch of A type, but without capitals. Part of the N arcade demolished in 1817 for an extension to the W gallery. Restored and reseated in 1868 by *Ashworth*. A further restoration took place in 1901, when the roofs were renewed, and PULPIT, FONT and CLERGY DESK by *H. Hems* added.

BRIDGE over the Axe. 1877 by *Philip Brannon*. One of the first concrete-arched bridges. Three arches, classical detail.

The medieval settlement by the seafront declined because of a pebble ridge across the mouth of the Axe. Seaton remained a fishing village until the mid C19, when a modest resort developed slowly, encouraged by the Trevelyans, the local landowners. It is now swamped by a sprawl of C20 chalets and amusements at the E end of the town, but retains some of its character to the W.

In the centre, the narrow winding FORE STREET running steeply down to the sea recalls the pre-resort settlement. At the top, MANOR HOUSE, a nice urban Georgian house of red brick, three storeys, windows with triple stone keystones, Doric doorway. Further down the TOWN HALL, the former Masonic Hall, C19 debased classical with steep pediment, and a number of early Victorian houses. Nothing much along the seafront; the ROYAL CLARENCE, stuccoed, six bays, is the largest hotel. Further E a good Edwardian terrace in the Arts and Crafts tradition, rendered, with Tudor doorways, large external stacks, and gabled roof-line. Up the hill to the W the superior end of the town, with individual villas (the most prominent CLIFF CASTLE and ST ELMO, a castellated pair, rather altered) and a good early Victorian terrace off QUEENS ROAD facing a communal garden.

A special detour is recommended to the W along OLD BEER ROAD, where CHECK HOUSE was built as Calverley Lodge in 1865–6 for

W. C. Trevelyan and his wife Pauline, patrons of the Pre-Raphaelites. Now a hotel. Designed by Ruskin's protégé *Benjamin Woodward* (of Deane & Woodward, architects of the Oxford Museum), just before his early death. The executive architect was *C. F. Edwards* of Axminster. Memorable for its fresh and original structural polychromy. Walls of small squared greenish-blue stone interspersed with large white squares; chimneys and strainer arches of red brick. Emphatic windows with shouldered heads; roofs of variegated slates. Not large – only two storeys. To the garden the spreading gabled composition is somewhat undisciplined, with a surprising rounded corner and pretty veranda. Inside, staircase with wrought-iron balustrade with gilded lilies and much solid joinery with trefoil motifs.

SEAFORTH LODGE, Old Beer Road. By *Henry Clutton*, 1864–5, for Lady Ashburton, a friend of the Trevelyans. Dull in comparison. Conservative stuccoed design, with shallow pedimental gables and bracketed eaves. Nice veranda and balcony.

WESTCLIFFE TERRACE, E of Check House. Attractive stuccoed C19 terrace of eight houses, with simple cast-iron railings. Backs of red brick with upper bows to catch the evening sun.

RYALL'S COURT, Marlpit Lane, off Beer Road. A large house in its own grounds, much extended. Originally of *c.* 1840, stuccoed, with embattled parapet and a projecting porch with ogee-arched doorway and oriel above, i.e. one of the larger types of *cottages ornés* as found in Sidmouth.

MANOR ROAD, off the N end of Fore Street. A curiosity: 1920s free-Gothic suburban houses (cf. Budleigh Salterton for this kind of taste), rubble stone, mullioned windows, with picturesque turrets at the corner of Meadow Road.

ROMAN VILLA, near Seaton Down House. Parts of a villa and a possibly Roman military complex have been excavated.

SHARPHAM HOUSE
Ashprington

8050

Sharpham is a good example of patronage by a member of a pro-fessional class of rising importance in Georgian Devon: the naval officer. The estate, which had once belonged to the Yarde family of Bradley, was bought in 1765 by Captain Philemon Pownall, who had acquired a fortune of £64,963 through the capture of a Spanish galleon in 1762. He employed *Sir Robert Taylor* to transform the house, one of the rare cases of a London architect working in Devon at this time. (Pownall may have known of Taylor through his work for Lord Howe, Treasurer of the Navy.) Work began *c.* 1770, but Pownall died at sea in 1780, and the house was com-pleted by his daughter Jane, who married Edmund Bastard.

The house is admirably sited on a promontory overlooking the river Dart, approached by a long and dramatically hilly drive. From the E it has the appearance of a Palladian villa built *de novo*, with characteristic Taylor features: impeccable ashlar detail, care-fully proportioned astylar elevations, full-height central canted bay. But as C18 pictures in the house confirm, there was an earlier house, part of which survives at the back, although the red sandstone Tudor door in the irregular W front is the only easily recognizable feature remaining. Taylor's addition, at first only one room deep, was later extended in a matching style (the pediment over the central window on the N side was moved to the W; a second pediment was added on the longer S side).

As the old house could be adapted for service rooms, there are no basements (unlike most of Taylor's villas). The living rooms occupy both ground and first floor, with the more important ones upstairs. Taylor's skill in combining spaces of different shapes is displayed at once in the entrance hall. It is octagonal (fitting into the canted bay), with eight Doric columns; the patterned floor has a compass design in allusion to Pownall's profession. A low unassuming doorway frames a glimpse of the half-landing of the staircase beyond, with a cast-iron balustrade with intertwined initials. The true nature of the staircase hall comes as a shock of a high 128 order. It is an elongated oval, top-lit, around which the stairs rise up to the second floor in a dizzy and alarming cantilever. Little ornament, the balustrades plain apart from the landings; the geometry is everything. The mathematical key to the oval is indeed set out in the marble pavement. It is one of the most spectacular and daring later C18 staircase designs anywhere in England.

On the first floor an octagonal drawing room above the entrance hall, with original door surrounds and cornices but C19 wall decoration, and a N drawing room with restrained plasterwork on the walls. The SE room has a coved ceiling with original cornice. On the second floor Taylor's virtuoso handling of spaces is demonstrated *en miniature* by the little groin-vaulted apsed lobbies to the corner bedrooms, and the charming pair of small oval rooms over the octagonal space below, very similar to those at his Asgill House, Richmond, London.

W of the house, C19 service wings with laundry and larders. Further W, STABLES, probably by Taylor, one-storeyed around a courtyard, an elegant design with an arch in the centre of each range.

The GROUNDS are laid out in the picturesque manner, with lawns coming up close to the house, replacing the formal parterres shown on the C18 paintings. To the SW a Victorian arboretum, to the S Edwardian terraces, both created for the Durants; near the house, SCULPTURE by *Moore* and *Hepworth* added by the Ash family. By the Dart, an octagonal SUMMER HOUSE of c. 1720.

SHAUGH PRIOR
5060

ST EDWARD. The attraction of this church – apart from its situation on the SW edge of Dartmoor – is the late medieval FONT COVER discovered in a cattle shed by *Hems* in 1871 and sensitively restored by him. It is an octagon of lantern shape, two-storeyed, with a steep conical top surrounded by little figures. The ornament is similar to motifs on rood-screen cornices. The rest not out of the ordinary. Arcade of the usual regional type: A type piers, depressed arches. W tower of Ashburton type but with the big octagonal crocketed pinnacles of West Devon. Two-storeyed embattled and vaulted porch. S windows with renewed C14 tracery supposed to be original in design. – (BRASS of c. 1855 to the Munford family.)

CHURCH HOUSE, by the churchyard, has old chimneys and a staircase projection. In the village, terraced COTTAGES of c. 1830 onwards, built for china-clay workers.

PORTWORTHY. A typical South West Devon farmhouse: a longhouse much rebuilt and extended in the C16–17. The original house (at the upper end of the present building) has an entrance passage (not a through route) retaining a door to the shippon and another to the hayloft from the chamber above. The C17 additions include the parlour cross-wing, two-storey bay to the inner room, and possibly the porch and staircase beside the hall fireplace.

The Plym valley has some of the densest ARCHAEOLOGICAL REMAINS of Dartmoor. Along both sides evidence remains of intensive occupation and industrial activity over many centuries. From the Bronze Age, fields, hut circles, and enclosures abound; also parts of a reave system all along the valley. Fragments of prehistoric field systems and settlements survive on SADDLESBOROUGH (surrounded by clay extraction), together with a stone row. There are two more stone rows N of Wotter and others on the SW side of GREAT TROWLESBURY TOR. At BRISWORTHY a good-looking but vigorously restored stone circle.

GRIM'S GRAVE. A mounded barrow with a circle of stone slabs.

Streamworks and openworks of the TIN INDUSTRY follow the valley (documented from the C12 at BRISWORTHY), with two blowing houses remaining upstream of Plym Steps. A RABBIT WARREN existed from the C12 at TROWLESWORTHY, where a later warren house and kennel field with an 8-ft wall remain; prominent earthworks from other warrens survive at WILLINGS WALLS and HENTOR.

At LEE MOOR the waste heaps of the CHINA CLAY WORKINGS, which started in the early C19 and still continue, form a vast lunar landscape. Part of the route of the TRAMWAY which ran from here down to the Cattewater can be traced; the winding-house still stands at the top of the second incline.

4000   SHEBBEAR

ST MICHAEL. Norman S doorway more ambitious than in the neighbouring villages: one order of colonnettes, but three orders of arch voussoirs, including beak-heads and zigzag. The S aisle arcade has odd square piers with chamfered angles and double-chamfered arches. They could be early C14, the likely date for the tracery of the N and S windows. But the windows are all renewed. Do they represent original evidence? W tower with angle buttresses only at the foot, no W door, and low pinnacles. S chancel chapel of two bays with the usual A piers of granite with capitals only to the main shafts. Original wagon roofs in nave, chancel, and chancel chapel. – PULPIT. Elizabethan, elaborate, with crude figures in the usual arched panels. – MONUMENTS. Unknown lady, said to be Lady Prendergast of Ludford, perhaps late C14. Not good sculpturally, and not well preserved. – William Rigsby †1699. Nice slate plate with coat of arms, skulls, and hourglass.

LAKE FARM. The home of some of the earliest leaders of the Bible Christians, the Methodist group established in 1815. The EBENEZER CHAPEL of 1841 (much altered) stands on the site of the Bible Christians' very first chapel of 1818, within a graveyard with the C19 slate slabs of the leaders of the denomination. The farmhouse is now the chaplain's house of SHEBBEAR COLLEGE, the Methodist boys' boarding school across the playing fields. The school was founded in the 1830s in the still existing house of James Thorne, the Bible Christians' printer. The later school buildings are by *James Crocker* of Exeter, 1877–8.

See also Durpley Castle.

SHEEPSTOR

The church is splendidly situated between the granite rocks and the large lake of the Burrator reservoir.

ST LEONARD. Unbuttressed W tower with the polygonal pinnacles of Plympton and Plymouth. Granite S arcade, A type piers, depressed arches. Restored in 1862 for Sir Massey Lopes (*see* Maristow) by *Blachford* of Tavistock. – SCREEN. 1914, based on a fragment of the one destroyed in 1862. – STAINED GLASS. E and nave N by *Hardman*. – MONUMENT. Elizabeth Elford † 1641. Small, of alabaster, with the lady semi-reclining, her baby by her side on the couch, three kneeling daughters by her bedside. Above, curtains drawn apart. A charmingly intimate atmosphere despite indifferent workmanship. – In the churchyard, C18 slate gravestones, and a big red Aberdeen granite sarcophagus to James Brooke, first Rajah of Sarawak, † 1868, who bought the Burrator estate in 1858. – Also a cyclopic Dartmoor granite boulder to the second Rajah † 1917.

CHURCH HOUSE, by the lychgate. Given by John Elford in 1570. With the date 1658, but obviously older.

MANOR HOUSE of the Elford family, now on the shore of the lake, ½ m. N. In ruins, but the porch and hall still clearly recognizable.

YEO FARM OLD HOUSE. An excellent small early C17 house (datestone 1610), on a symmetrical plan, with a two-storeyed central porch and end stone stacks, all in granite with ovolo-moulded windows and smooth arched doors. Now used as a farm outbuilding.

W of the Plym at DITSWORTHY WARREN, extensive evidence of BRONZE AGE SETTLEMENT, with enclosed and unenclosed hut groups, fields, and reaves. W of WHITTENKNOWLES ROCK a particularly complex enclosed settlement. At DRIZZLECOMBE very fine stone rows run parallel with the river, two single, one partly double, each with a barrow at one end and a standing stone at the other. Other barrows nearby. *See also* Shaugh Prior.

Medieval and later TINWORKING has also left remains in the valleys at Ditsworthy, and so has the post-medieval RABBIT FARM, with its pillow mounds or buries, late C16 warren house served by a leat, large kennel field with boundary wall and three doghouses built into it, and funnel-shaped walls which are the remains of vermin traps, some with their granite and slate traps remaining.

Further S, where Legis Lake joins the Plym, another very extensive

BRONZE AGE SETTLEMENT may be seen, again completely inter-mingled with later tinworking, fields, and the pillow mounds and vermin traps of LEGIS TOR WARREN. The hut settlement was one of the earliest Dartmoor sites to be excavated (in 1896) by the Dartmoor Exploration Committee. A stone row runs N to the summit of RINGMOOR DOWN, with a retaining circle at the s end.

In DEANCOMBE, where Narrator Brook runs down to Burrator Reservoir, the small prehistoric fields and hut circles have been much altered by later tinworking. Streamworks, shafts, adits, and a blowing house can be seen. To the w, remains of the large C19 EYLESBARROW mine can be seen, including the pit for the 50 ft waterwheel, the granite bearings that carried pumping rods, the base of a reverberatory furnace, and a series of six stamping mills with dressing floors and buddles set into the hillside.

The BURRATOR RESERVOIR was made in 1891 to provide a water supply for Plymouth, and later enlarged to 150 acres. As it appears now, it is a natural spectacle as good as any on Dartmoor. The English are usually much too timid about creating landscape on a large scale.*

SHEEPWASH

4000

ST LAWRENCE. 1879–80 by *J.F.Gould*, tower 1889 by *Webb* of Barnstaple. – FONT. Square, of block-capital shape, one of the semicircular surfaces with foliage, the other plain.

The church lies behind the village square, with thatched COTTAGES mostly built to the same design.

TOTLEIGH BARTON. An early site of some importance, once with a chapel. The present house, thatched, of rendered rubble, is mostly C16 and C17, with a few medieval features. It is on the usual three-room plan, but the cross-passage has solid walls and is exceptionally spacious. So is the high-ceilinged hall, with a large fireplace with fragments of earlier masonry including a re-used corbel and an altered timber two-light window with four-centred head; another single-light window on the first floor. The much renewed roof (one A-frame truss with carved feet, another over the porch) is of interest for its local technique of thatching directly on to broad horizontal battens without purlins or rafters. Opposite the house, a BARN of unrendered yellow cob on a high rubble plinth.

BRIDGE. Five pointed arches and cutwaters.

SHELDON

1000

ST JAMES. Medieval w tower, unbuttressed, battlemented; three-light Perp w window. Nave, chancel, and s porch rebuilt on old foundations in 1871 by *Hayward*, in a plain E.E. – Some old fragments of a SCREEN incorporated in the furnishings.

*A lake like this is well worth the sacrifice of an odd village or church (Pevsner 1952).

SHERFORD

7040

ST MARTIN. Perp W tower with diagonal buttresses, stair-turret in the middle of the S wall, no pinnacles. S side embattled, with S porch and rood-stair turret. N side with NW turret, N door through one of the buttresses (cf. Kingsbridge, Ugborough). Two N aisle windows have the motif of the five-branched star, as found e.g. at Staverton, Torbryan, Ipplepen, and Littlehempston. Four-bay arcades with octagonal piers with double-chamfered arches, the third bay higher, as if for transepts. In the chancel a pointed-trefoiled PISCINA. – SCREEN. The top very badly reconstructed; well carved cornice, Dartmouth type tracery, wainscot paintings. – The PULPIT incorporates Perp panelling. – MONUMENT. Elizabeth Reynell †1662. Small tablet in classical surround.

KEYNEDON, 1 m. S. Farmhouse, the former medieval manor house of the Halls family, once on a quadrangular plan, now mostly C16 and later. Large porch with very thick walls, arches on three sides. Granite entrance archway with four-centred head. Tudor windows in the r. wing. Responds remain from a gatehouse.

RANSCOMBE. A large, symmetrical C17 house of high quality, rather untypical of the South Hams. It is nevertheless on the typical three-room cross-passage plan with cross-wings at either end and a two-storey porch. Good C17 fittings, including the front door, five interior door frames, and fireplace lintels. Granary in the grounds, with pigeon holes, perhaps originally a dovecote.

SHILLINGFORD

9080

Not far from the fringes of Exeter, but still rural. The small church stands alone in a field.

ST GEORGE. W tower low and unbuttressed, of red sandstone ashlar with corner turret. Around the W window the arms of Sir William Huddesfield †1499, Attorney-General under Edward IV, and of his wife, Katharine Courtenay. Their MONUMENT is in the church: a N chancel wall recess of Easter Sepulchre type, remade in the C19, but preserving an unusual small rectangular brass plate against the back wall, showing them kneeling with their children under depressed ogee arches. As for the church, nave, transepts, and S porch were all largely rebuilt in 1856 by *David Mackintosh*, the old masonry re-used, but clinically recut. Continuous wagon roof with some old bosses; shallow transepts under low arches. – FONT. Perp, with Huddesfield arms. – BENCH ENDS. Some of the C16, restored. – STAINED GLASS. C16 shields (sanctuary S).

RECTORY. 1812–13, broad-eaved and rendered, re-using some material from the Huddesfield manor house on the site. Reduced in size in 1964–5.

SHIRWELL

5030

The church lies in the old village, among scattered houses on the edge of the hill, away from the main road.

ST PETER. The core is a C13 cruciform church with short unbuttressed S transept tower with one lancet window. Perp the belfry
windows and pinnacles, and the W porch of timber (much restored)
on a stone base, unusual for Devon. From the C13 church the plain
chamfered W doorway with original door and ironwork, and, inside,
the low arch between tower and nave, possibly the similar one
between the tower and the S aisle (implying an earlier aisle than the
present Perp one), and the low unmoulded chancel arch of rubble
(probably reworked in the C19). The chancel itself is C14, see the
Dec single-light window visible from the vestry, and the trefoil-
headed PISCINA with carved face between the drainage holes.
From the Perp period the N vestry, with restored E window and
original door to the chancel, and the low three-bay S arcade with B
type piers and standard capitals. The oddest feature of the church is
the rough timber pier of square section by the N transept, as if for a
hagioscope from the nave. The nave wall projects beyond it. N
transept with open wagon roofs; good moulded ribs and bosses. The
entrance to this transept and the nave roof were redone in *White*'s
restoration of 1873–89. White also renewed all the window tracery
and provided the chancel furnishings: good COMMUNION RAILS,
IRONWORK, and TILES. – REREDOS and SCREEN by *Herbert
Read*, 1912.

   FONT. Norman, square, of the table-top type, with four flat
blank arches to each side. – STAINED GLASS. E window by *Kempe
Studios*, 1898, with delicate flowered quarries. – MONUMENTS.
Effigy of a lady on a tomb-chest with quatrefoil decoration, said to
be Blanche St Leger † 1483, in a recess in the chancel N wall, much
too low for the figure. – Above, Lady Anne Chichester † 1723, with
two standing figures holding an oval inscription plate under a
baldacchino; quality poor. – Frances Lugg † 1712, with bust at the
top, also poor. – Mary Stucley † 1705. Cartouche with elaborate
floral decoration. – Good early C19 slate tombstones in the
churchyard.

ALMSHOUSES. Early C19, with recessed porches and Gothick windows.

See also Youlston Park.

8000   SHOBROOKE

ST SWITHIN. W tower old (Perp panelled tower arch), N arcade old (B
type piers, standard capitals), N and E walls old. S door reset, but
C12, with scalloped capitals to the shafts, a plain outer order, and a
hoodmould with head at the apex. The rest the result of restorations
of 1840, and of 1879 by *Ashworth*, when the S aisle was added to
match the N aisle. Exterior of random purple ashlar. – Two C17
PEWS. – Heavy stone REREDOS. – Low iron SCREEN. – STAINED
GLASS. One outstanding S aisle window, to Sir Frederick Shelley
† 1869: St Cecilia and angel musicians, 1881 by *W. F. Dixon*, showing Pre-Raphaelite influence, especially that of Frederick Shields in
the elegantly draped figures. – Other good but more conventional
windows, especially the chancel E, Last Supper by *Clayton & Bell*,
c. 1876. – In the N aisle Faith, Hope, and Charity, and two windows
with scenes from the life of Christ, all by *Lavers & Westlake* († 1893,

1898, 1900); two others by *Heaton, Butler & Bayne* (†1898, 1908).
The church stands on its own by a farm with long cob-walled
outbuildings. Up the nearby lane a HOLY WELL with low round-
headed arch.

SHOBROOKE HOUSE. Burnt out and demolished in 1947. An indifferent modern house stands on the site of the mansion remodelled
c. 1850 in an ambitious Italianate for J. H. Hippesley Tuckfield by
Professor *James Donaldson*. But the large mid C19 terraced gardens
remain, with classical canopied garden seat; also the grand gatepiers
and the SOUTH LODGE, of ashlar, two-storeyed, with bracketed
eaves. The EAST LODGE, a thatched *cottage orné*, must be earlier.

GREAT GUTTON. A C17 farmhouse exterior at its most impressive. A
large, tall house developed from a C15–16 three-room-and-cross-
passage plan. Porch, gable-end wing, three rear wings, a forest of
brick chimneystacks. The front elevation unusually showy for a
Devon farmhouse, even at this period, with its three- and four-light
ovolo-moulded oak mullion-and-transom-windows. Similar windows at the rear. Rooms on either side of the cross-passage with
C16–17 panelling. Attractive C19 railings and mounting block.
Nearby, BARN with three-bay jointed-cruck-truss roof, probably a
C17 remodelling of a larger, older building.

UPPINCOTT. A typical but unusually instructive farming hamlet.
BARTON is a remarkably well preserved early C17 farmhouse, E-
plan, with two-storey porch, two rear lateral stacks, and oak-
mullioned windows (four lights to the ground floor, three above).
Original panelled and studded front door, stud-and-panel screen
between hall and cross-passage, kitchen with bread-oven and walk-
in smoking-chamber. FARM is a house of c. 1600 extended and
partly rebuilt in the C19. Its outbuildings exemplify the later
planned farmstead, with ranges of linhays, barn, granary, byres,
and haylofts grouped around a courtyard.

SHUTE   2090

There are three buildings at Shute, in addition to the church. The
Elizabethan gatehouse, extended into a mock fortification in the C19,
provides a show entrance to the N. Beyond lies a substantial fragment
of the medieval house of the Bonvilles, who held the manor from 1295.
Through the C15 Bonville heiress Cicely it passed in 1476 to the Greys.
It was forfeited to the Crown after the death of Lady Jane Grey
(Cicely's great-granddaughter), and by the later C16 belonged to the
Poles (the first Pole here was William †1587). In 1787 Sir John
William de la Pole built a new house to the S on the slopes looking out
towards Colyton, and pulled down part of the old mansion, which
remained a humble farmhouse until given to the National Trust in
1959.

GATEHOUSE. For all its romantic fortified appearance, this is not a 63
medieval building. The battlemented centre with polygonal corner
turrets, built of local chert, is late C16. It bears the Pole arms and the
initials WP. Above the archway, two storeys of mullioned-and-
transomed windows. Restoration work revealed that the top one was
originally broader, forming a continuous band of lights with the

windows in the turrets, a typically late Tudor motif. The prominent, well carved gargoyles must be medieval work re-used; the wooden archway is made up of old arch-braced collar-beams. Perhaps these features were brought from the old house after 1787. The low battlemented walls and the symmetrical one-room pavilions at their ends may be C16 in origin but have been improved later. In the l. gatehouse turret a stair to the upper room, which has a plain four-centred fireplace and an excellent plaster ceiling installed in 1981, as part of the conversion by *Pearn & Procter* for the Landmark Trust. The ceiling was originally in a house in Cross Street, Barnstaple. It fits remarkably well. Enriched ribs, and decoration including fishes, thistles, and roses, implying a date soon after 1601.

SHUTE BARTON. The surviving parts consist of a U shape of three rubble stone ranges: a low entrance block with archway facing SW, a tall battlemented wing parallel to this, and another tall linking range running NE–SW. The house originally extended considerably further, beyond what is now the external NE wall propped by buttresses. The surviving parts, their evocative character preserved by a sensitive S.P.A.B. restoration in 1955–9, are difficult to interpret. The easiest explanation is that we have the storeyed wings from one end of a medieval house of which the hall has disappeared, all very much altered after the house became a farmhouse (date plaques of 1840 and 1855). Tantalizingly, there is no proof that any of the existing building is the house referred to in Sir William Bonville's will of 1308, which mentions a house with hall, chamber, pantry, kitchen and pastry.

The NE–SW wing has the most rewarding features. Irregular straight-headed windows on three levels, mostly of two lights. The top windows on the courtyard side and the slightly larger ground-floor windows on the SE side are cusped, i.e. medieval; the others are insertions or replacements. Indeed, the whole middle floor appears to be an insertion, with consequent alteration of ceiling levels inside. The ground-floor ceiling, of re-used beams, cuts across the cusped windows. In this room the whole end wall is filled by an enormous fireplace, carefully constructed of dressed stone, an insertion perhaps of the C16. Its triangular arched head is 18 ft wide. At the other end remains of a stud-and-panel screen. The top floor is reached by a tiny newel stair projecting into the courtyard. Did the upper room to which it leads once have other means of access? It is a grand and spacious chamber with an impressive C15 arch-braced roof (with later tie-beams), but curiously near the floor, if this is at its original level. Two sets of purlins and two tiers of curved wind-braces. The later chimneystack from the ground floor projects into the end bay; a garderobe has been fitted in next to it.

The NW–SE range has a variety of late medieval and Tudor mullioned-and-transomed windows, suggesting that there was a large medieval first-floor chamber in this wing. In the NW end wall is a tall cusped two-light transomed window next to a polygonal battlemented stair-turret with gargoyles. At the opposite end is a square tower with late medieval quatrefoiled battlements. In this tower later C17 windows with stone surrounds and Georgian sashes. The only notable interior remaining is a late C17 panelled first-floor room extending with a closet into the square tower. Fireplace with voluted surround and eared overmantel. The rest largely reconstructed in the C20. The modest low wing with the archway looks C16, but is unlikely to have been the main entrance. Upper room with arch-braced roof, a fireplace, and two-light cusped windows. Archway below with depressed arch and original door.

SHUTE HOUSE. One would like to know the architect of this handsome late Palladian composition of 1787. Three-storey centre, the S front with two full-height bows; low arched quadrant links to pavilions. In the quadrants, niches; on one side two *Coade* urns with spiral tops. Now divided into flats. (Fine ceilings, mostly with delicate neo-classical ornament in the Adam tradition, but one with a roundel with a charming rustic contemporary agricultural scene, very unmetropolitan.)

ST MICHAEL. Close to Shute Barton. Crossing tower, unbuttressed, on C14 piers and arches (cf. Axminster). Masonry of transept and S wall perhaps contemporary. N aisle added 1811. All much restored by *Ashworth* in 1869, with new roofs, new NE vestry, and renewed tracery. The NE chapel has a broader band of foliage in the capitals of its piers. – In the chapel the very grand MONUMENT to Sir William Pole, Master of the Household of Queen Anne, †1741, made in 1746, probably by *Richard Hayward* in the studio of *Sir Henry Cheere*. No religious content; it might stand in a public square or garden. He wears fashionable clothes, holds the thin long staff of his office, and stands on a pedestal against a Gothic arch. – Hon. Mrs Cocks †1805 by *R. Westmacott Sen.* – Sophia Lady Pole †1801 by *Peter Rouw*; an angel points the aspirant Lady Pole heavenwards. – Other minor early C19 monuments also by *Rouw*. – Margaret Lady Pole †1890 by *Hems*, conceived as a pendant to the Rouw sculpture, this one accompanied by equally aspirant infants. Central panel with classical frame in veined brown marble. – FONT. With quatrefoil panels, much repaired. – SCREEN. Wrought-iron grille between NE chapel and chancel; striking work by the local blacksmith *James White*. – STAINED GLASS. E window by *Powell*, c. 1869. – In the NE chapel window, C17 and C18 armorial glass, in a brightly coloured setting of 1808; other panels in S aisle windows.

SIDBURY   *1090*

ST GILES. An unusual and rewarding church with medieval work of all periods. The first impression is of an attractively textured and richly decorated Perp building: two-storey porch, S aisle, and two stair-turrets all embattled; W tower with Perp W window and W door with fleurons. But the tower itself is Norman, with shallow buttresses without offsets, i.e. like pilaster strips, and a pilaster strip up the middle of the sides. Two twin bell-openings high up. There was originally a pyramidal stone spire, whose weight was causing structural problems by the late C18. It was removed during the restoration of 1843 by *John Hayward*, who rebuilt the upper part of the tower. His wooden spire (all that a tight-fisted vestry would allow) was removed in the restoration of 1884 by *J. T. Micklethwaite & G. S. Clarke Jun.*, who erected the present needle spire and the Perp battlements with shields, pinnacles, and tracery frieze. The two full-length STATUES now in niches in the W wall were discovered in 1843. They appear to be C12: a saint and a bishop (heads restored?). Inside the tower on the ground floor, most unusually, there is a rib-vaulted room, the ribs broad, unmoulded, and without keystone, resting on four early C12 carved corbels: two lion masks, one rampant lion, and one atlas figure.

The chancel also is Norman, see the plinth and the ashlar work of the E wall with a chequer pattern cut into it *in situ*. Transepts of rubble with ashlar quoins and buttresses of the same date as (or earlier than?) the C13 windows. These have an early type of bar tracery with three grouped lancets. The aisled nave also has a plinth, but is clearly later than the tower, and indeed, when one goes inside, one finds a chancel arch and two arcades of the Transitional period: the S one of *c.* 1200, with circular piers, pointed chamfered arches, and moulded capitals, the N one similar, but perhaps a little later. These rest, as was found in the C19, on the foundations of an aisleless nave. The clustered N pier is an embellishment of 1884.

Earlier still is the puzzling CRYPT beneath the chancel, discovered in 1898. It was filled when the Norman chancel was built, and its upper part destroyed. It is about 10ft square, completely plain; a little worked ashlar at the edge of the steps. It perhaps originated as a free-standing mausoleum before being incorporated in an early church, but its early history is entirely unknown. The only other Saxon survival is a small fragment of a cross with interlace decoration, perhaps C10 (cf. Colyton), now built into the exterior of the S transept W wall. Could a tradition of an early cult centre explain the ambitious nature of the work of later periods? The Perp work inside includes the vaulted porch with big boss, arches from aisles to transepts, their soffits richly carved with a foliage trail, and the wagon roofs with moulded ribs over nave, aisles, and transepts. The Dec E window and the roof of the chancel date from *Micklethwaite & Somers Clarke*'s restoration of 1898–9. Squints to the chancel from both transepts.

WEST GALLERY. 1620, extended forward for the organ in 1754. – FONT. Perp, octagonal, with quatrefoil panels on the bowl and tracery panels on the pillar. – Chancel FITTINGS. A most attractive set by *Walter Cave*, whose family lived at Sidbury Manor: CHOIR STALLS 1899 with boldly profiled ends and small inset gesso panels; ALTAR 1899, in the form of a Jacobean table, with green silk ALTAR FRONTAL of 1905, also designed by *Cave*; REREDOS 1904, Crucifixion and gesso panels. – ALMSDESK and BOX also by *Cave*, 1899. – WALL PAINTINGS. Many fragmentary remains, especially interesting those around the C13 windows in the chancel N wall: remains of painted columns with stiff-leaf capitals. Another similar window surround, more worn, in the N transept. – St Christopher(?) on the tower arch. – Chancel arch gable with C16 vine-scroll. – STAINED GLASS. Windows of 1899, 1902, and 1906 by *Kempe Studios*: small figures, sombre colours, and a great deal of white glass. – E window 1913, the Transfiguration, designed by *Cave*. – MONUMENT. John Stone †1617, a quarryman, possibly Nicholas Stone's father, with a punning inscription.

CONGREGATIONAL CHAPEL. 1820. Broad rendered front; arched

openings with moulded labels and intersecting tracery. Set in a walled burial ground. Gate with overthrow.

Sidbury is an attractive village, once more important. A market and fair were granted here in 1290. Nice rows of cob houses in CHURCH STREET and BRIDGE STREET. VILLAGE HALL by *Walter Cave*, 1924, very simple; just a few Arts and Crafts touches such as the tiles under the eaves. Square POUND, now a bus shelter, with tall random stone walls. Set back from the street, COURT HOUSE, much rebuilt in 1856, but the garden front C16–17, with plain mullioned three- and four-light windows, symmetrically arranged, and a central door; and at right angles to this, facing the street, an C18 extension with segmental pediment over the central window.

SIDBURY MANOR. Mansion in free Jacobean Renaissance style; 1879 by *David Brandon* for Sir Stephen Cave M.P., a member of Disraeli's cabinet. He died before the house was completed. The former house, acquired by Cave's father, a Bristol merchant, stood to the S across the valley, near the present farm buildings. For the new house a site was cut into the hill, so that the S front overlooks terraced gardens. Entrance from the E, through a gravelled forecourt enclosed by good low iron railings and gates in C18 style. To the r., STABLES with shaped gable and cupola over the central archway, dated 1879. Both house and stables of red brick with Ham Hill dressings, in places very yellow. Asymmetrical entrance front, with gables of different shapes and a turret-like bay-window with conical roof as the main accents. Transomed windows with arched uncusped lights. The garden front is more regular, except at the l. corner, where there is an open loggia, a nicely detailed corbelled-out oriel, then the conservatory, and behind this a large wing with château roof (containing the master bedroom suite), the whole making an effectively varied composition when seen from the SW. A N service wing was demolished *c.* 1960.

Straightforward plan: axial corridors to E and S ranges; staircase in the angle, a huge hall with stairs rising on two sides; on the corridor sides bold round-headed arcades on both floors with naturalistic versions of Corinthian capitals. Good stained glass in the large landing window: the Cave arms surrounded by pale quarries alternating with roundels displaying a comprehensive interest in the natural world. Tall reception rooms with Jacobean-style single-rib ceilings. Dining hall with elaborately panelled walls and carved overmantel with hunting relief and quotation from Shakespeare; library in the SE corner, with built-in shelves and two deep bay-windows for desks; morning room on the E front with pale green *Morris* wallpaper.

Further up the hill a walled GARDEN. Three LODGES, the main one near the village with half-timbering, dated 1884. Stone gate-piers with balls.

On the Sidbury estate *Walter Cave* designed for his family an interesting variety of turn-of-the-century buildings. The first and most eccentric is MOUSEPLATT, of 1890, up a lane N of the village. A small house breathlessly crammed with Arts and Crafts detail. Brick striped with stone, half-hipped gables, two big battered chimneys. Porch with three brick and stone arches, and its own tiled roof with tiny eyebrow windows. To the r. the staircase windows are curiously expressed as rectangles rising beneath a curved strainer arch. Interior altered; additions of 1965 at the back. CASTLE HILL HOUSE, S of the Manor, for the estate manager is a more staid and mature work of 1910, L-shaped, with large eaves and casement windows. Of brick, dignified by rusticated brick quoins and door surrounds. At the N end of HARCOMBE, a pretty hamlet with some old houses on the E side of the valley, BEACONSGATE, 1894, this time in a Voyseyish white roughcast with battered buttress and deep eaves, but without Voysey's smoothness of handling. *Cave* also remodelled PACCOMBE FARMHOUSE.

SIDBURY CASTLE. Fine early Iron Age hillfort sited on a promontory. Other earthworks, apparently related, radiate from the site.

SIDFORD

1090

A main-road hamlet of Sidbury, now on the fringe of suburban Sidmouth.

ST PETER. 1867–73 by *C.F.Edwards*. Decidedly urban and hard-edged, of red brick with black mortar and Bath stone detail. Tall aisled clerestoried nave with bellcote, chancel, S porch. – REREDOS. 1873, executed by *Hems*, peculiar, with disembodied heads of evangelists poking out of quatrefoils. – STAINED GLASS. E window 1873, N and S aisle E windows 1901, all by *Clayton & Bell*.

72 In SCHOOL STREET an impressively long row of altered but basically early C17 houses, distinguished by prestigious detailing of their several prominent lateral stacks in variations of local ashlar stone and flint. One is in a chequered pattern, a speciality of East Devon.

BRIDGE. Said to date from the C12. Widened, but with the original parapets left in position.

See also Sand.

SIDMOUTH

1080

Until the early C19 Sidmouth was a small fishing town at the mouth of the river Sid. Its popularity as a holiday place began to develop at the end of the C18. 'The town is of late tolerably frequented in the bathing season,' wrote the *Copper Plate Magazine* in 1796, and already in 1792 it was sufficiently well known for a London speculator to plan the ambitious formal layout of Fortfield Terrace. But this grand crescent overlooking the sea was never completed, later terraces are few and short, and the speciality of Sidmouth became – and remains – the *cottage orné*. Butcher and Haseler's *Sidmouth Scenery* of 1816–17 has individual illustrations of no less than nineteen houses and cottages of gentlemen and aristocrats, and Rowe's collection of lithographs of 1826 was able to add a further dozen newly built examples, picturesquely scattered around the fringes of the old settlement. Enough remains of these to illustrate effectively the change from the earliest cottages (or cottage conversions), with their haphazardly quaint agglomerations of thatched roofs, ornamental gables, eccentrically detailed Gothick windows, and delicate Regency ironwork (Cliff

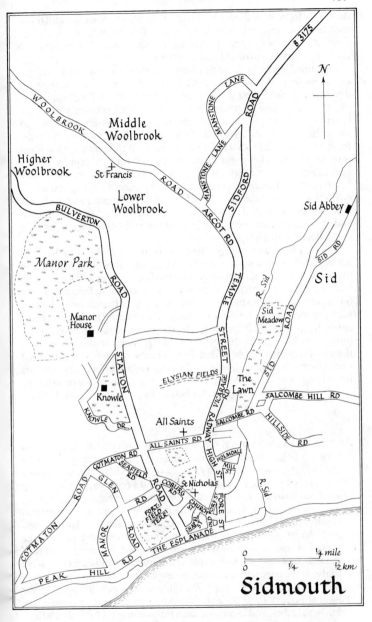

Sidmouth

Cottage, Royal Glen), to the more solid and capacious pattern-book 140 villas of the 1820s onwards. Two types were specially popular: the broad-eaved house prettified by Gothic windows, and the gabled house with Tudor detail, the 'house Gothic' style which was advocated by Lugar. An excellent group of the 1820s, including both types, remains in the idyllically secluded and aptly named Elysian Fields, on the slopes to the N of the town. To the NW there were earlier and more ambitious houses, but these have nearly all been radically altered or demolished; today's impression is, a little misleadingly, of an early C19 garden suburb of small villas and cottages.

Contained between the cliffs rising on either side, Sidmouth did not grow rapidly in the C19. The main landowners were less interested in development than their counterparts at Exmouth or Torquay, and so the town retained its modest main streets (embellished with some handsome C19 shops), and its ample pleasure grounds N of these and along the river Sid. Efforts to build an improved harbour in 1811 came to nothing, and the railway did not arrive until 1874, at a station some way to the N. The population, which had grown rapidly at the beginning of the century (1801: 1,252; 1831: 3,126), was still only 3,360 in 1871. Extensive (and mostly undistinguished) expansion did not take place until the C20; the urban district now embraces the main-road village of Sidford (q.v.) and the smaller hamlets of Woolbrook and Bulverton, and even incorporates the still largely rural Sidbury and Salcombe Regis (qq.v.).

The C19 villas and cottages have for the most part been well looked after, and the seafront and the town centre have remained remarkably unspoilt, free from the garish commercialism of most seaside resorts, due in part to the vigilance of the Sid Vale Association, founded (as the Sidmouth Improvement Committee) as early as 1846, one of the first amenity societies in the country. Early C20 building in the centre was generally in a tactful Regency spirit, the better suburban houses in an innocuous Arts and Crafts tradition. In the later C20 this haven from the modern world is now in danger from its own popularity: the chief visual threat is from inappropriately large groups of housing and flats for retired people, spreading over former gardens and wrecking the small-scale delight of the original houses (see e.g. All Saints Road).

CHURCHES

St Nicholas with St Giles. Perp W tower with buttresses of type C, belfry windows with Somerset tracery, polygonal stair-turret to the S side. The rest of 1859–60 by *William White*, re-using the original ground plan, but adding N and S porches, transepts, and an aisled chancel. The nave clerestory, which creates rather a lanky internal space, was an afterthought. Well managed external rhythm, quickening towards the densely massed E end; character-istic White detailing in the double-hipped transept gables, the squeezed tracery in some of the windows, and the heavy cusping of the aisle roof timbers. Other internal features – including the marble shafts to the nave with excellent foliage capitals, and the diapering of the nave E end (now swamped by whitewash) – were designed by the local antiquary *Peter Orlando Hutchinson* (who rescued some of the medieval fabric and incorporated it into a house for himself nearby – *see* Perambulation 3). The interior generally has suffered woefully from unsympathetic alterations and additions.

PULPIT. Stone, polygonal, with polychromatic tracery patterns. 1866, designed en suite with the similarly detailed CHANCEL SCREEN. – REREDOS. Coloured stone and marble, now covered with grey paint; evangelist symbols under arcading with inventive geometric cresting. Designed by *S.S. Teulon* (are screen and pulpit also by him?). – STAINED GLASS. C15 shield showing the five wounds (N chancel chapel). – An interesting collection of the 1860s. First the E window, 1860 by *Wailes*. – W window 1867 by *Hughes*: Suffer Little Children and the Corporal Works of Mercy, opulently coloured, with well designed figure groups, the gift of Queen Victoria in memory of her father, the Duke of Kent, who died at Sidmouth in 1820. – S transept to Bacon † 1859 by *A. Gibbs*. – S aisle to Gutteres † 1864 and to Pennant † 1869, all by *Ward & Hughes*, important examples of their range and variety before their later often over-sweet pictorialism. – S aisle W to Ord, by *Wailes*. – MONUMENTS. In the S chapel a draped urn to Mary Lisle of Northumberland † 1791, with a telling epitaph:

> Blest with soft airs from health-restoring skies
> Sidmouth to thee the drooping patient flies;
> Ah! not unfailing is thy port to save
> To HER thou gavest no refuge but a grave ...

– A large number of mural tablets, mostly minor C19.

ALL SAINTS. 1837 by *J. H. Taylor*, to serve the growing suburbs. Pre-ecclesiological Gothic, cruciform, with lancets and oddly clumsy pinnacles. Galleries to transepts and W end on iron columns. Elaborate roof. REREDOS and embellishment of E end *c.* 1870; other fittings of 1899; nave reseated 1901.

ST FRANCIS, Woolbrook. 1929 by *W. D. Caröe*. Simple Perp in Salcombe Regis stone, nave and chancel under one roof; later W end.

CONGREGATIONAL CHAPEL, Chapel Street. Dated 1820. Stucco with Gothic windows.

UNITARIAN CHAPEL, High Street. The oldest Nonconformist chapel in Sidmouth, established in 1710 by the Presbyterians, but much rebuilt in 1884, when the entrance was changed from the back lane to the main road, and new windows and porch were added. Stuccoed, with bargeboards. E gable with octagonal window. Good C18 fittings: gallery, hexagonal PULPIT with sounding-board, CLOCK dated 1767.

CONVENT OF THE ASSUMPTION (R.C.), NW of the town. Convent buildings by *G. Goldie*, 1884, church 1895, with several windows by *Scoles*. A picturesque group, the church with octagonal turret and Dec windows, the convent with tall chimneystacks.

PUBLIC BUILDINGS

HOSPITAL, E off the High Street. Low, rambling, tile-hung buildings by *Walter Cave*, the earliest parts of 1892, much enlarged since. MAY COTTAGE to the N, C17, much altered in 1830, was used as an earlier cottage hospital in 1885.

STATION (former). 1874. Substantial red brick station house with yellow brick dressings. Entrance with valanced canopy; station canopies on cast-iron brackets.

NORMAN LOCKYER OBSERVATORY, Salcombe Hill. One-storey administrative block of concrete, with two domes, *c.* 1912; a third dome of *c.* 1932.

PERAMBULATIONS

1. The Seafront

The sea wall and promenade along THE ESPLANADE were built only
in 1835–8 (by *G.H.Julian*), but Butcher's guide of 1810 refers
already to the grand public mall along the beach, 'railed and rolled
in very good style', a shelter containing a billiard room, which was
the main social centre, and fifteen lodging houses upon the beach.
Some of the houses remain, most of them by the 1830s converted to
hotels, and in the case of the ROYAL YORK and the FAULKNER
embellished later by Edwardian bays and tented balconies. To their
E Nos. 8–10, of 1909, in a plain Regency style, and Nos. 11–12, of
*c.*1911, CARLTON MANSIONS, the first purpose-built flats in the
town, quite an interesting attempt to be in keeping, a rather
crowded Regency composition in red brick, with two full-height
bows and a central tented first-floor bay. Further E WYNDHAM
HOUSE HOTEL has an original balcony and arched ground-floor
windows.

Now to the W. The gem is BEACH HOUSE, three storeys, with giant
Ionic corner pilasters, but charming Gothick windows with
marginal glazing (a Sidmouth speciality). On the r. a shallow bow
with tented balcony; porch with clustered columns. Now flats (but
good interior features preserved). Then the DEVORAN HOTEL,
1891, quite boldly gabled, with sgraffito decoration, its red brick
chastely whitened since, and the older BEDFORD HOTEL, plain
and rendered, which continues round the corner with another block
which breaks out with an upper bay and tented balconies, now
facing an uninspiring car park. From here one has a fine view of
FORTFIELD TERRACE, set back some distance from the sea. This
grand stuccoed composition was begun in 1792 as a speculation by
the lord of the manor, the antiquary Thomas Jenkins. The architect
was a Polish émigré, *Michael Novosielski*, best known as a London
developer and theatre designer. He died in 1795, and the l. side of
the shallow crescent was never completed. Three storeys, with the
restrained detail typical of 1790s classicism: arched doorways,
continuous tented balconies. The two end houses are set forward;
the centre pair is separated from the terraces by short colonnades
and distinguished by a pediment.

Continuing W along the seafront, the next landmark is the castellated
gateway of the BELMONT HOTEL, shown in 1817 by Haseler as the
entrance to Belmont House, built by Sir Joseph Scott. From here
PEAK HILL ROAD climbs up past several typical Sidmouth cottages perched romantically on the cliffs. The best are THE BEA-
CON, quite large, three storeys, thatched, with curvaceous
bargeboards, and CLIFTON COTTAGE, very pretty, with its
irregular composition of thatched roofs, clustered chimneys, and
original glazing. Inland from here, in a more retiring position,
ROYAL GLEN HOTEL, formerly Woolbrook Glen, where the
Duke and Duchess of Kent stayed with the infant Princess Victoria
in 1819–20. Stuccoed and castellated front, with especially
elaborately glazed Gothic windows; to the W, at first-floor level, a
delicate trellised and tented veranda around a shallow bow opens on
to an upper lawn. On the E side a pretty cast-iron porch, an early

addition, concealing a doorway of rustic flintwork with bark posts.
Tactful extensions in the same castellated style. The surrounding
area built up in the early C20; good small houses in the Arts and
Crafts tradition to the N in GLEN ROAD and MANOR ROAD.

2. *The Old Town*

Starting from The Esplanade, FORE STREET leads N, narrow and
winding, early C19 stucco with a few older and lower pre-resort
buildings. Near the start, on the E side, KNIGHTS, three-storeyed
with bowed windows; and opposite, the ROYAL LONDON
HOTEL, with a rusticated stuccoed front, the most important inn
in early C19 Sidmouth, with assembly rooms (much altered)
already in 1810. It occupies part of the triangle between Fore
Street, Old Fore Street, and the High Street, once no doubt an
open market place. The broader HIGH STREET starts with
several grander houses: on the W side, one of 2–3–2 bays, projecting centre, doorway with broken pediment; then POTBURY'S,
with an excellent sequence of Victorian shop windows within two
large houses, the first stuccoed, the second C18 red brick. Opposite, WARWICK HOUSE, a long, low C17 front, much altered,
with stone panels of club, heart, and diamond between ground-
and first-floor windows, the centre one cut by a later doorcase.
Then ALBION HOUSE, with a rainwater head dated 1820 and a
late Georgian pedimented doorcase. Several more late Georgian
houses across the road, after the C20 classical LLOYDS BANK in
Portland stone. In contrast, a low thatched survival, gable end to
the road, at the corner of HOLMDALE (much restored).

From here, a detour E to the area around the river, past POTBURY'S
AUCTION ROOMS in a former National School, and FEOFFEES
ALMSHOUSES, 1802, tall and gaunt. Further on, by the ford, a
pretty spot, OLD MILL HOUSE and BRIDGE HOUSE, of four
and three bays, the end windows bowed. To the S was an early C19
artisan area of little streets built on the formerly swampy flat land
around the river, now mostly erased for car-parking. By the car
park at the bottom of MILL STREET, the SWAN INN with tented
porches. Back up Mill Street to the High Street, past a few
thatched houses and a former chapel with tall arched windows.

OLD FORE STREET, narrow, has another typical mixture: the OLD
SHIP on the W side, with broad C17 pedimented doorcase and
early C17 panelling inside; SEFTON ANTIQUES and its neighbour, with two bowed shopfronts, one late Georgian, one Victorian; and the WOOLWICH BUILDING SOCIETY, with Gothic
glazing to the fanlight and upper arched windows. The MARKET
HOUSE, red brick with quoins, occupies the triangular space at
the end. Stone centrepiece with two large arched windows. Off
Church Street to the W, CHAPEL STREET, with the oldest relic in
the town: TUDOR COTTAGE, formerly a late medieval hall house,
with a lateral stack and the remains of a stud-and-panel screen
painted with the royal arms and with a remarkably bold design of
flowers and early Renaissance fantastic beasts.

3. The Regency and Victorian suburbs (roughly W–E)

CHURCH STREET leads N from the old town centre, a quiet scene, with late Georgian terrace houses with small shops below. By the church, HOPE COTTAGE, now the museum, c. 1830, with trellis porch, and immediately to the N AMYATT'S TERRACE of the same date, a well-proportioned stucco group looking out over a generous bowling green. At the end, the OLD CHANCEL, built by the local antiquary *Peter Orlando Hutchinson*, from materials which he rescued during the drastic restoration of the church in 1860. Perp E window. In 1864 he added a taller part to the W to serve as a house for himself. Picturesque gabled roofs, Gothic entrance with corbelled-out oriel, mullioned windows. Entrance hall with fan-vault, staircase with wrought-iron balustrade to Hutchinson's own design, study with painted heraldic ceiling. N of the bowling green COBURG TERRACE, c. 1830, a group rather than a terrace, with castellated parapets rising to a central pediment (cf. the C18 Gothic Tawstock Court, North Devon), but with characteristic early C19 Tudor windows with dripstones and marginal glazing.

In COBURG ROAD, CHURCH HOUSE and AURORA, formerly one house, of c. 1820, in the alternative style to the Gothic *cottage orné* – a distinguished red brick front with two shallow full-height bows and central door with entablature bowed out as a porch. Tented balconies at the side. Along Coburg Road a miscellany of small genteel dwellings: ALMA TERRACE, red brick, MAGNOLIA COTTAGE, specially attractive, and PEBBLESTONE COTTAGE, faced with local stones, at a fork of the roads. The neat flint garden walls are a typical Sidmouth feature. Further on, at the junction with Station Road, the more flamboyant WOODLAND HOTEL. In its present form it is largely of c. 1850, when a new owner (Mr Johnston) replaced a thatched roof by the octagonal slates, and added the gables extravagantly decorated with seaweed. Formerly Old Hayes, the house was converted from a thatched cob building to a gentleman's residence by the Rev. J. Copleston, father of the Bishop of Llandaff (*see* Offwell), and was enlarged with a new W front by Lord Gwydir c. 1810. The grounds, once famous for a rustic 'cloister' of pollarded oaks, have been reduced in size, but still have some exotic planting and a stream.

w along COTMATON ROAD are several charming thatched cottages: COTMATON COTTAGE, with eyebrow dormers and trellised ver-anda, the WHITE COTTAGE, originally one-storeyed, with Gothic casements and trellised porch, and the most endearing PAUNT-LEY COTTAGE, well maintained, octagonal, with domical roof and rustic veranda all around. In 1816 it was the lodge to a house called Marino belonging to the Rev. J. Hobson. A detour s can take in some later villas in SEAFIELD ROAD: LITTLECOURT, with bows and trellis balcony, SEAFIELD and SEACOURT (a pair) and EGLANTYNE, all with decorative bargeboards typical of c. 1830–40.

There were grander houses in large grounds on the slopes further N, but little remains in its early C19 state. POWYS, E of Station Road, now enlarged out of all recognition as retirement homes, is shown in 1819 as a double thatched villa, the two parts linked by a conservatory. NW off Station Road, KNOWLE (East Devon

Council Offices), now nondescript later C19 and C20, was once one of the most famous houses in Sidmouth. The long thatched 'cottage' with forty rooms, built in 1810, under Lord Le Despenser's close personal supervision (Hutchinson tells us that he inspected the work every evening and that what he disliked had to be undone), was owned by the collector and connoisseur T.L. Fish from 1836 to 1861. He made picturesque improvements, and opened his 'Marine Villa' to the public. But later rebuilding and alterations for a hotel (from 1882) have not left any recognizable early features. Something of the fine grounds remains, although diminished by council car parks, with some garden structures around KNOWLE DRIVE (Gothic arch, the footings of a grotto, derelict flint Gothic summer house).

The mid C19 LODGE to Knowle in STATION ROAD, random rubble and traceried bargeboards, makes a good contrast with its neighbour, the later C19 tile-hung LODGE to the MANOR HOUSE up a drive further N. This is a substantial Jacobean composition of red brick, gabled, with a display of bay-windows, 1869 by *G. Somers Clarke*. Now divided into flats. Good balustraded terrace.

Back to Woodlands and along ALL SAINTS ROAD. On the N side a good sequence of medium-sized villas in their own grounds, starting with CEDAR SHADE, a delightful scene with its garden with cedar trees and polygonal conservatory, now sadly viewed against the bulky additions in the grounds of Powys. The house has deep eaves, low-pitched roofs, and Gothic windows. Formerly L-shaped; sensitive additions of 1952 to the W. Then GREEN GABLES, with scalloped boarding but altered ground floor. All Saints' church follows (q.v.) and a SCHOOL, plain apart from tripartite end windows; c. 1850 by *S.S. Teulon*, enlarged 1867. Then SIDLANDS LODGE, a stuccoed urban pair at the corner of Radway, Ionic porch at the side.

Further N is the discreet turning off Vicarage Road into ELYSIAN FIELDS, a winding private drive laid out in the 1820s along the edge of the ridge overlooking the town, with stuccoed villas well hidden in large gardens. The most interesting is SIDHOLME (formerly Richmond House), built in 1826 for the Duke of Buckingham, enlarged soon after by a capacious music room, intended as a chapel, nearly the size of the house. The entrance was moved to the side at this time. Front with prettily ornamented gables, windows with dripstones and marginal glazing, continuous balcony, all still with the delicacy of the early C19. The music room, stepping out at the back with a large canted bay on each side and an organ recess at the end, is in a different spirit, with large arched windows. Its interior is a surprise: eclectic classical-Rococo, with marble fireplaces, mirrors and chandeliers, and a domical ribbed vault painted with *grottesche* above the cornice and putti on a blue sky in the centre. Other early C19 features elsewhere, especially an upstairs boudoir with ribbed vault. Attractive grounds with gravel and pebble walks though shrubberies and pine trees. At the end of Elysian Fields LONG ORCHARD, also with patterned bargeboards, balconies, and gables of different sizes. The other villas are of the broad-eaved type, either with classical detail (Camden, Fairlawn) or with Gothic windows (Somerton).

The final suburban villa excursion is to the NE, along SALCOMBE

ROAD with its terraces and BARRINGTON VILLA with cuspy bargeboards, to the river, where there is a tiny TOLL HOUSE with miniature Greek Doric columns and pediment. In this neighbourhood several houses enjoying picturesque river views. At the beginning of HILLSIDE ROAD, SALCOMBE COTTAGE and two more thatched cottages. Off SID ROAD, beautifully sited looking down the valley, HUNTER'S MOON, formerly Salcombe House, not a typical Sidmouth building, but a dignified late C18 five-bay stuccoed front with Ionic porch. Windows with keystones, reeded cornice. Tall hipped roof with later dormers. Low side wing with Gothic windows and clock tower. Built for Sir James Cockburn, Dean of York. Some way further N, SID HOUSE, red brick, late Georgian, and to the W, set back behind a lawn, SALCOMBE LODGE, typical of the delightfully naive builder's Gothic of the early C19. Long two-storey flat stucco front of five bays, with two-centred windows with dripstones; very pretty patterned glazing. SID ABBEY, shown on an engraving of 1816, is of a different and more ambitious type: probably an older building remodelled, two-storey Gothic bay-windows, steep crow-stepped gables. Finally SIDCLIFFE, down a lane to the W, a trim villa with specially intricate window patterns and veranda.

4. Outliers (roughly W–E)

PEAK HOUSE, Cotmaton Road. On the hill overlooking the sea. 1904 by *Evelyn Hellicar* for Sir Thomas Dewey, the founder of Commercial Union. Accomplished neo-Baroque. Garden front of ashlar, 3–2–1–2–3 bays, the ends with canted bay-windows with hipped roofs, the centre pedimented. Bold Baroque doorway, rusticated quoins, Gibbsian windows. Good interiors in early C18 style. The house replaces one of the late C18 enlarged in the early C19 for E. D. Lousada by *G. Julian*.

WOOLBROOK. Within the outer NW suburbs, remains of a main-road village, with a row of cottages at LOWER WOOLBROOK, another at HIGHER WOOLBROOK, and, near the Exeter road junction, BOWD, an attractive thatched cluster, with inn (much altered), farm, and outbuildings round a courtyard.

MANSTONE OLD HOUSE, Manstone Lane. Unhappily hemmed in by a housing estate. Interesting small late medieval stone cross-passage-hall-and-parlour house; kitchen and dairy (rebuilt later) beyond the cross-passage. Well repaired by *William Weir* in 1915. On both floors two-light cinquefoil-headed windows in square heads, suggesting that a ground-floor hall already existed *c.* 1500. The lateral stack is a later insertion (dated 1589?). Unusual separate N entrance to the parlour, by a two-centred doorway, quite elaborately moulded. The chamber above the parlour has a bracket carved with a green man, and a medieval arch-braced roof with two tiers of wind-braces. Arch-brace with ogee apex, as at Sand (q.v.), not far away.

WINDMILL HOUSE (formerly Home Orchard), Hillside Road. 1909 by *M. H. Baillie Scott*. A good example of the architect's classic Arts and Crafts style of the early C20, compact, slightly asymmetrical, with two big gables, sturdy chimneys, and sweeping tiled roofs. Large arched opening on the r. for a garden room (now glazed in), a typical Scott feature. Half-timbered porch at the back; the rest of flint with random brick and stone, instead of the more usual roughcast, showing how Scott was moving away from the tradition of Voysey towards an interest in local materials and variety of texture. Comfortably set at the end of a long terraced front garden, and approached through a matching entrance arch with its own tiled roof and original wooden gate.

SILVERTON

ST MARY. Perp nave, N and S aisles. The S aisle and S porch embattled. W tower with buttresses, battlements, and four pinnacles. The S door has a cinquefoil ogee arch; nook-shafts inside the windows. Aisles of four bays, the piers of standard section with boldly carved standard capitals. Three of the piers have image niches. Medieval wagon roof. Two known dates refer to the building history: the N aisle was erected out of funds left by a rector who died in 1479, and on the E respond of the N arcade is a rebus of a rector of 1519–31. Restoration of 1861–3 by *Edward Ashworth*; chancel largely rebuilt, Perp; interior reseated; new stone PULPIT. – ORGAN CHAMBER 1880, now morning chapel. – WEST GALLERY. 1734. – NORTH PARCLOSE SCREEN contemporary with the building. – Iron-clamped CHEST. – ALMSBOX. C17.

Quite a large village, extended by an estate of the 1970s towards Killerton. At the central crossroads former village SCHOOL, reconstructed in the C19, but with foundation plaque of 1732. FORE STREET leads N with an interesting group. Nos. 6–12 (and probably also Nos. 2–4) are a late medieval terrace of cob and thatched houses of one build. Hall and service room front on to the street, with an inner room to the rear, an adaptation of the usual plan to a tight site. Prominent lateral stacks added later. Opposite, some good individual houses: OLD CHURCH HOUSE GALLERY, cob, C16, with a wooden first-floor four-light ovolo-moulded oriel, and a simple single-rib plaster ceiling in a later extension; No. 3, early C19, with a pretty pattern-book doorcase and a porch on iron columns; and the NEW INN, painted brick, three storeys. Other good houses in the HIGH STREET, and a late Georgian row in the road S of the crossroads.

DUNSMOOR. Farmhouse, once a grander late medieval house, of which part of the much altered hall remains, its smoke-blackened roof now concealed. Two early C17 cross-wings at the upper end, the front one with mullioned windows, ground-floor main room with moulded beams, and a good first-floor chamber with its complete early C17 decoration: single-rib plaster ceiling, plaster frieze with cornucopias, chimneypiece flanked by fluted pilasters, elaborately panelled overmantel, original doors. A simpler ceiling in a smaller adjoining room. C16 arched garden entrance. Good C19 outbuildings.

HAYNE HOUSE. Early C19 three-storey, three-window front, stuccoed.

PARK FARM. The monumental pedimented composition comprises the STABLES of SILVERTON PARK. Formerly stuccoed, now very dilapidated. The palatial Grecian mansion was designed in 1838 for the fourth Earl of Egremont († 1845) by *J. T. Knowles* but never completed. It was dismantled *c.* 1892 and demolished *c.* 1900. It was an extraordinary design, entirely clothed in colonnades, Corinthian above Ionic.*

PRISPEN HOUSE. The former rectory. 1839 by *Richard Carver*. The usual type, stuccoed, with deep bracketed eaves.

CLYSTHAYES. A substantial late medieval farmhouse with rich late C16 and early C17 interior decoration. Smoke-blackened roof on jointed cruck-trusses with wall-posts to the ground: closed truss over the inner room with framed ladder/stair access in the joists of the inner-room ceiling. In the late C16 a rear wing was added (now demolished), and the lateral wall was partly rebuilt in timber-framing as a stud-and-panel screen at ground-floor level with close-studding above, incorporating a staircase to give separate access to chambers above. Late Elizabethan panelled screen between hall and inner room, the designs to either side similar but varied in detail, with geometric patterns and cornices. Chamber over the hall with Elizabethan plaster ceiling, single-ribbed, with very large central pendant.

PAPER MILLS. A large group of stone, brick, and corrugated-iron-clad buildings of various dates. Slim modern steel chimney and metal-plate water tank.

SLAPTON

ST JAMES. Low W tower with plain broach-spire, unbuttressed, and early. Chancel with Dec windows. There was a dedication in 1318. Two-storey N porch. Perp arcades with A type piers, capitals to the shafts only. Restoration 1885–1905. – SCREEN. Removed during the Second World War, and reassembled clumsily. Standard tracery; the top and wainscoting not original. – PULPIT. The stem is medieval.

COLLEGE. A collegiate chantry was founded by Guy de Brien in 1372. From this the ruin of an 80-ft tower survives, dominating the little village, and a few fragments incorporated in the house called THE CHANTRY, which is probably medieval and part of the collegiate buildings, but now looks late Georgian. On the E side of the tower are to be seen a two-centred arch and the roof-line of a building.

The village lies hidden inland, away from the little resort that developed close to the sea at the end of the remarkable shingle beach with lake behind. On the causeway beside the beach, an OBELISK commemorating the American landings of 1944, a trial run for the Normandy invasions.

POOL. A farmhouse on the site of the manor house of the de Briens and later the Hawkins. In the late C18 Polwhele described 'noble buildings of a vast extent, now crumbling to dust'.

DEERBRIDGE MILL. A watermill now converted to a house.

SLAPTON CASTLE. *See* Stokenham.

* See P. Metcalf in H. Colvin and J. Harris, eds., *The Country Seat* (1970), 234–6.

SOURTON

On the NW edge of Dartmoor.

ST THOMAS. Partly rebuilt in 1847, restored in 1881. Chancel with
one early C14 lancet. W tower with buttresses and obelisk pinnacles.
Granite arcade of two bays, A type piers; the chancel arch similar. –
ROYAL ARMS of Charles II.

Former VILLAGE HALL, converted to a Disneyland *cottage orné* in
1978. Rubble walls, coy undulating eaves, Gothic windows.

BEARSLAKE. The Dartmoor building tradition at its most picturesque. An exceptionally elongated range of granite and thatch
sweeping downhill, unifying a much altered structure of several
periods. In the upper end (which has been almost entirely
reconstructed) a late C15 pointed granite arch, leading now into the
baffle entry against a large stack. One granite mullioned window is
all that remains of an extensive cross-wing. The lower end of the
house is least altered, though even here the original plan is obscure.
It was of longhouse form (the shippon at the lower end has been
incorporated into the house), with two large stacks in the centre,
and another cross-wing, this time towards the road. Over the centre
a section of the earlier roof.

On SOURTON DOWN behind the hotel are the remains of an
extensive FIELD SYSTEM of unknown date. A large earthwork
consisting of a sub-square platform surrounded by a ditch is
probably either a Roman SIGNAL STATION or a small Civil War
battery or redoubt. The modern A30 in all likelihood represents the
Roman road to Cornwall.

SOURTON CONSOLS MINE. Of *c.* 1853. The chimneystack stands at
the junction of the A30 and the A386.

SOURTON ICE WORKS, on Okehampton Common, NE of Sourton
Tors. Remains of shallow ponds and trenches and the ruins of a C19
storehouse, all much damaged in the Second World War.

SOUTH BRENT

ST PETROCK. A South Western dedication. The church stands at the
NW end of the little town, right above a weir of the river Avon. Much
evidence of an original cruciform Norman church. What survives is
its crossing tower, now the W tower of the later church. The low
round-headed openings to the N and S are still clearly discernible.
The E is still open, the tower arch to the present church; this is
pointed. On the W side also the joint with the Norman nave can be
discerned. The tower itself consists of two kinds of masonry, flat
and slaty below, larger blocks above where a corbel-table carries the
battlements. No buttresses. In 1436 three altars were dedicated.
The date represents probably the body of the church: nave and two
aisles of six bays, tall octagonal granite piers with limestone capitals
and double-chamfered arches. The general impression is uncommonly roomy, thanks chiefly perhaps to the absence of a screen. The
church also has N and S transepts with very large windows, S porch,
and two later chancel chapels. Restored by *Hine & Odgers* in 1870,
when the tower arch was revealed and PULPIT and TILES were

added. – FONT. Circular, Norman, with three bands of decoration: cable, palmette, zigzag, similar to Blackawton and Buckfastleigh. – STAINED GLASS. N aisle W by *Heaton, Butler & Bayne*. – MONUMENT. William Cuming †1824, by *Kendall* of Exeter, with a mourning female bent over an urn. Shop production.

CHURCH HOUSE with porch, SE of the churchyard.

BOARD SCHOOL. 1875 by *James Hine*.

PACKHORSE BRIDGES. Brent Mill Bridge, ½ m. S of the railway station, and Lydia Bridge, ½ m. N of the side road up to Dartmoor, both widened.

HILLFORT, exploiting the natural eminence of BRENT HILL. Multiple ramparts, with additional outworks on the S and SW. On the summit, within the earthworks, building platforms much disturbed by quarrying. The CHAPEL also on the summit was founded in the C14; an C18 account describes a corbelled roof.

On DOCKWELL RIDGE and BRENT MOOR, on both sides of the river Avon, between Shipley Bridge and the Avon Reservoir, are prehistoric cairns, fields, and settlements. RIDERS RINGS, an enclosed settlement above the river, is a particularly large and well preserved Bronze Age 'pound' with houses and little stock enclosures or gardens inside, and a large annexe.

THREE BARROWS HILL. A group of massive barrows (*see* p. 27) and reave along the parish boundary with Ugborough.

At CORRINGDON BALL GATE a large long barrow, with small round cairns and a stone row nearby.

Above Lydia Bridge are the remains of a SAIL CLOTH MILL which operated until the 1870s. The leat and wheel pit are visible.

GLAZEBROOK VIADUCT. Of *Brunel*'s time the granite piers in pairs joined at the top by cross arches, alongside the later granite and brick viaduct. The striking pair of Brunel-type HOUSES with Venetian windows at the approach to the railway bridge may have been associated with the railway.

HENGLAKE BLOWING HOUSE, on the l. bank of the Avon. One of forty-three sites listed in Worth's *Dartmoor*. 17 ft 6 in. by 12 ft.

AVON DAM. A massive concrete dam, about 115 ft high and 330 yds long at the crest, was built in 1956 by *Lemon & Blizard* to impound the Avon.

6040   SOUTH HUISH

By Court Barton the ruins of the OLD CHURCH, dismantled after a new church was built at Galmpton (q.v.) in 1867–8. W tower with type B buttresses going up part of the way. S porch attached to the S aisle. The first window on the N side deeply splayed and small. The S arcade went to Dodbrooke, the font to Galmpton, the rood screen was reassembled in the house at Bowringsleigh, and the bench ends were given to the Earl of Devon and are probably those in the chapel at Powderham.

COURT BARTON. Double courtyard of stone farm buildings, sensitively converted to holiday cottages by. *Harrison Sutton Partnership*, 1984. Old roofs and openings retained.

JARVIS TENEMENT. A typical C17 South Hams farmhouse. Stone under a thatched roof. Two-room plan without cross-passage. Two-

storeyed porch and stair-turret. Inside, a large hearth incorporating two ovens: to its l. the stair, to its r. a large smoking-chamber.
Three bee boles in the base of the stair-turret.

See also Bowringsleigh.

SOUTHLEIGH

2090

ST LAWRENCE. Sheltered in a dip between the hills. The low w
tower medieval; s doorway very plain Norman, N arcade with
circular piers. The chancel arch is probably of *c.* 1300. s aisle added
in 1827, chancel rebuilt in 1852–4 by *T. T. Bury*, general restoration 1880 by *Hayward*. – MONUMENTS. R. Drake † 1600, without
effigy; for the style cf. Branscombe. – Plain big sarcophagus in the
churchyard to H. Willoughby, 1616.

WISCOMBE PARK. Pretty provincial Gothic by *Joseph Power* of
Colyton for C. Gordon, 1826. Two parallel blocks, stucco, slate
roofs, crenellated parapets. Five windows with trefoil heads. Porch
with cinquefoil head and fluted columns. Buttresses with Gothic
pinnacles.

BLACKBURY CASTLE, 2½m. SW. Fine late Iron Age hillfort with
complex earthwork entrance. To the s there was until recently a
massive earthen dyke, presumably associated with the hillfort.

SOUTH MILTON

6040

ALL SAINTS. w tower with tall polygonal pinnacles, stair-turret in
the middle of one side, and type B buttresses. Nave, s transept
(with two renewed small lancet windows, i.e. early; and a squint),
and N aisle. The arcade with A type piers with thin capitals to the
shafts only and nearly semicircular arches. The arch from nave
into s transept of the same type. – FONT. Circular, big, very
elementary early Norman; above a thick cable moulding a main
frieze, zigzag with staring faces, and above this a narrower frieze
with two animals and a woman falling back; the meaning not clear.
– The former REREDOS, painted, has big, hefty Baroque figures of
Moses and Aaron of 1792 (now on the N wall), and nice, varied,
typically early C19 lettering. – SCREENS. Interesting for the painted decoration of different dates, revealed in recent cleaning by
Anna Hulbert. Rood screen with late medieval painted figures in
white clothes in the wainscoting; well preserved. Standard tracery,
no coving, and only one strip of decoration in the cornice (the paint
here of *c.* 1800). – The parclose screens more unusual, late Perp,
with the curves of the Gothic arches all straightened out; painted
and grained in the late C19. – STAINED GLASS. E window *c.* 1960
by *James Paterson* of Bideford. – (Small bronze CRUCIFIX, C12.
Found in a field.)

CHURCH HOUSE. Early C16. Set into a slope; on the s side upper
windows of granite with elliptical heads, a blocked upper doorway,
and two round-headed doorways below.

ROSE COTTAGE, immediately below the Church House. A small
two-room-plan house of rubble walls under slate. Inside, carpentry
exceptional for the South Hams: four jointed-cruck roof trusses

with slightly cranked collars and three through purlins, all smoke-blackened. Also cross-beams with wide chamfers and drawer and bar stops, close-set joists, also chamfered, and wooden spiral stair. Was it connected with the Church House?

HORSWELL HOUSE. Good C18 double-pile house, five bays, two storeys, with dormers. Shell-hooded porch. The seat of the Roopes, inherited by the Ilberts in 1761.

SOUTH MOLTON

ST MARY MAGDALENE. The exterior of the church is distinguished by a tall w tower of four stages, 107 ft high and until 1751 crowned by a spire, with type B buttresses and tall pinnacles on the battlements. On its s side a niche with three heads above. Bell-openings with reticulated tracery. The w door has fleuron decoration, the w window is of four lights. Nave, aisles, transepts, and chancel all embattled, the s transept singled out by quatrefoil decoration of the battlements. The interior unusually light (as Devon churches go) because of the addition of a clerestory to the nave in 1864 by *C.E. Giles*. Arcades of five bays with type B piers, standard Devon capitals with figure as well as leaf carvings, and depressed arches. The aisles and shallow transepts are comfortably wide and well lit. The aisles in their present form date from 1825–9, when they were widened by *C. Hedgeland*, and the windows enlarged to allow for galleries (now removed). One original window remains behind the organ.

The chancel in its masonry is older than the rest of the church and narrower than corresponded to the later proportions. Thus the chancel arch is not wide enough and rests on big corbels to make up for the difference. One of them is a human figure. The chancel chapels, opening into the chancel with wide, low arches, are so deep, owing to the thickness of the older chancel walls through which they had to be broken, that they could be panelled and provided with corbels (reworked in the C19) for statues against the E jambs. E window renewed in 1858. Unceiled wagon roof in the chancel. Other roofs renewed by *Giles*.

FONT. Perp, octagonal, shaft panelled, bowl with elaborately cusped quatrefoils. – PULPIT. Perp, stone, octagonal, with exceptionally lavish narrow leaf-framed panels and engagingly crude figures standing in them under triangularly projecting canopies. – MACE RESTS. Two in the N transept. – REREDOS. Spiky Victorian; 1864. – TOWER SCREEN. 1903, a lush piece in polished marble, Caen stone, and mahogany, still seriously Gothic. – Much Victorian and Edwardian STAINED GLASS. An instructive sequence by *Hardman*: E window 1859, s chapel Smyth memorial 1867, s transept Brown memorial 1881. – Also N aisle to Kingdon †1898 by *Swaine Bourne & Son* of Birmingham, and s aisle w by the same firm, less good. – N aisle to Merson †1911 by *A. L. Moore*. – s aisle Mardon memorial 1912 by *Joseph Bell & Son* of Bristol. – MONUMENTS. Two good late C17 architectural tablets. – Joan Bawden †1709. Cartouche with cherub's head.

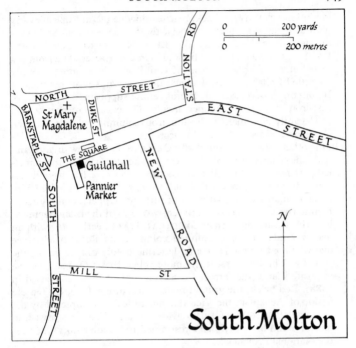

South Molton

ST JOSEPH (R.C.), East Street. 1863. Plain gabled front with plate tracery.

NONCONFORMIST CHURCHES. *See* Perambulation.

South Molton, a main-road market town, was a borough by the C14, and a centre of the woollen industry. The town grew until the mid C19, and remains attractively unspoilt, with a very satisfying central group of buildings. EAST STREET, the long main thoroughfare, broadens into the former market place, called THE SQUARE from the C19 after it had been dignified by the removal of the shambles. Island sites remain at either end, creating a pleasantly informal atmosphere. The church lies secluded at the end of a path to the N, approached through a delightful neo-Grecian cast-iron gateway with overthrow. Directly opposite, on the s side, the GUILDHALL, designed in 1739–41 by Mr *Cullen*, 115 re-using stonework and other materials bought at the sale of Lord Bath's house at Stow, Kilkhampton (North Cornwall). A friendly provincial Palladian design with three open rusticated arches on the ground floor, the upper floor with Corinthian pilasters and central niche, in which there is a later bust of Hugh Squier, the local benefactor (†1710), carved by *Hems*. Pediment, clock cupola, and balustraded parapet. A good mid C18 staircase leads up to two first-floor rooms embellished with excellent fittings from Stow. COURT ROOM at the front, with bolection-moulded panelling, acanthus cornice, and coved ceiling. C18 seating and carved royal arms; elegant candle sconces. The MAYOR'S PARLOUR has enriched panelling, four pedimented doorcases, and chimneypiece and overdoors painted with rustic scenes. Assembly room added behind in 1772. At the back, reached down a picturesque alleyway with a big arch on heavy corbels, the former Sergeant at Mace's quarters, now the LOCAL MUSEUM. Next to the Guildhall the PANNIER MARKET, 1863 by *W. F. Cross* of Exeter. The front is a little taller and grander than the Guildhall's, in a more forcefully modelled Italianate (vermiculated quoins, ram's-head keystones). It contains a new assembly room (ceiling supported by decorative cast-iron arches) over an open arcade. The covered market behind is elegantly minimal, with slim iron columns below a wooden clerestory, and a roof with thin iron ties.

On the other side of the Guildhall a good C18 house (now divided and with shopfronts inserted), six segment-headed windows, channelled quoins; next to it the GEORGE HOTEL, a five-bay, three-storey front of *c.* 1800, with *Coade* stone keystones. Chinese Chippendale staircase with alternating patterns. Upper assembly room behind (used as a theatre in the early C19). On the island facing W into the square the former MEDICAL HALL, early C19, with an iron veranda on Ionic unfluted columns, its Regency elegance overwhelmed by the later gold lettering boldly draped across the balcony. The house faces the more sober POST OFFICE on the opposite island (the former Corn Exchange of 1809, converted in 1888). Red brick, the ground-floor arches originally open. On the N side of the square the Victorian amenities are completed by the CONSTITUTIONAL CLUB, with ornate Victorian cast-iron balcony, and one of *Gibson*'s restrained Italianate banks (1865 for the National Provincial).

The lesser buildings of the town are mostly white or colour-washed and quite modest in scale, stretching for a considerable way along SOUTH STREET and EAST STREET and up the narrow lanes off them. First down SOUTH STREET: pleasant inserted Victorian shopfronts, and some good Georgian doorcases (Nos. 69–71, 24). The larger accents are the DEVON CONSTABULARY of 1894, lumpish brick Tudor, and No. 27, with an altered ground floor but apparently a substantial five-bay house of *c.* 1700, with rusticated pilasters, coved cornice, and hipped roof. Beyond Mill Street GOSPEL HALL, 1840, with narrow pointed windows, set in a yard, and WOODVILLE, tall and stuccoed, earlier C19, with remarkably sinuous vine-scroll bargeboards. No. 32 opposite is treated similarly.

Back up to BARNSTAPLE STREET to the NW, where BIDDERS COURT (Abbeyfield Homes) in red and cream brick, 1981–5 by *Michael J. Smith*, picks up the colours of the late C19 housing. Residential accommodation around a small courtyard; one-storey houses tucked away up a lane behind. Further on, three-storey rubble warehouses. Across the road at the beginning of NORTH STREET the former NATIONAL SCHOOLS, 1834 in origin, but with a later front with plate-tracery windows in the end gables. Further on up North Street to the back of the churchyard, with the CONGREGATIONAL CHURCH boldly outfacing the parish church. The coarse later C19 eclectic front (traceried round-arched windows, Doric pilasters, pedimented doorway) conceals a building of 1834 on the site of an earlier meeting house. Equally confident is the WESLEYAN CHAPEL, on a fine site looking down Duke Street, with its busy Dec front of 1883 with three porches and polygonal side adjuncts. Stone manse to the E. DUKE STREET, a narrow lane with some good C18 houses, leads back to the square.

Along EAST STREET plenty of modest Georgian frontages and some tactful infilling, notably ELYSIAN COURT (1981–4 by *Philip G. Brown*) behind the Health Centre on the N side, with arches leading through a series of small courtyards stepping up the hill. Unfortunately drab grey rendered walls. Further on, the BAY HOUSE, broad three-bay late Regency, and the OLD RECTORY, with two ground-floor Venetian windows, dentilled cornice, and a long side wing, slate-hung, with two more Venetian windows on the upper floor. On the other side, EASTLEIGH, a stuccoed villa with a gargantuan granite Doric porch. Minor houses stretch further down the hill; on the N side the former HUGH SQUIER SCHOOL, a small rectangle of 1684 with a four-centred doorway flanked by large Gothic windows (inserted later).

In NEW ROAD to the S, FREEMASONS' HALL, late C19, with two arched upper windows and a frivolous parapet, INFANTS' SCHOOL, 1861, a pleasant Gothic composition with teacher's house at one end, and the BAPTIST CHAPEL of 1843, rubble, with gables and lancets. Ornate slate gravestone on the chapel wall to Sarah Badcock †1853, signed with a flourish by '*Thomas, engraver*'.

N up STATION ROAD, some way out of the town, the former STATION. Two-storey gabled stone station house with offices attached, 1873 with later brick additions. To the W a large stone goods shed with a canopy over the side doors. To the SW the goods yard with warehouses, stone with brick dressings, following the curve of the former sidings.

S of the town, the Exeter Gate TOLL HOUSE, single-storey, with a round central projection.

(SOUTH COCKERHAM, Hacche Lane. Mid C18 rendered, three bays plus one. Pedimented projecting centre with Venetian window, doorway with open pediment and mask keystone.)

(KINGSLAND BARTON, Nadder Lane. Good C17 plaster ceiling.)

HONITON BARTON, 2 m. SW. A substantial E-plan house, now a farmhouse, in an attractive setting with a duckpond in front. Rendered, with modest wooden casements, but a good C17 moulded stone doorway to the porch and an inner wooden doorway also moulded. Datestone 1676 to Anthony and Elizabeth Paul. Early C17 dado panelling in the hall. End stack with two diagonally set chimneys. In the C18 the seat of the Southcombes. At the back a detached CHAPEL, now ruinous, rebuilt by Lewis Southcombe, the C18 rector of Rose Ash and Kings Nympton (qq.v.).

SOUTH POOL   7040

ST NICHOLAS AND ST CYRIACUS. Big W tower of Ashburton type with short polygonal pinnacles. The church itself small compared with the tower: two aisles, two transepts; porch at the W end of the S aisle. Granite window tracery, granite A type piers with capitals to the shafts only, moulded arches. – FONT. Circular, Norman, with the same curious decoration as at Dittisham. – SCREENS.

Rood screen with four-light tracery of Dartmouth type. Three cornice friezes with leaf etc. decoration, reset. Coving to the aisles only. Wainscoting with interesting early Renaissance arabesques (cf. Chivelstone), grey monochrome on coloured grounds. – Simpler parclose screens, the detail as at Stokenham. – EASTER SEPULCHRE, N chancel wall. Recess with tomb-chest (probably re-used) with badly damaged weepers. The recess has a Tudor arch and cresting, and in the spandrels the initials of Thomas Bryan, rector of South Pool and Portlemouth in 1536. On the back wall and soffit elementary panelling and a relief of the Resurrection, defaced, but with the elaborate C16 armour of the soldiers still visible. The effigy of a priest now on the tomb-chest cannot belong. – Other MONUMENTS. Effigy of a lady, the head very worn, S transept. – Leonard Darre †1615 and his wife, the daughter of a London alderman, †1608. Standing wall-monument, two alabaster kneeling figures, five children, high-quality work of London standard, in a simple surround with black columns and entablature.

COURT BARTON, S of the church. A much renewed stone farmhouse with good outbuildings round a large yard.

(RECTORY. 1828 by *Joseph Lidstone*.)

SCOBLE. Tall stone house in a remote position. Probably an C18 remodelling of an older core. Three storeys, stone modillioned cornice, good C18 panelling.

SOUTH TAWTON

ST ANDREW. Large, mostly of granite. Ashlar-built W tower of three stages with buttresses of type B, battlements, and obelisk pinnacles. Embattled S aisle with S turret and embattled porch. S aisle windows Perp, of granite, cusped. Chancel also of ashlar, but rougher work, perhaps earlier. N aisle not ashlar, but also embattled, the window tracery renewed (correctly) in the restoration of 1881 by *Hayward*. Interior with tall Beer stone piers of A type with capitals only to the shafts. N chancel chapel with granite arch to the nave. S chancel chapel of Beer stone with decorated capitals. Original wagon roofs, now unceiled, restored in 1881. One roof boss with a sheila-na-gig carving. – PULPIT. Charming early C18 work with inlay figures of the Evangelists and foliage. – SCREEN. 1902, part of several embellishments by *G.H.Fellowes Prynne*. Tall, with intricate tracery; a rood above. – ALTAR RAILS. Very elegant. Partly 1675, partly 1903, with twisted balusters. – BENCH ENDS. A few. – STAINED GLASS. Bliss, Weekes, and Lethbridge windows by *Clayton & Bell*, all 1881; Dunning-Cann window 1921. – In the N aisle an unusual late C19 window with figures on white glass. – Chancel E and S aisle E 1965 by *M. Meredith Williams*. Good bold colours. – MONUMENTS. John Wykes of North Wyke †1591. Recumbent figure under a low tester with three low Ionic front columns; bad. – Robert Burgoyne, erected 1651. A curiously composed tablet with two main figures kneeling l. and r. above a steep pediment, and a slate plate below with kneeling parents and children.

The E end of the church is raised above the winding village street and forms a beautiful group with the LYCHGATE of 1903, attached to

the CHURCH HOUSE, close to the stump of the village elm. The 69
Church House, built of exceptionally large granite blocks, is of the
early C16. Perp E gable window with tracery under a square head.
The upper floor is reached by a very ingenious series of outer
staircases which cut across a ground-floor window. Upper and
lower doorways with depressed arches. Very large internal stack
with two fireplaces on each floor, partly reconstructed in 1742;
jointed-cruck roof.

South Tawton is a large parish on the fringes of Dartmoor, with
much evidence for ancient settlement. S of the village is the
medieval new town of South Zeal (q.v.). Even for Devon, it is an
extremely rich area for large C15–18 farmhouses, and is of outstanding interest because it shows the intermingling of the longhouse and the three-room-and-cross-passage-plan traditions. Of
the longhouses, excellent examples are POWLESLAND, a cob
house with shippon still in agricultural use (as a stable), and still
occupied by the Powlesland family; WELL, a sophisticated
example with porch dated and inscribed 1660 I(E?)N, and IN 1641;
and the impressively long LOWER SESSLAND, one of the best of
the large longhouses on a five-room-and-cross-passage plan. The
shippon and hayloft are still in original use. Apart from Higher
Shilstone (*see* Throwleigh), perhaps the most attractive of all
surviving longhouses. EASTWEEK COTTAGE is another longhouse, with a lateral stack and a four-light granite mullioned hall
window.

WEST WEEK (or WEST WYKE) is yet another large medieval to
C17 house which evolved from a longhouse. Grand gateway to the
forecourt with crenellated parapets, dated 1656. Cross-wing and
two-storeyed porch. Medieval core with original roof at the lower
end. The upper end is apparently late C16. Very confusing
exterior: the ashlar granite blocks of the central section relate
oddly to the porch, and lead into a tall lateral stack, also of ashlared
granite. At the upper end, various good details, with datestone of
1585 and dripstones with the initials of William Battishill (†1615)
and his wife Jane. The house has however been sadly mutilated in
recent years. Good linhays in the farmyard on a courtyard plan;
walled garden.

Of the other type of farmhouse a good example is HENDICOTT,
which hides its C15–17 structure behind a C19 front. The medieval
roof has unusual carpentry (jointed crucks with face pegs augmented by slip tenons). The roof of BLACK STREET HOUSE is
unusually sophisticated: three bays with ovolo-moulded arch-
braced trusses, intermediate trusses, and inverted wind-braces.

At EAST WEEK, PUMPY COTTAGE is a small late medieval house.
Hall and inner room survive of a three-room-and-cross-passage
plan. Smoke-blackened roof of two bays, a third now occupied by
an inserted axial stack. Jointed crucks with early yoked apex;
upper-chamber partition smoke-blackened on the hall side only.
The ground-floor partition with round-headed C16 door frame
seems to have been rebuilt further back into the inner room,
perhaps replacing an original low partition, though the small scale
of the building also suggests that this house might originally have
been an example of a long hall, i.e. without a partition between hall
and inner room.

WICKINGTON. Now a small farmhouse of the usual three-room-
and-cross-passage type, but once a grander building. Remains of
an unusually elaborate hall screen with moulded uprights. The
most remarkable feature is the late medieval porch, no doubt once
taller. Ground floor with a two-centred moulded archway; ribbed
barrel-vault inside. Broached octagonal first floor with square-
headed window with two arched lights.

OXENHAM. Georgian front of 1714, two storeys, six bays. Classically
ordered windows, but two irregularly placed doorways, so perhaps
a remodelling. The seat of the Oxenhams from the C13 to 1814.

On SOUTH TAWTON COMMON and COSDON HILL are numerous
small enclosed Bronze Age settlements, cairns, reaves, a stone
circle, and a stone row. The existing field system on the side of the
moor between Cosdon and South Zeal is prehistoric in origin;
many hut circles survive in the modern fields.

Above BELSTONE CLEAVE, hut circles and cairns survive inter-
mingled with the later pillow mounds for the rabbits of SKAIGH
WARREN.

At the head of IVY TOR WATER one of Dartmoor's most spectacular examples of medieval alluvial TINWORKING remains, showing
the ridged spoil heaps left by the systematic working of the surface
tin deposits. A tin mill lies to the side of this great working.

See also North Wyke, South Zeal, Sticklepath, *and* Wood.

6090   SOUTH ZEAL

Formerly on the main Exeter–Okehampton road, now happily bypassed. A medieval new town, probably created in the mid C13.
Robert de Tony of South Tawton established a market and two
fairs in 1299, but the settlement never grew to much more than a
single village street running up and down the hill (cf. Newton
Poppleford) and widening around the market place. The medieval
layout is remarkably well preserved: substantial stone houses lie
back from the road, with long narrow burgage plots behind, the
occasional lane in between leading to the former open fields.

The grandest house, the OXENHAM ARMS, formerly belonged to
the Burgoynes. Two storeys, exterior details of c. 1600: stone
mullioned windows of three and four lights, two on each side of the
porch; to the l. a coachway with four-centred arch and straight
label. The two-storey porch of carefully jointed ashlar is an addition; are its two-centred archway and three-ribbed stone barrel-
vault re-used?

At the top of the hill the KINGS ARMS, thatched and roughcast,
with remains of one stone mullioned window. Many of the other
houses are earlier than they appear from their modest and rather
uninformative fronts to the streets. Several have large axial stacks;
some roofs preserve smoke-blackened medieval thatch and C15
carpentry. The modest rendered and slate-roofed exterior of
CROSSWAYS conceals a good late medieval house on a three-room
cross-passage plan with inserted axial stack. The upper end has a
good late medieval roof, smoke-blackened over the hall, and a
chamber jettied out over the stud-and-panel partition of the inner
room. MOORSIDE is on a two-room plan, built partly floored

towards the end of the C16, but quickly provided with a chimney and floored hall. Nos. 1 and 2 MILL HOUSE comprise a heavily disguised C16 house with arch-braced roof.

ST MARY. A small chapel of medieval origin in the centre of the old market place. Large granite blocks on lower courses of rubble; a plain rectangle with rudely hewn W bell-gable with battlements and four corner obelisks. The date 1713 on a plaque on the E wall. Perp windows, restored in 1877. The building had been a schoolhouse from 1773.

SCHOOL. In a side street, the new school of 1873–4, by *Charles Pinn*. Enjoyably hefty neo-Norman detail, the largest gable with a giant arch framing triple lights and oculus, and supporting a pyramid-topped bell-turret.

RAMSLEY COPPER MINE, above South Zeal to the S. A C19 stone chimney with brick cap remains, and the spoil heaps, still too toxic to support vegetation.

SOWTON

ST MICHAEL. The medieval church was rebuilt in 1844–5 at the expense of John Garratt, the High Church patron and owner of Bishop's Court (q.v.). The architect was *John Hayward*, then in the forefront of the ecclesiological revival. Hayward kept the Perp N arcade, with piers of unusually complex section and capitals with shield-bearing angels. But the importance of Sowton is as a rare survival of an early Victorian Tractarian village church, complete with its fittings. Red sandstone with Bath stone dressings; long and quite low, with well demarcated chancel, two-light Dec windows to the nave, cusped lancets to the chancel. Splendid W tower, late C14 in style rather than Camdenian Middle Pointed, of three stages, with diagonal buttresses to the tall first stage, a polygonal stair-turret clasping the SW angle, battlements, and big corner pinnacles ornamented with vigorous grotesques.

Inside, wagon roofs to nave and aisle. Open benches throughout, the ends with tracery patterns and symbols of the Passion; at the E end of the aisle the Garratt seats, with taller ends and poppyheads. Well moulded chancel arch with clustered shafts, the floor one step up from the nave, the sanctuary three further steps up. The chancel roof is an open wagon, with cross-members and an elaborate wall-plate, all painted and gilded; delicate stencilling to the walls. Sanctuary floor TILES; elaborate tiled dado behind the altar. – SEDILIA. Double, under multi-cusped arches, their faces flush with the sanctuary S wall. – Wooden ALTAR, the intricate front of three bays filled with diapered and painted panels, the altar top held on angel corbels. – COMMANDMENT PANELS. Tall Gothic frames flanking the E window, the texts gorgeously illuminated on porcelain panels. – COMMUNION RAIL. Panels of slender openwork tracery in brass and cast iron, an unusual design, still rather Georgian in character; it bears the maker's stamp *Lydach*. – PULPIT. Stone polygonal drum, buttressed and decorated with dense foliage; figures of the evangelists under nodding ogees by *John Thomas*, then in charge of the figure carving at the new Palace of Westminster. – FONT. Devon Perp style, with octagonal bowl and stem. Tall openwork tracery FONT COVER of 1848, designed by *Hayward*.

STAINED GLASS. A complete set by *Willement*, integral with the design of the church. In the E window the Crucifixion; Moses and Aaron facing each other in the sanctuary N and S; Last Judgement text in the W window, with St Michael and other archangels dramatically posed in bright gold armour against a dark blue ground. Through the windows of nave and aisle, quarry glass carrying the running text of the Creed, finishing with symbols of the evangelists behind the Garratt seats. – MONUMENT. John Garratt †1859, a foliated brass cross on a simple marble slab, by *Waller* of London, dignified and consciously reticent in the manner advocated by *Instrumenta Ecclesiastica*. – LYCHGATE in memory of Sarah Garratt †1852, with heavy roof of Salcombe Regis stone slabs.

OLD RECTORY. Five-bay brick front with rainwater head dated 1722. Only one room deep.

Sowton is now on the edge of Exeter, with a growing industrial estate off the motorway (so far with nothing of architectural interest), for which two good farmhouses were destroyed. The parish is important for the study of Devon's local building traditions, for it was the subject of a pioneering study by Alcock in 1962 and a later one by Laithwaite (*see* Further Reading). Interesting among the survivors is DYMONDS, later C17, on a four-room plan without cross-passage, with two good rooms at the W end, kitchen and service room at the E. Ovolo-moulded windows. Plasterwork in the hall and outside above the main door, the latter dated 1676 and initialled RB, probably for Richard Bevis, the son of the then owner of Bishop's Court.

IVINGTON FARM. The home farm of Bishop's Court (q.v.), built by the Garratts in 1846. Brick farmhouse, three bays, hipped roof, with central open pediment, on one side of a well-preserved planned farmyard. Tall bank barn on the SW, with two openings, the ground floor with three elliptical arches. Detached brick granary in the centre, with circular upper windows.

A small hamlet with a C19 church, within the old parish of Cornwood, now nearly on the edge of Plymouth.

ALL SAINTS. Late C19 nave and transept, SW turret, Dec windows. Chancel 1904 by *E. H. Sedding*. – STAINED GLASS from 1876.

BEECHWOOD. Large, irregular stuccoed house, the core built in 1779 for Richard Rosdew, since enlarged. Interior mostly C19. Later C19 top-lit staircase. The drawing room was enlarged by John Colborne, first Lord Seaton, the first Governor-General of Canada. The elaborate fireplace was brought in from Bert, Co. Kildare, in the 1890s by the third Lord Seaton. Library and small drawing room with late C19 *Walter Crane* wallpaper. STABLES with castellated wall with large archway; walled garden, also castellated. Late C18 landscaped PARK.

HEMERDON. An estate plan diverting the road is dated 1795. The house, built for James Woollcombe around the same time, was probably completed only gradually – see the irregular window levels on the two main fronts. These are of five and seven bays, three storeys, rendered, each with a central pediment. Simple staircase with tall arched window and stick balusters. The library was probably fitted up in the later C19: rich cornice, marble chimneypiece.

BORINGDON CAMP, in the NE of the parish. A substantial circular univallate HILLFORT, probably of Iron Age date. In the plantation outside, fieldwork has identified complex outworks to the entrance.

CROWNHILL DOWN. On the summit a fine linear barrow cemetery consisting of a variety of round barrow types. Other small cairns are dotted on the W slopes of the down; also a medieval longhouse and field system and, running E–W across the S end of the down, a major tinworking which exhibits medieval and post-medieval tin extraction by streaming, opencast, and deep-shaft methods. On the N side of the openwork a circular whim platform where the horizontal winding wheel was powered by an animal. Leats for the more recent WHEAL FLORENCE, whose chimney can still be seen, run across Crownhill Down.

See also Boringdon *and* Newnham.

SPREYTON

6090

ST MICHAEL. On a hill (as so many churches of St Michael are) and in an exposed position. An ashlar-built granite church, as befits its proximity to Dartmoor. The tower has buttresses of B type. Straight-headed windows, the tracery elementary. The piers of the arcade inside of A type, with plain unmoulded capitals as in Cornwall. Wagon roofs to nave and aisle and a much more elaborate one for the chancel, with an inscription recording the names of Henry le Maygne, Vicar, 'a native of Normandy who caused me to be built A.D. 1451' and 'wrote all this with his own hand' (an interesting fact), and Robert of Rouen of Becdenne, Prior of Cowick, near Exeter, and Richard Talbot, Lord of Spreyton, who 'gave of their goods to my building'. Restored by *James Crocker*, 1913; his fittings since replaced. – FONT. Norman, octagonal, with the most primitive gingerbread-like figures in relief on the pillar and a quincunx ornament on the panels of the bowl. – The WALL PANELLING of the nave is probably early C19.

Among many farmhouses, outstanding are THE BARTON, a large C15–18 house on a U-shaped plan, and COMBE, on a four-room-and-cross-passage plan adapted from a former longhouse, with arch- and wind-braced roof. CROFT has a similar roof, and good internal joinery. Lower room demolished; the upper end became a kitchen in the C17, with a full-width hearth incorporating a smoking chamber.

STARCROSS

9080

Close to the Exe estuary, a riverside hamlet which grew up by the ferry. The COURTENAY ARMS is Georgian; shallow-arched windows with keystones, broad arched front to the road. Bow-fronted villas opposite of the earlier C19; also the STRAND HOTEL, set back, a tall, two-bay house, and other modest early C19 villas looking across the water. The church lies a little inland.

RAILWAY MUSEUM. Built as an engine house for the short-lived South Devon Atmospheric Railway, 1845–7 by *I. K. Brunel*. Robust Italianate, with heavy corbels under the eaves and bold window surrounds with big keystones. Taller tower, consisting of a chimney surrounded by a staircase.

ST PAUL. Built as a wide rectangular box in the Grecian style by *Charles Hedgeland*, 1826, entirely remodelled in the Romanesque manner by *David Mackintosh* in 1854. Mackintosh added a chancel with E triplet; replaced the original sashes with large round-headed windows; and built quite an imposing W belfry. Wide tie-beam roof; pendants added in 1854. – WEST GALLERY. 1826, on Tuscan piers, converted to a social area in 1985. – STAINED GLASS. E window 1858 by *J. Bell* of Bristol, a bright, unsophisticated mosaic with small neo-Romanesque figure medallions. – S windows of 1856, 1859, and 1861 also by *Bell*.

STAVERTON

7060

ST PAUL DE LEON. Thin, early W tower with much batter, low polygonal stair-turret, no pinnacles, and an unmoulded tower arch. Nave and two aisles of five bays, earlier than the standard Perp design and in an unusual mixture of materials: moulded arches of red sandstone and white Beer stone, on granite octagonal piers with capitals decorated with fleurons. The second N pier from the E continues up above the capital. Chancel S window with star-shaped tracery (cf. Ipplepen, Torbryan). Perp the S chapel, vestry door, and two-storey porch. The nave windows were all renewed in the restoration of 1873–82 by *Ewan Christian*, with very wilful plate tracery on the S side (plainer geometric on the N). Old aisle roofs with bosses. – ALTAR. 1949, replacing the C19 one designed by the Rev. *H. Froude* now in the Lady Chapel. – ROOD SCREEN, across nave and aisle. Much restored in 1891–3 by the expert on Devon screens, *F. Bligh Bond*, the work executed by *H. Hems*, with advice from S. Baring-Gould, whose family came from Staverton. The pier casings are additions, and so is the rood loft, based on Atherington, and intended to have paintings, as at Lew Trenchard. The tracery original, type A standard; one painted wainscot panel remains. – Good PARCLOSE SCREENS. – MONUMENTS. Worth family, 1629. Kneeling figures, the children above the parents. – Thomas Bradbridge of Kingston House †1815. Neo-classical with urn. – Edward Bovey of Badaford. Unusual cut-out marble urn, white on black. '*Coulman* fecit.' – Minor monuments to the Goulds. Others were rescued by Baring-Gould from destruction during the restoration, and installed at Lew Trenchard. – BRASS to John Rowe †1592, oddly placed on the exterior of the church.

STAVERTON BRIDGE. 1413. Seven obtusely pointed arches and cutwaters. One of the oldest and most impressive Devon bridges.

KINGSTON HOUSE. A grand mansion of the C18 (dated 1743), built by John Rowe, who later went bankrupt. By 1784 the house was owned by Thomas Bradbridge, from whose time some of the interior alterations may date. Many windows blocked later. Restored in the 1980s. Austere but well-proportioned four-square exterior of rubble stone, well dressed window heads and cornices, seven and five bays, all four fronts well finished. Three storeys above capacious vaulted cellars. Main entrance on the E side, a sober Doric doorcase.

Inside, a surprising range of unusual C18 fittings. Large central stone-paved hall, with awkwardly sited staircase behind, which does not fit properly, occupying two instead of three bays. Was it brought from elsewhere? It is a very fine piece of C18 joinery, with exquisite marquetry on both steps and a dado in five different woods. Three slim balusters to the tread. Dado panelling, oddly detailed around fluted pilasters on the landing. Off the later axial corridor, SE room (truncated from its original size) with panelling and giant fluted pilasters flanking door and fireplace. The arrangement of the first-floor rooms probably not as originally planned (were they altered when the staircase was added?). First-floor E room with plasterwork overmantel: the Flight into Egypt in a pedimented frame on which two fat putti recline. Hanging garlands on either side; also busts on brackets, supposed to be St Peter and St Paul. The Rowes were Catholics, and this room is said to have been used as a chapel. In the NW bedroom, panelling with traces of original graining, and some most unusual painted decoration in two closets: one with large lions and birds, the other with landscapes, roughly done in a sketchy technique. More grained panelling on the second floor; also a room with *trompe l'œil* panelling painted on a wall.

Walled garden to the W, outbuildings to the N, one with elegant keystones.

PRIDHAMSLEIGH. A large former manor house around three sides of a courtyard. Unusually tall (two and a half storeys over a cellar). Double-gabled front decorated with (decaying) patterned slate-hanging. Much is C17 work for the Gould family, probably around an earlier house. Arched cellar door with blocked round-headed openings. Inside, bolection and ovolo mouldings and a niche with fluted pilasters. Late C17 gatepiers with ball finials. Fine DOVE-COTE on a circular plan with conical slate roof (corbelled stone inside) surmounted by a conical latern. Interior lined with nesting-holes with slate ledges.

See also Landscove.

STEDCOMBE HOUSE
Near Axmouth

2090

An excellent if somewhat conservative example of the compact post-Restoration house with belvedere, a rarity in Devon. Built *c.* 1697 by Richard Hallett. Solidly constructed, of brick with Portland stone dressings: bold quoins, moulded window surrounds. Four show fronts, each five windows wide, to the N with original sashes with thick glazing bars. Hipped roof with dormers, big square belvedere with round-arched windows. This, most unusually, is also of brick, and incorporates four chimneystacks. Much of the interior was gutted in the late 1970s because of dry rot, and remained unrepaired until 1988, when plans were made by *C. Rae-Scott* to restore the building as far as possible to its original appearance.* Principal rooms to S and W; W–E axial stair hall. Of the original main stairs, altered in the C19, only a few thick twisted balusters survive, but to its N an excellent lesser stair rises round a small well, from basement to attic. A tiny steep flight leads to the belvedere (unsuitable for large parties). Bolection-moulded panelling in the ground-floor SW room; on the first floor simpler panelled S and W bedrooms, with closets. A later addition is a remarkably exuberant Rococo chimneypiece, derived from Lock and Copland's *New Book of Ornament*, 1752.

STEVENSTONE
E of Great Torrington

5010

The principal Devon estate of the Rolles, one of the leading county families in the C18 and C19. Approached from the W past LITTLE SILVER COTTAGE, one of six lodges around the estate, 1879, of stone, with decorative bargeboards. The great house, already truncated *c.* 1914, is now a romantic ruin drowned in brambles and wistaria. The core was C16, remodelled *c.* 1709 by Sir Robert Rolle M.P. and later transformed into a mansion in the Franco-Italian style, as the *Building News* called it, by *Charles Barry Jun.* in 1869–73 for the Hon. Mark Rolle, who built so extensively on his properties (*see* Bicton, Otterton). The long, quite low ranges were given French mansard windows, and corner towers with château roofs were added. On the S side a two-storey bay-window and a tower are recognizable; to the E was the entrance front, reconstructed from old materials *c.* 1914. Formerly the house extended the length of the balustraded S terrace, and had several internal courtyards.

112 W of the house a walled garden with two C18 pavilions, an ORANGERY and a LIBRARY (so called by 1796). The library was converted to a house in the 1950s and (like the orangery) adapted by *Philip Jebb* for the Landmark Trust in 1978. Handsome red brick building with three arches to the ground floor, three tall arched windows above. Stone fluted Ionic giant pilasters on tall plinths; dentilled cornice. On a central cartouche the arms of John Rolle (who succeeded in 1726 and died in 1730). In a first-floor room a richly carved fireplace surround, brought from the dining room of the main house.

To the E, the OLD LAUNDRY, with at its S end a still recognizable tall Victorian roof. Beyond, two parallel ranges of older stables were turned into neat neo-Georgian residences in the 1950s; two storeys, with a lower link building. Other C20 detached houses scattered about the GROUNDS, which were landscaped in the 1870s by *Milner*, and still retain many fine specimen trees.

---

*This includes replacement of later sash-windows by windows based on those of the N front; reconstruction of dormers (whose original appearance is unknown); and the reinstatement of a W entrance doorway removed in the C19.

STICKLEPATH 6090
wsw of South Tawton

FINCH FOUNDRY. Really an edge-tool works. Founded in 1815, in operation until 1966, and now a museum. A group of modest structures, the main building (originally a cloth mill) single-storey, of stone, with a fan room attached. Nearby is the grinding house. Inside, the water-drive tilt-hammers survive, and each of the three sections has a waterwheel to provide power. To the road, in front of the foundry, a two-storey range of stone with a slate roof. Foundry cottage and foundry house adjacent.

Behind the foundry a QUAKER BURIAL GROUND.

METHODIST CHAPEL. 1816, enlarged in 1838. Small bell-tower at the side.

WESTERN AND CARNALL MILLS. Stone, of two storeys, converted to a dwelling in 1948. A waterwheel installed in 1971 generates electricity for the house.

STOCKLAND 2000

ST MICHAEL. A proud, tall, and slim C15 W tower, not as inconspicuous as they mostly are in East Devon. The W door with an elaborate foliage and fruit scroll along jambs and voussoirs. A proud Perp N aisle facing the village, with large three-light windows, buttresses, gargoyles, and battlements with pierced quatrefoils. In addition an equally embattled N chancel chapel and an embattled stair-turret between aisle and chapel. The whole is an excellent composition. N arcade of three broad arches, then two narrower ones, on B type piers with well carved capitals, all different. On the W respond a Courtenay coat of arms. Tower arch and chancel arch without capitals. S transept with one early C14 lancet. Restored in 1860, with new roofs, in the chancel on stone corbels, in the nave with central pendants below kingposts, and extensively refitted in a further restoration of 1866–8 by *E. Ferrey*. – MONUMENTS. Amos Collard †1747. Small, architectural, of grey veined marble. – Rev. William Keate †1777. Grey marble pediment against an obelisk; eloquent inscription.

BRIDGE. Early C19, small, single-arched; with cast-iron plaque warning that wilful damage will be punished by transportation.

The parish is typical of this area of East Devon for its wealth of C15–17 farmhouses and other small local buildings. Near the church, backing on to the churchyard, the two-storeyed CHURCH ALE HOUSE, on a miniature scale but with a C16 round-headed door probably re-used, as were the original roof and first floor. Extensively repaired and the roof entirely reconstructed by *A. Howard* in 1983, but faithful to the original in every detail, including the unusual tapered blocks at the foot of the trusses to prevent movement. In the village is TOWNSEND, of excellent quality throughout, showing a typical sequence of C15–17 farmhouse development. Chert walls under thatch. Original three-room cross-passage plan supplemented by a C17 rear kitchen and store and two-storeyed front and rear porches. Four jointed cruck trusses (one replaced); the hall truss has a cambered collar, arch-bracing and wind-braces in the upper bay. Smoke-blackened roof, the thatch on wattling, with inserted partitions smoke-blackened only on the hall side: thus the hall was originally open throughout, but chambers were partitioned off before the open hearth was abandoned in the late C16. Hall ceiling with intersecting beams, C17 ovolo-moulded windows and doors, and remnants of a stud-and-panel screen.

LOWER LYE,* ½m. N. The archetypal medieval farmhouse on a three-room cross-passage plan with a later cross-wing at the lower end. Rendered rubble walls under a hipped thatched roof. Smoke-blackened roof, on jointed crucks and with unusually broad and flat rafters which are widely spaced, carrying the thatching battens. Two stud-and-panel screens, the one between hall and inner room probably an original low partition. Fireplace in the inner room, inserted axial stack in the hall, and two staircases added in characteristic bulges beyond the line of the original walls.

KITES. An exceptionally small late medieval house, with original internal jetty to carry the upper chamber. Three-bay roof with one jointed cruck-truss and one true cruck. Kitchen/bakehouse added at the rear.

PENNYHILL.* An early example (datestone 1704) of a farmhouse on a symmetrical plan, with parlours at the front and service rooms at the rear. Good range of farm outbuildings around the yard facing the house.

OWL'S CASTLE. A late medieval house with an early stud-and-panel screen. Two-centred door frame to the small inner room; inserted jettied chamber; late C16 fireplace and ceiling.

GREAT CAMP, ¾m. N of Stockland Hill. A substantial, irregularly shaped Iron Age enclosure on a gentle hill-slope. Massive defences remain on the N side, but on the S only a low earthwork.

LITTLE CAMP, ½m. N of Great Camp. A circular earthwork which may be either prehistoric or medieval.

An exceptional quantity of MESOLITHIC material has been found in the parish and in neighbouring Membury.

STOCKLEIGH ENGLISH

ST MARY. Perp. Unbuttressed W tower with small pinnacles. Aisleless interior with lower, narrower chancel. Restored piecemeal in 1878–83, with a new chancel arch. – Minor MONUMENTS to the Bellews of Stockleigh Court, the best to William Bellew †1789, coloured marble with cartouche.

ST MARY'S COTTAGE. An early C16 church house, much altered.

STOCKLEIGH COURT. The late Georgian house of the Bellews. Stuccoed, five-window front of three storeys. Grecian one-storey addition on the l.

---

*For plans of Lower Lye and Pennyhill see pp. 68 and 69.

STOCKLEIGH POMEROY

ST MARY. From a Norman building the s door has been reset in fragmentary form. w tower with unmoulded tower arch on the plainest responds. Chancel rebuilt from original materials in 1841, the lancet windows (a group of three at the E end) no doubt from the building consecrated in 1261. Restored in 1861–3 by *William White*, who rebuilt the s side and porch, and added an impressively muscular arch-braced roof, in the nave with tie-beams, over the chancel arch and in the chancel on braced hammerbeams. But the N arcade is latest Perp; B type piers with standard capitals of special interest because they have symmetrical motifs and little figures in the new Renaissance fashion. – Contemporary BENCH ENDS, many with foliage motifs clearly of the 1530–50 style, besides initials, heraldry, two-tier tracery, and medallion profiles. – PULPIT made up of Renaissance panels from bench ends or backs. – Fragments of an earlier ROOD SCREEN, now under the tower arch.

CHURCH COTTAGE. The former early C16 church house.

STOCKLEIGH HOUSE. The former rectory, of the usual early C19 type, stuccoed, with broad bracketed eaves.

MILL. Two-storey, thatched, of cob; remodelled in the C18, but with one medieval jointed cruck truss.

STOKE CANON

A main-road village just N of Exeter.

ST MARY MAGDALENE. Perp w tower with diagonal buttresses; the church of 1835 by *John Mason* of Exeter, spacious and aisleless, with embattled roof. – FONT. C12, a single block of volcanic stone, carved in the most elementary style, but with quite a sophisticated design of four figures against the stem, and four atlas figures at the corners – an Italian concept – holding the bowl on their angularly raised arms. From the bowl four beasts crouch down to bite off their heads. – PULPIT. Jacobean, with the usual blank arch in each panel, exceptionally slim and tall. – ALTAR PAINTING by *John King* of Bristol, 1841. – Other FITTINGS by *Ashworth*, 1875.

OLD VICARAGE, High Street. 1848–51 by *St Aubyn*.

CULM VALE. Remodelled in 1863–70 for William Deudney, proprietor of the Stoke Canon paper mills. Two storeys; bold projecting eaves. Contemporary marble fireplaces. Nearby, a striking HOUSE by *Peter Blundell Jones* and *Gillian Smith*, 1976–7, with the type of modern organic plan more common across the Atlantic than in England. Circular, the curved living room with a hearth, the other rooms spiralling around it. Brick, with shallow-pitched roofs.

BRIDGE AND CAUSEWAY. Of late C13 origin. The present bridge, late C18 with early C19 flood arches, is over 800ft long.

SIGNAL BOX. 1874, with timber-framed upper storey. The last surviving Bristol–Exeter signal box of this type.

HILLFORT, Stoke Hill. Strongly sited overlooking the Exe valley. Univallate; one side intact, the s side still visible in a cultivated field.

STOKE FLEMING

s of Dartmouth, the church sited high above the coast.

ST PETER. Fine Perp w tower of Ashburton type, with a turret up the
centre of the N side. The body of the church early, and an interesting
archaeological puzzle. The three w bays are similar to those of St
Clement and St Saviour at Dartmouth, and of the same blue stone:
octagonal piers, slightly concave, with shafts in the diagonals; ill-
fitting moulded capitals, i.e. not later than the C14. Steeply pointed
arches of red sandstone, double-chamfered. Fourth pier of buff
limestone, and an odd shape: four main shafts, with in the diagonals
three steps. Standard Devon capitals, the arches moulded and taller
– these bays were evidently heightened in the C15 to take a rood loft.
E responds with the Carew arms. Behind the fourth bay are
transepts, perhaps left over from an older plan. Low chancel with
chancel arch. Restoration 1871 by St Aubyn (roofs and windows
renewed). – PULPIT. 1891 by Violet Pinwell, elaborately carved
with narrative scenes. – STAINED GLASS of 1866 onwards; Christ
with Angels by H. Holiday, 1880. – MONUMENTS. Stone effigy of a
lady, c. 1300, badly preserved. – Large brass to John Corp and his
granddaughter Eleanor who † 1391. One of the best early brasses in
Devon. Whole figures, hers a little smaller, and therefore placed on
a pedestal. Originally with a thin architectural frame.
BOWDEN HOUSE. The seat of the Nethertons from the mid C18.
Well sited, with a good view E. C18 rendered front of seven bays, the
central three slightly projecting. Modillioned eaves; good doorcase.
GREAT COMBE. In its present form a late C16 and C17 farmhouse
adapted from an earlier and possibly larger building. The lower end
was rebuilt above a cellar in the C18, but the two-storey porch with
richly moulded doorcase and contemporary door are of c. 1600.
Large ground-floor room with moulded plaster ceiling and overmantel with royal arms dated 1640. In the chamber above another
overmantel with a curiously grotesque head (a Medusa?) in a
strapwork frame with monster heads, flanked by terms. Remnants
of floral plasterwork on the roof trusses.
SANDERS. Early C19, with later embattled tower.
STOKE LODGE. Early C19, rendered, with veranda.

STOKE GABRIEL

ST MARY AND ST GABRIEL. w tower with much batter, and
buttresses only low down. Unmoulded tower arch probably older
than the rest of the church. Elaborate Perp N doorway in a square
frame. N and s aisles with piers of B type and standard capitals
distinguished where the screen runs across by figures of flying
angels with shields (renewed). Broad aisle windows with elementary
tracery. Restored by Hayward & Son, 1878–9 (new roofs and E
window). – Perp FONT. – Mid C19 REREDOS with evangelist
symbols and painted texts. – PULPIT. Foot spreading palm-like,
panels with thick nodding canopies, uprights between the panels
thickly ornamented (cf. Torbay: Paignton). – SCREEN. Much re-

done. The paintings in the wainscoting indicate a date not later than 1450. Restored by *Herbert Read*, 1930. – Three medieval BENCH ENDS; a few BOX PEWS; other seating made up of C18 panelling. – STAINED GLASS. E window 1879 by *Clayton & Bell*.

The pretty, intricate village centre in a valley close to the river Dart is now swamped by new houses on the surrounding slopes. The church stands high up, close to a yew tree a thousand years old.

CHURCH HOUSE INN. A well preserved church house, with a pentice along the front, as at Widecombe. Lateral and end stacks, a projection perhaps for an early staircase, and an upper round-headed doorway at the E end. Screen and moulded beams inside.

WADDETON. A small hamlet with cottages around a minute green. Gatepiers with griffins at the start of the drive to WADDETON COURT, a large manor house, the property of the Studdys from the early C19 to 1916. Seven-bay front with off-centre two-storey porch. The exterior detail dull Victorian Tudor (1844 according to Snell). By the drive the CHAPEL, rebuilt in 1868–9 by *Thomas Lidstone* of Dartmouth. Red sandstone. Nave and apsed sanctuary; quirky W buttress and bellcote. The apse has an internal arcade of marble colonnettes flanking the nine windows, which have excellent STAINED GLASS. – Painted sanctuary roof. – Brass TABLETS to the Studdys, including Eleanor Holdsworth, *née* Studdy, who rebuilt the chapel.

MAYPOOL (Youth Hostel). A solid stone and tile-hung house in an enviable position above the Dart. Built in 1883 by *R. Medley Fulford* for F. Simpson, engineer and boatyard owner. River front with two gabled wings and arcaded veranda; an angled bay-window to the S wing exploits the view downstream. Picturesquely grouped half-hipped and gabled roofs. Large top-lit hall with staircase up to a wooden gallery; stone Gothic fireplace. Another room with stained glass with musical figures.

TIDE MILL. The dam with mill pool and sluices remains.

See also Sandridge.

STOKEINTEIGNHEAD

ST ANDREW. The chief interest of the church is its SCREEN, Dec rather than Perp, and of a design very different from the standard type. The rood loft was not carried on a coving, but had a flat underside partly preserved. It is decorated with quatrefoils with big leaves in their centres. The panels are straight-headed too and only of three lights. Their tracery is elementary but much cusped. The central entrance has a heavily crocketed, very depressed ogee arch. W tower with diagonal buttresses and stair-turret. Interior with four-bay N and S aisles. The piers are red sandstone, B type, the capitals of Beer stone, standard on the S side, but on the N with shield-holding angels and little saints in ogee niches between them. Chancel rebuilt in 1865, incorporating a Dec PISCINA. Roofs largely medieval. Modest restoration in 1894 by *Tait & Harvey*. – BRASSES. In the sanctuary, Thomas Taggell, a priest, † 1375, the earliest in Devon, a whole figure. – In the nave, Elizabeth Furlong † 1641, heart-shaped.

– MONUMENT. Large early C19 tablet to members of the Graeme family, 'nine of whom all suffered in their country's cause', by *Faulkner* of Exeter.

CHURCH HOUSE, now an inn. The interior well preserved, with stud-and-panel screens, beams, and a lateral stack.

STOKENHAM

ST MICHAEL. A remarkably large church, and lying so that its whole length can be taken in from a distance. s aisle, s porch, s transept, projecting chancel, large four-light Perp windows, a usual but here spectacular sight. W tower of Ashburton type, rebuilt in 1636. The date is in cast-iron figures on the W door. N and s arcades of six bays; B type piers with standard capitals and moulded, nearly semicircular arches. The interior restored in 1874 by *Thomas Lidstone* of Dartmouth (walls scraped, roof repaired); the chancel refurbished in 1890 (marble panelling). – Double PISCINA with crocketed ogee arches. – SCREEN. Much restored, the wainscot paintings redone, the tracery type A standard, the cornice with only one frieze of decoration. – PARCLOSE SCREEN. The sections straight-topped, of four lights, with intersecting semicircular arches as the basic motif of the tracery. – PULPIT. Perp of 1874, with painted shields. – STAINED GLASS. E window 1875, with geometric patterns. – MONUMENTS. Minor tablets to John Somaster †1681, with a scrolled and floral surround, and to the Holdsworths of Widdicombe, governors of Dartmouth Castle. – Good CHURCHYARD RAILINGS and GATE with overthrow.

Stokenham is a large coastal parish whose s apex is Start Point with its LIGHTHOUSE. In addition to the village, with a pretty row of cottages NW of the church, there are several other settlements.

At CHILLINGTON, a METHODIST CHAPEL with Gothick windows and an oval datestone of 1850.

STOKELY BARTON, s of the village. A plain five-bay farmhouse of early C18 type, with a hipped roof. Impressive stone farm buildings around a courtyard.

COLERIDGE HOUSE. C19, neo-Elizabethan.

WIDDICOMBE HOUSE. On the site of an older house which belonged to the Heles. The main range, of coursed stone, facing NE, probably built by Arthur Holdsworth (†1726), is still in the manner of the late C17 gentleman's house: seven bays and two storeys, with alternating triangular and segmental pedimented dormers. At the s end a further bay with Venetian windows, the end of a Regency wing which has to the NE a broad bay-window with tented balcony. Good early C18 staircase with twisted and fluted balusters. C18 landscaped grounds.

TOLL HOUSE, guarding the road into Stokenham, ¾m. from Torcross. Rectangular, of two storeys, with a porch on the l.

SLAPTON CASTLE, on a spur between Stokenham and Slapton. A once substantial Iron Age hillfort, now only partially visible as an earthwork. The strength of its situation can still be appreciated from the road passing through it, which probably makes use of the two original entrances to the site.

ST BARTHOLOMEW. Tall W tower with diagonal buttresses, polygonal SE stair-turret, and no pinnacles (modern top). Straight-headed N and S windows. Arcade between nave and S aisle of four bays, the piers of B type with crude block-like capitals. Roofs of 1832, plastered over inside, and provided with cornices. – FONT COVER. Concave, with finial, C17? – PULPIT with early Renaissance panels. – PANELLING of the C18 along nave and aisle walls. – TILES. A number of Barnstaple type by the font. – Much good late Perp and early Renaissance WOODWORK is said to have been ripped out in 1832, when the chancel was lengthened, and installed in Weare Giffard house and church (q.v.).

BAPTIST CHAPEL. Two pairs of trefoil-headed windows.

NEWHOUSE. A C17 farmhouse around three sides of a courtyard, with good contemporary joinery inside. W range with early C19 symmetrical front and windows. C19 kitchen and dairy fittings.

GLEBE HOUSE. The former rectory. Mostly Gothic of 1855; C17 back wing. In the grounds an APIARY, a sweet thatched building with Gothick windows, polygonal, with a conical roof.

EARTHWORK ENCLOSURE, on a hilltop 1 m. E. Small and univallate, and probably prehistoric. The road rises up as it passes over the rampart.

ST MARGARET. W tower with diagonal buttresses at the foot, no pinnacles, polygonal NE stair-turret. The medieval church, of three bays with the sanctuary in the E one, was transformed in 1879–80 by *Henry Woodyer* for Thomas Carew Daniel of Stoodleigh Court. The two W bays of the S arcade are original (A type piers, standard Devon leaf capitals); also much of the wagon roofs. The third bay was rebuilt, and a new chancel and S chapel added, with a re-used Perp panelled arch between them. Not one of Woodyer's most interesting buildings, although his imprint is seen on the two-centred chancel arch, crisply moulded, with naturalistic capitals, the bold S porch, and the diverse tracery: Dec in the aisles, Flamboyant in the E window. – FONT. Circular, Norman but retooled, plain bowl, two quaint faces sticking out from the stem. – REREDOS. Chunky, polychromatic, with evangelist symbols. – Other furnishings and fittings by *Woodyer*, the door furniture especially characteristic. – STAINED GLASS by *Hardman*: E window 1880–2; others ranging from 1879 to 1910.

STOODLEIGH COURT (Ravenswood School). Hidden in large grounds. Rebuilt for Thomas Carew Daniel in 1883–4 by *Ernest George*, in partnership with *H. A. Peto*. Earlier plans for a neo-Tudor house by *L. P. Crace* were rejected. Smaller and plainer than George's Rousdon (q.v.), but in a similar style, derived from Shaw's early country houses. Local rubble stone with Ham Hill dressings, with a little half-timbering in the gables to add interest. L-shaped plan, mullioned windows, the roofs picturesquely grouped. N front with porch and large oriel window to the l., lighting the medievalizing double-height hall, as at Rousdon. But this is more a communication area than a living space: the staircase rises from one end, and divides, with one wing leading to an upper passage which looks down on the hall through large stone arches on the s side. By deft placing of corridors, the main living rooms and all the bedrooms face s. Much oak dado panelling, stone fireplaces, dining room with bold timber-rib ceiling in octagons and lozenges. Pretty SERVICE COURTYARD with a little timber cloister and tile-hung gables. In the entrance court, diagonally opposite the house, a charming ornamental DOVECOTE. Good contemporary LODGES.

BRIDGE over the Exe, humped, with two different-sized semi-circular arches. 1790, together with the thatched two-storey TOLL HOUSE with projecting front.

8070   STOVER HOUSE
                                 Teigngrace

A large house in ample grounds, a school since 1932. 1776–80, built and very likely designed by *James Templer*, who began his career apprenticed to an Exeter architect called John Bickley, and made his fortune erecting government buildings in India and Plymouth in partnership with Thomas Parlby and Henry Line. The young Thomas Hardwick (born 1752) drew plans and elevations of the house, but most likely after it was completed.

Stover stands on high ground, the entrance on the s side originally approached from a long drive from the lodge now isolated beside the main road (*see* below). It is an austere Palladian villa in granite ashlar, 1–3–1 bays, with a canted centre to both back and front and a rusticated basement (cellars below). The E side is also carefully composed, four bays, with a central raised-up attic window. To the w the lopsided feature of a quadrant wing connecting to a two-storey pavilion with service rooms, presumably an addition. No sign of a corresponding block to the w. The s entrance is obscured by an incongruous addition of the early C19: a grand portico with six Greek Doric columns (probably re-used, see the weathering on the inner face) connected by curving brick walls to the canted bay. Double flight of balustraded stairs. These additions probably date from after 1829, when the spendthrift George Templer had to sell the estate to the eleventh Duke of Somerset.

Excellent original interiors, in a restrained Adamish taste (cf. the elegant Templer monuments in the church at Teigngrace). In the entrance hall an overmantel with a plaster medallion with a classical scene surrounded by garlands. Two fluted columns with palm-leaf capitals; frieze with festoons. Axial corridor behind, with staircases at either end. Three main rooms along the s front, their delicate chimneypieces, ceilings, and overdoors with fans, swags, and festoons in the Adam style (cf. Saltram*), combined with heraldry and robust personal devices in the less refined tradition of provincial craftsmanship. In the centre room Roman profile heads on the outer ring of medallions on the ceiling. In the NW

---

* It is worth noting that Templer's associate *Thomas Parlby* designed the kitchen at Saltram in 1778.

room a specially attractive fireplace with yellow marble columns and a relief of sheep and shepherd; a large classical scene in a medallion on the overmantel. Another good fireplace in the central s room upstairs. According to Polwhele the fireplaces were designed to display local marbles. Curved stone cantilevered staircase; iron balustrade with a design of circles in ovals. Upstairs corridor with three little domes.

STABLES, W of the house. On a courtyard plan, and quite a sophisticated composition: 3–2–1–2–3-bay front in banded ashlar. Archway with two receding tiers above. N and s ranges with brick arched loggias to the courtyard (filled in on the s side); E and W sides with Georgian sashes. The centres step forward with shallow gables.

SCHOOL BUILDINGS. Confined to the w of the house, and not too intrusive. The most recent is a large but not unpleasant multipurpose octagonal wooden hall like an inflated summer house, by *Pinelog Ltd, c.* 1980.

James Templer laid out extensive GROUNDS, including a large lake with an island to the N near the low-lying site of the former mansion (now within Stover Country Park). Moore's *Devonshire* (1831) singled out for special praise the improvements achieved by irrigation and drainage by means of the Stover Canal (*see* Teigngrace), begun by the second James Templer in 1790 (although possibly conceived by his father) with the main object of improving transport of granite and clay.

The land around the house is built up in a terrace. At the end of the E terrace walk a TEMPLE, pedimented, with two Ionic columns *in antis*. Almost directly below this, dug into the side of the hill close to the old drive, a curious GROTTO, a monumental undulating range built of cyclopean ashlar blocks, the approach now very overgrown. 4–2–4 bays plus one, the central two with doorways, the others with rectangular windows with circular ones above, framed in giant arches. Rubble barrel-vault. NW of Higher Lodge, an ICE HOUSE.

LODGES and ENTRANCE GATES, stranded beside the A38. 143 Greek Doric, like the portico, and presumably of the same date, an accomplished neo-classical composition (cf. the White Lodge to Winslade Manor) which one would like to associate with *Foulston*. One-storey lodges of channelled ashlar, with a four-column link.

STOWFORD 4080

ST JOHN BAPTIST. Unbuttressed w tower handsomely built with alternating bands of red sandstone and granite. Battlements and big pinnacles. Nave and s aisle separated by a granite arcade of three plus two bays, the piers of A type, with capitals only to the main shafts, decorated abaci, and depressed pointed double-chamfered arches. The chancel arch and s chapel arches are probably older, although with Perp alterations. Plain Perp windows. Restoration and traditional Perp N aisle by *Sir G. G. Scott*, 1874. Medieval wagon roofs in nave, s aisle, and s chapel; chancel roof of 1874, with painted celure over the altar. – WOODWORK. A complete set of 1874 fittings, studiously historical, by *Hems*. The details were taken from some three hundred casts of medieval Devon woodwork. – STAINED GLASS. Chancel E and N aisle E and NE 1874 by *Lavers & Barraud*.

The chancel chapel was the family chapel of Haine (q.v.), and a tabard and gauntlet are exhibited in it. – FONT. Octagonal and odd, as if it were the late medieval recarving of a Norman font. – MONUMENTS. Two to members of the Harris family of Haine, of an ambitiousness unusual in this district. First Christopher Harris and wife, erected in accordance with a will of 1726. Two life-size standing figures with a sarcophagus and obelisk between. The figures are of decidedly provincial workmanship with painfully short legs, but the man is all the same in full Roman attire. – John Harris †1770. Sarcophagus in front of an obelisk, and on the pedestal below two portrait medallions. – In the chuchyard a C6 inscribed MEMORIAL STONE.

SHEPHERDS, just below the church porch. The general layout and the slightest indications inside testify to a Tudor past. Thatched roof and two picturesquely irregular gables.

STOWFORD HOUSE. Originally the rectory. Early C19, by *J. Powning*, with ambitious neo-Gothic parts of *c.* 1860–70.

See also Haine.

8040   STRETE

ST MICHAEL. A chapel of ease to Blackawton. Medieval tower with diagonal buttresses and no pinnacles. The rest of 1836 by *Joseph Lidstone*: tall quatrefoil shafts, tall lancet windows. – (STAINED GLASS. E window possibly by *Powell* of Whitefriars.)

3010   SUTCOMBE

ST ANDREW. W tower older and narrower than the nave; no buttresses or W door; unmoulded pointed tower arch. In the S chancel doorway a reset C12 head; the S nave door also possibly C12 reused. The rest Perp. Nave and two aisles, the N and S windows very late, without tracery. N arcade of five bays with the usual granite piers of A type with strip capitals and depressed pointed arches. The S arcade of only three bays has the same type of pier, but of limestone, and concave octagonal capitals to the main shafts only. Careful restoration by *Bodley & Garner*, 1876. – FONT. Octagonal, granite, Perp, with elementary designs. – PULPIT. With long narrow early Renaissance panels as at Welcombe. – SCREEN. Only the wainscoting survives (partly), of an unusual design, with long narrow panels showing a scroll of broad leaves or a number of square leaves. – BENCH ENDS. Plenty, with initials, coats of arms, mildly Flamboyant tracery, and early Renaissance motifs. – TILES. Of the familiar Barnstaple ware, in nave, chancel, and S aisle, some larger than usual. – STAINED GLASS. E window with medieval tracery lights with evangelists' symbols, the lower parts *c.* 1876 by *Burlison & Grylls*. – MONUMENTS. Jonathan Prideaux and Clement Davie, both of the 1760s, and both to the same pretty design.

Close to the church the six ALMSHOUSES founded by Sir William
   Morice, 1674, of stone, with casement windows.
MATCOTT. C18 front, of stone, five windows, modillion cornice.
THUBOROUGH BARTON, 1 m. S. A Prideaux mansion from *c.* 1500.
   Georgian five-window front of granite ashlar. Ionic porch.

SWIMBRIDGE

ST JAMES. A small church, but one of considerable interest, especially in its furnishings. The oldest part of the building is the W
tower, short and slim, narrower than the nave in front of which it
stands. It is unbuttressed, with an unmoulded, battered plinth.
Probably somewhat later it was provided with a broach-spire, lead-
covered, like those of Barnstaple and Braunton. The church itself,
mostly rebuilt in the C15 and C16 with N and S aisles and chancel
chapels, was restored by *J. L. Pearson* in 1879–82. He lowered the
aisle walls, rebuilt the parapets, and removed a nave dormer. The
N arcade of three bays has piers of the usual Devon B type and
standard leaf capitals, the S arcade the same piers but capitals only
to the main shafts. The chancel arcades, past the chancel arch, also
differ: the one on the N is like the N nave arcade, only deeper in the
arch-width (cut into the thickness of a pre-existing chancel wall)
and more ornate (with figures, for example) in the capitals; the one
on the S has responds of A type with small capitals. The arch
between N aisle and N chancel chapel has one big expressive head-
corbel. The chapel was connected with the chancel by a wide
hagioscope, where now the vestry has been built in. Externally the
S aisle and S porch are embattled; the S and E windows have Perp
tracery (S aisle straight-headed), the N windows are of three lights,
straight-headed and with mullions to the tops (no arches at all). In
his will of 1422 John d'Abernon stated that he wished to be buried
in the newly built aisle. This is supposed to refer to the N aisle, but
in that case the windows must be a much later alteration.
   ROOFS. The wagon roofs of Swimbridge are specially varied.
The oldest is in the chancel, unceiled and undecorated. The nave
roof has bosses (before the restoration of 1880 it was ceiled) and
over the rood screen a four-bay-wide CELURE with cross-ribs. In
the S aisle and S chancel aisle there are also bosses and there is even
another CELURE, but only above the E bay. The N aisle has bosses
too, and the N chancel chapel a flat ceiling with bosses and cross-
ribs repainted in 1727, as a date shows.
   FURNISHINGS. Uncommonly lavish, perhaps because the
church belonged to the Deans of Exeter Cathedral. – FONT. A
most extraordinary contraption, probably put together in the C18: 40
a lead bowl in an octagonal panelled early C18 casing, with folding
cupboard doors with early Renaissance panels between the case
and the cover. The cover is an odd mixture of C16 Renaissance
and Gothic elements (much renewed). Above it a canopy with Perp
leaf motifs and cross-ribbed and starred ceiling. – PULPIT.
Stone, cup type, like, for example, Dartmouth, with figures of
saints (of indifferent sculptural value) under nodding ogee
canopies in narrow leaf-framed panels. – Iron PULPIT STAIR by
Pearson.

33   SCREEN. One of the most glorious of Devon screens, partly (but carefully) restored. 44 ft long, right across nave and aisles, with tracery of B type, the mullions unusually richly carved, wainscoting of unusual design with leaf decoration in all its parts, and a completely preserved coving with ribs on angel corbels and panels between the ribs which have on the W side finely designed leaf and scroll motifs, not yet in the Italian taste, and on the E side coarser, broader Perp motifs. The cornice a close tangle of knobbly, bossy leaf forms. Where the screen crosses the arcade an opening is left, probably for a side altar with its reredos, and above this there is a plain forward-curved coving, also with leaf panels. The one on the N side is original, the other restoration. – BENCH ENDS. A few with rather summary tracery (leaf panels) and others imitating them. – REREDOS. Marble and alabaster, the figures carved by *Hems*, 1894. – STAINED GLASS. E window 1880 and S chapel E by *Clayton & Bell*, with much white canopy-work.

MONUMENTS. Tristram Chichester † 1654. Frontal demi-figure, cheek in hand, in an oval niche; deplorably bad. – Tablet to John Rosier † 1658, a member of Lincoln's Inn. Therefore the inscription reads:

> Loe with a Warrant sealed by God's decree
> Death his grim Seargant hath arrested me!
> No bayle was to be given: no law could save
> My body from the Prison of the Grave,
> Yet by the Gospell my poore soul hath got
> A Supersedeas, and Death seezed it not, etc.

– Charles Cutliffe † 1670. Tablet with a well-painted protrait in an oval at the top. – Large churchyard with many good slate tombstones, e.g. by *Vickery* of Barnstaple. It is entered through an archway in an attractive mixture of Ham Hill and local purple stone, no doubt by *Pearson*.

The VILLAGE HALL nearby, formerly a school, may have started as a church house. External stair to the upper floor.

BAPTIST CHAPEL, above the road, behind a steep burial ground. 1837, gabled, with Gothick windows.

SCHOOL and schoolhouse. 1866, extended 1926. Stone rubble with polychrome dressings.

The village lies in a valley, stretching along the main road between South Molton and Barnstaple, with the church as its centrepiece, and terraces of cottages on either side. The extensive parish embraces several hamlets (two with their own C19 chapels) and a remarkable number of good houses, many of medieval origin, but, as so often, most notable for their display of C17 wealth in the form of good joinery and plasterwork. The early C19, also a prosperous period, is the date of Bydown (q.v.), the grand mansion just S of the village.

In the village, COB COTTAGE and THE COTTAGE, a former farmhouse, are of late medieval origin; two late C17 ceilings with centre roundels. Other buildings are listed roughly clockwise from the centre.

At GUNN, a hamlet 2 m. N, the CHAPEL OF THE HOLY NAME, 1873, built by J. Pyke-Nott of Bydown. Simplest Gothic. – PULPIT with three re-used late medieval panels.

DEAN HEAD, ½m. W of Gunn. A late medieval farmhouse (remains of a smoke-blackened jointed-cruck roof) modernized in the early C17 (inserted floors, paired diagonal brick stacks, stair-turret added to the rear of the through passage), with excellent early C17 fittings. Parlour with moulded stud-and-panel screen and geometric ribbed plaster ceiling, divided by beams decorated with the popular winged horse motif. Demi-figures with swags above the screen; also on the overmantel. In the room above a plaster overmantel with the seasons in a strapwork cartouche. Good joinery throughout.

MIDDLE YARNACOTT, 1m. NNE of Swimbridge. C15 originally, with a two-bay open hall and a smoke-blackened roof. Before modernization in 1977 the house had the unusual plan of hall, inner room, dairy, and integral shippon, but (because it is set laterally on a hillside) no through-passage. Ladder access to a C16 jettied chamber at the W end of the hall with a chamber screen of wide panels and thin studs. The E end is a C17 addition. The chamber fireplace had at the back five C17 Barnstaple lead-glazed relief tiles.

YEOLAND HOUSE, 1m. NE. Of c.1830; three bays, hipped roof with small cupola, Tuscan porch. Contemporary bank barn behind, of rubble with dressed stone openings.

KERSCOTT, 1m. SE. The usual three-room farmhouse plan, much extended and altered. Two early C17 plaster ceilings, the parlour one with enriched ribs, the upper-chamber one with single ribs and cornice. Staircase with thick turned balusters.

STOWFORD, East Stowford, 2½m. SSE. A rendered stone and cob farmhouse with two lateral stacks. Through-passage, hall and inner chamber, the lower end demolished; two rear wings and two stair-turrets. A remarkable quantity of well preserved C17 fittings, including many doors and stopped door surrounds, moulded beams and bressumer to the inner room, and a plaster overmantel in the first-floor chamber with a scene of the sacrifice of Isaac in a cartouche.

DINNATON, 1m. S. A good example of a planned farm: buildings of rubble and brick of 1853 arranged around a yard; symmetrically-fronted farmhouse.

COBBATON, 2½m. S. The former chapel of ST THOMAS, of 1866–7, was converted to a house in 1982 and sympathetically extended, with an enclosing wall of rubble and a variegated tiled roof to the N, in keeping with the original materials. On the S side, dormers added above the plate-tracery windows. The former SCHOOL of 1876 at Cobbaton Cross is also now a house: one-storeyed, gabled, with an extraordinary slim chequered stone chimneystack.

At HANNAFORD, 1m. W, HANNAFORD HOUSE, an C18 stuccoed three-window front with Ionic corner pilasters. Central Venetian window with head keystones; pedimented doorway. In the ground-floor room on the r. a ceiling with Rococo flourishes and a marble fireplace in Adam style. Staircase with turned balusters.

TANNERY HOUSE, Hannaford Lane. Stuccoed, c.1830, four bays. Doric porch with two columns in antis; recessed entrance.

See also Bydown.

SYDENHAM
Marystow

The seat of the Wise family from the C14. The present house is one of the few of the C17 in Devon that are really imposing. It is chiefly the work of Sir Thomas Wise, Sheriff of Devon (†1630), with embellishments by his grandson Sir Edward Wise from *c.*1655.*

drawing rooms   hall   dining room   kitchen

15m
50ft

N →

Sydenham: plan

In 1675 it passed by marriage to the Tremaynes of Collacombe Manor (q.v.), who made some minor improvements *c.*1700. From 1809 it was used only as a shooting box by the Cornish branch of the family, and so survived little altered into the C20. The house was sympathetically restored for James Despenser-Robertson by *Philip Tilden*, 1938, when the roof was repaired. Some less happy internal alterations date from the 1960s.

The house stands quite close to the road, a symmetrical front of two storeys and gables facing E, with the projecting wings embracing a small courtyard closed by a good early C18 wrought-iron gate. The side wings have the unusual feature of gabled projections to the courtyard, echoing the central porch. Four-light mullioned windows of granite, with a single transom, very simply moulded, the ground-floor ones with dripstones. The upper windows of the gable ends of the wings, with wooden casements with the Palladian motif of a central arch, are presumably mid C17 alterations, and the pretty leaded lozenge casements in the side gables are perhaps of the same date. The porch, dignified by ashlar masonry, has a

---

*A Mr *Batley* made estimates for alterations in 1654–5.

broad entrance archway in the characteristically mixed style of the early C17: flattened Tudor arch with carved spandrels; classical Doric columns with broken-forward entablature.

The less regular N and W sides of the house suggest that the formal Jacobean front was an extension to an older building whose core may have been the N range adjoining the Jacobean N wing, where the back door leads to a passage between the kitchen and the present dining room. At the NW corner a picturesque but historically confusing composition builds up: a projecting newel stair on the N side, and along the W front facing the garden a succession of tall irregular projecting bays now capped rather awkwardly by slate-hung gables (perhaps late C17 or C18 modifications of a design that was once taller: Risdon wrote that Sir Thomas Wise's work was 'of such height as the very foundation is ready to reel under the burden'). The bays themselves are not all of one build, for the canted bay of the dining room is cut into by the broader projection housing both the large staircase window (four lights, two transoms) and a room off the hall.

Further S the W front has a two-storey porch with a re-used two-centred arch, corresponding to the porch on the entrance side. The hipped roof with sprocketed eaves at the S end of the W range indicates a late C17 remodelling of this part of the house, with Georgian sashes inserted later. The adjoining mullioned window was reinstated in the 1930s, and the little oriel on the S side is an addition of the same time.

The hall was refitted by Edward Wise in 1656, the date on the large and handsome fireplace with stone columns and open pediment filled by an exuberant achievement. The carved beam across the opening to the room next to the fireplace was probably brought in during the 1930s when a partition was removed. The staircase 93 beyond is in the more fantastic Netherlandish style of the earlier C17, excellently carved. The rather cramped dog-leg plan was probably dictated by existing walls. The compensation is the stately ascent achieved by the introduction of an intermediate landing on each flight in addition to the half-landing in the projecting bay built out for this purpose. Elaborately fluted and scrolled square tapering balusters, repeated along the dado; two exotic terms against the newels. The work was perhaps one of Sir Edward Wise's last improvements, for the fitting up of the top landing was left until the time of his grandson. This has a plaster ceiling with a circle of flowers and fruit in the C17 court style, and a cornice with festoons. The three pedimented and eared doorcases must also be mid C17.

The planning of the N end of the house is puzzling, no doubt the result of successive remodellings. In the NW corner is the dining room, with specially fine panelling of c.1600 which, like the adjoining staircase, seems too grand for the space it occupies. Intermittent fluted Corinthian pilasters, a frieze of enriched arches with delicate white inlaid scrollwork, similarly decorated top frieze and cornice, and an overmantel to match. In the N wing, an oddly large back hall with an L-shaped stair with plain turned balusters and newels decorated with strapwork which continues up to the attics. Adjoining are the former kitchen and servants' hall, with no features of note except for a secret room over the back entrance, said to have been approached originally from the kitchen chimney-stack.

In the main range, s of the hall, in the part of the house remodelled in the late C17, two drawing rooms, the first with good C18 fielded panelling and an inlaid panel to the overmantel, the second with slightly earlier bolection-moulded panelling and fluted pilasters. The s wing, left untouched by these improvements, and derelict in the C19, retains from the early C17 two doorways with stopped mouldings and a small back stairs. No cellars beneath this part of the house.

The upstairs rooms have an assortment of panelling from the C16 to the early C18 (some of it removed or altered in the 1960s). In the E porch room and bedrooms in the N wing, panelling of c.1600; at the end of the N wing a suite of bedroom, lobby, and closet fitted up in the early C18. Gallery over the hall with panelling of c.1600, but the grand pilastered door surrounds at either end added c.1700.

STABLES, N of the house. Late C17. Central cupola with bell dated 1676. Excellent original fittings.

GARDENS. The informally planted terrace on the w side is a creation of the 1960s; the regular raised beds to the s were made in the 1980s.

SYDENHAM DAMEREL

4070

ST MARY. W tower with B type buttresses and big polygonal pinnacles. The church was burnt down in 1957 and rebuilt on a smaller scale, without the s aisle. Perp windows to the N, straight-headed. – MONUMENT. Nice slate plate to John Richards †1634, with the Cornish kind of folk engraving.

SCHOOL. 1820s, the traditional local two-storeyed type, with master's house on the ground floor.

MILL LODGE (former rectory). Handsome early C19 five-bay, two-storey stone house with deep eaves and panelled brick chimneys.

HORSEBRIDGE. The BRIDGE has six semicircular arches and cutwaters.

ROYAL INN, Horsebridge. Jolly front of three bays with large arched windows with Gothic glazing.

SYON ABBEY

7060

Rattery

Formerly Marley House, owned by the Palk family and then inherited in 1806 by the Carews of Haccombe. It became a convent in 1935. A fine neo-classical house, but altered and added to. The N front is unattractively pebbledashed. Nine bays, with a Greek Doric pedimented portico of four very tall columns, the proportions distorted by the filling in of the basement level on this side. U-shaped plan: the small back courtyard now built over. On the s and w sides the arcaded basements, still exposed, project as terraces in front of the house. Elegant entrance hall, divided from the staircase on the r. by two Ionic marble columns. Good cornices, the one to the staircase of an unusual design with fluting and little pendant scrolls. Dining room to the l. of the hall with good marble fireplace. The light and elegant details suggest a late C18 rather than an early C19 date. Plain convent wing to the W by *Benedict Williamson*, with cloister on the garden side.

TACKBEARE MANOR   2000
1 m. SW of Bridgerule

A small former manor house which belonged to the Gilberts from the late C16 was improved by Colonel George Harwood c.1820, truncated when it became a farmhouse in the mid C19, and confusingly reinstated and extended after 1896 by Albert de C. Glubb († 1946). S-facing hall range with Georgian windows, the porch now central. W wing demolished, E wing extended N and remodelled in 1936–7. Re-used granite Tudor doorway added on the E side, leading into a new stair-hall; other re-used openings elsewhere. The new beams, shutters, and mantelpieces were carved by *Glubb* himself. In the hall range, one ground-floor room with a simple ceiling of c.1700 (an oval of oakleaves); also a good cornice and panelled doors. In the dining room in the E range a plaster overmantel with two figures and the Gilbert arms in strapwork, although dated as late as 1693. In the room above, a bolection-moulded fireplace with two profile heads and arms, and on the same floor to the N, in a room with much Glubb carving, a hilarious piece of rustic political comment of the early C18: an overmantel with a robust Father Time with scythe and hourglass, a crown descending upon a grandly dressed George I on his right, and a discomfited Old Pretender running away naked.

TALATON   0090

ST JAMES. Perp W tower with diagonal buttresses, and at the angles high up, as on the stair-turret, niches for figures with most of the statues preserved (an unusual thing): Virgin and Child, Evangelists, St Michael. The date may be that of the early C15 BELL preserved in the tower, which was given by Johanne de Beauchamp († 1435). Perp two-bay S aisle of B type piers with standard capitals and four-centred arches. S door with C15 tracery; S porch enrichments dating from 1859–60, when the church was restored by *Edward Ashworth*, who added the N aisle and reconstructed the roofs, re-using the medieval bosses and complementing the medieval screen by a rich celure and a painted chancel roof. – FONT. C12, the table-top type, with four blank arches on each side. – SCREEN. Splendid, with coving to E and W; standard type. – Some late medieval BENCH ENDS incorporated in C19 seating. – STAINED GLASS. An interesting collection of c.1860 by *Henry Hughes* (working separately from his partner, Ward): E window with pictorial Crucifixion, chancel N with medallions (and an unusual inscription below in ceramic tiles), three N aisle windows, and the W window with a dramatic Last Judgement. – S aisle 1923 by *A.K.Nicholson*. – MONUMENTS. John

Leach †1613. Architectural, with strapwork, crude putti, and acrostic verse. – Charles Harwood †1718. Latin inscription on feigned drapery. – Plain tablet to Charlotte Augusta Harwood of Hayne House, †1848, the daughter of the architect Sir William Chambers.

The church is tucked away down a slope below the rest of the village. Nearby, two good examples of the early use of brick in this part of East Devon: Harris Farm, and the more complex Old Manor.

THE OLD MANOR is a large farmhouse whose S and W fronts of c.1700, in smart chequered Flemish-bond brickwork with many ovolo-moulded timber-mullioned windows, disguise a complex, rather puzzling older L-shaped structure. Its core is a late medieval house. At the W end of the front range, jointed crucks and end-cruck, all smoke-blackened, with an exceptionally narrow ground-storey room over which a larger chamber was jettied out into the open hall; a stud-and-panel screen with early C16 painted floral decoration is carried up over the internal jetty. Early on this range was extended E, possibly as a kitchen, with cruck trusses (also smoke-blackened). Excellent stud-and-panel screens to both sides of the cross-passage, with blocked doors on the E side. Geometric single-rib plaster ceiling in the upper chamber of the added N cross-wing; overmantel dated 1639, with arms of the Davy family. There was yet another extension E c.1700, coeval with the S and W fronts. Georgian staircase, and other later staircases.

HARRIS FARM, further down the lane, has an almost symmetrical late C17 front in brickwork similar to that at the Old Manor.

LARKBEARE. Georgian, seven bays, the centre three slightly projecting. Two storeys with quoins and parapet; dormers and end gables.

RYDON HALL. Three by four bays, late Georgian, stuccoed, with Ionic porch.

TAPELEY PARK
Westleigh

Set in a commanding position above the Torridge estuary, looking out towards Bideford over splendid terraced gardens. The stately neo-Renaissance appearance of the three-storey exterior is due to *John Belcher*, who transformed the earlier house for Augustus and Lady Rosamond Christie from 1898 to 1916. Behind Belcher's grander frontages lies the original house built c.1700 for William Clevland, a naval officer, and the C18 extensions made by later Clevlands: S wing with dining room, N wing with drawing room (now music room) and a low service range behind (the central courtyard is now filled in). The back wing is still of stone; the rest was given a harsh mid C19 casing of red brick with stone stripes. Belcher retained only the brick, enriching the entrance front with Portland stone porch, pilasters, and pediment, and the garden front with a long, single-storey colonnade. Inside, his chief alteration was the creation of a large staircase hall out of two rooms, with a mullioned landing window to the central court; the addition of the sumptuous Baroque fireplace in the music room; and the redecoration of the S wing, where the dining room has a ceiling in late C17 style and a heavy marble fireplace brought from Hamilton, Scotland. From the earlier house several good C18 fireplaces of coloured marble remain, a room with mahogany panelling, and some excellent C18 ceilings, notably one in the large music room with Rococo motifs, and one in the NW room (probably the earlier music room – see the plaster musical instruments) with boldly modelled flowers and fruit, in the tradition of late C17 work by John Abbot, mixed with more up-to-date C18 motifs.

Belcher's Italian terraced GARDENS adjoin earlier gardens including a walled kitchen garden, a brick ice house, and a circular shell-lined grotto with diamond windows and a pointed door. Adjoining the house the Georgian brick DAIRY with bell-turret, still with its interior tiles. Excellent early C19 neo-Grecian LODGE and gatepiers, with sphinxes and Greek-key decoration.

Base of a granite OBELISK of 1855 to Archibald Clevland, the last of the Clevlands, who died in the Crimean War. The obelisk itself was struck by lightning in 1932.

TAVISTOCK

4070

Tavistock is one of the most interesting and attractive of Devon's inland towns. The distinctive character of its spacious centre beside the river Tavy, with its picturesque grouping of low, castellated buildings in grey-green Hurdwick stone, is the legacy of its two successive landowners: the Benedictine abbey around which the town grew, and the Russell family, later Earls of Bedford, who acquired the monastic estates after the Dissolution, and remodelled the town in the C19 around the abbey remains.

The abbey was a royal foundation with a charter of 981. By the end of the Middle Ages it was the wealthiest and most important Benedictine house in the South West, in 1517 exempted from episcopal visitation and famous as an early centre of printing. The abbey church, known only from fragmentary excavations, was rebuilt in the C13 and described by Bishop Grandison as 'edificia pulcherrima'. It lay immediately S of the parish church of St Eustace, and was longer by about a third, its chancel extending E across what is now Bedford Square nearly to the town gate. Of the domestic buildings, which appear to have been largely rebuilt in the C15, more substantial fragments remain (*see* Perambulation 1). The cloister lay across Plymouth Road (the Bedford Hotel is on the site of the refectory in the S range). Further S there was a smaller cloister, probably with the infirmary, and to the E an irregular outer court, now Abbey Place. The present Abbey Bridge is post-medieval; the main town bridge lay further N.

The town developed around the abbey precinct. By the early C12 there was a market and annual fair, by the later C12 the town was incorporated as a borough, and in 1305 it became one of the four Devon stannary towns. Unlike most urban centres in the county, it had a steady history of prosperity, derived first from early medieval tin-mining, then from the cloth trade, and in the earlier C19 from the copper boom which continued until its abrupt collapse in the 1870s. During this last period the population rose from 3,420 in 1801 to a

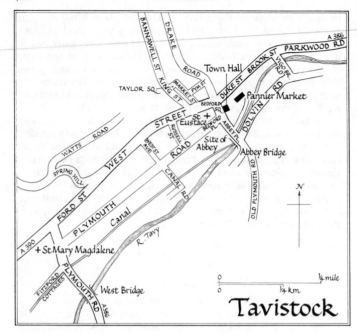

Tavistock

peak of 8,965 in 1861. The town expanded with genteel villas to E and W and more crowded working-class streets to the N, while around the fringes of the town the Duke of Bedford built about 300 model cottages (an exceptional gesture), provided a second church and cemeteries, and gradually transformed the town centre.

The old market area is still recognizable in the wedge-shaped Market Street, running N from West Street, the main thoroughfare N of the parish church. Here a few C17 houses remain, together with the early C19 Corn Exchange. To the S the abbey ruins mouldered until the C19. John Swete deplored their condition, and in 1797 wrote in his diary: 'I would have them neither laid desolate by the hand of Avarice or subject to the trim decorations of a capricious fancy.' In fact the Duke's first improvements, which started with the restoration of the gatehouse from 1822 to 1824, were conscientious rather than capricious, following the pinnacled and castellated style of the medieval survivals around the outer court. More radical change came after 1859, when part of the town E of the precinct was swept away for a new pannier market on a generous scale, the river banks were altered, Duke Street was created as a new E–W thoroughfare, and a grand Town Hall rose as a showpiece opposite the parish church. The town has retained its trim and confident C19 character with remarkable success. C20 eyesores are few, and even the car-parking has been arranged discreetly.

CHURCHES

ST EUSTACE. A Perp church on the large scale which befitted the prosperity of the Tavistock cloth trade. There was a dedication in

1318, but from this time the only likely remains are an ogee-arched recess in the N aisle, and perhaps the small arch at the E end of the N aisle and the base of the tower. The rest is late Perp. There are references to building work in 1352 and 1380, and to donations for the Clothworkers' Aisle in 1442, but it seems likely that nearly all of what we see now is early C16: upper parts of tower, nave with N and S aisles of five bays, chancel with two-bay N and S chapels, and an outer S aisle (the Clothworkers' Aisle). The W tower, with B type buttresses and tall pinnacles, was originally open to N and S, no doubt because the abbey was so close as to restrict space for processions. It also functioned as the town gateway to the abbey cemetery. Large four-light aisle windows with the simplest Perp tracery. The E end, in typical South-West-Country fashion, has no projecting chancel, and three gables in a row, all with five-light windows. Tall, slender nave arcades, with four-centred moulded arches. The outer S aisle alone is distinguished by a little decoration in the abaci, and by a more elaborately ceiled roof embellished with angels. Carved bosses to all the roofs. The spatial impression of the interior is of great amplitude without any surprises. General restoration and reseating 1844–5 by *John Hayward*.

FONT. The usual C15 octagonal type: shields in quatrefoils. – CHEST. Iron-bound; perhaps C14. – ORGAN CASE. 1845, without pipes. Covered with statues in 1879. – STAINED GLASS. A fine varied C19 collection. N aisle E 1876 by *Morris & Co.*, in memory of J.H. Gill of Bickham, Morris's brother-in-law. Evangelists, prophets, and scenes from the life of Christ. – N aisle second from E by *Kempe Studios*, third by *Fouracre*, fourth by *Dixon*. – S aisle E by *Wailes*, second from E by *Ward & Hughes*, third from E by *Fouracre*. – Clothworkers' Aisle E by *Powell*, first from E by *Mayer* of Munich, second by *Bacon*, third by *Clayton & Bell*. – Central E window 1949 by *Powell's* of Whitefriars. – PAINTINGS. Madonna and children, by *Deschwanden*, 1876. – Christ raising the daughter of Jairus, Dutch, Rembrandt school. – (CURIOSUM. Mrs Esdaile refers to a WALL PAINTING of Queen Elizabeth's tomb, a subject known to have been depicted in numerous London churches.)

MONUMENTS. John Fytz †1590, with wife and son †1605. Large standing wall-monument with recumbent effigies on a tomb-chest behind columns. The son kneels behind the couple, smaller, in profile against the back wall. The whole under an ornamental superstructure; not specially good. – Much better the alabaster monument, also standing against the wall, of John Glanville †1600 and wife. Tomb-chest on which he lies half-reclining, propped up on one elbow. She kneels quite separate in front on the floor, in profile, away from him and facing the altar. Two columns on the chest support an arch and two small allegorical figures. The portraits are uncommonly excellent. – B. Carpenter †1782 and his family. Large wall-monument with a long list of members of the family, and at the top the usual female standing by an urn, in this case with large ornamental palm-branches l. and r. By *J. Francis* of Clapham. – Bredall family (all surgeons). 1890 by *Hems*, with relief of Christ the healer. – In the churchyard, by the remains of the abbey cloister, an eloquent monument to John Gill †1811 and family; square concave-sided urn on a tall plinth with pilasters.

ST MARY MAGDALENE, Fitzford. Far more conspicuous in the

general picture of the town than the lower-lying St Eustace. Provided by the Duke as a chapel of ease for the w suburbs, reopened as an R.C. church in 1952. Built by *Henry Clutton* in 1865–7, exactly contemporary with his equally original church for the Duke at Woburn. The style is a most successful blend of Lombardic Romanesque and Transitional Gothic. Almost detached campanile-like NW tower, with very tall belfry windows and pinnacles, and a pyramid roof. Splendid s porte-cochère, with double flight of steps, and a rib-vault inside. The rest of the exterior plain, with lancet windows and parapet. Inside, an effective contrast of Hurdwick stone walls and Bath stone dressings. Lofty nave arcade with paired columns and nearly semicircular arches; blind arcading above in the chancel. Nave roof with tie-beams in the Italian manner. – FONT and PULPIT. Both of stone, on Devonshire marble columns.

CHRISTIAN BRETHREN CHAPEL, Abbey Place. *See* Perambulation 1.

METHODIST CHURCH, West Street Avenue and Chapel Street. 1856. Unecclesiastical Gothic: rendered, the w end with triple lancets and spindly turrets, the sides with an arched corbel table between buttresses.

UNITED REFORMED CHURCH, Russell Street. Gothic lancets; simple.

GOSPEL HALL (former), Bannawell Street. Even simpler, with big bracketed eaves and three arched windows.

CEMETERY, Plymouth Road. A Bedford gift. By *Henry Clutton*, 1881, the GATEWAY with large segmental arch and the tall, picturesque CHAPEL, with a rose window in the gable and Perp side windows above a high basement, all strongly buttressed.

PUBLIC BUILDINGS

TOWN HALL, GUILDHALL, and other public buildings in the town centre: *see* Perambulations.

GRAMMAR SCHOOLS. DRAKESMEAD SCHOOL, Russell Street, was the grammar school from 1837 to 1895, rebuilt for the Duke by *Edward Blore*. Plain Tudor: diagonal chimneys, gabled wings, stone mullioned windows. Its larger successor was the ALEXANDER SCHOOL (now part of Tavistock Primary School) at the w end of Plymouth Road, 1895 by *F. Bligh Bond*, Gothic, one-storeyed, with parapet and central bell-turret. Rear wings with covered cloister. This in turn was replaced by a new grammar school at Crowndale in 1931 (central courtyard, neo-Romanesque detail), by *J. Kerswill & Sons*.

ST RUMON'S C OF E SCHOOL, Dolvin Road. Built as a National School in 1847; Tudor.

TAVISTOCK COUNTY PRIMARY SCHOOL, Plymouth Road. 1856 by *E. Rundle*, built as the British School. One-storeyed, gabled, with large mullioned windows.

RUSSELL COURT, Drake Road. Now flats. Built as the workhouse, *c.* 1835, one of *Scott & Moffat*'s neat classical compositions, better preserved than most (cf. Bideford, Tiverton). Stuccoed, with the usual octagonal pedimented centre block, three-storey ranges on either side, one-storey entrance block with a large and dignified granite archway with channelled voussoirs and a pediment.

BRIDGES over the Tavy. The main bridge existing in the C13 was the East Bridge lying NE of the abbey precinct. ABBEY BRIDGE was built in 1763, and the East Bridge demolished in 1764. VIGO BRIDGE, built in 1773 for the new turnpike road, is especially handsome, with three round-headed arches and pointed cutwaters. WEST BRIDGE, originally of 1540, was replaced by a single span of concrete in 1939–40 (county architect *R. M. Stone*).

TAVISTOCK CANAL. Built in 1803–17 by *John Taylor*, to link the Tavy to Morwellham (q.v.), the river port on the Tamar. The basin lies off Canal Road, S of Plymouth Road (*see* Perambulation 3). The two-mile TUNNEL begins 3m. to the SW.

PERAMBULATIONS

1. The abbey precincts

A tour should start by the river in ABBEY PLACE. The approach to the bridge was cut through the abbey precinct in the C18, but the irregular shape of the outer court is still recognizable, with its gatehouse to the N and a range at an angle to it curving round to follow the original line of the river. The irregular pinnacled and castellated buildings, part C19, part medieval, make a pleasingly informal backdrop to the STATUE of Francis, seventh Duke of Bedford (1864 by *E. B. Stephens*). The GATEHOUSE is the most [151] substantial of the medieval survivals, with a late C12 core: one large and one small arch, round-headed with plain chamfers, in a two-storey later casing with pointed archways of two orders. Above these, two-light windows with square-headed dripstones, castellated gables, and corner pinnacles, all characteristic features of the late medieval domestic buildings of the abbey. The restoration of the gatehouse was the first of the sixth Duke's improvements, carried out in 1824 by *John Foulston*, hitherto esteemed for his neo-classical buildings at Plymouth, but at this moment becoming interested in a variety of styles (cf. Plymouth: Devonport). This is his first Gothic enterprise. He removed later windows to create a homogeneous late Gothic elevation, and reconstructed the upper parts, reasonably accurately, as drawings show. The interior was fitted up in 1829 for the Tavistock Library (founded 1799, and previously in a short-lived classical building opposite, designed by *Foulston*, which was disliked by the Duke). Bookshelves and a simple Gothic marbled fireplace remain in an upper room (now subdivided). To the E a wing was added by *Foulston* as the librarian's residence, with an upstairs lecture hall used in the C19 by the Freemasons (their throne remains; original panelling removed in 1983). Bust of the Duke of Bedford by *Francis*, given in 1839. The adjoining building on the site of the medieval domestic range with its picturesque little tower also had its windows regothicized by *Foulston*, and became a police station. Next to it is the GUILDHALL, now Magistrates' Court, constructed in 1848 in a matching Tudor style by the Bedford estate surveyor *Theophilus Jones*, on the site of medieval outbuildings. On the opposite side of Abbey Place the abbey buildings have gone, apart from a late medieval hall, set back from the road, possibly either part of the infirmary or the abbot's lodging. Used as a Presbyterian meeting house from 1691, it is now a CHRISTIAN BRETHREN CHAPEL. Polygonal castellated and pinnacled turrets, doorway with a square hood with quatrefoil spandrels. Interior all renewed. Adjoining to the N a small tower, the ground floor with an eight-rib vault with bosses. Between the chapel and the bridge two plain stuccoed houses; to the N, prominent at the corner of Bedford Place, the one-storeyed BEDFORD OFFICE, with Tudor windows and battlements in a monastic spirit. Next door, in BEDFORD PLACE, the BEDFORD HOTEL, its E part built between 1716 and 1725 as a private house for Jacob Saunders, a wealthy Presbyterian, on the site of the abbey refectory and acquired by the Duke of Bedford in 1752. The five-bay front was Tudorized by *Sir Jeffrey Wyatville* in 1822–9, when the building was converted to a hotel. Further work of 1830 by *Foulston* included a plaster-vaulted ballroom. The main entrance is through a generous one-storey porch. The interiors are much altered, but some attractive C19 Gothic cornices remain (cf. Warleigh House). In the older part, front rooms and hall have been united as a large dining room. Some C18 panelling and a simple stair with turned balusters survive. W of the main building an outbuilding with cupola, now the Bedford Bar.

Across Bedford Place, on the edge of the churchyard of the parish church (q.v.), a few relics of the medieval CLOISTER, a nearly straight-sided multi-moulded arch framing trefoil-headed blank arcading, in the style of *c.* 1240. W of the hotel the VICARAGE, of *c.* 1830. In its grounds the so-called BETSY GRIMBAL'S TOWER, the battered remains of a low W gatehouse, its broad moulded archway flanked by polygonal turrets. Hoodmoulded windows: quatrefoil peepholes at ground level. Preserved inside, various architectural fragments, including medieval timbers from the roof of the building now the Christian Brethren Chapel (*see* above), and (brought from elsewhere) three very early MEMORIAL STONES, probably C6, with inscriptions in Latin, two of them in ogham as well. The precinct wall S of the gatehouse has gone, but a good stretch survives alongside the pleasant RIVER WALK (reached by a path from Plymouth Road). At the SW corner a small battlemented tower with cusped single-light windows in square heads, called the STILL HOUSE.

2. The rest of the town centre

BEDFORD SQUARE, adjoining Abbey Place to the N, evolved after Foulston's work of the 1820s described above. It was part of a much more ambitious piece of urban replanning whose chief object was to free the area around the gatehouse from market use. Schemes had been discussed in the 1820s, but only a Corn Market in West Street was built (*see* Perambulation 3). The new plan of 1859 broadened the road E of the parish church into a square, with a new Town Hall on its E side, and swept away everything between this and the river for a new market bounded on the N side by Duke Street. To the S a service road (an afterthought) was built along a newly embanked riverside. The buildings are all by the Bedford surveyor *Edward Rundle*.

The TOWN HALL of 1860 reflects in its larger scale and bolder detail 151 the change from Regency to mid Victorian, although its castellated parapet and chimneys pay homage to the Perp spirit of the earlier Tavistock buildings. Symmetrical centre, an oriel over the archway to the market. Large Gothic mullioned-and-transomed windows light the first floor. Taller pinnacled tower on the r. The PANNIER MARKET, approached through the Town Hall or by the excellent cast-iron market gates to the S, is austerely robust, the aisles divided by granite segmental arches on solid pieces of wall rather than by iron columns. Wooden tie-beams with iron struts; central roof-lights. One-storey stalls to the S; to the N a taller range with the shopfronts to Duke Street making a show, set within segmental Gothic arches.

On the N side of Bedford Square two enjoyably self-conscious BANKS: the MIDLAND, with free-standing corner arcade and crowstepped gables, 1895, and LLOYDS, 1909, with more alien French château motifs (curved corner turret, oval windows). Above the part of the Midland Bank in DRAKE ROAD the CONSTITUTIONAL CLUB, with shallow corbelled-out oriel, then the town COUNCIL OFFICES in a stiffer Tudor Gothic, symmetrical, with two gables. To the l., in PYM STREET, former purpose-built printing works, KINGDON HOUSE, a remarkable Arts and Crafts 174 building by *Southcombe Parker*, *c*. 1906. An ingenious treatment of the ground floor to fit the sloping site. On the W side large arches with pronounced keystones; uphill to the N a lunette instead. Broad eaves on the N side, bold Art Nouveau lettering on the parapet round the corner. Opposite, the FRANCIS DRAKE, built as a temperance hotel, mostly bald late C19 Tudor, but incorporating parts of a C17 house, with a large four-centred granite archway, possibly brought from the abbey.

MARKET STREET, at the W end of Pym Street, is the main route from the town centre up the valley to the N, a broad wedge-shaped street, no doubt once an open market area, but now dividing in two at the S end, with two attractive islands of houses. In this area some of the oldest houses in the town. On the W side No. 22, with a jettied front; also several good early C19 shopfronts. Opposite, No. 4 Market Street, with C16 corbelled-out party-walls visible, and on the first floor fragmentary remains of late C16 ceilings and some bolection-moulded panelling. A side wall incorporates a small medieval two-light window. No. 5 is also a town house of the South Western type, with jettied timber front, now stuccoed over and classicized by a Venetian window in the dentilled gable. Separate back block with a jointed-cruck roof. No. 7 has a handsome Corinthian-columned shopfront. At the corner of Pym Street No. 9, the former UNION SAVINGS BANK, with early C19 channelled ground floor, and formerly a lettered parapet, applied to an C18 house. Then one of the town's few C20 commercial eyesores, the appallingly ugly COOP building of the 1960s. To the E, dug into the hill, a tall rubble stone MALTINGS; on its S side, deep down, remains of a water wheel fed from a tank by Drake Road; on the other side, narrow steps and the sites of cottages, recalling the overcrowded town of the C19. Here Market Street splits into

TAYLOR SQUARE and KING STREET, which later becomes
BANNAWELL STREET, with simple unspoilt terraces continuing
up the valley below the mighty VIADUCT of 1890 built for the
Plymouth, Devonport and South West Junction Railway: eight
arches of rough-faced granite (engineers *W. R. Galbraith* and *J. W.
Szlumper*).

3. W *of the town centre*

The two main roads leading W demonstrate planned and unplanned
growth. WEST STREET, the old road, has a haphazard mixture of
small houses with rendered fronts and windows of the C18–19;
some slate-hung fronts introduce a Cornish element. Two grander
exceptions: first a neo-classical building elegantly curving round
the corner of Market Street, with pairs of engaged Ionic columns
to the upper part; then the former CORN MARKET at the corner
of King Street, by *Charles Fowler*, 1835, with granite Doric columns to the once open ground floor, and good lettering on the
King Street frontage. Further on, No. 59 is a small neo-classical
house with a good interior: curved staircase, hall with fluted columns. In FORD STREET the FORD STREET CHARITY, found-
ed 1762, much restored. Central pediment; the details otherwise
very vernacular.

PLYMOUTH ROAD, parallel to West Street, was laid out by the
Duke of Bedford in the early C19, running past the Bedford Hotel,
and continuing with genteel villas. First a detour up CHURCH
LANE to take in No. 1, a small but distinguished neo-Grecian
house, plausibly attributed to *Foulston*. Pediments on both S and E
sides; S front with four Doric pilasters and a recessed tripartite
centre with a little incised ornament. Then, in Plymouth Road,
Nos. 1–6 BEDFORD PLACE, a restrained group by *Edward Blore*,
1836, still classical; channelled stucco ground floor, low linked side
porches. On the S side beyond the vicarage more picturesque pairs,
with three-storey towers over the recessed side entrances, and
hipped roofs over small bay-windows. Beyond these, CANAL
ROAD leads to the Tavistock Canal basin (*see* Public Buildings)
and an attractive group of early C19 low rubble stone warehouses
and cottages with round-arched windows, Nos. 2–3 Canal Road
unusually elaborate, with windows in giant arches, and slate-hung
fronts. Further W in Plymouth Road later stucco houses in groups
of four.

FITZFORD, at the W end of Plymouth Road, is a centre of its own,
with a church provided by the Duke (*see* St Mary Magdalene,
above), the additional landmark of the DRAKE MEMORIAL of
1883 by *Boehm*, the original of the one at Plymouth, and the Tudor
GATEHOUSE of the Fitz mansion, moved from further NE when it
was restored in 1871. The top stage reduced in height. Plain,
crenellated, with mullioned windows under straight dripstones;
large four-centred archway, a smaller granite doorway within it.

FITZFORD COTTAGES, built in 1862 facing the canal, form one of
the larger groups of the planned housing which the Duke of Bedford built on the fringes of Tavistock and in the neighbouring
countryside between the 1840s and the 1860s to alleviate the overcrowding caused by the mining boom. Thirty-six rubble-stone

cottages in groups of four, of two storeys, with a gable over each upper window and gabled projecting porches. Other groups of similar design e.g. across the river at Westbridge (the Bedford showpiece, sixty-four cottages built in 1850), in Dolvin Road (eighteen cottages, 1845–8) and in Parkwood Road (six blocks, 1859). The designer of them all – a total of about three hundred – was the architect-surveyor *Theophilus Jones*. Others, with yellow brick quoins and bay-windowed ends, at Kilworthy, Trelawny Road (ten blocks of flats). The standards were high for the time, and impressed contemporary commentators; each house has two or three bedrooms, and gardens with outbuildings including a pigsty.

On the slopes above the W end of the town, villas in their own grounds, taking advantage of the views. In SPRING HILL, BEDFORD VILLAS, two pairs of handsome plain stuccoed houses with hipped roofs; higher up in WATTS ROAD more varied designs with gables, bays, and towers (the N side built up only in the 1860s).

4. E *of the town centre*

In PARKWOOD ROAD Bedford cottages (*see* Perambulation 3). On the N side, BROOKLANDS, early C19, with tented balconies at the side; No. 15 (FERRUM HOUSE) is also early C19, with a rendered front with quoins and a porch canopy on iron supports. No. 41a was built as Gill & Rumble's FOUNDRY. Dated 1866. Later a wool-combing factory. Two storeys, rubble with granite dressings, round-arched windows.

5. *Outside the town*

The medieval parish was large; its area outside the town is now known as TAVISTOCK HAMLETS.

MOUNT TAVY, off Princetown Road. Now Mount House School. Early C19 three-bay garden front in pale brick; central bow with a delightful iron veranda. Three big arched windows on the ground floor. At the far end a conservatory. Entrance side of five bays, with a large Edwardian stone porte-cochère. The interiors also Edwardian, the main room roof-lit with a balustraded gallery. Behind the house an unusual former STABLE BLOCK of *c.* 1800; two concentric half-circles of stone buildings, a cobbled way between them, now converted to classrooms, with later slate-hanging. The centre has a gable, and circular windows flanking the doorway.

Further up Princetown Road OLD LODGE, an angle-fronted one-storeyed TOLL HOUSE of great charm, and an early pair of Bedford cottages, dated 1847.

KELLY COLLEGE, off Parkwood Road. Founded in 1867 by Admiral Kelly of Kelly House. Main buildings of 1872–4 by *C. F. Hansom*. An imposing institutional-Gothic front of Hurdwick stone with Bath dressings. Tall, symmetrical buttressed centre with six square-headed traceried upper windows. To the l. a short Gothic cloister leads to the gabled schoolrooms; beyond, the W wing, 1897 by *H. J. Snell*. The whole is less ambitious than planned; there were to have been dormitory blocks on the hill behind, and a separate chapel. The present chapel in the main block was originally the library: hammerbeam roof, iron columns along one side, organ recess with tall Dec stone arch. Library adjoining, also with hammerbeam roof, and an oriel window. Behind are later additions: science buildings of 1936 by *A.J.Parker*, of concrete blocks, but in a semi-Tudor style with mullioned windows; and theatre and assembly hall of 1962, portal-framed, faced with Hurdwick stone, by *L.Rossington*, who also designed the girls' dormitory in 1977, a tactful extension of a house of *c.*1930. Headmaster's house by *A.Kaldor*, 1979, pleasant, rendered, with tiled roof and wooden mullioned windows overlooking the valley.

The most distinguished adjunct to the school is NEWTON HOUSE, formerly Parkwood, by *Foulston*, of before 1836. 1–3–1 bays, Greek Doric, with four-column porch (probably re-used from Tavistock Library); tripartite windows (one blind). Some honey-suckle and incised line decoration. Good plasterwork inside, with delicate friezes; groin-vaulted central passage.

In the college grounds, the TRENDLE (from the Anglo-Saxon word for circle), an Iron Age enclosure.

LITTLECOURT, at the s end of Down Road. Originally a moderate-sized stone house by *Lutyens* for Major Gallie, 1910–14. The upper parts were demolished after a fire in 1935.

HAZELDON, off Okehampton Road. Asymmetrical Tudor Gothic. Two-storeyed porch with four-centred arch and quatrefoil parapet. Built for C.V.Bridgeman by *George Wightwick*, 1833–4.

TREE VIEW AND WOODLAND VIEW. Two mid C19 mine-captains' houses, the latter with a good central Doric porch.

NEW BRIDGE. Early C16; six pointed arches with cutwaters and refuges.

MINES. The C19 mines in the Tamar valley in Tavistock Hamlets were among the richest sources of copper in the world. As the copper became exhausted, many turned to the production of the arsenic found in association with copper. Among the most famous was the GREAT CONSOLS MINE in Blanchdown Wood, opened in 1844 and closed in 1901, but there is little to see except for heaps of waste. It had its own railway, opened in 1859, ending in a steep incline down to Morwellham quay (q.v.). Further s, at GAWTON MINE near the Tamar, there are remains of flues and chambers from the arsenic works.

See also Morwell Barton, Morwellham, *and* Walreddon.

TAWSTOCK

ST PETER. The church lies on its own in the grounds of Tawstock Court right below the lawn which extends in front of the house. It is one of the architecturally most interesting churches of North Devon. The fact alone that it possesses a tall tower over the cross-ing singles it out. There are parallels in South East Devon (Crediton, Colyton, Axminster, etc.), but even there only a few. Most of the visible evidence is early C14; exceptionally, the Perp style did only a little to improve or enlarge the church. The core may indeed be a cruciform building of the C12. The Dec arches appear to have been pierced through older walls, leaving solid

unmoulded chunks of masonry. Mouldings are applied only superficially: N and S arcades, for example, have square piers only
slightly chamfered, with C14 mouldings at the angles; the arches
have an unmoulded main part with much thinner moulded inner
arches resting on separate corbels, some with leaves in early C14
style, but the majority with heads. The crossing arches die into the
walls, without corbels. As for windows, the N transept N and the S
transept S windows have ogee reticulation typical of *c.*1320, and
the chancel E window has an octofoil above three cusped lights,
again early C14. The chancel N windows are in the same style.

The view up inside the crossing tower is most remarkable. The
square is by squinches of rather plain arches across the corners
converted into an octagon, and then again higher up by arches
across the angles into a square smaller than the crossing. This area
is then covered by a timber rib-vault with a star pattern. The top
stage of the tower has two-light Perp bell-openings and thin pinnacles on the battlements. Also Perp are the two-storeyed vestry
and alterations to the aisles and W windows. The S chapel, built of
carefully coursed ashlar, is late Perp: B type piers, standard leaf
capitals, and depressed pointed arches; straight-headed four-light
granite windows. Notable roofs: unceiled wagons in nave, chancel,
and S chapel. The S porch also has a wagon roof, boarded and with
cross-ribs, and in addition, in the place of the S doorway tympanum, a pattern of timber cross-ribs with stars of leaves at the
intersections. Where does it come from? The aisle ceilings are of
flat pitch with cross-ribs and bosses. They lie higher up than the
ceilings or roofs of the early C14, which must have rested on the
lower corbel-heads still visible. The wagon roofs of the transepts
were plastered over in the C18 and decorated each with a pretty
and very large star of long foliage trails. There was a tactful
restoration in 1867 by *Baker-King*, under *G.G.Scott*.

ALTAR, N transept. With an elementary kind of linenfold panelling in the front. Perhaps not originally an altar. The date must be
*c.*1500. – ROOD SCREEN of unusual design (cf. the parclose
screen at North Molton). Instead of sections of four lights, there
are here on each side of the doorway six individual tall narrow
lights, each with its own arched and traceried top. The screen has a
square framing and no coving. – PARCLOSE SCREEN with
standard tracery, but the doorway with spandrels decorated with
coarsely carved Renaissance profiles in roundels. – MANORIAL
PEW, N transept. A very remarkable object, small, with two solid
back walls panelled, and a complete ceiling with rosettes. The
decoration, which includes the Bourchier knot, especially the thick
balusters, is decidedly in the Franco-Flemish early Renaissance
taste, no doubt earlier than 1550. – TOWER GALLERY high up in
the transept, to connect the stair-turret with the central tower. The
parapet with good Perp decoration, but probably not originally in
that position. – BENCH ENDS. Not many, all with early Renaissance motifs, one with the arms of Henry VIII, others with monsters. – PULPIT. Wood, octagonal, on stumpy shafts, incorporating Perp panelling. – HOURGLASS STAND. In the form of
an arm (cf. Pilton). – LECTERN. An eagle of wood, on a robust
column. – FONT COVER. Crocketed, incorporating some medieval
detail. – ALTAR CLOTH. Embroidered; 1697. – TILES. Of Barn- 48

staple type (S chapel). – STAINED GLASS. N aisle W: C15 shields. –
N transept: C15 lights. – Chancel E: 1867, old-fashioned.

MONUMENTS. The best collection in the county, apart from
those in the cathedral. – Fine wooden C14 effigy, one of those
attributed to a Bristol workshop. Perhaps Eleanor or Margaret
Martin, from the family who owned Tawstock Court before the
Bourchiers. – Frances Lady Fitzwarren, 1589, S chancel chapel.
Six-poster (the earliest in Devon) with recumbent effigy and good
strapwork decoration. – Sir John Wrey †1597, N transept. Slate-
covered tomb-chest with large slate back-plate showing kneeling
figures, cartouche, and achievement. The monument was transferred to Tawstock from St Ive, near Callington in Cornwall, in
1924, a Wrey having married a Bourchier in 1652. The Wreys were
the successors of the Bourchiers at Tawstock. – Thomas Hinson
†1614 and wife, S chancel chapel. Wall-monument with the usual
kneeling figures facing each other. Hinson was Surveyor and
Receiver General to the third Earl and married a 'Cosyne
Germain'. – William Bourchier, third Earl of Bath, †1623,
chancel. A sumptuous standing wall-monument of alabaster, with
recumbent effigies on a sarcophagus, frontally kneeling smaller
figures to heads and feet, a big strapwork cartouche with inscription behind, and a far-projecting cornice with semicircularly rising
centre. Of excellent quality, perhaps London work; the ribbonwork on the pilasters, and trails of leaves around the inscription,
are both familiar motifs of the 'Southwark School'. – Mary St John
†1631, chancel, and William Skippon †1633, S chapel. Both with
kneeling figures. Skippon was steward and treasurer to the third
Earl. – Peter Gold, servant of the Bourchiers, erected 1666.
Unusual painted slate tablet with heraldic detail. – Henry Bourchier, fifth Earl of Bath, †1659, S chapel. Erected by his widow
before 1680. A splendid, relatively restrained free-standing monument of white and black marble. Big base on which four seated
dogs support a big square bulging sarcophagus. At the four corners
four black obelisks. – Lady Rachel Fane, wife of the above, †1680,
S chapel. Life-size standing figure of white marble, in heavy robes,
by *Balthazar Burman*. The monument is an exact copy of the statue
of the Countess of Shrewsbury at St John's College Cambridge,
made in 1672 by Burman's father, Thomas.

Lady Rolle †1705. Pretty cartouche by *Thomas Jewell* of Barnstaple. – Sir Henry Northcote †1729, N transept. By *T. Jewell Jun.*
Architectural, with cherubs. – Mary Lady Wrey †1751, S transept.
With white and pink marble sarcophagus on rocaille feet, very
handsome. – Ann Chilcot †1758, wife of Thomas Chilcot, organist
of Bath, N transept. Also a fine piece of its date, in coloured
marbles, with the inscription surmounted by a tondo with a seated
allegorical figure, and above that the usual obelisk with the profile
portraits of husband and wife in one roundel. The inscription plate
commemorating him was never filled in. – Sir Bourchier Wrey
†1784, S transept. Stately, absolutely plain free-standing urn on a
big square pedestal. – Ann Lady Wrey †1791, by *King* of Bath.
With a standing woman by an urn below two sprigs of weeping
willow. – Ann Bourchier Wrey †1813. Also with a female by an
urn. – Lady Marianne Wrey, by *H. Hems*, 1896 (S transept). Oval
tablet with naturalistic rose. – Numerous minor cartouches and

tablets of the late C17 and early C18 and other later ones, by e.g. *Gould* and *Youing* of Barnstaple and *Stephens* of Exeter; also many good slate LEDGER STONES in the s chapel.

Outside the s porch, SUNDIAL by *John Berry*, 1753, one of his most elaborate, showing the time in the principal capitals of Europe, and also, for example, at Cairo, Babylon, and Port Royal.

TAWSTOCK COURT. From 1940 St Michael's School. In a magnificent position above the church, overlooking the Taw valley. Of the mansion held by the Bourchiers from the mid C15 the GATE-HOUSE remains, s of the house: two polygonal turrets and a four-centred arch. Above this a little classical aedicule with arms. If the date 1574 above refers to the whole building, it is yet another example of the persistence of the tradition of the medieval gate-house in Devon in the later C16 (cf. Shute). In the turrets single-light windows with the usual Perp foliage in the spandrels.

The house of the Bourchiers, later Earls of Bath, may have faced the gatehouse. But the main front is now to the E, rebuilt by *Sir* 127 *Bourchier Wrey* after a fire in 1787, it is said to his own design, although *Sir John Soane* visited in 1789, and provided drawings for the finishing details, chiefly for the interior. The carpentry was carried out by a local man, *Edward Boyce* (contract in the Soane Museum). The long, immaculate stuccoed front is in the Gothic of the moment, not dissimilar in effect from Hartland Abbey (q.v.) rebuilt a few years earlier. Symmetrical and castellated, the two-storey canted bays carried up as slightly taller polygonal angle-turrets. Arched windows with Gothic glazing. In the centre a castellated pediment and projecting porch.

The house extends back with two long wings, the s one possibly incorporating older work, and embellished by C19 stone mullioned bay-windows. The porch on this side was moved from the s front, and corresponds to drawings in the Soane Museum. The N wing is largely masked by a one-storey extension of 1978. From the W the house has a quasi-Elizabethan aspect, the result of extensive 'improvements' of 1885. The additions at the back are of dark stone; many mullioned windows with red terracotta dressings probably from *Lauder & Smith*'s Barnstaple pottery. The long, narrow courtyard is closed by an entrance archway complete with portcullis.

The C18 plan of the interior is still recognizable: a central hall with corridors off to l. and r. providing access to the main rooms. The fittings are predominantly C19. Large panelled hall, incorporating some old woodwork, e.g. in the grand overmantel with coat of arms, motto, and panels with Adam and Eve, Abraham and Isaac. More re-used panelling in the NW room. The corridors with Greek-key motif must belong to the late C18 work, as does Soane's top-lit stair-hall in the N wing. The stairs have been renewed, but Ionic columns remain on the landing, with matching pilasters against the opposite wall; from a flat ceiling pendentives rise to carry an elliptical glazed oval lantern. The other C18 room is the library in the s wing, with built-in bookcases with open pediments and Ionic pilasters and a fireplace to match. The ceiling has a quilt-like pattern. Frieze of hanging garlands.

Close to the W entrance, two former STABLE BLOCKS face each other, both pedimented: the W one of stone with brick arches, early C18; the larger E one stuccoed, perhaps of the same date as the rebuilding of the house.

Good GATEPIERS. Near the entrance to the drive a delightful rustic LODGE with tree-trunk veranda and Gothic windows.

FOLLY TOWER. Circular, with stair-turret. Gothic windows.

BRETHREN CHAPEL, Eastacombe. Built by the local evangelist Robert Gribble c. 1817–18. Tall rendered front with windows of two heights.

PROVIDENCE METHODIST CHAPEL, Hiscott. Built by the Bible Christians in 1845. Low and rendered; round-arched openings.

CORFFE HOUSE AND LITTLE CORFFE. Tall three-storeyed Regency stuccoed front with deep bracketed eaves. At the side a shallow bow-window with pretty tented balcony. (Good Adam-style decoration in the main reception room: swagged medallions on the walls, ceiling with oval centrepiece. Older W wing with C16 moulded beams.)

FISHLEIGH BARTON. A large farmhouse. The medieval core is the centre of the present house, with a smoke-blackened common-rafter roof, very unusual for Devon. To the E a kitchen with a large fireplace roofed on trusses with short curved feet. To the W, the C17 house, essentially on a three-room and cross-passage plan, but with the room beyond the hall expanded into a cross-wing on jointed-cruck roof-trusses. Excellent C17 details include an original door and ovolo-moulded door frame with the initials LI and the date 1627, and two good plaster ceilings in first-floor rooms, one with intersecting ribs and pendants. To the W of the house a BARN with cruck trusses.

WICK. Early C15 (smoke-blackened roof of jointed crucks with square-set ridge; evidence for a louvre), remodelled and enlarged by C17 rear wings. Inner-room fireplace dated 1638.

See also Harracott.

8090   TEDBURN ST MARY

The main settlement is now along the Exeter–Okehampton road; the church lies away to the NW, where the old village used to be.

ST MARY. Roughcast, apart from the tower, which is of ashlar volcanic trap, and the chancel, which was rebuilt in the Dec style in the restoration of 1868 by *Ashworth*. W tower with diagonal buttresses and polygonal stair-turret. S porch with four heads in the corners for projected vaulting. The rest an intriguingly complicated story. S doorway, round-headed with dripstone, perhaps C12. S transept with lancets and ogee-headed recess in the S wall (*c.* 1300?). N aisle with odd tracery in the straight-headed W window. Could it be C14? The N arcade has been reconstructed: the W and E responds of volcanic stone, with carved angels, remain from a C14 arcade; in between there are tall arches on Beer stone piers. One capital with carved figures, others standard. The N chapel is also early – see the arches and E respond of *c.* 1300. Restored wagon roofs to nave and aisle. – BENCH ENDS with tracery panels and shields. – C19 TILES and patterned GLASS in the chancel, all that remains of an elaborate decorative scheme. – BRASS. Jane Gee † 1613, wife of Edward Gee, rector. Kneeling figures above a long English and Latin verse of unusual quality. – MONUMENT to the Langdon family. Perp aedicule, probably of *c*. 1854.

RECTORY. Early C19 three-bay stuccoed front; Doric porch. Older parts behind.

THORNWOOD HOUSE. An early Victorian Italianate villa, stuccoed, the wings with two shallow pedimented gables, the centre recessed, with Ionic porch.

LITTLE HACKWORTHY, Hackworthy Lane. A formerly prestigious house (Hockworthy Barton in the C17) which declined into a modest farmhouse and is now disguised by a C19 front and surrounded by cob farm buildings. Three-room cross-passage plan, the smoke-blackened roof on jointed crucks and end-crucks. The upper end was possibly always two-storeyed, as it is subdivided from the hall by a solid cross-wall with a C16 door frame at first-floor level. In the rear wall, magnificently preserved, a four-light oak hall window with cusped trefoil heads. The lower room has a rare type of early C17 plasterwork ceiling with frieze, the dominant motif double-headed eagles with lions, dogs, and two heraldic shields. At the rear, opposite the cross-passage and contained by the courtyard walls, a detached kitchen block with large brick stack and integral oven: a rare survival (cf. North Morte, Mortehoe) of a type of building which may once have been much more common on the Devon farm.

In the parish a large number of similarly substantial cob farmhouses with well-preserved internal features of the early C16 to late C17. Among them are GREAT HUISH, Huish Lane, with an early C16 screen with carving; HIGHER BROOK; LILLYBROOK, Six Mile Hill; VENNEMILE, Church Hill; and WINDOUT, Windout Lane, with a simple plaster ceiling similar to the one at Little Hackworthy.

EARTHWORK, at the extreme NW corner of the parish. Small, triangular, of the Iron Age. The name Shilstone a little to the S suggests the former existence of the stone structure of a burial mound.

TEIGNGRACE

ST PETER AND ST PAUL. Rebuilt in 1786 by the Templers of Stover House (q.v.). The Templers were people of taste, as is clear from the building and their monuments. The church is Gothic outside, with a short W tower and pointed windows, their casements imitating the plain intersecting kind of tracery which was what appealed most to the late C18. But the interior is cruciform with arms all of equal length, i.e. a central plan – an utterly un-Gothic concept. The E wall only has a slight extension, an apse with a pointed head. Above the centre of the little building a shallow unlighted dome, perfectly circular. Here the adopted Gothic idiom is entirely forgotten. – The elegant MONUMENTS are both interesting and varied. They have eloquent inscriptions, but are not of an excessive size. The earliest are two wall-monuments flanking the chancel arch, to James Templer †1782 and his wife Mary †1784, the first with a mourning figure at an urn, in a roundel, the second with a similar theme in a lunette at the top. – Charles Templer †1786 has a delicate shipwreck relief; Captain William Templer †1805 and his brother, both also drowned at sea, have the only signed tablet, a fat weeping angel by an urn above a Gothic fan coving, by *Coade & Sealy*. – The NELSON MEMORIAL, of 1805, is also of *Coade* stone. It has the unusual form of a figure of Fame above a globe, inscribed 'slain in battle'. – James Templer †1813 has another *Coade* monument: a female figure reclining on an urn, a standard type. – Other simpler tablets include two to naval associates, Cornwallis Viscount Hawarden †1803 and Captain Richard Dalling Dun †1813, both with chaste urns, and one to the Rev. John Templer †1832 (the first of two Templer rectors) with draped urn on sarcophagus. – The FURNISHINGS are simple. Two FONTS, a small C18 bowl on a hexagonal baluster, and a more generously sized carved marble one of the C19. – Two C18 PAINTINGS, a large and dramatic Pietà above the apse, by *Barry*, and a monk kneeling before the Virgin in the S transept. – Contemporary ORGAN CASE by *James Davis*.

The STOVER CANAL, constructed by the Templers in 1790–2 under the engineer *Thomas Gray*, runs for two miles from Jetty Marsh at Newton Abbot (q.v.) to Ventiford in the parish. It was intended to continue to Bovey Tracey. It served to irrigate the land around Stover (q.v.), but was used chiefly for the export of local ball clay to the Staffordshire potteries, and after 1820, when the Haytor tramway was built, for transporting granite. At VENTIFORD BASIN a derrick remains; at LOCKSBRIDGE a granite lock with top gates, beam, and paddle gear, and stone buildings in a former maintenance yard. Another lock at GRAVING DOCK LOCK, and at TEIGNBRIDGE CROSSING a canal BRIDGE dated 1798 and low stone buildings for storing ball clay.

9070

TEIGNMOUTH

Teignmouth was famous as a port and shipbuilding centre long before it became known as a resort. The town originated as two settlements, each with its own parish church: East Teignmouth with St Michael overlooking the sea, West Teignmouth with St James above the harbour on the Salty, the large expanse of water at the mouth of the estuary. The French found it worth while to attack harbour and town on two notorious occasions: in 1340 and 1690. The port prospered in the C18 with the growth of Newfoundland trade, and in the C19 as an important exporting point for Dartmoor granite and local ball clay.

Meanwhile the resort developed. Shaldon, across the estuary, already in Polwhele's time had 'several neat cottages and some new built houses in a decent style'; Teignmouth itself was called 'a fashionable watering place' in 1803. Major expansion came a little later. Both churches were rebuilt soon after 1815, and and in 1826, coinciding with the creation of George Templer's New Quay, and the bridge linking Teignmouth and Shaldon, the formal composition of Den Crescent, with its central assembly rooms, was laid out on the sandspit at the head of the estuary. Encouraged by the arrival of the railway in 1846, the resort remained popular into the C19; the sea front was embellished by an esplanade and pier, in the town centre modest Regency buildings were supplemented by quite presumptuous mid C19 urban terraces, and villas dotted the hills beyond.

The C20 has not been kind to Teignmouth. The damaging gaps

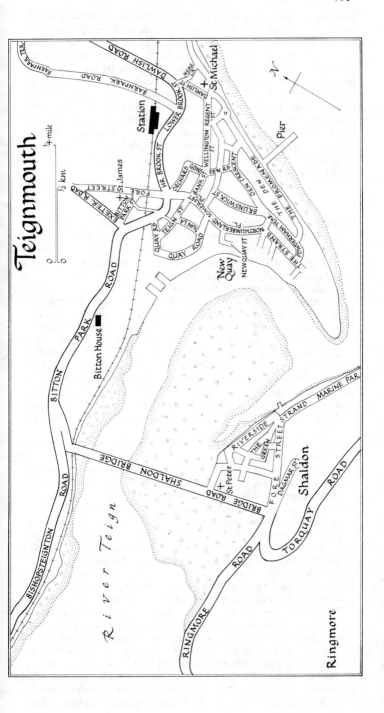

Teignmouth

made by Second World War air raids have been filled, but many of the stuccoed buildings have lost their original detail. The old warehouses around the quays have largely given way to indifferent modern structures, and, most disastrously, a destructive inner ring road has completed the fragmentation of the town begun by the C19 railway line. The centre, freed from through traffic, still has charm, although the splendid sweep of Den Crescent would be much enhanced if it could be freed from its mediocre clutter of C20 amenities. One major mansion in its grounds, Bitton House, still overlooks the estuary, but the hills behind the town are now covered by ever-expanding in-different C20 suburbs. In contrast, across the water, Shaldon and Ringmore still retain something of their early C19 character, with a pretty sprinkling of *cottages ornés*.

CHURCHES

ST JAMES, Bitton Park Street. W tower of red sandstone, unbuttress-ed, with small lancets, supposed to be of 1268 and part of the town defences. The body of the church is an octagon, designed by *W.E. Rolfe* of London, a pupil of Soane, and built by the Exeter architect *A. Patey*, 1817–21. An undogmatic but most successful building. Battlemented, with long thin windows and polygonal buttresses to each corner; octagonal central lantern, battlemented and slate-hung, with lace-like window tracery. Light, airy interior, with tall clustered cast-iron piers and thin cast-iron rib-vaulting. Originally with galleries on three sides; those to N and S were removed during remodelling in 1889–90 by *W.H. Lloyd* of Birmingham. – REREDOS. The centre is medieval: five bays of Dec canopy-work. Sold for £1 when the old church was demolished; reinstated and restored in 1891, with additional side panels. The texts come from the altarpiece of 1821. – CHEST. With figures of St Peter and St Paul from a pulpit of 1735. – The present PULPIT is of 1900.

ST MICHAEL. The parish church of East Teignmouth, directly above the beach. The cruciform core of *Andrew Patey*'s rebuilding of 1823 survives between E and W additions: engagingly naïve neo-Norman, entirely unworried by archaeological accuracy. Symmetrical S front, with entrance by a Norman doorway in the S transept. The windows tall and round-arched but filled with fancy Perp tracery. Inside, tall polygonal piers and block capitals, but wagon roofs. The exag-geratedly muscular chancel is of 1875 by *Frederick C. Deshon*: grey limestone, but with an E window of five trefoiled lancets in Ham Hill stone. Heavily moulded chancel arch, steeply stepped up sanctuary, S windows high up with outsize rere-arches and splayed sills. Grey limestone W front and tower 1887–9 by *R.M. Fulford*; a rather cramped W porch, but a satisfying five-stage tower with elongated belfry windows, openwork battlements, and big polygonal pin-nacles, an important accent in the Teignmouth townscape. At the W end, piers and springers show that Fulford planned to rebuild the nave as well. S chapel 1925–7 by *Sir Charles Nicholson*, grey limestone, orthodoxly well-mannered Perp. – REREDOS. 1875 by *Deshon*, stone with mosaic panels, angels under gables, trefoil canopies under little Byzantine domes. – FONT by *Fulford*, 1887. A rich composition in coloured and polished marbles, clearly

influenced by Butterfield. – PAINTING. Ecce Homo by *King* of
Exeter, 1821, originally the altarpiece, now in the N aisle. –
STAINED GLASS. Several of the late C19 and early C20 by the Drake
firm: *Frederick Drake* was a churchwarden. By the S door a lancet to
him of 1921, showing him as St James of Ulm, patron of glaziers, by
Maurice Drake.

ST PETER, Shaldon. 1893–1902 by *E.H.Sedding*, the site given by
the Rev. R. Marsh-Dunn. A superlative example of Arts and
Crafts inventiveness. Exterior of red sandstone and grey limestone,
striped. The long river front strong and uniform, firmly articulated
by flying buttresses (added in 1932 by *Caröe*) carried up above the
parapet. Variety is provided at either end. Apsed chancel, N transept and low vestry, SE apsed chapel. W front with a low baptistery
between two lobbies, pierced buttresses, and a large W window with
exuberantly imaginative flowing tracery, deeply recessed within
a shady Gothic arch, favourite devices of the architect's uncle,
J.D. Sedding (cf. e.g. Holy Trinity, Sloane Square, London).
Powerful interior, dominated by the great W window. Nave with
tall octagonal piers, two-centred arches with alternating blocked
voussoirs – no doubt intended to be carved like the ones in the
chancel – small clerestory, and a mighty panelled barrel-vault on
big transverse arches (cf. Caröe's St David, Exeter). The Blessed
Sacrament Chapel makes a delightfully intimate contrast, also
vaulted, with its own little S aisle.

The FURNISHINGS in a great variety of materials are also outstanding – so much so that their entrancing detail distracts from
the architecture. The ensemble around the chancel arch is especi-   164
ally effective. – Huge SCREEN with very wilful stone tracery, good
ironwork in between; two kneeling angels flanking the entrance. –
PULPIT. A splendid piece of *c.* 1910. Coloured marbles and alabaster; stylized foliage and bird carving in a Romanesque style. –
Bronze LECTERN with pelican and snake. – FONT. Octagonal
corner shafts with free Gothic foliage. – ALTAR FRONTAL and
RAILS likewise with foliage. – CHOIR STALLS also inventively
carved. – The S chapel is divided off by excellent IRON SCREENS
and has good STAINED GLASS designed by *Sedding*.

ST NICHOLAS, Ringmore Road. A small C13 chapel, rebuilt in
1622, largely reconstructed in 1894 by *E.H.Sedding*. – Plain tall
goblet-shaped Norman FONT.

OUR LADY AND ST PATRICK (R.C.), Dawlish Road. 1878 by
J.A.Hansom & Son, quite large and ambitious, in Hansom's
characteristically jerky and earnest Gothic. W front with NW turret
and a SW baptistery with thin buttresses with niches, rising to a
pinnacle. Tall S aisle with transverse gables. Lower N aisle with
stilted arcade arches and clerestory with spherical triangles (cf.
Abbotskerswell). Canted apse, with some good STAINED GLASS.

UNITED REFORMED CHURCH, Dawlish Road. Built as a Congregational chapel in 1882. A pendant to the R.C. church on the other
side of the railway line, also on a prominent hillside site. A fine,
complex composition from the SW: tall, polygonal W end with
large geometric traceried windows, generous porch, corner turret
with niche, and, rising behind, a central flèche. Much good carved
detail, of a higher standard than on average Nonconformist churches, see especially the shafts ending at eaves level with capitals,

and the foliage around the W doorway. Schools and church hall of
1903 adjoin; mullioned-and-transomed windows.

GOSPEL HALL, Bitton Park Street. Built as Ebenezer Chapel *c.* 1800
by a congregation which had George Muller as its pastor in the
1830s. A charming stuccoed front with the ogee-headed windows
and blank quatrefoils typical of unscholarly medievalizing designs
of the late C18–early C19. Tall interior with former gallery.

METHODIST CHURCH, Somerset Place. 1845, of stone, three
gables, arched openings, quatrefoils above side lancets.

WESLEYAN METHODIST CHAPEL, Shaldon. 1867. Tall, round-
arched windows; large roundel in the gable.

ST SCHOLASTICA'S ABBEY, Dawlish Road. Built for a community
of Benedictine nuns founded at Dunkirk in 1622, which moved to
Hammersmith in 1793. Established here through the patronage of
Isabella English, a sister of one of the nuns, and Bishop Vaughan
of Plymouth, in buildings of 1861–3 by *George Goldie*. Imposingly
sited three-storeyed convent buildings, grey limestone with lively
use of Bath stone for window dressings, and red sandstone for
banding and voussoirs. Priest's house at the corner. An irregular
cloister with corridors on two sides. Chapter house to the E (1872),
distinguished on the cloister side by an upper arcade of red and
white stone arches on detached columns.

CHAPEL with polygonal W turret, the interior narrower than
Goldie first intended, plain apart from some foliage carving in the
apsed sanctuary. All redecorated in pale colours in 1962. – Large
alabaster REREDOS added in 1932. – Sanctuary CEILING painted
at the same time by *Elphege Pippet* of *Hardman*'s. – Some original
grisaille STAINED GLASS. – Side ALTARS with marble columns,
by *Hansom*. – W gallery on large stone columns.

Immediately N of the convent, DUNESK, now an old people's
home, the house of Isabella English. Mid C19 stuccoed Tudor. A
pretty cast-iron footbridge over the drive.

PUBLIC BUILDINGS

BITTON HOUSE, Bitton Park Road. Now council offices. Well sited
in its own grounds (now a public park), on the N slope above the
estuary. The late C18 house was owned from 1812 to 1833 by
Admiral Pellew (*see* Canonteign), then by the poet Winthrop
Mackworth Praed (†1839), for whom it was remodelled by Soane's
pupil *George Basevi*. Stuccoed, and now garishly painted. Long S
front overcrowded with Grecian trimmings, the original house
probably the centre, with two full-height bows. W side with two
canted bays and tented veranda; entrance side with projecting
wings and canted porch with a little fan-vault. Elegant curved
staircase with stick balusters. Over an inner door, painted glass
portrait of Admiral Pellew. Some good cornices, but the interior
altered. Early C19 ORANGERY, of wood, with a hipped glazed
roof. A forceful design, with tall round-headed openings in groups
of three, between octagonal corner columns. Canted ends.
Restored in 1984.

LIBRARY, Bitton Park Road. By *Narracott, Tanner & André*,
c. 1966–70. Grey concrete blocks; prominent boat-profiled roof. A

brave Corbusian effort on an awkward left-over site above the disruptive inner ring road.

TRINITY SCHOOL, Buckeridge Road. Early C19 stuccoed villa with veranda; red brick additions of 1881 by *Goldie, Child & Goldie*.

STATION. 1884. One-storeyed, with three iron-crested pavilions (cf. Torquay). Limestone with blue brick dressings. Long canopy to the road.

SHALDON BRIDGE. Originally built of timber in 1825–7 by *Roger Hopkins* of Plymouth, 1,671 ft long, a record at the time. Rebuilt in 1930, with twenty-three fixed spans of varying width, concrete decks on steel girders, and a central drawbridge. Pretty Grecian angle-fronted two-storey TOLL HOUSE at the W approach.

PIER. 1865–7 by *J. W. Wilson*. Wood and iron, originally 600 ft long, now shorter.

LIGHTHOUSE. Small limestone tower of 1845. Octagonal metal lantern with weathervane.

PERAMBULATION

The grandest display of the early C19 resort is DEN CRESCENT, looking out to sea from the sandspit (the den or dune) at the head of the estuary. 1826 by *Andrew Patey* of Exeter. Still an impressive composition, despite the loss of some original balconies, ugly roof excrescences on the centrepiece, and a deplorable assortment of C20 clutter between the crescent and the sea, including an ill-placed theatre. Detached centre block, built as assembly rooms, now a cinema, with projecting ground floor with low, severe, unfluted Greek Doric columns; elegant Ionic columns above; pedimented centre; still a stately centrepiece despite the strip of ground-floor shops, crying out for sympathetic restoration. The flanking houses, all stuccoed, have round-arched ground-floor windows. Rusticated doorcases still in the late C18 manner, but Grecian ornament to the first-floor balconies. The flank wall facing the centre block is treated handsomely, with a Grecian porch and incised pilasters. The surrounding streets are less ambitious. To the W, POWDERHAM TERRACE, no longer Grecian, but early Victorian mixed Italianate, with pedimented upper windows and a lively roof-line with bracketed gables and dormers. In BRUNS-WICK STREET behind, modest early Victorian terraces; also DOLPHINS, a two-bay house with pretty ogee-shaped windows with Gothick glazing (cf. Gospel Hall).

Further E in REGENT STREET a few buildings remain to show the modest scale of the early resort, notably the ROYAL LIBRARY (W. H. Smith built out on the ground floor) of 1815 by *W. E. Rolfe* of London (*see* St James). Three bays with a shallow central bow; eclectic details: colonnettes within recessed panels, windows with intersecting glazing bars. The adjoining Nos. 1–2, of *c.* 1820, have a nice bulging series of full-height Regency bows. To the E, LLOYDS BANK is a dignified intruder of *c.* 1900, limestone with sandstone dressings and a corner entrance with bulgy columns. A little further on MERE LANE, still picturesque and winding, leads down from Dawlish Road to the sea, past St Michael's church (q.v.) and CLIFTON HOUSE, three storeys with central pediment and Soanian pilasters. In DAWLISH ROAD the villas begin: the best is CLIFFDEN (old people's home), with bow-windows facing w across its large grounds.

For the older town centre one must retrace one's steps along Regent Street to its continuation: WELLINGTON STREET–BANK STREET–TEIGN STREET, the line of the old main thoroughfare. WELLINGTON STREET has one grand terrace on the N side (Nos. 14–16), in stuccoed Kensington-Italianate, four storeys high, as are the more busily designed groups up the hill in ORCHARD GARDENS, some with bay-windows with triple windows above, others with hooded windows and bracketed cornices. The inner ring road abruptly terminates this detour, so back s now to SOMERSET PLACE, the main N–S route, leading into the broad and pleasant NORTHUMBERLAND PLACE. Plenty of early C19 bow-windows and Victorian shopfronts, especially good No. 51 with two curved upper bows; also the DEVON ARMS with Tuscan porch. Further s, where the street narrows, several houses with emphasized quoins.

Off to the w, NEW QUAY STREET leads to the NEW QUAY built in 1820 by George Templer of Stover (q.v.) for the export of Hay Tor granite, with the NEW QUAY INN with Greek Doric porch overlooking the harbour, and a two-storey stone warehouse on the jetty. Between the quays and Northumberland Place several small lanes, among them SUN LANE, with the interesting survival of a FISH SMOKING HUT: two upper weatherboarded storeys over a rubble stone ground floor, one wooden-mullioned window to the street. Now to TEIGN STREET, mostly modest and haphazard, but including some nice two-storey stucco houses, 'the house of Luny, marine artist †1837', three bays, set back behind an archway, and No. 25 at the end, taller, with angle pilasters. Opposite, QUAY ROAD, with one old four-storey warehouse amidst indifferent C20 buildings.

The upper end of West Teignmouth around St James has been brutally sliced off from the centre by the double barrier of railway and inner ring road. One can reach it on foot in the complicated fashion beloved by road engineers by underpass and bridge at the N end of PELLEW ARCADE, off Teign Street. This is a well-intended but tatty pedestrian precinct incorporating a few older buildings among new flats. When one has reached St James one can enjoy a little oasis with the Gospel Hall (q.v.) and a few simple stuccoed houses in BITTON PARK STREET EAST.

Teignmouth suburbs stretch uphill far inland. The larger C19 villas have mostly given way to later C20 estates, and only a few items need be mentioned in addition to those included under Public Buildings above. BARNPARK ROAD NE of the station has a good series of Victorian villas, and at the end, BARNPARK TERRACE, once a handsome secluded group with its own lodge, now messed about, with the Grecian detail mostly stripped off. In FERNDALE ROAD, further N, No. 30, a *cottage orné*, thatched, with Gothick glazing. Further down, paired stuccoed and gabled houses.

SHALDON, across the estuary, is more intimate and less spoilt than Teignmouth itself, but beginning to be threatened by late C20 development, especially in Fore Street. In BRIDGE ROAD Nos. 6–9, two storeys, incised pilasters. At the corner, a simple SCHOOL HALL, minimal Gothic. Opposite, in FORE STREET, HUNTERS

LODGE, a highly ornamented early C19 *cottage orné*: three gables, canted bow-windows, Gothick windows with much intricate glazing, oddly juxtaposed with the classical features of vermiculated quoins and doorway. The central gable has a circular chimney pot.

Further on one soon arrives at a pleasant informal cluster of small streets in the village centre with some pretty groups of thatched cottages, smartened up, e.g. in DAGMAR STREET, and in CROWN SQUARE, around the Wesleyan Methodist chapel (q.v.). Surrounding the wedge-shaped GREEN small early C19 houses; an incongruous and rather feeble little clock tower of 1919 at one end. Other good houses face the estuary along RIVERSIDE and the STRAND, e.g. SOUTHWOOD COTTAGE with pediment with circular window, and MARINE PARADE, a terrace of *c.*1830, partly earlier salt cod warehouses remodelled. Further on under the cliff in NESS DRIVE, NESS HOUSE HOTEL, early C19 stuccoed, with veranda and delicate trellised covered balcony on three sides; later C19 extension at the back. Also NESS COTTAGE, with an early C19 core, one-storeyed, with steeply pitched thatched roof with bargeboarded dormer. Doorway altered to a window.

TOLL HOUSE. An eccentric two-storey design, probably of 1828, to take account of the different levels of the Torquay and Newton Abbot roads.

RINGMORE, a nearby settlement upstream, also has a sprinkling of pretty cottages overlooking the river. By the STRAND a little late C18 group, and nearby, in RINGMORE ROAD, THE HERMITAGE, with a row of Gothick arched upper windows under a thatched roof, and THE PRIORY, with a Gothick window. Up HIGHER RINGMORE ROAD, OLD STOKE HOUSE, C17 or earlier, but also with pretty Gothick windows and a thatched roof, and other carefully cherished picturesque cottages. Back near Shaldon Bridge the more ostentatious RINGMORE TOWERS, mostly later C19, red sandstone, but with turrets added between the wars.

On the hills above Ringmore the extensive and well preserved remains of a medieval STRIP FIELD SYSTEM, fossilized in the modern hedge pattern.

TEMPLETON   *8010*

A neat little hamlet with a few thatched houses around the churchyard, which is entered through what was the medieval priest's house.

ST MARGARET. Modest: a low unbuttressed w tower of volcanic trap, possibly C13; aisleless nave with square-headed C15 S windows; chancel. Restored in 1877, when the S porch and top stage of the tower were rebuilt, and the arch-braced roof was erected. – FONT. Octagonal granite bowl on Victorian stem. – FONT COVER. Tall, pyramidal, C17. – CHOIR STALLS. Incorporating C17 panels. – STAINED GLASS. A few medieval fragments; the rest by *Drake*. – MONUMENT. Daniel Cudmore † 1679. Two crude allegorical figures, broken pediment, old-fashioned black-letter inscription.

TETCOTT

No village; church and house lie close together on their own.

HOLY CROSS. Unbuttressed W tower with cusped pinnacles. Red stone with an occasional band of granite. On the N side of the church several narrow C13 windows. In the S transept also a narrow cusped lancet. Restored in 1890. – FONT. Norman, circular, with a top border of crosses saltire. The base more elaborate than the bowl (cf. Clawton); corner faces and half-rosettes between, as if it had originally been a font of the Cornish St-Thomas-by-Launceston type. – PEW RAILS of the Arscott Chapel, fine openwork carving of c.1700. – BENCH ENDS. Broader than usual, with elementary decoration.

TETCOTT MANOR. The manor house of the Arscotts until 1788, then of the Molesworths of Pencarrow, Cornwall. A picturesque cluster of roofs of different heights, four ranges around a courtyard. Long two-storey rubble stone S front with a large two-storey porch with a round-headed arch and a straight gable with an C18 slate sundial. The 1603 datestone was brought in the C20 from Tetcott Mill. Three bays to the l. of the porch, four to the r., Georgian sash-windows. The W front more irregular, with a taller hipped-roofed centre with a lateral stack, and a fine brick end stack. (Inside, good early C17 joinery, hall with heavily beamed ceiling, dog-leg stairs with turned balusters. Above the hall a room with coved plaster ceiling and panelling of the later C17. In the E range the court room, with a late C17 plaster heraldic overmantel and ceiling with a trumpeting angel.)

Good outbuildings, including a BARN, a brick GRANARY, and attractive STABLES of brick with mullioned-and-transomed windows. The stables have loose-boxes behind a Tuscan colonnade. The brick buildings, and the garden walls to N and E, appear to have been associated with a new brick house of c.1700, demolished in 1831. Another stable block, of two storeys, with rusticated quoins, may be built of materials from this lost house. Nice early C18 ashlar GATEPIERS.

LOWER LANA. Tetcott estate farm and farm buildings of 1857, red brick, probably built of re-used materials from the house of c.1700.

THELBRIDGE

ST DAVID. Tower and chancel of rock-faced volcanic stone, rebuilt on a tight budget in 1871–2 by *Packham & Croote* of Exeter, the medieval masonry largely re-used and the Perp E window reset. Nave masonry also tidied up. Plastered nave roof and plain tower and chancel arches, perhaps pre-Victorian renovations. Chancel fittings poor but honest. – REREDOS. 1872. Cheap wooden-framed zinc panels, prettily painted with flowers. – FONT. Norman. Square scalloped bowl.

THELBRIDGE HALL. A late medieval to early C17 house refurbished in 1852 for the Rev. R.T. Bradstock. Two parallel ranges. Four-room and cross-passage plan with lateral stack. Victorian interior.

THORNBURY

4000

ST PETER. A good deal of the early medieval church remains. Unbuttressed low w tower a little narrower than the nave. Nave, s transept, chancel. Mid C12 s doorway with two orders of colonnettes with spur bases (cf. Buckland Brewer). Capitals partly scalloped, partly with volutes. The arch with two roll-mouldings. A Perp N chancel chapel added to the chancel somewhat later (octagonal piers, double-chamfered arches), and a N aisle later still, in the C15: two bays with the usual granite piers of A type. Restoration 1876. – FONT. C13 bowl. – Bits from SCREEN and BENCH ENDS re-used in the chancel seats. – (STAINED GLASS. Two windows by *Wailes*.) – Spicott MONUMENT, probably to Sir John Spicott † 1641. Sadly mutilated; only the recumbent figures, in bad preservation, four kneeling smaller figures, and two relief medallions survive.

THORVERTON

9000

ST THOMAS OF CANTERBURY. Interesting s porch, vaulted, with blind arcading against the W and E walls (cf. Crediton). The central boss with a weird representation of the Holy Trinity (cf. a boss in Exeter Cathedral); the others with carvings of the four Fathers of the Church and the four Evangelists. W tower with buttresses of B type, low stair-turret, and straight-headed bell-openings. The rest much altered in the C19. The aisles have embattled lean-to roofs of 1834. E window of the same date. Unusually tall piers between nave and s aisle, of B type, with all the capitals decorated by figures of angels. The piers were raised in 1834 to accommodate galleries. N transept 1864, when the church was restored. – An interesting collection of Victorian FITTINGS. – REREDOS. 1840, stone; trefoiled arcade; Commandment panels flanking the E windows. – LECTERN. 1843 by *W. & J. Cooper* of King's Lynn, a bronzed iron eagle, a copy of the medieval one at King's Lynn. – PULPIT. 1864, polygonal, with good architectural detail. – STALLS and PEWS with elaborately pierced backs, also of 1864, by *Rattee & Kett* of Cambridge, the stall ends with carved angels. – CORONAE. In the chancel 1858 by *Skidmore*; in the chancel aisle 1875 by *Willey* of Exeter. – STAINED GLASS. E window of the 1840s, undoubtedly by *Beer*, lively figured medallions on an intense blue and red lattice ground. – s aisle E to Luke Herman Coleridge † 1848. Vigorous, crudely drawn scenes, with unusually heavy lettering. – MONUMENTS. Roger Tuckfield of Raddon Court † 1683 and wife † 1677. Ionic columns flanking an inscription. – Elizabeth Tuckfield of Little Fulford † 1807. Neo-classical; mourning female figure with cross.

BAPTIST CHAPEL, in a small burial ground. Built in 1833–4. Three-bay rendered front with central pediment; four-centred windows. Gate with overthrow.

Quite a large village, with an attractive main street with plastered cottages, cobbled side walks, and a railed green and stream. BRIDGE HOUSE has a large porch with the date 1763, but is older. ACORN COTTAGE, nearby, has internal walls of cob bricks. At the crossroads, the DOLPHIN INN, early C19, and the former vicarage, 1840 by *Hayward*, with three broadly spaced windows below generous eaves. Some way on, the former station buildings, now a house, a grey limestone group with striking zigzag-patterned bargeboards.

TRAYMILL. A modest, plain rendered and thatched farmhouse incorporating parts of a late medieval manor house. Impressive medieval roof consisting of eight trusses (six smoke-blackened) of false hammerbeam type – the straight post upward from the hammerbeam here replaced by arch-bracing – with a smoke-blackened closed truss at the lower end, and two tiers of curved wind-braces on alternate trusses. In the walls of the former open hall there also survive two lights, with cusped heads, of a former four-light mullioned-and-transomed stone window, and a large door with a pointed head.

Among other early houses in the parish, DUNSALLER, with a main range of medieval origin (smoke-blackened roof on either side of an original partition, suggesting two open hearths). Richly moulded C17 main doorway. The rear parlour is also probably C17.

RADDON COURT. A substantial early C19 Italianate exterior, stuccoed, with bracketed eaves. Three-window entrance front; porch with blocked columns. S front with two canted bays. Older parts behind.

THORVERTON MILL. The largest working flour-mill in Devon (original turbines). The oldest part of 1898, four storeys and five bays, grey limestone with red brick dressings; later additions. Grain silos of granolithic (a patent cement of crushed granite).

BRIDGE. A single span over the Exe, 1908 by the County Surveyor, *S. Ingram*, and a very early example of reinforced concrete construction. Four arched ribs of 84 ft span carry a cantilevered deck.

THROWLEIGH

ST MARY. All-granite, all-ashlar, on the E slopes of Dartmoor. Three-stage W tower with B type buttresses. S side with S porch, low rood-loft turret, remarkably decorated S chancel doorway (scrolls in jambs and voussoirs, leaf decoration on spandrels), and granite window tracery. N arcade on A type piers; depressed arches. Wagon roofs to chancel (with bosses) and aisle. Restorations 1859–60, 1884, 1890, all discreet. – FONT. Perp, on a heavily moulded pillar; low bowl with compressed quatrefoil decoration. – Wainscot of a ROOD SCREEN, much restored by *Herbert Read*. – PULPIT made up of other rood-screen fragments. The screen was dated 1544. – The most interesting feature is the EASTER SEPULCHRE (reset), a coarsely modelled granite recess without figural decoration, the upper part missing. Depressed arch with scrollwork between two thick diagonal buttresses. – (STAINED GLASS. E window, 1912, and one S window by *Comper*.)

CHURCH HOUSE, by the lychgate. An attractive thatched group. The house is two-storeyed, of large irregular granite blocks. In the E gable wall an upper stone two-light window; at the opposite end the large chimneystack of an inserted fireplace. Inside, an old staircase doorway next to the fireplace. But the smoke-blackened arch-braced roof, with no evidence for partitions, suggests that the house was originally a single open chamber, unlike the two-storeyed church houses of the early C16.

PROVIDENCE METHODIST CHAPEL, Providence Place. Built by the Bible Christians in 1839. Rendered, with a gabled porch with datestone. Granite boundary wall; gate with lampholder.

On THROWLEIGH COMMON, on the N flank of Dartmoor, a good complex of irregular prehistoric fields and huts can be seen, with traces of a reave system. There is abundant evidence for tinstreaming. Higher up on the moor are complex agglomerated enclosures and the odd round barrow.

There are many good farmhouses in this parish on the fringe of Dartmoor. THROWLEIGH BARTON is larger than average, with an early C16 arch-braced roof over the inner parlour. WONSON MANOR has good C17 work, and a late medieval doorway in an outbuilding. CLANNABOROUGH and WAYE COTTAGE are both former longhouses. But the outstanding longhouse deserves a special description.

HIGHER SHILSTONE. A farmhouse, set into the hillside just below 81 the open moor, which expresses Devon's local building traditions as perfectly as any one structure can: perhaps also the most architecturally distinguished of all surviving Dartmoor longhouses. To a fine two-room medieval hall house with cross-passage and shippon a rear service wing and sophisticated exterior were added in the late C16 and C17. Later still, a shippon and stable block was built in two stages at the front, at right angles to the longhouse shippon. Front of large squared ashlar blocks; smaller blocks at the upper end, the courses disrupted by the later windows. Large round-headed granite doorway to the cross-passage with a roll-moulding enclosing stylized foliage decoration of oakleaves in lugged spandrels; hoodmould with labels; above the door, RT 1656. Adjacent, the separate shippon entrance, a plainer chamfered round-headed granite door frame, and granite steps to the hayloft door. Hollow-moulded mullions to every window in the house, including the cross-wing, the front boasting a particularly impressive range, with two four-light windows with king mullions and hoodmoulds, and three windows of two lights. At the rear end of the cross-passage, another round-headed granite door; off the passage, through the solid granite cross-wall, a door similar to the shippon's but in timber with mason's mitres. The shippon was apparently always so divided from the house, as the smoke-blackened roof of the late medieval hall and the un-smoke-blackened shippon roof survive unaltered: a great rarity in a longhouse. The shippon roof is on short raised crucks with through purlins and an end-cruck; the central drain, dunghole, and splayed slit windows also survive.

The house has a two-bay open hall roof, defined by good, solid cross-walls in small granite blocks at the upper end of the hall and the lower side of the cross-passage, with an arched collar to the central truss; all rafters, thatch, and ties survive completely smoke-blackened. Later on the hall was partially floored. The upper chamber projected out over the cross-passage so far into the hall that the axial stack was later inserted between the cross-passage and the cross-beam that marks the extent of the projection. Massive fireplace with hollow-chamfered lintel. At the upper end of the hall, another room, exceptionally spacious, heated by a gable-end stack. Double door off the hall to the unheated service cross-wing.

Across the yard a BARN, again in small squared blocks, its oak threshing-floor intact; stables and linhay with jointed cruck-trusses side-lapped on top of granite uprights; and in the centre of the whole group a dung-pit lined with massive granite boulders.

THRUSHELTON

4080

ST GEORGE. Formerly a chapel of Marystow. In a pretty, sheltered position just above a stream. Unbuttressed W tower; rectangular NE stair-turret. S aisle C14, with reticulated tracery to the W window, but the S windows all late Perp, straight-headed. Chancel E window C19 Dec. C14 S arcade of two bays, with octagonal piers, the plainest capitals, and double-chamfered arches. Chancel arch with the same mouldings. The S chapel arches late Perp, with A type piers and decorated abaci. Late medieval roofs: in the S aisle and S chapel ceiled wagons with carved wall plates and bosses, in the chancel with an additional rib E of the chancel arch. Plain early C19 chancel fittings. Churchyard with good slate tombstones.

CHURCH COTTAGE. Early and later C17 poorhouse and sexton's house, partly remodelled in early C19 Tudor.

See also Orchard.

THURLESTONE

6040

25 ALL SAINTS. Impressive C15 tower of unusual silhouette, since the stair-turret, placed in the middle of one side in the Ashburton manner, is markedly higher than the tower. Battlements but no pinnacles. The oldest part of the church is the chancel, with three deeply splayed small lancet windows, and a double piscina with pointed trefoil-headed niches and a pierced pointed quatrefoil above as tracery. Perp S aisle, with two-storey embattled S porch with some very rudimentary carving. Four-light windows with four-centred arches and no tracery; on the N side the same windows, rebuilt in 1685, but of three lights. Priest's door through a S chapel buttress (cf. Kingsbridge). S arcade with double-chamfered arches on A type piers. – FONT. Circular, Norman, of red sandstone, a usual type, with palmette frieze and cable moulding above, zigzag below. – S chapel ALTAR made up of bits of the screen. – STAINED GLASS.* Several windows by *A.J.Davies* of the Bromsgrove Guild: N aisle 1920, S aisle 1929 (two) and 1932, S chapel 1934. – MONUMENTS. H. Luscombe, rector, †1634. Kneeling figure. – Thomas Stephens †1658 and family. Also still in the old tradition of the Elizabethan wall-monument with kneeling figures.

The village is unusually picturesque, ón the plain above and close to Bigbury Bay. In the main street CHURCH HOUSE, a row of four rubble stone cottages, the church house itself probably the E part,

---

*Information from Robert C. Clements.

with a stone staircase within the back doorway, and a stud-and-panel screen inside. Land was given for it to be built on in 1536. Another good house is THATCHWAYS, rubble with thatched roof, a three-room cross-passage house with lateral stack on the front wall, and a rear outshot extended to an upper floor, as the ground rises behind.

BANTHAM HAM, at the mouth of the river Avon, a sheltered place for beaching ships, appears to have been used as a post-Roman trading post and settlement.

TIPTON ST JOHN
Ottery St Mary

0090

A pretty Victorian chapel and school; one quite grand house in the hamlet, with a big stone porch.

ST JOHN. 1839–40 by *John Hayward*, his first church, built under the patronage of the Coleridges of Ottery St Mary. Lancet style, with bellcote and shallow chancel. From the E the composition is symmetrical. Interior with W gallery. – STAINED GLASS. Two N nave windows by *Ward & Hughes*, 1889, one of them the Light of the World after Holman Hunt.

TIVERTON

9010

Tiverton, or Twyford (two fords), lies on a narrow spit of land between the rivers Exe and Lowman. The oldest settlement may be at the N end where the castle and church are sited, but the Exe Bridge, in existence by the C14, lies further S, and here the main streets developed. There were a market and three fairs already in 1200. By the C16 and C17 Tiverton was one of the chief centres of the cloth trade in the county, and the wealth of the great merchants – Greenway, Blundell, Slee – is reflected in the rebuilding of the church and the establishment of schools and almshouses on an especially generous scale. But apart from these, and one substantial stone house, few buildings remain from this time; the rest disappeared in a series of fires: 1598, 1612, 1661, 1726, 1730, 1731 – the last especially disastrous, after which an Act was passed ordering that all roofs should be of lead, slate, or tile.

In the early C18 Defoe could still describe Tiverton as the greatest manufacturing centre in the county, and surviving good C18 and early C19 houses show that the town remained comfortably prosperous. A second church was built, the town was paved throughout (Act of 1794), and in 1830 the market was removed from the main street to a purpose-built market house (cf. Exeter, Barnstaple, Crediton). By then the Industrial Revolution had arrived in the shape of John Heathcoat's lace factory, rescuing Tiverton from the decline that was overtaking other Devon cloth towns. The West Exe suburb expanded with well planned artisan housing; a works outing for Heathcoat employees and their families in 1836 involved 2,300 people. Lewis's Topographical Dictionary (1849) wrote of the 'imposing effect' of the lofty factories on the W bank of the Exe, and the population, estimated by the local historian Dunsford at 5,343 in 1790, had increased to

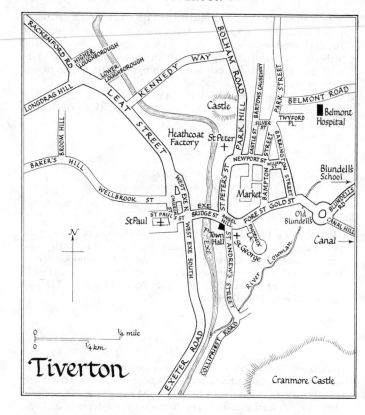

Tiverton

10,877 by 1891. Civic pride demanded a Victorian town hall of a grandeur unparalleled outside Exeter and Plymouth.

The Heathcoat factory still functions – one of the few in the county with such a continuous history – but the main impression of Tiverton now is of a local market town. The population in 1981 was 16,539. The contributions of the later C20 to the visual scene are largely negative; the destruction of many good houses in Fore Street, a punishing quantity of traffic gyrating round the town centre, and shopping developments of a dismal mediocrity distract one from the quality of surviving buildings. A few enterprising restorations, and some recent sympathetic infilling in West Exe, can be noted on the credit side.

CHURCHES

ST PETER. At the N end of the town, close to the castle. A gorgeously ostentatious display of civic pride. Facing the river, a tall slim red sandstone W tower with eight pinnacles; facing the town, and startlingly white since limewashing after restoration in 1985–6, a limestone S porch, chapel, and aisle, all embattled. The buttresses are decorated with the ships that brought Tiverton merchants their wealth. The richest of these, John Greenway, was responsible for the S porch and S chapel, built in 1517. They are real showpieces, almost as thickly encrusted with decoration as Launceston church in Cornwall. The battlements of the chapel are double-stepped and all pierced in ornamental filigree. Below them, heraldic panels, and a string course with small, exquisitely carved scenes of the Passion of Christ. Around the windows, blank tracery (cf. the porch of the Greenway almshouse chapel), and above, a frieze of ships. The s porch has pinnacled niches flanking the doorway, and heraldic panels above. The limewash disguises the fact that much of the stonework has been replaced or restored. The porch was taken down and reconstructed in 1825; its buttresses are largely c19, and its friezes and battlements entirely so, to a new design; the figural scenes of the frieze date from 1908. But the sculpture inside the porch is original: a beautiful stone vault panelled with ogee reticulation and motifs such as eagles, fishes, etc., in the panels, the details very close to the Oldham Chantry in Exeter Cathedral.* Above the inner doorway the Assumption of the Virgin flanked by the kneeling donor and his wife, and the initials I G. The Greenways were not squeamish about showing who had paid for all this work. In the E wall a small doorway into the chapel, apparently made in 1825. Its DOOR has a telling combination of Gothic tracery above early Renaissance pilasters; what is its history?

The N side of the church is less spectacular. It dates from 1853–6, when *Edward Ashworth* doubled the width of the N aisle, added a double transept to balance the Greenway Chapel, and rebuilt the chancel. Good gargoyles and grotesques. The N aisle is of limestone, the chancel red sandstone. The only older remains are those of a simple Norman doorway with zigzag decoration on jambs and voussoirs, built into the N aisle. No trace remains of the medieval Courtenay Chapel, which stood NE of the church until the early C18.

The roomy interior is in its present form largely Ashworth's apart from the panelled tower arch and the chancel arcades, which are medieval. He rebuilt the nave arcades, copying the medieval originals, but using Bath stone instead of Beer stone. The piers are an enriched variety of combined A and B types; standard capitals interspersed with angels; on the E faces, niches for statues. Ashworth also restored all the window tracery, rebuilt the clerestory and chancel arch, and provided new roofs and seating throughout. Little trace remains of an extensive early C17 restoration (although see the NW nave piers and the W tower doorway), and nothing of a thorough internal refitting of 1821–2. The Greenway Chapel was restored in 1829 by *G. A. Boyce*. It is separated from the s aisle by a low stone screen; capitals only to the shafts of the piers. The shallow vault is delightfully panelled, with pendants. Of the Greenway MONUMENT (†1529) only two large brasses remain, now mounted on the w wall.

CANDELABRA. Large and splendid, of brass, bought in 1709. – ORGAN. 1696 by *Christian Smith*, with rich foliage-scroll carving. – PAINTINGS. Large Adoration of the Magi by *Gaspar de Crayer*. – Liberation of St Peter by *Cosway*, a native of Tiverton, 1784. – Other FURNISHINGS largely C19 and later. – TILING. Chancel floor 1853–6, as also the dado under the E window, stretching the

*See S. Blaylock in *Devon Arch. Soc. Proc.*, 44 (1986).

width of the wall and incorporating symbols of the evangelists and monograms; sanctuary floor 1895, when the sanctuary was raised: the whole sequence lavish and large-scale, but now hidden behind puritan carpets and curtains. – PULPIT. Stone, with stem and polygonal drum decorated with tracery; by *Ashworth*, 1853–6. – FONT. 1909, designed by *E.H.Harbottle*: octagonal bowl and stem with figures under nodding ogees. – MAYOR'S PEW. C19, with C17 lion and unicorn. – SCREEN. First World War memorial screen to the N chancel chapel 1920, designed by *Sydney K.Greenslade* and executed by *Herbert Read*, as also the reredos in the chapel.

STAINED GLASS. An extensive and important collection of Victorian and Edwardian windows, of which only a selection is noted here. E window, the Ascension, 1856 by *Wailes*: a most successful and original composition. Christ in the centre light is dramatically haloed in white glass, and separated from the disciples across the base of the window by a band of celestial blue with receding lines of white cloud; interwoven foliage instead of canopies. – The more conventional W window is also of 1856 and by *Wailes*; so too are the somewhat later windows at the W end of the S aisle. – N aisle W window by *Drake & Son*, designed by *Maurice Drake* – as also probably the S aisle E window. – S aisle to J.Carew 1882 by *Hardman*. – S aisle to Scott 1905 by *Bell & Sons* of Bristol. – N aisle Sanders memorial 1906 by *Fouracre & Watson*, the four evangelists in a manner clearly influenced by the Arts and Crafts movement. – MONUMENTS, S side of chancel. John Waldron † 1579. Tomb-chest, still entirely Gothic, with black-letter inscription, large quatrefoils, pinnacled niches. – Opposite, as a classical pendant, George Slee † 1613. Tomb-chest with large strapwork cartouches and bad caryatids, the same detail as one finds on contemporary plasterwork. – Roger Giffard † 1603. Elaborate architectural wall-monument in two tiers with paired columns. – Richard Newte † 1678. Large, with open segmental pediment. – John Newte † 1792. Oval tablet in an architectural frame.

ST GEORGE, Fore Street. Devon's best C18 town church. Designed by the London architect *John James*, the designer of St George, Hanover Square. Begun in 1714–16, with the intention of accommodating Dissenters, used as a warehouse for several years, and completed in 1727–33. Dignified exterior of yellow sandstone with rusticated quoins and round-headed upper windows. The plan made symmetrical in the way popular in the early C18, with N and S doors, originally with semicircular flights of steps. Chancel balanced by a W extension for a bell-turret. Harmonious interior, little disturbed by minor later alterations. Segmental barrel-vault, the part above the altar with coffering.* Galleries supported on piers, with Ionic columns above. W gallery added in 1842, when the levels of the N and S galleries were raised and the seating was altered. The bell-turret was also altered at this time (it was formerly arched, a favourite James motif). Original cartouche, now on the W gallery, with diocesan arms and lion's-head mask. – Handsome PANELLING around the chancel: Ionic pilasters flanking pedimented panels with inscriptions. – ALTAR RAILS on three sides, with twisted and turned balusters. – STAINED GLASS. E

116

* Alternate ribs of the vault are of cast iron, presumably added in the C19 restoration (information from A.Harrison).

window by *J. Bell* of Bristol, 1846, large figure of St Andrew in a painterly style.

ST ANDREW, Blundells Road. 1971 by *Anthony Rome*. A rectangular block of reddish stone. Crucifix on the N wall. Windows on the s side, away from the road.

ST PAUL, West Exe. By *Manners & Gill* of Bath, 1854–6, supervised 136 by the local architect *G. A. Boyce*. The site given by John Heathcoat, and the church paid for by his son-in-law Ambrose Brewin of Hensleigh. Red sandstone with Bath stone dressings. Spreading triple-gabled E front to St Paul's Street. s tower with broach-spire; N vestry. Dec tracery, rather skimpily moulded. Spacious interior with six-bay arcades, octagonal columns, no chancel arch or clerestory. – MONUMENT. Small aedicule to Ambrose Brewin †1855 and his wife Caroline † 1877.

ST JOHN (R.C.), Longdrag Hill. An interesting group of 1836–9 by *G. A. Boyce*, built soon after Catholic emancipation, on land given by the Chichesters of Calverleigh Court, whose chaplain, the Abbé Moutier, bequeathed money for the buildings. Simple nave and chancel, completed in 1839, the style an odd mixture: correct geometric two-light windows with coloured glass borders; ceiling with shallow four-centred arch-braces. Former PRESBYTERY, symmetrical; large straight-headed Gothic windows with a centre band of flamboyant tracery disguising the upper-floor level. Former SCHOOL, 1836, with upstairs schoolroom.

BAPTIST CHAPEL, Newport Street. 1877 by *G. S. Bridgman*. A largish town chapel with rubble limestone gabled front and staircase wings. Brick Sunday school and hall of 1859 and 1897; finial of a small child reading.

WESLEYAN CHAPEL, St Peter's Street. 1814, on the site of an older preaching house. Originally approached by a narrow passage, now behind a forecourt. Quiet five-bay front with central pediment and swept parapets, partly rendered. Ionic balustraded porch added in 1904. Original galleries on three sides, on iron columns; late C19 organ recess with two Ionic columns *in antis*. Schools of 1876 and small burial ground behind.

UNITED REFORMED CHURCH, St Peter's Street. Built by the Congregationalists in 1831 on the site of their 1689 meeting house. Cheerfully eclectic, grey ashlar front with pediment and traceried round-arched windows. The interior is an irregular polygon with a continuous gallery with late C19 cast-iron front: pulpit (altered) and seating also late C19. The typical attendant buildings step down the hill: tall granite Gothic Memorial Rooms, three storeys of lancet windows under a steep gable, and a robust neo-Tudor manse.

TIVERTON CASTLE

Until 1539 Tiverton Castle was a major residence of the Courtenays, created Earls of Devon in 1335. They inherited a manor house from the de Redvers family in the 1290s, and Hugh Courtenay (d. 1340) seems to have rebuilt the property. In 1308–9 there was expenditure on the 'new hall and chamber', and there are close architectural similarities between the surviving work and Hugh's more ambitious contemporary work at Okehampton. The plan appears to have been a courtyard with ranges of domestic buildings, a gatehouse on the E, and defensive mural towers. The GATEHOUSE is the most striking feature. An entrance passage with two bays of quadripartite vaulting is flanked by two ground-floor rooms, with a large chamber above reached by two first-floor entries on N and S (the N one now enclosed in the later house). Later the gatehouse was extended forward by a single bay (note the different vaulting and the Perp outer archway with fleurons); the innermost arch of the original gateway was rebuilt at the same time. The first-floor room in this addition has massive moulded beams; they have been dated by dendrochronology to the C14. Are they re-used? The outer wall with its gateway can hardly be so early. A projecting staircase gives access to the roof of the extension (crenellations rebuilt).

At the SE corner of the site is a circular tower, probably remodelled in the C16, and restored and re-roofed in the 1970s. It has a well-preserved garderobe. A doorway at second-floor level suggests a former wall-walk to the gatehouse. Substantial ruins remain of the C14 DOMESTIC S RANGE, although interpretation is problematic. It clearly included a series of grand first-floor rooms, of which some good details remain: a piscina or laver, two-light windows with quatrefoils, and a single lancet. A transverse wall cutting across the W end of this section may be older. Further W, beyond the remains of an entrance facing the churchyard, is a square chamber block with the remains of a projecting corner staircase, and at first-floor level a fireplace, a trefoiled lancet, and a tall two-light window with shoulder-arched transom and quatrefoil head. The site of the C14 hall is unclear. Did it stand parallel to the gatehouse, adjoining the S range, and projecting into the courtyard? On the W side the course of the former courtyard wall overlooks a steep drop to the river Exe. It has the foundations of a square tower with garderobe shoot at its mid-point, and of a circular tower at the N end.

The castle was modernized in the later C16 by Roger Giffard, and in the C17, after the Civil War, by Peter West, a rich Tiverton merchant, from whom it passed by descent to the Carews. A long two-storey battlemented range adjoins the gatehouse to the N, its upper floor with six three-light Tudor windows. Similar windows on the inner side of the gatehouse. The date 1588 and the initials R.G. on a projecting NW corner. Adjoining this, projecting into the courtyard, is a late C17 double-pile wing with hipped roof, considerably altered, but still with its mullion-and-cross windows on the S side, and an attractive two-storey porch of chequered brickwork. Inside, in the angle of this wing and the gatehouse is a large late C17 well staircase rising to the second floor.

PUBLIC BUILDINGS

TOWN HALL. By *Henry Lloyd* of Bristol, winner of a competition in 1864. An enjoyable, coarse and confident Franco-Venetian composition, with a polygonal end neatly turning the awkward corner of Fore Street, and bulgy bows and fat columns to add interest to the St Andrew's Street front. Tall French château roof with jolly ironwork. The interior rather gaunt; steep staircase with cast-iron balustrade, council chamber with armorial glass.

LIBRARY, adjoining the Town Hall. Established as a War Memorial Library in the Angel Hotel in 1920; extended on the site of the hotel in 1927–9 by *Dixon & Bamsey*. In a quiet and pleasant free Tudor, with a slightly concave front to fit the street, and a projecting porch with stumpy Tuscan columns.

MARKET. Established on this site, the former bowling green, in 1830. Low, clerestory-lit covered market with clock cupola, much rebuilt in 1876; one-storey open stalls on one side. Now surrounded by car parks and an indifferent shopping precinct.

EAST DEVON COLLEGE OF FURTHER EDUCATION. A large campus N of the town. The only forceful contribution is the LIBRARY and ADMINISTRATION BUILDING of 1980 by *Thomas Davis* of the County Architect's Department, a four-square, deep-plan block of brown brick, with heavily splayed lower windows recessed between trapezoidal piers; well detailed corners. Other college buildings of 1960 (*R. N. Guy*) and 1970 (*Frank Rogers*). Behind is TIVERTON SCHOOL, 1958 by *R. N. Guy*, remodelled with additions in 1974 by the *Louis de Soissons Partnership*, the SPORTS HALL of 1974 with gable wall patterned in brick and concrete in an effort to be interesting.

BLUNDELL'S SCHOOL, Blundells Road. The old school buildings of 1604 are near the Lowman Bridge (*see* Perambulation 1). The school moved to its present site E of the town centre in 1882. There were then *c.* 100 pupils. There are now 450, and the school has extended on both sides of the road. To the S the OLD SCHOOL by *John Hayward*, an irregular group of severe red sandstone Tudor buildings whose main feature is a big battlemented clock tower with a taller stair-turret, viewed across a large lawn. Behind is the first-floor schoolroom with mullioned windows and hammerbeam roof (now the Peter Blundell Room, with gallery divided off). Adjoining LIBRARY with oriel window. Plain former boarding house, with bay-windows. A further block, now demolished, completed a quadrangle with the CHAPEL, apsed, and with rather a mean W tower; Perp detail. Bold arch-braced roof; stalls with open tracery. N aisle 1887; polygonal Lady Chapel 1980, pleasantly finished with a wooden slatted ceiling and abstract glass. To the W and S SCIENCE BUILDINGS and SPORTS HALL of the 1980s. Across the road, the BIG SCHOOL of 1964, by *Raglan Squire*. Dining hall with a multi-gabled front to the road and quite a dramatic folded roof; main hall plainer, with a segmental barrel roof. Workshops behind of 1974.

BELMONT HOSPITAL, Belmont Road. The former workhouse, rebuilt in 1837–8 by *Scott & Moffat*. Badly treated, but the dignified classical composition still recognizable (cf. Bideford, Tavistock). Half of the low entrance block remains, still with its late Georgian sashes; also the main range, with central octagonal tower with pedimented sides, but the windows all altered. Nice pedimented pedestrian entrance gateway to the W.

STATION. The railway arrived at Tiverton Junction, some way from the town, in 1848. The new PARKWAY station at the meeting of the M5 and the North Devon motorway dates from 1986. Pleasant top-lit waiting-area-cum-ticket-hall.

The GRAND WESTERN CANAL was constructed from Tiverton to Lowdwells, a distance of 7¾m., in 1810–14 and completed to Taunton in 1838. The later section was disused in 1867, but the Tiverton end is maintained for pleasure use. The wall of the embankment at the BASIN contains thirteen LIMEKILNS, two of them restored. The two-storey thatched LIMEBURNER'S COTTAGE adjacent is now a café.

PERAMBULATIONS

1. *Fore Street and Gold Street*

FORE STREET starts with the monster Town Hall (q.v.), opposite the curved terrace of Angel Hill, then continues as a broad street (the market was here until 1830), much disfigured by C20 shopfronts. Above these are a few remnants of the dignified terrace houses built after the fire of 1731. First a handsome couple on the N side: above the Trustee Savings Bank, C19 giant pilasters and round-headed windows; then a simpler C18 front of red and blue brick, segment-headed windows with keystones. Opposite, much was destroyed in the 1960s–70s. No. 5 is early C19: shopfront with two Greek Doric columns, giant pilasters above. Similar pilasters to the house at the corner of Phoenix Lane.

s from here, facing HAMMETS SQUARE, two major Georgian houses restored as offices after long neglect, although in an unfortunate setting of mediocre buildings near the bus station. Facing W, first RAYMOND PERRY HOUSE, tall and stuccoed, possibly a conversion of an older building, with a late C18 pedimented porch with reeded capitals. At the back an arched staircase window, and a second porch added at the time of the conversion in 1971. GOTHAM HOUSE, restored in 1962, faces N across a forecourt (now alas used as a car park) enclosed by iron railings and gatepiers with urns. An excellent early C18 brick front in the Baroque tradition, a rarity in Devon. Four Doric pilasters each with their own entablature; stone cornice, separate attic pilasters above. The central attic window is a showpiece in rubbed brick, with curly lintel and its own entablature. Other windows more restrained, segment-headed, with brick or stone keystones, all with aprons. Doric doorcase with fluted pilasters. The back also elegantly done, with central arched window with pilasters and rustication. Generous staircase, around a well; two twisted and one fluted baluster to each tread.

Further E in Fore Street a few more Georgian upper storeys visible, and a couple of nice cobbled alleys on the s side (SOUTH VIEW, STRATFORD PLACE). Then comes the junction with Gold Street and Bampton Street, a hideous jumble of angular frontages of the 1960s which replaced the Lord Palmerston, a dignified coaching inn.

GOLD STREET continues towards the Lowman Bridge. On the s side GREENWAY'S ALMSHOUSES, founded in 1517 by John Greenway to provide for five men (each to have two rooms and a garden). Originally with galleries, like the later Slee and Waldron almshouses (*see* Perambulations 2 and 3), but rebuilt in brick after

1731, and again, in stone, in the C19 to provide nine single rooms on three storeys. The tiny early C16 chapel survives at the end, much restored. Elaborately decorated. A single Perp window on each side; quatrefoil parapets with shields on the show side to the street and over the porch. Outer porch doorway basket-arched with coats of arms above, inner door more traditionally Perp, with niche with statue above. Restored niches with statues reset in the almshouse wall. On part of the back gardens simple stone ranges of further dwellings of 1838, converted to flats in 1952–5.

At the bottom of Gold Street several pleasant Georgian houses, especially the LOWMAN RESTAURANT, five plus one bays, two storeys, windows with keystones. The BRIDGE over the Lowman has iron railings attractively set back in a semicircle around the STATUE of Edward VII by *H. Hems*. On the far side a triangular CLOCK TOWER of 1908 by *J. Donkin*, a very debased descendant of an Eleanor Cross; Gothic windows, Art Nouveau leaded glass, pinnacled buttresses, and rather Baroque figures of Faith, Hope, and Charity.

Further on, within a large walled enclosure, OLD BLUNDELLS, 71 now flats, founded as a school by Peter Blundell, a wealthy Tiverton merchant. Built in 1604. Planned for 150 boys, a quite exceptional size for a school of this date. What is notable is the care taken to make the whole composition symmetrical. Yet apart from the round-arched doorways, the architectural details are entirely unclassical. Ashlar front with nine large windows, each of four arched lights. They were extended downwards, very tactfully, with a second transom, and buttresses added when the flats were made in 1882. The windows, divided into groups of three by two identical porches, originally lit the dining hall and two other open halls used for the higher and lower schools. C19 drawings show that these were divided from each other by screens, and had seats ranged along the long walls, exactly as specified in Blundell's will of 1599, and as found in contemporary schools such as Harrow. The back wings contained the two-storey master's house, the kitchens, and an usher's room. Cupola (reconstructed in 1840) between the two schoolrooms.

2. Streets N and S of Fore Street

BARRINGTON STREET has modest red brick back-street terraces of the C19, still in the Georgian tradition. On the E side former SCHOOL of 1894, low and gabled, by *Chester & Perkins*, with additions of 1911. *E.S. Perkins*, the local Director of Education, built the neighbouring pair of houses, THE HAVEN and THE WILDERNESS, the latter for himself, in 1908–9. Plain rendered fronts, The Wilderness with two-storey side porch with slightly Voyseyesque battered buttresses, a large window with coloured glass, and an inscribed door lintel carved by the architect's wife, *Isabel Perkins*. Set back, the former MIDDLE SCHOOLS, 1902 by *William Ashford*, extended 1909. Handsome red brick and stone Wrenaissance S front in the tradition of later London Board Schools; two-storeyed, the ends pedimented, with carved wreaths.

W to BAMPTON STREET, the main route N until St Peter's Street was extended in 1802. At the S end, near Fore Street, three-storey

early C19 frontages, e.g. Nos. 14–16 with incised pilasters. Next
door, the OLD MARKET HOUSE, built as the corn market in
1699 and rebuilt after the 1731 fire. Open ground floor, with
sturdy wooden Tuscan columns, nicely restored in 1970, with
modern shops set back behind. Upper floor of brick, with casement windows; bell-turret. Further N, No. 27 incorporates an
early C17 red sandstone archway, said to come from an earlier
market building. Nos. 29 and 31 are handsome corner buildings of
the earlier C19, with recessed rounded corners, a Tiverton feature
of this period. A similar house at the corner of William Street. At
the start of the more modest continuation of Bampton Street, No.
57, the Old Brewhouse, a low C17 stone building with handsome
original door and C19 patterned cast-iron windows.

Now W along NEWPORT STREET. At the corner the BLACK
HORSE, low and stuccoed, facing a good red brick house (No. 62
Bampton Street) with two Gibbsian doorcases. CLARE HOUSE,
by the entrance to the car park and market, worthy of a better
setting, is an elegant Regency villa of 1816, built as one of the
Tiverton vicarages; stuccoed, with Doric loggia curved at one end.
CASTLE STREET leads N, wide and attractive, with the town leat
(created in the C13) still running down its centre, as it once did
down all the main streets. Simple early to mid C19 two-storey
terraces, not uniform, some with Doric doorcases. On the E side
ST PETER'S HALLS, 1842 by G. A. Boyce, built for the Blue Coat
School founded in 1713. Tudor, stone, one window still with its
patterned glazing. In BARTOWS CAUSEWAY, the lesser continuation of Castle Street, ROSEBANK, a surprisingly tall late
Georgian house, and some attractive minor Georgian cottages near
the end. E from here one can explore a variety of low density
suburban developments of the early C19. At the junction of Silver
Street and PARK STREET, three Tivertonian curved corners and
one older timber-framed house with later stucco. To the E, TWY-
FORD PLACE, a pretty terrace of six houses with simple Grecian
verandas, and two larger houses with bracketed eaves and panelled
pilasters. On the W side of Park Street quite a grand, irregular
pedimented Italianate house, and opposite, VILLA FRANCA,
with an old core but chiefly of c. 1820, front with broad eaves and
veranda.

Now back to Newport Street, and down ST PETER'S STREET,
running from the church to the Exe Bridge. The street would be a
delight were it not for the traffic. First a pleasant mixture of quite
substantial stuccoed and brick frontages, C18–19; among them
Nos. 48–50, doorway with Soanian incised pilasters; Nos. 38–40,
red brick with large stone keystones; and No. 23, especially grand,
with a central archway, channelled ground floor, and giant pilasters with honeysuckle motif. Then, after several late Georgian
plainer fronts, the excellent early C18 AMORY HOUSE. Small but
quite elaborate. Five-window red brick front, two storeys over a
basement, hipped gambrel roof. All the windows have curly lintels
(cf. Gotham House, Perambulation 1). Aprons below the upper
windows, quoins to the corners and marking out the central bay,
coved cornice breaking into a little pediment, narrow doorcase
with bold scrolled open pediment.

CHILCOT SCHOOL, on the W side of St Peter's Street, was built in

1611 from a bequest by Robert Chilcot, clerk and nephew of Peter Blundell. The school was to teach 100 boys English and writing, probably in preparation for Blundell's School. Round-arched entrance with hoodmould ending in lozenges; original studded door. Within the passage, the door to the schoolroom still Perp four-centred. Schoolroom (49 by 20ft) with four windows on each side, mullioned with single transom, and a continuous hoodmould. Interior with barrel roof, and W gallery. At the back the schoolmaster's house, with mullioned windows.

Opposite, the GREAT HOUSE OF ST GEORGE, the early C17 house of George Slee († 1613), now council offices. A rarity among merchants' houses of this date, in having a wide frontage all of stone. Round-arched off-centre doorway, hoodmould ending in curls, neither Tudor nor classical in style (but a more elaborate back doorway to the screens passage with egg-and-dart moulding). Much restored mullioned windows of four and six lights, the lower ones with hoodmoulds, the upper ones with a more up-to-date continuous string above. Two straight gables flanking a smaller shaped central feature. Large rear wing with staircase(?) projection. Original stud-and-panel partitions in the screens passage, and another in the rear wing between a corridor and the rooms to the S. The unusual plan may be explained by part-commercial use; the house is also said to have been used for guild meetings. Large first-floor chamber, now subdivided; two ground-floor rooms with bolection-moulded panelling, one with an older Jacobean overmantel, one with a chimneypiece painting. Next door, the SLEE ALMSHOUSES, founded 1613, for six women. Much altered, but restored in 1981. Two storeys with wooden galleries, now glazed.

The S end of St Peter's Street is dominated by the C19 UNITED REFORMED CHURCH and its associated buildings (see Churches, above). They face across the steep triangular space of ANGEL HILL to a late Georgian curved terrace on a raised footpath, probably dating from after a fire of 1794. Its grandest house is No.9, red brick, three storeys, with round-headed upper windows. Down by the Exe Bridge, No.16, a substantial house of c.1800, four storeys, now rendered, front door with Coade stone surround, approached by a first-floor balcony overlooking the river.

From Fore Street a final excursion s down ST ANDREW'S STREET, an early suburban extension alongside the river. First C19 terraces; then, beyond a cobbled forecourt, the MUSEUM, built as the National Schools in 1844: the schoolrooms formerly in the two gabled wings, teachers' accommodation in the centre. Nicely textured purple stone, plain Tudor detail. Opposite, a good late Georgian terrace, Nos. 26–29, three-storeyed, with early C19 doorcases. Further on, the OLD POLICE STATION and BRIDEWELL of 1846, now two houses. Quite small, but in a surprisingly eloquent Piranesian classical; channelled ground floor, tall projecting centre with dentilled cornice, large arched doorway with concave rusticated arch. Small stone FIRE STATION next door.

3. West Exe

West Exe was linked to the town by a bridge from the C14 or earlier, and developed as an industrial suburb with fulling-mills on the leats of the river. Dunsford's map of 1790 shows the Waldron Almshouses on the edge of the built-up area. Then, in 1816, the suburb was transformed by the arrival of John Heathcoat, who set up a machine lace factory here, equipped with his own patented bobbin net machines, after the Luddites had destroyed his factory at Loughborough.

Close to the river, the pleasant short Georgian BRIDGE TERRACE faces the water. The stuccoed houses of BRIDGE STREET probably date from after the fire of 1794. The HEATHCOAT FACTORY lies to the N, off LEAT STREET. It still has its one-storey LODGES of c. 1816, as if to a country house, a symmetrical brick pair, with dentilled pediments. To their r. the former SCHOOL for the children of the factory workers, the first of its kind in the West Country. By G.A.Boyce, its date 1841 set on carved lace drapery. Coursed red sandstone, gabled wings, mullioned windows with patterned leading. The main factory, plain, five storeys, red brick, is a rebuilding by H.S.W.Stone after a fire of 1936. The original factory which Heathcoat took over had been built as a cotton mill in 1792. To the r. a four-storey extension which survived the fire; straight-headed windows, a possibly earlier part adjoins, segment-headed windows, brick bands between the floors. Close to the river, now within the factory grounds, EXELEIGH HOUSE, Heathcoat's own home, an elegant early C19 stuccoed villa with a porch with paired Ionic columns. The gardens have gone; the private bridge to the church was swept away in 1960.

Opposite the factory entrance housing and shops by *Frank Rogers* of the *Mid Devon District Council*, 1985, nicely in scale with the neighbouring buildings: pale machine-made bricks, some tile-hanging. On the corner of CHURCH STREET, as part of the same redevelopment, a funeral parlour given some presence by its coloured and patterned brickwork in the post-modern manner. Around the factory still some of the planned housing built by Heathcoat for his workers: some of the earliest is in HEATHCOAT SQUARE to the W, two plain ranges facing each other across gardens (flats above two-storey houses). In WELLBROOK STREET, HEATHCOAT HALL, built as a working men's institute, 1876, with five large arched windows and projecting wings. Further on the only older buildings, the WALDRON ALMSHOUSES, built by John Waldron in 1579, the best preserved of the almshouse groups of Tiverton. A stone range with wooden gallery at two levels, four dwellings on each floor, each with four-centred entrance with black-letter inscription (stone ground floor, timber above). At the back later extensions, but original chimney-stacks. The CHAPEL at the end similar to the earlier Greenway Almshouse chapel, but less elaborately carved; quatrefoil parapets, Perp windows, completely traditional apart from the rather odd lights of the W window. Four-centred doorway with the Waldron arms within the tiny porch; wagon roof. Around the corner, C20 almshouses in orange brick by *H.S.W.Stone*, 1968, well detailed; later additions behind by *Dixon & Pritchard* of Tiverton.

From here one can return to St Paul's church (q.v.) looking obliquely down ST PAUL'S STREET, the most coherent piece of town planning in Tiverton, with low, generously scaled terraces still in the Georgian tradition, of c. 1850. Each house of three bays, doorways with intermittent rustication, broad eaves, end houses with rounded recessed corners. Similar but simpler terraces in WEST EXE NORTH and LEAT STREET. Beyond these, SHILLANDS, Heathcoat factory housing of between the wars, well spaced neo-Georgian terraces around large lawns. In the opposite direction, WEST EXE SOUTH, widened in the 1950s. Post-war council housing on the w: flats of the 1960s, followed by quite pleasant earlier garden-suburb terraces.

Further out, quite on its own by a leat, an early but much altered row of cottages, significantly named LOUGHBOROUGH. At the corner of LONGDRAG HILL a turnpike cottage with wavy bargeboards, built in 1844 to command two gates.

Several good outlying houses w of the Exe of the C18 to early C19. Among them, off Crediton Road, ST AUBYN'S (formerly Howden Court), and, up a long drive off the Exeter Road, past a pretty bargeboarded lodge, ASHLEY COURT, an attractive Regency villa, three wide bays, broad eaves, delicate iron veranda. Older parts behind.

ASHLEY HOUSE. Past another former lodge. A small late C18 house on a remarkable plan: L-shaped, with top-lit quadrant containing hall and staircase linking the two wings. Round-headed doorway in the centre of the quadrant, approached up a double flight of steps, and flanked by windows in arched recesses. Both curved wall and arched windows are very reminiscent of Kenbury House, Exminster (demolished), the home of the gentleman architect Philip Stowey (see Exeter Sessions House). Is this also by *Stowey?*★ Wings with two-storeyed canted bays with Gothick glazing. The room in the r. wing has a curved end. The staircase starts with a straight flight on one side of the hall, then describes two curves around the centre of the quadrant.

BROOM HILL, off Baker's Hill. Stuccoed, Regency, with veranda, looking E across the valley, in its own grounds.

HENSLEIGH HOUSE, Longdrag Hill. A handsome, compact red brick front of *c.* 1700, five windows wide, with wooden eaves cornice and central pedimented door (restored after removal of Victorian alterations). Hensleigh belonged in the C19 to Ambrose Brewin (cf. St Paul). Two later canted bay-windows on the S side, flanked by blind narrow windows of *c.* 1700. In the SE room bolection-moulded panelling and a good plaster ceiling of the same date, a plain quatrefoil central panel surrounded by foliage scrolls, the corners with two elegant putti with trails of flowers, and two eagles with laurel wreaths. NE room with neat neo-Grecian cornice of the early C19, but panelling in the style of *c.* 1600, incorporating some genuine pieces; and a moulded beam, possibly not *in situ*. The thick back wall of this room suggests an older core. Staircase around a well, with oval roof-light, probably early C19, but the stairs remade. Some back parts demolished in the 1960s. C18 WALLED GARDEN to the NE. Two LODGES, simple one-storey Regency.

BOLHAM. A small hamlet to the N on the edge of the Knightshayes estate, with some pretty C19 estate housing. BOLHAM HOUSE is late Georgian, stuccoed, with two bow-windows and a veranda on

★I owe this comparison to Alastair Forsyth.

the garden side. Further N, HAYNE, three-storeyed, early C19, centre with pediment and round-headed windows.

N of Bolham, iron bowstring BRIDGE with struts and trellis infill.

See also Collipriest *and* Knightshayes.

TOPSHAM
Exeter

Topsham, the chief port on the Exe estuary and probably an early Roman beachhead, was important already in the Middle Ages. It was especially prosperous from the C17, when new quays were built and the town expanded S with gabled merchants' houses along the Strand, still one of the most delightful urban groups in Devon. The centre of the old town is the long N–S line of High Street and Fore Street on the cliffs above the river. Its old character is well preserved, the handsome frontages of the C17–19 often concealing older fabric, as one might expect. Little intrudes from the C20, for there is no through traffic – the narrow streets are indeed totally unsuited to modern vehicles – and the town is fortunate in being close enough to Exeter to have survived without large shopping developments.

St Margaret. In a large churchyard on the cliff above the river. The unbuttressed red sandstone medieval tower with stair-turret rises on the S side of the church rebuilt in 1874–6 of randomly coursed limestone by *Edward Ashworth*. Quite a picturesque group of E gables facing the street. Spacious if dull interior, with a variety of Dec windows and a ceiled and traceried chancel roof as the chief ornaments. Much naturalistic carving by *Hems*. W bays divided off tactfully in the 1970s by a wooden screen. – REREDOS. Stone, with canopies. – CHOIR FURNISHINGS. 1935. – FONT. Norman, circular bowl with large fluted zigzag motif, and in one place an animal, its head looking backwards, its mouth holding an apple(?). – FONT COVER. Brass, C19. – STAINED GLASS. A complete but not outstanding Victorian assortment. – E and W windows 1876 and 1877 by *F. Drake*. – N transept N 1876 by *Beer & Driffield*, coarse and colourful. – S transept S 1907 by *Burlison & Grylls*, in C16 Flemish style, one of their best in Devon. – MONUMENTS. Admiral Sir John Duckworth †1817 by *Chantrey*, a bust and a lively scene of a naval battle. – Lieut. Col. G. H. Duckworth †1811, also by *Chantrey*. He is shown in uniform, with an elaborately draped Victory.

Congregational Chapel, Victoria Road. 1839, Sunday school 1897. Tall, rendered, square, with hipped roof. Three-bay sides with gable and quatrefoil in the centre; W entrance flanked by niches. Good interior and gallery.

Methodist Church, Fore Street. 1867, built by the Wesleyans. Sunday school and caretaker's house 1909. Like no other chapel in Devon. Tall grey gabled limestone with sandstone dressings, large rose window, and rather dumpy circular corner tower with conical spire. The interior has apsidal chancel and transepts. This essay in Early English was by *J. R. N. Haswell* of North Shields.

Primary School, Majorfield Road. One-storeyed, with four arched windows. The N wing was built as a Quaker meeting house

soon after 1713. It became a Wesleyan chapel in 1811 and a school
in 1852.

PERAMBULATION. A tour of Topsham can start from the churchyard. First to the N, down FORE STREET towards the High
Street. Here there is a mixture of buildings of all dates, starting
with the visibly oldest, Nos. 61 and 62 on the w side. No. 61 is a
tiny medieval house with one room on each floor. The front is
timber-framed and jettied (built out underneath) between stone
walls; in a side wall a simple two-centred stone archway. A stone
fireplace on each floor – the upper one with wave-moulded surround and joggled lintel – probably added in the C16 (their stacks
interfere with the older roof of No. 62). No. 62 has a mid C17 part
to the road, the upper fireplace with the black and white sgraffito
decoration found elsewhere in Devon c. 1660–70. Behind this, two
trusses remain of a medieval roof (a rarity in a Devon town). Each
is an arch-braced jointed cruck, with lower wind-braces. There
was formerly a two-storey wing behind. No. 63 is clearly an altered
timber-framed jettied house of the C16 or C17.

Then the SALUTATION INN, with a curious combination of
Venetian window and broken pediment to the former assembly
room of 1768 above the projecting porch on the l. The main range
three-storeyed, with dentilled cornice, perhaps also a rebuilding of
the C18, although the large panelled door to the archway and other
parts of the building may be older. Rubble stone former warehouses behind. No. 70 has been sadly messed about. Built as the
Market House in 1791, its open ground floor with seven shallow
brick arches with keystones was altered in 1867, when part was
converted as police station and constable's house. Beside it, EXE
STREET, with former warehouses of stone, leads to the river.
Continuing along Fore Street, Nos. 71–73, with a long front to the
road, was until a fire in 1976 the most complete of the earlier
Topsham houses. The l. wing, rebuilt in the C17, survives. The
earlier part to the r. was reconstructed after the fire; below the
projecting room supported by a C17 column the screens passage
remains, with a post-and-panel partition. No. 74 is a gable-ended
house, distinguished by a double jetty. (Late C17 bolection-
moulded fireplaces.)

On the E side of Fore Street there is less to see (No. 11, Westaways,
has a spacious stone cellar, probably medieval). On this side
MAJORFIELD ROAD, one of the narrow alleys of old cottages off
Fore Street, is worth a look: on the s side dormers with original
leading and glass, and further on the school (q.v., above). Back on
the w side of Fore Street, by No. 82, a pleasant court perhaps of
late C17 date, the back house with segment-headed windows. Nos.
92–94, much altered and divided, has a large C16 hall fireplace but
the rest is late C17, including a good stair in a rear turret. Then two
grand C18 houses on the E side. GROVE HOUSE is of red brick:
three storeys, five windows, arched ground-floor windows, parapet.

BROADWAY HOUSE in HIGH STREET (the continuation of Fore
Street) is also of red brick and of similar proportions. It looks
earlier because it has a dentilled cornice, not a parapet, but is
known to have been built in 1776 by a merchant named Fryer.
Excellent Ionic doorcase with fluted pilasters and pediment. Orig-

inal iron railings and gates with overthrow. Well preserved
interior: the usual symmetrical layout with two rooms on either
side of passage-hall and staircase. In the passage-hall embossed
Spanish leather set in bolection-moulded panelling, clearly older
than the house, brought from elsewhere in Topsham. Large
Venetian staircase window, stairs with three thin turned balusters
to each tread and an elegantly scrolled rail. Good plaster cornices
to the ground-floor rooms. At the back the rear offices (back
kitchen, brewhouse, etc.) with a colonnade in front (both mentioned in sale particulars of 1782).

Further N cottages continue along the road to Exeter, but one can
now turn W down FOLLETT ROAD towards the river. On the r.
CLARA PLACE, built on the site of the workhouse, and described
in 1833 as 'a neat building erecting for the accommodation of
decent folks'. A formal group of three white rendered ranges
around a grassed court, set high above the road behind iron railings. Each block with pedimented projecting centre, the middle
one taller than the rest, with windows within a segmental arched
recess.

Along FERRY ROAD by the river, FOLLETT LODGE, a curious
1920s multi-period pastiche by *H. W. Holman*, a plain house which
has been embellished with everything from Tudor doorway to
shaped gable and tile-hung Regency bow-window. Near the ferry a
group of gabled houses and the PASSAGE INN with pedimented
centre doorcase, slate-hung first floor, and a plaque with the date
1788. In this area many relics of the maritime past. The HAR-
BOURMASTER'S HOUSE AND WORKSHOP was once the
CUSTOM HOUSE, originally late C17 but rebuilt after a fire in
1971; two storeys and gables. On the quay opposite is the cast-iron
KING'S BEAM for weighing dutiable goods. FURLONG, a long
two-storey limestone house, was a SAIL LOFT; a SLIPWAY
remains at the end of the garden. WIXELS is a similar building
with walls of the old QUAY projecting into the river. Several
WAREHOUSES of *c.* 1800: May & Simeons, two storeys with limestone below and weatherboarding above under a hipped slate roof.
UNDERHILL TERRACE is a conversion from another two- and
three-storey brick warehouse. In EXE STREET, an early C19 two-
and three-storey warehouse, limestone with brick dressings under
a slate roof. Part of this was once the MALTHOUSE for the Salutation Hotel in Fore Street. Further along the quay another gabled
group by *Holman*. W up the steps one can return to the churchyard.

S from the churchyard along Fore Street to the Strand, the chief
points of interest are of the C17 onwards. First Nos. 27–29, a late
example of a tall multi-gabled group. Three terraced houses (with,
confusingly, four gables in front, five behind). The l. house has a
side entrance with the date 1693. All three have back-to-back
central chimneystacks, with small well staircases fitted in alongside, indicating the move in the late C17 towards a standard terrace
house plan. In the centre house a ground-floor ceiling with a
simple plaster oval. Nos. 30–31 also are gabled, formerly a single
house of earlier C17 date (moulded brick fireplace on the first
floor). Then the attractive white-rendered GLOBE HOTEL, late
Georgian in its exterior features, but proved by its long, low pro-

portions and the remains inside of a screens passage and of a lateral stack to be a much older structure. Good late C17 staircase, fitted in tightly at the back. It divides in two, the minor portion with splat instead of turned balusters. Up an alley S of the Globe, CHAPEL COURT, late C17, a similar type to the houses in the Strand (*see* below), with Dutch brick used for chimneys and dressings. Staircase with closed string; bolection-moulded rib ceiling in the parlour. Opposite the Globe, No.51, C18, set at an angle to the road, makes a delightful contrast with its red and vitrified brick chequerwork. Beside it a cobbled side alley leads round to Church Cottage overlooking the churchyard, and opposite there is another cobbled lane by No.36, a long C17 house with a gable to the road.

Further S these intricacies cease for a while and the STRAND starts with a plain row of former warehouses, mostly grey limestone (although the first one, built into the cliff, has upper parts of brick in English bond). No.101, of three storeys, was converted to a house by the addition of a projecting brick wing. It uses the small imported 'Dutch' bricks for window heads. Rainwater head 1719. Just S of Holman Way, DUTCH COURT, near the old quay, late C17, entirely of Dutch brick. It is set at right angles to the road, like the similar houses along the Strand. Simple late C17 ribbed ceiling in the central room; closed string staircase with heavy turned balusters, an arch to the stairs with carved cherub's-head keystone. The best part of the Strand starts with SHELL HOUSE, ostensibly late C17, with a charming shell porch and later Georgian sashes, although the low proportions again suggest an earlier core. Now five windows wide, but possibly once incorporating the adjoining two-bay house to the r. In the room to the l. of the hall fielded oak panelling with heavily moulded frames, and an excellent plaster ceiling in the Abbot tradition with a quatrefoil decorated with a wreath of flowers and leaves. Dog-leg stairs (two turned balusters to the tread), probably C18, and a little later than the large archway on the first-floor landing which has been cut through the back wall of the original house.

No.25 the Strand (Topsham Museum) is one of the late C17 merchants' houses running back from the road (of which more below).* It was modernized in the C18, when the upper floors were heightened (rainwater head 1739), but the original plan is still recognizable, with staircase hall behind the front room (the staircase itself C18, with twisted and turned balusters, and an open string). In the front room a bolection-moulded fireplace surround flanked by later fluted pilasters; in the back room C18 fielded panelling and a contemporary corner cupboard. No.26, Old Court, is of similar type, with a later bow-window on the gable end. Fine brick piers with urns to the courtyard entrance. Then No.27, Dyke House, the first to display its original shaped gable and elevation of two windows to each floor with small central attic window above. No.28 was its counting-house across the courtyard (the only surviving example of this typically C17 Topsham arrangement), a two-storey building with a prettily detailed wooden fascia. Then Nos. 30–32, a long range along the street, probably an older building converted to cottages, and No.33,

---

*For a plan of No. 25 *see* p. 84.

another typical Strand house, modernized in the C18: good Doric
doorcase on the l., staircase with twisted balusters inside, C19
additions on the r. No.34* is another gabled house, the exterior
now rendered and pebbledashed, but with its original window
arrangement. Long C19 veranda along the flank. A well-preserved
example of the distinctive long thin Topsham plan: staircase
behind the front room (turned balusters, open string, suggesting
an early C18 date); then two intercommunicating rooms, and
beyond them the kitchen with back stairs. No.35, also gabled, has
a different plan, possibly a conversion. Opposite, it is regrettably
difficult to ignore STRAND COURT, 1964–70, banal flats blocking
the view of the river, built on the site of dry docks, both feebly
designed and inappropriately sited.

Further along the Strand one can turn to the attractive series of
gables of No.38 (with projecting room added over a porch and
early C19 Gothic French windows); No.39, unusual because L-
shaped (the gable is a modern addition); and No.40 with a later
bow-window, gatepiers with balls, and two original mullioned
windows on the long side. No.41, rather grander, facing a N
instead of a S courtyard, is supposed to be the earliest of the late
C17 Strand houses. Symmetrical front of five bays, originally
flanked by slightly projecting two-storey wings (the r. one rebuilt
single-storeyed), stuccoed later, with rusticated ground floor
(brick beneath). The room to the l. of the hall has an excellent
plaster ceiling with a circle of flowers and fruit, very similar to that
of Shell House; bolection-moulded fireplace surround. The staircase with closed string and thick turned balusters has the special
feature of a cluster of three newels with balls (instead of the usual
two or one) on the half-landing. It continues up to the attic floor.
In the l. first-floor room bolection-moulded and fielded panelling
and coved wooden cornice (secondary to the house, as there is an
earlier plaster ceiling visible in a cupboard). A few more houses
follow before one reaches the very end of the promontory: No.43,
early C19 and of 1876 (extraordinary pyramid-roofed water tower,
but perhaps basically late C17; and No.44, refronted c. 1800, with
round-headed ground-floor windows. The owner then was a
retired sailor, Thomas Paine, who among his building speculations
also extended No.45, with its pilasters with Grecian honeysuckle.

Returning back along the Strand one can explore the great variety of
good houses in the small streets off to the E. In LOWER SHAPTER
STREET, Nos. 1–2 have good C18 fronts of red brick with blue
headers, each three windows wide; in HIGHER SHAPTER
STREET a pleasant mix of houses and cottages (note the old glazing-bars to No.14). Then by Shell House up MONMOUTH HILL,
where No.11 is L-shaped, with a corner entrance and dentilled
cornice. In MONMOUTH STREET much to enjoy, especially Nos.
36–37, and Nos. 38–39, built in 1715; two storeys, with a continuous coved cornice. Formerly two single houses each of five
bays with a broad pedimented doorcase and Tuscan columns. A
similar doorcase to No.33 (Tincombe House). No.30 (Salisbury
House) has a lateral chimneystack, suggesting an older house
incorporated in the picturesque rendered front with early C19

*For a plan of No. 34 see p. 84.

porch with bowed window above. No.29 has end stacks of Dutch brick. Finally No.19, with a curious neo-classical-cum-Gothic doorcase with plaster decoration and the inscription 1818 JW (for *John Wish*, a local plasterer). Further N WHITE STREET, a nice narrow lane with a good row of houses on the l.: HOLME COT-TAGE and MALTSCOOP COTTAGE (somewhat altered) are a modest pair of red and blue chequer brick, with a central cluster of diagonal stacks.

THE RETREAT, off Topsham Road. A tall, handsome stuccoed house overlooking the river, its grounds partly built up after 1938, when it was divided into flats. According to Polwhele, converted from a sugar warehouse into a mansion by Captain Robert Orme (before 1775), and substantially remodelled by Sir Alexander Hamilton, High Sheriff of Devon, c.1790–5. Entrance front of seven bays with pediment over the central three, decorated with an Adamish roundel and garlands of husks. Large dummy Venetian window below, within an arch filled by a fan motif. Wooden Ionic porch, now glazed. Two Venetian windows on the s side. The w side facing the river, where the basement is exposed as a third storey, has been somewhat altered, but has a very pretty early C19 balcony and veranda; good railings also between the garden and the river. To the N a former C19 ballroom, now a separate house, and coach house and outbuildings, now a boatbuilding yard. Two small square LODGES flank the entrance drive, the N one with an Ionic porch.

Close by is the huge M5 VIADUCT, eleven spans, twin box girder construction, the total length 689 yards.

BRIDGE MILL, a two-storey stone tidemill, part C18, part early C20, worked until c.1960, when the machinery was removed and the mill pool filled in. Adjacent is a three-storey brick steam mill. The dam across the Clyst remains.

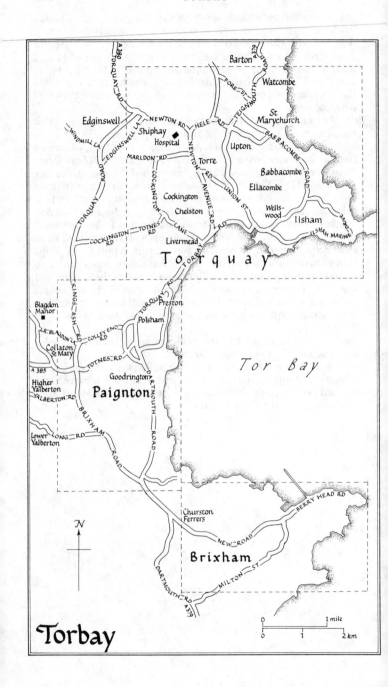

Torbay

TORBAY

INDEX OF STREETS

For localities within Torbay, *see* Index of Places at the end of the book.
B Brixham   C Cockington   CF Churston Ferrers   P Paignton
T Torquay

Torbay is an administrative creation of 1968, embracing the seaside resorts and other smaller settlements around Tor Bay. The unusually mild climate of this region encouraged early habitation, but it was only in the later C20 that the built-up area along the seafront became virtually continuous. The history and nature of the development of the three main constituents – Brixham, Paignton, and Torquay – are however quite distinct, and so each must be treated separately, as must the two main villages that lie within the area (Churston Ferrers and Cockington).

BRIXHAM

Brixham was once two places, Higher Brixham – the village with the parish church on the hill (cf. Dartmouth) – and the little fishing town by the harbour. The two are connected by Bolton Street, a distance of well over half a mile. Both centres have been enveloped by C20 suburban sprawl which extends still further out. Upper Brixham still has a recognizable village street with a few old houses and some delightful Regency villas. Lower Brixham was a port already in the Middle Ages, and William of Orange landed here in 1688. Of all that its present appearance tells us nothing. The present harbour was made in the C18, the pier was built in 1799–1804, and most of the houses around the little harbour also look early C19. The effects of C20 tourism are a little too visible, but generally the architectural character is still early Victorian, small houses painted cream and brown or in other colours, the delight of painters inspired by Christopher Wood.

CHURCHES

ST MARY, Higher Brixham. In a commanding position on a bleak hill now covered on more than one side by suburban houses. Sturdy big W tower with buttresses of type B. Largely cemented because so exposed. S side castellated, including the transept and the S porch, which has inside a complex lierne star vault, with a central boss with the Virgin and angels. N and S aisles of five bays with thin, tall piers: a version of the B type, very similar to Totnes, and so probably of the early C15. Moulded capitals, depressed arches with moulded profiles. The tower arch of the same style as the arcades. Re-roofed by *Ashworth* in 1867; restored by *Tait & Harvey* in 1905, when the galleries were removed. Most of the tracery renewed, but the E window supposed to be original. Recesses for funeral monuments open from the chancel into the N and S chancel chapels, the former ogee-arched, much cusped, the latter Tudor-arched with canopies and a little vault inside, panelled and with pendants (cf. Paignton). The shell PISCINA in the chancel has the coat of arms of Bishop Courtenay of Exeter (1478–87). In the N transept (the former Churston family pew), a SCREEN made up from part of the S gallery erected in 1792 for the use of the growing population of Lower Brixham. – FONT. Early C14, which is a rare date in fonts. Square base with dogs at the corners, octagonal pillar leading into the bowl by means of nodding-ogee canopies on angel brackets – an original, very pretty design. – ALTAR CLOTH. Made from pre-Reformation copes (cf. Culmstock, Holcombe Burnell). In the centre Virgin and Angels, on the borders thirteen Saints (from the orphreys). – CLOCK, in the church. 1740 by *William Stumbels* of Totnes. – MONUMENTS. Coffin lid with foliated cross. – Anne Stucley, *c.* 1720, with skulls at the bottom – could it be by *Weston*? – Minor monuments to the Uptons of Lupton House.

ALL SAINTS, Lower Brixham. A Commissioners' church built by *Thomas Lidstone* of Dartmouth, *c.* 1819–24, in 'modern Gothic style' (*Gentleman's Magazine*, 1830); extensively rebuilt in the late C19. S aisle 1885, N aisle and W front 1892 by *G. Somers Clarke*; tower and Lady Chapel 1900–6 by *Micklethwaite*.

OUR LADY STAR OF THE SEA (R.C.), New Road. 1967 by *Evans &*

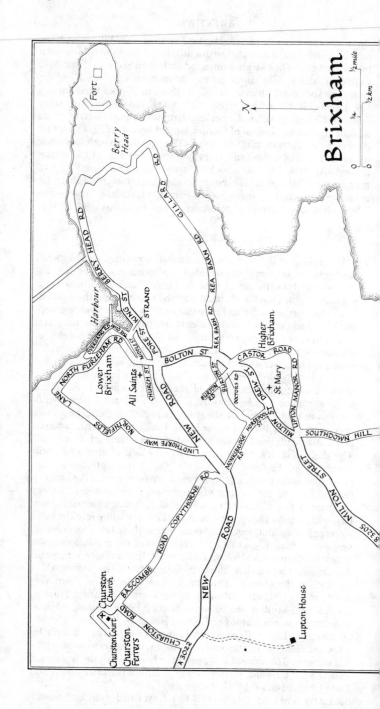

Brixham

Fort

Berry Head

BERRY HEAD RD

GILLARD RD

REA BARN RD

Harbour

THE QUAY

KING ST

STRAND

MIDDLE ST

FORE ST

OVERGANG RD

NORTH FURZEHAM RD

LANE

Lower Brixham

All Saints

CHURCH ST

NORTHFIELDS

LINDTHORPE WAY

NEW ROAD

BOLTON ST

REA BARN RD

CASTOR ROAD

Higher Brixham

BURTON ST

DOCTORS RD

BURTON ST

DREW ST

St Mary

MILTON ST

LIPTON MANOR RD

SOUTHDOWN HILL

MONKSBRIDGE RD

HORSEPOOL ST

MILTON STREET

B 3205

COPYTHORNE RD

BASCOMBE ROAD

Churston Church

Churston Court

Churston Ferrers

CHURSTON ROAD

NEW ROAD

A 3022

Lupton House

N

0 ¼ ½ km

0 ¼ ½ mile

Powell. Ingeniously planned on an awkward site (roof car park, church at first-floor level), but not attractive outside. Plain rendered rectangles; facing the road, large windows with coloured glass in small panes, double-glazed so the exterior effect is dingy. Semi-circular seating. Cornish granite altar and altar rail. – Blessed Sacrament Chapel with STAINED GLASS by *Moira Forsyth*.

CONGREGATIONAL CHAPEL, Bolton Street. Rendered chapel of 1843 with three-bay front; hall of the 1870s, behind a small walled yard. A striking contribution to the street scene.

METHODIST CHURCH. *See* Perambulation 1.

PUBLIC BUILDINGS

EDEN PARK JUNIOR SCHOOL. By *Stillman & Eastwick-Field*, 1968–70.

BERRY HEAD FORT, Berry Head Common. The site of an Iron Age cliff castle, but more prominent now are the remains of extensive Napoleonic fortifications, built in 1794–1804 by *Alexander Mercer*. Batteries, stores, and barracks on the tip of the headland were protected by a dry ditch and typical battered walls with roll-moulded string. Within the enclosure remains of an artillery store and an octagonal sentry box. The barracks have disappeared; they were prefabricated structures. Separate SW landward redoubt.*

WINDMILLS. Five were built around Torbay during the Napoleonic wars. The one in Windmill Hill Road retains a stone rubble base with the date 1797. Another at Galmpton Warborough has the tower complete to the curb; built *c*. 1810.

LIGHTHOUSE, Berry Head. Built in 1906, and at 200 ft, the highest above sea level. Remote-controlled. A small circular building, glazed, with a conical roof topped by a wind vane. Reputedly the smallest lighthouse in Great Britain.

PERAMBULATIONS

1. *Lower Brixham*

Apart from the busy little harbour surrounded by low houses of the early C19, the best streets are KING STREET, with three-storey stucco houses above a high retaining wall, the STRAND, with a former market of 1799, and OVERGANG ROAD to the N of the harbour. FORE STREET leading up from the harbour also has little that jars. The GLOBE, with carriageway, fits in well, as does the METHODIST CHURCH of 1816, enlarged in 1871, five bays, with round-arched windows, and a prominent porch on two columns. Branching off Fore Street, endless steps lead up the steep hill to the S. The long flight of TEMPERANCE STEPS is worth a special mention.

In BERRY HEAD ROAD, leading E from the harbour, BRITISH SEAMEN'S BOYS' HOME, C19 Gothic of various dates, by *E. Appleton*. The original house quite forceful, tall and gabled, with lancets under an arch, and corbelled-out dormers. Low chapel, the W part originally a schoolroom of 1875, given by Angela Burdett

---

* See D. Evans, *Devon Buildings Group Newsletter*, 5 (April 1988).

Coutts. Further s large houses above the road and, some way on, BERRY HEAD HOUSE HOTEL, built as a military hospital during the Napoleonic wars. Plain grey stone seven-window front. (For the contemporary fort *see* Public Buildings, above.)

N of the harbour, above the valley that was once a creek (now filled by an unappealing bus station and car park), MIDDLE STREET, with old cottages above in CHURCH STREET. From the crossroads by the head of the former creek, BOLTON STREET climbs up to Higher Brixham with some terraced houses (Nos. 36–42) with vermiculated doorways as at Southernhay in Exeter, etc., and a chapel of 1843 (q.v.). NEW ROAD leads N out of the town, with villas of the 1830s. N of New Road, among indifferent suburbia, one development worth a glance: COOMBE BANK in LINDTHORPE WAY, sheltered housing of c. 1981 by *Anthony Pearson* of *Wyvern Partnership*, an ingeniously undulating range with a pleasantly varied front with boxed and tile-hung bay-windows, overlooking a lawn with a tree. On the A3022 at Monksbridge a fine slate-hung two-storey TOLL HOUSE with angled front.

2. Higher Brixham

The centre of the village of Higher Brixham is at the crossroads by St Mary's church. The main route, DREW STREET–MILTON STREET, still has a convincingly village aspect, continuously built up with cottages and a few larger houses. The most interesting of these are the pretty villas built for the daughters of the Gillard family in the early C19. From NW to SE, first AYLMER, down a drive to the N of Milton Street. A pretty stucco front with concave-headed windows with marginal glazing; three bays to the two-storey centre, with a formerly one-storey bay with a blind arch on either side. The swept-roof trellis veranda was restored in 1988. Elegant interior, with groin-vaulted entrance hall; cantilevered staircase in a bowed projection to the garden, main ground-floor rooms with curved corners. Further on, the former town manor house of the Gillards (now subdivided), consisting of a large main range (BLACK HOUSE), probably C16 in origin, with an end stack on the r. and a l. wing projecting forward. The exterior all stuccoed. Early C19 porch with thin Doric columns. (In the main range an C18 staircase and panelling.) Opposite, NORTON, another Gillard villa, end-on to the road, similar but not identical to Aylmer; a slightly more sophisticated elevation, with the ogee-headed windows of the ground floor within arches. An older cottage at the back adapted as a service wing. Elliptical staircase, good interior detail. Two more similar villas off Drew Street to the N: EVELEIGH, in Doctors Road, and BURTON VILLA round the corner in Burton Street, with especially good ironwork, sadly swamped by the later housing which extends endlessly to the N. Also, in Burton Road, BURTON COURT, set back and looking down Doctors Road, a symmetrical early C19 stuccoed three-storey, three-bay house.

In HORSEPOOL STREET, N from the village centre crossroads, three former farmhouses remain: GOAT HOUSE, GREENOVER FARM, and HILL HOUSE; also, up the hill to the W, a cheerful flat-roofed effort of the 1930s, No. 1 SUNPARK. To the S, UPTON MANOR, Upton Manor Road, C18 but remodelled in the early C19, with a stuccoed, ogee-roofed veranda, deep bracketed eaves, and an entrance with Doric columns *in antis*.

LIMEKILN, almost on Mansands Beach. Large and rounded, with good features.

PREHISTORIC REMAINS. Palaeolithic and later material has been found in a number of caves, including Ash Hole and Windmill Hill Cave.

3. *Lupton House*

LUPTON HOUSE is the remains of an elegant Palladian mansion (now a school) built for Charles Hayne, sheriff in 1772, remodelled in a more stodgy neo-classical style *c.* 1840 by *George Wightwick* for Sir J. B. Yarde Buller. *Salvin* was paid for further alterations in 1862, since demolished. The house was gutted by fire in 1926 and reconstructed without the top floor. The s front, facing a garden sadly derelict at the time of writing, still makes a handsome show, with a lively rhythm of 2–1–1–1–2 bays, although the wings have lost their distinctive pedimented Palladian gables, and so appear weak when compared with the centre. This is enriched with pedimented windows above Venetian windows, all with false balustrades. In the centre a Doric doorcase treated as a single unit with the window above, which has carved volutes. The flat-fronted three-bay w front was remodelled by *Wightwick* when the main entrance was moved to this side. Roman Doric porte-cochère, windows with some Grecian detail.

The surviving interiors include *Wightwick*'s entrance hall with square piers and marble fireplace and a large seated statue of Mr Rowe by *E. B. Stephens*, and, facing the garden, *Wightwick*'s former library, divided by stocky Ionic marble columns; green marble fireplace with Greek key ornament. To the w a room with a ceiling which has late C18 Adamish swags and fan shapes (now subdivided), and between this and the library the C18 entrance hall (headmaster's study) with two busts on pedestals.

STABLES. The r. wing only remains, pedimented, with pilasters and lunette, of a large U-shaped group altered and improved by *Wightwick*.

LODGES. A neat neo-classical pair by *Wightwick*, pedimented, with Doric pilasters, originally cruciform in plan, tactfully doubled in depth in 1983–5 by *Keith Proctor*.

CHURSTON FERRERS

Church and manor house still stand alone in a rural enclave between Paignton and Brixham.

CHURCH. Not much atmosphere, owing primarily to extensive restoration of 1864–6 (all tracery renewed, roofs replaced), and also to the large clear-glass windows. Nave and aisles of five bays; thin piers of B type with capitals in which the arms of the Yarde family and also animals appear. Two-storeyed s porch at the w end of the s aisle (the Crucifixion above the entrance originally, one would presume, the head of a cross). Squint from the upper room through a quatrefoil opening in the reveal of a window in the s aisle. Low, small w tower with diagonal buttresses. – PULPIT. C18, cut down in 1863; inlaid tester. – SCREEN. Fragments incorporated in the vast Victorian contraption which now fills the tower arch. – BENCH ENDS. With leaves in diaper panels. – STAINED GLASS. In the s aisle easternmost window, armorial panels, some medieval. – MONUMENT. W. Farquharsen † 1813. Seated mourning female by an urn.

CHURSTON COURT (now a hotel), the former seat of the Yardes, of which the church was originally the private chapel, lies immediately w. Two-storey, symmetrical early C17 rendered front with low ovolo-moulded stone four-light windows. Higher gabled wing on the l. Remodelled inside in the late C17; entrance hall with bolection-moulded panelling, a large room on either side. Remains of a good staircase with spiral balusters and closed string, the lower flights destroyed to provide access to back extensions in 1985–7.

Along CHURSTON ROAD, between the church and the main road, C19 estate housing – a modest terrace and some pairs of cottages.

STATION (now Dartmouth Steam Railway). 1861 for the Dartmouth and Torbay railway. One-storeyed, random stone with ashlar quoins, simple flat awning. Two nearby HOTELS, simple late Georgian style.

RAILWAY VIADUCTS. Two most impressive structures, one at Hookhills of nine graceful arches of 40ft span, another at Broadsands of four arches. Rock-faced limestone. They carry the single track of the Torbay and Dartmouth line of the Dart Valley railways.

BROADSANDS ROAD. Near the top, an estate planned in 1933–4 by *Lescaze* (cf. Dartington), easily distinguished from the conventional suburban houses in the neighbourhood. Intended for retired business and professional people. Detached houses in Broadsands Road and ROCK CLOSE; also groups of three tucked into the slope, entered at first-floor level. All rendered, with flat roofs, sun terraces, and progressive features such as corner windows, grouped in some variety, although later additions have obscured the play of geometric asymmetry. No. 3 Rock Close is among the least altered. The site plan was by *Henry Wright*, the landscaping by *Beatrix Farrand*. The estate was described in *Building* in 1935 as 'probably the most ambitious attempt to build a comprehensive modern scheme to a uniform style'. Nearby an alternative aesthetic is provided by Tor Close, with small, sparely detailed pitched-roofed houses, in the manner of *de Soissons*.

At Elbury Farm, Goodrington, the Broadsands CHAMBERED CAIRN (*see* Introduction: Prehistory).

COCKINGTON

The grounds in which lie Cockington Court, Cockington church, and the Drum Inn are beautifully kept by Torbay Borough Council and make an extremely pleasing picture. Approaching the house the inn appears in a hollow below to the r., the E end of the church behind a sturdy oak tree.

26 ST GEORGE AND ST MARY. A typical Devon Perp exterior. Red

sandstone. E end with three gables, the chancel slightly projecting; Perp windows throughout. Low, broad W tower with diagonal buttresses and a stair-turret attached to the middle of the N side. Low obelisk pinnacles. Unmoulded round arch inside towards the nave. Nave and two aisles of five bays. No transepts. The piers of B type, the capitals left undecorated on the N, with standard decoration on the S. Restoration 1882–3 by *Hine & Odgers*, and by *Charles Nicholson*, when the woodwork was restored by *Herbert Read*. – FONT. C15, slim pillar, wide octagonal bowl with quatrefoil and heraldic decoration. – SCREEN. Very renewed, standard A tracery, carving entirely new. – PULPIT (from Torre church, i.e. the parish church of the village of Torquay). The most interesting piece in the church, wholly early Renaissance in its decoration. Baluster colonnettes flank the panels. In these the late medieval nodding ogee canopies are replaced by canopies with the new foliage, and the Perp angels by putti. The bracket opens out fan-wise to support the pulpit proper. – ALTAR RAILS. C17. – CHANCEL STALLS with a few misericords; also two earlier ones against the wall, said to come from Torre Abbey. – BENCH ENDS. A few under the tower. – STAINED GLASS. Figures of apostles in a S window (C15) and one St Paul (early C14) in a N window. – BELL, in the church. C17, with inscription reversed.

COCKINGTON COURT. The seat of the Carys from the C14 to 1654, when it was bought by Roger Mallock, an Exeter merchant. Parts of the Tudor house of the Carys survive, disguised by an extensive remodelling by Rawlin Mallock, c. 1673. Projecting wings (the date 1577 on the S wing) with broad, many-mullioned windows; now with wooden casements. Two-storey classical centre of seven bays; central doorway with Corinthian fluted columns. A top floor was removed and the interiors remodelled c. 1820 by the Rev. Roger Mallock. The hall was divided up and a staircase inserted. At the entrance to the grounds, an eminently picturesque LODGE with a rustic veranda on tree-trunks supporting the thatched roof, and Gothic windows with straight-sided heads instead of arches. Built shortly before the road was altered in 1838.

The Mallocks resisted the temptation to develop their estate on the edge of expanding Torquay until the 1930s, when the Cockington Trust was formed, aiming to preserve 'entire and unchanged the ancient amenities and character of the place and in developing its surroundings to do nothing which may not rather enhance than diminish its attractiveness'. The one-storey thatched FORGE and cottages of the village were assiduously preserved (and are a little too perfectly kept to satisfy). The Trust planned to complement these with a model village centre, designed by *Lutyens*, illustrated in a brochure of 1935. The inspiration was the C18 planned village rather than local vernacular tradition: a village green with estate office was to be flanked by thatched rows of cottages with shops. The only part of the scheme built was the DRUM INN. This also is thatched, the deep eaves taking in the central bay-windows in the main range. Two not quite symmetrical lower wings come forward, anchored by tall battered chimneys of brick. A further l. wing was planned but not built. At an angle to the forecourt, curved steps lead down to a garden, with an answering flight at its far end beside the millrace and remains of the mill.

At the same time groups of new houses were planned on different parts of the estate, away from the village, so that their designs did not have to conform to old-world principles. The first ones included semi-detached and terrace houses by *Gerald Lacoste* (Burridge Road and Sherwell Valley) with corner windows and colour-glazed pantiles as well as more traditional types, e.g. by *Bridgman & Bridgman* in Herbert Road.

PAIGNTON

Among the seaside developments of Torbay, Paignton on first acquaintance appears a poor relation, a scruffy low-key early C20 resort surrounded by indifferent suburbs, lacking the charm of Brixham or the leisured elegance of the best parts of Torquay. This is unfair: behind the tourist clutter near the seafront is a spacious, well-laid-out late Victorian town centre, developed by the local architect *G.S.Bridgman*; and adjoining this, a much older settlement, still traceable by its narrow streets. Until the Reformation Paignton was one of the richest manors of the Bishop of Exeter. Scanty remnants of the Bishop's Palace survive close to the substantial parish church; not far off is Kirkham House, a carefully restored small late medieval house. Around this old centre a few genteel villas began to appear from the early C19. Instead of the uniformity encouraged by the ground landlords of Torquay, one has several engagingly eccentric examples: Barcombe Hall,* an eclectic *villa rustica* of 1838, Redcliffe Towers of 1853, a Hindu fantasy, and the staggering Oldway mansion (now Council Offices) transformed in the early C20 by the Singers into a vision of Versailles.

CHURCHES

CHRIST CHURCH, Polsham. 1886–8 by *E.Gabriel* (or *J.R.Gates*, according to B.F.L. Clarke). Impressively scaled E.E., red sandstone, cruciform, with tall clerestory and apsed E end. A SW tower was planned. – Brass eagle LECTERN.

ST ANDREW, Sands Road. 1892–7 by *Fulford, Tait & Harvey*; a large red sandstone clerestoried town church in the manner of James Brooks (cf. St Matthew, Newtown, Exeter, by the same firm). Simplified French Gothic detail. Effective E end with a circular window high up, and an apsed NE chapel (the intended tower above it not executed). The W end completed by *Caröe* to a simplified plan in 1929–30. The interior with a generous number of polished shafts. Moulded arches in Ham Hill stone. – Good STAINED GLASS in the E windows (Lady Chapel E 1897). – Leafy CHURCHYARD with handsome lychgate, Victorian lamp standards, and schoolrooms of 1906 by *E.Appleton*.

ST GEORGE, Goodrington. 1939 by *E.Maufe*, the nave built in 1962 to a simplified version of Maufe's plans. Sacristy 1965. Plain rendered exterior, a little gaunt in its detail: the original plans had gables to the N vestries and tracery to the nave windows. The best

---

*To be demolished, alas.

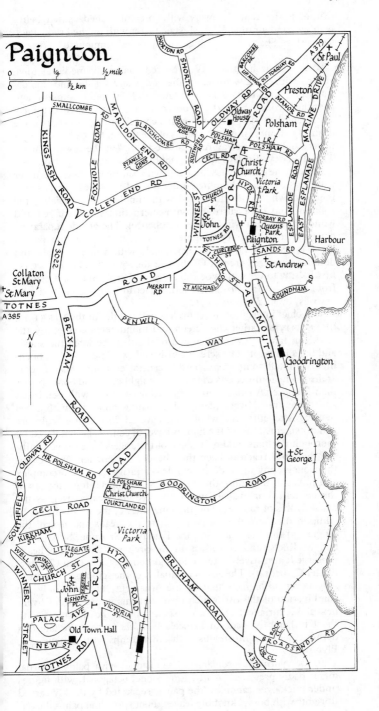

feature is the central tower, with forceful arched slatted belfry windows and a rather Scottish stair-turret with pitched roof. Passage aisles. Spacious crossing with pointed unmoulded crossing arches.

ST JOHN, Church Street. A large red sandstone medieval town church with a big w tower, embattled N and S aisles and N and S transepts, four-light aisle windows and five-light transept and chancel E windows, and a S porch with a low vaulted entrance. Total length, 193 ft. Of the Norman church of Paignton only some chancel masonry, the foundations of the w wall 6 ft E of the present tower, and the doorway reset in the w wall of the tower remain. The doorway displays quite a sophisticated use of polychrome masonry: the outer voussoirs red with saltire crosses, the inner white with zigzag; the outer order on red scalloped capitals, the inner on white ones decorated with simple foliage; finally, the columns and door surround with alternating stripes of red and white. E.E. lancet windows in the chancel. The arcade separating nave and aisles late C13, heightened in the C15. Only the E pair of piers is entirely C15: red, octagonal, with white capitals and double-chamfered arches. Of the C14 the S porch. The rest is C15, first half: w tower with type B buttresses, Perp windows. Restored from 1864 by E. Christian; another tactful restoration, and new vestries, by W. D. Caröe, 1912–14.

49   The chief interest of the church is without doubt the KIRKHAM CHANTRY, or rather the screen and monuments erected by the Kirkham family towards the end of the C15, between the S aisle and the S transept. The screen consists of two Tudor-arched openings with tall tomb-chests and a central entrance, also Tudor-arched. The tomb-chests each have a knight and a lady on top, less than life size. All three openings are fan-vaulted with pendants, and there are or were plenty of crowning pinnacles with angel figures. Altogether the whole was covered with figure sculpture and ornament. Most of the figures have, of course, been defaced by thorough Puritans, and only some of the angels have proved sufficiently out of reach to keep their heads. But enough survives for the iconography to be decipherable – a rarity. It is both complex and unusual, including the nine orders of angels, four doctors of the church, four evangelists, the twelve apostles, as well as the usual figures of mourners on the long sides of the tomb-chests. In addition there are four large panels to the heads and feet of the effigies, of the Visitation and the Family of St Anne, St Anthony and St Roch, and the Mass of St Gregory (with some heads preserved; a relatively rare subject, although cf. Oldham Chantry, Exeter Cathedral). The aesthetic quality of the sculpture was probably never as high as that of the ornament, but it is only the combination of the two which results in this impression of liveliness and luxuriance. There are no inscriptions; the identification to the Kirkhams is made in Prince's *Worthies* (1701); the late C15 dating rests on comparisons with other tombs with armour (e.g. Plympton).

FONT. Norman, circular, red sandstone, with palmette ornament; badly preserved. – PULPIT. Stone, octagonal, with figures under thick ogee canopies, the panels separated by thickly carved uprights with bossy, knobbly leaves. Foot spreading palm-like (cf.

Harberton, etc.). – SEDILIA. Reconstructed in 1870 from old fragments. Ogee-crocketed arches. Elaborate flamboyant Gothic. – ORGAN CASE by *M. Mowbray*, 1889, given by Paris Singer. Formerly below the tower. – MONUMENTS (other than those already mentioned). C15 cadaver in a recess in the S aisle. – Similar recess in the N aisle without effigy. – Two large kneeling figures facing each other, in the Kirkham Chapel, under two flat arches, badly preserved.

ST MARY, Collaton St Mary. 1864–6 by *J. W. Rowell*. Evocative Victorian group of small village church, school, and vicarage, built by the Rev. J. R. Hogg of Blagdon in memory of his daughter, who died in 1864. SW red sandstone tower with short pinnacles, lean-to porch, windows with red and white alternating voussoirs, all glimpsed beyond the steep yew-lined approach from the lychgate. – Rich furnishings: stone REREDOS, 1865 by *Earp*, with a relief of the Last Supper carved by *Phyffers* of Teignmouth; texts painted on the walls; splendid marble FONT on a high plinth, also by *Earp*, with elaborate suspended canopied FONT COVER. – STAINED GLASS. Good E window and chancel S windows, 1865 and 1867, designed by *Bentley*, executed by *Lavers, Barraud & Westlake*.

ST PAUL, Preston. 1939 by *N. F. Cachemaille Day*. Cruciform, with a prominent NE tower of red sandstone with angular fins, typical of this architect's modern reinterpretation of Gothic. The interior is less interesting, apart from the feature of an upper chapel above the vestry beneath the tower. Passage aisles, wooden-vaulted nave, no clerestory. Totally unsympathetic church hall attached at the W end, 1968–9.

BIBLE CHRISTIAN CHAPEL, Southfield Road. Built as an Independent Chapel in 1823, complete with caretaker's house – the oldest Nonconformist chapel in the area. Bought by the Bible Christians in 1884, altered in 1901. Plain rendered front, sides of red sandstone with pointed windows; low-pitched roof with projecting eaves. Porch of 1903. Interior with memorials from the mid C19.

UNITED REFORMED CHURCH, Dartmouth Road. Ambitious limestone group by *G. S. Bridgman*: chapel and halls of 1876, schools of 1887. Corner tower with octagonal spire; freestone and red sandstone dressings; sides with buttresses and gabled dormers.

ST MICHAEL'S METHODIST MISSION, Merritt Road. In the ground floor of a block of flats of 1906, built by Washington Singer (cf. Oldway) to relieve unemployment. Intended as a working men's club, but converted to a mission room in 1911.

PUBLIC BUILDINGS

OLDWAY HOUSE (now council offices). The original house was built in 1873 by the local architect *G. S. Bridgman* for Isaac Singer, founder of the sewing-machine company. Singer called the house 'the wigwam', and specified French Renaissance detail. Its fussy nature – brick with stone dressings, heavy cornice, prominent chimneys and dormers – can still be glimpsed on the W side. In 1904–7 a drastic remodelling was undertaken for Isaac Singer's son Paris, inspired by Versailles. Two stunningly bombastic fronts were added to N and E, both clothed with a giant Ionic order.

Along the whole of the E front a nine-column loggia, the irregular number perhaps an indication that this was not the design of a classically trained architect. N front with projecting pedimented portico. Quieter S front, also French C18 in style, with channelled ground floor, pedimented centre with niches flanking larger windows, canted one-storey pavilions. Inside, lavish decoration from both periods, but the *pièce de résistance* is Paris Singer's magnificent imperial stair (inserted on the site of his father's private theatre), with sumptuous marble cladding, bronze balusters, and a very accomplished coved illusionistic painted ceiling, based on one by Lebrun at Versailles. On the half-landing there used to be *David*'s painting of Napoleon crowning Josephine. On the first floor a broad gallery overlooking the stair with enriched Ionic columns, and a ballroom with Rococo-style panels and chimneypiece.

Sober classical ARCHWAY N of the house. Nearby the former RIDING SCHOOL, 1873 by *Bridgman* for Isaac Singer, an eccentric circular building, red brick, two storeys of windows, clerestory, low conical roof. Fine formal GROUNDS, laid out by the leading French formal landscape architect *A.Duchesne*. They include lakes, rock garden, grotto, and Italian garden, and also some delightfully haughty sphinxes in C18 style to the S of the house.

SCHOOL OF ART AND SCIENCE, Bishops Place and Gerston Place. 1908. Good free Baroque front. Doorway and upper windows with Gibbs rustication. On the flank wall a very large sgraffito panel, in bad condition.

BOARD SCHOOLS, Curledge Street. A handsome group of grey limestone buildings. On the W side the GROSVENOR BOARD SCHOOL, 1885, and BOARD ROOM; opposite, the GIRLS' SCHOOL, 1895, with three gables and white stone dressings, and the TEACHERS' CENTRE (the domestic end of the demolished Infants' School?).

FESTIVAL HALL, Esplanade. 1962 by *C.F.J.Thurley*. An ugly terminus to Torbay Road. A blank wall unfeelingly cutting off a view of the sea. The show front faces E to the green, with glazed upper parts. A restaurant on stilts looks out to sea.

PIER, Esplanade. 1878–9. A modest example, refurbished from 1981 by *E.Narracott, Tanner & André* with jazzy cladding and rooflights; triangular motifs in primary colours.

TORBAY LEISURE CENTRE, Dartmouth Road. 1978 by the Borough Architect, *Ray Banks*. Prominent but undistinguished large boxes.

POLICE STATION, Southfield Rise. 1968 by *Dawes Dingle*. The front block of two storeys on stilts, running back into the hill, successfully conceals the bulkier parts behind.

PERAMBULATIONS

1. The Old Town

The present seaside resort developed only from the later C19 on the salt marshes and sand dunes that separated the old settlement from the sea. The town has a more venerable history than Torquay. In the Middle Ages the manor belonged to the bishops of Exeter, who built a palace here to the s of the parish church, close to their deer park. The main thoroughfare of the old town was Winner Street (named after the bishops' vineyard), running N–S to the W of the church.

BISHOP'S PALACE, s of the churchyard. All that remains is a rectangular enclosure bounded by high walls, on the s and e sides with battlements, and one tower at the SE corner, with two storeys of two-light windows, trefoil-cusped and ogee-headed.

PRINCESS STREET, N of the church. The start of an intricate pattern of small streets, their character diminished by haphazard clearance, but from c. 1980 much improved by sensitive infilling and restoration by the *Borough Architectural Services Group*, chief architect *Austen Bond*. Facing Church Street, first the VICTORIA INN, stuccoed, and the former mid-C19 BREWERY, sturdy red stone buildings of three and four storeys, with a prominent ventilating tower, embellished by white and green paintwork since conversion to offices and housing by the Devon Historic Buildings Trust in 1981–2. In the streets behind, simple white-walled terraces, a tactful mixture of old and new. Round the corner in LITTLEGATE ROAD, in a pedestrian alley, the tiny stone CLINK with one slit window. Further on at the corner of KIRKHAM STREET Kirkham House, the most complete medieval secular building in Paignton.

KIRKHAM HOUSE is late medieval, restored by the Department of the Environment in 1960, when alterations dividing it into two cottages were removed. The house is now displayed to the public. Red sandstone, wooden mullioned windows all restored, but original ogee-headed oak front doorway. Traditional three-room plan, as found in rural farmhouses, but with details suggesting that this was a house of superior status. Screens passage with pebble floor and well preserved stud-and-panel screens with shouldered-headed arches. On either side, hall and parlour. The moulded beams and stone-hooded fireplaces with embattled cresting (also originally a stone laver in each room) are all signs of a house of some consequence. Part of the open hall is filled by an upper chamber jettied out over the screens passage, probably a later addition. The room beyond the hall is unheated; the kitchen was a separate building at the back of which foundations remain. The three chambers on the upper floor are reached by a reconstructed staircase and timber gallery in an extension along the back of the house. The room over the parlour has a hooded fireplace, the room at the opposite end a simpler fireplace on the end wall, and a corner garderobe. Roof much restored. The house was imaginatively furnished in 1980–1 with modern craftsman's work, commissioned to display traditional English timber and joinery techniques.

Also in KIRKHAM STREET a C19 stone warehouse, and two pretty cottages – MYRTLE COTTAGE, with a C19 frontage with an elegant Doric porch, and KIRKHAM and CHANTRY COTTAGES, a picturesque but over-restored composition with thatched roofs – before the street ends abruptly at a busy traffic junction. From here WELL STREET, with modest terraces, returns s to Church Street.

CHURCH STREET broadens at its higher N end as it meets WINNER STREET. No individual building to pick out, but several are probably older than their early C19 plastered frontages, e.g. Nos. 48–50

Church Street, low with undulating roof, and the GLOBE INN, Winner Street.

Further s, in FISHER STREET, the continuation of Winner Street, along what was the main Paignton to Dartmouth Road until the mid C19, several older houses, especially MERRICOTE, late Georgian, with coved eaves and porch with big fanlight, an irregular group nearby with Georgian sashes, and further on the TORBAY INN, a long rendered front, two doors with pedimented hoods, black and white detail.

TOWER HOUSE SCHOOL, e of Fisher Street. A grand mansion in a debased French classical style of c. 1890, brick and stone, with a balustraded central tower and a rounded corner.

2. The C19 and C20 Resort

A few handsome villas in the Torquay style of c. 1830–50 are to be found on the slopes to the NE of Winner Street, e.g. in SOUTH-FIELD ROAD. In SOUTHFIELD RISE the villas have recessed pedimented entrance wings to each pair, and the weird feature of an arched porch on paired Greek Doric columns. At the bottom of the road a polygonal Tudor TOLL HOUSE. But these are less typical of Paignton than the more urban developments which took place in the later C19, heralded by NEW STREET, between Winner Street and the New Torquay Road, with its stuccoed terraces, a quirky design with the central unit carried up from the bay-window through a first-floor arch, with projecting dormer above.

PALACE AVENUE, N of New Street, is a little later, an admirable urban ensemble of the 1890s by the local architect *G.S.Bridgman*, who was responsible for much of later C19 Paignton. The avenue divides around the trim oval gardens in the centre. On the s side the PALACE THEATRE, a public hall of 1890 with shaped gables at the ends and on the two projecting wings. The s side of the avenue has a terrace of houses with half-timbering. The rest is more formal, each side starting with a more presumptuous building: on the N side a former BANK in free classical style, on the s side a POST OFFICE (1888) with a confident rounded corner with Baroque doorway and a ground floor of red stone. This material is repeated for the piers between the ensuing shops. On the upper floors plenty of typically seaside bays; on the N side balconies recessed beneath large top-floor arches.

At the corner of Palace Avenue and Torquay Road LLOYDS BANK, a showy front with three colours of stone and polished marble columns at the corner entrance. Around TORQUAY ROAD a slightly earlier phase of development (c. 1860–70), stuccoed, with arched upper windows. Ingenious entrances from GERSTON PLACE to the domestic residences over the shops facing the main road. VICTORIA STREET, with the GERSTON HOTEL (1870) at the corner of HYDE ROAD, continues towards the sea in similar style to Palace Avenue.

Across the railway line first the lavish TORBAY CINEMA (opened as the Paignton Picture House in 1914), engagingly combining angular free Baroque (giant Ionic pilasters framing a concave centre with bow-windows) with art-nouveau details (see the sinuous door handles and the stained glass in the upper foyer). To the N VICTORIA SQUARE, 1983–6 by *Ardin & Brooks*, a shopping square with canopied arcades on two sides; quite playful gables above; white render and red woodwork. It has the merit of concealing an older multi-storey car park behind.

TORBAY ROAD continues towards the sea, beginning grandly on the r. with tall turn-of-the-century scrolly-gabled terracotta-trimmed terraces. At the back they have a profusion of balconies overlooking QUEENS PARK (opened 1901). This has quite a festive pavilion in QUEENS ROAD; tower with balustraded top.

Facing the Green along the sea front, gabled villas and hotels. At the W end a handsome classical CLUB of 1882, with a colonnade of fat Ionic columns and a bow at either end. Nearby, at the start of Roundham Road, a much restored group of thatched cottages, pre-dating the resort, then the little HARBOUR (constructed in 1837, enlarged 1938–9). ROUNDHAM ROAD circles the rising ground above, with a sprinkling of villas, mostly stuccoed (and mostly altered and extended). Occasional later examples, e.g. CONISTON in SANDS ROAD, 1902, in a free French Renaissance. In the opposite direction, to the E along the ESPLANADE, the best hotel building is the PALACE, with porte-cochère at the side, and a front room facing the sea with good Rococo-style plasterwork and a wooden chimneypiece to match.

Further N, at the beginning of MARINE DRIVE, the REDCLIFFE HOTEL, built in 1853–6 as Redcliffe Towers. An astonishing creation by a retired Indian engineer, *Robert Smith*, who bought the site in 1853 and transformed an earlier building into a castellated Indian fantasy. Large central tower with three added wings (for picture galley, conservatory and billiard room, and servants). Ogee 'Hindu' battlements with ogee machicolation; elaborate curvy plastered window surrounds. The tower has bay-windows with sea views on three sides, and is decorated with circular plaques and St John's crosses. A tunnel once existed, leading to a plunge bath on the beach directly below. The interiors much altered after 1902, when the house was acquired by the Singers (cf. Public Buildings: Oldway House). Further alterations in 1960. A new wing with echoes of the original style was added in 1986.

From the E end of the Esplanade LOWER POLSHAM ROAD, with some good early C19 villas (e.g. PARKFIELD, in large grounds), winds towards the old settlement of Polsham. Nearby, attractive GLASSHOUSES of the 1980s by the *Borough Architectural Services Group*, chief architect *Austen Bond*. The POLSHAM ARMS is an old house with lateral stack, ineptly clothed with fake timbers. N of Torquay Road a few more early C19 villas in HIGHER POLSHAM ROAD. Further E OLD TORQUAY ROAD, as the name might suggest, still has a few cottages and the MANOR INN, hidden away to the N of the present busy route leading to Torquay.

BARCOMBE HALL, Barcombe Drive.* A substantial villa in an asymmetrical picturesque Grecian-Gothic-Italianate, interesting as a very early example of its type in the Torbay area. Shown on a map of 1840, when it stood quite alone in its own grounds to the N of the town, and therefore identifiable with the house designed for N. H. Nugent by *Edward Davis* of Bath, a pupil of Soane, for

*Scandalously, not listed by the Department of the Environment, and threatened with demolition at the time of writing.

which drawings were exhibited at the Royal Academy in 1838. Not of stucco, like the early Torbay villas, but red sandstone with Bath stone dressings. An eclectic entrance front: shallow Gothic arched windows and doors, but a Doric four-column porch, with Doric triglyphs repeated along the cornice. To the l. a more Italianate campanile with round-arched upper windows and dentilled cornice. The garden elevation is also irregular. No Gothic detail: tripartite windows on the l., a canted bay near the centre, and on the r. a wing with a broad projecting shallow gable and a second thinner campanile. Remains of a formal Italianate garden with balustrades.

(THE COACH HOUSE, Steartfield Road. C19 coach house with little clock tower, pleasantly converted to cottages and flats, with two tactful new wings, by *Keith Proctor*, 1983–6.)

BLAGDON MANOR, off Totnes Road. The seat of the Kirkhams from the C13 to the C17. Much altered. A remodelling dated 1567 may account for the three-light transomed windows of the hall, with dripstones above, and the two-light window over the porch. The hall roof has been renewed. Above the fireplace a plasterwork panel dated 1708 with the arms and initials of Edward Blount. One pre-Tudor doorway visible in the hall: two-centred with hollow chamfer. In the room to the S a large four-centred fireplace in an unusual position backing on to the site of the screens passage.

S.T.C. FACTORY, Yalberton. An extensive, utilitarian range of 1957 by *J. Francis Smith*, with large glazed areas and a control tower like an airport.

9060   TORQUAY

Torquay's development as a seaside resort began at the end of the C18 when the south coast of Devon began to be exploited for the new fashion of sea bathing. The area's special asset was the mild climate, which encouraged winter visitors. Before this, the most important building was Torre Abbey, which lay some way from the sea, above Torre Abbey Sands W of the present harbour. The village of Tormohun (named from the Mohuns, Lords of the Manor from the C13) lay further N, with its parish church of St Saviour.

At the end of the C18 the land along the sea front was divided between the Carys of Torre Abbey and the Palks (*see* Lawrence Castle, Dunchideock) who owned Torre Manor and Torwood further E across the Fleet Brook. The first step towards the creation of the town was taken on the Cary side when in 1794 some houses called New Quay (later Cary Parade) were built by a local architect called *Searle*. In 1803 Sir Lawrence Palk obtained an Act of Parliament for the improvement of the harbour; the initial plans were by *Rennie*. Terraces on the steep hills to the E followed, the first ones by *Joseph Beard*, then by *Jacob Harvey* and his sons. The completion of the harbour and the further development of much of the town appears to have owed much to the expertise of the Devonian Dr Henry Beake (professor of history and Dean of Bristol and a national authority on financial matters). From the 1820s the chief entrepreneur was William Kitson, local banker and solicitor, and steward to the Palk estates from 1833. The Palks continued to control much of Torquay until the death of Lord Haldon fifty years later; after 1894, when the estates were sold off, the growth of the town became more haphazard.

The earliest of the new buildings were terraces in the Georgian urban tradition; but with a few exceptions (especially the splendid set piece of Hesketh Crescent of the 1840s at Meadfoot) the speciality of Torquay is not the square or crescent, as found for example at Brighton, but the stuccoed Italianate villas in their own grounds which stud the dramatic little hills that frame the harbour and are approached by picturesque winding carriage drives. From the 1830s development was rapid. Princess Victoria paid a visit in 1833, and the aristocracy followed. The Bishop of Exeter built himself a palatial *villa rustica* (now the Palace Hotel, and much altered) between the old settlement of Ilsham and the new one of Babbacombe, and the Cary lands were opened up for building first by the new Torbay Road to Brixham and Paignton (1842), then by the extensions of the railway from its first terminus at Torre (1848) to Torquay Station nearer the sea (1859). Meanwhile, Ellacombe, the valley between Babbacombe and the town centre, was developed by the Palks as a working-class area to serve the wealthier suburbs. The later suburbs have greater variety, not least in their wealth of High Victorian Gothic churches, many by major architects. Among domestic buildings, the dominance of the stuccoed Italianate begins to falter from the 1860s. The new Palk manor house on Lincombe Hill (1862), by the estate architect of the later C 19, *J. W. Rowell*, is grey limestone Tudor Gothic. Picturesque Old English, generally an alien style in Devon, is represented by one early example, a house on Babbacombe Cliff by *Nesfield* of 1878. Then, in the C 20, as expanding Torquay threatened to drown the surrounding countryside, the thatched cottage became precious; the vernacular revival (combined with formal gardens) was demonstrated influentially by the work of *Lutyens* at Cockington (q.v.) in the 1930s and (a little earlier) by his pupil *Fred Harrild*.

The town centre, lying in the valley between the Cary and Palk estates, was never of great significance, although there was some effort at municipal improvement when the Fleet Brook was culverted in 1865. The town became a borough in 1892, but its twin expressions of civic pride, the Town Hall and the Pavilion, were built only in 1911. By then Torquay embraced not only Ilsham and Babbacombe, but (from 1900) the old parish of St Marychurch to the NE, and on the NW side first Chelston, then (from 1928) Cockington, as well as several small settlements.

The C 19 charm of Torquay survived relatively unspoilt until after the Second World War. Today the visitor familiar with the older eulogies will be disappointed: one's first impression is shock at such callous destruction of the delicate Victorian balance between scenery and architecture. The little hills to the E of the harbour are dwarfed by ungainly towers of flats of the 1960s, while to the W the clean lines of the villas near the sea are almost universally swamped by clumsy hotel excrescences and a superfluity of signboards. Yet away from the centre, the separate parts of Torquay retain much of their appeal. Romantic drives still wind around the hills, with villas glimpsed through dense shrubberies. Clusters of cottages from old settlements remain, and despite suburban growth open stretches survive: the broad expanses of Torre Abbey Gardens to the W, Daddyhole Plain to the E, the unspoilt coastline of Anstey's Cove between Babbacombe

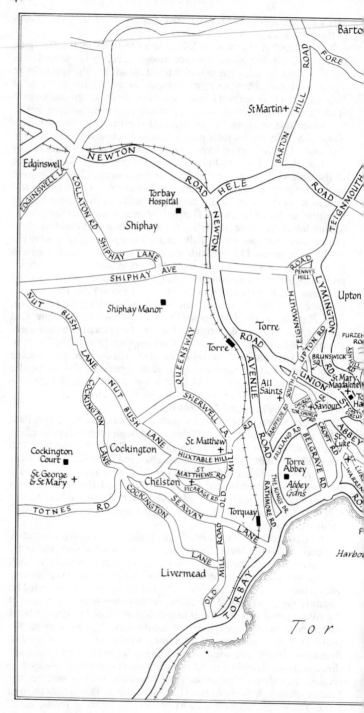

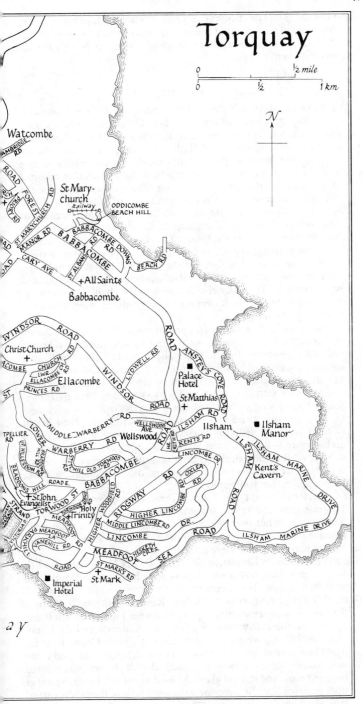

Torquay

0 ½ mile
0 ½ 1 km

N

Watcombe

St Mary-church

Railway ODDICOMBE
BEACH HILL

BABBACOMBE DOWNS

St Albans BEACH RD

+All Saints

Babbacombe

WINDSOR ROAD

Christ Church +

Ellacombe

LWR ELLACOMBE RD
PRINCES RD

WINDSOR ROAD

LYDWELL RD

ANSTEY'S COVE ROAD

Palace Hotel

St Matthias +

MIDDLE WARBERRY RD

WELLSWOOD AVE

Wellswood

ILSHAM RD

Ilsham

Ilsham Manor

TPELLIER RD

LOWER WARBERRY RD

UP HILLESTON RD

OLD TORWOOD

ILSHAM RD

KENTS RD

LINCOMBE DR

Kent's Cavern

ILSHAM MARINE DRIVE

BEADONS HILL ROAD E.

BABBACOMBE

RIDGWAY RD

LINCOMBE RD

OXLEA RD

+St John Evangelist

TORWOOD ST

Holy Trinity

MEADFOOT

HIGHER LINCOMBE RD

MIDDLE LINCOMBE RD

LINCOMBE DR

ILSHAM MARINE DRIVE

JANEHILL RD

MEADFOOT

SEA ROAD

HESKETH CRES.

ST MARK'S RD

+St Mark

Imperial Hotel

a y

and Ilsham. So if one chooses one's area carefully, it is still true to say, as Pevsner did in 1950, that much of Torquay retains that feeling of garden city which had been an English ideal ever since Nash's original plans for Regent's Park.

CHURCHES

ALL SAINTS, St Alban's Road, Babbacombe. By *William Butterfield*, nave 1865–7, E end and tower 1872–4. One of Butterfield's most important churches, and especially in its interiors extremely characteristic of this most wilful of High Church architects. Structurally quite simple, broad in the proportions, the interior with a surface treatment both fascinating and repellent. Short, circular polished marble piers. In the spandrels septfoils. The walls above them are of red and dark grey stone, patterned in grey and buff with a web of odd diaper lines. Brick and tiles with incised elementary ornament set in odd patterns behind the diapers. Cambered roof with quatrefoil clerestory windows cut into it. The chancel 'beyond all praise in its inspired strangeness' (Goodhart-Rendel). The polychrome treatment of the walls continues, but the patterns are tighter and more intricate, and there is also a carved foliage frieze. Ceiled roof painted with roundels. The chancel aisles open to the chancel in one oversized two-light arch with oversized tracery above, gargantuan and really uncommonly ugly.

Butterfield's FURNISHINGS are an integral part of the design and reflect equally strongly his interest in structural polychromy and sharp geometric forms. FONT and PULPIT both of brilliantly varied coloured marbles, both with overlapping arcading. Chancel FLOOR also of marble, in crisp, subtly coloured abstract patterns. LECTERN, CANDLESTICKS, and ALTAR CROSS 1871 by *Butterfield*. Chancel MOSAICS by *Salviati*. – STAINED GLASS. E window of 1874 and one S and two N windows by *A. Gibbs*, their bright colours and rich patterns perfectly appropriate to Butterfield's architecture. – BRASS. Anna Maria Hanbury † 1877, by *Butterfield*. – After all this the exterior is disappointingly reticent, grey stone with buff dressings and much diapering, dull E.E. detail, W tower with a tall, rather spiky spire.

ALL SAINTS, Bampfylde Road, Torre. 1883–9 by *J. L. Pearson*. Exterior grey and rather smooth, interior cream and red stone. Transverse arches over the nave; crossing, transepts, wide polygonal apse, geometric tracery. Only the aisles rib-vaulted. Entrance by a W narthex with a triple arcade.

CHRIST CHURCH, Ellacombe Church Road. By *Habershon, Brock & Webb*, 1868. Dec, with a SW tower-porch which turns octagonal and ends with a spire. No clerestory.

HOLY TRINITY, Torwood Gardens Road. 1894–6 by *J. Watson*. Striking NW tower with tall spire, its corner pinnacles with flying buttresses. Big Dec W window; the rest a conservative E.E. Limestone rubble. Converted to the Breakaway Sports Centre in 1982. The chancel now has a bar made up from the organ case and other woodwork, but preserves its stencilled wall decoration, painted boarded roof, and stained glass. Aisles divided off. From the upper floor inserted into the nave one has a good view of the boldly carved stiff-leaf capitals to the marble shafts supporting the roof, and of the

STAINED GLASS of the W window, 1907 by *Drake & Son*, designed by *Maurice Drake*. Very large, with three tiers of figure designs in aesthetic colours against clear glass, the clarity of the leading characteristic of the best work of the firm.

ST JOHN BAPTIST, Shiphay. Very minor. Built in 1897 for W. H. Kitson of Shiphay Manor by *E. H. Harbottle* as 'a place of public worship and entertainment', with a chancel, nave-cum-schoolroom, and classroom and vestry in the domestic-looking S transept with two storeys of rectangular windows. Nave adapted for worship in 1924. Pointed arches, no capitals, large S aisle windows.

ST JOHN EVANGELIST, Montpellier Road. 1861–73, a fine church by *G. E. Street*, replacing a small Greek Revival chapel of ease by *John Lethbridge* of 1822–30, built at the same time as the neighbouring terraces. Street's dominant building is prominent in all the views from the harbour, a tall, relatively plain exterior, except for the top of the W tower with its distinctive saddleback roof and wheel tracery in the gables (completed in 1884–5 by *A. E. Street* to his father's design). Statues above the SW door designed *c.* 1885 by *J. D. Sedding*. Interior with clustered shafts of polished Devon marble with bands of differently coloured marble. Broad chancel arch, stone-vaulted chancel, and large Dec E window.

The church was one of the leading centres of late C19 Anglo-Catholicism – hence the exceptionally rich furnishings. REREDOS by *Earp*; N aisle MOSAICS by *Salviati* (scenes from the life of St John); characteristically excellent IRONWORK by *Street* (LECTERN, CANDLESTICKS; the FONT COVER by *A. E. Street*); and, especially impressive, STAINED GLASS by *Morris & Co.*, E window 1865, some of their best work, with ten figures against foliage, Christ in Majesty in the roundel above, surrounded by angels, W window 1888 (designed by *Burne-Jones*). – Other windows by *Clayton & Bell* (S aisle, S clerestory). – ORGAN CASE by *A. G. Hill.* – At the W end the surprising feature of a full-size IMMERSION FONT, of marble (part of the original design). – LADY CHAPEL decorated by *J. D. Sedding*, 1888, converted to a columbarium in 1969.

ST LUKE, St Luke's Road, Warren Hill. 1863 by *A. Blomfield*, then still a young and daring architect. Random limestone with Bath stone dressings. The W side very successful with an oddly shaped NW turret to which an outer staircase leads up. Polygonal porch, very castle-like, and with a splendid view towards Torre Abbey Sands. Gabled N aisle with buttresses with evangelists. Good interior with short iron columns and tall arches. – Contemporary STAINED GLASS and chancel decoration by *Heaton, Butler & Bayne.* – Porch window of St Luke 1892 by *Kempe Studios*.

ST MARK, St Mark's Road, Torwood. Redundant. Insensitively converted to a theatre in 1986–7. One of *Salvin's* Torquay churches, 1856–7. Quite a hefty cruciform building, with shallow chancel, mostly E.E. in its details. Paired trefoil windows to the aisles; Dec E window. The central tower collapsed in 1856 before the church was completed, and was never rebuilt. On the W wall two carved evangelist symbols. E.E. arcades, and some good carving, e.g. the chancel arch corbels. For the theatre conversion, the aisles have been divided off and the nave has been converted to a raked auditorium. Most of the fittings and the stained glass remain, incongruous survivals. The chancel was restored in 1890–1 by *Fulford, Tait & Harvey*, with E window masonry and SCREENS by *J. D. Sedding*. – Alabaster REREDOS by *Hems*. – Tiled sanctuary DADO of art nouveau character, 1891 by *Powell & Sons*. – The good STAINED GLASS includes an E window of 1891 by *Hardman*, pictorial; chancel S by *Kempe Studios*; S chapel E 1892 by *Burlison & Grylls*. These make an interesting contrast with the earlier windows: in the N chapel, one in *Hardman*'s earlier style to the Rev. J. R. Hogg †1867, with figure medallions on foliage; in the aisles, several windows of the 1870s by *Clayton & Bell*, all with small figure groups.

ST MARTIN, Barton Hill Road. 1938 by *N. F. Cachemaille Day*. Stuccoed neo-Romanesque of the 1930s. Inside, over-strident red brick piers. Flat ceiling, striking baldacchino. Lower E chapel, W baptistery.

ST MARY, St Marychurch. The indifferent church by *J. W. Hugall*, 1856–61, was blandly rebuilt in 1952–6 after serious war damage. – FONT. C12, with interesting scenes: man on horseback with bugle; man with dog; man falling, his sword in his hand; boar and dog; harp-player. – Other furnishings by *Herbert Read*, post-war, apart from the rood screen.

ST MARY MAGDALENE, Union Street, Upton. 1843–9 by *Salvin*. Early Gothic out of the Lincolnshire Fens. The *Ecclesiologist* approved. Tall trefoiled lancets at the W end, circular windows above. S transept tower with spire and pinnacles, completed 1862. Apsed E end. Plain nave with columns and moulded capitals, but a riotous chancel, the result of embellishments in typical late Victorian High Church taste, begun under *G. G. Scott* in 1881–2. The first work was the ORGAN SCREEN with carved figures above a fine slab of local marble. Low marble CHOIR SCREEN; a series of carved panels over the choir stalls (an odd selection of subjects). Pretty carved and gilded ORGAN CASE. All this, as well as the REREDOS carved with the Crucifixion and scenes with St Mary Magdalene, dwarfed by an overpowering openwork superstructure to the reredos, completed in 1906, with overlifesize statue of Christ and Old Testament figures. More figures below canopies on the apse walls. The coving of the apse roof is decorated with stencilled patterns; the walls have unfortunately been repainted a shrieking red. – PULPIT. By *Temple Moore*, *c.* 1905, the traditional Devon Perp type, apart from its marble base. – N chapel furnished in 1927 with a mammoth wooden altar with two carved kneeling angels and a large PAINTING: Salvator Mundi, by *T. Mostyn*. – STAINED GLASS. Circular W windows by *Wailes*.

ST MATTHEW, Old Mill Road, Chelston. 1895–1904 by *Nicholson & Corlette*, excellent work of those imaginative though at that time still traditional church designers. Exterior with SE tower, very modest. W front with three gables, chiefly depending on the contrast between rock-faced and smooth sandstone. The interior of obvious Devon type, low and wide, with wagon roofs with carved bosses, type B piers, and an Arts and Crafts version of standard Devon capitals. – Contemporary furnishings: CHOIR STALLS 1904, SCREEN 1906. – The exceptional piece is the highly original FONT and FONT COVER. The font is a completely plain black bowl of polyphant on octagonal shafts. The cover has a circle of kneeling angels. It is suspended from a massive framework like a wellhead, made and given by *Gerald Moira*. On the cross beam Crucifixion and angels; low relief carving up the sides. Flanking this, two groups of figures by *F. Lynn Jenkins*: St George and children (exhibited 1899) and the Virgin and children. – STAINED GLASS all by *A. K. Nicholson*; E window 1903, nave windows mostly 1908–12.

ST MATTHIAS, Ilsham. Low, of grey stone, with a turret to the N transept. The original church of 1858 by *Salvin* comprised nave, N aisle, N transept, and chancel. S aisle and S transept added in 1865, chancel lengthened in 1882–5 by *J. L. Pearson*, who also raised the nave arcades and provided a clerestory and parapets in place of the earlier side gables. W bay and triple arcaded porch also by *Pearson*, 1894. – Sanctuary with lavish fittings and decoration of 1882, the carving executed by *Hems*: mosaic-lined walls, marble PULPIT and REREDOS. – Wooden W SCREEN also carved by *Hems*. – STAINED GLASS. W window Te Deum 1894 by *Powell & Son*. – Small window by *Charles Norris*. – CHURCH HALL to the S, quite tactful, by *Narracott, Tanner & André*, 1985–6.

ST MICHAEL, Chapel Hill, Torre. Chapel of 36 by 15 ft, perched on top of a precipitous rock N of the old village of Tormohun, and no doubt originally right away from human habitation. The floor is of solid rock, not evened out, the covering a pointed barrel-vault. Small window openings. Hard to date.

ST SAVIOUR, Tor Church Road. The medieval parish church of Tormohun, now the Greek Orthodox church of St Andrew. The W tower, without buttresses and pinnacles, has the marked batter of early building. Perp arcades, the SW arch on a carved bust instead of a respond; ceiled wagon roofs; but both exterior and interior so heavily restored that the atmosphere is chiefly early Victorian. Main restoration 1849, chancel extended and rebuilt 1873–4, W gallery rebuilt 1830. – Carved oak REREDOS by *Hems*, 1885. – PEWS of Spanish mahogany, 1850. – STAINED GLASS. E windows probably *c*. 1850, chancel N and others in the style of *Clayton & Bell*, S aisle first from E by *Wailes*. – MONUMENTS. Thomas Cary †1567, interesting because a very complete example of the Devonian tomb before the Elizabethan strapwork came in. The decoration a mixture of Perp and early Renaissance. Tudor arch to the recess, back wall with large, ungraceful Perp tracery, but wildly Flamboyant balusters flanking the recess, and delicate Renaissance motifs in the spandrels. – Wilmot Cary †1581. Palimpsest brass, the remains of two Flemish brasses of *c*. 1400 on the back. – Thomas Ridgeway †1604. Alabaster effigy in armour, propped up on elbow, piers and columns l. and r., obelisks and achievement on the cornice. – George Cary †1758. Grand wall-monument with swags and urns. – Many minor tablets of the early C19, when this was the only church serving the growing resort.

ASSUMPTION OF OUR LADY (R.C.), Abbey Road. By *J. Hansom*: nave, N aisle, chancel, and W turret 1853; S aisle and Lady Chapel added 1858. Dec, gabled aisles, with cusped lancets and spherical-triangle windows, a favourite of the architect (cf. Abbotskerswell). A bellcote instead of a tower. – Grey limestone PRESBYTERY to match.

OUR LADY HELP OF CHRISTIANS (R.C.), Priory Road, St Mary-church. 1865 by *Hansom*. An impressive group consisting of large

church, presbytery, and former orphanage. sw tower and spire
E.E., elaborately pinnacled. Long nave with quatrefoil piers and
clerestory. The N arcade lower than the s, where there is a gallery
for the orphanage children. – Lavish carved stone furnishings
including REREDOS and several ALTARS; PULPIT with marble
shafts. – In the sw chapel large BRASS to William John Potts
Chatto † 1882, who founded and paid for the church; another to his
son † 1913.

CENTRAL CHURCH. By *Narracott, Tanner & André*, 1970. Polygonal, all of concrete, the nearly windowless walls relieved by a
forceful but rather crude pierced screen wall rising up above roof
level to support a cross. – STAINED GLASS by *Peter Tysoe*.

METHODIST CHURCH, Old Mill Road, Chelston. Built by the
Wesleyans in 1908. Local red sandstone, octagonal spire.

UNITED REFORMED CHURCH, Furrough Cross, Babbacombe
Road. Built as a Free Episcopal Church in 1853 for parishioners
incensed by local ritualistic clergy. Fussy gabled limestone building with chancel; gabled porch with belfry above. Schools behind
of 1854. Over the hall door the Gladstone arms: the first minister
was a cousin of the Prime Minister.

UNITY CHURCH (Unitarian), Montpellier Road. 1912 by *Bridgman
& Bridgman*. A diminutive limestone cathedral for liberal
Christianity. Quirky free Perp, gabled and buttressed, with
tower-porch.

WESLEYAN METHODIST CHURCH, Babbacombe Road. 1873–4
by *G.S.Bridgman*, Dec, with a fine spire with tall lucarnes. It
makes a telling contrast with the former Presbyterian church
(below), its neighbour across the park.

FIRST CHURCH OF CHRIST SCIENTIST, Torwood Gardens Road.
Built in 1862 as St Andrew's Presbyterian church, a Kirk glower-
ing over the grass of Torwood Gardens. The Scottish connection
is stressed by an obsessive use of crow-stepped gables. Dark rubble
limestone, tower on the r., a weird flying buttress on the l., plate
tracery.

TORRE ABBEY

The abbey was founded in 1196 by William de Brewer as a thank-
offering for the safe return of his son from Austrian captivity.
Premonstratensian canons from Welbeck Abbey in Nottinghamshire were established here, and the abbey became the wealthiest
of the order's houses in England. Its position so close to the sea is
unusual. After the Dissolution much was left to collapse and decay,
but the s and w ranges of the domestic buildings were converted
to a residence by Thomas Ridgeway, after 1598. The Cary family,
owners from 1662, enlarged and altered the house in the late C17–
18, remodelling the entrance front in the s range facing the sea.
So the present impression is Georgian from the sea, and vaguely
late medieval from the w.

Approaching from the w, the most coherent feature is the
GATEHOUSE, slightly at an angle to the rest. Red sandstone, C14,
one large and one small arch; rib-vaults with very weathered arches
on corbels, and circular bosses with simple star decoration. Arms

of the abbey, and of the Brewers and their heirs the Mohuns. To the l. of the gateway the W range, from which the medieval ABBOT'S TOWER projects (cf. Buckfast). In its S wall a late C12 window. Passing through the gateway one comes to the S front of the range S of the cloister. Here was the medieval refectory, entirely transformed by the Carys, and now rendered and creeper-covered. Three storeys and seven bays. Stone porch on Doric columns, with segmental pediment. The bays were formerly divided by pilasters, of which the bases remain, removed in a late C18 remodelling when the windows were enlarged and a top storey added. On either side lower two-storey wings, the r. one an C18 addition, the l. one on the site of the monastic kitchens, linking up with the gatehouse. The crenellations were added in the later C18. At the opposite end, to the NE, two small late Tudor towers.

The interior of the S range, now a museum, is disappointing: no visible medieval remains apart from an undercroft with groin-vaults on columns. Later ground-floor partitions have been removed. In the angle between S and W ranges an C18 staircase with turned balusters and carved tread-ends. The W range also preserves its medieval undercrofts: a plain one with groin-vaults on square piers, and a larger one with circular piers with moulded capitals. On the first floor of both ranges a suite of reception rooms was created in the later C18. The best survival is the DINING ROOM in the W range, with neo-classical cornice, coved ceiling, and fireplace with marble columns. Opening off it is a chamber in the abbot's tower. The main part of the W range is occupied by the medieval guest hall which the Carys converted to an R.C. CHAPEL in 1779, adding an apse and large straight-headed windows with Gothick glazing. Late medieval plastered wagon roof with small bosses, visible only in the chapel, but continuing along the whole length of the range. In the chapel, altar by *Kendall* of Exeter, and many monuments to the Carys, the most elaborate a pair erected by George Cary to his father, another George Cary, †1805 and to his nephew Henry Franklin †1810, lost at sea aged eighteen, both with mourning figures by urns, against grey marble. The SW wing adjoining the gatehouse is on monastic foundations and has a medieval stair. Inside, it is largely Victorian (kitchens with bed-rooms above).

On the E side of the cloister the ruins of the CHAPTER HOUSE. Its entrance is the most architecturally worthwhile part of the medieval abbey to survive, a round-headed, transitional Gothic, richly moulded archway of five orders. Badly preserved shafts with crocket capitals. Flanking round-headed windows. To the N the remains of the SACRISTY adjoining the S transept of the church, with possible MUNIMENT ROOM further E.

The ABBEY CHURCH lay N of the house. It was 168 ft long. Its cruciform plan can still be clearly recognized, the N and S transepts with two square-headed E chapels each, and a straight-ended chancel – the type of E end usual in Cistercian and Premonstraten-sian churches. Excavations in 1987–8 established that the N aisle was part of the original plan. The masonry of the crossing piers has fallen, and some of it lies in massive fragments on the ground. In one of the SE chapels the piscina can still be seen, in the SE corner of the choir the fine ashlar facing. The choir stalls extended into the first two bays of the nave. Excavations have revealed the footings of the screen to their W, and of another screen further W, later replaced by enclosures for two chapels. The lidless coffin in the choir is supposed to have contained the body of William de Brewer's son.

Further E, puzzling remains of a rectangular building, at an angle to the rest of the domestic buildings, possibly the infirmary.

SW of the gatehouse a splendid medieval BARN, possibly C13, 124 ft long, buttressed, with a gabled central gateway. Restored slit windows, reconstructed roof. Named the Spanish Barn because an Armada crew was imprisoned here. Later used as stables and coach house.

To the NW in Falkland Road a picturesque tile-hung LODGE of c. 1900.

PUBLIC BUILDINGS

TOWN HALL, Castle Circus. 1911 by *Thomas Davison*. Long stone façade – too long for its Baroque centrepiece to be effective. It has a square tower like a city church, with diminishing storeys, rising behind a Doric porch.

OLD TOWN HALL, Union Street. *See* Perambulation 2.

173 PAVILION, by the harbour. By the Borough Engineer and Surveyor *H. A. Garrett*, 1911. A more enjoyable expression of civic pride than the Town Hall. A steel frame disguised by *Doulton* stoneware, cream with green panels. Copper roof; delightful corner domes with pretty art-nouveau ironwork around the roof promenades. E side remodelled in keeping, with a new entrance, in 1986–7, after removal of ugly theatre extensions of 1939. Interior, now subdivided for shops and restaurant, with elaborately plastered barrel-vault and central dome.

HARBOUR. Original enclosure 1803 by *Rennie*; outer breakwater 1867 by *J. P. Margery*. Promenade Pier 1890.

MUSEUM, Babbacombe Road. 1874–6 by *William Harvey* for the Torquay Natural History Society (among the founders in 1844 was William Pengelly, the explorer of Kent's Cavern, q.v. below). Handsome symmetrical five-bay Ruskinian front with Gothic upper windows, two decorated with allegorical figures (the arts and nature) in buff terracotta, a local product. Grand staircase inside, dividing in two up to the main display area on the first floor (now altered, with an inserted ceiling at the former gallery level). Back extensions with lecture room 1894–6.

COUNTY COURT OFFICES (Castle Chambers). Grand Gothic, gabled, with Tudor mullioned-and-transomed windows; octagonal central tower.

POST OFFICE, Union Street. Grand Edwardian Baroque.

MARKET, Market Street. 1850. Pedimented central entrance with paired Doric columns, flanked by round-headed openings. Altered by later shops. Refurbished in bold colours by *Narracott, Tanner & André*, 1983.

POLICE STATION, South Street. 1940s red brick. Traditional symmetry, but progressively plain (or just the result of wartime austerity?).

TORQUAY GRAMMAR SCHOOLS, Shiphay. Two schools in the

spacious grounds of SHIPHAY MANOR. The manor house, now part of the girls' school, was rebuilt for W. H. Kitson by *E. H. Harbottle* in 1884. Red sandstone, well grouped gables, plain apart from an arched doorway with stepped dripstones. Behind is the shell of a large medieval BARN with low entrance and slit windows, once a possession of Torre Abbey. The GIRLS' SCHOOL, of 1939, straightforward and compact, with flat-roofed, white-rendered ranges around a courtyard, makes an interesting contrast with the more informally grouped BOYS' SCHOOL, completed 1983, with its pale brick buildings with sweeping roofs. Both by the *County Architect's Department*.

WATCOMBE PRIMARY SCHOOL. An example of Devon County Council's progressive school design of the 1930s, white-rendered and flat-roofed.

TORBAY HOSPITAL, Newton Road. Large and confusing. The core is the hospital given in 1926 by Mrs Ella Rowcroft (foundation stone by *Eric Gill*), built in the grounds of a red brick Victorian villa called Hengrave House, which became a nurses' home. To this were added ward blocks by *Adams, Holden & Pearson*, on three sides of a courtyard, in a neo-Georgian style. (In the children's ward, TILES with nursery rhymes etc. by *Simpsons*.) The most interesting building is *Charles Holden*'s CHAPEL of 1930, long and thin, an austere understated exterior of white Portland stone, relieved only by plain raised panels. Tall, quite domestic segment-headed windows with small-paned metal frames; solid parapet. Interior with open coved timber roof. Around the perimeter of the site, much larger later C20 additions. To the N a long curved block with ribbon windows, *c.* 1968 by *Fry, Drew & Partners*, following the line of the hill, and a projecting five-storey block above operating theatres. In the outpatients' entrance, mosaic mural by *Arthur Goodwin*. To the S, the well-sited dining hall and kitchen, overlooking Tor Bay, 1982 by *Pearn & Procter*, red brick, with an attractive profile, stepped and chamfered to incorporate solar panels. On the slopes, staff housing of the 1980s by *Percy Thomas Partnership*.

TORQUAY STATION. 1878 by the Great Western Railway (*J. E. Danks* and *W. Lancaster-Owen*, engineers), built to replace the South Devon Railway's station of 1859, and to provide a grander introduction to the flourishing resort. Long and low, but effectively punctuated by four towers with steep slate roofs and iron cresting. Original platform canopies. Extended 1912.

TORRE STATION, Newton Road. 1848 for *Brunel*'s South Devon Railway, enlarged in 1882. Original timber-clad centre with hipped slate roof and large bracketed eaves. Platform with good cast-iron detail; lattice footbridge.

ATMOSPHERIC ENGINE HOUSE for the South Devon Railway. Now No. 16 Newton Road. 1847–8. Tapering campanile of limestone (cf. Starcross). Never used for its intended purpose.

PREHISTORIC REMAINS

KENT'S CAVERN, off Ilsham Road, is one of the most important archaeological sites in Britain, with evidence of human activity in Lower, Middle, and Upper Palaeolithic periods and later. The well

recorded excavations by William Pengelly in the 1850s–60s in this
limestone cave system, and at Windmill Hill Cave Brixham, were
crucial to the debate then taking place on the antiquity of man; the
discovery of human artefacts sealed with the bones of extinct
animals provided powerful confirmation of the theories of Lyell
and Darwin.

On the limestone WALL'S HILL, above Anstey Cove, remains of a
probably Iron Age lyncheted field system.

PERAMBULATIONS

1. The Harbour Area

Around the harbour every stage in the development of Torquay can be
seen, from the low, much altered two-storey cottages that still appear
here and there on the Strand and Victoria Parade, to the hotels and
towers of flats of the 1960s onwards which loom up on the steep slopes
directly above, amid the remnants of more genteel terraces and villas.

From W to E, first the Pavilion (*see* Public Buildings), close to the
unfortunately bulky two-storey car park of 1987; then, facing the
inner harbour, VAUGHAN PARADE, a plain stuccoed terrace of
c. 1830 (ground floor altered), the five bays at the r. end grander (for
a library), once with giant Ionic columns, but now crudely
rendered. Beyond this the more demonstratively classical later C19
LLOYDS BANK, with limestone rock-faced plinth and roof
balustrade, and the CARY ESTATE OFFICE, a pleasantly polychrome mixture mostly of red sandstone and marble.

In the STRAND, much haphazard rebuilding and refronting, unified
only by pretty cast-iron covered arcades. At the junction with
TORWOOD STREET the NATIONAL WESTMINSTER BANK,
enriched Italianate, a little frieze below the cornice, pepperpot
acroteria. The ROYAL HOTEL, with a simple stuccoed front
curving round the corner, was so named after the visit of Princess
Victoria in 1833. It was formerly the London Inn, the only hotel in
the town. Much reduced since the C19, the ballroom by *Foulston*
demolished. The corner is marked by the triangular MALLOCK
CLOCK TOWER, Gothic, with conical top (1902). Opposite the
Royal Hotel the VICTORIAN ARCADE in Torwood Street, 1909–
15 by *P. R. Wood*, built as a theatre but never completed. Grand
stone-faced exterior with giant Ionic columns, large upper
windows, and a parapet with sculptured groups. Doric entrance on
a canted corner. The interior prettied up with pseudo-Georgian
shopfronts in the 1970s.

VICTORIA PARADE, the third side of the harbour, has two confident
inter-war intrusions: the QUEENS HOTEL, quite a lively refronting of 1937, with its contrast between smooth continuous balconies
and glazed windshields with oblong panes, and HARBOURPOINT
at the other end, a more staid stone-faced 1920s front of five storeys,
with neo-Grec balconies. In between, the lower scale of the C19
remains, with nothing special, except perhaps No. 23, very boldly
Italianate, with pilasters and balustraded parapet. At the corner the
stuccoed Hotel Regina curves around to BEACON TERRACE,
stepping up Beacon Hill, one of the earlier Torquay terraces (1833

by *Harvey*), very attractively detailed. Incised Soanian pilasters alternating with different types of delicate balconies – an ingenious solution to the problem of creating a unified design on a slope. At the top, the ROYAL TORBAY YACHT CLUB, an irregular two-storeyed stucco composition of *c.* 1840, somewhat altered. Entrance between bold giant pilasters; dentilled chimneys. Opposite, project-ing into the sea, was the Marine Spa, an unsuccessful venture of 1857 by *G. H. Julian*, replaced, alas, by CORAL ISLAND, a crudely designed amusement and leisure centre of 1967 by the Borough Architect's Department (*Ray Banks*), built on the older founda-tions. Top-floor sun terrace with clumsy concrete arches.

2. *The Central Area*

The main shopping street of Torquay runs up from the harbour to the Town Hall at Castle Circus. It begins as FLEET STREET (laid out by the local Board of Health after the Fleet Brook – the boundary between Palk and Cary estates – was culverted in 1865), and is continued by UNION STREET (a new turnpike road of the 1820s). On the steep slope directly above and to the E of Fleet Street THE TERRACE, 1811, the first houses to be built on the Palk estate, a very handsome smooth white stucco terrace on a shallow curve, excellently maintained. Nine houses, the ends and centre set forward; *Coade* stone detail, continuous balconies. On the hill above, HIGHER TERRACE in MONTPELLIER ROAD, smaller stucco houses of *c.* 1820 (later heightened to three storeys) in a fine position overlooking the harbour, and the remains of another terrace (TORBAY VIEW), partly destroyed when St John's church (q.v.) replaced a more modest chapel of ease. Beyond the church a terrace by *Sidell Gibson*, 1987; rounded bows in a neo-Regency spirit, machine-made detail. At the S end of the road a CAR PARK, one of the first efforts to be more tactful after the excesses of the 1960s, 1972 by *Dawes Dingle*, two storeys of white vertical panels, skilfully tucked into the hillside.

Returning to THE TERRACE further downhill, and continuing N, HAGLEY HOUSE (Nos. 38–40), three storeys, Tuscan porch with barrel-vault, and smaller houses with Greek Doric porches. At the junction with Fleet Street the TRUSTEE SAVINGS BANK (built as the Devon and Exeter Savings Bank), 1889, a very festive classical front, Ionic and Composite, with enriched attic and a pedimented corner entrance. The W side of FLEET STREET was built up *c.* 1865 with a pleasant but unambitious serpentine brick shopping front-age. After lengthy discussion, this was demolished in 1987 and replaced in 1988–9 by a large new shopping development by *Dyer Associates*. The two-storeyed N part, with arched openings, is inspired by the façade of the original building. The longer S part has a Venetian-arched first-floor pedestrian arcade over ground-floor shops, and at the end a circular copper-roofed rotunda. A cable-stayed bridge leads, by way of a landscaped ramp, down to Long Green, linking the pedestrianized Fleet Street area to Harbourside, from which at long last traffic has also been excluded.

UNION STREET continues N from Fleet Street, very minor Victorian, interrupted by indiscriminate commercial buildings of the 1960s. The large HALDON SHOPPING CENTRE of 1980–2 (*Bernard*

Engle Partnership) marks a change of approach; discreetly low, with
its multi-storey car park tucked away behind. At the corner of Rock
Road there remains an austere Italianate villa of roughly coursed
ashlar (Torquay Disabled Fellowship), and opposite the OLD
TOWN HALL, in a similar style, 1851–2 by Mr *Dixon*, the Town
Surveyor, embellished only by a campanile, and by tripartite
windows in the front to Union Street. The prominent flats for old
people, by *Mervyn Seal* and *Baldock, Benns & Heighway*, date from
1988. Further on, characteristic contributions of the 1930s.
CASTLE CIRCUS HOUSE is of 1935 by *Stewart L. Thompson*, tall,
faced with thin slabs of travertine marble, with plain bands of
windows and a relief mural by *Oliver Skeaping*. Beyond the present
Town Hall, ELECTRIC HOUSE, a progressive period piece of 1935
by *William Marsden*. Former electricity showrooms; office entrance
in a taller l. projection. Plenty of streamlined details inside, well
preserved when converted to council offices in 1985. Further N,
GARDENS with nice railings, given to Torbay Hospital in 1897.

3. The Eastern Suburbs

3a. Park Hill

The outer areas of Torquay are extensive and cannot easily be covered
on foot, but one walk can be recommended. Starting from the
Strand, up PARK LANE, with old pubs on a scale with the former
fishing village, then via a flight of steps to PARKHILL ROAD. This
has an untypical but appealing building, a MASONIC HALL of
1857, an early work by the Torquay architect *Edward Appleton*, of
local limestone, with lively brick detail in red, yellow, and black
around the Gothic windows and angled entrance. THE RIVIERA is
a villa with a big Frenchy roof with cast-iron cresting, much added
to. Behind are the three tower blocks which form the most disastrous addition to the Torquay skyline of the 1960s: SHIRLEY
TOWERS (the three ugly sisters), 1962 by *Alec C. French & Partners*. In front of them, the prominent white EDENHURST COURT
by *Evans Powell Associates* shows that the lesson had not yet been
learnt by 1971. But above them on the crest, reached by another of
those steep flights that are a characteristic of the Torquay hills, an
unspoilt patch of C19 villas survives. (The steps are older than the
villas; they belonged to a path through the large grounds of
Woodbine Cottage, a picturesque *cottage orné* of *c.* 1820 attributed to
Foulston, demolished when its grounds were split up in the 1850s.)
First VANE TOWER and VILLA LUGANO (1871) with an Italianate tower, but unusual in having applied terracotta ornament, then
other Italianate stuccoed houses of the more usual type. By a footpath through St John's Wood one reaches the W end of Parkhill
Road and the group of the DEVONSHIRE HOTEL (two villas of the
1860s with a later link), SUNDIAL LODGE (symmetrical, with two
towers), and GEORGIAN HOUSE (a misnomer). Also part of the
group, down a drive, the PRINCES HOTEL, built *c.* 1860 as
Rockwood by *Harvey* for John Boyle, Earl of Cork and Orrery,
gabled Tudor, stuccoed, with a magnificent view over the sea.
Extension of 1909. By the drive a lodge, L-shaped, with a porch in
the angle. More villas lower down towards the sea; also the

IMPERIAL HOTEL, horribly altered and added to, but in its core still the first major hotel in Torquay, begun in 1863. Original five-storey staircase around a well; ornate classical plasterwork in the entrance hall and in the furthest reception room to the l. From here one can return via Beacon Hill to the harbour.

3b. Torwood, the Braddons, and the Warberrys

TORWOOD GARDENS, off Torwood Street, were laid out as public gardens on the edge of the town by 1850. Around the fringes several contemporary villas, e.g. GREENWOOD in Torwood Gardens Road; the spires of no less than three Victorian churches; the museum (q.v.); and along the N side a fine display of turn-of-the-century taste, when both classical stucco and Gothic detail had given way to tall half-timbered or crowstepped gables. To the N the steep slopes of Braddons Hill, built up with terraces already from the 1820s (see Perambulation 2, above). Higher up, in BRADDONS HILL ROAD EAST and WEST and along the roads above, separate villas in more spacious settings. 1960s redevelopment eroded some of the character of the area, but good survivals include Nos. 30 (Mount Braddon) and 34 (Braganza), both plain villas of the 1820s, and COLLINGWOOD in between, a little later in date. Among the newcomers, BRADDONS CLIFFE, by *Mervyn Seal*, 1974, with its chunky white balconies, has a little more character than the dismal new intrusions on the upper slopes of the hill. An earlier replacement is LITTLE TOR, No.45 Braddons Hill, an attractive house in the Arts and Crafts tradition, 1932 by Lutyens's pupil *Fred Harrild*. Trim, symmetrical garden front, rendered, with casement windows with small panes, and a steep hipped Westmorland slate roof. The front door is approached picturesquely by a wooden bridge over a basement court at the back, created from the cellar of an older house on the site. Heavily beamed drawing room; dining room with pretty Jacobean-style plasterwork.

Further E, off the main Babbacombe Road, in OLD TORWOOD ROAD, MANOR BARN COTTAGES and CLIFTON COTTAGES, much altered outbuildings, are reminders of the old manor house of the Palks, which stood here until 1843. They are incongruously squeezed by busily detailed late C19 stucco terraces and ugly C20 flats. Above, to the N, another sequence of winding drives around WARBERRY HILL, laid out in the 1840s by the *Harveys*. The 1960s have not improved the scene, but several good houses remain. KATHLEEN COURT, Stitchill Road, has a bowed Ionic portico to the garden and an Ionic porch *in antis* on the entrance front. NORMOUNT (now named Bishops Court), Lower Warberry Road, of 1844, is especially handsome, this time with a Doric porch and Ionic pilasters on the garden front. (Well-preserved interior: hall with Ionic columns, top-lit staircase. Octagonal garden pavilion.) Also in Lower Warberry Road, AUDREY COURT and DUNSTONE (formerly one house), c.1860, altered, and WARBERRY COURT, c.1840s; and in Wellswood Avenue, DAPHNE COURT, with a shallow gable over the entrance. More of c.1850 on the slopes above (e.g. NEWBURN, GARDENHURST, and TAPLOW COURT), well hidden up long drives from Middle Warberry Road.

3c. The Lincombes

LINCOMBE HILL, rising between Meadfoot and the Ilsham valley, was developed by the *Harveys* from the 1840s. DADDYHOLE PLAIN provides an excellent vantage point from which to survey their achievements – also the extent to which they have been eroded by strident C20 insertions. LINCOMBE DRIVE circles the hill, the most extensive of the Torquay villa drives, with dramatic panoramic sea views for most of its length. The houses are cunningly laid out; they are sited close to the upper roads, where the service entrances are, but the main approaches are from below, up long leafy drives which give the illusion of much larger estates. The steep flights of steps linking the roads, the high revetting walls, and the mature trees and shrubberies add much to the labyrinthine effect. Among the villas in Lincombe Drive, HATLEY ST GEORGE is one of the best preserved, 1846, characteristic restrained Italianate, with a handsome pedimented gable and Doric porch. E elevation with pedimented windows. (Good interiors; elegant staircase with oval roof-light.) Also of *c.* 1840–50 the group of HOLMWOOD, WOODEND, and GLEN ANDRED, and, in MIDDLE LINCOMBE ROAD, ST ELMO, AMERICA LODGE, MERTON, etc.

MINTON'S (formerly Iona), in Higher Woodfield Road, is a well restored villa of the usual type, of 1835, with pretty plaster ceilings preserved, but of especial interest for the tiles added after it was acquired by *Herbert Minton* in 1856. Hall with black and white Roman mosaic patterned floor, and glazed maroon and green dado; former kitchen with pretty blue and white stencilled wall tiles to a *Pugin* design; an upstairs bathroom with green and red stencilled pattern. The party piece is the SUMMER HOUSE of 1876, colourfully tiled all over; even the openwork seats are of glazed pottery.

At the end of Middle Lincombe Road, cocooned by neighbouring grounds, the MANOR HOUSE (now the Royal Institute for the Blind Rehabilitation Centre), built in 1862–4 by *J. W. Rowell* for the younger Sir Lawrence Palk, who had inherited in 1860. No longer stucco, but grey limestone in random courses. A pinched, vaguely Tudor gabled garden front, not quite symmetrical; a rather more successful W approach, past the pretty stables to an angled porch with an eclectic concentration of Gothic motifs: polychrome arch, plate tracery, and ballflower-studded balustrade. Grand but gawky top-lit inner hall, galleried, with a hooded fireplace and an imperial staircase with a large Gothic window. Substantial Gothic fireplaces in other rooms.

On the upper levels of Lincombe Hill, among C20 replacements, ROZEL, Middle Lincombe Road, is an ingenious layout of flats with a stepped profile and roof patios, 1959–61 by *Michael Lyell Associates*; one of the first post-war attempts to impose a new pattern on the Torquay hills, disruptive to the original villa-and-garden scheme, but much less so than later developments. LINCOMBE CRESCENT, Higher Lincombe Road, 1973 by *Mervyn Seal*, is an effort at a formal composition, with flats set back over two storeys of garages. Crudely detailed, especially at the back.

CASTLE TOR, off OXLEA ROAD, is another relative latecomer, but of quite a different calibre. The special feature is the remarkable sequence of terraced gardens, designed in 1930–4 by *Fred Harrild*, a pupil of Lutyens, for H. Pickersgill. The house itself, low and unassuming in the Arts and Crafts manner, is unfortunately considerably altered. The hors d'œuvre to the gardens starts at the top with a series of nearly circular arches leading the eye down to the lower terraces, but the subtlety lies in the way in which the parts are only gradually revealed. At the level of the house is a square sunken garden with charming corner pergolas with Tuscan columns; and from here there is just a ravishing view of the sea far below. Hidden below the balustrade lies a broad terrace with a formal basin of water, curved at the ends, and crossed by formal stepping-stones in front of a conservatory with Tuscan colonnade and half-glazed barrel roof. On either side, gentle cascades descend into the basin. At the far end, glimpsed beyond a short avenue, is a circular lawn. The interplay of cross axes and the strong architectural forms in this area are very reminiscent of Lutyens. The lower levels are more whimsical, and possibly not part of the original conception, as they do not appear on an early perspective view by Cyril Farey. They are reached by steps in a circular tower, and include a charming well head with an arch with a little carved figure. At the level of Lincombe Drive, the termination is a castellated entrance gateway complete with working portcullis.

3d. Wellswood and Ilsham

In BABBACOMBE ROAD a regular sequence of double villas, followed by larger detached ones, broken by WELLSWOOD PARK, a more unusual development on the N side, 1853 by the *Harveys*, quite modest two-storey houses in blocks of five, backing on to two sides of a generous private park (a similar arrangement to that adopted for parts of North Kensington at just this time). Four-bay garden fronts divided by pilasters; elegant trellis verandas. The front doors and lesser tradesmen's entrances both open directly on to the road, at the same level. A little further on is the centre of ILSHAM, with St Matthias (q.v.), and nearby a pleasant two-storey mid-C19 shopping parade. The mews behind also serves the contemporary terrace in KENT'S ROAD to the s. From here HIGHER ERITH ROAD, with separate villas, leads to Lincombe Drive (*see* Perambulation 3c, above).

ILSHAM MANOR, W of the junction of Ilsham Road and Ilsham Marine Drive. The remains of a medieval house are hidden behind a school attached to Stoodleigh Knowle Convent. A small tower now stands alone. It has an undercroft, a first-floor chapel with a Perp window of two lights, and on the other side a wooden doorcase, previously internal. Small room above. Several small slit windows. The building may date from soon after 1489, when the manor was acquired by Torre Abbey. Partial remains of a few outbuildings. Close by, a reticent convent building in 1920s Tudor, with a tactful extension of the same height with white-rendered walls. The main buildings of STOODLEIGH KNOWLE CONVENT are further up the hill; a C19 house much enlarged. Additions by *Evans & Powell*, 1966. Chapel with stained glass by *Charles Norris* of Buckfast (Crown of Thorns, above entrance).

ILSHAM MARINE DRIVE, looping around the headland, opened in

1924, was barely touched by residential development until the mid
C20, but the adjacent hilltop has since become dismally suburban-
ized. The few early houses were more sympathetic to the setting.
The most distinguished is MONKSWELL PARK, near Richmond
Close, formerly two houses, tucked into the slopes overlooking
Hope Cove. 1924–5 by *H.T.North*, a clever design in the Arts and
Crafts tradition, with wings angled to create a protected terrace
with veranda facing the sea. Rendered walls, grey-tiled roofs.

PALACE HOTEL, Babbacombe Road. This unprepossessing monster between Ilsham and Babbacombe began as Bishopstowe, built
by *E.W.Gribble* of Torquay in 1841–2 as a residence for Bishop
Phillpotts of Exeter. The original house – a picturesque asymmetrical rustic Italianate villa with campanile and shallow gabled
wing flanking the three-bay centre to the garden – was extended
after 1921, when the house became a hotel; the original variations
in height have been swamped by third-floor extensions. A few
plastered ceilings inside. Terrace garden and fine grounds with
plenty of Victorian specimen trees.

3e. Ellacombe

The valley N of Braddons and Warberry Hills was developed by *J.W.
Rowell* for the Palk estate from 1859 as a working-class suburb.
Palk presented ELLACOMBE GREEN as a recreation area. Much
of the housing dates from after 1890. Modest terraces run up and
down the steep hills, mostly of plain grey limestone. In UPTON
ROAD some taller villas with cuspy bargeboards, now Winter
Gardens Hotel.

3f. Babbacombe

For the architectural visitor Babbacombe is famous for its Butterfield
church (All Saints, q.v.). The Victorian tourist was attracted to
this small fishing hamlet of St Marychurch by its dramatic cliff
scenery. Along the clifftop route of BABBACOMBE DOWNS
ROAD a few older cottages survive among the seaside villas. At the
N end, the CLIFF RAILWAY, with straightforward concrete
station buildings of 1926, descends to ODDICOMBE BEACH; at
the S end BEACH ROAD winds down to the sea. On the precipitous slopes the BABBACOMBE CLIFF HOTEL, built as a
private house in 1878 for Lord Mount Temple by *W.E.Nesfield*. A
demonstration of the Old English style; L-shaped, picturesquely
grouped, with big chimneys and an arched entranceway into the
courtyard. A side opening within the archway gives a breathtaking
framed view of the sea. Stone ground floor, grey tile-hanging
above, Tudor detail. Further down the wooded slopes a scatter of
small cottages, all rather too altered. The group was called a Swiss
Village in the 1840s, and was much illustrated as one of the sights
of Torbay. In BABBACOMBE ROAD, ST ANNE'S HALL, a good
C19 composition, with sweeping roofs with half-hipped end and
tall chimney. All Saints' church lies further N, on the edge of
CARY PARK, a spacious development of villas undertaken by the
Cary estate.

3g. St Marychurch

St Marychurch is an old village whose parish originally included much of the Torquay suburbs, developed in the C19 by the Cary estate. The old centre is still recognizable along FORE STREET (now pedestrian). Near the church, AVON HOUSE HOTEL, black and white stucco, with bracketed eaves and emphasized quoins. In PARK ROAD, the continuation of Fore Street, and in the streets off, e.g. CAMBRIDGE ROAD, modest stuccoed terraces with gables to the road, in groups of two; other villas in CHURCH ROAD. CARY CASTLE further W is grander, with a Gothic battlemented tower over the porch. ST MARYCHURCH TOWN HALL at the corner of Fore Street and Manor Road, with a prominent circular corner tower with a conical roof and crazy-paving walls, dates from 1883. A large C20 contribution is the GENERAL ACCIDENT OFFICES by *Narracott, Tanner & André*, 1979–80, two storeys of ribbed concrete with a rather heavy arched porch, the frontage quite sensitively following the curve of ST MARY-CHURCH ROAD.

3h. Outer Areas N, NW, and E of St Marychurch

Remnants of several rural settlements lie hidden in the folds of the downs. At BARTON, old houses remain in Church Street, and the thatched OLD MANOR FARMHOUSE in Fore Street. E of the main road MAIDENCOMBE VILLAGE and BRIM HILL are still country lanes with clusters of cottages. Discreet mid-C19 additions include ROCK HOUSE, Rock House Lane, with gatepiers to match the rambling villa made from two older houses. WASHINGTON HOUSE (Watcombe Court), off Watcombe Beach Road, is a more formal unspoilt stucco house with splendid sea views. On a larger scale, also hidden in generous grounds, SLADNOR PARK, down a long drive E off Teignmouth Road, C19 Tudor, gabled. By the road a FOLLY, a castellated bastion of red sandstone.

BRUNEL MANOR (formerly Watcombe Park) in Teignmouth Road is a substantial stone house built *c.* 1870 by *J. Watson* for J.R. Crompton, a Lancaster paper manufacturer. It stands on the foundations of a house begun for himself by I.K. Brunel on an estate which he acquired from 1847. The house was left uncompleted at his death in 1859. Symmetrical garden front with plenty of spiky gables and dormers, a sprinkling of Gothic arches, and an angular wooden veranda on one side. The extensive terraced gardens S and W of the house were laid out for Brunel by *Nesfield*; the well preserved arboretum on the higher ground was planted by his head gardner, *Alexander Forsyth*. WATCOMBE COTTAGE, also in Teignmouth Road, a one-storey building with some pointed windows, was built as a chapel for Brunel's estate workers.

The HERALD EXPRESS OFFICES in Barton Hill Road (1978 by *Kenneth W. Reed & Associates*) are a rude shock compared with all this, but quite elegant in their own way; dark brick, tinted glass, recessed centre. Returning W along TEIGNMOUTH ROAD into Torquay, the highlights are a thatched cottage at PENNY'S HILL and a good group of villas with tented verandas.

4. The Western Suburbs

4a. Torre and Livermead

The W part of Torquay belonged to the Carys; development took
place mostly after 1849. At the start of TORBAY ROAD, facing the
Pavilion, the TORBAY HOTEL, 1866 by *J. & W. Harvey*,
extended later into a terrace of tall houses of the same date.
WALDON HILL, climbed by winding roads, still has a ring of
Italianate villas at the top, although its crowning feature, Waldon
Castle, towered and embattled, has gone. On its site the poorly
detailed KINGSDALE COURT, 1987 by *Michael Aukett &
Partners*, completed by *Robert J. Wood*, and nearby other, earlier
large blocks, one group with pagoda roofs in an effort to leaven
the lump. CROFT ROAD and BELGRAVE ROAD, the main
thoroughfares of the Cary estate, run inland beyond Waldon Hill.
Large villas near the sea; then more urban terraces, quite handsome, but too altered or cluttered with signs to be enjoyable. The
side streets are more rewarding, e.g. CHURCH STREET near the
former parish church of the old village of TORMOHUN (*see* St
Saviour, above). Near the N end of Union Road, BRUNSWICK
SQUARE, with a few early villas of *c.* 1830, and PORTLAND TER-
RACE, with early C19 *Coade* stone decoration. Elsewhere, many
inept C20 replacements. The most ludicrous is ROEBUCK HOUSE
in ABBEY ROAD, a tower of offices replacing one half only of a
semi-detached villa.

Along the seafront, first in the shadow of Waldon Hill the curving
stucco frontage of the PALM COURT HOTEL and the low former
TOLL HOUSE of *c.* 1842 to the Torbay Road. Then the prospect
broadens, with the ABBEY GARDENS stretching inland towards
the remains of Torre Abbey (q.v.). Elegant pedestrian BRIDGE of
1971. At the entrance to the gardens delightful late C19 polygonal
gatepiers-cum-kiosks with exotic roofs. To the N of the abbey a
large but quite discreetly sited CONFERENCE CENTRE, 1987 by
Module 2, a double cube with angled corner towers, plainly faced
with grey concrete panels. Adjacent lower swimming pool. Near
the station, the stately GRAND HOTEL, with two towers, and
SEAWAY COURT, the most accomplished of the later C20 flats, an
uncluttered, gleaming white six-storey sweep on a gentle curve,
1972 by *Evans Powell Associates*.

Further on, LIVERMEAD, linking Torquay and Paignton, was built
up only between the wars; villas in every style, thatched to
modernistic. The THATCHED HOUSE, Mead Road, is one of the
earliest and most ambitious houses in Livermead, 1925 by *Fred
Harrild*, interesting because, like his houses at Holne (q.v.), it
anticipates his master Lutyens's vernacular *cottage-orné* work at
Cockington. An irregular thatched and rendered house, the roof extending over a generous, stoutly timbered veranda on the seaward
side (now glazed). Walled entrance yard with thatched cottage and
an open timber loggia to the front door; gardens altered.

THE RAINBOW, on a hill W of Avenue Road, Torre. Built in 1937
by the Torquay benefactor Mrs E. M. Rowcroft, daughter of Sir
Edward Wills of Bristol, in the grounds of an older house called
Pilmuir. An exceptionally lavish but rather vulgar villa in a

debased classical style. Copper-roofed belvedere. Expensive fittings inside.

4b. Chelston

At the bottom of OLD MILL ROAD the relics of an old settlement. The CHELSTON MANOR HOTEL has a regular three-storey early C19 front with Tudor hoodmoulds and paired octagonal corner chimneys, probably concealing an older core. Converted outbuildings nearby; also CHELSTON COTTAGE, picturesquely thatched. Further s St Matthew's church (q.v.), spaciously set out on a green between Old Mill Road and Vicarage Road, the focus of an unspoilt late Victorian and Edwardian area with villas of modest size.

MANOR HOUSE HOTEL, Seaway Lane. An eccentrically detailed asymmetrical villa on a knoll overlooking the sea, built for the engineer and naval architect William Froude (1816–79), who constructed the world's first experimental ship tank when he lived here from 1867 to 1879. Red stone, brick trimmings, picturesque belvedere tower, clustered chimneystacks. The *pièce de résistance* is the hall, entered through a Gothic porch set at an angle. It has an open timber roof, and an even more remarkable wooden staircase with an upper flight soaring dizzily across from a gallery to a cantilevered second-floor landing. It was constructed on the suspension principle with the advice of *R.E.Froude* and the engineer *H.M.Brunel*. STABLES with spiky dormers, wrapped tightly round the N side of the house.

N of Chelston the old hamlet of SHIPHAY, with St John Baptist (q.v.), the Grammar Schools (q.v.) in the grounds of the manor house, and WATER LANE, with thatched cottages. Still further N, in EDGINSWELL LANE, on the edge of open country, a FARM-HOUSE with a good group of outbuildings, and EDGINSWELL HOUSE, stuccoed, mid C19.

TORBRYAN

HOLY TRINITY. Now maintained by the Redundant Churches Fund. Interesting as a uniform Perp church of the C15. W tower of Ashburton type, i.e. with central stair-turret. On the s buttresses, not very high up, two niches for figures on head corbels. Very low pinnacles. Exterior all rendered. Projecting chancel. The E windows of the chancel chapels have the star tracery found also at Ipplepen and elsewhere, a Dec form, but clearly here of the Perp period. s side with large four-light windows and embattled two-storey porch; N side with embattled rood-loft staircase. The s porch is beautifully fan-vaulted. Large airy interior. Arcades of five rather steeply pointed arches on enriched B type piers (cf. Powderham); standard capitals. Plastered wagon roof to the nave, flat roofs to the aisles (above these, lean-to roofs resting on the nave principals, an odd arrangement).

REREDOS. C19 Gothic, with Commandment panels. – ALTAR. Made from panels of a pulpit of local type (cf. Ipplepen). – PULPIT. Made from parts of the screen encasing the nave piers (cf. Dunchideock, Kenn). – SCREEN. Right across nave and aisles. Painted figures of saints in the wainscoting; tracery of type A standard; only one strip of decoration in the cornice; coving not preserved. – BOX PEWS. With candleholders; the pews enclose the original benches. – STAINED GLASS. Much medieval glass remaining in the tracery lights: E window with saints and heraldry (De Bryan and Wolston); chancel S with saints; aisle windows with angels with shields. – MONUMENTS. William Peter †1614 and wife †1600. Slate tablet with skulls, torches, and strapwork. – Several good LEDGER STONES, the one to the Goswells (†1630, 1662) the former altar, with consecration crosses. – LYCHGATE. Picturesque, rubble with pitched roof, possibly C16.

TORNEWTON HOUSE. The seat of the Peters from the C14 to the C17, then of the Wolstons. Main range early C19, rendered, five windows wide, with incised end pilasters. Older parts behind.

TOR COURT. Now a farmhouse. Date plaques 1677 and 1761. Three-window front with coved wooden eaves cornice; double-pile rear range with hipped roof.

EAST DOWNE. Farmhouse dated 1826. Quite a smart three-window front, ashlar dressings, vermiculated doorway. Flanking walls with swept parapets.

See also Denbury.

TOTNES

Totnes is one of the most rewarding small towns in England, appealing in the visual variety of the small buildings close-packed within the framework of its medieval street plan, intriguing in the exceptional quantity of wealthy merchants' houses surviving from the C16 and early C17. Already established before the Conquest (it had a mint in the C10), the town consists principally of a single main street running up a sloping ridge above the former marshes around the river Dart, at the river's highest navigable point and lowest bridging place. William I granted the town to Judhael of Totnes (q.v., Barnstaple), who built a castle at the highest point within the walls and founded a small Benedictine priory. The walls, which were probably only earthen ramparts, had already disappeared by the mid C16. Their line is still traced by North Street and South Street. Houses were being built outside the E and W gates (in Fore Street and at the upper end of High Street, beyond the castle) in the C13, and the Fore Street suburb was walled on the S side, along what is now Victoria Street. There was a bridge already in the C13, when Bridgetown, a rival borough on the opposite bank, was established by the lords of Berry Pomeroy.

The time of greatest prosperity for Totnes seems to have been the C15 to the mid C17, when the town's merchants dominated the overseas trade of the port of Dartmouth, exporting tin and cloth to France in return for linen and manufactured goods. It has been deduced from the subsidy rolls of 1523–5 that Totnes was then nearly four times as wealthy as Dartmouth, and ranked fifteenth among all English provincial towns. But apart from the C15 rebuilding of the church, the architectural survivals which testify to this wealth are largely of the later C16 and early C17, when so many of the houses along High Street and Fore Street were entirely rebuilt. According to

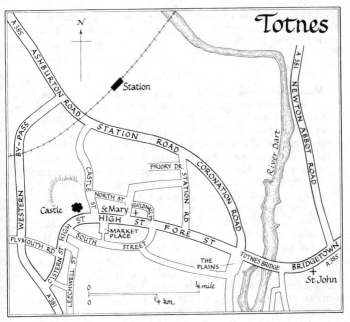

the most recent research,★ sixty-six existing houses are datable to before 1700 – a remarkable survival, and one of the best earlier groups in any town in England. Alteration and modernization have been only superficial. The houses are of the urban type characteristic of the South West, consisting of a two- or three-storey front block, only one room wide and one or two rooms deep – if two, with a shop on the ground floor and a hall behind – linked by a gallery across a courtyard to a two-storey back block containing the kitchen. Plenty of panelling and plaster ceilings remain to show that the merchants were up-to-date in their tastes. There is one exceptional classically ornamented stone front of 1585, but generally the frontages between the stone party walls were timber-framed, no doubt once as exuberantly decorated as those of Dartmouth, but now mostly hidden behind later plaster or the attractive small local slates that were popular in the C18 and C19.

From the mid C17 the merchant community of Totnes declined, and the town was left to rely on its strength as a local market centre. Houses tended to be remodelled rather than rebuilt. There was some effort to revive trade in the early C19, when, partly through the enterprise of the Duke of Somerset, there were improvements to the river navigation, some elegant new building on both banks, and a new bridge, but no major industry developed, and the population grew only slowly: in 1801 2,503 (probably no more than in the early C17), in 1871 (including Bridgetown) 4,073, in 1981 5,627. Later C20 suburban growth has happily left the old centre largely unscathed. A ring road has removed much of the traffic, and attempts are being made to revitalize the long-decayed riverside, although large-scale shopping

★ M. Laithwaite, 'Totnes Houses, 1500–1800', *The Transformation of English Provincial Towns*, ed. P. Clark, paperback ed., 1985, 62–98. This account of Totnes is much indebted to Michael Laithwaite's work.

development and car parking remain a continuing threat to a town whose character depends on a close-knit texture of small buildings and narrow streets.

CHURCHES

ST MARY. The broad red W tower, 120ft high, with big polygonal pinnacles, stands up high near the top of the hill, a beacon from afar, although as one climbs the High Street the church is hidden, and one comes upon it suddenly, set back a little from the narrow thoroughfare. The W tower is out of the ordinary in design, a rare thing. The remarkable feature is that it turns a real façade towards the street, i.e. S. Here a symmetrical composition is made of the two buttresses (of type B) and the central stair-turret. All three have a niche high up. In the central one appears a bearded mitred head with the inscription 'I made this tore'. It is supposed to refer to Bishop Lacy of Exeter. To l. and r. seated figures, identified tentatively as Prior Stoke (who gave money in 1445) and the then Earl of Devon. The tower is well dated. In 1449 the masons to the town were sent out to study towers at Ashburton, Buckland, Callington (in Cornwall), and Tavistock. In 1451 and 1452 parishioners were asked for help in the building of the tower. The master mason in charge was *Roger Growdon*. Ashburton was the model chosen; the forceful design with central stair-turret was taken up elsewhere as well (e.g. Ipplepen, Littlehempston). The church itself is a little earlier, and also approximately dated: 1432 Bishop Lacy's letter of indulgence to all who would contribute to the erection of the church; 1445 agreement that the parishioners should build a new chancel, and the Prior of Totnes keep it in repair. The last arrangement resolved a longstanding dispute. The tower of the priory, which lay immediately to the N of the parish church, had to be demolished for the new chancel, and a diagonal passage carved out between the two churches to allow for processions (still visible at the E end of the chancel).

Nave and embattled aisles, the S aisle also with pinnacles. An outer N aisle was added in 1824 and made larger and more correct in 1869. The S porch has a ceiling with ribs and bosses, outer and inner doorways with decoration in jambs, voussoirs, and spandrels, and a fine inner DOOR with early Renaissance ornament (candelabra, grotesques, etc.) perhaps of c. 1550–60. Interior with aisles of five bays. The piers are more elaborate than the usual type, perhaps a long-distance echo of the Dec piers of Exeter Cathedral: four major shafts with minor shafts in the hollows (as at Brixham). Continuous capitals, and nearly semicircular arches. Tower arch similar. The four-light windows also have nearly semicircular heads. The E window is of 1874, designed by *G. G. Scott Jun.* and *J. O. Scott*. Ceiled wagon roofs with bosses in nave and chancel.

The outstanding feature of the interior is the STONE SCREEN, one of the most perfect in England. Its erection was resolved on in 1459–60. It runs right across the church and is continued into parclose screens to separate the N and S chancel chapels from the chancel. The design is different in nave and aisles. The nave part has eight narrow two-light panels, plus two for the doors, the aisle parts three broader panels with depressed ogee arches of which the middle ones serve as entrances. But above each of these broad arches are two narrow tracery panels identical with those in the nave, and the same narrow coving and thin cornice ties them all together. Much enrichment to the basic design: canopies for statues on the mullions, and against the narrow panels at the top, ogee crocketed arches ending in leafy finials. Remains of colour and gilding. The rood loft was removed in the restoration of 1867–74 by *G. G. Scott* despite the protests of his assistant, *C. Baker-King*. N and W galleries were removed at the same time. – ROOD-STAIR TURRET. A singular and very successful feature in the chancel, a shallow 3/8 shape, with tall shallow niches and a heavy cornice.

FONT. The usual octagonal C15 type, except that the quatrefoil panels are rather more richly cusped. – PULPIT. Stone, and surprisingly simple, just two tiers of cusped blank arches. – CANDELABRA. Brass, acquired in 1701. – ORGAN GALLERY, classical, by *W. H. R. Blacking*. – MONUMENTS. Walter Smith †1555 (S chancel aisle). A popular early C16 type: an ogee recess for a small tomb-chest with quatrefoil decoration. No effigy. – Christopher Blackhall (N aisle), kneeling, in an arched recess, with his four wives, stiff but not identical figures, kneeling against the plinth below. – Walter Venning †1821 at St Petersburg, 'founder of the prison society', and his brother †1858. Later terracotta portrait, with a prisoner.

ST JOHN, Bridgetown. 1832, of good solid stone, with a big tower and originally W, N, and S galleries. Tall, pointed windows. The church of the evangelical fighter and martyr, James Shore. Gutted by fire in 1976, restored in 1980 with an inserted floor. – STAINED GLASS. E window by *Peter Tysoe*, abstract.

TOTNES CASTLE

The castle is a large motte-and-bailey, with the possible fragment of a second bailey to the N, established after the Norman Conquest at the highest point of the town, visibly intruding into the Anglo-Saxon street plan. The founder was almost certainly Judhael of Brittany, Lord of Totnes, who was also active at Barnstaple (q.v.). Later the castle was held by the de Nonants, de Cantilupes, and de la Zouches. Most of the visible remains are on the summit of the motte, which is exceptionally large (cf. Barnstaple, Okehampton). The bailey is surrounded by a wall, late medieval in origin but with extensive modern additions, which also ascends the sides of the motte. Nothing is known of the domestic buildings which once occupied the bailey (we have references to the hall, chamber, and chapel), although an exploratory excavation c. 1950 produced some fine stone fragments. The granite pillars at the bailey entrance came from one of the covered walks in the High Street.

The visitor climbs the motte by a winding path which leads to the door of the shell keep, and which presumably succeeded earlier routes. The motte ditch has not been excavated, but its course is clearly visible at the foot of the path. The motte top was excavated c. 1950, and the fabric of the two most substantial building periods is displayed. The shell keep, of limestone rubble with sandstone dressings, dates from the early C14 (the site is described as ruinous in 1273 but was defended again in 1326), and was the only part of the castle still maintained in Leland's day. It is one of England's best preserved structures among this relatively rare type (cf. Restormel, Cornwall). An irregular circle in plan, it is defended by a wall-walk with over thirty crenellations, most of them with arrowslits. Two stairways in the wall thickness give access to the parapet. The domestic range seems to have stood on the NW, where there is a garderobe block within the wall (projecting externally), and a row of corbels for the roof of a lean-to structure. The foundations of one cross-wall are also visible. The rest of the enclosed area may have been an open courtyard.

This shell keep was successor to an earlier C13 one, some of whose fabric may have been incorporated in the rebuild, but the major survival of early date is the quadrangular (originally dry-stone) foundation, found within the top 10 ft of the motte, and possibly built up from the ground surface below (a natural rock outcrop?). It was built with the motte, not inserted into it, and is therefore of the late C11 (cf. structures of this date but different character at Okehampton and Exeter, qq.v.). The narrowness of the foundations (less than 3 ft) led the excavator to suggest that they may have carried a timber superstructure. There was apparently a buttress at the NE corner, and the stone foundation extending eastward marks the limit of a small associated platform. We have here a tantalizing glimpse of part of one of the many varieties of early motte structure.

PUBLIC BUILDINGS

GUILDHALL, Guildhall Yard, N of the church. Erected c. 1553 on the site of the N range of the former priory cloister. A lowly building, its chief exterior feature is an open loggia added in 1897, using octagonal granite piers from the Fruit Market House built on the S side of the church in 1611. They bear the date and the name of Rychard Lee, who paid for their erection. The rectangular guildhall itself, rubble patched with red sandstone, may have been formed from the priory refectory. Early C19 Perp windows, but one good Tudor wooden doorway towards the W end, with heavily moulded four-centred arch and jambs. Inside, the COURT ROOM, with some linenfold panelling, a painted plaster coat of arms dated 1553 over the mayor's chair with elaborate canopy, and a W gallery with turned symmetrical balusters. To the W, first-floor COUNCIL CHAMBER with central lantern, another canopied chair, an enriched frieze, and a strapwork plaster overmantel dated 1624. Below this room the town prison, rebuilt in 1624: a wainscoted cell with barred window and original prison door. Guildhall Cottage to the W, of 1897, incorporates parts of C17 prison buildings, and some more granite columns. To the E, Nos. 5–5a, the old grammar school, which was converted from another priory building c. 1553, partly rebuilt in 1630, and remodelled in the C19, keeping the straight hoodmoulds of stone over the first-floor windows. Medieval undercroft (vault removed in the C19), with slit windows on the N side.

CIVIC HALL, Market Square. *See* Perambulations.

MAGISTRATES COURT, Ashburton Road. An early example of the

self-effacing white-walled style which became popular in the 1970s. Floor-length windows; shallow hipped roof with set-back clerestory. 1972 by the *County Council Architect's Department*.

KING EDWARD VI SCHOOL, Ashburton Road. Large extensions by *Stillman & Eastwick-Field*, 1971. An attractive cluster of white walls and pitched roofs at different angles, in a similar idiom to the Magistrates Court.

HOSPITAL, Plymouth Road. The long S range with central three-storey canted bay was the middle part of the workhouse of 1838–9.

BRIDGE over the River Dart. 1826–8 by *Charles Fowler*. Very handsome: three arches with vermiculated voussoirs; pedimented ends. A further arch to the W. Built by public subscription as part of the improvements to the riverside. At the NW corner a TOLL HOUSE (the upper storey a later addition). On the upstream side, bases of the cutwaters of the previous bridge are visible at low tide.

BRUTUS BRIDGE. A slender structure of reinforced concrete, 1982, upstream from the old bridge.

TIDEMILL. A site of medieval origin, truncated by the construction of Coronation Road. Within Harris's factory, leats and two buildings, one barely recognizable.

ATMOSPHERIC RAILWAY PUMPING ENGINE HOUSE. Never used for its intended purpose. Pump and boiler houses, much altered, now part of Unigate Dairy, near the railway station.

PERAMBULATIONS

FORE STREET climbs uphill from The Plains. The first accents are early C19, and then C18. On the N side the ROYAL SEVEN STARS HOTEL, a broad early C19 stuccoed front with generous porch with room above, and an intriguing interior with stair-hall in the glazed-over courtyard between two long back wings. C18 staircase in the r. hand one. Opposite is a stuccoed neo-classical corner terrace with plain acroteria on the parapet and a pediment on the end wall to Fore Street; built in 1836 by a local carpenter, *Henry Webber*. Then Nos. 4–6, C18 or early C19, stuccoed, giant Ionic pilasters. The earlier houses at this end of Fore Street are modest, and all heavily disguised, but of good quality; Nos. 20–22, e.g. (with mock timber-framing), have two good carved C16 fireplaces. A little further up, set back and spanning an alley that passes beneath, the pretty GOTHIC HOUSE, with a narrow castellated front and two upper canted bays. Facing on to the alley a broad house of three storeys, of early C19 appearance, but probably a remodelling. Paired brackets to deep eaves; windows in the rounded corner. In the alley behind, a C16–17 cottage, perhaps the original detached kitchen.

On the other side of Fore Street the POST OFFICE of 1928, tall and gabled, all clothed in attractively mottled Delabole slates, is a sensitive C20 contribution. Also on the N side No. 29 (Presto), rebuilt in 1737, with Doric first-floor pilasters, and LLOYDS BANK, 1862 by *Hine* of Plymouth, a rather large and clumsy palazzo, but no larger than No. 36 opposite, a tall, three-storey, brick-fronted house built between 1795 and 1808 for the merchant Giles Welsford, the grandest of its date in the town. Stately hooded porch on Corinthian columns, delicate fanlight, the five-bay front with a minimum of ornament, just recessed round-arched windows with stone impost-bands on the ground floor, one stone band at first-floor level, and a stone top cornice. Good fireplace in the l. front room; staircase with wrought-iron balustrade rising at r. angles to the central passage.

On the N side of Fore Street Nos. 35 and 37 are late examples of traditional houses with back blocks, built between 1789 and 1809. The plain Delabole slates on No. 37 are a modern replacement of the smaller, more attractive local slates. Set back by Station Road, No. 47, a more unusual type for Totnes, faced with red brick, of two bays, doorway with good fanlight, ground-floor Venetian window – a conservative feature it seems, for the house was described in 1812 as lately rebuilt.

On the S side is the first interesting group of C17 houses of the characteristic South Western type: Nos. 48–56. They are all jettied, were probably originally gabled (although occasionally with a hip, instead of a gable), and all have detached back blocks, mostly with galleries linking them to the main house. Nos. 48 (Luscombe's) and 50 were built as a pair with matching granite corbels, and inside, on the second floor, matching single-rib ceilings. Very fine ceilings on the first floor, No. 48 broad-ribbed with rich overall decoration, No. 50 equally good but with double-moulded ribs. No. 52, its front block rebuilt in 1692 to a remarkably old-fashioned design, has superficial C19 alterations, but a piece of cornice and dragon-corbel below the l. end of the gable suggest an ebullient original façade. Late C17 first-floor ceiling consisting of a simple oval with a loose wreath of leaves and winged cherubs' heads in the centre. Heavy framed staircase with turned balusters (the earliest of this type in the town). No. 54 has carved corbels and bressumers, the gable, originally with patterned timber-framing, carved (obscurely) with the date 1607. Good corbelled fireplaces in the shop.

Another fine group at Nos. 62–70 Fore Street, all with detached back blocks except No. 64 (altered), most with galleries. No. 62, unusually, has a dormer gable. At No. 64 (gas showrooms) another richly decorated broad-ribbed ceiling upstairs, with CP and Prince of Wales feathers, probably of c. 1616, but possibly as late as c. 1638. No. 66 preserves its original stud-and-panel partition in the side passage, and a moulded beam supporting the gallery across the courtyard. No. 68, jettied, refronted in the C18, is remarkable for its two-room-deep back block (visible from the museum courtyard) originally containing kitchen and dining room.

Still in Fore Street, the MUSEUM (No. 70),* impressively tall, is the most easily recognizable and best preserved example of a Totnes house of traditional type, restored in 1961 and 1971. It probably dates from the late C16; it was the home of Geoffrey Babb (†1604), an important merchant. Four-storey timber-framed front with two jetties, between massive stone party walls. In the main range between front room (shop) and back room (hall), staircase in its own square well; the window of an earlier and more typical stair survives in the passage wall. Across the cobbled courtyard a first-floor gallery (reconstructed in the 1970s) to the back block; there is

*For a plan of No. 70 Fore Street see p. 81.

evidence for another, two-storeyed stone gallery to a further block beyond, now demolished. Both surviving blocks have fireplaces with sgraffito geometric patterns inside, a mid C17 Devon fashion.

On the N side one can make a little detour down an alley to see how a large development with supermarket has been fitted quite tactfully into the tight urban fabric (1986), although the detail is pathetically crude. Covered walks with concrete columns supposed to be in keeping with the Guildhall, the usual gaping car park at the back. W of this site, LITTLE PRIORY, once the detached back block of a house in Fore Street, converted to a separate house in the C19. On the ground floor remains of a surprisingly fine hooded granite C16 fireplace with flanking columns and carved brackets. The front block was rebuilt as two houses c. 1600; in the surviving W house (No. 65), a simple single-rib ceiling.

The EASTGATE marks the boundary of the inner, probably Saxon, town, the point where Fore Street becomes High Street. It was remodelled in 1837 by the builder *Henry Webber*. Gothic battlements and cupola, an oriel window on the E side. HIGH STREET, dramatically steep and narrow, begins on the S side with Nos. 3–5, tall slate-hung houses with mansards, by *John Hannaford*, builder, c. 1782. Opposite, Nos. 8–10 have early bolection-moulded panelling on the exterior, a rare survival. The rear of No. 8, rebuilt c. 1719, was the medieval guildhall. No. 10 has single-rib ceilings and roughly contemporary panelling on ground and first floors. A detached rear kitchen was submerged in extensions when the house became an inn in the early C18.

Further on, where the High Street opens out towards the church, No. 16, with classical stone front dated 1585, remarkable not only for the use of stone rather than timber-framing, but for its style at a time when most English houses were still essentially medieval in form. An originally open arcade on the ground floor, flat rusticated Doric and Ionic pilasters with decorated entablatures above; the front probably originally finished with a gable. Nicholas Ball, the merchant who built it, was mayor in 1585. Vying in importance is the house opposite, Nos. 11–13 (Bradford and Bingley), an impressively long timber-framed frontage of 1586, also built for Nicholas Ball, originally with an oriel the whole length of the first floor, which has a single-rib ceiling.

An excellent sequence of later fronts follows on the S side in the prime position opposite the church. Nos. 18 and 22 are both jettied, their party walls hidden by later rusticated plaster. The plastered timber-framed fronts of Nos. 26 and 28, of c. 1700, are up-to-date in being classical, but still have traditional gables. No. 26 has sober giant pilasters, No. 28 fantastic mask-keystones to the windows on the first floor, and bold flanking scrolls to those on the floor above. No. 32 (Hodges) looks modest, but is of particular interest as a gallery-and-back-block house with quite elaborate panelling dated 1577 (now in the ground-floor room of the back block, formerly upstairs), a slightly earlier hooded granite fireplace in the same room, and two single-rib ceilings. The owner in 1577 was probably Nicholas Brooking, mayor in that year.

The BUTTERWALK begins further up on the N side of the High Street, opposite the market place. This picturesque series of houses with upper storeys projecting over the pavement was prob- 97 ably built piecemeal (first reference 1532; evidence for a jetty earlier than the walk at No. 51). Columns were replaced in the C18 or C19; but those of Nos. 35–37 are early C16. No. 47 may once have had wooden columns. Behind and above the walk the houses are very largely of the C16 and C17, mostly with detached back blocks, some with galleries. No. 39 and its neighbour No. 41, formerly a single large house, are now much subdivided, with detached back block containing kitchen and dining room or parlour. Four ceilings with small bosses, Tudor roses and single ribs. One ceiling includes roundels with WD and ID, probably for Walter Dowse (†1580) and his wife Joan (†1574). This is among the earliest convincingly dated plasterwork extant in Devon, and suggests that Totnes merchants were as progressive in their tastes as the country gentry. No. 43, BOGAN HOUSE, is even more rewarding, with similar plasterwork datable to the 1580s (initials of William and Elizabeth Bogan †1580 and 1583), although the house itself is mid C16, with moulded beams hidden beneath the plaster in the ground-floor back room. Good granite hooded fireplace (restored) in the same room; pole staircase; unusual C16 Beer-stone fireplace on the first floor with simple frieze of circles and lozenges, no doubt from a pattern book (cf. similar examples in Rye, Sussex). Other good features in the Butterwalk include a single-rib ceiling at No. 33; corbelled fireplaces in the restaurant at No. 49; and at No. 55 a good panelled and studded early C17 door with moulded frame, with stud-and-panel partition inside, moulded towards the entrance passage (now a staircase).

The Butterwalk faces the MARKET SQUARE, originally the Flesh Shambles, enlarged when the CIVIC HALL was built at its far end in 1958–61 (by *G.A. Jellicoe & Partners*). Bland, with shallow pitched roof, but less painful than most urban buildings of this time. Slate-hung first-floor hall on columns, approached by a spiral ramp. The High Street continues uphill with the POULTRY WALK, a smaller version of the Butterwalk, then swings to the l. along the ridge of the hill. Several good houses in the Poultry Walk. No. 44 (Birwood House), remodelled probably c. 1719, has two detached back blocks visible from the market place; one has panelled timber-framing of the late C16 or early C17. No. 50 has an early C19 shopfront; No. 52, dated 1815, retains its original small-scale slate-hanging.

The rest of the High Street, known for obvious reasons as The Narrows, looks superficially less interesting; there are, however, many C16 to C17 jettied houses. Beneath the plaster at No. 70 is a superb carved oriel with dragon-corbel. Nos. 64 and 90 are good small craftsmen's houses of similar date (corbelled fireplaces inside); Nos. 83 and 88 have nice early C19 slate-hanging (the latter with fish-scale panels). Half way down on the l., by the junction with South Street, is the site of the old West Gate. Next to it the only surviving conduit of the town's C16 water supply, with plaque of 1607. At the far end High Street divides into LEECH-WELL STREET and CISTERN STREET, with the Rotherfold (the old cattle market) between them. This was always the poorer end of the town, but again, many of the houses are older than they seem: Nos. 1, 22 and 24 Leechwell Street all have corbelled fireplaces; the KINGSBRIDGE INN is a C17 house with a panelled front door; and in Cistern Street No. 18 has a detached back block and corbelled fireplaces.

PLYMOUTH ROAD, leading r. from the top of the High Street, is mainly an earlier C19 creation, with a terrace of houses followed, beyond the bypass, by some good neo-classical villas. The most interesting aspect of the lesser terraces of cottages in the few side streets of the town is the way they outline the medieval town plan: CASTLE STREET hugging the castle earthwork; NORTH STREET and SOUTH STREET following the lines of the town ramparts.

THE RIVERSIDE. Early C19 improvements on land reclaimed much earlier from the river marshes resulted in THE PLAINS, running s from Fore Street, parallel with the river, a broad street with early C19 houses on the w side, Nos. 6–8 especially pretty, with end bows and a pair of Doric porches. Beyond is the three-storeyed DARTMOUTH INN, set further back, and, opposite, a former Methodist Chapel of 1861, polygonal, with coloured brick trim. Alongside, grey rubble limestone warehouses and industrial buildings, a picturesque composition especially when seen from the river, but with an uncertain future. Next to the bridge an intriguing group, enterprisingly converted for the local preservation trust: TOTNES WATERSIDE, by *Harrison Sutton Partnership*, 1986–7. Its core is a long, narrow, two-storey range of chequered brick, with coved eaves and domestic windows of the early C18. It runs back from the river, and perhaps was a merchant's house (cf. the Strand, Topsham). Parallel to it a rubble warehouse and, linking the two, a house 'lately erected' in 1824, its handsome five-bay frontage reinstated, and accessible from a new promenade above the river.

BRIDGETOWN to the E of the river was a medieval foundation, an attempt by the de Pomeroys of Berry Pomeroy to intercept some of Totnes's trade (cf. Barnstaple and Newport). Its present appearance is predominantly early C19. A good terrace, DEVON PLACE, opposite St John's church. One well-preserved C16 house, No. 5 Bridgetown, with oriel window. Overlooking the river, the former Seymour Hotel, now flats, c. 1830, much altered.

THE PRIORY, hidden away off Priory Drive, in the former orchard of Totnes Priory. Five-bay rubble stone front with stone keystones to regular Georgian sash-windows – probably a remodelled older house. Good C18 staircase with unusual plaster cornice of rather Gothic-looking large pendants. Ground-floor room on the r. with an accomplished C18 ceiling, a quatrefoil on which four well-modelled eagles are perching, holding a garland in their beaks (cf. Gatcombe, near Littlehempston). Centrepiece with profile head of Charles I (an addition?), in a sunburst. Fireplace flanked by Doric pilasters.

CONSERVATIVE CLUB, Station Road. Stuccoed, c. 1892, quite handsome, with round-arched window, pilasters, rusticated quoins, and large porch. Built as the Totnes Club.

(HOME MEADOW. Friendly, two- and three-storey sheltered housing on a courtyard plan, in a sympathetic local idiom. Rendered walls and pitched roofs. 1984 by *South Hams District Council*, principal architect *Alfred Johnson*.)

See also Bowden House *and* Follaton House.

TRENTISHOE

ST PETER. A minute church, especially before the present chancel was built in 1861. It stands in no village, just by a farmstead in a sheltered fold below the bare downs, with the sea less than ½ m. away to the NW. Tiny narrow W tower, rebuilt in 1638, narrower than the nave and now almost merging into the hillside. No aisles. Inside, there is a musicians' gallery, with a hole in the parapet where the double bass needed space beyond the narrow confines of the gallery. The tympanum which formerly existed between nave and chancel (cf. Molland, Parracombe) has been replaced by a chancel arch on corbels.

On TRENTISHOE DOWN a prominent ROUND BARROW.
Circular LIMEKILN by the beach at Heddon's Mouth.

TRUSHAM

ST MICHAEL. Unbuttressed, unpinnacled W tower. Three-bay N aisle, the piers B type but of granite (as are the windows in the tower). The tower arch extremely elementary – not necessarily a sign of great age. Restored by *J. W. Rowell*, 1865, and in 1890. The chancel now whitewashed, although the prettily painted ceiled wagon roof and two angels remain from a Victorian decorative scheme. Elaborate sanctuary TILES. – REREDOS. 1865, flanked by Commandments in Gothic niches. – FONT. Circular, Norman, plain. – PILLAR PISCINA. Also Norman; a scalloped capital. – SCREEN. Only the main uprights seem to be genuine. The rest by *Herbert Read*, as also the PULPIT. – STAINED GLASS. In the E window the Crucifixion, by *Beer*, 1865, figures on quarries, coarse. – In the N aisle, three windows of the 1890s by *Clayton & Bell*. – MONUMENTS. Two of unusual materials. In a recess in the chancel a painting commemorating the Staplehill family, late C16, all kneeling, with a brass below. – John Stooke † 1697 and wife. A large architectural wall-monument, all of wood, painted to simulate marble, with two painted portrait medallions.

The small church stands on the hillside W of the Teign valley amidst a scrappily expanding village. Among the C20 buildings several old houses to note.

OLD RECTORY. A large thatched complex below the church, probably in origin a late medieval farmhouse. There are two windows of *c.* 1500, one of them with a cusped head, and two C17 timber windows.

CRIDEFORD INN. A four-room-plan late medieval house altered in the C20. One late medieval oak mullioned window with four ogee-headed lights remains; also inserted C16–17 floors with moulded beams.

CHICKS, Greenhill. Thatched and rendered former forge and farmhouse remarkable for its completely smoke-blackened medieval roof.

ALMSHOUSES, Higher Town. A late C17 pair built by John Stooke. Short wings with gabled ends; windows renewed.

TUCKENHAY
Near Cornworthy

8050

Established on a creek at the head of the river Dart in 1806 by Abraham Tucker, who built quays and warehouses along the W bank. Now a charming backwater, with plenty of evidence of the industrial past. Numerous LIMEKILNS in the banks on the S side of the creek. Along the quay below the Maltster's Arms, three blocks of CIDER FACTORY and WAREHOUSES, one and two storeys in rubble stone, now converted to dwellings. On the S side another former warehouse of 1818, with a vaulted ground floor and two upper storeys. In the garden the small rectangular GAS HOUSE, with red corrugated-iron roof and double doors at the N end, built by Tucker to light the village. Further W, the CORN MILL with mill house attached, a two-storey stone building with a 10-ft overshot wheel at the S end.

Rising up the hillside at the S end of the village early C19 woollen MILLS, converted to paper mills in 1829 and enlarged in 1889 by the addition of a substantial H-plan building of stone with brick dressings, with a clock turret. Closed in 1970, and converted to holiday cottages. Late C19 workers' terraces of the same materials.

TWITCHEN

7030

In a lonely position, high up, and facing Exmoor, ST PETER, much rebuilt in 1844 by *Hayward*, except for the low unbuttressed W tower. – FONT. Norman, circular, with elementary zigzag decoration.

WESLEYAN CHAPEL. Early C19; forecourt with railings.

UFFCULME

0010

ST MARY. Medieval W tower and nave. Chancel rebuilt and refitted in 1843 by *John Hayward*, who in 1847–9 also added the outer S aisle and rebuilt the spire, which had fallen in the early C18; an ambitious early Tractarian restoration, financed chiefly by Richard Marker of Yondercott and the News of Craddock House. C19 Dec detail; broach-spire with crocketed corner pinnacles set diagonally. Inside, the earliest medieval part is the three-bay N arcade, of local red sandstone, with circular piers, moulded capitals, and double-chamfered arches, C13 or C14. Further E the arcades are Perp, like those of the S aisle (type A piers, with capitals only to the shafts). The C19 outer aisle similar. The S arcade whitewashed when the nave was reordered in 1973 (an early example in Devon) with nave altar, carpeted floor, and radially set benches (brought from Bradfield chapel). The plastered wagon roofs of nave and N aisle look C18. Over the chancel a plaster barrel-vault (repainted).

Hayward's chancel FITTINGS of 1843 survive: stone ALTAR, daring for its date; stone Gothic REREDOS (unfortunately painted); both (like the FONT) made by *Samuel Knight*. – PULPIT. 1719, in a not at all local Wren–Gibbons style, incorporating a panel of the Ascension (foreign?). – SCREEN. The most impressive feature of the church: early C15, reaching all across nave and aisles, with fan-vaulted coving on both sides (the N and S sections remade in 1847–9). At 67 ft, the longest in Devon. Openings of six lights each, B type tracery. Some red and green original colour revealed by recent cleaning. – SOUTH PARCLOSE SCREEN. Free Gothic of 1909, from Pennycross, Plymouth, installed in 1986. – TOWER SCREEN. Made up of fragments said to come from an organ gallery of 1629 (cf. Cullompton). – ALTAR, NE (Walrond) chapel. Made up of C16 bench ends or domestic panelling (?). – Painted ROYAL ARMS by *Robert Beer*, 1839. – STAINED GLASS. The E window a brightly coloured mosaic of 1843. – S aisle 1902 by *Lavers & Westlake*. – MONUMENTS. Two to the Walrond family, of bad workmanship. A tomb-chest with two relief busts in roundels, flanked by figures of Faith, Hope and Charity. On the chest free-standing busts of a man, a woman, and a boy, *c.* 1650. Probably not in its original arrangement (same hand at Bickleigh). – Of the other Walrond monument, of *c.* 1700, only the reclining figure of a man in armour and wig remains. – Other minor tablets.

Uffculme was once an important centre of the woollen trade. The VILLAGE SQUARE is an uneven wedge-shape on a slope, pleasantly surrounded by unassuming early C19 frontages. The SHAMBLES in the centre is a wooden construction like a lychgate. Close by, AYSHFORD HOUSE, formerly the grammar school founded by Nicholas Ayshford in 1701, a plain, orderly brick building with a wooden cross window and a cupola, much added to. In the village, a five-storey long narrow red-brick BREWERY (now a community centre), with a squat octagonal tower at the E end and round-headed windows.

At COLDHARBOUR WOOLLEN MILL, a variety of buildings dating from the late C18 to the C20 centred around a three-storey stone MILL of fireproof construction, built by Thomas Fox in 1799, and now a working museum. Brick additions, separate ranges of lower outbuildings, and a fine octagonal brick chimney, 127 ft high. Power was supplied by a 15 ft by 18 ft waterwheel, probably of 1885, and a 320 h.p. Pollet & Wigzell horizontal cross compound steam engine of 1910, both still operating.

BAPTIST CHAPEL, Chapel Hill. Rebuilt in 1815; later C19 extensions and alterations. Rendered front, walled burial ground with some elegant C18 monuments.

BOARD SCHOOL. 1874 by *J.H. Mooney* of Newbury.

See also Bradfield, Bridwell, *and* Craddock House.

6050

UGBOROUGH

A village on a hill, with the look of a town that never grew. Formerly cattle fairs were held here. Spacious village square with a conduit in the middle, the big church high up above the S side.

ST PETER. Castellated N side facing the village. W tower 94 ft high, of granite ashlar, with buttresses of type B, three-light bell-openings, and polygonal pinnacles corbelled out from the bell stage. Two-storeyed N porch, N transept, and E of it a Perp chapel and N vestry of the same date (see the continuous plinth). The vestry has a little bay-window to the E. S aisle of granite ashlar, also castellated, also with porch, transept, and chapel, but details simpler than on the N side. Priest's door cut into a chancel buttress (cf. Kingsbridge, Thurlestone). Perp windows originally of the typical granite pattern with depressed arches, mullions, and no tracery. Other windows look as if they may have been replaced c. 1800. The E window is C19. Six-bay arcades, the short octagonal piers of the same odd design as Modbury. The transept aisles are larger and taller, then two-bay chancel chapels. These E parts are of a different, later design: A type piers with tall moulded arches. The joints between W and E transept bay clearly visible. N aisle ceiling with panels with diagonal ribs, Perp, but perhaps reset as a ceiling c. 1800 from parts of a wagon roof. Excellent large wooden bosses of C14 type with heads, foliage, etc.; also one with sow and piglets (St Brannock, cf. Branscombe) and another with a blacksmith (St Eloy). Restoration 1867–8.

FONT. Norman, chalice-shaped, of red sandstone. Plain except for about a fifth, which has a pattern of palmettes; the rest probably cut back. – PULPIT. Stone, the curving-out foot with panels decorated with rib-vaulting patterns. – SCREEN. Badly treated but still impressive. Across nave and aisles, but only the wainscoting with painted figures of c. 1525 is complete. Among the representations the Annunciation, Assumption of the Virgin, Martyrdom of St Sebastian, etc. The upper parts cut down in the nave and only preserved in the aisles. They have tracery of the Dartmouth type and are deprived of their coving. Pieces of the cornice are stuck on to the spandrels. – PARCLOSE SCREEN. With tracery similar to Holbeton. – STAINED GLASS. S aisle second from E by *Powell & Son*, 1864, two medallions against quarries (Annunciation to the Shepherds, Nativity). – Similar window in the N aisle, 1863. – Other simpler windows of the 1860s in the N chapel. – BRASS. Lady, early C16. – MONUMENTS. Minor tablets only. Thomas and John King †1792, 1795, by *Richard Isbell* of Stonehouse. – Richard King †1811. Small figure mourning over an urn, by *Tyley* of Bristol. – On the N chancel wall inscribed oval tablets and shelf (remains of a larger monument?) to members of the Fownes family (1680, 1706, 1712) with some well carved foliage. – CURIOSUM. Village stocks.

EAST PEAK FARM. A late C17–early C18 farmhouse on a symmetrical plan with end stacks, probably a remodelling of an earlier structure, with service rooms and a staircase block integral at the rear. Inside, the house is somewhat altered, but flat balusters survive in the attic. First-floor granary and kitchen added later at the road end. C19 Gothick window tracery at the front. Opposite the house a bank BARN built into the hillside, with a shippon below, dated 1755.

FILHAM. S of Filham House (C18, altered in the C19), the remains of a medieval chapel (licensed 1400) adapted as a folly by the addition of a tall narrow polygonal tower in 1742.

(VENN HOUSE. Stone, Georgian, three bays, two storeys.)

VIADUCT. The stone piers remain from *Brunel*'s timber viaduct of 1848.

PREHISTORIC REMAINS. On Dartmoor, close to the long barrow at Corringdon Ball (*see* South Brent) but lying between the East and West Glaze Brooks, is a group of three stone rows, identified by Worth as one single and two triple rows. Cairns were recorded nearby, and recently two multiple stone rings have been found (cf.

Shovel Down, Gidleigh). Other stone rows on the sides of GLASS-COMBE BALL and on PILES HILL. Enclosed settlements lie along the valley sides, and cairns on the hilltops, with large summit cairns on UGBOROUGH BEACON and BUTTERDON HILL, and a ruined chambered long cairn on CUCKOO BALL.

TRAMWAY. The dismantled line leading from Redlake china clay works (Lydford) runs across almost the whole length of the parish.

EARTHWORK, S of Langford Barton. Possibly the remains of a mutilated motte-and-bailey castle.

See also Fowelscombe.

8070

UGBROOKE
Chudleigh

Ugbrooke is set in a valley. It is surrounded by the exquisitely landscaped park with its two lakes, given its present form by *Capability Brown* in the 1770s. The house at first sight appears unpromisingly C19, but is in fact chiefly of the C18, rebuilt for the fourth Lord Clifford (†1783) by *Robert Adam*. The estate had belonged to Exeter Cathedral in the Middle Ages, then to the Courtenays, and passed by marriage to the Cliffords in the C16. Baron Clifford, Charles II's Lord Chancellor, who retired to Devon after refusing to take the Test Act and died in 1673, left money to finish the house 'according to the model', but nearly all the evidence for his building, apart from some changes of floor levels and ceilings in the lesser rooms, was removed in Adam's remodelling. This began in 1763 and was largely complete by 1766. It was a frugal exercise, less ambitious than earlier schemes which had been proposed to Clifford by Adam as well as by other architects – *Brown, Paine Sen.* and *Jun.*, and *Carr*.*

The main building is almost square; rendered walls, ten by eleven bays, round three sides of a courtyard. The corner blocks rise to three storeys and have battlements, so that the house qualifies as the first of Adam's rather dull castle exteriors. All the other details are entirely domestic. Round-headed windows on the ground floor. Their coarse and heavy surrounds and other minor alterations date from 1874. To the E, linked to the main house by a C19 arch with conservatory above, is a projecting wing, dating from 1767–8, which incorporates the older chapel (consecrated 1671). This wing still has its elegant Adam appearance, with a shallow bow-fronted centre and battlements. The parts of the older house which lay behind were taken down by Adam, and when the main house was restored in 1957 after use as an agricultural store, the Victorian additions which filled its courtyard were demolished.

Simple Adam interiors in the S and W ranges: plain staircase, with a little plaster ornament around the roof-light; the decoration of the hall and the large, well-proportioned drawing room and dining room confined to simple fireplaces and good Adam cornices and overdoors. *William Spring* was clerk of the works. Adam's drawings show more elaborate details than those executed. The chapel wing is a little more ornate, with an attractive library, with original bookcases, filling the bow-fronted centre of the first floor.

*For these see A. Rowan, *Country Life*, 20 July 1967.

The CHAPEL (used as an R.C. parish church from the late C17) has a sumptuous Italian Renaissance interior, the result of much C19 attention, quite a surprise after the demure Adam front. Converted to a Greek-cross plan in the 1840s, with a new vault and a cupola over the crossing. Baptistery and Lady Chapel 1866. The walls lined with coloured marble; giant pilasters below the crossing. Tablet in coloured marbles to the eighth Lord Clifford † 1880, with putti and bay-leaf frieze.

STABLES. By *Joseph Rowe*, 1793. Away from the house; courtyard plan, one storey in front, two behind.

GROUNDS. No garden buildings apart from a few cottages and lodges (among them SMOOTHWAY LODGE, a small *cottage orné* with Gothic windows). DRYDEN'S SEAT is simply a grassy bank. So their charm lies entirely in Brown's skill:

> To shade the hill, to scoop and swell the green
> To break with wild diversities the scene
> To model with the Genius of the place
> Each artless feature, each spontaneous grace . . .*

At the top of the park, CASTLE DYKE, an Iron Age univallate hillfort, with outwork still surviving to the S (a defensible annexe for stock?). Within this annexe cropmarks of possibly earlier small enclosures.

UP EXE

CHAPEL. The same elementary shape as at Nether Exe. Undivided nave and chancel; C13-style windows. A pair of cottages until reconstructed as a chapel in 1888 by *R.M. Fulford*; now converted back again to a house.

UPLOWMAN

ST PETER. Medieval W tower, unbuttressed and embattled, without pinnacles, probably C14. From a C14 church one capital preserved in the S porch. The rest rebuilt *c.* 1500 by Lady Margaret Beaufort (q.v., Sampford Peverell) and almost completely reconstructed in 1863–6 by *Hayward*, who added a new chancel and renewed all the roofs. Across the chancel arch C19 wrought-iron cross with foliage trails. The S arcade, with B type piers and standard capitals, looks genuine Perp; likewise the broad arch for a tomb between chancel and S chapel, with a bracket for a statue between the two E responds, and a coat of arms. – (STAINED GLASS. Chancel windows by *Wailes*.)

UPLOWMAN COURT. Immediately N of the church, attached to the E end of a farmhouse (C19 externally but C17 or earlier inside), is an intriguing rubble-walled remnant: the solar end of a medieval house, now partly derelict. Probably C14 – see the windows and traces of a base-cruck roof. E wall with one partly blocked tall two-light window with shouldered lights below a transom (the top

* From 'A Poem on Ugbrooke' by Father Joseph Reeve, Lord Clifford's chaplain († 1820).

destroyed); to its S, a room with framed and moulded ceiling. An arched wooden doorway opens from this to the projecting chapel with remains of a traceried two-light E window. Another wooden doorcase in the N wall of the main block.

There are many large C15–18 farmhouses in the parish.

WIDHAYES is a late C16-early C17 farmhouse, refurbished in 1880. However, it still has its large C17 gateway with hoodmoulded round-headed arch, in which there is a splendid faceted and studded original door surmounted by a shell hood. Wicket gate with lozenge-shaped plaque above. The farmstead group includes an eleven-bay C17 linhay and a double barn.

SPALSBURY. Good late medieval farmhouse with two stud-and-panel screens, one carried up to the ridge.

80 MIDDLECOMBE. A classic C17 farmhouse – render, thatch, projecting porch – still happily with many of its original front windows: mullioned-and-transomed and richly ovolo-moulded to hall, parlour, and chamber, and especially handsomely moulded over one first-floor window. Inside, in the chamber above the hall, is some Jacobean panelling, in all likelihood re-used. There was obviously a rear cross-wing (or perhaps a detached kitchen block), as proved by the large stack/oven complex. The smaller house in front is probably late medieval in origin (see the small reset window at the back), indicating that the main house is a rebuilding on a substantial medieval farmstead site.

UPLOWMAN HOUSE. Regular three-storey late C18 stuccoed range of five bays, one room deep, overlooking a pretty valley E of the church. Doorcase with fluted pilasters and fanlight; corner quoins. Rear staircase projection. Earlier W range of two storeys above a basement.

UPLYME

ST PETER AND ST PAUL. Medieval W tower, battlemented, with square NE stair-turret; also medieval the N arcade with octagonal piers. The rest largely early C19 and of 1875, when the church was restored by *G. L. Bather* of Shrewsbury. Long, unbuttressed and embattled S side. The N side a surprise: a tall aisle with two tiers of windows and a W stair bay, all embattled, dating from 1829, when the still-existing N gallery was built. Nave wagon roof with C19 painting. Chancel floor steeply stepped up in 1875. – PULPIT. Cut-down Jacobean, its sounding-board now the vestry table. – SCREEN. C19, stone; elaborate, sharply cut Perp tracery (cf. the E window). – PANELLING in the chancel, apparently made up from the medieval screen. – Other fragments in the CHOIR STALLS. – STAINED GLASS. Nave S, the empty tomb, by *Hardman*, to the vicar's son Wilfred Parke †1912, 'killed at Wembley by the fall of his aeroplane'.

SCHOOL, near the church. Mid C19 Tudor.

WOODHOUSE. 1880 for Sir George Baker by *George & Peto*. Picturesquely set on a hill with views of the sea, approached up a long drive. Now an old people's home. A compact, quite tall house, attractively varied in its materials and its elevations. Patterned tile-hanging above a stone ground floor; half-timbered gables. The main, s-facing front with two-storey bay-windows with rounded corners; on the E side a polygonal bay with tented lead roof, on the W side a wooden porch with carved figures. Plain interiors, apart from a neo-Jacobean ceiling in the main s room. Low service court to the N, tied to the house by stone walls.

CANNINGTON VIADUCT. Mass concrete, completed in 1903, for the Axminster–Lyme Regis light railway. Ten elliptical arches, 610ft long, maximum height 93ft. The third arch from the W supported by brick infilling soon after completion.

One of Devon's few ROMAN VILLAS was excavated at HOLCOMBE in the C19 and again in the 1950s. A tessellated pavement was found, but little survives.

UPOTTERY   2000

ST MARY. The insensitive renewal of 1875 by *B. Ferrey* predominates. Medieval W tower with diagonal buttresses. Remains of a Norman corbel-table on the N wall (visible from the N chapel). In the same wall a piscina of *c.* 1250. Perp N arcade with B type piers and standard capitals. Panelled arch to the N chapel. Extensive repairs and refitting in 1826–7 by the builder-architects *J. & W. Lee* of Honiton, paid for by the former Prime Minister, Henry Addington, Viscount Sidmouth (who lived at the manor), included repewing and the removal of the rood screen, but most of this work disappeared in 1875 (windows renewed, new chancel arch, new nave roof, new seating). Carving by *Hems*. Organ chamber and vestry by *E.H. Harbottle*, 1898. The thin classical W organ gallery added by *W.H. Randoll Blacking* in 1927. – FONT. Perp, octagonal, with quatrefoil panels. – STAINED GLASS. Small medieval and other fragments in a s window. – MONUMENTS. John Hutchins †1709; architectural. – Minor tablets to the Addingtons.

RECTORY. 1843, Tudor Gothic, by *Hayward*.

Lord Sidmouth's early Victorian Tudor manor house has been demolished, but the former LODGE and STABLES remain; also estate housing and a SCHOOL in the village.

At the hamlet of RAWRIDGE a former C18 TUCKING MILL.

At NEWHOUSE, close to the county boundary, is a little group of buildings on a site dating from the C17. The present Baptist chapel was built in 1859 on the site of a C17 meeting-house. It has rendered walls, porch, lancet windows, and a slate roof with stone copings and ball finials. Inside, the box pews are original. The adjacent Sunday school and manse were built in 1913. Monuments in the burying ground also date from the C17.

UPTON HELLIONS   8000

ST MARY. Surrounded by only a few houses. Unbuttressed, unpinnacled W tower with NE stair-turret. C12 nave and lower chancel, of rubble with volcanic stone quoins. s door Norman, simple, of one order, the capitals scalloped. Unmoulded tower arch, unmoulded chancel arch. Late Perp s aisle, with s porch added at its W end. A puzzling low opening in a quatrefoil surround in the W wall of the aisle. The windows also mostly late Perp: three-light, straight-headed. The s arcade has piers of unusual section: lozenge-shaped, with four shafts in the main directions; very plain capitals. Ceiled wagon roofs, the one in the aisle more elaborately carved. – In the tower, C15 BELL in the original bell-frame. – FONT. Norman, in the shape of a big block-capital. – REREDOS. *Minton* tiles of *c.* 1875. – BENCH ENDS. The usual South Western type, with foliage motifs. On one a lion couchant. – Small ROYAL ARMS of painted and moulded plaster. – MONUMENTS. Richard Reynell †1631 and wife, of Lower Creedy, with the traditional kneeling figures facing each other. – Rev. James Carington †1794, with vase above pediment.

RECTORY (former). Early C18, remodelled in the C19. Brick, an irregular four-window front.

UPTON HELLIONS BARTON. Three ranges around a courtyard, rubble stone, the front plastered. A handsome exterior with tall lateral stacks. C16 front range with three-room-cross-passage plan, late C17 rear stair projection, dating respectively from the time of Dr George Carew (1566) and Richard Read (*c.* 1692). Good C16 doorway with elliptical head and ornate stops, studded door. Late C17 dog-leg stair with turned balusters.

BUCKSTONE COTTAGE, Church Lane. The former dower house of Creedy Park. Stuccoed two-storey, three-window front of *c.* 1820, with a Tuscan porch. Contemporary interiors; top-lit geometric stair with delicate plaster frieze around the cupola.

See also Creedy Park.

UPTON PYNE

OUR LADY. C14 w tower distinguished by an unusual display of statuary in cusped niches (doubtless influenced by the cathedral w front): King David in the stair-turret, four more smaller niches with the Evangelists high up above the diagonal buttresses in the corners of the battlements below the pinnacles, and a figure of Christ over the w window. Large bell-openings, two lights, one transom. Inside, the low, narrow, pointed, double-chamfered chancel arch remains from an aisleless C13 church. Perp s arcade with B type piers; capitals standard except that the E bay is distinguished as a chantry chapel by angels on the capitals, and leaves and shields on jambs and voussoirs. In this chapel two recesses with Tudor arches; in one an effigy in early C16 armour, probably Edmund Larder †1521. N arcade piers rebuilt 1833 by *John Ware* of Exeter. Perp capitals re-used, the arches reconstructed in the restoration of 1874–5 by *William White*. White also rebuilt the chancel (retaining a Perp N window), added the organ chamber to the N, with moulded arches to chancel and aisle, renewed all the roofs, and – a typical White touch – provided the small diagonal SE arch framing his new PULPIT. – REREDOS by *R.M.Fulford*, designed 1875, executed 1887 as part of a refitting of the sanctuary, framing an C18 Italian PAINTING of the Last Supper. – WEST GALLERY in the tower arch with C18 balustrade. – STAINED GLASS. German fragments dated 1630 in the s aisle SE window. –

Chancel E 1875 by *Ward & Hughes*. – N aisle E 1851 by *Hardman*,
to a *Pugin* design.

GLEBE HOUSE. Late C18, red brick, two storeys, three bays, with
bracketed eaves and a Tuscan porch. (Good hall with internal
fanlight; staircase with wrought-iron balusters, roof-light with
plasterwork frieze.)

PYNES. The grand mansion built by Hugh Stafford (1674–1734),
probably *c.* 1700, although altered, is still an excellent example of
the stately double-pile house that became popular after the Restoration but is relatively rare in Devon. Two show fronts of red
brick to S and W, each of seven bays, two storeys above a tall
basement, with dormers in the hipped roof. The former entrance
side to the S is distinguished by a centre of three projecting bays
with intermittently balustraded parapet. Corners emphasized by
giant brick pilasters on tall plinths of volcanic stone (now
rendered). Doorway converted to a balconied window in the C19,
its stone pediment perhaps original. The present W entrance also
with pilasters, the central ones now covered by channelled stucco.
A bold pedimented doorway has been inserted rather awkwardly at
basement level. To the N a restrained later C18 extension, red brick
with stone bands, containing justice room and kitchen. The E front
plain, five bays only, with a lower service wing to the N. It ends in a
water tower (*c.* 1879 by *James Jerman*) at the corner of the kitchen
courtyard.

The C19 entrance leads into a remarkably ceremonial entrance
hall created in 1852 by *Ambrose Poynter* for Sir Stafford Henry
Northcote, later Earl of Iddesleigh (1819–87). Stone stairs, rising
from the former basement level to a landing with heavy stone
interlacing balustrade on three sides. Eclectic detail: niche with
classical statue facing the entrance; ceiling cove embellished with
arms in strapwork. The rest of the house, with only minor alterations (C18 shutters, C19 fireplaces and some ceilings), is essentially of *c.* 1700, with an enfilade of reception rooms along the S
front, and behind them a stately, handsomely proportioned well
staircase, of transitional type, with closed string but balusters with
thick spiral above a ball, and ramped rail. Large arched landing
window with a C19 arrangement of stained glass, including some
C17 German roundels. Splendid ceiling with an oval of robustly
modelled fruit and flowers and mask heads in the local late C17
tradition. Cornice with egg and dart. On the first floor, S bedroom
with a plain moulded ceiling of the typical square-plus-semicircles
pattern, and pretty leaves and shells around the cornice. An octagonal ceiling in the adjoining closet. Main W bedroom with full-
height pine panelling with large raised panels.

Formal terraced GARDEN s of the house, shown on an C18
survey by *B. Langley*, remodelled in 1852 with a FOUNTAIN by
Charles R. Smith, who also provided bronze stags for the W
entrance piers.

HOME FARM. Early C19 STABLES with clock tower above the
arched carriageway.

ROUND BARROWS. One of lowland Devon's largest groups, centred
around the crossroads ¾ m. W of Brampford Speke village. Mostly
under cultivated farmland; other ritual sites in the area are indicated by cropmarks of ring ditches. The one barrow excavated this

century was shown to be of turf and earth construction with an apparently primary deposit of cremated bone in a collared urn, and later deposits of cremated bones, collared urns, and Trevisker pots. Outliers of this barrow group can be seen in the Exe valley and on the Raddon Hills.

See also Cowley.

VENN OTTERY

0090

St Gregory. Medieval w tower, low, unbuttressed, with paired square-headed belfry windows. The rest much restored by *Packham & Croote* of Exeter in 1882, when nave and chancel were stripped of roughcast, new windows inserted, and new roofs built. – BENCH ENDS. Some late medieval, with large foliage forms filling the ends; Victorian replacements by *Hems* to match.

VENN OTTERY COMMON. *See* Newton Poppleford.

VIRGINSTOW

3090

Close to the Cornish border.

St Bridget. Completely rebuilt in the lancet style in 1851 by *William Rundle* for the Rev. P. Cann. Nave with w bellcote on paired buttresses, s porch, chancel. Modest and old-fashioned. – FONT. Norman. Simple bowl on stem with recut cable moulding.

OLD RECTORY. 1845 for Mr Cann. Stone rubble, late Georgian in style. Stair-hall with plaster groin-vault.

WALKHAMPTON

5060

CHURCH (no dedication). All alone, except for the church house, on a hill on the edge of the moor $\frac{1}{2}$m. w of the village, a spectacular sight, with its big granite ashlar w tower. The buttresses diagonal, replaced at the bell stage by the polygonal supports of the big polygonal crocketed pinnacles (cf. Plymouth, Plympton). The church itself is small in comparison with the tower. Late Perp s aisle of granite ashlar; an earlier gabled s porch adjacent. The N aisle and its windows look earlier than the s aisle. Inside, both arcades similar: four bays, A type piers, depressed arches. The squint from the transept originally had a free-standing corner column as one finds them occasionally in Cornwall. Tower arch on big head-corbels. Restored in 1860–1; walls scraped. Sanctuary tiled in memory of Lady Lopes †1872. – FONT. Octagonal, Perp, with shields. – WOODWORK by the Rev. *Charles Walker* (†1909). – STAINED GLASS. s aisle E by *Ward & Hughes*. Others by *Powell* of Whitefriars.

CHURCH HOUSE. On the E boundary of the churchyard. Now two houses, formerly an inn. A small but quite complex building, a good deal altered (restoration date 1698) but basically C16. Granite rubble, two storeys. The most revealing side the s gable-end where the C16 openings have been exposed: on each floor two square-headed windows with two arched lights, and between the upper ones a Tudor doorway to the large first-floor room, presumably once approached by an outer stair. On the W side a large projection housing an internal stone stair. Inside, the ground floor is divided into two main rooms and a small central room by two stone cross-walls. Several stone doorways. Large fireplace in the N gable wall. Ground-floor rooms with chamfered beams on large stone corbels.

LADY MODYFORD'S SCHOOL. In the village. Founded 1719. A charming Victorian group with bell and clock tower, gabled school buildings, partly of 1863, and nearby a separate teacher's house of 1895. Brown stone with granite and red brick dressings. Decorative ridge tiles.

HUCKWORTHY BRIDGE. *See* Sampford Spiney.

WELLTOWN. A thoroughly confusing exterior, especially at the front, gives no hint of the outstanding interest of this fully developed C17 farmhouse with its many specialist rooms. Here is recorded the social progression from farmers to minor gentry of the Atwills, the owners from the early C14 until the late C18, who prospered from local tin-mining in the later C16 and early C17. The earliest house was on a N–S axis; its gable end is incorporated in the S front. Internally the evidence is confusing, but from this phase remain a two-centred door frame, a large axial stack, and a granite door frame with spandrels with stiff foliage decoration, which leads into a room with closely spaced heavy joists suggesting former service use, or even a shippon with hayloft above. Late C16 and early C17 extensions were added to E and N, and a long cross-wing to the W, so that the main house faced S. Of fireplaces of this period, one in the W cross-wing has a roll-moulding carried around a central semicircular recess with the initials RA and GA for Robert and Grace Atwill, who were here from 1580 to 1620. Off the present kitchen the dairy, with water channels in slate slabs and a floor for cooling. Opposite the house a substantial C19 fowlhouse.

EARLY SETTLEMENT. The extensive archaeological remains to the N and S of the Two Bridges–Tavistock road at MERRIVALE are some of the most readily accessible on Dartmoor for the less agile visitor. On both sides of the road runs a series of massive hut circles and enclosures, interspersed with abandoned moorstone workings of a later age, including half-finished cider millstones. Traces of a parallel reave system run across the area. S of the road, some well preserved stone rows, one single and two double; uniquely on Dartmoor, one of the double rows incorporates a retaining kerb and small barrow. There are also cairns, cists, a stone circle, and a tall standing stone. Other fine examples of Bronze Age settlement – cairns and stone rows – are to be seen on WALKHAMPTON COMMON and BLACK TOR, SW of Princetown.

At MERRIVALE also much evidence of tinworking; N of the road a series of blowing houses survives at intervals beside the river Walkham. There are also tinworking remains in the midst of prehistoric settlement in the S of the parish, in the valley of Newleycombe Lake next to Burrator Reservoir at NORSWORTHY, where beside the road was a medieval tinner's mill of which some mortar-stones and the base of a crazing mill survive.

At FOGGINTOR, apart from moorstone working, are the substantial remains of large granite quarries, with the railway that served them. The quarry at MERRIVALE still operates.

4070

WALREDDON
Whitchurch, 2 m. s of Tavistock

A medium-sized manor house of medieval origin, with a projecting porch dated 1596, one projecting wing, and on the other side a long detached buttressed barn, probably also C16. The back of the house is essentially Tudor; the front and sides have been regularized by Georgian windows. The result is a seven-bay front with segment-headed sash-windows and a modillion cornice. Inside, much Tudor panelling and joinery, and, in the parlour, a late C18 fireplace. From the C18 to the early C19 the house belonged to a junior branch of the Courtenays.

6020

WARKLEIGH

St John the Evangelist. Not in a village – close only to a substantial Rolle estate farm and farmhouse (dated 1876). Tallish W tower with diagonal buttresses and pinnacles. s aisle with piers of B type with capitals only to the main shafts. Three of the bays open into the nave; the fourth is the entrance to the s chancel chapel, a family chapel, with larger windows than the rest of the church. The arch to the chancel is broader than the others, so that a large squint can go through its W pier. Chancel rebuilt 1850, restored in 1883. Nave roof C19 with applied medieval bosses (the genuine roof survives above). An inscribed slate slab records the contributors, headed by the Hon. Mark Rolle. – BENCH ENDS with Renaissance foliage and profile heads in medallions, the usual motifs; made into a screen under the W tower arch. – PULPIT.
C18. – PYX CASE. A most interesting object, of a kind very rare, if not unique, in England – a late medieval wooden box to carry the Blessed Sacrament for administration to the sick. It measures $7\frac{3}{4}$ by $7\frac{1}{4}$ in., on a moulded base. The sides are painted with roses, a sun in a circle, and, typically, Perp leaves in spandrels. The colours are green, red, white, and gold, not at all faded. The box was discovered by Sabine Baring-Gould in the small OAK CHEST. – Tiled REREDOS of 1888. – STAINED GLASS. Chancel E and s aisle E by *Heaton, Butler & Bayne*, Resurrection and Ascension, *c.* 1892, animated figures in pale colours. – Contrast the small, stiff scenes in the medevalizing medallions of the s aisle s (formerly in the w window) of *c.* 1859. – Pretty LYCHGATE of 1908, with good leadwork.

Warkleigh House. A handsome small early Victorian Tudor house (1843 by *Abbott* of Barnstaple) built as the rectory for the Rev. Mr Thorold and retained as a family house; hence the later OLD RECTORY across the road, *c.* 1870, in a more ecclesiological Gothic.

WARLEIGH HOUSE
Tamerton Foliot, Plymouth

On a wonderful site overlooking the Tamar, still just outside the built-up area of Plymouth. A large rambling house in its own grounds, of medieval origin, but chiefly Tudor and early C19; now divided up as retirement flats. The manor was held by the Foliots in the early Middle Ages, then by Gorges, Bonvilles, Coplestones, and Bampfyldes before it was sold to the Radcliffes in 1741. The s front looks straightforward mid to late Tudor: E-plan, two storeys plus attics with straight gables, nearly symmetrical, porch with granite doorway in a full-height centre projection. Large, dominating Georgian sashed windows. Their Tudor dripstones and the rendering of the walls probably date from the improvements carried out for the Rev. Walter Radcliffe by *John Foulston* (1825–32). The long N range backs on to the eastern two-thirds of the s range. It is lower and in part probably of medieval origin, but much altered. Two- and three-light Tudor mullioned windows; renewed Perp window to the former chapel at the E end. In the NW corner an embattled addition by *Foulston*, with canted bays on both sides.

The double-height great hall survives on the l. of the porch, with C16 stone fireplace, doorway opposite the entrance, and stone arch to the oriel room off the SW corner. The C18 contributed the delightful gallery on s and E sides, the latter breaking forward in a double curve at each end. It is approached from the C18 staircase in the N wing. Good C18 fielded panelling in the room E of the hall. In Foulston's spacious living room to the N, a marble Gothic fireplace with matching grate, and a pretty cornice with little Gothic pendants (cf. Bedford Hotel, Tavistock). The N wing has been too much altered for its history to be clear; several stone doorcases survive, and the large stack of the kitchen fireplace to the E of the main stairs.

Near the house a good circular brick DOVECOTE and a large stone BARN. Close to the river a pleasingly quirky little Gothick CHAPEL with castellated gables; a boathouse tucked in beneath.

WASHFIELD

ST MARY. The usual w tower of the district, with diagonal buttresses, NE stair-turret, and no pinnacles. Arcade of three bays with A type piers and capitals only to the four main shafts, plus one arch from chancel into chancel chapel with standard leaf capitals. Extensively restored in 1875 to the designs of the rector, the Rev. *W. Lloyd-Jones*. s side rebuilt, with new vestry and organ chamber; medieval wagon roofs renewed; celure added over the screen; new chancel roof (but still with its C19 painted decoration). – FONT. Norman, square, of table-top type, two sides with six blank arches, the others with similarly elementary zigzag decoration. – SCREEN. 1624, of unusually rich Jacobean workmanship; the openings divided by Corinthian columns, not by balusters, the cornice decoration with animal and foliage motifs, not with strapwork; crowning Royal Arms. – STAINED GLASS. s aisle to the Rev. Mr Govett, 1900 by *Lavers & Westlake*. – N aisle w 1905 by

Powell & Sons. – MONUMENTS. Brass plate to Henry Worth †1606, with kneeling figures, the small plate in a stone frame with coupled columns.

THE WEECHES. Possibly a former church house. Wooden windows on the N side.

BROOK. Farmhouse, the s side with small mullioned straight-headed windows, and, high up, an oriel window boldly inscribed and dated 1565. Possibly the three-storey solar wing of a larger house.

WASHFORD PYNE

8010

ST PETER. Small and remote. Rebuilt – apart from the base of the W tower – in 1882–4 by *R.M.Fulford*. Characteristically inventive, with a picturesque variety of windows to N nave and s transept, and an effective mixture of building stones (local brownstone, purple-red sandstone, ochre Ham Hill). Tile-hung upper storey of tower and spire. Atmospheric interior with contemporary fittings: dado tiles, brass lamps, stained glass by *Drake*. – Elaborately carved LECTERN of 1893. – A traditional SCREEN added in 1922. – MONUMENT. Agnes Lambe †1807. Neo-classical, marble.

(PYNE FARMHOUSE. Four-room-and-cross-passage plan; good late C17 fittings.)

WONHAM. Of the manor house, nothing survives; of the chapel, just two sharply pointed window heads with two-light Perp tracery.

WATERMOUTH CASTLE
Berrynarbor

5040

A big castellated mansion with a splendid wide view over the Bristol Channel. Begun in 1825, but *c.*1845 'taken in hand, a mere shell. Furnishings mostly new' by *George Wightwick*, as his annotated drawings tell us, for Arthur Basset. The house stands on a high artificial platform surrounded by battlements, possibly originally a gun-emplacement (see the cross-shaped foundations in the cellars). Symmetrical W front, a toy fort with polygonal corner turrets. The s front embellished by one off-centre bay-window and a larger SE tower. Plain service wing to match, and extensive battlemented walls around the service courtyards. Within these, new buildings have been added for the 'entertainment centre' which occupies the castle, but the main house itself is little altered. Simple plan, with entrance hall and staircase running through the centre of the house, minstrels' gallery, Gothic fireplace, and flat framed ceiling all by *Wightwick*. The Georgian-Gothic screen dividing off the stairs is said to have been brought from another Basset property. The room to the l. with a rather feeble neo-Jacobean ceiling and a very lush marble fireplace. The best feature remaining in the s-facing rooms is the ceiling of the former library (the room with the bay-window), with its oval wreath of carved wooden oakleaves.

Little remains of the grounds, but further up the valley, at the entrance to the remnants of the subtropical gardens, an ARCH consisting of elaborately decorated stonework panels from the porch of Umberleigh House, Atherington. One panel has a coat of arms and the date 1525; others with Flamboyant wheels, shields, etc. The original porch must have been quite an exceptional show-piece.

WEARE GIFFARD

The church lies close to the manor house, away from the village.

HOLY TRINITY. W tower with diagonal buttresses and no pinnacles. Nave and S aisle. Five-bay Perp arcade, quite uncommon in the neighbourhood; piers of B type, with concave capitals. N and S windows with tracery of the unusual type found at Atherington and Monkleigh, i.e. with the lights linked by round-headed arches within the outer window frames. The S chapel E window is of a different design, five lights, the outer four ogee-headed, each pair with a quatrefoil above, the centre one with its mullions continuing to the top of the window. The chancel roof has sturdy moulded collars on slightly arched braces, kingposts, and traceried spandrels, an uncommon type for Devon (by the carpenter of the Hall roof?). The S aisle has the more usual wagon roof. – Medieval SOUTH DOOR with plain vertical panels. – FONT. Square, Norman, scalloped underside. – BENCH ENDS. A few of the usual type and design, one with Fortescue initials (after 1510). – WALL PAINTING (S wall). Martyrdom of St Sebastian, with two archers, C15; in good condition (cleaned in 1978). – STAINED GLASS. Many old bits in the window tracery. – S aisle E with remains of a C15 Jesse window. – E window 1864, pictorial, the Ascension against a vivid blue sky, spread over three lights. – MONUMENTS. Cross-legged knight, lady wearing a wimple, attributed to a Bristol workshop, c. 1300. Both slim and probably of high quality when their original surface still existed. – Four generations of Fortescues, 1638. Wall-monument with two frontally kneeling figures, two kneeling figures in profile above, and masses of children in small panels and medallions by the side. – Eleanor Fortescue †1847. Tomb-chest with brass cross and inscription on the lid.

WEARE GIFFARD HALL. A substantial late medieval and C16 manor house with a quite exceptional hall roof. The history of the building is much confused by antiquarian restorations and importations during the C19. The manor belonged to the Fortescues, together with Castle Hill (q.v.), from 1454, the year when the Weare heiress Elizabeth Denzil married the second son of Sir John Fortescue. The house was neglected from the later C17, when Castle Hill was rebuilt as the main Fortescue residence, but restored from 1832 by a younger son, George Matthew Fortescue. No details are known about this work: the earliest description is by Edward Ashworth in 1858, when the house appears to have been much as it is now.* Improvements to the grounds were in progress in 1842 (letter from the future third Earl Fortescue to his aunt, Eleanor Fortescue).

The plan of the house is not at once apparent; the modern entrance is in the E wing, which lies end on to the entrance drive so that one sees at first only an uneventful grey stone rubble range of

*E. Ashworth, *The Ancient Manor House of Weare Giffard*, 1858; see also *Country Life*, 2 January 1915.

two storeys, with irregular two-light square-headed windows. To the l. as one approaches is a three-storey GATEHOUSE, with a steep drop to the S, the only indications remaining of outer fortifications. The gatehouse is battlemented, with cusped two-light, straight-headed windows, and a depressed round-headed archway, a C16 form, containing a splendid original door with lozenges in a grid of rectangular panels, and lions with shields in the upper parts.

The late medieval hall range faces S. It is flanked by two far-projecting E and W wings which may have been rebuilt and extended later (the renewal of much of their window tracery makes dating difficult). The S range has windows (C19 improvements?) similar to those of the hall, but cuts awkwardly into the hall doorway at the E end of the main range. This doorway is exquisitely carved, with a tree-trunk instead of the usual tendril, with leaves scrolling around it. Above it is a square-headed two-light window, to its l. a large chimneystack, and at the W end the longer dais window, square-headed with ogee lights, and with a transom. On the W side of the house equally good detail is to be found in the two large arches of the W porch, presumably constructed in the C19 from C15 parts. Their original position is a puzzle. The W arch has excellently undercut foliage trails; the Weare fishes, and also the Courtenay arms (a Denzil connection), appear in the spandrels. The S arch has more conventional fleurons. On the N side of the house later additions butt up against the hall, which originally had windows on this side facing a courtyard.

The present entrance is through a modest C19 porch on the E side. The first impression is of a tantalizing jumble of woodwork, just close enough to what the house originally might have contained to deceive even a canny observer. Some panelling from North Aller Manor previously at the Sham Castle at Castle Hill is said to have been taken to Weare Hall already in 1812 (Chronicles of Castle Hill). The staircase hall in the E wing is an obviously C19 creation, with its bedpost newels, and large Flemish C16 carving with the Nativity and the Resurrection over the fireplace.

The outstanding interior is the hall, with its splendid original hammerbeam roof of four bays. There is nothing in Devon secular architecture to emulate it, although the roof at Orleigh Court (q.v.) is a close, though plainer, relation. The hall is not large (33 by 19 ft), and the luxuriousness of the roof is all the more impressive. The wall-plate has a broad band of magnificent foliage. The hammer-beams have seated animals (greyhounds and dragons, the support-ers of Henry VII) above pendants; the arched braces are heavily cusped, a unique feature in Devon. The taste for cusping and pendants appears in wood in London c. 1460 with the roof of Crosby Hall (although of a different type of construction) and in stone at around the same time at the Oxford Divinity Schools. Here the date must be after 1485, if the heraldic supporters are taken as evidence. Between the principals and the richly moulded purlins are straight wind-braces, forming a pattern in each bay of six cusped squares with diagonal crosses. The virtuosity of the hammerbeam roof is therefore combined with the all-over surface patterning popular in contemporary ceiled wagon roofs.

The hall fireplace has a basket arch with the Weare fishes and a Tudor rose in the spandrels. On the overmantel late C16 plasterwork with strapwork and royal arms dated 1599; more plaster decoration of the same period, with arms in relief, on the upper walls of the hall. Much excellent woodwork, mostly brought in. Apparently original is the lower part of the screen, with its robust cylindrical uprights with traceried panels in between (solid at the bottom, openwork above a horizontal rail 6 ft high). The gallery above has on the E face late Elizabethan panelling, on the W face imported woodwork with well carved C16 busts of bishops, etc., probably not English (said to come from Stoke Rivers church). Along the N wall linenfold panelling with a medley of reset early Renaissance panels above the usual medallions with heads, some in high relief; also the arms of Henry VII. On the W wall a set of misericords which look C17 Flemish. In the windows, especially the N window above the gallery (the only one remaining on this side), and elsewhere in the house, many small fragments of stained and painted glass, antiquarian miscellanies including Flemish roundels and a few English late medieval heads and quarries mixed up with characteristic early C19 blue and orange borders. In the hall window also the initials I F, assigned to John Fortescue (†1503), the most likely builder of the hall.

The other rooms also have much imported woodwork. In the W wing an early Jacobean fireplace and overmantel with royal arms of James I, obviously not *in situ*. Another of similar date in the SW room also brought in, according to Ashworth in 1858. This has Samson and Hercules on the jambs and vigorous but crude smaller figures above. Original ceiling with moulded beams. The corresponding room in the E wing has complete late Tudor panelling with arched panels between two tiers of pilasters and a plaster ceiling with single ribs in a large quatrefoil pattern. The great chamber above is a remodelling of similar date, with a coved ceiling with plaster frieze, and the Fortescue arms in a strapwork surround over the fireplace.

WELCOMBE

2010

The remotest setting, S of Hartland; entirely North Cornish, with church dedicated to St Nectan and the little HOLY WELL in its own roofed enclosure to the SE. The church was a medieval chapel of Hartland Abbey.

ST NECTAN. Early W tower, i.e. low, without buttresses and W door, and with tiny round-arched bell-openings. Aisleless, but with N and S transepts. All windows altered. Wagon roof, the part with richly decorated wall-plate and bosses indicating the original position of the screen. – The SCREEN is the best feature in the church, a primitive design with tall single-light panels arranged in sections of four, each light round-headed and round-cusped, but the date not likely to be earlier than the C14 – see the knobbly Dec foliage on the cusps. Straight top. The foliage friezes of the present cornice a later addition. The wainscoting incorporates old bench ends – PULPIT with narrow early Renaissance panels, as at Sutcombe. – LECTERN. Jacobean, quite a rarity. – READER'S DESK. Interesting, with tracery ends and simple poppy–heads. – TRIPTYCH. Amateur

painting by the Rev. *John Power* (†1903). – STAINED GLASS. N
transept by *Morris & Co.*, 1929, pictorial: Christ in a landscape.
EMBURY BEACON. *See* Hartland.

WEMBURY

The surrounds of the village now on the edge of Plymouth are much
built up, but the position of the church remains magnificent.

ST WERBURGH. No other South Devon church faces the open sea so
squarely. The visual contrast between the square tower and the
triangular outline of Great Mew Stone, the cliff off Wembury Point,
is singularly moving. The tower has diagonal buttresses climbing up
with several set-offs; the stair-turret a little higher than the battlements; no pinnacles. Square-headed Perp W doorway. Inside, four-
bay arcades, the piers of A type, the depressed arches with moulded
profiles. S aisle and S porch with late medieval ceiled roofs with
bosses. Restored in 1885 by *Hine & Odgers*, the chancel under the
supervision of *E. Christian*. – REREDOS, PULPIT, and FONT
(especially elaborate: polished marble, with angels) all designed by
Hine & Odgers; executed, like most of the woodwork, by *Hems*. –
STAINED GLASS. S chancel window 1905 by *Kempe Studios*.

The modest church contains two major MONUMENTS, as monuments go in Devon. First, Sir John Hele †1608 and his family.
Large standing wall-monument of limestone. Columns support an
entablature. Inside, a coffered arch with small figures in the
spandrels (cf. Cadeleigh). Sir John semi-reclining, propped up on
one elbow. Below and in front of him his wife recumbent, with her
little girl seated on a chair by her feet, frontal (cf. Marystow).
Against the base the usual kneeling figures of children. – Lady
Narborough †1678 (daughter of a Calmady of Langdon Court) is
uniquely ambitious for Devon in its intention, but sadly deficient in
execution. Free-standing black and white marble monument. Tall
bases, the Baroquely bulging sarcophagus supported by four white
lions. On it kneels the small figure of the lady at a *prie-dieu* – as if she
were Cardinal Mazarin. The monument is surrounded by contemporary iron railings. – Elizabeth Calmady †1694. Inscription on
feigned drapery beneath fringed canopy.

HELE ALMSHOUSES. Six rubble-stone almshouses with one room on
each floor, and a central chapel, built by Sir Warwick Hele in 1682.
Each house with two-light mullioned window under a gable, still in
the late Tudor tradition, but with a centrally placed door flanked by
small windows.

WEMBURY HOUSE. An attractive simple house of 1803 built for
Thomas Lockyer. Five bays plus one, two storeys, rubble with
ashlar dressings, rusticated quoins, a big hipped roof. Tuscan porch
with cast-iron balcony; garden front with central window flanked by
niches. It replaces an earlier house built by John Pollexfen in the
late C17, which itself was a rebuilding or remodelling of a house of
legendary grandeur created from the remains of a cell of Plympton
Priory by the wealthy lawyer Sir John Hele (†1608). Prince described it as 'beyond all others of those days in all this county and
equal to the best now'. All that survives of this is a mighty rubble

rampart at the opposite end of the lawn in front of the house, buttressed on the W side.

LANGDON COURT (now a hotel). A complicated house of medieval origin, on a courtyard plan; rebuilt in 1577 and remodelled in 1707 by the Calmadys, owners from 1564 to 1876. Altered and extended in 1877. Inner courtyard now roofed and the interiors much altered. The main C18 front faces W. Centre of three bays, filling the space between earlier gabled wings. Modillion cornice, mullion-and-transom windows on the ground floor, early C18 sashed windows above, the central one with a mask keystone. Broad central door with pilasters and heavy segmental pediment. S front of nine bays with five-bay dormered centre between earlier ends with straight gables. Two early C18 doorways with scrolled open pediments and segment-headed windows with keystones. E front with two-storeyed porch, largely C19. At the NE corner a battlemented tower dated 1877. The best interior features are in the S range: staircase hall with two later C18 overdoors, the staircase itself early C18 in style, with thick spiral balusters. C19 stained glass in the landing window. In the adjoining room a good early C18 plain marble fireplace, bolection-moulded panelling, and three doorcases with excessively bold voluted open pediments. The early C18 cellars below this range have elegant groined brick vaults on Tuscan columns. Such cellars are a feature of other C18 houses in the area (cf. Mothecombe, Puslinch).

COASTGUARD COTTAGES. In Bovisand Lane a mid C19 terrace of four, of stone rubble with a slate-hung front. At Warren Point, a row of three of the early C19: two storeys, stone rubble, with low-pitched roof. To the NE their similarly constructed BOATHOUSE.

OVERSOUND HOUSE, Down Thomas. 1930 by *William Wood* for himself. An early example of a determinedly Early Modern house: small, flat-roofed, of concrete blocks. Symmetrically planned, with a large living room overlooking Plymouth Sound. SEATHWAITE, in similar style, L-shaped, with a first-floor terrace, is also by *Wood*, 1932.

WEMBWORTHY

6000

ST MICHAEL. Much rebuilt in 1840 by *Thomas Parish* of Tiverton, except for the tower at the W end of the S aisle which is of 1626, unpinnacled, with buttresses at the foot of 1840. N arcade also of 1840; octagonal piers, stilted, almost triangular-headed arches. Chancel 1869, Perp. Parts of the ceiled wagon roofs in nave and aisle late medieval. Restored in 1902 by *E.H.Harbottle*. – STAINED GLASS. N aisle E: fragments of late C15 canopy-work and some figures in the Doddiscombsleigh style. – MONUMENTS. Mary Bury †1651 and Lawrence Clotworthy of Rashleigh Barton †1655. Both architectural: Ionic columns, broken pediments, and arms.

OLD RECTORY. The core probably C16, with the usual three-room-cross-passage plan; early C19 extensions (partly demolished in 1962).

HEYWOOD HOUSE. Mid C19 Tudor Gothic *cottage orné*, built in the grounds of Eggesford House (q.v.); extended sympathetically in the 1930s.

CASTLES. Two medieval EARTHWORKS in the parish: one in Heywood Wood, the other to its S, both adjacent to the Taw. It is uncertain whether they are successive or contemporary. The N one is a motte and bailey of usual form, the S one a ringwork and bailey with natural defences on the river side. The manor was held by the lords of Okehampton.

See also Eggesford and Rashleigh Barton.

₃₀₈₀   WERRINGTON

Since 1974 just over the Cornish border.

WERRINGTON PARK. A residence of the Abbots of Tavistock, given by Henry VIII, like other Tavistock property, to John Lord Russell, acquired and rebuilt by the Drakes. In 1651 it came into the hands of Sir William Morice, later Charles II's Secretary of State. His family added the C18 front range. The rooms here are listed in an inventory of 1763, but the excellent interior decoration may only have been completed after 1775, when the estate was bought by the Duke of Northumberland.

The house is admirably sited on an eminence overlooking a landscaped valley. The C18 part is the most interesting, a crisp white stucco front of seven bays with a canted centre. Ornament is confined to a little restrained stonework: pediment over the central garden door, two side windows with flat architraves and false balconies. Such features betray an awareness of mid C18 Palladian practice, but in Palladian terms the balance is odd, chiefly because there is no basement. The main rooms are at ground-floor level; the first-floor bedroom windows are low, of attic proportions. It is almost as if the top half only of an architect's elevation was used – service rooms at ground level being superfluous because the older house behind served for the purpose (cf. Sharpham). The large hipped roof above a dentilled cornice also appears incongruous. Entrance at the side, through a later porch.

The plan of the C18 range is eminently simple: three front rooms, a wide corridor or gallery behind, ending in a Venetian window, with the stair-hall at the end near the entrance. The corridor has a shallow barrel-vault. It was intended as a gallery for sculpture, as the 1763 inventory makes clear. At either end screens of green marbled wooden Ionic columns; above them medallions of the Duke and Duchess of Northumberland, which must have been added after 1775. The staircase is arranged around a rectangular well. It has a wrought-iron balustrade with lyre pattern, and plasterwork panels in the style of the mid C18 with a lively variety of devices: musical instruments, brushes and palettes, hawking trophies, and below these winged and bearded heads with garlands of flowers. The three reception rooms have exquisite plaster ceilings in a more delicate Rococo style, in which the French rocaille motif appears, together with musical instruments (central room) or cornucopias with flowers in high relief (corner rooms). Excellent fireplaces in the Kent style, especially the one in the central room, with voluted jambs, frieze of red marble, and richly ornamented overmantel with panting of the Judgement of Paris. Enriched doorcases and shutters. In the SW room a showy Italian fireplace, a late C19 import. First-floor passage with attractive overdoors with pulvinated friezes; at the ends, overdoors with open pediments.

Behind this c18 range, three wings around a small courtyard. The w one has the oldest visible fabric, with a wall not at right angles to the rest; it incorporates a massive stone stack adjacent to the present kitchen, and several late medieval granite doorways. The back wing was the 'old house' of the c18 inventories, i.e. late Tudor to early c17. Now very plain, gutted by fire in 1974, and with few features of interest left. Three-storey porch with the date 1641; projecting crude early c19 Gothic corridor on either side. Behind this, three storeys to the l. with large kitchen at the end; two-storeyed part to the r., with ground-floor old hall, which remained the main dining room until it became the servants' hall in the later c19. Remains of early c18 panelling, an c18 staircase, and a room with fielded panelling E of the hall. The low E range was remodelled after 1882 for the Williams family to provide for typical late Victorian needs. It houses a library with mullioned windows (original fittings, including an c18 fireplace brought from Italy), a small smoking room, and a billiard room beyond, also very complete.

Landscaped GROUNDS with a lake, four LODGES, and the c18 WHITE BRIDGE over the river Attery, carrying one of the drives. On a hill an eye-catcher, a FOLLY with a seat in a deep round-arched recess and with three Indian sugar-loaf excrescences on top. The former may well be derived from the Daniells' Indian drawings and aquatints, which would date this addition to the alterations of Werrington Park c. 1800 or shortly after.

St MARTIN. Built on a new site in 1742, as part of the replanning of house and park. The old tower was re-used (diagonal buttresses and pinnacles) but the façade was considerably widened by a screen-wall with angle turrets, all castellated and provided with the typical blank quatrefoils of c18 Gothicism. In niches in the façade and on the other sides of the church contemporary statues of the crudest style, yet at the same time quite impressive in their wild attitudes. The interior completely altered in a disastrously thorough restoration of 1891 by *St Aubyn*. – FONT. Norman, undecorated, but on a base with heads at the corners. – Another FONT with a small bowl on a baluster shaft is contemporary with the building of the church, as is the PULPIT. – MONUMENT to members of the Drake family: kneeling figures in relief in a strapwork frame, early c17.

YEOLM BRIDGE. Late medieval(?); ribbed pointed arches.

WEST ALVINGTON

The church lies high above the Kingsbridge estuary; the little port was established in the corner of this older parish.

ALL SAINTS. w tower with characteristic silhouette of big polygonal pinnacles; buttresses of type B. Far-projecting chancel, Dec (pointed trefoil head to the piscina); Perp s aisle and two-storey s porch embattled. Inside the porch a fireplace (cf. Wolborough, Newton Abbot). Tall Beer stone arcades of six bays, with moulded arches of shallow profile; A type piers with plain capitals to the four shafts, but carved abaci. Restored by *Richard Coad*, 1866. – FONT.

Octagonal, of the usual Perp type, but with leaf decoration in the eight panels which looks C17 rather than C15. – SCREENS. Restored by *Herbert Read*, 1914. Only the aisle parts of the rood screen are original. The s parclose has circles at the top of square-headed tracery, continental Flamboyant forms (cf. Colebrooke, Holbeton, etc.). – MONUMENTS. C16 Easter Sepulchre tomb in the chancel N wall, originally with brasses on the back. Tomb-chest with cusped quatrefoils in lozenges, diapered columns supporting a canopy with three ogee arches with little vaults inside; a common Purbeck marble type of *c.* 1520–30, but rare in Devon. – W. Bastard † 1703. Large, with coupled black columns, a big broken pediment with seated putti, angels' heads, and a skull as a tail-piece.

Near the church, PAY COTTAGE, the C16 church house. Doorways with pointed arches, Stone ovolo-moulded mullioned windows, and traces of shouldered-headed windows. An upper round-headed opening, probably for a door from external stairs.

LONGBROOK. A grey stone rubble farmhouse close to the road, smartened in the C18 by handsome gateposts with pyramid caps and balls. One room with simple C18 plasterwork: a ceiling with circles with flowers; shell-headed cupboards.

GERSTON. The seat of the Bastards before they moved to Kitley. Early C17, remodelled in the C18; a fine group of substantial stone outbuildings. Good classical gatepiers.

COMBE ROYAL. A Victorian house of the Luscombe family. Two-storey bow, heavy porch with paired pilasters.

See also Bowringsleigh.

ST PETROCK. Small, with W tower (diagonal buttresses, no pinnacles, NE polygonal stair-turret). Perp N arcade with A type piers and standard Devon leaf capitals. The rest extensively restored in 1887 by *William White*. He replaced all the windows in Geometric Dec, using Ham Hill stone, very striking against the dark purple rubble masonry of the walls. Inside, his roofs are on the tie-beam and kingpost pattern (cf. his work at e.g. Stockleigh Pomeroy). He also replaced a solid wall between chancel arch and N pier by the ingenious quadrilateral of piers around the pulpit. – FONT. Norman, of tub shape, with saltire cross and palmette decoration similar to Bishopsteignton. – BENCH ENDS. A few of the usual South Western type. – REREDOS, low SCREEN, STALLS, and BENCHES all by *White*, 1879. – (TOWER SCREEN. A fragment brought from a chapel at Town Farm.) – STAINED GLASS. Medieval fragments in chancel s (Crucifixion etc.).

CHURCH HOUSE, by the churchyard; much altered.

West Anstey is a typical parish of the Exmoor foothills, with good C15–17 farmhouses of which the following are among the earliest.

BADLAKE. A small late medieval house. Mid C15 entrance door frame; slightly later the two-storey porch with a small wooden window with a trefoil head. A larger window of four lights with cinquefoil heads and octagonal mullions also survives *ex situ*. Jointed cruck trusses; the centre truss of the hall, with cranked collar, chamfered arch-braces, and two tiers of wind-braces, is also mid C15. C16 flooring-in, represented by massive axial beams with heavy unmoulded joists, closely set. Staircase in a projection to the rear. Later C18 extension of the inner room and C19 widening of the kitchen end.

BUNGSLAND. A medieval house with an exceptional roof, externally completely disguised by later alterations and additions. Three-room cross-passage plan with an early arched door to the hall from the cross-passage, and a C17 inserted stack and ceiling in the hall. Excellent medieval roof on jointed cruck trusses, with clasped purlins, and one closed truss with substantial curved braces, both very unusual in Devon. Cranked collars and lower wind-braces. All the roof of massive timbers.

WEST BUCKLAND   6030

ST PETER. 1860 by *R.D.Gould*, apart from the Perp W tower with diagonal buttresses and no pinnacles. Simple exterior with trefoiled lancets and a tiny clerestory, but quite enterprising polychromy inside: S arcade of yellow and buff stone on blue marble columns; bands of tiles above; tiles also round the chancel arch and the E window. – FONT. Perp, octagonal, with quatrefoils. – STAINED GLASS. Good C19 E window with Nativity. – In the churchyard, close to the S porch, a set of early C19 HEADSTONES with very pretty inscriptions (by *T.Britton*).

WEST BUCKLAND SCHOOL. Founded as Devon County School in 1858 by the Rev. *J.L.Brereton* of West Buckland, and Lord Ebrington, the future Earl Fortescue, of Castle Hill, a pioneer effort in the campaign for more middle-class education. Main building of red brick and stone, with three-storey central tower and Gothic windows, by *R.D.Gould*, 1861; to the l., dining hall and dormitories, 1878, large, with mullioned windows; to the r., battlemented hall, 1934. Many later additions. In the school, busts of the two founders by *E.B.Stephens*, 1861.

METHODIST CHAPEL, in the hamlet. 1829, and typical of many of that date in villages or by the roadside. Severe, with rendered walls, round-arched windows, and gabled porch with ornamental bargeboards. In front, an irregular walled burial ground.

STOODLEIGH FARM. Good, plain, five-bay Georgian front of ashlar. In the r. room a chimneypiece dated 1731 with the initials of William and Grace Buckingham. Ceiling with plaster ovals; in the l. room, one with a quatrefoil centre. C18 stair with dado panelling.

WEST DOWN   5040

ST CALIXTUS. An early plan, not enlarged by Perp aisles. N and S transepts, the S one opening into the nave by an unmoulded pointed arch. The N transept has a more ambitious heavy double-hollow-chamfer arch and a good open wagon roof of trefoil section. In its N wall, a three-light early C14 window with ogee reticulation (just like Tawstock); below it, a low tomb recess, decorated with ballflower and containing a wooden EFFIGY, attributed to a Bristol workshop, of a man with folded hands in lawyer's robes, very worn. It probably commemorated Sir John Stowford, Chief Justice of the Common Pleas, *c.* 1290–after 1372. Of the same date as the effigy the fine pointed cinquefoil-cusped PISCINA, transferred, it is said, from the transept to the chancel. The chancel was 'rebuilt in 1675' (inscription) but is now largely of 1841. Restoration of 1872 by *William White*, who replaced most of the windows, raised the chancel floor, and reroofed and reseated throughout. The W tower alone looks decidedly Perp, but is a rebuilding of 1711–12. Buttresses of B type; pinnacles. – FONT. Norman, a scalloped capital, raw, as if the decoration had been hacked off. – REREDOS. Painted panels and mosaic dado, 1881. – STAINED GLASS. E window and chancel S good, possibly by *Clayton & Bell*, *c.* 1872.

West Down is quite a large village of substantial farmhouses and smaller cottages, packed tightly together around the church. To the W the OLD VICARAGE, with a stuccoed early C19 front. To the E the MANOR HOUSE, a modest early C17 symmetrical five-bay front with three- and four-light granite mullioned windows and a projecting porch. (In the l. room, fireplace with a four-centred arch. The r. room has a good geometric plaster ceiling; three panels between plastered beams, dated 1624. Good contemporary joinery; dog-leg stairs. Upper rooms with plaster friezes; also an elaborately decorated W gable wall with figures supporting a strapwork cartouche.) Nearby, TOWN ESTATE FARM, with porch dated 1669, and a good group of outbuildings.

LOWER AYLESCOTT. A three-room-and-cross-passage house on an unorthodox plan, the end rooms both heated by external stacks, but the central room unheated. From the middle chamber stairs rise in a turret leading into a jettied first-floor rear corridor continued along a rear side wing to connect with a contemporary block housing kitchen and dairy with chambers above. Datestone of 1606; contemporary detailing.

WESTHILL
Near Ottery St Mary

ST MICHAEL. A new church of 1845–6, by *Wollaston*, in the lancet style. S porch, nave and chancel, with large roofs, a strong archbraced roof to the nave. Unsympathetic W extension of 1978 in artificial stone, by *Anthony Hollow*. – STAINED GLASS. E triplet 1846 by *Wailes*, good, in C14 style.

WESTLEIGH

Overlooking the Taw estuary above Barnstaple.

ST PETER. W tower with thick buttresses covering the angles, polygonal stair-turret on the S side close to the E angle, no pinnacles. The chancel windows look *c.* 1300 but are renewed. S porch and S door a little later. N aisle Perp, with granite piers of A type, capitals only to the main shafts, and depressed pointed arches. Restored by *J.F.Gould*, 1879. – TILES. In nave and aisle; not only the usual

Barnstaple designs. – PAINTINGS. Christ, *c*. 1830, by *Harlow*. – 'Rizpah' by *Lord Leighton*, exhibited at the Royal Academy in 1893, and the typical Chantrey Bequest picture. – (Much Victorian STAINED GLASS, the most ambitious the Life of David in the N aisle E, 1856 by *Warrington*. – S transept E 1857 by *T. Wilmhurst*. – N aisle N 1883 by *Lavers & Westlake*. – W tower 1894 by *Clayton & Bell*. RH) – MONUMENTS. Several to the Clevland family of Tapeley, especially John † 1763 (profile in medallion above a flat very classical urn), and Augustus † 1849 (with a large weeping figure on her knees below a weeping willow) by *M. W. Johnson* of New Road, London – his worst work, according to Gunnis. – Good slate HEADSTONES in the churchyard.

EASTLEIGH. Substantial rubble stone house, belonging to the Berry family from *c*. 1500 to 1802. Late medieval core, much remodelled. The front now with Georgian Gothick sash-windows, Tuscan porch, and hipped roof, the S side also Georgianized. But traces of earlier stone windows remain, and in the gable end, two complete ones with three and four cusped ogee-headed lights, still with some old glass. C17 and C18 rear wings, the l. one with a massive kitchen fireplace. Castellated courtyard walls. (Inside, good joinery both of *c*. 1600 and *c*. 1800.)

(SOUTHCOTT BARTON. A good early C17 house, E-plan, with two-storey porch. Front with Georgian sashes. Massive early C17 door and elaborately moulded and stopped doorcase. Excellent joinery of the same date inside: enriched stud-and-panel screen between passage and hall; C17 dog-leg stair in the rear wing, with turned balusters. Some excellent contemporary plasterwork also: above the stairs, with pendant, and especially in the two main upper chambers, each with a coved ceiling with double-ribbed geometric design round the central pendant, and an overmantel with strapwork cartouche.)

See also Tapeley Park.

WEST OGWELL   8070

Church and manor house lie hidden away on their own, although only three miles from Newton Abbot.

CHURCH (vested in the Redundant Churches Fund since 1982). Of exceptional interest, both for its early structure undisturbed by the usual Perp remodelling and because its simple and charming late Georgian interior has escaped radical Victorian restoration. Built *c*. 1300, it is cruciform and aisleless, the windows with tracery of late C13 type, intersected and cusped into the shape of pointed trefoils and quatrefoils. Long chancel; sedilia also with three pointed-trefoil heads. S transept with two Perp windows inserted. The tower probably added *c*. 1400: unbuttressed, with granite dressings. The W window with its early tracery perhaps re-used. Inside, round-headed arches to tower and transepts; plastered barrel-vault of the early C19. The chancel roof-trusses must be of *c*. 1600 (see the decoration of the wall-plate). – PULPIT. Plain C17. – ALTAR RAILS. Of *c*. 1800, of the simplest, with curved central part. – High

BOX PEWS to nave and N transept, the S transept provided with a fireplace, probably for a pew now removed.

MANOR HOUSE, now CONVENT of the Companions of Jesus the Good Shepherd. Founded 1920, established here in 1943. An overwhelmingly plain exterior of 1790, built for Pierce Joseph Taylor, just seven bays of windows, two and a half storeys high. No decoration whatever. Stables and outbuildings of 1589 for Sir Thomas Reynell. Chapel of 1955.

WEST PUTFORD

3010

ST STEPHEN. An early plan, as is more common in North than in South Devon. Nave and chancel perhaps early C14, see the two-light SW nave window; N and S transepts added in the later C14, see the S transept piscina. The N transept has a window with Y tracery and a late medieval panelled ceiling. Unbuttressed W tower also later C14, the upper stage probably C16 (round-arched belfry windows, stunted pinnacles); rebuilt with old masonry in 1883. C19 chancel roof, E window, and S porch. Late medieval door with knocker. – FONT. Norman, a rather shapeless oval, with one cable-moulding between bowl and shaft. – PULPIT and COMMUNION RAILS. Both C18, with twisted balusters. – BENCH ENDS. Only a few old bits. – TILES. An exceptionally large collection of the usual C16 Barnstaple designs, relaid in the chancel in 1930. – Good slate LEDGER STONES of the C17 and C18 in the church, and an excellent collection of later inscribed slate HEADSTONES in the churchyard.

CHURSTON HOUSE. Manor house built by a member of the Prideaux family some time between 1576 and 1611. Hall with four-light window, original screen, and overmantel with two allegorical figures in Elizabethan dress, representing Peace and Plenty, sculpturally very crude (cf. Boringdon). Another plaster overmantel in an upper room. The granite porch is an incongruous addition from Ashbury House, where it was a gateway. It was removed to Churston in 1934.

CORY BARTON. A C16 farmhouse, the former seat of the Corys.

WESTWARD HO!

4020

A modern planner's nightmare. Around the beach a spatter of chalets, amusements, and one-storey shops fill the spaces between the Victorian villas, whose gardens are given over to car parks or weeds. The C19 hotels have become tatty self-catering flats. Yet the bones of the Victorian development remain. Charles Kingsley's novel of 1855 made this remote part of the coast famous. The resort was developed by a private company. In 1872, Murray's Handbook says 'Westward Ho! consists at present of two or three rows of terraces, many scattered villas, a single line of shops, and a church nearly opposite the principal hotel.' Set into the slopes above, the tall terraces and spiky villas are still there, the earliest of stucco, the later ones of the pale yellow brick of North Devon (cf. Ilfracombe). In KIPLING TERRACE the United Service College, a public school for sons of servicemen, was established in 1874 (see Kipling's *Stalky & Co.*).

HOLY TRINITY. 1867 by *W. C. Oliver*. Coarse Gothic, local stone with granite dressings, circular clerestory windows, no tower.

The site of Mesolithic occupation (*see* Introduction: Prehistory) has been almost eroded by the sea.

WESTWOOD
Broadclyst

0090

ST PAUL. Small chapel of ease, 1873 by *Ashworth*; of the local purple volcanic stone with Bath stone dressings. Quite elaborate Dec windows. Chancel arch with carved corbels by *Hems*; otherwise plain.

HAY HOUSE. Handsomely sited. Two early C19 stuccoed fronts of three bays, moulded window surrounds.

WEST WOOLFARDISWORTHY
Near Bideford

3020

Also known as Woolsery.

HOLY TRINITY. W tower with thick buttresses hiding the angles, an unmoulded pointed arch towards the nave, and a centrally placed polygonal stair-turret on the S side, unusual in North Devon but not infrequent in the south of the county. Witnesses of the Norman church are the surviving S transept and the S door with one order of colonnettes and decorated arch orders, the central one with beak-heads, the inner one with zigzag (exactly as at Shebbear). Interior with wide nave and a five-bay arcade to the N aisle which has granite piers of A type, capitals only to the main shafts, decorated abaci, and unusually wide depressed pointed arches. An inscription records a rebuilding of 1648. This is probably responsible for the cornices of the completely plastered-over wagon roofs. Restored in 1872. – FONT. Square, Norman, undecorated, on five shafts of blue stone. – BENCH ENDS. Of the usual Devon and Cornwall type, a good many of them. Decorated with shields with arms or with initials, figures of saints, Christ crucified (very unusual), and also some of the Instruments of the Passion (ladder, nails, scourge, etc.). – MONUMENTS. Richard Cole † 1614. Standing wall-monument with semi-reclining figure, propped on elbow, columns to l. and r., and obelisks and achievement on top; sculpturally not good. – Several later wall-monuments, e.g. Richard Hammett and wife, with a plain urn against an obelisk; anonymous, *c.* 1790.

METHODIST CHAPEL, in the centre of the little hamlet. Built by the Bible Christians, 1858, schoolroom 1887; a typical group of humble rendered buildings stepping down the street.

LEWORTHY MILL. A house of late medieval origin, remodelled in 1684, the date of the overmantel in the now subdivided upper chamber. Initials of the Knill family. Remains of a coved ceiling with cornice of trailing leaves, and other plasterwork fragments.

WEST WORLINGTON

Finely sited above the valley of the Little Dart, in the centre of what there is of a village.

ST MARY. Picturesque access to the churchyard under the archway of the former church house. Picturesque, crooked, shingled spire on the short unbuttressed tower stump. Nave and s aisle separated by a three-bay arcade with B type piers with standard Devon capitals with figures (angels) as well as the usual leaf decoration. s aisle and s porch with original wagon roofs. Chancel restored in 1881, the rest, tactfully, in 1905–13. – PARCLOSE SCREEN with standard A type tracery and spandrel decoration. – BENCH ENDS. C16, traceried. – STAINED GLASS. s aisle E 1908 by *Fouracre & Watson*. – MONUMENT. Sir Thomas Stucley of Affeton †1663. – Lt. Lewis Stucley †1870 by *Gaffin*. Sword and hanger with inscription, still classical.
VICARAGE. 1847 'in the Italian style' according to White.
AFFETON CASTLE, 1 m. W. The C15 GATEHOUSE of the fortified manor house of the Affetons survives, much altered by their Stucley descendants in 1868. Main gateway with depressed arch, filled in. Three-storey NE tower. Ruins of other buildings.

WEYCROFT
1½ m. N of Axminster

The manor house of the Brooke family from the C15 to the early C17. They received a licence to crenellate in 1427, but the only fortified element surviving is a tower-porch, which now looks largely C19, attached to one side of the house now called WEYCROFT HALL. This consists of a two-storeyed range with the tower-porch, and an open hall, tactfully restored in the later C19 after being used as farm buildings. The hall is medieval, large and lofty, with a later roof (tie-beams and queenposts), but the windows at least in part of c. 1400: tall, of two lights with a transom, the lower lights with cusped arches, the upper ones straight-headed (restored?). Blocked opening to a lost E wing; four-centred doorway at the W end. The W wing much rebuilt; a three-storey part has late Tudor windows, but a lower wing has a gable-end window with reticulated tracery, now divided by a floor. In a passage, door with painting of Moses, a pair with one in Weycroft Manor, no doubt re-used church furnishings.
WEYCROFT MANOR is a remodelled outbuilding, with an early roof concealed beneath the present one, and some exposed timber partitions. Mostly 1930s neo-Georgian inside. Hall door with painting of Aaron (cf. above). Adjoining at the end, WELL HOUSE, another former outbuilding. It has two puzzling triangular arches in the wall, their tympana prettily decorated with flint and limestone chequerwork, an East Devon speciality. Many fragments of worked stone in the gardens, including arched windows, perhaps from the chapel licensed in 1417.
By the road, WEYCROFT MILL and MILL HOUSE, C18 and C19 on an earlier site. Mid C19 steam mill at the back (original

machinery but wheels removed), and a two-storey rubble-stone range of stores and granaries.

WHIMPLE

ST MARY. The tower is low, ashlar-built, with stunted pinnacles on the battlements. The rest of the church much rebuilt by *Hayward* in 1845, when it was extended E and a S aisle added to match the existing Perp N arcade. No chancel arch; short chancel because of the restricted site. – REREDOS. 1882 by *Fulford*, large and complex, with cusped central canopy and openwork gables, all in front of a traceried gable with carved finial of Christ and angels. Flanking Commandment boards, Gothic, of 1845. – SCREEN. Eight painted panels remain, early C16, not of special aesthetic merit. – MONUMENT. Canon E. Heberden † 1843. Inscription in finely detailed Dec surround, by *Hayward*, executed by *Simon Rowe*.

STRETE RALEIGH. Stuccoed C19 Tudor front. The house belonged to the Bullers in the C19. Now flats.

FORDTON, The Green. A late medieval farmhouse. The exceptional feature is in the back wall of the hall (now within the outshot): a three-light late medieval window in timber with trefoil heads, with a later, lower tier of similar heads.

KNOWLE CROSS. Several good C18 and early C19 cob cottages around the road junction, survivals of simple one-room and two-room ground-floor plans, with hipped thatched roofs; probably squatters' cottages, as they are built right on the road and have no land behind.

WHITCHURCH

S of Tavistock, on the W fringes of Dartmoor.

ST ANDREW. Norman S door, undecorated. Chancel of *c.* 1300 (see the one remaining N window). Easter Sepulchre recess inside. The rest late Perp granite ashlar: W tower, S transept, N aisle. Arcade with tall piers of A type with four-centred moulded arches. S transept arch in the same style. Chancel lengthened in the restoration of 1879 by *Hayward* (with *Eliot* of Plymouth); E window with intersecting tracery (re-used?), S porch and E chapels rebuilt. – FONT. Plain, octagonal, with shields in the panels. – STAINED GLASS. E and W windows 1879 by *Fouracre & Watson*. – MONUMENTS. In the Easter Sepulchre recess, to Paschaw Allyn † 1626, with a long row of kneeling children on a slate plate. The tomb-chest still has very much the Perp character, though the panels are now separated by short columns. – Francis Pengelly † 1722, by *Weston*, with this sculptor's characteristic oval relief of the Raising of the Dead, extremely vivid. The small free-standing figures to the l. and r. of the relief and the two still smaller reclining figures on the pediment much less lively.

CHURCH HOUSE, now an inn. Granite mullioned windows; staircase projection facing the churchyard.

In the parish several larger houses of ancient origin. THE PRIORY

(Tiddybrook) is L-shaped, with a medieval three-storey battle-mented porch with angle buttresses and two-centred arch. The rest Victorianized with decorative bargeboards and cusped windows. SORTRIDGE retains one range from a once quadrangular house. Mullioned windows, two-storey porch; granite doorways and C18 panelling inside. GRENOFEN is stuccoed Georgian, with a front with two full-height bows built for J.M. Knighton, and an older wing behind. HOLWELL incorporates part of the manor house of the Glanville family.

HIGHER GRENOFEN. A longhouse, with the hall and inner room above the cross-passage, the shippon below. The house itself is of one build, late C16 or early C17, with fireplace, projecting window bay, and spacious staircase wing as well as a heated inner room. The shippon is interesting for its separate entrance for cattle from the N. Its upper floor was in domestic use from the C17: access is obtained by a staircase in a projection from the S wall leading off the cross-passage.

AVONDALE (the old mine house), Sortridge. Striking early C19 slate-hung exterior, tall, with two projecting wings with canted bays.

See also Walreddon.

WHITESTONE

The church stands high above Nadderwater, overlooking Exeter and the estuary.

ST CATHERINE. Red sandstone, mostly roughcast. W tower with polygonal stair-turret and diagonal buttresses. Perp windows to N aisle and S transept, but a pre-Perp plan, with two-bay N arcade on octagonal pier, chancel arch, and separate arch to N chapel. Primitive octagonal capitals; plain double-chamfered arches of red sandstone. Restored in 1866–8 by *R.M. Fulford*, who partly rebuilt the chancel, inserting the deeply moulded free-Dec S windows. Further restoration 1915 by *Fellowes Prynne*, who re-used the remains of a W gallery to make the W SCREEN. It has a front painted with shields, dated 1621, still entirely Elizabethan in style, on turned baluster columns. – PARCLOSE SCREEN. Plain Jacobean; small columns with a decorative band below and a strapwork cornice. – PULPIT. Hourglass type, of wood, the stem medieval, the rest by *Fulford*, 1886, its stair attached to his elaborately fronted CLERGY STALLS. – REREDOS. 1915 by *Fellowes Prynne*, together with linenfold sanctuary panelling minutely inscribed with the Commandments. – STAINED GLASS. Late C15 Virgin and Five Wounds, reset in a N window. – Other medieval fragments in the S transept. – Remains of bright patterned glass of 1811. – E window 1874 and S chancel patterned glass all by *Drake*. – Three WOODWIND INSTRUMENTS (bassoon and two oboes), a rarity, preserved in the S transept.

GLEBE HOUSE. A clergy house which became the rectory. A classic history of gradual transformation. The S front of 1775, five bays, Georgian sashes, with two further bays and a Tuscan porch added after 1830, is an extension of the lower end of a late medieval hall-house, remodelled in the later C16 as a ground-floor hall. In the old part a C16 fireplace and moulded beams, and two stud-and-panel screens, the one at the inner end with some original colour. The medieval roof survives, smoke-blackened, with arch-braced jointed crucks and curved wind-braces, the collar to the central truss distinguished by a pendant. A first-floor chamber was jettied out into the open hall. A four-light trefoil-headed wooden window from this room is now in an outbuilding, together with the large wooden main outer doorway from the hall.

WHITESTONE HOUSE. Early C19, rendered, with deep eaves and Corinthian porch. Good oval entrance hall with open-well stair behind.

HURSTON HOUSE. Irregular, stuccoed, with nice Georgian Gothick windows and a curve between the two wings.

See also Oldridge.

WIDECOMBE-IN-THE-MOOR   7070

The church lies in a wonderful position, a sheltered hidden-away valley in the folds of Dartmoor.

ST PANCRAS. Nowhere else in Devon can the typical South West English contrast between tower and church be seen so uncompromisingly. The w tower is late Perp, tall and imposing, of granite ashlar, with buttresses of type B, three-light bell-openings, and big polygonal pinnacles. The body of the church, earlier than the tower, is long and low, with aisles, transepts, and s porch. The six bays have low octagonal granite piers with double-chamfered arches, their handsome proportions revealed by the absence of pews at the w end. The roofs over the three w bays are taller than the others, presumably the result of rebuilding in phases; see also the change in window heights. – SCREEN. Only the wainscoting remains, with painted panels of saints, early C16. – PAINTINGS. Moses and Aaron, rather lovable examples of folk art, with a lot of gold. – CURIOSA. In the tower, four painted boards dated 1786, with verses describing a thunderstorm of 1638.

The small village is over-visited in the tourist season, but the tearooms and parking areas have fortunately been restricted to its N end. So the w approach to the church remains unspoilt: a little square with a central tree, the GLEBE HOUSE on the r., the CHURCH HOUSE (now National Trust shop) on the l. The church house is the grandest in the county, two-storeyed, all of granite ashlar, and unique in having a loggia with seven octagonal columns. One original four-centred doorway, upper windows of two and three arched lights, covered staircases at rear and E end. The ground floor has a fine early C16 ceiling with moulded beams and counter-changed joists.

Widecombe is a large parish, with numerous small hamlets and single farmhouses tucked into the slopes of the sheltered valleys overlooking the open moor. They include an exceptional number of the LONGHOUSES characteristic of the Dartmoor area, a few of them still in their original form, others illustrating progressive adaptation, as the shippon end was appropriated for domestic use (*see* Uppacott, below). Some are distinguished by C17–18 granite door frames of especially high quality, often dated, so that one sees how long the traditions of Tudor ornament continued. These range from a simple type, e.g. BONEHILL (N of the village), with door frame in a wide two-storeyed porch wing, with roll-moulding, initials IS, and the date 1682, to more elaborate forms, for example LAKE, near Poundsgate, 2½m. s, where the doorway in a similar porch wing has the roll-moulding carried round the spandrels to enclose highly stylized oak leaves, initials TH and the date 1661, and CORNDON-FORD, 1½m. SW, where the roll-moulding rises from moulded bases, again enclosing spandrel decoration, this time of fleur-de-lys and shields carrying the initials RW and the date 1718.

COCKINGFORD, 1m. S. Former MILL and MILLHOUSE of c.1800, with machinery, and cast-iron waterwheel by *Willcocks & Son* of Buckfastleigh; nearby an early C19 BRIDGE into the parish of Buckland-in-the-Moor.

WINDWHISTLE, SW of Cockingford. A small, deliberately picturesque early C20 house, right on the road, the front entirely slate-hung. Big thatched roof; round-arched granite doorway.

PONSWORTHY, 2m. SW. An especially attractive hamlet, with its group of simple rubble stone houses, MILL, and OLD BAKEHOUSE (tactfully converted to a house in 1976 by *Anthony Adcock*) retaining an impressive oven complex. PONSWORTHY HOUSE is of c.1800, with a porch with granite Doric columns.

ST JOHN, at LEUSDON, s of Ponsworthy. 1863 by *J.W.Rowell*, simple Dec: nave, chancel, s porch, and s tower with parapet and small pyramid roof. – Good Arts and Crafts STAINED GLASS s window (Sir Galahad) to Lieut. W.T.M.Bolitho †1915, by *A.A. Orr*.

At LOWER TOWN, s of Leusdon, CRESSENHAYES, an early C16 house, much altered (beam with early C16 painted decoration at the upper end of the hall).

SPITCHWICK MANOR, ½m. E of Poundsgate. Two lodges (early and late C19) survive at the entrances to the large estate where in the C18 a house was built by the first Lord Ashburton, who was responsible for the extensive plantations in this area. The house itself now later C19.

UPPACOTT, 1m. E of Poundsgate. Along the same lane at Uppacott and Tor, a particularly rewarding and instructive series of four longhouses. HIGHER UPPACOTT must claim distinction, not least because it has been purchased by the Dartmoor National Park Authority in an imaginative attempt to preserve and display the longhouse tradition. The original front on the road is disappointing mostly because of a poorly detailed conversion of a later building at the upper end joining the cross-wing to the original house. But the moorland side is compelling in its perfect marriage of building and landscape, the longhouse tradition at its most pure and simple. The walls scarcely rise above ground level, so deeply is the house dug into the hillside. The thatch sweeps down to hide the house from the view of the visitor and from the moorland weather: there are no first-floor windows, and only two small ones on the ground floor, one with re-used hollow and straight chamfered granite mullions. Inside, the longhouse is virtually unaltered: the cross-passage still gives common access to house and shippon, with no separate shippon entrance, and the shippon is subdivided from the cross-passage only by a flimsy late partition. The shippon still has its central drain in the cobbled floor, dung-hole, splayed slit windows, and hayloft beams. At the original front end (the roadside end) of the cross-passage, a round-headed door with mason's mitres. An inserted stack in ashlar granite blockwork, with moulded base and corbelled head, shows well in the cross-passage. On the door frame over the entrance to the hall a re-used stud. The hall itself was open, and the smoke-blackened roof survives, complete with original thatch. The late C16-early C17 flooring-in is simple but effective, with cross-beams and every joist stopped and chamfered. A blocked hall window-opening survives on the inner face. In the wall of the first-floor chamber a framed timber partition with stud, wattle, and cob infill. Compared to this, LOWER UPPACOTT (opposite, down-hill) is much altered, the shippon now incorporated into the house; but it too has a smoke-blackened roof, and an upper chamber jettied out over the former inner room. Late C16 cross-wing at the upper end.

Further along the lane, another typical moorland group. First HIGHER TOR. The house faces a farmyard: a medieval two-room, cross-passage and shippon plan with added dairy outshot. Until a recent fire, smoke-blackened thatch survived over the hall and inner room: now there are only the roof-trusses, jointed crucks with a square-set ridge on a yoked apex. A stack was inserted and the house floored probably in several stages from the late C16: the position of the stack between the oddly cramped hall and the inner room is very unusual for Devon. Hall fireplace inscribed RH 1632. The shippon was incorporated into the house, and its roof rebuilt, in 1974. LOWER TOR, also late medieval, also has a much altered shippon end, this time showing a progressive separation from the house, for it has its own cross-passage and separate entrance. Porch at the front dated 1707.

HANNAFORD MANOR, 1 m. s of Poundsgate. Quite an ambitious Arts and Crafts manor house (subdivided c. 1950), built in 1904–11 by *A. Wickham Jarvis* for Major Bolitho, with terraced gardens by *Thomas Mawson*. (The Bolithos, a banking family, were also responsible for the fine gardens at Trengwainton House, Cornwall.) The house is a carefully detailed multi-gabled composition of dressed granite, with broad-eaved slated roofs, a variety of tall chimney-stacks, and simple mullioned windows. The main room is a double-height panelled hall looking s over the main terrace. Large inglenook fireplace, gallery, and a little internal oriel window at one end, a feature that the architect must have liked, as it appears in two other places as well. Good simple panelling in the other main living rooms. Attractive service courtyard with thatched corner summer house. Mawson's GARDENS, although on a much smaller scale than his work at Wood (q.v.), similarly exploit the site by terraces connected by ample curved steps. Simple granite balustrading; delightful semicircular basin with carved dolphin spout against the wall to the E of the house, gateway to the kitchen garden beyond, oval pool at a lower level (not as on Mawson's original plan). To the W a small, stocky dovecote as a corner feature.

The valleys of the parish are spanned by numerous picturesque BRIDGES. DARTMEET BRIDGE, at the boundary with Lydford parish, is an especially attractive spot, with a bridge of 1792 and the remains of the earlier clapper bridge close by. Many other CLAP-

PER BRIDGES of undefinable date elsewhere, e.g. over the East and West Webburn.

EARLY SETTLEMENT. Traces of parallel reave systems can be seen throughout much of the parish, e.g. on CORNDON TOR and YAR TOR, which form part of the Dartmeet or Holne Moor system (*see* Holne). The settlement of FOALES ARRISHES belongs to another major system across RIPPON TOR and MOUNTSLAND COMMON (*see* Ilsington), with smaller fields and hut settlements interspersed within it. There are in the parish several prominent ridge-sited Bronze Age cairns, some of which have yielded Wessex-type grave goods.

WIDWORTHY

The small church lies close to the old manor house; the early C19 mansion is a little way off down a drive.

ST CUTHBERT. The usual W tower with diagonal buttresses, no aisles, but transepts separated from the nave by Perp arches. Low recess in the S transept. Simple interior, restored and refitted in 1785–7. – MONUMENTS. Knight in armour, *c.*1400, well preserved. He wears a bascinet on his head; angels support his pillow. – Alice Isack †1685, architectural, and another illegible scrolly C17 tablet. – The later monuments are chiefly to the Marwoods. James Marwood †1767 (possibly made later) is a first-rate piece by *John Bacon*, with two of his richly draped female allegories to the l. and r. of a richly garlanded urn. It is a variant of the monument to Elizabeth Draper at Bristol Cathedral (1778). – Robert †1783, Sarah †1797, James †1811. An unusually ambitious effort for *Peter Rouw* of London, with three figures. – Sarah †1787. Female figure and two putti against a grey pyramid, by *W. Pinder*. – Also by *Rouw*, Thomas White, steward of the manor, †1838, with neo-classical bust, and the Rev. Thomas Tucker †1830.

WIDWORTHY BARTON. Close to the church; an attractive small rubble stone manor house on a courtyard plan, with no major alterations since the early C17. It belonged to the Chichesters, who sold it to the Marwoods in the C18. Restored sensitively in the 1960s by *Pearn & Procter*, who eliminated some less desirable changes made in the 1930s. The core of the house is late medieval (back range with one smoke-blackened arch-braced truss; front range with four surviving arch-braced trusses, unblackened). But the interesting period is of *c.*1600, when the front range was given its present regular, but not symmetrical fenestration: large four-light transomed windows, two for the hall, one for the parlour, tied together by a hoodmould-cum-string-course which also runs around the two-storey porch between the two rooms and is carried around the W end of the hall. In this gable wall a six-light transomed window lighting the hall – an unusual arrangement (no solar wing). Running back, a W range symmetrically composed, with three large transomed windows to a long gallery; lower windows and central four-centred doorway on the ground floor. The gallery is also lit by a large window in the S gable-end. In the rest of the S range the former kitchen (large stack and brick-lined oven) on the ground floor.

Service rooms also on the ground floor of the E range; dovecote in the SE gable.

The most unusual feature of the interior is the hall screen, made up of early C17 square panels in sets of three, divided by Ionic pilasters, on the hall side painted with simple trompe l'oeil chamfers in cream and black around a brown centre (cf. the geometric sgraffito fireplaces of the mid C17). The panels at the W end are original; the others were made to match in the 1960s. The other special feature of the hall, apart from the simple four-centred fireplace against the back wall, is the remains of a small gallery above what may have been a dais room, between hall and long gallery. Plasterwork frieze; two delicate plaster angel corbels in costumes that can be precisely dated to the early C17, and with Italian hairstyles. (A similar frieze in the hall was destroyed by a fire in the C20.) Access to the gallery, and also to the long gallery beyond, was probably by a newel stair in the re-entrant angle, of which traces remain. It was replaced by a larger staircase of the 1930s projecting into the courtyard. In the long gallery, set back at the far end, a handsome overmantel of stone, wood, and plaster, brought in. It bears the arms of Bluett and Rowe (cf. Holcombe Rogus) in strapwork, and the date 1591.

At the E end of the house, the window of the parlour suggests that there was at first no upper floor (as with the hall), but the ceiling with chamfered beams must have been inserted by the early C17, as the room above has panelling of this date. Around its top a frieze with inlaid lozenge pattern, and a fragmentary inscription referring to John Chichester. The adjoining bedroom in the E range has an exposed post-and-panel partition.

WIDWORTHY COURT. Built in 1830 by *G. S. Repton* for Sir Edward Marwood Elton, in place of the old manor house. An up-to-date stone block with Tuscan four-column porch on the N side; the W side of 1–3–1 bays, with the main reception rooms looking out over a terrace. A giant Ionic portico was projected but not built. The Court was an 'elegant mansion' in White's time; after later disfigurement it was restored to its former splendour in 1987. Hall with high coved ceiling; grand staircase beyond (*Willement* supplied glass for the landing window in 1835); dining room with two Ionic columns, and good cornices. Handsome service court at the back, the stables with clock and bell under a little pediment and on either side lunette windows with big keystones.

WILMINGTON HAYES. Substantial neo-Tudor, of flint and stone, *c.* 1911. S and W sides each with gables and canted bays.

WILLAND

ST MARY. Very small unbuttressed W tower, probably early Gothic. A low church with a N aisle, the piers of type B section, the capitals standard, but with heraldry besides foliage. S porch with decorated top and inscription. – PULPIT. Early C19 two-decker. – SCREEN. Painted, with very simple tracery, and a flat coving, i.e. an early type, say *c.* 1400 (cf. Stokeinteignhead). Later straight cresting with vine scroll.

The village lies away from the main road. On a simple cottage a plaque for the Willand National School, erected in 1844. On the road to Kentisbeare a good red brick C18 house of three bays, with arched ground-floor windows and a pedimented Tuscan porch.

VERBEER MANOR HOTEL. Five-window, late C18 front; projecting pedimented centre with Venetian window and Tuscan porch.

WINKLEIGH

The large village was once more important than now, and it retains the feeling of a small town, with its pleasant broad main street with an inn at one end, and a pyramid-topped conduit of 1832. Intricate side streets of white-walled houses, the church tucked away among them.

ALL SAINTS. Perp throughout. w tower with buttresses only at the foot. Top with cusped pinnacles. The body of the church outside was much renewed in 1871–3 by *R.D.Gould* in an expensive restoration paid for by G.H.Pinckard of Godalming (see s nave window). The good carved detail is by *Hems*. Built into the s wall a Norman(?) head. The N aisle is the show front to the town: big windows of three lights, buttresses between them; the N transept embattled. The s transept (Gidley Chapel) was added in the C17. N arcade of five bays, the granite piers of A type, with capitals only to the main shafts; nearly semicircular arches. An additional bay to the chancel chapel, the piers here with a more elaborate moulding which is repeated in the chancel arch and on one side of the N transept arch (four main shafts with four minor ones in the diagonals). Original wagon roofs to nave and aisles (repaired in 1871–3). The gorgeous ceiled chancel roof is by *Gould*, enriched by diagonal ribs and intricate wall-plates with shield-bearing angels, the carving by *Hems*, the whole painted and gilded. The interior walls are decorated throughout with sgraffito patterns, increasingly elaborate towards the E.

Very complete C19 fittings. – REREDOS. Designed in 1873 by *Gould*; not erected until the 1880s. Carving by *Earp*. Veined brown alabaster, with mosaic inlay. Central demi-figure of Christ flanked by elegant free-standing angels; expressive demi-figures of saints in quatrefoils. – PULPIT. A polychromatic tour-de-force in polished marbles by *Gould* and *Hems*. – Nave BENCHES 1872–3 by *Hems*; a complete set, their traceried ends of more complex design than their medieval prototypes. – ROOD SCREEN. Intricate tracery; bressumer and tall cross painted and gilded. Later than Gould's work – who was the designer? – Good IRONWORK throughout by *Letheren* of Cheltenham (door furniture, font cover, etc.). – STAINED GLASS. N aisle W: late C15 angels with shields in the tracery heads. – E window 1873 by *Clayton & Bell*, very good small Passion scenes. – s window, Raising of Lazarus, 1873 by *W.F.Dixon*.

By the C12 there were two manors at Winkleigh; the castles at either end of the town may represent the centre of each.

CROFT CASTLE, at the SW end of the town, has been largely destroyed by a modern building. It was a ringwork, with no obvious bailey. At COURT CASTLE, now bisected by a road following the motte ditch on the bailey side, the bailey is occupied by a C17–18 house; the large, flat-topped motte has been landscaped, with a folly.

PENIEL METHODIST CHAPEL, Stable Green. Long, low and rendered, with typical arched windows with intersecting glazing-bars. Built by the Bible Christians in 1840.

(SOUTHCOTT BARTON. Now a farmhouse, with some traces of the manor house of the Southcotts. A chapel was licensed in 1427.)

WINSLADE MANOR
Clyst St Mary

9090

Since 1975–7 the headquarters of the London and Manchester Assurance – the first prestige offices of this kind to arrive in Devon. The house, previously neglected and unsympathetically extended for a school, was restored, and behind it are some of the best later C20 office buildings in the county. Both the restoration and the first phase of new offices are by *Powell & Moya*, 1974–7.

180

Despite the extensive additions, the mansion is still successfully dominant, raised up on a grassy plinth and connected only by a discreet glazed link to the lower offices. The house was built on a new site probably soon after 1782, the year when the estate was acquired by Edward Cotsford, M.P. and Sheriff of Devon, who had made his fortune in the East Indies. It is a plain but well proportioned rendered block, five by six bays, of two storeys, with basement and attics. The s front (originally facing the gardens, now with steps down to a new sunken drive) is divided into 1–3–1 bays by channelled pilasters, an original feature, as they are visible on a distant view of the house in a portrait of Cotsford by L. F. Abbott. The pediments to the ground-floor windows, and the balustraded terrace and parapet, may belong to mid C19 improvements for Henry Porter. Later alterations in 1879 for Josiah Dixon were by *W. T. Sams*. Most of the C19 and C20 additions have been removed, apart from the square w bay-window and the N porch with paired Doric columns.

Inside, the main elements of the late C18 house remain. The most remarkable is the spacious full-height top-lit central hall, strikingly redecorated in blue, white, and dark red. It has two sets of galleries on four sides: fluted Ionic columns on the ground floor, composite columns and fluted square piers above. At the upper levels the NE and NW supports are, very oddly, set in from the corners. The plasterwork is handsome but eclectic, in the typically Devonian pre-neo-classical phase: a Vitruvian scroll above the Ionic columns, Greek-key fret on the floor above, and on the ceiling around the domed lantern delicate Adamish garlands of husks, with corner medallions. Adamish decoration also on the walls of the dog-leg staircase in the centre of the E side, with stone treads with moulded soffits and S-shaped iron balusters. The staircase is connected to the hall and galleries by large paired arches. In the main rooms several good cornices; the best ceiling, with a fan-shaped centre and bucrania, is in the SE (conference) room on the ground floor. The conversion added a new back stairs and transformed the service basement for conference facilities.

129

The additions of 1974–7 are self-effacing, in the manner of *Powell & Moya*'s college buildings at Oxford and Cambridge. Their visibly open structure of floors on concrete columns tellingly underlines the solidity of the older house. The colouring also is tactful: a variety of neatly finished white and grey concrete surfaces. The chief visual interest is the chiaroscuro achieved by the deeply recessed windows which run behind the set-back white columns, leaving the broad floor bands uninterrupted. The shallow split-pitched roofs save this horizontal emphasis from being too abrupt. The offices, planned for a staff of 600, form a long backdrop to the house, with a lower computer block projecting to the W near one end, and a larger wing extending to the E. Double-height entrance hall; elsewhere the interiors are subdued – open-plan, with movable partitions in black and white.

The expansion of the staff to 850 called for additions in 1982–3. The separate deep-plan air-conditioned block to the E, by *Marshman Warren Taylor*, is less satisfying than the earlier buildings – a three-storey steel-framed structure with glazing recessed behind a self-consciously vertical grid of brick-faced piers. Nearby, the former STABLES, gutted to provide squash courts, swimming pool, and other staff facilities; U-shaped, covered in rather raw pink render, with large extensions behind. Close by, the former walled garden, converted to a car park. To the S, carefully preserved planting, with a small lake.

WHITE LODGE, on the old Exeter Road to the N. A distinguished Greek Doric design of *c.* 1820 (cf. Stover), a composition worthy of an architect like Burton or Wilkins. One-storeyed, three bays divided by pairs of fluted columns. The centre is pedimented; at the ends the entablature projects above the columns in an almost Baroque manner.

RED LODGE, Church Lane. One-storeyed; central pediment on two sides.

GREENDALE. Early C19, 1–2–1 bays, stuccoed, with a central pediment above the tripartite Doric entrance.

WITHERIDGE

A compact village, the most important settlement between Tiverton and South Molton, with market and fairs already in the C13.

ST JOHN BAPTIST. Quite large compared with most of the churches in this barren neighbourhood. Fragments of simple Romanesque carving built into the masonry. W tower Perp, the W window a characteristic example of latest Perp tracery. Upper parts rebuilt in 1841, with crude round-headed windows and obelisk pinnacles. Originally there was a shingled spire. Of 1841 also the battlements to the body of the church, the slightly funny embattled priest's door, and the generally much-renewed-looking appearance of the church. N and S arcades of four bays, quite tall; B type piers, standard capitals. Squint from the S aisle. The chancel earlier, separated by a chancel arch, and with an E.E. S window (the E window is of 1877). In the S chapel, remains of a canopied niche in a S window jamb. Nave with ceiled wagon roof. S doorway elaborately decorated with fleurons on jamb and arch; niche for an image above. – FONT. Perp, octagonal, quite richly decorated, mainly with quatrefoils. – PULPIT. Stone, Perp, with figures in narrow panels under nodding-ogee canopies. In one panel a badly carved Crucifixion, probably early C16. – Chancel FITTINGS mostly from a restoration of 1882–3; elaborate TILES.

BRADFORD TRACY HOUSE. A picturesque early C19 front with scalloped bargeboards, arched windows, and a veranda with tented canopy. Contemporary LODGE, also with decorative bargeboards.

COLLETON FARM. Irregular early C19 Gothic. Later garden room at the end, Gothic, with conical roof. Entrance hall with Gothic plaster ceiling.

PILLIVEN. This exceptionally large and much rebuilt farmhouse is important for the early carpentry of the roof to its medieval core. One true cruck truss of massive size survives, the face of the cruck blade decorated with triple roll-mouldings. It is all heavily smoke-blackened, and possibly as early as the C14. The roof is of the early ridge type (square-set, carried on a yoke), with straight collar and braces and curved wind-braces, all joined by notched halvings.

BERRY CASTLE. A well preserved earthwork enclosure. The hilltop site suggests a Roman military origin.

WITHLEIGH
2½ m. W of Tiverton

9010

ST CATHERINE. A small chapel of 1846 by *Hayward*. Nave and chancel, S porch, W bellcote on big buttresses. E window of three trefoiled lights. Other windows with plate tracery, those of the chancel flush and without hoodmoulds, as if in anticipation of the High Victorian stylistic vocabulary. Brutally modernized inside; the fittings have been destroyed, apart from the FONT, a precocious effort in polychrome consisting of an arcaded bowl on Purbeck shafts.

WITHYCOMBE RALEIGH

0080

Now a suburb of Exmouth.

ST JOHN IN THE WILDERNESS. At the N end of the village, still just in a country setting. Originally a medieval chapel of ease to East Budleigh, called St Michael. Low, broad W tower with diagonal buttresses of orange rather than the usual red sandstone. Panelled tower arch. N aisle with a Perp E window and piers of B type with standard capitals. Neglected after a new chapel was built in the village in 1720; only the tower and the N aisle escaped demolition in 1788. The church was rebuilt on old foundations in 1925 by *Ralling & Tonars*.

ST JOHN THE EVANGELIST. 1862–4 by *Ashworth*, an ambitious church on a new site, to serve the growing suburb, replacing the C18 'new chapel'. Mature Dec throughout, with a variety of windows; clerestoried and aisled nave, transepts, S tower. Disappointing interior: painted, fittings removed. – SCREEN by *Charles Norris*,

1964, with his typical coloured glass set in resin. – STAINED
GLASS. Several good windows. E window *c.* 1872 by *Clayton & Bell*,
pictorial Ascension. – s aisle w 1865 by *Hardman*. – s transept, Shaw
memorial, by *Morris & Co.*, 1919, saints under canopies, pale
aesthetic colours with red accents.

ALL SAINTS. *See* Exmouth.

6090
WOOD
South Tawton

The house is in a quiet but accomplished version of the Arts and
Crafts style, built for William Lethbridge by a little known architect, *Daniel Gibson*, who had been in partnership with the eminent
landscape architect *Thomas Mawson*. Mawson laid out the spectacular formal grounds; he was invited to advise before building
began in 1900, and the work was largely complete in 1905. They
are one of his major achievements, much illustrated in the later
editions of his book *The Art and Craft of Garden Making*.

All is hidden down a long drive, although a small group of
gabled and roughcast estate cottages on the road, and the fine
wrought-iron gates between pyramid-topped gatepiers set in a
semicircular wall, provide a foretaste both of Gibson's Voyseyesque manner and of Mawson's ability to handle formal approaches. There was an older house on the site, but nothing
remains of it except the basic form of hall between two wings,
facing SE. This was made into the garden front and now looks out
over Mawson's spacious lawn. Broad gabled wings reaching far
forward; large stone mullioned windows. The symmetry is a little
dull, but given interest by the small twin-gabled projecting bays
facing each other across the paved terrace and by the use of granite
ashlar for the central hall range, in contrast to the roughcast
elsewhere.

The entrance side faces SW towards the carriage drive that had
to be cut into the slope of the hill. Here the composition is more
relaxed: a two-storey porch with Tudor door, a big tapering stack
to its r. with a circular chimney, long, low mullioned windows
under the eaves, and running out at a r. angle a service wing with
carriage arch flanked in a spirited manner by two further stacks
with tall round chimneys. Two similar chimneys on the NE side of
the house have been removed (one rebuilt as a square turret).
Behind the main range further wings around a small courtyard.
Excellent detailing throughout, the exterior with a minimum of
ornament, the granite mullions barely moulded, the lesser windows just with functional slate dripstones, the restraint relieved
only by the prettily decorated lead guttering and downpipes.

Well preserved interior. The double-height hall is quite austere,
with bold exposed timbering. Inglenook fireplace; an open gallery
(now glazed) looks down from the staircase landing. The staircase,
also with exposed timbers, rises around a solid core in the C16
manner. The main reception rooms in the wings with more traditional panelling and fireplaces; but their little bays to the terrace
are a delight, with their simply ornamented plaster ceilings.
Indeed, the plasterwork throughout the house is worth a special

look, most of it with charmingly naïve flowers and foliage in the Jacobean vernacular manner so popular with Arts and Crafts architects. Excellent door ironwork and Art Nouveau light fittings.

The sloping site made it necessary for Mawson to lay out the GROUNDS on several levels, and to make much use of retaining walls. He was keen to demonstrate that this could be achieved with local granite rubble, and in the more informal parts of the grounds furthest from the house used plants in crannies as the sole ornament. The formal garden buildings and balustrading are in a similar mood, simple robust forms, with only the most elemental dressed granite detail, typical of Mawson's early style. The carefully grouped farm buildings behind the house are similarly plain and robust. Yet a study of the paving shows that every stone must have been chosen and laid with immense care. It is the combination of a complex and subtle formal layout with an enthusiasm for the rigorous spirit of local materials that gives these gardens their special character, one that is so different both from the mellower contemporary work of Lutyens, and from the Mawson firm's later Beaux-Arts manner.

The centrepiece is the long lawn the width of the house, flanked by paved walks leading to gazebos. At the end is a circular pool presided over by a small bronze helmeted figure by *Derwent Wood*. Behind is an exedra defined by sturdy granite posts linked by iron bars, intended as a rose pergola. Steps lead down to an oval lawn (the sundial from this is now near the tennis lawn), beyond which the ground slopes away gently to an older lake glimpsed beyond Victorian specimen trees. To the w, at a lower level, extensive kitchen gardens adapted from older ones. Between them and the house, a semicircular dipping pond, a favourite Mawson feature. Behind the house (overlooked by the billiard room at the back), a small garden enclosed on two sides by walls of irregular granite blocks with simple arched niches for sculpture (now empty). Above the entrance drive to the E, tennis and bowling lawns with pavilion, and a long vista to a summer house framed by yew hedges.

WOODBURY
0080

A large village between Exeter and East Budleigh, which had a fair and a market in the C 13.

ST SWITHIN. A consecration in 1409 is recorded. The tall grey W tower has buttresses of type B and the unusual motif of several small two-light windows on top of each other. The W door with a foliage scroll in jambs and arch, the W window still with many cusps and some ogee or pointed quatrefoils in the tracery. The piers of the N aisle are an unusual variety of the B type: four shafts, and in the diagonals two wavy lines instead of one. The capitals standard, the arches depressed. The aisle was completed in the 1530s. Between chancel and N chapel a panelled depressed arch, probably intended as a canopy to a monument to Richard Haydon † 1533, whose arms appear on a capital. The arch is combined with a squint. Panelled tower arch. Wagon roofs in chancel and S porch. The later C 19 saw a succession of repairs and improvements under the Rev. J. L.

Fulford, vicar from 1846 to 1898 and a High Church leader in the county. His son was the architect R. M. Fulford. Chancel windows renewed 1852; chancel E gable rebuilt and new window inserted 1853; screen rebuilt and newly painted 1862. A major restoration by R. M. Fulford took place only in 1893, when most of the window masonry of the N side was replaced, the arcade rebuilt, a new nave roof provided, and W gallery and box pews were removed.

FONT. The usual octagonal Perp type with quatrefoil panels, but the pillar nicely decorated with vaulting-rib patterns. – Much good minor woodwork. – SCREEN. Much renewed in 1862. – ALTAR RAILS and FONT RAILS. Elizabethan; sturdy fluted columns instead of balusters, and strong posts with thick balls on top. Bought in 1678; said to have come from a church in Exeter. Late C16 ornament of Exeter type. – PANELLING. Plain C18; now placed all along nave and aisle walls. – PULPIT. The usual early C17 motif of stumpy blind arches in the panels. Made in 1635 by *Thomas Crutchard* of Woodbury. The trumpeting angel from the sounding-board, of 1777 by *Peter Daley*, is now on the organ screen. – Some chancel STALL ENDS and some decayed BENCH ENDS of the same type as at East Budleigh. – STAINED GLASS. In the S transept E fragments, not Devonian, inserted in 1963, including a demi-figure of a bishop and a layman's head, C16, of high quality. – E window 1893 by *Kempe Studios*. – MONUMENTS. Recumbent figures of husband and wife, possibly of the Prideaux family, late C16(?), on a tomb-chest with Ionic pilasters and strapwork. – Samuel Trancott Gruttner of Elbing, Prussia, † 1813 and wife. By *J. Kendall*. Mourning woman by urn.

VICARAGE, ½ m. N. 1849 by *John Hayward*. Irregular front of stone (partly re-used from a barn which had belonged to the Vicars Choral); square-headed windows with cusped lights. The back with some re-used medieval windows probably from the priest's house.

SCHOOL. 1870 by *R. M. Fulford*, on a site given by the Rolles. A very attractive asymmetrical composition, with the taller teacher's house at one end (and, alas, some unfortunate extensions). Red brick with blue brick patterns, stone plate-tracery windows, low pebbled garden walls.

CHRIST CHURCH. Established in the village in 1851 in protest against the High Church practices of the Vicar, Mr Fulford. By *William Phillips*, opened in 1861. A plain brick box (disfigured by C20 extensions), with pedimented gables, the windows along the sides framed by brick arches.

The large, rather straggling village centre includes in addition to older cottages much C19 Rolle ESTATE HOUSING, the earliest of 1877, in the Broadway. Also earlier houses in a late Georgian style by the local builder *William Phillips*, among them ROSEMARY COTTAGE of 1833, with an elaborate porch made up of older pieces, with two dolphins (perhaps from a ship?) under a steep pediment, and CLAREMONT COTTAGES of 1839. In Globe Hill, the OLD COURT HOUSE, built as magistrates' court and police station in 1860–1, a red brick, five-window front. In Greenway, WOODBURY HOUSE, three bays, two storeys, of brick with tripartite windows, built in 1781 for Philip Lemprière, former Attorney-General of Jersey.

OAKHAYES, Oakhayes Lane. Stuccoed Regency three-bay front with

a Tuscan porch. Longer garden front with central canted bay. Built
c. 1830 for the Rev. Francis Filmer. Well landscaped small grounds.
On the Exeter and Exmouth Road the hamlets of Exton and Ebford.
At EXTON, a pretty C19 tile-hung SCHOOL, the church of ST
ANDREW, 1962, neat red brick, with a C19 FONT from the previous
church, and EXTON HOUSE, late Georgian, rendered. At
EBFORD, by the main road, EBFORD MANOR HOTEL, early C19,
five-bay front, stuccoed, with quoins, and to its S the excellent
EBFORD MANOR, rebuilt by Robert Venn, a Woodbury clothier
(†1729). It is a tall, three-storey house of double depth, brick with
stucco quoins, 1–3–1 bays, parapet and central pediment. Later
Greek Doric porch. Large ground-floor room with good C18
fittings: unusual trompe l'œil panelling and a marble chimneypiece
with mirror (altered for a later window). The grounds were remodelled by Venn's nephew Matthew Lee after 1756. Good wrought-
iron gate with overthrow. MOUNT EBFORD was built in the early
C19 by T. H. Lee on the site of a garden building. Stuccoed, five
bays, a three-storey bow at the r. end.

GULLIFORD BURIAL GROUND, further S on the Exeter–Exmouth
Road. The first chapel here was established in 1689; its successor
has been demolished. Monuments from the C18 remain, within a
large walled enclosure with tall brick gatepiers, in an atmosphere of
gentle melancholy and decay.

GULLIFORD, on a symmetrical plan with gable-end stacks, one in
'Dutch' bricks, is a good example of later farmhouse traditions; so is
EXTON FARM, on a three-room plan, with heated principal rooms
at either end.

(LOWER BAGMOLES. A farmhouse with a floor of local 'popples',
laid in fan shapes.)

WOODBURY COMMON is a reservoir of upstanding archaeological
sites of all periods. WOODBURY CASTLE, on the site of an earlier
defended settlement, is a substantial Iron Age HILLFORT, protected by outworks on the N and W. There are also a number of large
Bronze Age BARROWS, FIELD SYSTEMS of dates ranging from
probable prehistoric to modern, and extensive relics of the use of the
common for military training from the C18 to the C20.

See also Lympstone *and* Woodbury Salterton.

WOODBURY SALTERTON   *0080*
1 m. N of Woodbury

A hamlet of Woodbury, where 'the eye is gladdened by a group of
ornamental buildings' (Freeman's *Exmouth*). They were the gift of
Miss Marianne Pidsley of Greendale.

HOLY TRINITY. 1843–4. Nave with bellcote, chancel, S porch; built
largely of stone from the Vicars Choral barn at Woodbury. Tall, Dec
detail, very Puginian. Was *Hayward* the architect (cf. Woodbury
vicarage)? Steep slate roofs in two colours (the nave slates renewed).
Chancel arch with sharp wiry mouldings. Chancel refitted 1899, but
the nave BENCHES with sharp Gothic profiles, and the READING
DESK with C17 panels from the chapel at Nutwell (*see* Lympstone),
date from 1843–4. – The STAINED GLASS (mostly removed) was
hand-painted by the *Pidsley* sisters.

The SCHOOL has a very slim clock-cum-bell-turret dated 1847, an elaborate Gothic niche, fishscale-slate roofs, and an open wooden porch: still *cottage orné* tradition rather than domestic ecclesiological. Nearby WELL HOUSE and CONDUIT with trefoiled arch. The bargeboarded OLD VICARAGE of the same date completes the group.

BROWN'S FARMHOUSE. C17, a rare Devon example of a lobby-entry house.

WOODLAND

ST JOHN. Small unbuttressed tower with strong batter, central polygonal stair-turret, and low pinnacles. Small church; nave and N aisle of three bays with granite piers of A type with capitals only to the shafts and nearly semicircular arches. – FONT. Octagonal, granite. – ALTAR CLOTH. Made from an early C16 English cope. – STAINED GLASS. In the E window tracery the Four Doctors of the Church, late C15, by the 'Doddiscombsleigh workshop' (cf. Dunsford). – MONUMENT. Thomas Culling †1670. Brass with cherubs' heads.

(GURRINGTON HOUSE. Built for Thomas Abraham (†1818) of the East India Company. Late Georgian, rendered, four-window garden front; large mid C19 porch.)

WOODLEIGH

A small village above the South Hams Avon valley.

ST MARY. Low, early, unbuttressed W tower with renewed battlements on corbel-table. The plan of the rest of the church also early: nave, no aisles, but two transepts, and chancel. The transept arches look indeed as if they might be contemporary with the tower. No early window, but one in the S transept with three pointed lights below a hoodmould and a date above of 1647. Restoration 1890 by *G. Fellowes Prynne*. – FONT. Octagonal, Norman; two very shallow blank pointed arches on each panel (cf. Kingsbridge). – EASTER SEPULCHRE combined with MONUMENT (cf. the Easter Sepulchre at West Alvington). Tomb-chest with the usual quatrefoil decoration in an ogee-arched recess. Against the back wall three poorly carved reliefs: Pietà, Resurrection, and the Angel and the three Marys. In the cresting, inscription: 'Orate pro anima Thome Smith, rectoris huius ecclesie.' He died in 1526 or 1527. – (Good minor later wall-monuments.)

CHURCH HOUSE, at the SE corner of the churchyard. Formerly an inn. Rubble stone; front projection for a stone semicircular stair.

WOOD BARTON. Formerly a Fortescue mansion, now reduced to a rubble stone farmhouse. Two-storey C16 porch with four-centred inner and outer doorways. In the grounds, a gaunt three-storey stone range with brick dressings, built in 1902–5 by *Scoles & Raymond* for a short-lived monastery, now farm buildings.

WOOLACOMBE

4040

Woolacombe Bay was laid out for building by *Arnold Thorne* of Barnstaple in the 1880s. It did not grow fast. Along the seafront a fringe of Victorian and Edwardian villas; behind them a formless spread of C20 seaside flats, an insult to the glorious sweep of the bay. On the slopes above, the only redeeming features: the church and its vicarage, enveloped in C20 expansion but still prominent from afar.

ST SABINUS. 1910 by *W.D.Caröe*. Small, but quite worthy of the architect of St David at Exeter. Red sandstone, with an asymmetrically placed tower stump covered by a saddleback roof, and a big roof covering the nave and narrow lean-to aisles. The N aisle was added after 1952 by *Oliver & Dyer* of Barnstaple. The aisles have low cusped three-light windows; the chancel, slightly narrower than the nave, also has aisles, separated by oak posts stained green. Nave piers with dying arches. Fine open roof with big semicircular braces, lit by dormers on the N side. Sacristy 1925. – Free Perp FONT, 1916. – Tall chancel SCREEN and other furnishings, 1929. – STAINED GLASS. Much by *Kempe & Co.*, 1919–30. – In the W windows, four flame-like figures of the Evangelists, 1983 by *Charles Norris*.

VICARAGE, N of the church. Perhaps by *Caröe*. Bold roofs and tall tapering chimneys; one wing at an angle. Roughcast and slate-hung.

HEALTH CENTRE, E of the church. Very modest, and quite pleasing, with its white walls and monopitch roofs in deliberate contrast to the church; *c.* 1982.

WOOLFARDISWORTHY

8000

Near Crediton

ST MARY. Tower basically medieval, but the whole church largely rebuilt in 1845 by *Hayward*. (Chancel with much restored wagon roof with richly moulded wall-plate. Painted texts around the chancel arch. – BRASSES. H.R.Beer † 1911. With angels in low relief. – Rev. A.Bell † 1904.)

OLD RECTORY. Mid C19 Tudor Gothic. Nice iron gatepiers and gates.

See also West Woolfardisworthy (near Bideford).

WORTHAM

3080

Lifton

One of the most remarkable and appealing small manor houses in Devon. It became the chief seat of the Dinhams after 1501. Their early C16 remodelling of the medieval house was unusually elaborate in its detail, and is exceptionally well preserved. Moreover, Wortham has been fortunate in its C20 owners, first *Philip Tilden*, who restored the house after 1945, and more recently the Landmark Trust, for whom it was repaired sensitively by *Paul Pearn* in 1969–75.

The house is L-shaped, with a main range facing N and a long E wing to the rear. The front is largely an early C16 rebuilding, mostly of ashlar, local sandstone with some granite dressings. Two storeys throughout, mullioned windows with slightly ogee-headed arched lights, not quite symmetrically arranged. The hall window immediately to the l. of the central porch is a restoration, as is the far l. ground-floor window and the end gable of the E wing above it. But the front is still very close to an early C18 Prideaux drawing, apart from the disappearance of the battlements over the hall. The porch is surprisingly grand, two and a half storeys, ending in a gable, with an ornate first-floor window with cusped lights and hoodmould incorporated into a string course. The entrance is emphasized by a moulded arch with a heavy dripstone with square ends, character-istic of Perp in the granite areas. It frames the more usual square-headed doorway. In the tympanum between them, coarse rope-like tracery and roundels with wheel (or sun?) and star. The hall range itself is older than the early C16; the back wall is of rubble with some slatestone. The sturdy polygonal stair-turret is clearly an addition. It has a square top, corbelled out, with a little ogee-headed window. The long E rear wing probably dates from the early C16, and was extended a little later. On the E side two hefty lateral stacks, one of them for the kitchen (oddly sited at the opposite end of the hall from the screens passage, and perhaps not in its original position). Above the C20 kitchen entrance there is another cusped window, possibly reset.

The ground-floor hall was created in the early C16. The joinery is excellent. The inserted ceiling has moulded beams and joists; the carved foliage of the stops runs into the wall-plate. At the E end, a stone arched doorway to the staircase. The four-centred fireplace is not original: it was brought by Philip Tilden from Antony in Cornwall. What is the history of the screen? It is a remarkable piece of woodwork, a little cousin of the free-standing screen at Rufford Old Hall, Lancs, but unparalleled in Devon, and clearly not made for its present position. Could it be monastic loot installed after the Reformation? Three sections, with pairs of tall linenfold panels between thick moulded posts ending in carved pinnacles. The uprights nearest to the walls appear not to have been end pieces, the pinnacles have been truncated and are nailed to the beam above, and the base may have been reduced in size – so the whole may once have been larger.

On the other side of the screens passage the parlour, fitted up in the early C17 with panelling with pilasters, and a naïve but vigorously carved wooden overmantel with foliage and caryatids, but with an earlier (restored) ceiling with thin wooden ribs and well carved bosses similar to the carving in the hall. Stone doorway and original door to the stair-turret. In the great chamber over the hall the C15 roof is visible (it was formerly concealed by a later ceiling). Arch-braces, three tiers of purlins, and pairs of thin crossed wind-braces, all the timbers moulded. Between chamber and closet an early C16 post-and-panel screen, and another between closet and porch room, with a peephole window looking out over a passage. Other C16 timber partitions and stone fireplaces in the E wing. Remains of an arch-braced truss suggest that a large room was added against the S wall in the C16.

YARCOMBE

2000

ST JOHN. Quite large, with the usual W tower (low stair-turret), two embattled aisles, and an embattled S porch. Built partly of dressed flint. The usual arcades: A type piers, capitals to the shafts only, two-centred arches, those to the transepts on angel corbels. The windows Perp, the roofs all old, partly wagon, partly lean-to, partly flat. Chancel rebuilt in 1890–1, at the expense of the Eliot-Drakes (of Nutwell, Lympstone (q.v.) and Sheafhayne in this parish), the architect apparently *C.H.Samson* of Taunton, although the style and the use of Ham Hill stone is reminiscent of *R.M.Fulford*. Ceiled wagon chancel roof with carving by *Hems*.

CHURCH HOUSE, now an inn, abutting the churchyard.

BAPTIST CHAPEL. 1829. A simple rendered building with hipped roof; doorway with scrolled brackets and flat hood.

LIVENHAYES. A late medieval house with original jettied chamber: its arched door preserved in the centre of the partition at first-floor level. Good early C16 modernization of the hall, with a ceiling of intersecting moulded beams. Typical later C16–17 improvement at the kitchen end, with the local type of full-width fireplace incorporating a walk-in smoking chamber: stack dated 1662.

SHEAFHAYNE MANOR. Tudor in origin, much reworked *c.* 1900.

YARNSCOMBE

5020

ST ANDREW. Low N transept tower with Norman masonry (see the small window in the E wall) – cf. other North Devon towers in this position, e.g. Braunton. Later angle buttresses, low pinnacles, and polygonal W stair-turret. The arch to the nave low, pointed, and unmoulded. Perp S aisle, with granite windows and four-bay granite arcade, A type piers, depressed pointed arches. Old ceiled wagon roofs. Restored in 1888–9 by *Gould & Webb*. – FONT. Octagonal, Perp, with tracery and quatrefoil patterns. – CHEST. Early, iron-bound. – TILES. Of the usual Barnstaple designs (S aisle, E end). – STAINED GLASS. S aisle E: late medieval angel with shield. – MONUMENTS. Two low Perp recesses, one in the aisle S wall, one in the chancel N wall, both with depressed pointed arches. The chancel one is the more elaborate, probably intended as an Easter Sepulchre. Panelled and cusped arch, an early C16 type, with battered carving of a Trinity at the back, within an ogee arch. Slab with long black-letter inscription to John Cockworthy †14?? and his wife; possibly earlier and re-used. – John Pollard †1667 and family, with frontal heads in roundels. – Good LEDGER STONES.

YEALMPTON

5050

ST BARTHOLOMEW. An early church by *William Butterfield*. Plans for piecemeal rebuilding were exhibited in 1848, and the church was finished, except for the chancel decoration, in 1850, when work ceased, as the patron, G.R.P.Bastard of Kitley, became a Roman Catholic. W tower added only in 1914–15, by *Charles King* of Plymouth. The exterior is conventional late C13 to early C14, not specially impressive or Butterfieldian. But the interior has many of this remarkable architect's qualities and foibles, and is an important early instance of his use of constructional polychromy. (His earliest plans for All Saints Margaret Street were of 1849.) The chancel arch has another slightly lower arch set in and the space between the two filled with a multi-coloured diaper pattern; low N chancel chapel; and above again a diaper or criss-cross of dark marble. Piers octagonal with alternation of lighter and darker grey marble. Aisle walls with inscriptions in circular frames and once more a somewhat jarring linear pattern, this time trefoil, surrounding them. This decoration dates from 1863; it was intended to frame painted scenes. The Butterfield furnishings display the same delight in coloured materials. – FONT. Octagonal, of polished red and black Kitley marble. – Old FONT, Norman, with crude wavy decoration. – Low SCREEN, a chunky design of purple marble, with buttresses, tracery, and fleurons. – The chancel, with good STAINED GLASS (E window by *Hardman*), TILES, and colourful roof, still has a richly Butterfieldian atmosphere. – BRASSES. Flemish(?) palimpsest, *c.* 1400, cut down and re-engraved on the back to a Coplestone. – Sir John Crocker, in armour, 1508. – MONUMENTS. Mary Coppelston †1630. Arched recess with kneeling figures against the tomb-chest; no effigy. – Edward Pollexfen of Kitley †1710. Bust on top of a large architectural surround. – Pollexfen Bastard †1732, with urn. – Several other Bastards: Edmund and Baldwin Pollexfen both †1773; two female figures. – Thomas Veale †1780. – In the churchyard W of the tower an early INSCRIBED STONE of sponge-finger shape with the word TOREUS, probably C6–7. – Good LYCHGATE by *Butterfield*; half-hipped roofs, the truss piercing the slates as a little dormer.

E of the church, SCHOOL and SCHOOLHOUSE, 1852, also by *Butterfield*. Stone, very simple, with steep slate roofs of differing heights. Not completed; now a house.

YEALM BRIDGE. Early C19, a single wide segmental arch. Small TOLL HOUSE with Gothick windows, and a more unusual TOLL KEEPER'S SHELTER, a small stone rubble hut with steeply pitched corbelled roof and a circular interior.

LIMEKILNS. A single semicircular example E of Yealm Bridge on the river bank. At Kitley Caves, another, and a pair with three round-arched openings.

PUSLINCH BRIDGE, over the Yealm at the head of the creek. Three pointed arches, one cutwater and refuge; possibly C17.

BOWDEN. The old manor house of the Coplestones. Now a farmhouse, largely rebuilt in the early C19. Good group of outbuildings.

See also Kitley *and* Lyneham.

YELVERTON
N of Plymouth

The church lies on a curious plateau where main moor-roads meet.

ST PAUL. 1910–14 by *Nicholson & Corlette*. The exterior – with

steeply gabled nave, lean-to aisles, and battlemented NE tower –
promises much less than the excellent interior has to give: early C20
at its best, before it quite abandoned traditions. The type of the
interior is Devonian, but the sharp angular forms of the shafts of the
compound piers, the painting of the wagon roofs, and especially the
sense of smooth surfaces as something pleasurable in itself belong to
our century. The whole church is lined with slabs of buff-coloured
Ham Hill stone.

Near the main road a Second World War AIRFIELD, with grass-
banked Spitfire shelters around the edges.

(Among the many individual dwellings scattered over the moorland
here, two small houses were built in the Arts and Crafts tradition by
Minoprio & Spenceley, 1936, one thatched, one slated, L-shaped,
with an angled wing; simple casement windows.)

YEOFORD
Near Crediton

7090

The tiny chapel of HOLY TRINITY, built in 1891, is little more than
a red brick shed with a bellcote, but the SCHOOL is a bold effort
by *Charles Pinn* for Crediton School Board (cf. South Zeal), 1877.
Brick and stone, neo-Saxo-Norman. Were the arched and triangular-
headed windows inspired by Rougemont Castle, Exeter?

YOULSTON PARK
Shirwell

5030

The manor house of the Raleighs, which passed by marriage to the
Chichester family in the early C16. They sold the house in 1920.
The unassuming Georgian exterior conceals a house of complex
development: one of the most rewarding in North Devon. The r.
half is a courtyard house with projecting wings and, in the centre
of the front range, a hall whose fabric is basically medieval, as the
rubble walling here suggests. To the l. a long projecting wing with
late C17 interiors of the time of Sir Arthur Chichester, who 'hath
made a very noble dwelling of Youlston' (Prince, 1701). The wing
may be on older foundations (see the thick wall at the back). The
windows now all Georgian sashes, with lunettes in the gables of the
hall range, and a Palladian window in the E side lighting a staircase. Slate roof, no parapets.

The present entrance is by a porch with four Tuscan columns
attached to the projecting l. wing of the main range. It leads into an
entrance hall, formerly two rooms, which appear to have been
fitted up around 1800 with an assortment of C16–18 panelling now
all painted white, and an C18 ceiling with a quilted pattern. On the
l. wall an early C19 Gothic fireplace with a late C17 overmantel. To
the r. is the hall, now rather disappointing, as the great coved
ceiling is bare except for a rich cornice of thick leaves in late C17
style: all that remains of more elaborate plasterwork. Below this is
white-painted C18 fielded panelling, with pilasters and a segmental
pediment around the fireplace. Above the panelling circular plaster

wreaths with hanging swags, and one earlier square stone panel with a mythological scene. Marble fireplace with long scrolls.

This late C17 and C18 refurbishing conceals a much older building, for which the evidence is the relieving arches of windows, revealed on the courtyard side, and, especially, the impressive medieval roof preserved above the present coved ceiling of the hall. The date is perhaps c. 1400. Unusually for Devon, it is a crown-post roof, although the visual emphasis is not on the crown-posts, which are short and unmoulded, but on the massive base crucks meeting below the collar, a construction generally considered earlier than the arch-braced roof with jointed crucks or full-length principals, which became the most common late medieval types in Devon. Five trusses remain, smoke-blackened throughout, with traces of a louvre in the centre bay, where the rafters have been cut back. Hollow-chamfered collar purlin, two sets of side purlins, with wind-braces in the lower section. On the main square-set purlins a moulded plate carries short uprights to the common rafters; there are other vertical struts between wall and rafters and between collar-beams and principals.

To the r. of the hall the corner room has a ceiling divided geometrically: beams with Greek key and other ornament of c. 1800. Double doors to the hall, Corinthian doorcase; enriched dado. Behind this room is an C18 well staircase lit by the Palladian window on the E side: square fluted newels, turned balusters, open string. But the most impressive interiors are in the wing on the other side of the house, dating from c. 1680 onwards, after Youlston had become the main Chichester seat. The first section is taken up by a generous late C17 staircase, ascending around an open well up to the second floor. Richly carved string; urn-shaped balusters decorated with acanthus and with egg and dart round the necking (cf. Great Potheridge, and Royal Hotel, Bideford). The staircase is now incongruously painted white. The sloping ceiling has plasterwork with festoons hanging from masks. It may date from a mid C18 remodelling of the top floor.

Next to the stairs a large saloon with a splendid ceiling with daring relief figures of putti, and the Chichester heron and other birds among scrolls and garlands, in the tradition of the third John Abbot (cf. his work of 1681 at Exeter Custom House). The style is very close to the ceilings of the Royal Hotel, Bideford, although one of the coats of arms (Leigh), perhaps a later addition, refers to a marriage of 1715. The walls are covered with excellent Chinese wallpaper of the second half of the C18, with large figures on a buff ground. (Similar papers at Avebury Manor, Wilts, and in the Victoria and Albert Museum.) Bolection mouldings to doors and fireplace. The end room of this wing has an even more virtuoso display of the plasterer's art, with central oval relief, and embellished coats of arms with herons in the corners. Good wooden overmantel with fruit, flowers, and lions' masks. Below this wing very simple cellars. Behind the main block with the hall, a courtyard, with a range at the back housing the former kitchen, with rough chamfered beams and the remains of a large fireplace, smoking chamber, and oven. In the room over the entrance hall a simple early C19 marble fireplace.

STABLES, late C18, on three sides of a courtyard, the entrance flanked by piers topped by balls. Stuccoed over rubble; upper lunette windows.

LODGES. A very handsome late C18 pair, one-storeyed, with hipped roofs with a pediment on each side, and niches with urns. Stuccoed over brick.

ZEAL MONACHORUM

ST PETER. W tower with diagonal buttresses at the foot; no pinnacles. Perp S aisle, much renewed outside, inside with granite arcade on A type piers, capitals only to the main shafts. Earlier far-projecting N transept. – FONT. Norman, of tub shape, with a little zigzag and cable decoration. – Iron SCREEN. – STAINED GLASS. E window designed in 1851 by *F. W. Oliphant*, made by *Hardman*. Figures under canopies; stylized colours. – Chancel S: sepia Virgin and Child, a curious piece, photographically reproduced from an engraving.

A tight village of thatched houses. Near the church HERON COURT, with bulging projection and late Georgian window.

REEVE CASTLE. Built by *William Carter Pedler* for himself in 1900. A late fling at a Gothic folly. Octagonal, with top-lit central hall, taller polygonal tower, and projecting bays of various shapes to take advantage of the splendid views. Large moulded pointed and round-arched openings throughout, elaborate cornices and pierced balustrade, all of glazed yellow brick. Best seen from a distance.

INDEX OF PLATES

INDEX OF ARTISTS

INDEX OF PATRONS AND RESIDENTS

Indexed here are the names/titles of families and individuals (not of bodies or commercial firms) recorded in this volume as having owned property and/or commissioned architectural work. It includes monuments to members of such families, but not those to other individuals.

INDEX OF PLACES

Bold figures indicate main entry. * indicates entries in which reference is made to Dartmoor.

THE BUILDINGS OF ENGLAND

COMPLETE LIST OF TITLES

Northamptonshire *1st ed. 1961 Nikolaus Pevsner, 2nd ed. 1973 revised Bridget Cherry*

Northumberland *1st ed. 1957 Nikolaus Pevsner with Ian A. Richmond, revision in progress*

Nottinghamshire *1st ed. 1951 Nikolaus Pevsner, 2nd ed. 1979 revised Elizabeth Williamson*

Oxfordshire *1st ed. 1974 Jennifer Sherwood and Nikolaus Pevsner*

Shropshire *1st ed. 1958 Nikolaus Pevsner*

Somerset, North, and Bristol *1st ed. 1958 Nikolaus Pevsner, revision in progress*

Somerset, South and West *1st ed. 1958 Nikolaus Pevsner*

Staffordshire *1st ed. 1974 Nikolaus Pevsner*

Suffolk *1st ed. 1961 Nikolaus Pevsner, 2nd ed. 1974 revised Enid Radcliffe*

Surrey *1st ed. 1962 Ian Nairn and Nikolaus Pevsner, 2nd ed. 1971 revised Bridget Cherry*

Sussex *1st ed. 1965 Ian Nairn and Nikolaus Pevsner, revision in progress*

Warwickshire *1st ed. 1966 Nikolaus Pevsner and Alexandra Wedgwood*

Wiltshire *1st ed. 1963 Nikolaus Pevsner, 2nd ed. 1975 revised Bridget Cherry*

Worcestershire *1st ed. 1968 Nikolaus Pevsner*

Yorkshire: The North Riding *1st ed. 1966 Nikolaus Pevsner*

Yorkshire: The West Riding *1st ed. 1959 Nikolaus Pevsner, 2nd ed. 1967 revised Enid Radcliffe*

Yorkshire: York and the East Riding *1st ed. 1972 Nikolaus Pevsner with John Hutchinson, revision in progress*